# MANHATTAN PREP

# 5 lb. Book of GRE® Practice Problems

## GRE® Strategy Guide Supplement

GRE success lies in consistent performance, which requires the deep
familiarity with GRE questions that can only be gained with practice.
This guide provides that practice.

5 lb. Book of GRE® Practice Problems, Second Edition

ISBN-13: 978-1-5062-3444-1

10 9 8 7 6 5 4 3 2 1

Layout Design: Dan McNaney
Production Manager: Derek Frankhouser
Production Designers: Cathy Huang and Belen Ferrer
Cover Design: Dan McNaney and Frank Callaghan

Printed in India

# *INSTRUCTIONAL GUIDE SERIES*

# *SUPPLEMENTAL MATERIALS*

June 15, 2015

Dear Student,

Thank you for picking up a copy of 5 lb. Book of GRE® Practice Problems. We hope this book provides just the right practice as you prepare for the GRE.

A great number of people were involved in the creation of the book you are holding. First and foremost is Zeke Vander-hoek, the founder of Manhattan Prep. Zeke was a lone tutor in New York when he started the company in 2000. Now, well into its second decade, the company contributes to the successes of thousands of students around the globe every year.

Our Manhattan Prep Strategy Guides are based on the continuing experiences of our instructors and students. Jen Dziura was the primary author and editor of the original edition of this book, with editorial support from Chris Ryan and Emily Meredith Sledge. Questions were written not only by Jen, Chris, and Emily, but also by many other instructors, including Roman Altshuler, Chris Berman, Faruk Bursal, Dmitry Farber, Stacey Koprince, David Mahler, Seb Moosapoor, Stephanie Moyerman, Michael Schwartz, Tate Shafer, Tommy Wallach, and Ryan Wessel.

The Second Edition that you are holding brought even more talent to the table. This update was authored by Liz Moliski and Emily Meredith Sledge and edited by Whitney Garner, Stacey Koprince, and Stephanie Moyerman. New content was written by Liz and Emily, as well as by Roman Altshuler, Chris Berman, Brian Birdwell, Josh Braslow, Ceilidh Erickson, Rina Goldfield, Joe Lucero, Ryan Starr, Neil Thornton, and Julia Van Dyke.

Meanwhile, Dan McNaney, Derek Frankhouser, Cathy Huang, and Belen Ferrer provided design and layout expertise as Dan and Derek managed book production. Liz Krisher made sure that all the moving pieces, both inside and outside of our company, came together at just the right time. Finally, we are indebted to all of the Manhattan Prep students who have given us feedback over the years. This book wouldn't be half of what it is without your voice.

At Manhattan Prep, we aspire to provide the best instructors and resources possible, and we hope that you will find our commitment manifest in this book. We strive to keep our books free of errors, but if you think we've goofed, please visit manhattanprep.com/GRE/errata. If you have any questions or comments in general, please email our Student Services team at gre@manhattanprep.com. Or give us a shout at 212-721-7400 (or 800-576-4628 in the U.S. or Canada). I look forward to hearing from you.

Thanks again, and best of luck preparing for the GRE!

Chris Ryan
Vice President of Academics
Manhattan Prep

# HOW TO ACCESS YOUR ONLINE RESOURCES

## IF YOU PURCHASED A PHYSICAL COPY OF THIS BOOK

1. Go to: **www.manhattanprep.com/gre/access**
2. Follow the instructions on the screen.

Your one year of online access begins on the day that you register your book at the above URL.

You only need to register your product ONCE at the above URL. To use your online resources any time AFTER you have completed the registration process, log in to the following URL:

**www.manhattanprep.com/gre/studentcenter**

Please note that online access is nontransferable. This means that only NEW and UNREGISTERED copies of the book will grant you online access. Previously used books will NOT provide any online resources.

## IF YOU PURCHASED A DIGITAL VERSION OF THIS BOOK

1. Create an account with Manhattan Prep at this website:
**www.manhattanprep.com/gre/register**

2. Email a copy of your purchase receipt to **gre@manhattanprep.com** to activate your resources. Please be sure to use the same email address to create an account that you used to purchase the book.

For any technical issues, email **gre@manhattanprep.com** or call **646-254-6479**.
Please refer to the following page for a description of the online resources that come with this book.

# YOUR ONLINE RESOURCES

## YOUR PURCHASE INCLUDES ONLINE ACCESS TO THE FOLLOWING:

## CHALLENGE PROBLEM ARCHIVE

The challenge problem archive included with the purchase of this book is available online in Manhattan Prep's student center. The archive includes more than 180 extremely challenging GRE® practice problems written by Manhattan Prep's expert instructors, plus an additional 12 problems (1 new problem each month) posted throughout the next year. These original problems are designed to mimic the most advanced math questions on the GRE. All questions include answers and comprehensive explanations. This question bank serves as a supplement to the problem sets in Manhattan Prep's 5 lb. Book of GRE Practice Problems.

## VIDEO INTRODUCTION TO THE 5 LB. BOOK

Learn from one of Manhattan Prep's expert instructors how to best study for the GRE. The video includes general GRE tips and study schedules as well as specific ways to work through the vast number of problems included in the 5 lb. Book of GRE Practice Problems.

## SUPPLEMENTAL QUESTION BANKS

Take your studies even further with our question banks. These banks include extra GRE practice problems fine-tuned by our curriculum team to simulate real exam questions. Every question comes with a detailed answer explanation. These problems are an excellent practice resource for dedicated GRE students.

## ONLINE UPDATES TO THE CONTENT IN THIS BOOK

The content presented in this book is updated periodically to ensure that it reflects the GRE's most current trends. You may view all updates, including any known errors or changes, upon registering for online access.

**The above resources can be found in your Student Center at manhattanprep.com/gre/studentcenter**

# TABLE of CONTENTS

# TABLE *of* CONTENTS

# Chapter *of* 1

5 lb. Book of GRE® Practice Problems

# Verbal Diagnostic Test

# In This Chapter...

*Verbal Diagnostic Test*

*Verbal Diagnostic Test Answers*

# Verbal Diagnostic Test

**20 Questions**
**Time: 30 Minutes**

> **For each of Questions 1 to 6, select <u>one</u> entry for each blank from the corresponding column of choices. Fill in the blank in the way that best completes the text.**

1. In interviews, despots are often surprisingly _____; this helps to explain how seemingly awful people are able to command so many followers.

   | |
   |---|
   | malign |
   | indignant |
   | forgiving |
   | personable |
   | munificent |

2. The thriving health food company sells _____ meat products so meat-like that vegetarians sometimes call the phone number on the box to make sure that the product is really animal-free.

   | |
   |---|
   | mendacious |
   | nugatory |
   | ersatz |
   | parallel |
   | clandestine |

3. The successful tech company faces an ironic problem in the fall quarter; people are so excited about the next (i) _____ of its product, which will be released over the holidays, that they refuse to purchase the (ii) _____ version.

   | Blank (i) | Blank (ii) |
   |---|---|
   | ingenuity | obsolete |
   | implication | current |
   | iteration | practical |

4.  Newborn babies are perfectly (i) _____ , as yet unable to be concerned for others, or even to understand a difference between themselves and the world around them. As young children mature, they make the (ii) _____ discovery that other people exist and have their own needs and desires—in other words, that the entire world is not about them.

| Blank (i) | Blank (ii) |
|-----------|------------|
| solipsistic | arresting |
| sophomoric | selfish |
| quixotic | undue |

5.  Historically, arguments against women's suffrage (i) _____ from the claim that women would cancel out their husbands' votes to the charge that women would merely (ii) _____ their husbands' preferences, thus making their votes redundant. Such arguments, while once convincing, today seem (iii) _____ indeed.

| Blank (i) | Blank (ii) | Blank (iii) |
|-----------|------------|-------------|
| ran the gauntlet | override | ponderous |
| ran the gamut | ape | shabby |
| held the line | disclaim | cogent |

6.  His theory purported that "proper" enjoyment of art was a matter of pure aesthetics—it is surely, he says, a baser pleasure being enjoyed by the untrained (i) _____ , the museum "tourist" with (ii) _____ sensibilities, and even the art theorists and art historians who simply appreciate cultural referents or narratives in art, a predilection he thinks leads to (iii) _____ view of any art that includes such elements.

| Blank (i) | Blank (ii) | Blank (iii) |
|-----------|------------|-------------|
| cabal | incendiary | a facile |
| literati | parochial | an urbane |
| hoi-polloi | dulcet | a painstaking |

**MANHATTAN**
PREP

**Question 7 is based on the following reading passage.**

During an economic depression, it is common for food prices to increase even as incomes decrease. Surprisingly, however, researchers determined that during a depression, for every 5 percent increase in the cost of bread, the lowest socioeconomic class actually increases the amount of bread purchased per capita by 3 percent.

7.   Which of the following hypotheses best accounts for the researchers' findings?

(A)   Not all food costs increase during a depression; some food items actually become less expensive.

(B)   Because bread consumption does not increase by the same percentage as the cost does, people are likely consuming more of other food items to compensate.

(C)   When incomes decrease, people are typically forced to spend a larger proportion of their income on basic needs, such as food and housing.

(D)   People who suddenly cannot afford more expensive foods, such as meat, must compensate by consuming more inexpensive foods, such as grains.

(E)   During a depression, people in the lowest socioeconomic class will continue to spend the same amount of money on food as they did before the depression began.

**Question 8 is based on the following reading passage.**

Bedbug infestations have been a problem in major cities for years. The pesticide DDT has been found to be useful in killing bedbugs. However, DDT was banned in the United States and has been replaced by weaker pesticides. Thus, there is no effective means for eradicating bedbugs in the United States.

8.   Which of the following, if true, most weakens the conclusion?

(A)   Bedbugs resemble other small insects in their appearance and behavior.

(B)   Bedbugs have largely been eradicated in other parts of the world.

(C)   Some treatments that do not include DDT have proven effective against bedbugs in other parts of the world.

(D)   Bedbugs are resistant to the types of pesticides used to treat cockroach and ant infestations.

(E)   The number of bedbug infestations has risen significantly in the 21st century.

---

**Questions 9 to 12 are based on the following reading passage.**

---

Dan Flavin's *alternate diagonals of March 2, 1964 (to Don Judd)*, an 8-foot-long diagonal beam of light set at a 45-degree angle, is a colorful sculpture of light that is visually arresting, even from across the room. As one approaches the work, it is difficult not to become almost blinded by the intensity of the light and the vivacity of the colors. Though it may strike one as

5  garish on first glance, a more lengthy perusal reveals a delicate interplay between the red and yellow beams, giving the work a visual richness.

*Alternate diagonals* was made by Flavin in response to one of his own previous works, *the diagonal of May 25, 1963 (to Constantin Brancusi)*. His first piece composed solely of light, *the diagonal of May 25, 1963* was also an 8-foot-long fluorescent light sculpture (though Flavin

10 never liked to call them sculptures—he referred to them as "situations") hung at a 45-degree angle, and also included a yellow fluorescent light tube. *Alternate diagonals* seems almost more of an evolution of the former work than a response to it, but regardless of the exact nature of the intended interplay between the two, it is important to frame *alternate diagonals* as a companion work.

15    *Alternate diagonals* known as a ready-made, a work of art composed entirely of objects that anyone could find and put together as the artist has. This is precisely what is so intriguing about the work—it toys with the boundaries of what we can define as a ready-made in contemporary art and, perhaps, within the field of art production itself. It forces a spectrum to be employed instead of a black-and-white categorization of the ready-made—a spectrum

20 stretching between the "pure" ready-made (any work that essentially could be transferred straight from anyone's garage to a gallery, such as Duchamp's *Bottle Rack*), all the way to a contemporary two-dimensional work where the artist's canvas and paints were purchased from an art supply store in an infinitely more manipulated but still semi-"ready-made" fashion. Flavin's piece, it seems, is situated somewhere in the center of such a spectrum, and raises the

25 question of where the "ready" ends and the "made" begins.

9.   The main point of the passage is to

(A)  assert the superiority of ready-made art
(B)  decry the broadening of the definition of art
(C)  discuss a work in context and its effect on the discipline
(D)  explain the relationship between two works of art
(E)  praise an artist and his creations

**MANHATTAN**
PREP

10.  According to the passage, both "diagonal" works could best be described as

    (A)  using red and yellow light

    (B)  initially striking the viewer as garish

    (C)  toying with boundaries of art

    (D)  running through the plane at a particular slope

    (E)  identical in concept

11.  The author's tone could best be described as

    (A)  admiring and supportive

    (B)  enthusiastic and fawning

    (C)  respectful and distant

    (D)  obligatory and unenthused

    (E)  erudite and objective

12.  The passage implies which of the following?

    (A)  Conventional two-dimensional work is a thing of the past.

    (B)  Flavin is one of the most important artists of his time.

    (C)  *Bottle Rack* has very little artistic manipulation.

    (D)  Flavin disliked the word "sculpture" because of the Renaissance association.

    (E)  The best art work is in the center of the artistic spectrum of art production.

---

**For each of Questions 13 to 16, select the <u>two</u> answer choices that, when used to complete the sentence, fit the meaning of the sentence as a whole <u>and</u> produce completed sentences that are alike in meaning.**

---

13.  Many young employees actively seek out mentors, but when managers attempt to mentor young employees who have not sought out mentoring, the help often comes across as presumptuous and _____.

    ☐  baneful

    ☐  noxious

    ☐  patronizing

    ☐  amenable

    ☐  pragmatic

    ☐  condescending

14. In previous decades, it was simply assumed that fathers of young children would work full-time and at the same intensity as they did before becoming parents, but today, increasing numbers of men—wanting to further their careers but also wanting to spend time with their children—are more _____ about this arrangement.

    ☐  stolid

    ☐  ambiguous

    ☐  whimsical

    ☐  ambivalent

    ☐  equivocal

    ☐  officious

15. The slipstream is a partial vacuum created in the wake of a moving vehicle that allows for "drafting," whereby a racecar can _____ another and win the race by taking advantage of reduced wind resistance.

    ☐  supersede

    ☐  assume

    ☐  overtake

    ☐  champion

    ☐  collide

    ☐  outstrip

16. While the celebration of the artist's work was pure paean—nothing but plaudits and tributes—many of those in the art world feel that an acknowledgment of the artist's _____ would help to humanize the artist and make the art more accessible.

    ☐  faculties

    ☐  poultices

    ☐  foibles

    ☐  mores

    ☐  aptitudes

    ☐  peccadilloes

**MANHATTAN**
PREP

> **Questions 17 and 18 are based on the following reading passage.**

      In keeping with the notable incorporation of operatic elements into the rock music lexicon, the genre in the 1970s experienced a significant shift in emphasis away from recording and toward music performance itself. Several factors effected this change. First, the extended length and the moralizing subject matter of songs of the era rendered them less appropriate
5  for radio play and more suitable for public presentation. Additionally, the advent of the concept album, in which multiple tracks revolved around a single unifying narrative or theme, furnished a basis upon which similarly calibrated performances could be enacted. Finally, as PA system technology improved, it became possible to hold concerts with 100,000 people or more, which encouraged artists to craft concerts that diverged from the merely musical toward
10  the experiential. Bands began conceiving of their performances as *shows*, more akin to musical theater guided by plot and setting than to the traditional concert guided by the omnipresent set-list. Instead of simply playing one song after another, therefore, bands developed full performance medleys revolving around specific motifs, and punctuated by bombastic light shows, costume changes, and other massive stunts. For example, the popular British band
15  Pink Floyd famously built a barrier in the middle of stage during one performance then had it dramatically knocked down mid-show as a promotion for their new album *The Wall*.

17.  The passage cites all of the following as reasons for the inclusion of operatic elements into the rock music genre in the 1970s EXCEPT:

    (A)  Changes in concert equipment changed the way shows could be delivered.

    (B)  Pink Floyd's dramatic staging served to promote an influential album.

    (C)  Shifts in the content of the music contributed to the songs having a more "story-telling" quality.

    (D)  One medium through which rock songs had typically been delivered to the public became less conducive to the genre.

    (E)  Artists altered their performances to reflect changes in the modern concert ambiance.

18.  In the context of the passage, the word "effected" (line 3) most nearly means

    (A)  influenced

    (B)  moved forward

    (C)  transformed

    (D)  determined

    (E)  brought about

---

**Questions 19 and 20 are based on the following reading passage.**

---

In 1977, the Community Reinvestment Act (CRA) was passed for the purpose of reducing discriminatory credit practices in low-income neighborhoods. The act required Federal financing supervisory agencies to use their authority to encourage lending institutions to meet the credit needs of all borrowers in their communities. The CRA had little impact until 1993,

5 when the Department of Housing and Urban Development (HUD) initiated legal proceedings against lenders who declined too many applications from minority borrowers.

Some argue that, while providing equal access to credit is an important aim, pressure on lenders from HUD led to practices that later caused those same lenders to be assailed as "predatory." In *Housing Boom and Bust*, economist Thomas Sowell wrote that the CRA, far from

10 being as benign as it appeared, was based on a flawed assumption: that government officials were qualified to tell banks how to lend the money entrusted to them by depositors and investors.

---

Consider each of the answer choices separately and indicate <u>all</u> that apply.

---

19.  It can be inferred from the passage that

☐  the CRA was perceived by some as seemingly innocuous

☐  HUD had the ability to affect banking practices

☐  Thomas Sowell had asserted that a certain level of expertise is required to direct banks' lending activities

---

Consider each of the answer choices separately and indicate <u>all</u> that apply.

---

20.  Which of the following can be inferred about discriminatory credit practices?

☐  They are more common in middle-income neighborhoods than in high-income neighborhoods.

☐  Legislators who voted for the CRA did so because they were opposed to such practices.

☐  Critics allege that attempts to combat such practices can have unintended consequences.

**MANHATTAN**
PREP

# Verbal Diagnostic Test Scoring

| Question # | Your Answer | Correct Answer | Tally your correctly answered questions. *No partial credit!* | Find more questions like this in chapter: |
|:---:|:---:|:---:|:---:|:---:|
| 1 | | personable | | 3 |
| 2 | | ersatz | | 3 |
| 3 | | iteration, current | | 3 |
| 4 | | solipsistic, arresting | | 3 |
| 5 | | ran the gamut, ape, shabby | | 3 |
| 6 | | hoi-polloi, parochial, a facile | | 3 |
| 7 | | (D) | | 6 |
| 8 | | (C) | | 6 |
| 9 | | (C) | | 5 |
| 10 | | (D) | | 5 |
| 11 | | (A) | | 5 |
| 12 | | (C) | | 5 |
| 13 | | patronizing, condescending | | 4 |
| 14 | | ambivalent, equivocal | | 4 |
| 15 | | overtake, outstrip | | 4 |
| 16 | | foibles, peccadilloes | | 4 |
| 17 | | (B) | | 5 |
| 18 | | (E) | | 5 |
| 19 | | 1st, 2nd, and 3rd | | 5 |
| 20 | | 3rd only | | 5 |

**Raw Verbal Score:**
**(# of verbal questions answered correctly)**

## Verbal Diagnostic Test: Scoring Guide

| Raw Verbal Score | Verbal Reasoning Diagnostic Scaled Score |
|:---:|:---:|
| 20 | 169–170 |
| 19 | 168–170 |
| 18 | 166–168 |
| 17 | 163–165 |
| 16 | 161–163 |
| 15 | 159–161 |
| 14 | 157–159 |
| 13 | 156–158 |
| 12 | 154–156 |
| 11 | 152–154 |
| 10 | 150–152 |
| 9 | 149–151 |
| 8 | 147–149 |
| 7 | 145–147 |
| 6 | 143–145 |
| 5 | 140–142 |
| 4 | 137–139 |
| 3 | 133–136 |
| 2 | 130–132 |
| 1 | 130–131 |
| 0 | 130 |

NOTES:

Diagnostic Scaled Score is approximate.

(a) If your time for this diagnostic section exceeded the 30-minute guideline, this approximate score may not be indicative of your performance under standard time conditions.

(b) Scaled Score depends not only on how many questions were answered correctly (Raw Score), but also on the overall difficulty of the set of questions. This diagnostic test approximates the difficulty of the official GRE® revised General Test.

**MANHATTAN**
PREP

# Verbal Diagnostic Test Answers

1. **Personable.** The blank "helps to explain how seemingly awful people are able to command so many followers," so it needs to be a positive word. While both "forgiving" and "munificent," which means generous, are positive, both add meaning that isn't suggested by the given sentence. "Personable," meaning pleasant in appearance and manner, fits best. "Malign" (evil) and "indignant" (annoyed or angry) are both negative.

2. **Ersatz.** The words "vegetarians" and "animal-free" indicate that the meat products are fake, or "ersatz." Note the many trap answers: "mendacious" (lying), "nugatory" (without value), and "clandestine" (hidden), all of which are negative but do not describe fake meat. As a noun, a "parallel" can be a thing that is similar to or analogous to another, the way fake meat is analogous to real meat. However, when used as an adjective, as it is here, "parallel" only means aligned and equidistant.

3. **Iteration, current.** This sentence is comparing two "versions" of a product. The first blank requires a synonym of "version," such as "iteration." There's a bit of a theme trap in "ingenuity," which means innovation or creativity. An "implication" is either an insinuation or a consequence; neither makes sense in this context. The second blank describes a "version" that is contrasting with the "next iteration," so that would logically be the previous one. "Current" works well here (and "obsolete" is too judgmental; it's not outdated or out of production yet!). It might be true that the version is "practical," but the given sentence doesn't suggest this additional meaning; if anything, "refuse to purchase" disagrees with the idea of a practical version of the product.

4. **Solipsistic, arresting.** Solipsism is literally the theory that only the self exists or can be known to exist ("solipsistic" is sometimes used a bit figuratively to mean really selfish). Babies could be "sophomoric" (juvenile) or "quixotic" (idealistic or unrealistic), but neither answer choice relates to "unable to be concerned for others, or even to understand a difference between themselves and the world around them." For the second blank, the "discovery" in question is that "the entire world is not about them." That's a pretty earth-shaking discovery for someone who thought otherwise! "Arresting" (striking or dramatic) gets this across. Note the trap answer "selfish," which is related to the overall meaning of the sentence but does not describe the "discovery." There is no indication in the sentence that the discovery is "undue" (excessive or unwarranted).

5. **Ran the gamut, ape, shabby.** The first blank requires something that means ranged. The clue is the two very different beliefs described—that women's votes would be the opposite of their husbands', or that the votes would be the same and therefore "redundant." The idiom "ran the gamut" gets this across (much like the expression "from A to Z"). Though similar-sounding, "ran the gauntlet" means withstood an attack from all sides. "Held the line" has many meanings, some figurative and others more literal, but often is used to mean "imposed a limit." In the second blank, "ape" means mimic or copy, agreeing with "making their votes redundant." "Override" (cancel or negate) agrees with "cancel out their husbands' votes" but the second claim should be in contrast with the first. "Disclaim" means deny, which doesn't agree with "redundant." The phrase "while once" signals that the third blank requires something that goes against "convincing." Meaning mediocre or of poor quality, "shabby" fits. It can describe clothes or furniture, but is often used metaphorically (such as in the expression "not too shabby," which can describe any job well done). "Ponderous" (awkward or dull) does not oppose "convincing," and "cogent" is actually a synonym for "convincing."

6. **Hoi-polloi, parochial, a facile.** The theory described is a theory of incredible snobbery! First of all, the person described thinks that there is a "'proper' enjoyment of art" (and, presumably, an improper one as well). He thinks that "untrained" people viewing art enjoy only "a baser pleasure," and calls other people "museum 'tourists.'" In the first blank, "hoi-polloi" matches the idea of common people, the masses. A "cabal" is a secret political faction, so is unrelated to this sentence. "Literati" are well-educated people who are interested in literature; this is nearly opposite the meaning required in blank (i). The second blank is a description of the "sensibilities" of "the museum 'tourist,'" and "parochial" matches the idea of ordinary, low-class, unsophisticated. "Incendiary" can literally mean designed to cause fires, or can figuratively mean exciting or provocative. Neither meaning of "incendiary" works here. "Dulcet" means sweet and soothing, and typically refers to sound, not to a noun like "sensibilities." Finally, "the art theorists and art historians" are thought to have "a facile," or overly simple, view. The theorist seems to think that only "pure aesthetics" (principles of beauty) should matter; the theorists and historians he disdains are those who like "cultural referents or narratives"—that is, recognizable themes or figures, or stories. Both "an urbane" (suave or sophisticated) and "a painstaking" (meticulous or thorough) are positive, disagreeing with this person's attitude toward "art theorists and art historians."

7. **(D).** This Reading Comprehension question is really a Logic question. Such questions typically consist of a single paragraph with one question. First, analyze the argument: During a depression, it is normal for food prices to increase at the same time that incomes decrease. Logically, this would make it more difficult for people to afford the same food that they used to purchase prior to the depression. A study showed a surprising result, however: when the cost of bread went up during a depression, the poorest people actually bought more bread. Note that the argument doesn't say merely that more money is spent on bread; that would be expected if the price increased. The argument says that the actual amount of bread purchased increased. The correct answer will explain why people would buy more bread even though the cost has gone up and incomes have declined.

While choice (A) is likely true in the real world, it does not explain why people buy more bread when the cost of bread has increased and incomes have declined. Choice (B) is an example of faulty logic. It is true that the cost increase is a higher percentage than the consumption increase, but this does not mean that people are consuming less bread and therefore need to eat other things to compensate. In fact, the opposite is true: the argument explicitly states that people are buying more bread than they were! Choice (C) is tempting because it talks about people spending a "larger" proportion of income on food—but "proportion" is a value relative only to the person's income level. It does not indicate that the person is spending more money on a particular thing. More importantly, though, this choice does not answer the question asked. Correct choice (D), in contrast, provides a reason why an increase in the cost of one food item might cause people to consume more of that item despite a loss of income: other food items are even more expensive and are, thus, much less affordable. The people still need some amount of food to survive, so they purchase more of the food item that does not cost as much money. This accounts for the researchers' findings. Even if choice (E) were true (and this would be difficult if incomes are decreasing), it would not explain why people buy more bread at a time when the bread costs more and incomes are declining.

8. **(C).** This is a Logic question that asks you to weaken an argument. The author cites a problem: a pesticide that is effective in killing bedbugs is no longer available for use. Thus, the author claims, there is no effective means to kill the bedbugs in the United States. The problem here is that the author makes a very large jump between "replaced by weaker pesticides" and "there is no effective means." Finding something that attacks this assumption would be a good way to weaken the argument. Regarding choice (A), the behaviors of bedbugs have nothing to do with the ability to eradicate them. Choice (B) does not specify how bedbugs were eradicated in other parts of the world. It is possible that all successful eradications elsewhere relied on DDT. Correct choice (C) opens up the possibility that there might

be an approved means to eradicate the dreaded bedbug in the United States. It also calls the author's conclusion about there being "no effective means for eradicating bedbugs in the United States" into question. Choice (D), though largely out of scope, might be viewed as strengthening the author's conclusion, as it points to more evidence that existing pesticides are not effective on bedbugs. However, eliminating one possibility is not the same as eliminating *all* possibilities, which is what the author does in the conclusion. As for choice (E), the number of infestations has nothing to do with the ability to eliminate bedbugs in the United States.

9. **(C).** After describing Flavin's work, the author compares it to another work in the second paragraph, then goes on to discuss its effect on the definitions of a type of art. Choice (A) is a distortion as "superiority" is not mentioned. Choice (B), if anything, is backwards, as the author seems to approve of the broadening. Choices (D) and (E) ignore the significant part of the passage that discusses the broadening of definitions.

10. **(D).** Both works are said to be set at 45-degree angles (thus, "at a particular slope," which incidentally would happen to be 1 or −1). Choices (A), (B), and (C) are only explicitly mentioned in connection with *alternate diagonals*. Choice (E) is incorrect, as the concept of the works is not discussed; furthermore, the author writes "Alternate diagonals seems almost more of an evolution of the former work than a response to it." If the second work is an "evolution," the two works cannot be "identical."

11. **(A).** The passage teems with positive words—"visually arresting," "vivacity," "intriguing," to name just a few—and this indicates the author is biased in favor of the works. Thus, the neutral aspect of choices (C), (D), and (E) is incorrect. As for choice (B), "fawning" has a negative connotation.

12. **(C).** Choice (C) must be true as the author cites *Bottle Rack* as an example of the extreme end of the ready-made spectrum, and contrasts it with a type of "infinitely more manipulated" work. As for choice (A), the passage only mentions such conventional work in passing and does not predict its future. The passage does not rank Flavin, as choice (B) suggests, nor does it explain why he disliked the word "sculpture" for his works, as choice (D) does. Similarly, the passage only suggests that Flavin's work is in the center, not that such location is a virtue—the "best art work," as in choice (E).

13. **Patronizing, condescending.** The blank describes "help" offered by managers to "young employees who have not sought out mentoring." Furthermore, the help "comes across as presumptuous." Giving arrogant, unwanted help is "patronizing" or "condescending." Note that "baneful" (harmful) and "noxious" (poisonous) are similar to each other, but are much too negative. "Amenable," which means cooperative or compliant, is too positive, and the word generally applies better to people than to a noun like "the help." Similarly, "pragmatic" (sensible or practical) is both too positive and unpaired with any other choice.

14. **Ambivalent, equivocal.** Today, some men are "wanting to further their careers but also wanting to spend time with their children," so their feelings about the traditional working arrangement are mixed or complex. "Ambivalent" and "equivocal" match the idea of mixed feelings. Note trap answer "ambiguous," which means "unclear" and is more appropriate for describing a situation or statement than a person. The remaining choices are each unpaired: "stolid" means unemotional, "whimsical" has a positive meaning (fanciful or playful) and a negative meaning (capricious or erratic), and "officious" means domineering or intrusive.

15. **Overtake, outstrip.** The slipstream allows a racecar to "win the race by taking advantage of reduced wind resistance." In other words, the trailing car would be able to go faster than the car in front of it, and therefore pass it. "Supersede" may look the part, but it's actually a figurative word meaning replace (e.g., I was superseded by younger workers at my job). Only "outstrip" and "overtake" carry the literal meaning of physically passing something. When X "assumes" Y, X accepts or seizes Y (e.g., a leader assumes power). It's strange to think of a racecar assuming another racecar. Winning the race may lead people to call the winner the "champion," but one car does not "champion" another. Similarly, "collide" might make you think of the car crashes that sometimes occur during car races, but a car cannot "collide another." Rather, a car would collide *with* another.

16. **Foibles, peccadilloes.** "Paean" is praise, as are "plaudits and tributes." The celebration was "pure" praise. "While" indicates that the rest of the sentence should go in the opposite direction. Acknowledging flaws and mistakes—that is, "foibles" and "peccadilloes"—could indeed "help to humanize" an artist. "Faculties" (inherent mental or physical powers) and "aptitudes" (natural ability) are similar, but are too positive. The remaining choices are unpaired and also off topic: "poultices" are soft, moist masses of material applied to the body to heal or relieve pain and "mores" are customs or traditions.

17. **(B).** While it is true that Pink Floyd's dramatic staging served to promote its album, this is not a "reason for the inclusion of operatic elements into the rock music genre in the 1970s." It is an example, not a cause. Choice (A) is incorrect because the passage states that PA systems (a type of concert equipment) changed. Choice (C) is incorrect because the passage states that concept albums contained "narrative" themes. Choice (D) is incorrect because the passage states that rock songs were less appropriate for radio play. Choice (E) is incorrect because the passage states that the larger concerts "encouraged artists to craft concerts that diverged from the merely musical toward the experiential."

18. **(E).** The passage discusses several phenomena occurring in the 1970s that were in part responsible for "a significant shift in emphasis away from recording and toward music performance itself." These factors thus "brought about," or "effected," this change. Don't get confused by "influenced," one synonym of which is affected.

19. **1st, 2nd, and 3rd.** Sowell wrote that the CRA was "far from being as benign as it appeared." Thus, the CRA "appeared" benign, or "innocuous," at least to some. The passage states that HUD exerted pressure on lenders, which led to practices that later caused those same lenders to be assailed as "predatory." Thus, HUD had the ability to affect banking practices. Finally, Sowell argued that the idea "that government officials were qualified to tell banks how to lend" was a "flawed assumption." If Sowell believed that the government officials were not "qualified" to advise the banks, it follows that some minimum level of expertise is necessary in order to be qualified to do so.

20. **3rd only.** The passage states that discriminatory credit practices existed in low-income neighborhoods. Do not assume that there is a linear relationship wherein such practices occur most in low-income neighborhoods, less in middle-income neighborhoods, and least in high-income neighborhoods. Maybe such practices exist *only* in low-income neighborhoods. The first choice is out of scope. The second choice is also out of scope—you have no way to know what legislators were thinking or feeling when they voted for the CRA. The passage does provide good proof for the third statement—since some argue that "pressure on lenders from HUD led to practices that later caused those same lenders to be assailed as 'predatory,'" you can safely conclude that some critics think that attempts to combat discriminatory credit practices (passing the CRA and enforcing it through HUD) can have unintended consequences—in this case, replacing a lack of lending with predatory lending.

**MANHATTAN**
PREP

# Chapter *of* 2

## 5 lb. Book of GRE® Practice Problems

# Math Diagnostic Test

# In This Chapter...

Math Diagnostic Test

Math Diagnostic Test Answers

# Math Diagnostic Test

**20 Questions**
**35 Minutes**

---

For questions in the Quantitative Comparison format ("Quantity A" and "Quantity B" given), the answer choices are always as follows:

(A)   Quantity A is greater.
(B)   Quantity B is greater.
(C)   The two quantities are equal.
(D)   The relationship cannot be determined from the information given.

For questions followed by a numeric entry box [＿＿], you are to enter your own answer in the box. For questions followed by fraction-style numeric entry boxes $\frac{\boxed{\phantom{xx}}}{\boxed{\phantom{xx}}}$, you are to enter your answer in the form of a fraction. You are not required to reduce fractions. For example, if the answer is $\frac{1}{4}$, you may enter $\frac{25}{100}$ or any equivalent fraction.

All numbers used are real numbers. All figures are assumed to lie in a plane unless otherwise indicated. Geometric figures are not necessarily drawn to scale. You should assume, however, that lines that appear to be straight are actually straight, points on a line are in the order shown, and all geometric objects are in the relative positions shown. Coordinate systems, such as *xy*-planes and number lines, as well as graphical data presentations, such as bar charts, circle graphs, and line graphs, *are* drawn to scale. A symbol that appears more than once in a question has the same meaning throughout the question.

---

|   | **Quantity A** | **Quantity B** |
|---|---|---|
| 1. | $0.0\overline{1410}$ | $0.0\overline{141}$ |

A certain bookstore sells only paperbacks and hardbacks. Each of the 200 paperbacks in stock sells for a price between $8 and $12, and each of the 100 hardbacks in stock sells for a price between $14 and $18.

|   | **Quantity A** | **Quantity B** |
|---|---|---|
| 2. | The average price of the books in stock at the bookstore | $9.99 |

$$2 < x < 4$$

|   | **Quantity A** | **Quantity B** |
|---|---|---|
| 3. | $\dfrac{x-3}{-x}$ | $\dfrac{3-x}{-x}$ |

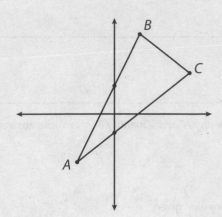

|  | **Quantity A** | **Quantity B** |
|---|---|---|
| 4. | The slope of line segment *AB* | The slope of line segment *AC* |

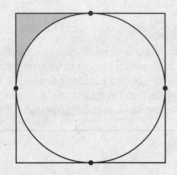

In the figure above, the circle is inscribed in a square that has area 16.

|  | **Quantity A** | **Quantity B** |
|---|---|---|
| 5. | The area of the shaded region | 1 |

$$a > 1$$
$$b > 5$$

|  | **Quantity A** | **Quantity B** |
|---|---|---|
| 6. | $(5b)^a$ | $\left(b^2\right)^a$ |

|  | **Quantity A** | **Quantity B** |
|---|---|---|
| 7. | $(5 + a)(3 + a)$ | $a^2 + 2a + 15$ |

In triangle *ABC*, *AB* = 12, *AC* = 10, and *BC* = 5.

|  | **Quantity A** | **Quantity B** |
|---|---|---|
| 8. | The measure of angle *A* | The measure of angle *C* |

**MANHATTAN**
PREP

9.   If $\dfrac{52}{x}$ is a positive integer, how many integer values are possible for $x$?

    (A)  5
    (B)  6
    (C)  7
    (D)  8
    (E)  10

10.  If $3x + 6y = 69$ and $2x - y = 11$, what is the value of $y$?

11.  If $7^9 + 7^9 + 7^9 + 7^9 + 7^9 + 7^9 + 7^9 = 7^x$, what is the value of $x$?

    (A)  9
    (B)  10
    (C)  12
    (D)  63
    (E)  $9^7$

12.  In a certain election race, all of the 8,400 votes were cast for either candidate A or candidate B. If votes for candidate A and votes for candidate B were cast in a 4 to 3 ratio, how many votes were cast for candidate A?

13.  What is the sum of all the integers from −457 to 459, inclusive?

14.  $a^3 b^4 c^7 > 0$. Which of the following statements must be true?

Indicate all such statements.

    ☐  $ab$ is negative
    ☐  $abc$ is positive
    ☐  $ac$ is positive

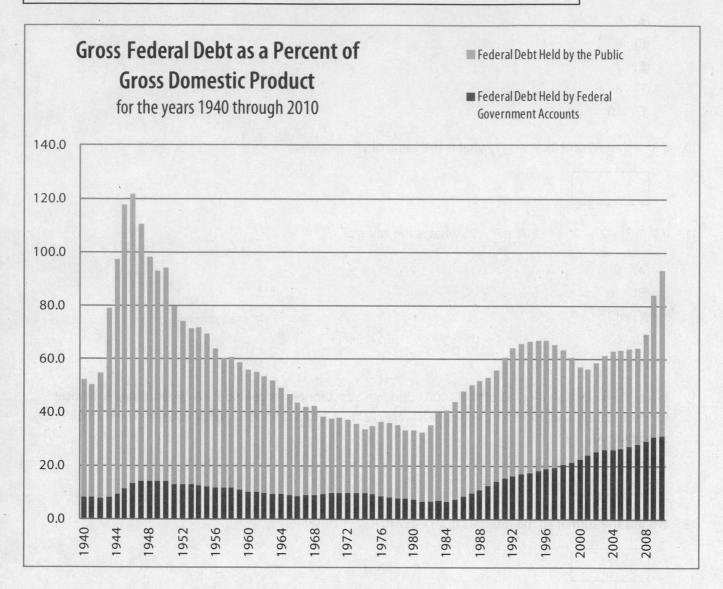

**Gross Federal Debt as a Percent of Gross Domestic Product**
for the years 1940 through 2010

■ Federal Debt Held by the Public

■ Federal Debt Held by Federal Government Accounts

15. In how many years between 1940 and 2010, inclusive, did the gross federal debt exceed the gross domestic product?

   (A)  Three
   (B)  Four
   (C)  Five
   (D)  Six
   (E)  More than six

**MANHATTAN**
PREP

16. During which decade was federal debt held by federal government accounts closest to half of all federal debt?

    (A) 1960s
    (B) 1970s
    (C) 1980s
    (D) 1990s
    (E) 2000s

17. At its highest point, what was the approximate ratio of federal debt held by the public to that held by federal government accounts?

    (A) 1:1
    (B) 2:1
    (C) 5:1
    (D) 8:1
    (E) 12:1

18. A number $x$ is 32% of a number $y$. If $y$ is 20% of $z$, what is $z$ in terms of $x$?

    (A) $0.064x$
    (B) $0.64x$
    (C) $6.4x$
    (D) $\dfrac{x}{0.064}$
    (E) $\dfrac{x}{0.64}$

19. If $S^2 > T^2$, which of the following must be true?

    (A) $S > T$
    (B) $S^2 > T$
    (C) $ST > 0$
    (D) $|S| > |T|$
    (E) $ST < 0$

20. In a certain nation, every citizen is assigned an identification number consisting of the last two digits of the person's birth year, followed by five other numerical digits. For instance, a person born in 1963 could have the identification number 6344409. How many identification numbers are possible for people born in the years 1980–1982, inclusive?

(A) 360
(B) 2,880
(C) 288,800
(D) 300,000
(E) 2,400,000

**MANHATTAN**
PREP

# Quantitative Diagnostic Test Scoring

| Question # | Your Answer | Correct Answer | Tally your correctly answered questions. *No partial credit!* | Find more questions like this in chapter: |
|---|---|---|---|---|
| 1 | | (C) | | 11 |
| 2 | | (A) | | 17 |
| 3 | | (D) | | 15 |
| 4 | | (A) | | 28 |
| 5 | | (B) | | 29 |
| 6 | | (B) | | 14 |
| 7 | | (D) | | 8 |
| 8 | | (B) | | 27 |
| 9 | | (B) | | 13 |
| 10 | | 7 | | 8 |
| 11 | | (B) | | 14 |
| 12 | | 4,800 | | 20 |
| 13 | | 917 | | 15 |
| 14 | | "*ac* is positive" only | | 15 |
| 15 | | (A) | | 24 |
| 16 | | (E) | | 24 |
| 17 | | (D) | | 24 |
| 18 | | (D) | | 12, 19 |
| 19 | | (D) | | 9, 15 |
| 20 | | (D) | | 23 |

**Raw Quantitative Score:**
(# of quant questions answered correctly)

# Quantitative Diagnostic Test: Scoring Guide

| Raw Quantitative Score | Quantitative Reasoning Diagnostic Scaled Score |
|:---:|:---:|
| 20 | 169–170 |
| 19 | 167–169 |
| 18 | 164–166 |
| 17 | 161–163 |
| 16 | 159–161 |
| 15 | 157–159 |
| 14 | 155–157 |
| 13 | 153–155 |
| 12 | 152–154 |
| 11 | 150–152 |
| 10 | 149–151 |
| 9 | 147–149 |
| 8 | 145–147 |
| 7 | 143–145 |
| 6 | 142–144 |
| 5 | 139–141 |
| 4 | 136–138 |
| 3 | 133–135 |
| 2 | 130–132 |
| 1 | 130–131 |
| 0 | 130 |

NOTES:

Diagnostic Scaled Score is approximate.

(a) If your time for this diagnostic section exceeded the 35-minute guideline, this approximate score may not be indicative of your performance under standard time conditions.

(b) Scaled Score depends not only on how many questions were answered correctly (Raw Score), but also on the overall difficulty of the set of questions. This diagnostic test approximates the difficulty of the official GRE® revised General Test.

**MANHATTAN**
PREP

# Math Diagnostic Test Answers

1. **(C).** In a repeating decimal, the portion under the bar repeats without end. In Quantity A, the portion "1410" repeats, after an initial 0.0 that does not repeat. In Quantity B, the portion "0141" repeats, starting immediately after the decimal. To compare, write out more digits of each decimal:

Quantity A:     0.0141014101410 …
Quantity B:     0.0141014101410 …

The two quantities are equal; Quantity A and Quantity B are just different ways of writing the same number.

2. **(A).** Because there are twice as many paperbacks as hardbacks in stock, the overall average price will be closer to the price of the paperbacks than the price of the hardbacks. However, the fact that the problem gives price *ranges* instead of prices complicates matters a bit. Calculate the lowest possible overall average and the highest possible overall average to see whether that average can be both lower and higher than $9.99.

To calculate the lowest possible overall average, assume the lowest price for all paperbacks and all hardbacks ($8 and $14, respectively). Note that there are twice as many paperbacks as hardbacks, which essentially double-weights the $8:

$$\frac{200(\$8)+100(\$14)}{200+100} = \frac{2(\$8)+1(\$14)}{3} = \frac{\$30}{3} = \$10$$

This minimum price is already greater than $9.99, so the maximum price would also be greater and there is no need to calculate it.

Quantity A is greater.

3. **(D).** Since $2 < x < 4$, test values between 2 and 4 in both quantities to see which quantity is larger for each example. On Quantitative Comparison questions, try to prove (D), or at least test whether it's possible.

If $x = 2.5$, Quantity A $= \frac{2.5-3}{-2.5} = \frac{-0.5}{-2.5} = \frac{5}{25} = \frac{1}{5}$ and Quantity B $= \frac{3-2.5}{-2.5} = \frac{0.5}{-2.5} = \frac{-5}{25} = \frac{-1}{5}$. In this case, Quantity A is greater.

Before just randomly trying other values between 2 and 4, try to strategize: is there an example in which Quantity B is greater? Since the two quantities have the same denominator, focus on the numerators. $x - 3$ is positive when $x > 3$ and negative when $x < 3$. Since the first number tested was less than 3, next try something greater than 3.

If $x = 3.5$, Quantity A $= \frac{3.5-3}{-3.5} = \frac{0.5}{-3.5} = \frac{-5}{35} = \frac{-1}{7}$ and Quantity B $= \frac{3-x}{-x} = \frac{3-3.5}{-3.5} = \frac{-0.5}{-3.5} = \frac{5}{35} = \frac{1}{7}$. In this case, Quantity B is greater. (Note: you could have stopped calculating the exact values of Quantity A and Quantity B for this example once it became clear that Quantity A was negative and Quantity B was positive.)

Alternatively, it would also be strategic to think about what number, if any, could make the two quantities equal. If $x = 3$, Quantity A = Quantity B = 0, because both numerators will be 0, and 0 divided by any non-zero number is just 0.

Since Quantity A is greater than Quantity B for some values of $x$ between 2 and 4, but Quantity B is greater than Quantity A for other values of $x$ between 2 and 4, the relationship cannot be determined from the information given.

4. **(A).** While there are no numbers on the graph, both lines have positive slopes (the lines rise upward when reading from left to right) and segment $AB$ is steeper than segment $AC$. Thus, segment $AB$ has a greater slope.

While you should be cautious about making assumptions on the GRE, the fact that the two lines form two sides of a triangle and meet at vertex $A$ shows that the lines are not parallel, and segment $AB$, which rises above segment $AC$ to the right of their meeting point, is definitely steeper.

5. **(B).** If the area of the square is 16, then the side of the square is 4. Since the circle is inscribed in the square, its diameter is 4 and its radius is 2. Since the area of a circle is $\pi r^2$, the area of this circle is $4\pi$. Thus, the combined area of the four "corners," outside the circle but inside the square, is $16 - 4\pi$. The shaded region is one of these four identical "corners," so the area of the shaded region is $\dfrac{16 - 4\pi}{4} = 4 - \pi \approx 4 - 3.14 = 0.86$, which is less than 1.

Quantity B is greater.

6. **(B).** Since both quantities have the same exponent as well as at least one $b$ inside the parentheses, one way to compare the quantities is to distribute that exponent:

   Quantity A:    $(5b)^a = 5^a b^a$

   Quantity B:    $(b^2)^a = (b \times b)^a = b^a b^a$

Because $b^a$ is positive (i.e., a positive base to a positive power) and common to both quantities, it can be ignored or canceled from both:

   Quantity A:    $5^a$

   Quantity B:    $b^a$

Because the positive exponent is common to both quantities, a larger positive base indicates the greater quantity. Because $b > 5$, Quantity B is greater.

7. **(D).** FOIL the terms in Quantity A:

   $(5 + a)(3 + a) = 15 + 5a + 3a + a^2 = a^2 + 8a + 15$

Since $a^2$ and 15 appear in both quantities, eliminate them:

   Quantity A:    $8a$

   Quantity B:    $2a$

**MANHATTAN**
PREP

If *a* is positive, Quantity A is greater. If *a* is negative, Quantity B is greater. If *a* is zero, the two quantities are equal. Without information about *a*, the relationship cannot be determined from the information given.

(Note also, because neither quantity is set equal to zero or any other number, it is impossible to actually "solve" either quantity to get roots or solutions for *a*.)

8. **(B).** Begin by drawing the triangle described by the text and labeling the sides:

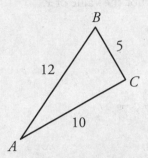

According to the properties of triangles, the longer the side opposite an angle, the larger the angle itself must be. Since angle *A* opens to the shortest side, length 5, but angle *C* opens to the longest side, length 12, it must be true that angle *C* is greater than angle *A*. Thus, Quantity B is greater.

9. **(B).** If $\dfrac{52}{x}$ is a positive integer, then *x* is a positive factor of 52 (i.e., *x* divides evenly into 52). This question can most easily be solved by listing positive factor pairs for 52, as listing in pairs will help prevent omissions. Each pair multiplies to 52.

The factors of 52 are:

    1 & 52
    2 & 26
    4 & 13

Check to make sure this list is complete. Looking down the left column, 1 and 2 made the list, then 3 didn't divide evenly into 52, then 4 did. Since 4 pairs with 13, check the other integers between 4 and 13. Since 5, 6, 7, 8, 9, 10, 11, and 12 don't divide evenly into 52, this list is complete. There are 6 factors, so the answer is (B).

10. **7.** Multiply each term of the second equation by 6: $12x - 6y = 66$. Why do this? Because the first equation has a $6y$, and the *y* terms will now cancel when the equations are added:

| | | |
|---|---|---|
| New second equation: | $12x - 6y$ | $= 66$ |
| + First equation: | $3x + 6y$ | $= 69$ |
| Sum: | $15x$ | $= 135$ |
| | $x$ | $= 9$ |

Plug $x = 9$ back into an original equation to get $y$:

$$2x - y = 11$$
$$2(9) - y = 11$$
$$18 - 11 = y$$
$$y = 7$$

In summary, $x = 9$ and $y = 7$. Be sure to use the value of $y$ to select your answer, and not the value of $x$.

11. **(B).** Factor $7^9$ out of $7^9 + 7^9 + 7^9 + 7^9 + 7^9 + 7^9 + 7^9$ to get:

$$7^9 (1 + 1 + 1 + 1 + 1 + 1 + 1) = 7^9 (7)$$

Or, just count that there are seven $7^9$'s in the original sum, which can be written as $7 \times 7^9$.

Since $7^9 (7)$ is the same as $7^9 (7^1)$, simplify further: $7^9 (7^1) = 7^{(9 + 1)} = 7^{10}$. Thus, $x = 10$.

Note: it is *not* correct to simply add the original exponents together. When adding or subtracting exponential expressions with the same base, it is not possible to directly combine exponents. Factoring out is the correct procedure.

12. **4,800.** If votes for candidate A and votes for candidate B were in a 4 to 3 ratio, then for every 4 votes candidate A got, candidate B got 3. You can think of these votes as existing in "sets" of 7 votes.

Divide 8,400 by 7 to get 1,200. Thus, the votes were cast in 1,200 "sets" of 7. In each "set," the votes went A A A A B B B (4 votes for A, 3 for B). Thus, the total number of votes for A is $1,200 \times 4 = 4,800$.

13. **917.** There must be a trick to this, as it would be impossible to sum so many numbers under GRE time constraints, even with a calculator. To see the trick, try an example with much smaller numbers. For instance, what is the sum of all the integers from $-2$ to 4, inclusive?

New example:    $\cancel{-2} + \cancel{-1} + \cancel{0} + \cancel{1} + \cancel{2} + 3 + 4 = 7$

That is, $-2$ and 2 cancel, $-1$ and 1 cancel, and 0 has no impact on the sum. So the sum is just the leftover numbers at the end, $3 + 4 = 7$.

Similarly, in the set $-457, -456 \ldots 0 \ldots 456, 457, 458, 459$, all the integers from $-457$ to 457 cancel each other out. Only 458 and 459 remain. The sum is $458 + 459 = 917$.

14. **"*ac* is positive" only.** Since $b^4$ must be positive, if $a^3 b^4 c^7$ is positive, $a^3 c^7$ must also be positive. Since putting an *odd* exponent on a number doesn't change whether the number is positive or negative, $ac$ must be positive, so the third statement is true. The other statements require knowledge of the sign of $b$, which is not known here, since the even exponent "hides" whether the underlying base is positive or negative.

15. **(A).** The chart expresses gross federal debt as a percent of gross domestic product, so federal debt exceeded gross domestic product in any year in which the value of the graph rose above 100. Only during three years in the 1940s does the graph extend above 100.

**MANHATTAN**
PREP

16. **(E).** Federal debt held by federal government accounts would be half of all federal debt in any year in which the dark, bottom portion of the bar equaled the lighter, top portion. Although it never actually reached 50% of the total federal debt, the dark portion of the bar came closest to equaling the light portion during the 2000s.

17. **(D).** The ratio of federal debt held by the public to that held by federal government accounts for any given year would be the measure of the lighter, top bar over the measure of the darker, bottom bar for that year. (To get the measure of the lighter, top bar, you must subtract the value of the darker, bottom bar.)

While the federal government accounts percent hovered near the low teens throughout most of the graph, debt held by the public rose above 100% during portions of the 1940s. Identify the year in which the lighter, top bar is the largest in comparison to the darker, lower portion. In this chart, it happens to be the tallest bar overall, which was 1946, although it's not necessary to identify the exact year:

> Total bar: 120 (actually a bit more)
> Dark, bottom bar: 15 (or a bit less)
> Light, top bar: 120 (or more) − 15 (or less) = 105 (or a bit more)

The ratio is thus 105 (slightly more) : 15 (maybe less), which is $7:1$ (or a bit higher). Among the given options, this ratio is closest to $8:1$.

18. **(D).** Translate the percent relations in the problem into algebraic statements. First, "a number $x$ is 32% of a number $y$" becomes:

> $x = 0.32y$

Similarly, "$y$ is 20% of $z$" becomes:

> $y = 0.2z$

Substituting for $y$ from the second equation into the first eliminates $y$ and gives the following relationship between $x$ and $z$:

> $x = 0.32(0.2z)$
> $x = 0.064z$

Finally, the problem asks for $z$ in terms of $x$, so isolate the variable $z$ by dividing both sides of the equation by 0.064:

> $z = \dfrac{x}{0.064}$

19. **(D).** The square root of a squared variable is equal to the absolute value of that variable: $\sqrt{x^2} = |x|$, not $x$. So, taking the square root of both sides of this inequality results in $|S| > |T|$. Answer choice (A) does not have to be true because $S$ could be negative while $T$ is positive. For example, if $S = -5$ and $T = 4$, then $S^2 > T^2$. Testing fractions in answer choice (B) shows that it does not have to be true. If $S^2 = \dfrac{1}{9}$ and $T^2 = \dfrac{1}{16}$, then $T = \dfrac{1}{4}$ or $-\dfrac{1}{4}$. $\dfrac{1}{4}$ is greater than $\dfrac{1}{9}$, which means that $T$ can be greater than $S^2$. Answer choice (C) does not have to be true because $S$ and $T$ could have opposite signs. Answer choice (E) does not have to be true because $S$ and $T$ could have the same sign.

20. **(D).** This is a combinatorics problem in which *order matters* (as it always does with passcodes, ID codes, etc.). Since the identification numbers each have 7 digits, draw 7 slots. In each slot, list the number of possibilities for that slot.

Since the question asks only about identification numbers for people born in 1980, 1981, and 1982, the identification numbers must begin with 80, 81, or 82. Thus, only 8 (1 option) can go in the first slot. Only 0, 1, or 2 (3 options) can go in the second slot:

$$\underline{\quad 1 \quad} \;\; \underline{\quad 3 \quad} \;\; \underline{\quad\quad} \;\; \underline{\quad\quad} \;\; \underline{\quad\quad} \;\; \underline{\quad\quad} \;\; \underline{\quad\quad}$$

Note that there is no rule against repeating a number in an identification number (the problem gives the example "a person born in 1963 could have the code 6344409"), so each remaining slot can each contain any of the digits 0–9 (10 options):

$$\underline{\quad 1 \quad} \;\; \underline{\quad 3 \quad} \;\; \underline{\quad 10 \quad} \;\; \underline{\quad 10 \quad} \;\; \underline{\quad 10 \quad} \;\; \underline{\quad 10 \quad} \;\; \underline{\quad 10 \quad}$$

This fundamental counting principle states that the total number of choices is equal to the product of the independent choices. To calculate the answer, multiply $1 \times 3 \times 10 \times 10 \times 10 \times 10 \times 10 = 300{,}000$.

Alternatively, note that for each birth year, the part of the identification number unique to the individual is a 5-digit number. These could be 00000–99999 (99,999 + 1 = 100,000 options). There are 100,000 possible numbers for each of 3 years, or 300,000 identification numbers possible.

**MANHATTAN**
PREP

# Chapter 3

## of

### 5 lb. Book of GRE® Practice Problems

# Text Completions

# In This Chapter...

# Text Completions

> **Select one entry for each blank from the corresponding column of choices. Fill in the blank in the way that best completes the text.**

1.  In Europe, football, otherwise known as soccer, is the most popular sport by several orders of magnitude, whereas in the United States of America, fandom is fairly evenly _____ among a few different sports.

    | |
    |---|
    | regarded |
    | inspired |
    | enjoyed |
    | measured |
    | apportioned |

2.  The astrophysicist argues that our books and films about interstellar space travel are a form of mass _____ , and that only a miracle on a scale heretofore unseen could allow a human being to voyage to even the closest star in another solar system.

    | |
    |---|
    | innovation |
    | delusion |
    | dementia |
    | catastrophe |
    | hysteria |

3.  Peculiarly enough, Shakespeare has been often (i) _____ as the best English language playwright, and often (ii) _____ as a man lacking the education to write those plays.

    | Blank (i) | Blank (ii) |
    |---|---|
    | crowned | demonized |
    | stigmatized | dismissed |
    | castigated | deified |

4.  While far from the bane that some scholars have declared them to be, (i) _____ versions of novels and essays do indeed excise essential elements; students would have to supplement their reading with (ii) _____ sources to fully understand the intent of the original.

    | Blank (i) | Blank (ii) |
    |---|---|
    | annotated | complementary |
    | abridged | complimentary |
    | antedated | compelling |

5.  Even the _____ and alluring charms of Paris were not sufficient to cure the young expatriate of his yearning for the simple and quaint charms of his rural American home.

| lascivious |
| --- |
| sophisticated |
| foreign |
| alien |
| alienating |

6.  The fact that the average life expectancy ten thousand years ago was so much shorter than it is now is often (i) _____ as evidence supporting the notion that the world always improves with time. However, if you (ii) _____ for the fact that most children in that epoch died in childbirth, life expectancy for those who survived birth was nearly the same then as it is now.

| Blank (i) | Blank (ii) |
| --- | --- |
| cited | prepare |
| disregarded | read |
| embodied | correct |

7.  On an aptitude test in 1986, an argument posited that the possibility of conducting banking transactions from home was as likely as flying cars, an argument that sounds _____ today, when such transactions are commonplace.

| prescient |
| --- |
| preternatural |
| preordained |
| preposterous |
| pithy |

8.  The widespread tendency to _____ retired political leaders who were successful stems from an arguably primal human need to venerate both men and gods.

| castigate |
| --- |
| remember |
| lionize |
| appreciate |
| indemnify |

9.   Academic work can be as taxing as manual labor. The misconception that (i) _____ work strains the mind less than physical work strains the body has been proven wrong by scientific investigation as well as by anecdotal evidence. It is simply not true that the (ii) _____ musings of a mathematician are necessarily easier than the physical labor of, say, a carpenter.

| Blank (i) | Blank (ii) |
| --- | --- |
| cerebral | quotidian |
| intense | extraordinary |
| actuarial | intellectual |

10.  Known for her humorous but acerbic wit, the fashion doyenne commented, in her usual, simultaneously (i) _____ and (ii) _____ manner, that in Los Angeles, "the women dressed like men and the men dressed like boys."

| Blank (i) | Blank (ii) |
| --- | --- |
| slanderous | considerate |
| amusing | hysterical |
| serious | caustic |

11.  Every generation is accused of slacking by the preceding ones, before in turn calling its own progeny lackadaisical; such is the _____ of life.

| |
| --- |
| vicissitude |
| irony |
| circle |
| serendipity |
| comedy |

12.  Although retired, the professor takes pains to remain _____ the latest developments in her field.

| |
| --- |
| akimbo to |
| abreast of |
| obtuse to |
| subservient to |
| askance to |

13.  She was not the only (i) _____ of the long-proposed legislation, but she was the (ii) _____ who finally got the bill onto the legislative agenda.

| Blank (i) | Blank (ii) |
| --- | --- |
| apologist | catalyst |
| critic | mercenary |
| proponent | lackey |

14. Jeremy was not one to (i) _____ his success, let alone talk much at all, so his family was shocked when they finally discovered that their (ii) _____ son was a Rhodes Scholar.

| Blank (i) | Blank (ii) |
|---|---|
| demarcate | improvident |
| whitewash | taciturn |
| trumpet | dissolute |

15. In his youth, Oscar Wilde catapulted to sudden fame both because of and despite his (i)_____ witticisms; however, the cutting remarks that won him renown also led to his financial and physical ruin, and he died (ii)_____ and sickly in a shabby Parisian hotel.

| Blank (i) | Blank (ii) |
|---|---|
| innovative | pallid |
| acerbic | aghast |
| inimical | impecunious |

16. Hursthouse, (i) _____ virtue ethicists in general, argues that ethics is properly neither situational nor utilitarian and that one ought to seek out virtue and emulate it rather than base one's judgments on subjective concerns or a (ii) _____ weighing of pain and pleasure likely to result from a given action; critics, of course, tend to (iii) _____ that Hursthouse and other virtue ethicists who seek to define virtue merely seek to enshrine their own prejudices under the guise of theory.

| Blank (i) | Blank (ii) | Blank (iii) |
|---|---|---|
| enigmatic to | pragmatic | posit |
| breaking away from | quixotic | deny |
| emblematic of | grandiloquent | cajole |

17. The film was (i) _____ (ii) _____ by critics; rightfully, not a single reviewer had any positive thing to say about it.

| Blank (i) | Blank (ii) |
|---|---|
| warily | lauded |
| mendaciously | panned |
| roundly | venerated |

18. The distinction between architecture and the engineering professions that it resembles is that the former must consider (i) _____ as well as functionality, as clients often base their decisions more on the beauty of the project than its practicality.

| |
|---|
| insouciance |
| utility |
| price |
| aesthetics |
| profundity |

19. Once considered able to only _____ emulate actions without understanding the action's deeper significance, bearded dragons have recently been observed copying non-instinctive actions of other bearded dragons, prompting scientists to question whether other reptiles might also be capable of genuine imitation.

| |
|---|
| attentively |
| insensibly |
| listlessly |
| actively |
| consciously |

20. December's earthquake was but a _____ to a terrible year for a small island nation recently wracked by civil strife and devastating tropical storms.

| |
|---|
| prologue |
| catharsis |
| coda |
| homily |
| rampage |

21. Although they had never met, the two writers felt they were of one mind, each (i) _____ anticipating the contents of the other's letters; never had two intellectuals been more (ii) _____.

| Blank (i) | Blank (ii) |
|---|---|
| ominously | providential |
| anachronistically | shrewd |
| presciently | simpatico |

22. After many years of war and bloodshed, some became _____ suffering, casting a blind eye to scenes of misery around them.

| inured to |
|---|
| exempted from |
| dominant over |
| effusive towards |
| maudlin over |

23. After a brief initial struggle over power, the group elected a leader and _____ into a surprisingly harmonious team.

| fractured |
|---|
| syncopated |
| coalesced |
| agglomerated |
| amortized |

24. The highly anticipated finale of the TV series was divisive: newcomers to the show found the fast-paced action enjoyable while long-time fans _____ the storyline unfinished.

| appreciated |
|---|
| generated |
| examined |
| considered |
| secured |

25. The author was far from (i) _____ the novel. While most of the book was already written, he knew that it would take innumerable hours to review and edit. This was going to be (ii) _____, not only because of the book's length, but also because of the convoluted plot.

| Blank (i) | Blank (ii) |
|---|---|
| finishing | hardy |
| inscribing | trying |
| rejecting | redundant |

**MANHATTAN PREP**

26.  During his sales pitch, the car salesman attempted to _____ the young couple into purchasing the luxury automobile, despite the pair's obvious indifference to his flattery.

| support |
| --- |
| inveigle |
| deliberate |
| marginalize |
| hector |

27.  Just as reminiscences of a childhood spent in rural Mexico color the poet's work, so too does the experience of war _____ her poetry.

| inform |
| --- |
| mimic |
| invalidate |
| defer |
| presage |

28.  The peanut is often (i) _____ referred to as a nut; (ii) _____ to such people, it is actually a legume.

| Blank (i) | Blank (ii) |
| --- | --- |
| archaically | unbeknownst |
| erroneously | abhorrent |
| deftly | consanguineous |

29.  The (i) _____ child approached the diving board; (ii) _____ water in the first place, he found the prospect of jumping into it from some height even more frightening.

| Blank (i) | Blank (ii) |
| --- | --- |
| tremulous | beguiled by |
| coltish | chary of |
| cumbersome | repulsed by |

30.  Soldier ants are wingless, sterile females that guard the colony and supply it with food, thus acting as both (i) _____ and laborers as the (ii) _____ queen produces enough (iii) _____ to continually populate the colony.

| Blank (i) | Blank (ii) | Blank (iii) |
| --- | --- | --- |
| sentries | fecund | forebears |
| sages | efficacious | progeny |
| sycophants | imperious | harbingers |

31. The Paris Commune was a government that ruled France for about two months in 1871; despite its (i) _____ reign, it was at the time (ii) _____ as a sign of the emergence of a powerful working class.

| Blank (i) | Blank (ii) |
|-----------|------------|
| equivocal | discounted |
| ephemeral | recanted |
| omnipotent | heralded |

32. While taller wind turbines would allow more areas of the country to provide cost-effective alternative energy, there are several (i) _____ that engineers are currently facing while trying to build such turbines. Taller towers necessitate (ii) _____ bases, requiring the current width to be nearly doubled. This leads to (iii) _____ issue: these wider sections would be too large to travel on modern highways, meaning that the taller turbines would need to be constructed at the location where they are to eventually stand.

| Blank (i) | Blank (ii) | Blank (iii) |
|-----------|------------|-------------|
| flaws | equitable | a concomitant |
| supplements | unobtrusive | a theoretical |
| complications | stouter | an objective |

33. During the prolonged and elaborate farewell tour, no one thought the plaudits heaped upon him were _____ , since his heroics were well documented and admired by all.

| |
|---|
| obsequious |
| derivative |
| deserved |
| vestigial |
| antiquated |

34. He has such a pleasingly (i) _____ personality that it's hard to be bothered by the (ii) _____ in his past.

| Blank (i) | Blank (ii) |
|-----------|------------|
| sanguine | peccadilloes |
| high-handed | incendiaries |
| evanescent | achievements |

**MANHATTAN PREP**

35. The Tasmanian devil is not considered (i) _____, since only a few of its confrontations with humans have been (ii) _____.

| Blank (i) | Blank (ii) |
|---|---|
| adverse | premature |
| menacing | quixotic |
| unpredictable | unprovoked |

36. The (i) _____ young employee was soon (ii) _____ for making a serious mistake that cost the company thousands of dollars.

| Blank (i) | Blank (ii) |
|---|---|
| banal | enamored |
| sagacious | castigated |
| verdant | deposed |

37. The beauty pageant contestant told the judges she wanted world peace, but her suggestion to bring about world peace was _____—apparently, she naïvely thinks everyone could just be told to "love one another" and all the world's disagreements would fade away.

| |
|---|
| convoluted |
| facile |
| impeccable |
| amicable |
| dulcet |

38. In front of her parents, adults euphemistically referred to the overly talkative young girl as precocious, though they privately found her to be _____.

| |
|---|
| garrulous |
| skittish |
| solicitous |
| endearing |
| naïve |

39. While the author's first collection of short stories presented a (i) _____ hodgepodge of voices, the second collection presents a remarkably (ii) _____ set of tales presented by a (iii) _____ narrator.

| Blank (i) | Blank (ii) | Blank (iii) |
|---|---|---|
| motley | insightful | lonely |
| variable | even | disingenuous |
| homogeneous | facetious | sole |

40. In contrast to environmental economics, an older field that concerns itself with the monetary valuation of natural resources, the emergent field of ecological economics positions the human economy as a subsystem of natural ecologies, thus _____ environmental economists' subordination of the natural world.

| |
|---|
| circumscribing |
| corroborating |
| refuting |
| ameliorating |
| reversing |

41. Today's highly partisan political environment is far from _____; not so long ago, ideological opponents were still able to set aside differences and work across party lines, as is typically necessary to pass productive legislation.

| |
|---|
| civil |
| immutable |
| polemical |
| efficacious |
| enjoyable |

42. The virtual (i) _____ of John F. Kennedy focuses on his presidential achievements, legend, and assassination; similarly, during his candidacy, verbal and written (ii) _____ were laid at the altar of his wartime exploits.

| Blank (i) | Blank (ii) |
|---|---|
| deification | calumnies |
| excoriation | garlands |
| praise | obloquies |

43. For centuries, commercial portrait painters have employed a bifurcated aesthetic: like other artists, they strive to represent the truth that gives their works life, but commerce dictates that they simultaneously employ subtle _____ that make the likeness more attractive than the sitter.

| |
|---|
| palettes |
| aesthetics |
| artifacts |
| artifices |
| sentiments |

**MANHATTAN**
PREP

44. Dogmatic professors often alienate their classes because they fail to realize that their _____ enervates rather than inspires students.

| |
|---|
| wisdom |
| pedantry |
| parsimony |
| pulchritude |
| wit |

45. General McClellan focused so intently on the petty, logistical details of the upcoming campaign that Lincoln felt that said attention to _____ , however necessary, had superseded more lofty goals.

| |
|---|
| irrelevancies |
| tactics |
| minutiae |
| strategy |
| peccadilloes |

46. Jimmy Stewart, the actor, spoke with an (i) _____ that (ii) _____ audiences; through hesitancy and understatement, he was at least as captivating as his flamboyant peers.

| Blank (i) | Blank (ii) |
|---|---|
| awkward lisp | enthralled |
| overwhelming passion | repelled |
| appealing shyness | amused |

47. Given the (i) _____ of the book, the critical reception was surprisingly (ii) _____ ; reviewers who usually pounce on the slightest orthodoxy met the text with unabashed approbation.

| Blank (i) | Blank (ii) |
|---|---|
| ingenuity | tepid |
| tortuousness | laudatory |
| conventionality | deprecating |

48. Ironically, the commentator who so roundly condemned personal (i) _____ was (ii) _____ to the point of bankruptcy—he himself was a reflection of an aspect of the ills that, in other areas, he railed against.

| Blank (i) | Blank (ii) |
|---|---|
| indolence | profligate |
| probity | antediluvian |
| dissipation | ascetic |

49. For all the student's meticulous preparation, he received _____ grade on his final exam.

| a passable |
|---|
| a deplorable |
| an exacting |
| a surprising |
| an outstanding |

50. Just as ancient Greek culture in some ways provided the Romans with a model, the remnants of Roman culture _____ the development of medieval European mores.

| duplicated |
|---|
| curbed |
| foresaw |
| informed |
| hindered |

51. As an evolutionary adaptation, cats have developed a mechanism whereby their heads are measuring devices, as their bodies can fit through any space that their heads can, and this physiology is a safeguard that _____ their success as a species.

| reproduces |
|---|
| ensures |
| enhances |
| mitigates |
| inundates |

52. Far from the (i) _____ novice that he made himself out to be, the new teacher was in fact quite (ii) _____: within a week of arrival, he understood the school's byzantine power structures and was using the dysfunctional administration to his advantage.

| Blank (i) | Blank (ii) |
|---|---|
| cunning | canny |
| guileless | unseemly |
| capricious | desultory |

53. Since there are significant (i) _____ in the flawed methodologies of the studies upon which it is based, the meta-analysis is anything but (ii) _____.

| Blank (i) | Blank (ii) |
|---|---|
| irregularities | unreliable |
| subtleties | intelligible |
| consistencies | credible |

**MANHATTAN**
PREP

54. Crane Brinton argued that the middle phases of revolutions are especially (i) _____ because the unleashed force of social momentum transfers power inexorably from more stable (if oppressive) forces to less temperate ones. Yet, he then goes on to say that the excesses (ii) _____ and a more peaceful period ensues.

| Blank (i) | Blank (ii) |
|-----------|------------|
| brusque | metastasize |
| berserk | grow |
| pacific | recede |

55. The Donner party made a _____ choice to try to cross the Sierra Nevada too late in the season, and they paid dearly for that dangerous decision.

| |
|---|
| prudent |
| parlous |
| suicidal |
| semiotic |
| providential |

56. The engineer is not interested in developing products to meet market needs; her work is known for its technical brilliance much more than for its _____ potential.

| |
|---|
| scientific |
| ergonomic |
| commercial |
| academic |
| revolutionary |

57. Frederick the Great of Prussia was known for his (i) _____ under fire during his military victories; however, when confronting issues of domestic policy, this equilibrium sometimes failed him. He was often (ii) _____ with his ministers, who never knew when they might be subjected to one of his tirades.

| Blank (i) | Blank (ii) |
|-----------|------------|
| intrepidity | fascist |
| cruelty | mercurial |
| sangfroid | vainglorious |

58. In her opening remarks, the school's director empathized with the apparent (i) _____ of taking disciplinary action in the classroom; on the one hand, teachers can ill-afford to (ii) _____ indisputably disruptive behaviors, while on the other, overly strict administration can actually foster such behaviors.

| Blank (i) | Blank (ii) |
| --- | --- |
| necessity | fabricate |
| entreaty | brook |
| paradox | mitigate |

59. The library wing was first conceived merely as (i) _____ to address the problem of book overstock until a more permanent solution could be found. Ironically, it was the flimsy nature of the wing itself that attracted such architectural interest and ultimately led to its canonization as a (ii) _____ of its kind. Now a statute exists to protect this originally transient structure in (iii) _____ .

| Blank (i) | Blank (ii) | Blank (iii) |
| --- | --- | --- |
| a stopgap | paragon | consecration |
| an ornament | nadir | chronology |
| a modicum | catalyst | perpetuity |

60. Though the negotiation was initially expected to proceed smoothly, it soon became apparent that any semblance of (i) _____ between the parties was disingenuous or, at best, a superficial adherence to certain (ii) _____ .

| Blank (i) | Blank (ii) |
| --- | --- |
| duplicity | mores |
| amity | truisms |
| solace | plaudits |

61. Unable to eschew her well-known tendency toward (i) _____, the speaker effectively turned a five-minute policy brief into an hour-long (ii) _____ on the history of the region.

| Blank (i) | Blank (ii) |
| --- | --- |
| terseness | distension |
| precision | expatiation |
| elaboration | repertory |

62. The senator's _____ upbringing seemingly had no effect on his policy: he vociferously championed economic, political, and even cultural isolationism.

| cosmopolitan |
| bucolic |
| liberal |
| tendentious |
| opulent |

63. The plan, if it can be called that, has been more of (i) _____ vision than a concrete proposal; like many similarly (ii) _____ ideas, it is unlikely to ever come to fruition.

| Blank (i) | Blank (ii) |
| --- | --- |
| an oppositional | quixotic |
| a protean | pragmatic |
| a martial | unorthodox |

64. It was a fact that the region was both quiet and rural, but what the typically impoverished residents considered (i) _____ refuge was considered by the well-heeled visitors to be an intolerable (ii) _____ , and its residents' lifestyles unpleasantly (iii) _____ .

| Blank (i) | Blank (ii) | Blank (iii) |
| --- | --- | --- |
| a parochial | asylum | tony |
| an arcadian | utopia | spartan |
| a squalid | hinterland | rational |

65. Though many readers assumed that the (i) _____ depicted in her stories reflected the author's own lifestyle, in reality she was more prudish than (ii) _____ .

| Blank (i) | Blank (ii) |
| --- | --- |
| dissent | licentious |
| propriety | moralizing |
| debauchery | perspicacious |

66.  The club had been all male up until 1963, when it began to admit women, who now make up more of
     the membership; hence, the female club president was both annoyed and amused at an elderly male
     member's (i) _____ suggestion that women be shuffled off to (ii) _____ organization where they
     could play bridge and drink tea without having to worry about serious issues.

| Blank (i) | Blank (ii) |
|-----------|------------|
| regressive | an incendiary |
| rustic | an auxiliary |
| prudish | a hierarchical |

67.  Although this historical figure had been (i) _____ politician and a brilliant inventor, the professor
     found herself unable to (ii) _____ the interest of her students in the career of a man with such
     outdated views.

| Blank (i) | Blank (ii) |
|-----------|------------|
| an insipid | whet |
| a deft | accrue |
| an effete | tout |

68.  The comedian's _____ wit has long been the cause of the polarized sentiments she evokes in her
     audience; some adore her caustic sense of humor, while others abhor it.

| |
|---|
| ample |
| acerbic |
| anachronistic |
| abstruse |
| astounding |

69.  Contrary to the assumptions that many Westerners hold about mindfulness practices, meditation is often
     anything but _____; while using various methods to calm the mind, meditators frequently experience
     intense periods of restlessness and doubt.

| |
|---|
| beneficial |
| mystical |
| orthodox |
| benign |
| halcyon |

**MANHATTAN**
PREP

70. Faced with _____ job market, many young people are returning to graduate school rather than attempting to compete for the few available jobs.

| a myopic |
|---|
| an anemic |
| a botched |
| a booming |
| an educated |

71. Despite his longtime advocacy for campaign finance reform, the career politician was, in fact, far more (i) _____ corporate interests than his rival, whose relatively recent entry into the political arena meant that he had far fewer (ii) _____ to make good on.

| Blank (i) | Blank (ii) |
|---|---|
| leery of | affiliations |
| beholden to | dilemmas |
| apathetic about | obligations |

72. Far too (i) _____ to consider a career in the political limelight, the unassuming aide contented herself with a career behind the scenes, (ii) _____ supporting the political heavyweights of her day.

| Blank (i) | Blank (ii) |
|---|---|
| diffident | implicitly |
| apathetic | quietly |
| ideological | skeptically |

73. There are many good reasons to construct urban traffic lanes for cyclists: city infrastructure is already _____ under the strain of excess auto traffic, and the safety advantages of limiting road-sharing between cyclists and vehicles are all too clear.

| seething |
|---|
| waiting |
| groaning |
| baying |
| intensifying |

74. Though the professor had made her (i) _____ tendencies clear to the hiring committee, the extent and consistency of her (ii) _____ was still a surprise to many who had voted to approve her hiring: she persistently challenged the academic methods and the institutional procedures of her department and of the university as a whole, going so far as to advocate for the (iii) _____ of "inherently elitist" institutions of higher education in the name of democratizing education.

| Blank (i) | Blank (ii) | Blank (iii) |
|-----------|------------|-------------|
| intellectual | iconoclasm | abolition |
| illiberal | theories | enshrinement |
| heterodox | intelligence | mitigation |

75. The apparent simplicity of a cup of coffee _____ the dizzying number of hours of toil required to produce it, from months of cultivation of the bean tree to painstaking refinement in highly sophisticated machinery.

| |
|---|
| redresses |
| confirms |
| belies |
| furnishes |
| fosters |

76. Notwithstanding the mishmash of worn tools littering every surface of the artist's studio, the place exuded a certain sense of order manifest through the clutter; the décor was, if (i) _____ , (ii) _____ .

| Blank (i) | Blank (ii) |
|-----------|------------|
| unkempt | largely unsophisticated |
| dire | positively callous |
| arduous | surprisingly deliberate |

77. Two years after the legislature's (i) _____ approval of the community arts center, construction came to an equally public standstill, largely due to the unforeseen hemorrhaging of the (ii) _____ funds at the hands of spendthrift leaders.

| Blank (i) | Blank (ii) |
|-----------|------------|
| scorned | stolen |
| heralded | exacerbated |
| ratified | appropriated |

**MANHATTAN**
PREP

78. Incensed, and perhaps spooked, by the implications of the bureau's purportedly (i) _____ inquisitions, the Hollywood film director shuttered his studios, suspended production of numerous projects, and (ii) _____ with his wife to Europe.

| Blank (i) | Blank (ii) |
|-----------|------------|
| suspicious | immigrated |
| benign | decamped |
| risqué | pandered |

79. The relationship between the two leaders has gone from positively (i) _____ to chilly at best, not least because the recent arms scandal threatens to (ii) _____ the mutual trust that has been held on both sides for years.

| Blank (i) | Blank (ii) |
|-----------|------------|
| peaceful | bolster |
| reverent | erode |
| congenial | fester |

80. It is in no way shocking that scientific experiments sometimes lead to _____; however, in order for results to be deemed valid, peer review studies must consistently duplicate the normal pattern of the original study.

| |
|---|
| anxiety |
| malfunctions |
| anomalies |
| vaccines |
| paradigms |

81. Debates over free will have always focused on the extent to which humans may be said to be fully (i) _____ their actions. Dr. Wegner in his article deliberately and artfully (ii) _____ the traditional talking points of the controversy, instead asking a tangential, though possibly more (iii) _____, question: What effect does a person's belief in free will have on his or her well-being?

| Blank (i) | Blank (ii) | Blank (iii) |
|-----------|------------|-------------|
| responsible for | mitigates | fundamental |
| determined by | eschews | ideological |
| based on | contradicts | flashy |

82. Once the candidate established herself as the clear front-runner, it took but a brief interlude in the clamor for all her erstwhile (i) _____ to gather around her and to begin loudly proclaiming their (ii) _____ . It seemed, in other words, to cause these newcomers not an iota of discomfort to behave in a manner that a casual observer might have characterized as (iii) _____ outright hypocrisy.

| Blank (i) | Blank (ii) | Blank (iii) |
|-----------|------------|-------------|
| supporters | distaste | tantamount to |
| detractors | magnanimity | reciprocal with |
| zealots | fealty | hinging on |

83. Some substances toxic to humans induce lassitude and torpor, whereas others incite (i) _____ or (ii) _____ .

| Blank (i) | Blank (ii) |
|-----------|------------|
| convulsions | complaints |
| quarrels | retching |
| apathy | drowsiness |

84. Commentators and comedians had a field day with the widespread corruption in politics, so much so that one _____ defined a "gaffe" as a politician accidentally telling the truth.

| |
|---|
| wag |
| apologist |
| diplomat |
| egoist |
| transgressor |

85. Economists describe the low rate of growth in wages since the 2007 financial crisis as (i) _____ . Many cite examples of (ii) _____ , thus causing a corresponding decline in lifestyles. Unless this unfortunate trend is reversed, often blameless middle-class families will be (iii) _____ to years of poverty and deprivation.

| Blank (i) | Blank (ii) | Blank (iii) |
|-----------|------------|-------------|
| pathetic | real buoyancy | uplifted |
| promising | actual decreases | devoted |
| partisan | medical bills | sentenced |

**MANHATTAN**
PREP

86. Like Evelyn Waugh, Martin Amis infuses his prose with his own (i) _____ wit. His satiric novels are honeycombed with cutting jibes honed to razor sharpness, and consequently even his scenes chronicling grotesque tragedies often bring a (ii) _____ smile to the reader's lips.

| Blank (i) | Blank (ii) |
|---|---|
| sartorial | disapproving |
| scintillating | discreet |
| feckless | wry |

87. Ms. Llewellyn is known to gently _____ students who don't do their homework, but because of her generally amiable demeanor, she refuses to punish anyone, and seldom even raises her voice.

| |
|---|
| pillory |
| detest |
| malign |
| penalize |
| chide |

88. For eons, _____ was considered not only polite, but virtuous; now, fashionable behavior lauds laxity and tardiness, and arriving at a function an hour late is considered appropriate.

| |
|---|
| probity |
| parsimoniousness |
| prodigality |
| punctiliousness |
| panache |

89. The danger of giving too many long and bombastic speeches while on the campaign trail is that a politician can come off as _____ rather than eloquent.

| |
|---|
| unscrupulous |
| voluble |
| frank |
| hostile |
| languid |

90. It is strange to think that for the majority of the 1950s, the _____ of nuclear holocaust was a daily part of people's lives, so much so that elementary school students ran drills in which they had to dive under their desks and curl up into a ball.

| |
|---|
| specter |
| annihilation |
| brutality |
| detonation |
| arms race |

91. As opposed to the hedonism and (i) _____ of his undergraduate years, during his doctoral program Boehm became a model of (ii) _____, and his earnest devotion led to academic laurels.

| Blank (i) | Blank (ii) |
|---|---|
| apathy | diligence |
| studiousness | morality |
| duplicity | detachment |

92. The actress was desperate to (i) _____ the part in the new Michel Gondry film. It was (ii) _____ role, with lots of onscreen time and a number of long scenes that would allow the actress, usually cast as a vapid ingénue or bombshell, to truly show her dramatic range.

| Blank (i) | Blank (ii) |
|---|---|
| land | a grave |
| ascertain | a plum |
| ensure | a theatrical |

93. Nora Ephron's 1989 film, *When Harry Met Sally*, was more than a hit movie—for a generation, it was a cultural _____ regarding the often fraught relations between men and women.

| |
|---|
| rudder |
| bolster |
| touchstone |
| stanchion |
| cornerstone |

94. The professor explains the Efficient Market Hypothesis with _____ uncommon among business finance faculty: she is not fully convinced of the validity of the theory.

| an enthusiasm |
|---|
| a degree of humility |
| a thoroughness |
| a level of skepticism |
| an eloquence |

95. Some have argued that people who work in the service industry experience subtle psychological damage each time they (i) _____ their true emotions in order to put on a smile for the customer. Unfortunately, such efforts are (ii) _____ of the job, as no one wants to be served by a weepy waiter or an irate flight attendant.

| Blank (i) | Blank (ii) |
|---|---|
| masquerade | the apex |
| simulate | the conceit |
| mask | part and parcel |

96. In an age of near-instantaneous fact checking, political candidates must be careful of making spontaneous statements intended to appease a crowd, as any fictitious claim will inevitably be found to be _____.

| dull |
|---|
| bogus |
| genuine |
| unnecessary |
| unfamiliar |

97. His grandmother's house was always a bedlam of porcelain figurines, collector's spoons, and other (i) _____ doodads. But it hardly would have been (ii) _____ to tell her that he thought her choice of décor was vulgar; in fact, he had to think (iii) _____, because the avaricious youth was gunning for a big birthday present from her.

| Blank (i) | Blank (ii) | Blank (iii) |
|---|---|---|
| tacky | discerning | amicably |
| vitreous | rancorous | tactically |
| grizzled | doting | duplicitously |

98. The captain (i) _____ (ii) _____ for as long as he could, but eventually the crew became frustrated with the small portions of mead and the dearth of plunder, and decided to take matters into their own hands.

| Blank (i) | Blank (ii) |
|-----------|------------|
| dissuaded | sea change |
| warded off | mutiny |
| depreciated | helmsmanship |

99. Of course, we would all like to believe that our every success is of our own manufacture, but to believe that is to neglect the (i) _____ element present in all lives, beginning with a birth lottery that assigns to some such gifts as intelligence and to others such (ii) _____ as wealth.

| Blank (i) | Blank (ii) |
|-----------|------------|
| common | encumbrances |
| inchoate | dispensations |
| serendipitous | piques |

100. The eyes of the mantis shrimp have more types of photoreceptors, or color-detecting cells, than those of any other animal on the planet. While one would think that this would allow the mantis shrimp to better (i) _____ colors, researchers have found this to be (ii) _____.

| Blank (i) | Blank (ii) |
|-----------|------------|
| improve | baseless |
| discriminate | obvious |
| distort | illiberal |

101. Jackson's supporters praised his earthy speech as evidence of his common touch, while his (i) _____ condemned it as (ii) _____.

| Blank (i) | Blank (ii) |
|-----------|------------|
| interlocutors | vulgar |
| detractors | obtuse |
| contemporaries | genteel |

102. Economists have developed such sophisticated and (i) _____ mathematical tools for modeling human behavior that other social scientists often employ those tools to model and help (ii) _____ even decisions that have no obvious economic consequences.

| Blank (i) | Blank (ii) |
|-----------|------------|
| eclectic | interpolate |
| populist | extrapolate |
| versatile | explicate |

**MANHATTAN**
PREP

103. Patients who stop taking antibiotics when symptoms subside contribute to the evolution of drug-resistant strains, because an incomplete course of treatment spares the most _____ bacteria.

| widespread |
| immature |
| robust |
| benign |
| notorious |

104. Children who are recognized as preternaturally intelligent often go on to fulfill their early promise, contrary to the stereotype of maladjusted _____ wasting their gifts.

| prodigies |
| teenagers |
| cranks |
| theorizers |
| pragmatists |

105. Freud's structural model of the psyche should be understood as (i) _____ device, useful for inciting and guiding discovery, rather than as an attempt to (ii) _____ physical relationships among parts of the human brain.

| Blank (i) | Blank (ii) |
| --- | --- |
| a heuristic | dictate |
| a literary | ameliorate |
| an allegorical | represent |

106. The silent-film pioneer Harold Lloyd made a virtue of the (i) _____ limits of his day, playing men so (ii) _____ it was easy to imagine it was the character rather than the medium who lacked a voice.

| Blank (i) | Blank (ii) |
| --- | --- |
| artistic | avant-garde |
| commercial | diffident |
| technical | reluctant |

107. When first introduced by senior management, the new boss was viewed as a figurehead at best, but after months of watching him shake up the office hierarchy and double productivity, even the most _____ of his employees was astonished at what he was able to accomplish.

| |
|---|
| scrutinized |
| clueless |
| skeptical |
| senior |
| resolute |

108. Critics of media consolidation say that it has resulted in both a (i) _____ of unique viewpoints and a lack of local news coverage: conglomerates will often discuss the same issues and talking points across all platforms, while (ii) _____ events are no longer covered by smaller media organizations that can't afford to (iii) _____ enough full-time reporters.

| Blank (i) | Blank (ii) | Blank (iii) |
|---|---|---|
| banality | elaborate | staff |
| deviation | domestic | imply |
| scarcity | regional | broadcast |

109. Just as Philip K. Dick's acclaimed science fiction shows his gift for dystopian fantasy, so too his early efforts at mainstream novels (i) _____ his ability to represent the more (ii) _____ world.

| Blank (i) | Blank (ii) |
|---|---|
| attest to | ebullient |
| belie | quotidian |
| gainsay | fantastical |

110. The independent audit showed that the company was not _____, let alone flourishing, as its initial report to its stockholders tried to aver.

| |
|---|
| copious |
| evasive |
| thriving |
| unprecedented |
| solvent |

**MANHATTAN**
PREP

111. A business that, when it receives a requisite amount of regulatory pressure, (i) _____ its own non-compliance with industry safety standards with yet another series of suspect omissions, is of the most highly (ii) _____ variety.

| Blank (i) | Blank (ii) |
|---|---|
| imbues | laudable |
| verifies | contrived |
| supplants | contemptible |

112. Unfortunately for the young hire, the amiable, gregarious air of his boss during the initial interview belied a vastly more _____ style on the job, a fact that he learned to his chagrin within the first few days of employment.

| draconian |
|---|
| friendly |
| fatuous |
| illicit |
| nonplussed |

113. (i) _____ comprehension of the character of Italian wine is impeded not only by labyrinthine complexities of vineyards and varietals, but also by fluctuations in environmental conditions from year to year, which render even the most reliable vintages subject to (ii) _____.

| Blank (i) | Blank (ii) |
|---|---|
| An exhaustive | efficient taxonomy |
| A futile | remarkable variance |
| An irredeemable | mitigating circumstances |

114. Added to the (i) _____ with which the clerk seems to treat his clients is what appears to be a more general lack of respect for his office; he seems to treat the whole thing as if it were some grand (ii) _____.

| Blank (i) | Blank (ii) |
|---|---|
| casual nonchalance | gesture |
| profound meticulousness | farce |
| idle envy | tirade |

115. According to critics, the novelist's latest effort, with its dry pedantry and humorless presentation, managed to make a seemingly (i) _____ subject matter into (ii) _____ collection of poorly constructed sentences.

| Blank (i) | Blank (ii) |
| --- | --- |
| engaging | a worthy |
| affectless | a tired |
| dogmatic | an instructive |

116. The more deeply one delves into the relevant literature, the more apparent it becomes that psychoanalysis is a practice (i) _____ . Even tenets that some might deem (ii) _____ to the general philosophy, such as the notion that the human psyche is primarily governed by conflicting desires and is formed in large part by early childhood experiences, are by no means accepted as gospel, even by some of its most (iii) _____ .

| Blank (i) | Blank (ii) | Blank (iii) |
| --- | --- | --- |
| teeming with ridicule | critical | esteemed beneficiaries |
| devoid of substance | immaterial | quarrelsome factions |
| rife with contention | anathema | seasoned practitioners |

117. The pair's apparent antagonism could easily be written off as (i) _____ pure and simple, but further scrutiny should render (ii) _____ the fact that the rivalry also confers a fair amount of (iii) _____, insofar as it provides each an opportunity to derive inspiration and motivation from the other.

| Blank (i) | Blank (ii) | Blank (iii) |
| --- | --- | --- |
| hypocrisy | useless | worthless pride |
| antipathy | patent | mutual benefit |
| flagrancy | spurious | tacit disagreement |

118. In this day and age, side show barkers, competing with the unfathomable number of spectacular oddities daily displayed on the internet for free, must increasingly lard their pitches with flights of fancy and soaring _____ , arching far beyond reality, to fill the seats in their arcades.

| |
| --- |
| tit-for-tat |
| parables |
| conundrums |
| innuendos |
| hyperboles |

**MANHATTAN**
PREP

119. (i) _____ the law had little impact, but it was (ii) _____ by subsequent legislation providing funding and enforcement.

| Blank (i) | Blank (ii) |
|-----------|-------------|
| Justifiably | rendered moot |
| Unbelievably | given teeth |
| Initially | kept at bay |

120. Evoking both horror and joy in its audience in equal measure, the opera became an instant classic of _____ technique.

| |
|---|
| macabre |
| figurative |
| articulate |
| counterpoint |
| contrived |

121. The famous Notre Dame cathedral in Paris took almost 200 years to complete; this immense architectural effort included the first notable use of a flying _____ , but this renowned feature was not part of the original design and was only employed when the walls forming the nave began to crumble and needed additional support.

| |
|---|
| partition |
| albatross |
| hallmark |
| buttress |
| trademark |

122. While no single empirical investigation can ever conclusively prove the (i) _____ of a theory, the fact that the data are (ii) _____ findings from over a dozen independent labs worldwide bodes well for the framework's resilience.

| Blank (i) | Blank (ii) |
|-----------|-------------|
| rationality | consistent with |
| veracity | founded on |
| candor | antithetical to |

123. A full account of the complexities of sleep, sought after by scientists, philosophers, and mystics for millennia, continues to elude us. That we are still so ignorant about a topic so (i) _____ to our daily lives is at once fascinating and (ii) _____ .

| Blank (i) | Blank (ii) |
| --- | --- |
| mysterious | deeply humbling |
| obscure | fully impenetrable |
| pertinent | totally blatant |

124. Mozart's brief life exemplified a discrepancy between fame and means: as his musical star (i) _____ beyond measure, his income (ii) _____ .

| Blank (i) | Blank (ii) |
| --- | --- |
| abated | grew exponentially |
| waxed | remained exorbitant |
| dwindled | barely stirred |

125. Finally, after refusing for a decade, the family patriarch, weakened by age and infirmity, surrendered to the impassioned pleas of his avaricious nieces, and gave his _____ to the risky investment stratagem.

| |
| --- |
| assent |
| ascent |
| dissent |
| descent |
| assertion |

126. Even thrill-seeking visitors to amusement parks will avoid those attractions with a reputation for real (i) _____ , like those at the now-shuttered Action Park. These patrons want not danger but its (ii) _____ , a ride that (iii) _____ but is in fact perfectly safe.

| Blank (i) | Blank (ii) | Blank (iii) |
| --- | --- | --- |
| peril | complement | satisfies |
| titillation | simulacrum | mollifies |
| lavishness | abettor | terrifies |

127. Desktop publishing allows (i) _____ to do for themselves the work once reserved for professionals whose (ii) _____ or other training developed design skills along with narrow technical mastery.

| Blank (i) | Blank (ii) |
| --- | --- |
| dilettantes | sensibility |
| artisans | acumen |
| idealogues | apprenticeship |

**MANHATTAN**
PREP

128. There was much to admire about the singer's voice, but her abilities as a performer were not as
     (i) _____ as those of the singer who followed, whose stage presence was far more (ii) _____.

| Blank (i) | Blank (ii) |
|-----------|------------|
| unremarkable | charismatic |
| hackneyed | pedestrian |
| arresting | experienced |

129. The contradictions in the philosopher's life were more (i) _____ because he was celebrated for his
     prodigal intellectual (ii) _____ that led to his profound insights.

| Blank (i) | Blank (ii) |
|-----------|------------|
| insightful | acumen |
| confounding | vacuity |
| unpremeditated | veracity |

130. If impact on one's contemporaries is the test of (i) _____ , Flann O'Brien's *The Third Policeman* cannot
     be said to be among the most significant postmodern novels, as it went unpublished and unread for
     27 years. The literary theorist Keith Hopper, though, appeals to standards other than peer (ii) _____ when
     he argues persuasively that *The Third Policeman* is among the most important of early postmodern works,
     not least because of its deep subversion of both enlightenment and modern traditions in literature.

| Blank (i) | Blank (ii) |
|-----------|------------|
| eminence | currency |
| modishness | influence |
| conversance | dissolution |

131. One liberal activist asserts that politicians' tendency to (i) _____ talk of class warfare stems largely
     from a communal state of denial, a refusal to accept that we already occupy a highly (ii) _____ society.

| Blank (i) | Blank (ii) |
|-----------|------------|
| denigrate | socialized |
| besmirch | balkanized |
| encourage | politicized |

132. In the course of a transatlantic voyage following the First World War, he magically acquired an honorific title of "Count" as well as a "von" in his name, a development due to his aquiline nose and social (i) _____ rather than his (ii) _____ genetics, which lacked any distinction, and he (iii) _____ successfully enough in New York City to parlay this charade into a small fortune.

| Blank (i) | Blank (ii) | Blank (iii) |
|-----------|------------|-------------|
| arrogance | peasant | coalesced |
| deftness | patrician | dissembled |
| maladroitness | perturbing | disseminated |

133. There is little agreement among specialists about whether the Second Amendment to the United States Constitution provides _____ guarantee of a right to bear arms for private citizens, or whether it was instead meant to allow the populace to protect itself in lieu of a military.

| |
|---|
| an earnest |
| an amended |
| a questionable |
| a defeasible |
| an ironclad |

134. The writer Lillian Hellman honestly called her disingenuous argumentative strategy "the nobility racket": a _____ that involved taking the moral high ground no matter how removed from the subject at hand.

| |
|---|
| philosophy |
| sophistry |
| sinecure |
| volubility |
| serendipity |

135. The fitness guru, seemingly an advocate of overall salubrious living, often, late at night and behind closed doors, _____ his integrity by consuming vast quantities of sugar and chemical-riddled junk food.

| |
|---|
| ridiculed |
| restored |
| undermined |
| redacted |
| insinuated |

**MANHATTAN**
PREP

136. The recent discoveries of unexploded World War II munitions buried just beneath houses and roads in European cities is very (i) _____, since one can easily imagine becoming a (ii) _____ of a war that ended decades ago.

| Blank (i) | Blank (ii) |
|-----------|------------|
| exhilarating | hero |
| disquieting | martyr |
| demeaning | casualty |

137. It may be surprising that even perennially (i) _____ reporters have had misgivings about entering the war zone; their (ii) _____ at the prospect can only be a reflection of the heightened (iii) _____ that pervades the region.

| Blank (i) | Blank (ii) | Blank (iii) |
|-----------|------------|-------------|
| professional | trepidation | rhetoric |
| dauntless | excitement | peril |
| foreign | skepticism | awareness |

138. One does not generally associate teenagers with (i) _____. Jean, however, exercises a self-discipline that verges on (ii) _____. It is unclear whether this is a testament to a particularly conservative upbringing or a reaction against an excessively (iii) _____ one.

| Blank (i) | Blank (ii) | Blank (iii) |
|-----------|------------|-------------|
| silent obedience | asperity | illiberal |
| polished urbanity | punishment | permissive |
| practiced restraint | asceticism | meddlesome |

139. Unexpectedly, the actor's (i) _____ behavior did little to (ii) _____ his reputation as a family man, a reputation (iii) _____ by his exceptionally skilled team of publicists.

| Blank (i) | Blank (ii) | Blank (iii) |
|-----------|------------|-------------|
| dissolute | assuage | cleverly subverted |
| impudent | damage | easily refuted |
| paternal | temper | carefully cultivated |

140. Now that fresh produce has become (i) _____—markets and stands in cities throughout the world boast dozens of varieties of fruits and vegetables for customers to choose from—many (ii) _____ that were once the inevitable result of nutritional deficiencies are now entirely (iii) _____.

| Blank (i) | Blank (ii) | Blank (iii) |
|-----------|------------|-------------|
| salubrious | maladies | organic |
| ubiquitous | reactions | dietetic |
| comestible | cultivars | preventable |

141. Despite her (i) _____ position on tax reform, the senator was not (ii) _____ to strike a concessionary tone when she debated the issue with her opponents.

| Blank (i) | Blank (ii) |
|---|---|
| conservative | loath |
| fiduciary | permitted |
| hardline | qualified |

142. There seems to be (i) _____ the practice of medicine in the United States: while it is the duty of medical professionals to maintain the health of their patients, the same professionals stand to profit more from their patients' (ii) _____ .

| Blank (i) | Blank (ii) |
|---|---|
| a protest against | infirmity |
| an aversion to | inattentiveness |
| a paradox in | uncertainty |

143. Whereas early work in the field of spectroscopy (i) _____ the dispersal of visible light by a prism, the concept was later (ii) _____ to (iii) _____ any and all interactions with radiative energy, including electromagnetic radiation, pressure waves, and the kinetic energy of particles.

| Blank (i) | Blank (ii) | Blank (iii) |
|---|---|---|
| contrasted with | expanded | affirm |
| arose from | transformed | endure |
| focused on | amended | include |

144. While Abdul's _____ with his children made him well loved, he worried what too much laxity might cost him in their teenage years.

| |
|---|
| complacence |
| sternness |
| satisfaction |
| equanimity |
| permissiveness |

# Text Completions Answers

**1. Apportioned.** You are told that football is by far the most popular sport in Europe. The word "whereas" then creates a contrast: the U.S. fans are evenly split among their many sports. "Regarded," "inspired," and "enjoyed" are all traps related to sports or fandom, but don't properly express the sentence's intention that the popularity is split. "Measured" is close, but doesn't quite divide things appropriately. "Apportioned" means divided and allocated; it is the correct answer.

**2. Delusion.** The second half of the sentence states that it would take a miracle for a person to get to another solar system. In other words, it's more or less impossible. "Dementia," "catastrophe," and "hysteria" do not reflect this meaning. And while space travel would be an incredible "innovation," innovation also doesn't express the proper meaning of this sentence. "Delusion," meaning a belief that is maintained despite being contradicted by reality, is the best fit.

**3. Crowned, dismissed.** "Peculiarly enough" indicates that the blanks oppose each other, and "best English language playwright" indicates that blank (i) must be positive, so blank (ii) must be negative. "Crowned" is the only positive word choice for the first blank and is the correct answer; "stigmatized" means condemned, and "castigated" means scolded. In the second blank, "deified" has a positive tone and doesn't express the contrast that the sentence suggests, while "demonized" is much too strong an attitude to direct towards someone for lacking education; "dismissed" is a more appropriate word and the correct answer.

**4. Abridged, complementary.** Certain "versions of novels and essays" cut out important parts, or "excise essential elements." Then, "to fully understand the intent of the original," students would have to "supplement," or add to, "their reading with [some type of ] sources." So the text versions described by blank (i) are lacking parts of the original and the reading sources described by blank (ii) provide some of what is lacking. An "abridged" source is one that has been shortened, and "complementary sources" would enhance or support this shortened version. Be careful of the homophone "complimentary," which means either admiring or given free of charge, neither of which works in blank (ii). "Compelling" sources would either evoke interest or inspire conviction. While the supplemental reading might do so, no indication of either additional meaning is given in the sentence, and this choice fails to address the problem that "abridged versions" create for students. "Annotated versions" have additional notes of explanation; such versions would be *less* likely to require supplementation to understand, not more. Finally, there is no indication that the "[blank (i)] versions of novels and essays" are "antedated," or dated prior to their actual date.

**5. Sophisticated.** The blank should be a positive word to accompany "alluring." What's more, it should be something that contrasts the "simple and quaint" nature of rural America. Given this, you need a positive word for something not simple. "Lascivious" means overtly and often inappropriately sexual; this doesn't fit the sentence. "Foreign" may appear to go along with "expatriate;" it's easy to fall into such a theme trap if you are not in the habit of pointing to explicit clues in the sentence ("simple and quaint," in this case). "Alien" is similar in meaning to "foreign" and is also a slightly negative word. Likewise, "alienating" is not a positive word—in this case, it would lead to an impression that the young lad felt unwelcome in Paris. "Sophisticated," with its sense of polished culture, offers the best contrast to "simple and quaint."

6. **Cited, correct.** The first sentence states a fact about life expectancy that relates to the claim that the world is improving with time. Clearly this would be true if life expectancies have increased with time, making "cited" a perfect fit for blank (i). Neither "disregarded" nor "embodied" fits with the idiom "as evidence." The second blank, however, says that this statistic is slightly misleading if one considers a second fact (i.e., that most children died in childbirth). While you might "prepare" for the fact or "read" for the fact, that does not change the fact. But if you "correct" for the fact that most children died in childbirth, then the new life expectancy statistic would change.

7. **Preposterous.** The sentence states that two things were thought to be equally unlikely in 1986. But today, while one of those events still seems quite far-fetched, the other is commonplace, making the argument sound absurd or "preposterous." "Preternatural" means what is beyond normal or natural and is used to express mysterious or exceptional events. This argument isn't really mysterious as much as it is wrong. Note that "prescient" (ability to foretell the future) is the opposite of what the sentence requires—because the prediction about the future was entirely wrong, it does not sound "prescient." To "preordain" is to decide or determine an outcome in advance. While the fact that banking transactions from home are commonplace now could possibly imply that the transactions were "preordained," the argument against such a possibility would neither be preordained nor sound preordained. Finally, "pithy" means concise, and nothing in the sentence suggests that the argument is concise.

8. **Lionize.** The bad news: there are a lot of hard words in this question. The good news: the sentence itself is relatively straightforward. There is a "widespread tendency" to do something, and that tendency "stems from [a] need to venerate" somebody. So the tendency described by the blank should be similiar to "venerate." "Castigate" means to punish or reprimand—the opposite of what you need. "Remember" and "appreciate" both seem to work, if somewhat imperfectly, but neither is strong enough to match "venerate" (treat with deep respect or awe). These are spin traps—close, but not quite right. "Indemnify" is a complicated word. It can mean to free someone from responsibility for some as yet uncommitted wrongdoing—sort of like handing someone a "Get out of jail free" card. It can also mean to promise money against a potential loss, as is the case with insurance. Fortunately, neither of these meanings, complicated though they are, aligns with "venerate." Only "lionize"—to grant someone celebrity status—works in this context.

9. **Cerebral, intellectual.** From the beginning, the passage sets up a dichotomy between the work of the brain and the work of the body. The second sentence compares how "[blank] work strains the mind" to how "physical work strains the body," and so blank (i) should be a word describing the "musings of a mathematician" as they compare to "the physical labor of a carpenter." Here, again, the word should be something that goes along with academic and "cerebral." "Quotidian" means everyday, common, or unextraordinary. "Extraordinary" is the opposite of "quotidian" and doesn't offer the counterpoint to "physical labor" necessary for this blank. "Intellectual," however, fits blank (ii) perfectly.

10. **Amusing, caustic.** The clue "usual" means that the two blanks must match "humorous" but acerbic—and in that order. "Slanderous" and "serious" are, respectively, unrelated to and the opposite of humorous, making "amusing" the only possible answer choice for the first blank. Similarly, "acerbic" needs to pair with a word that means something similar to sharp or sarcastic. "Caustic" is a perfect synonym, while "considerate" is the opposite of what is needed and "hysterical" might match the first blank but not the second.

**MANHATTAN**
PREP

11. **Circle.** The clue "in turn" suggests that the event occurs continuously, making "circle" the best answer choice in this sentence. Incorrect answers "irony" and "comedy" add an idea—humor—that was not indicated by the sentence. Finally, "serendipity" and "vicissitude" are somewhat antonyms of one another with the first being a happy occurrence and the second being an unhappy one. However, the sentence does not suggest that the accusing done by each generation is anything other than matter-of-fact.

12. **Abreast of.** The word "although" indicates that what the professor is doing is unusual or not required of a retired person. "Takes pains" also indicates that what she is doing is difficult. To keep "abreast of" a topic is to remain current and is therefore the correct answer. "Akimbo" means in a hands-on-hips stance, which would probably be a pain but isn't something the professor could do "to the latest developments in her field." "Obtuse" (slow-witted) does not fit the desired meaning. There's no reason to believe that the professor is "subservient to" the developments in her field. And finally, "askance" means with a look of disapproval, which also doesn't fit in this sentence.

13. **Proponent, catalyst.** The woman in this sentence "finally got the bill onto the legislative agenda," so she is definitely an advocate, or "proponent," of the legislation. She's not a "critic" of the legislation, but she's also not an "apologist" since there's no clue in the sentence to believe that the legislation is controversial. In blank (ii), "mercenary" means she would be paid for her efforts and "lackey" means she would be doing this subserviently for someone else. Either option might work if there were additional clues about the subject, but without those clues, "catalyst," someone who creates change, is the best option and the correct answer.

14. **Trumpet, taciturn.** Jeremy is successful, but it takes his family a long time to discover his accomplishments. Thus, Jeremy does not brag—or even report the facts! To "trumpet" is to talk loudly or report something to everyone and is a better option than "demarcate," set the boundaries of, or "whitewash," cover up some unpleasant facts. In the second blank, only "taciturn," which means quiet, works, Jeremy doesn't talk much at all. "Improvident" means not providing for the future, and "dissolute" means lax in morals or licentious. Nothing in the sentence indicates either description.

15. **Acerbic, impecunious.** Standing alone, any of the choices for the first blank could describe "witticisms," which are witty remarks. Remarks could be "innovative" (original or creative), "acerbic" (sharp or sarcastic), or "inimical" (harmful or hostile). However, the remarks are described as "cutting remarks" after the semicolon, so the first blank should match that characterization. "Cutting" is a synonym for "acerbic," so this is the best choice. "Inimical" is too negative, conflicting with the idea that "Wilde catapulted to sudden fame both because of and despite" his remarks. The second blank is part of a two-part list: "he died _____ and sickly." The cause is given in the preceding two-part list: "the cutting remarks … led to his financial and physical ruin." A two-by-two structure like this stays in order, meaning that "financial … ruin" is related to the blank, just as "physical ruin" is related to "sickly." Only "impecunious," which means poor or destitute, fits. Neither "pallid" (pale) nor "aghast" (horrified) fits with "financial ruin."

16. **Emblematic of, pragmatic, posit.** The end of the sentence states that Hursthouse puts forth the same views as many other virtue ethicists. So in the first blank, the sentence requires something like representative of. "Emblematic of" is a perfect fit here and the correct answer. "Breaking away from" conveys the opposite meaning and "enigmatic to" (difficult to understand) also does not fit the desired meaning. It's later stated that Hursthouse thinks ethics is neither situational nor utilitarian—the next part of the sentence will have a first part that matches up with situational and a second part that matches up with utilitarian. (GRE sentences often use a pattern of mentioning two things, and then giving more information about those two things in the same order.) For example, "Base one's judgments on subjective concerns" refers back to a situational approach to ethics and a "_____ weighing of pain and pleasure" refers back to a utilitarian (or practical) approach. Thus, "pragmatic," which means practical, matches better than "quixotic," which means impractical, or "grandiloquent," which means pretentious. Finally, critics agree with the idea that virtue ethicists seek to enshrine their own prejudices, so in the third blank, the sentence needs a word like say or claim. "Posit" is the only match since "deny" is the opposite of what the sentence intends and "cajole" (persuade) does not fit the context.

17. **Roundly, panned.** The sentence indicates that there wasn't a single positive comment from any critic; in other words, the film was unanimously criticized or 100% disliked. "Mendaciously" means dishonestly, and there's no clue to indicate that the critics were being dishonest. Similarly, there's no clue in the sentence to suggest that anyone was "warily" suggesting anything. "Roundly" means emphatically or so thoroughly as to leave no doubt. "Panned" means reviewed negatively and is almost always used to refer to plays, movies, etc., so the word is a perfect match here—to be roundly panned would mean reviewed 100% negatively, which is exactly what the sentence suggests. "Lauded" and "venerated" are both positive and would indicate that the critics enjoyed the movie; clearly that's not the case here.

18. **Aesthetics.** The sentence states that "the distinction between architecture and engineering professions" is that architecture must consider something in addition to "functionality." Later, the sentence indicates that architectural clients base decisions more on beauty than practicality, so architecture must consider visual appeal as well as functionality. The word that best fits this meaning is "aesthetics." "Insouciance," meaning carelessness or indifference, does not fit. "Utility," "price," and "profundity" are all characteristics that architects might consider, but they don't take into account the fact that clients base their decisions on beauty.

19. **Insensibly.** The phrase "once considered" suggests that whatever follows is no longer thought to be true, so the blank will oppose the clue "capable of genuine imitation" and go along with the idea that the bearded dragons were thought to be acting "without understanding the action's deeper significance." An appropriate choice, then, will mean something like "mindlessly." "Listlessly" means unenergetically, while "actively" means the opposite. "Consciously" is a reversal trap. To do something "attentively" means to do so with great interest. This leaves "insensibly," which means unaware or incapable of perception.

20. **Coda.** There are two possibilities for the blank: something like a bad ending (yet another bad event occurred in December) or something like an inconvenience (relative to the other "devastating" events). A "coda" is an ending that sums up what came before, which, in this case, was pretty bad. A "rampage" is bad but does not fit grammatically before the word "to," nor does it correctly describe an earthquake—rather, murderers or mobs go on rampages. A "prologue" would be at the beginning of the year, not at the end. "Catharsis" means an emotional release and doesn't fit the context of a natural disaster, which would build up emotional distress rather than release it. And finally, "homily" is a lecture, sometimes religious, but this doesn't fit the context of a natural disaster.

**MANHATTAN**
PREP

**21. Presciently, simpatico.** The sentence indicates that the two writers very much thought alike. "Presciently" means seeing into the future or as though seeing into the future, which is exactly what the writers were able to do while anticipating each other's letters. "Ominously" puts too negative of a spin on the anticipation, and "anachronistically," which means out of time, does not fit the context of the sentence. "Simpatico" matches the idea of being of one mind better than "providential," favorable or auspicious, or "shrewd."

**22. Inured to.** "Casting a blind eye to" suffering means that these people ignore or pretend not to see the suffering. Thus, they are "inured to" suffering—they are hardened and desensitized as a result of seeing so much of it. Trap answer "exempted" would mean that the people described are no longer personally subject to the suffering, which the sentence does not indicate. Because they ignore suffering, they also wouldn't be "maudlin" or "effusive," which are about expressing strong feelings. Finally, "dominant over" does not fit idiomatically since you can't become dominant over suffering.

**23. Coalesced.** Since the group overcame the "struggle over power" and became "a harmonious team," the blank needs a word that means came together. "Coalesced" matches perfectly and is the correct answer. "Agglomerated" is a bit of a trap—to agglomerate is to collect or form into a mass or group. Since the people were already in a group, the word is inappropriate (agglomerate is also used more for things than for people). "Fractured" is the opposite of coming together. The other options are difficult words but are used in contexts very different than group harmony: "syncopated" means either the shortening of a word or the displacement of beats in a musical piece and "amortized" means reducing a debt.

**24. Considered.** The newcomers and the long-time fans are divided in their opinions. The newcomers were happy with the show, so the long-time fans must have been unhappy: they thought that "the storyline" was "unfinished." Only "considered" matches this meaning. "Appreciated" is a reversal trap. The fans did not "generate," "examine," or "secure" the storyline.

**25. Finishing, trying.** Since the novel will take "innumerable hours to review and edit," the author is far from completing, or "finishing," it. "Inscribing" (writing) is a theme trap and "rejecting" does not convey the desired meaning. The second blank will agree with the clue that immediately follows: "the book's length" and its "convoluted plot." Therefore, it will be hard, or "trying," to finish the book. "Hardy" (strong, resilient) and "redundant" do not match the required meaning.

**26. Inveigle.** The word "despite" indicates that there is a contrast between what the salesman is attempting to do and how the couple is responding. The salesman is attempting to give them false compliments in order to get the couple to buy a car, but his tactic isn't working. "Inveigle" means to flatter or charm someone into doing something and is the correct answer. "Support," "deliberate," "marginalize" (relegate to an unimportant position), and "hector" (to bully, torment) do not convey this same meaning.

**27. Inform.** The poet's childhood memories color, or influence, her work. The sentence needs a similar word for how war influences her poetry. "Inform"—to give substance, character, or distinction to—can be used in this way. "Mimic" is a trap answer choice: it may be possible to say that her poetry mimics her experiences, but not that her experiences mimic her poetry (rather, her experiences are mimicked in her poetry). "Invalidate" is too strong for this sentence nor does it indicate the proper meaning. "Defer" is not used properly (something defers *to* something else) nor would war likely defer to poetry. And "presage," which means to foreshadow, does not pair with color as well as "inform" does.

28. **Erroneously, unbeknownst.** Since the peanut is not really a nut (it is a legume), it is being erroneously, or mistakenly, referred to as such. "Deftly" is the opposite of what the sentence suggests, and "archaically" would mean that the peanut used to be referred to as a nut. "Unbeknownst to" means unknown by, which would explain why people are making this mistake. "Abhorrent" is too strong of a term for this sentence, nor does the sentence indicate that anyone is disgusted by peanuts. "Consanguineous" comes from the latin roots con- (with) and sanguis (blood) to mean of the same blood or related: it's hard to be blood-related to something that has no blood!

29. **Tremulous, chary of.** All of the clues in the sentence are about being scared, so "tremulous" matches best in blank (i). Neither "coltish" (playful) nor "cumbersome" (complicated, hard to handle) fix the meaning of the sentence. The sentence states that the child finds diving even more frightening than water in general, so "chary of" (suspicious or slightly scared of), a less extreme version of frightening, fits. "Repulsed by" is too strong of a word for blank (ii) and "beguiled by" would mean the child was deceived by the water.

30. **Sentries, fecund, progeny.** The sentence states that solider ants guard the colony and supply it with food, "thus acting as both _____ and laborers." In this sentence pattern, the first blank matches up with "guard the colony" and "laborers" matches up with "supply it with food." "Sentries," or guards, matches perfectly and is the correct word for blank (i). A "sage" is a wise scholar and a "sycophant" is a lackey or flatterer, neither of which fits the meaning of the sentence. The sentence then states that the queen can continually "populate the colony," so "fecund" (fertile) goes in blank (ii) and progeny (offspring) goes in blank (iii). "Efficacious" means effective and "imperius" means domineering, but the sentence does not indicate that this would describe the queen ant. "Forebears" means ancestors, which is the opposite of what blank (iii) requires. Finally, "harbingers" means a herald or a forerunner of something else, but producing signs of something else would not help to populate a colony.

31. **Ephemeral, heralded.** Since the government lasted only about two months, it was "ephemeral," or short-lived. "Equivocal," or ambiguous, and "omnipotent," or all powerful, could describe a government, but this sentence gives no such indication of either of these meanings. Despite the fact that it was short-lived, the government was regarded, or celebrated, as the emergence of a powerful working class: only "heralded" matches. The expression "discounted as X" might work if the final part of the sentence held a more negative tone: the idea was discounted as too impractical. But "the emergence of a powerful working class" has no such negative connotation. Similarly, "recanted," or renounced, would only work if the final part of the sentence was something that was being disavowed.

32. **Complications, stouter, a concomitant.** The first sentence says that taller turbines would be better, but there is some contrasting negative element. In other words, the "engineers are facing" some "complications." Neither "flaws" nor "supplements" conveys this idea of difficulty in building the turbines. In the second sentence, "Taller towers necessitate _____ bases, requiring the current width to be nearly doubled," suggests that the second blank should mean wider. The only choice for the second blank that can mean "wider" is "stouter." "Equitable," meaning fair, and "unobtrusive" do not mean anything like "wider." The final sentence says that the wider sections lead "to a(an) _____ issue" because they are too large to transport on modern highways. Therefore, the third blank has to mean something like additional. Although "a theoretical issue" has a nice sound to it, the problem is very real, so "theoretical" cannot be correct. "Objective" used as an adjective means unbiased, which does not fit the intended meaning. "Concomitant," which means accompanying (often in a subordinate way), matches well.

**MANHATTAN**
PREP

**33. Obsequious.** "Plaudits" are praise (note the similarity to "applause"), which matches the idea of praise being "heaped upon him" on a "prolonged and elaborate farewell tour." Additionally, the negative certainty of "*no one* thought the plaudits heaped upon him were _____" matches in degree the positive certainty of "admired *by all*." If he was admired by all, then no one would think that the praise was undeserved or inappropriate. Thus, "deserved" represents a reversal trap. "Obsequious," meaning attentive to an excessive degree, puts a negative spin on the praise, which is what "no one" would think; this is the answer. "Derivative" as an adjective has several meanings, depending on what it is describing: it is typically applied to people or the works of art they produce (imitative) or can apply to a financial product (having a value based on some asset). Here, "derivative" describes "plaudits," so it most likely means originating from or based on something. Because the blank is not getting at whether the praise is original, but rather whether it is appropriate, this choice is incorrect. Both "vestigial," residual or leftover, and "antiquated," old-fashioned or outdated, introduce additional meaning not indicated by the sentence.

**34. Sanguine, peccadilloes.** The sentence states that the man's personality is pleasing—so pleasing that "it's hard to be bothered by" something in his past. The first word should match pleasing, and the second should be something negative that others might overlook. "Sanguine" means cheerful and optimistic. Note that "high-handed" might sound positive, but actually means tactlessly overbearing. "Evanescent" (fading quickly, short-lived) is inappropriate to describe a personality. "Peccadilloes" are minor faults or sins—small enough that they might be overlooked if the person has other virtues. "Incendiaries" can mean either bombs or a person who stirs up conflict; the former definition is too strong for the blank, and the latter does not fit the meaning of the sentence. "Achievements" has a positive connotation, while the second blank should convey a negative connotation.

**35. Menacing, unprovoked.** The Tasmanian devil, a type of wild animal, is "not considered _____ since only a few of its confrontations," or hostile encounters, "with humans have been _____." The two blanks have to work together in this sentence, and the second blank is easier. "Unprovoked" is the only choice for the second blank that would reasonably describe hostile encounters with wild animals "Quixotic," which means idealistic or unrealistic, does not work because the sentence is talking about real encounters. "Premature" does not fit either. Given that the Tasmanian devil usually only confronts humans when provoked, it is not "menacing," which is the correct choice for blank (i). Because it is a wild animal, it cannot be considered predictable, so "unpredictable" is incorrect. "Adverse," which is used to describe something that is harmful because it prevents success, is inappropriate to use in describing a wild animal. You might say that the presence of wild animals is an "adverse" factor, but you could not say that the animals themselves were "adverse."

**36. Verdant, castigated.** The sentence indicates that the employee is young and makes mistakes. "Verdant" means either green and lush, like a forest, or new and inexperienced (the use of green as a metaphor, as in, she's still green at her job). "Banal" means unoriginal, which does not fit with the rest of the sentence, and "sagacious" means shrewd, which is the opposite of how the employee acted. Since the mistake was so expensive, it makes sense that the employee would be "castigated," or severely criticized. He wouldn't be "deposed"—that word is for kings, dictators, etc., forced out of power. And the employee would not be "enamored," or filled with a feeling of love, for the mistake he just made.

**37. Facile.** The sentence suggests that the idea of bringing about world peace by saying "love one another" is naïve, or oversimplified. "Facile" matches well and has the sense of superficial. Neither "convoluted" (difficult to understand, complicated) nor "impeccable" (flawless) fit the desired meaning. "Amicable," which means friendly, and "dulcet," which means sweet and soothing, have a similar problem: while the suggestion might be a friendly and sweet one, those definitions don't properly convey the idea that the suggestion is naïve.

**38. Garrulous.** A "euphemism" is a mild or indirect term substituted for one considered too harsh or blunt. Adults referred to the girl with the positive word "precocious," which means forward or advanced for her age, whereas she really was "overly talkative," so the blank should mean something like too talkative, or garrulous. "Skittish" could be cast as positive (excitable) or negative (unpredicable, jittery), but neither is a negative spin on "forward" nor "talkative." The other choices are either neutral, such as "naïve," meaning innocent or unworldly, or positive, such as "solicitous" (concerned or attentive) and "endearing" (lovable or charming). None of these choices would require a euphemistic replacement. "Garrulous," then, is the correct choice.

**39. Motley, even, sole.** This question is an excellent lesson in the principle: *don't add anything to your reading of the sentence that wasn't there already.* The sentence indicates that the first short story collection had many diverse voices and the second collection has "a _____ narrator"—in other words, just one speaker. The word "sole" fits the third blank; neither "lonely" nor "disingenuous" convey the idea of a single narrator. The first story collection was a "hodgepodge" (jumble), but the second was not a jumble; it was an "even" set of stories. "Insightful" and "facetious" (not serious) are not antonyms for a jumble. For the first blank, "motley" works because it means composed of diverse and often incongruous elements. "Variable" is a trap: a variable hodgepodge of voices would imply that the voices in the first collection can change over time, not that the voices were varied or diverse. And "homogenous" would indicate that the voices were all similar; this describes the second collection, not the first.

**40. Reversing.** The opening words, "In contrast," alert you to look for the opposition between "environmental economics" and "ecological economics." The latter field "positions the human economy as a subsystem of natural economies," which is the opposite of a system that "subordinates" nature to the economy. The new system is opposite, or "reversing," the way the old system thought of things. "Corroborating" is a reversal trap for those who missed "in contrast." "Circumscribing" means to enclose or encircle and is thus inappropriate. "Ameliorating" is the process of mitigating or making better and is not a good match. "Refuting," a spin trap, is the most tempting incorrect answer, but the sentence only provides evidence for opposition, not contradiction.

**41. Efficacious.** Because the semicolon indicates agreement, the blank will agree with "opponents were still able to set aside differences and work across party lines, as is typically necessary to pass productive legislation." In other words, political opponents were once able to govern effectively despite their differences but they can no longer do so today. "Efficacious" means effective as a means or remedy and so is a good match. "Polemical," meaning strongly opinionated, and "civil" are not justified by the clue. "Enjoyable" and "immutable," meaning unchangeable, do not match the desired meaning. Note that "enjoyable" introduces a new idea not present in the original sentence. Don't assume that the old days were necessarily enjoyable; all you know is that they were effective, or efficacious.

**42. Deification, garlands.** The straightforward structure and positive spin indicate positive choices for both blanks. "Excoriation" means harsh criticism and is the opposite tone of what the sentence requires. "Praise" is positive but doesn't match the clue "laid at the altar," which suggests a more extreme version of a positive word. That leaves the correct answer, "deification" for blank (i). The second blank has two words with negatives meanings: "calumnies" means slander and "obloquies" means abusive language. That leaves "garlands," the correct answer, a word that is most commonly used to describe a wreath of flowers and leaves worn as an honorable décoration, but can also mean a prize or distinction.

**43. Artifices.** The clues "bifurcated" and "but" signal a contrast: commercial portrait painters are similar to other painters in some ways, but the blank refers to how they are in some ways different than those other painters (they try to make the subject look more attractive in the painting). The correct answer, "artifices," means a trickery or deception and fits perfectly with the clue. Trap answers "palettes" and "aesthetics" are related to painting, but don't match the meaning of the blank. "Artifacts" is a trap word that looks similar to "artifices" but means a historic relic. "Sentiments" is an attitude, but the sentence provides no information about the painter's attitude or how that would make the subject of the piece more attractive.

**44. Pedantry.** The correct answer should parallel "dogmatic" and match the negative spin of "enervates rather than inspires." "Wisdom," "pulchritude" (beauty), and "wit" are all positive terms that don't match with the sentence structure. Only "pedantry" (being arrogant in relation to learning) and "parsimony" (stinginess) are negative, and only "pedantry" fits the idea of an uninspiring professor.

**45. Minutiae.** The correct answer must reflect the clue "petty" and oppose the idea of "lofty goals." Lincoln felt that McClellan paid so much attention to trivial details, or "minutiae," that he ignored the big picture. The trap answer "irrelevancies" is incorrect because the "logistical details" are not irrelevant; they are merely minor, or not worthy of so much attention. "Tactics" and "strategy" don't convey the idea of minor details. And nothing in the sentence suggests that attention was being placed on minor offenses or "peccadilloes."

**46. Appealing shyness, enthralled.** As is often the case, the second blank is easier; given the structure, it must match the clue "captivating" in meaning and spin. "Enthralled" is a perfect match here and the correct answer. "Repelled" is far too negative a tone, and "amused," while positive, does not match the idea of "captivating." The first blank must parallel "hesitancy and understatement" and also have a positive spin. "Awkward lisp" does not have a positive spin and "overwhelming passion" does not parallel "hesitancy and understatement." That leaves the correct answer "appealing shyness."

**47. Conventionality, laudatory.** The word "surprisingly" before blank (ii) indicates that the blanks will oppose each other in tone; since the reviewers gave "unabashed approbation," the second blank should be a positive word, such as receptive. "Laudatory" is a synonym for "approbation" and is therefore the correct answer. "Tepid," meaning lukewarm, and "deprecating," meaning to belittle or express disapproval, are not good matches. Given the oppositional structure, blank (i) should be negative. "Ingenuity" is too positive. "Tortuousness," meaning twisting or crooked, and "conventionality" both have negative connotations. The reviewers "usually pounce on the slightest orthodoxy," or widely accepted theory, so the best match is "conventionality."

**MANHATTAN**
PREP

**48. Dissipation, profligate.** "Ironically" is a good clue here—the commentator condemned a quality that he himself actually possessed! Both words should be negative, similar in meaning, and match the idea of bankruptcy. "Dissipation" and "profligate" are both related to wastefulness or irresponsible living. "Indolence" means laziness, "probity" means integrity, "antediluvian" means outdated, and "ascetic" means austere. Notice that while some of the other words do have a negative spin, none of the incorrect choices are similar in meaning or match the idea of bankruptcy.

**49. A deplorable.** This sentence begins with the expression "For all," an idiomatic way of saying "despite." The second half of the sentence, then, should contradict the "meticulous preparation" reported in the first half: the student's grade must have been bad. "Passable" wouldn't do the job here—it would suggest a decent but not fantastic grade—and "outstanding" is the exact opposite of what you want. "Exacting" means demanding, and while the test must have been exacting on the student, his grade could not be described as such. "Surprising" is the most pernicious option, because the student was likely very surprised by a grade that did not reflect the work he put into studying; this choice does not make clear, however, that the student's grade was terrible. "Deplorable," on the other hand, fits the bill—it means surprisingly bad.

**50. Informed.** The clue "Just as" indicates that the second part of the sentence will need to mirror the first part. Thus, the blank must match the meaning of "provided the Romans with a model." "Informed" can be used in this way and is the correct answer. Don't be tricked by "duplicate" (to provide a model isn't to make an exact copy) or "foresaw" (the remnants of Roman culture didn't tell the future). Both "curbed" and "hindered" have too strong of a negative spin and do not mirror the first part of the sentence.

**51. Enhances.** The sentence requires a word that means helps or strengthens—"enhances" is a perfect synonym for strengthen and the correct answer. Don't fall for "ensures," which is too extreme. Having a head that can measure spaces is cool, but hardly guarantees the success of a species. "Reproduces" is a word related to success as a species, but does not fit the blank. "Mitigate" means to make less severe, and "inundate" means to overwhelm, neither of which fit in the blank.

**52. Guileless, canny.** The sentence contrasts the teacher's "novice" appearance with what he in fact was. The second half of the sentence indicates that he understood the "byzantine" (complicated) power structures and was using the administration "to his advantage." This suggests that he was quite sharp, making "canny" a perfect fit for blank (ii). "Unseemly" means improper, and there's no clue in the sentence that suggests his behavior was inappropriate. "Desultory" would mean that the teacher lacked a plan, but his use of the administration would suggest otherwise. Blank (i) describes the word "novice" and helps to explain how the teacher made himself appear: the opposite of "canny." "Cunning" has a similar meaning to canny and might be selected by someone who misses the contrast between the two blanks. There's no reason to believe that the teacher was "capricious," or whimsical. That leaves "guileless," a synonym for innocent, and a perfect fit in this sentence.

**53. Irregularities, credible.** If the methodologies are "flawed," then there would be "significant irregularities" in the meta-study. Neither "subtleties" nor "consistencies" fits with the clue "flawed." If there are "significant irregularities," then the analysis is "anything but" good. For blank (ii) the best answer with a positive connotation is "credible," or believable. "Intelligible" is also positive, but does not fit the contrast with the first blank, and "unreliable" is negative.

54. **Berserk, recede.** There are two major clues about the middle phases of a revolution: transferring power to "less temperate" forces would cause chaos, and a more peaceful period follows the difficult times. Therefore, blank (i) needs a word that means the opposite of peaceful. "Brusque" means short but is not the opposite of peaceful, and "pacific" is a synonym of peaceful and the exact opposite of what the blank requires. That leaves "berserk," which is the correct answer. The second sentence states that a more peaceful time comes later, so the "excesses" should become more stable. "Metastasize" means to spread, which is the opposite of what the blank requires. "Grow" has the same problem. That leaves the correct answer "recedes." If the difficult times "recede," then a more peaceful time arrives.

55. **Parlous.** The correct answer must match dangerous—only "parlous" does this, and it is the correct answer. Note that "suicidal" is too extreme and not indicated by the sentence. Both "prudent" (wise) and "providential" (opportune) have the wrong tone for the blank. And "semiotic," which means related to signs and symbols, is not supported by the sentence.

56. **Commercial.** The sentence gives two clues about the engineer: she is not interested in making products that match "market needs," and her work is known more for "its technical brilliance" than for "its _____ potential." Her work is technically good, then, but does not necessarily match "market" or customer needs; that is, it lacks "commercial" potential. Work that has technical brilliance could very well have lots of "scientific," "academic," or possibly even "revolutionary" potential; therefore none of these answer choices can be correct, since they do not offer any contrast. "Ergonomic" is a tempting choice since a brilliant piece of engineering might be quite uncomfortable for its user, but an engineer who lacks interest in developing needed products would not necessarily think to create uncomfortable products.

57. **Sangfroid, mercurial.** The sentence says that Frederick the Great was known for "his _____ under fire," but goes on to say that his "equilibrium sometimes failed him." That is the clue. The blank must mean something like grace or calm. "Sangfroid" (composure) is the best fit. "Intrepidity" (bravery) and "cruelty" do not match the clue. The failed equilibrium and "tirades" are both clues for blank (ii), which describes the way he sometimes behaved with his ministers. "Mercurial" (temperamental) is the best fit. "Fascist" (despotic) and "vainglorious" (boastful) go too far.

58. **Paradox, brook.** This sentence gives you very little to go on for blank (i); as is often the case, the clue for the first part appears in the second part of the sentence. This second part presents a dilemma indicated by "on the one hand" and "on the other": "teachers can't ill-afford to _____ indisputably disruptive behaviors," but too much strictness can actually promote disruptions. So blank (ii) must be something like "tolerate," as being tolerant would contradict being "overly strict," and blank (i) needs a word that indicates a contradiction. Starting with blank (i), "entreaty" means a request, and so doesn't fit this phrase at all. The "necessity of taking disciplinary action" sounds good in general, but the word "necessity" does not convey the idea of a contradiction. Instead, "paradox," which means a seemingly self-contradictory situation, is the choice that best communicates the nature of the situation. Moving to blank (ii), "fabricate" means to make up, and "mitigate" means to lessen the impact of something; neither fits the idea of "tolerate." Here "brook," which means to tolerate or condone, is the best fit.

**59. A stopgap, paragon, perpetuity.** The implication of the phrase "a more permanent solution" is that the original building was not permanent: it was "a stopgap," or a temporary fix. "An ornament" and "a modicum" (a small amount) don't fit the desired meaning for the first blank. The clue for the second blank is "canonization." To canonize something literally means to declare to be a saint, but in its figurative sense, it means to hold up as an exemplar or a "paragon." The third blank gets its clue from "originally," which indicates that you are looking for an opposite of transient. "In perpetuity" means forever, which fits. "Consecration" (dedication to the sacred) is a theme trap for "canonization," a religious step to sainthood, but this word can also describe the process by which something comes to be regarded as figuratively saintlike, or as an ideal example. "Chronology" (order in time) is about time, but does not mean lasts forever.

**60. Amity, mores.** The word "though" indicates that the negotiation did not actually proceed smoothly. The first blank comes after "semblance of," which indicates an outward appearance, especially one different from the reality. The word "disingenuous" backs up that meaning. You need something positive—the parties are showing false "amity," or friendliness, out of "a superficial adherence to" (pretense of following) customs or rules—"mores." The other choices for the first blank, "duplicity" (deliberate deceptiveness) and "solace" (comfort or consolation in sorrow) don't fit logically with "disingenuous." Similarly, "truisms" (self-evident claims) and "plaudits" (expressions of praise) would create a nonsensical meaning in the second blank.

**61. Elaboration, expatiation.** "Eschew" means to avoid or abstain, thus the speaker was unable to resist something that lengthened her presentation. The correct answer, "elaboration," would lengthen a presentation. "Terseness" means brevity and is a reversal trap, and "precision" also is generally not something that would cause a presentation to become excessively long. For the second blank, the clue is "turned a five-minute policy brief into an hour-long," making "expatiation," which means to speak or write at length, the correct choice. Since the second blank must match the general meaning of the first blank, "elaboration," the answer for the first blank provides another clue. "Distension," the act of swelling, refers only to a physical swelling. Similarly, "repertory," a collection of information or examples, doesn't fit the context either.

**62. Cosmopolitan.** Because the clue is "no effect," the blank will oppose championing "economic, political, and even cultural isolationism." Isolationism is a policy of abstaining from relationships with other countries, so the senator's upbringing must have been non-isolationist, or worldly. "Cosmopolitan" means worldly and is therefore a good fit. "Opulent" (wealthy), "tendentious" (opinionated), and "liberal" are all theme traps that ignore the contrast between the senator's upbringing and his views. "Bucolic" refers to an idyllic rural life and does not match the sentence.

**63. Protean, quixotic.** The first blank needs an idea that contrasts with "concrete proposal." "Protean" matches nicely. "Oppositional" and "martial" (warlike) don't contrast with "concrete" and so aren't correct. For the second blank, you need a word that also represents the idea of not being "concrete," as well as the idea of being "unlikely to ever come to fruition." "Quixotic" matches perfectly. "Pragmatic" is the exact opposite, and the sentence does not indicate whether the idea is "unorthodox" (against tradition).

**MANHATTAN**
PREP

64. **An arcadian, hinterland, spartan.** A "refuge" is positive; you also have the clue "quiet and rural." "Arcadian" conveys a positive view of rural life. "Parochial" (provincial) has a similar meaning except that it is somewhat negative. "Squalid" (dirty and run down) is even worse. The clue for the second blank is the word "but," which indicates that the "well-heeled" (wealthy) visitors see the region very differently; the sentence requires a negative version of the first blank. "Hinterland" conveys the idea of a backwater or an undesirable place. Neither "asylum" (place of refuge) nor "utopia" (a perfect place) have the required negative spin. The wealthy visitors see life there as "unpleasantly _____," so a negative word is needed. The only choice that can be negative is "spartan" (simple, austere.) "Tony" (posh, stylish) and "rational" are both positive.

65. **Debauchery, licentious.** This sentence features a somewhat complex structure. "Though" indicates that both blanks will oppose "prudish," since her stories are very different than her life. "Debauchery" (referring to sexual excess) fits the first blank, and "licentious" (lewd or sexually unrestrained) fits the second blank. "Propriety" (proper behavior) and "moralizing" are reversal traps, as they are aligned with prudishness. "Dissent" and "perspicacious" (perceptive) do not match the meaning or structure.

66. **Regressive, an auxiliary.** Given the lengthy explanation of the club's history, the elderly male member's suggestion was backwards, or hopelessly old-fashioned. Only "regressive" matches. "Rustic" (rural) and "prudish" (excessively proper or modest) both add something to the description of the old man that is not in the original sentence. In the second blank, you want something that reflects the idea "play bridge and drink tea without having to worry about serious issues." "Auxiliary" has this sense of secondary or on the side. The word "incendiary" (flammable) is almost an opposite of the desired meeting. Although the proposed organization might be "hierarchical," there is nothing in the sentence that suggests that.

67. **A deft, whet.** "Although" indicates that the first blank must be something positive or interesting to the students. Only "deft" (skillful) works. "Insipid" (uninteresting) and "effete" (weak or ineffectual) are not positive ways of describing a politician. Despite the fact that the historical figure was so accomplished, he also had old-fashioned views; as a result, the professor hasn't been able to get the students interested in him. "Whet," which means stimulate, is the only word that fits. "Tout" is a bit of a trap—the professor could "tout" the historical figure as an interesting thing to learn about, but she can't "tout" someone's interest. Similarly, "accrue" means accumulate over time, which doesn't fit here; although interest (money earned on a loan or bank deposit) can be accumulated over time, people's interest in a topic is not said to accumulate.

68. **Acerbic.** The comedian has a "caustic" (critical or sarcastic) sense of humor. Also, she's polarizing, as some people adore her, and some hate, or "abhor," her. A good word for the blank would mean something like sharp or biting or controversial. "Acerbic" (sharp, sarcastic, or candid in an almost bitter way) is the best choice. "Ample" (big or large) doesn't explain why her wit is so controversial. "Anachronistic" means out of place in time, and "abstruse" means difficult to understand. An "astounding" sense of humor would probably cause everyone to feel the same way about her and so can be eliminated.

69. **Halcyon.** The opposition structure is complicated. "Contrary" followed by "anything but" functions as a double negative, so the blank will agree with the Western-held assumptions about mindfulness. Additionally, a semicolon followed by "while" indicates that the blank will agree with "calm the mind" and oppose "restlessness and doubt." "Mystical," then, does not match the meaning and might be considered a theme trap. "Beneficial" and "benign" both add a negative spin not justified by the the rest of the sentence. "Orthodox"also does not match the meaning. That leaves "halcyon" (calm or joyful) as the best choice.

**MANHATTAN**
PREP

70. **An anemic**. While anemia is a medical condition, "anemic" as a metaphor means weak or lacking vitality; the job market is weak, so young people are choosing graduate school instead. "Myopia," or nearsightedness, also makes a good metaphor, but describes people and their decisions. The job market hasn't been "botched" (who botched it?), and it isn't "booming" (the sentence says that there aren't many jobs available). "Educated" is a trap answer; the young people are going to graduate school because the job market is bad, not because the job market is "educated."

71. **Beholden to, obligations.** "Despite" the fact that the politician was in favor of "campaign finance reform," he was "_____ corporate interests." A clear contrast is indicated, but it's tough to fill in this first blank with this information. Start with the second. His opponent is relatively new to politics so he doesn't have as many campaign promises, or "obligations," to "make good on." It isn't possible to make good on "dilemmas" or on "affiliations." In contrast to the new politician, then, the "career politician" must must have had more obligations; in other words, he is "more beholden to corporate interests." If he were "leery of" these interests, then the word "despite" couldn't be used at the beginning of the sentence. The sentence doesn't contain any information to suggest that he is "apathetic about," or lacking interest in, "corporate interests."

72. **Diffident, quietly.** The initial "Far too" indicates that the first blank will oppose "limelight" (an old theatrical expression meaning to be in the spotlight) and agree with "unassuming" (shy). "Diffident" (shy or reserved) is a good match and is also a clue for the second blank, which must match the first one; "quietly" is the best choice. Neither "implicitly" nor "skeptically" matches the meaning of shy or reserved. "Ideologically" is a theme trap that ignores the objective clues. "Apathetic" (unenergetic, indifferent) is also a spin trap.

73. **Groaning.** You might feel stuck if the idiom "groan under the strain" isn't familiar to you, but process of elimination can still work here. The part of the sentence following the colon must be equivalent—either an example or a restatement—to the part before it. The word that fills the blank must make "city infrastructure is already _____ under the strain of excess auto traffic" a good reason to create bike lanes in the city. Since bike lanes would help to relieve the traffic burden, the blank must mean something like struggling. "Groaning," which is something that a person struggling with a heavy load would do, is used figuratively here. The words "seething" (very angry), "waiting," "baying" (yelling loudly), and "intensifying" don't create an image of a person struggling under a heavy load the way that "groaning" does and so are not correct.

74. **Heterodox, iconoclasm, abolition.** The first two blanks both describe the professor's tendencies and should have a similar meaning. The clue for those blanks follows the colon: "she persistently challenged the academic methods and the institutional procedures of her department and of the university as a whole." For the first blank, "intellectual" is a theme trap. "Illiberal" means narrow-minded and does not describe someone who challenges institutions and established procedures. "Heterodox" (unorthodox or not in accordance with established thought) is a good match. Similarly, for the second blank, "iconoclasm" (opposing established beliefs) fits, while "intelligence" is another theme trap and "theories" does not match the desired meaning. The last blank describes arguing for doing something to "inherently elitist institutions" to democratize education. Since getting rid of universities entirely would have that effect, "abolition" is a great fit. "Enshrinement" (to cherish as sacred) is a reversal trap and "mitigation" (make less severe) is too mild to match the language "going so far as."

**MANHATTAN**
PREP

75. **Belies.** The phrase "apparent simplicity" is the clue that indicates that there is more to coffee than meets the eye. This sentence sets up a contrast between the phrases ("apparent simplicity" and "dizzying number of hours of toil") that are both used to describe coffee; the word that fills the blank must be a contrast word. "Confirms," "furnishes," and "fosters" (supports) are all incorrect because those words would be used to connect two phrases that agreed with each other. "Redresses" (corrects or rights a wrong) could be used for an opposite connection but doesn't fit here because there is no sense that the "simplicity" is correcting all those hours of work. "Belies" (to be at odds with) is most appropriate here.

76. **Unkempt, surprisingly deliberate.** The tricky blank structure masks what is ultimately a not-so-tricky word relationship: that of opposites. The clues for this relationship are the words "notwithstanding" and "if." The first part of the sentence says that in spite of the clutter of tools lying about, the studio was orderly. The part after the semicolon talks about the décor, and the idiomatic structure "if X, Y" is used to show a similar contrast. The first blank must match "cluttered," and the second must match "orderly." The best match for cluttered is "unkempt," and the better match for orderly is "surprisingly deliberate," because something that is deliberate is not random and so must have a certain order to it. The words "dire" (dreadful or grim) and "arduous" (difficult) may describe the way some people feel about clutter, but do not describe a cluttered décor. Similarly, "unsophisticated" (simple) and "callous" (uncaring) do not describe an orderly décor.

77. **Heralded, appropriated.** The phrase "equally public" provides a clue that the legislator's approval was also highly publicized, or "heralded." "Ratified," which means officially approved, would be redundant in this context. The sentence does not indicate that anyone "scorned" (rejected or was disdainful of) the approval. The sentence doesn't provide much of a clue for the second blank. When this happens, only one answer choice will make sense (and usually that correct choice won't add much to the sentence), while the other, incorrect answer choices will drastically change the meaning. Here, "appropriated," which means allocated or assigned, fits nicely and doesn't add any unintended meaning. Neither "stolen" nor "exacerbated" (made worse) is an appropriate description of funding that was approved by a legislature.

78. **Benign, decamped.** The first blank hinges on the meaning of the word "purportedly," which means pretending to be, or masquerading as. The sentence implies that the bureau is pretending to be harmless, or "benign." It wouldn't make sense to say that the bureau pretended that its "inquisitions" (inquiries or questionings) were "suspicious"; that word is an opposite trap. The sentence does not suggest that the inquisitions were "risqué" (sexually suggestive). The second blank requires a word that means to leave hurriedly; "decamped" fits. The word "immigrated," though close in meaning, isn't quite right because it means to arrive at a country or region rather than to leave from it. "Immigrated" is especially tricky because is sounds very similar to the word emigrated, which does mean to leave a country or region and move to another one. "Pandered," which means indulged another's desire, is not appropriate in this sentence.

79. **Congenial, erode.** When a relationship goes from something to "chilly at best," the relationship used to be warm or cordial: "congenial" fits best for the first blank. "Peaceful" doesn't go far enough, and "reverent" goes too far. If the relationship has gotten worse, then there has been an undermining, or an eroding, of mutual trust. To "bolster" something is to support or to improve it, so this choice is opposite to the desired meaning. "Fester" (not improve and likely get worse over time) is a negative word; something positive, such as "trust," cannot be said to "fester." Only something negative, such as a wound or resentment, can be described as "festering."

80. **Anomalies.** The opening phrase "It is in no way shocking that" suggests that whatever follows will at first appear to be "shocking." The second part of the sentence provides another clue when it says "however" other scientists must be able to "duplicate the normal pattern" of the original experiment in order to consider its results valid. So the blank must be filled by a word that describes results that deviate from what is expected, such as the correct answer "anomalies." Although "anxiety" and "malfunctions" might be unexpected outcomes of scientific experiments, they do not fit with the second part of the sentence and so are not correct. "Vaccines" and "paradigms," or models, are expected outcomes of scientific experiments and so cannot be correct either.

81. **Responsible for, eschews, fundamental.** Your first clue is "free will." One can only be "responsible for" the things one decides, or freely wills, to do. Judgments of people might well be "determined by" or "based on" something that they have done, but such judgments would be an outcome of determining responsibility, not the responsibility itself. For the second blank, the word "instead," even though it occurs later in the sentence, implies that Dr. Wegner is avoiding "the traditional talking points of the controversy." He "eschews" them. There is nothing in the sentence to suggest that Dr. Wegner "mitigates" (reduces the severity of) or "contradicts" the points that are usually made when "free will" is discussed. The word "though" indicates that the third blank contrasts with the word "tangential." A "tangential" question is one that is related to the issue but not at its core, so such a question would usually be regarded as less important to answer. The third blank, then, should mean something like at the core of the issue, or "fundamental." There is nothing in the sentence to suggest that the question is "ideological" (strongly related to a particular belief system or ideology) or "flashy."

82. **Detractors, fealty, tantamount to.** "Erstwhile" means past or former, indicating that those who are now "gathering around" the candidate were once doing something different—that is, criticizing or detracting. The correct answer for the first blank must be "detractors." "Supporters" and "zealots" (fanatical supporters) are the reverse of what you want and are there to trap anyone who doesn't notice the word "erstwhile." These former "detractors" are "gathering around her" to proclaim their loyalty, or "fealty," in a way that is deeply inconsistent with their past actions, as they are "behaving in a manner" that one might call "outright hypocrisy." They are not proclaiming their "distaste" or "magnanimity," which means generosity, especially from a former opponent. Since the last sentence says that the former opponents didn't feel at all embarrassed about behavior that might be described "as _____ outright hypocrisy," the third blank must mean equivalent to or the same as, which is exactly what "tantamount to" means. Neither "reciprocal with" (an equal exchange with) nor "hinging on" (dependent on) fit the desired meaning here.

83. **Convulsions, retching.** This sentence contrasts various symptoms of exposure to toxic substances. The two blanks must contrast with "lassitude" (tiredness) and "torpor" (sluggishness) because of the word "whereas." Additionally, the word "incite" indicates that the blanks will contain words that are active rather than passive. Although "convulsions" (violent seizures) and "retching" are not opposites of "lassitude" and "torpor," these are the only choices that might be active symptoms of poisoning. "Quarrels" (arguments) and "complaints" are not symptoms of poisoning. Incorrect choices "apathy" and "drowsiness" are somewhat similar to "lassitude" and "torpor" and are therefore the opposite of what you want.

**MANHATTAN**
PREP

84. **Wag.** The sentence concerns "Commentators and comedians." Since defining a "gaffe" (a mistake) "as a politician accidentally telling the truth" is meant to be funny, the blank needs to be a word for a comedian. A "wag" is a joker, although not necessarily a professional one, and a decent match. An "apologist" would be a supporter who made excuses for the corrupt politicians; this doesn't fit the meaning of the sentence as a whole. A "diplomat" also wouldn't be likely to publicly say something so impolite about politicians. And finally, although a comedian could also be an "egoist" (self-centered person) or "transgressor" (violator of rules), these words are not synonyms for "commentators and comedians."

85. **Pathetic, of actual decreases, sentenced.** The first sentence alone provides little indication of what the first blank should be: there is a "low rate of growth" and "the 2007 financial crisis," which are both negative, but the blank isn't necessarily so. Economists describe the low rate of growth as surprising? Not surprising? Terrible? Normal? Read on for more context. Blank (ii) describes examples of something that causes "a corresponding decline in lifestyles." The best fit is "actual decreases," which refers back to the "wages" in the first sentence. "Medical bills" represent a cost, but this goes unquantified, so to claim "a corresponding decline in lifestyles" would be a stretch. "Buoyancy" when applied to the economy means a high level of activity, so this choice is the opposite of what is needed. With "actual decreases" in the second sentence, there is better context for the first blank. Economists (in general) describe a "low rate of growth in wages," and "many cite examples of actual decreases," which is even worse, so indeed the first blank should be something like "paltry" or "poor"; "pathetic" in this context is a synonym. "Promising" is opposite and "partisan," which means biased or prejudiced, is unrelated. The final sentence continues the negative characterization of this "unfortunate trend," predicting "years of poverty and deprivation" for an "often blameless" group. "Uplifted" and "devoted" are too positive, but "sentenced" to (i.e., punished with) "years of poverty and deprivation" works.

86. **Scintillating, wry.** The first blank describes Martin Amis's "wit." The second sentence describes Amis's novels as full of sharp "jibes," or insulting remarks; "scintillating," which means clever or amusing, describes such an author's wit quite well. "Sartorial" (relating to style of dress) and "feckless" (incompetent or good-for-nothing) are great GRE words, but don't describe a clever author's wit. The second sentence says that because of the author's wit, descriptions of sad and horrible scenes "often bring a _____ smile to the reader's lips." Why would a reader smile when reading about something awful? The smile must be ironic, because of the contrast between the tragic scene and the clever writing. The word that fits best is "wry," which can mean ironic. A "disapproving" smile doesn't make sense, and there is no need for a reader to be "discreet" or inconspicuous while reading a disturbing section of a book; no one else knows what the reader is smiling about anyway.

87. **Chide.** The sentence describes what the teacher "gently" does to "students who don't do their homework." She is too "amiable" (friendly or good-natured) to punish them, so the blank must mean something like lightly criticize, or "chide." The adverb "gently" is important here, because it's impossible to gently "detest" or "pillory" them (attack or ridicule publicly). "Malign" (say bad things about) is also too negative, and Ms. Llewellyn doesn't punish anyone, so "penalize" doesn't work.

88. **Punctiliousness.** What was the case "for eons" is contrasted with the situation "now," which is that "laxity and tardiness" are "fashionable" and "considered appropriate." So it must be that the blank is some behavior that is not lax or not tardy. "Punctiliousness," which is the state of being strict in observance of formalities, fits with the former, and with the latter, too, if punctuality is a formality. "Probity," which means integrity or honesty, certainly fits with "virtuous," but doesn't contrast with what is happening "now." Two of the choices are antonyms: "parsimoniousness" means frugality to the point of stinginess and "prodigality" is the quality or situation of spending money without care. Though opposite, both are negative and wouldn't be "considered not only polite, but virtuous," nor do they contrast with "laxity" or "tardiness." The final choice, "panache," meaning flamboyance or flair, is not indicated by the sentence—don't read too much into "fashionable."

89. **Voluble.** The first clues in this short sentence are "bombastic" (pompous and verbose) and "long," one of which should agree with the blank. The word "eloquent" should contrast with the blank due to "rather than." "Voluble," which is used to describe someone who talks incessantly, fits perfectly. "Unscrupulous" and "hostile" are negative but don't really relate to talking too much in a pompous way. "Frank," meaning direct and sincere in speech, is neither in direct agreement nor in direct disagreement with any of the clues. And finally, "languid," which means slow and relaxed, is not supported by the rest of the sentence.

90. **Specter.** If elementary school students ran drills in which "they had to dive under their desks and curl up into a ball," there was a fear or a threat that was a daily part of people's lives. A secondary meaning of the word "specter" (which can also mean ghost) is something widely feared as a dangerous occurrence. "Annihilation," "brutality," "detonation," and "arms race" all seem to fit with the theme of a nuclear holocaust, but these words do not mean fear or threat.

91. **Apathy, diligence.** "As opposed" indicates a reversal between what happened in Boehm's undergraduate years and during his doctoral program, which is also indicated by the switch from "hedonism," or pleasure-seeking, to "earnest devotion," probably to academic studies, as this devotion "led to academic laurels." The first blank should either match "hedonism" or contrast "devotion," and the second blank should match "earnest devotion" or be something related to academic success. The best answers are "apathy," indifference or lack of interest, and "diligence," commitment or hard work. "Studiousness" would be a good fit for the second blank, but is an opposite trap in the first blank. There are no clues to suggest that he was deceitful, or exhibiting "duplicity." In the second blank, "morality" might *feel* right: if your personal view is that "hedonism" is immoral, this would provide the contrast required. However, pleasure-seeking is not *by definition* immoral, any more than "morality" would necessarily lead to academic laurels. "Detachment" means indifference, so it's a near synonym of "apathy"; it's another opposite trap that would work well in the other blank, but not in blank (ii).

92. **Land, a plum.** The first blank needs to be a synonym of get. "Ascertain" does not fit that meaning, and "ensure" is used incorrectly—the actress might want to ensure that she gets the part, but it doesn't make sense to say that she wants to "ensure the part" itself. The second blank should describe a role with "lots of onscreen time" and good scenes; you need a synonym for good. That's exactly what "plum" means. "Grave" (important or harmful) and "theatrical" (relating to theater or overly dramatic in a negative way) do not fit the desired meaning.

**MANHATTAN**
PREP

93. **Touchstone**. You need a clue that matches "more than a hit movie" and goes with the idea of having meaning for a whole generation of people. "Touchstone," or something used to make judgments about other things, matches perfectly. "Cornerstone" doesn't work—a cultural touchstone is a single important event, place, work of art, etc. A "cultural cornerstone" would be something the whole society is built upon (like individualism, Islam, or the monarchy, depending on the society). A "rudder" is literally part of a ship related to steering; if you are lost in life, you are like a ship without a rudder. A "bolster" is pretty similar to a "stanchion," at least when used metaphorically to mean a support (literally, a "bolster" is a pillow, and a "stanchion" is an upright bar or post), so neither is the answer.

94. **A level of skepticism.** The colon means that the blank will agree with the clue "not fully convinced," so the correct answer is "a level of skepticism." "An enthusiasm" is the opposite of what would fit this blank. "Degree of humility," "thoroughness," and "eloquence" do not match the fact that she is "not fully convinced" about this theory.

95. **Mask, part and parcel.** The sentence says that people who work in the service industry "put on a smile for the customer," implying that they hide their true emotions in some way. "Masquerade" is close, but it means either to pretend to be someone or to be disguised as something else; neither meaning works for the first blank. To "simulate" emotions is to pretend to feel them, not to hide them, which doesn't work either, so the correct answer for the first blank is "mask." For the second blank, you need something like a requirement. "Apex" is a high point (i.e., The apex of my career was playing for the Knicks). "Conceit" means a fanciful notion. "Part and parcel," meaning an essential piece of something, is the correct phrase.

96. **Bogus.** "In an age of near-instantaneous fact checking," politicians need to be careful about what they say, "as" (which means "because" here) "any fictitious claim" will be proved fictitious or false. "Bogus" (not genuine) is an excellent match. "Genuine" is a reversal trap. "Dull" in this context means boring, which, although negative, is not the desired meaning. Neither "unnecessary" nor "unfamiliar" fit the desired meaning either.

97. **Tacky, discerning, tactically.** The judgmental mind behind this sentence finds his grandmother's décor "vulgar," so the first blank should be a synonym for that. "Tacky" fits the bill. Neither "vitreous" (made from glass) or "grizzled" (having gray hair) can reasonably describe the grandmother's decorating scheme. The second blank should be something like appropriate: it wouldn't be appropriate to tell his grandma what he really thinks. Neither "rancorous" (malevolent) or "doting" (to lavish attention on) fits this meaning. "Discerning," meaning having or showing good judgment or shrewd, fits perfectly. For the third blank, you need a word that describes being nice to someone in order to get a good birthday present. "Amicable" doesn't capture the strategy of the idea, but "duplicitous" is way too negative. It means deceitful, which is not really an apt description for the act of refraining from telling your grandma that she has terrible taste. "Tactically," meaning by way of showing adroit planning, is correct.

98. **Warded off, mutiny.** The second half of the sentence says that the crew became frustrated and "decided to take matters into their own hands," implying that they took over the ship. "Mutiny" fits perfectly. (A "sea change" is a profound transformation, while "helmsmanship" relates to helmsman, a person who steers a ship.) For the first blank, you need a word implying that the captain tried to fight off the mutiny. "Dissuading" is tempting, but it is something you can do only to people (e.g., I dissuaded the pirates from mutinying). "Warded off" means fended off or averted, which is perfect here. "Depreciated" (to cause to decrease in value) has the wrong meaning.

**99. Serendipitous, dispensations.** A "birth lottery" is offered as an example of the sort of element the first word describes. Since a lottery is random, based on chance, the first blank should be something like due to luck, and that is just what "serendipitous" means. Be careful of the trap answer "common." Although "common element" is a frequently used expression, it does not capture the correct meaning, which is random. "Inchoate" (incipient, only partially in existence) is a good GRE word, but it has the wrong meaning. The second blank looks to be roughly synonymous with gifts. "Dispensations" will work there, while "encumbrances" and "piques" are both negative.

**100. Discriminate, baseless.** The mantis shrimp has more color detecting cells than any other creature. "While one would think" indicates that the common or logical view will turn out to be incorrect. Certainly the logical deduction would be that these shrimp are good at seeing colors, so "discriminate" (which can mean to distinguish accurately) is the best choice for the first blank. The GRE will often use lesser known secondary meanings, as here with "discriminate." "Distort" is a reversal trap and "improve" does not fit the desired meaning. The second blank should contrast what "one would think." It turns out that they can't actually see more colors, so this claim is false, or "baseless" (without basis in fact). "Obvious" and "illiberal" (narrow-minded) do not mean false.

**101. Detractors, vulgar.** "While" indicates that the clause after the comma will oppose the clause before the comma. So instead of supporters, you want opposers. The word "condemned" further hints that the first blank will be something like opposers/condemners. Only "detractors" works. "Interlocutors" (go-betweens) and "contemporaries" (people who lived at the same time) do not fit the desired meaning. For the second blank, you want a description that a detractor would apply to "earthy speech." So you want earthy, but in a bad way—perhaps coarse or unrefined would serve. The word "vulgar" fits those descriptions. "Obtuse" (unintelligent or ignorant) is negative but does not match the clue "earthy." In contrast, "genteel" (polite) is almost the opposite of what you want.

**102. Versatile, explicate.** The first blank doesn't offer much of a clue, beyond the idea that the tools are "sophisticated" (and therefore positive). "Versatile" is the best fit. "Eclectic" (drawing from multiple sources) is neutral, not positive. "Populist" (a member of a political party claiming to represent the interests of the common people) is tricky because it looks similar to popular. Next, the social scientists are using these tools "to model and help _____ even decisions." "Explicate" (explain) is the best match. "Interpolate" means to estimate an intermediate point between two known points, or to insert new words into a text; decisions cannot be interpolated. Similarly, decisions cannot be extended by assuming that existing trends will continue, so "extrapolate" doesn't fit either.

**103. Robust.** The bacteria that survive antibiotics would presumably be those hardest to kill. You might also want a word that means something like drug-resistant. The only word that means anything like hard-to-kill is "robust." "Widespread," "immature," and "benign" (not harmful) do not indicate that the bacteria are inherently harder to kill. Although "notorious" (well known for something bad) is tempting, a "notorious" bacteria is not necessarily hard to kill; it could just be particularly infectious or toxic.

**104. Prodigies.** These very intelligent children actually do "fulfill their early promise," so the blank should indicate that they really are talented in some way. Such children are "prodigies." Although "teenagers" is tempting because children become teenagers, the sentence says that the children "go on to fulfill their early promise," implying that they lead extraordinary lives, and teenager-hood is only a short part of someone's life. The other answers, "cranks," "theorizers," and "pragmatists" (practical people), are not supported by the sentence.

**MANHATTAN**
PREP

**105. Heuristic, represent.** The first word is defined in the sentence as a device useful for "inciting and guiding discovery." That's one of the meanings of "heuristic," which is the correct answer. A "literary device" is a common expression and so sounds good, but the meaning is wrong because a "literary device" is a technique used in writing to produce a specific effect. An "allegorical" (symbolic or metaphorical) device is a specific type of "literary device" and so doesn't work either. If you are not meant to take the "model of the psyche" as a guide to the physical structure of the brain, then you want a word that means something like show or depict for the second blank. "Represent" is the closest choice. The word "dictate" is incorrect because a model of the brain doesn't determine the physical form of the brain. "Ameliorate" (make a bad thing better) also does not fit the desired meaning.

**106. Technical, diffident.** Since the "medium … lacked a voice," the technology of the day prevented Lloyd from speaking on film, so the first word should be something like technological. "Technical" will do. Neither "artistic" nor "commercial" describes the limits of films that lacked a voice. The second blank requires an adjective that would explain why a character would fail to speak, perhaps something like mute. "Diffident" means something like self-effacing or very shy and very shy people are often somewhat reluctant to speak; this is the best choice. "Reluctant" is a trap answer—it does not mean reluctant to speak (the similar-sounding reticent does, and the two words are often confused). "Avant-garde" (developing new or experimental artistic concepts) does not fit the desired meaning.

**107. Skeptical.** Follow the structure to unravel this sentence. The part before the semicolon says that the boss was considered a "figurehead." However, people slowly realized that he was actually getting a lot of stuff done! The employees were initially critical or doubtful; the best match among the answers is "skeptical." The other four answers, "senior," "clueless," "resolute" (determined), and "scrutinized" (closely observed) do not match the meaning.

**108. Scarcity, regional, staff.** "Critics" are complaining about something related to "a _____ of unique view-points." The sentence indicates that the "conglomerates will often discuss the same issues and talking points across all platforms," so there is a lack of, or "scarcity," of differing viewpoints. Neither "banality" (boring, ordinary) nor "deviation" (different from the norm) fits the desired meaning. The sentence also indicates that there is "a lack of local news coverage," so local "events are no longer covered by smaller media." The best match for local is "regional." "Domestic" is a good trap, but when applied to locations, this word typically refers to an entire country (domestic vs. international). "Elaborate" does not mean local. Finally, the smaller media groups can't afford to hire, or "staff," enough employees. "Imply" is a trap because it sounds very close to employ. "Broadcast" seems to go along with media, but does not fit the desired meaning of this blank.

**109. Attest to, quotidian.** "Just as … so too …" suggests that the mainstream novels show a gift, just as the science-fiction novels do. The first word should mean something like show, or display. Among these answers, only "attest" has that meaning. Incorrect choices "belie" and "gainsay" both indicate an opposite direction. The second word should describe the world of mainstream, rather than science-fiction, novels: something not fantastic, but just ordinary or everyday. "Quotidian" has just that meaning. "Fantastical" (odd and bizarre) and "ebullient" (cheerful and exuberant) don't, in general, describe the ordinary, everyday world.

**110. Solvent.** If a company is far from "flourishing" (prospering), it is not doing well, even if the report "avers" (swears) that it is. "Solvent" means profitable; a "not profitable" company is definitely not doing well. "Thriving" is very tempting but ignores the expression "let alone flourishing." The correct use of the expression "not X, let alone Y," requires that X be at a lower level or be an intermediate step towards Y, as in "The paper was not even comprehensible, let alone informative." Since "thriving" is on the same level as "flourishing," it can't logically be used here. "Copious" (detailed), "evasive," and "unprecedented" don't fit with "let alone flourishing" either.

**111. Supplants, contemptible.** "Requisite" means made necessary by circumstances or regulation, so "a requisite amount of regulatory pressure" is the normal, suitable, or necessary amount of pressure on "a business." But what does *this* business do? Regarding "pressure" about "industry safety standards," the business [does something to] "its own non-compliance … with yet another series of suspect omissions." The blanks must make the sentence generally read this way: A business that [replaces or substitutes = blank (i)] bad safety standards with "yet another" set of bad safety standards is very [bad = blank (ii)]. "Supplants" is a synonym for replaces and "contemptible" means despicable or deplorable, so these choices fit. "Imbue" means inspire or permeate with some characteristic or feeling. "Non-compliance" could be said to be imbued with "omissions" of compliance, but "yet another" separates and distinguishes the "omissions" from the original "non-compliance"; the context and structure of the sentence make this choice wrong. "Verifies" is too positive in the first blank and "laudable," or worthy of praise, is too positive in the second blank. There is no indication in the sentence that a business that behaves this way is "contrived," which means unrealistic or artificially created.

**112. Draconian.** "Belied" means contradicted or was at odds with. Thus, the boss's on-the-job style is contradicted by his "amiable," or warm, friendly style in the interview. The clue is that the young hire (the new employee) experiences "chagrin," which is mental distress or unease. "Draconian," which means harsh, strict, or severe, is best. Don't be confused by "nonplussed," the primary meaning of which is confused or surprised—it doesn't capture the boss's strictness. The answer "friendly" is a trap for anyone who doesn't notice the word "belied" earlier in the sentence. "Fatuous" (silly and pointless) is a great GRE word, but doesn't match the intended meaning. "Illicit" (illegal) goes too far: there is nothing in the sentence to suggest that the boss is behaving illegally.

**113. An exhaustive, remarkable variance.** The first blank is tricky; start with the second one. "Fluctuations" cause the "most reliable" wines to be something like unpredictable. Only "remarkable variance" fits. "Taxonomy" is a classification system and "mitigating circumstances" are circumstances that make something less severe or serious. If even the "reliable vintages" exhibit a large variance, then it must be difficult to have full, or "exhaustive," comprehension of Italian wines. "Futile" (ineffective) and "irredeemable" (unable to be saved or helped) do not fit the desired meaning.

**114. Casual nonchalance, farce.** If the clerk treats his office (a fancy way to say his job) with a general lack of respect, then he treats his clients with a similarly cool and distant manner, a manner of "casual nonchalance." "Meticulous" (careful and precise) is positive and "envy" is not indicated by the sentence. As for the second blank, knowing that "grand farce" is a common English idiom is helpful but is not essential—the word "farce," or mockery, is the only word that fits. A "grand gesture" would be positive (a "grand gesture" would be something like an elaborate marriage proposal, apology, etc.), and it is not possible to treat one's entire job like a "grand tirade" (angry speech).

**MANHATTAN**
PREP

115. **Engaging, a tired.** Since the critics viewed the book negatively, as evidenced by "dry pedantry" (a rigid over-emphasis on rules or details) and "humorless presentation," the author must have turned an interesting topic into a tedious one. Thus, the first blank will be positive in tone and the second negative. "Engaging" matches the tone and content. "Affectless," meaning showing a lack of emotion or sympathy, and "dogmatic," meaning opinionated or doctrinal, do not match the positive tone needed for the first blank. Similarly, for the second blank, only "a tired" matches the required negative tone; "a worthy" is positive and "an instructive" is neutral.

116. **Rife with contention, critical, seasoned practitioners.** This problem is best solved starting from the last blank. Certain "tenets" (principles important to a group of people) are not necessarily accepted as fact ("gospel") even by those who really believe in the practice of psychoanalysis. These people are "seasoned practitioners," experienced in psychoanalysis. "Quarrelsome factions" are the opposite of the intended meaning and while "beneficiaries" could work, the sentence does not provide any clues to justify use of the word "esteemed." Next, move to the second blank. The experts may question "even tenets" that are deemed central to the overall philosophy. The best match is "critical" (crucial). "Immaterial" (unimportant) and "anathema," used to describe something that is cursed or loathed, do not fit the idea of something that is crucial to the philosophy. Finally, the second sentence provides the necessary clues for the first blank: psychoanalysis is a subject of debate even among those who practice it; it is "rife with contention." The practitioners do not "ridicule" it or find it "devoid of substance" (lacking substance). Rather, they disagree with some of the principles even as they continue to follow the overall philosophy.

117. **Antipathy, patent, mutual benefit.** The first and third blanks are highly related, so consider them first. "Apparent antagonism" exists between two people; are they really so hostile to one another? The two individuals also "derive inspiration and motivation from the other." In other words, there is a "mutual benefit" to the seemingly hostile relationship, which otherwise might be "written off" as pure hatred, or "antipathy." Neither "flagrancy" (the act of being flagrant, offensive) nor "hypocrisy" fits the meaning of hatred. For the third blank, both "worthless pride" and "tacit disagreement" are negative in nature; they do not convey a "benefit." Now return to the second blank. The "apparent antagonism" can be "written off," so "further scrutiny should render" clear or apparent the fact that there is actually a positive to this "rivalry." The best fit is "patent" (obvious, evident). "Useless" and "spurious" (not genuine, insincere) do not fit the desired meaning.

118. **Hyperboles.** The answer must match the clues "flights of fancy" and "arching far beyond reality." "Hyperbole" is exaggeration and is the correct answer. "Tit for tat" (retaliation in kind), "parables" (stories with morals), "conundrums" (difficult questions), and "innuendos" (hint or insinuation, often negative) do not fit this meaning.

119. **Initially, given teeth.** First, or "initially," the law in question "had little impact," but "subsequent legislation" changed this. "Justifiably" and "unbelievably" are value judgments that are not supported by the rest of the sentence. In the second blank, you need something that will contrast with having little impact and will match the idea of a law now gaining "funding and enforcement." Only "given teeth" has this (metaphorical) meaning. "Rendered moot" and "kept at bay" go against the desired meaning.

120. **Counterpoint.** The blank requires a word that means having two distinct components, since the opera is capable of evoking two distinct emotions. "Counterpoint" (use of contrast in a work of art) is a good fit. "Macabre" is a trap, since it goes along with horror but leaves out joy. "Articulate" is related to speech and does not fit here. "Contrived" (not natural, planned) and "figurative" (using metaphor or other non-literal device to convey meaning) are not supported by any clues in the sentence

**121. Buttress.** "Buttress," as a noun or a verb, relates to support and is therefore justified by the clue "needed additional support." Note that you certainly do not need to memorize architectural terms for the GRE, but you should definitely know the metaphorical meaning of buttress (to support). A "partition" is tempting, but the purpose of such a feature is to divide or separate two things, not necessarily to support something. An "albatross" is a bird but is also used metaphorically to mean an ongoing problem. While "hallmark" and "trademark" can be synonyms, they don't mean to support.

**122. Veracity, consistent with.** No single experiment can ever prove the truth, or "veracity," of a theory. "Rationality" is close but connotes the idea of the theory being logical, rather than factual. "Candor" (honest and direct communication) is incorrect because the theory is not telling the truth; rather, a theory is true (or is not true). For the second blank, in order for the theory to be supported, or "resilient," the results from independent labs should agree with each other, or be "consistent with" each other. The results don't have to be "founded on" or "antithetical to" (opposed to) each other in order for the theory to be supported.

**123. Pertinent, deeply humbling.** Sleep is important, or relevant, to your daily life, making "pertinent" the best word for the first blank. The explanation in general may be "mysterious" or "obscure," but the topic is not "mysterious" or "obscure" "to our daily lives." Regarding the second blank, the expression "at once fascinating and _____" indicates at least a loose contrast, so you need something that could contrast with "fascinating." The clue "so ignorant" is a good indication that what you want is "deeply humbling." Don't fall for the trap answer "fully impenetrable." While the topic of sleep is presented as somewhat impenetrable (that is, hard to understand), the blank is not describing sleep, but rather human ignorance about it. "Totally blatant," which means obvious or not at all hidden, doesn't describe human ignorance about sleep either.

**124. Waxed, barely stirred.** There is a discrepancy or mismatch between Mozart's fame and his financial situation, so whatever happened to one did not happen to the other. The clue "beyond measure" indicates that his musical star must have grown, so "waxed" is the only possibility for the first blank; "abated" and "dwindled" both mean to get smaller. Mozart's income must have either gone down or remained low; "barely stirred" is the correct answer for the second blank. It could not be the case that his income "grew exponentially" or "remained exorbitant," or there would be no discrepancy.

**125. Assent.** While the structure might seem tricky, the blank must oppose "refusing for a decade" since the patriarch finally "surrendered." "Assent" is the best choice because it means agreement. "Ascent" (climb up), "dissent (disagreement), and "descent" (climb down) do not fit the text and are essentially phonetic tricks. "Assertion" does not fit because he cannot "give his assertion." Rather, he would "assert" something.

**126. Peril, simulacrum, terrifies.** "Even" suggests that the first blank describes the sort of thing you might otherwise expect a thrill seeker to find attractive. These patrons do not want "danger," so you could just reuse that word for the first blank. "Peril" is the best choice. Although "titillation" does describe a sort of thrill, it is not negative, nor does it suggest danger. "Lavishness" suggests luxury, not danger, and so does not fit either. The third word is probably easier to anticipate than the second, so skip ahead. "In fact" suggests that you want a word that means seems to be unsafe, and the description of the "thrill-seeking visitors" suggests that you want something, well, thrilling. "Terrifies" is the closest choice. "Satisfies" yields a perfectly fine sentence, but it does not contrast with "perfectly safe." "Mollifies," which means to sooth or pacify, is the opposite of what the thrill seekers want. The second blank, then, requires something like imitation, and "simulacrum" is the closest synonym among the answers. Using a "complement" here

**MANHATTAN**
PREP

would imply something that partners with danger, which doesn't match the meaning of imitation of danger. Similarly, an "abettor" of danger would be an aid or a helper, which doesn't fit the intended meaning either.

**127. Dilettantes, apprenticeship.** The first word should indicate an opposite of "professionals." The word that suggests itself is amateurs, and the closest answer to that is "dilettantes," which is roughly synonymous with dabblers. "Artisans" (skilled craftspeople) is a reversal trap and "ideologues" (uncompromising advocates of an ideology) is a great GRE vocabulary word that does not fit the meaning of this sentence. The second word should suggest a type of training, and among the options only "apprenticeship" does so. "Acumen" (sharp insight) and "sensibility" are not types of training.

**128. Arresting, charismatic.** The first singer is good "but" she is not as good as the next singer; the first blank requires a positive word. Only "arresting" (impressive) fits. Both "unremarkable" and "hackneyed" (trite or unoriginal) are negative. If the first singer is not as good, then the second singer is better, so the latter's stage presence must be much better. "Pedestrian" (unremarkable) doesn't fit, but both "charismatic" and "experienced" are fairly positive words. Here, there are two ways to eliminate "experienced." First, while you might call the singer herself "experienced," the target of this blank is the singer's "stage presence," which cannot be properly described as "experienced." Second, "arresting," the correct choice for blank (i), aligns very well with a "charismatic" stage presence.

**129. Confounding, acumen.** The "contradictions in the philosopher's life were more _____" given that the philosopher had some characteristic that led to "profound insights," meaning a very deep understanding or awareness. Since the second blank is that characteristic, start there. Although "prodigal" is often used to mean extravagant, here it means something more like abundant. The second blank must mean something like skill then, because a high level of intellectual skill would logically lead to deep understanding, and the first blank must mean surprising, because it would be surprising if someone who was very skilled at making good judgments had a lot of contradictions in his life. The correct answer to the first blank is "confounding," which means surprising. "Insightful" and "unpremeditated" are words associated with thought, but they do not fit the desired meaning for the first blank. The correct answer for the second blank, "acumen," is the skill of making good judgements. "Vacuity," which means empty-headedness, is the exact opposite of what is needed. "Veracity" means truthfulness, which is tempting, but doesn't quite fit with the clue. A truthful person is not necessarily going to have deep insights.

**130. Eminence, influence.** Borrowing another word from the sentence, the first word should be something like "significance." The closest option is "eminence," which suggests great importance. If Hopper argues that the book was among the most important in spite of the fact that it cannot have had an impact on O'Brien's contemporaries, then he must appeal to some standard other than impact. "Influence" is the word most nearly synonymous with impact. Because "currency" echoes the concern about how widely read the book was, it might appeal, but this word does not fit the earlier clue; he "appeals to standards other than" the one mentioned earlier, "impact on one's contemporaries." Finally, "dissolution" (dissolving or ending something) is not a type of standard.

**131. Denigrate, balkanized.** Start with the second blank. A society with "class warfare" is divided into hostile groups, or "balkanized," but it need not be either "socialized" or "politicized." Politicians who "refuse to accept" such talk would tend to dismiss or belittle, or "denigrate," it. "Besmirch" means to attack the honor of something—although the word is negative, it isn't quite appropriate here. "Encourage" is a reversal trap: since the sentence says that the politicians do not believe that society is experiencing "class warfare," they would not urge people to discuss it.

**MANHATTAN**
PREP

**132. Deftness, peasant, dissembled.** The subject "magically acquired an honorific title" and he was able to "parlay this charade into a small fortune." These hints suggest that his motive was to make himself look and sound more important than he actually was. Blank (i) and blank (ii) contrast how he was able to get away with this trick: because of his "aquiline," meaning regal, nose and his social tendencies, and despite his genetics. The best fit for blank (i) is "deftness," which means skilled or clever. The other options here both suggest something negative about his social abilities, be it "arrogance," meaning conceit, or "maladroitness," meaning ineffective or clumsy, the opposite of the meaning needed here. Blank (ii) describes his "genetics, which lacked any distinction." The best match is "peasant," or a farm worker with little social status. "Perturbing" is too negative in this context. And "patrician," which means characteristic of aristocracy, is the opposite of what the blank requires. Finally, blank (iii) calls for a word that indicates how he "successfully" was able to act in order "to parlay this charade into a small fortune." Of the answer choices, "coalesced" means to combine distinct elements, which does not fit in this context. Likewise, "disseminated" means to spread or disperse something, and also doesn't fit here. "Dissembled" (disguise or conceal) fits best: he successfully disguised his true identity.

**133. An ironclad.** Since the final part of the sentence is meant to go against the idea that the Second Amendment provides a guarantee of a private right, you need to fill the blank in the first part with something that reinforces the guarantee. "Ironclad" means rigid or fixed and does what you need here. "Defeasible" and "questionable" would undermine the guarantee. Nothing in the passage has any bearing on whether the guarantee is "earnest." "Amended" is a theme trap because the sentence is talking about the Second Amendment to the United States Constitution, but "amended" means added to and does not fit the desired meaning for the blank.

**134. Sophistry.** The sentence indicates that Lillian Hellman was being honest when calling her disingenuous, or deceitful, argumentative strategy "the nobility racket." The fact that she calls the deceitful strategy a "racket" indicates that she doesn't truly believe in the things she states while using this argumentative strategy. Therefore, the word that best fills the blank is "sophistry," which means the use of fallacious arguments, often with the intent to deceive others. If someone espoused a "philosophy," she would actually believe in what she was saying. "Sinecure" (a position that requires little work but provides financial benefit), "volubility" (talkativeness), and "serendipity" (fortunate accident) do not fit the desired meaning.

**135. Undermined.** The fitness guru seems to promote a healthy lifestyle ("salubrious" means healthy). On the other hand, when he's alone, he's not very healthy himself. These actions would do something like "corrupt" or "do bad things to" his integrity. The correct answer, "undermined," means to reduce the power of, undercut, or sabotage. He's not making fun of himself, so "ridiculed" doesn't quite work. "Restored" is the opposite of the intended meaning. "Redacted" means to draft or make ready for publication. The guru did not "insinuate," or subtly suggest, anything about his integrity.

**136. Disquieting, casualty.** The sentence claims that there are "unexploded World War II munitions," or bombs, buried in places where people live. This could be upsetting, dangerous, or some other negative word. Of the given options, "disquieting" (disturbing) fits. "Exhilarating" (exciting) is positive and "demeaning" (belittling or disdainful), while negative, does not match the meaning of the sentence. The situation is disturbing because someone could become a victim, or "casualty," of an old war. It wouldn't be disturbing to become a "hero" and "martyr" (someone who suffers or is killed for a cause) doesn't fit the intended meaning of an accidental death.

**MANHATTAN**
PREP

137. **Dauntless, trepidation, peril.** The first part of the sentence says that even "perennially," or enduringly, _____ reporters have had misgivings about entering a war zone. Since war zones are dangerous, the first blank is likely filled by a word that describes people who don't usually worry about danger. "Dauntless" and "professional" could both fit; "foreign" does not. The part after the semicolon says that "their [the reporters] _____ at the prospect" of entering a war zone must be a reflection of the _____ that "pervades," or spreads through, a war zone. People in a war zone are in danger and likely scared, not necessarily "professional," so the first blank must mean not scared, or "dauntless," the second blank must mean fear, and the third blank must mean fear or danger. The correct answer for the second blank, "trepidation" or sense of fear, fits perfectly. "Excitement" and "skepticism" don't mean fear. The correct answer for the third blank, "peril," means danger and so also fits perfectly. Although "awareness" is tempting because "heightened awareness" is often associated with dangerous situations, the meaning is wrong because fear is not "a reflection of the heightened awareness"; rather, "heightened awareness" is a result of fear. "Rhetoric," or persuasive speaking, is a great GRE word, but has the wrong meaning for the third blank.

138. **Practiced restraint, asceticism, permissive.** The word "however" in the second sentence indicates that Jean—who "exercises a self-discipline"—is very different from most teenagers. Therefore, teenagers are not associated with self-discipline. For blank (i), the phrase that most closely matches is "practiced restraint." "Silent obedience" doesn't quite match and "urbanity" means polite, confident, or polished. For blank (ii), the idiom "verges on" indicates that the word will mean some extreme form of self-discipline. The best word for that is "asceticism" (a lifestyle of extreme self-denial). "Asperity" (harshness in tone or temper) is tempting but usually refers more to emotions or weather conditions. For blank (iii), the words "whether" and "or" indicate that the blank will describe the opposite of a "conservative upbringing." The best match is "permissive." Jean might want to react to a "meddlesome," or very intrusive, upbringing, but it's not the opposite of conservative. Don't be tempted by "illiberal," which means narrow-minded or bigoted.

139. **Dissolute, damage, carefully cultivated.** The actor had some kind of behavior, but "unexpectedly" it "did little to _____ his reputation as a family man." The first two blanks must contrast and should be selected together. If his behavior was "dissolute," it was lax in morals, and thus surprising that it "did little to damage his reputation." While negative, "impudent" (impertinent or disrespectful) behavior isn't necessarily the same or the opposite of "family man" behavior. "Paternal" is exactly like fatherly, or "family man" behavior, so it would be unexpected only if "paternal behavior did little to help his reputation," but no such meaning exists among the blank (ii) choices. "Assuage" means to make something less painful or severe, while "temper" means to neutralize or alleviate; both unjustly imply that "his reputation as a family man" is something unpleasant. The last blank is what "his exceptionally skilled team of publicists" did to his reputation: they "carefully cultivated," or tried to develop (a quality, sentiment, or skill) his reputation. The team is "his," so they shouldn't work against his reputation, as both "cleverly subverted" (undermined) and "easily refuted" (discredited) would.

140. **Ubiquitous, maladies, preventable.** The information between the dashes provides extra information about the word just before: "fresh produce has become" available everywhere. The best match is "ubiquitous" (existing everywhere). Neither "salubrious" (healthful) or "comestible" (edible) fits the required meaning. For the second blank "were once the inevitable result of nutritional deficiencies," diseases, or "maladies," fits. Neither "reactions" nor "cultivars" (cultivated plants) would be "the inevitable result of nutritional deficiencies." Finally, these once "inevitable" diseases are now mostly avoidable because people have better access to fresh produce. The best match is "preventable." "Organic" and "dietetic" (relating to the diet) are both related to food but don't match the meaning of avoidable.

141. **Hardline, loath.** The sentence is tricky; you may need to fill the two blanks at the same time. Perhaps the senator is not willing to "strike a concessionary tone" or perhaps she is not reluctant to strike such a tone; which meaning is correct? "Concessionary" is the act of conceding a point, so the senator must have a particular position that differs from her opponents. If, in spite of her _____ position," she is not reluctant to concede a point, then her position must be quite strong, or "hardline." If, on the other hand, she is not willing to concede anything, then her position must be middle-of-the-road or undetermined. No choice fits this meaning, so "hardline" is the correct answer for the first blank. The sentence does not provide clues to tell whether her position is "conservative" or liberal. "Fiduciary," (relating to trust, especially with financial matters) does not fit here. For the second blank, the senator was ultimately not unwilling, or not "loath" to concede a point. "Not permitted" would refer to someone else restricting her; the sentence doesn't indicate this. "Not qualified" implies an outside value judgment; again, the sentence doesn't indicate this.

142. **A paradox in, infirmity** The colon in this sentence indicates that the second part is somehow equivalent to or an example of what is described in the first part. Although the duty of medical workers is to "maintain the health of their patients," they earn money from their patients' _____ . The second blank must be a word that is opposed to "health," such as illness. "Infirmity" (weakness, frailty) is a match; neither "inattentiveness" (lack of attention) or "uncertainty" fits this meaning. The first blank must be describing this contrast, or "paradox." Neither "a protest against" nor "an aversion to" describes a contrast.

143. **Focused on, expanded, include.** The sentence contrasts early and later work in the field of spectroscopy: "early work" had something to do with "visible light," while later work had something to do with "any and all interactions" of a certain type. The two blanks likely need to be filled together, so scan the answers. The options for the second blank are fairly similar: they all mean some form of broadened or changed. If the later work broadened or changed something for "any and all interactions," then the earlier work must have been more narrow in scope. The best pairing is "focused on" and "expanded": The early work "focused on" a more narrow area, while the later work "expanded" to "include" more interactions. For the first blank, "contrasted with" and "arose from" do not pair with the idea of broadened or changed to create a contrast between the first two blanks. For the second, "transformed" and "amended" both mean changed; "expanded" is a better match for the contrast with the first blank. Finally, "affirm" (assert, declare) and "endure" do not fit the full phrase: "the concept was expanded to affirm any and all interactions" or "the concept was expanded to endure any and all interactions."

144. **Permissiveness.** The "while" that starts this sentence sets up a contrast: Abdul is worried that he's being too "lax," or easy-going; this same laxness is why his kids love him so much. "Permissiveness" (providing a lot of freedom, possibly too much) matches this meaning. "Complacence" (self-satisfaction), "satisfaction," and "equanimity" (calmness) don't mean easy-going and "sternness" (very serious, expressing disapproval) is the opposite.

**MANHATTAN**
PREP

# Chapter 4 *of*

## 5 lb. Book of GRE® Practice Problems

# Sentence Equivalence

# In This Chapter . . .

# Sentence Equivalence

> **Select the two answer choices that, when used to complete the sentence, fit the meaning of the sentence as a whole and produce completed sentences that are alike in meaning.**

1. While the colonists would eventually push westward, first, they were in for a long, difficult winter, and the main challenge was to _____ their existing resources.

   ☐ sell
   ☐ peddle
   ☐ steward
   ☐ upend
   ☐ husband
   ☐ procure

2. James Joyce, the author of many novels, including *Finnegans Wake*, saw deeply into the hearts of his characters, but, in a life irony as subtle yet piercing as those endured by his characters, he himself could barely _____ text well enough to proof his own galleys.

   ☐ see
   ☐ feel
   ☐ walk
   ☐ move
   ☐ distinguish
   ☐ interpret

3. At work, she is far less _____ than she is around her friends, but from time to time her staff sees her in a volatile state.

   ☐ pretentious
   ☐ capricious
   ☐ informal
   ☐ fickle
   ☐ direct
   ☐ explicit

4.  Forty years ago, anthropologists firmly believed that Neanderthals and modern *homo sapiens* had never mated, but advances in genetic testing have since proven that incorrect—such is the _____ nature of science.

    ☐  fallacious
    ☐  evolving
    ☐  counterfactual
    ☐  advancing
    ☐  vacillating
    ☐  indeterminable

5.  The music of the late '70s is often described as _____, despite the notable exception of a few innovators in the budding punk and hip-hop scenes.

    ☐  derivative
    ☐  trite
    ☐  inspired
    ☐  visionary
    ☐  enigmatic
    ☐  cerebral

6.  A field trip was arranged so that this troupe of _____ dancers could observe the real masters of their art.

    ☐  seasoned
    ☐  fledgling
    ☐  expert
    ☐  torpid
    ☐  novice
    ☐  lithe

7.  The exhibit is not so much a retrospective as a _____ ; the artist's weaker, early work is glossed over, and any evidence of his ultimate dissolution is absent entirely.

    ☐  paean
    ☐  polemic
    ☐  tirade
    ☐  panacea
    ☐  tribute
    ☐  critique

**MANHATTAN**
PREP

8. After a long, hard practice in the summer sun, the players were visibly _____.

☐ flagging
☐ hale
☐ lissome
☐ loathsome
☐ vigorous
☐ enervated

9. Nothing evoked memories of her grandmother's house like the _____ of scents associated with the variety of dishes at the holiday feast.

☐ paucity
☐ anomaly
☐ medley
☐ mélange
☐ dearth
☐ rarity

10. Unlike the politician's earlier evasions and equivocations, this latest statement is _____ lie.

☐ a bald
☐ a tacit
☐ an overt
☐ a didactic
☐ a rhetorical
☐ an implicit

11. Possessed of a lighthearted approach to life, Winnie thought that those who were _____ in regards to values and mores missed out on a certain liveliness and spontaneity.

☐ lax
☐ equable
☐ priggish
☐ auspicious
☐ impious
☐ punctilious

12. Where gay and lesbian individuals and couples were once ignored, at best, by mainstream media and marketing companies, they are now being _____ as the new frontier in consumer spending.

   ☐ touted
   ☐ subverted
   ☐ revered
   ☐ scrutinized
   ☐ promoted
   ☐ predicted

13. For most of the 20th century, American political contentions reflected pragmatic rather than ideological differences; candidate debates centered around whether programs were _____.

   ☐ partisan
   ☐ voluble
   ☐ feasible
   ☐ innocuous
   ☐ prejudiced
   ☐ viable

14. Though considered a somewhat somber drama at the time of its release in 1975, the film *Shampoo*, about a philandering hairdresser, now seems more the _____ comedy.

   ☐ puckish
   ☐ inhibited
   ☐ prurient
   ☐ wry
   ☐ dated
   ☐ puritanical

15. With almost 40 titles to her name, the popular novelist has _____ imagination and is never at a loss for new ideas, though the quality of her works is far from consistent.

   ☐ a prolix
   ☐ a prolific
   ☐ an exemplary
   ☐ a fecund
   ☐ an ingenious
   ☐ a profligate

**MANHATTAN**
PREP

16. Representative government arose in part from dissatisfaction with too many monarchs making _____ decisions without regard for precedents.

   - ☐ capricious
   - ☐ considered
   - ☐ malicious
   - ☐ pessimistic
   - ☐ insidious
   - ☐ erratic

17. Because the Lewis and Clark expedition through the West was conceived primarily as a mapping project, government officials were _____ by the wealth of information on a myriad of topics that the explorers gathered.

   - ☐ aggravated
   - ☐ flabbergasted
   - ☐ crushed
   - ☐ bedazzled
   - ☐ bored
   - ☐ disappointed

18. Many people erroneously believe that humans are naturally _____ to distrust or even fear those outside of their social or cultural group; anthropologists and social scientists, however, have consistently shown that xenophobia is a learned behavior.

   - ☐ indoctrinated
   - ☐ proven
   - ☐ prone
   - ☐ disposed
   - ☐ taught
   - ☐ compelled

19. Geneticists find Iceland a living laboratory for the study of _____ because virtually all of its current 300,000 citizens descend from less than a thousand Icelanders who survived the medieval Black Death.

   - ☐ diversity
   - ☐ revivification
   - ☐ therapy
   - ☐ history
   - ☐ mutation
   - ☐ rejuvenation

20. Given the influx of information via social media, the only way that a person can function effectively is to _____, to metaphorically separate the wheat from the chaff.

    ☐ delete
    ☐ triage
    ☐ prioritize
    ☐ respond
    ☐ requite
    ☐ eliminate

21. Although accommodating in person, George Orwell _____ defended his political positions in print.

    ☐ tenaciously
    ☐ obsequiously
    ☐ inadvertently
    ☐ doggedly
    ☐ sycophantically
    ☐ idiosyncratically

22. Although historically, paints were often tinted with toxic elements such as lead, cadmium, and mercury, _____ number of painters lived to be seventy, eighty, and even ninety.

    ☐ an incomprehensible
    ☐ a flabbergasting
    ☐ an impossible
    ☐ a confounding
    ☐ a dismaying
    ☐ an enlightening

23. The phrase "gilding the lily" is a late 19th-century expression that was first coined to describe the ostentatious gestures of some of the newly rich, such as applying gold gilt to the carved lilies on the entrances of their Beaux Arts homes; it still serves as a shorthand for any _____ and showy behavior.

    ☐ gauche
    ☐ eccentric
    ☐ idiosyncratic
    ☐ prosperous
    ☐ affluent
    ☐ uncouth

**MANHATTAN PREP**

24. While she still advocated for the wholesale restructuring of society based on principles of equity and sustainability, the radical blogger-turned-essayist had to _____ the expression of her views in order to appeal to the more middle-of-the-road sensibilities of the publishing market.

   □  abridge
   □  moderate
   □  amalgamate
   □  undermine
   □  galvanize
   □  temper

25. A "Mycenaean waist" refers to the taut, impossibly small waists characteristic of people depicted in certain ancient drawings found on Crete, and it certainly does not _____ any characteristic of most people in modern, overweight Western societies.

   □  deify
   □  depict
   □  denigrate
   □  mirror
   □  defame
   □  distort

26. The commentator's analysis of the recent conflict was anything but _____; he parroted his ideological compatriots, adding nothing new or insightful to the discussion.

   □  novel
   □  derivative
   □  tendentious
   □  fresh
   □  evenhanded
   □  hackneyed

27. In uncertain times, _____ theories often gain greater and faster adherence among the populace than proven ones do.

   □  corroborated
   □  putative
   □  conjectural
   □  incorrect
   □  irrefutable
   □  irreconcilable

28. Each civil engineer in the firm acted as _____ the others: no one submitted a construction project proposal if another expressed concerns about either the feasibility of the project or the cost estimates.

☐  a go between for
☐  a reviewer for
☐  an estimator for
☐  a negotiator for
☐  a hindrance to
☐  an overseer to

29. Arthur Conan Doyle's upstanding hero Sherlock Holmes engages in just as much clever deception as his nemesis, Professor Moriarty, proving that _____ is not inherently evil.

☐  immorality
☐  brilliance
☐  cunning
☐  subterfuge
☐  wrongdoing
☐  judgment

30. The etymologies of the words *alpha* and *omega* couldn't be more different; the former is obscure—the original symbol for *alpha* was an ox's head, and an ox is *'alp* in Phoenician—while the latter is _____ , as *omega* simply means "big O."

☐  transparent
☐  complicated
☐  overt
☐  erudite
☐  abstruse
☐  scholarly

31. While the muted colors do suggest a certain sobriety, the overall effect is undeniably _____ .

☐  vivacious
☐  poignant
☐  dull
☐  lackluster
☐  mirthful
☐  benign

**MANHATTAN**
PREP

32. Although the system's _____ is not currently in dispute at the national level, increasing local allegations of preferential treatment are threatening to change the situation.

   ☐ unfairness
   ☐ solemnity
   ☐ probity
   ☐ equity
   ☐ partiality
   ☐ solicitousness

33. Response to the provocative proposal was predictably _____: little care was given to the concealment of dislike for its aims or scorn for its authors.

   ☐ inscrutable
   ☐ polemical
   ☐ iconoclastic
   ☐ scathing
   ☐ fictitious
   ☐ impenetrable

34. The prime minister affected empathy for the impoverished citizenry, but most economic historians believe that her austerity measures, which were unduly _____, further injured them.

   ☐ arduous
   ☐ commercial
   ☐ mercantilist
   ☐ onerous
   ☐ strict
   ☐ venal

35. While traveling to the spa's remote location could be hectic, visitors more than made up for the stress by unwinding in a supremely _____ environment.

   ☐ effusive
   ☐ pacific
   ☐ elegant
   ☐ luxurious
   ☐ placid
   ☐ blithe

36.  The man looked much older than his 70 years, his _____ frame looking as though it had endured at
     least 40 years in the desert; although the casting director had initially pictured a more physically robust
     Moses, the actor was, in the end, perfect for the role.

     ☐   fetid
     ☐   vigorous
     ☐   desiccated
     ☐   wizened
     ☐   arid
     ☐   hale

37.  The children's attempt at a Mother's Day brunch was _____; soggy French toast, lukewarm coffee,
     and a syrup fight in the kitchen that would inevitably end up being cleaned up by the very recipient of
     the brunch.

     ☐   convivial
     ☐   amiable
     ☐   comical
     ☐   satirical
     ☐   farcical
     ☐   labile

38.  Many major websites today have _____ privacy policy: written by lawyers to protect the website that
     hired them, the language in the document is so abstruse that most consumers could not read it even if
     they tried to.

     ☐   an inscrutable
     ☐   a decipherable
     ☐   a repetitive
     ☐   a lucid
     ☐   a sanctioned
     ☐   an unreadable

39. Though chronicling the heroism and sacrifice of the common soldier, Erich Remarque's classic novel, *All Quiet on the Western Front*, is profoundly _____ and thus was banned by the Nazis since it implicitly opposed their vision of armed conquest.

- ☐ inspirational
- ☐ pacific
- ☐ prescient
- ☐ conciliatory
- ☐ prophetic
- ☐ clairvoyant

40. Just months from retirement, the disgraced executive was forced to make _____ exit from the company.

- ☐ a glorious
- ☐ a triumphant
- ☐ a boorish
- ☐ an ignominious
- ☐ a defiled
- ☐ an unseemly

41. _____ in scandal, the company could regain favor with customers only through mass firings of guilty executives.

- ☐ Wallowing
- ☐ Stoic
- ☐ Bogged down
- ☐ Brave
- ☐ Mired
- ☐ Besotted

42. By framing the new law as a question of urgent safety rather than of privacy, the government obviated the need to pass through the standard channels of legislation, effectively _____ all formal dissent and relegating any would-be naysayer from a position of engaged activist to that of powerless bystander.

- ☐ curtailing
- ☐ undermining
- ☐ targeting
- ☐ lobbying
- ☐ instigating
- ☐ facilitating

43. Exactly which bird species fell victim first to the deadly virus is the subject of ongoing controversy; what is known, however, is that it took but a slight mutation in the pathogen's genetic constitution to render it lethal to _____ of related species.

☐   a contraband

☐   a surplus

☐   an aurora

☐   a myriad

☐   a pantheon

☐   a plethora

44. Although known for bon mots such as, "If you don't have anything nice to say about anybody, come sit next to me," Alice Roosevelt Longworth was said to be very kind; her circulated _____ did not reflect vindictiveness.

☐   vituperations

☐   rants

☐   witticisms

☐   zeal

☐   quips

☐   taciturnity

45. Always on the lookout for a shady deal or quick con, she became known and scorned as an _____ opportunist.

☐   unqualified

☐   unprincipled

☐   alluring

☐   unprecedented

☐   attractive

☐   unscrupulous

46. After many hours of debate, things seemed to have reached _____ , as neither side was willing to give so much as an inch, and no one had anything new to offer.

☐   an impasse

☐   a pause

☐   a timeout

☐   a confrontation

☐   an engagement

☐   a stalemate

47. While kidney stones are known to produce a truly _____ sensation, often compared to the agony of childbirth, they are almost never fatal.

   ☐ anodyne
   ☐ inoffensive
   ☐ painstaking
   ☐ tortuous
   ☐ excruciating
   ☐ torturous

48. Given the breadth and speed of social media, the only way celebrities can hope to conceal their foibles is by employing practices as _____ as those of a spy ring.

   ☐ draconian
   ☐ arduous
   ☐ conspicuous
   ☐ duplicitous
   ☐ fanciful
   ☐ cloaked

49. The director of the musical admitted that while he was very good with characterization, scenery, lighting, and music, choreography was not at all his _____ .

   ☐ strong suit
   ☐ weakness
   ☐ forté
   ☐ hobby
   ☐ deficiency
   ☐ pastime

50. Though most technology used in the manufacture of bicycles is either decades old or adapted from other industries, the advent of carbon fiber frames brought with it genuine _____ .

   ☐ innovation
   ☐ antiquity
   ☐ flexibility
   ☐ venerability
   ☐ transformation
   ☐ seriousness

51. Through _____ antics that flouted the conventions of the establishment, the Yippies of the late 1960s impressed themselves into the public consciousness; their behavior culminated in the instigation of riots in Chicago during the Democratic convention in 1968.

    ☐  fastidious
    ☐  socialist
    ☐  brazen
    ☐  anarchist
    ☐  communist
    ☐  insolent

52. Sometimes _____ comes at a price; research suggests that among first-generation Chinese Americans, those who embrace the traditional Confucian values of their homeland are more likely to succeed academically than are those who do not.

    ☐  acculturation
    ☐  assimilation
    ☐  investiture
    ☐  alienation
    ☐  indebtedness
    ☐  estrangement

53. Many Enlightenment philosophers viewed Machiavelli's book as a satire meant to expose and caricature the _____ claims to power of the very figures Machiavelli pretended to endorse.

    ☐  sarcastic
    ☐  specious
    ☐  spurious
    ☐  squalid
    ☐  stolid
    ☐  stoic

54. The defendant impressed the jurors as _____; they did not believe that a woman of her education and experience could possibly be as naïve as she acted.

    ☐  disingenuous
    ☐  guileless
    ☐  innocent
    ☐  accomplished
    ☐  artful
    ☐  culpable

**MANHATTAN**
PREP

55. Crucial to fostering a realistic understanding of the potential boons—and perils—of the new drug will be a concerted effort to _____ the specific contexts and symptoms that render its use appropriate.

☐ furnish
☐ delineate
☐ outlaw
☐ transmute
☐ stipulate
☐ proscribe

56. Millions of dollars over budget and months late, the planned software was finally ready for release, much to the chagrin of its original investors; although it actually had all of the capabilities that the original specification _____, the delay meant that it had already been surpassed by competitor's products.

☐ possessed
☐ boasted of
☐ predicted
☐ updated
☐ enhanced
☐ promised

57. Robert Gottlieb, who otherwise found much to admire in John Steinbeck, argued that Steinbeck was politically _____, offering an adolescent disaffection in place of settled judgment.

☐ naïve
☐ perspicacious
☐ contemptible
☐ keen
☐ callow
☐ disinterested

58. The mayor's _____ speech turned the bipartisan issue—traffic reduction—into a three-month-long fight between former allies.

☐ alienating
☐ honest
☐ refreshing
☐ plodding
☐ divisive
☐ conventional

59. In his writings after visiting New York, Albert Camus expressed more of an inkling rather than a
_____ understanding of what he found lacking in American culture.

- ☐ elementary
- ☐ shrewd
- ☐ penetrating
- ☐ inchoate
- ☐ sinuous
- ☐ dialectical

60. Technological advances in communication—such as computers and texting—have caused the teaching
of cursive writing in school to become so exceptional that, if the trend continues, original source texts,
minutes from historic meetings, diaries, and even letters from ancestors will become _____ to future
generations.

- ☐ unintelligible
- ☐ intellectual
- ☐ meaningless
- ☐ humdrum
- ☐ quotidian
- ☐ indecipherable

61. It is in the best interest of criminal defendants to appear _____ in front of the judge, showing that not
all moral sympathy is lost on them.

- ☐ callous
- ☐ vindicated
- ☐ contrite
- ☐ penitential
- ☐ messianic
- ☐ pious

62. After 25 years as an emergency room surgeon, his reaction during nearly any emergency could only
be described as _____: he would evenly address the paramedics, evaluate the situation, and
methodically work through his normal routine.

- ☐ qualified
- ☐ premeditated
- ☐ phlegmatic
- ☐ unflappable
- ☐ enraptured
- ☐ enthusiastic

**MANHATTAN
PREP**

63. Despite the blandishments of the real estate con artist, the intended mark remained _____ about the value of the plot for sale, as, on the map, it seemed to border a swamp.

☐ optimistic
☐ enthused
☐ irascible
☐ skeptical
☐ jaundiced
☐ leery

64. In response to a recent editorial slamming the agency's newest advertising campaign, the agency spokesman denounced the piece as _____ adversarial motives, due to the editorialist's position on the board of the agency's primary competitor.

☐ stemming from
☐ producing
☐ typifying
☐ epitomized by
☐ engendered by
☐ creating

65. In the week that followed the climber's disappearance, Internet rumor mongers blogged a myriad of _____ reports of her demise, only to be embarrassed by the release of a dramatic video that showed her celebrating on the summit.

☐ apocryphal
☐ apocalyptic
☐ sentimental
☐ spurious
☐ saccharine
☐ scandalous

66. That investments abated so dramatically in the final quarter of last year is surprising given the many clear indications that the company would soon be _____.

☐ profitable
☐ bankrupt
☐ subsidized
☐ insolvent
☐ acquired
☐ thriving

67. The tragedy—and the resultant horrific loss of life and damage to property—occurred because of his _____ approach to his duties, evinced by his slouching posture and cavalier attitude.

   ☐ murderous
   ☐ petty
   ☐ lax
   ☐ aristocratic
   ☐ barbarous
   ☐ slack

68. The _____ that marks the composer's more recent work represents a major departure from the experiments in dissonance represented by her early compositions.

   ☐ disparity
   ☐ stridency
   ☐ creativity
   ☐ harmony
   ☐ harshness
   ☐ euphony

69. Although they were already late for the formal reception, the couple continued to _____ because they preferred to lounge about and bask in each other's company.

   ☐ lurk
   ☐ dally
   ☐ tarry
   ☐ skulk
   ☐ embrace
   ☐ equivocate

70. The player's exploits both on the field and in the finest night clubs around the world earned him many _____ from his legions of staunch admirers—so many, in fact, that his given name was all but forgotten.

   ☐ similes
   ☐ appellations
   ☐ sobriquets
   ☐ misnomers
   ☐ accolades
   ☐ kudos

71.  To the casual observer, the desert appears _____ place; those who look deeper, however, discover that it supports a vibrant ecosystem teeming with life.

    ☐  a verdant
    ☐  an arid
    ☐  a desolate
    ☐  a desiccated
    ☐  an inhospitable
    ☐  a lush

72.  The presidential candidate, known not only for the deeply reasoned content of his prepared speeches but also for the fiery brilliance of his delivery, badly miscalculated his ability to perform equally successfully when delivering _____ answers to unexpected queries from the media.

    ☐  extemporaneous
    ☐  capricious
    ☐  lubricious
    ☐  disingenuous
    ☐  impromptu
    ☐  premeditated

73.  While her friends agree that she projects an air of affability, they are of two minds about whether this friendliness is in fact _____.

    ☐  amiable
    ☐  unaffected
    ☐  genial
    ☐  magnanimity
    ☐  sincere
    ☐  vexing

74.  To avoid a lengthy prison term, the convicted financier signed a binding document, delineating the millions in fines and restitution that she must pay, as well as another legal memorandum in which she _____ her role and financial interest in the hedge fund she had founded.

    ☐  abjured
    ☐  jeopardized
    ☐  reneged
    ☐  deposed
    ☐  censured
    ☐  forwent

75. Some religious adherents follow the letter of their particular tradition while simultaneously _____ its most basic ethical tenets, a fact that may explain why so much violence is perpetrated in the name of love of and obedience to a faith.

☐ breaching
☐ obeying
☐ surpassing
☐ heeding
☐ contravening
☐ contracting

76. It is perplexing that the number of PhD applicants in linguistics, so obviously a _____ field, has either grown or held steady in each of the past fifteen years.

☐ moribund
☐ waxing
☐ burgeoning
☐ waning
☐ dissolute
☐ debased

77. Writers, particularly those of the contemplative persuasion, have always found the _____ nature of the mind—with its passing thoughts and inconstant moods—difficult to convey in language.

☐ inchoate
☐ essential
☐ vestigial
☐ ephemeral
☐ evasive
☐ fleeting

78. Though the majority of rules in sports are enumerated in rulebooks, there is _____ code of conduct that relates to sportsmanship.

☐ a tacit
☐ an evanescent
☐ an incorrigible
☐ an unambiguous
☐ a blatant
☐ an implicit

**MANHATTAN**
PREP

79. Many people think that antibiotics are a cure-all, but these medications can actually _____ the problem; taken inconsistently, antibiotics can in fact strengthen bacterial strains.

    ☐ exacerbate
    ☐ ameliorate
    ☐ differentiate
    ☐ distort
    ☐ pathologize
    ☐ magnify

80. Sandra was entirely _____ by the crossword puzzle that, unlike the simple fill-in-the-blanks published on weekdays, was one of the more difficult cryptic crosswords only published on weekends.

    ☐ confounded
    ☐ flummoxed
    ☐ enraged
    ☐ smitten
    ☐ incensed
    ☐ impressed

81. While many teachers say they are keen on the idea of participatory pedagogy, they often have little understanding of what participatory practices entail, and are, in fact, _____ to change; even when they think they are doing otherwise, observations show that teachers perpetuate the teacher-centered classroom practices to which they have been habituated.

    ☐ amenable
    ☐ impervious
    ☐ inimical
    ☐ prone
    ☐ reconciled
    ☐ resigned

82. The subject of the documentary was not bothered that the filmmaker received such _____ from the critics, but that none of the acclaim filtered down to him.

    ☐ opprobrium
    ☐ wealth
    ☐ fulmination
    ☐ approbation
    ☐ plaudits
    ☐ capital

83.  *The Thin Blue Line*, a documentary by Errol Morris, is one of a very few movies that has had a tangible effect on the real world; the film managed to _____ its subject, who had been on death row for a crime that Morris demonstrated that the man did not commit.

☐   exculpate

☐   incarcerate

☐   inter

☐   excuse

☐   manumit

☐   vindicate

84.  Most people expect to see straightforward and direct cause-and-effect relationships between actions and reactions; this contributes to making _____ one of the most difficult concepts to really understand.

☐   causality

☐   randomness

☐   intentionality

☐   happenstance

☐   mathematics

☐   science

85.  The professor's belief that all of the students admitted to the university were well-qualified academically led her to assume some degree of _____ in every student who was doing poorly in her class.

☐   moral turpitude

☐   ineptness

☐   amorality

☐   laziness

☐   incompetence

☐   sloth

86.  In a way, the environmental movement can still be said to be _____ movement, for while it has been around for decades, only recently has it become a serious organization associated with political parties and platforms.

☐   an incipient

☐   a disorganized

☐   a nascent

☐   a nebulous

☐   an inconsequential

☐   an immaterial

87. Einstein's idea that electromagnetic radiation was divided into a finite number of "energy quanta" was purely experiential until it was theoretically _____ by the work of physicists such as Louis de Broglie and Werner Heisenberg.

- ☐ bolstered
- ☐ undermined
- ☐ condoned
- ☐ pardoned
- ☐ sabotaged
- ☐ buttressed

88. The plan, according to law enforcement and judicial officials, was to keep the prisoner _____ during his court appearances, but the defense attorney argued that restraints would prejudice the jury.

- ☐ manacled
- ☐ malleable
- ☐ nettled
- ☐ fettered
- ☐ incensed
- ☐ incomparable

89. The painter was just as famous for his personality as for his work; unlike the many pretentious and egotistical men in his field, he was known to be entirely _____ .

- ☐ artless
- ☐ shrewd
- ☐ ingenuous
- ☐ selfless
- ☐ adroit
- ☐ artful

90. The newest romantic comedy wasn't exactly bad, but simply _____ ; it had laughs, but they were all jokes most audience members had heard before.

- ☐ atrocious
- ☐ amusing
- ☐ trite
- ☐ hackneyed
- ☐ witty
- ☐ egregious

91. An obsession with aesthetics _____ all of the work of the computer company; even their unsuccessful products manage to look like winsome pieces of modernist sculpture.

    ☐   underpins
    ☐   irradiates
    ☐   underserves
    ☐   overwhelms
    ☐   undergirds
    ☐   saturates

92. Oftentimes, when administrators force teachers to cleave too closely to a federal curriculum, those teachers feel _____ , because the mandatory curriculum curbs their sense of being creative and dynamic educators.

    ☐   crushed
    ☐   confounded
    ☐   thwarted
    ☐   undermined
    ☐   tormented
    ☐   walloped

93. The federal government knows that a certain level of financial stability can be attained by lowering interest rates, yet if it overuses this power, it risks losing its most reliable means of _____ a crisis.

    ☐   interring
    ☐   exacerbating
    ☐   annihilating
    ☐   palliating
    ☐   compounding
    ☐   assuaging

94. Even though Mariposa loved taking on roles that involved a lot of lines, she was excited to be playing a more _____ character, requiring her to focus more on gesture and expression.

    ☐   laconic
    ☐   dramatic
    ☐   dejected
    ☐   curt
    ☐   mute
    ☐   melancholy

**MANHATTAN**
PREP

95. Because the United States has become a mature, established nation, the _____ nature of Thomas Paine's political diatribes is now downplayed by government officials, who would vociferously denounce a contemporary version as seditious.

    ☐ pallid
    ☐ incendiary
    ☐ antithetical
    ☐ anemic
    ☐ demagogic
    ☐ deferential

96. A professional spy, he always affected a _____ demeanor, but those who disliked him often characterized it as taciturn or brusque.

    ☐ phlegmatic
    ☐ histrionic
    ☐ hirsute
    ☐ melodramatic
    ☐ melancholic
    ☐ dispassionate

97. Though Hamlet is famous for being _____ , he still manages to go on something of a killing spree in Shakespeare's play, proving that he is hardly paralyzed with depression.

    ☐ indecisive
    ☐ melancholy
    ☐ monological
    ☐ morose
    ☐ violent
    ☐ barbaric

98. It's worth wondering whether the increase in diagnoses of psychological disorders has caused us to see certain behaviors that were once considered normal as _____ .

    ☐ importunate
    ☐ mythical
    ☐ unfortunate
    ☐ anomalous
    ☐ aberrant
    ☐ fabulous

99. Proust proved that the _____ can be the domain of the novel every bit as much as the fantastical can be.

- ☐ mundane
- ☐ literary
- ☐ bombastic
- ☐ cosmopolitan
- ☐ belletristic
- ☐ quotidian

100. The magazine's editor was known to be a very busy woman, so it was important when speaking with her to get right to the _____ of the issue.

- ☐ pith
- ☐ conclusion
- ☐ gist
- ☐ apex
- ☐ genesis
- ☐ culmination

101. The reclusive boy was thought to be less than clever, but at sixteen he wrote a complex and beautiful symphony that at long last revealed him to be _____.

- ☐ dim
- ☐ musical
- ☐ monastic
- ☐ exceptional
- ☐ hermetic
- ☐ precocious

102. Many poets _____ the primacy of meter over words: Stephen Fry, in his book, *The Ode Less Traveled*, argues that rhythm is essential in poetry, whereas deeper meaning is less important.

- ☐ stress
- ☐ acknowledge
- ☐ allow
- ☐ immolate
- ☐ underscore
- ☐ decry

**MANHATTAN**
PREP

103. The saying "Time stops for no man" also applies to rock and roll; once the rebellious sound of the young, it _____ became part of the culture of the old, as had every preceding style of music.

    ☐   inevitably
    ☐   accidentally
    ☐   deliberately
    ☐   unavoidably
    ☐   resolutely
    ☐   painfully

104. Isherwood's sympathy for communism during the interwar period was not only a reaction against fascism, but also a mark of his fellow feeling for the laboring classes and his _____ to engage as an equal with working people.

    ☐   disinclination
    ☐   hankering
    ☐   proclivity
    ☐   implacability
    ☐   unwillingness
    ☐   joviality

105. Academic freedom does not protect a professor's classroom remarks on matters irrelevant to his subject, though it guarantees the professor considerable liberty of speech about matters _____ to his or her academic work.

    ☐   germane
    ☐   indifferent
    ☐   mimetic
    ☐   disinterested
    ☐   congruent
    ☐   pertinent

106. Unbridled passion, whether rage or ardor, gives way to the sort of rash declarations that too often end in _____ and sorrow.

    ☐   disdain
    ☐   pity
    ☐   rue
    ☐   affinity
    ☐   remorse
    ☐   contempt

**MANHATTAN**
PREP

107. The tremendous wealth of ancient life on display as part of the Ancient Life of New York exhibit—billion-year-old blue-green bacteria from the Adirondacks, fossilized tree stumps and spiders from Schoharie County, trilobites from Oneida County, and armored fish from throughout the state—represents only a tiny fraction of the New York State Museum's _____ collection of over one million specimens.

☐ piecemeal
☐ voluble
☐ exhaustive
☐ evergreen
☐ sweeping
☐ commanding

108. The representative's violent ascension to prominence began with a _____ attack on the comparatively conciliatory leaders of his own party.

☐ truculent
☐ partisan
☐ savage
☐ biased
☐ imperious
☐ dissembling

109. Even from a distance, the man could see that the tornado had _____ from the site all but the most basic elements of his childhood home; nothing but traces of the original foundations remained.

☐ tethered
☐ extirpated
☐ recapitulated
☐ interred
☐ obliterated
☐ hallowed

110. By the third quarter, the home team had lost any chance of emerging victorious, the game becoming an utter _____, a fact made most evident, perhaps, by the escalating jeers coming from the nearby bleachers.

☐ debacle
☐ rout
☐ boondoggle
☐ forgery
☐ fallacy
☐ infirmity

**MANHATTAN**
PREP

111. Only by disregarding the warning signs—equivocations, unexplained absences, disinterest—could the young husband continue to _____ his partner's fidelity.

   - ☐  suspect
   - ☐  aver
   - ☐  dismiss
   - ☐  disparage
   - ☐  assert
   - ☐  doubt

112. The _____ between parties is rapidly becoming insurmountable, as a lack of faith on both sides creates conditions where issues once considered incontrovertible are becoming subject to contention.

   - ☐  accord
   - ☐  prevalence
   - ☐  rift
   - ☐  breach
   - ☐  travesty
   - ☐  piety

113. The influence of Bennett's research can hardly be understated, but what is surprising is that his ideas have given birth to two related, yet _____ systems of thought within the same field.

   - ☐  suitable
   - ☐  divergent
   - ☐  impactful
   - ☐  complementary
   - ☐  distinguished
   - ☐  incongruous

114. In many pre-agrarian societies, the shaman or medicine-woman was considered the most _____ member of the group: indeed, her knowledge seemed to include every subject, from history and healing to parenting and spirituality.

   - ☐  perspicacious
   - ☐  mendacious
   - ☐  superfluous
   - ☐  sagacious
   - ☐  duplicitous
   - ☐  mellifluous

115. Wilderness first-aid trainers often assert that certain life-saving procedures must be _____ when the situation demands, notwithstanding the presence of minor contraindications.

   ☐ utilized
   ☐ medicated
   ☐ contrived
   ☐ employed
   ☐ created
   ☐ disputed

116. The judge's keen eye for sussing out the pretension of the lawyers in her courtroom was surpassed only by the _____ wit with which she castigated them for it.

   ☐ sedulous
   ☐ mordant
   ☐ obtuse
   ☐ jurisprudent
   ☐ trenchant
   ☐ assiduous

117. The amount of self-abasement with which the inmate _____ the probation panel to be set free verged on the humiliating; nevertheless, the judges remained unmoved and he was ultimately sent back to his cell to serve another three years.

   ☐ beseeched
   ☐ chided
   ☐ snubbed
   ☐ conceded
   ☐ received
   ☐ supplicated

118. The cult members treated their leader with _____ loyalty that verged on the obsessive and made them willing, should the need ever arise, to do so much as lay down their lives for him.

   ☐ a fanatical
   ☐ an arbitrary
   ☐ a fickle
   ☐ a mortifying
   ☐ a zealous
   ☐ an indeterminate

**MANHATTAN**
PREP

119. Jefferson regarded sumptuous living as among the most _____ evils to threaten the young republic, more pernicious even than loyalty to the deposed empire.

  ☐  reactionary
  ☐  venerable
  ☐  epicurean
  ☐  grievous
  ☐  baneful
  ☐  fastidious

120. Theology was once regarded as the "Queen of the Sciences," because every subject eventually had to meet its demands, but two hundred years ago that honor and title fell to mathematics, which enjoys _____ over not only physical science but social science as well.

  ☐  mayhem
  ☐  credence
  ☐  hegemony
  ☐  autonomy
  ☐  dominance
  ☐  independence

121. The new particles produced by CERN's Large Hadron Collider are _____, lasting a millionth of a billionth of a billionth of a second before disintegrating into photons, quarks, or other particles.

  ☐  ephemeral
  ☐  infinitesimal
  ☐  myriad
  ☐  poignant
  ☐  fleeting
  ☐  countless

122. While the professor first achieved renown for the theory he devised single-handedly during the early days of his career, his later contributions were achieved in a more _____ manner.

  ☐  solitary
  ☐  collaborative
  ☐  synergetic
  ☐  exegetic
  ☐  unilateral
  ☐  collusive

**MANHATTAN**
PREP                139

123. Although the media's coverage of the event was lackluster, the organizers still felt it was _____; what mattered, they said, was not the piddling number of talking heads who turned out to comment, but rather the mass of everyday people who came to register their disapproval of the proposed oil pipeline.

- ☐ a blemish
- ☐ an exception
- ☐ a coup
- ☐ a debacle
- ☐ a miracle
- ☐ an achievement

124. Lady Astor once commented to Winston Churchill, "If I were married to you, I'd put poison in your coffee." Churchill's famous _____: "Nancy, if you were my wife, I'd drink it."

- ☐ anecdote
- ☐ aphorism
- ☐ retort
- ☐ recrimination
- ☐ rejoinder
- ☐ maxim

125. The teacher was well-loved by students, but he never _____ the work of teaching; in fact, planning lessons and facilitating group process only exacerbated his deep-seated anxieties about preparation and public speaking.

- ☐ appreciated
- ☐ fancied
- ☐ abhorred
- ☐ relished
- ☐ detested
- ☐ ascertained

126. The teacher was no _____, although she felt she had to maintain the appearance of an authority figure; in truth, she couldn't care less whether students ate food in her class or doodled during lectures.

- ☐ stickler
- ☐ educator
- ☐ delinquent
- ☐ scholar
- ☐ luminary
- ☐ disciplinarian

**MANHATTAN**
PREP

127. The actress was young but not _____; she knew manipulation when she saw it, and she resisted being swayed by her crafty handlers.

   ☐ guileless
   ☐ disingenuous
   ☐ naïve
   ☐ cunning
   ☐ talented
   ☐ sophisticated

128. The _____ of recent national political discourse is matched only by the seriousness of the problems, which such hateful rhetoric is impotent to address.

   ☐ virulence
   ☐ acrimony
   ☐ shortsightedness
   ☐ partisanship
   ☐ miscalculation
   ☐ intransigence

129. Martin Luther King, Jr. was more _____ than is commonly thought today; it was only in the posthumous process of canonization that his more palatable, less far-reaching political and social visions became prominent.

   ☐ ineffective
   ☐ radical
   ☐ politic
   ☐ immoderate
   ☐ incongruous
   ☐ raucous

130. While it would help to offset a portion of the expenses of the renovation project, which had been far more _____ than initially anticipated, the proposed tourism fee was never enacted by the city council, who thought that a more complete solution was necessary.

   ☐ fortuitous
   ☐ unexpected
   ☐ costly
   ☐ subtle
   ☐ timely
   ☐ dear

131. Aviation authorities at one time issued _____ guidelines for hobbyists flying model airplanes, but in the absence of definitive laws, some individuals have chosen to ignore the recommendations.

- ☐ regular
- ☐ discretionary
- ☐ voluntary
- ☐ firm
- ☐ insufficient
- ☐ unvarying

132. The so-called "reality" television show claimed to display the _____ side of the starlet's life, but her daily routines were far too sensational for the claims to hold true.

- ☐ unusual
- ☐ predictable
- ☐ quotidian
- ☐ exotic
- ☐ mundane
- ☐ plastic

133. The problem with listening to prognosticators—especially in an age when no one seeks to hold them accountable—is that for every accurate prediction made, there are several others that turn out to be _____.

- ☐ mistaken
- ☐ unforeseen
- ☐ hasty
- ☐ misleading
- ☐ untrue
- ☐ surprising

134. If the allegations turn out to be true and the school's administrators are found to be _____, the university may lose its accreditation and the administrators might never be able to be employed in higher education again.

- ☐ repentant
- ☐ culpable
- ☐ synoptic
- ☐ contrite
- ☐ complicit
- ☐ unsound

**MANHATTAN**
PREP

135. The author's characterization of unions as always inimical to economic growth is too _____ for even his adherents to take seriously.

☐ temperate
☐ immoderate
☐ impressive
☐ lax
☐ splendid
☐ extreme

136. Thomas Pynchon became a renowned writer despite the glaring eccentricity of his work; he seemingly ignored the sensibilities of the general public rather than _____ them.

☐ recoiling from
☐ catering to
☐ coping with
☐ commiserating with
☐ pandering to
☐ cowering to

137. Many, if not most, sociologists subscribe to the idea that humans are _____, but the public reaction to the Ebola outbreak so mirrors the flailing hysteria recorded during the medieval plague outbreaks that it could be concluded that human nature is largely immutable.

☐ homogenous
☐ heterogeneous
☐ malleable
☐ monolithic
☐ pliant
☐ variegated

138. In romance novels, a strapping hero often _____ a rapier in the service of an ennobled yet submissive woman; this display of force carries the day but, despite the popularity of such books, some pundits bemoan the passive portrayal of women.

☐ sheathes
☐ brandishes
☐ wields
☐ promulgates
☐ disseminates
☐ cauterizes

139. Mr. Gupta announced that his centrist party would pursue prudent policies, courses that were progressive, while remaining _____ about imposing drastic social changes.

- ☐ passionate
- ☐ fervent
- ☐ cautious
- ☐ concerned
- ☐ congealed
- ☐ conservative

140. A problem in modern industrial nations—a designation that now encompasses more than the United States and Europe—is that when the wages of the middle class are stagnant, the economy expands at a _____ pace.

- ☐ plodding
- ☐ normal
- ☐ lucrative
- ☐ pedestrian
- ☐ profitable
- ☐ exponential

141. The abilities of microorganisms to adapt to sweeping environmental changes are more _____ than is commonly thought: from self-induced rapid mutations that allow them to utilize novel nutrient sources, to the appropriation of other microbe communities, their innovative capabilities know no end.

- ☐ ineffectual
- ☐ profuse
- ☐ advantageous
- ☐ prolific
- ☐ beneficial
- ☐ accommodating

142. Despite her reputation for conservative play, as of late, Polgar's chess has been full of _____ gambits.

- ☐ atypical
- ☐ treacherous
- ☐ abstruse
- ☐ anomalous
- ☐ studious
- ☐ impractical

**MANHATTAN**
PREP

143. Only by overlooking the grievances frequently expressed by her constituency could the incumbent think that the pandering advertisements would do anything but _____ her campaign.

- ☐ bolster
- ☐ aggrieve
- ☐ encourage
- ☐ hobble
- ☐ hamstring
- ☐ restore

144. Though often equivocal in making decisions, he was _____ in his resolve upon reaching a verdict.

- ☐ steadfast
- ☐ vacillating
- ☐ vague
- ☐ unwavering
- ☐ apprehensive
- ☐ critical

145. The expansion proposal, which the school board affirms will maximize efficiency while maintaining _____ class sizes, has nevertheless been resoundingly opposed by parent groups and the teachers union.

- ☐ remedial
- ☐ manageable
- ☐ flexible
- ☐ deficient
- ☐ reasonable
- ☐ unwieldy

146. The bridge player's frequent errors, although frustrating for his partner, were _____ his defeat, since none of the competing players could determine, from the cards he played, what cards he likely held—a necessary prerequisite to figuring out how to block his plays.

- ☐ an insurance against
- ☐ the reason for
- ☐ an indication of
- ☐ an obstacle to
- ☐ a hurdle for
- ☐ the guarantee of

147. The medical study contains a glaring deficiency: it assumes that the results are _____, however, the experimental participants were exclusively men between the ages of 30 and 60 with no significant co-morbidities.

     ☐  positive
     ☐  generalizable
     ☐  promising
     ☐  singular
     ☐  exceptional
     ☐  universal

**MANHATTAN**
PREP

# Sentence Equivalence Answers

1. **Steward, husband.** The "While" indicates that the second part of the sentence will contrast with pushing forward—due to the approaching winter, the colonists need to stay put and conserve what they have. Only "steward" and "husband" mean this. "Sell" and "peddle" don't work because there's nothing in the sentence to indicate that they need to sell or buy anything. (And why would you sell your resources when a hard winter is coming?) "Procure," which means get or acquire, doesn't work because the sentence references their "existing resources." "Upend" also doesn't work because of its meaning; the colonists do not need to stand their resources on end!

2. **See, distinguish.** This sentence is worded in a tricky way, as the words "but" and "barely" negate each other. Thus, the blank parallels "saw deeply." ("Proof" here means proofread or edit, and galleys are drafts of a book about to be published.) How ironic that an author who sees into the hearts of his characters is practically blind in real life! "Interpret" is an attractive trap, but Joyce had a vision problem, not an intellectual one. "Feel," "walk," and "move" are not correct because they don't mean to see.

3. **Capricious, fickle.** The first part of the sentence describes a woman as "less _____" at work "than she is around her friends," "but" her staff at work occasionally does see her "in a volatile state," or a temperamental state that is likely to change quickly. Given the "but," the blank must be a synonym for "volatile." "Capricious" and "fickle" can both mean temperamental and likely to change quickly and so are the correct answers. Although "direct" and "explicit" form a pair, they are not synonyms for "volatile" and so are not correct. "Informal" and "pretentious" also do not fit "volatile."

4. **Evolving, advancing.** Sometimes a seeming theme trap ("evolving") is not a trap—this sentence is literally about evolution, and also uses "evolving" or "advancing," the correct answers, metaphorically. "Fallacious" and "counterfactual" form an incorrect pair; the sentence doesn't say that all science is wrong, just that it is constantly revised to account for new information. "Vacillating" is tempting because it can also mean changing, but it implies going back and forth, which is not the correct meaning. "Indeterminable" is similarly tempting because it means incapable of being decided, but the sentence isn't really saying that; it is saying that science changes over time.

5. **Derivative, trite.** The blank is supposed to describe the music, "despite the notable exception of a few innovators," so the blank must be something that is the opposite of innovative. "Derivative" means based on another source and "trite" means overused and lacking in freshness, making these two the correct answers. "Visionary" and "inspired" are tempting choices because they both can mean innovative, but the sentence calls for something that is not innovative. "Enigmatic" means hard to understand or mysterious, and although some might consider the music of the '70s to be "enigmatic," this word, along with "cerebral," does not fit with the idea of not being innovative.

6. **Fledgling, novice.** Because the dancers are going to observe the "real masters of their art," they themselves are not masters. "Fledgling" and "novice" both mean inexperienced. "Seasoned" and "expert" form a pair, in agreement with "real masters" but opposite the blank in meaning. "Torpid," which means sluggish, might describe novice dancers, but can't be correct because it doesn't have a match. Similarly "lithe," which means supple and graceful, is a great word for describing dancers, but lacks a match.

**MANHATTAN**
PREP    

7. **Paean, tribute.** A "retrospective" would be an exhibit that shows the history and progression of the artist's work, but this exhibit only shows the good parts (it "glossed over" the weaker work and omits the artist's "dissolution," which literally means ending, but metaphorically could mean his failure at the end). Thus, the blank needs a word that has something to do with praising. "Paean" and "tribute" are the only matches. A "paean" is generally a song or speech of praise and is used metaphorically here. "Polemic" and "tirade" both mean a long angry speech, and so do not fit the blank." "Panacea," which means a cure-all, also has the wrong meaning, as does "critique."

8. **Flagging, enervated.** After "a long, hard practice" in hot weather, naturally the players would be tired. "Flagging" and "enervated" both mean tired. Although the players who withstood such a demanding practice likely are "hale" and "vigorous," it wouldn't make sense to say that they "were visibly" healthy or energetic after working very hard. "Lissome," which means slim and graceful, and "loathsome," which means repulsive, are great GRE words, but they don't fit the meaning of this sentence

9. **Medley, mélange.** The feast includes a "variety of dishes," so the sentence requires a word that means mixture or multitude. "Medley" and "mélange" both mean mixture. "Paucity" and "dearth" both mean scarcity, so that pair is at odds with the idea that there are many different dishes. "Rarity" could perhaps refer to the scent of dishes that are only made once a year, but "anomaly" refers to something that deviates from the norm, so these two words can't be the correct pair.

10. **A bald, an overt.** The earlier "evasions and equivocations" are ways to avoid a question or flip-flop on an issue. The latest statement is "unlike the politician's earlier evasions and equivocations" because it is an explicit, clear, or obvious lie. "Bald" and "overt" both match. The trap answers "tacit" and "implicit" (hinted at, unspoken) are synonyms that mean the opposite of what the blank requires. "Didactic" and "rhetorical," which could both describe a speech that is intended to instruct, are near synonyms that form a pair. However, they don't fit the meaning of the sentence.

11. **Priggish, punctilious.** The blank requires a word that is the opposite of the words "lighthearted" and "liveliness and spontaneity," so something like strict would match. "Priggish," which means self-righteous, and "punctilious," which means conscientious, are not quite synonyms, but are both related to taking the rules much too seriously. "Lax" is a reversal trap, as is "impious," which means irreverent; both words are possible antonyms for strict. Neither "equable," which means even-tempered, nor "auspicious," which means favorable or promising, fits the desired meaning nor have matches, so they are also incorrect.

12. **Touted, promoted.** The sentence says that certain people "were once ignored" but are "now being _____ as the new frontier." The blank, then, has to mean something like not ignored in a new or novel way. If something is "touted" or "promoted," someone is trying to sell it, at least figuratively, which fits with the idea that mainstream media and marketing companies are trying to promote gays and lesbians as the new frontier in consumer spending. "Scrutinized" is tempting, because it could be regarded as the reverse of being ignored, but it has no match and thus cannot be a correct answer. "Revered" is similarly tempting, but again it does not have a match and so cannot be the answer. "Subverted," or undermined, is a good GRE vocabulary word, but it can't be the answer because, like "predicted," it doesn't fit the sentence.

**MANHATTAN**
PREP

13. **Feasible, viable.** The blank requires two words that are like "pragmatic," which means practical. "Feasible" and "viable" relate to the practical considerations of whether the plan is workable or likely to succeed. The pairing "partisan" and "prejudiced" is a trap; the words mean biased and fit with "ideological," not "pragmatic." Neither "voluble," which means talkative, nor "innocuous," which means harmless, fits the intended meaning.

14. **Puckish, wry.** You need two words that are the opposite of "somewhat somber." Only "puckish" and "wry" have the sense of being funny or playful and so are the correct answers. Although "prurient," meaning having an excessive interest in sexual matters, might describe a comedy about a "philandering hair dresser," it doesn't have an answer match. "Inhibited" and "puritanical" form a pair, but have the wrong meaning—they are too similar to "somber." Finally, "dated" might be used to describe an old movie, but it doesn't have a match.

15. **A prolific, a fecund.** The novelist is described as "never at a loss for new ideas," so she must have a very active imagination. "Prolific" and "fecund" both mean fertile, or very productive, and thus fit this clue perfectly. "Profligate" is almost a match for "prolific" and "fecund" because it means wildly extravagant, and a person who produces a lot of ideas of varying quality could be described as having a "profligate" imagination. However, "profligate" has a distinctly negative spin (it implies wastefulness) that "prolific" and "fecund" do not have and so does not match them in meaning as well as they match each other. "Prolix" is a trap because it looks similar to "prolific," but it means tediously lengthy. "Exemplary" and "ingenious" form a tempting wrong answer pair, because the writer's imagination does appear to be outstanding, but the sentence specifically says that "the quality of her works is far from consistent," which makes "prolific" and "fecund" much better matches.

16. **Capricious, erratic.** The clue is "without regard for precedents"—that is, the monarchs made decisions based on their own whims or desires, ignoring any preexisting standards. "Capricious" and "erratic" can both mean changeable and unpredictable, describing such monarchs perfectly. "Considered" is the opposite of the desired meaning, and "malicious," "pessimistic," and "insidious," which means stealthy, while appropriately negative, add new ideas that are not indicated by the sentence.

17. **Flabbergasted, bedazzled.** Since the expedition "was conceived primarily as a mapping project," the officials could be amazed or surprised at the "wealth of information on a myriad of topics that the explorers gathered." Both "flabbergasted" and "bedazzled" convey surprise or awe. While the officials might have been "aggravated" that the explorers returned with too much information, another word with similar meaning doesn't exist to pair with "aggravated." "Crushed," "bored," and "disappointed" don't appropriately describe the situation; the explorers brought back even more information than they were originally planning.

18. **Prone, disposed.** "Xenophobia," which means dislike or fear of people from other social or cultural groups, is described in the sentence as "a learned behavior." The "however" marks this view as opposed to the preceding part of the sentence, which then must be saying that "many people erroneously believe" that xenophobia is not a learned behavior. If a behavior is not learned, it must be inborn or innate. The correct answers are "prone" and "disposed," which mean inclined or willing. "Compelled" and "indoctrinated" form a pair that suggests that force or manipulation are used to get people to be xenophobic, which does not fit with the idea of it being an innate behavior. "Taught" cannot be correct because if something is "taught," it is not innate. "Proven" is a theme trap because scientists often try to prove theories, but it cannot be correct because it does not have a match.

19. **Diversity, mutation.** The geneticists mentioned are studying a population descended from a rather small number of people a rather long time ago. Geneticists—who study genes, of course—would be interested in how the genes of this population changed over time. Therefore, "the study of" both genetic "diversity" and genetic "mutation" appropriately fit the blank. "Revivification," which means the restoration of life, and "rejuvenation" do not fit because this sentence is not about bringing ancient people back to life. "Therapy" and "history" have the wrong meanings.

20. **Triage, prioritize.** The words for the blank should match the clue "to metaphorically separate the wheat from the chaff." (Chaff is the inedible part of wheat that is discarded before the wheat can be made into flour, so this expression means to separate out the useful and non-useful, or important and unimportant, parts of something.) You can also use the clues regarding "the only way that a person can function" given an "influx of information." "Delete" and "eliminate" are attractive traps but don't match the idea of separating the important parts from the unimportant. Only "triage" (think of what emergency nurses do) and "prioritize" match. "Respond" and "requite," which means to reciprocate, are not good fits.

21. **Tenaciously, doggedly.** The word "Although" indicates that the correct pair must contrast "accommodating." Both "tenaciously" and "doggedly" convey the idea that Orwell refused to back down. The pair "obsequiously" and "sycophantically," which both mean fawning or in an excessively deferential manner, are the opposite of what the blank requires. "Inadvertently," which means accidentally, and "idiosyncratically," which means individualistic, can't be correct because they don't have matches.

22. **A flabbergasting, a confounding.** The word "Although" indicates that the blank will convey something that contrasts with the main clause of the sentence, which says that "_____ number of painters lived" to an old age. Since the sentence also says that paints contained poisons, you need two words that mean something like surprising or surprisingly large. The correct answers, "a flabbergasting" and "a confounding" both mean surprising. Trap answers "incomprehensible" and "impossible" go too far—it's interesting that many painters had long lives, but it's not beyond all comprehension. "Dismaying" is incorrect because it isn't upsetting that many painters lived long lives. Although apparently contradictory information might be "enlightening," that word has no match and cannot be correct.

23. **Gauche, uncouth.** The two words must match the words "ostentatious" and "showy." Both "gauche" and "uncouth" convey the idea of showing off in a vulgar way. Remember not to insert your own opinions—"eccentric" and "idiosyncratic" are near-synonyms, but are a trap. "Prosperous" and "affluent" also form a tempting trap, because they could both describe someone who is "newly rich," but they do not mean "showy."

24. **Moderate, temper.** The sentence describes the blogger as "radical" and says that, "in order to appeal to the more middle-of-the-road sensibilities," she had to do something to "_____ the expression of her views"; in other words, she had to alter them in some way. "Moderate" and "temper" are the correct answers because both mean to make something less extreme. "Undermine," a synonym for sabotage, is tempting, but the usage is incorrect here because one does not deliberately undermine one's own views. To "galvanize" is to shock or excite into action and to "amalgamate" is to combine, so neither of these words fits with the idea of moderating. To "abridge" is to shorten, but shortening the expression of one's views does not make them more moderate.

25. **Depict, mirror.** The image of people with "small waists" is contrasted with that of people in "overweight Western societies." The word "not" before the blank indicates that the blank should mean represent or portray. To "mirror" means to "depict" or portray, and thus both correct answers are good matches. "Distort" is a trap answer, because although an image can be distorted, the sentence is not saying that modern people are distorted. "Denigrate" and "defame" are both very strong words that mean to criticize or disparage, but there is no criticism of modern people in this sentence, just a comparison. "Deify," which means to treat as godlike, neither has a match nor fits the meaning of the sentence.

26. **Novel, fresh.** The sentence says the commentator "parroted his ideological compatriots," people who think the same way that he does; his commentary was the same as theirs. However, "anything but" reverses the direction, so if his commentary was the same as someone else's, it was anything but "novel" or "fresh," the correct answers. If something is "tendentious," it is intended to promote a particular viewpoint, so that is not the right answer. Although "evenhanded" is tempting, it cannot be the correct answer because it does not have a good match. "Derivative" and "hackneyed" form an incorrect trap pair; both of these words mean imitative or unoriginal, the opposite of what the blank requires.

27. **Putative, conjectural.** The structure of the sentence indicates that the blank opposes the word "proven"; it should be something like unproven or not necessarily proven. The correct answers, "putative" (generally thought to be) and "conjectural" (hypothetical, speculative) both match this meaning. "Corroborated" and "irrefutable" are an incorrect pair of words that have meanings similar to "proven." "Incorrect" could also be seen as an opposite of "proven," but it does not have a match (and note that an unproven theory is not necessarily wrong). "Irreconcilable," which means incompatible or conflicting, also cannot be correct because it neither has a match nor fits the intended meaning.

28. **A reviewer for, an overseer to.** The sentence says that "no one submitted a construction project proposal if another expressed concerns." Each of the engineers could look over a proposal before submission, and thereby act as "an overseer to" the others. The only other option that gives that same meaning is "a reviewer for," since reviewers check for issues. "A go between for" and "a negotiator for" are an incorrect pair, since there is nothing in the sentence that suggests that the engineers negotiate with each other. A "hindrance to" is tempting but has a negative spin, and there is nothing in the sentence suggesting that the relationship is negative. Similarly, "an estimator for" is attractive because construction project proposals involve estimates, but the second part of the sentence says that the issue was only whether other engineers "expressed concerns" about project feasibility or cost estimates. It does not say that the engineers performed each others' cost estimates, so "an estimator" is going too far.

29. **Cunning, subterfuge.** Both Sherlock Holmes and Professor Moriarty engage in "clever deception," though one of them is ethical and the other is not. The blank requires a synonym for "clever deception." "Cunning" and "subterfuge" can both mean "clever deception" and so are the correct answers. "Immorality" and "wrongdoing" do not imply anything clever, and "brilliance" and "judgment" do not imply deception.

30. **Transparent, overt.** The etymology, or origin, of the word "alpha" is described as "obscure," and the word "while" implies that the blank, which describes the etymology of "omega," will be not obscure. Both "transparent" and "overt" carry this meaning. "Complicated" and "abstruse" are the opposite of the desired meaning, and neither "erudite" (learned, scholarly) nor "scholarly" fits the meaning of the sentence.

31. **Vivacious, mirthful.** In this case, "sobriety" means grave or serious, so the blank requires an antonym, something like happy or lively. "Vivacious" means lively and "mirthful" means full of joy. These are correct answers. "Dull" and "lackluster" are the opposites of the desired meaning. "Poignant" (touching in a sad way) also does not mean happy or lively. "Benign" can mean kindly, but has no connotation of joyous or lively and so does not fit.

32. **Probity, equity.** There are "allegations of preferential treatment," or unfairness, at the local level, and these are threatening to spill over into criticisms that the system is unfair or partial at the national level. The sentence indicates, however, that the system's fairness is "not currently in dispute" at that level, so the blank requires synonyms for fairness or impartiality. The correct answers are "equity" and "probity" (integrity, honesty). The words "unfairness" and "partiality," which means favoritism, are opposite the desired meaning. "Solemnity," which describes a serious and proper state of being, and "solicitousness," which means hovering attentiveness, are not correct because they do not fit the desired meaning and do not have a match.

33. **Polemical, scathing.** The sentence says that "little care was given to the concealment of dislike … or scorn." "Scathing" is a good description of such a response. "Polemical" also fits the blank, as a polemic is a scathing text or speech. An iconoclast is someone who attacks beliefs or institutions that are widely accepted, so a predictable response to a "provocative proposal" would not be described as "iconoclastic." "Inscrutable" and "impenetrable" both mean impossible to understand, but, since the criticism here was unconcealed, these don't work. "Fictitious" cannot be correct, because there is nothing to suggest that the response was imaginary, although the authors might have wished that it were.

34. **Arduous, onerous.** The prime minister "affected empathy for the impoverished citizenry," meaning that she acted as if she understood and shared the emotions of the poor citizens. However, the word "but" after the comma changes the direction, suggesting that she didn't actually feel that way. The sentence goes on to say that most historians think that her "austerity measures," meaning cost-saving measures, further harmed the poor citizens. The measures are described as "unduly _____," so the blank must be filled by something that an empathetic person would not impose on citizens struggling with poverty. The correct answers are "arduous" and "onerous," which both mean overly difficult or unpleasant. "Strict" is almost a match, but strict is used to describe rules that must be obeyed, not rules that are overly harsh. "Commercial" and "mercantilist" form a pair that means having to do with the buying and selling of goods and services, but this is a trap because the sentence talks about "economic historians." "Venal" is an excellent GRE word that means capable of being bought or bribed, but does not work here.

35. **Pacific, placid.** Getting to the spa is "hectic," but this "stress" is "more than made up for" once visitors reach the spa. The spa's environment, then, is the opposite of hectic or stressful; it is calm or soothing. The correct answers, "pacific" and "placid," both match this meaning. Although spas are often "elegant" or luxurious," this pair does not match the meaning of calm or soothing. "Effusive," which means gushing, and "blithe," which means cheerfully indifferent or happy, are also not good matches for the desired meaning.

36. **Desiccated, wizened.** The man looks even older than his actual age of 70, as though he had "endured at least 40 years in the desert." "Desiccated" means dried out and "wizened" means old and withered. The trap answer "arid," which means dry, is a good word to describe a desert, but cannot describe a person. "Vigorous" and "hale" are both used to describe strong and healthy people, so they do not fit the intended meaning. "Fetid," which means foul smelling, does not fit the desired meaning.

**MANHATTAN**
PREP

**37. Comical, farcical.** The "children's attempt at a Mother's Day brunch" went pretty badly—so badly that it actually made more work for Mom. What a joke! Correct choices "comical" and "farcical" both mean laughable. The brunch was not "satirical," because it was not making fun of a preexisting work of art, situation, etc. Although the brunch likely was "convivial" and "amiable," which both mean warm and good-humored, this pair doesn't fit with the idea of children creating a minor disaster while trying to do something nice for their mother. "Labile," which can mean unstable or moody, is used to describe a person or a chemical reaction, not a brunch.

**38. An inscrutable, an unreadable.** The language of the privacy policy "is so abstruse that most consumers could not read it," indicating that the privacy policy must be hard to read, and indeed "abstruse" means difficult to comprehend. The correct answers, "inscrutable" and "unreadable," although not perfect synonyms for each other, also both mean difficult to comprehend or understand. "Decipherable" and "lucid," meaning clear and understandable, are the opposite of what the blank requires. "Sanctioned," which in this context means officially approved of, and "repetitive" are not synonyms for hard to read and so cannot be correct.

**39. Pacific, conciliatory**. The opening "Though" foreshadows a twist. The sentence means that although the novel describes "the heroism and sacrifice of the common soldier," it is "profoundly _____," where the blank is something that would be unexpected in a novel about brave soldiers. The sentence also says that the novel was banned because it "implicitly opposed," or was against, "their vision of armed conquest." Therefore, it must have an anti-armed conquest theme, something peaceful. "Pacific" and "conciliatory," which both mean anti-war, are the correct answers. "Prescient," "clairvoyant," and "prophetic" all mean able to foresee the future, a trap related to the Nazis's "vision of armed conquest." The sentence isn't talking about a supernatural vision, but rather about an overarching goal. It is true that "prophetic" can also mean "characteristic of prophets," and many prophets in various religious traditions spoke out against what they saw as evil governments. However, the interpretation of "prophetic" as "resisting evil authority" is not what is found as even a secondary definition in standard dictionaries. More importantly, even if you accepted this definition, there is no synonymous or near-synonymous partner among the answer choices. Sentence Equivalence questions require two answers that produce equivalent sentences. Only "pacific" and "conciliatory" work.

**40. An ignominious, an unseemly.** The blank should match "disgraced." "Ignominious" and "unseemly" work well. Trap answer "defiled" does not appropriately describe an action (you could defile a holy place by doing something very inappropriate, but for a place or thing to be defiled, it should be very pure beforehand.) "Glorious" and "triumphant" do not match the idea that the executive was "disgraced." "Boorish," which means ill-mannered, is incorrect because it doesn't have a match.

**41. Bogged down, mired.** The scandal is so severe that the company can save itself only through the rather extreme measure of "mass firings." "Bogged down" and "mired" have the sense of being stuck in something (a bog and a mire are both physical things—swampy, quicksand-like patches). Note trap answer "wallowing" (indulging oneself)—only a person or animal can wallow (and anyone wallowing wouldn't want to regain favor anyway). "Stoic" and "brave" are used to describe people who calmly face danger or hardship, but do not fit the idea that the company is in a "scandal." "Besotted," which means infatuated, has the wrong meaning and no match.

**42. Curtailing, undermining.** The government "obviated" or avoided, the traditional "channels of legislation," and by doing so is making "formal dissent" impossible. In other words, the government is "curtailing" or "undermining" such disagreement—words that both mean to prevent or undercut. "Targeting" is tempting, but the government isn't aiming at or attacking formal dissent; rather, it is preventing or avoiding it entirely. "Lobbying," "instigating," and "facilitating," although all words associated with political actions, do not have the correct meaning.

43. **A myriad, a plethora.** The virus spread to a large number ("myriad," "plethora") of bird species. Watch out for trap answers "surplus," which means an excess and would not be appropriate to describe bird species, and "pantheon," which means all of the gods in a particular religion and also would not be appropriate to describe a number of bird species. "Contraband," meaning illegal goods, and "aurora," used to describe the dawn or other lights in the sky, are great GRE words, but not good fits for the blank.

44. **Witticisms, quips.** The first part of sentence says that, even though Longworth was known for "bon mots," which literally means "good words" in French and is generally used to describe wisecracks or one-liners, she was actually a "very kind" person. Given that her "_____ did not reflect any vindictiveness," or meanness, the blank must be another word for "bon mots," such as "witticisms" or "quips." Although "vituperations," meaning verbally abusive language, and "rants" also form a pair, they are much more negative than "bon mots" and therefore not a match. "Taciturnity" describes the state of being taciturn, or untalkative, and so has the wrong meaning. "Zeal" which means fervor or enthusiasm, doesn't have the correct meaning either, and also isn't used quite correctly in this expression. Although "zeal" can be passed from person to person, it isn't explicitly circulated, the way that one-liners are.

45. **Unprincipled, unscrupulous.** The woman is looking for "a shady deal or quick con," making her someone who is looking to make money by any means necessary. While "alluring" and "attractive" are a pair of words with similar meanings, there is nothing in the sentence that suggests she is pleasing to the eye. Of the remaining words, "unprecedented" does not work, since there is no clue that she is the first opportunist, and "unqualified" fails as well, since there is no clue that she is not qualified as an opportunist. This leaves the correct pair of "unprincipled" and "unscrupulous," both of which mean not acting with moral principles.

46. **An impasse, a stalemate.** If neither side of the debate is willing to give an inch to the other, then it would be impossible for a solution to be found. The debate is more or less frozen. Both "a confrontation" and "an engagement" imply some kind of clash, but the sentence implies that any kind of serious clashing is now over (no one had anything new to offer). "An impasse" and "a stalemate" reflect the static nature of the conflict. "A pause" and "a timeout" are not correct because there is no indication that the debate will continue.

47. **Excruciating, torturous.** The sensation produced by kidney stones is compared to "the agony of childbirth," so the blank must be a word that means extremely painful. "Painstaking" (done with great care) and "tortuous" (full of twists and turns) are both traps. The correct answers, "excruciating" and "torturous," describe terrible pain. "Anodyne" and "inoffensive" are similar to each other but mean the opposite of what the blank requires.

48. **Duplicitous, cloaked.** The sentence begins by suggesting that social media has fast and far-reaching effects, so celebrities wanting to "conceal their foibles" would need to do something that would resemble what a spy ring would do: be unobserved or deceitful. The correct answers are "duplicitous" and "cloaked," both of which mean deceitful or concealed. While a spy ring might act in a way that is "draconian" (excessively harsh) or "arduous" (difficult or tiring), these words don't fit with the sentence, nor do they have matching words among the answer choices. Both "conspicuous" (noticeable) and "fanciful" (overimaginative or unrealistic) describe practices that are the opposite of what a spy ring would employ.

**MANHATTAN**
PREP

49. **Strong suit, forté.** The sentence lists the many things that the director is good at, but the word "while" in this expression suggests that choreography was a weakness. The phrase "not at all" twists the meaning back in the opposite direction, so the blank requires a word like strength. "Strong suit" and "forté" both fit perfectly. "Hobby" and "pastime" are a pair, but they don't work here, as this is clearly the director's job. Similarly, "weakness" and "deficiency" are a pair but mean the opposite of what the sentence suggests.

50. **Innovation, transformation.** "Though" indicates that the advent of carbon fiber brought something opposite to "old or adapted" technology. The blank should mean originality or change—"innovation" and "transformation" match that meaning. The opposite of a new item is an "antiquity." The other answer choices could each be considered a positive value brought about by carbon fiber frames, but without a clue about the bike's "flexibility," "venerability," or "seriousness," none of those answer choices would fit, nor do they have a pair word.

51. **Brazen, insolent.** The sentence says that the "_____ antics" of the group "flouted" (openly ignored or disobeyed) "the conventions of the establishment." "Brazen" and "insolent" can both mean to openly ignore or disobey and they are the correct answers. "Socialist" and "communist" form a tempting pair because people who adhere to either socialist or communist beliefs might well have disagreed with "the conventions of the establishment" in the United States in the 1960s, but neither term means to disobey. "Anarchist" is perhaps the most tempting wrong answer because anarchists do not believe in formal governments and are sometimes described as agitators or insurgents, but there is no match for "anarchist" among the choices, so it cannot be correct. "Fastidious," or particularly concerned about detail or cleanliness, most certainly does not describe the behavior of the Yippies.

52. **Acculturation, assimilation.** The structure of this sentence demands a little extra attention. Those who do not "embrace the … values of their homeland" do worse academically, so they will be the ones to pay the "price." What comes at a price, then, is embracing the culture of the new home. "Acculturation" and "assimilation" both mean exactly this. The incorrect pair, "alienation" and "estrangement" (separation from a group), have the opposite meaning. "Indebtedness" does not fit this sentence, since there is no reason to believe that someone owes someone else. And "investiture," which means the act or formal ceremony of conferring rank on a person, also does not fit in this sentence.

53. **Specious, spurious.** If Machiavelli only pretended to endorse "the _____ claims to power," and if they were subject to "exposure and caricature," they must have been not only illegitimate but ridiculous. None of the answers suggests ridiculousness, but two answers—"specious" and "spurious"—mean the claims are false. While not synonyms, both words describe claims that are superficially attractive, but in fact false. "Sarcastic" (mocking) might be a trap for someone who misses that the claims referred to by the blank are not made by Machiavelli but by those who originally made the claims to power. "Squalid" (dirty or dishonest) doesn't fit the sentence or match any other answer choice. And while "stolid" and "stoic" both mean unemotional, the sentence offers no reason to believe that the claims are unemotional.

54. **Disingenuous, artful.** This sentence is difficult because the word "impressed" is used to refer to making an impression in a negative way. The defendant did not make a positive impression; rather, the sentence suggests that she came across as not as naïve as she pretended to be. "Disingenuous" means precisely that and one meaning of "artful" is deceptive. The sentence does not suggest that the woman was "innocent," and while she might have been "accomplished," that's not how the jurors thought of her actions. "Guileless" is a trap since it is a synonym of both ingenuous and artless, all three of which mean innocent and without deception; this meaning, however, is the opposite of what

the blank requires. Finally, "culpable" means guilty and is an attractive trap, but goes further than the clues in the sentence; the woman was not naïve, but she was not necessarily guilty.

55. **Delineate, stipulate.** A "realistic understanding of the potential boons—and perils," or advantages and disadvantages, of the new drug requires that people know when they should and should not use it. In other words, the "contexts and symptoms" that are "appropriate" for taking the drug should be "delineated" or "stipulated," both of which mean spelled out or specified. "Furnish," which means to provide or to be a source of, might seem close, but one would not provide the times when the drug's use is appropriate. Instead, the sentence suggests that people need to provide appropriate information about when the drugs should be used. "Outlaw" and "proscribe" form a pair, but one would be unable to ban or forbid "the contexts," much less "the symptoms," for using the drug. Finally, "transmute," meaning to change in form, does not fit the context.

56. **Boasted of, promised.** If you don't know the meaning of "chagrin," or embarrassment, this problem could be challenging. The investors were embarrassed that, when the software got to market, it had already been surpassed! Here is a great opportunity to recycle other words from the sentence to fill in the blank: a "specification" must specify, or call for or describe. "Possessed" is a tempting choice here, but a specification is just a description of a planned product or project and therefore can't possess the actual capabilities of the software. "Updated" and "enhanced" form a nice equivalent pair, but they don't quite fit the meaning. Finally, "predicted" does not accurately describe what the "original specification" would do—it wouldn't forecast the capabilities of the software, it would just describe what they were supposed to do. That leaves "boasted of" and "promised" as the correct answer pair.

57. **Naïve, callow.** "Otherwise" suggests that Gottlieb did not find Steinbeck's political views admirable. "Adolescent disaffection" suggests that Gottlieb found Steinbeck's views in some sense immature, so look for negative words that mean something like unsophisticated. "Naïve" and "callow" are the best options. "Perspicacious" and "keen" both suggest insight, nearly opposite of what the sentence suggests. "Disinterested" is a tricky word here. It most commonly means unbiased, though it can also mean not interested (two very different meanings). Neither option makes a great sentence here, but just as important, none of the other answer choices has a similar meaning to either definition. "Contemptible" is negative, but with no suggestion of immaturity—make sure to use the clues provided without adding your own ideas.

58. **Alienating, divisive.** "Bipartisan" in this context means an issue on which both sides agree. If the speech turns that issue into a "three-month-long fight," then the word in the blank, which describes the speech, must be something pretty negative, pitting both sides against each other. "Alienating" and "divisive" are great matches, suggesting estrangement and hostility. A "refreshing" speech would have woken everyone up and a "plodding" speech would have put everyone to sleep, but neither would have turned friends against each other. "Conventional" and "honest" are both incorrect as well, since neither matches another answer choice.

59. **Shrewd, penetrating.** The blank should be an antonym for "inkling," which means only a hint of something. Camus had only a hint of understanding "rather than" a thorough or complete "understanding." Both "shrewd" and "penetrating" fit this idea. "Elementary" and "inchoate" are a pair of words that mean simple-minded or still developing, and are the opposite of what the sentence suggests. Finally, "sinuous" means containing many curves and "dialectical" means related to discussion of ideas and opinions. These words do not form a pair and do not fit the intended meaning of the sentence.

**60. Unintelligible, indecipherable.** Fewer and fewer people are learning to write (or read) cursive, and it may become true that no one will learn it in the future. If that's the case, no one will be able to read the documents written in cursive, rendering them unreadable. The two most closely matched answers are "unintelligible" and "indecipherable." "Intellectual" does not fit the required meaning. "Meaningless" is a tempting answer, but the documents *do* have meaning—it's just that no one will be able to determine what that meaning is. "Humdrum" and "quotidian" have similar meanings, but there's no indication that the sources will be boring, so these answers are also incorrect.

**61. Contrite, penitential.** Criminal defendants want to look good in front of the judge by "showing that not all moral sympathy is lost on them." The defendants are not necessarily innocent, so "vindicated" doesn't work. Neither would "pious," meaning devoutly religious, or "messianic," meaning fervent or passionate. And "callous" has the opposite tone of the intended meaning; a defendant appearing callous in front of a judge would be showing insensitivity for his or her actions. That leaves the correct answers, "contrite" and "penitential," both of which mean remorseful or apologetic.

**62. Phlegmatic, unflappable.** The surgeon worked "methodically" and addressed paramedics "evenly," so his reactions in an emergency would be calm, cool, and in control. "Phlegmatic" means not excitable, calm, and composed, so it's a good fit. "Unflappable" means not easily upset or perturbed, especially in a crisis. "Qualified" is a bit of a trap: he's a qualified doctor, but to say that his reactions were "qualified" would imply that they were limited or restricted in some way. Someone methodical might be "premeditat[ing]" about certain things, but how can a reaction be "premeditated"? He couldn't pre-plan his response to an emergency. "Enraptured" and "enthusiastic" would indicate emotional responses, but, in fact, the opposite was true: he showed little emotion and retained composure.

**63. Skeptical, leery.** The word "Despite" at the beginning of the sentence indicates that the blank must oppose the encouragement of a con artist (someone who tricks people out of money)—that is, the "mark" is doubtful about the con artist's claims. (A mark is someone who is a target of a criminal or con artist.) "Skeptical" and "leery" match this meaning. "Optimistic" and "enthused" create a pair, but do not fit the required meaning of the sentence. And the remaining words neither fit the intended meaning of the sentence nor form a pair: "irascible" means easily angered, while "jaundiced" most commonly means yellow in complexion (from the medical condition) but can also mean bitter or envious.

**64. Stemming from, engendered by.** If the editorialist is "on the board of the agency's primary competitor," then any attack on the ad campaign was probably written with ulterior motives. The blank should mean something like "coming from." "Stemming from" and "engendered by" would both fit this meaning ("engendered" means created or produced). "Producing" and "creating" are a trap here; they would suggest that the editorial itself *created* the adversarial motives, which isn't the case. The fact that the writer was on the board suggests that the adversarial motives led to the editorial, not vice versa. "Typifying" and "epitomized by" both suggest "being the ideal example of." The sentence doesn't suggest that the editorial is the *perfect* example of adversarial motives; it just implies that the piece was spawned by them.

**65. Apocryphal, spurious.** The sentence states that "rumor mongers" were writing about the climber's "demise" but were later embarrassed to discover she made it to the summit. This would suggest that the reports were untrue, which both "apocryphal" and "spurious" mean. The sentence does not support the idea that the reports were "sentimental," "saccharine" (excessively sweet), or "scandalous." Trap answer "apocalyptic" ignores the clues in the sentence and is inappropriate for an event involving only one person, even if the outcome was tragic.

66. **Profitable, thriving.** Investments in the company "abated"—diminished or fell—dramatically, but this was "surprising." Given this, the expectation must have been that any investments would either hold steady or increase, suggesting that the company had been expected to do well. "Profitable" and "thriving," though not exact synonyms, both fit the meaning that the company was expected to do well. "Bankrupt" and "insolvent" are both traps; they are opposite the required meaning. "Subsidized" would add meaning not present in the sentence; perhaps the company will receive subsidies, but there is nothing in the sentence to suggest it. Likewise, it's certainly possible that the company might have been "acquired," but choosing that answer would mean creating a new narrative not present in the original sentence.

67. **Lax, slack.** The answers must parallel "slouching posture and cavalier attitude." Note that cavalier is used here to mean offhand or disdainful. Thus, "aristocratic" is a bit of a trap answer, as are "murderous" and "barbarous," which don't match the clues—while this person's actions caused horrific loss of life, it doesn't sound as though that was his intention. "Petty" (of secondary or little importance) also doesn't fit here. Thus, the correct answers are "lax" and "slack," both of which mean not careful.

68. **Harmony, euphony.** If the composer's latest work is a "major departure from" the "dissonance represented by her early compositions," then the blank should be a word that means harmony or pleasant sound. In addition to the word "harmony" itself, "euphony" means pleasant sound, so these would both stand in contrast to "dissonance." "Harshness" and "stridency," on the other hand, are synonyms for "dissonance" and would therefore not be a departure at all. Neither "disparity" nor "creativity" contrasts with "dissonance," nor does either choice have a pair among the other answers.

69. **Dally, tarry.** They were "already late" but still "preferred to lounge about," or delay their departure for the party. Therefore, they continued to "dally" or "tarry." The incorrect pair "lurk" and "skulk" has a negative, furtive connotation—the words are related to hanging around for some bad reason. Neither "embrace" nor "equivocate," meaning to be vague in order to conceal some truth, has a pair, nor are there any hints in the sentence that would suggest that the couple did either of these.

70. **Appellations, sobriquets.** The spin of this sentence is positive—"staunch admirers"—and the player's "given name was all but forgotten" (the expression "all but" means something like 99%). In other words, the player was given many nicknames; "appelations" and "sobriquets" both fit. Although "kudos" and "accolades," which both mean praise, form a tempting theme trap because the sentence talks about the player's admirers, neither captures the idea of a nickname. A "misnomer" is something of a nickname, but a false one, so it doesn't fit either. "Similes" is tricky because is sounds like "similar," but it is a figure of speech used to describe something by comparing it to something else, not a nickname.

71. **A desolate, an inhospitable.** The desert "supports a vibrant ecosystem teeming with life." "Teeming" means full of, so the desert is full of life, but only people who look deeply see that. The blank, then, must be filled by words that mean the opposite of full of life. "Desolate," which means bleakly empty, and "inhospitable," which when describing an environment means hard to live in, both fit: casual observers don't see much life in deserts. Although "arid" and "dessicated" both mean dried up and seem like good descriptions of a desert, they are not correct because they are not opposites of "teeming." "Verdant" and "lush" are a reversal trap, as both are used to describe an environment that is full of greenery and plant life.

**MANHATTAN**
PREP

72. **Extemporaneous, impromptu.** "Badly miscalculated" indicates that there are two opposing parts of the sentence: the candidate's "prepared speeches" are good, but some other form of communication is bad. You need two words that mean improvised or off-the-cuff: "extemporaneous" and "impromptu" are a perfect fit. "Capricious" (whimsical or variable) is tempting but doesn't pair as well as the two correct answers. "Lubricious" and "disingenuous" form a pair relating to dishonesty that is unrelated to the clues and might be a trap (if you insert your own, negative ideas about politicians). Finally, "premedititated" would apply to the "prepared speeches," not the off-the-cuff communication.

73. **Unaffected, sincere.** Her friends think that she "projects an air of affability," but this choice of words suggests the appearance of something that is not necessarily genuine. She appears affable, or friendly, but her friends have mixed feelings about this. The blank must mean something like genuine. "Sincere" isn't too hard to spot as a match, but the other correct answer, "unaffected," is a trickier word, used to describe someone who is genuine and sincere. "Amiable" and "genial" both mean friendly, and thus are trap answers that fit with the first half of the sentence but not the blank in the second half. "Magnanimity," which means generosity, and "vexing," which means annoying, are also not good fits.

74. **Abjured, forwent.** The founder did something bad enough to be threatened with a prison term. She is paying "fines and restitution" and she must also have to do something else negative (for her) relative to her role in the company. "Abjured" and "forwent" both work here; she is giving up her position and financial stake in the company. "Reneged" means to break a promise; she can't "renege a role." Similarly, a leader can be "deposed," but you don't depose a role. The hedge fund founder may be "censured" (probably worse), but it doesn't make sense for her to "censure" (disapprove of, reprimand) her role. Finally, her actions may have "jeopardized" her role, but she wouldn't sign a legal memorandum to do so.

75. **Breaching, contravening.** The sentence sets up a contrast: "adherents follow the letter of their particular tradition while" doing something else. This contrast is reinforced in the second half of the sentence, which points to a contradiction between "violence" and "love." The blank must mean something like going against "the most basic ethical tenets," making "breaching" and "contravening" correct. "Obeying" and "heeding," which both mean follow, are trap answers and are opposite the required meaning. Neither "surpassing" nor "contracting" fits the required meaning, nor do these choices have a pair among the other answers.

76. **Moribund, waning.** The sentence indicates that the number of PhD applicants in linguistics "has either grown or held steady in each of the past fifteen years" while also suggesting that this fact is surprising. This could be surprising for a number of reasons, but the only words that would pair in this sentence are "moribund," which means dying, and "waning," which means growing smaller. "Waxing" and "burgeoning" do form a pair, but if the field were growing, it would not be a surprise that the number of applicants has also grown. Neither "dissolute" nor "debased," which both mean lacking in morals, fits the desired meaning of the blank.

77. **Ephemeral, fleeting.** This sentence is about writers of the "contemplative persuasion," meaning writers who are pensive and spend a lot of time in thought, and who have a tough time writing about a certain state of mind. The biggest clue to that state of mind is the phrase "passing thoughts and inconstant moods," which means the answer will mean changeable, impermanent, or inconsistent. The best answers are "ephemeral" and "fleeting." "Vestigial," or a remnant of something, does not fit. "Essential" might work, but there's no indication that the changeable aspects of the mind are necessary. "Evasive" (trying to avoid something) does not have the right meaning. "Inchoate," meaning not fully formed, is tempting but does not form a pair with any other answer.

78. **Tacit, implicit.** The word "Though" sets up a contrast, so the blank needs to be something that means the opposite of "enumerated in rulebooks." Both "tacit" and "implicit" mean implied but not plainly expressed and are the correct answer. "Unambiguous" and "blatant" do form a pair, but have the opposite meaning of the one required for the blank. Finally, "evanescent," which means short-lived, and "incorrigible," which means not able to be corrected, do not form a pair, nor do they fit the meaning of the sentence.

79. **Exacerbate, magnify.** While many people think antibiotics are great for everything ("a cure-all"), they can "actually" make the problem worse: they could "strengthen bacterial strains," which is a bad thing. The two best answer choices are "exacerbate" and "magnify." "Ameliorate," or make better, is the exact opposite and so is incorrect. "Differentiate," to distinguish, doesn't fit the meaning either. "Distort" would mean that the problem is changed but not necessarily made worse. "Pathologize," which means to view something as medically or psychologically unhealthy, is a tempting trap, as a bacterial infection is a an unhealthy condition, but the meaning doesn't match the idea of making a problem worse.

80. **Confounded, flummoxed.** The puzzle in question is one of the "more difficult cryptic crosswords," so one would expect Sandra to be, well, puzzled by it. "Enraged" and "incensed" are an intriguing pair, but there is no reason to believe Sandra was made angry by the puzzle. "Smitten" can't work here because the correct idiom is smitten with. "Impressed" might work, but it doesn't have a pair word (since "smitten" can't be correct). "Confounded" and "flummoxed" both mean perplexed and are correct.

81. **Impervious, inimical.** The "while" at the beginning of this sentence indicates that the opening phrase, "teachers say they are keen on the idea of participatory pedagogy," will be contrasted with the second idea, that teachers "often have little understanding of what participatory practices entail." The part of the sentence following the semicolon confirms this reality with observations of how teachers actually act in classrooms. The blank, then, must be filled with a word describing how teachers are "in fact" likely to behave: not able or likely to change. Both "impervious" and "inimical" fit this meaning. "Amenable" and "prone" are not a true pair, nor do they match with the observations of how teachers actually behave. "Reconciled" and "resigned" are a pair that would mean the teachers are changing their behavior, but the sentence indicates that this is not so.

82. **Approbation, plaudits.** The filmmaker received "acclaim," while the subject of the documentary did not. "Approbation" and "plaudits" are both synonyms for acclaim and are correct. "Opprobrium" and "fulmination," which both mean strong criticism or protest, reflect the opposite of the required meaning, while "wealth" and "capital" don't fit the meaning of the sentence.

83. **Exculpate, vindicate.** Morris's film demonstrated that its subject "did not commit" the crime in question; in other words, the film demonstrated his innocence. Both "exculpate" and "vindicate" mean to clear someone of blame or suspicion and are a perfect match. "Incarcerate" is the opposite of what the sentence suggests, while "inter" means to place in a grave or tomb. "Excuse" means to lessen the blame or forgive someone for a fault, but not to prove they were not at fault in the first place. Finally, of the incorrect answer choices, "manumit" is closest in meaning, but is the act of freeing a slave, not a prisoner.

**MANHATTAN**
PREP

84. **Randomness, happenstance.** The subject matter of this sentence, "cause-and-effect relationships," makes "causality" and "intentionality" very tempting answers. However, most people *do* understand causality (or at least think they do) so the blank, which represents something that people don't understand, is going to mean the exact opposite of "straightforward and direct" causality, such as "randomness" or "happenstance." "Mathematics" and "science" may be difficult for some people to understand, but a solid understanding of causality would actually help people understand those subjects, so they are incorrect choices.

85. **Laziness, sloth.** On the one hand, the professor believes that all her students are "well-qualified academically." On the other hand, some students do poorly in the professor's class. So if they're doing poorly despite being qualified, she assumes that each of these students isn't trying hard. "Ineptness" and "incompetence" make for a really appealing pair here, as both could describe a student who is doing poorly in a class. However, this pair does not also account for the fact that the students are "well-qualified" and, therefore, can't be considered inept. "Laziness" and "sloth," which means laziness or a reluctance to work, both fill this blank nicely and are the correct answers. It's worth noticing the other pair here, "moral turpitude" and "amorality," both of which mean a lack of morals. While the students might be lazy, there is no evidence that their poor performance has anything to do with their morals.

86. **An incipient, a nascent.** While the environmental movement has been around awhile, it has only recently become a "serious organization." In other words, the movement can be said to be relatively new, in a way. The answer choices "disorganized" and "nebulous" don't fit that meaning. The other pair, "inconsequential" and "immaterial," is needlessly negative. "Incipient" and "nascent" capture the idea that, while the movement has been around for a while, it is only just now becoming a serious and relevant organization.

87. **Bolstered, buttressed.** It is critical to work out here whether the physicists mentioned at the end of the sentence were for or against Einstein's theory. The sentence suggests that the idea went from "purely experiential" to "theoretically" something. There's a contrast here, and the contrast is not between right and wrong. It is between something that has been shown by experiment and something that has been understood theoretically. The later scientists are providing support for Einstein. "Undermined" and "sabotaged" are negative, while "condoned" and "pardoned" don't fit the meaning. Only "bolstered" and "buttressed" correctly express the idea of support.

88. **Manacled, fettered.** They wanted to "keep the prisoner _____," but the "restraints would prejudice the jury." So the plan must have been to keep this prisoner restrained. "Manacled" and "fettered" are very close synonyms that mean chained or restrained and are, therefore, the correct pair. "Incensed," meaning "angry," pairs somewhat nicely with "nettled," meaning irritated or annoyed. While they make a good pair, they do not mean restrained. Neither "malleable," meaning bendable or easily influenced, nor "incomparable" fit the context of the sentence.

89. **Artless, ingenuous.** The painter is "unlike" others who are "pretentious and egotistical." In other words, he is not pretentious or egotistical. "Artless" and "ingenuous," meaning without effort or pretentiousness, are perfect. "Shrewd," "adroit," and "artful" each mean clever or skillful and "selfless" means unselfish; none of these four traits contrasts with "pretentious and egotistical."

90. **Trite, hackneyed.** The movie "had laughs" but the jokes were old or unoriginal. The jokes, then, were not *bad* so much as "trite" or "hackneyed," both of which mean unoriginal. "Atrocious" and "egregious" mean the same thing as bad, so they don't work. And while "amusing" and "witty" make a pair, they are the opposite of what the sentence intends to say.

**91. Underpins, undergirds.** The company's "unsuccessful products manage" to look very good, so this "obsession with aesthetics" is found throughout or permeates the company's work. Both "underpins" and "undergirds" fit this meaning. "Irradiates" means either to expose to radiation or to illuminate. "Underserves" means to fail to provide adequate services and does not make sense here. "Saturates" and "overwhelms" might be thought of as a pair, but would not be used in the same context, nor would these extreme words best fit the sentence.

**92. Thwarted, undermined.** The end of this sentence makes it clear that the teachers in question are not happy about having to "cleave," or stick, to a prescribed curriculum because it prevented them from teaching in a "creative and dynamic" way. "Crushed," "confounded," "walloped," and "tormented" are all negative, but all of them miss the meaning of the sentence (and no two of them make a good pair). On the other hand, "thwarted" and "undermined" fit the context: the teachers were prevented from teaching in the way they felt best.

**93. Palliating, assuaging.** The government can lower interest rates to maintain "a certain level of financial stability," but it can't do so too often or it may not be able to handle or manage a future crisis. "Interring" is a difficult GRE word meaning to place a corpse in a grave or tomb. "Exacerbating" and "compounding" are the opposite of the desired meaning. Only "palliating" and "assuaging," both of which mean easing or diminishing, correctly fit the meaning here; "annihilating" goes too far.

**94. Laconic, curt.** The words "[e]ven though" set up a contrast: Mariposa's latest character does not have a lot of lines, so she will need to rely more on physical acting. Mariposa's character might be quite "dramatic," but that would not contrast with the roles that involved many lines. "Melancholy" and "dejected" imply sadness, but not necessarily a refusal to speak (Hamlet is pretty depressed and he talks all the time). "Mute" goes too far: one can't be more mute; rather, one would be mute if that person had no lines at all. "Laconic" and "curt" both match the idea that her character is not very talkative. Note that "curt" has the sense of being rudely short with people, whereas "laconic" is not necessarily negative, and while they aren't perfect synonyms, the two correct answer choices do provide a similar meaning to the sentence.

**95. Incendiary, demagogic.** The sentence is quite complex. It can often be helpful to reduce such a sentence down to its main core—eliminating the tacked-on modifiers—and then add the extra information back in as needed. Doing so here leaves you with: "The _____ nature of Thomas Paine's political diatribes is now downplayed by government officials." The word "diatribes" denotes strongly negative speech or writing, and, as such, their "nature" would more likely be controversial or fiery than understated or restrained. "Pallid," which means pale or weak, forms a close, but incorrect, pair with "anemic." "Antithetical" works superficially—it means directly opposed or mutually incompatible but it doesn't connote a nature that would need to be downplayed. "Deferential," meaning respectful, is the opposite of the needed meaning. That leaves the correct pair: "incendiary," which means inflammatory and provocative, and "demagogic," which refers to verbiage intended to arouse strong negative sentiments (usually against an established power).

**MANHATTAN**
PREP

96. **Phlegmatic, dispassionate.** The people who disliked the spy thought his demeanor was "taciturn," meaning reserved or uncommunicative, or "brusque," meaning abrupt or blunt. Because those descriptives are given from the people who dislike the spy, look for words that describe those same qualities in a more neutral, or even positive, manner. "Histrionic" and "melodramatic" are a great pair, but, as is so often the case, they mean exactly the opposite of what the blank needs: overly theatrical and exaggerated. "Hirsute" is a tough word that actually means hairy, and there's nothing to suggest that the spy is feeling "melancholic," or sad. That leaves just two words. "Phlegmatic" means calm, cool, and collected, and "dispassionate" means unemotional and composed; both are more positive versions of "taciturn or brusque."

97. **Melancholy, morose.** The key to this sentence comes at the very end, when the sentence says that Hamlet is not "paralyzed with depression," or generally depressed. "Indecisive" and "monologic" both fit the famous character of Hamlet, but they don't fit the sentence (nor do they make a pair). Similarly, "violent" and "barbaric" would be accurate in describing someone who committed a "killing spree," but they don't fit the blank. Only "melancholy" and "morose" match the idea that he was depressed.

98. **Anomalous, aberrant.** The word "once" signals a change in the direction of meaning. As the sentence ends with the idea that the behaviors in question "were once considered normal," you need something for the blank that means uncommon. "Mythical" and "fabulous" may seem to fit, but they're too extreme. "Anomalous" and "aberrant," which both mean deviating from an expected standard, fit. "Importunate," meaning persistent, may rhyme with "unfortunate," but that's about all they have in common.

99. **Mundane, quotidian.** While things that are "fantastical" can be "the domain of the novel," Proust proved that other things can also be. The blank needs to contrast with "the fantastical." "Mundane" and "quotidian" are the correct answer pair. "Cosmopolitan" means cultured or glamorous and is the opposite of what the sentence requires. "Bombastic" and "belletristic," both of which mean pompous or ostentatious, do not contrast with "fantastical." Finally, "literary" is a trap since a novel is a piece of literature.

100. **Pith, gist.** In this sentence, the key words are "very busy woman," implying that the editor doesn't have a lot of free time. It would be necessary to get right to the most important part of the issue. "Conclusion" and "culmination" are a pair, but they mean the end, which isn't quite right. "Pith" and "gist" (the essence of something) are a much better match for the blank. "Apex," or climax, and "genesis," or beginning, not only do not form a pair, but also do not fit the meaning.

101. **Exceptional, precocious.** Though people used to believe the boy was "less than clever," the "but" indicates that he actually was clever. In fact, he wrote a "complex and beautiful symphony" at the young age of 16, which suggests he is a prodigy, or child genius. "Precocious," meaning advanced for his age, and "exceptional," or extraordinary, are good descriptions for a child prodigy. "Musical" is a tempting answer, but the word doesn't have anything to do with his cleverness, nor does it have a matching answer choice. "Monastic" and "hermetic" might appeal as answer choices, due to his "reclusive" nature, but they do not fit with other clues in the sentence. Note that "hermetic" doesn't actually mean "like a hermit"; it means "airtight."

102. **Stress, underscore.** The part of the sentence after the colon is an example illustrating the point made in the first part of the sentence. Since Fry "argues" that rhythm is more important than deeper meaning, the corresponding first part, "meter," is more important than "words." These poets are proclaiming "the primacy of meter over words." The correct answers "stress" and "underscore" convey this meaning. The much milder pair, "acknowledge" and "allow," doesn't fit because their intensity doesn't match that of "argues." "Immolate" is a great GRE vocabulary word that means to burn as a sacrifice, which, although interesting, is definitely not the desired meaning here. "Decry" is another great word that means to publicly denounce, but it also does not fit.

103. **Inevitably, unavoidably.** The clues here—"Time stops for no man" and "as had every preceding style of music"—suggest that rock and roll suffered the same fate that all music and all people eventually do. It "inevitably" or "unavoidably" joined the "culture of the old." The sentence does not provide information to believe that this happens "accidentally" nor its opposite, "deliberately." Similarly for "resolutely" and "painfully," the sentence does not provide a clue to suggest that this is how it became "a part of the culture of the old."

104. **Hankering, proclivity.** The word "and" signals agreement between two parts of the sentence. Isherwood had "fellow feeling for the laboring classes"; that is, he was sympathetic with working people and so had a desire to engage as an equal with them. "Hankering" and "proclivity" are the nearest synonyms. "Disinclination" and "unwillingness" are the opposite of the required meaning and "implacability," which means not able to be appeased, also suggests a negative tone that is opposite what the sentence requires. "Joviality" (friendliness) is tempting because it is positive, but it does not fit the meaning of the blank.

105. **Germane, pertinent.** "Though" implies that the matters about which a professor enjoys "liberty of speech" are opposite those "irrelevant to his subject," so the blank might mean something like relevant. "Germane" and "pertinent" are the best synonyms. "Mimetic" and "congruent" are slightly related to the idea at hand—the former means copying (like a mime, for instance) and the latter means something like similar or in agreement. "Indifferent" and "disinterested" might seem like a pair, but "indifferent" means uninterested or apathetic, while "disinterested" means unbiased. Neither word fits nor do they form a pair.

106. **Rue, remorse.** The sentence states that uncontrolled passion can lead to something bad. The answer should be close to sorrow, perhaps something like regret. "Rue" and "remorse" are the nearest synonyms and are therefore the correct answer pair. "Disdain" and "contempt" are also synonyms, but anger and sorrow do not pair as well as regret and sorrow. "Pity" might work if it had a pair in the answer choices, while "affinity" has no pair and also doesn't have the same negative tone that the other answer choices have.

107. **Exhaustive, sweeping.** Since the tremendous wealth on display represents only a tiny fraction of the collection, and since the collection has "over one million specimens," it is a very large collection indeed. You might anticipate an answer like huge. "Exhaustive," which means including everything, and "sweeping," which means extensive, both fit. If a collection is "piecemeal," it would have been acquired piece by piece over time. Likely as that might be, there's no clue in the sentence that would suggest this. "Voluble" means talkative and does not fit, nor does "evergreen," which means fresh or popular. Finally, "commanding" means authoritative or imposing, and there's no reason to believe that the collection commands authority over other collections.

**MANHATTAN**
PREP

108. **Truculent, savage.** The blank requires a word that contrasts with "comparatively conciliatory" and modifies the word "attack," something like a strong attack. "Truculent" and "savage" both suggest a disposition to fight and are therefore the correct answer. The word "imperious," meaning arrogant and domineering, is close, but doesn't have the same strength as the correct answers do. "Partisan" and "biased" do form a pair, but do not contrast with "conciliatory." Finally, an attack that is "dissembling" would be sneaky or bluffing, but the sentence does not suggest that the attack was meant to be sneaky.

109. **Extirpated, obliterated.** This sentence is about as purely definition-based as you can get: the house was torn from the ground and utterly destroyed. "Extirpated" and "obliterated" both fit. "Tethered" means tied to something. "Recapitulated" means to summarize and is better known by its shortened version: recap. "Interred" means to place in a grave or tomb. And "hallowed" means to make holy or to be greatly revered. None of the latter four options form a pair, nor do any of them fit the context of this sentence.

110. **Debacle, rout.** If the team has no chance of winning the game in the third quarter, the game must have been a crushing failure or a drubbing. "Debacle" and "rout" fit well. Note that a "boondoggle" is certainly bad, but it is an unnecessary and wasteful project. "Forgery" means fake and there's nothing fake about a bad loss. "Fallacy" means a mistaken belief and "infirmity" means a physical or mental illness, neither of which fits this sentence.

111. **Aver, assert.** The young husband is ignoring certain warning signs regarding his partner's fidelity. This would suggest that he believes his partner to be faithful. Of the answer choices, "aver" and "assert" are near synonyms that would complete the sentence in a similar way. "Suspect" could possibly work here, but there is no other word that produces a sentence with the same meaning. The remaining options all provide opposite tones for the sentence. If he paid attention to the warning signs mentioned, the husband might "doubt" or "dismiss" his partner's fidelity, or he might even "disparage," or belittle, his partner for the lack of fidelity.

112. **Rift, breach.** "Incontrovertible" indicates that there were issues that were once totally accepted by both parties. Now they are "subject to contention," indicating that there is a widening gap, or fissure, between the parties: a "rift" or "breach" between them. Note that the other four answer choices do not have a pair among them, nor do their meanings reflect the intended meaning of the sentence. An "accord," or treaty, would be the opposite of what the sentence suggests. And though the fissure between the parties might be considered by some to be upsetting, there is not a "travesty" between the parties. "Piety" can mean either the quality of being religious/reverent or a belief that is held with reverence, but neither meaning fits here. And finally, "prevalence," which means commonplace, also does not fit with the clues in the sentence.

113. **Divergent, incongruous.** The word "yet" indicates that the words that fill the blank will contrast with "related." While not perfect synonyms, "divergent," which means developing in different directions, and "incongruous," which means not in harmony, would make sentences that are alike in meaning, so they are the correct pair. "Suitable," "impactful," "complementary" (working well together), and "distinguished" do not contrast with the word "related."

114. **Perspicacious, sagacious.** The colon signals that the second part of the sentence agrees with the first part, so the blank must express how the shaman's knowledge seems "to include every subject." The only pair of words that would match in this sentence are "perspicacious" and "sagacious," both of which mean wise or astute. "Mendacious" and "duplicitous" both mean dishonest or deceitful, but nothing in the sentence suggests that the shaman would be the most untruthful member of the group. "Superfluous" means unnecessary and "mellifluous" means sweet-sounding, neither of which fits in the context of this sentence.

115. **Utilized, employed.** The sentence suggests that despite certain minor "contraindications," which are specific situations in which a procedure should not be performed, life-saving procedures should be performed when the situation demands. Though first-aid might include medication, procedures would not be "medicated." And "disputed" does not have a pair in the answer choices, nor would it make sense to dispute any life-saving procedures. While it might be possible for life-saving procedures to be "contrived" or "created," there is no clue in the sentence to suggest that trainers think that these procedures should be made up. Thus, the correct answers are "utilized" and "employed."

116. **Mordant, trenchant.** The best clue in this sentence is its parallel structure. The judge's keen eye "was surpassed only by the _____ wit with which she castigated them." Keen means sharply discerning, so look for words that denote a sharpness, or bitingness, of wit. "Mordant" and "trenchant," both of which are close in meaning to sharp and discerning, are best. Don't be confused by the other set of synonyms, "assiduous" and "sedulous," both of which have meanings close to diligent. "Jurisprudent," which means skilled in the principles of law, is a trap for those thinking about words that might describe a judge. And someone who is "obtuse" would be slow-witted, a word that is the opposite of what the sentence intends.

117. **Beseeched, supplicated.** The inmate is begging, pleading, imploring the probation panel to be set free. "Beseeched" and "supplicated" are closest to this meaning. A person might "receive" a group of individuals if he or she were welcoming them, but this doesn't match the intended meaning of the sentence, nor does it match with any other of the answer choices. "Conceded" isn't the right word either, nor would you concede a group of people (unless you were giving them away to someone else). Finally, both "chided" and "snubbed" have a negative connotation and are the opposite of how the inmate was acting towards the probation panel.

118. **A fanatical, a zealous.** The loyalty of the cult members "verged on the obsessive"; use that same description to fill the blank. "Fanatical" and "zealous" are best here. An obsessive loyalty would definitely not be "arbitrary" or "fickle," nor would it be "indeterminate," or undefined. Finally, while others might be mortified by such loyalty, the loyalty itself would not be "mortifying."

119. **Grievous, baneful.** The evils described by this word are more "pernicious," or harmful, than ... well, it doesn't even really matter—you want a word like "pernicious." Perhaps very bad. "Grievous," which means causing grief or very harmful, will work. "Baneful" is an even closer synonym to "pernicious." Note that you could also find the correct answer by noticing that none of the other four options have a pair in the sentence. "Venerable" means respected, "epicurean" means related to fine food and wine, and "fastidious" means very attentive to detail, all of which have the incorrect tone for the blank. Finally, "reactionary" means opposed to political or social reform, which also doesn't fit the sentence.

**MANHATTAN**
PREP

120. **Hegemony, dominance.** Just as once "every subject eventually had to meet theology's demands," both physical science and social science must now meet mathematics' demands. This suggests that mathematics enjoys something like rule over these fields; the phrase "Queen of the Sciences" suggests the same. "Hegemony" usually describes the dominance of one state over others, but can also mean the dominance of one social group, political party, etc. "Dominance" will also work. If you anticipated the word autocratic, "autonomy" might be attractive, especially as a pair with "independence," but autocratic describes government by a single person with unlimited powers, while autonomy means self-governance. Finally, neither "mayhem" nor "credence" have a pair in the answer choices with a similar meaning, nor do they convey a meaning that matches with the clues in the sentence.

121. **Ephemeral, fleeting.** Something "lasting a millionth of a billionth of a billionth of a second" is very short-lived. "Ephemeral" and "fleeting" have just this meaning. In real life, the particles may be small ("infinitesimal"), there may be a lot of them ("myriad," "countless"), and they may bring a tear to the eye of a few scientists ("poignant"), but none of these are indicated by clues in the sentence.

122. **Collaborative, synergetic.** The word "While" indicates that the "later contributions" were achieved in a manner opposite to "single-handedly." Both "collaborative" and "synergetic" mean working together or in a group. Note that trap answers "solitary" and "unilateral" are the opposite of the required meaning, and "collusive" has the wrong spin—to collude is to cooperate for illegal or fraudulent purposes. Finally, "exegetic" means explanatory or interpretive, which isn't the right meaning, nor does it have a pair in the answer choices.

123. **A coup, an achievement.** The sentence suggests that despite the unimpressive media coverage of the event, the organizers were still pleased. The second part of the sentence states one specific positive aspect of the event: a "mass of everyday people" attended. Therefore, the best pair of words here would be "coup" and "achievement," both of which can mean a successful move, and both of which match the positive feelings that the organizers felt. A "miracle" (a highly improbable event that can't be explained by science) is too strong. Of the remaining options, "blemish" and "debacle" form a pair, but they contradict the intended meaning of the sentence. Finally, "exception" does not work since it does not have a pair.

124. **Retort, rejoinder.** Churchill makes a witty comeback. "Retort" and "rejoinder" are perfect. "Recrimination," meaning an accusation, does not fit. A witty reply is not an "anecdote," nor is it an "aphorism" or "maxim" (both of which mean a short statement containing some general truth or wisdom).

125. **Fancied, relished.** The teacher was "well-loved by students" but didn't love or enjoy "the work of teaching." In fact, he had "deep-seated anxieties" about certain aspects of teaching. "Fancied" and "relished" are the correct pair. Of the incorrect answer choices, "appreciated" is most similar to the correct answers, but there is no clue in the sentence that would suggest that the teacher did not appreciate the work he did. While "abhorred" and "detested" are synonyms, their meaning is the opposite of what the clues suggest. Finally, "ascertained" does not fit the required meaning, nor does it have a pair among the answers.

126. **Stickler, disciplinarian.** Pay close attention to the directional words "no," "although," and "in truth." "Although" suggests a turn in the sentence; the teacher had to "maintain the appearance of," or pretend to be, "an authority figure," while, in reality, she was "no" strict person. Both a "stickler" and a "disciplinarian" are strict people, so these are the correct answer choices. "Educator" and "scholar" are words that are associated with teachers, but they don't mean strict. A "luminary" is a prominent and inspiring person, but there is no evidence in the sentence that the teacher is such a person. "Delinquent" is also not a good match for strict.

127. **Guileless, naïve.** If the actress can recognize when people are trying to trick her or manipulate her, she's definitely not overly innocent, gullible, or easily fooled. The two best answers that mean innocent and gullible are "guileless" and "naïve." "Disingenuous" and "cunning" would be more appropriate in describing her "crafty handlers," while "talented" and "sophisticated" don't have pairs among the other answers and don't match the desired meaning.

128. **Virulence, acrimony.** The blank in this sentence describes "recent national political discourse," which is referred to as "hateful rhetoric" at the end of the sentence. While the other options in this question could possibly describe a person's opinion on political discourse, the only words that could match "hateful" are "virulence" and "acrimony," both of which mean harsh or full of malice. "Partisanship" and "intransigence" form a pair, since each means biased or unlikely to compromise, but without anything in the sentence suggesting that people are not willing to compromise, the pair does not work here. Neither "shortsightedness" nor "miscalculation" mean "hateful," nor do these two words form a pair.

129. **Radical, immoderate.** There is a contrast between what Martin Luther King, Jr. was really like and how he is generally perceived today. The sentence contains two important clues. First, he went through a "process of canonization" posthumously (after his death), meaning that he was turned into a saint-like figure in the popular imagination. Second, during the process, his "more palatable" (pleasing or easy to agree with) "and less far-reaching political and social visions became prominent." It must be true, then, that he had less palatable, more far-reaching visions that are now overlooked. The word in the blank should mean something like revolutionary or boundary-pushing. "Radical" and "immoderate" both fit this meaning. Ineffective," "politic" (sensible), "incongruous" (not in harmony with the surroundings), and "raucous" (very loud or harsh) do not fit the required meaning.

130. **Costly, dear.** The council was looking to "offset … expenses," so the renovation project must have been more expensive than planned. "Costly" fits, as does "dear," which can indeed mean expensive. Using secondary definitions is one of the GRE's favorite traps. "Fortuitous" and "timely" could make a reasonable pair, but those two, along with "subtle," don't fit the meaning of the sentence. "Unexpected" could fit the meaning but it does not have a pair among the answers.

131. **Discretionary, voluntary.** "Aviation authorities" issued "guidelines," or "recommendations," but there is an "absence of definitive laws." The guidelines are not legally required; rather, they are "voluntary" or "discretionary." "Firm" and "unvarying" are the opposite of what is needed. "Insufficient" goes too far—there is no judgment that the guidelines were "not enough," just that they weren't definitive. "Regular" is a versatile word that can mean everything from constituting a pattern to happening habitually or happening frequently.

**MANHATTAN**
PREP

**132. Quotidian, mundane.** The show "claimed to display the _____ side of the starlet's life," but those claims cannot be true because "her daily endeavors were far too sensational." The blank needs to say something along the lines of "unsensational." The pair "unusual" and "exotic" means the opposite. "Plastic" has many meanings, none of which apply very well here, and it doesn't have a pair. Finally, when down to "predictable," "quotidian," and "mundane," choose the best pair. "Predictable" is a near miss here. It doesn't necessarily mean "unsensational" because things could be predictably sensational. "Quotidian" means unsensational, everyday, or ordinary, just like "mundane," so these are the best answer choices.

**133. Mistaken, untrue.** Prognosticators are people who predict the future, and, according to the sentence, listening to them is a "problem" because no one holds them accountable for their predictions today. This idea is echoed in the idiomatic phrase "for every X there are Y," where X and Y contrast. So, for every "accurate prediction" there are "several others" that are *not* accurate. "Mistaken" and "untrue" fit this definition. A false or inaccurate prediction might be unintentionally "misleading," but describing a statement as "misleading" typically implies lack of clarity or deliberate deception; this goes too far, and "mistaken" and "untrue" pair better with each other than either does with "misleading." Both "unforeseen" and "surprising" mean unexpected, so these form an answer pair. However, the context is wrong: an inaccurate prediction might make the ultimate outcome unexpected, but this blank describes the other predictions themselves. A hurried, or "hasty," prediction might or might not turn out to be inaccurate, but there are no indications of prediction speed in the sentence.

**134. Culpable, complicit.** "Allegations" are unproven claims that someone has done something wrong or illegal, so if they "turn out to be true," the administrators would be found to be guilty or deserving of blame. This is further supported by the negative results: "the university may lose its accreditation" and the perpetrators "might never be able to be employed in higher education again." The answers "culpable" (deserving blame) and "complicit" (collaborating with others in an illegal activity or wrongdoing) both fit the meaning of the sentence and produce sentences that are alike in meaning. "Repentant" and "contrite" are an answer pair meaning remorseful or guilt-ridden, which is close, but goes a bit too far: the sentence indicates they may be "found" guilty but not necessarily that they feel badly about it. The remaining choices are unpaired and not a good fit for the blank anyway. "Synoptic," which is related to the word "synopsis," means forming a summary. When referring to people, "unsound" means unreliable or not competent.

**135. Immoderate, extreme.** In this sentence, the author has described unions as "always inimical" (meaning harmful or hostile) to economic growth. If even his "adherents," his devoted followers or admirers, could not take this claim seriously, then this claim must be too far-fetched to believe. "Immoderate" (exceeding reasonable limits) and "extreme" both fit this meaning well. "Temperate" and "lax" would both indicate the opposite—a relaxed or balanced position. And though the author's writing might be "impressive" or "splendid," neither of those would make the characterization hard to take seriously.

**136. Catering to, pandering to.** Pynchon "ignored the sensibilities of the general public rather than" paying attention to them. "Catering to" and "pandering to" best match this meaning. "Cowering to" and "recoiling from" are a little too dramatic and extreme for this sentence. Neither "coping with" nor "commiserating with" fits the intended meaning (nor do they have a pair among the answers).

137. **Malleable, pliant.** "Many sociologists" think "humans are _____," "but" a certain event leads the writer to conclude that "human nature is immutable," or unable to change. Therefore, the blank needs to mean changeable. "Monolithic" means large and indivisible and "homogenous" means uniform or unvaried, so neither of these match the desired meaning. "Heterogeneous" and "variegated" (having a lot of variety) are tempting, but variety is not the same thing as change. The best choices are "malleable" and "pliant," which each mean physically bendable and, secondarily, easily influenced or changeable.

138. **Brandishes, wields.** Note that all the choices are verbs, so "a strapping hero often [does something to/with] a rapier," which is a thin pointed sword used for thrusting; the hero's action is later referred to as a "display of force." The blank might be something like uses, or some verb more specific to how a rapier is used, such as thrusts. To "sheathe" a weapon is to put it away (in a sheath, which is a cover for a blade); this is the opposite of using it in a "display of force." Ideas or information can be "promulgated" or "disseminated," meaning spread, communicated, or publicized, so these choices form an answer pair. However, swords cannot be "promulgated" or "disseminated," so the answer pair doesn't work in this context. To "cauterize" is to burn skin or flesh to stop bleeding or seal a wound, so this choice is unpaired and does not match the required meaning. The synonyms "brandish" and "wield" in this context indicate that the hero held and waved the rapier as a threat. These choices agree with the "display of force" characterization of the action.

139. **Cautious, conservative.** Gupta's policies are "prudent," meaning thoughtful, and "progressive," while also "remaining _____ about imposing drastic social changes." The word "while" indicates a contrast, so the party is likely being careful not to do anything drastic. Both "cautious" and "conservative" fit well. "Passionate" and "fervent" are a great pair, but the meaning is the opposite of what you want. "Congealed" (took shape or coalesced) does not match the required meaning and "concerned," while tempting, does not have a pair among the answers.

140. **Plodding, pedestrian.** That the economy expands at a certain pace is described as "a problem." This happens when "wages of the middle class are stagnant," showing no activity or only sluggishly growing. The blank, then, likely refers to a sluggish or slow pace of economic expansion. "Lucrative" and "profitable" are synonymous with each other, but imply economic growth, which would not be a problem. An "exponential" pace would be one that increases at a faster and faster rate, which is opposite the idea of "stagnant" wages or a "problem" with the economy. If the economy expands at a "normal" pace, the expansion is typical or expected, which is not negative enough. Only "plodding," which means slow-moving, and "pedestrian," which means dull, fit the meaning of the sentence and produce sentences that are alike in meaning.

141. **Profuse, prolific.** First, examine the structure of the sentence to determine the role of the blank. "The abilities of microorganisms to [do something] are more _____ than is commonly thought: from [X], to [Y], their innovative capabilities know no end." The blank describes the "abilities." The colon indicates that examples will follow of what is meant by the first part of the sentence. In the idiom "from X, to Y," the examples X and Y are just two abilities, and the idiom suggests a range of other abilities in between. This is further supported by "their innovative capabilities know no end." Thus, the blank should be a synonym for unlimited. The synonyms "profuse" and "prolific" mean abundant or plentiful, which fits the desired meaning. "Advantageous" and "beneficial" are synonyms meaning favorable or leading to good results. "Accommodating" forms something of a false triple with the previous pair: it means obliging someone else's wishes and, like "beneficial," is a synonym for helpful. Any of these could describe "abilities," but none of the three address the meaning of the idiom or of capabilities that "know no end." Finally, "ineffectual" means unproductive, so this choice is not only unpaired, it is also nearly opposite the intended meaning.

**MANHATTAN**
PREP

142. **Atypical, anomalous.** In chess, a "gambit" is an opening move that sacrifices something (such as a pawn) in exchange for some other competitive advantage; such a move typically involves some risk. "Gambit" is also used outside of chess to mean a tactic or calculated move. (This is not the only chess term that can also be used figuratively: "pawn" is another.) Polgar has a "reputation for conservative," or non-risky play, but lately she has been using a lot of "gambits." The blank requires an adjective to describe these "gambits," and might be filled with something like risky. "Treacherous" can mean deceitful or it can mean hazardous or risky, either of which could apply to "gambits" intended to take some advantage from an opponent. However, no other choice matches either definition. "Abstruse," meaning difficult to understand, is not the same as risky. Polgar might be "studious" about determining which gambits to use, but "studious" is both out of context in the blank and unpaired. "Atypical" and "anomalous" both mean unusual or different from what is expected. This pair works because Polgar has a reputation for one type of play, but has been exhibiting another type. "Impractical" on its own is quite tempting, because "impractical" play seems almost opposite "conservative play," but it does not have a match among the other choices and so cannot be correct.

143. **Hobble, hamstring.** The politician who currently holds office would have to be deep in denial about the dissatisfaction of her constituency to to think that "pandering advertisements would do anything but _____ her campaign." When a politician's communications are described as "pandering," it means that they are intended to please the group that they are trying to appeal to and are not sincere. A group that has been upset with a politician for a while is not likely to be impressed by this, so her campaign would likely be harmed by such advertisements. The correct answers, "hobble" and "hamstring," literally mean to cripple the legs of an animal, and are used figuratively to mean to prevent the campaign from being able to take off. "Bolster," which means to support or strengthen, "encourage," and "restore" are almost opposites of the desired meaning and so are not correct. "Aggrieve" is tricky because it is negative, but it means to make resentful and so does not quite fit.

144. **Steadfast, unwavering.** A person who is "equivocal in making decisions" is uncertain; he keeps changing his mind or not making a final decision. The phrase "Though often" in this sentence indicates that the blank will contrast with "equivocal." In addition, the nouns "resolve," which means firm determination or decision, and "verdict," a decision or judgment, reinforce the idea that the blank should be something like definite. The two answers that best match are "steadfast" and "unwavering," which are synonyms meaning resolute or not wavering. "Vague" means uncertain or indefinite and "vacillating" means wavering or alternating between different options. These form an answer pair, but one that is the opposite of what the blank requires. "Apprehensive" is similar to, though not exactly a synonym of, "vague" or "vacillating": someone who is fearful that something bad will happen might hesitate to make a decision, but not necessarily. "Critical" doesn't directly address the question of decisiveness implied by the sentence, and has a negative connotation not supported by the sentence.

145. **Manageable, reasonable.** The proposal will "maximize efficiency" and do something to class sizes, but surprisingly parents and teachers are "resoundingly opposed." Both items, then, must be positive: despite the fact that they will "maximize efficiency" and have good "class sizes," people still don't like the plan. Both "manageable" and "reasonable" fit. "Flexible" is probably the word most similar, but "flexible" class sizes are not necessarily a positive; it could be tough if students kept coming and going. "Remedial" (intended to fix or cure) does not fit, nor does it have a pair. And while classes might be considered "unwieldy" or "deficient," those words are not similar nor do they fit the required meaning.

**146. An obstacle to, a hurdle for.** The blank in this sentence is describing the bridge player's errors and the effect that they had on his defeat. These errors are "frustrating for his partner," but his competitors were unable to determine "what cards he likely held" or "how to block his plays." These two clues suggest that the bridge player was doing something helpful for himself or his team, thereby preventing defeat. The best pair of words, then, is "an obstacle to" and "a hurdle for," suggesting that the errors prevented his (immediate) defeat. The other four options all give opposite meaning to this sentence, though in different degrees of certainty. "An insurance against" and "the guarantee of" would indicate that defeat was imminent, while "the reason for" and "an indication of" would suggest it was likely.

**147. Generalizable, universal.** The colon in this sentence introduces an illustration of how or why the medical study is deficient. The study "assumes" one thing about the results, "however" something else is actually true. The blank, then, must contrast with "experimental participants were exclusively men between the ages of 30 and 60 with no significant co-morbidities." It helps to know that "co-morbidities" are multiple diseases present simultaneously in a patient, but if you didn't, the sentence provides enough other clues to answer correctly. The "glaring deficiency" is that the "experimental participants" included no females, no under-30- or over-60-year-olds, and no people with "significant co-morbidities." In other words, the study was limited to a pretty specific group, so the contrasting blank should be something like "not limited." Results that are "generalizable" can be broadly applied; "universal" results are applicable to all cases. These synonyms correctly allude to the study flaws that follow "however." The adjective "positive" can mean a variety of things, including good, affirmative, optimistic, useful, or definite. When describing "results," none of those meanings addresses the study flaws listed. A similar choice is "promising," or showing signs of future success. While it would be wrong to assume that "results are promising" when the "study contains a glaring deficiency," such an assumption is not itself an example of the deficiency. "Singular" and "exceptional" both mean remarkable or unusual—almost the opposite of "universal."

# Chapter 5
## *of*
### 5 lb. Book of GRE® Practice Problems

# Reading Comprehension

# In This Chapter...

Reading Comprehension

Reading Comprehension Answers

# Reading Comprehension

> **Questions 1–3 are based on the following reading passage.**

   While new census data reveals that unemployment numbers are more dire than was previously suspected, it is not clear that the forecast for American entrepreneurship is equally alarming. An article in a major national newspaper suggests that the contraction in hiring at existing companies might result in more new companies being founded. College graduates,
5  unable to find traditional jobs, instead opt to start their own businesses. Where a recession may seem an unpropitious time for such a historically risky endeavor, with no better options, would-be entrepreneurs have little to lose. Unfortunately, this situation does not necessarily impact the economy positively. Though the average number of new businesses started per year has been higher during the recession than it was before, the proportion of high-value businesses
10  founded each year has declined. So even if a business manages to stay solvent, it may not bring significant returns. Also, because of an inevitable dearth of angel investors and venture capitalists, many new entrepreneurs are putting their own money on the line. In certain ways, the choice between accepting a traditional job and starting a business is not unlike the choice between renting and buying property. The latter requires a significant initial outlay and carries
15  heavier risks, but the rewards can be equally substantial.

1.  The primary purpose of the passage is to

   (A)  propose changes in the way the public generally interprets census data

   (B)  maintain that college students should form their own companies, especially during economic recessions

   (C)  present a nuanced view of a contemporary economic issue

   (D)  evaluate the viability of low- versus high-value businesses under various environmental conditions

   (E)  draw an analogy between career decisions and real estate decisions, specifically the choice to rent or buy property

2.  According to the passage, the reason that many college graduates are choosing to launch their own companies in the present economic climate is that

   (A)  they are hampered by the difficulty of finding outside investors

   (B)  they cannot easily find positions typically open to workers of their experience

   (C)  the prevalence of low-value companies has increased

   (D)  they are forced to decide between renting and buying property

   (E)  forecasts of the unemployment rate are likely to become less dire in coming years

3.   It can be inferred from the passage that over the course of the recent recession, the number of American high-value businesses founded per year

    (A)   has fallen sharply

    (B)   has fallen moderately

    (C)   has risen sharply

    (D)   has risen moderately

    (E)   may have either fallen or risen

**Question 4 is based on the following reading passage.**

According to Mercy Amba Oduyoye in *Daughters of Anowa: African Women and Patriarchy*, the women of the Asante people of Ghana participated in war as nurses or as providers of supplies, but only those who had not yet reached or who were past childbearing age did so. If such women died in battle, they died "as individuals and not as potential sources of human

5   life." As such, many old women engaged in valiant acts, sometimes sacrificing their own lives, to defend those they had given life to.

4.   Which of the following can be inferred from the passage?

    (A)   The deaths of Asante women of childbearing age were lamented more than were the deaths of other women.

    (B)   Older Asante women were more courageous than younger Asante women.

    (C)   Some of those who worked as nurses or as providers of supplies died in battle.

    (D)   Old women were accorded special status above other women and men.

    (E)   Men could not be considered potential sources of human life.

**MANHATTAN**
PREP

---

**Questions 5–7 are based on the following reading passage.**

The past decade has seen a statistically significant uptick in reports of the bacterial strains known as "super-bugs," so called not because of enhanced virulence, but because of their resistance to many antimicrobial agents. In particular, researchers have become alarmed about NDM-1 (New Delhi metallo-beta-lactamase), which is not a single bacterial species, but a

5   transmittable genetic element encoding multiple resistance genes. A resistance "cocktail" such as NDM-1 could bestow immunity to a bevy of preexisting drugs simultaneously, rendering the bacterium nearly impregnable.

However, in spite of the well-documented dangers posed by antibiotic-resistant bacteria, many scientists argue that the human race has more to fear from viruses. Whereas

10   bacteria reproduce asexually through binary fission, viruses lack the necessary structures for reproduction, and so are known as "intracellular obligate parasites." Virus particles called virions must marshal the host cell's ribosomes, enzymes, and other cellular machinery in order to propagate. Once various viral components have been built, they bind together randomly in the cellular cytoplasm. The newly finished copies of the virus break through the cellular

15   membrane, destroying the cell in the process. Because of this, viral infections cannot be treated ex post facto in the same way that bacterial infections can, since antivirals designed to kill the virus could do critical damage to the host cell itself. In fact, viruses can infect bacteria (themselves complete cells), but not the other way around. For many viruses, such as that responsible for the common cold sore, remission rather than cure is the goal of currently

20   available treatment.

While the insidious spread of drug-resistant bacteria fueled by overuse of antibiotics in agriculture is nothing to be sneezed at, bacteria lack the potential for cataclysm that viruses have. The prominent virologist Nathan Wolfe considers human immunodeficiency virus (HIV), which has resulted in the deaths of more than thirty million people and infected twice that

25   number, "the biggest near-miss of our lifetime." Despite being the most lethal pandemic in history, HIV could have caused far worse effects. It is only fortunate happenstance that this virus cannot be transmitted through respiratory droplets, as can the viruses that cause modern strains of swine flu (H1N1), avian flu (H5N1), and SARS.

5. The main purpose of the passage can be expressed most accurately by which of the following?

    (A) To contrast the manner by which bacteria and viruses infect the human body and cause cellular damage

    (B) To explain the operations by which viruses use cell machinery to propagate

    (C) To argue for additional resources to combat drug-resistant bacteria and easily transmissible pathogenic viruses

    (D) To highlight the good fortune experienced by the human race, in that the HIV pandemic has not been more lethal

    (E) To compare the relative dangers of two biological threats and judge one of them to be far more important

6. According to the passage, infections by bacteria

    (A) result from asexual reproduction through binary fission

    (B) can be treated *ex post facto*

    (C) can be rendered vulnerable by a resistance cocktail such as NDM-1

    (D) are rarely cured by currently available treatments, but rather only put into remission

    (E) mirror those by viruses, in that they can both do critical damage to the host cell

7. According to the passage, intracellular obligate parasites

    (A) are unable to propagate themselves on their own

    (B) assemble their components randomly out of virions

    (C) reproduce themselves through sexual combination with host cells

    (D) have become resistant to antibiotics through the overuse of these drugs

    (E) construct necessary reproductive structures out of destroyed host cells

**MANHATTAN**
PREP

---

**Questions 8–10 are based on the following reading passage.**

---

A supernova is a brief stellar explosion so luminous that it can briefly outshine an entire galaxy. While the explosion itself takes less than fifteen seconds, supernovae take weeks or months to fade from view; during that time, a supernova can emit an amount of energy equivalent to the amount of energy the sun is expected to radiate over its entire lifespan.

5 Supernovae generate enough heat to create heavy elements, such as mercury, gold, and silver. Although supernovae explode frequently, few of them are visible (from Earth) to the naked eye.

In 1604 in Padua, Italy, a supernova became visible, appearing as a star so bright that it was visible in daylight for more than a year. Galileo, who lectured at the university, gave several lectures widely attended by the public. The lectures not only sought to explain the origin of

10 the "star" (some posited that perhaps it was merely "vapour near the earth"), but seriously undermined the views of many philosophers that the heavens were unchangeable. This idea was foundational to a worldview underpinned by a central and all-important Earth, with celestial bodies merely rotating around it.

8.  The primary purpose of the passage is to

    (A)  give the history of supernovae

    (B)  describe a shift in thought as a result of a natural event

    (C)  juxtapose two opposing views about supernovae

    (D)  corroborate the view that the earth is not central to the universe

    (E)  explain how science and philosophy interrelate

---

Consider each of the answer choices separately and indicate all that apply.

---

9.  Which of the following can be inferred by the passage?

    ☐  Supernovae can take over a year to fade from view.

    ☐  Prior to 1604, no one had ever seen a supernova.

    ☐  Galileo convinced philosophers of the incorrectness of their views.

10.  The author mentions which of the following as a result of the supernova of 1604?

    (A)  The supernova created and dispersed the heavy elements out of which the Earth and everything on it is made.

    (B)  Galileo explained the origin of the supernova.

    (C)  The public was interested in hearing lectures about the phenomenon.

    (D)  Galileo's lectures were opposed by philosophers.

    (E)  Those who thought the supernova was "vapour" were proved wrong.

---

**Question 11 is based on the following reading passage.**

---

    *A Small Place* is Jamaica Kincaid's memoir of growing up in Antigua as well as an indictment of the Antiguan government and Britain's colonial legacy in Antigua. Kincaid blames colonial rule for many of Antigua's current problems, including drug dealing and selling off land for tourist properties. Kincaid's critics question why, if the British are responsible for
5  the Antiguan government's corruption, the British government itself isn't more corrupt. Kincaid has responded that there must have been some good people among the British, but that they stayed home.

---

Consider each of the answer choices separately and indicate <u>all</u> that apply.

---

11.  Based on the information in the passage, with which of the following would Kincaid be likely to agree?

    ☐  A government can bring about a degree of corruption abroad that the government itself does not suffer from at home.

    ☐  Britain has caused corruption in governments throughout its former colonial empire.

    ☐  The British who colonized Antigua were more likely to be corrupt than the general British population.

---

**Questions 12–14 are based on the following reading passage.**

---

    By 1784, Wolfgang Amadeus Mozart was internationally renowned as the composer of *The Marriage of Figaro*, and consequently received a commission from the Prague Opera House to compose another opera. The resulting product was *Don Giovanni*, which tells the tale of a criminal and seducer who nevertheless evokes sympathy from audiences, and whose behavior
5  fluctuates from moral crisis to hilarious escapade.
    While *Don Giovanni* is widely considered Mozart's greatest achievement, eighteenth century audiences in Vienna — Mozart's own city — were ambivalent at best. The opera mixed traditions of moralism with those of comedy — a practice heretofore unknown among the composer's works — resulting in a production that was not well-liked by conservative Viennese
10 audiences. Meanwhile, however, *Don Giovanni* was performed to much acclaim throughout Europe.

12.  The primary purpose of the passage is to

    (A)  relate the story of a somewhat likable antihero

    (B)  discuss how a work of art was met by diverging responses

    (C)  give a history of the work of Mozart

    (D)  make a case for the renown of *Don Giovanni*

    (E)  emphasize the moral aspects of a musical work

**MANHATTAN**
PREP

13. The author mentions the mixing of "traditions of moralism with those of comedy" (line 8) primarily in order to

    (A) explain a work's lackluster reception among a particular group of people

    (B) remind the reader of the plot of *Don Giovanni*

    (C) highlight a practice common in contemporary opera

    (D) argue for an innovative approach to opera

    (E) undermine a previously presented assertion

14. It can be inferred from the passage that which of the following is true about the response of Viennese audiences to *Don Giovanni*?

    (A) The audiences preferred purely moralistic works.

    (B) The response was unequivocally positive.

    (C) They did not know that the composer was attempting to mix musical styles.

    (D) The play's moral themes were offensive to Viennese audiences.

    (E) They preferred operas that followed existing stylistic conventions.

---

**Questions 15–17 are based on the following reading passage.**

---

      In the 1960s, Northwestern University sociologist John McKnight coined the term redlining, the practice of denying or severely limiting service to customers in particular geographic areas, often determined by the racial composition of the neighborhood. The term came from the practice of banks outlining certain areas in red on a map; within the red outline,

5  banks refused to invest. With no access to mortgages, residents within the red line suffered low property values and landlord abandonment; buildings abandoned by landlords were then more likely to become centers of drug dealing and other crime, thus further lowering property values.

      Redlining in mortgage lending was made illegal by the Fair Housing Act of 1968, which

10  prohibited such discrimination based on race, religion, gender, familial status, disability, or ethnic origin, and by community reinvestment legislation in the 1970s. However, redlining has sometimes continued in less explicit ways, and can also take place in the context of constrained access to health care, jobs, insurance, and more. Even today, some credit card companies send different offers to homes in different neighborhoods, and some auto insurance companies

15  offer different rates based on zip code.

      Redlining can lead to reverse redlining, which occurs when predatory businesses specifically target minority or low income consumers for the purpose of charging them more than would typically be charged for a particular service. When mainstream retailers refuse to serve a certain area, people in that area can fall prey to opportunistic smaller retailers who sell

20  inferior goods at higher prices.

> Consider each of the answer choices separately and indicate __all__ that apply.

15. Which of the following can be inferred from the passage?

☐ Redlining ceased with the passing of the Fair Housing Act in 1968.

☐ Providing services based on zip code may be a form of redlining.

☐ Access to mortgages is related to higher property values.

16. Which of the following, not mentioned in the passage, would qualify as an example of reverse redlining as defined in the passage?

(A) A bank refuses to offer mortgages to consumers in certain neighborhoods.

(B) Residents of low-income neighborhoods are less likely to be hired for positions than residents of higher-income neighborhoods, even when the applicants have the same qualifications.

(C) Police respond to reports of crimes more quickly in some neighborhoods than in others.

(D) A grocery store in a low-income neighborhood sells low-quality produce for high prices, knowing that most residents do not have the ability to buy elsewhere.

(E) An auto insurance company hires an African American spokesperson in a bid to attract more African American consumers.

17. Which correctly describes a sequence of events presented in the passage?

(A) Subprime mortgages lead to widespread defaults, which lead to landlord abandonment.

(B) Reverse redlining leads to landlord abandonment, which leads to the use of buildings for crime and drug dealing.

(C) Landlord abandonment leads to redlining, which leads to crime and drug dealing.

(D) Redlining leads to reverse redlining, which leads to constrained access to health care, jobs, insurance, and more.

(E) Redlining leads to landlord abandonment, which leads to the use of buildings for crime and drug dealing.

**MANHATTAN**
PREP

---

**Question 18 is based on the following reading passage.**

---

Premastication is the practice of a mother pre-chewing food before feeding it, mouth-to-mouth, to her baby. While germophobic Western society eschews this practice, it is not only common in the developing world, but provides benefits to a developing baby. Babies are not born with digestive bacteria; they get some from passing through the birth canal, but continue
5  to encounter the beneficial bacteria during breastfeeding and while being handled, in general, by adults. Throughout most of human history, in fact, babies have received disease-fighting antibodies and digestive bacteria from the mother's saliva, transmitted via premasticated food. In some cultures, fathers also premasticate food for babies; sometimes even entire family groups will do this—a toddler at a family meal might wander from person to person, being fed
10  by many adults.

---

Consider each of the answer choices separately and indicate <u>all</u> that apply.

---

18.  Based on the information in the passage, the author of the passage would most likely agree that

☐  Germophobia can contribute to depriving babies of a health benefit.

☐  Premasticating food for babies is done only in the developing world.

☐  Adult saliva has benefits for babies in addition to the transmission of beneficial digestive bacteria.

Questions 19–22 are based on the following reading passage.

Matisse and Picasso; Picasso and Matisse. Throughout the twentieth century, this pairing has been touted as the quintessential artistic rivalry. In *Matisse and Picasso*, Yve-Alain Bois follows Hubert Damisch in proposing that the interaction between Picasso and Matisse should be seen as a dynamic game rather than a static conflict of artistic polarities. Bois employs the
5  metaphor of chess, arguing that the game represents the artists' exchange as "a competitive rivalry and a complex temporality" that can be viewed both as a linear process and a simultaneous structure.

But the metaphor of a competitive sport, however complex and intellectually rich, is misleading. The two artists were engaged not just in competition (even friendly competition)
10  but also in friendly dialogue. The two men were more than rivals: they were colleagues, critics, teachers, and occasional friends. A better model, though perhaps one with less flash, is that of a simple conversation, with all the rich variation and shifts in motivation and tone that are possible.

Picasso's *Large Nude in a Red Armchair* marks the extremes of the artist's combativeness
15  towards Matisse. The painting is a clear parody of Matisse's earlier *Odalisque with a Tambourine*. The composition of the figures is strikingly similar: a woman lounges in an armchair at the center of the painting, arm raised above her head, decorative wallpaper behind her. Both paintings feature vivid color contrasts, with green wallpaper, vivid reds, glaring yellows, and rich browns. But Picasso's painting, finished in 1929, mocks the achievements of Matisse's
20  earlier work. The sensuous, rich mood of Matisse's painting has been transformed in Picasso's work into something harsh and grotesque.

The other extreme of the dialogue between the two artists can be seen in Picasso's *Woman with Yellow Hair* and Matisse's response, *The Dream*. The exchange begins with Picasso's work, in 1931. The painting depicts a woman asleep on her arms, resting on a table. She is full,
25  rich, warm, and curved, her head and arms forming a graceful arabesque. This image seems a direct attempt to master Matisse's style and to suggest to the older artist new directions for his work. While there may well be an edge of competitiveness to the painting, a sense that Picasso was demonstrating his ability to do Matisse's work, it remains in large part a helpful hint.

Matisse, nearly a decade later, continues the conversation in a similar tone. In *The Dream*
30  of 1940, he proposes a revision of Picasso's work. Again, a woman lies asleep on a table, her arm tucked beneath her head. Matisse accepts Picasso's basic suggestions for his style: sinuous curves, volumes, and shocking uses of color to express an effect. But Matisse also modifies the earlier work significantly. Color is no longer rigidly tied to form, as bits of fuchsia seep outside the thick black line marking the outline of the table and the patch of yellow on the woman's
35  blouse refuses to be contained by the drawn line. Matisse uses Picasso's same palette of red, purple, white, black, and yellow to create this revision, editing out only the garish green, as if to chide Picasso for the choice. The brilliant interplay of colors in Matisse's work is far more sophisticated and subtle than that offered by Picasso. "Thank you," Matisse seems to be saying, "but you missed a few spots."

**MANHATTAN**
PREP

19. The primary purpose of the passage is to

    (A) discuss the two best painters of an epoch
    (B) evaluate a theory and endorse a revision
    (C) compare selected works of two masters
    (D) show that Matisse's work is more sophisticated
    (E) illustrate how Picasso taught Matisse

20. The author would most likely agree with which of the following statements?

    (A) Artistic rivalries are more like Olympic competitions than professional sports.
    (B) Artistic mastery is best demonstrated by employing multiple styles.
    (C) Artists must be good conversationalists.
    (D) Artistic rivalries can actually be reciprocally nourishing.
    (E) Artistic rivalries generally last for decades.

21. According to the passage, which of the following describes *Woman with Yellow Hair*?

    (A) It was parody of a work by Matisse.
    (B) Its colors were not rigidly tied to its form.
    (C) Its color palette was larger than that of *The Dream*.
    (D) It was a response to a work by Matisse.
    (E) It was harsh and grotesque.

22. Which of the following, had it actually occurred during the artists' lifetimes, would further support the author's thesis?

    (A) A joint exhibition of the two artists' work
    (B) A radio broadcast of the two artists discussing painting
    (C) A movie that dramatized the competition between the two artists
    (D) A play that depicted the two artists playing chess
    (E) A painting of the two artists

**MANHATTAN PREP**

---

**Questions 23–27 are based on the following reading passage.**

---

Timelines are one of the most commonplace classroom tools used to teach history. They present a concise chronology with dates and events listed in a linear narrative, forming a skeletal story of history. Despite their usefulness in allowing students to gain a cursory knowledge of many key moments in the past, their bare-bones, fact-centered structure is

5 symptomatic of the myopic character of curricula that emphasize the What, When, and Who and eclipse the significance of Why and How.

In the United States, by far the most common brand and format of timeline is the World Almanac for Kids US History Timeline—a banner set of 8 horizontal panels each with 8 events, beginning with Columbus's voyage in 1492 and ending with Clinton's election in

10 1993. This timeline has photos accompanying it—about 5–6 per panel—next to most of the dates, and below each date is a 1–2 line description of an event that took place in that year. What immediately commands one's attention when looking at this timeline are the dates themselves. Bolder and more prominently placed than anything else, they seem to be the most important feature of the timeline—even more so than the events' descriptions. The way the

15 dates line up in perfect order presents the viewer with a rigid historical narrative, complete with a beginning and end.

To analyze any particular timeline, it is important to recognize what the timeline expresses implicitly. The first implicit message transmitted by the World Almanac for Kids US History Timeline is that each event listed on the timeline's face must hold some kind of particular

20 historical significance to qualify as one of only 64 pieces of American history presented, though no event's entry gives even a vague explanation as to why it merits this. The second message the timeline conveys, simply by hanging in the classroom, is that this version of history is an "official" one. Third, that each of these events happened totally independently of one another. Fourth, that, at most, only one significant event occurred in any given year. And finally, that

25 American history is entirely made up of wars and minor battles, punctuated by the occasional presidential election and technological innovation. Now, certainly, one can easily surmise that the timeline authors are not consciously promoting these implications, and instead assume that the viewer will automatically acknowledge that it is not a comprehensive history but rather a simple summary of selected events through time. The danger of using the timeline as

30 a teaching tool, of course, lies squarely in that assumption.

23. The author implies which of the following?

    (A) Dates are not important in history.

    (B) Historical events are not interconnected.

    (C) Implicit messages can be as important as explicit ones.

    (D) A study of American history that does not include women and minorities is incomplete.

    (E) American history is best thought of as a linear continuum of events.

24. The author's attitude toward timelines can best be described as

    (A) condescending and impertinent

    (B) tolerant and bemused

    (C) suspicious and resigned

    (D) wary and critical

    (E) negative and complacent

25. The author would most likely agree with all of the following EXCEPT:

    (A) There are more than 64 important events in American history.

    (B) Some students ascribe importance to prominent graphic position.

    (C) Timelines have some positive uses.

    (D) Timelines have no subliminal effects.

    (E) Demonstrating how events interconnect has merit.

26. According to the passage, a problem with timelines is

    (A) their prominent placement in classrooms

    (B) their lack of context

    (C) their infinite nature

    (D) their factual inaccuracy

    (E) their inclusion of photos

27. Which of the following could be substituted for the word "myopic" (line 5) without changing the meaning of the passage?

    (A) ignorant

    (B) bigoted

    (C) purblind

    (D) astigmatic

    (E) mordant

Questions 28–33 are based on the following reading passage.

As queen of France, Marie Antoinette suffered what were likely the harshest criticisms ever laid against any queen or mistress in France's long history. There were two major factors that combined to propagate this dark new level of acidic criticism—one was the blooming public sphere, and the second was the scandalous "Diamond Necklace Affair."

5      Literacy rose greatly over the course of the 18th century and, not coincidentally, the annual output of printed publications tripled by the end of Louis XV's reign and expanded exponentially throughout Louis XVI's kingship. Royal censorship had also been greatly reduced by this time, and a massive "black market" for books and extremely popular underground publications flourished during this period. Also, coffeehouse culture and print culture collided 10  during the mid-to-late 1700s, giving Parisians open forums in which to share the gossips and criticisms circulating via the underground pamphlets.

Having endless numbers of pamphlets and an equally infinite number of readers eager to snap them up would be no good without a juicy story, however. This, of course, was exactly what the people received with the Diamond Necklace Affair. On August 11th, 1784, a social 15  climber named Rohan and a prostitute named Nicole Leguay met in the gardens of Versailles. Nicole was a stunning look-alike of Marie Antoinette, and she was indeed believed to be the queen by Rohan that night. To get on Marie's good side—a necessary evil for anyone with social ambitions at Versailles—Rohan was led to believe that if he procured a fabulously bejeweled necklace on her behalf, it would be a great favor.

20      The scam was revealed when jewelers Boehmer and Bossange inquired directly to Marie Antoinette over payment for the grandiose diamond necklace. They presented her with an invoice that she had apparently signed (though it was actually a clever forgery). The queen was furious and had Rohan arrested and marched off to the Bastille. Yet, in addition to the countless aristocrats who sued to the king on Rohan's behalf, at one point over 10,000 people came to 25  the doors of the Bastille demanding Rohan's release. He was eventually acquitted, much to the queen's dismay.

The consequences of this affair were severe for Marie Antoinette. The mere fact that a common street prostitute—one who engages in underhanded, nocturnal dealings to obtain absurdly expensive jewelry—could be so easily mistaken by a nobleman for the queen of 30  France was incredibly damaging to the queen's already blackened reputation. Furthermore, as this hatred of the queen began to boil over, it became inevitable that it would spill onto the monarchy itself. Though Marie would always be the ultimate villainess, she could never be completely untangled from Louis and, thus, from the monarchy itself. She was not a mistress who could be surreptitiously cut away or a political advisor who could be dismissed. She was a 35  queen, and this fact had inescapable consequences.

28. The second paragraph of the passage serves to

   (A) elucidate further the mechanisms by which disdain for a public figure grew
   (B) contrast two factors that spurred criticism of the queen
   (C) explain the endemic corruption of the French court
   (D) discuss the results of a famous scandal
   (E) detail reasons for Marie Antoinette's unpopularity as well as the consequences

29. The passage implies that a significant proportion of the French aristocracy

   (A) was jealous of the queen's riches
   (B) read coffee house pamphlets
   (C) proved more loyal to Rohan than to the queen
   (D) were less literate than the general populace
   (E) became leaders of the Revolution

30. According to the passage, readership of books and pamphlets increased in the late 18th century because

   (A) the education of women nearly doubled the number of readers
   (B) the literacy rate tripled during the reign of Louis XV
   (C) there were more exciting scandals to write about than there had been in previous times
   (D) government censorship had relaxed
   (E) the number of coffee houses increased

   Consider each of the answer choices separately and indicate all that apply.

31. According to the passage, Rohan

   ☐ committed forgery
   ☐ had social ambitions
   ☐ had support from the populace

   Consider each of the answer choices separately and indicate all that apply.

32. The author suggests that Marie Antoinette

   ☐ caused problems for the monarchy
   ☐ never met Rohan
   ☐ had unlimited legal power

33.  The author's tone could best be described as

  (A)  arrogant and supercilious
  (B)  prim and meretricious
  (C)  thoughtful and disinterested
  (D)  sober but lascivious
  (E)  analytical but enthusiastic

---

**Questions 34–37 are based on the following reading passage.**

---

In John D'Emilio's essay "Capitalism and Gay Identity," D'Emilio argues that the emergence of industrial capitalism led to new opportunities for "free laborers" in the United States, leading to various beneficial changes in social conditions. The overarching themes emerge from D'Emilio's argument about the effects of the onset of industrial capitalism: the new abundance
5   of independence, and choice for "free laborers." He implies throughout that these—independence and choice—are the distinct new markers of the social conditions resultant from this economic shift.

   D'Emilio argues that capitalism empowers laborers as "free" in the sense that they are free to look for jobs and to negotiate contracts and terms of labor. D'Emilio's critics suggest
10  that he largely sidesteps the problems that confound free labor ideology and limit the ability of workers to openly negotiate contracts with employers and to accept or reject the conditions offered. The "contract negotiations" cited as a sign of freedom by D'Emilio are often hardly negotiations at all, but rather highly exploitative arrangements that workers have little ability to affect. From the first Lowell Girls all the way to the modern third world garment workers
15  described by Enloe's "Blue Jeans and Bankers," it is clear that for many—particularly women, minorities, and immigrants—free labor has hardly been free at all.

   Such critics also suggest that D'Emilio misrepresents the historical and continued significance of the home. The shift from a home-based to an industrial economy—though indeed very drastic—was hardly as absolute as D'Emilio suggests. Indeed, from nannying, to
20  housekeeping, to even the "home-based jobs" described in "Blue Jeans and Bankers," labor is still a very active part of the home even today.

   In the essay "The Approaching Obsolescence of Housework: A Working-Class Perspective," Davis spends a great deal of time discussing the continuation of labor in the home in stark contrast to the assertions of D'Emilio. Where D'Emilio argues that industrial
25  capitalism equated to freedom from the home, Davis argues that it actually equated to thickening the bars that caged housewives to the home as productive and reproductive labor split further and more distinctly apart. Davis argues that women "were the losers in a double-sense: as their traditional jobs were usurped by the burgeoning factories, the entire economy moved away from the home, leaving many women largely bereft of significant economic
30  roles."

34.  Which of the following statements is the best description of the structure of the passage?

   (A)  A theory is described and supported by additional studies.

   (B)  A theory and a screed against it are provided.

   (C)  A theory is presented, followed by opinions that impugn it.

   (D)  A theory is discussed and its author's credentials questioned.

   (E)  A theory is presented and ridiculed.

35.  In the second paragraph, the author mentions the Lowell Girls in order to

   (A)  illustrate how industrial capitalism eroded women's economic position

   (B)  challenge an assertion about the importance of home-based economies

   (C)  rebut the arguments of D'Emilio's critics

   (D)  favorably contrast their position to that of Third World garment workers

   (E)  support an assertion that workers' autonomy is more myth than reality

36.  The passage suggests that Davis would be most likely to agree with which of the following?

   (A)  Industrial capitalism leads to independence and choice.

   (B)  Minorities in particular had little freedom of choice.

   (C)  People without economic roles are disadvantaged.

   (D)  Home-based jobs still account for a significant percentage of the overall economy.

   (E)  Domestic work should be paid.

37.  Which of the following would provide the best title for the passage?

   (A)  Industrial Capitalism and the Oppression of Labor

   (B)  D'Emilio, Enloe, and Davis: A Reconciliation

   (C)  A Rejection of D'Emilio's Account of "Free Labor"

   (D)  Women's Sacrifices for Industrial Capitalism

   (E)  Industrial Capitalism and Freedom for All

> **Questions 38–40 are based on the following reading passage.**

Henri Matisse's *The Ochre Head* represents the artist's exuberant display of his new mastery of a technique once peculiar to Picasso. Matisse has learned to artfully separate color and drawing. The painting depicts a head and shoulders, a bouquet of red flowers in a dark blue vase sitting upon a bench, a framed drawing of a woman's head, and an unframed
5  painting or drawing, also of a woman. But what is most striking about the painting is the way Matisse has begun to allow his colors and his forms to play freely, even while they are coordinated. The ochre of the head runs out past the form. Bits of blue from the bench appear in the man's neckline or along his shoulder. The colors of the various frames and surfaces of the drawing on the wall overlap and refuse to be constrained by definite lines of form. Although
10  this technique is not given the kind of free reign Picasso allows it in his Cubist period or in works such as *Minotaur*, it is still a stunning development for Matisse. And he seems aware of this fact. The painting's composition references Picasso's *Still Life with Ancient Head* from 1925, signaling Matisse's awareness that he is borrowing from his younger colleague.

38. The author uses the word "peculiar" (line 2) to mean which of the following?

    (A)  strange
    (B)  abstract
    (C)  unknown
    (D)  unique
    (E)  appealing

39. The main idea of the passage is to

    (A)  describe an artistic work and its inspiration
    (B)  describe how Matisse surpassed Picasso
    (C)  describe how Matisse developed his style
    (D)  describe a representative example of Matisse's work
    (E)  describe the influence of Picasso on the art world

40. According to the passage, all of the following are true of *The Ochre Head* EXCEPT:

    (A)  The artist did not color between the lines.
    (B)  Its arrangement is similar to that of a piece by Picasso.
    (C)  It is considered among the best of Matisse's work.
    (D)  Its use of technique is more constrained than that of *Minotaur*.
    (E)  It depicts household objects.

Questions 41–45 are based on the following reading passage.

History textbooks in the United States are far too fact-based and even have the ability to make students feel as though all history is made up of "Quick-Facts" and diagrams, not dynamic events to be critically analyzed. Furthermore, it is often the case that textbooks are given undue authority in determining the curriculum; many teachers simply "teach the book."

5    This is particularly disturbing when considering the fact that state committees for choosing textbooks often treat them, in the words of Sandra Wong, "more like encyclopedias of facts than as cultural products that convey values and perspectives" when deciding which ones to pick. In her article "Evaluating the Content of Textbooks: Public Interests and Professional Authority," Wong discusses how textbook committees are rarely concerned with
10  the actual substance of the writing in the textbooks they evaluate, and are far more interested in things like "charts, illustrations, and introductory outlines."

What, then, would be a better tool to use in the high school classroom than textbooks or timelines for creating an effective learning environment that could reflect the dynamic nature of historical study? Out of all the various alternatives—going to plays, hearing speakers,
15  listening to music, using interactive online resources, elucidating connections to students' personal lives by going to local history museums or having students write autobiographical essays, etc.—the most promising is, by far, film. Movies are a magnificent way into history for even the most resistant naysayer of historical study. Film is a hugely popular medium with endless numbers of historically based works —everything from documentaries to dramas—
20  that not only present facts, but dramatize the human relations behind those facts.

The main critique presented against the use of historical film in the classroom is, of course, the existence of rampant inaccuracies and biases laced throughout these films, not to mention the agendas of the filmmakers themselves. However, some historians believe that these seeming flaws are actually part of the reason why film is an ideal teaching tool—not only
25  does it allow students to see history come to life, and thus interact with it dynamically, as well as make history immediately accessible to a modern audience because of the techniques used in filmmaking, but it can also foster deep critical thinking skills if instructors lead dialogues after film viewings about the inaccuracies, the biases, and all of the things that make the film not just a record of a historical event, but also a reflection of the modern moment.

41. Which of the following is <u>not</u> cited by the passage as an alternative method for historical study?

    (A)  Listening to music
    (B)  Attending a lecture
    (C)  Volunteering at an archeology dig
    (D)  Writing a personal statement
    (E)  Watching a film

42. The purpose of the passage is to

    (A) support the film industry

    (B) criticize government education policies

    (C) advocate a new process for textbook adoption

    (D) propose increased use of a particular didactic tool

    (E) denigrate an established philosophy

43. According to the passage, a problem with state committee textbook selection is

    (A) the lack of education of the committee members

    (B) misplaced priorities

    (C) the dominance of larger states

    (D) valuing perspectives instead of facts

    (E) personal prejudices

44. The purpose of the last paragraph is to

    (A) acknowledge an insurmountable obstacle

    (B) raise and undermine an objection

    (C) reassert the need for alternative educational tools

    (D) admit a flaw in a preferred alternative

    (E) advocate more interactive instruction

45. The passage implies which of the following?

    (A) Students can benefit from exposure to inaccurate accounts of history.

    (B) Students today prefer music to film.

    (C) Students today are functional illiterates.

    (D) Students today prefer charts to opinions.

    (E) Students today should not be exposed to political agendas.

> **Questions 46–47 are based on the following reading passage.**

From assemblages of found objects to bizarre video installations and digital interactive experiments, much of contemporary art has been criticized as cold, unapproachable, impersonal, and emotionless. One link between the immediately appealing, expressive paintings that are often the most popular museum attractions and the "brainy" constructivist
5  school of art pioneered in the early twentieth century is the notion of *gesture* as an expressive tool.

Mark di Suvero's *Iroquois* (1983–1999) is composed of several industrial-sized I-beams. The materials are so heavy and large the artist used cranes and other construction tools to manipulate and connect the beams, all of which have been painted a bright red-orange. The
10  result is an intruding work of almost architectural dimensions that one can immediately sense is terribly heavy and somewhat precarious, yet stable and balanced. As one contemplates *Iroquois*, walking in and around its structure, backing away to see it from a distance, the linear forms become considerably more complex than one might presume. The tangled steel was obviously constructed with great care, yet each piece seems to threaten the viewer with its
15  weight and size, jutting out away from the central nexus, daring the entire form to topple over. At the same time, the piece seems to exude stability, balance, even serenity. *Iroquois* resonates with an energy born not of the physical quality of the sculpture, which is quite passive and stable, but rather of the *gestural* quality of the forms.

---

Consider each of the answer choices separately and indicate <u>all</u> that apply.

46.  Which of the following can be inferred from the passage?

☐  Some of the most popular museum attractions are contemporary art installations.

☐  Expressive paintings have been considered "brainy."

☐  Seemingly cold and cerebral art can nevertheless make use of certain expressive tools.

---

Consider each of the answer choices separately and indicate <u>all</u> that apply.

47.  Which of the following does the author assert about *Iroquois*?

☐  Paradoxically, it appears to be both stable and unstable.

☐  It uses gesture to evoke a sense of energy.

☐  Some interpret it as simpler than it really is.

Questions 48–51 are based on the following reading passage.

In his *Discourse on Inequality*, Rousseau posits that early social contract theories establish unjust social and political arrangements that provide only the appearance of legitimacy and equality.

In Rousseau's accounting, the beginnings of the social contract lie in the fears of the rich.
5 In a state of nature, one in which there is no government or law to control the interactions of people, the rich would have great difficulty protecting the property that they possess. Thus, the rich turn to the mechanism of the social contract to shore up the holdings Rousseau views as "hoarded." The concept of a social contract is appealing to the poor, because the poor fear death in a state of lawlessness and thus seek protection. To obtain assent to the contract, the
10 rich focus their rhetoric on a seeming equality of obligation by creating rules that apply equally to all members of society. This system, however, simply systematizes the "theft" the rich had perpetrated on the poor in the pre-law state of nature.

Rousseau then begins to develop his own vision of a social contract, through which he attempts to right these injustices. His first departure from earlier theorists is in the formation of
15 the sovereign. Rather than members of the state surrendering their rights to another person—an irrational course of action tantamount to surrendering oneself into slavery—they surrender their right to all members of the society and thus to no one. Rousseau refers to this sovereign as the "general will" and it has the task of legislating for the new civil society that is created in the contract.

20 Unlike early social contract theories, Rousseau's version conceives of property rights that allow for rights of first occupancy to justify claims, rather than rights of the strongest. In this system, property can be taken only if it has not been previously occupied and only to the degree necessary for the subsistence of those taking it, measures intended as a check to the hoarding of property by force enshrined in earlier contract theory.

**MANHATTAN**
PREP

48.  Which of the following societies would Rousseau be likely to endorse?

   (A)  A society in which there is no government or law to control how people interact with each
        other.
   (B)  A society in which a primary leader is elected through a fair democratic process.
   (C)  A society in which there is only communal property, rather than private property.
   (D)  A society in which the social contract has been dismantled and replaced with rights of first
        occupancy.
   (E)  A society in which a homeless family could legally move into an empty house they did not
        purchase.

49.  It can be inferred from the passage that Rousseau would believe which of the following of a society of
     men and women living without the primary structures of civilization?

   (A)  Their wealth would inevitably be equally distributed across the population.
   (B)  Those with more wealth would be at risk of losing it to those with less.
   (C)  Property would not be hoarded by those who had the most power.
   (D)  The social contract would be created in order to protect and support the poor.
   (E)  Property would only be taken if it had not been previously occupied and was necessary
        for the subsistence of those taking it.

50.  Select the sentence in the second paragraph that explains the mechanism by which a privileged group is
     able to secure widespread approval for the systematized "theft" it achieves through hoarding.

51.  In the context in which it appears, "subsistence" (line 23) most nearly means

   (A)  survival
   (B)  enrichment
   (C)  protection
   (D)  help
   (E)  opposition

> **Questions 52–53 are based on the following reading passage.**

      The African American writer and social critic James Baldwin grew up as an outsider to both the language and the culture of power, and yet achieved a balance between self-expression and the language of power. As a child in the 1930s, Baldwin felt acutely separated from a culture of power in which Hollywood movies portrayed an optimistic, capitalist, white
5  America that dealt with white issues and employed white actors. In "Congo Square," Baldwin opens his essay with an important idea: "A child is far too self-centered to relate to any dilemma which does not, somehow, relate to him." Watching the films of the dominant culture, Baldwin attempted to relate the information to his own life, connecting with it however he could. Rather than blindly accept the storylines in the movies, when Baldwin saw a staircase in *A Tale*
10  *of Two Cities*, he thought, "I knew about staircases."

      At the same time, Baldwin distrusted the culture of power: "The civilized … do not intend to change the *status quo* … these people are not to be taken seriously when they speak of the 'sanctity' of human life, or the 'conscience' of the civilized world."

> Consider each of the answer choices separately and indicate <u>all</u> that apply.

52. It can be inferred from the passage that Baldwin would agree with which of the following about a 1930s film that dealt only with African American issues and employed only African American actors?

    ☐  It would be significantly better than most Hollywood movies from the 1930s.

    ☐  It would suffer from the same kind of problems as the more typical 1930s Hollywood movies.

    ☐  It would be less likely than most other 1930s Hollywood movies to reinforce the predominant culture.

53. Baldwin's quotation from "Congo Square" is used primarily in order to illuminate what aspect of 1930s America?

    (A)  The culture of power that Baldwin mistrusted

    (B)  The fact that Hollywood movies were primarily optimistic and centered on white culture

    (C)  The idea that America was hungry for a writer such as Baldwin, because its films focused only on white America

    (D)  The alienating effect of films of the era on black children

    (E)  The concept that children are incapable of deriving any educational value from films they can't relate to

**MANHATTAN**
PREP

> **Questions 54–56 are based on the following reading passage.**

   The Parthenon has long been regarded as one of the great architectural and artistic products of the High Classical Period. Yet, scholars have struggled to reach a consensus interpretation for the meaning of the Parthenon frieze. The study of this particular sculptural element of the Parthenon, a continuous band of sculpture that ran round the top of the
5 building's temple-chamber, has proven quite difficult.

   Today only 423 feet of the original 524 survive, and of those, 247 feet are housed in the British Museum in London. Another large section is now in the Acropolis Museum in Athens, and still other pieces reside in exhibits throughout Europe, making it a difficult task to discuss, let alone experience the unified whole the designers wished the audience to witness—a key
10 element in deciphering any work of art.

   Denied the opportunity to study the frieze as it existed in antiquity, scholars are faced with the burden of reconstructing the visual experience of the monument before they can even begin interpreting it. To do so, an inventory is taken of characters and figure-types represented on the frieze and their arrangement. Then this inventory is compared to historical
15 precedents and placed in its contemporary context in the hopes of using prior examples to decipher its meaning. Considering the various fragments of the Parthenon frieze as a whole and comparing it to other Greek artworks, two aspects of the arrangement immediately strike the informed viewer.

   First, it is clear that the frieze is meant to be thought of as a continuous whole. This is
20 particularly interesting because it is completely unprecedented in Greek art. Continuous friezes on the faces of Greek temples generally depicted single subjects, but if continued over all four sides of a building, the four stretches of the frieze would generally be thematically separate.

   The second unique aspect of the Parthenon frieze has to do with the fundamental nature of Greek art: namely that all works of art prior to the Parthenon frieze depicted only scenes
25 from myth and legend. Yet, in this relief, for the first time in the history of Greek art, we find mortals, leading some scholars to the conclusion that what is depicted is a specific event that actually took place at a particular time and place.

54. In the context in which it appears, the word "informed" (line 18) most nearly means

    (A) assiduous
    (B) artistic
    (C) unique
    (D) erudite
    (E) scientific

55. Which of the following would be the best title for the above passage?

    (A) The Parthenon Frieze: An Insoluble Sculptural Mystery
    (B) The Parthenon Frieze and Methods of Artistic Interpretation
    (C) The Parthenon Frieze: Idiosyncratic Stonework
    (D) Mortals in Greek Art
    (E) The Parthenon Frieze: Continuity of Character

56. According to the passage, each of the following is true about the Parthenon EXCEPT:

    (A) It was constructed in the High Classical Period.
    (B) It has been seen as a great work of art.
    (C) It featured a temple-chamber.
    (D) It is not known how it looked at the time of its construction.
    (E) It contained a one-of-a-kind sculptural element.

> **Questions 57–58 are based on the following reading passage.**

A single short story can suggest a desired response from the reader. It is a difficult task, though, to create a world within a single short story and then repeat this world again in other stories while maintaining a consistent flow of ideas. Many authors prefer to use the same setting, indeed, often the same characters in each story. Isabel Allende's *Diez Cuentos' de Eva*
5   *Luna* comes to mind. In these stories, Allende uses the small town of Agua Santa as the setting for the entire collection.

*Woman Hollering Creek* is a collection of short stories by Sandra Cisneros. Rather than using the same characters or setting throughout the collection, Cisneros takes a different approach to relating her stories to one another. Much of the burden, in fact, is placed on
10  the reader, for the characters change each time, as does the setting. Furthermore, while the characters are largely Mexican American immigrant women, each character presents a distinct style and literary voice. What these works have in common is more intuitive; mood, circumstance, time, tone, and imagery all play a role in creating the world in which the stories take place.

57. The author of the passage would be most likely to agree with which of the following statements?

(A) Short story collections depend on the reader to find the common thread that ties the stories together.
(B) Isabel Allende uses the same setting for the majority of her fiction.
(C) It is possible to create a coherent short story collection if the stories take place in vastly different times and places.
(D) Intuition is a more important aspect of Sandra Cisneros's writing than the characters or the setting.
(E) The best short story collections feature some through line that the reader can follow and that connects the various stories.

58. According to the passage, which of the following characterizes both short stories by Isabel Allende and short stories by Sandra Cisneros?

(A) Similarities in tone among the stories
(B) Similarities in time among the stories
(C) Similarities in characters among the stories
(D) Similarities in setting among the stories
(E) None of the above

> **Questions 59–60 are based on the following reading passage.**

Scottish economist Adam Smith's *The Wealth of Nations* heralded the market-based economic system that has increasingly become the norm since the book's publication in 1776. Some say that Smith's magnum opus was to economics as Newton's *Principia Mathematica* was to physics or as Darwin's *On the Origin of Species* was to biology. Certainly the book made its
5   impact in the western world.

1776 predates wide usage of the term *capitalism*, now commonly associated with Smith, and which Smith refers to as a "system of natural liberty." Smith presented what we today consider Economics 101: supply and demand, and the importance of specialization and the division of labor. He also posited that individuals pursuing their own self-interest could
10  unintentionally create a more just society by so doing—an idea sometimes referred to as the "Invisible Hand."

Even Smith's critics do not deny the book's immense influence. Murray Rothbard levels the criticism that *The Wealth of Nations*, in fact, eclipsed public knowledge of all economists— better ones, he says—before Smith.

> Consider each of the answer choices separately and indicate <u>all</u> that apply.

59. Which of the following statements is <u>not</u> in contradiction with the opinions of Murray Rothbard as expressed in the passage?

☐ Smith was possibly the third best economist of all time.

☐ *The Wealth of Nations* should not have been as influential as it was.

☐ Adam Smith was not particularly influential.

60. Which of the following would be an example of the "Invisible Hand" as described by Adam Smith?

(A) A group of moviegoers who are able to get cheaper tickets for a film by buying their tickets as a group

(B) A society in which the division of labor frees certain people to pursue careers that might seem impractical in a non-capitalist society

(C) A university in which classes are first-come, first-served, thereby equitably distributing courses according to the passion and dedication of students

(D) A market in which there are more buyers than sellers, thus forcing the price of goods upwards

(E) A stock exchange in which each trader acts according to a different set of information, such that certain commodities become hyped and their prices overinflated

**MANHATTAN**
PREP

Questions 61–62 are based on the following reading passage.

Fame and fortune are often associated with virtue, industry, and a host of other attributes. However, random strokes of fate often determine such success and said commonly perceived virtues prove irrelevant. For instance, decades after her death, Coco Chanel remains the epitome of French fashion and her name, as well as the company she founded, is known
5   throughout the world. Yet, few realize that she, while undeniably talented, initially succeeded by leveraging her status as a courtesan. As a company owner, it would be an understatement to say that she was not known for her generous treatment of her employees. During the Nazi occupation, she lived a privileged life at the Hotel Ritz and her lover at the time was a German intelligence operative.
10      Conversely, there is the example of Madeleine Vionnet, a professional contemporary of Chanel. She is often credited with permanently transforming fashion through her use of the bias cut—cutting material against the grain of the fabric. In the 1930s, her gowns were worn by Hollywood stars, and her standing was second to none. She was also, in many ways, an early feminist, establishing largely unheard of employee benefits—such as day care and medical
15   care—for her largely female staff. In addition, she lobbied for fashion copyright protections. When the Second World War broke out, she closed her business and simply retired. Today, she is largely unknown outside of the fashion industry.

61.  The author wrote the passage to posit which of the following?

   (A)  That the relationship between virtue and success is inverse
   (B)  That an inferior designer was more successful than a superior one
   (C)  To contrast the aesthetic of Chanel to that of Vionnet
   (D)  To suggest that no causal relationship exists between personal qualities and professional legacy
   (E)  To contrast the difference between transitory and lasting success

62. The author discusses the employee benefits offered by Vionnet in order to

   (A)  emphasize Vionnet's anti-Nazi politics
   (B)  illustrate Vionnet's admirable qualities
   (C)  highlight Chanel's reputed drug use and collaboration
   (D)  demonstrate the economic burden of French socialist policies
   (E)  provide details that bolster Vionnet's feminist credentials

> **Questions 63–64 are based on the following reading passage.**

During the 1960s and '70s, scientists were concerned and puzzled by a large gap in the human fossil record. The "aquatic ape theory" gained prominence as an explanation for this gap. This theory posited that primitive humans were forced toward a littoral lifestyle by competition for arboreal resources. Analogies were made to seal populations, who sleep on
5 land at night but spend most of their days in coastal waters. Proponents pointed to various physiological human attributes, such as bipedalism and the webbing between human toes, as extant adaptations.

However, the aspect of the theory that captured the public imagination and undoubtedly boosted its standing was the point that this hypothesis explained human hairlessness; as with
10 dolphins, this streamlining would facilitate swimming and diving. Proponents noted that the remaining body hair would match the flow of water, and extreme advocates explained the gender difference in hair by suggesting that females much more rarely ventured out of the shallows and into the putatively more dangerous forests and savannahs.

Nonetheless, despite the popular stature of the theory, the scientific community almost
15 unanimously rejects it as mere conjecture not only because of the lack of supporting evidence but also because its claims do not withstand scrutiny. While bipedalism does facilitate swimming, it is even more of an advantage in terrestrial pursuits. Further, biomechanical analysis indicates that humans remain such inadequate swimmers that they could not so succeed. As for hairlessness, critics point out that other semi-aquatic mammals actually
20 have dense fur and/or barrel shaped torsos for heat retention. Today, the theory, while still championed by a prominent writer but non-scientist, has no serious support among mainstream-trained paleoanthropologists.

63. The passage implies that, according to the theory, a male aquatic ape would most likely do which of the following?

   (A)  Spend almost all of its time in the water
   (B)  Spend its nights in the water, but its days partly on land
   (C)  Spend its days partly in the water, but its nights partly on land
   (D)  Spend its days mostly in the water, but its nights on land
   (E)  Spend almost all its time on land

64. The author describes a remaining proponent of the theory as a "non-scientist" (line 21) in order to do which of the following?

   (A)  Cast doubt upon her objectivity
   (B)  Tout the superiority of common sense over academics
   (C)  Cast doubt upon her expertise
   (D)  Cast doubt upon mainstream paleoanthropologists
   (E)  Illustrate the sexism of mainstream scientists

Questions 65–66 are based on the following reading passage.

The Tokugawa period (1603–1867) in Japan serves as a laboratory for organizational behavior historians for the same reason that Iceland works for geneticists—isolation removes extraneous variables. The Tokugawa shoguns brought peace to a land of warring feudal lords. To preserve that tranquility, the Tokugawa shogunate forbade contact with the outside world,
5 allowing only a few Dutch trading ships to dock at one restricted port. Domestically, in pursuit of the same goal, the social order was fixed; there were four classes—warriors [samurai], artisans, merchants, and farmers or peasants—and social mobility was prohibited. The ensuing stability and peace brought a commercial prosperity that lasted nearly two hundred years.

However, as psychologists, social historians, and Biblical prophets have all observed, in
10 varying ways, humans inevitably fail to anticipate unintended consequences. In the Tokugawa period, the fixed social hierarchy placed the samurai on top; they and the government were essentially supported by levies on the peasantry, as the other two classes were demographically and economically inconsequential. However, prosperity brought riches to the commercial classes and their numbers burgeoned. Eventually, their economic power dwarfed
15 that of their supposed superiors, the samurai. Simultaneously, the increasing impoverishment of the samurai adversely affected the finances of the peasantry and the government. By the early 19th century, this imbalance between social structure and economic reality eroded the stability of the society. This condition, in conjunction with increasing pressure for access from foreigners, such as Admiral Perry in 1853, led to the collapse of the shogunate in 1867. In short,
20 the success of this imposed order led to its undoing through consequences that were beyond the ken of the founders.

65. The primary objective of the passage is to

   (A) compare the Tokugawa period to modern Iceland
   (B) demonstrate the folly of imposing a social order
   (C) show how American naval power ended Japan's isolation
   (D) illustrate how a society can model a common human failing
   (E) argue that commerce is more successful than militarization

66. Which of the following would provide further support for the main reason cited for the decline of the Tokugawa period?

   (A) A samurai becomes a successful merchant.
   (B) A successful artisan becomes a samurai.
   (C) A samurai must work as a bodyguard for an artisan.
   (D) A severe drought causes widespread famine.
   (E) A military invasion by American marines occurs.

> **Questions 67–68 are based on the following reading passage.**

   The War of the Spanish Succession, 1701–14, began as a quarrel over whether an Austrian
Habsburg or French Bourbon would succeed the childless Charles II of Spain. The conflict
eventually embroiled most of Europe, with Austria, England, Holland, and Prussia the major
powers opposing France, Spain, and Bavaria. For centuries afterward, school children learned
5 of the Duke of Marlborough's victory at Blenheim and the military brilliance of Prinz Eugen
of Savoy, an independent territory east of France, as well as the opposing brightness of Louis
XIV of France, known as the Sun King, who also built the famous palace at Versailles. Today,
however, virtually all those names would elicit only blank stares.
   Although this war and its personages have now vanished into obscurity, its effects greatly
10 affected the course of European and world history. The Treaty of Utrecht, which ended the
war in 1714, ceded the Spanish island of Gibraltar to England. The "Rock of Gibraltar" became
an invincible British fortress that controlled the Mediterranean and thus was of paramount
importance in both world wars. Conversely, the same treaty elevated Prussia to a kingdom,
thus setting in motion a chain of events that led to a unified Germany under a Prussian Kaiser
15 instead of one governed by the Austrians, arguably making the bloodshed that consumed the
20th century more likely.

67. The author implies that a possibly negative aspect of the Treaty of Utrecht was

   (A)  awarding Gibraltar to the British
   (B)  reducing the Duke of Marlborough to obscurity
   (C)  elevating Prussia to a kingdom
   (D)  failing to resolve the Spanish succession
   (E)  providing the impetus for the eventual world wars

68. Which of the following must be true, according to the passage?

   (A)  Not all of the important military personages were from major powers.
   (B)  The battle of Blenheim was the most important engagement of the war.
   (C)  England was the victorious power.
   (D)  France was defeated in the war.
   (E)  The transfer of Gibraltar was the most important result of the war.

**MANHATTAN**
PREP

Questions 69–70 are based on the following reading passage.

Michael Lewis, the American journalist and non-fiction writer, originally studied art history as an undergraduate and worked for a prominent art dealer before obtaining a masters degree in economics at the London School of Economics. After a short stint at Salomon Brothers, he wrote *Liar's Poker*, which became a tremendous success. However, his fame and
5   fortune continued to arc upward with the publication of *Moneyball* and *The Big Short*. Some argue that his education in the humanities, in addition to finance, greatly contributed to the popularity of his work.

An alternative explanation exists. Although baseball and Wall Street are not commonly associated, Lewis's works concerning both those topics share more than the common
10  theme of lucre. All the books cited above focus on mavericks "gaming the system." Lewis's protagonists, such as Billy Beane of the small market Oakland Athletics and the small, out of the establishment traders that bet against mortgage derivatives, are smart non-conformists who rebel against monolithic systems by exploiting inherent inconsistencies. Such a theme echoes the American nation-building construct—lone, free individuals winning against great
15  odds by employing common sense and ingenuity. This is a story line that Americans hear from birth; it is no wonder that Lewis's books are popular despite subjects that are not necessarily of universal interest. Further support for this thesis is that *Moneyball* became a major motion picture and a film of *Liar's Poker* is in development. Of course, unlike baseball games, such debates can never be definitively scored.

69.  The author primarily does which of the following?

(A)  Contrasts two opposing theories for a process
(B)  Discusses two suppositions and implicitly favors the latter
(C)  Details two programs and definitively prefers the latter
(D)  Describes a writer's work and its dearth of popularity
(E)  Outlines the biography of a writer and critiques his work

70.  The author does all of the following EXCEPT

(A)  employ an idiomatic expression
(B)  describe the protagonists in question
(C)  reference popular culture as evidence
(D)  discuss the parallels shared by Lewis's two professions
(E)  mention his subject's formative influences

---

**Questions 71–72 are based on the following reading passage.**

---

The term "free rider" originates from the idea of someone who rides public transportation without paying the fare. The "free rider problem" is what results when too many people do this: the transit system will go bankrupt. More broadly, the free rider is someone who uses or enjoys the benefits of something without paying, or takes more than his or her proper share of
5  a publicly shared good that is limited in supply. Free riders can cause others to curtail their own contributions, not wanting to be taken advantage of, or can result in the excessive depletion of the common resource.

In some cases, the free rider problem is viewed as a necessary cost of government. When citizens pay for national defense or environmental protection, everyone benefits, even those
10  who evade paying taxes.

---

Consider each of the answer choices separately and indicate __all__ that apply.

---

71. Which of the following examples clearly match the definition of a free rider problem as described in the passage?

    ☐  The population of game birds in a state park declines sharply when hunting quotas are observed by only some hunters.

    ☐  A senior citizen pays less for a movie ticket than do the other people in the theater.

    ☐  A yearly school bake sale based on the honor system is suspended when too many people take food without paying.

72. The author of the passage would be most likely to agree with which of the following statements?

    (A)  Free riders cannot be blamed for their actions, because they are an inevitable part of any government.

    (B)  Free rider problems are not worth worrying about, because they are an inevitable part of any government.

    (C)  There are at least some situations in which the free rider problem should not be viewed as an inevitable part of government.

    (D)  National defense is a perfect example of why free rider problems need to be stamped out as quickly as possible.

    (E)  Free riders are morally at fault, and ought to be punished.

---

**Questions 73–74 are based on the following reading passage.**

---

In 2010, a team of biologists led by Svante Paabo announced evidence that modern humans interbred with Neanderthals some 60,000–100,000 years ago. These researchers compared the full sequence of Neanderthal DNA to that of five modern humans from China, France, sub-Saharan Africa, and Papua New Guinea, and looked for DNA shared by both
5   Neanderthals and non-African modern humans, but not by sub-Saharan Africans. Because Neanderthals and modern humans are known to have diverged hundreds of thousands of years before modern humans left Africa, Paabo attributed any such common DNA to interbreeding in Eurasia. Paabo's team announced that the modern humans from China, France, and Papua New Guinea all have the same proportion of Neanderthal DNA, and inferred
10   that interbreeding with Neanderthals must have taken place before the ancestor population of those Eurasians divided. Paabo maintained that these two events, the migration of modern humans out of Africa and the division of the Eurasian population, mark the interval during which the interbreeding must have taken place, and that for roughly forty thousand years of that window, Neanderthals and modern humans lived near one another in the Middle East.
15      The team's conclusions were answered with skepticism on a number of fronts. Critics pointed out that an earlier report reached similar conclusions based on Neanderthal samples later found to be contaminated with DNA from modern humans. Paleontologists and archaeologists charged that the conclusion was unsupported by archaeological evidence. Further, Paabo's team found evidence only of Neanderthal DNA in modern humans, not of
20   modern human DNA in Neanderthals, but critics claim that interbreeding would result in gene flow in both directions.

---

Consider each of the answer choices separately and indicate <u>all</u> that apply.

---

73.  The passage implies that which of the following claims is true?

☐   Modern humans and Neanderthals share a common ancestor.

☐   Modern humans and Neanderthals interbred.

☐   Modern humans and Neanderthals lived near one another approximately 80,000 years ago.

---

Consider each of the answer choices separately and indicate <u>all</u> that apply.

---

74.  The passage suggests which of the following is true of Paabo's critics?

☐   They doubt Paabo's integrity.

☐   They ignore DNA evidence.

☐   They sometimes appeal to archaeological evidence.

**MANHATTAN**
PREP

---

**Questions 75–76 are based on the following reading passage.**

---

Though an echo is a fairly simple acoustic phenomenon—a reflection of sound waves off some hard surface—it occurs only under very specific circumstances. Imagine a listener standing at the sound source. The reflecting object must be more than 11.3 meters away from the sound source, or the echo will return too soon to be distinguishable from the
5   original sound. A reflecting object more than about 170 meters, on the other hand, will rarely produce an audible echo, since sound dissipates with distance. Further, multiple surfaces each reflecting the same original sound to the same listener will likely not produce an echo, but a reverberation, a persistent sound gradually decreasing in amplitude until the listener can no longer hear it. Common though echoes are then, it is unsurprising that some sounds seem to
10  produce no echo.

A centuries-old tradition holds that a duck's quack does not echo. Scientists in the Acoustics Department of the University of Salford set out to test and explain this claim. They recorded a duck, Daisy, first in an anechoic chamber filled with sound-absorbing fiberglass wedges, then in an echo chamber with the acoustical properties of a small cathedral. The
15  sound of the duck quacking in the anechoic chamber was clearly different from the sound of the duck quacking in the echo chamber, but the researchers acknowledged that it would be very hard to recognize an echo in the latter recording without having very recently heard the former. Partly this is because a quack isn't a single burst of sound, but fades in and out, so that the beginning of the echo might blend with the end of the original sound. Partly it is because
20  a quack is just not very loud. The Salford researchers also speculate that most people may simply not encounter ducks in proximity to reflectors such as buildings or mountains. A further complication, though one the researchers leave unremarked, is that people generally hear ducks in flocks, where one quack might be indistinguishable from the echo of another.

75.  According to the passage, all of the following make an audible echo unlikely EXCEPT

    (A)   a reflecting surface too close to the original sound
    (B)   a reflecting surface too far from the original sound
    (C)   multiple reflecting surfaces
    (D)   multiple listeners
    (E)   sound-absorbing materials

---

Consider each of the answer choices separately and indicate <u>all</u> that apply.

---

76.  The passage suggests that which of the following would propagate echoes?

    ☐   An anechoic chamber
    ☐   A cathedral
    ☐   A mountain

---

**Questions 77–79 are based on the following reading passage.**

---

Simone de Beauvoir's feminism was heavily informed by existentialist ethics. Within this frame of thought, good and evil are expressed in human beings' transcendence and "immanence," respectively. Human existence can only be justified via continually expanding into the future by engaging in freely chosen projects—i.e., transcendence. Transcendence
5  is thus a general goal for human beings, while its opposite—immanence—is considered a degradation of existence, from "liberty into constraint." Freely chosen, immanence is a moral fault, but when inflicted, it is described as "oppression." In a social environment in which women are prevented from choosing and engaging in serious projects because of their status as women, their ability to transcend is systemically thwarted, so transcendence becomes a
10  specifically feminist goal. De Beauvoir explains that women are viewed as intrinsically passive and immanent, in opposition to men who are meant to be active and transcendent.

In the society observed by de Beauvoir, "[women] live … attached through residence, housework, economic condition, and social standing to certain men—fathers or husbands … " It is specifically women who are attached to men—not men to women nor women and men
15  to each other. As de Beauvoir notes, the nature of this relationship, overlapping the assumption that men are the active transcendent half of humanity, leaves women in a position of forced immanence.

---

Consider each of the answer choices separately and indicate <u>all</u> that apply.

77. According to the passage, Simone de Beauvoir believed which of the following?

☐  In society, women are attached to men.

☐  Women are intrinsically passive and immanent.

☐  Self-constraint is worse than imposed constraint.

---

Consider each of the answer choices separately and indicate <u>all</u> that apply.

78. According to the passage, immanence is always

☐  a moral fault

☐  a degradation of existence

☐  oppression

79. The passage could best be described as which of the following?

    (A) An explanation of existentialist ethics and transcendence

    (B) An explanation of feminist theory and female immanence

    (C) A diatribe about immanence and a social injustice

    (D) A description of a philosopher's influences and framework

    (E) An outline of social structure and conflicts

---

**Questions 80–81 are based on the following reading passage.**

---

What differentiates science and non-science? According to the modern definition of science, the Ancient Greeks were not scientists but rather philosophers. Their investigations were performed in an unscientific manner, as is illustrated by Aristotle and his conclusions about the properties of water. Before studying water, Aristotle discovered that matter existed in
5  three main categories: solid, liquid, and gas. He concluded that a solid was the least expanded of the three and verified this by seeing that a solid always sank in a liquid of the same type. However, when Aristotle encountered water, he saw that it had properties that contradicted his previous categorization. In order to reconcile this disparity, he postulated that water was an exception and that the shape of solid water caused it to stay afloat. This, of course, is incorrect.
10     To the contrary, the studies of Galileo Galilei followed a certain self-made doctrine for gathering data and performing scientific experiments. Galileo's method forced one to first form a hypothesis, then design an experiment to confirm or deny this hypothesis, and then accept or discard the hypothesis based on one's findings. Using this method, Galileo disproved many commonly held misconceptions about the rules of physics. In one of his more
15  famous experiments, Galileo hypothesized that the Earth's gravitational field resulted in the same acceleration of all objects, regardless of mass. To prove this, he dropped two iron balls of different masses from an elevated place and showed that gravity pulled on both masses evenly. This experiment disproved the commonly held belief (at the time) that an object with greater mass would fall to the ground more quickly.

80. The author's primary purpose in writing this passage is to

    (A) explain the modern distinction between science and non-science via historical examples

    (B) criticize the research methods employed by the Ancient Greek philosophers

    (C) illustrate the importance of following the scientific method as invented by Galileo Galilei

    (D) compare and contrast the historical definition of science with the modern-day definition

    (E) argue that the findings of Galileo are more important than those of Aristotle

81.  Which of the following can be properly inferred from the passage?

   (A)  Solid water has the same shape as other solid forms of matter.

   (B)  When dropped from the same height, an object with greater mass will fall to the ground more quickly than an object with less mass.

   (C)  One cannot be both a scientist and a philosopher.

   (D)  If Aristotle had followed Galileo's method, he would have rejected his hypothesis that solids were the least expanded form of matter.

   (E)  In the absence of the scientific method, one cannot disprove commonly held misconceptions about the rules of physics.

---

**Questions 82–84 are based on the following reading passage.**

Lousia May Alcott's *Little Women* opens to a common scenario—the women knitting at home and waiting for news from the man of the family, who is at the war front. The family dynamics of *Little Women*, as a microcosm of the larger society, are marked by explicitly articulated male dominance. The division of labor has it so that women are confined to
5   the domestic sphere while men step into the public sphere and engage in activities there, returning to the domestic sphere at night to be cared for by their spouse or female children. Alcott describes the character of Meg, a young wife, as "often … lonely," with her husband "absent till night, and nothing to do but sew, or read, or potter about."

Marmee later tells Meg that she ought to "take [her] part in the world's work," even
10  though she is a woman. Ultimately, however, "taking her part in the world's work" meant no more than talking to her husband about politics whilst remaining at home, allowing him to continue to be the mediator between Meg's individuality and the world at large. Chapter 38 of the novel wraps up the issue by concluding that "a woman's happiest kingdom is home, her highest honor the art of ruling it [as a] wise wife and mother," such position being "the sort of
15  shelf on which young wives and mothers may consent to be laid, safe from the restless fret and fever of the world." Some have read Alcott's romantic glorification of women's confinement as sarcastic, but either way, her loving readers must have agreed with the statement, for the novel has never been out of print.

82.  The primary purpose of the passage is to

   (A)  explain the continued popularity of a novel

   (B)  detail the domestic confinement of 19th century women

   (C)  analyze the sociological implications of a work of art

   (D)  argue for the emancipation of women

   (E)  indict the politics of a literary work

83. The passage implies that for a woman to effectively "take [her] part in the world's work," she must do which of the following?

    (A) Talk to her husband about politics

    (B) Rule her home

    (C) Sew, read, and potter about

    (D) Find a mediator to interact with the world at large

    (E) Leave the house

Consider each of the answer choices separately and indicate all that apply.

84. The passage implies which of the following about American society at the time that *Little Women* depicts?

    ☐ It was wartime.

    ☐ It glorified women's confinement.

    ☐ The vast majority of public activities took place during the day.

Questions 85–86 are based on the following reading passage.

"Falsifiability" is the term coined by Karl Popper for the idea that a hypothesis or theory addresses the observable world only insofar as it can be found false as the result of some observation or physical experiment. For instance, the proposition "all cats have fur" can easily be proven false with the observation of a single hairless cat. The proposition "the world will
5  end in the year 3035" is impractical to falsify, but still passes the test of falsifiability in that there exists the logical possibility that 3035 will come and go without the world ending. To the contrary, it is possible to posit that everything that happens is the will of Zeus. No matter what experiment we design—such as praying to Zeus to give us the answer or daring Zeus to strike us with lightning—we can always infer that the result is the will of Zeus. Such a proposition, as
10  conceived here, is not falsifiable. Popper claimed that a falsifiable theory is the only kind that can truly be scientific, or at least useful to the scientific community.

    By that logic, we can also say that no theory should be formed that has no chance of being true. However, seeing as that kind of theory is much less likely to be formed, it is understandable that Popper does not devote that much time to the criterion of
15  "confirmability."

85. According to the passage, which of the following does not meet the criteria for falsifiability?

    (A) All birds are black.

    (B) Earth is the only planet in the universe with intelligent life.

    (C) It rains on Mars every day.

    (D) The sun will explode in 100,000 years.

    (E) No human being lives forever.

86. To which of the following is the author most likely to agree regarding "confirmability"?

    (A) It is a more important theory than falsifiability.

    (B) It does not have much practical, scientific use.

    (C) It applies to a broad range of theories.

    (D) It is an unreasonable idea.

    (E) Popper should have developed this idea along with falsifiability.

---

**Questions 87–90 are based on the following reading passage.**

---

    A dictionary definition of the term "political" might read something like, "of or concerned with government, political parties, or politicians." Such a definition is not precisely wrong, but rather is outdated and falls short by not accounting for what Nancy Fraser calls "the shift from a repressive model of domination to a hegemonic one." If at some point we believed
5  governments to operate exclusively through law and the threat and enforcement of concrete punishment, such as imprisonment, monetary penalties, etc., and called this and everything that directly influenced it "politics," we have now acknowledged the role of hegemony, which legitimizes law and supports the exercise of power.

    This is significant because, under the first definition, the only cultural products that can
10  be said to be political must explicitly address issues of political partisanship or governance, while under the second definition, all cultural objects can be traced to a certain ideology—in accordance, negotiation, or opposition to hegemony—and therefore be political.

    But we do not feel that we are discussing politics or viewing politics all the time, even if we are, according to our definition of "the political." This is because even if all subject matter is
15  (at least potentially) political, not all talk is so. When conducting her study on political talk, Nina Eliasoph focused not as much on what people talked about, but rather on how exactly they talked about things: "whether speakers ever assume that what they say matters for someone other than themselves, ever assume that they are speaking in front of a wider backdrop." She cited Hanna Pitkin in concluding that "public-spirited conversation happens when citizens
20  speak in terms of 'justice'." To use an example from the theater, then, we can say that when a director decides to frame her production of *A Streetcar Named Desire* as the story of a woman who is losing her mind and does not get along with her aggressive brother-in-law, she is actively depoliticizing the story, whereas she is actively politicizing it if she decides to frame the narrative as one example of the devastating effects of an old bourgeois morality, a changing
25  economic system, and the social valuing of an abusive model of masculinity.

87. The second paragraph of the passage serves to

    (A)   offer an alternative to the definitions previously presented

    (B)   discuss a revision of the definitions previously presented

    (C)   delineate the distinction between the definitions previously presented

    (D)   delineate an exception to the definitions previously presented

    (E)   describe the inadequacy of the definitions previously presented

88. The author cites *A Streetcar Named Desire* (line 21) in order to

    (A)   provide a counterpoint to the thesis of the passage

    (B)   illustrate an aspect of the subject under discussion

    (C)   advocate politicizing a work of art

    (D)   illustrate the universality of politics

    (E)   illustrate a fallacy of a definition

89. According to a theory presented in the passage, a person is engaging in public interest conversation if that person discusses which of the following?

    (A)   Justice

    (B)   Theater

    (C)   Sexism

    (D)   Economics

    (E)   Politicians

90. Select a sentence from the first or second paragraph that levels an explicit criticism.

Questions 91–92 are based on the following reading passage.

Explanationism is the idea that prediction is, in itself, insufficient to confirm a theory. To adequately confirm a theory, according to an explanationist, is to see how well it describes events and phenomena that have already been observed. Stephen Brush, a staunch explanationist, would say that a correct prediction does not necessarily confirm the truth of a
5   theory; it could be the case that a theory predicts something and yet does not provide the best explanation of it. Take, for example, the difference in the perspectives of Copernicus and Brahe on the solar system. Copernicus's model of the solar system was heliocentric, positing that all of the planets revolved around the sun. Brahe's theory stated that all of the planets revolved around the sun, *except* the earth, which was immobile, and that the sun actually revolved
10  around the earth. Even if both accurately predicted future movements of the planets, it is easy to see how Copernicus's theory has less of an "ad hoc" quality—and, of course, provides a superior explanation of the mechanisms of the solar system. It is certainly true that a theory can successfully predict a certain event, yet fail to provide an adequate explanation for why it happened, or perhaps even stumble on the prediction more by accident than by manner of
15  understanding the mechanism behind the event.

A predictionist would argue that while a theory can provide a perfect explanation for something happening, a theory cannot be tested for understanding or explaining the underlying mechanism of a phenomenon unless it can also predict some event that confirms that exact mechanism at work. For instance, a physicist might study the formation of solids and
20  posit that all solids will sink if they are placed in a liquid of the same element, because the solid is denser than the liquid. Given this premise, we discover that the physicist's prediction is true, and even once he stages an experiment with ice and water, he will not be proven wrong, but rather will have discovered a unique property of solid water.

91.  Which of the following best expresses the main idea of the passage?

(A)  Explanationism is a superior theory to predictionism.

(B)  Two very different ideas can both be used to successfully investigate scientific theories.

(C)  Copernicus's model of the solar system was more accurate than Brahe's due to explanationism.

(D)  One cannot posit a physical theory without predictive power or previous observations.

(E)  A predictionist and an explanationist will always diverge on whether a scientific theory is correct.

92. Which of the following most accurately states the author's reason for citing the Copernicus and Brahe models of the solar system?

    (A) It shows that a theory without predictive power can never be tested and verified.

    (B) It reveals that some theories can have more or less of an "ad hoc" quality.

    (C) It shows that two different theories can never yield the same predictions for future events.

    (D) It is used to support the idea that a more complicated model will always fail to a simpler model.

    (E) It provides an example of when a theory can correctly predict future events but not offer the best explanation.

---

**Questions 93–98 are based on the following reading passage.**

---

Subatomic particles can be divided into two classes: fermions and bosons, terms coined by physicist Paul Dirac in honor of his peers Enrico Fermi and Satyendra Bose. Fermions, which include electrons, protons, and neutrons, obey the Pauli exclusion principle, according to which no two particles can inhabit the same fundamental state. For example, electrons cannot circle
5  the nuclei of atoms in precisely the same orbits, loosely speaking, and thus must occupy more and more distant locations, like a crowd filling seats in a stadium. The constituents of ordinary matter are fermions; indeed, the fact that fermions are in some sense mutually exclusive is the most salient reason why two things composed of ordinary matter cannot be in the same place at the same time.
10      Conversely, bosons, which include photons (particles of light) and the hitherto elusive Higgs boson, do not obey the Pauli principle and in fact tend to bunch together in exactly the same fundamental state, as in lasers, in which each photon proceeds in perfect lockstep with all the others. Interestingly, the seemingly stark division between fermionic and bosonic behavior can be bridged. All particles possess "spin," a characteristic vaguely analogous to that
15  of a spinning ball; boson spins are measured in integers, such as 0 and 1, while fermion spins are always half-integral, such as ½ and 1½. As a result, whenever an even number of fermions group together, that group of fermions, with its whole-number total spin, effectively becomes a giant boson. Within certain metals chilled to near absolute zero, for instance, so-called Cooper pairs of electrons form; these pairs flow in precise harmony and with zero resistance
20  through the metal, which is thus said to have achieved a superconductive condition. Similarly, helium-4 atoms (composed of 2 electrons, 2 protons, and 2 neutrons) can collectively display boson-like activity when cooled to a superfluid state. A swirl in a cup of superfluid helium will, amazingly, never dissipate.
        The observation that even-numbered groups of fermions can behave like bosons raises
25  the corollary question of whether groups of bosons can ever exhibit fermionic characteristics. Some scientists argue for the existence of skyrmions (after the theorist Tony Skyrme who first described the behavior of these hypothetical fermion-like groups of bosons) in superconductors and other condensed-matter environments, where twists in the structure of the medium might permit skyrmions to form.

Consider each of the answer choices separately and indicate all that apply.

93. The example of "a crowd filling seats in a stadium" (line 6) is intended to

   ☐  expand upon one consequence of the Pauli exclusion principle

   ☐  illustrate a behavior of certain fermions

   ☐  describe how electrons circle the nuclei of atoms in concentric, evenly spaced orbits

94. The author's primary purpose in writing this passage is to

   (A)  explain the mechanism by which fermions can become bosons

   (B)  describe the two classes of subatomic particles

   (C)  provide examples of the different forms of matter

   (D)  explain the concept of particle "spin"

   (E)  argue that most matter is composed of one type of particle

95. Which of the following is not mentioned as a characteristic of bosons?

   (A)  They can be composed of groups of fermions.

   (B)  They are measured in integer spin.

   (C)  They are the constituents of ordinary matter.

   (D)  They tend to bunch together in the same fundamental state.

   (E)  They lead to phenomena such as superconductors and superfluids.

96. Which of the following can be properly inferred from the passage?

   (A)  An atom composed of two protons and a neutron would be considered a boson.

   (B)  Skyrmions have been discovered in superconductors and other condensed matter environments.

   (C)  Two electrons in an atom cannot circle the same nucleus at exactly the same distance.

   (D)  A current through a superconducting wire will never dissipate.

   (E)  Fermions cannot behave as bosons unless they are cooled to a temperature near absolute zero.

97. According to the passage, which of the following describes a difference between fermions and bosons?

   (A)  Fermions cannot inhabit the same fundamental state, whereas bosons bunch together in the same state.

   (B)  Fermions contain many more types of particles than bosons.

   (C)  Fermions exist in groups, but bosons do not.

   (D)  Fermions have integral spin values, whereas Bosons have half-integer spin.

   (E)  Fermions do not obey the Pauli principle, whereas bosons do.

98.  Based on the information in the passage about the Pauli exclusion principle, to which one of the following situations would this principle be most relevant?

(A)  Fermi Energy: The maximum energy that electrons in a solid will contain in order to avoid having identical energy levels

(B)  Particle Accelerators: Devices that will accelerate charged particles to very high speeds through the application of an external magnetic field

(C)  Quantum Entanglement: When particles interact physically and then become separated but still have interdependent properties

(D)  Double Slit Experiment: An experiment that revealed the particle and wave duality of photons

(E)  The Higgs Field: The field produced by the conjectured Higg's particle that would explain why matter has mass

---

**Questions 99–101 are based on the following reading passage.**

---

*Homo economicus*, or economic human, denotes the idea of human beings as rational, narrowly self-interested agents who, given total information about opportunities and possible constraints, seek to obtain the highest possible well-being for themselves at the least possible cost. In the late 19th century, a host of economists built mathematical models based on the
5  conception of real humans as *Homo economicus*.

Exponents of *Homo economicus* tend to acknowledge that total information is not possible in the real world; thus, breakdown in models based on the concept are due to imperfect information held by the self-interested economic actors. Amartya Sen has pointed out that *Homo economicus* ignores that people can and do commit to courses of action out of
10  morality, cultural expectations, and so forth. Veblen and Keynes allege that *Homo economicus* assumes far too great an understanding of macroeconomics on the part of humans. Tversky puts forth that investors are not rational: they are unconcerned by small chances of large losses, but quite risk-averse regarding small losses. Bruno Frey points out that humans are often intrinsically motivated, and that such motivation explains heroism, craftsmanship, and other
15  drives that do not fit neatly into the model of a narrowly focused gain-seeker. Critics of the psychoanalytic tradition point out, somewhat obviously, that humans are frequently conflicted, lazy, and inconsistent.

**MANHATTAN**
PREP

Consider each of the answer choices separately and indicate all that apply.

99. Which of the following phenomena would exemplify Bruno Frey's critique of *Homo economicus*?

☐ A woodworker spends months on the delicate inlay of a door, knowing that his many hours of hard work will inevitably result in a higher price when he comes to sell the piece.

☐ A television journalist often travels to dangerous countries all over the world because he is contractually obligated to do so, and his ratings are higher the more dangerous his exploits appear to be.

☐ An economist dedicates her career to illustrating a fundamental flaw in a particular theory, though she knows there will be no tangible reward for her efforts.

100. Which of the following best describes the main idea of the passage?

(A) *Homo economicus* is a useful, if theoretical, actor to use in the formation of mathematical models.

(B) *Homo economicus* is a fundamentally flawed and thus theoretically useless construction, for a host of reasons.

(C) *Homo economicus* is often criticized by those who don't fully understand its function in economic theory.

(D) *Homo economicus* is a problematic construction, because it simplifies human motivations and is overly optimistic about human understanding.

(E) *Homo economicus* fell out of favor with most economists in the 20th century due to its many incorrect assumptions about humanity.

Consider each of the answer choices separately and indicate all that apply.

101. Which of the following is a complaint leveled against the theory of *Homo economicus* posited by certain economists in the late 19th century?

☐ It assumes that the average person knows a lot more about the general workings of the economy than he or she actually does.

☐ It assumes that humans experience a proportional and linear emotional response to all risks and rewards.

☐ It assumes that the primary impetus behind human decision making is not predicated on ethics or cultural mores.

> **Questions 102–103 are based on the following reading passage.**

     While critics contend that the views expounded on in *Against Method* are tantamount to scientific anarchism, its author Paul Feyerabend maintains that his views stem not from a desire to promote scientific chaos so much as from a recognition that many of the fundamental tenets of science—rationality, empiricism, and objectivity, for example—are as seriously flawed

5 as the "subjective" paths to truth that scientists are quick to repudiate. Feyerabend goes further by arguing that many methods that are now condemned in the scientific community played a critical role in historical moments of scientific progress. The fact that these methods helped science advance in the past indicates that scientists should think twice before they condemn them.

10      Much of *Against Method* is a case study of the events surrounding Galileo's single-handed rejection of the geocentric cosmological model in favor of the updated heliocentric model. Feyerabend goes to lengths to point out that what ultimately allowed Galileo to succeed in convincing the Western world that the earth revolved around the sun (and not the other way around) was the use of methods most modern scientists would deem highly suspect. For

15 example, in attempting to explain why the rotation of the earth did not cause a rock dropped from a tower to follow a curved, rather than a straight, path, Galileo relied on several as-yet unproven hypotheses about the laws of motion, essentially begging the question for his own position. Additionally, his published works display a rhetorical style that reads more like propaganda than like scholarly work. By showing that these methods were critical to a crucial

20 scientific advancement, Feyerabend casts doubt on whether these "unscientific" practices really deserve the criticism they so often garner.

102. Replacement of the word "repudiate" (line 5) with which of the following words would result in the LEAST change in meaning in the passage?

    (A)  overrule

    (B)  embrace

    (C)  underscore

    (D)  decry

    (E)  debate

103. The passage implies that Feyerabend makes use of a case study primarily in order to

(A) demonstrate that since a canonical example of scientific progress itself made use of practices now deemed unscientific, scientists ought to revise their account of what is and is not acceptable scientific practice

(B) show that Galileo, in his attempt to prove that a rock dropped from a tower followed a straight, not a curved, path, was guilty of many of the same errors in reasoning that make science controversial today

(C) underscore the notion that if science wants to keep thinking of itself as a field that is open to "subjective," as well as "objective," paths to truth, it needs to adopt some of the techniques that were prevalent in Galileo's time

(D) back up the claim that tautological reasoning is acceptable only when used in the service of supporting hypotheses that have yet to be proven

(E) demonstrate that any endeavor in the philosophy of science that uses examples from history to support its claims is ultimately doomed to failure

Questions 104–108 are based on the following reading passage.

In traditional theater forms, the roles of performer and audience are completely separate, so that performance space can be said to encompass an actors' sphere and a spectators' sphere. Even when performers move out into the audience or when there is scripted audience interaction, spectators do not become performers. Finally, while stories may open up the
5  imagination or excite audiences, according to Augusto Boal, they discourage political action by providing catharsis. The passive spectator follows the play's emotional arc and, once the action concludes, finds the issue closed. Boal reminds us that our theater etiquette creates a kind of culture of apathy where individuals do not act communally, despite shared space, and remain distanced from art.
10      Workshop theater, such as Boal's Image Theatre and Forum Theatre, is a response to that. In the workshop form, performance space is created for a select group of people, but the performers' sphere and the audience's sphere are collapsed: everyone is at once theater maker and witness. In Image Theatre, participants will come up with a theme or issue and arrange themselves into a tableau that depicts what that issue looks like in society today, versus
15  what the ideal situation would be. They then try to transition from the current image to the ideal image in a way that seems plausible to all the participants. Forum Theatre, on the other hand, creates a narrative skit depicting a certain problem. After the actors have gone through the action of the play once, a facilitator, known as the joker (like the one in a pack of cards), encourages those who have watched the story to watch it again and to stop it at any time to
20  take the place of the protagonist. The aim is to find a solution to the problem, realizing along the way all of the obstacles involved. In Forum Theatre, just as in Image Theatre, there is not always a solution. The main goal of this form, then, is to engage in the action, to reflect, and to understand particular issues as being part of a larger picture, thus using art to re-cast what seem like private troubles in a public, political light.
25      The main reason Boal developed these workshop styles was to grant audiences agency so that they may create ways to free themselves of oppression. Because he found theater audiences to be locked into a passive role—just like he found the oppressed coerced into a subservient role in relation to their oppressors—he created the "spect-actor," or someone who simultaneously witnesses and creates theater.

104. The second paragraph of the passage serves to

(A)  elaborate on the topic of the first paragraph
(B)  provide a rationale for an artistic endeavor
(C)  discuss an artistic answer to a passive culture
(D)  explain the theater's lack of appeal
(E)  evaluate two contrasting styles of theater

105. The author uses the word "agency" (line 25) to mean

    (A)  profit

    (B)  organization

    (C)  publicity

    (D)  power

    (E)  hegemony

106. Which of the following would Boal consider a "spect-actor"?

    (A)  a person who engages in political action

    (B)  an audience member who finds catharsis in a play

    (C)  any person placed in a subservient role

    (D)  any actor

    (E)  a participant in an Image workshop

107. According to Boal, all of the following are disadvantage of traditional theater forms EXCEPT:

    (A)  Such productions prevent the actors from going into the audience.

    (B)  Such productions provide catharsis.

    (C)  Such productions discourage communal activity.

    (D)  Such productions obstruct political change.

    (E)  Such productions distance the audience from the art.

108. All of the following would be characteristic of a Forum workshop EXCEPT:

    (A)  Productions begin with a narrative script.

    (B)  Different people often play the protagonist.

    (C)  Some performances do not achieve catharsis.

    (D)  Participants arrange themselves into a tableau.

    (E)  Performances are guided by a mediator.

Questions 109–111 are based on the following reading passage.

Stars create energy through the process of fusion. When a star explodes—a phenomenon called a supernova—so much energy is released that heavy metals such as iron and gold are formed, seeding surrounding hydrogen clouds. Newer stars therefore contain more heavy elements in their atmospheres. Heavy elements form the materials that make up our planet
5 (and even human bodies). It is believed that for a system of planets such as our solar system to form around a star during cloud contraction, the presence of these heavy elements in the cloud is a necessity.

A molecular cloud can become unstable and collapse by the force of gravity, overcoming outward thermal pressure of the constituent gases. At a given temperature and density, two
10 critical measures of size, Jeans mass and Jeans length, can be calculated. If the size of the cloud exceeds either of these critical values, gravity will ultimately win, and the probability of eventual cloud contraction is high.

However, some outside influence is still evidently required for a theoretically unstable cloud to initiate collapse. The natural rotation of a galaxy can slowly alter the structure of a
15 cloud, for instance. Surrounding supernovae can generate shockwaves powerful enough to affect the debris in other clouds, forcing the debris inward and possibly causing contraction to begin. One theory states that density waves propagating through spiral structures can also sufficiently stimulate clouds to cause contraction.

Consider each of the answer choices separately and indicate all that apply.

109. The author of the passage suggests that cloud contraction may begin in which of the following ways?

- ☐ Through the process of fusion
- ☐ Explosions of stars within a close enough proximity, generating shockwaves that prompt contraction in nearby clouds
- ☐ Debris forced outwards from a cloud

110. Which of the following inferences about our solar system is best supported by the passage?

(A) Life in the solar system depends on energy from the sun.

(B) When the system reaches a particular size, it can become unstable and begin to collapse.

(C) The natural rotation of the galaxy can alter the galaxy's structure.

(D) It is believed to have been formed from materials "seeded" into hydrogen clouds.

(E) It produced so much energy when it was formed that heavy elements were generated.

111. It can be inferred from the passage that which of the following inhibits interstellar cloud collapse?

    (A)  Supernova explosions

    (B)  Galactic rotation

    (C)  Thermal pressure

    (D)  Gravitational force

    (E)  Density waves

---

**Question 112 is based on the following reading passage.**

---

    The Norton-Polk-Mathis House in San Antonio displays an integrated design well-suited to the primary purpose of the building: to impress. This is evidenced by the fact that the building was designed with the street it faces in mind. Only the South façade is architecturally interesting or involved—the sides of the building are flat, featureless, and uninteresting.

5  The house was designed not only as a living area, but also as a structure to be seen from the street. The building reflects typical Renaissance ideals of order and weight, and, while it is asymmetrical, it is well balanced and stable. The choice of materials also reflects the "re-discovery" of antiquity prevalent in the Italian Renaissance. The white stone lends an elegant simplicity to the building yet it radiates an air of strength and mass reminiscent of the

10  Parthenon or the Athenian temples—especially when juxtaposed with the other, seemingly fragile brick and wood homes of the neighborhood.

---

Consider each of the answer choices separately and indicate <u>all</u> that apply.

112. Which of the following can be inferred about the Norton-Polk-Mathis House?

    ☐  It was built during the Italian Renaissance.

    ☐  Its primary purpose was utilitarian in nature.

    ☐  It appears stronger than other nearby homes.

> **Questions 113–114 are based on the following reading passage.**

After 22 years of observations in Shark Bay, Australia, behavioral biologist Janet Mann and her colleagues have discovered that certain bottlenose dolphins, known as spongers, form social networks, showing the first hints of culture among non-human animals. Spongers are dolphins that wear marine basket sponges on their beaks as hunting tools, using them to
5 root around on deep sandy bottoms and find fish concealed below the sand. Sponging is a complex hunting technique passed on from mother to offspring. A sponger must know where the sponges grow, how to pick the right sponge, how to remove the sponge intact from the ocean floor, and how and where to properly hunt.

Spongers typically live solitary lives, but over 22 years of observation, a pattern
10 emerged. The 28 female spongers formed cliques with other female spongers that were not necessarily genetically related to them. This behavior differs from other animal behavior where circumstances, such as genetics or food sources, dictate the formation of groups. The fact that these spongers chose to associate based upon similar, socially learned behaviors makes their cliques a cultural first among animals.

113. Which of the following expresses the main idea of the passage?

(A) Sponging is a complex behavior used by some dolphins as a hunting technique.

(B) Any study of animal behavior must take place over an extended period of time in order for patterns to emerge.

(C) A small set of non-human animals has been found to form social networks.

(D) Studying how animals form groups is important to our understanding of nature.

(E) Only humans can form social networks.

> Consider each of the answer choices separately and indicate <u>all</u> that apply.

114. Which of the following can be properly inferred from the passage?

☐ Groups formed by genetic bonds or food supplies do not qualify as social networks.

☐ All spongers of Shark Bay, Australia, form social networks.

☐ Spongers can only be found in Shark Bay, Australia.

---

**Questions 115–116 are based on the following reading passage.**

---

For years, the idea that blind people can hear better than sighted people was considered something of an old canard. However, functional brain imaging now has allowed us to look inside the brains of blind people who possess what can only be termed cerebral superpowers—the ability to understand speech at up to 25 syllables per second, a speed
5  that sounds like "noise" to sighted people (a typical sighted person understands closer to 10 syllables per second). As it turns out, a brain region called V1, situated at the back of the skull and which normally only responds to light has actually been rewired in the brains of blind people—and now processes auditory information. This is truly a stunning example of the brain's plasticity, a topic of cardinal importance in designing educational experiences and
10  materials to best engage the brains of students.

Of course, in discussing the brain's amazing plasticity, modern thinkers take for granted something that would have been shocking to thinkers from Aristotle (who posited a holistic, non-corporeal mind in *De Anima* in the 4th century, BC) through Descartes (who argued, in the 17th century, for mind-body dualism)—the idea that the mind is physically located in the brain
15  and that our intellect, personality, and selfhood are attributable to physical processes in the brain and can be altered by brain injuries.

115. According to the passage, the belief that blind people can hear better than sighted people

    (A)   is untrue

    (B)   was not a matter of contention, but was then shown to be true

    (C)   was, for years, thought to be true, but is now up for debate

    (D)   is put forth by the scientific community, but this evidence is contested by many

    (E)   was, for years, thought by many to be false, and then was shown to be true

---

Consider each of the answer choices separately and indicate <u>all</u> that apply.

---

116. According to the passage, Aristotle would NOT have thought that

    ☐   the mind is separate from the body

    ☐   the mind exists in parts or modules, rather than as one entity

    ☐   blind people can hear better than sighted people

**MANHATTAN**
PREP

Questions 117–118 are based on the following reading passage.

The atrocities committed during the Second World War by the National Socialists are well known and have been meticulously documented by historians. Far less known, however, are the mass deportations that took place almost two years after the conclusion of the war, this time orchestrated by the Allied governments. In the years after 1945, over 12 million German-
5  speaking citizens of Czechoslovakia, Hungary, Romania, and Poland were dispossessed, packed into trains, and left to fend for themselves in a newly defeated and impoverished Germany. What allowed for this mass exile—the largest forced migration in history—was the confluence of political motivations on the part of the key players. The expelling countries of Eastern and Central Europe were especially keen on punishing Germans for the horrors of the war—though,
10  of course, their own German-speaking populations were hardly responsible for Germany's actions—and on increasing the ethnic homogeneity within their borders. The Allied powers, too, had something to gain. The Soviet Union, intent on capitalizing politically on Germany's defeat, aimed to irrevocably undermine relations between Germany and Poland, especially by ceding German territory to Poland and emptying it of its inhabitants. Britain, weary from the
15  war, hoped the resulting mass suffering would reinforce the completeness of Germany's defeat. And the United States, in turn, was attempting to cozy up to the nations of Eastern and Central Europe in the hopes of keeping them away from Soviet influence.

The result of the deportations, however, was the death of at least 500,000 people and Germany's acquisition of a homeless population far greater than that of any other industrialized
20  country. The death toll was not far worse, furthermore, only because the Soviets' ambition to cripple Germany was unsuccessful. Following the war, Germany underwent what is known as its "economic miracle," which made it possible to house, feed, and employ the mass of exiles. That this episode is practically excised from the history books in some countries, however, is surely corroboration of the platitude that history is written by the victors.

Consider each of the answer choices separately and indicate all that apply.

117. Which of the following can be inferred from the passage?

☐  Some events that occurred during World War II do not appear in history books.

☐  The Allied powers included the Soviet Union, Britain, the United States, and Poland.

☐  The Allied powers were not entirely unified on political matters.

Consider each of the answer choices separately and indicate all that apply.

118. Which of the following, if true, would weaken the claim that the Allied powers had something to gain from the deportations?

☐ The United States believed that the Eastern and Central European powers hoped to create more multicultural, ethnically mixed societies.

☐ The Soviet Union wanted to profit from post-war trade between Germany and Poland.

☐ Britain, weary of the killing during the war, pledged itself to preventing suffering.

**Questions 119–121 are based on the following reading passage.**

Quantum mechanics is a relatively new field of physics that was developed in the early 1900s. Although we classically think of a particle as a fixed object, quantum mechanics describes particles as waves using properties such as position and energy. The quantum mechanical wave describes the probability that the particle's properties take on certain values.

5  Take, for example, the analogy of rolling a six-sided die. For each roll there is a one-in-six chance that any single number will result. After rolling, however, only one single number will be observed. If the die is rolled enough times, one can deduce that the die has six sides and that each side is equally likely. However, one can never be completely sure, because rolling dice is probabilistic in nature. Quantum mechanics states that the same is true of the position (and

10  other properties) of a particle. A particle trapped in a closed box has some finite probability of being at any location within the box. Open the box once and you'll find the particle at only one location. Open the box enough times and you'll see all the particle locations and the frequency at which they are achieved. From this, one can deduce the original properties of the quantum mechanical wave, just as one could deduce the properties of the die.

15  The counterintuitive properties of quantum mechanics, that the attributes of a particle cannot be known in advance of measurement, initially provoked many strong philosophical debates and interpretations regarding the field. In fact, Einstein was deeply troubled by the idea of nature being probabilistic and commented famously that, "God does not play dice with the universe." Over the last 70 years, however, irrefutable evidence has abounded that verifies

20  the truth of the theory of quantum mechanics.

119. Which of the following best expresses the main idea of the passage?

(A) Particles are not fixed objects but rather exist in the form of waves.

(B) Controversial theories are often found to be correct.

(C) Quantum mechanics correctly postulates the probabilistic nature of particles.

(D) Many questions still exist about the nature of particles and quantum mechanics.

(E) Experiments can be designed to test the quantum mechanical nature of particles.

120. Based on the information in the passage, which of the following would best explain Einstein's motivation for stating that "God does not play dice with the universe"?

(A) Einstein did not believe that particles should be governed by probability as in a game of dice.

(B) Einstein believed that God should control the fate of the universe.

(C) Einstein was opposed to the theory of quantum mechanics on the grounds that it violated causality.

(D) Einstein's religious beliefs did not allow him to fully understand the theory of quantum mechanics.

(E) Einstein believed that God created the universe such that particles would be modeled probabilistically as in quantum mechanics.

Consider each of the answer choices separately and indicate all that apply.

121. Which of the following can be properly inferred based on the information in the passage?

☐ The location of a particle within a closed box cannot be known for certain without observing the particle.

☐ Properties such as position and energy of a particle can never be measured.

☐ Particles can be properly described as quantum mechanical waves.

**MANHATTAN**
PREP

---

> **Questions 122–126 are based on the following reading passage.**

Invisible theater and guerrilla theater are two forms of street theater with similar origins but very different approaches. Both forms take place exclusively in public places, but invisible theater conceals its performative nature whereas guerrilla theater flaunts it. While invisible theater creates a performance space unbeknownst to its audience, guerrilla theater actively
5   seeks the attention of an audience by explicitly imposing a performance space onto a public place.

Starting in the early 1970s, Augusto Boal and fellow actors have staged scenes regarding social issues in public or semi-public places (e.g., restaurants), crafting their dialog and action to get a verbal reaction from bystanders. Because performers and non-performers remain
10  distinct, invisible theater returns somewhat to the model set up by traditional theater. However, there are a few key differences. The performance space is created in public places without the awareness of non-performers. For non-performers, being beyond the performative space allows them to avoid the etiquette of theatergoing and removes that "lens" that unavoidably emerges when we feel we are viewing art or performance. If people do not suspect that they
15  are viewing art, however, they are free to engage with the action and concepts of an unfolding drama as if these actions and concepts were real.

Boal has documented various successful instances of invisible theater in which non-performers actively listen, participate in public-spirited discussion, and even take unplanned public-minded action in response to the dialogue and events set up by invisible theater
20  performers. Because onlookers think they are witnessing real life events, because the performers are bold in their statements, because the scripted characters are very vocal about what they are doing and experiencing, invisible theater is able to instigate political conversation within an everyday context; it successfully creates public forums out of thin air.

Guerrilla theater creates surprise performances in public but is driven by the forceful
25  imposition of "traditional" (if we can call anything about guerrilla theater "traditional") theater. One example includes two professors of Galway's University College who dressed in their robes and went out to the street, questioning pedestrians and awarding diplomas to the ones least able to provide good answers, as a way to protest their university's decision to grant Ronald Reagan an honorary doctorate in law.

30  A large part of the goal of guerrilla theater is to get publicized, its message echoed over and over in our ever-expanding network of technology-interface mass media. Guerrilla theater knows it may antagonize its direct audience—it often hopes to, because conflict is more likely to be broadcast, and the goal of guerrilla theater is to get people talking publicly.

---

Consider each of the answer choices separately and indicate all that apply.

---

122. Which of the following can be inferred from the passage?

☐ When people are unaware that they are viewing a performance, they tend to act more naturally.

☐ Invisible theater is best described as improvisational.

☐ One measure of the success of a theatrical performance can be the actions taken by the audience once the performance is over.

123. The main point of the passage could best be described as

(A) a discussion of two different but aligned artistic currents

(B) an examination of which of two art forms is more effective at prompting political action

(C) a synopsis of the evolution of theater

(D) a presentation of two theatrical concepts that conceal their performative nature

(E) an overview of artistic life in public places

---

Consider each of the answer choices separately and indicate all that apply.

---

124. Which of the following is true of both invisible theater and guerrilla theater?

☐ Both have a goal of encouraging discourse.

☐ Both impose performance space onto public location.

☐ Both antagonize their audience.

125. The passage implies that the Galway professors believed which of the following?

(A) Guerrilla theater was superior to invisible theater.

(B) Protesting an honor could result in the revocation of the award.

(C) Granting Ronald Reagan a degree demeaned the intellectual standard of the university.

(D) Handing out diplomas was a legal activity.

(E) Ronald Reagan's foreign policy had deleterious effects.

---

Consider each of the answer choices separately and indicate all that apply.

---

126. Which of the following, if true, would undermine the principle of invisible theater?

☐ When people knowingly view art, their heightened attention increases their perception and involvement.

☐ Audience members watch a performance and later report to others what happened, still not knowing that the event was a theater piece.

☐ A lively debate about public issues is brought to a halt by the imposition of scripted characters inserting theatrical dialogue.

---

**Questions 127–131 are based on the following reading passage.**

---

Cells employ many strategies to avoid genetic mutation. From the high fidelity of DNA-synthesizing enzymes to the pro-death signaling that accompanies mutagenic stimuli such as UV radiation, cellular mechanisms that stymie genetic changes are ubiquitous throughout the natural world. These mechanisms are critical because widespread genomic changes would
5    wreak physiological havoc; indeed, malfunctions in molecular players that safeguard against mutagenesis, such as the protein p53, have been implicated in diseases such as cancer.

Yet despite the criticality of preventing and eliminating DNA mutations to avoid deleterious changes in cells, in specific contexts many organisms have also adapted beneficial mechanisms to induce genetic changes.
10    One such instance is observed in vertebrate immune systems: white blood cells such as T cells recognize invading pathogens through receptors on their surfaces. In order to recognize a wide variety of pathogens, these cells must generate a large repertoire of receptors. Relying only on a genetically encoded repertoire would be disadvantageously limiting—analogous to having only a few dozen language phrases with which to respond to the nearly infinite
15    potential combinations of words in a conversation. Instead, the repertoire is generated by a process of genetic recombination, in which T cells "cut-and-paste" the DNA encoding their microbe-recognizing receptors. Many of these genetic rearrangements produce cells bearing non-functional proteins; such unproductive cells are eliminated through senescence. Nevertheless, this seemingly haphazard process of programmed genetic mutation is crucial to
20    generating immunological diversity, as individuals with defects in this pathway exhibit clinical immunodeficiency. How this process is regulated by T cells to prevent harmful mutations remains the subject of ongoing research.

---

Consider each of the answer choices separately and indicate <u>all</u> that apply.

127. Which of the following is true of genetic changes in cells?

    ☐   They can cause serious problems to body systems.

    ☐   They can provide benefits to the immune system.

    ☐   Some genetic mutation is regulated by T cells.

128. The phrase "seemingly haphazard" (line 19) is meant to indicate that

    (A)  the process of programmed genetic mutation deserves further study

    (B)  the production by T cells of "unproductive cells" is wasteful

    (C)  genetic recombination may appear random, but is not

    (D)  T cells are essential to proper immune system functioning

    (E)  programmed genetic mutation can be dangerous to an organism

Consider each of the answer choices separately and indicate <u>all</u> that apply.

129. Which of the following can be inferred from the first paragraph of the passage?

☐ Pro-death signaling is a mechanism that hinders genetic changes.

☐ Cellular mechanisms that safeguard against mutagenesis are very common.

☐ Protein p53 may play a role in preventing cancer from forming.

130. The analogy regarding "a few dozen language phrases … conversation" (lines 14–15) is meant to elucidate

(A) why genetic recombination is important to T cell functioning

(B) the need for numerous means of fighting cancer and other diseases caused by cell mutation

(C) why white blood cells such as T cells rely on a genetically encoded repertoire

(D) how language use is like "cutting and pasting"

(E) the mechanism by which mutagenesis can compromise physiological functioning

Consider each of the answer choices separately and indicate <u>all</u> that apply.

131. In the analogy in the third paragraph, the "nearly infinite potential combinations of words in a conversation" represent

☐ pathogens

☐ receptors

☐ T cells

**Questions 132–133 are based on the following reading passage.**

Martin Haberman pulls no punches in his scathing critique of the insensitive and unjust treatment received by children in poverty in the public school system. He focuses the brunt of his criticism on teachers who have been insufficiently trained for the realities of the modern school environment and whose prejudices, lack of deep content knowledge, and excessive
5 focus on order and discipline profoundly limit their effectiveness. Haberman writes, "the principles and theories we call child and adolescent development were all developed to explain the middle-class experience," and that everyone else in public schools, including non-white, immigrant, or non-English-speaking children, are considered somehow anomalies, thus leading to the absurd situation in which a teacher completes teacher training and is put in front
10 of a class of students she considers to be made entirely of "exceptions."

**MANHATTAN**
PREP

> Consider each of the answer choices separately and indicate <u>all</u> that apply.

132. According to Haberman, a teacher's effectiveness can be compromised by

    ☐   insufficient attention to order and discipline

    ☐   insufficient knowledge of the material being taught

    ☐   personal bias

133. In the last line of the passage, the word "exceptions" is in quotes to make the point that

   (A)   the idea of "exceptions" is crucial to effective education

   (B)   the quote is taken verbatim from a teacher

   (C)   students who perform well academically are an aberration, not the reverse

   (D)   certain teachers inappropriately consider "non-white, immigrant, or non-English-speaking children" to be other than the norm

   (E)   teachers versed in the principles and theories of child and adolescent development are actually the norm

> **Questions 134–135 are based on the following reading passage.**

        Naturalism, arising in the 19th century as a literary response to Darwin's account of evolution, focused on describing everyday reality but differed from realism in its attempts to provide a "scientific" foundation for its depictions of characters, stressing the influence of environment and heredity upon the individual psyche. Émile Zola, in particular, saw his craft
5  as an extension of the scientific method into the domain of art. The 19th century, perhaps in opposition to naturalism, saw the rise of the Decadent movement, embracing artifice over nature in writing, championed by Zola's erstwhile protégé, Joris-Karl Huysmans. The protagonist of his masterpiece, *Á rebours* (literally, *Against the Grain*, but more commonly translated as *Against Nature*), removes himself from society—viewing it as the product of
10  a nature long surpassed by human ingenuity—and surrounds himself exclusively with art, perfume, literature, and technology.

> Consider each of the answer choices separately and indicate <u>all</u> that apply.

134. Which of the following can be inferred from the passage about perfume?

    ☐   Some followers of the Decadent movement considered it to be an example of human artifice.

    ☐   Some followers of the Decadent movement considered it to be superior to natural entities.

    ☐   Some followers of the Decadent movement enjoyed surrounding themselves with it.

Consider each of the answer choices separately and indicate all that apply.

135. Which of the following, if true, would undermine the claim that the Decadent movement was opposed to naturalism?

    ☐   Decadent authors intended to use literature as a vehicle for the scientific method.

    ☐   Decadent authors focused on the effects of environment on shaping character.

    ☐   Decadent authors elaborated on the way inherited traits influenced human behavior.

---

**Questions 136–137 are based on the following reading passage.**

---

    For many years, biological scientists have sought to decipher cellular function by quantifying the degrees of protein and mRNA expression within populations of their cells of interest. Classically, these measurements required combining many cells into a single sample and rupturing their membranes, thus exposing pooled quantities of the target molecule for
5  detection. One limitation of these techniques is the reliance on average measurements: it is impossible to distinguish a uniform population of cells expressing intermediate quantities of a molecule from a population composed of separate low and high expressers. The distinction has proven to be important, particularly in the context of drug targeting of cancer cells; prescribing a dose to hit the "average" cell may completely miss the more aggressive "one
10 percent."
    The advent of single-cell measurement technology such as flow cytometry and RNA FISH has made it possible to capture not only a population's average levels of a molecule, but also the distribution of the molecule's expression within the population. As a result, researchers are increasingly investigating the sources and significance of variability within populations that
15 were previously assumed to be identical.

136. According to the passage, the limitation of combining many cells into one sample and then rupturing their membranes in order to detect a target molecule is that

    (A)   variability exists within cell populations

    (B)   some cells in the sample may contaminate others

    (C)   this method cannot single out the cells that express more of a certain molecule

    (D)   the rupture of cell membranes is implicated in the formation of cancer

    (E)   it is preferable to capture a population's average levels of a molecule

Consider each of the answer choices separately and indicate <u>all</u> that apply.

137. Which of the following can be inferred from the passage regarding flow cytometry and RNA FISH?

☐   Both technologies allow researchers to quantify properties of individual cells.

☐   Using these technologies, it is impossible to distinguish a uniform population of cells expressing intermediate quantities of a molecule.

☐   Both technologies allow researchers to measure variability of molecule expression within cell populations.

---

**Questions 138–139 are based on the following reading passage.**

---

The Portuguese began to enter Angola in the 16th century, and over the next three hundred years slowly pushed into the interior of the sizable nation located in Southern Africa, finally achieving complete occupation by the 1920s. Following Angolan independence in 1975, and despite a bloody civil war that lasted until 2002, the Angolan economy has grown at a
5  double-digit pace since the 1990s, due largely to expansive mineral and petroleum reserves. Conversely, Portugal is now broke and in debt, its economy shrinking by full percentage points every year. In a grand stroke of irony, Portugal's Prime Minister Pedro Passos Coelho in 2011 suggested to Angola's President Jose Eduardo dos Santos that "We should take advantage of this moment … to strengthen our bilateral relations." President dos Santos replied, "We
10  are aware of Portugal's difficulties and we are open and available to help." This "help" will likely come in the form of Angola's investment in Portuguese industries that the International Monetary Fund has ordered be privatized as a condition of a 78 billion dollar bailout. Already, the country that once mined Angola for slaves and raw material is now virtually helpless as Angola purchases Lisbon's prime real estate, using much of it to build luxury resorts where
15  Angolan officials go for holidays.

Despite the stunning reversal of fortune, Angola is not without its difficulties. Corruption is rampant, and Angola has one of the highest levels of income inequality in the world—in the capital city of Luanda, hamburgers go for 50 dollars and designer jeans cost twice what they do in London or New York, while two-thirds of the population lives on less than 2 dollars a day.

138. Which of the following is <u>not</u> stated as a component of Portugal and Angola's historical relationship?

(A)   Portuguese traders sold Angolan slaves.

(B)   Raw material was taken from Angola by the Portuguese.

(C)   The two nations were at war.

(D)   The Portuguese increasingly dominated Angola over a period of several hundred years.

(E)   Angola achieved independence from Portugal in the 20th century.

139. The "grand stroke of irony" (line 7) is best described as

   (A)   two countries dedicated to strengthening bilateral relations share economic problems
   (B)   a former colonial possession is now being called upon to assist its former possessor
   (C)   slavery has ended, and yet people still live in poverty
   (D)   the cost of living in Luanda is very high, and yet most people are poor
   (E)   the Portuguese economy was once thriving and is now dwindling

---

**Questions 140–142 are based on the following reading passage.**

---

For as long as humans have been philosophizing about the mind, virtually every thinker has conceived of the mind as a unitary entity. In fact, such a view was crucial to both Aristotle's and Descartes's view that the mind (or the soul) survived death. Surely the self cannot be subdivided; surely one cannot have half a mind?

5      Indeed, the final evidence that one can, in fact, have "half a mind" came in the 1960s, from the famous studies for which Roger Sperry was awarded the Nobel Prize in 1981 for his discoveries about the functional specialization of the cerebral hemispheres. Working with epileptics who had been treated via the cutting of the *corpus callosum*, or division between the two hemispheres, Sperry was able to observe "odd behavior" in these patients—each half of
10   the brain could gain new information, but one hemisphere was entirely unaware of what the other had learned or experienced.

Restak, in *The Modular Brain*, posits that the brain is not centrally organized (some prior theories of mind had actually posed the existence of a "director" in the brain, begging the question of who directs the director's brain) but, alternatively, that different parts of the brain
15   control different abilities, and that those "modules" can operate independently. As we can easily see from patients with brain damage, there is no "unified mind and personality"—part of ourselves, centered in different parts of the brain, can change or be obliterated entirely as a result of physical changes to the brain. Consider the case of Phineas Gage, a rail worker who, in 1848, while attempting to compress explosive powder with a tamping rod, literally blew a
20   hole in the front of his brain. While Gage was ultimately able to function fairly normally, his personality was markedly changed; he became boorish and irresponsible. Gage's case was well documented, allowing modern reconstructions to show that his injury affected areas of the brain that we now know to be related to moral sensibilities and their expression. That is, Phineas Gage literally lost one (or more) of the modules in his modular brain system.

140. The case of Phineas Gage is presented as evidence that

   (A)   the modular brain system has a central "director"
   (B)   people who lose parts of the brain are usually able to function normally
   (C)   brain injury is a serious risk in certain types of work
   (D)   splitting the *corpus callosum* can result in marked changes in personality
   (E)   aspects of personality can be physically located within the brain

**MANHATTAN**
PREP

Consider each of the answer choices separately and indicate all that apply.

141. In lines 13–14, the phrase "begging the question of who directs the director's brain" is meant to emphasize that

- ☐ the problem of a "director" in the brain is recursive
- ☐ whether there is such a "director" of the brain is an open question
- ☐ Restak has both asked and answered a question about the brain's organization

Consider each of the answer choices separately and indicate all that apply.

142. Which of the following can be inferred about thinkers who conceive of the mind as a unitary entity?

- ☐ They believe that the mind survives death.
- ☐ Their views are incompatible with modular brain theory.
- ☐ They are unaware that certain aspects of personality are known to be controlled by certain areas of the brain.

---

**Questions 143–145 are based on the following reading passage.**

---

Most mental health disorders and cases of drug abuse tend to diminish a person's ability to recognize other people's feelings. A recent study in Norway suggests, however, that these effects can be bolstered by a nasal spray puff of the brain hormone oxytocin, which is known to increase feelings of calm and social bonding. Although oxytocin is already prescribed for
5  certain disorders that affect social function, such as autism, these treatments are often tried in isolated cases, leaving the overall effects of the drug without evaluation.

The Norwegian experiment focused on 40 students, each of whom was given either a control dose of salt water or the drug oxytocin. After the nasal dose, the students were shown faces of happy, angry, or neutral expressions, some of which were subtler than others. The
10  researchers found that after a nasal spray dose of oxytocin, the students' awareness of the expressions was intensified. Further, the experiment showed that the oxytocin had the greatest effect on those who were least able to evaluate emotions properly when given the control.

Although the results of this study seem promising, Leknes, the lead scientist in the investigation, cautions that the hormone would not be a "cure-all" for mental illness or drug
15  addiction. Rather, he suggests, the hormone might help some individuals better interpret the social cues from the world around them.

143. The author of the passage would most likely agree with which of the following statements about the brain hormone oxytocin?

   (A)  Its overall effects require further evaluation.

   (B)  In the future, it will be used to cure mental illness and drug addiction.

   (C)  It is not useful for people who are already able to interpret social cues.

   (D)  Its effects on the brain are unknown.

   (E)  It is more effective when dosed via nasal spray than orally.

144. The passage lends the most support to which of the following conclusions about the nasal spray study of oxytocin?

   (A)  The results of the study are inconclusive because a sample set of 40 students is not substantial.

   (B)  The nasal spray of oxytocin increased feelings of calm and social bonding for the students.

   (C)  Many students were unable to recognize the expressions shown to them when given only the control dose of salt water.

   (D)  The students who might need oxytocin most are the ones who appear most responsive to the hormone.

   (E)  The subtler the expression, the more difficult it was for the students to identify.

145. Which of the following is not mentioned in the passage regarding the Norwegian study on oxytocin?

   (A)  The study showed that oxytocin made students more able to distinguish faces from one another.

   (B)  Leknes was the lead scientist in the investigation.

   (C)  A control dose of salt water was used to gauge normal student ability to recognize facial expressions.

   (D)  Students who participated in the study were shown happy, angry, or neutral expressions.

   (E)  Oxytocin had the greatest effect on students who were least able to evaluate emotions properly when given the control dose.

---

**Question 146 is based on the following reading passage.**

---

Ever-present in Jamaican folklore and storytelling is the character of the trickster Anansi, an African spider-god who regularly outsmarts other animal-god characters. Also known as Kwaku Ananse, 'Nancy Spida,' and Aunt Nancy in the Southern US, the character of Anansi originated with the Ashanti people in Ghana. In Jamaican culture, as well as throughout the
5 Caribbean, Anansi has been a symbol of slave resistance. Just as Anansi uses cunning and subterfuge to achieve victories over his oppressors, so too did slaves employ such strategies within the power structure of the plantations.

**MANHATTAN**
PREP

Consider each of the answer choices separately and indicate <u>all</u> that apply.

146. Which of the following can be inferred from the passage?

☐ Anansi originated in Jamaican folklore.

☐ Jamaican folklore features other characters that have both divine and animal characteristics.

☐ Anansi is known on at least two continents.

---

**Questions 147–149 are based on the following reading passage.**

---

The cosmic microwave background is a uniform 2.7 Kelvin radiation that permeates the entire universe. Although it was postulated almost 50 years before, Penzias and Wilson discovered the cosmic microwave background accidentally in the 1970s. Working at Bell Labs, these two scientists were using a radio telescope to observe distant stars. They found, however,
5 that no matter where they pointed their telescope they observed an approximately 3 Kelvin background signal. After convincing themselves that this signal was real and not some artifact of their instrument, they consulted with a team at Princeton University that had been searching for the cosmic microwave background. The Princeton team confirmed what Penzias and Wilson had found. Apparently, Penzias and Wilson had accidentally stumbled upon the oldest
10 observable relic of the early universe.

Why does the cosmic microwave background exist and permeate all of space? Just an instant after the Big Bang, all matter in the universe was so energetic, or hot, that it existed as free particles known as "quarks." In the fractions of a second following, the universe expanded and cooled until the quarks lost enough energy to form electrons, protons, and neutrons,
15 the building blocks of ordinary matter. Photons, the smallest particles of light, also filled the universe and were so energetic that they "bounced" off electrons, keeping the electrons and protons from forming atoms. After approximately 400,000 more years, the photons lost enough energy that atoms could form readily. Without any lone electrons off of which photons could "bounce," the photons began streaming unimpeded all through the universe, mostly
20 unchanged but for one exception. Due to the further expansion and cooling of the universe, these photons have cooled to just 2.7 degrees above absolute zero. It was these same photons that Penzias and Wilson observed approximately 13.6 billion years later here on Earth.

147. Which of the following most accurately expresses the author's intent in writing the passage?

(A) To describe the discovery and reason for the cosmic microwave background

(B) To explain how science discoveries can be made accidentally

(C) To argue that the cosmic microwave background is the oldest observable relic of the universe

(D) To defend the work of Penzias and Wilson

(E) To support the theory of the Big Bang using the cosmic microwave background

148. According to the passage, which of the following events occurred first after the Big Bang?

    (A) The universe expanded and cooled until atoms formed.

    (B) Photons streamed unimpeded through space.

    (C) All matter existed as particles known as "quarks."

    (D) The cosmic microwave background cooled to 2.7 Kelvin.

    (E) Atomic nuclei, composed of protons and neutrons, formed.

149. According to the passage, with which of the following would the author most likely agree regarding the discovery of Penzias and Wilson?

    (A) It was not as important as the signal for which they were originally searching.

    (B) The telescope belonging to Penzias and Wilson was more sensitive than that of the Princeton team.

    (C) Penzias and Wilson would not have discovered the cosmic microwave background if it had been more than 3 Kelvin in temperature.

    (D) Penzias and Wilson did not initially understand the implications of their results.

    (E) Penzias and Wilson did not believe that their signal was real when they took their discovery to the Princeton team.

---

**Questions 150–151 are based on the following reading passage.**

---

    American composer and conductor John Philip Sousa viewed the increasing popularity of the phonograph with deep dismay. He suggested that it would "reduce the expression of music to a mathematical system of megaphones, wheels, cogs, disks, cylinders, and all manner of revolving things, which are as like real art as the marble statue of Eve is like her beautiful,
5 living, breathing daughters." Such "mechanical" music was not sincere, according to Sousa: "The nightingale's song is delightful because the nightingale herself gives it forth. The boy with a penny whistle and glass of water may give an excellent imitation, but let him persist, he is sent to bed as a nuisance."

    Sousa further decried a "decline in domestic music," noting the decline of musical
10 instrument purchases and predicting that when music comes so easily out of a phonograph, mothers will not bother to sing lullabies to their babies. He opined that when music is so readily playable, musical and vocal instruction as a normal part of education will fall out of fashion, the "tide of amateurism" receding, and music will become the province of machines and professional singers only. "What of the national throat?" asked Sousa. "Will it not weaken?
15 What of the national chest? Will it not shrink?"

Consider each of the answer choices separately and indicate all that apply.

150. Which of the following, if they occurred, would contradict Sousa's arguments?

    ☐   A private school that once demanded two semesters of vocal instruction as a requirement
        for graduation now offers the same classes as electives.

    ☐   A young boy in an isolated rural area during the Great Depression hears a professional
        bluegrass band for the first time on a phonograph, and it inspires him to ask his
        grandfather to teach him to play the family banjo.

    ☐   A modern recording artist comments that, because of her terrible stage fright, her live
        performances are less genuine than the recordings she is able to produce when she feels
        comfortable in the studio.

151. In the context in which it appears, "national chest" (line 15) most nearly refers to

    (A)   the performances of professional singers
    (B)   the US Treasury
    (C)   the phonograph
    (D)   the vocal abilities of amateur American singers
    (E)   musical instruments found in American homes

**Questions 152–153 are based on the following reading passage.**

        In thermodynamics, an idealized blackbody is an object that reflects zero incident
    electromagnetic radiation, absorbing all such radiation instead and consequently warming
    up. The blackbody emits just as much energy per unit time as it absorbs; the electromagnetic
    spectrum of the emitted energy, however, is completely determined by the temperature of
5   the blackbody and by no other properties thereof, such as material composition or structure.
    In contrast, reflected radiation undergoes no fundamental change in its original spectral
    characteristics, other than a possible Doppler shift created by the motion of the reflector
    relative to an observer. Researchers have recently discovered that a microscopic "forest" of
    vertically aligned single-wall carbon nanotubes of varying heights applied to a surface has
10  extremely low reflectance across a wide range of wavelengths of visible light, the closest
    scientists have come thus far to creating a perfectly dark material.

152. Which sentence in the passage states the variables that define the electromagnetic spectrum of a
    blackbody?

---

Consider each of the answer choices separately and indicate __all__ that apply.

---

153. Which of the following can be properly inferred from the passage?

☐ An object that reflects incident electromagnetic radiation is not an idealized blackbody.

☐ Reflected radiation always exactly matches the spectral characteristics of the original incident radiation.

☐ A microscopic "forest" of vertically aligned single-wall carbon nanotubes of varying heights applied to a surface will absorb all incident electromagnetic radiation.

---

**Questions 154–156 are based on the following reading passage.**

---

For many years, most physicists supported one of two cosmological theories: the steady-state universe, and the Big Bang. The theory of the steady-state universe states that the universe has always existed exactly as we observe it at present, whereas the Big Bang theory postulates that the universe was conceived from a singularity in space-time that has expanded
5  into the current universe. The validity of either theory was not tested until 1929, when Edwin Hubble famously discovered what is now known as Hubble's Law.

Hubble's experiment is now a famous benchmark in modern physics. Hubble, using the Mount Wilson Observatory, observed a class of stars known as Cephied variables, luminous stars that blink and flicker with a rate that depends on their distance from the observer. Using
10  this relation and over years of observation, Hubble calculated the distance to many of these variable stars. Milton Humason, a fellow astronomer, helped Hubble to calculate the stars' relative velocities to Earth. When Hubble combined the two data sets he found an interesting relationship: all the stars appeared to be moving away from us! In fact, the speed at which they were moving increased with an increasing distance from Earth.
15  Hubble realized, from this small set of data, that the earth was a part of the expanding universe. As the universe expands outward in all directions, any observer from a fixed vantage point will look out and see everything running away from them. The further away any two points are, the more the expansion affects them, and the faster they appear to be moving away from each other. Hubble's result was the first experimental proof that we do not live in a
20  steady-state universe, but rather a dynamic and expanding one.

154. Which of the following best expresses the main idea of the passage?

    (A)  Edwin Hubble discovered Hubble's Law, a benchmark in modern physics.

    (B)  Hubble discovered that the universe is expanding, disproving the theory of the steady-state universe.

    (C)  Before 1929, most physicists supported one of two theories of the universe.

    (D)  All objects in space are receding from each other because of the expansion of the universe.

    (E)  Modern physics would not have progressed without Hubble's discovery of the expanding universe.

155. Which of the following is not mentioned in the passage regarding Hubble's experiment in which he deduced Hubble's Law?

    (A)  It used years of data on Cepheid variable stars.

    (B)  Hubble accumulated data using the Mount Wilson Observatory and help from a fellow astronomer.

    (C)  Hubble found that all the observed stars appeared to be moving away from Earth.

    (D)  Hubble deduced the distance to Cepheid variable stars based on the rate at which they blinked and flickered.

    (E)  Hubble deduced the velocity of Earth to find the stars' absolute velocities.

---

Consider each of the answer choices separately and indicate <u>all</u> that apply.

---

156. Which of the following can be properly inferred from the passage?

    ☐  The steady-state universe theory does not allow for an expanding universe.

    ☐  The closer any two points in the universe are, the less expansion affects them, and the slower they appear to be moving apart.

    ☐  After Hubble's discovery of the expanding universe, the Big Bang was the only cosmological theory that could be valid.

Questions 157–159 are based on the following reading passage.

Homer's *The Odyssey* is an epic poem that put a popular oral myth into writing for the first time. *The Histories* is an attempt by its author Herodotus to provide an unbiased account of historical conflicts in the Hellenistic world. These two works share two important motifs: the interference of the gods in the events of the mortal world, and the concept of a
5  predetermined and unavoidable destiny. One might assume that these two themes are one and the same—a predetermined fate set forth by the gods. However, Homer's and Herodotus's gods are presented as acting in a political fashion—each one acting within certain boundaries to accomplish his or her own agenda. As such, the wills of the gods do not coincide to allow for the formulation of a cohesive "master plan." Instead of destiny created by the gods, Homer
10  and Herodotus present fate as something beyond the gods—a driving force under which the actions of gods and mortals lead to the realization of destiny. In *The Odyssey* and *The Histories*, the idea of gods with limited power leads to a conception of fate wherein the gods act not as the creators of destiny, but as agents of its fulfillment.

157. Which of the following, if true, would most strongly support the assumption rejected by the argument of the passage?

    (A) The gods pursue their agendas by conferring with other gods to ensure that their agendas serve a common goal.

    (B) The agendas of gods and mortals frequently coincide with the demands of fate.

    (C) Homer and Herodotus disagree strongly about the motives and agendas of the gods, as well as about the nature and severity of their conflicts.

    (D) Destiny would be fulfilled regardless of what activities gods and mortals engaged in.

    (E) In both Homer and Herodotus, gods and mortals frequently examine their motives and goals and are capable of making their own decisions about what to do.

158. The author most likely uses the term "unbiased" (line 2) to convey which of the following ideas?

    (A) The historical conflicts are presented in a way that precludes religious explanation.

    (B) The historical conflicts are presented in a way that does not favor any particular party to the conflicts.

    (C) The subjects of the histories are not restricted to any particular ethnic, social, religious, or geographical group.

    (D) The historical conflicts are explained entirely by reference to the actions of the people and states involved in them.

    (E) The histories are written in such a way as to challenge the sensibilities of their readers.

Consider each of the answer choices separately and indicate all that apply.

159. Which of the following can be inferred about the gods in *The Odyssey* and *The Histories*?

☐ There are limits to what the gods can accomplish.

☐ The gods, like human beings, pursue their own interests.

☐ The gods do not control the final outcomes of their actions.

**Questions 160–162 are based on the following reading passage.**

The goal of a sunscreen chemical is simple—to prevent harmful UVB (and in some cases UVA) radiation from penetrating the skin. There are two main ways in which this goal can be accomplished—by reflecting (physically blocking) ultraviolet light or by absorbing UV light. Sunscreen chemicals are therefore put into two groups based on which method they employ;
5    they are classified as either *physical blockers* or *chemical absorbers*. Physical blockers, the most common of which is titanium dioxide, scatter all radiation in the UVB and UVA range. Titanium dioxide reflects light waves in the 290–770 nm range. However, the vast majority of commercial sunscreens are chemical absorbers.

Chemical absorbing sunscreens work on the principle of photo-excitation of electrons.
10   They absorb photons of light of specific wavelengths and use the energy to promote electrons between energy levels. When the electrons later return to the ground energy state, they emit light at longer wavelengths (lower energies). Chemical species that exhibit this behavior are called chromophores. The specific wavelength absorbed by a given chromophore is determined by the discrete quantal amounts of energy that are required to excite electrons
15   between the energy levels or its molecules. Since the primary objective of an absorbing sunscreen is to absorb UVB light (290–320 nm), the best sunscreens are those that absorb most heavily in this range. The chromophores that most readily fit this requirement are those with conjugated pi-bonding systems.

160. Which of the following best summarizes the distinction between physical blockers and chemical absorbers?

(A) Physical blockers darken their target light waves while chemical absorbers lighten them.

(B) Physical blockers convert their target light waves into radiation while chemical absorbers convert them into a different kind of radiation.

(C) Physical blockers disperse their target light waves while chemical absorbers convert them into light with a longer wavelength.

(D) Physical blockers scatter their target light waves while chemical absorbers convert them into radiation.

(E) Physical blockers prevent light waves from reaching the skin while chemical absorbers absorb them into the skin.

161. Based on the passage, which of the following can be inferred about the chromophores referred to in the final sentence of the passage?

    (A)  If exposed to light with wavelengths of approximately 300 nm, they will scatter the radiation.

    (B)  If exposed to light with wavelengths in the 290–320 nm range, they will lower the energy level of some of their constituent electrons.

    (C)  If exposed to light waves in the 290–770 nm range, they will absorb the photons and emit them as light of longer wavelengths.

    (D)  If exposed to light with wavelengths of approximately 300 nm, some electrons in their component molecules will switch to higher energy levels.

    (E)  If exposed to light waves in the 290–320 nm range, they will promote the discrete quantal amounts of energy that are required to excite electrons between energy levels.

162. Select the sentence in the second paragraph that explains the physical feature on the basis of which one could select a chromophore for a sunscreen that would protect against UVA radiation.

---

**Questions 163–165 are based on the following reading passage.**

---

The story of *Sir Gawain and the Green Knight* has its foundation in Arthurian legend as formulated and passed down by the pagan oral tradition. In its written form, however, the tale bears the marks of Christian influence—it contains numerous scriptural and doctrinal references to Christianity. Since the author of *Sir Gawain and the Green Knight* is unknown,
5   it is difficult to determine with any certainty the extent to which he was responsible for the incorporation of Christianity into the legend. For all we know, the story may have been "Christianized" in its oral form long before the poet set it into writing. The poet himself supports this possibility by writing in the opening lines that he will tell "anew" the tale "as I heard it in hall." If this is the case (and even if it is not), it is distinctly possible that the heroes of
10   the Arthurian tradition represent in the written form a pagan interpretation of Christian ideals, rather than an externally imposed Christianization of pagan codes of behavior.

While it could certainly be argued that the poet portrays Sir Gawain as a good Christian hero in an attempt to infuse the story with Christian values, the critical tone of the narrative seems to suggest a different conclusion—that by critically editorializing the paganized form of
15   Christianity embodied by Sir Gawain, the poet is trying to correct what he sees to be the flaws of that form. From the perspective of this conclusion it is clear that the poet only "Christianizes" the traditional legend to the extent that he *criticizes* the pagan interpretation of Christianity that is inherent in the behavior of its heroes.

Those who would argue that the poet intends to portray Sir Gawain as the perfect
20   Christian hero would point to the descriptions of his chivalric qualities. The poet does indeed describe Gawain's Christian virtues generously; he even makes a special aside early in the second fit to describe the significance of the pentangle embossed on Gawain's shield, and to explain "why the pentangle is proper to that peerless prince." The author then delves into a lengthy enumeration of Gawain's Christian virtues. What is more, the fact that he uses the
25   pentangle—a pagan symbol—to do so would seem to suggest that the author does indeed intend to add a Christian interpretation to the pagan legend he is retelling. Viewed in its larger context, however, this passage takes on a different significance. In further examination of the poet's descriptions of Sir Gawain, it becomes apparent that the knight's seemingly perfect Christian behavior is superficial. A contrast can be observed between his "Christian"
30   words and actions and his decidedly un-Christian motives. One theory is that, by emphasizing this contrast, the poet intends to denounce the pagan "misunderstanding" of the Christian message.

Consider each of the answer choices separately and indicate all that apply.

163. Which of the following can be inferred about the pagan and Christian origins of *Sir Gawain and the Green Knight*?

  ☐   As an orally-handed-down tale, it was pagan, but as a written tale, it was Christian.

  ☐   Sir Gawain was a knight in King Arthur's court.

  ☐   *Sir Gawain and the Green Knight* contains both Christian and pagan elements, although it is not clear that either perspective is dominant.

164. Which of the following can be inferred from the author's interpretation of the Christian aspects of the poem, presented in the third paragraph?

  (A)   Pagans and Christians differ in their interpretations of the Christian symbolism in the story.

  (B)   A pagan cannot have motives that are acceptable from a Christian perspective.

  (C)   A pagan story cannot be used to convey a Christian attitude.

  (D)   Christianity was absent in Arthurian stories before such stories were written down.

  (E)   Being a good Christian involves having both the right actions and the right motives.

165. Which of the following, if true, would most undermine the "theory" mentioned in the final sentence of the passage?

  (A)   Sir Gawain is portrayed as disingenuous in his exercise of "Christian virtues."

  (B)   Another character in the story is also associated with pagan symbols and is praised straightforwardly for her Christian virtues.

  (C)   Sir Gawain, in the story, prays to God to help him in battle.

  (D)   Another character in the story is associated with pagan symbols but is portrayed as having no Christian virtues whatsoever.

  (E)   A group of people in the story are portrayed as "barbarians" who are neither pagan nor Christian.

**MANHATTAN**
PREP

<hr>

**Questions 166–167 are based on the following reading passage.**

Various tales in Herodotus's *The Histories* display a circular means of the realization of fate. In one story involving the birth of Cyrus and his rise to power in Asia, Herodotus tells us that the Median king Astyages was having disturbing dreams about his daughter Mandane. We are told that his first dream, in which Mandane's urine flooded all of Asia, was interpreted
5  ominously by the Magi. As a consequence, when the time came to marry Mandane off, Astyages made what turned out to be a fatal mistake. While there were plenty of wealthy and powerful Medes eligible for marriage, "his fear of the dream made him refuse to marry her to any of them; instead, he gave her to a Persian called Cambyses, whom he found to be of noble lineage and peaceful behavior, although he regarded him as the social inferior by far of a Mede
10  of the middle rank." Essentially, Astyages altered what would be a normal treatment of the marriage in order to marry his daughter to someone less threatening. This attempt to avoid the prophesy of the first dream backfired however, and when Mandane became pregnant, Astyages had another foreboding dream. This second dream was interpreted to mean that Mandane's son would rule in Astyages's place. Herodotus tells us that "[the prophecy of the
15  second dream] was what Astyages was guarding against" when he again took action, telling his advisor Harpagus to kill the baby. This plan backfired as well since Harpagus refused to kill the baby, leading to a complicated chain of events whereby the child—later to be named Cyrus—survived and returned to conquer his grandfather's kingdom. In this story, Astyages's downfall is depicted as resulting directly from two major mistakes—marrying Mandane to
20  Cambyses and telling Harpagus to kill their offspring. These mistakes in turn are shown to be motivated by fear of the prophesies of his downfall. Had not some divine force planted the dreams in his head, he would not have taken the steps necessary to fulfill those prophesies. Through this circular path, destiny is unavoidably realized.

<hr>

Consider each of the answer choices separately and indicate <u>all</u> that apply.

166. Which of the following can be inferred from the passage about Astyages's view of the Median socio-political structure?

    ☐  As a result of his first dream, Astyages believed the threat his daughter posed to him could be through her husband.

    ☐  Astyages believed that it is always best to observe the recommendations of the Magi.

    ☐  Astyages believed that a Persian noble was less of a threat to his position than a Median noble.

167. Which of the following, if true, would most strongly undermine the claim that Astyages's downfall proceeded from two major mistakes?

    (A)  Mandane's son would have conquered his grandfather's kingdom regardless of who his father was.

    (B)  Astyages's first dream was in fact a warning against allowing his daughter to marry.

    (C)  Harpagus would not have killed the baby regardless of whether he knew the prophecy.

    (D)  Mandane's husband would have deposed Astyages if he had known why his son was killed.

    (E)  Astyages's dreams were better interpreted as advising him not to do anything out of the ordinary.

---

**Questions 168–170 are based on the following reading passage.**

---

Nineteenth century painter Albert Bierstadt's view of his artistic skill as a vehicle for self-promotion was evident in his choices of style and subject matter. From the debut of his career with the exhibition of *Lake Lucerne* (1856), he developed a fixed style that was most easily recognizable for its size—the largest of the 636 paintings on display at the exhibition, it
5  was over three meters wide. This, coupled with the artist's ability to represent the optimistic feeling in America during the westward expansion, is what led to Bierstadt's explosive growth in popularity during the 1860s. Bierstadt deliberately appealed to those rich patrons—railroad tycoons and financiers—whose nearest substitute to making the arduous journey out West was to purchase a hyperbolized replica of a Western vista.
10       But trends following the Civil War produced a drastic shift away from the adventurous optimism of the pre-war era and toward a more subdued appreciation for the details of American life. In this new social context, the paintings now seemed too decadent, too gaudy, for the new philosophy taking root in the country following the horrors of war. As one commentator in 1866 put it, Bierstadt's work "may impose upon the senses, but does not affect
15  the heart." In a sense, then, that same American pride upon which Bierstadt had capitalized to advance his success was now, in its fickleness, the source of his downfall.

168. According to the passage, the new philosophy taking root in America after the Civil War would be best described as

    (A)  justifiable pessimism
    (B)  somber realism
    (C)  restrained minimalism
    (D)  prideful idealism
    (E)  stubborn dogmatism

**MANHATTAN**
PREP

169. The passage quotes the commentator (lines 14–15) primarily in order to

    (A)  challenge a prevailing thesis

    (B)  point out an erroneous assertion

    (C)  provide expert testimony

    (D)  highlight a controversy

    (E)  offer evidence supporting a claim

170. All of the following are mentioned as contributors to Bierstadt's success EXCEPT

    (A)  the dimensions of his paintings

    (B)  his ability to convey auspicious feelings

    (C)  subdued appreciation for the details of American life

    (D)  catering to the preferences of the wealthy

    (E)  portrayals of exaggerated landscapes

# Reading Comprehension Answers

1. **(C).** The passage presents positive and negative views on the "forecast for American entrepreneurship." The author is careful to present his or her arguments fairly and with some reservations (e.g., "it is not clear that," "suggests that," "may seem"). Ultimately, the view is balanced, or "nuanced," so choice (C) is correct. Regarding choice (A), the author does not "propose changes." Regarding (B), the author never argues that any group of college students should (or should not) form their own companies. If anything, the author offers both sides of the issue, leaving it up to individuals to decide. Regarding (D), the author offers one fact about the varying rates at which businesses of two types (low value and high value) are founded. However, the author never evaluates the viability (or likelihood of success) of these types. As for (E), the analogy drawn in the last two sentences is not the main point of the passage; it is a final observation, one that sheds light on the issue, but this analogy is not the primary purpose for which the passage was written.

2. **(B).** The question asks what is true "according to the passage." There should be direct proof for the correct answer in the passage text. Specifically: "College graduates, unable to find traditional jobs, instead opt to start their own businesses," (lines 4–5). Correct choice (B) matches the idea that college graduates are "unable to find traditional jobs." Regarding (A), college graduates who start their own businesses may indeed be hampered by a lack of access to outside investment, but this is not offered as the reason that they start such businesses. Be careful of answer choices that restate truths from the passage but do not answer the specific question posed! As for (C), it may be true that low-value companies have become more prevalent, but again, this does not answer the specific question. Regarding (D), the choice between renting and buying property is offered only as an analogy, not as a literal choice for college graduates (let alone as the reason for their entrepreneurial decisions). Regarding choice (E), the passage says nothing about how forecasts of the unemployment rate are likely to evolve.

3. **(E).** This question asks what "can be inferred" about the number of American high-value businesses; that is, what else must be true based upon the evidence given in the passage? The answer choices all have to do with how this number has changed (or may have changed) during the course of the recent recession. In particular, when you encounter mathematical language, take extra care to make the argument airtight mathematically. Search for the key phrase "high-value businesses": the passage states that "the proportion of high-value businesses founded each year has declined." Watch out! A proportion is not the same as a number. The proportion has fallen, but the overall number of new business starts has been higher over recent years. If the overall number is up, but the proportion is down, it is unknown whether the absolute number of high-value businesses is up or down; this is exactly what choice (E) indicates.

4. **(C).** The passage states that some women went to war to nurse others or to provide supplies and that "such women," including many old women, died in battle. Therefore, it can be inferred that "some of those who worked as nurses or in providing supplies died in battle," which makes choice (C) correct. Regarding choice (A), the passage does not address how people lamented the deaths of anyone who died in battle. The passage also does not address the courageousness of younger women, choice (B), or the status of men in Asante culture, choices (D) and (E).

5. **(E).** The first paragraph introduces bacterial "super-bugs" with some alarm. The second paragraph increases the alarm, noting that "many scientists argue that the human race has more to fear from viruses." This paragraph describes how viruses hijack the cell in order to illustrate how tough viruses are to treat. The last paragraph continues the comparison and puts a stake in the ground: "bacteria lack the potential for cataclysm that viruses have." The point is further illustrated by the "near-miss" of the HIV pandemic. As for choice (A), it is unknown how bacteria

infect the body. Regarding (B), the hijacking process is certainly described, but to make a larger point: why it's hard to eradicate viruses in comparison with bacteria. As for (C), after reading this passage, you may want to call up the CDC and donate money, but the passage itself only raises a warning, if even that—it is not a call to action. Regarding choice (D), the last paragraph does highlight the human race's good fortune, but this is not the larger point of the whole passage. Choice (E) is correct—the passage compares the two threats (bacteria and viruses) and judges viruses to be far more important (after all, viruses have the "potential for cataclysm").

6. **(B).** Focus on the keywords "infections by bacteria" (which can be rearranged to "bacterial infections"). What does the text say about bacterial infections? The second paragraph gives a direct clue: "viral infections cannot be treated ex post facto in the same way that bacterial infections can." In other words, bacterial infections can be treated "ex post facto" (which means "after the fact"). Choice (B) matches this idea. Regarding (A), the second paragraph states that bacteria themselves "reproduce asexually through binary fission," but that isn't necessarily true about *infections* by bacteria. Regarding (C), the first paragraph notes that resistance "cocktails" such as NDM-1 actually make bacteria "nearly impregnable." As a result, an infection by bacteria that have this cocktail would be less vulnerable, not more vulnerable. Choices (D) and (E) are true about viral infections, but not bacterial infections.

7. **(A).** This Specific Detail question asks what is true about "intracellular obligate parasites" (or IOPs, to give them a temporary abbreviation). The second paragraph states: "Whereas bacteria reproduce asexually through binary fission, viruses lack the necessary structures for reproduction, and so are known as 'intracellular obligate parasites.'" The word "so" toward the end indicates that viruses are called IOPs because they "lack the necessary structures for reproduction." Choice (A) captures this idea.

8. **(B).** Articulate the main idea before reading the choices. Is the passage really about supernovae, or is it about Galileo, the philosophers, and the ideas being discussed? The fact that the "twist" occurs in the second paragraph (the passage is not talking just about science—now it's talking about history and philosophy) supports the position that the second paragraph is more central to the main idea and that the first paragraph is background information. Choice (A) is wrong because it does not mention the main content of the second paragraph, the ideas and assumptions that became controversial. It is also too broad—giving a history of supernovae would take a lot more than two paragraphs. Choice (B) is correct—the passage does describe a "shift in thought" (from the unchangeable "heavens" to a more scientific view), and this shift was prompted by a "natural event" (the supernova). Choice (C) is attractive but does not describe the main idea. While Galileo and the philosophers certainly had different views about the bright light they saw in the sky, it's not clear that philosophers had "views about supernovae" in general. Choice (D) can be stricken due to "corroborate" (to prove true or support with evidence). The passage is describing, not making an argument. Finally, choice (E) is too broad. One could spend an entire career discussing how science and philosophy interrelate. This passage covers a much more narrow topic.

9. **1st only.** The first sentence of the second paragraph proves the first statement: "In 1604 in Padua, Italy, a supernova became visible, appearing as a star so bright that it was visible in daylight for more than a year." Since this supernova was visible for more than a year, it is possible for supernovae to "take more than a year to fade from view." (Note that if the first statement said "Supernovae *always* take more than a year to fade from view," it would be wrong.) The second statement cannot be proven. Just because a supernova in 1604 caused a stir does not mean no one else had ever seen one before. The third statement also cannot be proven. Galileo disagreed with the philosophers, but those particular philosophers may never have changed their minds.

10. **(C).** As a result of the supernova in 1604, Galileo gave popular lectures in which he "sought to explain the origin of the 'star'" and which "undermined the views" of some philosophers. Choice (A) mixed up some wording from the first paragraph to set a trap; the earth was not made after the supernova of 1604. Choice (B) is too extreme—Galileo "sought to explain" the origin of the supernova, but it is unclear whether he succeeded. Choice (C) is true—the lectures were "widely attended by the public." (A very picky person might point out that just because people go to a lecture doesn't mean they are interested, but all of the other answers are definitely wrong, so that confirms that this is a reasonable—that is, very tiny—inferential leap.) Choice (D) is attractive, but is a trap answer. Galileo, in his lectures, "undermined" (weakened) the views of the philosophers. But the passage doesn't say what the philosophers' responses were or whether the philosophers were opposed to the lectures themselves (a person could be opposed to the ideas in a lecture but still think the lecturer should be allowed to lecture). Choice (E) is also attractive because the modern reader knows this to be true in real life. However, the question does not ask, "What really happened?" It asks: "The author mentions which of the following as a result of the supernova of 1604?" The author does not mention that the philosophers were "proved wrong." Their views were "undermined," which is much less extreme.

11. **1st and 3rd only.** Kincaid's critics point out that Britain's government is not as corrupt as Antigua's. Kincaid makes a witty rejoinder, but does not deny that the British government is less corrupt than Antigua's. This, coupled with her stated belief that Britain is responsible for corruption in Antigua, justifies the first and third statements. As for the second statement, no governments of the "former colonial empire" are discussed in the passage except Antigua's.

12. **(B).** In main idea questions, you can often eliminate one or more answers just based on the first word or phrase in the answer: *relate, discuss, give a history, make a case, emphasize.* Does the passage "make a case"? It doesn't—like almost all GRE passages, it is merely reporting facts and/or the opinions of others, so (D) is wrong. "Emphasize" in choice (E) is also a bit strange—usually, the purpose of a passage is something a little bigger than just "emphasizing" something. The first paragraph gives background information about *Don Giovanni*, while the second paragraph gives the "twist"—even though almost the whole world loved *Don Giovanni*, people in Mozart's own hometown were less enthusiastic about it. Choice (B) matches this—the passages discusses how the opera *Don Giovanni* was met by "diverging" (differing) opinions, specifically those of Viennese audiences versus those of everyone else.

13. **(A).** The second paragraph states that "[t]he opera mixed traditions of moralism with those of comedy—a practice heretofore unknown among the composer's works—resulting in a production that was not well-liked by conservative Viennese audiences." The language "a practice heretofore unknown" indicates that Mozart had not done this before. Correct answer (A) is a good match—a "lackluster reception" means that those who "received" something (the audience) were unimpressed. Note that the GRE is trying to hide the correct answer a little bit by saying "a particular group of people" for "Viennese audiences." Also note that (D) and (E) are incorrect because the author does not "argue" or "undermine" at any point. Talking about moralism and comedy doesn't address the plot, as mentioned in choice (B), and the passage does not mention what is common in contemporary (modern) opera, so choice (C) is out of scope.

14. **(E).** According to the passage, "conservative" Viennese audiences did not like *Don Giovanni*'s "heretofore unknown" mixing of moralism and comedy. It can be inferred that Viennese audiences disliked the opera's adventuresome genre-blending and preferred works that kept to "stylistic conventions," as noted in choice (E). Choices (A) and (B) contain extreme language ("purely," "unequivocally"). Choices (C) and (D) go too far. The passage offers no indication that audiences were confused or offended, merely that they didn't like or had mixed feelings about a work of art.

**MANHATTAN**
PREP

15. **2nd and 3rd only.** Redlining never "ceased"; rather, as noted in the second paragraph, it "has sometimes continued in less explicit ways." The second paragraph also states that "even today … auto insurance companies offer different rates based on zip code." Such a practice, then, may be a form of redlining. In addition, the first paragraph notes that "with no access to mortgages, residents within the red line suffered low property values." Thus, access to mortgages is related to higher property values.

16. **(D).** The third paragraph states that "reverse redlining … occurs when predatory businesses specifically target minority or low income consumers for the purpose of charging them more than would typically be charged for a particular service." Choices (A) and (B) describe *regular* redlining, the practice of denying service or constraining access to something like jobs. Redlining is about businesses, not police, so (C) is out. Choice (E) does mention targeting minority consumers, but does not give an example of offering inferior products or overcharging. Choice (D) is a good example of what is described in the third paragraph.

17. **(E).** The first paragraph states that "[w]ith no access to mortgages, residents within the red line suffered low property values and landlord abandonment; buildings abandoned by landlords were then more likely to become centers of drug dealing and other crime, thus further lowering property values." The lack of access to mortgages is due to redlining. Thus, redlining causes landlord abandonment and the resultant effects—(E) is a perfect match. Note that (A) mentions "subprime mortgages" and "defaults," which are never mentioned in the passage. Choice (B) incorrectly cites reverse redlining rather than redlining. Choice (C) gets the relationship between redlining and landlord abandonment backwards. In Choice (D), "constrained access to health care, jobs, insurance, and more" is not just a potential consequence of reverse redlining; these negatives are mentioned in context with redlining.

18. **1st and 3rd only.** "Germophobic" Western society avoids "premastication," which provides "beneficial bacteria," so the first statement is true. The word "only" eliminates the second statement—watch out for extreme language! If just one person outside of the developing world premasticates food for a baby, this statement is false, so it cannot be inferred. Finally, since "babies have received disease-fighting antibodies and digestive bacteria from the mother's saliva," saliva has at least one benefit (antibodies) aside from digestive bacteria.

19. **(B).** The author discusses Bois and Damisch's metaphor ("a dynamic game"), calls it misleading, and proposes an expansion beyond the competitive aspect. This matches choice (B). Choice (A) is incorrect, as the author does not claim that the two artists were the best. Choice (C) only addresses the details and evidence presented in the passage but not the main point. Choices (D) and (E) are both distortions because the passage does not rank the painters, and these issues are again not the point.

20. **(D).** This question type asks for a combination of the point, tone, and, perhaps, structure. The author expresses the point at the end of the first paragraph by suggesting that the rivalry between Picasso and Matisse was more of a dialogue, or "exchange." This would match choice (D), that "rivalries can be reciprocally nourishing." Choice (A) is an incorrect comparison because the passage rejects the idea that such rivalries are mere competitions. Choice (B) distorts a detail by adding an opinion not stated in the passage. The author writes about the artists employing multiple styles, but never implies they are masters *because* they employ multiple styles. Choice (C) is a distortion based on a misreading of the "conversation" metaphor. Choice (E) is incorrect, as the word "generally" is a claim that the author does not make; the passage concerns one particular rivalry.

21. **(C).** The last paragraph states that Matisse used the same palette in his work but omitted the green, so Picasso's *Woman with Yellow Hair* had a larger color palette, as noted in choice (C). Choices (A), (D), and (E) are incorrect because they cite comments about *Large Nude in a Red Armchair*, not *Woman with Yellow Hair*. Choice (B) is backwards—the passage states that Matisse's response, as opposed to Picasso's work, did not rigidly tie color to form.

22. **(B).** The author's point is that the rivalry was more of a dialogue than a competition, so "a radio broadcast" as offered in choice (B) would further support this thesis. Choices (A) and (E) are not correct because those choices do not say anything about the nature of the rivalry. Choice (C) is wrong because the author's point is that their relationship was more than a competition. Choice (D) misconstrues the metaphor that the author rejects.

23. **(C).** The last paragraph devotes itself to highlighting the problematic implicit messages of timelines. Choice (A) is a distortion; the author does not claim dates are unimportant but that historical study should go beyond mere dates. Choices (B) and (E) are backwards, as these are two of the implicit messages that the author rejects. Choice (D), while quite likely in the real world, does not have to follow from the passage—the author implies that there is more to history than "wars and minor battles, punctuated by the occasional presidential election and technological innovation" but does not specify what that is.

24. **(D).** The author argues that timelines are simplistic and misleading; the author is "wary and critical" of the devices, choice (D). The words "condescending and impatient" in answer choice (A) would never describe a GRE author. Regarding choice (B), the author is not "bemused," or amused, at all. Nor is the author "negative or complacent," as stated in choice (E).

25. **(D).** The last paragraph discusses the negative implicit—or subliminal—issues with timelines, so (D) is the correct answer to this Except question. Since the author indicates that an implicit flaw is showing "only" 64 events, it must follow that there are more, so (A) is incorrect. In the second paragraph, the author worries that the prominence of the dates will draw too much attention, so eliminate (B). In the first paragraph, the author says, "[d]espite their usefulness in allowing students to gain a cursory knowledge … " In other words, timelines have some positive uses; cross off (C). As for (E), the third criticism is that the events appear to have occurred completely independently of one another; the author believes, then, that showing how some events affected or influenced others would be beneficial.

26. **(B).** In the last paragraph, a listed implicit flaw is that the events are presented as independent—without context, which matches choice (B). The passage mentions the prominent placement of timelines, choice (A), and use of photos, choice (E), but does not suggest that these are problems. Choice (C) is false, as the passage states that these timelines had beginnings and ends. Regarding (D), the author does not challenge the factual accuracy of timelines.

27. **(C).** "Myopic" means nearsighted, and the author employs it to describe the inability of some curricula to show the big picture. Similarly, "purblind," choice (C), means "partially blind or deficient in understanding." Choices (A), (B), and (D) are not justified by evidence from the passage. Ignorance and bigotry are not mentioned as problems. "Astigmatic" indicates visual distortion, but the passage spoke of missing elements. "Mordant," meaning caustic or corrosive, has no connection to the passage.

28. **(A).** The second paragraph further describes "the blooming of the public sphere," one of the two factors named in the first paragraph. It details how literacy and printing allowed gossip to circulate more widely, describing "the mechanisms by which disdain … grew," choice (A). Choice (B) is incorrect because the passage does not contrast the

**MANHATTAN**
PREP

factors (the second paragraph does not even mention the Diamond Necklace Affair). Choice (C) is out of scope and irrelevant as the passage is about Marie Antoinette's unpopularity, not the court or corruption. Choice (D) is incorrect; the last paragraph discusses the results. Choice (E), while arguably the main point of the passage, goes beyond that of the second paragraph, which does not discuss consequences.

29. **(C).** The fourth paragraph mentions "countless aristocrats who sued to the king on Rohan's behalf," so it must be true that a significant proportion was more loyal to the accused, which matches (C). Nothing in the passage refers to jealousy and nothing imputes that the queen's wealth was the cause of the aristocrats' dislike, so (A) can be eliminated. Choice (B) does not have to follow; the passage only says pamphlets were popular with the general public. Similarly, the passage does not provide literacy rates so (D) is out. The Revolution is not mentioned, so choice (E) is out of scope.

30. **(D).** This Detail question concerns the second paragraph, which cites a reduction in royal censorship as a cause. Choice (D) is therefore correct. Choice (A) is out of scope; the education of women is never mentioned. Choice (B) is a distortion; the passage says publications, not the literacy rate, tripled. Choice (C) is incorrect, as the passage does not discuss the number of scandals over time. Choice (E) is not mentioned in the passage.

31. **2nd and 3rd only.** The first statement can't be proven—the passage does not indicate who the clever forger was. The second statement is correct—the third paragraph identifies Rohan as a "social climber." In the fourth paragraph, the author states that "10,000 people came to the doors of the Bastille demanding Rohan's release," which supports the third statement.

32. **1st only.** The point of the final paragraph is that the queen's unpopularity caused significant problems for the monarchy. The passage does not say whether the queen met Rohan; she wouldn't have to meet someone personally to order that he be punished. The third statement is backwards: the queen's power must have had limits since Rohan was released despite her prosecution.

33. **(C).** This is essentially a vocabulary question. "Disinterested" does not mean uninterested—it means unbiased. GRE authors are never described as "arrogant" or "supercilious," as these words are too negative (and inappropriate), so eliminate (A). It is also very unlikely that "prim" and "meretricious" or "sober" and "lascivious" would be correct for the same reason, so eliminate (B) and (D). As for (E), the author is "analytical," but no phrases or adjectives in the passage justify "enthusiastic."

34. **(C).** After the theory is described, the remainder of the passage cites studies and opinions that disagree in part or in whole, making (C) the correct choice. Choice (A) is incorrect because no additional support is provided. Choice (B) is incorrect, because the criticisms are not a "screed," which is a long diatribe. Choice (D) is incorrect because it is not the author's credentials that are questioned. Choice (E) is wrong—there is no ridicule. Note that (B), (D), and (E) all express inappropriate attitudes for a GRE author. While authors can certainly argue for or against something, or express some enthusiasm or support, GRE authors do not rant and rave, and only very, very rarely "ridicule" or question the integrity of those with whom they disagree.

35. **(E).** The Lowell Girls are mentioned to show that historically "free labor has hardly been free at all." This supports choice (E). Choice (A) is incorrect—that is the subject of the fourth paragraph, but does not concern the Lowell Girls. Choice (B) is incorrect—that is the subject of the third paragraph, but does not concern the Lowell

Girls. The answer must come from the part of the passage referenced. Choice (C) is backwards—this argument is put forth by D'Emilio's critics. Choice (D) is a distortion; the reference is to show how historically normal this situation was, not to contrast two supposedly parallel groups of unempowered workers.

36. **(C).** The answer has to be something that *must* follow from the discussion of Davis in the last paragraph, not something that Davis could or likely would agree with. Choice (C) is correct because Davis argues that women "were the losers in a double-sense ... leaving many women largely bereft of significant economic roles." If being "bereft" of an economic role makes one a "loser," it is not going too far (in fact, it is less extreme) to say that "[p]eople without economic roles are disadvantaged." Choice (A) is wrong as it is an opinion of D'Emilio's mentioned in the first paragraph. Choice (B) is wrong as it is an opinion of Enloe's mentioned in the second paragraph. Choice (D) is incorrect because, in the last sentence of the passage, Davis states that the "entire economy" has left the household. Finally, choice (E) is out of scope as nothing is said about pay for domestic work.

37. **(C).** A "best title" question asks for the main point. The point of this passage is to highlight trenchant criticisms of D'Emilio's work—the lack of any rebuttal of these points indicates that the author sympathizes with them. This supports choice (C). Choices (A), (D), and (E) are incorrect because they ignore that the passage concerns scholarly opinions rather than the history itself. Choice (B) is incorrect, as no reconciliation is attempted. Additionally, (E) is closer to D'Emilio's view than the author's.

38. **(D).** "Unique," choice (D), is a secondary meaning of "peculiar." The author uses it in the context of Matisse learning something that Picasso had done. Of the wrong answers, (B) and (E) at best come from prohibited outside knowledge, whereas (A) and (C) are the opposite of the intended meaning—anything "strange" or "unknown" to Picasso would be something he doesn't do; "peculiar to Picasso" means something that he's known for doing.

39. **(A).** The author describes both the work (*The Ochre Head*) and the inspiration for that work (*Still Life with Ancient Head*), which matches choice (A). Choice (B) is a distortion as the passage does not rate the painters. Choice (C) is a distortion as the passage describes a painting but not how the artist developed his style. Choice (D) is incorrect as the passage indicates that this was a new direction rather than a representative work. Choice (E) is out of scope because the passage only discusses two painters, not the art world.

40. **(C).** While the author clearly appreciates the work, its place in the hierarchy of all of Matisse's works is not discussed, so (C) is the correct answer to this Except question. The four wrong answers can all be found in the passage. For choice (A), the passage states that "colors ... refuse to be constrained by definite lines of form." For choice (B), the end of the passage states that the painting's composition references a Picasso work. For choice (D), the passage says the technique is not employed with the "free reign" used in *Minotaur*; that is, *The Ochre Head* is more constrained in its use of the technique. For choice (E), the passage says a vase of flowers and a bench are depicted.

41. **(C).** To answer a question of this type, find the other four choices in the text. In the third paragraph, (A) is mentioned verbatim. Choice (B) is justified by "hearing speakers," and (D) by "write autobiographical essays." Choice (E) is mentioned explicitly. Therefore, (C) is the correct answer to this Except question.

42. **(D).** The passage, after establishing problems with textbooks, proposes film as a vehicle for teaching history. Since film is mentioned as a current alternative, it is being used now to teach history, but the author would like to expand this use. "Didactic" means "intended to instruct," so films used to teach history would certainly qualify as a "didactic

**MANHATTAN**
PREP

tool." Thus, (D) is correct. Choice (A) is out of scope and ignores the educational thrust. Choices (B) and (C) are out of scope and do not include the bulk of the passage, which propose film as a learning tool. Choice (E) is too negative—a GRE author would not "denigrate"—and "philosophy" is an inappropriate word for the passage (using textbooks is hardly a "philosophy" so much as just a common practice).

43. **(B).** The answer to Detail questions must be found in the text. The second paragraph quotes Wong to assert that committees wrongly value facts over perspectives, thus justifying "misplaced priorities," which matches (B). Leaving aside their merits, (A), (C), and (E) are not mentioned in the passage and outside knowledge is not allowed. Choice (D) is the opposite of the correct answer.

44. **(B).** The final paragraph begins by mentioning the main criticism of this proposal but then argues that this supposed flaw is in fact a virtue and a golden opportunity. Thus, choice (B) is correct. Choices (A) and (D) ignore the author's rebuttal to the criticism. Choice (C) is problematic as the paragraph is concerned with one particular tool—film. Choice (E) ignores both the criticism and rebuttal and merely mentions an out-of-context detail.

45. **(A).** In the last paragraph, the passage states that the main critique of the use of films to teach history is their "rampant inaccuracies and biases." Then, the author goes on to argue that this can be a positive: "these seeming flaws are actually part of the reason why film is an ideal teaching tool," because teachers can lead discussions of the film's problems and biases. Thus, the author certainly argues that students can benefit from exposure to inaccurate accounts of history (not that students would *always* benefit, but that students *can* benefit when the inaccurate film is accompanied by critical analysis). The other choices cannot be justified. Choice (B) does not have to follow; the passage only lists music and film as alternatives. Choice (C) is too extreme. Choice (D) is a preference of the state committees, not the students. Choice (E) is backwards—the last paragraph states that students can benefit by such exposure.

46. **3rd only.** The first statement is wrong, because the passage contrasts "appealing, expressive paintings that are often the most popular museum attractions" with "constructivist" art. The second statement is also wrong—the constructivist art, not the expressive paintings, is referred to as "brainy" in the passage. Note that these first two statements may very well be true in real life, but that is not what the question asks. The question asks which statements can be inferred *from the passage*. The third statement is true—contemporary art is called "cold" in one sentence and "brainy" (or "cerebral") in another sentence. The final sentence of the paragraph links this brainy constructivist art to the use of gesture as an expressive tool.

47. **1st, 2nd, and 3rd.** The author describes *Iroquois* as "precarious, yet stable and balanced," which is a good match for the first statement. The second statement matches the final sentence, which states that *Iroquois* "resonates with an energy born not of the physical quality of the sculpture … but rather of the gestural quality of the forms." The third statement is a good match for the sentence, "[a]s one contemplates *Iroquois* … the linear forms became considerably more complex than one might presume." If the forms are more complex than one might think, it follows that some find the forms simpler than they really are.

48. **(E).** Choice (A) is wrong because Rousseau did argue for a social contract, meaning there should be some kind of law. Choice (B) is wrong because Rousseau did not think members of a state should surrender their rights to a single person. Choice (C) is wrong because Rousseau did argue that people could claim property if they needed it, implying the existence of private property in his ideal society. Choice (D) is wrong because Rousseau did not want to dismantle the social contract entirely, but to replace it with his own ideal social contract. Choice (E) is the answer because Rousseau desired a society where "property can be taken … to the degree necessary for the subsistence of those taking it."

49. **(B).** Choice (A) is incorrect because the passage states that "[i]n a state of nature … the rich would have great difficulty protecting the property that they possess." Even if the rich were to lose their property, nothing indicates that this property would end up evenly distributed among everyone. Choice (B) is correct because this is precisely what the sentence cited above says. Choices (C), (D), and (E) are wrong because they point to Rousseau's vision for a perfect society, rather than a pre-law society.

50. "To obtain assent to the contract, the rich focus their rhetoric on a seeming equality of obligation by creating rules that apply equally to all members of society." This sentence from the second paragraph shows the mechanism by which the wealthy are able to convince the poor to agree to a social contract that will allow them to be defrauded. Be careful not to go looking in the passage for specific language mentioned in the question (like "hoarding" or "systematized"). More often than not, that will lead you to the wrong sentence.

51. **(A).** Choice (A) is correct because the passage says that people should only take something if they need it (i.e., for survival). Choice (B) is wrong because it is the exact opposite of what the passage says, in that people should *not* simply enrich themselves with property. Choice (C) is wrong because though a house could be protection, that's not what "subsistence" means. Choice (D) is wrong because it isn't specific enough. Choice (E) does not fit the meaning of the sentence.

52. **3rd only.** The first statement is wrong because, while Baldwin takes issue with the average 1930s Hollywood movie for failing to represent anything other than the dominant culture, that doesn't mean he would find an individual film focused on African American culture "significantly better." Such a film could be bad for other reasons. The second statement is wrong because even though a film that focused only on African American issues could be just as limited as one that failed to focus on such issues, there is a significant difference: one would be reinforcing the dominant culture, while the other would be presenting an alternative culture. Baldwin would thus be unlikely to find them equally problematic. The third statement is correct because the predominant culture in the 1930s was white, so the film in question would be less likely to reinforce that culture, given that it would feature only African American issues and actors.

53. **(D).** Choice (A) is wrong because the quotation has to do with children and their ability to relate to a given work of art, rather than the culture of power. Choice (B) is wrong because the quote does not discuss white culture specifically. Choice (C) is wrong because the passage never says that America was hungry for a writer like Baldwin. Choice (D) is correct because even though the quote doesn't explicitly mention black children, the point is that children in general can't relate to a dilemma that doesn't relate to them. Because the passage indicates that Hollywood films of the era "dealt with white issues and employed white actors," these films would not have related to black children, who would have thus been alienated from mainstream culture. Choice (E) is wrong because the passage doesn't say that children can't derive *any* educational value from films they can't relate to, only that they might feel alienated.

54. **(D).** Choice (A) is wrong because "assiduous" means diligent, which is irrelevant here. Choice (B) is wrong because the people studying art do not have to be "artistic." Choice (C) is a trap built on the uniqueness of the Parthenon, but "informed" is not describing the Parthenon. Choice (D) is correct because "erudite" means knowledgeable, and knowledge would allow someone viewing the frieze to recognize its unique qualities. Choice (E) is wrong because this is a question of knowledge, not applying technical, or "scientific," skills.

**MANHATTAN**
PREP

55. **(C).** Choice (A) is wrong because many of its characteristics have in fact been worked out. Choice (B) is wrong because the passage is not primarily about artistic interpretation. Choice (C) is correct because "idiosyncratic" is a synonym for unique, and the frieze is said to be unique in two ways. Choice (D) is incorrect because only one paragraph discusses the existence of mortals in the frieze and because this title is much too broad. Choice (E) is a trap: all sides of the frieze are continuous, not the individual characters.

56. **(D).** Choice (A) is incorrect because the first sentence indicates that the Parthenon was constructed in the "High Classical Period." Choice (B) is incorrect because the same sentence says that the Parthenon was "regarded as a great architectural and artistic product." Choice (C) is incorrect because the frieze is said to have come from the "temple-chamber" of the Parthenon. Choice (D) is correct because the passage says only that it is "difficult to study" the frieze because not all of it survives "today" and the surviving parts are in different locations. This doesn't necessarily mean that today's scholars don't know what the missing portions looked like at the time of construction (perhaps drawings of the Parthenon survive, for example). Choice (E) is incorrect because the frieze is described as "unique" and defined as a "structural element" of the Parthenon.

57. **(C).** Choice (A) is wrong because the passage only discusses the ways in which Sandra Cisneros's work puts the burden on the reader. Choice (B) is wrong because the passage only discusses a single one of Isabel Allende's books. Choice (C) is correct because the second paragraph says that Sandra Cisneros's short story collection does have inter-related stories, but they do not use the same characters or setting in each story. Choice (D) is wrong because intuition is not discussed as a part of Sandra Cisneros's writing. Choice (E) is wrong because the passage does not assess what would make the "best short story collections."

58. **(E).** Choice (A) is wrong because while tone is mentioned in relation to Sandra Cisneros's work, it is not mentioned in relation to Isabel Allende's work. Choice (B) is wrong because while time is mentioned in relation to Sandra Cisneros's work, it is not mentioned in relation to Isabel Allende's work. Choice (C) is wrong because while similarities in characters are mentioned in relation to Isabel Allende's work, they are directly said not to exist in Sandra Cisneros's work. Choice (D) is wrong because while setting is mentioned in relation to Isabel Allende's work, it is directly said not to exist in Sandra Cisneros's work. Therefore, (E) is the correct choice.

59. **1st and 2nd only.** The first statement is correct because Rothbard says that there were "better [economists] before Smith." This means that at least two were better than Smith, but Smith could still have been the third best (the passage does not directly state that Rothbard thinks that Smith comes in third place, but the question asks for statements that do not contradict Rothbard's remarks). The second statement is correct because Rothbard says that Smith's book "eclipsed public knowledge" of better economists, meaning it had an influence that it shouldn't have. The third statement is not correct because, according to the first line of the third paragraph, "[e]ven Smith's critics do not deny the book's immense influence."

60. **(C).** The "Invisible Hand" is described in the second paragraph as the idea that "individuals pursuing their own self-interest could unintentionally create a more just society." Choice (A) is wrong because the final result is not particularly just—this would be a better choice if the moviegoers' actions somehow caused a benefit to people other than themselves. Choice (B) is wrong because it has little to do with selfishness or justice, but with another aspect of Smith's writings. Choice (C) is correct because this system promotes selfishness (each student tries to sign up as quickly as possible for each class, without thinking of others), but those classes are then said to be "equitably

distributed." Choice (D) is wrong because raising prices isn't inherently selfish, no one appears to be competing, and the end result is not particularly just. Choice (E) is wrong for the same reasons as (D).

61. **(D).** The passage indicates that Chanel and Vionnet are examples illustrating a theory that personal virtues are "irrelevant" to material success. This matches choice (D). Choice (A) is a distortion, as "irrelevant" indicates no relationship, not an inverse one. Choice (B) confuses an example given in the passage with the purpose of the passage and creates a hierarchy that the passage did not. Choice (C) again confuses example and purpose; furthermore, the passage does not focus on aesthetics. Choice (E) is an irrelevant comparison and also confuses example and purpose.

62. **(B).** When a question uses the phrase "in order to," the correct answer will address the author's purpose for inserting the detail rather than the literal meaning. Choice (A) is at best unknown, as her company was in operation before the war. Choice (B) is correct because the information supports the author's theory that personal virtue is irrelevant to material success. Choice (C) comes from the wrong paragraph, as this information about Vionnet does not "highlight" anything about Chanel. Choice (D) is not supported by anything in the passage. Choice (E) is a distortion; the author mentions that Vionnet could be so thought of, but his point is merely about her personal integrity and does not address her feminist credentials.

63. **(D).** In the first paragraph, the passage states that seals "who sleep on land at night but spend most of their days in coastal waters" are analogous. None of the other choices accurately follows the pattern of this analogy. Thus, (D) is correct.

64. **(C).** The author contrasts the proponent to trained scientists, enumerates criticisms of the theory, and sides with the critics. Thus, the author is casting "doubt upon her expertise," which matches choice (C). Choice (A) is incorrect because, as a "proponent," she is not objective by definition. Choice (B) is not addressed by the passage. Choice (D) is exactly backwards. Choice (E) brings up an issue that is not mentioned.

65. **(D).** The author states that the Tokugawa period in Japan was a model for patterns of organization, but "as psychologists, social historians, and Biblical prophets have all observed, in varying ways, humans inevitably fail to anticipate unintended consequences." This qualifies as a "common failing," which matches choice (D). Choice (A) is incorrect, as Iceland is only mentioned briefly as an analogy. Choice (B) is wrong both because the author does not express a point of view and because the issue is the result of rather than the imposition of a fixed order. Choice (C) addresses a very minor detail, not the purpose. Choice (E) is a comparison that the passage does not address and therefore cannot be inferred.

66. **(C).** The author states that the inversion of the financial and social rankings led to the decline of Tokugawa society. Choices (A) and (B) are both incorrect because the passage states that social mobility was prohibited. Choice (D) is incorrect because the main reason cited for the decline has to do with specific decisions made by the ruling clan, decisions that had unforeseen consequences. A drought is an act of nature. Choice (E) is also incorrect; while the author does mention foreign pressure as leading to the collapse of the government, the question concerns the decline of the society, which began long before Admiral Perry's arrival.

67. **(C).** The author states that unifying Germany under Prussian rather than Austrian rule made war more likely. Choice (A) is a result of the treaty but the author does not imply that it was negative. Choice (B) does not relate to the Treaty. Choice (D) is not mentioned in the passage and thus not correct. Choice (E) is wrong because it is a distortion

to state that the author thought the Treaty "provided the impetus," or reason, for later wars; the author mentions only that the Treaty increased the chances that war would occur.

68. **(A).** The passage mentions the military brilliance of Prinz Eugen of Savoy, "an independent territory east of France." Savoy is not mentioned among the "major powers" in the prior sentence, so choice (A) must be true and is correct. Choices (B) and (E) are both incorrect because the author does not create hierarchies of importance in either case; thus, no particular ranking must be true. Choices (C) and (D) are incorrect because the passage does not indicate who won and who lost.

69. **(B).** The author discusses two ideas, but subtly favors the latter; language such as "it is no wonder" indicates an implicit sympathy for the second suggestion. Thus, choice (B) is correct. Choice (A) distorts the point as "theories" are not the same as ideas, the two ideas are not exactly "opposing," and the issue is not a "process." Choice (C) is incorrect—the last sentence of the passage undermines "definitively" and "programs" are not the same as ideas. Choice (D) is wrong because "dearth" means lack, and Lewis's work is certainly very popular. Choice (E) is incorrect because, in addition to missing the point, there is no critique, only a very brief description.

70. **(D).** Lewis had jobs in the art and banking worlds; the passage draws no parallels between the two, so (D) is correct. (Some parallels are drawn between baseball and finance, but these were not Lewis's two professions.) Choice (A) is incorrect because "gaming the system" is idiomatic. Choice (B) is incorrect as the fourth sentence of the second paragraph describes Lewis's protagonists. Choice (C) is incorrect because movie making, used as evidence, is part of popular culture. Choice (E) is incorrect as the introductory discussion of Lewis's education can fairly be called a mention of "formative influences."

71. **1st and 3rd only.** The first statement is correct because some hunters are taking more game birds than they should, causing the population of those birds to decline. The second statement is wrong because the free rider problem concerns people enjoying benefits improperly, not people paying different but possibly proper amounts for the same service. The third statement is correct because in this instance, the action of many free riders leads to a systemic shutdown.

72. **(C).** Choice (A) is wrong because nowhere in the passage is it stated that free riders cannot be blamed. Choice (B) is wrong because nowhere in the passage is it stated that free rider problems are not worth worrying about. Choice (C) is correct because the first sentence of the last paragraph says that "[i]n some cases, the free rider problem is viewed as a necessary cost of government," implying that in other cases, it is not. Choice (D) is incorrect because national defense is cited as an example of the inevitability of free rider problems, not as proof that they need to be stamped out as quickly as possible. Choice (E) is incorrect because the passage does not discuss the morality of free riders.

73. **1st only.** Regarding the first statement, the first paragraph claims "modern humans are known to have diverged hundreds of thousands of years before modern humans left Africa." To say that they diverged is to say that two species share a common ancestry to that point. Regarding the second statement, whether modern humans and Neanderthals interbred is a matter of controversy ("The team's conclusions were answered with skepticism on a number of fronts,") and thus this answer cannot be definitely true. Finally, Paabo asserts that Neanderthals and modern humans lived near one another, but the rest of the passage says that his claims were "answered with skepticism." Though the passage does not say what his critics thought of that particular claim, there is not enough information to conclude that it is true.

74. **3rd only.** The second paragraph says that "[p]aleontologists and archaeologists charged that the conclusion was unsupported by archaeological evidence," so they appeal to archaeological evidence to criticize Paabo's conclusions, and this supports the third statement. The first statement is wrong because there is no suggestion that the contamination of Neanderthal DNA with modern human DNA was deliberate, nor even that it was done by Paabo, nor is any other reason offered to doubt his integrity. The second statement is wrong because there is no suggestion that they ignore DNA evidence, even if they are not as persuaded by it as Paabo and his team.

75. **(D).** The passage claims that the reflecting surface must be far enough away so that the sound of the echo is distinct from the original sound, but not so far away that the sound is completely dissipated. You can use that information to eliminate (A) and (B). The passage also claims that multiple reflecting surfaces are apt to produce a reverberation rather than an echo, so cross off (C). The anechoic chamber with "sound-absorbing fiberglass wedges" is presented as a contrast to an "echo chamber," so (E) is also out.

76. **2nd and 3rd only.** The second paragraph notes that the echo chamber is constructed with "the acoustical properties of a small cathedral" precisely in order to create echoes; this supports the second statement. Mountains, along with buildings, are offered in the second paragraph as examples of the sort of reflecting surface likely to bring about an echo, which supports the third statement. The first choice is wrong because the passage describes an "anechoic chamber" as filled with "sound-absorbing fiberglass wedges," which are the opposite of the sound-reflecting objects required to propagate echoes.

77. **1st only.** The first statement is justified because in the second paragraph, de Beauvoir is quoted as saying exactly so. The second statement is not justified because at the end of the first paragraph, de Beauvoir indicates that women "*are viewed as* intrinsically passive and immanent." This does not mean that de Beauvoir believes this (in fact, the second paragraph gives good evidence that she believes precisely the reverse). The third statement is not justified because, although de Beauvoir views both self-constraint and imposed constraint (oppression) as negative, she does not indicate which type she considers to be worse. Though the passage says that "immanence is a moral fault" when someone chooses it, the first paragraph does not indicate whether de Beauvoir believes this.

78. **2nd only.** The first paragraph states that immanence is considered "a degradation" before going back and forth between immanence as a freely chosen moral fault and immanence as the result of oppression. Thus, immanence is not always characterized as a moral fault or as oppression.

79. **(D).** The first sentence of the passage announces that existentialist ethics were a major influence on de Beauvoir's philosophy. Much of the rest of the passage is devoted to explaining that philosophy, which makes choice (D) correct. Choice (A) is too broad as the passage doesn't explain all of existential ethics, of which transcendence is just one concept. Similarly, (B) is too broad as the passage does not discuss all of feminist theory, just de Beauvoir's. Choice (C) is wrong—the passage is not a "diatribe," or bitter attack. Choice (E) is again too broad for the passage.

80. **(A).** The author's primary purpose in writing this passage is to explain the distinction between science and non-science via historical examples, such as those of Aristotle and Galileo. The author begins by positing the question of differentiating the two, and then goes on to use historical examples to explain why each does or does not meet the qualification for modern science. Thus, choice (A) is correct. Regarding (B), the author never criticizes the Ancient Greek philosophers, just labels their method unscientific. As for (C), nowhere does the author claim that it is important to follow Galileo's scientific method, just that this is now the modern definition of science. Regarding (D), the author never makes mention of the historical definition of science. Lastly, as for (E), the author never argues that the

**MANHATTAN**
PREP

findings of Galileo are more important than those of Aristotle. Further, the author only discusses one finding of each philosopher/scientist, so this answer is out of scope.

81. **(D).** As the second paragraph states, Galileo's method "forced one to first form a hypothesis, then design an experiment to confirm or deny this hypothesis, and then accept or discard the hypothesis based on one's findings." Aristotle's hypothesis was that solids were the least expanded form of matter, and the experiment he designed to prove this was to show that solids sank within liquids of the same type. As this did not hold true for water, under the Galilean method Aristotle would be forced to discard his hypothesis based on the results of his experiment. Thus, choice (D) is correct. Regarding (A), the passage does not contain any information about the shape of solid water or of other solid forms of matter, only about Aristotle's conjectures on the shape of solid water. Regarding (B), the passage claims the opposite of this fact: an object with larger mass will not fall to the ground more quickly than an object with lesser mass. As for (C), the passage states that the ancient Greeks were more philosophers than scientists, but never prohibits one from being both. As for (E), the passage states that Galileo used his scientific method to disprove many commonly held misconceptions about the rules of physics, but never states that one cannot do this in the absence of his method.

82. **(C).** The passage describes the role of Alcott's women in their society and briefly wonders about the author's motivation. Choice (A) concerns only the last sentence of the passage. Choices (B) and (D) ignore that the passage discusses a novel rather than reality. Choice (D) is also too broad and somewhat nonsensical since the passage concerns the past. Choice (E) misses the author's tone—there is no indictment, merely a discussion.

83. **(E).** In the second paragraph, the passage dismisses Meg's "taking part" by saying it "meant no more than" talking to her husband, "remaining at home," and allowing him to be a mediator between her and the world. This implies that she must "leave the house," which matches choice (E). Choice (A) misses the point of the passage and is almost backwards. Choices (B) and (C) are misplaced details about the alternative to "taking part." Choice (D) distorts the second paragraph, which says Meg's husband was her mediator to the world at large.

84. **1st and 3rd only.** The first statement is justified, as the first sentence states that the man of the house was at the war front. The third statement must follow, because the passage states that men went out in public to conduct activities and returned home at night. The second statement, while quite possibly true, is not mentioned in the passage. The passage only states that Alcott glorified this condition in her novel, not that the entire society did so.

85. **(E).** A "falsifiable idea" is "one that can be shown to be false." The statement in choice (E), "no human being lives forever," can only be shown to be false if one observes a human being that lives forever. However, this would be impossible (because of the word "forever"), and thus the idea is not falsifiable. In addition, answer choices (A) through (D) are incorrect. The statement "All birds are black" is falsifiable by identifying a single bird that is not black. The statement "Earth is the only planet in the universe with intelligent life" can be proven false by finding intelligent life on any planet in the universe except Earth. The statement "It rains on Mars every day" can be proven false by observing Mars on a single non-rainy day. The statement "The sun will explode in 100,000 years" can be proven false by waiting more than 100,000 years and verifying that the sun has not exploded. Note that choices (D) and (E) seem somewhat similar—however impractical it is to wait 100,000 years to falsify something, there is still a big difference between "100,000 years" and "forever."

86. **(B).** The author states in the last paragraph that a theory that is unable to be proven true is very unlikely to be formed. Therefore, it appears that the author believes that "confirmability" lacks a practical application. This supports choice (B). The author states in the second paragraph, "it is understandable that Popper does not devote that much time to the criterion of 'confirmability,'" implying that confirmability is less important that falsifiability, not more, so choice (A) is incorrect. Regarding choice (C), the author states that a theory that is unable to be proven true is unlikely to be formed. Therefore, it is unlikely that the author believes that confirmability applies to a broad range of theories. As for choice (D), the first sentence of the last paragraph states that confirmability follows the same logic as falsifiability ("By that logic, … ") and thus it appears the author believes that confirmability is reasonable. As for choice (E), the author states in the last sentence that "it is understandable that Popper does not devote that much time to the criterion of 'confirmability'." Thus, the author is unlikely to agree that Popper should have developed the idea of confirmability.

87. **(C).** The second paragraph focuses on the significance of the two definitions of "political," as (C) states. Choice (A) is incorrect because no alternative is offered in the second paragraph. Choice (B) is incorrect because there is no "revision"—this choice might describe the third paragraph. Similarly, in (D), there is no "exception." Choice (E) is closer to the point of the first paragraph.

88. **(B).** The author mentions the play as an example, or "illustration," of when speech is political, which is the aspect discussed in that paragraph. This matches choice (B). Choice (A) is incorrect as it is used as an example, not counter-point. Choice (C) is wrong because the passage does not advocate a position. Choices (D) and (E) miss the point of the example, which is neither about universality nor a fallacy.

89. **(A).** The answer to this type of question is always explicit in the passage. In the third paragraph, the passage cites Hanna Pitkin: "public-spirited conversation happens when citizens speak in terms of 'justice.'" None of the other choices is mentioned in this section of the passage. Choice (A) is correct.

90. "Such a definition is not precisely wrong, but rather is outdated and falls short … " (second sentence of first paragraph). This is the only one of the four sentences in paragraphs 1 and 2 that includes an explicit criticism.

91. **(B).** The passage describes two different ideas, explanationism and predictionism, that have both been used to verify or disprove different scientific theories. Thus, choice (B) is correct. As for (A), the passage never states that either theory is superior to the other. Although (C) is true, the passage only mentions the two models of the solar system as an example of the workings of explanationism. Therefore, it cannot be the main idea of the passage. Regarding (D), the passage does not describe what is required to posit a physical theory. As for (E), a predictionist and an explanationist may always diverge on how to prove that a scientific theory is true, but they might still agree on whether or not the theory is correct.

92 **(E).** Before citing the example of the Copernicus and Brahe models of the universe, the author states in the first paragraph that "it could be the case that a theory predicts something and yet does not provide the best explanation of it." The author goes on to use Copernicus and Brahe as an example, stating that both of their theories have predictive power, but Brahe's does not offer the best explanation for the workings of the solar system.  This supports choice (E). As for (A), the author is actually arguing the opposite: that predictive power alone is never enough to verify a theory. Regarding (B), the author does reveal that some theories have more or less of an ad hoc quality, but this is not the author's reason for citing this example. The main reason must be related back to explanationism. As

**MANHATTAN**
PREP

for (C), the example showed the opposite—both theories were found to accurately predict future events, and thus they must have both made the same predictions for those future events. Although it is true that the more complicated model failed, the author's intent was to show that an incorrect model can still make correct predictions; eliminate (D).

93. **1st and 2nd only.** The words "for example" at the beginning of the sentence containing the crowd analogy follow a sentence about the Pauli exclusion principle. This principle says that fermions cannot "inhabit the same fundamental state." Electrons, which are fermions, are likened to members of a crowd in a stadium; the fact that electrons cannot "circle the nuclei of atoms in precisely the same orbits" (just as crowd members cannot sit on top of one another) is a "consequence" of the Pauli exclusion principle. Thus, the first statement is justified. These electrons "must occupy more and more distant locations"; the crowd analogy certainly illustrates that behavior, so the second statement is justified. As for the third, incorrect statement, while it is true that electrons cannot occupy the same orbits as one another and must instead occupy more and more distant locations, you do not know that those orbits are "concentric" or "evenly spaced."

94. **(B).** The author begins by naming the two classes of subatomic particles, choice (B), and then divides the remainder of the passage into descriptions of each class and their relation to each other. Regarding (A) and (D), the author explains both of these concepts within the passage, but they are subordinate to the main idea of describing the two types of subatomic particles and thus are not the primary purpose of the passage. As for (C) and (E), the author's primary purpose in writing is not to provide examples or to argue.

95. **(C).** The author states that fermions, not bosons, are the constituents of ordinary matter. All other answers are mentioned in the second paragraph of the passage. Thus, (C) is the correct choice.

96. **(D).** The second paragraph states that Cooper pairs of electrons will "flow in precise harmony and with zero resistance through the metal." As an example of the same phenomenon, the second paragraph also states that a "swirl in a cup of superfluid helium will, amazingly, never dissipate." Therefore, it is correct to infer that "a current through a superconducting wire will never dissipate," as in choice (D). As for (A), the passage states that an even number of fermions (which, according to the first paragraph, "include electrons, protons, and neutrons") constitute a boson, but not an odd number (½ integer times an odd will not give an integer). The last paragraph states that "scientists argue for the existence of skyrmions" in a medium that might permit them to be formed, implying that they have not yet been discovered, so eliminate (B). In (C), the author states that two electrons cannot circle a nucleus in the same orbit, but they could spin in different orbits that are the same distance from the nucleus. Finally, in (E), the author gives two examples of fermions becoming bosons at cooled temperatures but does not say this is the *only* situation in which this can occur.

97. **(A).** The first paragraph states that fermions obey the Pauli principle, according to which no two particles can occupy the same fundamental state. The second paragraph states that bosons tend to bunch together in exactly the same state. This supports choice (A) and is the opposite of (E); thus, (E) is incorrect. Choice (D) is also the opposite of what the passage claims. Bosons have integral spin values and fermions have "half-integral" spin. Answer (B) is incorrect because the passage does not discuss the total number of particle types for bosons or fermions, and answer (C) is incorrect because the passage explicitly states that both fermions and bosons can exist in groups.

98. **(A).** The passage states that the Pauli principle prohibits any two particles from inhabiting the same fundamental state. Further, the Pauli principle should be applied to fermions, "which include electrons, protons, and neutrons,"

but not bosons (from the second paragraph). Answer choice (A) discusses electrons, which are fermions, avoiding occupation of identical energy levels, so (A) is relevant and thus the correct answer. As for (B), a charged particle in a magnetic field neither provides the criteria for a fermion nor references inhabitance of the same state. Answer (C) does not specify the type of particle. Answer (D) is about photons, which are described in the passage as bosons, to which the Pauli principle does not apply. Regarding (E), the passage explicitly states that the Higgs particle is a boson, so the Pauli exclusion principle doesn't apply here.

99. **3rd only.** Frey points out in the second paragraph that "humans are often intrinsically motivated, and that such motivation explains heroism, craftsmanship, and other drives that do not fit neatly into the model of a narrowly focused gain-seeker." The first statement is incorrect because the craftsman in question is working for money, rather than for the inherent love of the work. The second statement is incorrect because even though the journalist may appear to act heroically, his motivations are related to his career. The third statement is correct because the economist in question is working without hope of monetary reward.

100. **(D).** Choice (A) is incorrect because the passage never says that *Homo economicus* is a useful way to form mathematical models. Choice (B) is incorrect because the passage never says *Homo economicus* is a theoretically useless construction, only that it is a problematic one. Choice (C) is wrong because there's no reason to believe that the people who criticize the theory "don't fully understand its function." Choice (D) is correct because the second paragraph of the passage describes numerous problems with *Homo economicus*, all of which center around simplifying people's motivations and assuming they understand more than they actually do. Choice (E) is incorrect because the passage never says that *Homo economicus* fell out of favor or whether the handful of critics cited is representative of "most economists."

101. **1st and 3rd only.** The first statement is correct because Veblen and Keynes allege that "*homo economicus* assumes far too great an understanding of macroeconomics on the part of humans." The second statement is incorrect (and too extreme) because, although Tversky says that people are "unconcerned by small chances of large losses, but quite risk-averse regarding small losses," he does not imply that there is a broader linear pattern. The third statement is correct because Amartya Sen says that people "can and do commit to courses of action out of morality, cultural expectations, and so forth."

102. **(D).** The gist of this sentence is that while scientists condemn certain practices as flawed, the methods they themselves use are subject to many of the same flaws. The correct answer will be a word, synonymous with "repudiate," that means to condemn or denounce. Choice (D), "decry," is the right word.

103. **(A).** According to the passage, Feyerabend wants to demonstrate that historic instances of scientific progress were themselves marked by these flaws, and thus should not be seen as flaws at all. To this end, he describes a situation that any scientist would agree is an example of progress and shows how it made use of practices that are now condemned by scientists. Feyerabend basically implies that scientists have a choice between throwing this out as an example of good science or accepting these practices as part of good science. Since scientists are unlikely to say that the introduction of heliocentrism was a bad thing, they will be forced to "revise their account of what is and is not acceptable scientific practice." Thus, (A) is correct. Choice (B) is wrong because the point of the case study is that Galileo is a *good* example of science. As for choice (C), "subjectivity" is called "seriously flawed" in the first paragraph. Choice (D) says tautological reasoning is acceptable only when it's being tautological. This is not why Feyerabend makes use of a

case study. Choice (E) misses the point—Feyerabend is using an example from history to defend certain ways of doing science.

104. **(C).** The first sentence of this paragraph defines Boal's work as a response to a culture of apathy. This matches choice (C). Choice (A) is incorrect—the paragraph describes a response, not an elaboration. Choice (B) is incorrect because it is not until the last paragraph that the author provides a rationale for the two theatres. Choice (D) is beyond the scope of the passage. Choice (E) is incorrect because there is no evaluation.

105. **(D).** This is essentially a vocabulary question. "Power" is one meaning of "agency," and this is the only meaning that makes sense in the context of creating "ways to free themselves." Thus, choice (D) is correct. Choices (A) and (B) are other meanings of "agency" that do not fit the context of the passage. Choice (C) might be related to "agent," but it has no relationship to "agency" or the passage here. Choice (E) is incorrect as it implies domination over others.

106. **(E).** The last paragraph defines a "spect-actor" as "someone who simultaneously witnesses and creates theater." In the second paragraph, the passage states that at Image events "everyone is at once theater maker and witness." Thus, (E) is the correct choice. Choice (A) does not mention theater, so it is incorrect. As for choice (B), Boal specifically says that catharsis keeps people passive (also, the audience member is not acting, which is crucial to being a "spect-actor"). Choice (C) is incorrect and, to an extent, backwards—the passage said that Boal found that position analogous to that of a passive audience. Choice (D) is too broad, given the first paragraph about traditional theater.

107. **(A).** At the end of the first paragraph, the author paraphrases Boal: "theater etiquette creates a kind of culture of apathy where individuals do not act communally … and remain distanced from art." This supports choice (A). Choices (C) and (E) can be eliminated. Choices (B) and (D) are wrong because Boal states that traditional theater discourages political action by providing catharsis. Choice (A) is correct because Boal states that actors *do* go into the audience in traditional theater, so they are not prevented from doing so.

108. **(D).** This choice is a characteristic of an Image workshop, not a Forum workshop. In the second paragraph, the passage states that Forum workshops begin with a narrative skit, (A); then the facilitator—or mediator, (E)—encourages spectators to assume the role of the protagonist, (B). Choice (C) is justified as the paragraph states that performances do not always arrive at a satisfactory solution. Therefore, (D) is the correct answer to this Except question.

109. **2nd only.** In the third paragraph, "The natural rotation of a galaxy," "surrounding supernovae," and "density waves" are listed as examples of the outside influence "evidently required for a theoretically unstable cloud to initiate collapse." The first statement is a trap—fusion appears in the first paragraph and the author does not suggest that it leads to cloud contraction. (While the passage does suggest that fusion is related to supernovae and that supernovae can contribute to cloud collapse, don't fill in the gaps yourself—the passage simply does not provide enough information to infer that fusion is part of a series of events that begins cloud contraction.) The second statement is true (realizing this requires you to match up "explosions of stars" in the answer choice with "supernovae" in the third paragraph). The third statement is a distortion—forcing debris *inward*, not outward, may cause cloud contraction to begin.

110. **(D).** Choice (A) is true in real life, of course, but is not mentioned in the passage. Choice (B) refers to the molecular clouds in the second paragraph, not to our solar system. Choice (C) is reminiscent of this sentence in the

third paragraph—"The natural rotation of a galaxy can slowly alter the structure of a cloud"—but this does not refer to our solar system. Found in the first paragraph, correct answer (D) reflects that "for a system of planets such as our solar system to form around a star during cloud contraction, the presence of these heavy elements in the cloud is a necessity." The first paragraph additionally states that "heavy metals such as iron and gold are formed, seeding surrounding hydrogen clouds." Choice (E) gets the story backwards—heavy elements were needed to create the solar system, not vice-versa.

111. **(C).** The second paragraph states that "outward thermal pressure of the constituent gases [of the molecular cloud]" is what is "overcome" in the process of the collapse of the cloud. This is something that "inhibits," or holds back, cloud collapse. Thus, (C) is correct.

112. **3rd only.** The Norton-Polk-Mathis House uses typical Renaissance ideals as well as materials "prevalent in the Italian Renaissance." However, the passage certainly does not say that the house itself was built during the Renaissance. The first statement is not true. According to the passage, the primary purpose of the building is "to impress," so its purpose is not primarily utilitarian. The second statement is also not true. The author does write that the house "radiates an air of strength," especially when "juxtaposed with the other, seemingly fragile brick and wood homes of the neighborhood." This supports the third statement.

113. **(C).** The most important idea in the passage is that a small group of dolphins has been found to form social networks, which is a first among non-human animals. One indication of this is that both the first and last sentences in the passage highlight this fact, so (C) is correct. Answer choice (A) is stated in the passage, but is not the main idea; it explains the behavior of the animals that form social networks. Choice (B) is never stated in the passage, although this study did span a relatively long time. Choice (D) is a much bigger claim than the passage suggests; you are never given a motivation for this study. Finally, choice (E) goes against the main idea of the passage as the passage discusses how dolphins can form social networks.

114. **1st only.** The passage states that other animals aside from the sponger dolphins often form groups based on circumstances such as genetics or food sources. As the dolphins are the first to be categorized as "social networks," it must be true that groups formed under the previous circumstances would not qualify as social networks, supporting the first statement. As for the second statement, the passage does not state that all spongers of Shark Bay form social networks, only the females. As for the third statement, the passage does not comment on the location of spongers; it only mentions the spongers of Shark Bay. Thus, the third statement cannot be inferred.

115. **(E).** The passage describes this belief as an "old canard." A *canard* is a "rumor," or "a false or baseless story." An "old canard" is one that has been passed around for awhile—very much analogous to an "urban legend." The passage goes on to say that the blind people in the study have "cerebral superpowers" and that the discovery that blind people can hear better than sighted people is "a stunning example of the brain's plasticity." Thus, choice (E) is correct.

116. **2nd only.** According to the passage, Aristotle "posited a holistic, non-corporeal mind" and would have found "shocking" the idea that "the mind is physically located in the brain." Thus, the first statement is not correct, since Aristotle believed in a "non-corporeal" (not part of the body) mind. Since Aristotle believed in a "holistic" mind, he did NOT think that "the mind exists in parts or modules." Thus, the second statement is correct. As for the third statement, the passage does not indicate what Aristotle might have thought about blind people's hearing.

**MANHATTAN**
PREP

117. **3rd only.** The last sentence posits that the deportation of German-speaking citizens by the Allied powers is excised from history books because history is written by the victors—this makes the first statement look attractive, but the statement says "during World War II." The first paragraph is clear that the deportations "took place almost two years after the conclusion of the war." The third answer choice can be inferred from the claim that the United States hoped to keep Eastern and Central European nations away from Soviet influence, meaning that the United States and the Soviet Union were not fully aligned in their views. The passage lists the Allied powers as the Soviet Union, Britain, and the United States, but does not include Poland. The second statement cannot be inferred.

118. **1st, 2nd, and 3rd.** The second half of the first paragraph lists reasons why the Soviet Union, Britain, and the United States, respectively, had something to gain from the deportations. Each of the answer choices undermines one of these reasons.

119. **(C).** The passage describes how the theory of quantum mechanics models particles as probabilistic waves, and how the theory has been confirmed over the past 70 years. Answer choice (C) correctly incorporates all of these ideas into the main idea of the passage. Answer choice (A) is incorrect as it does not address the theory of quantum mechanics, which is the overarching idea of the passage. Choices (B) and (D) are both large claims that are out of the scope of the passage. Finally, although tests can be and have been designed to test quantum mechanics, choice (E) does not express the main idea of the passage.

120. **(A).** The passage states that Einstein was deeply troubled by the theory of quantum mechanics, and thus his quote must express that unsettlement. Further, his reference to dice implies that he did not believe the universe should be controlled by probability, but should be set. Therefore, (A) best expresses his motivation; Einstein worries that particles should not be probabilistic in nature. Choice (B) has no bearing on quantum mechanics, and thus cannot express Einstein's motivation. Choice (C) is out of scope because of the mention of causality. Choice (D) confuses Einstein's being troubled by quantum mechanics with a lack of understanding. Choice (E) makes a supposition that cannot be inferred from the passage about Einstein's religious beliefs.

121. **1st and 3rd only.** The first statement is a proper inference because the first paragraph states, "A particle trapped in a closed box has some finite probability of being at any location within the box. Open the box once and you'll find the particle at only one location." In other words, the exact location of the particle cannot be known until it is measured. The second statement is incorrect, as the passage actually states the opposite: that measurements of position can be taken. The third choice is a correct inference because the first paragraph states that "quantum mechanics describes particles as waves" and the conclusion notes that quantum mechanics has been verified as true.

122. **1st and 3rd only.** According to the second paragraph, not knowing that they are seeing a theater piece allows viewers to "avoid the etiquette of theatergoing" and "engage with the action and concepts of an unfolding drama as if these actions and concepts were real." This is a good match with the first statement. The third paragraph refers to "scripted characters" in invisible theater, so it cannot be inferred that "invisible theater is best described as improvised." Another reference to "dialogue ... set up by invisible theater performers" weighs against invisible theater being improvisational. The third paragraph begins, "Boal has documented various successful instances of invisible theater in which non-performers ... take unplanned public-minded action in response to the dialogue and events set up by invisible theater performers." The last sentence of the passage also states that "the goal of guerilla theater is to get people talking publicly." Thus, it can be inferred that "actions taken by the audience once the performance is over" can be one measure of success of a theater piece.

123. **(A).** In the first sentence, the author calls invisible theater and guerrilla theater "two forms of street theater with similar origins but very different approaches." This is a good match with choice (A). Choice (B) is incorrect because the passage doesn't say which form is more effective. Choice (C) is too broad and the evolution is not the focus. Choice (D) is incorrect because the first paragraph states clearly that "invisible theater conceals its performative nature whereas guerrilla theater flaunts it." Choice (E) is too broad as the passage does not cover all artistic life in public places.

124. **1st and 2nd only.** The first statement is true, as the third paragraph goes into great detail about invisible theater's goal of encouraging public-minded talk, and the passage ends with "the goal of guerrilla theater is to get people talking publicly." The second statement is justified because the first paragraph states that "[b]oth forms take place exclusively in public places." The third choice is mentioned only in regard to guerilla theater; invisible theater is only said to involve the audience.

125. **(C).** The professors gave diplomas to the people who were the least able to answer questions as a way to mock the university's decision. This matches choice (C). Choice (A) does not have to be true because the passage merely discusses the form of the professors' protest. Choice (B) cannot be justified since it doesn't have to be true that the professors believed that result would follow. Similarly, choice (D) is wrong because it is not certain that the professors considered the legality of their actions. Choice (E) is not justifiable—no information is given about any particular policies the professors decried.

126. **1st and 3rd only.** The first statement, if true, would contradict the assumption of invisible theater that removing the boundary between performer and audience encourages involvement. The second statement describes a very likely result, and a goal, of invisible theater, and thus would not "undermine" the principle of invisible theater. The third statement describes a situation where the goal of invisible theater—a lively debate about public issues—was already happening, and invisible theater ruined it! This would definitely undermine the principle of invisible theater.

127. **1st, 2nd, and 3rd.** The first paragraph states that "widespread genomic changes would wreak physiological havoc," such as cancer. The first statement is supported. The second paragraph adds that "many organisms have also adapted beneficial mechanisms to induce genetic change." In short, some genetic changes are bad, but others are beneficial. The third paragraph explains how genetic change is important to immune functioning; the second statement is supported. The last line of the passage states "this process is regulated by T cells to prevent harmful mutations." The third statement is also justified.

128. **(C).** The word "seemingly" indicates that the changes are not really haphazard. "Seemingly haphazard" refers to "programmed genetic mutation." The "this" in "this seemingly haphazard process of programmed genetic mutation" harks back to "genetic recombination," so choice (C) is a match.

129. **1st, 2nd, and 3rd.** Pro-death signaling is given in a list of "cellular mechanisms that stymie genetic changes." "Stymie" means "hinder." The first statement is true. These cellular mechanisms are called "ubiquitous," which means existing everywhere, so certainly they are "very common." The second statement is also true. The final sentence of the paragraph says that "malfunctions in molecular players that safeguard against mutagenesis, such as the protein p53, have been implicated in diseases such as cancer." Since the malfunction of p53 may cause cancer, it can be inferred that p53, when properly functioning, may work against cancer. The third statement is also true.

**MANHATTAN**
PREP

130. **(A).** According to the passage, T cells need a large repertoire of receptors in order to be able to recognize a wide variety of pathogens. The passage goes on to say that "[r]elying only on a genetically encoded repertoire would be disadvantageously limiting—analogous to having only a few dozen language phrases with which to respond to the nearly infinite potential combinations of words in a conversation. Instead, the repertoire is generated by a process of genetic recombination …" According to this analogy, the language phrases are the repertoire of receptors; just as a speaker must respond to a nearly infinite body of language combinations, T cells must also have a large repertoire so they can respond to a wide variety of pathogens. This repertoire is increased through genetic recombination. Choice (A) is correct. Note that choice (B) is out of scope, choice (C) is the exact opposite of what is being described, choice (D) is a distortion based on another analogy in the passage (also, an analogy on the GRE would not be "meant to elucidate" *another* analogy!), and choice (E) refers to the first paragraph, not the analogy in question.

131. **1st only.** In the analogy referenced, the "language phrases" are receptors that can respond to various pathogens. The "nearly infinite potential combinations of words" is what a speaker must respond to—the reason a speaker needs a wide repertoire of language. Similarly, the wide variety of pathogens is the reason T cells need such a wide variety of receptors. This supports the first statement only.

132. **2nd and 3rd only.** The passage contends that Haberman "focuses the brunt of his criticism on teachers who have been insufficiently trained for the realities of the modern school environment and whose prejudices, lack of deep content knowledge, and excessive focus on order and discipline profoundly limit their effectiveness." The word "compromise" in the question stem means something like hurt or limit. Note that Haberman thinks that *too much* order and discipline is hurting teachers' effectiveness, so the first statement is the opposite of what the passage says. The second and third statements respectively match up with "lack of deep content knowledge" and "prejudices."

133. **(D).** The quote marks are present to make the point that the students who are referenced—"non-white, immigrant, or non-English-speaking children"—are *not* exceptions. Rather, they are the norm. Haberman's point is that the teacher is the problem, not the students. Therefore, (D) is correct. Choice (E) seems to reflect a truth that Haberman is railing against, but has nothing to do with the question ("exceptions" refers to students, not teachers).

134. **1st and 2nd only.** The passage indicates that Decadent authors embraced artifice over nature. Huysmans's protagonist, in an example of Decadent writing, surrounds himself with perfume, among other items. It can be inferred that at least one follower of the Decadent movement considered perfume to be an example of artifice, and that he held it to have surpassed, or be superior to, natural entities. However, the passage does not say whether Huysmans enjoyed surrounding himself with the perfume—only that his character did, so the third statement is not supported.

135. **1st, 2nd, and 3rd.** All three of the features are listed as characteristic of the Naturalist movement. "Vehicle for the scientific method" matches "extending the scientific method," while "focused on the effects of environment on shaping character" and "elaborated on the way inherited traits influenced human behavior" both match the passage's claim that Naturalism stressed "the influence of environment and heredity upon the individual psyche." If Decadent authors embraced any of these literary practices, this would bring their work closer in line with Naturalism.

136. **(C).** The first paragraph states that "one limitation" of the classical method is "the reliance on average measurements: it is impossible to distinguish a uniform population of cells expressing intermediate quantities of a molecule from a population composed of separate low and high expressers." This is a good match for choice (C). Note that (A)

is precisely what scientists want to measure (not a limitation), and (E) is a distortion—it is *not* preferable to capture only average levels. This goes against the main point of both paragraphs.

137. **1st and 3rd only.** According to the second paragra[h, flow cytometry and RNA FISH are examples of "single-cell measurement technology," so the first statement is true. Much of the wording in the second statement—"it is impossible to distinguish a uniform population of cells expressing intermediate quantities of a molecule"—is lifted from a sentence in the first paragraph, talking about classical methods—not the newer, single-celled measurement technologies. Finally, the second paragraph states that flow cytometry and RNA FISH have "made it possible to capture … the distribution of the molecule's expression within the population," which is a good match for the wording in the third statement.

138. **(C).** This question asks for the choice *not* mentioned in the passage. The first paragraph states that Portugal "once mined Angola for slaves and raw material," so choices (A) and (B) are out. The beginning of the passage concerns Portugal taking over Angola over a period beginning in the 16th century and culminating in the 1920s, so eliminate choice (D). The passage refers to "Angolan independence in 1975"—since that date is during the 20th century, choice (E) is out. The passage says that a "civil war" in Angola lasted until 2002, not a war against the Portuguese, so choice (C) is the answer.

139. **(B).** The "grand stroke of irony" the author refers to is Angola helping Portugal. Why is this ironic? Because, as stated in the first paragraph, "The country that once mined Angola for slaves and raw material is now virtually helpless." Choice (B) is the best match. Choices (A) and (E) are not ironic. While choices (C) and (D) do present some kind of contrast, they are not the "stroke of irony" to which the author refers.

140. **(E).** According to the third paragraph, Gage's physical injury affected his personality. The part of his brain that was damaged is now known to be related to morality, and Gage "literally lost one (or more) of the modules in his modular brain system." Choice (E) is a good match. Choice (A) is the opposite of what is being argued. Choice (B) is not indicated by the passage. Choice (C) may be true but is not the reason the author presented the example. Choice (D) relates to the previous paragraph, not to Phineas Gage.

141. **1st only.** The author is saying that, if the brain has a director, then that director would need its own director—and, presumably, *that* director would need a director, etc. The expression "begging the question" isn't really about a question; the second and third statements are traps.

142. **2nd only.** A "unitary entity" would not be split into parts or modules. While Aristotle and Descartes believed that the mind survived death, and lived long enough ago that they couldn't have been aware "that certain aspects of personality are known to be controlled by certain areas of the brain," the question is not only about Aristotle and Descartes—it is about all advocates of a unitary view of the mind. The passage does not offer enough information about these thinkers to indicate whether they think the mind survives death, or whether some of them (more modern thinkers, presumably) are aware of current research into the brain. You can eliminate the first and third statements.

143. **(A).** The first paragraph of the passage states that oxytocin treatments are often tried in isolated cases and the overall effects are without evaluation. The passage then describes a small study that seems promising, but makes no definitive claims. Therefore, it is likely that the author would agree that the effects of oxytocin require further evaluation, supporting choice (A). Answer choice (B) is incorrect as the passage states the opposite, namely that oxytocin is

not a "cure-all." Although the author focuses on the effects of oxytocin for those who are not able to interpret social cues, answer choice (C) is incorrect as the author does not state that the drug would not be useful for those who can already do so. The author specifically addresses choice (D) in the passage, stating that the hormone oxytocin increases feelings of calm and social bonding. Finally, answer choice (E) is incorrect, as the author never addresses oxytocin as an oral treatment.

144. **(D).** The second paragraph states that "the experiment showed that the oxytocin had the greatest affect on those who were least able to evaluate emotions properly when given the control." Thus, it can be inferred that those with the least ability to naturally infer emotions, in other words, the ones who might need it most, reaped the greatest benefits of the hormone. This matches choice (D). Additionally, (A) is incorrect as the passage does not discuss inconclusiveness based on sample size. Choice (B) is incorrect as it incorrectly pairs the known effects of the hormone in the brain with the results of the student study. Choice (C) is incorrect as the passage does not address the ability of the students to recognize expressions, just the relative change between the controlled salt water dose and the oxytocin. Finally, choice (E) is incorrect for a similar reason: the passage does not state that the subtler the expression the more difficult it was for students to identify, just that some expressions that were used were subtler than others.

145. **(A).** The experiment was related to students' ability to recognize emotions from facial expressions, not their ability to tell faces apart. Therefore, (A) is the correct answer. Choice (B) is mentioned in the first sentence of the last paragraph of the passage. Choice (C) is addressed throughout the second paragraph, first when it is stated that "a control dose of salt water" was given, and then when awareness after exposure to oxytocin is compared to awareness after the controlled salt water dose. Choice (D) is explicitly stated in the second sentence of the second paragraph. Finally, choice (E) is explicitly addressed in the last sentence of the second paragraph.

146. **2nd and 3rd only.** According to the passage, "Anansi originated with the Ashanti people in Ghana," so the first statement is untrue. The passage also states that in Jamaican folklore, Anansi "outsmarts other animal-god characters," so those characters must exist, which supports the second statement. Finally, since Anansi is called "Aunt Nancy" in the United States and is from Ghana, Anansi is known on at least two continents. This supports the third statement.

147. **(A).** In the first paragraph of the passage, the author describes the discovery of the cosmic microwave background. The second paragraph explains why the cosmic microwave exists and its implications to science. Therefore, the author wrote this passage to describe the discovery and reason for the cosmic microwave background, which matches choice (A). Choice (B) is incorrect as the author cites one example of an accidental discovery, but does not explain how multiple discoveries can be made accidentally. Choices (C) and (D) are incorrect as the author does not argue or defend, respectively. Finally, the main theory presented in the passage is the cosmic microwave background, whereas (E) incorrectly makes it seem that the author's intent is to defend the Big Bang and that the cosmic microwave background is only a subordinate idea.

148. **(C).** The second sentence in the first paragraph states that "[j]ust an instant after the Big Bang, all matter in the universe was so energetic, or hot, that it existed as free particles known as 'quarks.'" The paragraph proceeds in sequential order, and thus this event happened soonest after the Big Bang, making (C) the correct choice. The events described in choices (A) and (B) are said to have happened approximately 400,000 years after the Big Bang. Answer choice (D) describes the present state of the cosmic microwave background, 13.6 billion years later. Answer choice (E) is never addressed in the passage.

149. **(D).** The passage states that Penzias and Wilson accidentally discovered the cosmic microwave background and did not even understand what they had found until after consulting the Princeton group. It can be inferred that they did not initially understand the implications of their result, matching choice (D). Choice (A) is incorrect as the passage does not describe the importance of the signal for which Penzias and Wilson were originally searching. Choice (B) is incorrect as the passage never discusses the Princeton instrumentation used for searching for the cosmic microwave background. The capabilities of the telescope used by Penzias and Wilson are never discussed, thus choice (C) is not supported. Finally, the opposite of choice (E) is stated in the passage, which says that Penzias and Wilson convinced themselves that their signal was real before approaching the Princeton team.

150. **2nd and 3rd only.** Sousa argues against mechanical music on the grounds that it is insincere, and that it will decrease music in the home and music played or sung by amateurs as well as music instruction in education. The first statement is an example of one of the things Sousa was afraid of—vocal instruction being less a "normal part of education"—and thus does not "contradict." The second statement is an example of the phonograph increasing amateur music playing and "domestic music," so this does contradict Sousa's point. Finally, the third statement is an example of recorded music being more sincere than live music, so this definitely contradicts Sousa's point.

151. **(D).** Here, "chest" really does mean a part of the human body not a trunk or treasury. The statement about the "national" throat and chest comes right after a worry that "music will become the province of machines and professional singers only." Thus, the "national chest" is a reference to amateur singers, which matches choice (D).

152. "The blackbody emits just as much energy per unit time as it absorbs; the electromagnetic spectrum of the emitted energy, however …" (second sentence). The second sentence of the paragraph, after the semicolon, states that the electromagnetic spectrum of the emitted energy of a blackbody is completely determined by temperature and no other properties. Therefore, the only variable that defines the electromagnetic spectrum of a blackbody is temperature, as stated in the second sentence.

153. **1st only.** The passage states in the first sentence that "an idealized blackbody is an object that reflects zero incident electromagnetic radiation." Therefore, if an object reflects incident electromagnetic radiation, it cannot be an idealized blackbody and the first statement can be properly inferred. The second statement, however, cannot be inferred as the passage states that "a possible Doppler shift" can cause a fundamental change in the original spectral characteristics of reflected electromagnetic radiation. Finally, for the third statement, the passage states that any object that absorbs all incident electromagnetic radiation is a perfect blackbody. However, the passage also states that "a microscopic 'forest' of vertically aligned single-wall carbon nanotubes of varying heights applied to a surface" is "the closest [that] scientists have come thus far to creating a perfectly dark material," implying that this material is not a perfect blackbody. Therefore, it cannot be inferred that this object will absorb all incident radiation.

154. **(B).** The passage highlights two key points as they relate to one another: the two competing theories of the universe and Hubble's discovery that the universe is expanding. The correct answer, (B), highlights both of these points and their relation to the other. Thus, (E) is correct. Choices (A) and (C) highlight only one of these points each. Choice (D) describes Hubble's law, which does not fully capture the main idea. Choice (E) is not an idea presented in the passage.

155. **(E).** The second paragraph states that "Milton Humason, a fellow astronomer, helped Hubble to calculate the stars' relative velocities to Earth," but nowhere in the passage does it say that Hubble deduced the velocity of Earth or the stars' absolute velocities. Choice (A) is mentioned at the beginning of the second paragraph. Choice (B) is

mentioned in the first and fourth sentences of the second paragraph. Choice (C) is stated in the second to last sentence of the second paragraph. Finally, (D) is addressed in the second and third sentences of the second paragraph.

156. **1st and 2nd only.** The last sentence states that Hubble's experiment was "proof that we do not live in a steady-state universe, but rather a dynamic and expanding one"; therefore it must be true that the steady-state universe theory does not allow for an expanding universe. The first statement can be inferred. The second paragraph also notes that the speed at which objects are moving away from each other in space increases with an increasing distance between the objects. Thus, the second statement can be properly inferred. Finally, the third statement incorrectly assumes that once the steady-state universe theory was disproved, the Big Bang was the only theory that remained. The first sentence of the passage states only that "most physicists supported one of two cosmological theories," leaving the possibility of other theories that might still agree with Hubble's discovery.

157. **(A).** The passage dismisses the assumption that the gods determine destiny by pointing out that they act "politically," and their agendas often conflict, so that they could not formulate a "master plan." But if the gods had a common goal, then this objection would no longer apply. Thus, (A) is the correct choice. On the other hand, if the agendas of the gods coincided with the demands of fate, that wouldn't support the idea that the gods were in charge of fate, so choice (B) would not support the assumption. If Homer and Herodotus disagreed about the motives and agendas of the gods, as choice (C) claims, that would not undermine the view that for both authors fate is beyond the gods. Nor would the claim that destiny would be fulfilled regardless of what the gods did—choice (D)—or the idea that the gods and mortals can make their own decisions—choice (E)—so long as these decisions ultimately led to the fulfillment of destiny.

158. **(B).** Choice (B) offers the most common sense of the term "unbiased," and the only one that fits in this context. Choice (A) is wrong since the passage indicates that the role of the gods is a motif in the *Histories*. Since Herodotus provides an account of conflicts in the Hellenic world, choice (C) is wrong. Choice (D) is wrong since the passage also states that the concept of destiny is part of Herodotus's history, so the actions of people and states by themselves cannot explain the events involved. As for choice (E), there is no indication that the histories were meant to challenge anyone's sensibilities.

159. **1st, 2nd, and 3rd.** The first statement paraphrases the claim that the gods act "within certain boundaries," while the second statement paraphrases the claim that they do so "to accomplish his or her own agenda." The third statement is the main point of the passage: that the gods act as agents of destiny, which they do not themselves control.

160. **(C).** Chemical blockers scatter, or disperse, light waves. Chemical absorbers use light waves to promote electrons which then release light waves with a longer wavelength as they return to their ground energy state. Thus, choice (C) is correct. Choice (A) makes a reference to lightening and darkening light waves, neither of which is mentioned in the passage. Choices (B) and (D) refer to converting light waves to radiation, which is not mentioned in the passage. And absorbers absorb the radiation into their molecular structure, not into the skin as in choice (E).

161. **(D).** The chromophores absorb light in the 290–320 nm range and use it to promote (or move up) electrons between energy levels. Since light with wavelengths of 300 nm falls in this range, their electrons should move up in energy levels when exposed to it. Thus, choice (D) is correct. Choice (C) would be correct if not for the range given: the author does not indicate how chromophores react to light above 320 nm. Choice (B) is the exact opposite of what the question asks for. Choice (A) applies to physical blockers but not to chemical absorbers.

162. "The specific wavelength absorbed by a given chromophore is determined by the discrete quantal amounts of energy that are required to excite electrons between the energy levels or its molecules." In order to select a chromophore for a particular sunscreen, you would need to know which light waves the sunscreen needs to block and which chromophore would block those waves. This sentence identifies which feature of a chromophore determines which light waves it absorbs. The next sentence in the passage might seem like a good match, but it only specifies how to select a chromophore that would absorb UVB radiation, not UVA radiation.

163. **3rd only.** The first statement is not true because the author points out in the first paragraph that "[for] all we know, the story may have been 'Christianized' in its oral form long before the poet set it into writing." The second statement is incorrect because the leap from "the story of Sir Gawain and the Green Knight has its foundation in Arthurian legend" to "Sir Gawain was a knight in King Arthur's court" is too large to make. The third statement is true, and a good match for the final sentence of the first paragraph, which posits that the tale may be "a pagan interpretation of Christian ideals" or "an externally imposed Christianization of pagan codes of behavior."

164. **(E).** Choices (C) and (D) are directly contradicted by the passage. Nothing suggests that the religious outlook of the interpreter influenced the interpretation of the story, so choice (A) is also wrong. Choice (B) is too strong: the passage only states that, according to its interpretation of the story, Gawain's motives are not Christian. But this doesn't show that they could not be. Choice (E), on the other hand, follows directly from the claim that while Gawain's actions and words are Christian, his motives are not.

165. **(B).** The theory in the final sentence is that the poet associates Gawain with a pagan symbol and then portrays his "Christian" virtues as superficial in order to criticize the pagan interpretation of Christianity. Choice (B), if true, would show that the poet was, at very least, inconsistent in this message (or, possibly, the part about Gawain being superficial in his virtues is really just about Gawain). Choice (A) is true and described in the passage, so it would not "undermine" the theory. Choices (C), (D), and (E) do not address the interplay between paganism and Christianity and thus have no bearing on the theory.

166. **1st and 3rd only.** Since Astyages reacted to his first dream by altering the marriage arrangements for his daughter (in order to select a less threatening husband), it can be inferred that he believed her husband could be a threat. Since he intentionally selected a Persian rather than a Median, it can additionally be inferred that he thought a Persian would be less of a threat. Thus, the first and third statements can be inferred. However, although Astyages' dream was "interpreted ominously by the Magi" and "as a consequence" he pursued a course of action, the passage does not indicate that he thought it was "always" best to obey the Magi, nor whether the Magi made "recommendations." Therefore, the second statement is not supported.

167. **(A).** One of the two mistakes referred to in the passage was marrying Mandane to Cambyses. But if her son would have deposed Astyages even if he had had a different father, then altering what would have been the normal treatment of her marriage was not a mistake that led to Astyages's downfall. This supports choice (A).

168. **(B).** The passage makes the case that Bierstadt's work, which represented the "optimistic feeling in America during the Westward expansion," was later considered "gaudy" and no longer suited for the prevailing trends in art in America after the war. The optimism that once characterized American preferences was tempered by the "horrors of war." The new American attitude, in other words, was one of "somber realism," choice (B). Don't get misled into picking (D), "prideful idealism," by the fact that the passage mentions American pride. The passage does not imply that

there was anything idealistic about the new American attitudes after the Civil War. Choice (A) may also be tempting but the author never makes any sort of claim as to whether the new American attitudes are misguided.

169. **(E).** A central thesis of the passage is that the same elements that initially made Bierstadt's work popular eventually contributed to its downfall. These elements were, in short, an emphasis on size and quantity rather than emotionality. The quoted phrase is a criticism of his work to this effect, providing a specific example of the opinion of the time. This supports choice (E). Choice (C) may be tempting, but this phrase may or may not be the opinion of an expert, plus to "provide expert testimony" is not the best description for the purpose of the phrase.

170. **(C).** The author argues in the first paragraph that Bierstadt "developed a fixed style that was most easily recognizable for its size," (A), that he had an "ability to represent the optimistic feeling in America," (B), that he "deliberately appealed to those rich patrons," (D), and that patrons could purchase a "hyperbolized replica of a Western vista," (E). The increasing attention to "subdued appreciation for the details of American life" is mentioned in the second paragraph as a trend that worked *against* Bierstadt. Therefore, choice (C) is the correct answer to this Except question.

# Chapter 6 *of*

## 5 lb. Book of GRE® Practice Problems

# Logic-Based Reading Comprehension

# In This Chapter...

Logic-Based Reading Comprehension

Logic-Based Reading Comprehension Answers

# Logic-Based Reading Comprehension

1.  The school board has responded to the new school lunch guidelines by replacing fried potatoes with fruit in a standard meal option that used to consist of a hamburger, fried potatoes, and milk. However, the guidelines specifically require that vegetables, not fruits, be included in every meal.

    The information above most strongly supports which of the following conclusions?

    (A)  Fruit provides just as much health value to students as vegetables.

    (B)  Students are more likely to eat fruit than vegetables.

    (C)  The school board is not following the new school guidelines.

    (D)  The school board is responsible for the health of the student population.

    (E)  The new school lunch guidelines are unnecessarily strict.

2.  While many people think of the lottery as a harmless way to have fun and possibly win some money, buying lottery tickets is a form of gambling. Therefore, public officials shouldn't buy lottery tickets.

    The argument above relies upon which of the following assumptions?

    (A)  Individuals who play the lottery are less likely to win a big payout than they are to be killed in a car crash.

    (B)  Some public officials are guilty of much more serious offenses than gambling.

    (C)  Public officials shouldn't gamble.

    (D)  Many public officials are easily tempted to violate rules governing their positions.

    (E)  Most lottery winners are not made as happy by their winnings as they expected.

3.  Some say that Saddlebrook College provides the best value in our state. Yet, students at our state's Tunbridge College pay less, enjoy newer buildings and smaller class sizes, and earn larger incomes after graduation.

    The information above, if true, most strongly supports which of the following judgments?

    (A)  Tunbridge College provides the best value in our state.

    (B)  Tunbridge College has more stringent entrance requirements than Saddlebook College, and thus attracts students of a higher caliber.

    (C)  It is not true that Saddlebrook College provides the best value in our state.

    (D)  Student income after graduation is a valid means of judging the value of a college education.

    (E)  Students at Tunbridge College report higher rates of satisfaction than students at Saddlebrook College.

4.  Studies have long shown that people who drive red cars receive more speeding tickets from the police than do those who drive cars of other colors. Researchers have thus concluded that the color of a car influences its driver's behavior.

    The researchers' conclusion depends upon which of the following assumptions?

    (A)  Drivers of black cars receive the second-most speeding tickets.

    (B)  Red cars do not attract more attention from the police than do cars of other colors.

    (C)  Police officers do not drive red cars.

    (D)  Red cars do not receive any more parking tickets, on average, than do cars of other colors.

    (E)  Drivers of red cars who are ticketed for speeding are able to appeal their tickets more often than drivers of other color cars.

5.  The headmaster at Leawood Day School noticed that scores on math tests were lower this year than in previous years. This year, all students took math courses during the first period of the school day; in years past, they had taken math during the final period of the day. Reasoning that the students perform better on math tests when they are fully awake, the headmaster concluded that test scores would be higher if math classes were moved to the end of the day.

    The headmaster's reasoning depends upon which of the following assumptions?

    (A)  It would be possible to reconfigure the school's schedule to accommodate having math classes in the afternoon.

    (B)  Several schools similar to Leawood Day School hold math classes in the afternoon.

    (C)  The quality of the teaching has little bearing on test scores.

    (D)  This year the math department started using new, unfamiliar curricular materials.

    (E)  Students are more likely to be fully awake during the final period of the day than they are during the first period of the day.

6.  Exterminator: Using poisoned food is the most effective tactic for combating a mouse infestation. The mouse will carry the food back to the nest, causing all of the mice to die, while a trap will kill only the one mouse that falls into it. If all signs of the mice disappear for three consecutive weeks after poisoned food is used, the homeowner can be sure that the poison was successful in eradicating the mice.

Which of the following, if true, most seriously calls into question the exterminator's claim that the absence of signs for three weeks means the mice have been eradicated by the poison?

(A)  Because mice hide whenever they sense humans, it is very difficult to see or hear mice even when there is an active infestation.

(B)  It is more humane to use "live-catch" traps that allow homeowners to release the still-living mice outside.

(C)  In the spring, many mice that nest in houses begin foraging for food outside and do not return to the comfort of the house until the fall or winter.

(D)  There are several different kinds of poison that could be used, some of which are more effective than others.

(E)  It sometimes takes longer than three weeks for all of the mice to ingest and die from the poison.

7.  The recent decline in the employment rate was spurred by predictions of slow economic growth in the coming year. However, those predictions would not have affected the employment rate if major industries had not lacked capital reserves. So if major industries increase their capital reserves, the employment rate will not decline in the future.

Which of the following, if true, casts the most doubt on the validity of the argument above?

(A)  Major industries foresaw the drop in employment.

(B)  Some major industries had appreciable capital reserves.

(C)  An increase in labor costs could adversely affect the employment rate.

(D)  The government could pass legislation mandating that major industries set aside a fixed amount as capital reserves every year.

(E)  The drop in the emloyment rate was more severe this year than last.

8.  New methods of math education in this country do a disservice to our children. In the lower grades, math instruction should focus on the basic skills that students will need to solve complex problems in higher grades. Learning basic math skills is like learning the scales and chords that one will later use to master complicated concertos and symphonies. Increasingly, math educators in this country seem to have it backward, emphasizing in higher grades the same narrow, skills-based approach that students learned in lower grades rather than the analytical tools that they will need to solve complex math problems.

Which of the following, if true, would most seriously weaken the conclusion drawn above?

(A)  While music courses are often included in elementary school curricula, such classes are rarely taught in high school.

(B)  On international tests of complex math skills, high school students in this country performed no worse than did their counterparts from countries in which problem solving is emphasized in higher grades.

(C)  When presented with a math problem to solve, students in higher grades are more likely to arrive at different answers than students in lower grades.

(D)  Older students tend to receive higher grades in math than younger students do.

(E)  Universities in this country report a steady increase in the percentage of first-year students who qualify to take courses such as engineering that require advanced math.

9.  **The fight against the drug trade in Country X should focus for the time being on tightening the country's borders and targeting major smugglers.** Wiping out poppy fields in rural areas means inflicting even greater hardship on an economically depressed farming population. **Rather, the United Nations and the government of Country X must carefully rebuild agricultural infrastructure in areas where the economy depends on these poppy fields.**

What purpose do the two boldface sentences serve in the passage?

(A)  The first is the conclusion drawn by the speaker; the second is the alternative to that conclusion.

(B)  The first is a short-term solution to a problem; the second is a long-term solution to the same problem.

(C)  The first presents a problem; the second poses an ideal solution to the problem.

(D)  The first presents a popular solution to a problem; the second presents a solution preferred by the author.

(E)  The first presents an argument; the second presents evidence to support the argument.

10. In the 18th and 19th centuries, it was believed by many in coastal cities of the United States that the waterfront was an undesirable location for residential buildings. As a result, much of the waterfront in these cities was never developed aesthetically and instead was left to industry and commerce. Today, however, waterfront properties are generally seen as prestigious, as evidenced by the large sums paid for homes along the beach front. A developer who wishes to make a large profit would be wise to buy urban waterfront lots and erect residential buildings on them.

Which of the following, if true, most strongly supports the claim made about urban waterfront properties?

    (A) People today have more money, relatively speaking, to spend on real estate than they did in previous centuries.

    (B) Homeowners will be willing to spend large sums on residential properties in traditionally industrial or commercial districts.

    (C) Many urban waterfront lots are available for purchase.

    (D) Many coastal cities are encouraging developers to rehabilitate the waterfront through tax incentives.

    (E) Properties in interior residential districts in coastal cities are significantly more expensive than those along the waterfront.

11. Psychiatric research has shown that receiving high-quality outpatient care, rather than being confined to an institution, produces the best quality of life for people who are mentally ill. Responding to this research, Congress in 1963 passed a law that released 95% of the mentally ill patients who had been confined to institutions. In 1983, however, researchers discovered that, on average, mentally ill people in the United States were faring worse than ever.

Which if the following, if true, best resolves the paradox in the above passage?

    (A) More people were diagnosed with psychiatric disorders in 1983 than in 1963.

    (B) In 1983, men who had been released from mental institutions fared worse than their female counterparts.

    (C) A number of psychiatric medications were discovered between 1963 and 1983, including some early antidepressants.

    (D) Congress never supplied the funding that would have been necessary to provide high-quality outpatient care to the newly released patients.

    (E) Most of the released patients who were doing badly in 1983 suffered from one of three mental illnesses.

12. In response to the increasing cost of producing energy through traditional means, such as combustion, many utility companies have begun investing in renewable energy sources, chiefly wind and solar power, hoping someday to rely on them completely and thus lower energy costs. The utility companies claim that although these sources require significant initial capital investment, they will provide stable energy supplies at low cost. As a result, these sources will be less risky for the utilities than nonrenewable sources, such as gas, oil, and coal, whose prices can fluctuate dramatically according to availability.

The claim of the utility companies presupposes which of the following?

(A) The public will embrace the development of wind and solar power.

(B) No new deposits of gas, oil, and coal will be discovered in the near future.

(C) Weather patterns are consistent and predictable.

(D) The necessary technology for conversion to wind and solar power is not more expensive than the technology needed to create energy through combustion.

(E) Obtaining energy from nonrenewable sources, such as gas, oil and coal, cannot be made less risky.

13. Inorganic pesticides remain active on the surfaces of fruits and vegetables for several days after spraying, while organic pesticides dissipate within a few hours after application, leaving the surface of the sprayed produce free of pesticide residue. Therefore, when purchasing from a farm that uses inorganic pesticides, one must be careful to wash the produce thoroughly before eating it to prevent the ingestion of toxins. But one need not worry about ingesting pesticides when purchasing from farms that use only organic pesticides.

The argument above assumes which of the following?

(A) Consumers are aware of the origins of the produce they purchase.

(B) Produce from farms that use organic pesticides reaches the consumer within hours after it is picked or harvested.

(C) No farm uses both organic and inorganic pesticides.

(D) Organic pesticides are incapable of penetrating the skin of a fruit or vegetable.

(E) The use of either type of pesticide does not increase the cost of produce.

**MANHATTAN**
PREP

14. Unlike juvenile diabetes, which is a genetic condition present from birth, type 2 diabetes is acquired later in life, generally as a result of obesity and inactivity. The number of cases of type 2 diabetes has been steadily increasing in the United States since 1970, indicating to many researchers that the U.S. population is becoming increasingly heavy and sedentary. If the government wishes to stem the spread of the disease, it should educate the public about the dangers of an inactive, calorie-laden lifestyle and promote healthful diets and exercise.

Which of the following, if true, provides the strongest reason to believe that the proposed education program will <u>not</u> be effective?

   (A)  School health programs already educate middle-school students about the issue.
   (B)  The public already has access to this information through the internet.
   (C)  Food companies encourage the public to indulge in unhealthful snacks.
   (D)  The government has not set aside money for such a program.
   (E)  Healthful foods and exercise programs are beyond the financial means of many people.

15. Every year, many people become ill because of airborne mold spores in their homes. After someone becomes ill, specialists are often hired to eradicate the mold. These specialists look in damp areas of the house, since mold is almost always found in places where there is substantial moisture. If one wishes to avoid mold poisoning, then, one should make sure to keep all internal plumbing in good condition to prevent leakage that could serve as a breeding ground for mold.

Which of the following is an assumption on which the argument depends?

   (A)  Mold itself does not create moisture.
   (B)  Most homeowners know enough about plumbing to determine whether theirs is in good condition.
   (C)  Mold cannot grow in dry areas.
   (D)  No varieties of mold are harmless.
   (E)  Mold spores cannot be filtered from the air.

16. To prevent overcrowding, last month the town zoning board limited the number of new buildings that can be constructed in the town in any given year. The board claims that doing so will preserve open spaces and lessen the strain on municipal resources such as schools and garbage disposal. Critics of the changes argue that the plan will harm the community or, at the very least, will fail in its purpose.

Which of the following, if true, most supports the claims of the critics of the plan?

(A) Other towns have had mixed success with similar zoning plans.

(B) No new schools have been built in the town in ten years.

(C) Property taxes in the town are higher than in neighboring towns.

(D) Under the zoning plan, new apartment buildings would be exempt from the limits on new construction.

(E) The nearest garbage dump is several miles away from the town.

17. Because of a rare type of fungus that killed off many cacao trees in Brazil, there was an unusually meager harvest of cacao beans this year. The wholesale price of cocoa solids and cocoa butter has increased significantly and is unlikely to fall in the foreseeable future. As a result, the retail price of chocolate is certain to increase within six months.

The answer to which of the following questions would provide information relevant to evaluating the argument above?

(A) Has the price of cocoa solids and cocoa butter remained steady during other periods of poor harvest?

(B) Are consumers willing to spend more for chocolate?

(C) Have the prices of other ingredients in chocolate decreased recently?

(D) What percentage of cacao trees in Brazil were affected by the fungus?

(E) Can the fungus be eliminated within the next six months?

**MANHATTAN**
PREP

18. Two years ago, the cost of the raw material used in a particular product doubled after an earthquake disrupted production in the region where the material is mined. Since that time, the company that makes the product has seen its profit margins decline steadily. Aiming to improve profit margins, the company's head of engineering has decided that he must find a new source for the raw material.

Which of the following, if true, would cast the most doubt on the validity of the head of engineering's decision?

(A) New competitors have entered the market every six months for the past two years, resulting in price wars that have progressively driven down revenues across the market.

(B) Although the earthquake occurred two years ago, the region's mines have still not recovered to pre-earthquake production capacity.

(C) There are several other regions in the world where the raw material is mined, but those regions do not produce as much of the raw material as the current source region.

(D) The company could use a completely different raw material to make its product.

(E) Recent advances in mining technology will make mining the raw material much more efficient and cost-effective in the future.

19. According to a recent research study, more than 90% of graduates of the private high schools in a certain county continue their education in college. By contrast, only 65% of graduates of the public high schools subsequently pursue college education. Therefore, if parents in the county wish to increase the likelihood that their children will attend college, they should send them to private rather than public schools.

Which of the following statements, if true, would most seriously weaken the argument above?

(A) Graduates of private schools typically score higher on standardized tests and other tests of academic achievement.

(B) While private schools are typically very expensive, attendance of public school is free for the residents of the county.

(C) In comparison with graduates of private schools, a substantially greater proportion of public school graduates receive need-based financial aid for their college education.

(D) In comparison with private schools, public schools provide more opportunities for student involvement in sports and other athletic activities, which almost always increase the likelihood of students' acceptance to colleges.

(E) Since most public schools are located in rural areas of the county populated primarily by farmers, nearly 30% of students from public high schools choose to pursue farming occupations rather than apply to colleges.

20. Due to high jet fuel costs, airline carriers are looking for new ways to increase revenues and thereby counteract declining profits. Airline A has proposed increasing the number of passengers that can fit on its airplanes by creating several standing room only "seats" in which passengers would be propped against a padded backboard and held in place with a harness. This proposal, since it relates to passenger safety, cannot be implemented without prior approval by the Federal Aviation Administration.

The above statements, if true, indicate that Airline A has made which of the following conclusions?

(A) The addition of standing room only "seats" will generate more revenue than the cost of ensuring that these seats meet safety standards.

(B) The Federal Aviation Administration will approve Airline A's specific proposal.

(C) The revenue generated by the addition of standing room only "seats" is greater than the current cost of jet fuel.

(D) There are no safer ways in which Airline A can increase revenues.

(E) Passenger safety is less important than increasing revenue.

21. A recent development in the marketplace for consumer technology goods has been the premium placed on design—products with innovative and appealing designs relative to competing products can often command substantially higher prices. **Because design innovations are quickly copied by other manufacturers though,** many consumer technology companies charge as much as possible when it comes to their new designs to extract as much value as possible from their new designs. But large profits generated by the innovative design will give competitors stronger incentives to copy the designs. **Therefore, the best strategy to maximize overall profit from an innovative new design is to charge less than the greatest possible price.**

In the argument above, the two portions in boldface play which of the following roles?

(A) The first is an assumption that assists a course of action criticized by the argument; the second provides a consideration to support the argument's recommended position.

(B) The first is a consideration that helps explain the appeal of a certain strategy; the second presents an alternative strategy endorsed by the argument.

(C) The first is an assumption that justifies a specific strategy; the second is that strategy.

(D) The first is a consideration presented to demonstrate that a particular strategy will not apply; the second is a factor cited to support the argument's main position.

(E) The first is a factor used to justify a particular strategy; the second is a factor against that strategy.

22. Smoking is a known cause of certain serious health problems, including emphysema and lung cancer. Now, an additional concern can be added to the list of maladies caused by smoking. A recent study surveyed both smokers and nonsmokers, and found that smokers are significantly more anxious and nervous than nonsmokers.

    Which of the following is an assumption on which the argument rests?

    (A) Anxiety and nervousness can lead to serious health problems.

    (B) Anxiety and nervousness do not make individuals more likely to start smoking.

    (C) Equivalent numbers of smokers and nonsmokers were surveyed for the study.

    (D) Smokers are aware of the various health problems attributed to smoking, including lung cancer and emphysema.

    (E) Smokers who had smoked a cigarette immediately before responding to the survey were more anxious and nervous than smokers who had not smoked for several hours.

23. The number of new cases of tuberculosis diagnosed in Country X increased dramatically this year. The country's news media have speculated that the sharp increase in new cases is the result of the tuberculosis outbreak that occurred in neighboring Country Y last year. Health officials in Country X have therefore proposed that all visitors from Country Y must submit to a medical examination before entering Country X.

    Which of the following, if true, most strongly suggests that the proposed medical examinations will <u>not</u> help curb the spread of tuberculosis in Country X?

    (A) Country Z, which also neighbors Country Y, has not experienced an increase in cases of tuberculosis.

    (B) Current medical technology is not capable of detecting all carriers of tuberculosis.

    (C) Country X does not have the resources to examine all visitors from Country Y.

    (D) Tuberculosis is not spread through human contact.

    (E) Citizens of Country Y will not travel to Country X if the proposal is implemented.

24.  The people of Prohibitionland are considering banning the service of alcoholic beverages in restaurants to curb unruly behavior on the part of its residents. Proprietors of restaurants in Prohibitionland are protesting the ban on the grounds that it will reduce their revenues and profits. However, several provinces in Prohibitionland enacted restrictions on alcoholic beverages last year, and the sales taxes paid by the restaurants in those provinces rose by an average of 50%. In contrast, the sales taxes paid by restaurants located in areas of Prohibitionland that did not have any restrictions rose by an average of 30 percent.

Which of the following, if true, supports the restaurant proprietors' economic stance against the ban?

(A)  In the provinces that restricted alcoholic beverages, there was a short-term negative impact on restaurant visitation in the beginning of last year.

(B)  The sales tax in Prohibitionland is lower on food and beverages than it is on other consumer goods, such as clothing.

(C)  The consumption of alcoholic beverages in Prohibitionland has been on a gradual decline the last 20 years.

(D)  The restrictions on alcoholic beverages enacted last year allowed for the service of alcohol beginning around dinner time each evening.

(E)  Overall sales tax revenue did not increase at a substantially higher rate in the provinces that enacted the restrictions on alcoholic beverages than in the rest of Prohibitionland last year.

25.  Serious individual art collectors are usually discreet when making significant purchases or sales related to their collections. At art auctions, for example, these collectors often place anonymous bids for major artwork. Therefore, the whereabouts of most of the world's most valuable artwork are probably unknown.

Each of the following, if true, would weaken the conclusion above EXCEPT:

(A)  The value of a piece of art is purely subjective.

(B)  Serious art collectors usually publicize their new artwork several months after making a purchase.

(C)  Museums own the vast majority of the world's most valuable artwork.

(D)  Of all the individuals in the world who own extremely valuable artwork, only a few are considered serious art collectors.

(E)  The private collections of most serious individual art collectors are often displayed in public settings.

26. Last January, in an attempt to lower the number of traffic fatalities, the state legislature passed its "Click It or Ticket" law. Under the new law, motorists can be pulled over and ticketed for not wearing their seat belts, even if no additional driving infraction was committed. Lawyers and citizens groups are already protesting the law, saying it unfairly infringes on the rights of the state's drivers. Law enforcement groups counter these claims by stating that the new regulations will save countless additional lives.

Which of the following inferences is best supported by the passage above?

(A) Prior to the "Click It or Ticket" law, motorists could not be stopped simply for not wearing a seat belt.

(B) The "Click It or Ticket" law violates current search and seizure laws.

(C) Laws similar to "Click It or Ticket" have effectively reduced traffic fatalities in a number of states.

(D) The previous seat belt laws were ineffective in saving lives.

(E) Law enforcement groups, rather than citizens groups, should determine how to best ensure the safety of motorists.

27. Calorie restriction, a diet high in nutrients but low in calories, is known to prolong the life of rats and mice by preventing heart disease, cancer, diabetes, and other diseases. A 6-month study of 48 moderately overweight people, who each reduced their calorie intake by at least 25%, demonstrated decreases in insulin levels and body temperature, with the greatest decrease observed in individuals with the greatest percentage change in their calorie intake. Low insulin level and body temperature are both considered signs of longevity, partly because an earlier study by other researchers found both traits in long-lived people.

If the above statements are true, they support which of the following inferences?

(A) Calorie restriction produces similar results in humans as it does in rats and mice.

(B) Humans who reduce their calorie intake by at least 25% on a long-term basis will live longer than they would have had they not done so.

(C) Calorie intake is directly correlated to insulin level in moderately overweight individuals.

(D) Individuals with low insulin levels are healthier than individuals with high insulin levels.

(E) Some individuals in the study reduced their calorie intake by more than 25%.

28. Recent research has indicated that married people are not only happier than unmarried people, but also healthier. This study has been widely reported by the media, with most commentators concluding that being married is good for one's health and attitude.

    The conclusion of the media commentators depends on which of the following assumptions?

    (A) The longer people are married, the happier and healthier they become.

    (B) Married couples who had a large, extravagant wedding are happier than those who had a small, simple ceremony.

    (C) Married people cannot get depressed.

    (D) Single people with depression or health problems are just as likely to get married as are other single people.

    (E) Some marriages are more harmonious than others.

29. For nearly a century, physiologists erroneously believed that a **buildup of lactic acid in muscle tissue was responsible for the soreness that many people experience after strenuous exercise**. The acid, they claimed, is the waste produced by metabolic activity in the muscle and reaches "threshold" levels, causing soreness, when the muscle has depleted its oxygen supply. **Researchers have recently discovered, however, that lactic acid is actually the fuel that powers muscular activity.** Therefore, the cause of muscle soreness remains unknown.

    In the argument above, the portions in boldface play which of the following roles?

    (A) The first is an assertion that the author accepts as true; the second is a consideration in support of that assertion.

    (B) The first is an assertion that the author accepts as true; the second describes a situation that the author posits as contrary to that assertion.

    (C) The first is an assertion that the author argues against; the second is evidence presented as contrary to the author's argument.

    (D) The first is evidence that the author believes is no longer valid; the second is additional evidence that the author uses to support his main point.

    (E) The first is a claim that the author believes to be invalid; the second is the author's main point.

**MANHATTAN**
PREP

30. An oil field prospector and developer reported a large oil deposit in southwestern Texas. As a result, a large oil and gas company purchased the field with the intention of drilling oil wells in the area soon afterwards. However, the company found that the oil deposit was actually much smaller than the prospector had indicated. Thus, the methods that the prospector had used to determine the size of the oil deposit must have been inaccurate.

Which of the following is an assumption on which the argument depends?

    (A) The company's methods of measuring the size of the oil deposit were determined by a third party to be more accurate than those used by the prospector.

    (B) The prospector did not purposefully fabricate or misrepresent the size of the oil deposit.

    (C) Though smaller than originally thought, the oil deposit contained enough oil to make drilling commercially feasible.

    (D) The prospector did not explore other oil fields and use the same methods to determine the magnitude of the oil present, if any.

    (E) The company had successfully drilled for oil in other large oil fields in Texas throughout the early twentieth century.

31. According to a recent study on financial roles, one-third of high school seniors say that they have "significant financial responsibilities." These responsibilities include, but are not limited to, contributing to food, shelter, or clothing for themselves or their families. At the same time, a second study demonstrates that a crisis in money management exists for high school students. According to this study, 80% of high school seniors have never taken a personal finance class even though the same percentage of seniors has opened bank accounts and one-third of these account holders has bounced a check.

Which of the following conclusions can be properly drawn from the statements above?

    (A) High schools would be wise to incorporate personal finance classes into their core curricula.

    (B) At least one-third of high school seniors work part-time jobs after school.

    (C) The number of high school seniors with significant financial responsibilities is greater than the number of seniors who have bounced a check.

    (D) Any high school seniors who contribute to food, shelter, or clothing for themselves or their families have significant financial responsibilities.

    (E) The majority of high school students have no financial responsibilities to their families.

32. Federal law prohibits businesses from reimbursing any employees for the cost of owning and operating a private aircraft that is used for business purposes. Thus, many companies in the United States themselves purchase private aircraft. The vast majority of the business aviation fleet is owned by small and mid-size businesses, and flights are strictly for business purposes, with mostly mid-level employees on board. These companies and their boards of directors are in full compliance with the law and with what is best for their businesses.

Which of the following can be most properly inferred from the statements above?

   (A)   The federal law in question costs businesses money.

   (B)   Most executives would rather fly on company owned planes than on commercial airlines.

   (C)   Large businesses usually have their executives fly first or business class on commercial flights.

   (D)   Upper-level executives are less often in compliance with the law.

   (E)   By not receiving any reimbursement for these flights, the mid-level executives on board are complying with the law.

33. Experts estimate that insurance companies' tardiness in paying doctors for legitimate medical claims adds approximately 10% in overhead costs for physicians. Insurance companies counter that the tardiness sometimes results from billing errors made by the doctors themselves. Since dealing with these billing errors costs the insurance companies time and money, it is clear that insurance companies do not have a significant economic incentive to delay claim payments to doctors.

Which of the following pieces of information, if true, weakens the conclusion above?

   (A)   Some doctors who submit accurate bills to insurance companies still receive tardy payments.

   (B)   The cost to the insurance companies to process incorrect bills from doctors' offices is roughly equivalent to the increased costs that physicians accrue as a result of tardy payments from insurance companies.

   (C)   A rising proportion of medical claims submitted by doctors to insurance companies are deemed illegitimate by those insurance companies.

   (D)   The billing errors made by doctors' offices are typically very minor, such as the submission of a claim with an outdated patient home address.

   (E)   The overhead costs incurred by doctors as a result of delayed insurance payments result in an increase in the premiums paid by consumers to health insurance companies that far exceeds any increase in the fees paid to doctors by insurance companies.

34. Farmers in developing countries claim that the U.S. government, through farm subsidies, is responsible for the artificially low global price of wheat. Because the U.S. government buys whatever wheat American farmers are unable to sell on the open market, American farmers have no incentive to modulate the size of their crops according to the needs of the global market. As a result, American farmers routinely produce more wheat than the global market can absorb and the global price of wheat is kept low. Without these subsidies, the farmers in developing economies claim, American farmers would produce only the amount of wheat that they could sell on the open market and the global price of wheat would rise.

Which of the following, if true, most weakens the claims of the farmers in developing countries regarding the price of wheat?

   (A) Wheat that is not processed for consumption is often used for certain industrial applications.
   (B) Non-governmental buyers of wheat and wheat products are able to predict how much wheat they will need several years in advance.
   (C) The U.S. government offers similar subsidies to soybean farmers, though the global price of soybeans is significantly higher than that of wheat.
   (D) Other countries, such as Canada and Russia, are likely to produce more wheat if the United States were to reduce its output.
   (E) The price of sorghum, a crop for which the U.S. government offers no subsidies, is lower than that of wheat.

35. Researchers studying the spread of the Black Plague in 16th-century England claim that certain people survived the epidemic because they carried a genetic mutation, known as Delta-32, that is known to prevent the bacteria that causes the plague from overtaking the immune system. To support this hypothesis, the researchers tested the direct descendants of the residents of an English town where an unusually large proportion of people survived the plague. More than half of these descendants tested positive for the mutation Delta-32, a figure nearly three times higher than that found in other locations.

The researchers' hypothesis is based on which of the following assumptions?

   (A) Delta-32 does not prevent a carrier from contracting any disease other than the plague.
   (B) The plague is not similar to other diseases caused by bacteria.
   (C) Delta-32 did not exist in its current form until the 16th century.
   (D) No one who tested positive for Delta-32 has ever contracted a disease caused by bacteria.
   (E) The plague does not cause genetic mutations such as Delta-32.

36. Implementing extensive wireless networks in cities would be a practical way to meet the needs of city households, schools, and businesses. Rural communities have found that wireless networks are both more reliable and cheaper than land-based networks.

    Which of the following would most likely be cited by a supporter of the argument?

    (A) Urban areas do not pose additional problems for the effective operation of wireless networks.

    (B) Wireless networks work far better where population density is low.

    (C) Iceland, a very rural country, successfully uses wireless networks.

    (D) The expense of wireless transmission in areas with large buildings is much higher than in areas without such buildings.

    (E) Poor neighborhoods have less access to internet services than do educators or businesses.

37. Studies have shown that **people who keep daily diet records are far more successful at losing weight than people who don't keep track of what they eat**. Researchers believe that many weight-loss efforts fail because people eat more calories than they intend to consume. One study followed a group of patients who reported that they could not lose weight when consuming only 1,200 calories a day. **The study found that the group consumed, on average, 47% more calories than it claimed and exercised 51% less.** In contrast, when dieters record what they eat, their actual consumption more closely matches their reported consumption.

    The two boldface portions in the argument above are best described by which of the following statements?

    (A) The first is a conclusion reached by researchers; the second is evidence that this conclusion is correct.

    (B) The first is an explanation of why a certain theory is thought to be true; the second is an example of research results that support this theory.

    (C) The first is an example illustrating the truth of a certain theory; the second is a competing theory.

    (D) The first is a premise upon which the researchers base their opinion; the second illustrates that their opinion is correct.

    (E) The first introduces a theory that the researchers have disproved; the second is the basis for the researchers' argument.

**MANHATTAN**
PREP

38.  The anticipated retirement of tens of thousands of baby boomers will create an unprecedented opportunity to move significant numbers of people into career-track jobs at family-supporting incomes. Major industries, from health care and construction to automotive repair, will soon face deep shortages of workers as a result of projected growth and boomer retirements. Fortunately, many of these jobs have relatively low barriers to entry and could be filled by out-of-work young people. To achieve this result, the city government should convene employers and educators to determine how best to create paths of upward mobility in these fields.

Which of the following, if true, most weakens the argument?

    (A)  Immigration reform will limit the pool of available workers.

    (B)  Government efforts have been shown to affect employment trends only rarely.

    (C)  The best available positions require skills not possessed by the vast majority of the unemployed.

    (D)  A small proportion of baby boomers will not retire as soon as is anticipated.

    (E)  Many out-of-work young people are unaware of these looming employment opportunities.

39.  The "Doppler effect" refers to the universally perceived change in the apparent pitch of a sound when that sound is approaching or receding from the listener. Specifically, whenever the distance between the listener and the source of the sound is decreasing, the sound will be perceived by the listener as higher than its true pitch; whenever that distance is increasing, the sound will be perceived by the listener as lower than its true pitch. If the distance between the listener and the source is not changing, the listener will perceive the true pitch of the sound.

If the above principle holds, which of the following should be observed as an eastward-traveling train is approached by a westward-traveling train that is blowing its horn?

    (A)  Passengers in the eastbound train should hear the true pitch of the horn; passengers in the westbound train will hear a sound lower than the true pitch.

    (B)  Passengers in the westbound train should hear the true pitch of the horn; passengers in the eastbound train will hear a sound lower than the true pitch.

    (C)  Passengers in the eastbound train should hear the true pitch of the horn; passengers in the westbound train will hear a sound higher than the true pitch.

    (D)  Passengers in the westbound train should hear the true pitch of the horn; passengers in the eastbound train will hear a sound higher than the true pitch.

    (E)  Passengers in both trains should hear a sound that is higher than the true pitch.

40. The popular notion that a tree's age can be determined by counting the number of internal rings in its trunk is generally true. However, to help regulate the internal temperature of the tree, the outermost layers of wood of the Brazilian ash often peel away when the temperature exceeds 95 degrees Fahrenheit, leaving the tree with fewer rings than it would otherwise have. So only if the temperature in the Brazilian ash's environment never exceeds 95 degrees Fahrenheit will its rings be a reliable measure of the tree's age.

Which of the following is an assumption on which the argument above depends?

   (A) The growth of new rings in a tree is not a function of levels of precipitation.
   (B) Only the Brazilian ash loses rings because of excessive heat.
   (C) Only one day of temperatures above 95 degrees Fahrenheit is needed to cause the Brazilian ash to lose one ring.
   (D) The internal rings of all trees are of uniform thickness.
   (E) The number of rings that will be lost when the temperature exceeds 95 degrees Fahrenheit is not predictable.

41. Celiac disease results from an inability of the digestive tract, specifically the small intestine, to absorb gluten, a protein found in wheat, barley, and certain other grains. The body's immune system attacks the gluten as if the protein were a harmful pathogen, often resulting in serious damage to the intestinal lining. People who suffer from celiac disease must eliminate gluten from their diets. Symptoms of the disease include abdominal cramps, bloating, and anemia.

If the statements above are true, which of the following assertions can be made on the basis of them?

   (A) Anyone who suffers from celiac disease will experience anemia.
   (B) Eliminating gluten from one's diet will cure celiac disease.
   (C) People experiencing abdominal cramps, bloating, and anemia have celiac disease.
   (D) Gluten is found only in grains.
   (E) The human body cannot always recognize harmless substances.

**MANHATTAN**
PREP

42. All languages that have exactly six basic color terms describe the same six colors—black, white, red, green, blue, and yellow—corresponding to the primary neural responses revealed in studies of human color perception. In addition, all languages that have only three basic color terms distinguish among black, white, and red. This evidence shows that the way in which the mind recognizes differences among colored objects is not influenced by culture.

Which of the following, if true, most seriously weakens the argument above?

  (A)  While languages differ in their number of basic color terms, no language has been conclusively determined to have more than 11 such terms.

  (B)  Every language contains mechanisms by which speakers who perceive subtle differences in hue can describe those differences.

  (C)  Among cultures employing only three color terms, the word red typically encompasses not only objects that would be called red in English but also those that would be called yellow.

  (D)  Several languages, such as Vietnamese and Pashto, use a single term to mean both blue and green, but speakers of such languages commonly refer to tree leaves or the sky to resolve ambiguous utterances.

  (E)  In a study of native speakers of Tarahumara, a language that does not distinguish between blue and green, respondents were less able to identify distinctions among blue and green chips than native speakers of Spanish, which does distinguish between blue and green.

43. In an attempt to discover the cause of malaria, a deadly infectious disease common in tropical areas, early European settlers in Hong Kong attributed the malady to poisonous gases supposed to be emanating from low-lying swampland. **Malaria, in fact, translates from the Italian as "bad air."** In the 1880s, however, doctors determined that *Anopheles* mosquitoes were responsible for transmitting the disease to humans. **The female of the species can carry a parasitic protozoa that is passed on to unsuspecting humans** when a mosquito feasts on a person's blood.

What functions do the two statements in boldface fulfill with respect to the argument presented above?

  (A)  The first follows from a mistaken conclusion about a topic in question; the second explicates the correct explanation of that topic.

  (B)  The first provides an initial conjecture; the second presents evidence that contradicts that conjecture.

  (C)  The first serves to illuminate a contested assumption; the second offers confirmation of that assumption.

  (D)  The first identifies the cause of an erroneous conclusion; the second develops a premise to support the correct conclusion.

  (E)  The first provides detail about the original, and incorrect, school of thought; the second provides the judgment later found to be true.

44. Government restrictions have severely limited the amount of stem cell research companies in the United States can conduct. Because of these restrictions, many scientists previously based in the United States and specializing in the field of stem cell research have signed long-term contracts to work for foreign companies. Recently, Congress has proposed lifting all restrictions on stem cell research.

Which of the following conclusions can most properly be inferred from the information above?

(A)   At least some foreign companies that conduct stem cell research work under fewer restrictions than some United States companies do.

(B)   Because scientists previously based in the U.S. are under long-term contracts to foreign companies, there will be a significant influx of foreign professionals into the United States.

(C)   In all parts of the world, stem cell research is dependent on the financial backing of local government.

(D)   In the near future, U.S. companies will no longer be at the forefront of stem cell research.

(E)   If restrictions on stem cell research are lifted, many of the scientists previously based in the United States will break their contracts to return to U.S. companies.

45. If life exists elsewhere in the solar system, scientists suspect it would most likely be on Europa, an ice covered moon orbiting Jupiter. However, NASA recently scrapped an unmanned science mission to Europa and reassigned most of the employees involved in the project to another project that concerns landing an astronaut on Mars. Polls show that Americans are far more fascinated by space travel than they are by discovering life elsewhere in the universe. Critics argue that NASA's decision-making process places a greater emphasis on public interest than it does on the importance of scientific research.

Which of the following, if true, would most strengthen NASA's contention that the critics are misinformed?

(A)   In 2013, NASA spent 30% of its total budget on developing a space shuttle that can travel to Mars. In 2018, that figure is expected to drop to 0%.

(B)   Studies have shown that Congress traditionally determines NASA's budget based on its perception of public interest in NASA's projects.

(C)   Some scientists are convinced that a mission to Europa would add immeasurably to our understanding of the universe; others believe that we will gain little insight from exploring Europa.

(D)   A new telescope that has been developed in Tokyo allows scientists to look at Europa in ways never possible before and promises to yield more information than the planned mission was designed to provide.

(E)   Most Americans feel that a shuttle to Mars is the next logical step in the development of a system that will eventually allow humans to travel to places as far away as Europa and beyond.

**MANHATTAN**
PREP

46. Dengue fever is a viral infection transmitted by the *Aedes* mosquito, whereas malaria is a parasitic infection transmitted by the *Anopheles* mosquito. Since both types of mosquito are prevalent on Nicaragua's "Mosquito Coast," anyone with a compromised immune system should not travel to this region, particularly during the rainy season.

All of the following, if true, strengthen the argument EXCEPT:

   (A) Medicines taken to prevent or treat malaria can cause serious health complications for people with weak immune systems.

   (B) The Nicaraguan government is trying to reduce the number of mosquitoes on the Mosquito Coast.

   (C) A compromised immune system has difficulty fighting either viral or parasitic infections.

   (D) During the rainy season, the populations of both *Aedes* and *Anopheles* mosquitoes multiply in the Mosquito Coast.

   (E) The most effective chemical insect repellent has been shown to cause brain damage upon repeated application to the skin.

47. In 2001, the Peruvian government began requiring tourists to buy expensive permits to hike the remote Inca Trail, which goes to the ancient city of Machu Picchu. The total number of permits is strictly limited; in fact, only 500 people per day are now allowed to hike the Inca Trail, whereas before 2001, visitors numbered in the thousands. The Peruvian government argues that this permit program has successfully prevented deterioration of archaeological treasures along the Inca Trail.

Which of the following, if true, most strengthens the argument above?

   (A) Since 2001, tourist guides along the Inca Trail have received 50% to 100% increases in take-home pay.

   (B) Villages near Machu Picchu have experienced declines in income, as fewer tourists means fewer sales of craft goods and refreshments.

   (C) Many of the funds from the sale of Inca Trail permits are used to staff a museum of Incan culture in Peru's capital city, Lima, and to hire guards for archaeological sites without permit programs.

   (D) Since 2001, Incan ruins similar to Machu Picchu but not on the Inca Trail have disintegrated at a significantly greater rate than those on the trail.

   (E) The total number of tourists visiting Peru has risen substantially since 2001, even as the number of tourists hiking the Inca Trail has remained constant.

48. The Farmsley Center for the Performing Arts, designed by a world-renowned architect, was built 10 years ago in downtown Metropolis. A recent study shows that, on average, a person who attends a performance at the Farmsley Center spends $83 at downtown businesses on the day of the performance. Citing this report, the chairman of the Farmsley Center's Board of Trustees claims that the Farmsley Center has been a significant source of the economic revitalization of downtown Metropolis.

Which of the following, if true, most strongly supports the chairman's contention?

    (A) The Metropolis Chamber of Commerce honored the Farmsley chairman this year for his contributions to the city.

    (B) Restaurants near the Farmsley Center tend to be more expensive than restaurants in outlying areas.

    (C) The Farmsley Center is the only building in Metropolis designed by a world-renowned contemporary architect.

    (D) For major theater companies on national tours, the Farmsley Center is the first choice among venues in downtown Metropolis.

    (E) Many suburbanites visit downtown Metropolis on weekends in order to see performances at the Farmsley Center.

49. One retirement account option allows a worker to save money without paying taxes, but requires the worker to pay taxes on funds withdrawn from the account upon retirement. A second option requires the worker to pay taxes upfront, but allows the worker to withdraw funds tax-free upon retirement. Assuming that the total amount available in the worker's retirement account at retirement is higher than the total amount contributed prior to retirement, workers can expect to pay less in taxes overall if they choose the second option.

Which of the following pieces of information would be most useful in determining whether the conclusion is valid for an individual worker?

    (A) The amount of money the worker will contribute to the retirement plan over his or her career

    (B) The amount that tax rates will increase in the future

    (C) Whether inflation will be lower than the retirement account's annual earnings

    (D) How the worker's tax bracket in retirement compares to his or her tax bracket while still employed

    (E) The dollar value of the worker's account upon retirement

50. In a recent poll, 71% of respondents reported that they cast votes in the most recent national election. Voting records show, however, that only 60% of eligible voters actually voted in that election.

Which of the following pieces of evidence, if true, would provide the best explanation for the apparent discrepancy?

(A) The margin of error for the survey was plus or minus five percentage points.

(B) Fifteen percent of the survey's respondents were living overseas at the time of the election.

(C) Prior research has shown that people who actually do vote are also more likely to respond to polls than those who do not vote.

(D) Many people who intend to vote are prevented from doing so by last-minute conflicts on election day or other complications.

(E) Some people confused the national election with other recent elections when responding to the poll.

51. Scientists recently documented that influenza spreads around the world more efficiently in the modern era due to commercial air travel. Flu symptoms are severe enough that the ill would likely cancel or reschedule air travel, but an infected person can travel across the globe before the first signs appear. Further, if symptoms develop while someone is on a plane, the infected person's cough can spread the virus easily in the enclosed and closely packed environment.

Which of the following would best minimize the role air travel can play in the spread of influenza during a pandemic?

(A) Installing air filtration systems in the planes to kill any flu virus particles flowing through the filters.

(B) Requiring air travelers to receive flu vaccinations far enough in advance of the trip to provide protection against the disease.

(C) Refusing to allow children, the elderly, or others who are especially vulnerable to flu to travel by air during a pandemic.

(D) Requiring all air travelers to wash their hands before boarding a plane.

(E) Conducting medical examinations during the boarding process and prohibiting passengers with flu symptoms from flying.

52. Male CEOs of major corporations are, on average, three inches taller than the average male. When data from the general population are analyzed and corrected for gender and age, a clear pattern emerges: for every extra inch of height, a person's annual salary increases by approximately $789. Citing these data, a prominent journalist claims that most employers have an unconscious bias in favor of tall people.

Which of the following considerations, if true, would most seriously undermine the journalist's argument?

   (A)   On average, a woman is shorter than her husband and earns less than he does.

   (B)   Socioeconomic status has been shown to have a strong positive correlation to both height and educational attainment.

   (C)   Professional basketball players, who are some of the tallest people in the labor force, have high incomes.

   (D)   Human resources professionals, who make many hiring decisions, are on average no taller than the general population.

   (E)   A tall person's tenure in a paid position is typically shorter than is the tenure of a person of average height.

53. Traditionally, public school instructors have been compensated according to seniority. Recently, the existing salary system has been increasingly criticized as an approach to compensation that rewards lackadaisical teaching and punishes motivated, highly-qualified instruction. Instead, educational experts argue that, to retain exceptional teachers and maintain quality instruction, teachers should receive salaries or bonuses based on performance rather than seniority.

Which of the following, if true, most weakens the conclusion of the educational experts?

   (A)   Some teachers believe that financial compensation is not the only factor contributing to job satisfaction and teaching performance.

   (B)   School districts will develop their own unique compensation structures that may differ greatly from those of other school districts.

   (C)   Upon leaving the teaching profession, many young teachers cite a lack of opportunity for more rapid financial advancement as a primary factor in their decisions to change careers.

   (D)   A merit-based system that bases compensation on teacher performance reduces collaboration, which is an integral component of quality instruction.

   (E)   In school districts that have implemented pay-for-performance compensation structures, standardized test scores have dramatically increased.

54. Network executives have alleged that television viewership is decreasing due to the availability of television programs on other platforms, such as the internet, video-on-demand, and mobile devices. These executives claim that **declining viewership will cause advertising revenue to fall so far that networks will be unable to spend the large sums necessary to produce programs of the quality now available**. That development, in turn, will lead to a dearth of programming for the very devices that cannibalized television's audience. However, technology executives point to research that indicates that **users of these devices increase the number of hours per week that they watch television** because they are exposed to new programs and promotional spots through these alternative platforms. This analysis demonstrates that networks can actually increase their revenue through higher advertising rates, due to larger audiences lured to television through other media.

In comparing the executives' arguments, the portions in boldface play which of the following roles?

(A) The first is an inevitable trend that weighs against the argument; the second is that argument.

(B) The first is a prediction that is challenged by the argument; the second is a finding upon which the argument depends.

(C) The first clarifies the reasoning behind the argument; the second demonstrates why the argument is flawed.

(D) The first acknowledges a position that the technology executives accept as true; the second is a consequence of that position.

(E) The first restates the argument through an analogy; the second outlines a scenario in which that argument will not hold.

55. According to a study of more than 50,000 Norwegian smokers, smokers who reduced their nicotine intake from cigarettes, even by up to 50%, did not achieve significant health benefits. The mortality rate for those who cut back on cigarettes was not lower than that for heavier smokers; moreover, the rate of cardiovascular disease was similar across all subsets of smokers in the study. As a result, the sponsors of the study claim that reducing nicotine intake does not improve one's health.

Which of the following, if true, most seriously jeopardizes the findings of the study described above?

(A) The majority of study participants minimized their nicotine withdrawal symptoms through the use of skin patches and chewing gum that provide nicotine to the body.

(B) Many of the study's participants periodically dined in restaurants in which smoking was permitted.

(C) The study's participants started smoking at different ages and had varied initial nicotine intake.

(D) Quitting smoking entirely results in a marked reduction in the ill effects of smoking.

(E) Men and women who smoked pipes and cigars were excluded from the study.

56. In developed countries, such as Canada, the percentage of the population diagnosed with clinical depression is much greater than that in developing countries. Researchers hypothesize that this difference is due to the increased leisure time afforded to residents of developed countries.

The hypothesis of the researchers depends on which of the following assumptions?

(A) Clinical depression is a genetically transmitted malady.

(B) Access to accurate diagnostic procedures for depression is equal for residents of developing and developed countries.

(C) Most activities characterized as "leisure time" in developed countries are inherently boring.

(D) Certain medications that effectively treat clinical depression are not readily available in developing countries.

(E) Few residents of developing countries dedicate any of their time to leisure.

57. Most cable television companies currently require customers to subscribe to packages of channels, but consumer groups have recently proposed legislation that would force the companies to offer à la carte pricing as well. Subscribers would pay less, argue the consumer groups, because they could purchase only the desired channels. However, the cable industry argues that under the current package pricing, popular channels subsidize less-popular ones, providing more options for viewers. For this reason, the industry claims that it is always cheaper for the consumer to purchase many bundled channels than to buy them individually.

Which of the following would be most important to determine before deciding whether to require cable television companies to offer à la carte pricing in order to reduce consumer costs?

(A) Whether the total number of channels offered to consumers would decrease, along with programming diversity, as a result of the à la carte pricing structure

(B) Whether advertising revenue for the cable television companies would decrease as a result of the à la carte pricing structure

(C) Whether a large number of consumers would, in fact, significantly reduce the number of channels purchased if given the option of purchasing them individually

(D) Whether the number of cable television consumers has been declining as a result of new avenues of content delivery, such as the Internet

(E) Whether à la carte subscribers would be required to have new television-set-top boxes

58.  A certain pharmaceutical firm recently developed a new medicine, Dendadrine, that provides highly effective treatment of severe stomach disorders that were previously thought untreatable. However, the company spent nearly $5 billion to research and develop the new medicine. Given the size of the market for Dendadrine and the amount of the initial investment, the company would need to sell Dendadrine at a price that is at least five times greater than its variable costs just to break even. Yet company management claims that Dendadrine will soon become the major driver of the firm's profits.

Which of the following statements best reconciles the management's claim with the evidence about the expenditures associated with the development of Dendadrine?

(A)  The pharmaceutical firm expects to be granted patent protection for Dendadrine; drugs under patent protection typically sell at prices that are approximately 10 times their variable costs.

(B)  The development of some pharmaceutical products involves substantial initial expenditures on research, testing, and approval.

(C)  In clinical tests, Dendadrine has proven far more effective at treating severe stomach disorders than any prior available treatments, without any serious side effects.

(D)  No competitors are developing or planning to develop new medicines that might compete with Dendadrine in the marketplace.

(E)  Millions of people suffer from severe stomach disorders, representing an estimated one to two billion dollars every year in revenue.

# Logic-Based Reading Comprehension Answers

1. **(C).** The given information "most strongly supports" one of the conclusions in the choices. When drawing a conclusion on the GRE, don't stray far from the passage. The guidelines call for including vegetables (not fruits) in every meal. The school board has replaced fried potatoes with fruit. While this does sound like a nutritional improvement, all you can infer for certain is that the guidelines are not being met.

(A) The passage states nothing about the relative health value of fruits and vegetables.

(B) The passage provides no information about how likely students are to eat any kind of food. Avoid bringing in outside knowledge or suppositions when drawing a conclusion from given information.

**(C) CORRECT.** This choice spells out the only inference you can legally make: the board is not following the guidelines.

(D) There is no information in the passage about whether the board is responsible for the health of the students.

(E) This opinion may seem reasonable, but it is not at all proven by the passage, which simply presents facts. In general, avoid making value judgments when drawing a conclusion when given only factual information. The premises would have to contain opinions as well.

2. **(C).** The correct answer is an assumption that the author believes to be true in drawing the conclusion, which is "public officials shouldn't buy lottery tickets" (as indicated by "therefore"). The argument claims that "buying lottery tickets is a form of gambling" and "therefore," a certain group shouldn't do so. The author must believe that this group, the public officials, should not gamble.

(A) People who play the lottery are not likely to win, it's true. This is a reason why people in general should not buy lottery tickets. However, the correct answer needs to address why "public officials" specifically "shouldn't buy lottery tickets."

(B) It's irrelevant whether some public officials are guilty of more serious offenses than gambling.

**(C) CORRECT.** This choice provides the necessary link between lottery tickets and public officials. Premise: "Buying lottery tickets" = "gambling." Conclusion: "Public officials shouldn't buy lottery tickets." The missing assumption, which this choice supplies word for word, is "public officials shouldn't gamble." If an argument says "certain people shouldn't do X because X is Y," then the assumption is that those certain people shouldn't do Y.

(D) It may be true that many officials are tempted to violate the rules, but this assumption does not have to be made in drawing the given argument.

(E) Like choice (A), this choice provides a reason why people in general shouldn't play the lottery, but it does not address why "public officials" specifically "shouldn't buy lottery tickets."

**MANHATTAN**
PREP

3. **(C).** The question asks what judgement, or conclusion, must follow from the exact words of the passage. Answers that could be true are incorrect.

(A) The argument states that "[s]ome say that Saddlebrook College provides the best value in our state," and then offers evidence opposing that statement. It does not have to be true that Tunbridge provides the best value in the state; there could be other colleges in the state.

(B) The passage provides no information about entrance requirements or the quality of the student body.

**(C) CORRECT.** The second sentence in the passage describes various ways in which Tunbridge is a better value than Saddlebrook, so it must follow that Saddlebrook is not the best value.

(D) This choice represents an assumption in the argument—that income after graduation is part of evaluating which college provides the best value—but the question asks for a conclusion, not an assumption within the argument.

(E) This choice is irrelevant—"satisfaction" is not the same as "value."

4. **(B).** The researchers have confused correlation with causation. If two traits X and Y are found together (in this case, red cars and speeding tickets), it does not mean that X causes Y. It could be that Y causes X, or that some third factor Z causes both. In addition, the researchers have made a second assumption—that the increased number of speeding tickets is the result of an increase in the number of speeding infractions (and not, say, the increase in attention that a red car might get).

(A) This choice regarding black cars is completely irrelevant to this argument.

**(B) CORRECT.** To move from correlation evidence to a cause/effect conclusion, the researchers must assume that no other cause is possible. In this case, they must assume that the color itself does not lead to tickets.

(C) What color cars police officers drive is irrelevant.

(D) This choice focuses on an entirely different type of ticket and thus is irrelevant.

(E) This choice is outside the scope of the argument as it deals with events after the act of speeding or the issuance of a speeding ticket.

5. **(E).** The headmaster's argument explicitly relies on the idea that students perform better on math tests when they are fully awake. Noting the drop in scores, the headmaster reasons that this drop is due to the change in class time as opposed to any other factor or combination of factors. The assumption must make a connection between the time of the class and the waking state of the students.

(A) The logistics of the schedule are irrelevant to the headmaster's position that scores would improve if the class time were moved.

(B) The time at which other schools hold math classes is irrelevant to the headmaster's argument, especially since the efficacy of that scheduling is not mentioned.

(C) While this choice could be assumed, it is not necessary to assume that the quality of teaching has little effect to conclude that a time change will raise scores.

(D) This choice provides an alternative reason for the lower scores that is contrary to the headmaster's conclusion. Thus, if anything, the headmaster would have to assume the opposite.

**(E) CORRECT.** This choice is the direct link needed between time of day and student wakefulness.

6. **(C).** The exterminator explains the effects of using poisoned food to combat a mouse infestation: mice will pick up the food and carry it to the nest, where all of the mice will eat the food and die as a result. The exterminator then claims that if X happens, then it will be certain that Y happened first. Specifically, he claims that if all signs of the mice disappear for three consecutive weeks after setting out poisoned food, then the mice all must have died as a result of that poisoned food. The correct answer will weaken this claim, for instance by showing that if X happens, it will not necessarily mean that Y happened; perhaps there is another reason why X happens.

(A) This choice is very tempting, but the exterminator argues that "all signs" of the mice "disappear"; this choice mentions only the difficulty of seeing and hearing mice. These do not represent "all signs" of an infestation; mice may leave droppings, chew things up, and so forth. Further, the mice are not harder to see and hear only after poison has been used. They are always hard to see and hear, so this does not provide an alternative explanation as to why signs might diminish or disappear after poison has been used.

(B) This choice may be true, but it does not address the exterminator's claim that if all signs disappear, then the *poison* must have killed the mice.

**(C) CORRECT.** This choice offers an alternative explanation for the absence of signs of an infestation. If the mice have left the house, then any signs of infestation would also cease because the mice are no longer there. However, the signs will have ceased because the mice left voluntarily, not because they have been eradicated by the poison, as claimed by the exterminator.

(D) It is likely true that different poisons have different levels of efficacy, but this argument does not distinguish between types of poison. The claim is simply that the poison must have killed the mice (as opposed to some other explanation for why the signs of mice would disappear).

(E) The exterminator does not claim that the poison will work within three weeks (or within any time frame at all). He only claims that if the signs disappear over three consecutive weeks, then that means that the poison worked. It might be the case that the signs don't disappear until weeks 3, 4, or 5, but the exterminator's claim would still hold: because the signs have disappeared for three consecutive weeks, the poison worked.

7. **(C).** The conclusion is that "if major industries increase their capital reserves, the employment rate will not decline in the future." Why? Because major industry did not have capital reserves. The author assumes that having capital reserves is sufficient to prevent a decline in the employment rate. Weakening that assumption would effectively cast doubt on the author's claim, and a choice that demonstrates that other factors are involved would do so.

(A) Whether the drop in employment was foreseen does not relate to the core of the argument, which is that capital reserves will prevent another decline in the employment rate.

(B) The fact that some major industries had appreciable capital reserves does not contradict the claim that an increase in these reserves would prevent a future drop in employment rates.

**(C) CORRECT.** The author neglects to take into account the fact that other factors, such as an increase in labor costs, could adversely affect the employment rate. For example, if the cost of labor becomes prohibitively expensive, even with increased reserves, the employment rate could decline.

(D) Legislation mandating a certain level of reserves does not contradict the claim that increased reserves would prevent a drop in employment rates.

(E) The fact that the drop in employment rate was more severe this year than last does not contradict the claim that an increase in reserves would prevent a drop in the employment rate.

8. **(E).** The conclusion of the argument is that "[n]ew methods of math education in this country do a disservice to our children." Why? Because math teachers emphasize "the same narrow, skills-based approach" in higher grades "that students learned in lower grades rather than the analytical tools that they will need to solve complex math problems." To weaken the conclusion, show that this approach has not had a negative effect on children's math skills.

(A) Music is used simply as an analogy in the argument. It has no effect on the conclusion.

(B) The argument suggests that students are getting worse at advanced math skills due to new methods of teaching. This answer choice provides no basis for evaluating students' math performance over time; performing "no worse than" students from other countries provides no information about students' performance prior to the introduction of the new teaching methods.

(C) The simple fact that older students arrive at different answers does not address the concerns of the argument, which is that students are not prepared for higher-level math.

(D) The fact that older students receive better grades in math does not address the concerns of the argument, which is that students are not prepared for higher-level math.

**(E) CORRECT.** This choice states that an increasing percentage of native first-year students qualify to take college courses requiring advanced math. This suggests that more children are prepared for advanced math than had previously been the case, thus weakening the conclusion of the argument.

9. **(B).** The first boldface sentence states that the fight against the drug trade in Country X "should focus for the time being on tightening the country's borders and targeting major smugglers." The second boldface sentence states that the United Nations and the government of Country X should eventually replace the poppy fields with other farming ventures ("agricultural infrastructure"). The correct choice will describe the function of each sentence in the argument. The first sentence is a shorter-term conclusion and the second sentence is a longer-term conclusion of the argument.

(A) This choice states that the first sentence is the conclusion and that the second sentence is an alternative to that conclusion. This misrepresents the relationship. The first sentence is a shorter-term conclusion and the second sentence is a longer-term conclusion of the argument.

**(B) CORRECT.** This choice states that the first sentence is a short-term solution to a problem and the second a long-term solution to the same problem. This accurately describes the relationship.

(C) This choice states that the first sentence presents a problem. According to the text, however, the first sentence is not a problem but rather is a solution to a problem.

(D) No information was given about the popularity of the solution, so this is incorrect.

(E) The first sentence does present an argument, but the second sentence, rather than providing evidence, presents a second argument.

10. **(B).** The conclusion is that a "developer who wishes to make a large profit would be wise to buy urban waterfront lots and erect residential buildings on them." The basis for that claim is that people pay large sums for beach front homes. The question asks for the choice that strengthens that conclusion.

(A) This choice states that people have more buying power today than in previous centuries. This does not strengthen the claim that a developer will make money on urban waterfront properties.

**(B) CORRECT.** This choice states that homeowners will be willing to spend large sums of money on residential properties in traditionally industrial or commercial districts. Since the argument states that urban waterfronts have traditionally been industrial, this fact strengthens the claim that a developer can make a profit on urban waterfront properties.

(C) This choice states that many urban waterfront lots are available for purchase. This does not suggest, however, that a developer will be able to sell them profitably.

(D) This choice states that many coastal cities are giving tax breaks to developers who rehabilitate the waterfront, but this does not suggest that anyone will buy the developed properties.

(E) This choice states that properties in the interior of cities are more expensive than those on the waterfront. Although waterfront properties are therefore cheaper to acquire, this does not necessarily mean that a developer can make a profit after buying such properties.

11. **(D).** The passage states that mentally ill people fare best when two conditions are met: 1) they are not confined to institutions, and 2) they receive high-quality outpatient care. When Congress allowed many mentally ill people to leave mental institutions, it ensured that condition 1 was met for those who were released. The passage does not state, however, whether Congress also ensured that condition 2 would be met. The plight of the mentally ill in 1983 would not be very surprising if those who had been released never received the high-quality outpatient care that they needed.

(A) An increase in the number of people diagnosed with psychiatric disorders does not explain why the average mentally ill person would be faring worse.

(B) The difference between outcomes for men and women, without additional assumptions or information, does not explain the decrease in average welfare for the mentally ill in the United States.

(C) The discovery of new medications does not explain why the mentally ill were doing worse in 1983; if anything, it makes their plight somewhat more surprising, since the new medications may have benefited some people with mental illness.

**(D) CORRECT.** This resolves the paradox by offering a plausible explanation of why the mentally ill were worse off in 1983. If Congress never supplied the funding that would have been necessary to provide high-quality outpatient care to the newly released patients, those patients did not fulfill condition 2 for improved welfare in psychiatric patients.

(E) The specific diagnoses of those who fared worst in 1983 cannot resolve the paradox under consideration, since those individuals may well have had the same illnesses before they were released.

12. **(C).** The conclusion of the argument is that renewable sources of energy, chiefly solar and wind, will be less risky for certain utilities than nonrenewable sources, such as oil and gas. The basis for this claim is that the renewable sources will provide stable, low-cost supplies of energy, whereas the prices for nonrenewable sources will fluctuate according to availability. You are asked to find an assumption underlying this argument. For this argument to be valid, it must in fact be true that these renewable sources of energy will provide stable, low-cost supplies.

(A) The utility companies' claim has to do with the supply risk of the new energy sources, not with how these sources are received by the public. Thus, this choice is irrelevant.

(B) If no new supplies of traditional energy sources are found, then it is true that perhaps these nonrenewable supplies will continue to fluctuate in price in a risky manner. However, the argument does not depend upon any assumption about the future discovery of oil and gas supplies.

**(C) CORRECT.** If it is assumed that weather patterns are consistent and predictable, then with the stated premises, the conclusion that solar and wind power will be less risky than oil and gas follows. If, on the other hand, weather patterns are not consistent and predictable, then solar and wind power are not reliable and thus will not "provide stable energy supplies at low cost." Therefore, the argument's conclusion directly depends on this assumption.

(D) To reach the required conclusion that renewable sources of energy, chiefly solar and wind, will be less risky for certain utilities than nonrenewable sources, it is not necessary to assume that the conversion technology for new sources is not more expensive than the present technology.

(E) This choice does not directly affect the argument. Whether energy produced through combustion can be made less risky is irrelevant; the new energy sources might still be less risky than the older sources.

13. **(D).** The conclusion of the argument is that one need not worry about ingesting pesticides when purchasing produce from farms that use only organic pesticides. The basis for that claim is that organic pesticides leave the surface of produce within a few hours of spraying. In order for this argument to be valid, one must assume that the organic pesticides do not harm the produce in any lasting way and that people aren't eating the produce within a few hours of the pesticide treatment.

(A) This is unrelated to the argument, since the conclusion speaks about not having to worry about ingesting produce on which only organic pesticides were known to be used.

(B) If anything, this statement runs counter to the argument. If produce that has been sprayed with organic pesticide reaches the final consumer within hours, it is possible that the pesticides are still present.

(C) The conclusion of the argument is already limited to those farms that use "only organic pesticides."

**(D) CORRECT.** If a pesticide is capable of penetrating the skin of a fruit or vegetable then, while the organic pesticide will dissipate from the surface of the fruit in a few hours, it might remain inside the fruit. The author of this argument assumes that the organic pesticides cannot penetrate the skin.

(E) The issue of cost is unrelated to the argument's conclusion about pesticide residues.

14. **(E).** The conclusion of the argument is that the government should educate the public about the dangers of inactivity and poor diet to stop the spread of type 2 diabetes. The correct choice will show that this plan likely will not work.

(A) The fact that schools educate middle school students about a disease that is generally "acquired later in life" does not address the effectiveness of a broad public education plan sponsored by the government.

(B) The fact that the public already has access to this information through the internet does not say anything predictive about the effectiveness of the plan. People may not actually be reading the information.

(C) Just because food companies encourage the public to indulge in unhealthful snacks does not mean that a program that teaches the public to do otherwise would not be successful.

(D) The argument recommends a specific plan; whether it eventually receives government funding is a separate issue.

**(E) CORRECT.** Even with the best planning, the program might not achieve its goals simply because people cannot afford to follow the program's advice.

15. **(A).** According to the argument, "mold is almost always found in places where there is substantial moisture," so therefore, to avoid mold and the resultant mold poisoning, people should take steps to prevent wet areas. This argument assumes that wet areas occur first, causing mold to grow. Conversely, this assumption requires that the mold growth itself does not occur first, creating wet areas as a result.

**(A) CORRECT.** The argument depends on the assumption that the reason mold and wetness are observed together is that wet areas cause mold growth. If the reverse causation (mold causes wetness) were true, then keeping all plumbing in good condition to prevent leakage would do little to prevent the growth of mold. This choice eliminates the alternative causation.

(B) The argument does not specify or assume that homeowners cannot hire experts to check their plumbing.

(C) Even if mold could grow in dry areas, the fact that mold is almost always found in wet areas is still valid. This is the fact upon which the argument is based, so the argument does not depend on the unnecessarily absolute assertion that mold cannot grow in dry areas.

(D) Even if some varieties of mold are harmless, the conclusion of this argument, that "one should make sure to keep all internal plumbing in good condition to prevent leakage" and minimize mold growth, could still be valid. Therefore, this argument does not depend on the unnecessarily absolute assertion that no varieties of mold are harmless.

(E) Whether mold spores can be filtered from the air may be relevant to a conclusion about the health effects of mold in the home, but it is not directly relevant to the given conclusion.

16. **(D).** This argument discusses a plan with the stated goal "to prevent overcrowding." Two points of view are represented in the argument: one is that of the town zoning board, the originators of the plan, and the other is that of critics of the plan. The question asks for information that would most support the claims of the critics of the plan.

(A) How other towns fared under similar zoning plans is irrelevant to this argument, unless additional information was presented to connect the situation of this town to those. There is no such connecting information, so this choice neither strengthens nor weakens either point of view.

(B) How long it has been since the construction of the last school in town is irrelevant to this argument. The argument addresses methods to prevent overcrowding, an issue that is not directly related to school construction.

(C) The argument never mentions property taxes, so how property taxes in this town compare to those in neighboring towns is irrelevant.

**(D) CORRECT.** The argument states that "the town zoning board limited the number of new buildings that can be constructed in the town in any given year." The goal of this plan is to prevent overcrowding, but only does so indirectly: the town zoning board plan limits the number of new buildings, except for apartment buildings. If many new residents move into town, then the strain on town services will not decrease and may, in fact, increase.

(E) The distance to the nearest garbage dump is irrelevant to an argument about how to prevent overcrowding.

17. **(C).** The conclusion of the argument is that "the retail price of chocolate is certain to increase within six months." This claim is based on the fact that the wholesale price of cocoa solids and cocoa butter has increased significantly and is likely to stay high. The argument assumes that the retail price of chocolate is driven by the wholesale price of cocoa and ignores the cost of the other ingredients in chocolate. To evaluate the conclusion of the argument, it is necessary to examine whether this assumption is valid.

(A) The price of cocoa solids and cocoa butter during other periods of poor harvest is irrelevant. There is no guarantee that the market for chocolate would respond the same way in this case.

(B) The willingness of consumers to spend more for chocolate is irrelevant when evaluating whether chocolate will be more expensive due to a shortage of cocoa beans.

**(C) CORRECT.** If the price of other ingredients in the chocolate has dropped, then the decrease could offset the higher price of cocoa, and the retail price of chocolate could remain steady.

(D) The percentage of cacao trees affected by the fungus is irrelevant. Regardless of the percentage, it would not change the fact stated by the argument that "there was an unusually meager harvest of cocoa beans this year."

(E) It may seem useful to determine whether the fungus can be eliminated within the next six months. However, the conclusion was not about the fungus or the cacao crop, but rather the retail price of chocolate. The time frame for the elimination of the fungus would only be relevant to the short-term retail price of chocolate if you make several additional assumptions: that the harvest immediately increases, that the resulting glut of cocoa beans immediately offsets the "unusually meager harvest of cocoa beans this year," that the wholesale price of cocoa immediately drops to its pre-fungus level, and that the retail price would not be affected in the meantime. You cannot make all of these assumptions, so the answer to this question is irrelevant to the conclusion.

18. **(A).** The argument rests on the assumption that there is a connection between the one-time raw material price increase and the two-year steady decline in profit margins. Alternatively, something else could have caused either a steady two-year decline in revenues or a steady two-year increase in costs; if so, this event is more likely to be the cause of a steady decline in profit margins over the same two-year period. As a result, this would weaken the engineer's conclusion that finding a new source for the raw material will improve profit margins.

**(A) CORRECT.** New competitors have caused a steady two-year decline in revenues. This weakens the engineer's assumption that the one-time doubling of costs for the raw material is the cause of the steady two-year decline in profit margins.

(B) The fact that the region's mines are producing less than they did before the earthquake does not indicate anything about the cost of the raw material; to weaken the engineer's conclusion, it would be necessary to show that cost is not reduced.

(C) The amount of raw material produced by other regions does not indicate anything about the cost of the raw material; to weaken the engineer's conclusion, it would be necessary to show that cost is not reduced.

(D) The use of a different raw material does not indicate anything about the cost of that raw material; to weaken the engineer's conclusion, it would be necessary to show that cost is not reduced.

(E) Although mining the raw material may become more cost-effective for the mine (that is, cheaper), this does not indicate what will happen to the price the mine charges for the material when selling to the company producing the product in question. To weaken the engineer's conclusion, it would be necessary to show that cost is not reduced.

19. **(E).** The argument concludes that children in this county are more likely to attend college if they attend private high schools instead of public high schools. The basis for this claim is that a higher percentage of graduates of private schools pursue a college education. It is assumed that public schools are inferior to private schools as a training ground for college. Any statement that provides an alternative explanation for the fact that public school graduates attend college at lower rates than private school graduates would weaken the argument.

(A) While higher test scores might increase students' chances of admission to college, this fact is unrelated to whether students will actually attend college. Even if one could prove that earning higher test scores makes a student more likely to attend college, this statement would not weaken the argument, but rather strengthen it.

(B) Since the conclusion centers on the likelihood of attending college, economic and financial considerations for high school are outside the scope of the argument.

(C) Since the amount of need-based aid is not directly related to whether a student will attend college, this statement is outside the scope of the argument.

(D) While better athletic opportunities could increase students' chances of admission to college, they are unrelated to whether students will actually attend college. Also, even though the advantages of public school mentioned in this statement were taken into account by the study, the proportion of graduates of public schools attending colleges remains substantially lower than the proportion of graduates of private schools.

(E) CORRECT. This answer choice demonstrates that the difference in the percentage of graduates attending colleges is not because of any advantage provided by private schools but because a subset of the graduates of public high schools simply choose to pursue a different career path. In other words, 30% of the graduates of public schools voluntarily choose not to pursue a college education. Yet 65% out of the remaining 70% of graduates end up in college. This statement indicates extremely high college matriculation rates for students who want to attend college after graduation from public high schools.

20. (A). Only two pieces of information are given about Airline A's standing room "seats" proposal. First, it is geared toward increasing revenue to counteract declining profits. Second, since the proposal relates to passenger safety, it must be approved by the Federal Aviation Administration. Airline A must have concluded that the cost of implementation of its proposal is less than the revenue that the new seats will generate.

(A) CORRECT. Since Airline A knows that its proposal would have to comply with safety standards, it must have concluded that the cost of compliance is worth it. In other words, the only way for Airline A to achieve its goal of increasing profit is to implement ideas that will generate more revenue than they cost. Airline A must therefore have concluded that the standing room only "seats" meet this criteria.

(B) The statements in the passage imply nothing about whether Airline A believes that the Federal Aviation Administration will approve the proposal. Although Airline A must believe that the proposal has a chance of approval (otherwise it's unlikely to have proposed it), the airline might have proposed its specific plan knowing that it might not be approved, or that it might have to be changed in certain ways.

(C) Airline A's goal is simply to "counteract declining profits" caused by the high cost of jet fuel. This does not mean, however, that the proposal must fully mitigate the cost of jet fuel. As long as the proposal increases revenue without an equal or greater increase in cost, it will in some way counteract declining profits.

(D) The passage does not mention any other ways that Airline A has considered increasing revenues. Therefore, it is impossible to relate Airline A's perception of its standing room "seats" proposal to any other proposals.

(E) The statements in the passage do not address Airline A's view regarding the safety of the standing room only "seats." It is very possible that Airline A views its proposal as safe and sees no conflict between passenger safety and increasing revenue, much less that it has made any determination about the relative importance of these two issues.

21. **(B).** This question is an Analyze the Argument Structure question; the best approach is to identify the conclusion, decide how each boldface portion of the question relates to the conclusion, and eliminate incorrect answer choices on that basis. Here, the second boldface is the conclusion of the argument, as highlighted by the use of the signal word "Therefore."

(A) The first boldface is not an assumption as assumptions are, by definition, unstated. Also, the second boldface does not just describe the argument's recommended position, it is itself the conclusion of the argument.

**(B) CORRECT.** The first boldface is a consideration that helps explain why companies charge as much as possible for new designs. The second boldface presents a different strategy endorsed by the argument, which is to charge less than the greatest possible price to maximize profit.

(C) The first boldface is not an assumption as assumptions are, by definition, unstated. The second boldface is not the strategy referenced in the first boldface.

(D) The first boldface does not demonstrate that the strategy of selling for the greatest price will not apply, but instead supports it. Also, the second boldface is the argument's conclusion, not a factor that supports it.

(E) The description of the first boldface is accurate; however, the second boldface is not a factor against the strategy of maximizing profits by charging the greatest possible price, but it is an alternative strategy altogether.

22. **(B).** Although the premises of this argument suggest only a correlation between smoking and anxiety or nervousness, the argument has a causal conclusion: it concludes that smoking causes individuals to become anxious and nervous (i.e., that A causes B). Often, assumptions support a causal conclusion either by eliminating an alternative cause for the conclusion (that C did not cause B) or by demonstrating that the causation, if one exists, is in the proper direction (that B did not cause A).

(A) The argument concludes that smoking causes anxiety and nervousness. Whether these maladies lead to more serious health problems is not relevant to the conclusion.

**(B) CORRECT.** For smoking to be the cause of anxiety and nervousness (A caused B), it must be true that these individuals were not more likely to be anxious and nervous before they started smoking. If smokers had these pre-conditions, which contributed to their decision to begin smoking (B caused A), the conclusion—that smoking causes these maladies—would be incorrect.

(C) The argument concludes that smoking causes anxiety and nervousness. The number of survey respondents is not relevant to the conclusion.

(D) The argument concludes that smoking causes anxiety and nervousness. The awareness of the health problems related to smoking is not relevant to the conclusion.

(E) The argument is not based on the immediate impact that smoking has on anxiety and nervousness. Moreover, the argument never compares some smokers to other smokers.

**MANHATTAN**
PREP

23. **(D).** Because of the speculation that the tuberculosis outbreak in Country X was the result of an outbreak of tuberculosis in Country Y, health officials in Country X have proposed requiring all visitors from Country Y to undergo a medical examination. You are asked to find a choice that suggests that this proposal will *not* have the desired effect of curbing the spread of tuberculosis in Country X.

(A) This has no bearing on the situation between Country X and Country Y.

(B) This suggests only that the proposal would not prevent ALL cases. But even if the proposal does not prevent all cases, it could help prevent many.

(C) This suggests only that the proposal would not catch ALL carriers of the disease from Country Y. But even if the proposal does not prevent all cases, it could help prevent many.

**(D) CORRECT.** This suggests that the visitors from Country Y are not the source of the disease. Thus, testing them would likely do little to curb the spread of the disease.

(E) If the visitors from Country Y are indeed carriers, then their refusal to visit Country X would help curb the disease.

24. **(D).** The argument concerns the economic impact on restaurants in Prohibitionland if the service of alcoholic beverages is banned. It presents evidence that, despite restrictions on the service of alcohol in certain areas of Prohibitionland, sales taxes in restaurants in those areas rose at a higher rate than for those in other parts of Prohibitionland. This evidence suggests that the ban would not have any adverse economic impact. To support the restaurant proprietors' claim, the correct answer choice will call the relevance of the seemingly contradictory evidence into question.

(A). This answer choice may seem to strengthen the argument that banning the service of alcoholic beverages would have an adverse impact on restaurants. However, as the evidence involves data for the entire year, citing a short-term negative impact on restaurant visitation at the beginning of the year does not measurably strengthen the argument.

(B) The relative tax rate on food and beverages as compared to other consumer goods is irrelevant.

(C) A gradual decline in alcohol consumption over the past 20 years would suggest that over time, any ban on alcohol would have an increasingly small impact on restaurant visitation, weakening the proprietors' argument.

**(D) CORRECT.** This statement calls the evidence into question by indicating that any measured increase in sales taxes and, presumably, revenues for restaurants that have been operating under the restrictions enacted last year is irrelevant, as the restrictions are arguably completely different than the total ban that has been proposed. This answer choice substantially strengthens the proprietors' argument by threatening to make the cited evidence irrelevant.

(E) That overall sales tax revenue did not increase at a higher rate in the provinces that enacted the restrictions on alcoholic beverages weakens the proprietors' argument, as it makes the cited evidence more compelling by ruling out the possibility of different growth rates in the different areas.

25. **(A).** The passage concludes that "the whereabouts of most of the world's most valuable artwork are probably unknown." The basis for this claim is that "serious art collectors are discreet" when purchasing or selling significant pieces of art. To weaken this claim, one would need information that demonstrated that serious art collectors, while discreet in purchasing and selling their artwork, were relatively open about the artworks in their possession. Alternatively, one could weaken this claim using information that showed that serious art collectors possessed only a small fraction of the world's most valuable art. The question asks you to find an answer choice that does <u>not</u> weaken the conclusion.

**(A) CORRECT.** That the value of a piece of art is subjective is irrelevant to the reasoning of the argument. This choice does not present any information that weakens the link drawn between the whereabouts of valuable artwork and the discretion employed by serious art collectors when purchasing or selling such artwork. Thus, this choice does NOT weaken the conclusion.

(B) That serious art collectors publicize their art shortly after purchasing it means that the whereabouts of their valuable art must be widely known. This choice makes clear that serious art collectors are discreet only in purchasing and selling their artwork, and that the location of newly purchased artwork is unknown, if at all, for only a short period of time. As such, this choice weakens the conclusion.

(C) If museums own the vast majority of the world's valuable artwork, then the practices of serious individual art collectors are essentially irrelevant to the location of most of the world's valuable artwork. Therefore, this choice weakens the conclusion since the public nature of museums means that the whereabouts of most of the world's valuable work are widely known.

(D) Since the majority of the world's valuable privately held artwork is owned by individuals who are not considered serious collectors, then the practices of serious art collectors are essentially irrelevant to the location of most of the world's valuable artwork. This choice weakens the conclusion by removing the link between serious art collectors and most of the world's valuable artwork.

(E) That the collections of most serious art collectors are often displayed in public settings means that the whereabouts of their valuable art must be widely known. This choice makes clear that serious art collectors are discreet only in purchasing and selling their artwork; once it is in their possession, the artwork is typically unveiled for the public.

26. **(A).** The argument explains that the new "Click It or Ticket" law is generating controversy. Under the new law, drivers can be cited for not wearing their seat belts, even in the absence of an additional driving infraction. Any acceptable inference must be directly supported by evidence from the text.

**(A) CORRECT.** The entire controversy is based on the new law that allows motorists to be cited even in the absence of an additional infraction. Thus, it follows that prior to the passage of this law, an additional driving infraction must have been necessary to stop and cite an individual for not wearing a seat belt.

(B) Search and seizure laws are never mentioned in the text. This answer choice is outside the scope of the argument.

(C) Laws in other states are never mentioned in the text. This answer choice is outside the scope of the argument.

**MANHATTAN**
PREP

(D) Though the text states that the new regulation might save countless additional lives, the effectiveness of the previous laws is never mentioned.

(E) The argument does not compare or otherwise evaluate the competency or authority of law enforcement groups and citizens groups.

27. **(E).** The passage provides some specific information about the effects of calorie restriction. In rats and mice, this diet is known to prolong life by preventing diseases. In a study of moderately overweight humans, insulin levels and body temperature decreased. A proper GRE inference must follow from the specific information provided, without relying on any significant assumptions.

(A) The passage states that calorie restriction in mice and rats prolongs life by preventing diseases. The human study had much more limited findings—that calorie restriction in moderately overweight humans decreases insulin levels and body temperature. While these traits are known to be associated with longevity, there is no data that links calorie restriction itself to prolonged human life. Additionally, calorie restriction may have other unstated effects, unrelated to longevity. There is no information in the passage that indicates whether these effects are the same in humans as in mice and rats. Finally, the use of the term "humans" is far too general; the study dealt only with moderately overweight humans and so any inference would need to be restricted to this subset of individuals.

(B) While the passage indicates that certain traits known to be associated with longevity are found in moderately overweight humans who reduce their calorie intake, this is far removed from the conclusion that calorie intake will actually increase a human's lifespan. Additionally, as with answer choice (A), the use of the term "humans" is far too general.

(C) The study observed that individuals with the greatest percentage decrease in their calorie intake demonstrated the greatest decrease in insulin levels and body temperature. This shows a strong correlation between calorie intake and insulin levels. However, this correlation is not necessarily direct. It is possible that this correlation holds, but only up to a point. For example, it might be the case that any reduction in calorie intake over 50% does not result in any additional insulin level decreases. Moreover, the passage only draws this correlation for individuals with the greatest percent decrease in calorie intake. It is very possible that individuals with a relatively low decrease in calorie intake exhibit the exact same decrease in insulin levels as individuals with a moderate decrease in calorie intake.

(D) The study makes no reference to the health of individuals who reduce their calorie intake. It tries to draw some connection to the longevity of those individuals, but longevity is not the same as health. An individual could live a very long, unhealthy life.

**(E) CORRECT.** The passage states that the greatest decrease in insulin levels was observed in individuals with the greatest percentage change in their calorie intake. This means that some individuals in the study reduced their calorie intake by a greater percentage than other individuals in the study. The passage also states that the study participants reduced their individual calorie intakes by "at least 25%." Thus, one can safely infer that there were some participants who reduced their calorie intake by more than 25%.

28. **(D).** Research indicates that there is a connection between marriage and happiness as well as health. Media commentators have concluded that marriage causes happiness and health. However, to do so, the commentators must reject the reverse causation: being happy and healthy makes a person more likely to marry.

(A) The research compared married people to unmarried people. Neither the researchers nor the media commentators made any distinction between newlyweds and those who had been married a long time, so this assumption is not necessary.

(B) The type of wedding is outside the scope of this argument. The research compared married people to unmarried people, but made no distinction based upon the type of wedding.

(C) At first, this statement may seem necessary—after all, if the commentators conclude that marriage causes happiness, a lack of depression in married people would certainly support that conclusion. However, the statement is too extreme. One depressed married person does not invalidate the research indicating that, on average, married people are healthier and happier than non-married people.

**(D) CORRECT.** This statement eliminates the alternative interpretation of the research findings—that being happy and healthy makes a person more likely to marry.

(E) The research compared married people to unmarried people. Neither the researchers nor the media commentators made any distinction between harmonious marriages and combative marriages, so this assumption is not necessary.

29. **(D).** The question concerns the structure of the argument. Here, the conclusion is the final sentence, which follows from the evidence previously presented. Therefore, the correct answer cannot describe either boldface portion as the author's final conclusion. The first section details an earlier, erroneous belief. Any answer choice that suggests that the author agrees with this first statement is incorrect. The second boldface statement shows that the earlier theory—that lactic acid causes soreness—was incorrect, and thus also provides evidence in support of the author's conclusion. So, the correct answer must describe the second boldface portion as supporting the conclusion.

(A) This choice misrepresents the first bolded portion by claiming that the author accepts it as true. The author presents it as an incorrect, outdated belief. The second portion is also incorrect because it indicates that the second bolded portion supports the first one.

(B) This choice also misrepresents the first portion, for the reason described above. It is correct that the second bolded portion is contradictory to the first portion.

(C) The first portion is correctly described as an assertion that the author does not believe to be true. Yet the second portion is incorrectly described as against the author's final conclusion.

**(D) CORRECT.** This choice correctly represents the first portion as a belief that the author considers erroneous. The second portion is correctly described as evidence in support of the author's conclusion.

(E) The first portion is correctly described as evidence the author considers invalid. However, this choice misrepresents the second portion as the conclusion, whereas it is evidence that supports the conclusion.

30. **(B).** The conclusion of the argument is contained in the last sentence: "Thus, the methods that the prospector had used to determine the size of the oil deposit must have been inaccurate." The evidence provided is that the prospector reported a large oil deposit that was later determined to be much smaller. The unstated assumption necessary for the conclusion is that there is not another reason why the prospector might have reported a larger oil deposit than actually existed.

(A) It is not necessary to the conclusion that a third party affirmed the company's determination because the conclusion accepts that the oil deposit was indeed smaller than indicated by the prospector and focuses on the cause of the discrepancy as opposed to the discrepancy itself.

**(B) CORRECT.** The argument concludes that the prospector's methods resulted in inaccurate measurements of the size of the oil deposit. This assumes that the prospector did not simply misreport or misrepresent the measurements, presumably for personal gain.

(C) The commercial feasibility or profitability of the oil deposit is not integral to the argument or its conclusion.

(D) Whether the prospector utilized the same methods to measure the oil deposits in other locations is not relevant to the argument or the conclusion.

(E) That the company has a long operating history and much experience drilling oil wells is not relevant because the company's measurements of the size of the oil field are accepted as a given.

31. **(C).** This passage relates information from two studies concerning high school seniors: the first discusses the financial responsibilities of high school seniors, while the second explains the coursework in finance taken by typical high school seniors. On the GRE, a proper response to a Draw a Conclusion question must directly follow from the evidence in the passage.

(A) Although it might be true that schools would be wise to educate students in finance, this is an opinion that does not have to be true based upon the given evidence.

(B) That one-third of high school seniors claim "significant financial responsibilities" to their families does not necessarily mean that these same students work "part-time jobs after school." There are many ways that these students might earn money for their families. If they do work, they might work on weekends or over the summer.

**(C) CORRECT.** The first study states that one-third of all high school seniors have significant financial responsibilities to their families. The second study states that 80% of seniors have opened a bank account, and of this 80%, one-third have bounced a check. The number of seniors that has bounced a check (one-third of 80%) is fewer than the number of seniors with significant financial responsibilities to their families (one-third of 100%).

(D) The passage states that certain high school seniors who contribute to the food, shelter, or clothing for themselves or their families "rate themselves" as having significant financial responsibilities. This does not mean that any high school senior who contributes to these categories has significant financial responsibilities.

(E) The passage states that one-third of high school seniors say that they have "significant financial responsibilities." This does not indicate that the other two-thirds have no responsibilities. Because no information is given about the other two-thirds of the students, no conclusion about them must follow.

32. **(E).** According to the statements, the companies that own private aircraft for business use are fully in compliance with the relevant law. A correct inference must follow from at least part of the premises given.

(A) It does not have to be true that the law costs the businesses money as no evidence about the relative costs is given.

(B) This choice is an irrelevant comparison as the preferences of the executives are not the concern of the statements.

(C) This choice does not have to follow as there is no information given about the travel arrangements made by large companies. The statements only indicate that the majority of private planes are not owned by large companies.

(D) There is no information given about the travel arrangements of upper level executives and no reason to believe that those with the companies discussed do not comply with their companies' policies.

**(E) CORRECT.** If, as the statements indicate, the companies are in full compliance with this law, it must be true that the executives following their guidelines also are.

33. **(E).** The conclusion of the argument is that insurance companies do not have a significant economic incentive to delay claim payments to doctors. To weaken this conclusion, an answer choice must provide some significant economic incentive for insurance companies to be tardy in paying doctors for legitimate medical claims.

(A) While the fact that some doctors who submit accurate bills to insurance companies still receive tardy payments seems to indicate that there must be something other than errors causing delayed payments, it fails to prove that the insurance company has an economic incentive to deliberately delay claim payments to doctors. For example, this fact could simply indicate that the insurance companies are inefficient at handling their paperwork.

(B) This choice compares the costs insurance companies must absorb due to incorrect bills to the costs physicians must absorb due to tardy payments. However, this information does not establish an economic incentive for insurance companies to delay claim payments to doctors.

(C) The argument is focused on the payment of legitimate claims; the rising proportion of illegitimate claims does not establish a clear economic incentive for insurance companies to delay payments of legitimate claims.

(D) The types of billing errors made by doctors' offices does not establish any economic motive for insurance companies to delay payments to doctors.

**(E) CORRECT.** This choice articulates a logical chain that establishes a clear economic motive for insurance companies to delay paying doctors for legitimate medical claims. If insurance companies delay payments to doctors, this results in a 10% increase in overhead costs for physicians. These costs ultimately result in higher fees that doctors charge to insurance companies. Insurance companies, in turn, raise the premiums that they charge consumers for health coverage. This choice states that the insurance companies increase their fees to consumers far more than the doctors increase their fees to insurance companies, enabling the insurance companies to pocket the difference; therein lies the economic motive for insurance companies to be tardy paying doctors for legitimate medical claims.

34. **(D).** Farmers in developing countries claim that the global price of wheat is low because American farmers produce too much of the grain. They also claim that American farmers produce too much wheat because they have

no incentive to manage their crops, since the U.S. government will buy any surplus wheat. The question asks which choice weakens the claim that removing the American subsidy would cause the price of wheat to rise.

(A) The fact that there are uses for wheat that is not eaten is irrelevant. This does not address the farmers' claims.

(B) That buyers of wheat can predict their needs in advance is irrelevant, because the text indicates that American farmers do not pay attention to actual demand for wheat.

(C) In this argument, the global market for soybeans is irrelevant to the global market for wheat, which is a different commodity with different demand, supply, and pricing structures.

**(D) CORRECT.** The farmers assume that the sole cause of the wheat surplus is the United States. This answer choice suggests that other countries would modify their output to counterbalance any reduction on the part of the United States, keeping prices constant rather than allowing them to rise.

(E) The price of another crop is largely irrelevant. Moreover, the fact that the price of sorghum, a non-subsidized crop, is lower tends to support, rather than weaken, the claims of the farmers.

35. **(E).** The researchers claim that Delta-32 prevents its carriers from contracting the plague. They support this claim by noting that a strikingly large percentage of descendants of plague survivors carry the mutation. The question asks for an assumption underlying the claim.

(A) The argument is specific to the relationship between Delta-32 and resistance to the plague. Other diseases are irrelevant.

(B) The argument is specific to the relationship between Delta-32 and resistance to the plague. Other diseases are irrelevant.

(C) If Delta-32 existed in its current form before the 16th century, the the conclusion would still stand, so this choice is not a necessary assumption.

(D) The argument does not claim that Delta-32 prevents all bacteria-caused disease.

**(E) CORRECT.** The researchers claim that Delta-32 prevented its carriers from contracting the plague on the basis of its presence in descendants of plague survivors. But it is theoretically possible that these descendants carry the mutation Delta-32 because the plague mutated the genes of their ancestors. In order to claim that the mutation prevented the plague, you must assume that the plague did not cause the mutation Delta-32.

36. **(A).** The argument claims that wide dissemination of wireless access would be a practical way to meet urban needs, based on the evidence of its successful use in rural areas. The author then must assume that urban areas provide no additional problems for wireless use.

**(A) CORRECT.** This choice confirms an assumption of the argument and thus strengthens the conclusion.

(B) This choice weakens the argument because it damages the assumption that urban areas pose no extra problems for wireless use.

**MANHATTAN**
PREF

(C) This choice is irrelevant because it provides information about another rural area; the conclusion concerns urban areas.

(D) This choice weakens the argument because it damages the assumption that urban areas pose no extra problems for wireless use.

(E) This choice is an irrelevant distinction. The argument mentioned all three groups as in need of this service. The suggestion that one group needs it more than the others is irrelevant to the conclusion.

37. **(D).** The conclusion of this argument is that "many weight-loss efforts fail because people eat more calories than they intend to consume." The first boldface portion is a factual premise ("Studies have shown …"). This premise indirectly supports the researchers' conclusion. The second boldface portion is another supporting premise, this one citing a specific study showing that dieters who do not keep a diet record eat more than they realize.

(A) The first boldface is not the conclusion; it is an observed fact. The second boldface is evidence that the researchers' conclusion is correct, but is not evidence that the first boldface is correct.

(B) The first boldface is a fact that supports the researchers' theory, but it does not explain why their conclusion is correct—the other premises do so.

(C) The first boldface is a fact that supports the researchers' theory, but it does not illustrate the truth of that theory—the second boldface does. The second boldface is a fact that supports the researchers' theory; it is not a competing theory.

**(D) CORRECT.** The first boldface (diet record = diet success) is a basis for the researchers' conclusion that many weight loss efforts fail because people consume more than they intended. The second boldface directly illustrates how weight loss efforts of a certain group failed for exactly that reason.

(E) The first boldface is a factual statement, not a theory. Furthermore, the first boldface supports the theory of the researchers; it is not something they have disproved.

38. **(B).** This argument concludes that the city should convene a conference of relevant parties to create opportunities for unemployed young people. The argument's premise is that the retirement of the baby boomers will create shortages. The argument assumes the efficacy of its conclusion—in other words, that the conference will actually be effective in creating job opportunities. Attacking an assumption is an effective way to weaken an argument.

(A) If anything, this choice strengthens the argument. If immigration does not provide a labor pool, it is more likely that a shortage will ensue.

**(B) CORRECT.** The argument assumes that it is feasible to affect employment patterns by government encouragement and/or action. If that assumption is denied, the conclusion is weakened, as the conference would be pointless.

(C) This choice makes an irrelevant distinction. It does not matter if the best positions require skills, as long as the majority are available to the unskilled unemployed in question.

**MANHATTAN**
PREP

(D) Knowing that a small proportion of baby boomers will not retire on schedule does not significantly weaken the argument. The argument relies on general estimates, not on exact numbers.

(E) If anything, this choice strengthens the argument. If these people are unaware of these opportunities, it would be positive to convene to plan how to reach them.

39. **(D).** Since the westbound train is blowing its horn, the westbound train is "the source of the sound." Therefore, the passengers on the westbound train are traveling along with the source of the sound, and thus are neither approaching the source nor receding from it. Hence, the westbound passengers should hear the true pitch of the sound.

According to the passage, the passengers in the eastbound train are approaching the source of the sound, the westbound train; the distance between the eastbound passengers and the sound is decreasing. Therefore, according to the given description of the Doppler effect, the eastbound passengers should perceive a sound that is higher than the true pitch.

(A) Passengers in the eastbound train do not hear the true pitch of the horn; passengers in the westbound train do.

(B) It is true that the westbound passengers hear the true pitch; the eastbound passengers, however, hear a sound that is higher than the true pitch.

(C) Passengers in the eastbound train do not hear the true pitch of the horn; passengers in the westbound train do.

**(D) CORRECT.** Westbound passengers do hear the true pitch of the sound. Eastbound passengers do hear a sound that is higher in pitch than the true sound.

(E) It is true that eastbound passengers hear a sound that is higher than the true pitch; the westbound passengers, however, hear the true pitch.

40. **(E).** The author concludes that one will only be able to determine the age of a Brazilian ash by counting its rings if the temperature in the tree's environment never exceeds 95 degrees Fahrenheit. The author bases this conclusion on the fact that the tree loses rings when the temperature exceeds that level. However, if the number of rings lost by a Brazilian ash at high temperatures can be predicted, it may be possible to determine the age of a tree even if the temperature exceeds 95 degrees.

(A) The argument says nothing about precipitation. This answer choice is out of scope since it would require a number of other assumptions to make it relevant to the argument's conclusion.

(B) Whether other trees share this feature is irrelevant; the argument focuses only on the Brazilian ash.

(C) If it is the case that one day above 95 degrees is equal to one ring lost, then it might still be possible to predict the tree's age, as long as it is known on how many days the temperature exceeded 95 degrees.

(D) The thickness of the rings is irrelevant.

**(E) CORRECT.** The conclusion is that the rings will be a reliable measure only if the temperature never exceeds 95 degrees. This is true only if there is no way to predict how many rings would be lost when the temperature does exceed 95 degrees. If it were possible to predict this, one might be able to assess the age of a tree using its rings even if the temperature had exceeded 95 degrees.

41. **(E).** The text states that celiac disease results when the body mistakes gluten for a harmful pathogen, causing damage to the intestine. It also says that gluten is a protein found in certain grains and that people suffering from celiac disease must eliminate gluten from their diets. The symptoms of the disease include cramps, bloating, and anemia. The correct answer choice must follow from these facts alone.

(A) Anemia is just one of several symptoms of the disease. It does not have to be true that everyone who has the disease will also develop anemia.

(B) It does not have to follow that eliminating gluten will cure the disease, only that people with the disease must not eat gluten. The disease could come back if people eat gluten again.

(C) It is not a certainty that the symptoms mentioned are also symptoms of other conditions.

(D) It is not known whether gluten is found only in grains. It may exist in other foods as well.

**(E) CORRECT.** If the body mistakes gluten for a harmful pathogen, then it must be true that the body cannot always recognize harmless substances.

42. **(E).** This argument proposes that culture does not influence the process by which the mind distinguishes colored objects. In support of the conclusion, the argument notes that all languages with six color terms name the same colors, as do all languages with three color terms. To weaken the conclusion, the correct choice will support the counter argument that culture does influence how the mind distinguishes colored objects. Notice the logical difference between distinguishing color names and distinguishing colored objects. For instance, a speaker of English can visually distinguish two objects with different shades of red, even if he or she cannot easily name the difference. Some of the wrong answers attempt to confuse these two processes.

(A) Irrelevant. It may be interesting to observe that no language has more than 11 basic color terms. However, this observation neither weakens nor strengthens the argument that culture influences how the mind perceives color variations.

(B) Irrelevant. In fact, this statement may slightly strengthen the argument: if every language permits speakers to describe subtle color variations, then it might be argued that human color perception is independent of language, since language would then not be "boxing in" the speaker.

(C) Irrelevant. The term red may encompass both red and yellow, but that doesn't mean that speakers of the language cannot see the difference between red and yellow. In the same way, the English word blue covers many shades that English speakers with normal vision can distinguish (sky blue, royal blue, etc.).

(D) Strengthens. If speakers of languages without a blue–green distinction refer to the sky or tree leaves to clarify their meaning, then they obviously see a difference between the sky and tree leaves. Using the sky or tree leaves as reference points is no different from using fruit names for colors (e.g., orange, peach). This evidence reinforces the idea that humans have a common basis for perceiving colors.

**(E) CORRECT.** If Tarahumara speakers are less able to identify differences between blue and green objects than Spanish speakers, then it can be argued that the lack of a blue–green distinction in the Tarahumara language influences how Tarahumara speakers actually perceive colors. It should be noted that this evidence does not completely prove the point—the causality could actually work the other way (e.g., Tarahumarans could share a genetic defect that causes blue–green color blindness, and so they never developed a distinction in their language). Also, if the experiment is not well designed, the difficulty in identification could simply come from the lack of a handy term to capture the difference between blue and green. However, the evidence as given does support the hypothesis that culture influences color perception.

43. **(A).** This question is an Analyze the Argument Structure question; the best approach is to identify the conclusion and then determine how each boldface portion of the argument relates to the conclusion. The conclusion of this argument appears in the third sentence: "doctors determined that *Anopheles* mosquitoes were responsible for transmitting the disease to humans." The first boldface statement indicates that malaria was named based upon the original, but incorrect, view that the disease was caused by "bad air"; the statement does not support the conclusion. The second boldface statement provides the specific mechanism by which the mosquito is responsible for human infection; it therefore supports the conclusion. More simply, the first statement does not support the conclusion, while the second statement does.

**(A) CORRECT.** The first statement does follow from the original, but incorrect, view that the disease was caused by "bad air." It weakens the conclusion by supporting an incorrect conclusion. The second statement is a supporting premise that explains why the conclusion is true.

(B) A conjecture is a hypothesis or supposition, but the first statement is not a conjecture; it is a fact. The second statement contradicts the original conclusion, but it does not contradict the fact provided by the first statement.

(C) To illuminate is to clarify or explain. The first statement does not explain any assumption (or the original conclusion, for that matter); it merely states a fact that follows from the original, erroneous conclusion. The second statement does not confirm anything in the first half of the argument; rather, it supports the later, correct conclusion.

(D) The first statement did not cause the erroneous conclusion; rather, it is a result of that conclusion. The second statement is a premise that supports the correct conclusion.

(E) The first statement does provide additional detail about the original, erroneous conclusion. The second statement is not the actual conclusion (or judgment); it is a premise in support of the later conclusion.

44. **(A).** In this argument, a cause and effect relationship is presented between scientists based in the U.S. who sign long-term contracts with foreign companies and the U.S. government's restrictions on stem cell research. This cause and effect relationship is the key to the correct answer.

**(A) CORRECT.** If scientists based in the United States signed the contracts because of restrictions in that country, it must follow that their new employers were under fewer restrictions. Therefore, at least some foreign companies must work under fewer restrictions than some U.S. companies do.

(B) While it is possible that once the restrictions are lifted, U.S. companies will want to hire more scientists and will seek them overseas, there are too many unknowns between the given premises and this conclusion. It is doubtful that an increase in the number of immigrating stem cell research scientists would have a "significant" impact on the number of "foreign professionals" overall.

(C) This passage is about government restrictions; no information is given about "financial backing." Beware of extreme statements such as "in all parts of the world."

(D) No information is given concerning the current or future position of the United States in terms of stem cell research. Though restrictions and scientists switching companies are two issues related to a company's prosperity, there is no information about how these issues directly affect the position of the United States.

(E) No information is given that would predict the behavior of the scientists in the future.

45. **(D).** In the argument, the critics mistake correlation for causation. While it is true that most employees were reassigned to the mission to Mars, it is not established that the mission to Europa was scrapped to move the employees to a different project; it's possible that some other motivation caused the demise of the Europa project. NASA claims that its critics are misinformed.

(A) Irrelevant. The conclusion is based on the critics' assumption of causation, and this choice fails to address the issue of the motivations underlying NASA's decision-making process. That the percentage of spending is going to decrease could indicate many possible scenarios, including that NASA is unhappy with the progress of the project and plans to cut future spending or that the organization expects the development of the shuttle to be completed by 2018.

(B) Weakens. If public interest determines its budget, NASA has strong motivation to keep public interest high. Additionally, "budget" is not mentioned in the original argument.

(C) Irrelevant. This statement differentiates between the opinions of some scientists and the opinions of others, but sheds no light on the motivations behind NASA's decisions.

**(D) CORRECT.** This answer choice provides an alternative explanation for the decision to abandon the attempt to send an unmanned vessel to Europa; the Tokyo telescope will provide the information that NASA would have obtained from the mission, making the mission unnecessary.

(E) Irrelevant. The conclusion concerns NASA's motivations; this statement is about the motivations of American citizens. There is no direct relationship between what Americans see as the future of space exploration and the motivations behind NASA's decision making.

46. **(B).** The argument claims that no one with a compromised immune system should travel to Nicaragua's "Mosquito Coast," due to the risk of contracting dengue fever or malaria. The correct answer choice is the choice that does not strengthen the argument. Therefore, the four wrong answers must each strengthen the argument.

(A) Strengthens. Since the method of preventing or treating one of the diseases can have adverse side effects, the danger is made worse, particularly for people with compromised immune systems.

**MANHATTAN**
PREP

**(B) CORRECT.** If the government were to succeed in this effort, there would be somewhat less risk to travelers with compromised immune systems. This would weaken the conclusion that such travelers should avoid the Mosquito Coast. If the effort were to fail, it would produce no change in the danger to such travelers. Either way, this answer choice does nothing to strengthen the argument that such travelers should avoid the Mosquito Coast.

(C) Strengthens. Since a compromised immune system doesn't effectively fight either dengue fever or malaria, people with such immune systems are at increased risk of infection by such diseases.

(D) Strengthens. The populations of both mosquitoes grow during rainy season; thus, the chance of contracting either disease also grows.

(E) Strengthens. The insect repellent may be the most effective available, but it can also have a terrible side effect. Using this repellent is one of the options for dealing with the risk of mosquito-borne disease. Since this option is more dangerous than before, the travel advisory is strengthened.

47. **(D).** According to the text, the Peruvian government claims that Inca Trail treasures would have deteriorated without a new permit program that has restricted the number of tourists. The correct answer will strengthen this claim.

(A) Irrelevant. The increase in pay may have resulted from the permit program, but there is no direct connection to preservation of the Inca Trail.

(B) Irrelevant. Local villages may have seen a drop in income as a result of the restrictions on tourist numbers, but this does not strengthen or weaken the claim that the permit program prevented Inca Trail ruins from deteriorating.

(C) Irrelevant. The funds are a positive result of the permit program, but if these funds are used to protect or preserve archaeology elsewhere, then they do not impact the preservation of ruins specifically on the Inca Trail.

**(D) CORRECT.** The more rapid deterioration of similar ruins elsewhere supports the claim that the permit program has helped prevent deterioration of Inca Trail ruins. Notice that this evidence does not rise to the level of absolute proof; other differences between the ruins might explain the different rates of deterioration. However, this evidence clearly supports the hypothesis that the permit program was successful.

(E) Irrelevant. Without the permit program, it is possible (though far from certain) that the number of tourists hiking the Inca Trail would have risen together with the total number of tourists visiting Peru. However, an increase in the number of tourists on the Inca Trail would not necessarily have led to greater deterioration of archaeological treasures on the trail.

48. **(E).** The chairman claims that same-day spending at downtown businesses by people attending performances at the Farmsley Center has contributed to the economic revitalization of downtown Metropolis. His argument depends on the assumption that this spending represents an increased flow of money into the economy of downtown Metropolis. If, for example, the $83 per visitor that he cites is money that would have been spent in downtown businesses even if the Farmsley Center had not been built, the chairman's argument would be unsound.

(A) Irrelevant. This choice does not specify the contributions to the city that led to the honor. Perhaps the chairman was honored for activities unrelated to the Farmsley Center, or perhaps he was honored simply because Metropolis residents feel civic pride at having a grand performance space downtown.

(B) Irrelevant. Expensive restaurants may be a sign of the economic revitalization of downtown Metropolis, but they do not indicate the causal factors that led to the revitalization.

(C) Irrelevant. In the absence of information specifically relating the architecture of the Farmsley Center to spending at downtown businesses, it does not have to follow that the architect's international standing has helped in the economic revitalization downtown.

(D) Irrelevant. The Farmsley Center may host performances that would otherwise have taken place at other downtown venues, but this does not mean that extra money is spent downtown.

**(E) CORRECT.** If suburbanites are coming to Metropolis to see performances at the Farmsley Center, they are bringing money from out of town and spending it in downtown Metropolis. This inflow of money supports the idea that the Farmsley Center has contributed to the economic revitalization of downtown Metropolis.

49. **(D).** The argument presents two retirement account options. In the first, taxes are paid when money is withdrawn upon retirement; in the second, taxes are paid when the money is initially deposited into the account. The author assumes that it is better to pay taxes on the contributions than on the withdrawals because the amount contributed will be smaller than the amount available for withdrawal. However, the amount paid in taxes, whether on contributions or withdrawals, depends on both the amount of money contributed or withdrawn and on the tax rates applied to those contributions or withdrawals. Thus, to evaluate the argument, it would be helpful to know the amounts of money involved and the relevant tax rates.

(A) It would be useful to know both the amount contributed and the value of the account upon retirement. Knowing just the first figure, however, does not allow the worker to figure out which retirement account option would result in a smaller tax bill.

(B) It might be useful to know when and how the tax rates would increase, but "in the future" is too vague. The tax rates may increase while the worker is still employed, or not until the worker has retired. Thus, no conclusion can be drawn concerning which plan is the better option.

(C) This choice provides no information about the tax consequences, which are the focus of the conclusion.

**(D) CORRECT.** If a worker knows the relative tax brackets to expect during the different stages, he or she can better predict whether it would be less expensive to pay taxes on the contributions or on the withdrawals.

(E) It would be useful to know both how much is contributed and the value of the account upon retirement. Knowing just the second figure, however, does not allow the worker to figure out which retirement account option would result in a smaller tax bill.

**MANHATTAN**
PREP

50. **(C).** The argument presents a discrepancy between the percentage of survey respondents who reported that they voted in an election (71%) and the percentage of eligible voters who did vote in that election (60%). An explanation of a GRE discrepancy explains why the apparent conflict does not apply.

(A) If the margin of error is ±5%, then the 71% figure could be as low as 66% (or as high as 76%). This accounts for less than half of the discrepancy between 71% and 60%.

(B) This choice does not address the stated discrepancy between the percentage of voters who said that they voted and the percentage of voters who actually did vote. No information is given concerning residency requirements so this information is irrelevant.

**(C) CORRECT.** One explanation for the discrepancy between these two results is the possibility that people who do vote will respond to surveys at a higher rate than people who do not vote; in other words, people who do vote are overrepresented in the survey's results. This is an additional premise that would explain the higher percentage of individuals polled indicating that they voted.

(D) While this may be true, the poll did not ask people if they intended to vote; rather, it asked people if they had already voted in a past election.

(E) While this may account for some percentage of the discrepancy, the numerical data is not sufficient to explain the entire discrepancy; "some" means "at least one." In addition, the confused people would not necessarily have responded that they did vote (when thinking about a different election) even though they did not vote in the national election. They could just as easily have reported that they did not vote (when thinking about a different election) even though they did vote in the national election.

51. **(B).** This question is a disguised inference question; when the passage consists of premises, the correct choice must follow directly from those premises and not require any additional assumptions. Here, the issue is how to minimize the spread of flu via air travel.

(A) The passage states that the infection can be spread by coughing. The flu virus, therefore, can reach the other passengers in the "closely packed environment" before it enters any filters that might kill the virus.

**(B) CORRECT.** Vaccines provide significant protection against developing the virus (not 100% protection, but the question concerns minimizing the impact of air travel, not eliminating it entirely). If all passengers are vaccinated against the virus, many of those who otherwise would have developed the disease will not, and, therefore, will not spread it to others.

(C) Anyone can contract the virus and subsequently spread it; the mentioned populations are merely "especially vulnerable" to it. Infected people traveling to another place can infect children, senior citizens, and others who have stayed in their home regions.

(D) The passage states that the infection can be spread by coughing; while it may be true that the virus can also spread via hand contact, this information is not stated in the passage.

**MANHATTAN**
PREP

(E) The passage states that people who develop symptoms before travel begins likely would not make the trip; banning those with observable symptoms will not "minimize" the role of air travel because there are not that many people in this category. The larger danger is those who may be infected but have not yet developed symptoms.

52. **(B).** The journalist cites data about the success of tall people, then concludes that employers have an unconscious bias in favor of tall people. The journalist assumes that employer bias is the only explanation for the data; the correct choice will question this explanation.

(A) Irrelevant. Gender comparisons are irrelevant to the journalist's data on CEOs, since those data are only about male CEOs. Likewise, gender comparisons are irrelevant in interpreting the journalist's data about the general population, since the passage says those data have been corrected for the influence of gender and age.

**(B) CORRECT.** If socioeconomic status is correlated to both height and educational attainment, you would expect taller people to be, on average, better educated. The economic success of tall people could then be attributed to their higher levels of educational attainment rather than to employer bias.

(C) Irrelevant. Professional basketball players, with their above average height and above average pay, only account for a small part of the correlation between height and pay. And insofar as height is useful in the game of basketball, the high wages of tall players can be explained without reference to any unconscious bias on the part of their employers.

(D) Irrelevant. An HR professional might unconsciously favor tall people (or good-looking people, or charismatic people, etc.) without being tall (or good-looking, or charismatic, etc.).

(E) Irrelevant. Without additional assumptions, a length of service differential neither bolsters nor undermines the journalist's argument.

53. **(D).** The argument concerns the compensation system for public school teachers. It suggests that educational experts believe that a system of teacher compensation based on performance rather than seniority would help to retain exceptional teachers and maintain quality instruction. The correct answer is the one that most undermines this contention of the educational experts.

(A) Irrelevant. That many factors contribute to job satisfaction and teaching performance neither weakens nor strengthens the argument for a performance-based pay structure for public school teachers.

(B) Irrelevant. Nothing in the argument indicates that one universal system of compensation must be adopted. It is very possible that several effective models of performance-based pay could be developed and implemented successfully.

(C) Strengthens. This choice indicates that many young teachers are extremely frustrated by the traditional pay structure in which financial advancement is directly tied to seniority. Thus, these teachers would likely welcome a change that allows them more rapid opportunity for financial advancement.

**(D) CORRECT.** Weakens. This choice indicates that collaboration among teachers is integral to high-quality instruction and that a system of compensation based on teacher performance reduces collaboration. Thus, the effect of a merit-based system of pay would be to undermine quality instruction, which is one of the two stated goals of the educational experts.

**MANHATTAN**
PREP

(E) Strengthens. The educational experts' argument in favor of performance-based compensation is bolstered if standardized tests scores have dramatically risen in school districts that have instituted such pay structures.

54. **(B).** This question asks for the choice that properly describes the role of the two boldfaced portions in relation to the conclusion: "networks can actually increase their revenue through higher advertising rates, due to larger audiences lured to television through other media." The first boldface portion opposes this position by predicting smaller audiences; the second lends support to it by citing evidence that alternative media devices lead their users to watch more television.

(A) The first boldface does weigh against the argument, but it is a prediction, rather than "an inevitable trend"; the second boldface supports the argument but is not the conclusion itself.

**(B) CORRECT.** The argument about potential increased network revenue is contrary to the first boldface's prediction about shrinking audiences and falling revenue; the argument indeed depends upon the second boldface's assertion that users of alternative devices will actually watch more hours of television.

(C) The first boldface opposes the argument, rather than clarifies it; the second would suggest that the argument is sound, rather than flawed.

(D) The technology executives do not accept the prediction of the network executives; the second boldface contradicts that prediction and is not a consequence of it.

(E) The first boldface does not use an analogy; the second is in agreement with, not opposition to, the argument.

55. **(A).** This is a Weaken the Conclusion question. The correct answer choice will cast doubt on the sponsors' claim that "reducing nicotine intake does not improve one's health."

**(A) CORRECT.** This answer choice indicates that most study participants did not actually reduce their overall nicotine intake; instead, they replaced the reduction in cigarette-based nicotine with nicotine from other sources.

(B) Although this choice does indicate that a number of study participants might have consumed nicotine from secondhand smoke, it does not undermine the idea that these individuals, by cutting back their smoking, have significantly reduced their nicotine intake. Before the study, the nicotine intake of these participants was smoking plus secondhand smoke; now, the only nicotine intake is secondhand smoke.

(C) This choice neither strengthens nor weakens the conclusion. The study only addresses the reduction of nicotine intake through smoking and never mentions these other factors. That the study used a diverse sample of smokers does not, in itself, undermine the validity of the conclusions.

(D) This answer choice is irrelevant. The study concerns the effects of reducing nicotine intake through smoking, not quitting smoking entirely.

(E) This choice is irrelevant. While it further details the methodology used in selecting subjects, it neither strengthens nor weakens the conclusion.

56. **(B).** The passage concludes that increased leisure time in the developed world causes an increase in the percentage of people diagnosed with clinical depression. To arrive at this causal conclusion, the argument must assume that alternative causes for this disparity are impossible.

(A) This statement weakens the hypothesis. If clinical depression were genetically transmitted, then the amount of leisure time would have no effect on the percentage of the population diagnosed with clinical depression.

**(B) CORRECT.** If individuals in the developing and developed worlds do not have equal access to accurate diagnostic procedures, it is possible that either frequent misdiagnoses or a lack of correct diagnoses causes the seeming disparity between the populations. Thus, for the argument to be valid, this assumption must hold true. Put another way, this assumption eliminates a possible outside cause (the difference in diagnostic techniques between the developing and the developed worlds).

(C) Nothing indicates that most leisure activities must be inherently boring. As long as more individuals in the developed world than in the developing world are experiencing boredom, the logic of the passage remains valid.

(D) This choice weakens the researchers' hypothesis. If fewer effective medications were available in the developing world, the incidence of clinical depression there should be higher than in developed countries.

(E) It is unimportant whether few residents of developing countries dedicate any of their time to leisure. The argument already states that residents of developed countries have increased leisure time relative to residents of developing countries, so this assumption is unnecessary.

57. **(C).** Two points of view are expressed in the argument: consumer groups claim that à la carte pricing will reduce consumer costs, while the cable television industry claims that the current package pricing structure is most cost effective for consumers. If the goal is to reduce the cost of cable television for consumers, it is critical to determine whether adding the option of à la carte pricing is likely to save consumers money.

(A) According to the argument, the decision revolves around the costs to consumers, not the number of channels available to them. If there were some pricing consequences as a result of this loss of diversity, the point might be relevant, but no such information is given.

(B) According to the argument, the decision is based only on the costs to consumers, not the advertising profits of the cable television companies.

**(C) CORRECT.** If consumers would not choose to order all of the channels they currently buy as part of a package subscription, then the television industries' claim that à la carte pricing would always be more expensive is suspect. If many consumers only watch and wish to pay for a few of their favorite channels, à la carte pricing could very well result in lower cable bills for those consumers.

(D) According to the argument, the decision concerns only the costs to consumers, not the number of consumers who subscribe. If there were some pricing consequences as a result of a loss of subscribers, the point might be relevant, but no such information is given.

**MANHATTAN**
PREP

(E) According to the argument, the decision is to be based only on the costs to consumers, not the technical equipment requirements a change in cost structure would require.

58. **(A).** The argument provides information about the substantial costs associated with the development of Dendadrine. Yet the management views Dendadrine as a highly profitable project. To reconcile these claims, the correct answer choice will demonstrate that the drug will generate profits that will more than compensate for the high initial expenditures associated with its development.

**(A) CORRECT.** If management expects to earn patent protection for the new drug, then the company can also expect to charge the unusually high prices that will more than compensate for the initial research and development costs.

(B) While this choice explains the high costs associated with the development of Dendadrine, it says nothing about how well such products do on the market and whether they subsequently become profitable.

(C) Although this choice supports the idea that Dendadrine will sell well, it does not specifically support the contention that the drug will be profitable in the face of unusually high costs.

(D) Although this choice supports the idea that Dendadrine will be the primary, if not only, treatment for this market segment, it does not support the contention that the drug will be profitable in the face of unusually high costs.

(E) Although this choice supports the idea that the market for Dendadrine is very large and will generate revenues in excess of $5 billion within a few years, it does not specifically support the contention that the drug will be profitable in the face of unusually high costs.

# Chapter 7
## *of*

5 lb. Book of GRE® Practice Problems

# Arithmetic

# In This Chapter...

# Arithmetic

For questions in the Quantitative Comparison format ("Quantity A" and "Quantity B" given), the answer choices are always as follows:

(A)   Quantity A is greater.
(B)   Quantity B is greater.
(C)   The two quantities are equal.
(D)   The relationship cannot be determined from the information given.

For questions followed by a numeric entry box [          ], you are to enter your own answer in the box. For questions followed by a fraction-style numeric entry box [ ▭/▭ ], you are to enter your answer in the form of a fraction. You are not required to reduce fractions. For example, if the answer is $\frac{1}{4}$, you may enter $\frac{25}{100}$ or any equivalent fraction.

All numbers used are real numbers. All figures are assumed to lie in a plane unless otherwise indicated. Geometric figures are not necessarily drawn to scale. You should assume, however, that lines that appear to be straight are actually straight, points on a line are in the order shown, and all geometric objects are in the relative positions shown. Coordinate systems, such as $xy$-planes and number lines, as well as graphical data presentations, such as bar charts, circle graphs, and line graphs, *are* drawn to scale. A symbol that appears more than once in a question has the same meaning throughout the question.

|   | **Quantity A** | **Quantity B** |
|---|---|---|
| 1. | $39 - (25 - 17)$ | $39 - 25 - 17$ |

|   | **Quantity A** | **Quantity B** |
|---|---|---|
| 2. | $14 - 3(4 - 6)$ | $(4)(-3)(2)(-1)$ |

|   | **Quantity A** | **Quantity B** |
|---|---|---|
| 3. | $-5 \times 1 \div 5$ | $-6 \times 1 \div 6$ |

4.   What is the value of $5 - (4 - (3 - (2 - 1)))$ ?

|   | **Quantity A** | **Quantity B** |
|---|---|---|
| 5. | $-\dfrac{2^3}{2}$ | $(-2)^2$ |

|   | **Quantity A** | **Quantity B** |
|---|---|---|
| 6. | $5^3 - 5^2$ | $5$ |

|   | **Quantity A** | **Quantity B** |
|---|---|---|
| 7. | $-10 - (-3)^2$ | $-[10 + (-3)^2]$ |

|  | **Quantity A** | **Quantity B** |
|---|---|---|
| 8. | (30,000,000)(2,000,000) | (15,000,000)(4,000,000) |

9. What is the sum of the numbers in the grid below?

| -2 | -1 | 1 | 2 | 3 | 4 |
|---|---|---|---|---|---|
| -4 | -2 | 2 | 4 | 6 | 8 |
| -6 | -3 | 3 | 6 | 9 | 12 |
| -8 | -4 | 4 | 8 | 12 | 16 |
| -10 | -5 | 5 | 10 | 15 | 20 |
| -12 | -6 | 6 | 12 | 18 | 24 |

10. Molly worked at an amusement park over the summer. Every two weeks, she was paid according to the following schedule: at the end of the first 2 weeks, she received $160. At the end of each subsequent 2-week period, she received $1, plus an additional amount equal to the sum of all payments she had received in previous weeks. How much money was Molly paid during the full 10 weeks of summer?

$ 

A book with 80,000 words costs $24 and a short story with 1,000 words costs $1.

|  | **Quantity A** | **Quantity B** |
|---|---|---|
| 11. | Cost per word of the book | Cost per word of the short story |

**Ticket Prices at the Natural History Museum**

|  | Weekdays | Weekends & Holidays |
|---|---|---|
| Child (ages 5–18) | $7 | $9 |
| Adult (ages 19–64) | $14 | $16 |
| Senior (ages 65+) | $8 | $10 |
| *Children under age 5 attend free | | |

|  | **Quantity A** | **Quantity B** |
|---|---|---|
| 12. | The price for tickets at the Natural History Museum on a weekday for one 12-year-old and one 39-year-old | The price for tickets at the Natural History Museum on a weekend for one 4-year-old, two 8-year-olds, and one senior over 65 years old, after applying a coupon for $10 off the total cost |

On a certain train, tickets cost $6 each for children and $9 each for adults. The total train ticket cost for a certain group of six passengers was between $44 and $50.

|  | **Quantity A** | **Quantity B** |
|---|---|---|
| 13. | The number of children in the group | The number of adults in the group |

14. If 617 is divided by 49, the sum of the tens digit and the tenths digit of the resulting number is what value?

   (A) 1
   (B) 5
   (C) 6
   (D) 7
   (E) 9

|  | **Quantity A** | **Quantity B** |
|---|---|---|
| 15. | The number of days between May 30, 1917, and May 15, 1996, inclusive | The number of days between May 15, 1912, and May 30, 1991, inclusive |

Alfred's Coffee Shop offers a "buy six cups of coffee, get one free" discount, and Boris's Coffee Shop offers 15% off all orders of six or more cups of coffee. At both shops, the regular price of a single cup of coffee is $2.60.

|  | **Quantity A** | **Quantity B** |
|---|---|---|
| 16. | The total cost for one order of seven single cups of coffee from Alfred's | The total cost for one order of seven single cups of coffee from Boris's |

17. In a certain ancient kingdom, the standard unit of measure was the "crown," equal to 10 standard modern inches. An alternative unit of measure was the "scepter," equal to 14 standard modern inches. If a tower measured 70 crowns tall, how many scepters tall was it?

   (A) 35
   (B) 49
   (C) 50
   (D) 75
   (E) 98

18. A total of $450 was donated to charity by 25 employees. If 15 employees donated at least $12 but less than $19 and 9 employees donated at least $19, what is the maximum amount, in dollars, that the last employee could have donated?

$ [ ]

19. A tank has a capacity of 200 pints. How many gallons of water would it take to fill the tank to $\frac{3}{10}$ of its capacity? (1 gallon = 8 pints)

[ ] gallons

1 kilogram = 2.2 pounds

|   | **Quantity A** | **Quantity B** |
|---|---|---|
| 20. | The number of kilograms in 44 pounds | The number of pounds in 44 kilograms |

21. If the formula for converting degrees Fahrenheit to degrees Celsius is $C = \frac{5}{9}(F - 32)$, what is the value of $F$ when $C$ is 30?

(A) $-\frac{10}{9}$

(B) $\frac{338}{9}$

(C) 86

(D) $\frac{558}{5}$

(E) 112

22. On a trip, Joe's car traveled an average of 36 miles per gallon of fuel. Approximately how many kilometers did the car travel on 10 liters of fuel? (5 miles = approximately 8 kilometers; 1 gallon = approximately 4 liters)

[ ] kilometers

**MANHATTAN**
PREP

23. How many 1-inch square tiles would it take to cover the floor of a closet that has dimensions 5 feet by 4 feet? (1 foot = 12 inches)

    (A)  20
    (B)  240
    (C)  1,440
    (D)  2,160
    (E)  2,880

Child A ate $\frac{3}{5}$ of a kilogram of chocolate and Child B ate 300 grams of chocolate. (1 kilogram = 1000 grams)

|  | **Quantity A** | **Quantity B** |
|---|---|---|
| 24. | The weight, in grams, of the chocolate that Child A ate | Twice the weight, in grams, of the chocolate that Child B ate |

25. Out of 5.5 billion bacteria grown for an experiment, 1 in 75 million has a particular mutation. Approximately how many of the bacteria have the mutation?

    (A)  7
    (B)  73
    (C)  733
    (D)  7,333
    (E)  73,333

26. A particular nation's GDP (Gross Domestic Product) is $4.5 billion. If the population of the nation is 1.75 million, what is the per capita (per person) GDP, rounded to the nearest dollar?

    (A)  $3
    (B)  $25
    (C)  $257
    (D)  $2,571
    (E)  $25,714

27. Global GDP (Gross Domestic Product) was $69.97 trillion in 2011. If the world population for 2011 was best estimated at 6,973,738,433, approximately what was the global GDP per person?

   (A) $10
   (B) $100
   (C) $1,000
   (D) $10,000
   (E) $100,000

28. The runners on a cross country team ran a 5-mile race at average (arithmetic mean) speeds ranging from 4 miles per hour to 7 miles per hour, inclusive. Which of the following are possible race completion times for individual members of the team?

   Indicate all such times.

   ☐  36 minutes
   ☐  48 minutes
   ☐  60 minutes
   ☐  75 minutes
   ☐  90 minutes
   ☐  120 minutes

# Arithmetic Answers

1. **(A).** First simplify inside the parentheses:

$$39 - (25 - 17) =$$
$$39 - 8 =$$
$$31$$

You could also distribute the minus sign to get $39 - 25 + 17$ if you prefer. Quantity B is equal to $-3$, so Quantity A is greater. If you noticed right away that the minus sign would distribute in Quantity A but not Quantity B, you could have picked (A) without doing any arithmetic.

2. **(B).** This question is testing PEMDAS (Parentheses/Exponents, then Multiplication/Division, then Addition/Subtraction), at least in Quantity A. Make sure that you simplify inside the parentheses, and then multiply, before subtracting:

$$14 - 3(4 - 6) =$$
$$14 - 3(-2) =$$
$$14 + 6 =$$
$$20$$

Quantity B is $(4)(-3)(2)(-1) = 24$.

3. **(C).** The two quantities are equal. Note that in Quantity A:

$$-5 \times 1 \div 5 =$$
$$-5 \div 5 =$$
$$-1$$

In Quantity B:

$$-6 \times 1 \div 6 =$$
$$-6 \div 6 =$$
$$-1$$

4. **3.** Make sure to begin with the innermost parentheses:

$$5 - (4 - (3 - (2 - 1))) =$$
$$5 - (4 - (3 - 1)) =$$
$$5 - (4 - 2) =$$
$$5 - (2) =$$
$$3$$

5. **(B).** In Quantity A, the exponent should be computed before taking the negative of the value—in accordance with PEMDAS. Thus, you get $-8/2 = -4$.

In Quantity B:

$$(-2)^2 =$$
$$(-2)(-2) =$$
$$4$$

6. **(A).** Do not make the mistake of thinking that $5^3 - 5^2 = 5^1$. You cannot just subtract the exponents when you are subtracting two terms with the same base! Instead, compute the exponents and subtract:

$$5^3 - 5^2 =$$
$$125 - 25 =$$
$$100$$

Quantity A is greater. Alternatively, you could factor out $5^2$ (this is an important technique for large numbers and exponents where pure arithmetic would be impractical):

$$5^3 - 5^2 =$$
$$5^2(5^1 - 1) =$$
$$5^2(4) =$$
$$100$$

7. **(C).** In Quantity A:

$$-10 - (-3)^2 =$$
$$-10 - (9) =$$
$$-19$$

In Quantity B:

$$-[10 + (-3)^2] =$$
$$-[10 + (9)] =$$
$$-19$$

8. **(C).** The GRE calculator will not be able to handle that many zeros. Start this calculation on paper. To make things easier, you could cancel as many zeros as you want, as long as you do the same operation to both quantities. For instance, you could divide both sides by 1,000,000,000,000 (just think of this as "1 with 12 zeros"), to get:

| **Quantity A** | **Quantity B** |
|:---:|:---:|
| (30)(2) | (15)(4) |

**MANHATTAN**
PREP

Or, just use a bit of logic: 30 million times 2 million is 60 million *million*, and 15 million times 4 million is also 60 million *million*. (A "million million" is a trillion, but this doesn't matter as long as you're sure that each Quantity will have the same number of zeros.)

9. **147.** There are several patterns in the grid, depending on whether you look by row or by column. Within each row, there are positive and negative terms at the beginning that cancel each other. For example, in the first row, you have $-2 + 2 = 0$ and $-1 + 1 = 0$. The only terms in the first row that contribute to the sum are 3 and 4, in the far-right columns. The same is true for the other rows.

Thus, the sum of the grid is equal to the sum of only the two far-right columns. The sum in the first row in those columns is $3 + 4 = 7$; the sum in the next row is $6 + 8 = 14$, etc. The sum in the final row is $18 + 24 = 42$. Add $7 + 14 + 21 + 28 + 35 + 42$ in your calculator to get 147.

10. **$2,575.** At the end of the first two weeks, Molly received $160. At the end of the fourth week, she received $1, plus $160 for the total she had been paid up to that point, for a total of $161. At the end of the sixth week, she received $1, plus ($160 + $161), or $321, for the total she had been paid up to that point, making the sixth week total $322. To keep track, put these values in a table:

| Week # | Paid This Week($) | Cumulative Pay Including This Week ($) |
|--------|-------------------|----------------------------------------|
| 2      | 160               | 160                                    |
| 4      | 160 + 1 = 161     | 160 + 161 = 321                        |
| 6      | 321 + 1 = 322     | 321 + 322 = 643                        |
| 8      | 643 + 1 = 644     | 643 + 644 = 1,287                      |
| 10     | 1,287 + 1 = 1,288 | 1,287 + 1,288 = 2,575                  |

11. **(B).** In Quantity A, $\dfrac{24}{80,000} = 0.0003$, or 0.03 cents per word. In Quantity B, $\dfrac{1}{1,000} = 0.001$, or 0.1 cents per word. Quantity B is greater. Note that the calculation was not strictly necessary—it would have been more efficient to notice that the book costs 24 times the story but has 80 times the words. (Then remember to choose the greater number!)

12. **(A).** The ticket for the 4-year-old in Quantity B costs $0 (children under age 5 attend free).

Quantity A: The price for tickets at the Natural History Museum on a weekday for one 12-year-old and one 39-year-old = $7 + $14 = $21.

Quantity B: The price for tickets at the Natural History Museum on a weekend for one 4-year-old, two 8-year-olds, and one senior over 65 years old, after applying a coupon for $10 off the total cost is equal to ($0 + $9 + $9 + $10) − $10 = $18.

Quantity A is greater.

13. **(D).** Even though the range of costs ($44 to $50) is fairly small, there is still more than one possibility. A good way to work this out is to start with the simplest scenario: 3 adults and 3 children. Their tickets would cost 3(9) + 3(6) = $45. That's in the range, so it's one possibility.

Since children's tickets are cheaper, you don't want to add more children to the mix (4 children, 2 adults will give you too small a total), but try switching out 1 child for 1 adult.

For 4 adults and 2 children, tickets would cost 4(9) + 2(6) = $48. Thus, Quantity A and Quantity B could be equal, or Quantity B could be greater, so the relationship cannot be determined from the information given.

14. **(C).** Divide 617 by 49 with the calculator to get 12.5918.... The **tens** digit is 1. The **tenths** digit is 5. The answer is 1 + 5 = 6.

15. **(B).** Calculating the number of days in each quantity would be time consuming; each date range includes a lot of days! Instead, a faster approach is to compare the starting and ending dates for the two quantities.

Quantity A: The number of days between May 30, 1917 and May 15, 1996, inclusive.

Quantity B: The number of days between May 15, 1912 and May 30, 1991, inclusive.

All of the start and end dates are in May, but both the starting and ending years in Quantity B are 5 years earlier than those in Quantity A. Thus, the approximate whole number of years in both ranges is the same (about 79 years). However, the range in Quantity A starts later in the month and ends earlier in the month than the range in Quantity B. Both differences mean that Quantity B includes a greater number of days.

Alternatively, consider the following: the date range in Quantity A is about half a month less than 79 years, while the date range in Quantity B is about half a month greater than 79 years. Quantity B is greater.

16. **(A).** At Alfred's, an order of 7 single cups of coffee would cost 6($2.60) = $15.60, because the 7th cup is free.

At Boris's, an order of 7 single cups of coffee would receive the 15% discount: 7($2.60)(0.85) = $15.47.

Alternatively, because the non-discounted price of a single coffee ($2.60) and the number of single cups of coffee ordered is common to both quantities, an actual cost calculation is optional. Instead, you could compare the discounts in percent terms. At Alfred's, "buy six drinks get one free" means that, for every seven drinks you purchase, the last one is free. That's one in seven drinks free, or $\frac{1}{7}$ off, which is about $\left(\frac{1}{7} \times 100\right)\% = 14.29\%$ off. This is smaller than the 15% discount at Boris's, so the total cost at Alfred's is greater. By the way, remember to pick the greater quantity (Quantity A), not the "better deal"!

17. **(C).** A tower that was 70 crowns tall was 70 crowns × 10 inches/crown = 700 inches tall. This same 700-inch tower, measured in scepters, would be $\frac{700 \text{ inches}}{14 \text{ inches/scepter}} = 50$ scepters tall. Also, note that since the scepter is longer than the crown in absolute terms, fewer scepters will "fit" in the height of the tower, so any choices 70 or greater could be eliminated right away.

**MANHATTAN**
PREP

18. **$99.** To maximize the last employee's contribution, minimize everyone else's. If 15 employees could have donated a minimum of $12 and 9 employees could have donated a minimum of $19:

$$15(12) + 9(19) = 180 + 171 = 351.$$

So, the minimum that all 24 of these employees could have given is $351. Therefore, the maximum that the 25th employee could have given is $450 - 351 = 99$, or $99.

19. **7.5 gallons.**

First find out how many pints $\dfrac{3}{10}$ of the capacity is:

$$200 \times \frac{3}{10} = \frac{600}{10} = 60$$

Now convert pints to gallons:

$$60 \text{ pints} \times \frac{1 \text{ gallon}}{8 \text{ pints}} = \frac{60}{8} = 7.5 \text{ gallons}$$

20. **(B).** To compare the values, convert the quantity on the left from pounds to kilograms and the quantity on the right from kilograms to pounds:

| **Quantity A** | **Quantity B** |
|---|---|
| $44 \text{ pounds} \times \dfrac{1 \text{ kilogram}}{2.2 \text{ pounds}}$ | $44 \text{ kilograms} \times \dfrac{2.2 \text{ pounds}}{1 \text{ kilogram}}$ |

Before actually multiplying, notice that the Quantity A is divided by 2.2, while the Quantity B is multiplied by 2.2. Quantity B will be greater.

You could also solve this by noticing that the two quantities involve reverse calculations, with the same number of units (44). Since a kilogram is heavier than a pound, it takes more of the lighter pounds to equal 44 heavier kilograms than it takes of the heavier kilograms to equal 44 of the lighter pounds.

21. **(C).** Start by plugging 30 in for $C$ in the equation:

$$30 = \frac{5}{9}(F - 32)$$

Now isolate $F$. Begin by multiplying both sides by $\dfrac{9}{5}$:

$$\frac{9}{5} \times 30 = F - 32$$

To multiply 30 by $\dfrac{9}{5}$ quickly, reduce before multiplying:

$$\frac{9}{1} \times 6 = F - 32$$
$$54 = F - 32$$
$$86 = F$$

22. **144 kilometers.** Convert miles per gallon to kilometers per liter by multiplying by the conversion ratios such that both the miles and gallons units are canceled out:

$$\frac{36 \text{ miles}}{1 \text{ gallon}} \times \frac{8 \text{ kilometers}}{5 \text{ miles}} = \frac{288 \text{ kilometers}}{5 \text{ gallons}}$$

$$\frac{288 \text{ kilometers}}{5 \text{ gallons}} \times \frac{1 \text{ gallon}}{4 \text{ liters}} = \frac{288 \text{ kilometers}}{20 \text{ liters}} = \frac{14.4 \text{ kilometers}}{1 \text{ liter}}$$

The car has 10 liters of fuel in the tank:

$$10 \text{ liters} \times 14.4 \text{ kilometers/liter} = 144 \text{ kilometers}$$

23. **(E).** There is a hidden trap in this question. Remember that the dimensions of this room are square feet, not feet (because 5 feet × 4 feet = 20 square feet). To avoid this trap, you should convert the dimensions to inches first, then multiply.

$$5 \text{ feet} \times 4 \text{ feet} = 60 \text{ inches} \times 48 \text{ inches}$$

The dimensions of the closet in inches are 60 inches by 48 inches, or $60 \times 48 = 2,880$ square inches. Each tile is 1 square inch, so it will take 2,880 tiles to cover the floor.

24. **(C).** $\frac{3}{5}$ of a kilogram is 600 grams. Twice 300 grams is also 600 grams. The two quantities are equal.

25. **(B).** One good way to keep track of large numbers (especially those that won't fit in the GRE calculator!) is to use scientific notation (or a loose version thereof—for instance, 5.5 billion in scientific notation is $5.5 \times 10^9$, but it would be equally correct for your purposes to write it as $55 \times 10^8$).

$$5.5 \text{ billion} = 5,500,000,000 = 5.5 \times 10^9$$
$$75 \text{ million} = 75,000,000 = 75 \times 10^6$$

Since 1 in 75 million of the bacteria have the mutation, divide 5.5 billion by 75 million:

$\frac{5.5 \times 10^9}{75 \times 10^6}$, which can also be written as $\frac{5.5}{75} \times \frac{10^9}{10^6}$. Only $\frac{5.5}{75}$ needs to go in the calculator, to yield 0.0733333…

Since $\frac{10^9}{10^6}$ is $10^3$, move the decimal three places to the right to get 73.333…, or answer choice (B).

Or, write one number over the other and *cancel out the same number of zeros from the top and bottom* before trying to use the calculator: $\frac{5,500,000,000}{75,000,000} = \frac{5,500,\cancel{000,000}}{75,\cancel{000,000}} = \frac{5,500}{75} = 73.333…$

**MANHATTAN**
PREP

26. **(D).** This problem is asking you to divide $4.5 billion by 1.75 million. When dealing with numbers that have many zeros, you can avoid mistakes by using scientific notation or by writing out the numbers and canceling zeros before using the calculator:

$$4.5 \text{ billion} = 4,500,000,000 = 4.5 \times 10^9$$
$$1.75 \text{ million} = 1,750,000 = 1.75 \times 10^6$$
$$\frac{4.5 \times 10^9}{1.75 \times 10^6} = 2.57142\ldots \times 10^3 = 2,571.42\ldots$$

The answer is (D). Alternatively, write one number on top of the other in fully-expanded form, and cancel zeros before using the calculator:

$$\frac{4,500,000,000}{1,750,000} = \frac{4,500,00\cancel{0,000}}{1,75\cancel{0,000}} = \frac{450,000}{175} = 2,571.42\ldots$$

27. **(D).** This problem is asking you to divide $69.97 trillion by 6,973,738,433. When dealing with numbers that have many zeros, you can avoid mistakes by using scientific notation or by writing out the numbers and canceling zeros before using the calculator.

Before doing that, however, look at the answers—they are very far apart from one another, which gives you license to estimate. GDP is about 70 trillion. Population is about 7 billion. Thus:

$$\frac{70,000,000,000,000}{7,000,000,000} = \frac{70,000,\cancel{000,000,000}}{7,\cancel{000,000,000}} = 10,000$$

28. **48 minutes, 60 minutes, and 75 minutes.** $\text{Rate} \times \text{Time} = \text{Distance}$, thus $\dfrac{\text{Distance}}{\text{Rate}} = \text{Time}$.

The race times range from a maximum time of $\dfrac{5 \text{ miles}}{4 \text{ miles/hour}} = 1.25$ hours $= 75$ minutes for the slowest runner to a minimum time of $\dfrac{5 \text{ miles}}{7 \text{ miles/hour}} = $ about $0.71429$ hours $=$ about $42.86$ minutes for the fastest runner. All answers between (and including) 42.86 minutes and 75 minutes are correct.

# Chapter 8 *of*

## 5 lb. Book of GRE® Practice Problems

# Algebra

# Chapter 8

## In This Chapter...

*Algebra*

*Algebra Answers*

# Algebra

For questions in the Quantitative Comparison format ("Quantity A" and "Quantity B" given), the answer choices are always as follows:

(A)  Quantity A is greater.
(B)  Quantity B is greater.
(C)  The two quantities are equal.
(D)  The relationship cannot be determined from the information given.

For questions followed by a numeric entry box [        ], you are to enter your own answer in the box. For questions followed

by a fraction-style numeric entry box ═══, you are to enter your answer in the form of a fraction. You are not required to

reduce fractions. For example, if the answer is $\frac{1}{4}$, you may enter $\frac{25}{100}$ or any equivalent fraction.

All numbers used are real numbers. All figures are assumed to lie in a plane unless otherwise indicated. Geometric figures are not necessarily drawn to scale. You should assume, however, that lines that appear to be straight are actually straight, points on a line are in the order shown, and all geometric objects are in the relative positions shown. Coordinate systems, such as $xy$-planes and number lines, as well as graphical data presentations, such as bar charts, circle graphs, and line graphs, *are* drawn to scale. A symbol that appears more than once in a question has the same meaning throughout the question.

1.  If $4(-3x - 8) = 8(-x + 9)$, what is the value of $x^2$?

2.  If $2x(4 - 6) = -2x + 12$, what is the value of $x$?

3.  If $x \neq 0$ and $\dfrac{3(6 - x)}{2x} = -6$, what is the value of $x$?

4.  If $x \neq 2$ and $\dfrac{8 - 2(-4 + 10x)}{2 - x} = 17$, what is the value of $x$?

−5 is 7 more than −z.

| Quantity A | Quantity B |
|:---:|:---:|
| $z$ | −12 |

5.

6.   If $(x + 3)^2 = 225$, which of the following could be the value of $x - 1$?

   (A)   13
   (B)   12
   (X)   −12
   (Δ)   −16
   (E)   −19

$$x = 2$$

| **Quantity A** | **Quantity B** |
|---|---|
| 7.    $x^2 - 4x + 3$ | 1 |

$$p = 300c^2 - c$$
$$c = 100$$

| **Quantity A** | **Quantity B** |
|---|---|
| 8.    $p$ | 29,000$c$ |

$$-(x)^3 = 64$$

| **Quantity A** | **Quantity B** |
|---|---|
| 9.    $x^4$ | $x^5$ |

10.   If $3t^3 - 7 = 74$, what is the value of $t^2 - t$?

   (A)   −3
   (B)   3
   (C)   6
   (D)   9
   (E)   18

11.   If $y = 4x + 10$ and $y = 7x - 5$, what is the value of $y$?

12.   If $x - y = 4$ and $2x + y = 5$, what is the value of $x$?

**MANHATTAN**
PREP

13.  $4x + y + 3z = 34$
     $4x + 3z = 21$

     What is the value of $y$?

     ┌─────────────┐
     │             │
     └─────────────┘

| **Quantity A** | **Quantity B** |
|---|---|
| 14. $(x + 2)(x - 3)$ | $x^2 - x - 6$ |

$$xy > 0$$

| **Quantity A** | **Quantity B** |
|---|---|
| 15. $(2x - y)(x + 4y)$ | $2x^2 + 8xy - 4y^2$ |

$$x^2 - 2x = 0$$

| **Quantity A** | **Quantity B** |
|---|---|
| 16. $x$ | 2 |

| **Quantity A** | **Quantity B** |
|---|---|
| 17. $d(d^2 - 2d + 1)$ | $d(d^2 - 2d) + 1$ |

| **Quantity A** | **Quantity B** |
|---|---|
| 18. $xy^2z(x^2z + yz^2 - xy^2)$ | $x^3y^2z^2 + xy^3z^3 - x^2y^4z$ |

$a = 2b = 4c$ and $a$, $b$, and $c$ are integers.

| **Quantity A** | **Quantity B** |
|---|---|
| 19. $a + b$ | $a + c$ |

$k = 2m = 4n$ and $k$, $m$, and $n$ are non-negative integers.

| **Quantity A** | **Quantity B** |
|---|---|
| 20. $km$ | $kn$ |

For the positive integers $a$, $b$, $c$, and $d$, $a$ is half of $b$, which is one-third of $c$. The value of $d$ is three times the value of $c$.

|  | **Quantity A** | **Quantity B** |
|---|---|---|
| 21. | $\dfrac{a+b}{c}$ | $\dfrac{a+b+c}{d}$ |

22. If $x^2 - y^2 = 0$ and $xy \neq 0$, which of the following must be true?

Indicate all such statements.

- ☐ $x = y$
- ☐ $|x| = |y|$
- ☐ $\dfrac{x^2}{y^2} = 1$

$$3x + 6y = 27$$
$$x + 2y + z = 11$$

|  | **Quantity A** | **Quantity B** |
|---|---|---|
| 23. | $z + 5$ | $x + 2y - 2$ |

24. If $(x - y) = \sqrt{12}$ and $(x + y) = \sqrt{3}$, what is the value of $x^2 - y^2$?

- (A) 3
- (B) 6
- (C) 9
- (D) 36
- (E) It cannot be determined from the information given.

$$a \neq b$$

|  | **Quantity A** | **Quantity B** |
|---|---|---|
| 25. | $\dfrac{a-b}{b-a}$ | 1 |

$$a = \frac{b}{2}$$
$$c = 3b$$

|  | **Quantity A** | **Quantity B** |
|---|---|---|
| 26. | $a$ | $c$ |

27. If $xy \neq 0$ and $x \neq -y$, $\dfrac{x^{36} - y^{36}}{\left(x^{18} + y^{18}\right)\left(x^9 + y^9\right)} =$

    (A)  1

    (B)  $x^2 - y^2$

    (C)  $x^9 - y^9$

    (D)  $x^{18} - y^{18}$

    (E)  $\dfrac{1}{x^9 - y^9}$

28. If $x \neq -y$, what is the value of $\dfrac{x^2 + 2xy + y^2}{2(x+y)^2}$ ?

    (A)  1

    (B)  $\dfrac{1}{2}$

    (C)  $\dfrac{1}{x+y}$

    (D)  $xy$

    (E)  $2xy$

$$x > y$$
$$xy \neq 0$$

|  | **Quantity A** | **Quantity B** |
|---|---|---|
| 29. | $\dfrac{x^2}{y + \dfrac{1}{y}}$ | $\dfrac{y^2}{x + \dfrac{1}{x}}$ |

30. If $x + y = -3$ and $x^2 + y^2 = 12$, what is the value of $2xy$?

31. If $x - y = \dfrac{1}{2}$ and $x^2 - y^2 = 3$, what is the value of $x + y$?

32. If $x^2 - 2xy = 84$ and $x - y = -10$, what is the value of $|y|$?

33. Which of the following is equal to $(x - 2)^2 + (x - 1)^2 + x^2 + (x + 1)^2 + (x + 2)^2$?

   (A) $5x^2$
   (B) $5x^2 + 10$
   (C) $x^2 + 10$
   (D) $5x^2 + 6x + 10$
   (E) $5x^2 - 6x + 10$

34. If $a = (x + y)^2$ and $b = x^2 + y^2$ and $xy > 0$, which of the following must be true?

   Indicate <u>all</u> such statements.

   ☐ $a = b$
   ☐ $a > b$
   ☐ $a$ is positive

35. $a$ is directly proportional to $b$. If $a = 8$ when $b = 2$, what is $a$ when $b = 4$?

   (A) 10
   (B) 16
   (C) 32
   (D) 64
   (E) 128

**MANHATTAN**
PREP

# Algebra Answers

1. **676.** Distribute, group like terms, and solve for $x$:

$$4(-3x - 8) = 8(-x + 9)$$
$$-12x - 32 = -8x + 72$$
$$-32 = 4x + 72$$
$$-104 = 4x$$
$$-26 = x$$

Then, multiply 26 by 26 in the calculator (or $-26$ by $-26$, although the negatives will cancel each other out) to get $x^2$, which is 676.

2. **−6.**
$$2x(4 - 6) = -2x + 12$$
$$2x(-2) = -2x + 12$$
$$-4x = -2x + 12$$
$$-2x = 12$$
$$x = -6$$

3. **−2.** $\dfrac{3(6 - x)}{2x} = -6$

Multiply both sides by $2x$, distribute the left side, combine like terms, and solve:

$$3(6 - x) = -6(2x)$$
$$18 - 3x = -12x$$
$$18 = -9x$$
$$-2 = x$$

4. **−6.** $\dfrac{8 - 2(-4 + 10x)}{2 - x} = 17$

Multiply both sides by the expression $2 - x$, distribute both sides, combine like terms, and solve:

$$8 - 2(-4 + 10x) = 17(2 - x)$$
$$8 + 8 - 20x = 34 - 17x$$
$$16 - 20x = 34 - 17x$$
$$16 = 34 + 3x$$
$$-18 = 3x$$
$$-6 = x$$

5. **(A).** Translate the question stem into an equation and solve for $z$:

$$-5 = -z + 7$$
$$-12 = -z$$
$$12 = z$$

Because $z = 12 > -12$, Quantity A is greater.

6. **(E).** Begin by square-rooting both sides of the equation, but remember that 225 could be the square of either 15 or −15. (The calculator will not remind you of this! It's your job to keep this in mind). So:

$$x + 3 = 15$$
$$x = 12$$
$$\text{so, } x - 1 = 11$$

OR

$$x + 3 = -15$$
$$x = -18$$
$$\text{so, } x - 1 = -19$$

Only −19 appears in the choices.

7. **(B).** To evaluate the expression in Quantity A, replace $x$ with 2.

$$x^2 - 4x + 3 =$$
$$(2)^2 - 4(2) + 3 =$$
$$4 - 8 + 3 = -1 < 1$$

Therefore, Quantity B is greater.

8. **(A).** To find the value of $p$, first replace $c$ with 100 to find the value for Quantity A:

$$p = 300c^2 - c$$
$$p = 300(100)^2 - 100$$
$$p = 300(10,000) - 100$$
$$p = 3,000,000 - 100 = 2,999,900$$

Since $c = 100$, the value for Quantity B is $29,000(100) = 2,900,000$. Quantity A is greater.

9. **(A).** First, solve for $x$:

$$-(x)^3 = 64$$
$$(x)^3 = -64$$

The GRE calculator will not do a cube root. As a result, cube roots on the GRE tend to be quite small and easy to puzzle out. What number times itself three times equals −64? The answer is $x = -4$.

Since $x$ is negative, Quantity A is positive (a negative number times itself four times is positive) and Quantity B is negative (a negative number times itself five times is negative). No further calculations are needed to conclude that Quantity A is greater. Notice that solving for the value of $x$ here was not strictly necessary. Knowing that the cube root of a negative number is negative gives you all the information you need to solve.

**MANHATTAN**
PREP

10. **(C).** First, solve for $t$:

$$3t^3 - 7 = 74$$
$$3t^3 = 81$$
$$t^3 = 27$$
$$t = 3$$

Now, plug $t = 3$ into $t^2 - t$:

$$(3)^2 - 3 = 9 - 3 = 6$$

11. **30.** Since each equation is already solved for $y$, set the right side of each equation equal to the other.

$$4x + 10 = 7x - 5$$
$$10 = 3x - 5$$
$$15 = 3x$$
$$5 = x$$

Substitute 5 for $x$ in the first equation and solve for $y$.

$$y = 4(5) + 10$$
$$y = 30$$

$x = 5$ and $y = 30$. Be sure to answer for $y$, not $x$.

12. **3.** Notice that the first equation has the term $-y$ while the second equation has the term $+y$. While it is possible to use the substitution method, summing the equations together will make $-y$ and $y$ cancel, so this is the easiest way to solve for $x$.

$$
\begin{array}{r}
x - \cancel{y} = 4 \\
2x + \cancel{y} = 5 \\
\hline
3x \quad\ = 9 \\
x \quad\ = 3
\end{array}
$$

13. **13.** This question contains only two equations, but three variables. To isolate $y$, both $x$ and $z$ must be eliminated. Notice that the coefficients of $x$ and $z$ are the same in both equations. Subtract the second equation from the first to eliminate $x$ and $z$.

$$
\begin{array}{r}
4x + y + 3z = 34 \\
-(4x \quad\ + 3z = 21) \\
\hline
y \quad\quad = 13
\end{array}
$$

14. **(C).** FOIL the terms in Quantity A:

$$(x + 2)(x - 3) = x^2 - 3x + 2x - 6 = x^2 - x - 6$$

The two quantities are equal.

15. **(B).** FOIL the terms in Quantity A:

$$(2x - y)(x + 4y) = 2x^2 + 8xy - xy - 4y^2 = 2x^2 + 7xy - 4y^2$$

Since $2x^2$ and $-4y^2$ appear in both quantities, eliminate them. Quantity A is now equal to $7xy$ and Quantity B is now equal to $8xy$. Because $xy > 0$, Quantity B is greater. (Don't assume! If $xy$ were zero, the two quantities would have been equal. If $xy$ were negative, Quantity A would have been greater.)

16. **(D).** Factor $x^2 - 2x = 0$:

$$x^2 - 2x = 0$$
$$x(x - 2) = 0$$
$$x = 0 \text{ OR } (x - 2) = 0$$

$x = 0$ or 2.

Thus, Quantity A could be less than or equal to Quantity B. The relationship cannot be determined from the information given.

(Note that you *cannot* simply divide both sides of the original equation by $x$. It is illegal to divide by a variable unless it is certain that the variable does not equal zero.)

17. **(D).** In Quantity A, multiply $d$ by every term in the parentheses:

$$d(d^2 - 2d + 1) =$$
$$(d \times d^2) - (d \times 2d) + (d \times 1) =$$
$$d^3 - 2d^2 + d$$

In Quantity B, multiply $d$ by the two terms in the parentheses:

$$d(d^2 - 2d) + 1 =$$
$$(d \times d^2) - (d \times 2d) + 1 =$$
$$d^3 - 2d^2 + 1$$

Because $d^3 - 2d^2$ is common to both quantities, it can be ignored. The comparison is really between $d$ and 1. Without more information about $d$, the relationship cannot be determined from the information given.

18. **(C).** In Quantity A, the term $xy^2z$ on the outside of the parentheses must be multiplied by each of the three terms inside the parentheses. Then simplify the expression as much as possible.

Taking one term at a time, the first is $xy^2z \times x^2z = x^3y^2z^2$, because there are three factors of $x$, two factors of $y$, and two factors of $z$. Similarly, the second term is $xy^2z \times yz^2 = xy^3z^3$ and the third is $xy^2z \times (-xy^2) = -x^2y^4z$. Adding these three terms together gives the distributed form of Quantity A: $x^3y^2z^2 + xy^3z^3 - x^2y^4z$.

This is identical to Quantity B, so the two quantities are equal.

**MANHATTAN**
PREP

19. **(D).** Since $a$ is common to both quantities, it can be ignored. The comparison is really between $b$ and $c$. Because $2b = 4c$, it is true that $b = 2c$, so the comparison is really between $2c$ and $c$. Watch out for negatives. If the variables are positive, Quantity A is greater, but if the variables are negative, Quantity B is greater.

20. **(D).** If the variables are positive, Quantity A is greater. However, all three variables could equal zero, in which case the two quantities are equal. Watch out for the word "non-negative," which means "positive or zero."

21. **(C).** The following relationships are given: $a = \dfrac{b}{2}$, $b = \dfrac{c}{3}$, and $d = 3c$. Pick one variable and put everything in terms of that variable. For instance, variable $a$:

$$b = 2a$$
$$c = 3b = 3(2a) = 6a$$
$$d = 3c = 3(6a) = 18a$$

Substitute into the quantities and simplify.

Quantity A: $\dfrac{a+b}{c} = \dfrac{a+2a}{6a} = \dfrac{3a}{6a} = \dfrac{1}{2}$

Quantity B: $\dfrac{a+b+c}{d} = \dfrac{a+2a+6a}{18a} = \dfrac{9a}{18a} = \dfrac{1}{2}$

The two quantities are equal.

22. $|x| = |y|$ **and** $\dfrac{x^2}{y^2} = 1$. Since $x^2 - y^2 = 0$, add $y^2$ to both sides to get $x^2 = y^2$. It might look as though $x = y$, but this is not necessarily the case. For example, $x$ could be 2 and $y$ could be $-2$. Algebraically, taking the square root of both sides of $x^2 = y^2$ does *not* yield $x = y$, but rather $|x| = |y|$. Thus, the 1st statement is not necessarily true and the 2nd statement is true. The 3rd statement is also true and can be generated algebraically:

$$x^2 - y^2 = 0$$
$$x^2 = y^2$$
$$\dfrac{x^2}{y^2} = 1$$

23. **(C).** This question may at first look difficult, as there are three variables and only two equations. However, notice that the top equation can be divided by 3, yielding $x + 2y = 9$. This can be plugged into the second equation:

$$(x + 2y) + z = 11$$
$$(9) + z = 11$$
$$z = 2$$

Quantity A is thus $2 + 5 = 7$. For Quantity B, remember that $x + 2y = 9$. Thus, Quantity B is $9 - 2 = 7$.

The two quantities are equal.

**MANHATTAN**
PREP                                      375

**24. (B).** The factored form of the Difference of Squares (one of the "special products" you need to memorize for the exam) is comprised of the terms given in this problem:

$$x^2 - y^2 = (x + y)(x - y)$$

Substitute the values $\sqrt{12}$ and $\sqrt{3}$ in place of $(x - y)$ and $(x + y)$, respectively:

$$x^2 - y^2 = \sqrt{12} \times \sqrt{3}$$

Combine 12 and 3 under the same root sign and solve:

$$x^2 - y^2 = \sqrt{12 \times 3}$$
$$x^2 - y^2 = \sqrt{36}$$
$$x^2 - y^2 = 6$$

**25. (B).** Plug in any two unequal values for $a$ and $b$, and Quantity A will always be equal to $-1$. This is because a negative sign can be factored out of the top or bottom of the fraction to show that the top and bottom are the same, except for their signs:

$$\frac{a - b}{b - a} = \frac{a - b}{-(a - b)} = -1$$

**26. (D).** To compare $a$ and $c$, put $c$ in terms of $a$. Multiply the first equation by 2 to find that $b = 2a$. Substitute into the second equation: $c = 3b = 3(2a) = 6a$. If all three variables are positive, then $6a > a$. If all three variables are negative, then $a > 6a$. Finally, all three variables could equal zero, making the two quantities equal.

**27. (C).** The Difference of Squares (one of the "special products" you need to memorize for the exam) is $x^2 - y^2 = (x + y)(x - y)$. This pattern works for any perfect square minus another perfect square. Thus, $x^{36} - y^{36}$ will factor according to this pattern. Note that $\sqrt{x^{36}} = \left(x^{36}\right)^{1/2} = x^{36/2} = x^{18}$, or $x^{36} = (x^{18})^2$. First, factor $x^{36} - y^{36}$ in the numerator, then cancel $x^{18} + y^{18}$ with the $x^{18} + y^{18}$ on the bottom:

$$\frac{x^{36} - y^{36}}{\left(x^{18} + y^{18}\right)\left(x^9 + y^9\right)} = \frac{\left(x^{18} + y^{18}\right)\left(x^{18} - y^{18}\right)}{\left(x^{18} + y^{18}\right)\left(x^9 + y^9\right)} = \frac{\left(x^{18} - y^{18}\right)}{\left(x^9 + y^9\right)}$$

The $x^{18} - y^{18}$ in the numerator will also factor according to this pattern. Then cancel $x^9 + y^9$ with the $x^9 + y^9$ on the bottom:

$$\frac{\left(x^{18} - y^{18}\right)}{\left(x^9 + y^9\right)} = \frac{\left(x^9 + y^9\right)\left(x^9 - y^9\right)}{\left(x^9 + y^9\right)} = x^9 - y^9$$

**28. (B).** First, recognize that $x^2 + 2xy + y^2 = (x + y)^2$. This is one of the "special products" you need to memorize for the exam. Factor the top, then cancel:

**MANHATTAN**
PREP

$$\frac{x^2 + 2xy + y^2}{2(x+y)^2} = \frac{\cancel{(x+y)^2}}{2\cancel{(x+y)^2}} = \frac{1}{2}$$

29. **(D).** It is possible to simplify first and then plug in examples, or to just plug in examples without simplifying. For instance, if $x = 2$ and $y = 1$:

Quantity A: $\dfrac{x^2}{y+\dfrac{1}{y}} = \dfrac{2^2}{1+\dfrac{1}{1}} = \dfrac{4}{2} = 2$

Quantity B: $\dfrac{y^2}{x+\dfrac{1}{x}} = \dfrac{1^2}{2+\dfrac{1}{2}} = \dfrac{1}{\dfrac{5}{2}} = \dfrac{2}{5}$

In this case, Quantity A is greater. Next, try negatives. If $x = -1$ and $y = -2$ (remember, $x$ must be greater than $y$):

Quantity A: $\dfrac{x^2}{y+\dfrac{1}{y}} = \dfrac{(-1)^2}{-2+\dfrac{1}{-2}} = \dfrac{1}{\dfrac{5}{-2}} = \dfrac{-2}{5}$

Quantity B: $\dfrac{y^2}{x+\dfrac{1}{x}} = \dfrac{(-2)^2}{(-1)+\dfrac{1}{-1}} = \dfrac{4}{-2} = -2$

Quantity A is still greater. However, before assuming that Quantity A is *always* greater, make sure you have tried every category of possibilities for $x$ and $y$. What if $x$ is positive and $y$ is negative? For instance, $x = 2$ and $y = -2$:

Quantity A: $\dfrac{x^2}{y+\dfrac{1}{y}} = \dfrac{2^2}{-2+\dfrac{1}{-2}} = \dfrac{4}{-\dfrac{5}{2}} = 4 \times -\dfrac{2}{5} = -\dfrac{8}{5}$

Quantity B: $\dfrac{y^2}{x+\dfrac{1}{x}} = \dfrac{(-2)^2}{(2)+\dfrac{1}{2}} = \dfrac{4}{\dfrac{5}{2}} = 4 \times \dfrac{2}{5} = \dfrac{8}{5}$

In this case, Quantity B is greater. The relationship cannot be determined from the information given.

30. **−3.** One of the "special products" you need to memorize for the GRE is $x^2 + 2xy + y^2 = (x + y)^2$. Write this pattern on your paper, plug in the given values, and simplify, solving for $2xy$:

$$x^2 + 2xy + y^2 = (x+y)^2$$
$$(x^2 + y^2) + 2xy = (x+y)^2$$
$$(12) + 2xy = (-3)^2$$
$$12 + 2xy = 9$$
$$2xy = -3$$

31. **6.** The Difference of Squares (one of the "special products" you need to memorize for the exam) is $x^2 - y^2 = (x + y)(x - y)$. Write this pattern on your paper and plug in the given values, solving for $x + y$:

$$x^2 - y^2 = (x + y)(x - y)$$
$$3 = (x + y)(1/2)$$
$$6 = x + y$$

32. **4.** One of the "special products" you need to memorize for the exam is $x^2 - 2xy + y^2 = (x - y)^2$. Write this pattern on your paper and plug in the given values:

$$x^2 - 2xy + y^2 = (x - y)^2$$
$$84 + y^2 = (-10)^2$$
$$84 + y^2 = 100$$
$$y^2 = 16$$
$$y = 4 \text{ or } -4, \text{ so } |y| = 4.$$

33. **(B).** First, multiply out (remember FOIL = First, Outer, Inner, Last) each of the terms in parentheses:

$$(x^2 - 2x - 2x + 4) + (x^2 - 1x - 1x + 1) + (x^2) + (x^2 + 1x + 1x + 1) + (x^2 + 2x + 2x + 4)$$

Note that some of the terms will cancel each other out (e.g., $-x$ and $x$, $-2x$ and $2x$):

$$(x^2 + 4) + (x^2 + 1) + (x^2) + (x^2 + 1) + (x^2 + 4)$$

Finally, combine:

$$5x^2 + 10$$

34. **$a > b$ and $a$ is positive.** Distribute for $a$: $a = (x + y)^2 = x^2 + 2xy + y^2$. Since $b = x^2 + y^2$, $a$ and $b$ are the same except for the "extra" $2xy$ in $a$. Since $xy$ is positive, $a$ is greater than $b$. The 1st statement is false and the 2nd statement is true.

Each term in the sum for $a$ is positive: $xy$ is given as positive, and $x^2$ and $y^2$ are definitely positive, as they are squared and not equal to zero. Therefore, $a = x^2 + 2xy + y^2$ is positive. The 3rd statement is true.

35. **(B).** To answer this question, it is important to understand what is meant by the phrase "directly proportional." It means that $a = kb$, where $k$ is a constant. In alternative form: $\dfrac{a}{b} = k$, where $k$ is a constant.

So, because they both equal the constant, $\dfrac{a_{old}}{b_{old}} = \dfrac{a_{new}}{b_{new}}$. Plugging in values: $\dfrac{8}{2} = \dfrac{a_{new}}{4}$. Cross-multiply and solve:

$$32 = 2a_{new}$$
$$a_{new} = 16$$

# Chapter *of* 9

5 lb. Book of GRE® Practice Problems

# Inequalities and Absolute Values

# In This Chapter...

Inequalities and Absolute Values

Inequalities and Absolute Values Answers

# Inequalities and Absolute Values

For questions in the Quantitative Comparison format ("Quantity A" and "Quantity B" given), the answer choices are always as follows:

(A)  Quantity A is greater.
(B)  Quantity B is greater.
(C)  The two quantities are equal.
(D)  The relationship cannot be determined from the information given.

For questions followed by a numeric entry box [＿＿], you are to enter your own answer in the box. For questions followed

by a fraction-style numeric entry box ▭, you are to enter your answer in the form of a fraction. You are not required to

reduce fractions. For example, if the answer is $\frac{1}{4}$, you may enter $\frac{25}{100}$ or any equivalent fraction.

All numbers used are real numbers. All figures are assumed to lie in a plane unless otherwise indicated. Geometric figures are not necessarily drawn to scale. You should assume, however, that lines that appear to be straight are actually straight, points on a line are in the order shown, and all geometric objects are in the relative positions shown. Coordinate systems, such as $xy$-planes and number lines, as well as graphical data presentations, such as bar charts, circle graphs, and line graphs, *are* drawn to scale. A symbol that appears more than once in a question has the same meaning throughout the question.

$$7y - 3 \leq 4y + 9$$

|  | **Quantity A** | **Quantity B** |
|---|---|---|
| 1. | $y$ | 4 |

$$3|x - 4| = 16$$

|  | **Quantity A** | **Quantity B** |
|---|---|---|
| 2. | $x$ | $\dfrac{28}{3}$ |

3.  If $b \neq 0$ and $\dfrac{a}{b} > 0$, which of the following inequalities must be true?

Indicate <u>all</u> such inequalities.

☐  $a > b$

☐  $b > 0$

☐  $ab > 0$

4.  If $6 < 2x - 4 < 12$, which of the following could be the value of $x$?

    (A)  4
    (B)  5
    (C)  7
    (D)  8
    (E)  9

5.  If $y < 0$ and $4x > y$, which of the following could be equal to $\dfrac{x}{y}$?

    (A)  0
    (B)  $\dfrac{1}{4}$
    (C)  $\dfrac{1}{2}$
    (D)  1
    (E)  4

$$3(x - 7) \geq 9$$
$$0.25y - 3 \leq 1$$

| Quantity A | Quantity B |
|:----------:|:----------:|
| $x$ | $y$ |

6.

7.  If $|1 - x| = 6$ and $|2y - 6| = 10$, which of the following could be the value of $xy$?

    Indicate all such values.

    ☐  −40
    ☐  −14
    ☐  −10
    ☐  56

8.  If $2(x - 1)^3 + 3 \leq 19$, which of the following must be true?

    (A)  $x \geq 3$
    (B)  $x \leq 3$
    (C)  $x \geq -3$
    (D)  $x \leq -3$
    (E)  $x < -3$ or $x > 3$

**MANHATTAN PREP**

9.  If $3p < 51$ and $5p > 75$, what is the value of the integer $p$?

    (A)  15
    (B)  16
    (C)  24
    (D)  25
    (E)  26

10. A bicycle wheel has spokes that go from a center point in the hub to equally spaced points on the rim of the wheel. If there are fewer than six spokes, what is the smallest possible angle between any two spokes?

    (A)  18°
    (B)  30°
    (C)  40°
    (D)  60°
    (E)  72°

$$|-x| \geq 6$$
$$xy^2 < 0 \text{ and } y \text{ is an integer.}$$

|     | **Quantity A** | **Quantity B** |
|-----|----------------|----------------|
| 11. | $x$            | $-4$           |

12. If $\dfrac{|x+4|}{2} > 5$ and $x < 0$, which of the following could be the value of $x$?

    Indicate <u>all</u> such values.

    ☐  −6
    ☐  −14
    ☐  −18

$$|x^3| < 64$$

|     | **Quantity A** | **Quantity B** |
|-----|----------------|----------------|
| 13. | $-x$           | $-|x|$         |

14. If $|3x + 7| \geq 2x + 12$, then which of the following is true?

   (A) $x \leq \dfrac{-19}{5}$

   (B) $x \geq \dfrac{-19}{5}$

   (C) $x \geq 5$

   (D) $x \leq \dfrac{-19}{5}$ or $x \geq 5$

   (E) $\dfrac{-19}{5} \leq x \leq 5$

$$|3 + 3x| < -2x$$

| Quantity A | Quantity B |
|:---:|:---:|
| $|x|$ | 4 |

15.

16. If $|y| \leq -4x$ and $|3x - 4| = 2x + 6$, what is the value of $x$?

   (A) $-3$

   (B) $-\dfrac{1}{3}$

   (C) $-\dfrac{2}{5}$

   (D) $\dfrac{1}{3}$

   (E) $10$

$x$ is an integer such that $-x|x| \geq 4$.

| Quantity A | Quantity B |
|:---:|:---:|
| $x$ | 2 |

17.

$$|x| < 1 \text{ and } y > 0$$

| Quantity A | Quantity B |
|:---:|:---:|
| $|x| + y$ | $xy$ |

18.

$$|x| > |y| \text{ and } x + y > 0$$

| Quantity A | Quantity B |
|:---:|:---:|
| $y$ | $x$ |

19.

**MANHATTAN**
PREP

x and y are integers such that $|x|(y) + 9 < 0$ and $|y| \leq 1$.

|  | **Quantity A** | **Quantity B** |
|---|---|---|
| 20. | $x$ | $-9$ |

$$p + |k| > |p| + k$$

|  | **Quantity A** | **Quantity B** |
|---|---|---|
| 21. | $p$ | $k$ |

$$|x| + |y| > |x + z|$$

|  | **Quantity A** | **Quantity B** |
|---|---|---|
| 22. | $y$ | $z$ |

$$b \neq 0$$

$$\frac{|a|}{b} > 1$$

$$a + b < 0$$

|  | **Quantity A** | **Quantity B** |
|---|---|---|
| 23. | $a$ | $0$ |

24. If $f^2 g < 0$, which of the following must be true?

(A) $f < 0$
(B) $g < 0$
(C) $fg < 0$
(D) $fg > 0$
(E) $f^2 < 0$

25. $\sqrt{96} < x\sqrt{6}$ and $\dfrac{x}{\sqrt{6}} < \sqrt{6}$ . If x is an integer, which of the following is the value of x?

(A) 2
(B) 3
(C) 4
(D) 5
(E) 6

$$|x|y > x|y|$$

|  | **Quantity A** | **Quantity B** |
|---|---|---|
| 26. | $(x+y)^2$ | $(x-y)^2$ |

27. Which of the following could be the graph of all values of $x$ that satisfy the inequality $4 - 11x \geq \dfrac{-2x+3}{2}$ ?

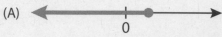

(A) ────────●────────→ 0

(B) ────────●────────→ 0

(C) ────●────────────→ 0

(D) ──●───●──────────→ 0

(E) ──●────●─────────→ 0

$$-1 < a < 0 < |a| < b < 1$$

|  | **Quantity A** | **Quantity B** |
|---|---|---|
| 28. | $\left(\dfrac{a^2\sqrt{b}}{\sqrt{a}}\right)^2$ | $\dfrac{ab^5}{\left(\sqrt{b}\right)^4}$ |

$$x > |y| > z$$

|  | **Quantity A** | **Quantity B** |
|---|---|---|
| 29. | $x+y$ | $|y|+z$ |

30. The integers $k$, $l$, and $m$ are consecutive even integers between 23 and 33. Which of the following could be the average (arithmetic mean) of $k$, $l$, and $m$?

(A) 24
(B) 25
(C) 25.5
(D) 28
(E) 32

**MANHATTAN**
PREP

31.

The number line above represents which of the following inequalities?

(A) $x < 1$

(B) $-6 < 2x < 2$

(C) $-9 < 3x < 6$

(D) $1 < 2x < 3$

(E) $x > -3$

32. For a jambalaya cook-off, there will be $x$ judges sitting in a single row of $x$ chairs. If $x$ is greater than 3 but no more than 6, which of the following could be the number of possible seating arrangements for the judges?

Indicate <u>two</u> such numbers.

- ☐ 6
- ☐ 25
- ☐ 120
- ☐ 500
- ☐ 720

33. Which of the following inequalities is equivalent to $-\dfrac{a}{3b} < c$ for all non-zero values of $a$, $b$, and $c$?

Indicate <u>all</u> such inequalities.

- ☐ $\dfrac{a}{b} > -3c$

- ☐ $-\dfrac{a}{3} < bc$

- ☐ $a > -3bc$

$$|x + y| = 10$$
$$x \geq 0$$
$$z < y - x$$

| **Quantity A** | **Quantity B** |
|:---:|:---:|
| $z$ | 10 |

34.

$$0 < a < \frac{b}{2} < 9$$

|  | **Quantity A** | **Quantity B** |
|---|---|---|
| 35. | $9 - a$ | $\dfrac{b}{2} - a$ |

For all values of the integer $p$ such that $1.9 < |p| < 5.3$, the function $f(p) = p^2$.

|  | **Quantity A** | **Quantity B** |
|---|---|---|
| 36. | $f(p)$ for the greatest value of $p$ | $f(p)$ for the least value of $p$ |

37. If $\left|\dfrac{a}{b}\right|$ and $\left|\dfrac{x}{y}\right|$ are reciprocals and $\dfrac{a}{b}\left(\dfrac{x}{y}\right) < 0$, which of the following must be true?

     (A) $ab < 0$

     (B) $\dfrac{a}{b}\left(\dfrac{x}{y}\right) < -1$

     (C) $\dfrac{a}{b} < 1$

     (D) $\dfrac{a}{b} = -\dfrac{y}{x}$

     (E) $\dfrac{y}{x} > \dfrac{a}{b}$

38. If $mn < 0$ and $\dfrac{k}{m} + \dfrac{l}{n} < mn$, which of the following must be true?

     (A) $km + ln < (mn)^2$

     (B) $kn + lm < 1$

     (C) $kn + lm > (mn)^2$

     (D) $k + l > mn$

     (E) $km > -ln$

39. If the reciprocal of the negative integer $x$ is greater than the sum of $y$ and $z$, then which of the following must be true?

     (A) $x > y + z$

     (B) $y$ and $z$ are positive.

     (C) $1 > x(y + z)$

     (D) $1 < xy + xz$

     (E) $\dfrac{1}{x} > z - y$

**MANHATTAN**
PREP

40.  If $u$ and $-3v$ are greater than 0, and $\sqrt{u} < \sqrt{-3v}$, which of the following cannot be true?

(A)  $\dfrac{u}{3} < -v$

(B)  $\dfrac{u}{v} > -3$

(C)  $\sqrt{\dfrac{u}{-v}} < \sqrt{3}$

(D)  $u + 3v > 0$

(E)  $u < -3v$

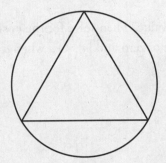

41.  In the figure above, an equilateral triangle is inscribed in a circle. If the arc bounded by adjacent corners of the triangle is between $4\pi$ and $6\pi$ long, which of the following could be the diameter of the circle?

(A)  6.5

(B)  9

(C)  11.9

(D)  15

(E)  23.5

# Inequalities and Absolute Values Answers

1. **(D).** Solve the inequality algebraically:

$$7y - 3 \le 4y + 9$$
$$3y - 3 \le 9$$
$$3y \le 12$$
$$y \le 4$$

Because $y$ could be less than or equal to 4, the relationship cannot be determined from the information given.

2. **(D).** Solve the inequality by first dividing both sides by 3 to isolate the absolute value. Then solve for the positive and negative possibilities of $(x - 4)$, using the identity that $|a| = a$ when $a$ is positive or zero and $|a| = -a$ when $a$ is negative:

$$3|x - 4| = 16$$

$$|x - 4| = \frac{16}{3}$$

$$+ (x - 4) = \frac{16}{3} \qquad \text{or} \qquad - (x - 4) = \frac{16}{3}$$

$$(x - 4) = \frac{16}{3} \qquad\qquad (x - 4) = -\frac{16}{3}$$

$$x - 4 = \frac{16}{3} \qquad\qquad x = -\frac{16}{3} + 4$$

$$x = \frac{16}{3} + 4 \qquad\qquad x = -\frac{16}{3} + \frac{12}{3}$$

$$x = \frac{16}{3} + \frac{12}{3} \qquad\qquad x = -\frac{4}{3}$$

$$x = \frac{28}{3}$$

Thus, $x$ could be $\frac{28}{3}$ or $-\frac{4}{3}$, making the two quantities equal or Quantity B greater, respectively. The relationship cannot be determined from the information given.

3. **$ab > 0$ only.** If $\frac{a}{b} > 0$, then both $a$ and $b$ must have the same sign. That is, $a$ and $b$ are either both positive or both negative. The 1st inequality could be true, but is not necessarily true. The relative values of $a$ and $b$ are not indicated by the inequality in the question stem. The 2nd inequality could be true, but is not necessarily true. If $a$ were negative, $b$ could be negative. The 3rd inequality must be true, as it indicates that $a$ and $b$ have the same sign.

4. **(C).** When manipulating a "three-sided" inequality, perform the same operations on all "sides." Therefore, the first step to simplify this inequality would be to add 4 to all three sides to get: $10 < 2x < 16$. Next, divide all three sides by 2. The result is $5 < x < 8$. The only answer choice that fits within the parameters of this inequality is 7.

**MANHATTAN**
PREP

5. **(A).** If $y$ is negative, then dividing both sides of the second inequality by $y$ yields $\dfrac{4x}{y} < 1$. Remember to switch the direction of the inequality sign when multiplying or dividing by a negative (whether that negative is in number or variable form). Next, dividing both sides by 4 changes the inequality to $\dfrac{x}{y} < \dfrac{1}{4}$. The only answer choice less than $\dfrac{1}{4}$ is 0.

6. **(D).** Solve each inequality algebraically:

$$3(x - 7) \geq 9$$
$$x - 7 \geq 3$$
$$x \geq 10$$

$$0.25y - 3 \leq 1$$
$$0.25y \leq 4$$
$$y \leq 16$$

Since the ranges for $x$ and $y$ overlap, either quantity could be greater. For instance, $x$ could be 11 and $y$ could be 15 ($y$ is greater), or $x$ could be 1,000 and $y$ could be −5 ($x$ is greater). The relationship cannot be determined from the information given.

7. **−40, −14, and 56 only.** Solve each absolute value, using the identity that $|a| = a$ when $a$ is positive or zero and $|a| = -a$ when $a$ is negative:

$$|1 - x| = 6$$

| $+ (1 - x) = 6$ | or | $- (1 - x) = 6$ |
|---|---|---|
| $(1 - x) = 6$ | | $(1 - x) = -6$ |
| $-x = 5$ | | $-x = -7$ |
| $x = -5$ | | $x = 7$ |

$$x = -5 \text{ or } 7$$

$$|2y - 6| = 10$$

| $+ (2y - 6) = 10$ | or | $- (2y - 6) = 10$ |
|---|---|---|
| $(2y - 6) = 10$ | | $(2y - 6) = -10$ |
| $2y = 16$ | | $2y = -4$ |
| $y = 8$ | | $y = -2$ |

$$y = 8 \text{ or } -2$$

Since $x = -5$ or 7 and $y = 8$ or $-2$, calculate all four possible combinations for $xy$:

$(-5)(8) = -40$
$(-5)(-2) = 10$
$(7)(8) = 56$
$(7)(-2) = -14$

Select $-40$, $-14$, and 56. (Do *not* pick $-10$, as $xy$ could be 10, but not $-10$.)

8. **(B).**   $2(x - 1)^3 + 3 \leq 19$
$2(x - 1)^3 \leq 16$
$(x - 1)^3 \leq 8$

Taking the cube root of an inequality is permissible here, because cubing a number, unlike squaring it, does not change its sign.

$x - 1 \leq 2$
$x \leq 3$

9. **(B).** Dividing the first inequality by 3 results in $p < 17$. Dividing the second inequality by 5 results in $p > 15$. Therefore, $15 < p < 17$. Because $p$ is an integer, it must be 16.

10. **(E).** In this scenario, if there are $n$ spokes, there are $n$ angles between them. Thus, the measure of the angle between spokes is $\dfrac{360°}{n}$. Since $n < 6$, rewrite this expression as $\dfrac{360°}{(\text{less than } 6)}$. Dividing by a "less than" produces a "greater than" result. Therefore, $\dfrac{360°}{(\text{less than } 6)} = $ greater than 60°. The only answer that is greater than 60° is (E). To verify, note that $n$ can be at most 5, because $n$ must be an integer. Because there are 360° in a circle, a wheel with 5 spokes would have $\dfrac{360°}{5} = 72°$ between adjacent spokes.

11. **(B).** First, solve the inequality for $x$, remembering the two cases that must be considered when dealing with absolute value: $|a| = a$ when $a$ is positive or zero and $|a| = -a$ when $a$ is negative:

$|-x| \geq 6$

$\begin{array}{ccc} +(-x) \geq 6 & \text{or} & -(-x) \geq 6 \\ -x \geq 6 & & x \geq 6 \\ x \leq -6 & & \end{array}$

$x \leq -6$ or $x \geq 6$

Because $xy^2 < 0$, neither $x$ nor $y$ equals zero. A squared term cannot be negative, so $y^2$ must be positive. For $xy^2$ to be negative, $x$ must be negative. This rules out the $x \geq 6$ range of solutions for $x$. Thus, $x \leq -6$ is the only range of valid solutions. Since all values less than or equal to $-6$ are less than $-4$, Quantity B is greater.

**MANHATTAN**
PREP

12. **−18 only.** Solve the absolute value inequality by first isolating the absolute value:

$$\frac{|x+4|}{2} > 5$$

$$|x+4| > 10$$

To solve the absolute value, use the identity that $|a| = a$ when $a$ is positive or zero and $|a| = -a$ when $a$ is negative. Here if $(x+4)$ is positive or zero that leaves:

$$x + 4 > 10$$
$$x > 6$$

This, however, is not a valid solution range, as the other inequality indicates that $x$ is negative.

Solve for the negative case, that is, assuming that $(x + 4)$ is negative:

$$-(x + 4) > 10$$
$$(x + 4) < -10$$
$$x < -14$$

Note that this fits the other inequality, which states that $x < 0$.

If $x < -14$, only $-18$ is a valid answer.

13. **(D).** First, solve the absolute value inequality, using the identity that $|a| = a$ when $a$ is positive or zero and $|a| = -a$ when $a$ is negative:

$$|x^3| < 64$$

$$+(x^3) < 64 \qquad \text{or} \qquad -(x^3) < 64$$
$$x < 4 \qquad\qquad\qquad x^3 > -64 \text{ (Flip the inequality sign when multiplying by } -1.)$$
$$x > -4$$

$$-4 < x < 4$$

$x$ could be positive, negative, or zero. If $x$ is positive or zero, the two quantities are equal. If $x$ is negative, Quantity A is greater. The relationship cannot be determined from the information given.

14. **(D).** Solve $|3x + 7| \geq 2x + 12$, using the identity that $|a| = a$ when $a$ is positive or zero and $|a| = -a$ when $a$ is negative:

$$+(3x + 7) \geq 2x + 12 \qquad \text{or} \qquad -(3x + 7) \geq 2x + 12$$

$$x + 7 \geq 12$$
$$x \geq 5$$

$$-3x - 7 \geq 2x + 12$$
$$-7 \geq 5x + 12$$
$$-19 \geq 5x$$
$$\frac{-19}{5} \geq x$$

$$x \leq \frac{-19}{5} \text{ or } x \geq 5$$

15. **(B).** Solve the absolute value inequality, using the identity that $|a| = a$ when $a$ is positive or zero and $|a| = -a$ when $a$ is negative:

$$|3 + 3x| < -2x$$

$$+(3 + 3x) < -2x \quad \text{or} \quad -(3 + 3x) < -2x$$
$$3 + 5x < 0 \quad\quad\quad\quad -3 - 3x < -2x$$
$$5x < -3 \quad\quad\quad\quad\quad -3 < x$$
$$x < -\frac{3}{5}$$

$$-3 < x < -\frac{3}{5}$$

Since $x$ is between $-3$ and $-\frac{3}{5}$, its absolute value is between $\frac{3}{5}$ and 3. Quantity B is greater.

16. **(C).** The inequality is not strictly solvable, as it has two unknowns. However, any absolute value cannot be negative. Putting $0 \leq |y|$ and $|y| \leq -4x$ together, $0 \leq -4x$. Dividing both sides by $-4$ and flipping the inequality sign, this implies that $0 \geq x$.

Now solve the absolute value equation, using the identity that $|a| = a$ when a is positive or zero and $|a| = -a$ when a is negative:

$$|3x - 4| = 2x + 6$$

$$+(3x - 4) = 2x + 6 \quad \text{or} \quad -(3x - 4) = 2x + 6$$
$$3x - 4 = 2x + 6 \quad\quad\quad\quad -3x + 4 = 2x + 6$$
$$x - 4 = 6 \quad\quad\quad\quad\quad\quad 4 = 5x + 6$$
$$x = 10 \quad\quad\quad\quad\quad\quad\quad -2 = 5x$$

$$x = 10 \text{ or } -\frac{2}{5}$$

If $x = 10$ or $-\frac{2}{5}$, but $0 \geq x$, then $x$ can only be $-\frac{2}{5}$.

17. **(B).** If $-x|x| \geq 4$, $-x|x|$ is positive. Because $|x|$ is positive by definition, $-x|x|$ is positive only when $-x$ is also positive. This occurs when $x$ is negative. For example, $x = -2$ is one solution allowed by the inequality: $-x|x| = -(-2) \times |-2| = 2 \times 2 = 4$.

**MANHATTAN**
PREP

So, Quantity A can be any integer less than or equal to −2, all of which are less than 2. Quantity B is greater.

18. **(A).** The inequality $|x| < 1$ allows $x$ to be either a positive or negative fraction (or zero). Interpreting the absolute value sign, it is equivalent to $-1 < x < 1$. As indicated, $y$ is positive.

When $x$ is a negative fraction:

> Quantity A: $|x| + y$ = positive fraction + positive = positive
> Quantity B: $xy$ = negative fraction × positive = negative
> Quantity A is greater in these cases.

When $x$ is zero:

> Quantity A: $|x| + y$ = 0 + positive = positive
> Quantity B: $xy$ = 0 × positive = 0
> Quantity A is greater in this case.

When $x$ is a positive fraction:

> Quantity A: $|x| + y$ = positive fraction + $y$ = greater than $y$
> Quantity B: $xy$ = positive fraction × $y$ = less than $y$
> Quantity A is greater in these cases.

In all cases, Quantity A is greater.

19. **(B).** In general, there are four cases for the signs of $x$ and $y$, some of which can be ruled out by the constraints of this question:

| $x$ | $y$ | $x + y > 0$ |
|-----|-----|-------------|
| pos | pos | True |
| pos | neg | True when $|x| > |y|$ |
| neg | pos | False when $|x| > |y|$ |
| neg | neg | False |

Only the first two cases need to be considered for this question, since $x + y$ is not greater than zero for the third and fourth cases.

If $x$ and $y$ are both positive, $|x| > |y|$ just means that $x > y$.

If $x$ is positive and $y$ is negative, $x > y$ simply because positive > negative.

In both cases, $x > y$. Quantity B is greater.

20. **(D).** If $y$ is an integer and $|y| \leq 1$, then $y = -1, 0$, or $1$. The other inequality can be simplified from $|x|(y) + 9 < 0$ to $|x|(y) < -9$. In other words, $|x|(y)$ is negative. Because $|x|$ cannot be negative by definition, $y$ must be negative, so only $y = -1$ is possible.

If $y = -1$, then $|x|(y) = |x|(-1) = -|x| < -9$. So, $-|x| = -10, -11, -12, -13$, etc.

Thus, $x = \pm 10, \pm 11, \pm 12, \pm 13$, etc. Some of these $x$ values are greater than $-9$ and some are less than $-9$. Therefore, the relationship cannot be determined.

21. **(A).** In general, there are four cases for the signs of $p$ and $k$, some of which can be ruled out by the constraints of this question:

| $p$ | $k$ | $p + |k| > |p| + k$ |
|-----|-----|---------------------|
| pos | pos | Not true in this case: For positive numbers, absolute value "does nothing," so both sides are equal to $p + k$. |
| pos | neg | True for this case: $p +$ (a positive absolute value) is greater than $p +$ (a negative value). |
| neg | pos | Not true in this case: $k +$ (a negative value) is less than $k +$ (a positive absolute value). |
| neg | neg | Possible in this case: It depends on relative values. Both sides are a positive plus a negative. |

Additionally, check whether $p$ or $k$ could be zero.

If $p = 0$, $p + |k| > |p| + k$ is equivalent to $|k| > k$. This is true when $k$ is negative.

If $k = 0$, $p + |k| > |p| + k$ is equivalent to $p > |p|$. This is not true for any $p$ value.

So, there are three possible cases for $p$ and $k$ values. For the second one, use the identity that $|a| = -a$ when $a$ is negative:

| $p$ | $k$ | Interpret: |
|-----|-----|------------|
| pos | neg | $p = \text{pos} > \text{neg} = k$ <br> $p > k$ |
| neg | neg | $p + |k| > |p| + k$ <br> $p + -(k) > -(p) + k$ <br> $p - k > -p + k$ <br> $2p - k > k$ <br> $2p > 2k$ <br> $p > k$ |
| 0 | neg | $p = 0 > \text{neg} = k$ <br> $p > k$ |

In all the cases that are valid according to the constraint inequality, $p$ is greater than $k$. Quantity A is greater.

**MANHATTAN PREP**

22. **(D).** Given only one inequality with three unknowns, solving will not be possible. Instead, test numbers with the goal of proving (D).

For example, $x = 2$, $y = 5$, and $z = 3$.
Check that $|x| + |y| > |x + z|$: $|2| + |5| > |2 + 3|$ is $7 > 5$, which is true.
In this case, $y > z$ and Quantity A is greater.

Try to find another example such that $y < z$. Always consider negatives in inequalities and absolute value questions.
Consider another example: $x = 2$, $y = -5$ and $z = 3$.
Check that $|x| + |y| > |x + z|$: $|2| + |-5| > |2 + 3|$ is $7 > 5$, which is true.
In this case, $z > y$ and Quantity B is greater.

Either statement could be greater. The relationship cannot be determined from the information given.

23. **(B).** If $\dfrac{|a|}{b}$ is greater than 1, then it is positive. Because $|a|$ is non-negative by definition, $b$ would have to be positive. Thus, when multiplying both sides of the inequality by $b$, you do not have to flip the sign of the inequality:

$$\frac{|a|}{b} > 1$$

$$|a| > b$$

To summarize, $b > 0$ and $|a| > b$. Putting this together, $|a| > b > 0$.

In order for $a + b$ to be negative, $a$ must be more negative than $b$ is positive. For example, $a = -4$ and $b = 2$ agree with all the constraints so far. Note that $a$ cannot be zero (because $\dfrac{|a|}{b} = 0$ in this case, not $> 1$) and $a$ cannot be positive (because $a + b > 0$ in this case, not $< 0$).

Therefore, $a < 0$. Quantity B is greater.

24. **(B).** Neither $f$ nor $g$ can be zero, or $f^2 g$ would be zero. The square of either a positive or negative base is always positive, so $f^2$ is positive. In order for $f^2 g < 0$ to be true, $g$ must be negative. Therefore, the correct answer is (B). Answer choices (A), (C), and (D) are not correct because $f$ could be either positive or negative. Answer choice (E) directly contradicts the truth that $f^2$ is positive.

25. **(D).** Solve the first inequality:

$$\sqrt{96} < x\sqrt{6}$$

$$\frac{\sqrt{96}}{\sqrt{6}} < x$$

$$\sqrt{16} < x$$

$$4 < x$$

Solve the second inequality:

$$\frac{x}{\sqrt{6}} < \sqrt{6}$$

$$x < \sqrt{6}\sqrt{6}$$

$$x < \sqrt{36}$$

$$x < 6$$

Combining the inequalities gives $4 < x < 6$, and since $x$ is an integer, $x$ must be 5.

26. **(B).** In general, there are four cases for the signs of $x$ and $y$, some of which can be ruled out by the constraint in the question stem. Use the identity that $|a| = a$ when $a$ is positive or zero and $|a| = -a$ when $a$ is negative:

| $x$ | $y$ | $|x|y > x|y|$ is equivalent to: | True or False? |
|-----|-----|------|------|
| pos | pos | $xy > xy$ | False: $xy = xy$ |
| pos | neg | $xy > x(-y)$ | False: $xy$ is negative and $-xy$ is positive. |
| neg | pos | $(-x)y > xy$ | True: $xy$ is negative and $-xy$ is positive. |
| neg | neg | $(-x)y > x(-y)$ | False: $-xy = -xy$ |

Note that if either $x$ or $y$ equals 0, that case would also fail the constraint.

The only valid case is when $x$ is negative and $y$ is positive:

Quantity A: $(x + y)^2 = x^2 + 2xy + y^2$
Quantity B: $(x - y)^2 = x^2 - 2xy + y^2$

Ignore (or subtract) $x^2 + y^2$ as it is common to both quantities. Thus:

Quantity A: $2xy = 2(\text{negative})(\text{positive}) = \text{negative}$
Quantity B: $-2xy = -2(\text{negative})(\text{positive}) = \text{positive}$

Quantity B is greater.

**MANHATTAN**
PREP

27. **(A).** First, solve $4 - 11x \geq \dfrac{-2x+3}{2}$ for $x$:

$$4 - 11x \geq \frac{-2x+3}{2}$$

$$8 - 22x \geq -2x + 3$$

$$5 - 22 \geq -2x$$

$$5 \geq 20x$$

$$\frac{5}{20} \geq x$$

$$\frac{1}{4} \geq x$$

Thus, the correct choice should show the gray line beginning to the right of zero (in the positive zone), and continuing indefinitely into the negative zone. Even without actual values (other than zero) marked on the graphs, only (A) meets these criteria.

28. **(A).** From $-1 < a < 0 < |a| < b < 1$, the following can be determined:

$a$ is a negative fraction,
$b$ is a positive fraction, and
$b$ is more positive than $a$ is negative (i.e., $|b| > |a|$, or $b$ is farther from 0 on the number line than $a$ is).

Using exponent rules, simplify the quantities:

Quantity A: $\left( \dfrac{a^2 \sqrt{b}}{\sqrt{a}} \right)^2 = \dfrac{\left(a^2\right)^2 \left(\sqrt{b}\right)^2}{\left(\sqrt{a}^2\right)} = \dfrac{a^4 b}{a} = a^3 b$

Quantity B: $\dfrac{ab^5}{\left(\sqrt{b}\right)^4} = \dfrac{ab^5}{\left(b^{1/2}\right)^4} = \dfrac{ab^5}{b^{\frac{1}{2} \times 4}} = \dfrac{ab^5}{b^2} = ab^3$

Dividing both quantities by $b$ would be acceptable, as $b$ is positive and doing so won't flip the relative sizes of the quantities. It would be nice to cancel $a$'s, too, but it is problematic that $a$ is negative. Dividing both quantities by $a^2$ would be okay, though, as $a^2$ is positive.

Divide both quantities by $a^2 b$:

Quantity A: $\dfrac{a^3 b}{a^2 b} = a$

Quantity B: $\dfrac{ab^3}{a^2 b} = \dfrac{b^2}{a}$

Just to make the quantities more similar in form, divide again by $b$, which is positive:

Quantity A: $\dfrac{a}{b}$

Quantity B: $\dfrac{b}{a}$

Both quantities are negative, as $a$ and $b$ have opposite signs. Remember that $b$ is more positive than $a$ is negative. (i.e., $|b| > |a|$, or $b$ is farther from 0 on the number line than $a$ is.) Thus, each fraction can be compared to $-1$:

Quantity A: $\dfrac{a}{b}$ is less negative than $-1$. That is, $-1 < \dfrac{a}{b}$.

Quantity B: $\dfrac{b}{a}$ is more negative than $-1$. That is, $\dfrac{b}{a} < -1$.

Therefore, Quantity A is greater.

29. **(D).** Given only a compound inequality with three unknowns, solving will not be possible. Instead, test numbers with the goal of proving (D). Always consider negatives in inequalities and absolute value questions.

For example, $x = 10$, $y = -9$, and $z = 8$.
Check that $x > |y| > z$: $10 > |-9| > 8$, which is true.
In this case, $x + y = 10 + (-9) = 1$ and $|y| + z = 9 + 8 = 17$. Quantity B is greater.

Try to find another example such that Quantity A is greater.
For example, $x = 2$, $y = 1$, and $z = -3$.
Check that $x > |y| > z$: $2 > |1| > -3$, which is true.
In this case, $x + y = 2 + 1 = 3$ and $|y| + z = 1 + (-3) = -2$. Quantity A is greater.

The relationship cannot be determined from the information given.

30. **(D).** The values for $k$, $l$, and $m$, respectively, could be any of the following three sets:

     Set 1: 24, 26, and 28
     Set 2: 26, 28, and 30
     Set 3: 28, 30, and 32

For evenly spaced sets with an odd number of terms, the average is the middle value. Therefore, the average of $k$, $l$, and $m$ could be 26, 28, or 30. Only answer choice (D) matches one of these possibilities.

31. **(B).** The number line indicates a range between, but not including, $-3$ and 1. However, $-3 < x < 1$ is not a given option. However, answer choice (B) gives the inequality $-6 < 2x < 2$. Dividing all three sides of this inequality by 2 yields $-3 < x < 1$.

32. **120 and 720 only.** If $x$ is "greater than 3 but no more than 6," then $x$ is 4, 5, or 6. If there are 4 judges sitting in 4 seats, they can be arranged $4! = 4 \times 3 \times 2 \times 1 = 24$ ways. If there are 5 judges sitting in 5 seats, they can be arranged

$5! = 5 \times 4 \times 3 \times 2 \times 1 = 120$ ways. If there are 6 judges sitting in 6 seats, they can be arranged $6! = 6 \times 5 \times 4 \times 3 \times 2 \times 1 = 720$ ways. Thus, 24, 120, and 720 are all possible answers. Only 120 and 720 appear in the choices.

33. $\dfrac{a}{b} > -3c$ **only.** For this problem, use the rule that multiplying or dividing an inequality by a negative flips the inequality sign. Thus, multiplying or dividing an inequality by a variable should *not* be done unless you know *whether* to flip the inequality sign (i.e., whether the variable represents a positive or a negative number).

1st inequality: TRUE. Multiply both sides of the original inequality by $-3$ and flip the inequality sign.

2nd inequality: Maybe. Multiply both sides of the original inequality by $b$ to get the 2nd inequality, but only if $b$ is positive. If $b$ is negative, the direction of the inequality sign would have to be changed.

3rd inequality: Maybe. Multiplying both sides of the original inequality by $-3b$ could lead to the 3rd inequality, but because the inequality sign flipped, this is only true if $-3b$ is negative (i.e., if $b$ is positive).

34. **(B).** From $z < y - x$, the value of $z$ depends on $x$ and $y$. So, solve for $x$ and $y$ as much as possible. There are two cases for the absolute value equation: $|x + y| = 10$ means that $\pm(x + y) = 10$ or that $(x + y) = \pm 10$. Consider these two cases separately.

The positive case:

$x + y = 10$, so $y = 10 - x$.
Substitute into $z < y - x$, getting $z < (10 - x) - x$, or $z < 10 - 2x$.
Because $x$ is at least zero, $10 - 2x \le 10$.
Putting the inequalities together, $z < 10 - 2x \le 10$.
Thus, $z < 10$.

The negative case:

$x + y = -10$, so $y = -10 - x$.
Substitute into $z < y - x$, getting $z < (-10 - x) - x$, or $z < -10 - 2x$.
Because $x$ is at least zero, $-10 - 2x \le -10$.
Putting the inequalities together, $z < -10 - 2x \le -10$.
Thus, $z < -10$.

In both cases, 10 is greater than $z$. Quantity B is greater.

35. **(A).** The variable $a$ is common to both quantities, and adding it to both quantities to cancel will not change the relative values of the quantities:

Quantity A: $(9 - a) + a = 9$
Quantity B: $\left(\dfrac{b}{2} - a\right) + a = \dfrac{b}{2}$

According to the given constraint, $\dfrac{b}{2} < 9$, so Quantity A is greater.

36. **(C).** If $p$ is an integer such that $1.9 < |p| < 5.3$, $p$ could be 2, 3, 4, or 5, as well as −2, −3, −4, or −5. The greatest value of $p$ is 5, for which the value of $f(p)$ is equal to $5^2 = 25$. The least value of $p$ is −5, for which the value of $f(p)$ is equal to $(−5)^2 = 25$. Therefore, the two quantities are equal.

37. **(D).** If $\dfrac{a}{b}\left(\dfrac{x}{y}\right) < 0$, then the two fractions have opposite signs. Therefore, by the definition of reciprocals, $\dfrac{a}{b}$ must

be the negative inverse of $\dfrac{x}{y}$, no matter which one of the fractions is positive. In equation form, this means $\dfrac{a}{b} = -\dfrac{y}{x}$,

which is choice (D). The other choices are possible but not necessarily true.

38. **(C).** In order to get $m$ and $n$ out of the denominators of the fractions on the left side of the inequality, multiply both sides of the inequality by $mn$. The result is $kn + lm > (mn)^2$. The direction of the inequality sign changes because $mn$ is negative. This is an exact match with (C), which must be the correct answer.

39. **(D).** The inequality described in the question is $0 > \dfrac{1}{x} > y + z$. Multiplying both sides of this inequality by $x$, the

result is $0 < 1 < xy + xz$. Notice that the direction of the inequality sign must change because $x$ is negative. Therefore:

    (A) Maybe true: true only if $x$ equals −1.
    (B) Maybe true: either $y$ or $z$ or both can be negative.
    (C) False: the direction of the inequality sign is opposite the correct direction determined above.
    (D) TRUE: it is a proper rephrasing of the original inequality.
    (E) Maybe true: it is not a correct rephrasing of the original inequality.

40. **(D).** When the GRE writes a root sign, the question writers are indicating a non-negative root only. Therefore, both sides of this inequality are positive. Thus, you can square both sides without changing the direction of the inequality sign. So $u < −3v$. Now evaluate each answer choice:

    (A) Must be true: divide both sides of $u < −3v$ by 3.
    (B) Must be true: it is given that $−3v > 0$ and therefore, $v < 0$. Then, when dividing both sides of $u < −3v$ by $v$, you must flip the inequality sign and get $\dfrac{u}{v} > −3$.
    (C) Must be true: this is the result after dividing both sides of the original inequality by $\sqrt{-v}$.
    (D) CANNOT be true: adding $3v$ to both sides of $u < −3v$ results in $u + 3v < 0$, not $u + 3v > 0$.
    (E) Must be true: this is the result of squaring both sides of the original inequality.

**MANHATTAN**
PREP

41. **(D).** Since each of the three arcs corresponds to one of the 60° angles of the equilateral triangle, each arc represents $\frac{1}{3}$ of the circumference of the circle. The diagram below illustrates this for just one of the three angles in the triangle:

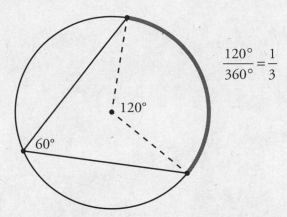

$$\frac{120°}{360°} = \frac{1}{3}$$

The same is true for each of the three angles:

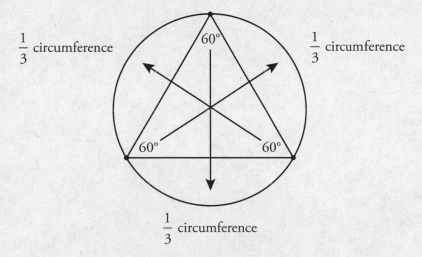

$\frac{1}{3}$ circumference

$\frac{1}{3}$ circumference

$\frac{1}{3}$ circumference

Since each of the three arcs is between $4\pi$ and $6\pi$, triple these values to determine that the circumference of the circle is between $12\pi$ and $18\pi$. Because circumference equals $\pi$ times the diameter, the diameter of this circle must be between 12 and 18. Only choice (D) is in this range.

# Chapter 10

*of*

5 lb. Book of GRE® Practice Problems

# Functions, Formulas, and Sequences

# In This Chapter...

Functions, Formulas, and Sequences

Functions, Formulas, and Sequences Answers

# Functions, Formulas, and Sequences

For questions in the Quantitative Comparison format ("Quantity A" and "Quantity B" given), the answer choices are always as follows:

(A)   Quantity A is greater.
(B)   Quantity B is greater.
(C)   The two quantities are equal.
(D)   The relationship cannot be determined from the information given.

For questions followed by a numeric entry box [      ], you are to enter your own answer in the box. For questions followed

by a fraction-style numeric entry box ⬚/⬚, you are to enter your answer in the form of a fraction. You are not required to

reduce fractions. For example, if the answer is $\frac{1}{4}$, you may enter $\frac{25}{100}$ or any equivalent fraction.

All numbers used are real numbers. All figures are assumed to lie in a plane unless otherwise indicated. Geometric figures are not necessarily drawn to scale. You should assume, however, that lines that appear to be straight are actually straight, points on a line are in the order shown, and all geometric objects are in the relative positions shown. Coordinate systems, such as $xy$-planes and number lines, as well as graphical data presentations, such as bar charts, circle graphs, and line graphs, *are* drawn to scale. A symbol that appears more than once in a question has the same meaning throughout the question.

1.   If $f(x) = x^2 + 1$, what is the value of $f(2) + f(-2)$?

    (A)   0
    (B)   1
    (C)   4
    (D)   5
    (E)   10

2.   If $h(x) = 2x^3 - 3$ and $h(m) = -19$, what is the value of $m$?

    (A)   −3
    (B)   −2
    (C)   2
    (D)   6,856
    (E)   6,862

3.   If $f(x) = x + 5$ and $f(2g) = 19$, what is the value of $f(3 - g)$?

4.   If $f(a, b) = a^2b^4$, and $f(m, n) = 5$, what is the value of $f(3m, 2n)$?

5.  If $f(x) = x^2 - 1$, what is the value of $f(y) + f(-1)$?

    (A) $y^2 - 1$
    (B) $y^2$
    (C) $y^2 + 1$
    (D) $y^2 - 2y$
    (E) $y^2 - 2y - 1$

6.  If $f(x) = \dfrac{x}{2} - 1$, what is the value of $f(f(10))$?

    ☐

7.  If $h(x) = 5x^2 + x$, then which of the following is equal to $h(a + b)$?

    (A) $5a^2 + 5b^2$
    (B) $5a^3 + 5b^3$
    (C) $5a^2 + 5b^2 + a + b$
    (D) $5a^3 + 10ab + 5b^3$
    (E) $5a^2 + 10ab + 5b^2 + a + b$

8.  If $\lceil x \rceil = 2x^2 + 2$, which of the following is equal to $\lceil 4 \rceil$?

    (A) $\lceil -1 \rceil$
    (B) $\lceil -2 \rceil$
    (C) $\lceil 2 \rceil$
    (D) $\lceil 17 \rceil$
    (E) $\lceil 34 \rceil$

9.  $\boxed{x}$ is defined as the least integer greater than $x$ for all odd values of $x$, and the greatest integer less than $x$ for all even values of $x$. What is the value of $\boxed{-2} - \boxed{5}$?

    (A) $-12$
    (B) $-9$
    (X) $-8$
    (Δ) $-7$
    (E) $3$

10. $g(x) = x^2 - 4$ and $g(c) = 12$. If $c < 0$, what is the value of $g(c - 2)$?

    ☐

11. If $h(x) = 2x - 1$ and $g(x) = x^2 - 3$, what is the value of $h(g(5))$?

12. If $h(x) = |3x| + 2$ and $g(x) = x^2 - 7$ and $g(m) = 29$, what is the value of $h(m)$?

13. If $*x$ is defined as the square of one-half of $x$, what is the value of $\dfrac{*5}{*3}$ ?

    Give your answer as a fraction.

14. If $\sim x = |14x|$, which of the following must be true?

    Indicate <u>all</u> such answers.

    ☐  $\sim 2 = \sim(-2)$
    ☐  $\sim 3 + \sim 4 = \sim 7$
    ☐  The minimum possible value of $\sim x$ is zero

15. If $\#x$ is defined for all $x > -2$ as the square root of the number that is 2 more than $x$, what is the value of $\#7 - \#(-1)$?

16. If $g(x) = \dfrac{x^2(4x + 9)}{(3x - 3)(x + 2)}$, for which of the following $x$ values is $g(x)$ undefined?

    Indicate <u>all</u> such values of $x$.

    ☐  $-\dfrac{9}{4}$
    ☐  $-2$
    ☐  $0$
    ☐  $1$
    ☐  $2$
    ☐  $\dfrac{9}{4}$

$$f(x) = 2x - 3$$
$$f(m) = -11$$

| **Quantity A** | **Quantity B** |
|---|---|
| 17.            $m$ | One-half of $f(m)$ |

18. The price of a phone call consists of a standard connection fee, which is constant, plus a per-minute charge. A 10-minute call costs $2.90 and a 16-minute call costs $4.40. How much does a 13-minute call cost?

    (A) $3.55
    (B) $3.57
    (C) $3.58
    (D) $3.65
    (E) $3.77

19. The first three terms in an arithmetic sequence are 30, 33, and 36. What is the 80th term?

    ☐

20. The sequence $S$ is defined by $S_n = 2(S_{n-1}) - 4$ for each integer $n \geq 2$. If $S_1 = 6$, what is the value of $S_5$?

    (A)  −20
    (B)   16
    (C)   20
    (D)   24
    (E)   36

21. The sequence $S$ is defined by $S_n = S_{n-1} + S_{n-2} - 3$ for each integer $n \geq 3$. If $S_1 = 5$ and $S_2 = 0$, what is the value of $S_6$?

    (A)  −6
    (B)  −5
    (X)  −3
    (Δ)  −1
    (E)   1

**MANHATTAN**
PREP

22. The sequence $S$ is defined by $S_n = S_{n-1} + S_{n-2} - 1$ for each integer $n \geq 3$. If $S_1 = 11$ and $S_3 = 10$, what is the value of $S_5$?

    (A)   0
    (B)   9
    (C)   10
    (D)   18
    (E)   19

23. The sequence $S$ is defined by $S_n = S_{n-1} + S_{n-2} + S_{n-3} - 5$ for each integer $n \geq 4$. If $S_1 = 4$, $S_2 = 0$, and $S_4 = -4$, what is the value of $S_6$?

    (A)   −2
    (B)   −12
    (X)   −16
    (Δ)   −20
    (E)   −24

24. The sequence $P$ is defined by $P_n = 10(P_{n-1}) - 2$ for each integer $n \geq 2$. If $P_1 = 2$, what is the value of $P_4$?

    ┌─────────┐
    │         │
    └─────────┘

25. The sequence $S$ is defined by $S_{n-1} = \dfrac{1}{4}(S_n)$ for each integer $n \geq 2$. If $S_1 = -4$, what is the value of $S_4$?

    (A)   −256
    (B)   −64
    (X)   $-\dfrac{1}{16}$
    (D)   $\dfrac{1}{16}$
    (E)   256

26. The sequence $A$ is defined by $A_n = A_{n-1} + 2$ for each integer $n \geq 2$, and $A_1 = 45$. What is the sum of the first 100 terms in sequence $A$?

    (A)     243
    (B)   14,400
    (C)   14,500
    (D)   24,300
    (E)   24,545

27. In a certain sequence, the term $a_n$ is defined by the formula $a_n = a_{n-1} + 10$ for each integer $n \geq 2$. What is the positive difference between $a_{10}$ and $a_{15}$?

   (A)   5
   (B)   10
   (C)   25
   (D)   50
   (E)   100

28. For a physical fitness test, scores are determined by the expression $2ps - 45m$, where $p$ and $s$ are the numbers of push-ups and sit-ups an athlete can do in one minute for each activity and $m$ is the number of minutes the athlete takes to run a mile. During the test, Abraham did 21 push-ups and 30 sit-ups and ran the mile in 10 minutes. Javed got the same score, but did 4 more push-ups and ran the mile in 12 minutes. How many sit-ups did Javed do in one minute?

   (A)  16
   (B)  19
   (C)  25
   (D)  27
   (E)  35

29. If $a\#b = a^2\sqrt{b} - a$, where $b \geq 0$, what is the value of $(-4)\#4$?

   (A)  −36
   (B)  −28
   (C)   12
   (D)   28
   (E)   36

30. The expression $x\$y$ is defined as $\dfrac{x^2}{y}$, where $y \neq 0$. What is the value of $9\$(6\$2)$?

   (A)  $\dfrac{1}{2}$

   (B)  $\dfrac{9}{4}$

   (C)  $\dfrac{9}{2}$

   (D)  18

   (E)  108

31. Amy deposited $1,000 into an account that earns 8% annual interest compounded every 6 months. Bob deposited $1,000 into an account that earns 8% annual interest compounded quarterly. If neither Amy nor Bob makes any additional deposits or withdrawals, in 6 months how much more money will Bob have in his account than will Amy have in hers?

    (A)  $40
    (B)  $8
    (C)  $4
    (D)  $0.40
    (E)  $0.04

32. The half-life of an isotope is the amount of time required for 50% of a sample of the isotope to undergo radioactive decay. The half-life of the carbon-14 isotope is 5,730 years. How many years must pass until a sample that starts out with 16,000 carbon-14 isotopes decays into a sample with only 500 carbon-14 isotopes?

    (A)       180 years
    (B)     1,146 years
    (C)     5,730 years
    (D)    28,650 years
    (E)   183,360 years

33. $f(x) = \dfrac{2-x}{5}$ and $g(x) = 3x - 2$. If $f(g(x)) = 1$, what is the value of $x$?

    (A)   $\dfrac{5}{3}$

    (B)   $-\dfrac{1}{3}$

    (C)   $\dfrac{2}{3}$

    (D)   $1$

    (E)   $\dfrac{5}{3}$

34. A certain investment doubled in value every 9 years. If Saidah had $25,125 in the investment when she was 27 years old, what was the value of the investment when she retired at 63 years old?

    (A)   $50,250
    (B)   $150,750
    (C)   $201,000
    (D)   $251,250
    (E)   $402,000

35. An archer's score is calculated by the formula $\dfrac{50b - 10a}{10 + s}$, where $b$ is the number of bull's-eyes hit, $a$ is the total number of arrows shot, and $s$ is the time in seconds it took the archer to shoot. By how many points would an archer who took 10 seconds to shoot 10 arrows and hit all bull's-eyes beat an archer who shot twice as many arrows and hit half as many bull's-eyes in 15 seconds?

   (A)  2
   (B)  7
   (C)  10
   (D)  18
   (E)  20

36. Each term of a certain sequence is calculated by adding a particular constant to the previous term. The 2nd term of this sequence is 27 and the 5th term is 84. What is the 1st term of this sequence?

   (A)  20
   (B)  15
   (C)  13
   (D)  12
   (E)  8

37. If $a\#b = \dfrac{1}{2a - 3b}$ and $a@b = 3a - 2b$, what is the value of $1@2 - 3\#4$?

   (A)  $-\dfrac{7}{6}$
   (B)  $-1$
   (X)  $-\dfrac{5}{6}$
   (D)  $\dfrac{2}{3}$
   (E)  $\dfrac{7}{6}$

38. In a certain sequence, the term $a_n$ is defined by the formula $a_n = a_{n-1} + 5$ for each integer $n \geq 2$. If $a_1 = 1$, what is the sum of the first 75 terms of this sequence?

   (A)  10,150
   (B)  11,375
   (C)  12,500
   (D)  13,950
   (E)  15,375

**MANHATTAN**
PREP

39. In a certain sequence, the term $a_n$ is defined by the formula $a_n = 2 \times a_{n-1}$ for each integer $n \geq 2$. If $a_1 = 1$, what is the positive difference between the sum of the first 10 terms of the sequence and the sum of the 11th and 12th terms of the same sequence?

    (A)      1
    (B)   1,024
    (C)   1,025
    (D)   2,048
    (E)   2,049

The operation @ is defined by the equation $a@b = (a - 1)(b - 2)$.
$$x@5 = 3@x$$

| Quantity A | Quantity B |
|---|---|
| $x$ | 1 |

40.

41. The wait time in minutes, $w$, for a table at a certain restaurant can be estimated by the formula $w = d^2 + kn$, where $d$ is the number of diners in the party, $k$ is a constant, and $n$ is the number of parties ahead in line at the beginning of the wait. If a party of 4 has an estimated wait time of 40 minutes when 6 other parties are ahead of it, how many minutes would the estimated wait time be for a party of 6 if there are 3 parties ahead of it?

    (A)  28
    (B)  33
    (C)  39
    (D)  42
    (E)  48

A certain sequence is defined by the formula $a_n = a_{n-1} - 7$.
$$a_7 = 7$$

| Quantity A | Quantity B |
|---|---|
| $a_1$ | −35 |

42.

43. Monthly rent for units in a certain apartment building is determined by the formula $k\left(\dfrac{5r^2 + 10t}{f + 5}\right)$ where $k$ is a constant, $r$ and $t$ are the number of bedrooms and bathrooms in the unit, respectively, and $f$ is the floor number of the unit. A 2-bedroom, 2-bathroom unit on the first floor is going for $800/month. How much is the monthly rent on a 3-bedroom unit with 1 bathroom on the 3rd floor?

   (A)   $825
   (B)   $875
   (C)   $900
   (D)   $925
   (E)   $1,000

|            **Quantity A**            | **Quantity B** |
| ------------------------------------ | -------------- |
| 44. The sum of all the multiples of 3 | 9,990 |
|     between 250 and 350              |                |

Town A has a population of 160,000 and is growing at a rate of 20% annually. Town B has a population of 80,000 and is growing at a rate of 50% annually.

|            **Quantity A**            | **Quantity B** |
| ------------------------------------ | -------------- |
| 45. The number of years until town   | 3              |
|     B's population is greater than    |                |
|     that of town A                   |                |

46. If $f(x) = x^2$, which of the following is equal to $f(m + n) + f(m - n)$?

   (A)   $m^2 + n^2$
   (B)   $m^2 - n^2$
   (C)   $2m^2 + 2n^2$
   (D)   $2m^2 - 2n^2$
   (E)   $m^2 n^2$

47. $S$ is a sequence such that $S_n = (-1)^n$ for each integer $n \geq 1$. What is the sum of the first 20 terms in $S$?

   [          ]

48. If $f(x, y) = x^2 y$ and $f(a, b) = 6$, what is $f(2a, 4b)$?

   [          ]

**MANHATTAN**
PREP

$f(x) = m$ where $m$ is the number of distinct prime factors of $x$.

|  | **Quantity A** | **Quantity B** |
|---|---|---|
| 49. | $f(30)$ | $f(64)$ |

50. The sequence $a_1, a_2, a_3, \ldots, a_n$ is defined by $a_n = 9 + a_{n-1}$ for each integer $n \geq 2$. If $a_1 = 11$, what is the value of $a_{35}$?

51. In sequence $Q$, the first number is 3, and each subsequent number in the sequence is determined by doubling the previous number and then adding 2. In the first 10 terms of the sequence, how many times does the digit 8 appear in the units digit?

52. For which of the following functions $f(x)$ is $f(a + b) = f(a) + f(b)$?

    (A)   $f(x) = x^2$
    (B)   $f(x) = 5x$
    (C)   $f(x) = 2x + 1$
    (D)   $f(x) = \sqrt{x}$
    (E)   $f(x) = x - 2$

Sam invests a principal of $10,000, which earns interest over a period of years.

|  | **Quantity A** | **Quantity B** |
|---|---|---|
| 53. | The final value of the investment after 2 years at 8% interest, compounded annually | The final value of the investment after 4 years at 4% interest, compounded annually |

54. The number of years it would take for the value of an investment to double, at 26% interest compounded annually, is approximately which of the following?

    (A)   2
    (B)   3
    (C)   4
    (D)   5
    (E)   6

55. An investment is made at 12.5% annual simple interest. The number of years it will take for the cumulative value of the interest to equal the original investment is equal to which of the following?

   (A)  4
   (B)  5
   (C)  6
   (D)  7
   (E)  8

56. If $f(2a) = 2f(a)$ and $f(6) = 11$, what is the value of $f(24)$?

   (A)  22
   (B)  24
   (C)  44
   (D)  66
   (E)  88

57. If $\frac{1}{2}f(x) = f\left(\frac{1}{2}x\right)$, which of the following is true for all values of $f(x)$?

   (A)  $f(x) = 2x + 2$
   (B)  $f(x) = 13x$
   (C)  $f(x) = x^2$
   (D)  $f(x) = x - 10$
   (E)  $f(x) = \sqrt{x - 4}$

**MANHATTAN**
PREP

# Functions, Formulas, and Sequences Answers

1. **(E).** Use the notation "$f(x)$" and "$f(2)$" as an indication to substitute 2 for $x$ in the given equation:

$$f(2) = (2)^2 + 1$$
$$f(2) = 5$$

Likewise, plug $-2$ in for $x$:

$$f(-2) = (-2)^2 + 1$$
$$f(-2) = 5$$

Now add: $5 + 5 = 10$.

2. **(B).** Be careful with the notation here. The problem indicates that $h(m) = -19$, *not* that $h(-19) =$ something else. Do not plug $-19$ in for $x$; rather, plug $m$ in for $x$ and set the answer equal to $-19$:

$$2m^3 - 3 = -19$$
$$2m^3 = -16$$
$$m^3 = -8$$
$$m = -2$$

3. **1.** The main function is $f(x) = x + 5$. The notation $f(2g)$ indicates that you should plug $2g$ in for all instances of $x$: $f(2g) = 2g + 5$, which is also given as 19. If $2g + 5 = 19$, then $2g = 14$, and $g = 7$.

The question asks for the value of $f(3 - g)$, which is $f(3 - 7) = f(-4) = -4 + 5 = 1$.

4. **720.** Plug $m$ and $n$ into the function in place of $a$ and $b$. If $f(m, n) = 5$, then:

$$m^2 n^4 = 5$$

This cannot be further simplified, so continue to the second part of the problem: plug $3m$ and $2n$ into the function for $a$ and $b$:

$$f(3m, 2n) = (3m)^2(2n)^4 = 9m^2 \, 16n^4 = 144m^2 n^4$$

Since $m^2 n^4 = 5$, $144m^2 n^4 = 144(5) = 720$.

5. **(A).** The question requires plugging $y$ into the function, then plugging $-1$ into the function, then summing the two results:

$$f(y) = y^2 - 1$$
$$f(-1) = (-1)^2 - 1$$
$$f(-1) = 0$$

Thus, $f(y) + f(-1) = y^2 - 1 + 0 = y^2 - 1$.

**6. 1.** When dealing with "nested" functions, solve the innermost function first:

$$f(10) = \frac{10}{2} - 1 = 4$$

$$f(4) = \frac{4}{2} - 1 = 1$$

Thus, $f(f(10)) = 1$.

**7. (E).** Replace each $x$ with the expression $(a + b)$ to solve for $h(a + b)$.

$$h(a + b) = 5(a + b)^2 + (a + b)$$
$$h(a + b) = 5(a^2 + 2ab + b^2) + a + b$$
$$h(a + b) = 5a^2 + 10ab + 5b^2 + a + b$$

**8. (A).** The question uses a made-up symbol in place of the traditional notation $f(x)$. To answer the question, "If $\lceil x = 2x^2 + 2$, which of the following is equal to $\lceil 4$ ?" plug 4 into the given function.

$$\lceil 4 = 2(4)^2 + 2$$
$$\lceil 4 = 34$$

Do not fall for trap answer choice (E). The correct answer is 34, which does not appear in the choices in that form. Trap choice (E) is $\lceil 34$, which equals $2(34)^2 + 2$; this is much greater than 34.

Instead, solve each answer choice until one equals 34. Choice (A), $\lceil\lceil -1$, uses the function symbol twice, so plug $-1$ into the function, then plug the resulting answer back into the function again:

$$\lceil -1 = 2(-1)^2 + 2 = 4$$

$$\lceil 4 = 2(4)^2 + 2 = 34$$

(Note: you do not need to complete this math if you notice that $\lceil 4$ must have the same value as the original $\lceil 4$ in the question stem.)

Thus, $\lceil\lceil -1 = 34$, choice (A), is correct. It is not necessary to try the other answer choices.

**9. (B).** This problem uses a made-up symbol that is then defined verbally, rather than with a formula. $\lceil x \rceil$ has two different definitions:

If $x$ is odd, $\lceil x \rceil$ equals the least integer greater than $x$ (e.g., if $x = 3$, then the "least integer greater than 3" is equal to 4).

If $x$ is even, $\lceil x \rceil$ equals the greatest integer less than $x$ (e.g., if $x = 6$, the "greatest integer less than $x$" is equal to 5).

Since $-2$ is even, $\lceil -2 \rceil =$ the greatest integer less than $-2$, or $-3$.

**MANHATTAN**
PREP

Since 5 is odd, $\boxed{5}$ = the least integer greater than 5, or 6.

Thus, $\boxed{-2} - \boxed{5} = -3 - 6 = -9$.

10. **32.** For the function $g(x) = x^2 - 4$, plugging $c$ in for $x$ gives the answer 12. Thus:

$$c^2 - 4 = 12$$
$$c^2 = 16$$
$$c = 4 \text{ or } -4$$

The problem indicates that $c < 0$, so $c$ must be $-4$.

The problem then asks for $g(c - 2)$. Since $c = -4$, $c - 2 = -6$. Plug $-6$ into the function:

$$g(-6) = (-6)^2 - 4$$
$$g(-6) = 36 - 4 = 32$$

11. **43.** The problem introduces two functions and asks for $h(g(5))$. When dealing with "nested" functions, begin with the innermost function:

$$g(5) = 5^2 - 3 = 22$$
$$h(22) = 2(22) - 1 = 43$$

Thus, $h(g(5)) = 43$.

12. **20.** The problem introduces two functions as well as the fact that $g(m) = 29$. First, solve for $m$:

$$g(m) = m^2 - 7 = 29$$
$$m^2 = 36$$
$$m = 6 \text{ or } -6$$

The question asks for $h(m)$:

$$h(6) = |3 \times 6| + 2 = |18| + 2 = 18 + 2 = 20$$
$$h(-6) = |3 \times -6| + 2 = |-18| + 2 = 18 + 2 = 20$$

The answer is 20 for either value of $m$.

13. $\dfrac{25}{9}$ **(or any equivalent fraction).** This function defines a made-up symbol rather than using traditional function notation such as $f(x)$. Since $*x$ is defined as "the square of one-half of $x$":

$$*x = \left(\frac{1}{2}x\right)^2$$

The question asks for *5 divided by *3:

$$*5 = (2.5)^2 = 6.25$$
$$*3 = (1.5)^2 = 2.25$$

Therefore, $\dfrac{*5}{*3} = \dfrac{6.25}{2.25} = \dfrac{625}{225} = \dfrac{25}{9}$.

Alternatively, you can reduce before squaring:

$$\frac{*5}{*3} = \frac{(2.5)^2}{(1.5)^2} = \left(\frac{2.5}{1.5}\right)^2 = \left(\frac{25}{15}\right)^2 = \left(\frac{5}{3}\right)^2 = \frac{25}{9}$$

14. **1st, 2nd, and 3rd.** This function defines a made-up symbol: ~$x$ is equivalent to $|14x|$. The question asks which statements must be true, so test each one:

$$\sim\!2 = \sim\!(-2)$$
$$|14(2)| = |14(-2)|$$
$$|28| = |-28|$$
$$28 = 28$$

This first statement must be TRUE.

Similarly, test the second statement:

$$\sim\!3 + \sim\!4 = \sim\!7$$
$$|14(3)| + |14(4)| = |14(7)|$$
$$42 + 56 = 98$$
$$98 = 98$$

This second statement must be TRUE.

Finally, the third statement is also TRUE. Since ~$x$ is equal to a statement inside an absolute value, this value can never be negative. If $x = 0$, then the value of $|14x|$ is also 0. The minimum possible value for ~$x$ is 0.

15. **2.** This function defines a made-up symbol, rather than using traditional notation such as $f(x)$. First, translate the function:

$$\#x = \sqrt{x+2}$$

The square root of any value greater than or equal to 0 is the *non-negative* square root of the value. That is, the square root of 4 is just +2, not −2. Thus:

$$\#7 = \sqrt{7+2} = \sqrt{9} = 3$$
$$\#(-1) = \sqrt{-1+2} = \sqrt{1} = 1$$

Finally, $\#7 - \#(-1) = 3 - 1 = 2$.

**MANHATTAN**
PREP

16. **−2 and 1.** The term "undefined" refers to the circumstance when the solution is not a real number—for example, division by 0 is considered "undefined." There aren't many circumstances that result in an undefined answer. Essentially, the GRE considers two main cases: the square root of a negative integer and division by 0. There are no square roots in this problem, but it's possible that 0 could end up on the denominator of the fraction. Set each of the terms in the denominator equal to 0:

$$3x - 3 = 0$$
$$3x = 3$$
$$x = 1$$

$$x + 2 = 0$$
$$x = -2$$

Thus, if $x = 1$ or $x = -2$, then the denominator would be 0, making $g(x)$ undefined. All other values are acceptable.

17. **(A).** The problem gives a function, $f(x) = 2x - 3$, and then indicates that, when $m$ is plugged in to the function, the answer is −11. Therefore:

$$2m - 3 = -11$$
$$2m = -8$$
$$m = -4$$

Quantity A is equal to −4. The problem indicates that $f(m) = -11$, so Quantity B is equal to $\dfrac{11}{2} = -5.5$. Quantity A is greater.

18. **(D).** Since "the price of a phone call consists of a standard connection fee, which is a constant, plus a per-minute charge," write a formula, using variables for the unknown information. Let $c$ equal the connection fee and $r$ equal the per-minute rate:

$$2.90 = c + r(10)$$
$$4.40 = c + r(16)$$

Now, either substitute and solve or stack and combine the equation. Note that there is one $c$ in each equation, so subtracting is likely to be fastest:

$$
\begin{array}{r}
4.40 = c + 16r \\
-\ (2.90 = c + 10r) \\
\hline
1.50 = 6r \\
r = 0.25
\end{array}
$$

The calls cost 25 cents per minute. Note that most people will next plug $r$ back into either equation to find $c$, but $c$ isn't necessary to solve!

A 10-minute call costs $2.90. That $2.90 already includes the basic connection fee (which is a constant) as well as the per-minute fee for 10 minutes. The problem asks how much a 13-minute call costs. Add the cost for another 3 minutes ($0.75) to the cost for a 10-minute call ($2.90): $2.90 + 0.75 = \$3.65$.

In fact, both the 10-minute and 16-minute calls include the same connection fee (which is a constant), so a shortcut can be used to solve. The extra 6 minutes for the 16-minute call cost a total of $4.40 − $2.90 = $1.50. From there, calculate the cost per minute ($1.5 \div 6 = 0.25$) or notice that 13 minutes is halfway between 10 minutes and 16 minutes, so the cost for a 13-minute call must also be halfway between the cost for a 10-minute call and the cost for a 16-minute call. Add half of $1.50, or $0.75, to $2.90 to get $3.65.

19. **267.** While the sequence is clear (30, 33, 36, 39, 42, etc.), don't spend time counting to the 80th term. Instead, find a pattern. Each new term in the list adds 3 to the previous term, so determine how many times 3 needs to be added. (By the way, the term "arithmetic sequence" means a sequence in which the same number is added or subtracted for each new term.)

Start with the first term, 30. To get from the first term to the second term, start with 30 and add 3 *once.* To get from the first term to the third term, start with 30 and add 3 *twice.* In other words, for the third term, add one fewer instance of 3: twice rather than three times. To write this mathematically, say: $30 + 3(n-1)$, where $n$ is the number of the term. (Note: it's not necessary to write this out, as long as you understand the pattern.)

To get to the 80th term, then, start with 30 and add 3 exactly 79 times:

$$30 + (79 \times 3) = 267$$

20. **(E).** The sequence $S_n = 2(S_{n-1}) - 4$ can be read as "to get any term in sequence $S$, double the previous term and subtract 4."

The problem gives $S_1$ (the first term) and asks for $S_5$ (the fifth term):

$$\frac{6}{S_1} \quad \frac{}{S_2} \quad \frac{}{S_3} \quad \frac{}{S_4} \quad \frac{}{S_5}$$

To get any term, double the previous term and subtract 4. To get $S_2$, double $S_1$ (which is 6) and subtract 4: $S_2 = 2(6) - 4 = 8$. Continue doubling each term and subtracting 4 to get the subsequent term:

$$\frac{6}{S_1} \quad \frac{8}{S_2} \quad \frac{12}{S_3} \quad \frac{20}{S_4} \quad \frac{36}{S_5}$$

21. **(A).** The sequence $S_n = S_{n-1} + S_{n-2} - 3$ can be read as "to get any term in sequence $S$, sum the two previous terms and subtract 3."

The problem gives the first two terms and asks for the sixth term:

$$\frac{5}{S_1} \quad \frac{0}{S_2} \quad \frac{}{S_3} \quad \frac{}{S_4} \quad \frac{}{S_5} \quad \frac{}{S_6}$$

**MANHATTAN**
PREP

To get any term, sum the two previous terms and subtract 3. So the third term will equal $5 + 0 - 3 = 2$. The fourth term will equal $0 + 2 - 3 = -1$. The fifth term will equal $2 + (-1) - 3 = -2$. The sixth term will equal $-1 + (-2) - 3 = -6$:

$$\frac{5}{S_1} \quad \frac{0}{S_2} \quad \frac{2}{S_3} \quad \frac{-1}{S_4} \quad \frac{-2}{S_5} \quad \frac{-6}{S_6}$$

22. **(D).** The sequence $S_n = S_{n-1} + S_{n-2} - 1$ can be read as "to get any term in sequence $S$, sum the two previous terms and subtract 1."

The problem gives the first term and the third term and asks for the fifth term:

$$\frac{11}{S_1} \quad \frac{}{S_2} \quad \frac{10}{S_3} \quad \frac{}{S_4} \quad \frac{}{S_5}$$

Within the sequence $S_1$ to $S_3$, the problem gives two values but not the middle one ($S_2$). What version of the formula would include those three terms?

$$S_3 = S_2 + S_1 - 1$$
$$10 = S_2 + (11) - 1$$
$$10 = S_2 + 10$$
$$0 = S_2$$

$$\frac{11}{S_1} \quad \frac{0}{S_2} \quad \frac{10}{S_3} \quad \frac{}{S_4} \quad \frac{}{S_5}$$

To get each subsequent term, sum the two previous terms and subtract 1. Thus, $S_4 = 10 + 0 - 1 = 9$ and $S_5 = 9 + 10 - 1 = 18$:

$$\frac{11}{S_1} \quad \frac{0}{S_2} \quad \frac{10}{S_3} \quad \frac{9}{S_4} \quad \frac{18}{S_5}$$

23. **(E).** The sequence $S_n = S_{n-1} + S_{n-2} + S_{n-3} - 5$ can be read as "to get any term in sequence $S$, sum the three previous terms and subtract 5."

The problem gives the first, second, and *fourth* terms and asks for the sixth term:

$$\frac{4}{S_1} \quad \frac{0}{S_2} \quad \frac{}{S_3} \quad \frac{-4}{S_4} \quad \frac{}{S_5} \quad \frac{}{S_6}$$

Within the sequence $S_1$ to $S_4$, the problem gives three values but not the fourth ($S_3$). What version of the formula would include those four terms?

$$S_4 = S_3 + S_2 + S_1 - 5$$
$$-4 = S_3 + 4 + 0 - 5$$
$$-4 = S_3 - 1$$
$$-3 = S_3$$

**MANHATTAN**
PREP                                        425

Fill in the newly calculated value. To find each subsequent value, continue to add the three previous terms and subtract 5. Therefore, $S_5 = -4 + (-3) + 0 - 5 = -12$. $S_6 = -12 + (-4) + (-3) - 5 = -24$:

$$\frac{4}{S_1} \quad \frac{0}{S_2} \quad \frac{-3}{S_3} \quad \frac{-4}{S_4} \quad \frac{-12}{S_5} \quad \frac{-24}{S_6}$$

24. **1,778.** The sequence $P_n = 10(P_{n-1}) - 2$ can be read as "to get any term in sequence $P$, multiply the previous term by 10 and subtract 2."

The problem gives the first term and asks for the fourth:

$$\frac{2}{P_1} \quad \frac{\phantom{2}}{P_2} \quad \frac{\phantom{2}}{P_3} \quad \frac{\phantom{2}}{P_4}$$

To get $P_2$, multiply $2 \times 10$, then subtract 2 to get 18. Continue this procedure to find each subsequent term ("to get any term in sequence $P$, multiply the previous term by 10 and subtract 2"). Therefore, $P_3 = 10(18) - 2 = 178$. $P_4 = 10(178) - 2 = 1,778$.

$$\frac{2}{P_1} \quad \frac{18}{P_2} \quad \frac{178}{P_3} \quad \frac{1,778}{P_4}$$

25. **(A).** The sequence $S_{n-1} = \frac{1}{4}(S_n)$ can be read as "to get any term in sequence $S$, multiply the term *after* that term by $\frac{1}{4}$." Since this formula is "backwards" (usually, later terms are defined with regard to previous terms), solve the formula for $S_n$:

$$S_{n-1} = \frac{1}{4}(S_n)$$
$$4S_{n-1} = S_n$$
$$S_n = 4S_{n-1}$$

This can be read as "to get any term in sequence $S$, multiply the previous term by 4."

The problem gives the first term and asks for the fourth:

$$\frac{-4}{S_1} \quad \frac{\phantom{2}}{S_2} \quad \frac{\phantom{2}}{S_3} \quad \frac{\phantom{2}}{S_4}$$

To get $S_2$, multiply the previous term by 4: $(4)(-4) = -16$. Continue this procedure to find each subsequent term. Therefore, $S_3 = (4)(-16) = -64$. $S_4 = (4)(-64) = -256$:

$$\frac{-4}{S_1} \quad \frac{-16}{S_2} \quad \frac{-64}{S_3} \quad \frac{-256}{S_4}$$

**26. (B).** The first term of the sequence is 45, and each subsequent term is determined by adding 2. The problem asks for the sum of the first 100 terms, which cannot be calculated directly in the given time frame; instead, find the pattern. The first few terms of the sequence are 45, 47, 49, 51, …

What's the pattern? To get to the 2nd term, start with 45 and add 2 once. To get to the 3rd term, start with 45 and add 2 twice. To get to the 100th term, then, start with 45 and add 2 ninety-nine times: $45 + (2)(99) = 243$.

Next, find the sum of all odd integers from 45 to 243, inclusive. To sum up any evenly spaced set, multiply the average (arithmetic mean) by the number of elements in the set. To get the average, average the first and last terms. Since $\frac{45 + 243}{2} = 144$, the average is 144.

To find the total number of elements in the set, subtract $243 - 45 = 198$, then divide by 2 (count only the odd numbers, not the even ones): $\frac{198}{2} = 99$ terms. Now, add 1 (to count both endpoints in a consecutive set, first subtract and then "add 1 before you're done"). The list has 100 terms.

Multiply the average and the number of terms:

$$144 \times 100 = 14{,}400$$

**27. (D).** This is an arithmetic sequence where the difference between successive terms is always +10. The difference between, for example, $a_{10}$ and $a_{11}$, is exactly 10, regardless of the actual values of the two terms. The difference between $a_{10}$ and $a_{12}$ is $10 + 10 = 20$, or $10 \times 2 = 20$, because there are two "steps," or terms, to get from $a_{10}$ to $a_{12}$. Starting from $a_{10}$, there is a sequence of 5 terms to get to $a_{15}$. Therefore, the difference between $a_{10}$ and $a_{15}$ is $10 \times 5 = 50$.

**28. (D).** First, calculate Abraham's score: $2ps - 45m, = 2(21)(30) - 45(10) = 1260 - 450 = 810$. Javed got a score of 810 also, but did 4 more push-ups than Abraham, or $21 + 4 = 25$ push-ups. So, the formula for Javed's score is:

$$810 = 2ps - 45m$$
$$810 = 2(25)s - 45(12)$$
$$810 = 50s - 540$$
$$1{,}350 = 50s$$
$$s = 27$$

**29. (E).** This problem defines a function for the made-up symbol #. In this problem $a = (-4)$ and $b = 4$. Plug the values into the function: $(-4)^2 \sqrt{4} - (-4) = 16 \times 2 + 4 = 36$. Do not forget to keep the parentheses around the $-4$! Also note that only the positive root of 4 applies, because the problem has been presented in the form of a real number underneath the square root sign.

**30. (C).** This problem defines a function for the made-up symbol \$. The order of operation rules (PEMDAS) stay the same even when the problem uses made-up symbols. First, calculate the value of the expression in parentheses, 6\$2.

Plug $x = 6$ and $y = 2$ into the function: $\frac{6^2}{2} = \frac{36}{2} = 18$. Replace 6\$2 with 18 in the original expression to give 9\$18.

Again, plug $x = 9$ and $y = 18$ into the function: $9\$18 = \frac{9^2}{18} = \frac{81}{18} = \frac{9}{2}$.

**MANHATTAN**
PREP                    427

31. **(D).** Both Amy and Bob start with $1,000 and earn 8% interest annually; the difference is in how often this interest is compounded. Amy's interest is compounded twice a year at 4% each time (8% annual interest compounded 2 times a year means that she gets half the interest, or 4%, every 6 months). Bob's interest is compounded four times a year at 2% (8% divided by 4 times per year) each time. After 6 months, Amy has $1,000 × 1.04 = $1,040.00 (one interest payment at 4%) and Bob has $1,000 × (1.02)² = $1,040.40 (two interest payments at 2%). The difference is $1,040.40 − $1,040.00 = $0.40.

Alternatively, Bob's interest could be calculated as two separate payments. After three months, Bob will have $1,000 × 1.02 = $1,020.00. After 6 months, Bob will have $1,020 × 1.02 = $1,040.40.

32. **(D).** After each half-life, the sample is left with half of the isotopes it started with in the previous period. After one half-life, the sample goes from 16,000 isotopes to 8,000. After two half-lives, it goes from 8,000 to 4,000. Continue this pattern to determine the total number of half-lives that have passed: 4,000 becomes 2,000 after 3 half-lives, 2,000 becomes 1,000 after 4 half-lives, 1,000 becomes 500 after 5 half-lives. The sample will have 500 isotopes after 5 half-lives. Thus, multiply 5 times the half-life, or 5 × 5,730 = 28,650 years.

Note that the answer choices are very spread apart. After determining that 5 half-lives have passed, estimate: 5 × 5,000 = 25,000 years; answer (D) is the only possible answer.

33. **(B).** Substitute the expression for $g(x)$ into the function for $f(x)$, and set the answer equal to 1. Since $g(x) = 3x - 2$, substitute the expression $3x - 2$ in for $x$ in the expression for $f(x)$:

$$f(g(x)) = \frac{2 - g(x)}{5} = \frac{2 - (3x - 2)}{5} = \frac{4 - 3x}{5}$$

Since $f(g(x)) = 1$, solve the equation $\dfrac{4 - 3x}{5} = 1$:

$$4 - 3x = 5$$
$$-3x = 1$$
$$x = -\frac{1}{3}$$

34. **(E).** The value of the investment doubled every 9 years. Calculate the amount of money at the end of each 9-year period:

| Age | Value |
|---|---|
| 27 | $25,125 |
| 27 + 9 = 36 | $50,250 |
| 36 + 9 = 45 | $100,500 |
| 45 + 9 = 54 | $201,000 |
| 54 + 9 = 63 | $402,000 |

At age 63, the investor had $402,000.

**MANHATTAN**
PREP

35. **(D).** Calculate each of the archer's scores by plugging in the appropriate values for $b$, $a$, and $s$. For the first archer, $b = a = s = 10$ and the score is $\dfrac{(50 \times 10) - (10 \times 10)}{10 + 10} = \dfrac{400}{20} = 20$. For the second archer, $b =$ half of $10 = 5$, $a =$ twice as many as $10 = 20$, and $s = 15$. The score for the second archer is $\dfrac{(50 \times 5) - (10 \times 20)}{10 + 15} = \dfrac{50}{25} = 2$. The difference in scores is $20 - 2 = 18$.

36. **(E).** Let $k$ equal the constant added to a term to get the next term. If the second term $= 27$, then the third term $= 27 + k$, the 4th term $= 27 + 2k$, and the 5th term $= 27 + 3k$. The 5th term equals 84, so create an equation:

$$27 + 3k = 84$$
$$3k = 57$$
$$k = 19$$

To find the first term, subtract $k$ from the second term. The first term $= 27 - 19 = 8$.

37. **(C).** This problem defines functions for the made-up symbols # and @. Substitute $a = 1$ and $b = 2$ into the function for $a@b$: $3(1) - 2(2) = -1$. Substitute $a = 3$ and $b = 4$ into the function for $a\#b$: $\dfrac{1}{2(3) - 3(4)} = \dfrac{1}{-6} = -\dfrac{1}{6}$. Now, subtract: $(-1) - \left(-\dfrac{1}{6}\right) = -1 + \dfrac{1}{6} = -\dfrac{5}{6}$.

38. **(D).** This is an arithmetic sequence: each new number is created by adding 5 to the previous number in the sequence. Calculate the first few terms of the sequence: 1, 6, 11, 16, 21, and so on. Arithmetic sequences can be written in this form: $a_n = a_1 + k(n - 1)$, where $k$ is the added constant and $n$ is the number of the desired term. In this case, the function is: $a_n = 1 + 5(n - 1)$. The 75th term of this sequence is $a_{75} = 1 + 5(74) = 371$.

To find the sum of an arithmetic sequence, multiply the average value of the terms by the number of terms. The average of any evenly spaced set is equal to the midpoint between the first and last terms. The average of the 1st and 75th terms is $\dfrac{1 + 371}{2} = 186$. There are 75 terms. Therefore, the sum of the first 75 terms $= 186 \times 75 = 13,950$.

39. **(E).** This is a geometric sequence: each new number is created by multiplying the previous number by 2. Calculate the first few terms of the series to find the pattern: 1, 2, 4, 8, 16, and so on. Geometric sequences can be written in this form: $a_n = r^{n-1}$, where $r$ is the multiplied constant and $n$ is the number of the desired term. In this case, the function is $a_n = 2^{n-1}$.

The question asks for the difference between the sum of the first 10 terms and the sum of the 11th and 12th terms. While there is a clever pattern at play, it is hard to spot. If you don't see the pattern, one way to solve is to use the calculator to add the first ten terms: $1 + 2 + 4 + 8 + 16 + 32 + 64 + 128 + 256 + 512 = 1,023$.

The 11th term plus the 12th term is equal to $1,024 + 2,048 = 3,072$. Subtract 1,023 to get 2,049.

Alternatively, look for the pattern in the first few terms (1, 2, 4, 8, 16...): every term is equal to 1 more than the sum of the ones before it. For example, $1 + 2 = 3$ and the next term is 4: $1 + 2 + 4 = 7$ and the next term is 8. Thus, the sum of the first 10 terms of the sequence is 1 less than the 11th term. The 11th term $= 2^{10} = 1,024$, so the sum of the first 10 terms $= 1,023$. and the difference between the 10th and 11th terms equals 1. Add the value of the 12th term or $1 + 2,048 = 2,049$.

40. **(B).** This problem defines a function for the made-up symbol @. Use the definition of the new symbol to rewrite the equation $x@5 = 3@x$ without the @ operator:

> For $x@5$, $a = x$ and $b = 5$: $x@5 = (x - 1)(5 - 2) = 3x - 3$.
> For $3@x$, $a = 3$ and $b = x$: $3@x = (3 - 1)(x - 2) = 2x - 4$.

Equating these two expressions gives you:

> $3x - 3 = 2x - 4$
> $x = -1$

Quantity B is greater.

41. **(E).** Start by solving for the constant, $k$. A party of 4 ($d = 4$) has an estimated wait time of 40 minutes ($w = 40$) when 6 other parties are ahead of it ($n = 6$). Plug these values into the formula:

> $w = d^2 + kn$
> $40 = 4^2 + k(6)$
> $40 = 16 + 6k$
> $24 = 6k$
> $k = 4$

Then solve for the wait time for a party of 6 ($d = 6$) if there are 3 parties ahead of it ($n = 3$), using the constant $k = 4$ determined above:

> $w = d^2 + kn$
> $w = 6^2 + 4(3)$
> $w = 36 + 12$
> $w = 48$ minutes

42. **(A).** The sequence $a_n = a_{n-1} - 7$ can be read as "to get any term in sequence $a$, subtract 7 from the previous term." The problem provides the 7th term; plug the term into the function in order to determine the pattern. Note that Quantity A asks for the value of $a_1$, so try to find the 6th term:

> $7 = a_6 - 7$
> $a_6 = 14$

**MANHATTAN**
PREP

In other words, each previous term will be 7 greater than the subsequent term. Therefore, $a_7 = 7$, $a_6 = 14$, $a_5 = 21$, and so on. The term $a_1$, then, is greater than the starting point, 7, and must also be greater than the negative value in Quantity B. Quantity A is greater. Note that the value in Quantity B is the result of incorrectly *subtracting* 7 six times, rather than adding it.

43. **(A).** First, solve for the constant $k$ using the price information of the 2-bedroom, 2-bath unit ($m = 800$, $r = t = 2$, and $f = 1$):

$$800 = k\left(\frac{5(2)^2 + 10(2)}{1+5}\right)$$

$$800 = k\left(\frac{20+20}{6}\right)$$

$$800 = k\left(\frac{20}{3}\right)$$

$$800\left(\frac{3}{20}\right) = k$$

$$40(3) = k$$

$$120 = k$$

Next, solve for the rent on the 3-bedroom, 1-bath unit on the 3rd floor ($r = 3$, $t = 1$, and $f = 3$):

$$m = 120\left(\frac{5(3)^2 + 10(1)}{3+5}\right)$$

$$m = 120\left(\frac{45+10}{8}\right)$$

$$m = 120\left(\frac{55}{8}\right)$$

$$m = 15(55)$$

$$m = 825$$

44. **(B).** First, find the smallest multiple of 3 in this range: 250 is not a multiple of 3 ($2 + 5 + 0 = 7$, which is not a multiple of 3). The smallest multiple of 3 in this range is 252 ($2 + 5 + 2 = 9$, which is a multiple of 3). Next, find the largest multiple of 3 in this range. Since 350 is not a multiple of 3 ($3 + 5 + 0 = 8$), the largest multiple of 3 in this range is 348.

The sum of an evenly spaced set of numbers equals the average value multiplied by the number of terms. The average value is the midpoint between 252 and 348: $(252 + 348) \div 2 = 300$. To find the number of terms, first subtract $348 - 252 = 96$. This figure represents all numbers between 348 and 252, inclusive. To count only the multiples of 3, divide 96 by the 3: $96 \div 3 = 32$. Finally, "add 1 before you're done" to count both end points of the range: $32 + 1 = 33$.

The sum is $300 \times 33 = 9,900$. Since 9,900 is smaller than 9,990, Quantity B is greater.

**45. (A).** Set up a table and calculate the population of each town after every year; use the calculator to calculate town A's population. If you feel comfortable multiplying by 1.5 yourself, you do not need to use the calculator for town B. Instead, add 50% each time (e.g., from 80,000 add 50%, or 40,000, to get 120,000).

|        | Town A | Town B |
|--------|--------|--------|
| Now    | 160,000 | 80,000 |
| Year 1 | $160{,}000(1.2) = 192{,}000$ | $80{,}000 + 40{,}000 = 120{,}000$ |
| Year 2 | $192{,}000(1.2) = 230{,}400$ | $120{,}000 + 60{,}000 = 180{,}000$ |
| Year 3 | $230{,}400(1.2) = 276{,}480$ | $180{,}000 + 90{,}000 = 270{,}000$ |

Note that, after three years, town A still has more people than town B. It will take longer than 3 years, then, for town B to surpass town A, so Quantity A is greater.

**46. (C).** The problem provides the function $f(x) = x^2$ and asks for the quantity $f(m + n) + f(m - n)$. Plug into this function twice—first, to insert $m + n$ in place of $x$, and then to insert $m - n$ in place of $x$:

$$f(m + n) = (m + n)^2 = m^2 + 2mn + n^2$$
$$f(m - n) = (m - n)^2 = m^2 - 2mn + n^2$$

Now add the two:

$$(m^2 + 2mn + n^2) + (m^2 - 2mn + n^2) = 2m^2 + 2n^2$$

**47. 0.** Adding 20 individual terms would take quite a long time. Look for a pattern. The first several terms in $S_n = (-1)^n$, where $n \geq 1$:

$$S_1 = (-1)^1 = -1$$
$$S_2 = (-1)^2 = 1$$
$$S_3 = (-1)^3 = -1$$
$$S_4 = (-1)^4 = 1$$

The terms alternate $-1$, $1$, $-1$, $1$, and so on. If the terms are added, every pair of $-1$ and $1$ will add to zero; in other words, for an even number of terms, the sum will be zero. Since 20 is an even number, so the first 20 terms sum to zero.

**48. 96.** The problem provides the function $f(x, y) = x^2y$ and also the fact that when $a$ and $b$ are plugged in for $x$ and $y$, the answer is 6. In other words:

$$f(x, y) = x^2y$$
$$f(a, b) = a^2b = 6$$

The problem asks for the value of $f(2a, 4b)$. First, plug $2a$ in for $x$ and $4b$ in for $y$:

$$f(2a, 4b) = (2a)^2(4b)$$
$$f(2a, 4b) = 4a^2(4b)$$
$$f(2a, 4b) = 16a^2b$$

**MANHATTAN**
PREP

The problem already provides the value for the variables: $a^2b = 6$. Therefore, $16a^2b = 16(6) = 96$.

49. **(A).** The problem indicates that $f(x) = m$ where $m$ is the number of distinct (or different) prime factors of $x$. For example, if $x = 6$, 6 has two distinct prime factors: 2 and 3. Therefore, the corresponding answer ($m$ value) would be 2.

For Quantity A, $f(30)$: 30 has 3 distinct prime factors (2, 3, and 5), so $f(30) = 3$.

For Quantity B, $f(64)$: 64 is made of the prime factors 2, 2, 2, 2, 2, and 2). This is only one distinct prime factor, so $f(64) = 1$.

Quantity A is greater.

50. **317.** Each term in the sequence is 9 greater than the previous term. To make this clear, write a few terms of the sequence: 11, 20, 29, 38, etc.

$a_{35}$ comes 34 terms after $a_1$ in the sequence. In other words, $a_{35}$ is $34 \times 9 = 306$ greater than $a_1$.

Thus, $a_{35} = 11 + 306 = 317$.

51. **9.** After the first term in the sequence, every term has a units digit of 8:

$Q_1 = 3$
$Q_2 = 2(3) + 2 = 8$
$Q_3 = 2(8) + 2 = 18$
$Q_4 = 2(18) + 2 = 38$
$Q_5 = 2(38) + 2 = 78$
$\ldots$

So 8 is the units digit nine out of the first ten times.

52. **(B).** The question asks which of the functions in the answer choices is such that performing the function on $a + b$ yields the same answer as performing the function to $a$ and $b$ individually and then adding those answers together.

The correct answer should be such that $f(a + b) = f(a) + f(b)$ is true for any values of $a$ and $b$. Test some numbers, for example $a = 2$ and $b = 3$:

|  | $f(a + b) = f(5)$ | $f(a) = f(2)$ | $f(b) = f(3)$ | Does $f(a + b) = f(a) + f(b)$? |
|---|---|---|---|---|
| (A) | $f(5) = 5^2 = 25$ | $f(2) = 2^2 = 4$ | $f(3) = 3^2 = 9$ | No |
| (B) | $f(5) = 5(5) = 25$ | $f(2) = 5(2) = 10$ | $f(3) = 5(3) = 15$ | Yes |
| (C) | $f(5) = 2(5) + 1 = 11$ | $f(2) = 2(2) + 1 = 5$ | $f(3) = 2(3) + 1 = 7$ | No |
| (D) | $f(5) = \sqrt{5}$ | $f(2) = \sqrt{2}$ | $f(3) = \sqrt{3}$ | No |
| (E) | $f(5) = 5 - 2 = 3$ | $f(2) = 2 - 2 = 0$ | $f(3) = 3 - 2 = 1$ | No |

Alternatively, use logic—for what kinds of operations are performing the operation on two numbers and then summing results the same as summing the original numbers and then performing the operation? Multiplication or division would work, but squaring, square-rooting, adding, or subtracting would not. The correct function can contain *only* multiplication and/or division.

53. **(B).** Solve this problem by applying the compound interest formula:

$$V = P\left(1 + \frac{r}{100}\right)^t$$

Since the principal $P$ is the same in both cases, leave it out and just compare the rest:

Quantity A: $\left(1 + \frac{r}{100}\right)^t = \left(1 + \frac{8}{100}\right)^2 = (1.08)^2 = 1.08 \times 1.08 = 1.1664$

Quantity B: $\left(1 + \frac{r}{100}\right)^t = \left(1 + \frac{4}{100}\right)^4 = (1.04)^4 = 1.04 \times 1.04 \times 1.04 \times 1.04 \approx 1.1699$

Quantity B is greater.

Alternatively, use logic. Notice that the *simple* interest in each case would be the same: 2 years of 8% *simple* interest (of an unchanging principal) is equal to 4 years of 4% *simple* interest of the same principal. Now go back to the compounded world. If the simple interest scenarios are the same, then it will always be true that the compounded scenario with *more frequent* compounding will result in greater principal in the end, because "interest on the interest" is earned more often:

| 2 periods of 8% compounded interest | < | 4 periods of 4% compounded interest | < | 8 periods of 2% compounded interest | < | 16 periods of 1% compounded interest |
|---|---|---|---|---|---|---|

The differences are small but real.

54. **(B).** Start with $1, and multiply by $\left(1 + \frac{26}{100}\right) = 1.26$ for each year that passes. In order for the amount to double, it would have to reach $2:

End of Year 1: $1 \times 1.26 = \$1.26$
End of Year 2: $1.26 \times 1.26 = \$1.5876$
End of Year 3: $1.5876 \times 1.26 = \$2.000376 \approx \$2.00$

It takes 3 years for the investment to double in value. In terms of *simple* interest, it would take about 4 years (since 26% is just a tiny bit more than 25% = 1/4). The compounded case earns "interest on the interest," though, so the investment grows more quickly.

**MANHATTAN**
PREP

55. **(E).** "Simple" interest means that the interest is calculated based on the initial amount every time; the interest earned is not included in future calculations. Each year, the investment pays 12.5%, or $\frac{1}{8}$, of the original investment as simple interest. As a result, it will take exactly 8 years for the cumulative interest to add up to the original investment.

Be careful not to apply the compound interest formula here. If the 12.5% interest is in fact compounded annually, it will take only about 6 years for the investment to double in value.

56. **(C).** This question concerns some function for which the full formula is not provided. The problem indicates that $f(2a) = 2f(a)$. In other words, this function is such that plugging in $2a$ is the same as plugging in $a$ and then multiplying by 2. Plug $f(6) = 11$ into the equation $f(2a) = 2f(a)$:

$$f(2(6)) = 2(11)$$
$$f(12) = 22$$

Use the same process a second time. If $a = 12$ and $f(12) = 22$:

$$f(2(12)) = 2(22)$$
$$f(24) = 44$$

Alternatively, use logic. Plugging in $2a$, yields the same answer as plugging in $a$ and then multiplying by 2. Plugging in 24 is the same as plugging in 6 a total of 4 times, and yields an answer 4 times as big as plugging in 6. Since plugging in 6 yields 11, plugging in 24 yields 44.

57. **(B).** The question is asking, "For which function is performing the function on $x$ and THEN multiplying by $\frac{1}{2}$ the equivalent of performing the function on $\frac{1}{2}$ of $x$?"

The fastest method is to use logic: since the order of operations says that order does not matter with multiplication and division but *does* matter between multiplication and addition/subtraction, or multiplication and exponents, choose a function that has only multiplication and/or division. Only answer choice (B) qualifies.

Alternatively, try each choice:

| | $\frac{1}{2}f(x)$ | $f\left(\frac{1}{2}x\right)$ | equal? |
|---|---|---|---|
| (A) | $\frac{1}{2}(2x+2)=x+1$ | $2\left(\frac{1}{2}x\right)+2=x+2$ | No |
| (B) | $\frac{1}{2}(13x)=\frac{13x}{2}$ | $13\left(\frac{1}{2}x\right)=\frac{13x}{2}$ | Yes |
| (C) | $\frac{1}{2}x^2$ | $\left(\frac{1}{2}x\right)^2=\frac{1}{4}x^2$ | No |
| (D) | $\frac{1}{2}(x-10)=\frac{x}{2}-5$ | $\frac{1}{2}x-10=\frac{x}{2}-10$ | No |
| (E) | $\frac{1}{2}\sqrt{x-4}$ | $\sqrt{\frac{1}{2}x-4}$ | No |

To confirm that the terms in choice (E) are equal, try plugging in a real number for $x$. If $x = 8$, then the left-hand value becomes 1 and the right-hand value becomes the square root of 0. The two values are *not* the same.

# Chapter 11 *of*

5 lb. Book of GRE® Practice Problems

# Fractions and Decimals

# In This Chapter...

Fractions and Decimals

Fractions and Decimals Answers

# Fractions and Decimals

For questions in the Quantitative Comparison format ("Quantity A" and "Quantity B" given), the answer choices are always as follows:

(A)  Quantity A is greater.
(B)  Quantity B is greater.
(C)  The two quantities are equal.
(D)  The relationship cannot be determined from the information given.

For questions followed by a numeric entry box [    ], you are to enter your own answer in the box. For questions followed by a fraction-style numeric entry box $\frac{\phantom{xxx}}{\phantom{xxx}}$, you are to enter your answer in the form of a fraction. You are not required to reduce fractions. For example, if the answer is $\frac{1}{4}$, you may enter $\frac{25}{100}$ or any equivalent fraction.

All numbers used are real numbers. All figures are assumed to lie in a plane unless otherwise indicated. Geometric figures are not necessarily drawn to scale. You should assume, however, that lines that appear to be straight are actually straight, points on a line are in the order shown, and all geometric objects are in the relative positions shown. Coordinate systems, such as $xy$-planes and number lines, as well as graphical data presentations, such as bar charts, circle graphs, and line graphs, *are* drawn to scale. A symbol that appears more than once in a question has the same meaning throughout the question.

1.  What is the value of $\dfrac{1}{2}+\dfrac{2}{3}+\dfrac{3}{4}+\dfrac{4}{5}+\dfrac{5}{6}$?

    Give your answer as a fraction.

|  | **Quantity A** | **Quantity B** |
|---|---|---|
| 2. | $-\dfrac{3}{4}+\dfrac{2}{3}$ | $-\dfrac{3}{4}\times\dfrac{2}{3}$ |

3.  At a convention of monsters, $\dfrac{2}{5}$ have no horns, $\dfrac{1}{7}$ have one horn, $\dfrac{1}{3}$ have two horns, and the remaining 26 have three or more horns. How many monsters are attending the convention?

    (A)  100
    (B)  130
    (C)  180
    (D)  210
    (E)  260

4.  Devora spends $\frac{1}{4}$ of her money on a textbook, and then buys a notebook that costs $\frac{1}{6}$ the price of the textbook. If there is no sales tax on the items and she makes no other purchases, what fraction of her original money does Devora have remaining?

Give your answer as a fraction.

5.  Which of the following are equal to 0.003482?

Indicate all such values.

☐   $-0.003482 \times 10^{-1}$

☐   $0.3482 \times 10^{-2}$

☐   $34.82 \times 10^{4}$

☐   $34.82 \times 10^{-4}$

☐   $3,482 \times 10^{-6}$

6.  Which of the following are equal to $12.12 \times 10^{-3}$?

Indicate all such values.

☐   $-1.21 \times 10^{3}$

☐   0.012

☐   $0.00001212 \times 10^{3}$

☐   $0.01212 \times 10^{3}$

7.  5 is how many fifths of 10?

(A)   2.5
(B)   5
(C)   10
(D)   20
(E)   50

| **Quantity A** | **Quantity B** |
|---|---|
| 8.  $\frac{75}{4^2} \times \frac{3^2}{45} \times \frac{2^4}{45}$ | $\frac{3^2}{4^2} \times \frac{2^2}{5^2} \times \frac{10}{3}$ |

**MANHATTAN**
PREP

9.  In a certain class, $\frac{5}{12}$ of all the students are girls and $\frac{1}{4}$ of all the students are girls who take Spanish. What fraction of the girls take Spanish?

    (A) $\frac{5}{48}$

    (B) $\frac{5}{12}$

    (C) $\frac{2}{5}$

    (D) $\frac{3}{5}$

    (E) $\frac{7}{12}$

10. $\frac{1}{5}$ of all the cars on a certain auto lot are red, and $\frac{2}{3}$ of all the red cars are convertibles. What fraction of all the cars are NOT red convertibles?

    Give your answer as a fraction.

    $$\boxed{\phantom{xxxx}}$$
    $$\boxed{\phantom{xxxx}}$$

11. Two identical pies were cut into a total of 16 equal pieces. If one of the resulting pieces was then split equally among three people, what fraction of a pie did each person receive?

    (A) $\frac{1}{48}$

    (B) $\frac{1}{24}$

    (C) $\frac{1}{16}$

    (D) $\frac{3}{16}$

    (E) $\frac{3}{8}$

$$xy \neq 0$$

| **Quantity A** | **Quantity B** |
|---|---|
| $2 + \dfrac{1}{xy}$ | $\dfrac{2xy+1}{xy}$ |

12.

|  | **Quantity A** | **Quantity B** |
|---|---|---|

13.

$$\frac{2}{3} - \frac{\frac{1}{4}}{\frac{1}{3}} \cdot \frac{1-2}{1}$$

$$\frac{1}{4} - \frac{\frac{1}{3}}{\frac{2}{3}} \cdot \frac{3-4}{1}$$

At store A, $\frac{3}{4}$ of the apples are red.

At store B, which has twice as many apples, 0.375 of them are red.

| **Quantity A** | **Quantity B** |
|---|---|
14. | The number of red apples | The number of red apples |
| at store A | at store B |

15. A pot of soup was divided equally into two bowls. If Manuel ate $\frac{1}{4}$ of one of the bowls of soup and $\frac{2}{5}$ of the other bowl of soup, what fraction of the entire pot of soup did Manuel eat?

Give your answer as a fraction.

16. Which of the following is equal to $\dfrac{\frac{ab}{c}}{\frac{cd}{a}}$ for all non-zero values of $a, b, c,$ and $d$?

(A) $ac$

(B) $bd$

(C) $\dfrac{1}{bd}$

(D) $\dfrac{a^2b}{c^2d}$

(E) $\dfrac{ab^2}{cd^2}$

**MANHATTAN**
PREP

17. Which of the following is equal to $\left(\dfrac{\sqrt{12}}{5}\right)\left(\dfrac{\sqrt{60}}{2^4}\right)\left(\dfrac{\sqrt{45}}{3^2}\right)$?

(A) $\dfrac{1}{12}$

(B) $\dfrac{1}{6}$

(C) $\dfrac{1}{4}$

(D) $\dfrac{1}{3}$

(E) $\dfrac{1}{2}$

18. Which of the following is equal to $\dfrac{-1}{2x} - \dfrac{1}{4y} + \dfrac{1}{xy} + \dfrac{1}{8}$ ?

(A) $\dfrac{(x-4)(2-y)}{8xy}$

(B) $\dfrac{(x-2)(y-4)}{8xy}$

(C) $\dfrac{(x-4)(y-2)}{8xy}$

(D) $\dfrac{(x+2)(4-y)}{8xy}$

(E) $\dfrac{(x-2)(4-y)}{8xy}$

$x$ is a digit in the decimal 12.15x9, which, if rounded to the nearest hundredth, would equal 12.16.

| Quantity A | Quantity B |
|:---:|:---:|
| $x$ | 4 |

19.

20. What is the value of $\dfrac{(17^2)(22)(38)(41)(91)}{(19)(34)(123)(11)(119)(26)}$ ?

Give your answer as a fraction.

21. In a decimal number, a bar over one or more consecutive digits means that the pattern of digits under the bar repeats without end. What fraction is equal to $7.58\overline{3}$?

Give your answer as a fraction.

|   | **Quantity A** | **Quantity B** |
|---|---|---|
| 22. | $\left(\dfrac{\sqrt{25}}{\sqrt{10}}\right)\left(\dfrac{\sqrt{8}}{\sqrt{15}}\right)$ | $\left(\dfrac{\sqrt{51}}{\sqrt{46}}\right)\left(\dfrac{\sqrt{23}}{\sqrt{34}}\right)$ |

23. What is the value of $\sqrt{\dfrac{3}{2}} - \sqrt{\dfrac{2}{3}}$ ?

(A) $\dfrac{\sqrt{3}-\sqrt{2}}{\sqrt{6}}$

(B) $\dfrac{1}{\sqrt{6}}$

(C) $\dfrac{\sqrt{3}}{3}$

(D) $\dfrac{\sqrt{3}}{2}$

(E) $\dfrac{\sqrt{5}}{\sqrt{6}}$

24.  In a certain box of cookies, $\frac{3}{4}$ of all the cookies have nuts and $\frac{1}{3}$ of all the cookies have both nuts and fruit. What fraction of all the cookies in the box have nuts but no fruit?

(A)  $\frac{1}{4}$

(B)  $\frac{5}{12}$

(C)  $\frac{1}{2}$

(D)  $\frac{7}{12}$

(E)  $\frac{5}{6}$

25.  $\frac{1}{4}$ of all the juniors and $\frac{2}{3}$ of all the seniors of a certain school are going on a trip. If there are $\frac{2}{3}$ as many juniors as seniors, what fraction of the junior and senior students are not going on the trip?

(A)  $\frac{4}{9}$

(B)  $\frac{1}{2}$

(C)  $\frac{2}{3}$

(D)  $\frac{1}{3}$

(E)  $\frac{5}{6}$

26.  $\frac{4}{5}$ of the women and $\frac{3}{4}$ of the men in a group speak Spanish. If there are 40% as many men as women in the group, what fraction of the group speaks Spanish?

Give your answer as a fraction.

$abcd \neq 0$

|  | **Quantity A** | **Quantity B** |
|---|---|---|
| 27. | $\dfrac{a^2b}{cd^2} \times \dfrac{d^3}{abc}$ | $\dfrac{d^2}{bc} \times \dfrac{ab^2}{bd}$ |

$$m \neq 0$$

|          **Quantity A**          |          **Quantity B**          |
|----------------------------------|----------------------------------|

28.  $\left(\dfrac{1}{2} + \dfrac{1}{m}\right)(m+2)$          $\dfrac{(m+2)^2}{2m}$

29. Which two of the following numbers, when added together, yield a sum between 1 and 2?

Indicate two such numbers.

☐ $\dfrac{7\left(2^3\right)}{3^3 - 7}$

☐ $\dfrac{2^4}{1+2+3+4}$

☐ $\dfrac{3}{11} \div \dfrac{6}{11}$

☐ $\dfrac{-2^3 3^2}{2^2 5^2}$

☐ $\dfrac{-11^2 - 11^3}{(30)(44)}$

30. Which three of the following numbers, when multiplied by each other, yield a product less than −1?

Indicate three such numbers.

☐ $\dfrac{-15}{17}$

☐ $\dfrac{-18}{19}$

☐ $\dfrac{23}{-22}$

☐ $\dfrac{17}{-16}$

31. What is the value of $(3 - \dfrac{1}{3})^2 + (3 + \dfrac{1}{3})^2$?

(A) $\dfrac{122}{9}$

(B) $\dfrac{164}{9}$

(C)  36

(D) $\dfrac{164}{3}$

(E)  162

**MANHATTAN**
PREP

32. If $\dfrac{3}{\dfrac{m+1}{m}+1}=1$, what is the value of $m$?

   (A)  −2

   (B)  −1

   (C)   0

   (D)   1

   (E)   2

$$rs=\sqrt{3}$$

|  | **Quantity A** | **Quantity B** |
|---|---|---|
| 33. | $\dfrac{2r\sqrt{12}}{r^2s\sqrt{72}}$ | $\dfrac{14rs^2}{42s}$ |

|  | **Quantity A** | **Quantity B** |
|---|---|---|
| 34. | $\dfrac{\sqrt{10}}{\sqrt{8}}\div\dfrac{\sqrt{9}}{\sqrt{10}}$ | $\dfrac{\sqrt{11}}{\sqrt{9}}\div\dfrac{\sqrt{10}}{\sqrt{11}}$ |

35. Which of the following fractions has the greatest value?

   (A)  $\dfrac{7}{(16)(25)}$

   (B)  $\dfrac{5}{(32)(5^4)}$

   (C)  $\dfrac{30}{(512)(5^3)}$

   (D)  $\dfrac{5}{(4^6)(5)}$

   (E)  $\dfrac{4}{(2^{11})(5^2)}$

$$\frac{m}{p}>\frac{n}{p}$$

|  | **Quantity A** | **Quantity B** |
|---|---|---|
| 36. | $m$ | $n$ |

37. If $2x \neq y$ and $5x \neq 4y$, then what is the value of $\dfrac{\dfrac{5x-4y}{2x-y}}{\dfrac{3y}{y-2x}+5}$ ?

   (A) $\dfrac{1}{2}$

   (B) $\dfrac{3}{2}$

   (C) $\dfrac{5}{2}$

   (D) $\dfrac{7}{2}$

   (E) $\dfrac{9}{2}$

38. What is the value of $\dfrac{39^2}{2^4} \div \dfrac{13^3}{4^2}$ ?

   (A) $\dfrac{13}{2}$

   (B) $\dfrac{9}{2}$

   (C) $\dfrac{3}{2}$

   (D) $\dfrac{3}{13}$

   (E) $\dfrac{9}{13}$

**MANHATTAN**
PREP

# Fractions and Decimals Answers

1. $\dfrac{71}{20}$ **(or any equivalent fraction).** Sum the fractions by finding a common denominator, which is a multiple of 2, 3, 4, 5, and 6. The smallest number that works is 60.

$$\frac{1}{2}+\frac{2}{3}+\frac{3}{4}+\frac{4}{5}+\frac{5}{6}=\frac{30}{60}+\frac{40}{60}+\frac{45}{60}+\frac{48}{60}+\frac{50}{60}=\frac{30+40+45+48+50}{60}=\frac{213}{60}=\frac{71}{20}$$

2. **(A).** In Quantity A, use a common denominator to add:

$$-\frac{3}{4}+\frac{2}{3}=-\frac{9}{12}+\frac{8}{12}=-\frac{1}{12}$$

In Quantity B, multiply straight across both top and bottom (common denominators are only needed for addition and subtraction). Cancel where possible:

$$-\frac{3}{4}\times\frac{2}{3}=-\frac{\cancel{3}}{4}\times\frac{2}{\cancel{3}}=-\frac{2}{4}=-\frac{1}{2}$$

Quantity A is greater. (Be careful with negatives! The closer to 0 a negative is, the greater it is.)

3. **(D).** This is a common GRE setup—the question presents several fractions and one actual number. First find what fraction of the whole that number represents, then solve for the total (call the total $m$). Notice that all the denominators are primes, so they don't share any factors. Therefore, the common denominator is their product: $5\times7\times3=105$.

$$\frac{2}{5}+\frac{1}{7}+\frac{1}{3}=\frac{42}{105}+\frac{15}{105}+\frac{35}{105}-\frac{92}{105}$$

The remaining 26 monsters represent $\dfrac{13}{105}$ of the total monsters at the convention:

$$26=\frac{13}{105}m$$

$$\frac{105}{13}\times26=m$$

$$105\times2=m$$

$$210=m$$

4. $\dfrac{17}{24}$ **(or any equivalent fraction).** The textbook costs $\dfrac{1}{4}$ of Devora's money. The notebook costs $\dfrac{1}{6}$ *of that amount,*

or $\dfrac{1}{6}\left(\dfrac{1}{4}\right)=\dfrac{1}{24}$ of Devora's money. Thus, Devora has spent $\dfrac{1}{4}+\dfrac{1}{24}=\dfrac{6}{24}+\dfrac{1}{24}=\dfrac{7}{24}$ of her money. Subtract from 1 to

get the fraction she has left: $1-\dfrac{7}{24}=\dfrac{24}{24}-\dfrac{7}{24}=\dfrac{17}{24}$ .

Alternatively, pick a value for Devora's money. (Look at the denominators in the problem—4 and 6—and pick a value that both numbers go into evenly.) For instance, say Devora has $120. She would spend $\frac{1}{4}$, or $30, on the textbook. She would spend $\frac{1}{6}$ *of that* amount, or $5, on the notebook. She would have spent $35 and would have $85 left, and thus $\frac{85}{120}$ of her money left. Reduce $\frac{85}{120}$ to get $\frac{17}{24}$, or enter $\frac{85}{120}$ in the boxes.

5. **$0.3482 \times 10^{-2}$, $34.82 \times 10^{-4}$, and $3{,}482 \times 10^{-6}$ only.** Note that the first answer is negative, so it cannot be correct. For the second answer, move the decimal 2 places to the left: $0.3482 \times 10^{-2} = 0.003482$ (correct). For the third answer, move the decimal 4 places to the *right* (since the exponent is positive)—this move makes the number much greater and cannot be correct. For the fourth answer, move the decimal 4 places to the left: $34.82 \times 10^{-4} = 0.003482$ (correct). For the fifth answer, move the decimal 6 places to the left: $3{,}482 \times 10^{-6} = 0.003482$ (correct).

6. **$0.00001212 \times 10^3$ only.** First, simplify $12.12 \times 10^{-3} = 0.01212$. Now, test which answers are equal to this value. The first answer is negative, so it cannot be correct. The second answer is 0.012 and is therefore incorrect (the end has been "chopped off," so the number is not the same value). The third answer is $0.00001212 \times 10^3 = 0.01212$ and is correct. The fourth answer is $0.01212 \times 10^3 = 12.12$ and is not correct.

7. **(A).** Translate the words into math. If $x$ means "how many," then "how many fifths" is $\frac{x}{5}$:

$$5 = \frac{x}{5} \times 10$$

$$5 = \frac{10x}{5}$$

$$25 = 10x$$

$$\frac{25}{10} = x$$

$$x = 2.5$$

8. **(A).** Simplify each quantity by breaking down to primes and canceling factors:

Quantity A: $\dfrac{75}{4^2} \times \dfrac{3^2}{45} \times \dfrac{2^4}{45} = \dfrac{3 \times 5 \times 5}{\left(2^2\right)^2} \times \dfrac{3^2}{3 \times 3 \times 5} \times \dfrac{2^4}{3 \times 3 \times 5} = \dfrac{2^4 \times 3^3 \times 5^2}{2^4 \times 3^4 \times 5^2} = \dfrac{1}{3}$

Quantity B: $\dfrac{3^2}{4^2} \times \dfrac{2^2}{5^2} \times \dfrac{10}{3} = \dfrac{3^2}{\left(2^2\right)^2} \times \dfrac{2^2}{5^2} \times \dfrac{2 \times 5}{3} = \dfrac{2^3 \times 3^2 \times 5}{2^4 \times 3 \times 5^2} = \dfrac{3}{2 \times 5} = \dfrac{3}{10}$

Since $\frac{1}{3} > \frac{3}{10}$, Quantity A is greater. You can compare these fractions by making a common denominator, by cross-multiplying, or by comparing the decimal equivalents 0.333 (repeating infinitely) and 0.3.

If there are identical factors in each quantity in the same position (e.g., $3^2$ on top or $4^2$ on bottom), then you can save time by canceling those factors first from both quantities.

**MANHATTAN**
PREP

9. **(D).** This question is *not* asking for $\frac{1}{4}$ of $\frac{5}{12}$. Rather, $\frac{1}{4}$ and $\frac{5}{12}$ are fractions of the same number (the number of students in the whole class). A good way to avoid this confusion is to plug in a number for the class. Pick 12, as it is divisible by both 4 and 12 (the denominators of the given fractions).

Class = 12
Girls = 5
Girls who take Spanish = 3 (which is $\frac{1}{4}$ of all the students in the class)

The question asks for the number of girls who take Spanish over the number of girls. Thus, the answer is $\frac{3}{5}$.

10. $\frac{13}{15}$ **(or any equivalent fraction).** If $\frac{1}{5}$ of all the cars are red, and $\frac{2}{3}$ of *those* are convertibles, then the fraction of all the cars that are red convertibles = $\left(\frac{1}{5}\right)\left(\frac{2}{3}\right) = \frac{2}{15}$. Since you want all of the cars that are NOT red convertibles, subtract $\frac{2}{15}$ from 1 to get $\frac{13}{15}$.

11. **(B).** If two pies are cut into 16 parts, each pie is cut into eighths. Thus, $\frac{1}{8}$ of a pie is was divided among three people. "One-third of one-eighth" = $\left(\frac{1}{3}\right)\left(\frac{1}{8}\right) = \frac{1}{24}$.

12. **(C).** Transform Quantity B by splitting the numerator:

$$\frac{2xy+1}{xy} = \frac{2xy}{xy} + \frac{1}{xy}$$

Next, cancel the common factor $xy$ from top and bottom of the first fraction:

$\frac{2xy}{xy} + \frac{1}{xy} = 2 + \frac{1}{xy}$, which is the same as Quantity A.

Alternatively, you can transform Quantity A by turning 2 into a fraction with the same denominator ($xy$) as the second term.

$2 + \frac{1}{xy} = \frac{2xy}{xy} + \frac{1}{xy} = \frac{2xy+1}{xy}$, which is the same as Quantity B. Thus, the quantities are equal.

13. **(B).** Simplify each quantity from the inside out.

$$\text{Quantity A: } \frac{\frac{1}{4}}{\frac{2}{3}-\left(\frac{1-2}{\frac{1}{3}}\right)} = \frac{\frac{1}{4}}{\frac{2}{3}-\left(\frac{-1}{\frac{1}{3}}\right)} = \frac{\frac{1}{4}}{\frac{2}{3}-(-3)} = \frac{\frac{1}{4}}{\left(\frac{2}{3}+3\right)} = \frac{\frac{1}{4}}{\left(\frac{2}{3}+\frac{9}{3}\right)} = \frac{\frac{1}{4}}{\frac{11}{3}} = \frac{1}{4}\times\frac{3}{11} = \frac{3}{44}$$

$$\text{Quantity B: } \frac{\frac{1}{3}}{\frac{1}{4}-\left(\frac{3-4}{\frac{2}{3}}\right)} = \frac{\frac{1}{3}}{\frac{1}{4}-\left(\frac{-1}{\frac{2}{3}}\right)} = \frac{\frac{1}{3}}{\frac{1}{4}-\left(\frac{-3}{2}\right)} = \frac{\frac{1}{3}}{\left(\frac{1}{4}+\frac{3}{2}\right)} = \frac{\frac{1}{3}}{\left(\frac{1}{4}+\frac{6}{4}\right)} = \frac{\frac{1}{3}}{\frac{7}{4}} = \frac{1}{3}\times\frac{4}{7} = \frac{4}{21}$$

Since Quantity B has a greater numerator *and* a smaller denominator, it is greater than Quantity A. This rule works for any positive fractions. You could also use the calculator to compute the decimal equivalents.

14. **(C).** Whether you choose fractions or decimals, put $\frac{3}{4}$ and 0.375 in the same form to more easily compare. Either way, 0.75 is double 0.375 (or $\frac{3}{4}$ is double $\frac{3}{8}$). Since store *B* has twice as many apples, 0.375 of store *B*'s apples is the same number as 0.75 of store *A*'s apples.

Alternatively, pick numbers such that store B has twice as many apples. If store A has 4 apples and store B has 8 apples, then store A would have $\left(\frac{3}{4}\right)(4) = 3$ red apples and store B would have $(0.375)(8) = 3$ red apples. The two quantities are equal.

15. $\frac{13}{40}$ **(or any equivalent fraction).** Manuel ate $\frac{1}{4}$ of one-half of the entire pot of soup and then $\frac{2}{5}$ of the other half of the entire pot of soup. As math:

$$\frac{1}{4}\left(\frac{1}{2}\right) + \frac{2}{5}\left(\frac{1}{2}\right) = \frac{1}{8} + \frac{1}{5} = \frac{13}{40}$$

Alternatively, pick numbers, ideally a large number with many factors. For example, say there are 120 ounces of soup. Each bowl would then have 60 ounces. Manuel ate $\frac{1}{4}$ of one bowl (15 ounces) and $\frac{2}{5}$ of the other bowl (24 ounces). In total, he ate 39 ounces out of 120. While $\frac{39}{120}$ would be counted as correct, reducing $\frac{39}{120}$ (by dividing both numerator and denominator by 3) yields $\frac{13}{40}$, the answer reached via the other method above.

16. **(D).** To divide by a fraction, multiply by its reciprocal:

$$\frac{\frac{ab}{c}}{\frac{cd}{a}} = \frac{ab}{c} \times \frac{a}{cd} = \frac{a^2 b}{c^2 d}$$

17. **(C).** Pull squares out of the square roots and cancel common factors:

$$\left(\frac{\sqrt{12}}{5}\right)\left(\frac{\sqrt{60}}{2^4}\right)\left(\frac{\sqrt{45}}{3^2}\right) = \frac{2\sqrt{3}}{5} \times \frac{2\sqrt{15}}{2^4} \times \frac{3\sqrt{5}}{3^2} = \frac{\sqrt{3}}{5} \times \frac{\sqrt{15}}{2^2} \times \frac{\sqrt{5}}{3}$$

Since $\sqrt{15} = \sqrt{3}\sqrt{5}$,

$$\frac{\sqrt{3}}{5} \times \frac{\sqrt{15}}{2^2} \times \frac{\sqrt{5}}{3} = \frac{\sqrt{3}}{5} \times \frac{\sqrt{3}\sqrt{5}}{2^2} \times \frac{\sqrt{5}}{3} = \frac{3 \times 5}{5 \times 2^2 \times 3} = \frac{1}{2^2} = \frac{1}{4}$$

**MANHATTAN**
PREP

Alternatively, in the calculator multiply $12 \times 60 \times 45 = 32{,}400$, then take the square root to get 180 for the numerator. The denominator is $5 \times 2 \times 2 \times 2 \times 2 \times 3 \times 3 = 720$. Finally, calculate $\dfrac{180}{720} = 0.25$, which is $\dfrac{1}{4}$.

18. **(C).** Combine the four fractions by finding a common denominator ($8xy$, which is also suggested by the answer choices):

$$\frac{-1}{2x} - \frac{1}{4y} + \frac{1}{xy} + \frac{1}{8} = \frac{-1(4y)}{2x(4y)} - \frac{1(2x)}{4y(2x)} + \frac{1(8)}{xy(8)} + \frac{1(xy)}{8(xy)}$$

$$= \frac{-4y}{8xy} - \frac{2x}{8xy} + \frac{8}{8xy} + \frac{xy}{8xy} = \frac{xy - 4y - 2x + 8}{8xy}$$

Now the key is to factor the top expression correctly:

$$xy - 4y - 2x + 8 = (x-4)(y-2)$$

It is a good idea to FOIL the expression on the right to make sure it matches the left-hand side. Or, FOIL the numerators of the choices to see which matches the distributed form of the numerator above.

Finally, $\dfrac{xy - 4y - 2x + 8}{8xy} = \dfrac{(x-4)(y-2)}{8xy}$.

19. **(A).** Since the decimal rounds to 12.16, the thousandths digit $x$ must be 5, 6, 7, 8, or 9. All of these possibilities are greater than 4.

20. $\dfrac{1}{3}$ **(or any equivalent fraction).** One option is to punch the whole numerator and the whole denominator into the calculator and submit each product. If you're very careful, that will work. However, it might be wise to try canceling some common factors out of the fraction, to save time and to avoid errors. It's fine to switch to the calculator whenever the cancelations aren't obvious:

$$\frac{(17^2)\cancel{(22)}\overset{2}{}(38)(41)(91)}{(19)(34)(123)\cancel{(11)}(119)(26)} = \frac{(17^2)(2)(\cancel{38})\overset{2}{}\,(41)(91)}{\cancel{(19)}(34)(123)(119)(26)}$$

$$= \frac{(17^2)(2)(2)(41)(91)}{(\cancel{34})\underset{2}{}(123)(119)(26)} = \frac{(17)(2)(2)\cancel{(41)}(91)}{(2)(\cancel{123})\underset{3}{}\,(119)(26)}$$

$$= \frac{(17)(2)(2)(\cancel{91})\overset{7}{}}{(2)(3)(119)(\cancel{26})\underset{2}{}} = \frac{\cancel{(17)}(2)(2)\cancel{(7)}}{(2)(3)(\cancel{17} \times \cancel{7})(2)}$$

$$= \frac{\cancel{(2)}\cancel{(2)}}{\cancel{(2)}(3)\cancel{(2)}} = \frac{1}{3}$$

21. $\dfrac{91}{12}$ **(or any equivalent fraction).** First, turn the decimal into a sum of two pieces, to separate the repeating portion:

$$7.58\overline{3} = 7.58 + 0.00\overline{3}$$

Deal with each piece in turn. Like any other terminating decimal, 7.58 can be written as a fraction with a power of 10 in the denominator:

$$7.58 = \frac{758}{100}$$

The repeating portion is similar to $0.\overline{3} = 0.3333... = \frac{1}{3}$

So $0.00\overline{3}$ is just $\frac{1}{3}$, moved by a couple of decimal places: $0.00\overline{3} = (0.\overline{3})(0.01) = \left(\frac{1}{3}\right)\left(\frac{1}{100}\right) = \frac{1}{300}$.

Finally, write the original decimal as a sum of fractions, and then combine those fractions:

$$7.58\overline{3} = 7.58 + 0.00\overline{3} = \frac{758}{100} + \frac{1}{300} = \frac{758 \times 3}{300} + \frac{1}{300} = \frac{2,275}{300}$$

Enter $\frac{2,275}{300}$ unreduced, or you can reduce it to $\frac{91}{12}$.

22. **(A).** Both quantities are positive square roots, so just compare the underlying numbers.

Quantity A: $\dfrac{(25)(8)}{(10)(15)} = 1.3\overline{3}$

Quantity B: $\dfrac{(51)(23)}{(46)(34)} = 0.75$

The square root of $1.3\overline{3}$ (or $\frac{4}{3}$) is greater than the square root of 0.75 (or $\frac{3}{4}$).

23. **(B).** The square root of a fraction is the square root of the top over the square root of the bottom:

$$\sqrt{\frac{3}{2}} - \sqrt{\frac{2}{3}} = \frac{\sqrt{3}}{\sqrt{2}} - \frac{\sqrt{2}}{\sqrt{3}}$$

Then make a common denominator: $\sqrt{3}\sqrt{2} = \sqrt{6}$.

$$\frac{\sqrt{3}}{\sqrt{2}} - \frac{\sqrt{2}}{\sqrt{3}} = \frac{\sqrt{3}\sqrt{3}}{\sqrt{3}\sqrt{2}} - \frac{\sqrt{2}\sqrt{2}}{\sqrt{3}\sqrt{2}} = \frac{3}{\sqrt{6}} - \frac{2}{\sqrt{6}} = \frac{1}{\sqrt{6}}$$

24. **(B).** Since $\frac{3}{4}$ of the cookies have nuts and $\frac{1}{3}$ of the cookies *also* have fruit, subtract $\frac{3}{4}$ from $\frac{1}{3}$ to get all the cookies with nuts but no fruit:

$$\frac{3}{4} - \frac{1}{3} = \frac{9}{12} - \frac{4}{12} = \frac{5}{12}$$

Alternatively, pick numbers. Since you will be dividing by 4 and 3, pick a number divisible by 4 and 3. If there are 12 cookies, then 9 have nuts and 4 of them have nuts *and* fruit, so 5—and thus $\frac{5}{12}$ of the total—would have nuts but no fruit.

**MANHATTAN**
PREP

25. **(B).** If a question refers to fractions of different numbers that are *also* related by a fraction, try plugging in numbers. Since there are $\frac{2}{3}$ as many juniors as seniors, some convenient numbers are:

Juniors = 20

Seniors = 30

Juniors going on trip = $\frac{1}{4}(20) = 5$

Seniors going on trip = $\frac{2}{3}(30) = 20$

Out of 50 total students, 25 are going on the trip, so 25 are NOT going on the trip. The answer is $\frac{25}{50} = \frac{1}{2}$.

26. $\frac{11}{14}$ **(or any equivalent fraction).** If a question refers to fractions of different numbers that are *also* related by a fraction or percent, try plugging in numbers. Since there are 40% as many men as women, some convenient numbers are:

Men = 40

Women = 100

Women who speak Spanish = $\frac{4}{5}(100) = 80$

Men who speak Spanish = $\frac{3}{4}(40) = 30$

The group has 140 total people and 110 Spanish speakers. The answer is $\frac{110}{140} = \frac{11}{14}$ (you are not required to reduce, as long as your answer is correct and fits in the box).

27. **(D).** Cancel factors on top and bottom of each product:

Quantity A: $\frac{a^2 b}{cd^2} \times \frac{d^3}{abc} = \frac{a^2 bd^3}{abc^2 d^2} = \frac{ad}{c^2}$

Quantity B: $\frac{d^2}{bc} \times \frac{ab^2}{bd} = \frac{ab^2 d^2}{b^2 cd} = \frac{ad}{c}$

The two quantities differ in the denominators: Quantity A has $c^2$, while Quantity B has $c$. It cannot be determined which quantity is greater, because for some values (e.g., $c = 2$) $c^2$ is greater than $c$, and for others (e.g., $c = 0.5$) $c^2$ is less than $c$.

28. **(C).** Simpler explanation could avoid FOILing. Consider simplifying within parentheses, then multiplying out.

$$\left(\frac{1}{2} + \frac{1}{m}\right)(m+2) = \frac{1}{2}(m) + \frac{1}{2}(2) + \frac{1}{m}(m) + \frac{1}{m}(2)$$

$$= \frac{m}{2} + 1 + 1 + \frac{2}{m} = \frac{m}{2} + 2 + \frac{2}{m}$$

Make a common denominator ($2m$) to sum these terms (also, note that this makes Quantity A similar in form to Quantity B):

$$\frac{m}{2} + 2 + \frac{2}{m} = \frac{m(m)}{2(m)} + 2\left(\frac{2m}{2m}\right) + \frac{(2)2}{(2)m} = \frac{m^2 + 4m + 4}{2m}$$

Since the quantities now have the same denominators and $(m + 2)^2 = m^2 + 4m + 4$, the two quantities are equal.

29. $\dfrac{7(2^3)}{3^3 - 7}$ **and** $\dfrac{-11^2 - 11^3}{(30)(44)}$ **only.** To start, compute each value:

$$\frac{7(2^3)}{3^3 - 7} = \frac{7 \times 8}{27 - 7} = \frac{56}{20} = 2.8$$

$$\frac{2^4}{1+2+3+4} = \frac{16}{10} = 1.6$$

$$\frac{3}{11} \div \frac{6}{11} = \frac{3}{11} \times \frac{11}{6} = \frac{3}{6} = \frac{1}{2} = 0.5$$

$$\frac{-2^3 3^2}{2^2 5^2} = \frac{-8 \times 9}{10^2} = \frac{-72}{100} = -0.72$$

$$\frac{-11^2 - 11^3}{(30)(44)} = \frac{-11^2(1 + 11)}{(30)(44)} = \frac{-121(12)}{(30)(44)} = \frac{-1,452}{1,320} = -1.1$$

The question asks for exactly two values that sum to a number between 1 and 2.

No two of the positive numbers sum to a number between 1 and 2. So the answers must be a positive and a negative. The only two possibilities that work are 2.8 and −1.1.

30. $\dfrac{-18}{19}$, $\dfrac{23}{-22}$, **and** $\dfrac{17}{-16}$ **only.** The product of three of the numbers must be less than −1. You can brute-force the calculation by trying all possible products, but use the relative size of the numbers to reduce the effort.

Notice that the four answer choices are all very close to −1, but some are greater than −1, and others are less than −1. To get the exact order, you can use the calculator, or you can think about the difference between each fraction and −1:

$$\frac{-15}{17} = \frac{-17}{17} + \frac{2}{17} = -1 + \frac{2}{17}$$

$$\frac{-18}{19} = \frac{-19}{19} + \frac{1}{19} = -1 + \frac{1}{19}, \text{ which is less than the previous number (since } \frac{2}{17} > \frac{1}{19})$$

$$\frac{23}{-22} = \frac{-23}{22} = \frac{-22}{22} - \frac{1}{22} = -1 - \frac{1}{22}$$

$$\frac{17}{-16} = \frac{-17}{16} = \frac{-16}{16} - \frac{1}{16} = -1 - \frac{1}{16}, \text{ a greater decrease from −1 than the previous number}$$

**MANHATTAN**
PREP

So the order of the original numbers relative to each other and to $-1$ is this: $\dfrac{17}{-16} < \dfrac{23}{-22} < -1 < \dfrac{-18}{19} < \dfrac{-15}{17}$.

Try multiplying the three lowest numbers first, since they will produce the lowest product. Only *one* product of the three numbers can be less than $-1$ (or there would be more than one right answer), so the three numbers must be as follows, as you can check on the calculator:

$$\frac{17}{-16} \times \frac{23}{-22} \times \frac{-18}{19} \approx -1.052... < -1$$

31. **(B).** First, simplify inside the parentheses. Then, square and add:

$$\left(\frac{8}{3}\right)^2 + \left(\frac{10}{3}\right)^2$$

$$\frac{64}{9} + \frac{100}{9}$$

The answer is $\dfrac{164}{9}$.

32. **(D).** If the left-hand side of the equation is equal to 1, then the numerator and denominator must be equal. Thus, the denominator must also be equal to 3:

$$\frac{m+1}{m} + 1 = 3$$

$$\frac{m+1}{m} = 2$$

$$m + 1 = 2m$$

$$1 = m$$

Alternatively, plug in each answer choice (into both instances of $m$ in the original equation), and stop as soon as one of them works.

33. **(B).** Cancel common factors in each quantity and substitute in for $rs$:

Quantity A: $\dfrac{2r\sqrt{12}}{r^2 s\sqrt{72}} = \dfrac{2\sqrt{12}}{rs\sqrt{72}} = \dfrac{2\sqrt{12}}{\sqrt{3}\sqrt{72}} = \dfrac{2\sqrt{4}}{\sqrt{72}} = \dfrac{2\times 2}{\sqrt{36}\sqrt{2}} = \dfrac{4}{6\sqrt{2}} = \dfrac{2}{3\sqrt{2}}$

Quantity B: $\dfrac{14rs^2}{42s} = \dfrac{14rs}{42} = \dfrac{14\sqrt{3}}{3\times 14} = \dfrac{\sqrt{3}}{3}$

At this point, use the calculator, or compare the two quantities with an "invisible inequality":

$$\frac{2}{3\sqrt{2}} \;\text{??}\; \frac{\sqrt{3}}{3}$$

Since everything is positive, it is safe to cross-multiply:

$$2 \times 3 \;\text{??}\; 3\sqrt{2}\sqrt{3}$$

Now square both sides. Since everything is positive, the invisible inequality is unaffected:

$$(2 \times 3)^2 \; ?? \; 3^2 \times 2 \times 3$$

$$36 \; ?? \; 54$$

Since $36 < 54$, Quantity B is greater.

34. **(A).** To divide fractions, multiply by the reciprocal:

Quantity A: $\dfrac{\sqrt{10}}{\sqrt{8}} \div \dfrac{\sqrt{9}}{\sqrt{10}} = \dfrac{\sqrt{10}}{\sqrt{8}} \times \dfrac{\sqrt{10}}{\sqrt{9}} = \dfrac{10}{\sqrt{72}} = \dfrac{10}{6\sqrt{2}} = \dfrac{5}{3\sqrt{2}}$

Quantity B: $\dfrac{\sqrt{11}}{\sqrt{9}} \div \dfrac{\sqrt{10}}{\sqrt{11}} = \dfrac{\sqrt{11}}{\sqrt{9}} \times \dfrac{\sqrt{11}}{\sqrt{10}} = \dfrac{11}{3\sqrt{10}}$

Square both quantities to get rid of the square roots:

Quantity A: $\left(\dfrac{5}{3\sqrt{2}}\right)^2 = \dfrac{5^2}{3^2 2} = \dfrac{25}{18}$

Quantity B: $\left(\dfrac{11}{3\sqrt{10}}\right)^2 = \dfrac{11^2}{3^2 10} = \dfrac{121}{90}$

At this point, use the calculator. Quantity A is approximately 1.389, whereas Quantity B is approximately 1.344.

35. **(A).** To determine which fraction is greatest, cancel common terms from all five fractions until the remaining values are small enough for the calculator. Note that every choice has at least one 5 on the bottom, so cancel $5^1$ from all of the denominators.

Note also that every fraction has a power of 2 on the bottom, so convert 16, 32, 512, $4^6$, and $2^{11}$ to powers of 2. Since $16 = 2^4$, $32 = 2^5$, $512 = 2^9$, and $4^6 = (2^2)^6 = 2^{12}$, the modified choices are:

(A) $\dfrac{7}{(2^4)(5)}$

(B) $\dfrac{5}{(2^5)(5^3)}$

(C) $\dfrac{30}{(2^9)(5^2)}$

(D) $\dfrac{5}{(2^{12})}$

(E) $\dfrac{4}{(2^{11})(5)}$

Since every choice has at least $2^4$ on the bottom, cancel $2^4$ from all 5 choices:

(A) $\dfrac{7}{5}$

(B) $\dfrac{5}{(2)(5^3)}$

(C) $\dfrac{30}{(2^5)(5^2)}$

(D) $\dfrac{5}{2^8}$

(E) $\dfrac{4}{(2^7)(5)}$

Note that the numerators also have some powers of 2 and 5 that will cancel out with the bottoms of each of the fractions. In choice (C), $30 = (2)(3)(5)$:

(A) $\dfrac{7}{5}$

(B) $\dfrac{1}{(2)(5^2)}$

(C) $\dfrac{3}{(2^4)(5)}$

(D) $\dfrac{5}{2^8}$

(E) $\dfrac{1}{(2^5)(5)}$

These values are now small enough for the calculator. Note that the GRE calculator does not have an exponent button—to get $2^8$, you must multiply 2 by itself 8 times. This is why you should memorize powers of 2 up to $2^{10}$, and powers of 3, 4, and 5 up to about the 4th power.

(A)  1.4

(B)  0.02

(C)  0.0375

(D)  0.01953125

(E)  0.00625

Alternatively, you might notice in the previous step that only the choice (A) simplified fraction is greater than 1; in all the others, the denominator is greater than the numerator.

36. **(D).** Without knowing the signs of the variables, do not assume that $m$ is greater than $n$. While it certainly *could* be (e.g., $m = 4$, $n = 2$, and $p = 1$), if $p$ is negative, the reverse will be true (e.g., $m = 2$, $n = 4$, and $p = -1$).

37. **(A).** This expression is complicated, but the answer choices are just numbers, so the variables must cancel. This, and the relative lack of constraints on the variables, suggests that you can plug in values for $x$ and $y$ and then solve.

Try $x = 2$ and $y = 3$. For these numbers, $2x \neq y$ and $5x \neq 4y$ as required. Any other numbers that also follow those constraints would yield the same result below:

$$\frac{\frac{5x-4y}{2x-y}}{\frac{3y}{y-2x}+5} = \frac{\frac{5(2)-4(3)}{2(2)-(3)}}{\frac{3(3)}{(3)-2(2)}+5} = \frac{\frac{10-12}{4-3}}{\frac{9}{3-4}+5} = \frac{\frac{-2}{1}}{\frac{9}{-1}+5} = \frac{-2}{-9+5} = \frac{-2}{-4} = \frac{1}{2}$$

38. **(E).** To divide fractions, multiply by the reciprocal of the divisor:

$$\frac{39^2}{2^4} \div \frac{13^3}{4^2} = \frac{39^2}{2^4} \times \frac{4^2}{13^3}$$

Now break down to primes and cancel common factors:

$$\frac{39^2}{2^4} \times \frac{4^2}{13^3} = \frac{(3 \times 13)^2 \times (2^2)^2}{2^4 \times 13^3} = \frac{3^2 \times 13^2 \times 2^4}{2^4 \times 13^3} = \frac{3^2}{13} = \frac{9}{13}$$

**MANHATTAN**
PREP

# Chapter 12 *of*

5 lb. Book of GRE® Practice Problems

# Percents

# In This Chapter...

# Percents

For questions in the Quantitative Comparison format ("Quantity A" and "Quantity B" given), the answer choices are always as follows:

(A)   Quantity A is greater.
(B)   Quantity B is greater.
(C)   The two quantities are equal.
(D)   The relationship cannot be determined from the information given.

For questions followed by a numeric entry box [          ], you are to enter your own answer in the box. For questions followed

by a fraction-style numeric entry box $\frac{\boxed{\phantom{xx}}}{\boxed{\phantom{xx}}}$, you are to enter your answer in the form of a fraction. You are not required to

reduce fractions. For example, if the answer is $\frac{1}{4}$, you may enter $\frac{25}{100}$ or any equivalent fraction.

All numbers used are real numbers. All figures are assumed to lie in a plane unless otherwise indicated. Geometric figures are not necessarily drawn to scale. You should assume, however, that lines that appear to be straight are actually straight, points on a line are in the order shown, and all geometric objects are in the relative positions shown. Coordinate systems, such as $xy$-planes and number lines, as well as graphical data presentations, such as bar charts, circle graphs, and line graphs, *are* drawn to scale. A symbol that appears more than once in a question has the same meaning throughout the question.

|  | **Quantity A** | **Quantity B** |
|---|---|---|
| 1. | 50 as a percent of 30 | The percent increase from 30 to 80 |

2.  If Ken's salary were 20% higher, it would be 20% less than Lorena's. If Lorena's salary is $60,000, what is Ken's salary?

    (A)  $36,000

    (B)  $40,000

    (C)  $42,500

    (D)  $42,850

    (E)  $45,000

Greta's salary was $x$ thousand dollars per year, then she received a $y$% raise.

Annika's salary was $y$ thousand dollars per year, then she received an $x$% raise.

$x$ and $y$ are positive integers.

|  | **Quantity A** | **Quantity B** |
|---|---|---|
| 3. | The dollar amount of Greta's raise | The dollar amount of Annika's raise |

Roselba's annual income exceeds twice Jane's annual income and both pay the same positive percent of their respective incomes in tranportation fees.

|  | **Quantity A** | **Quantity B** |
|---|---|---|
| 4. | The annual amount Jane pays in transportation fees | Half the annual amount Roselba pays in transportation fees |

An item's price was discounted by 16%. Later, the discounted price was increased by 16%.

|  | **Quantity A** | **Quantity B** |
|---|---|---|
| 5. | The original price | The price after the discount and increase |

6.  12 is 5 percent of what number?

7.  7 percent of 9 is what percent of 7?

%

8.  What percent of 13 is 20 percent of 195?

%

9.  25 percent of 30 is 75 percent of what number?

10. What is the percent increase from 50 to 60?

%  increase

11. If x were reduced by 30%, the resulting number would be 63. What is the value of x?

12. What is 230% of 15% of 400?

**MANHATTAN**
PREP

13. 45% of 80 is $x$% more than 24. What is the value of $x$?

    ┌─────────────┐
    │             │
    └─────────────┘

14. 10 percent of 30 percent of what number is 200 percent of 6?

    ┌─────────────┐
    │             │
    └─────────────┘

15. If $y \neq 0$, what percent of $y$ percent of 50 is 40 percent of $y$?

    ┌─────────────┐
    │             │ %
    └─────────────┘

16. If $a \neq 0$, 200 percent of 4 percent of $a$ is what percent of $\frac{a}{2}$?

    ┌─────────────┐
    │             │ %
    └─────────────┘

17. If positive integer $m$ were increased by 20%, decreased by 25%, and then increased by 60%, the resulting number would be what percent of $m$?

    ┌─────────────┐
    │             │ %
    └─────────────┘

|  | **Quantity A** | **Quantity B** |
|---|---|---|
| 18. | The price of an item after five consecutive 10% discounts are applied | 50% of the price of the item |

19. Raymond borrowed $450 at 0% interest. If he pays back 0.5% of the total amount every 7 days, beginning exactly 7 days after the loan was disbursed, and has thus far paid back $18, with the most recent payment made today, how many days ago did he borrow the money?

    (A)   6
    (B)   8
    (C)   25
    (D)   42
    (E)   56

At a warehouse, an order was shipped out, reducing the number of parts in inventory by half. Then a shipment of parts was received, increasing the current number of parts in inventory by 50%.

|  | **Quantity A** | **Quantity B** |
|---|---|---|
| 20. | The number of parts in inventory before the two shipments | The number of parts in inventory after the two shipments |

A house valued at $200,000 two years ago lost 40% of its value in the first year and a further 20% of that reduced value during the second year.

|  | **Quantity A** | **Quantity B** |
|---|---|---|
| 21. | The current value of the house | $100,000 |

22. 1% of 200% of 360 is what percent of 0.1% of 60?

[    ] %

23. If Mary has half as many cents as Nora has dollars, then Nora has what percent more cents than Mary does? (100 cents = 1 dollar)

(A)    100%

(B)    200%

(C)    1,990%

(D)    19,900%

(E)    20,000%

24. The number that is 50% greater than 60 is what percent less than the number that is 20% less than 150?

(A)    5%

(B)    10%

(C)    15%

(D)    20%

(E)    25%

25. A cockroach population doubles every 3 days. In 30 days, by what percent would a cockroach population increase?

(A)       900%

(B)     1,000%

(C)     9,999%

(D)   102,300%

(E)   102,400%

26. After a 15% discount, the price of a computer was $612. What was the price of the computer before the discount?

    (A) $108.00
    (B) $520.20
    (C) $703.80
    (D) $720.00
    (E) $744.00

At the end of April, the price of fuel was 40% greater than the price at the beginning of the month. At the end of May, the price of fuel was 30% greater than the price at the end of April.

| **Quantity A** | **Quantity B** |
|---|---|
| The price increase in April | The price increase in May |

27.

28. Aloysius spends 50% of his income on rent, utilities, and insurance, and 20% on food. If he spends 30% of the remainder on video games and has no other expenditures, what percent of his income is left after all of the expenditures?

    (A) 30%
    (B) 21%
    (C) 20%
    (D) 9%
    (E) 0%

29. In 1970, company X had 2,000 employees, 15% of whom were women, and 10% of these women were executives. In 2012, the company had 12,000 employees, 45% of whom were women. If 40% of those women were executives, what was the percent increase in the number of women executives from 1970 to 2012?

    [       ] %

30. 75% of all the boys and 48% of all the girls at Smith High School take civics. If there are 20% fewer boys than there are girls in the school, what percent of all the students take civics?

    [       ] %

Airline A and airline B both previously charged $400 for a certain flight. Airline A then reduced its price by 25%. Airline B responded by reducing its price by 55% but adding $150 in fees. Then, airline A increased its reduced price by 10%.

|  | Quantity A | Quantity B |
|---|---|---|
| 31. | The final price of the flight on airline A | The final price of the flight on airline B |

$p$ is 75% of $q$ and $p$ equals $2r$.

|  | Quantity A | Quantity B |
|---|---|---|
| 32. | $0.375q$ | $r$ |

$0 < x < 100$

|  | Quantity A | Quantity B |
|---|---|---|
| 33. | $x$% of 0.5% of 40,000 | 0.05% of 2,000% of $40x$ |

**Profit Per Student (in Dollars) at Dan's Dojo, 2000–2004**

| 2000 | 60 |
|---|---|
| 2001 | 80 |
| 2002 | 80 |
| 2003 | 100 |
| 2004 | 162 |

34. At Dan's Dojo, the percent increase from 2004 to 2005 (not shown) was the same as the percent increase from 2000 to 2001. What was the profit per student for 2005?

$ ☐

35. If $x$ is 0.5% of $y$, then $y$ is what percent of $x$?

    (A)     199%

    (B)     200%

    (C)     2,000%

    (D)     19,900%

    (E)     20,000%

**MANHATTAN**
PREP

Bill pays 20% tax on his gross salary of $5,000 each month and spends 25% of the remaining amount on rent.

|  | **Quantity A** | **Quantity B** |
|---|---|---|
| 36. | The monthly tax paid on Bill's salary | The rent paid monthly by Bill |

37. Four people shared a dinner with an $80 bill and tipped the waiter 15 percent of this amount. If each person contributed equally to paying the bill and tip, how much did each person pay?

    (A) $20.00

    (B) $23.00

    (C) $23.75

    (D) $24.00

    (E) $25.00

The price of a certain stock rose by 25 percent and then decreased by $y$ percent. After the decrease, the stock was back to its original price.

|  | **Quantity A** | **Quantity B** |
|---|---|---|
| 38. | $y$ | 25 |

39. A chemist is mixing a solution of acetone and water. She currently has 30 ounces mixed, 10 of which are acetone. How many ounces of acetone should she add to her current mixture to attain a 50/50 mixture of acetone and water if no additional water is added?

    (A)   2.5

    (B)   5

    (C)   10

    (D)   15

    (E)   20

By the end of July, a certain baseball team had played 80% of the total games to be played that season and had won 50% of those games. Of the remaining games for the season, the team won 60%.

|  | **Quantity A** | **Quantity B** |
|---|---|---|
| 40. | Percent of total games won for the season | 52% |

|  | **Quantity A** | **Quantity B** |
|---|---|---|
| 41. | 0.4 percent of 4 percent of 1.25 | 0.002 |

42. Jane has a 40-ounce mixture of apple juice and seltzer that is 30% apple juice. If she pours 10 more ounces of apple juice into the mixture, what percent of the mixture will be seltzer?

   (A)  33%
   (B)  44%
   (C)  50%
   (D)  56%
   (E)  67%

Half of the shirts in a closet are white and 30% of the remaining shirts are gray.

|   | **Quantity A** | **Quantity B** |
|---|---|---|
| 43. | The percent of the shirts in the closet that are not white or gray. | 20% |

The length and width of a painted rectangle were each increased by 10%.

|   | **Quantity A** | **Quantity B** |
|---|---|---|
| 44. | The percent increase in the area of the painted rectangle | 10% |

45. If 35% of x equals 140, what is 20% of x?

   (A)   9.8
   (B)   39.2
   (C)   80
   (D)   320
   (E)   400

46. A population of a colony of bacteria increases by 20 percent every 3 minutes. If at 9:00am the colony had a population of 144,000, what was the population of the colony at 8:54am?

   (A)  100,000
   (B)  112,000
   (C)  120,000
   (D)  121,000
   (E)  136,000

The price of an item is greater than $90 and less than $150.

|              | **Quantity A** | **Quantity B** |
|---|---|---|
| 47. | The price of the item after a 10%-off discount and then a $20-off discount | The price of the item after a $10-off discount and then a 20%-off discount |

48. The number that is 20 percent less than 300 is what percent greater than 180?

   (A)  25

   (B)  $33\frac{1}{3}$

   (C)  50

   (D)  $66\frac{2}{3}$

   (E)  75

49. A tank that was 40% full of oil was emptied into a 20-gallon bucket. If the oil fills 35% of the bucket's volume, then what is the total capacity of the tank, in gallons?

   (A)   8.75

   (B)  15

   (C)  16

   (D)  17.5

   (E)  19

50. If 150 were increased by 60% and then decreased by $y$ percent, the result would be 192. What is the value of $y$?

   (A)  20

   (B)  28

   (C)  32

   (D)  72

   (E)  80

51. If $x$ is 150% greater than 200, $x$ is what percent greater than 50% of 500?

   (A)    0

   (B)   20

   (C)   50

   (D)  100

   (E)  200

52. 16 ounces of birdseed mix contains 10% sesame seed by weight. How much sesame seed must be added to produce a mix that is 20% sesame seed by weight?

    (A)  1 ounce
    (B)  1.6 ounces
    (C)  2 ounces
    (D)  2.4 ounces
    (E)  4 ounces

*a*, *b*, and *c* are positive.

|  | **Quantity A** | **Quantity B** |
|---|---|---|
| 53. | $(a + b)\%$ of $c$ | $c\%$ of $(a + b)$ |

| Conference Ticket Advance Discounts ||
|---|---|
| 5–29 days in advance | 15% |
| 30–59 days in advance | 30% |
| 60–89 days in advance | 40% |

54. Helen paid $252 for a conference ticket. If she had purchased the ticket one day later, she would have paid $306. How many days in advance did she purchase the ticket?

    (A)   5
    (B)  30
    (C)  59
    (D)  60
    (E)  89

# Percents Answers

1. **(C)**. 50 as a percent of 30 is $\left(\frac{50}{30} \times 100\right)\% = 166.\overline{6}\%$. (Note: it's incorrect to calculate "50 percent of 30," which is 15. This asked for 50 *as a percent* of 30, which is equivalent to asking, "What percent of 30 is 50?")

To find the percent increase from 30 to 80, use the percent change formula:

$$\text{Percent Change} = \left(\frac{Difference}{Original} \times 100\right)\%$$

$$\text{Percent Change} = \left(\frac{80-30}{30} \times 100\right)\% = 166.\overline{6}\%$$

The two quantities are equal. Note that doing the final calculation in each quantity is not necessary, because both equal $\frac{50}{30} \times 100$.

2. **(B)**. The question asks for Ken's salary, so set a variable: call Ken's salary $k$. Lorena's salary is $60,000. Now, translate the equation in the first sentence.

"If Ken's salary were 20% higher" can be translated as Ken's salary + 20% of Ken's salary, or $k + 0.2k$. "It would be 20% less than Lorena's" can be translated as (Lorena's salary − 20% of Lorena's salary), or $60,000 − (0.2)(60,000)$. This is equivalent to $(0.8)(60,000)$. Now solve:

$$1.2k = 0.8(60,000)$$
$$1.2k = 48,000$$
$$k = 40,000$$

Ken's salary is $40,000.

3. **(C)**. Because the problem never indicates real values, pick your own smart numbers. If $x = 100$ and $y = 50$, then:

Greta's salary was $100,000 and she received a 50% raise. Greta's raise, therefore, was $50,000.
Annika's salary was $50,000 and she received a 100% raise. Annika's raise, therefore, was $50,000.

The two quantities are equal. This holds true for any positive numbers chosen for $x$ and $y$, because $x$ percent of $y = y$ percent of $x$. Thus, any two numbers can be used—just as 50% of 100 = 100% of 50, it is also true that 1% of 2,000 = 2,000% of 1, or $a$% of $b = b$% of $a$.

4. **(B).** Roselba's income is more than twice as great as Jane's income. If both pay the same percent of income in transportation fees, that means Roselba must pay *more* than twice as much as Jane in transportation fees. Therefore, half of Roselba's fees will still be greater than Jane's fees. Quantity B is greater.

Alternatively, use smart numbers. Call Jane's income $100. Roselba's income, then, is greater than $200. If both pay 10% in transportation fees, then Jane pays $10 and Roselba pays more than $20. Half of Roselba's amount equals more than $10.

5. **(A).** The problem doesn't indicate any specific values, so pick a smart number. Because this is a percent problem, call the original price $100. Quantity A equals $100.

Decreasing a value by 16% is the same as taking $(100 - 16)\% = 84\%$ of the number: so $(0.84)(100) = \$84$. To increase the value by 16%, take 116% of the number, or multiply by 1.16: $(1.16)(84) = \$97.44$.

Quantity A is greater.

6. **240.** Translate the question as $12 = 0.05x$ and solve on the calculator: $x = 240$. Alternatively, translate the question as $12 = \dfrac{5}{100}x$ and solve on paper:

$$12 = \frac{1}{20}x$$

$$(12)(20) = x$$

$$x = 240$$

7. **9.** Always translate the phrase "what percent" as $\dfrac{x}{100}$. Translate the question as:

$$0.07(9) = \frac{x}{100}(7)$$

$$0.63 = \frac{7x}{100}$$

$$63 = 7x$$

$$9 = x$$

Incidentally, the pattern "$x$ percent of $y = y$ percent of $x$" always holds true! Here, 7% of 9 = 9% of 7, but it is also true that 2% of 57 = 57% of 2, etc. This works with any two numbers. If you notice this, then you can "fill in the blank" on the answer immediately: "what percent" must be 9%.

Finally, notice that the answer is 9 and not 0.09 or 9%. The question asks "what percent," so the percent is already incorporated into the sentence — the "what" by itself represents only the number itself, 9.

**MANHATTAN**
PREP

8. **300.** Always translate the phrase "what percent" as $\dfrac{x}{100}$. Translate the question as:

$$\frac{x}{100}(13) = 0.2(195)$$

$$\frac{13x}{100} = 39$$

$$13x = 3,900$$

$$x = 300$$

Alternatively, take 20 percent of 195 ($0.2 \times 195 = 39$) and rephrase the question: "What percent of 13 is 39?" Since 39 is three times as big as 13, the answer is 300.

9. **10.** Translate the question as $0.25(30) = 0.75x$ and solve on the calculator: $x = 10$.

Alternatively, write the percents in simplified fraction form and solve on paper:

$$\frac{1}{4}(30) = \frac{3}{4}x$$

$$30 = 3x$$

$$x = 10$$

10. **20% increase.** Use the percent change formula:

$$\text{Percent Change} = \left( \frac{Difference}{Original} \times 100 \right)\%$$

$$\text{Percent Change} = \left( \frac{60-50}{50} \times 100 \right)\% = \left( \frac{10}{50} \times 100 \right)\% = (0.2 \times 100)\% = 20\%$$

11. **90.** Because 30% less than $x$ is the same as 70% of $x$, translate as follows: $0.7x = 63$. Use the calculator to get $x = 90$. Alternatively, solve on paper:

$$\frac{7}{10}x = 63$$

$$x = (63)\left( \frac{10}{7} \right)$$

$$x = (9)(10)$$

$$x = 90$$

12. **138.** Translate into decimals (for the percents, move the decimal two places to the left) and use the calculator to solve:

$$x = 2.3(0.15)(400)$$
$$x = 138$$

Alternatively, translate into fractions and solve on paper:

$$\frac{230}{100} \times \frac{15}{100} \times 400 =$$

$$\frac{23}{10} \times \frac{15}{1} \times 4 =$$

$$\frac{23}{2} \times \frac{3}{1} \times 4 =$$

$$\frac{23}{1} \times \frac{3}{1} \times 2 = 138$$

13. **50.** The left-hand side of the equation is given: 45% of 80 is $(0.45)(80) = 36$. The problem then becomes: "36 is $x\%$ more than 24." From this step, there are two possible approaches.

One approach is to translate the equation and solve:

$$36 = 24 + \frac{x}{100}(24)$$

$$12 = \frac{24x}{100}$$

$$12\left(\frac{100}{24}\right) = x$$

$$50 = x$$

Alternatively, the increase $(36 - 24)$ is 12, so rephrase the statement as "12 is $x\%$ of 24." Recognizing that 12 is half of 24, $x$ must be 50. Or, translate and solve:

$$12 = \frac{x}{100}(24)$$

$$12\left(\frac{100}{24}\right) = x$$

$$50 = x$$

**MANHATTAN**
PREP

14. **400.** Translate as decimals and use the calculator to solve, keeping in mind that taking 200% of a number is the same as doubling it, or multiplying by 2:

$$0.10(0.30)x = 2(6)$$
$$0.03x = 12$$
$$x = 400$$

Alternatively, translate as fractions and solve on paper:

$$\left(\frac{1}{10}\right)\left(\frac{3}{10}\right)x = 2(6)$$

$$x = 12\left(\frac{100}{3}\right)$$

$$x = 400$$

15. **80.** The question already contains a variable ($y$). Use another variable to represent the desired value. Represent "what" with the variable $x$, and isolate $x$ to solve. Notice that by the end, the $y$ variables cancel out:

$$\left(\frac{x}{100}\right)\left(\frac{y}{100}\right)50 = \left(\frac{40}{100}\right)y$$

At this point, there are *many* options for simplifying, but do simplify before multiplying anything. Here is one way to simplify:

$$\left(\frac{x}{100}\right)\left(\frac{y}{2}\right) = \left(\frac{2}{5}\right)y$$

$$x = \frac{2y(100)(2)}{5y}$$

$$x = 80$$

16. **16.** 200% of 4% is the same as $2 \times 4\%$ (note that 200% equals the plain number 2), or 8%. Rephrase the question as "8% of $a$ is what percent of $\frac{a}{2}$?" Without translating to an equation, this can be simplified by multiplying both sides of the "equation" by 2 (remember that "is" means "equals"):

8% of $a$ is what percent of $\frac{a}{2}$?

16% of $a$ is what percent of $a$?

Thus, the answer is 16.

Alternatively, translate the words into math:

$$\left(\frac{200}{100}\right)\left(\frac{4}{100}\right)a = \left(\frac{x}{100}\right)\left(\frac{a}{2}\right)$$

$$\left(\frac{2}{25}\right)a = \frac{xa}{200}$$

$$\left(\frac{2}{25}\right)a\left(\frac{200}{a}\right) = x$$

$$16 = x$$

17. **144.** If $m$ were increased by 20%, decreased by 25%, and then increased by 60%, it would be multiplied by 1.2, then 0.75, then 1.6. Since $(1.2)(0.75)(1.6) = 1.44$, doing these manipulations is the same as increasing by 44%, or taking 144% of a number (this is true regardless of the value of $m$).

Alternatively, pick a real value for $m$. Because this is a percent problem, 100 is a good number to pick. First, 100 is increased by 20%: $(100)(1.2) = 120$. Next, 120 is decreased by 25%, which is the same as multiplying by 75%: $(120)(0.75) = 90$. Finally, 90 is increased by 60%: $(90)(1.6) = 144$. The new number is 144 and the starting number was 100, so the new number is $\left(\frac{144}{100}\right)$ % of the original number, or 144%.

18. **(A).** Say the item costs $100. After the first 10% discount, the item costs $90. After the second, the item costs $81 (the new discount is only $9, or 10% of 90). After the third discount, the item costs $81 − $8.10 = $72.90. What is the trend here? The cost goes down with each discount, yes, but the discount itself also gets smaller each time; it is only a $10 discount the very first time. The total of the five discounts, then, will be less than $50.

If the item costs $100 to start, then the value for Quantity B will be $50, or a total discount of $50. This is greater than the total discount described for Quantity A.

Finally, make sure to answer (A) for the higher price—don't accidentally pick (B) for the "better deal"!

19. **(E).** 1% of $450 is $4.50, so 0.5% is $2.25. That's the amount Raymond pays back every week. Because he has paid back $18 in total, divide 18 by 2.25 to determine the total number of payments: $\frac{\$18}{\$2.25} = 8$.

So Raymond has made 8 payments, once every 7 days. The payments themselves spread over only a 7-week period (in the same way that 2 payments spread over only a 1-week period). Raymond waited 1 week to begin repayment, however, so a total of 8 weeks, or 56 days, have passed since he borrowed the money.

20. **(A).** The number of parts in inventory first decreased by 50%, then increased by 50%. If the initial number of parts in inventory was $x$, the number after both shipments was $x(0.50)(1.5) = 0.75x$. The number of parts after the shipments was 75% of the number before, which is fewer. Quantity A is greater.

Alternatively, choose a smart number to test. If $x = 100$, then the inventory first decreased to 50, and then increased from 50 to 75. Quantity A is 100 and Quantity B is 75.

**MANHATTAN**
PREP

Finally, it is possible to solve this question using logic. The 50% decrease is taken as a percent of the original number. The 50% increase, however, is taken as a percent of the new, *smaller* number. The increase, therefore, must be smaller than the decrease, making the final value smaller than the original.

21. **(B).** To reduce $200,000 by 40%, multiply by 0.6 (reducing by 40% is the same as keeping 60%): $200,000(0.6) = $120,000.

To reduce $120,000 by 20%, multiply by 0.8 (reducing by 20% is the same as keeping 80%): $120,000(0.8) = $96,000. Quantity B is greater.

22. **12,000%.** Translate the statement into an equation. Since one of the percents is a variable, fractions are preferable to decimals:

$$\frac{1}{100} \times \frac{200}{100} \times 360 = \frac{x}{100} \times \frac{0.1}{100} \times 60$$

Because 100 appears twice on the bottom of both sides of the equation, multiply each side of the equation by 10,000 (or 100 twice) to cancel the 100's out:

$$\frac{1}{\cancel{100}} \times \frac{200}{\cancel{100}} \times 360 = \frac{x}{\cancel{100}} \times \frac{0.1}{\cancel{100}} \times 60$$

$$200 \times 360 = x(0.1)(60)$$

$$\frac{200 \times 360}{60} = x\left(\frac{1}{10}\right)$$

$$200 \times 6 \times 10 = x$$

$$x = 12,000$$

The answer is 12,000%. (The phrase "what percent" translates into math as $\dfrac{x}{100}$. Additionally, $\dfrac{12,000}{100}$ is the same thing as 12,000%, just as $\dfrac{50}{100}$ is equal to 50%. While 12,000% may seem quite large, it is correct.)

Alternatively, use decimals, while still writing "what percent" as a fraction. Then, use the calculator to solve:

$$(0.01)(2)(360) = \frac{x}{100}(0.001)(60)$$

$$7.2 = \frac{x}{100}(0.06)$$

$$120 = \frac{x}{100}$$

$$12,000 = x$$

23. **(D).** Because no actual amounts of money are stated in the question, use smart numbers to solve this problem. If Mary has half as many cents as Nora has dollars, then, as an example, if Nora had $10, Mary would have 5 cents. Nora's $10 equals 1,000 cents. To determine what *percent more* cents Nora has, use the percent change formula:

$$\text{Percent Change} = \left( \frac{Difference}{Original} \times 100 \right) \%$$

$$\text{Percent Change} = \left( \frac{1,000 - 5}{5} \times 100 \right) \% = 19,900\%$$

Any example in which "Mary has half as many cents as Nora has dollars" will yield the same result. Note that the percent change formula is required—a percent *more* (or percent increase) is not the same as a percent *of* something.

To do the problem algebraically (which is more difficult than using a smart number, as above), use $M$ for Mary's cents and $N$ for Nora's cents. Divide $N$ by 100 in order to convert from cents to dollars, $\frac{N}{100}$, and set up an equation to reflect that Mary has half as many cents as Nora has dollars:

$$M = \frac{1}{2} \left( \frac{N}{100} \right)$$

$$M = \frac{N}{200}$$

$$200M = N$$

Therefore, Nora has 200 times as many cents. 200 times *as many* is 199 times *more*. To convert 199 times *more* to a percent, add two zeros to get 19,900%.

24. **(E).** Rather than trying to write out the whole statement as math, note that "the number that is 50% greater than 60" can be calculated: 1.5(60) = 90. Similarly, "the number that is 20% less than 150" is 0.8(150) = 120. The question can be rephrased as "90 is what percent less than 120?" Use the percent change formula. Since the question specifies a "percent *less*," the "original" number is 120:

$$\text{Percent Change} = \left( \frac{Difference}{Original} \times 100 \right) \% = \left( \frac{30}{120} \times 100 \right) \% = 25\%$$

25. **(D).** The percent increase is the difference between the amounts divided by the original, converted to a percent. If the population doubles, mathematically the increase can be written as a power of 2. In the 30-day interval, if the original population is 1, it will double to 2 after three days—so, $2^1$ represents the population after the first increase, the second increase would then be $2^2$ and so on. Since there are 10 increases, the final population would be $2^{10}$ or 1,024. Therefore, the difference, 1,024 − 1, is 1,023. Use the percent change formula to calculate percent increase:

$$\text{Percent Change} = \left( \frac{Difference}{Original} \times 100 \right) \% = \left( \frac{1,023}{1} \times 100 \right) \% = 102,300\%$$

Note that the new number *is* 102,400% of the original, but that was not the question asked—the percent *increase* is 102,300%.

**MANHATTAN**
PREP

26. **(D).** Call the original price $x$. That price is discounted by 15% to get 612:

$$0.85x = \$612$$
$$x = \$720$$

Do not add 15% of \$612 to \$612. The 15% figure is a percent of the unknown original number, not of \$612.

27. **(B).** Call the original price $x$. At the end of April, the total price was $1.4x$. The price increase in April was $1.4x - 1x = 0.4x$.

In May, the price increased an additional 30% over April's final price of $1.4x$. Thus, the price at the end of May was $(1.3)(1.4)x$, or $1.82x$. The price increase in May was $1.82x - 1.4x = 0.42x$.

Since $x$ is positive, $0.42x$ (42% of $x$) is greater than $0.4x$ (40% of $x$). Quantity B is greater.

Alternatively, use smart numbers. If the original price was \$100, April's increase would result in a price of \$140 and May's increase would be $(1.3)(140) = \$182$. Thus, April's increase was \$40 and May's increase was \$42. May's increase will be greater no matter what number is used as the starting price (it is reasonable in GRE problems to assume that a price must be a positive number).

28. **(B).** The 50% spent on rent, utilities, and insurance and the 20% spent on food are both percents of the total, so sum the percents: 50% + 20% = 70%. After these expenditures, Aloysius has 30% left. He then spends 30% *of the remaining 30%* on video games. 30% of 30% = $0.30 \times 0.30 = 0.09$, or 9% of the total, so 30% − 9% = 21% of his income remains.

Alternatively, use smart numbers. If Aloysius's income is \$100, he would spend \$50 on rent, utilities, and insurance, and \$20 on food, for a total of \$70. Of his remaining \$30, he would spend 30%, or \$9, on video games, leaving \$21, or 21%, of the original amount.

29. **7,100%.** In 1970, company X had $0.15(2,000) = 300$ female employees. Of those, $0.10(300) = 30$ were female executives.

In 2012, company X had $0.45(12,000) = 5,400$ female employees. Of those, $0.40(5,400) = 2,160$ were female executives.

$$\text{Percent Change} = \left( \frac{Difference}{Original} \times 100 \right)\%$$
$$\text{Percent Change} = \left( \frac{2130}{30} \times 100 \right)\% = 7,100\%$$

30. **60%.** Use smart numbers. There are 20% fewer boys than girls, so choose 100 for the number of girls (100 is a good number to pick for percent problems). Thus, there are $(100)(0.8) = 80$ boys in the school. If 75% of all the boys take civics, then $0.75(80) = 60$ boys take civics. If 48% of all the girls take civics, then $0.48(100) = 48$ girls take civics.

Therefore, $60 + 48 = 108$ students take civics and there are 180 total students:

$$\left(\frac{108}{180} \times 100\right)\% = 60\%$$

31. **(C).** Airline A reduced its price by 25% to ($400)(0.75) = $300, but then increased that price by 10% to ($300) (1.1) = $330. Airline B reduced its fare to ($400)(0.45) = $180, but added $150 in fees, bringing the total price to $180 + $150 = $330. The two quantities are equal.

32. **(C).** Write an equation from the first part of the given information: $p = 0.75q$. Since $p = 2r$, substitute $2r$ for $p$ in the first equation:

$$2r = 0.75q$$
$$r = 0.375q$$

The two quantities are equal.

Alternatively, use smart numbers. If $q$ is 8, then $p$ is $(8)(0.75) = 6$. (Note: because you have to multiply $q$ by 0.75, or $\frac{3}{4}$, try to pick something divisible by 4 for $q$, so that $p$ will be an integer.) Therefore, $r$ is $\frac{6}{2} = 3$.

Since $0.375q = (0.375)(8) = 3$, the value for $r$ is also 3. The two quantities are equal.

33. **(A).** When a percent contains a variable, use fractions to translate. Quantity A is:

$$\frac{x}{100} \times \frac{0.5}{100} \times \frac{40{,}000}{1} = x(0.5)(4) = 2x$$

Quantity B is:

$$\frac{0.05}{100} \times \frac{2{,}000}{100} \times \frac{40x}{1} = (0.05)(2)(4x) = 0.4x$$

Since $x$ is positive, Quantity A is greater (this is true even if $x$ is a fraction).

Alternatively, use smart numbers. If $x = 50$, then Quantity A equals:

$$\frac{50}{100} \times \frac{0.5}{100} \times \frac{40{,}000}{1} = (0.5)(0.5)(400) = 100$$

Quantity B equals:

$$\frac{0.05}{100} \times \frac{2{,}000}{100} \times \frac{(40)(50)}{1} = (0.05)(2)(4)(50) = 20$$

Quantity A is greater.

**34. 216.** The percent increase from 2000 to 2001 is:

$$\text{Percent Change} = \left( \frac{Difference}{Original} \times 100 \right)\%$$

$$\text{Percent Change} = \left( \frac{20}{60} \times 100 \right)\% = 33.\overline{3}\%$$

Now, apply a $33.\overline{3}\%$, or $\frac{1}{3}$, increase to 2004's figure. The GRE calculator cannot accept a repeating decimal; instead, divide 162 by 3 to get the amount of increase, and then add 162 to get the new profit per student in 2005: $162 \div 3 + 162 = 216$.

**35. (E).** First, write "$x$ is 0.5% of $y$" as math. Make sure you don't accidentally interpret 0.5% as 50%!

$$x = \frac{0.5}{100} \times y$$

The question asks "$y$ is what percent of $x$?", so solve for $y$:

$$100x = 0.5y$$
$$200x = y$$

If $y$ is 200 times $x$, multiply by 100 to convert to a percent:

$$\frac{200x}{1} \times \frac{100}{100} = \frac{20,000x}{100}$$

The answer is 20,000%. (For reference, if one number is 2 times as big as the other, it is 200% the size—add two zeros. So, 200 times as big = 20,000%.)

Alternatively, use smart numbers. If $y = 100$, then $x = \frac{0.5}{100}(100) = 0.5$. Next, answer the question, "100 is what percent of 0.5?" Pick a new variable to translate the "what percent" portion of the sentence:

$$100 = \frac{n}{100} \times 0.5$$
$$10,000 = 0.5n$$
$$20,000 = n$$

(In translating percents problems to math, always translate "what percent" as a variable over 100.)

**36. (C).** Bill's tax is $(0.20)(\$5,000) = \$1,000$. Thus, his remaining salary is $4,000. His rent is therefore $(0.25)(\$4000) = \$1,000$. The two quantities are equal.

**37. (B).** If four people shared the $80 bill equally, then each person paid for one-quarter of the bill, or $\frac{\$80}{4} = \$20$.

The tip is calculated as a percent of the bill. Because the question asks about the amount that each (one) person paid, calculate the 15% tip based solely on one person's portion of the bill ($20): (0.15)(20) = $3.

In total, each person paid $20 + $3 = $23.

Alternatively, find the total of the bill plus tip and take one-fourth of that for the total contribution of each person. The total of bill and tip is $80 + (0.15)($80) = $80 + $12 = $92. One-fourth of this is $\frac{$92}{4} = $23$.

38. **(B).** Use a smart number for the price of the stock; for a percent problem, $100 is a good choice. The price of the stock after a 25% increase is (1.25) × $100 = $125.

Next, find the percent decrease ($y$) needed to reduce the price back to the original $100. Because $125 − $25 = $100, rephrase the question: 25 is what percent of 125?

$$25 = \frac{x}{100}(125)$$

$$\frac{2,500}{125} = x$$

$$x = 20$$

You have to reduce 125 by 20% in order to get back to $100. Therefore, Quantity A is 20%, so Quantity B is greater.

39. **(C).** The chemist now has 10 ounces of acetone in a 30-ounce mixture, so she must have 20 ounces of water. The question ask how many ounces of acetone must be added to make this mixture a 50% solution. No additional water is added, so the solution must finish with 20 ounces of water. Therefore, she also needs a total of 20 ounces of acetone, or 10 more ounces than the mixture currently contains.

Note that one trap answer is (B), or 5. This answer is not correct because the final number of ounces in the solution is *not* 30; when the chemist adds acetone, the amount of total solution also increases—adding 5 ounces acetone would result in a solution that is $\frac{15}{(30+5)}$ acetone, which is not equivalent to a 50% mixture.

40. **(C).** Choose a smart number for the total number of games; for a percent problem, 100 is a good number to pick. If the total number of games for the season is 100 and the team played 80% of them by July, then the team played (100)(0.8) = 80 games. The team won 50% of these games, or (80)(0.5) = 40 games.

Next, the team won 60% of its *remaining* games. As there were 100 total games and the team has played 80 of them, there are 20 games left to play. Of these, the team won 60%, or (20)(0.6) = 12 games.

Therefore, the team has won a total of 40 + 12 = 52 games out of 100, or 52% of its total games. The two quantities are equal.

Alternatively, this problem could be done using weighted averages, where the total percent of games won is equal to the sum of all of the individual percents multiplied by their weightings. In this case:

Total Percent Won = (50%)(80%) + (60%)(100% − 80%) × 100%

Total Percent Won = [(0.5)(0.8) + (0.6)(0.2)] × 100%

Total Percent Won = [(0.4) + (0.12)] × 100%

Total Percent Won = 0.52 × 100%

Total Percent Won = 52%

41. **(B).** In order to compare, use the calculator to find 0.4 percent of 4 percent of 1.25 (be careful with the decimals!):

$$0.004 \times 0.04 \times 1.25 = 0.0002$$

Or, as fractions:

$$\frac{0.4}{100} \times \frac{4}{100} \times 1.25 = \frac{2}{1,000} = 0.0002$$

Quantity B is greater.

42. **(D).** Originally, Jane had a 40-ounce mixture of apple and seltzer that was 30% apple. Since 0.30(40) = 12, 12 ounces were apple and 28 ounces were seltzer.

When Jane pours 10 more ounces of apple juice into the mixture, it yields a mixture that is 50 ounces total, still with 28 ounces of seltzer. Now, the percent of seltzer in the final mixture is $\frac{28}{50} \times 100 = 56\%$.

43. **(A).** Choose a smart number for the total number of shirts in the closest; this is a percent problem, so 100 is a good number to pick. Out of 100 shirts, half, or 50, are white.

You know 30% of the *remaining* shirts are gray. If there are 50 white shirts, there are also 50 remaining shirts and so (0.3)(50) = 15 gray shirts. Therefore, there are 50 + 15 = 65 total shirts that are white or gray, and 100 − 65 = 35 shirts that are neither white nor gray. Since 35 out of 100 shirts are neither white nor gray, exactly 35% of the shirts are neither white nor gray.

Alternatively, use algebra, though that is trickier on a problem such as this one. Set a variable, such as $x$, for the total number of shirts. The number of white shirts is $0.5x$ and the remaining shirts would equal $x − 0.5x = 0.5x$. The number of gray shirts, then, is $(0.5x)(0.3) = 0.15x$. Thus, there are $0.5x + 0.15x = 0.65x$ white or gray shirts, and $x − 0.6x = 0.35x$ shirts that are neither white nor gray. Therefore, $0.35x \div x = 0.35$, or 35%.

44. **(A).** Choose smart numbers for the dimensions of the rectangle—for instance, length = 20 and width = 10.

The original area of the rectangle = length × width = 200

After a 10% increase for both the length and the width, the area becomes 22 × 11 = 242.

Use the formula for percent change:

$$\text{Percent Change} = \left(\frac{\text{Difference}}{\text{Original}} \times 100\right)\%$$

$$\left(\frac{242-200}{200} \times 100\right)\% = \left(\frac{42}{200} \times 100\right)\% = \left(\frac{21}{100} \times 100\right)\% = 21\%$$

Quantity A is greater.

Alternatively, use logic. The formula for area requires multiplying the length and the width. If just one side is increased by 10%, then the overall area will increase by 10%. If two sides are increased by 10%, then the overall area will increase by more than 10%.

45. **(C).** Translate the given information into math:

$$\frac{35}{100}x = 140$$

$$x = 140 \times \frac{100}{35}$$

$$x = 400$$

Next, find 20% of $x$, or 0.20(400) = 80.

46. **(A).** Every 3 minutes, the population increases by 20% (which is the same as multiplying by 1.2). Beginning at 8:54am, this change would occur at 8:57am and again at 9:00am. Use the variable $x$ to represent the original quantity. Note that the 20% increase occurs twice:

$$x(1.2)(1.2) = 144,000$$
$$x = 100,000$$

Note that you cannot just reduce 144,000 by 20% twice, because 20% is not a percent of 144,000—it is a percent of the unknown, original number.

Alternatively, begin from 144,000 and calculate "backwards":

From 8:57am to 9:00am: $y(1.2) = 144,000$, so $y = \dfrac{144,000}{1.2} = 120,000$.

From 8:54am to 8:57am: $z(1.2) = 120,000$, so $z = \dfrac{120,000}{1.2} = 100,000$.

47. **(D).** Reducing a number by a percent involves multiplication; reducing a number by a fixed amount involves subtraction. The order of operations (PEMDAS) will make a difference.

One possible value for the item is $100. In this case, the value of Quantity A = ($100)(0.9) − $20 = $70. The value of Quantity B = ($100 − $10)(0.80) = $72. Here, Quantity B is greater.

**MANHATTAN**
PREP

However, a greater starting value may change the result, because a 20% discount off a greater starting value can result in a much greater decrease. For a $140 item, the value of Quantity A = ($140)(0.9) − $20 = $106. The value of Quantity B = ($140 − $10)(0.80) = $104. Here, Quantity A is greater. The relationship cannot be determined from the information given.

48. **(B).** 20% less than 300 is the same as 80% of 300, or 0.80(300) = 240. The question is "240 is what percent greater than 180?"

$$\text{Percent Change} = \left( \frac{Difference}{Original} \times 100 \right)\%$$

$$\text{Percent Change} = \left( \frac{60}{180} \times 100 \right)\% = 33.\overline{3}\%$$

49. **(D).** First find the volume of oil in the bucket. The oil fills 35% of the bucket's 20-gallon volume, or (20)(0.35) = 7 gallons of oil.

These 7 gallons originally filled 40% of the tank. If $T$ is the volume of the tank, $T(0.4) = 7$, so $T = 17.5$ gallons.

50. **(A).** First, find the value of 150 increased by 60%: (150)(1.6) = 240. If 240 were then decreased by $y$ percent, the result would be 192. Because 240 is decreased by 48 to get 192, the question can be rephrased: 48 is what percent of 240?

$$48 = \frac{x}{100}(240)$$

$$48\left(\frac{10}{24}\right) = x$$

$$x = 20$$

51. **(D).** "150% greater than 200" means 150% of 200, or 300, *added back to* 200. This is the not the same figure as 150% *of* 200. Thus, 150% greater than 200 is 200 + (200)(1.5) = 500.

50% of 500 = 250. Translate the question as "500 is what percent greater than 250?" Since 500 is twice 250, it is 100% greater than 250.

Alternatively, use the percent change formula.

$$\text{Percent Change} = \left( \frac{Difference}{Original} \times 100 \right)\%$$

$$\text{Percent Change} = \left( \frac{500 - 250}{250} \times 100 \right)\% = 100\%$$

52. **(C).** A 16-ounce mix that contains 10% sesame by weight has 1.6 ounces of sesame. It might be tempting to think that adding another 1.6 ounces would make a mixture that is 20% sesame. However, this is incorrect—adding 1.6 ounces of sesame will also add 1.6 ounces to the total amount of seed in the jar, reducing the concentration of sesame in the mix: $\left( \frac{3.2 \text{ ounces sesame}}{17.6 \text{ ounces total}} \times 100 \right)\% = 18.18\%$.

Instead, write an equation expressing the ratio of sesame to the total mixture, where $x$ is the amount of sesame to add; this equals the desired 20% (or $\frac{1}{5}$) figure:

$$\frac{1.6 + x}{16 + x} = \frac{1}{5}$$

Cross-multiply and solve for $x$:

$$5(1.6 + x) = 16 + x$$
$$8 + 5x = 16 + x$$
$$4x = 8$$
$$x = 2$$

**53. (C).** It is always the case that, for two positive quantities, $M$% of $N = N$% of $M$. In this case, $(a + b)$ makes the problem appear more complicated, but the principle still applies. Algebraically:

| **Quantity A** | **Quantity B** |
|:---:|:---:|
| $\dfrac{(a+b)}{100} \times c$ | $\dfrac{c}{100} \times (a+b)$ |

Both quantities can be simplified to $\dfrac{c(a+b)}{100}$. The two quantities are equal.

**54. (B).** Helen bought a ticket for $252; if she had bought it one day later, she would have paid $54 more. There are three possibilities that represent the dividing lines between the given discount levels:

Possibility 1: She bought the ticket 60 days in advance for a 40% discount (if she'd bought it one day later, or 59 days in advance, she would have received a 30% discount instead).

Possibility 2: She bought the ticket 30 days in advance for a 30% discount (if she'd bought it one day later, or 29 days in advance, she would have received a 15% discount instead).

Possibility 3: She bought the ticket 5 days in advance for a 15% discount (if she'd bought it one day later, or 4 days in advance, she would not have received any kind of discount).

This question is harder than it looks, do not calculate a percent change between $252 and $306. The discounts are *percents of the full-price ticket*, which is an unknown value. Call it $x$.

Note that the only three possible answers are 5, 30, and 60 (answers (A), (B), and (D), respectively); 59 days ahead and 89 days ahead do not represent days for which the next day (58 and 88 days ahead, respectively) results in a change in the discount.

Possibility 1 (60 days in advance): $252 would represent a 40% discount from the original price, so the original price would be $252 = 0.6x$, and $x$ would be $420.

If the full ticket price is $420, then buying the ticket 1 day later would result in a 30% discount instead, or ($420)(0.7) = $294. The problem indicates, however, that Helen would have paid $306, so Possibility 1 is not correct.

Possibility 2 (30 days in advance): $252 would represent a 30% discount from the original price, so the original price would be $252 = 0.7x and x would be $360.

If the full ticket price is $360, then buying the ticket 1 day later would result in a 15% discount instead, or ($360)(0.85) = $306. This matches the figure given in the problem, so Possibility 2 is correct; you do not need to test Possibility 3. Helen bought the ticket 30 days in advance.

# Chapter 13

## of

5 lb. Book of GRE® Practice Problems

# Divisibility and Primes

# In This Chapter...

Divisibility and Primes

Divisibility and Primes Answers

# Divisibility and Primes

For questions in the Quantitative Comparison format ("Quantity A" and "Quantity B" given), the answer choices are always as follows:

(A)    Quantity A is greater.
(B)    Quantity B is greater.
(C)    The two quantities are equal.
(D)    The relationship cannot be determined from the information given.

For questions followed by a numeric entry box [    ], you are to enter your own answer in the box. For questions followed

by a fraction-style numeric entry box [    ], you are to enter your answer in the form of a fraction. You are not required to

reduce fractions. For example, if the answer is $\frac{1}{4}$, you may enter $\frac{25}{100}$ or any equivalent fraction.

All numbers used are real numbers. All figures are assumed to lie in a plane unless otherwise indicated. Geometric figures are not necessarily drawn to scale. You should assume, however, that lines that appear to be straight are actually straight, points on a line are in the order shown, and all geometric objects are in the relative positions shown. Coordinate systems, such as xy-planes and number lines, as well as graphical data presentations, such as bar charts, circle graphs, and line graphs, are drawn to scale. A symbol that appears more than once in a question has the same meaning throughout the question.

1.    For how many positive integer values of $x$ is $\frac{65}{x}$ an integer?

[    ]

2.    If $x$ is a number such that $0 < x \le 20$, for how many values of $x$ is $\frac{20}{x}$ an integer?

(A)    Four
(B)    Six
(C)    Eight
(D)    Ten
(E)    More than ten

|  | **Quantity A** | **Quantity B** |
|---|---|---|
| 3. | The number of distinct factors of 10 | The number of distinct **prime** factors of 210 |

|  | **Quantity A** | **Quantity B** |
|---|---|---|
| 4. | The least common multiple of 22 and 6 | The greatest common factor of 66 and 99 |

5.  The number of students who attend a school could be divided among 10, 12, or 16 buses, such that each bus transports an equal number of students. What is the minimum number of students that could attend the school?

    (A)  120
    (B)  160
    (C)  240
    (D)  320
    (E)  480

|  | Quantity A | Quantity B |
|---|---|---|
| 6. | The number of distinct prime<br>factors of 27 | The number of distinct prime<br>factors of 18 |

7.  How many factors greater than 1 do 120, 210, and 270 have in common?

    (A)  One
    (B)  Three
    (C)  Six
    (D)  Seven
    (E)  Thirty

8.  Company H distributed $4,000 and 180 pencils evenly among its employees, with each employee getting an equal integer number of dollars and an equal integer number of pencils. What is the greatest number of employees that could work for company H?

    (A)  9
    (B)  10
    (C)  20
    (D)  40
    (E)  180

9.  $n$ is divisible by 14 and 3. Which of the following statements must be true?

    Indicate all such statements.

    ☐  12 is a factor of $n$.
    ☐  21 is a factor of $n$.
    ☐  $n$ is a multiple of 42.

**MANHATTAN**
PREP

10. Positive integers $a$ and $b$ each have exactly four factors. If $a$ is a one-digit number and $b = a + 9$, what is the value of $a$?

        ┌──────────────┐
        │              │
        └──────────────┘

11. Ramon wants to cut a rectangular board into identical square pieces. If the board is 18 inches by 30 inches, what is the least number of square pieces he can cut without wasting any of the board?

    (A)   4
    (B)   6
    (C)   9
    (D)  12
    (E)  15

12. When the positive integer $x$ is divided by 6, the remainder is 4. Each of the following could also be an integer EXCEPT

    (A)  $\dfrac{x}{2}$

    (B)  $\dfrac{x}{3}$

    (C)  $\dfrac{x}{7}$

    (D)  $\dfrac{x}{11}$

    (E)  $\dfrac{x}{17}$

13. If $x^y = 64$ and $x$ and $y$ are positive integers, which of the following could be the value of $x + y$?

    Indicate all such values.

    ☐   2
    ☐   6
    ☐   7
    ☐   8
    ☐  10
    ☐  12

14. If $k$ is a multiple of 24 but not a multiple of 16, which of the following cannot be an integer?

(A) $\dfrac{k}{8}$

(B) $\dfrac{k}{9}$

(C) $\dfrac{k}{32}$

(D) $\dfrac{k}{36}$

(E) $\dfrac{k}{81}$

15. If $a = 16b$ and $b$ is a prime number greater than 2, how many positive distinct factors does $a$ have?

16. If $a$ and $b$ are integers such that $a > b > 1$, which of the following cannot be a multiple of either $a$ or $b$?

(A) $a - 1$

(B) $b + 1$

(C) $b - 1$

(D) $a + b$

(E) $ab$

17. 616 divided by 6 yields remainder $p$, and 525 divided by 11 yields remainder $q$. What is $p + q$?

18. If $x$ is divisible by 18 and $y$ is divisible by 12, which of the following statements must be true?

Indicate all such statements.

☐  $x + y$ is divisible by 6.

☐  $xy$ is divisible by 48.

☐  $\dfrac{x}{y}$ is divisible by 6.

**MANHATTAN**
PREP

19.  If $p$ is divisible by 7 and $q$ is divisible by 6, $pq$ must have at least how many factors greater than 1?

     (A)  One
     (B)  Three
     (C)  Six
     (D)  Seven
     (E)  Eight

20. If $r$ is divisible by 10 and $s$ is divisible by 9, $rs$ must have at least how many factors?

     (A)  Two
     (B)  Four
     (C)  Twelve
     (D)  Fourteen
     (E)  Sixteen

21.  If $t$ is divisible by 12, what is the least possible integer value of $a$ for which $\dfrac{t^2}{2^a}$ might not be an integer?

     (A)  2
     (B)  3
     (C)  4
     (D)  5
     (E)  6

22.  If $a$, $b$, and $c$ are multiples of 3 such that $a > b > c > 0$, which of the following values must be divisible by 3?

     Indicate all such values.

     ☐  $a + b + c$
     ☐  $a - b + c$
     ☐  $\dfrac{abc}{9}$

23.  New cars leave a car factory in a repeating pattern of red, blue, black, and gray cars. If the first car to exit the factory was red, what color is the 463rd car to exit the factory?

     (A)  Red
     (B)  Blue
     (C)  Black
     (D)  Gray
     (E)  It cannot be determined from the information given.

24. Jason deposits money at a bank on a Tuesday and returns to the bank 100 days later to withdraw the money. On what day of the week did Jason withdraw the money from the bank?

   (A) Monday
   (B) Tuesday
   (C) Wednesday
   (D) Thursday
   (E) Friday

25. $x$ and $h$ are both positive integers. When $x$ is divided by 7, the quotient is $h$ with a remainder of 3. Which of the following could be the value of $x$?

   (A)  7
   (B)  21
   (C)  50
   (D)  52
   (E)  57

26. When $x$ is divided by 10, the quotient is $y$ with a remainder of 4. If $x$ and $y$ are both positive integers, what is the remainder when $x$ is divided by 5?

   (A)  0
   (B)  1
   (C)  2
   (D)  3
   (E)  4

27. What is the remainder when $13^{17} + 17^{13}$ is divided by 10?

   ┌─────────────┐
   │             │
   └─────────────┘

28. If $n$ is an integer and $n^3$ is divisible by 24, what is the largest number that must be a factor of $n$?

   (A)   1
   (B)   2
   (C)   6
   (D)   8
   (E)   12

**MANHATTAN**
PREP

10! is divisible by $3^x 5^y$, where $x$ and $y$ are positive integers.

|  | **Quantity A** | **Quantity B** |
|---|---|---|
| 29. | The greatest possible value for $x$ | Twice the greatest possible value for $y$ |

|  | **Quantity A** | **Quantity B** |
|---|---|---|
| 30. | The number of distinct prime factors of 100,000 | The number of distinct prime factors of 99,000 |

31. Which of the following values times 12 is <u>not</u> a multiple of 64?

    Indicate <u>all</u> such values.

    ☐    $6^6$

    ☐    $12^2$

    ☐    $18^3$

    ☐    $30^3$

    ☐    222

32. If $3^x(5^2)$ is divided by $3^5(5^3)$, the quotient terminates with one decimal digit. If $x > 0$, which of the following statements must be true?

    (A) $x$ is even

    (B) $x$ is odd

    (C) $x < 5$

    (D) $x \geq 5$

    (E) $x = 5$

33. *abc* is a three-digit number in which $a$ is the hundreds digit, $b$ is the tens digit, and $c$ is the units digit. Let &(*abc*)& = $(2^a)(3^b)(5^c)$. For example, &(203)& = $(2^2)(3^0)(5^3)$ = 500. For how many three-digit numbers *abc* does the function &(*abc*)& yield a prime number?

    (A) Zero

    (B) One

    (C) Two

    (D) Three

    (E) Nine

# Divisibility and Primes Answers

1. **4.** If $x$ is a positive integer such that $\dfrac{65}{x}$ is also an integer, then $x$ must be a factor of 65. The factors of 65 are 1, 5, 13, and 65. Thus, there are four positive integer values of $x$ such that $\dfrac{65}{x}$ is an integer.

2. **(E).** Notice that the problem did *not* say that $x$ had to be an integer. Therefore, the factors of 20 will work (1, 2, 4, 5, 10, 20), but so will 0.5, 0.1, 0.25, 2.5, etc. It is possible to divide 20 into fractional parts—for instance, something 20 inches long could be divided evenly into quarter inches (there would be 80 of them, as $\dfrac{20}{0.25} = 80$). There are an infinite number of $x$ values that would work (it is possible to divide 20 into thousandths, millionths, etc.), so the answer is (E). It is very important on the GRE to notice whether there is an integer constraint on a variable or not! Any answer like "More than 10" should be a clue that this problem may be less straightforward than it seems.

3. **(C).** The *factors* of 10 are 1 & 10, and 2 & 5. Since there are four factors, Quantity A is 4.

The *prime factors* of 210 are 2, 3, 5, and 7:

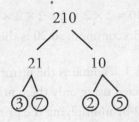

Because 210 has four prime factors, Quantity B is also 4. The two quantities are equal.

4. **(A).** The least common multiple of 22 and 6 is 66. One way to find the least common multiple is to list the larger number's multiples (it is more efficient to begin with the larger number) until reaching a multiple that the other number goes into. The multiples of 22 are 22, 44, 66, 88, etc. The smallest of these that 6 goes into is 66.

The greatest common factor of 66 and 99 is 33. One way to find the greatest common factor is to list all the factors of one of the numbers, and then pick the greatest one that also goes into the other number. For instance, the factors of 66 are 1 & 66, 2 & 33, 3 & 22, and 6 & 11. The greatest of these that also goes into 99 is 33. Thus, Quantity A is greater.

5. **(C).** The number of students must be divisible by 10, 12, and 16. So the question is really asking, "What is the least common multiple of 10, 12, and 16?" Since all of the answer choices end in 0, each is divisible by 10. Just use the calculator to test which choices are also divisible by 12 and 16. Because the question asks for the minimum, start by checking the smallest choices. Since $\dfrac{120}{16}$ and $\dfrac{160}{12}$ are not integers, the smallest choice that works is 240.

6. **(B).** "Distinct" means different from each other. To find distinct prime factors, make a prime factor tree, and then disregard any repeated prime factors. The integer 27 breaks down into $3 \times 3 \times 3$. Thus, 27 has only 1 distinct prime factor. The integer 18 breaks down into $2 \times 3 \times 3$. Thus, 18 has 2 distinct prime factors.

**7. (D).** Pick one of the numbers and list all of its factors. The factors of 120 are: 1 & 120, 2 & 60, 3 & 40, 4 & 30, 5 & 24, 6 & 20, 8 & 15, 10 & 12. Since the problem specifically asks for factors "greater than 1," eliminate 1 now. Now cross off any factors that do *not* go into 210:

$$\cancel{120},\ 2\ \&\ \cancel{60},\ 3\ \&\ \cancel{40},\ \cancel{4}\ \&\ 30,\ 5\ \&\ \cancel{24},\ 6\ \&\ \cancel{20},\ \cancel{8}\ \&\ 15,\ 10\ \&\ \cancel{12}$$

Now cross off any factors remaining that do *not* go into 270. Interestingly, all of the remaining factors (2, 3, 5, 6, 10, 15, 30) *do* go into 270. There are 7 shared factors.

**8. (C).** In order to distribute $4,000 and 180 pencils evenly, the number of employees must be a factor of each of these two numbers. Because the question asks for the greatest number of employees possible, start by checking the greatest choices:

(E) $4,000 could not be evenly distributed among 180 employees (although 180 pencils could).
(D) $4,000 could be evenly divided among 40 people, but 180 pencils could not.
(C) is the greatest choice that works—$4,000 and 180 pencils could each be evenly distributed among 20 people.

Alternatively, find the greatest common factor (GCF) of the two numbers. Factor: $4,000 = 2 \times 2 \times 2 \times 2 \times 2 \times 5 \times 5 \times 5 = 2^5 \times 5^3$ and $180 = 2 \times 2 \times 3 \times 3 \times 5 = 2^2 \times 3^2 \times 5$. These numbers have $2 \times 2 \times 5$ in common, so 20 is the GCF.

**9. "21 is a factor of *n*" and "*n* is a multiple of 42" only.** Since $n$ is divisible by 14 and 3, $n$ contains the prime factors of both 14 and 3, which are 2, 7, and 3. Thus, any numbers that can be constructed using only these prime factors (no additional factors) are factors of $n$. Since $12 = 2 \times 2 \times 3$, you *cannot* make 12 by multiplying the prime factors of $n$ (you would need one more 2). However, you *can* construct 21 by multiplying two of the known prime factors of $n$ ($7 \times 3 = 21$), so the second statement is true. Finally, $n$ must be at least 42 ($= 2 \times 7 \times 3$, the *least common multiple* of 14 and 3), so $n$ is definitely a multiple of 42. That is, $n$ can only be 42, 84, 126, etc.

**10. 6.** Start by considering integer $a$, which is the most constrained variable. It is a positive one-digit number (between 1 and 9, inclusive) and it has four factors. Prime numbers have exactly two factors: themselves and one, so only look at non-prime one-digit positive integers. That's a short enough list:

1 has just one factor
4 has three factors: 1, 2, and 4
6 has four factors: 1, 2, 3, and 6
8 has four factors: 1, 2, 4, and 8
9 has three factors: 1, 3, and 9

So the two possibilities for $a$ are 6 and 8. Now apply the two constraints for $b$. It is 9 greater than $a$, and it has exactly four factors. Check the possibilities:

If $a = 6$, then $b = 15$, which has four factors: 1, 3, 5, and 15.
If $a = 8$, then $b = 17$, which is prime, so it has only has two factors: 1 and 17.
Only $b = 15$ works, so $a$ must be 6.

11. **(E).** Cutting a rectangular board into square pieces means that Ramon needs to cut pieces that are equal in length and width. "Without wasting any of the board" means that he needs to choose a side length that divides evenly into both 18 and 30. "The least number of square pieces" means that he needs to choose the largest possible squares. With these three stipulations, choose the largest integer that divides evenly into 18 and 30, or the greatest common factor, which is 6. This would give Ramon 3 pieces going one way and 5 pieces going the other. He would cut $3 \times 5$ = 15 squares of dimension 6" $\times$ 6". Note that this solution ignored squares with non-integer side length for the sake of convenience, a potentially dangerous thing to do. (After all, identical squares of 1.5" by 1.5" could be cut without wasting any of the board.) However, to cut squares any larger than 6" $\times$ 6", Ramon could only cut 2 squares of 9" or 1 square of 18" from the 18" dimension of the rectangle, neither of which would evenly divide the 30" dimension of the rectangle. The computed answer is correct.

12. **(B).** When dealing with remainder questions on the GRE, the best thing to do is test a few real numbers:

Multiples of 6 are 0, 6, 12, 18, 24, 30, 36, etc.

Numbers with a remainder of 4 when divided by 6 are those 4 greater than the multiples of 6:

$x$ could be 4, 10, 16, 22, 28, 34, 40, etc.

You could keep listing numbers, but this is probably enough to establish a pattern.

(A) $\dfrac{x}{2}$ $\longrightarrow$ ALL of the listed $x$ values are divisible by 2. Eliminate (A).

(B) $\dfrac{x}{3}$ $\longrightarrow$ NONE of the listed $x$ values are divisible by 3, but continue checking.

(C) $\dfrac{x}{7}$ $\longrightarrow$ 28 is divisible by 7.

(D) $\dfrac{x}{11}$ $\longrightarrow$ 22 is divisible by 11.

(E) $\dfrac{x}{17}$ $\longrightarrow$ 34 is divisible by 17.

The question is "Each of the following could also be an integer EXCEPT." Since four of the choices could be integers, (B) must be the answer.

13. **7, 8, and 10 only.** If $x^y = 64$ and $x$ and $y$ are positive integers, perhaps the most obvious possibility is that $x = 8$ and $y = 2$. However, "all such values" implies that other solutions are possible. One shortcut is noting that only an even base, when raised to a power, could equal 64. So you only have to worry about even possibilities for $x$. Here are all the possibilities:

$$2^6 = 64 \quad \longrightarrow x + y = 8$$
$$4^3 = 64 \quad \longrightarrow x + y = 7$$
$$8^2 = 64 \quad \longrightarrow x + y = 10$$
$$64^1 = 64 \quad \longrightarrow x + y = 65$$

The only possible values of $x + y$ listed among the choices are 7, 8, and 10.

14. **(C).** If $k$ is a multiple of 24, it contains the prime factors of 24: 2, 2, 2, and 3. (It could also contain other prime factors, but the only ones for certain are the prime factors contained in 24.)

If $k$ were a multiple of 16, it would contain the prime factors of 16: 2, 2, 2, and 2.

Thus, if $k$ is a multiple of 24 but *not* of 16, $k$ must contain 2, 2, and 2, but *not* a fourth 2 (otherwise, it would be a multiple of 16).

Thus: $k$ definitely has 2, 2, 2, and 3. It could have any other prime factors (including more 3's) *except* for more 2's.

An answer choice in which the denominator contains more than three 2's would guarantee a non-integer result. Only choice (C) works. Since $k$ has fewer 2's than 32, $\dfrac{k}{32}$ can never be an integer.

Alternatively, list multiples of 24 for $k$: 24, 48, 72, 96, 120, 144, 168, etc.

Then, eliminate multiples of 16 from this list: 24, ~~48~~, 72, ~~96~~, 120, ~~144~~, 168, etc.

A pattern emerges: $k = $ (an odd integer) $\times$ 24:

  (A) $\dfrac{k}{8}$ can be an integer, for example when $k = 24$.

  (B) $\dfrac{k}{9}$ can be an integer, for example when $k = 72$.

  (C) $\dfrac{k}{32}$ is correct by process of elimination.

  (D) $\dfrac{k}{36}$ can be an integer, for example when $k = 72$.

  (E) $\dfrac{k}{81}$ can be an integer, for example when $k = 81 \times 24$.

15. **10.** Because this is a numeric entry question, there can be only one correct answer. So, plugging in any prime number greater than 2 for $b$ must yield the same result. Try $b = 3$.

If $a = 16b$ and $b = 3$, then $a$ is 48. The factors (*not* prime factors) of 48 are: 1 & 48, 2 & 24, 3 & 16, 4 & 12, and 6 & 8. There are 10 distinct factors.

16. **(C).** Since a positive multiple must be greater than or equal to the number it is a multiple of, answer choice (C) cannot be a multiple of $a$ or $b$, as it is smaller than both integers $a$ and $b$.

Alternatively, try testing numbers such that $a$ is larger than $b$:

  (A)   If $a = 3$ and $b = 2$, $a - 1 = 2$, which is a multiple of $b$.
  (B)   If $a = 3$ and $b = 2$, $b + 1 = 3$, which is a multiple of $a$.
  (C)   Is the correct answer by process of elimination.
  (D)   If $a = 4$ and $b = 2$, $a + b = 6$, which is a multiple of $b$.
  (E)   If $a = 3$ and $b = 2$, $ab = 6$, which is a multiple of both $a$ and $b$.

**MANHATTAN**
PREP

17. **12.** Remember, remainders are always whole numbers, so dividing 616 by 6 in the GRE calculator won't yield the answer. Rather, find the largest number less than 616 that 6 *does* go into (not 615, not 614, not 613 … ). That number is 612. Since $616 - 612 = 4$, the remainder $p$ is equal to 4.

Alternatively, divide 616 by 6 in your calculator to get 102.66…. Since 6 goes into 616 precisely 102 whole times, multiply $6 \times 102$ to get 612, then subtract from 616 to get the remainder 4.

This second method might be best for finding $q$. Divide 525 by 11 to get 47.7272…. Since $47 \times 11 = 517$, the remainder is $525 - 517 = 8$.

Therefore, $p + q = 4 + 8 = 12$.

18. **"$x + y$ is divisible by 6" only.** To solve this problem with examples, make a short list of possibilities for each of $x$ and $y$:

$x = 18, 36, 54 …$
$y = 12, 24, 36 …$

Now try to *disprove* the statements by trying several combinations of $x$ and $y$ above. In the 1st statement, $x + y$ could be $18 + 12 = 30$, $54 + 12 = 66$, $36 + 24 = 60$, or many other combinations. All of those combinations are multiples of 6. This makes sense, as $x$ and $y$ individually are multiples of 6, so their sum is, too. The first statement is true.

To test the second statement, $xy$ could be $18(12) = 216$, which is *not* divisible by 48. Eliminate the second statement.

As for the third statement, $\dfrac{x}{y}$ could be $\dfrac{18}{12}$, which is not even an integer (and therefore not divisible by 6), so the third statement is not necessarily true.

19. **(D).** This problem is most easily solved with an example. If $p = 7$ and $q = 6$, then $pq = 42$, which has the factors 1 & 42, 2 & 21, 3 & 14, and 6 & 7. That's 8 factors, but read carefully! The question asks how many factors *greater than 1*, so the answer is 7. Note that choosing the smallest possible examples ($p = 7$ and $q = 6$) was the right move here, since the question asks "at least how many factors …?" If testing $p = 70$ and $q = 36$, many, many more factors would have resulted. The question asks for the minimum.

20. **(C).** This problem is most easily solved with an example. If $r = 10$ and $s = 9$, then $rs = 90$. The factors of 90 are 1 & 90, 2 & 45, 3 & 30, 5 & 18, 6 & 15, and 9 & 10. Count to get a minimum of 12 factors.

21. **(D).** If $t$ is divisible by 12, then $t^2$ must be divisible by 144 or $2 \times 2 \times 2 \times 2 \times 3 \times 3$. Therefore, $t^2$ can be divided evenly by 2 at least four times, so $a$ must be at least 5 before $\dfrac{t^2}{2^a}$ might not be an integer.

Alternatively, test values. If $t = 12$, $\dfrac{t^2}{2^a} = \dfrac{144}{2^a}$. Plug in the choices as possible $a$ values, starting with the smallest choice and working up:

(A)   Since $\dfrac{144}{2^2} = 36$, eliminate.

(B)   Since $\dfrac{144}{2^3} = 18$, eliminate.

(C)   Since $\dfrac{144}{2^4} = 9$, eliminate.

(D)   $\dfrac{144}{2^5} = 4.5$. The first choice for which $\dfrac{t^2}{2^a}$ might not be an integer is (D).

22. $a + b + c$, $a - b + c$, and $\dfrac{abc}{9}$. Since $a$, $b$, and $c$ are all multiples of 3, $a = 3x$, $b = 3y$, $c = 3z$, where $x > y > z > 0$ and all are integers. Substitute these new expressions into the statements.

First statement: $a + b + c = 3x + 3y + 3z = 3(x + y + z)$. Since $(x + y + z)$ is an integer, this number must be divisible by 3.

Second statement: $a - b + c = 3x - 3y + 3z = 3(x - y + z)$. Since $(x + y + z)$ is an integer, this number must be divisible by 3.

Third statement: $\dfrac{abc}{9} = \dfrac{3x\,3y\,3z}{9} = \dfrac{27xyz}{9} = 3xyz$. Since $xyz$ is an integer, this number must be divisible by 3.

23. **(C).** Pattern problems on the GRE often include a very large series of items that would be impossible (or at least unwise) to write out on paper. Instead, try to recognize and exploit the pattern. In this case, after every 4th car, the color pattern repeats. By dividing 463 by 4, you find that there will be 115 cycles through the 4 colors of cars—red, blue, black, gray—for a total of 460 cars to exit the factory. The key to solving these problems is the remainder. Because there are $463 - 460 = 3$ cars remaining, the first such car will be red, the second will be blue, and the third will be black.

24. **(D).** This is a pattern problem. An efficient method is to recognize that the 7th day after the initial deposit would be Tuesday, as would the 14th day, the 21st day, etc. Divide 100 by 7 to get 14 full weeks comprising 98 days, plus 2 days left over. For the two leftover days, think about when they would fall. The first day after the deposit would be a Wednesday, as would the first day after waiting 98 days. The second day after the deposit would be a Thursday, and so would the 100th day.

25. **(D).** Division problems can be interpreted as follows: dividend = divisor × quotient + remainder. This problem is dividing $x$ by 7, or distributing $x$ items equally to 7 groups. After the items are distributed among the 7 groups, there are 3 items left over, the remainder. This means that the value of $x$ must be some number that is 3 larger than a multiple of 7, such as 3, 10, 17, 24, etc. The only answer choice that is 3 larger than a multiple of 7 is 52.

26. **(E).** This is a bit of a trick question—any number that yields remainder 4 when divided by 10 will also yield remainder 4 when divided by 5. This is because the remainder 4 is less than both divisors, and all multiples of 10 are also multiples of 5. For example, 14 yields remainder 4 when divided either by 10 or by 5. This also works for 24, 34, 44, 54, etc.

27. **0.** The remainder when dividing an integer by 10 always equals the units digit. You can also ignore all but the units digits, so the question can be rephrased as: *What is the units digit of $3^{17} + 7^{13}$?*

The pattern for the units digits of 3 is [3, 9, 7, 1]. Every fourth term is the same. The 17th power is 1 past the end of the repeat: $17 - 16 = 1$. Thus, $3^{17}$ must end in 3.

**MANHATTAN**
PREP

The pattern for the units digits of 7 is [7, 9, 3, 1]. Every fourth term is the same. The 13th power is 1 past the end of the repeat: $13 - 12 = 1$. Thus, $7^{13}$ must end in 7. The sum of these units digits is $3 + 7 = 10$. Thus, the units digit is 0.

28. **(C).** Start by considering the relationship between $n$ and $n^3$. Because $n$ is an integer, for every prime factor $n$ has, $n^3$ must have three of them. Thus, $n^3$ must have prime numbers in multiples of 3. If $n^3$ has one prime factor of 3, it must actually have two more, because $n^3$'s prime factors can only come in triples.

The question says that $n^3$ is divisible by 24, so $n^3$'s prime factors must include at least three 2's and a 3. But since $n^3$ is a cube, it must contain at least three 3's. Therefore, $n$ must contain at least one 2 and one 3, or $2 \times 3 = 6$.

29. **(C).** First, expand 10! as $10 \times 9 \times 8 \times 7 \times 6 \times 5 \times 4 \times 3 \times 2 \times 1$.

(Do *not* multiply all of those numbers together to get 3,628,800—it's true that 3,628,800 is the value of 10!, but analysis of the prime factors of 10! is easier in the current form.)

Note that 10! is divisible by $3^x 5^y$, and the question asks for the greatest possible values of $x$ and $y$, which is equivalent to asking, "What is the maximum number of times you can divide 3 and 5, respectively, out of 10! while still getting an integer answer?"

In the product $10 \times 9 \times 8 \times 7 \times 6 \times 5 \times 4 \times 3 \times 2 \times 1$, only the multiples of 3 have 3 in their prime factors, and only the multiples of 5 have 5 in their prime factors. Here are all the primes contained in $10 \times 9 \times 8 \times 7 \times 6 \times 5 \times 4 \times 3 \times 2 \times 1$ and therefore in 10!:

$10 = 5 \times 2$
$9 = 3 \times 3$
$8 = 2 \times 2 \times 2$
$7 = 7$
$6 = 2 \times 3$
$5 = 5$
$4 = 2 \times 2$
$3 = 3$
$2 = 2$
$1 = $ no primes

There are four 3's and two 5's total. The maximum values are $x = 4$ and $y = 2$. Therefore, the two quantities are equal.

30. **(B).** Since only the number of *distinct* prime factors matter, not what they are or how many times they are present, it is possible to tell on sight that Quantity A has only 2 distinct prime factors, because 100,000 is a power of 10. (Any prime tree for 10, 100, or 1,000, etc. will contain only the prime factors 2 and 5, occurring in pairs.)

In Quantity B, 99,000 breaks down as $99 \times 1,000$. Since 1,000 also contains 2's and 5's, and 99 contains even more factors (specifically 3, 3, and 11), Quantity B is greater. It is not necessary to make prime factor trees for each number.

31. **$18^3$, $30^3$, and 222 only.** Because $64 = 2^6$, multiples of 64 would have at least six 2's among their prime factors.

Since 12 (which is $2 \times 2 \times 3$) has two 2's already, a number that could be multiplied by 12 to generate a multiple of 64 would need to have, at minimum, the *other* four 2's needed to generate a multiple of 64.

Since you want the choices that don't multiply with 12 to generate a multiple of 64, select only the choices that have *fewer than four 2's* within their prime factors.

| | | | |
|---|---|---|---|
| $6^6$ | $= (2 \times 3)^6$ | six 2's | INCORRECT |
| $12^2$ | $= (2^2 \times 3)^2$ | four 2's | INCORRECT |
| $18^3$ | $= (2 \times 3^2)^3$ | three 2's | CORRECT |
| $30^3$ | $= (2 \times 3 \times 5)^3$ | three 2's | CORRECT |
| $222$ | $= (2 \times 3 \times 37)$ | one 2 | CORRECT |

32. **(D).** When a non-multiple of 3 is divided by 3, the quotient does not terminate (for instance, $\frac{1}{3} = 0.333...$).

Since $\dfrac{3^x (5^2)}{3^5 (5^3)}$ does *not* repeat forever, $x$ must be large enough to cancel out the $3^5$ in the denominator. Thus, $x$ must be at least 5. Note that the question asks what *must* be true. Choice (D) must be true. Choice (E), $x = 5$, represents one value that would work, but this choice does not *have* to be true.

33. **(B).** Since a prime number has only two factors, 1 and itself, $(2^a)(3^b)(5^c)$ cannot be prime unless the digits $a$, $b$, and $c$ are such that two of the digits are 0 and the third is 1. For instance, $(2^0)(3^1)(5^0) = (1)(3)(1) = 3$ is prime. Thus, the only three values of <u>abc</u> that would result in a prime number &(<u>abc</u>)& are 100, 010, and 001. However, only one of those three numbers (100) is a three-digit number.

**MANHATTAN**
PREP

# Chapter 14

## of

5 lb. Book of GRE® Practice Problems

# Exponents and Roots

# In This Chapter...

Exponents and Roots

Exponents and Roots Answers

# Exponents and Roots

For questions in the Quantitative Comparison format ("Quantity A" and "Quantity B" given), the answer choices are always as follows:

(A)   Quantity A is greater.
(B)   Quantity B is greater.
(C)   The two quantities are equal.
(D)   The relationship cannot be determined from the information given.

For questions followed by a numeric entry box $\boxed{\phantom{xxx}}$, you are to enter your own answer in the box. For questions followed

by a fraction-style numeric entry box $\dfrac{\boxed{\phantom{xx}}}{\boxed{\phantom{xx}}}$, you are to enter your answer in the form of a fraction. You are not required to

reduce fractions. For example, if the answer is $\dfrac{1}{4}$, you may enter $\dfrac{25}{100}$ or any equivalent fraction.

All numbers used are real numbers. All figures are assumed to lie in a plane unless otherwise indicated. Geometric figures are not necessarily drawn to scale. You should assume, however, that lines that appear to be straight are actually straight, points on a line are in the order shown, and all geometric objects are in the relative positions shown. Coordinate systems, such as $xy$-planes and number lines, as well as graphical data presentations, such as bar charts, circle graphs, and line graphs, *are* drawn to scale. A symbol that appears more than once in a question has the same meaning throughout the question.

|  | **Quantity A** | **Quantity B** |
|---|---|---|
| 1. | $25^7$ | $5^{15}$ |

$$216 = 2^x 3^y$$
$x$ and $y$ are integers.

|  | **Quantity A** | **Quantity B** |
|---|---|---|
| 2. | $x$ | $y$ |

|  | **Quantity A** | **Quantity B** |
|---|---|---|
| 3. | $\sqrt{9}\sqrt{25}$ | $\sqrt{15}$ |

|  | **Quantity A** | **Quantity B** |
|---|---|---|
| 4. | $\sqrt{3}+\sqrt{6}$ | $\sqrt{9}$ |

5.   If $5{,}000 = 2^x 5^y$ and $x$ and $y$ are integers, what is the value of $x + y$?

$\boxed{\phantom{xxxxxxxx}}$

6. If $3^2 9^2 = 3^x$, what is the value of $x$?

    (A)  2
    (B)  3
    (C)  4
    (D)  5
    (E)  6

    80 is divisible by $2^x$.

    **Quantity A**          **Quantity B**

7.          $x$          3

8. If $17\sqrt[3]{m} = 34$, what is the value of $6\sqrt[3]{m}$?

    _____

9. $\dfrac{\dfrac{1}{1}}{\dfrac{1}{5^{-2}}}$   is equal to which of the following?

    (A)  $\dfrac{1}{25}$
    (B)  $\dfrac{1}{5}$
    (C)  1
    (D)  5
    (E)  25

10. $\sqrt{2+\sqrt{2+\sqrt{2+\sqrt{4}}}}$  is equal to which of the following?

    (A)  $\sqrt{2}$
    (B)  2
    (C)  $2\sqrt{2}$
    (D)  4
    (E)  $4\sqrt{2}$

    **Quantity A**          **Quantity B**

11.          $10^6 + 10^5$          $10^7 + 10^4$

**MANHATTAN**
PREP

12. For which of the following positive integers is the square of that integer divided by the cube root of the same integer equal to nine times that integer?

    (A)   4

    (B)   8

    (C)   16

    (D)   27

    (E)   125

13.

    0               $\sqrt[3]{p}$  2

If the hash marks above are equally spaced, what is the value of $p$?

    (A)   $\dfrac{3}{2}$

    (B)   $\dfrac{8}{5}$

    (C)   $\dfrac{24}{15}$

    (D)   $\dfrac{512}{125}$

    (E)   $\dfrac{625}{256}$

14. What is the greatest prime factor of $2^{99} - 2^{96}$?

    ☐

15. If $2^{k} - 2^{k+1} + 2^{k-1} = 2^{k}m$, what is the value of $m$?

    (A)   $-1$

    (B)   $-\dfrac{1}{2}$

    (C)   $\dfrac{1}{2}$

    (D)   1

    (E)   2

16.  If $5^{k+1} = 2{,}000$, what is the value of $5^k + 1$?

   (A)   399
   (B)   401
   (C)   1,996
   (D)   2,000
   (E)   2,001

17.  If $3^{11} = 9^x$, what is the value of $x$?

18.  If $\sqrt[5]{x^6} = x^{\frac{a}{b}}$, what is the value of $\frac{a}{b}$?

   Give your answer as a fraction.

19.  Which of the following is equal to $\dfrac{10^{-8}25^7 2^{16}}{20^6 8^{-1}}$?

   (A)   $\dfrac{1}{5}$
   (B)   $\dfrac{1}{2}$
   (C)   2
   (D)   5
   (E)   10

20.  If $\dfrac{5^7}{5^{-4}} = 5^a$, $\dfrac{2^{-3}}{2^{-2}} = 2^b$, and $3^8(3) = 3^c$, what is the value of $a + b + c$?

21.  If $12^x$ is odd and $x$ is an integer, what is the value of $x^{12}$?

**MANHATTAN**
PREP

22. What is the value of $\dfrac{44^{\frac{5}{2}}}{\sqrt{11^3}}$?

    ```
    ┌─────────────┐
    │             │
    └─────────────┘
    ```

$$\frac{(10^3)(0.027)}{(900)(10^{-2})} = (3)(10^m)$$

| **Quantity A** | **Quantity B** |
|:---:|:---:|
23.
| $m$ | 3 |

24. Which of the following equals $\dfrac{2^2 + 2^2 + 2^3 + 2^4}{(\sqrt{5}+\sqrt{3})(\sqrt{5}-\sqrt{3})}$?

    (A)  2

    (B)  4

    (C)  8

    (D)  16

    (E)  32

25. If $\dfrac{0.000027 \times 10^x}{900 \times 10^{-4}} = 0.03 \times 10^{11}$, what is the value of $x$?

    (A)  13

    (B)  14

    (C)  15

    (D)  16

    (E)  17

26. Which of the following equals $\left(\sqrt[2]{x}\right)\left(\sqrt[3]{x}\right)$?

    (A)  $\sqrt[5]{x}$

    (B)  $\sqrt[6]{x}$

    (C)  $\sqrt[3]{x^2}$

    (D)  $\sqrt[5]{x^6}$

    (E)  $\sqrt[6]{x^5}$

$$n = 0.00025 \times 10^4 \text{ and } m = 0.005 \times 10^2$$

| **Quantity A** | **Quantity B** |
|---|---|
| 27. $\dfrac{n}{m}$ | 0.5 |

28. If $2^2 < \dfrac{x}{2^6 - 2^4} < 2^3$, which of the following could be the value of $x$?

Indicate all such values.

- ☐  24
- ☐  64
- ☐  80
- ☐  128
- ☐  232
- ☐  256

29. Which of the following is equal to $x^{\frac{3}{2}}$?

   (A)  $x^2\sqrt{x}$
   (B)  $x\sqrt{x}$
   (C)  $\sqrt[3]{x^2}$
   (D)  $\sqrt[3]{x}$
   (E)  $(x^3)^2$

30. If $125^{14}48^8$ were expressed as an integer, how many consecutive zeros would that integer have immediately to the left of its decimal point?

   (A)  22
   (B)  32
   (C)  42
   (D)  50
   (E)  112

# Exponents and Roots Answers

1. **(B).** If a problem combines exponents with different bases, convert to the same base if possible. Since $25 = 5^2$, Quantity A is equal to $(5^2)^7$. Apply the appropriate exponent formula: $(a^b)^c = a^{bc}$. Quantity A is equal to $5^{14}$, thus Quantity B is greater.

2. **(C).** Construct a prime factor tree for 216:

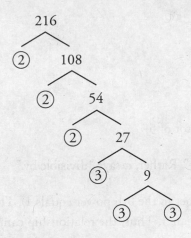

$216 = 2^3 3^3$, so $x = 3$ and $y = 3$.

3. **(A).** In Quantity A, $\sqrt{9}\sqrt{25} = 3 \times 5 = 15$. Since 15 is greater than $\sqrt{15}$, Quantity A is greater.

4. **(A).** You may *not* add $\sqrt{3}$ and $\sqrt{6}$ to get $\sqrt{9}$, but you can put each value in the calculator. $\sqrt{3} = 1.732...$ and $\sqrt{6} = 2.449...$, and their sum is about 4.18. Since Quantity B is $\sqrt{9} = 3$, Quantity A is greater.

5. **7.** Construct a prime factor tree for 5,000:

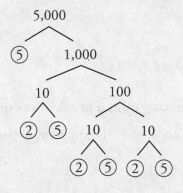

Thus, $5,000 = 2^3 5^4$, therefore $x = 3$ and $y = 4$, and the answer is $3 + 4 = 7$.

6. **(E).** In order to compare or combine exponents with different bases, convert to the same base if possible. Since $9 = 3^2$:

$$3^2(3^2)^2 = 3^x$$

Multiply exponents in accordance with the exponent formula, $(a^b)^c = a^{bc}$:

$$3^2 3^4 = 3^x$$

Add the exponents to multiply numbers that have the same base:

$$3^6 = 3^x$$

Therefore, $x = 6$.

7. **(D).** Construct a prime factor tree for 80; it has four factors of 2 and one factor of 5.

That doesn't mean $x$ is 4, however! The problem does not say "80 is equal to $2^x$". Rather, it says "divisible by."

80 is divisible by $2^4$, and therefore also by $2^3$, $2^2$, $2^1$, and $2^0$ (any non-zero number to the 0th power equals 1). Thus, $x$ could be 0, 1, 2, 3, or 4, and could therefore be less than, equal to, or greater than 3. Thus, the relationship cannot be determined.

8. **12.** This question looks much more complicated than it really is—note that $\sqrt[3]{m}$ is in both the given equation and the question. Just think of $\sqrt[3]{m}$ as a very fancy variable that you don't have to break down:

$$17\sqrt[3]{m} = 34$$

$$\sqrt[3]{m} = \frac{34}{17}$$

$$\sqrt[3]{m} = 2$$

Therefore, $6\sqrt[3]{m} = 6(2) = 12$.

9. **(A).** This question requires recognizing that a negative exponent in the denominator turns into a positive exponent in the numerator. In other words, the lowermost portion of the fraction, $\frac{1}{5^{-2}}$, is equal to $5^2$. The uppermost portion of the fraction, $\frac{1}{1}$, is just equal to 1.

Putting these together, the original fraction can be simplified. $\dfrac{\frac{1}{1}}{\frac{1}{5^{-2}}} = \frac{1}{5^2} = \frac{1}{25}$, which is the final answer.

**MANHATTAN**
PREP

10. **(B).** To solve, start at the "inner core"—that is, the physically smallest root sign:

$$\sqrt{2+\sqrt{2+\sqrt{2+\sqrt{4}}}} =$$
$$\sqrt{2+\sqrt{2+\sqrt{2+2}}} =$$
$$\sqrt{2+\sqrt{2+2}} =$$
$$\sqrt{2+2} = 2$$

11. **(B).** Be careful! These quantities are not equal! When *multiplying* exponents with the same base, it is correct to add the exponents:

$$10^6 \times 10^5 = 10^{11}$$

However, numbers raised to powers cannot be directly combined by addition or subtraction. Instead, sum this way:

Quantity A $= 10^6 + 10^5 = 1,000,000 + 100,000 = 1,100,000$

Quantity B $= 10^7 + 10^4 = 10,000,000 + 10,000 = 10,010,000$

Thus, Quantity B is greater.

Alternatively, you can do some fancy factoring. The distributive property is a big help here: $ab + ac = a(b + c)$. In other words, factor out the $a$.

Factor out $10^5$ in Quantity A:

$$10^6 + 10^5 = 10^5\left(10^1 + 1\right) = 10^5\left(11\right) \cong 10^6$$

Factor out $10^4$ in Quantity B:

$$10^7 + 10^4 = 10^4\left(10^3 + 1\right) = 10^4\left(1,001\right) \cong 10^7$$

The approximation in the last step is just to make the point that you don't have to be too precise: Quantity B is about 10 times greater than Quantity A.

12. **(D).** To solve this question, translate the text into an equation. Call "the square of that integer" $x^2$, "the cube root of the same integer" $\sqrt[3]{x}$, and "nine times that integer" $9x$:

$$\frac{x^2}{\sqrt[3]{x}} = 9x$$

Test the answers; doing so shows that choice (D) is correct:

$$\frac{27^2}{\sqrt[3]{27}} = 9(27)$$

$$\frac{27^2}{3} = 9(27)$$

$$27^2 = 9(27)(3)$$

$$27 = 9(3)$$

Choices (A) and (C) are not likely to be correct because the cube roots of 4 and 16, respectively, are not integers; test the others first:

Choice (B): $\frac{64}{2} = 9(8)$? No.

Choice (D): Correct as shown above.

Choice (E): $\frac{15,626}{5} = 9(125)$? No.

13. **(D).** To determine the distance between hash marks, divide 2 (the distance from 0 to 2) by 5 (the number of segments the number line has been divided into). The result is $\frac{2}{5}$. Therefore:

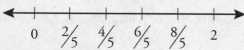

Note that 2 is equal to $\frac{10}{5}$, so the number line is labeled correctly.

Since $\sqrt[3]{p}$ marks the same hash mark on the number line as $\frac{8}{5}$:

$$\sqrt[3]{p} = \frac{8}{5}$$

$$p = \left(\frac{8}{5}\right)^3$$

$$p = \frac{512}{125}$$

The answer is (D). Watch out for trap answer choice (B), which represents $\sqrt[3]{p}$, not $p$.

14. **7.** You cannot subtract $2^{99} - 2^{96}$ to get $2^3$! You cannot directly combine numbers raised to powers when adding or subtracting. (As it turns out, the difference between $2^{99}$ and $2^{96}$ is much, much greater than $2^3$.) Instead, factor out the greatest common factor of $2^{99}$ and $2^{96}$:

$$2^{99} - 2^{96} = 2^{96}(2^3 - 1) = 2^{96}(7)$$

Since $2^{99} - 2^{96}$ is equal to $2^{96}7^1$, its greatest prime factor is 7.

**MANHATTAN**
PREP

15. **(B).** First, factor $2^{k+1}$ into $2^k 2^1$ and $2^{k-1}$ into $2^k 2^{-1}$:

$$2^k - 2^k 2^1 + 2^k 2^{-1} = 2^k m$$

Factor out $2^k$ from the left, then cancel $2^k$ from both sides:

$$2^k(1 - 2^1 + 2^{-1}) = 2^k m$$

$$1 - 2^1 + 2^{-1} = m$$

$$1 - 2 + \frac{1}{2} = m$$

$$-\frac{1}{2} = m$$

16. **(B).** The key to solving this problem is to understand that $5^{k+1}$ can be factored into $5^k 5^1$. (Exponents are added when multiplying numbers with the same base, so the process can also be reversed; thus, any expression with the form $x^{a+b}$ can be split into $x^a x^b$.) Thus:

$$5^{k+1} = 2{,}000$$

$$5^k 5^1 = 2{,}000$$

Now divide both sides by 5:

$$5^k = 400$$

So, $5^k + 1 = 401$.

Notice that you can't solve for $k$ itself—$k$ is not an integer, since 400 is not a "normal" power of 5. But you don't need to solve for $k$. You just need $5^k$.

17. **5.5.** Begin by converting 9 to a power of 3:

$$3^{11} = \left(3^2\right)^x$$
$$3^{11} = 3^{2x}$$

Thus, $11 = 2x$ and $x = 5.5$.

18. $\dfrac{6}{5}$. The square root of a number equals that number to the $\dfrac{1}{2}$ power, so too is a fifth root the same as a $\dfrac{1}{5}$ exponent. Thus:

$$\sqrt[5]{x^6} = (x^6)^{\frac{1}{5}} = x^{\frac{6}{5}}$$

Since $x^{\frac{6}{5}} = x^{\frac{a}{b}}$, $\dfrac{a}{b} = \dfrac{6}{5}$.

19. **(B).** Since $10^{-8} = \dfrac{1}{10^8}$ and $\dfrac{1}{8^{-1}} = 8^1$, first substitute to convert any term with negative exponents to one with a positive exponent:

$$\frac{10^{-8}25^7 2^{16}}{20^6 8^{-1}} = \frac{25^7 2^{16} 8^1}{10^8 20^6}$$

Then, convert the non-prime terms to primes, combining and canceling where possible:

$$\frac{25^7 2^{16} 8^1}{10^8 20^6} = \frac{\left(5^2\right)^7 2^{16} \left(2^3\right)^1}{\left(2^1 5^1\right)^8 \left(2^2 5^1\right)^6} = \frac{5^{14} 2^{16} 2^3}{2^8 5^8 2^{12} 5^6} = \frac{5^{14} 2^{19}}{2^{20} 5^{14}} = \frac{1}{2}$$

20. **19.** To solve this problem, you need to know that to divide numbers with the same base, subtract the exponents, and to multiply them, add the exponents. Thus:

$$\frac{5^7}{5^{-4}} = 5^{7-(-4)} = 5^{11}, \text{ so } a = 11.$$

$$\frac{2^{-3}}{2^{-2}} = 2^{-3-(-2)} = 2^{-1}, \text{ so } b = -1.$$

$$3^8(3) = 3^8(3^1) = 3^9, \text{ so } c = 9.$$

Therefore, $a + b + c = 11 + (-1) + 9 = 19$.

21. **0.** This is a bit of a trick question. $12^x$ is odd? How strange! $12^1$ is 12, $12^2$ is 144, $12^3$ is 1,728 ... every "normal" power of 12 is even. (An even number such as 12 multiplied by itself any number of times will yield an even answer.) These normal powers are 12 raised to a positive integer. What about negative integer exponents? They are all fractions of this form: $\dfrac{1}{12^{\text{positive integer}}}$.

The only way for $12^x$ to be odd is for $x$ to equal 0. Any non-zero number to the 0th power is equal to 1. Since $x = 0$ and the question asks for $x^{12}$, the answer is 0.

22. **352.** A square root is the same as a $\dfrac{1}{2}$ exponent, so $\dfrac{44^{\frac{5}{2}}}{\sqrt{11^3}} = \dfrac{44^{\frac{5}{2}}}{\left(11^3\right)^{\frac{1}{2}}} = \dfrac{44^{\frac{5}{2}}}{11^{\frac{3}{2}}}$.

The common factor of 44 and 11 is 11, so factor the numerator:

$$\frac{44^{\frac{5}{2}}}{11^{\frac{3}{2}}} = \frac{11^{\frac{5}{2}} 4^{\frac{5}{2}}}{11^{\frac{3}{2}}}$$

When dividing exponential expressions that have a common base, subtract the exponents:

$$\left(\frac{11^{\frac{5}{2}}}{11^{\frac{3}{2}}}\right)4^{\frac{5}{2}} = \left(11^{\frac{5}{2}-\frac{3}{2}}\right)4^{\frac{5}{2}} = \left(11^{\frac{2}{2}}\right)4^{\frac{5}{2}} = \left(11^{1}\right)4^{\frac{5}{2}}$$

Now simplify the 4 term, again noting that a $\frac{1}{2}$ exponent is the same as a square root:

$$\left(11^{1}\right)4^{\frac{5}{2}} = (11)\left(4^{\frac{1}{2}}\right)^{5} = (11)\left(\sqrt{4}\right)^{5} = (11)\left(2^{5}\right) = 352$$

23. **(B).** Since $(10^{3})(0.027)$ is 27 and $(900)(10^{-2})$ is 9:

$$\frac{27}{9} = (3)(10^{m})$$

$$3 = 3(10^{m})$$

$$1 = 10^{m}$$

You might be a little confused at this point as to how $10^{m}$ can equal 1. However, you can still answer the question correctly. If $m$ were 3, as in Quantity B, $10^{m}$ would equal 1,000. However, $10^{m}$ actually equals 1. So $m$ must be less than 3.

As it turns out, the only way $10^{m}$ can equal 1 is if $m = 0$. Any non-zero number to the 0th power is equal to 1.

24. **(D).** You could factor $2^{2}$ out of the numerator, but the numbers are small enough that you might as well just say that the numerator is $4 + 4 + 8 + 16 = 32$.

FOIL the denominator:

$$(\sqrt{5} + \sqrt{3})(\sqrt{5} - \sqrt{3})$$
$$\sqrt{25} + \sqrt{3}\sqrt{5} - \sqrt{3}\sqrt{5} - \sqrt{9}$$
$$\sqrt{25} - \sqrt{9}$$

$$5 - 3 = 2$$

$$\frac{32}{2} = 16 \text{ is the final answer.}$$

25. **(A).** One good approach is to convert 0.000027, 900, and 0.03 to powers of 10:

$$\frac{27 \times 10^{-6} \times 10^{x}}{9 \times 10^{2} \times 10^{-4}} = 3 \times 10^{-2} \times 10^{11}$$

Now combine the exponents from the terms with base 10:

$$\frac{27 \times 10^{-6+x}}{9 \times 10^{-2}} = 3 \times 10^{9}$$

Since $\frac{27}{9} = 3$, cancel the 3 from both sides, then combine powers of 10:

$$\frac{10^{-6+x}}{10^{-2}} = 10^{9}$$

$$10^{-6+x-(-2)} = 10^{9}$$

$$10^{-4+x} = 10^{9}$$

Thus, $-4 + x = 9$, and $x = 13$.

26. **(E).** A good first step is to convert to fractional exponents. A square root is the same as the $\frac{1}{2}$ power and a cube root is the same as the $\frac{1}{3}$ power:

$$x^{\frac{1}{2}} x^{\frac{1}{3}} = x^{\frac{1}{2}+\frac{1}{3}} = x^{\left(\frac{3}{6}+\frac{2}{6}\right)} = x^{\frac{5}{6}} = \sqrt[6]{x^{5}}$$

27. **(A).** To simplify $0.00025 \times 10^{4}$, move the decimal in $0.00025$ four places to the right to get $2.5$. To simplify $0.005 \times 10^{2}$, move the decimal in $0.005$ two places to the right to get $0.5$. Thus, $n = 2.5$, $m = 0.5$, and $\frac{n}{m} = \frac{2.5}{0.5} = 5$.

28. **232 and 256 only.** The inequality could be simplified using exponent rules, but all the numbers are small enough either to have memorized or to quickly calculate:

$$2^{2} < \frac{x}{2^{6} - 2^{4}} < 2^{3}$$

$$4 < \frac{x}{64 - 16} < 8$$

$$4 < \frac{x}{48} < 8$$

To isolate $x$, multiply all three parts of the inequality by 48:

$$192 < x < 384$$

The only choices in this range are 232 and 256.

29. **(B).** Since a number to the $\frac{1}{2}$ power equals the square root of that number, $x^{\frac{3}{2}}$ could also be written as $\sqrt{x^{3}}$. This, however, does not appear in the choices. Note, however, that $\sqrt{x^{3}}$ can be simplified:

$$\sqrt{x^{2} \times x}$$

**MANHATTAN**
PREP

$$\frac{\sqrt{x^2} \times \sqrt{x}}{x\sqrt{x}}$$

This matches choice (B). Alternatively, convert the answer choices. For instance, in incorrect choice (A),

$x^2 \sqrt{x} = x^2 x^{\frac{1}{2}} = x^{\frac{5}{2}}$. Since this is not equal to $x^{\frac{3}{2}}$, eliminate (A). Correct choice (B) can be converted as such:

$x\sqrt{x} = x^1 x^{\frac{1}{2}} = x^{\frac{3}{2}}$.

31. **(B).** Exponents questions usually involve prime factorization, because you always want to find common bases, and the fundamental common bases are prime numbers. Test some values to see what leads to zeros at the end of an integer.

$$10 = 5 \times 2$$
$$40 = 8 \times 5 \times 2$$
$$100 = 10 \times 10 = 2 \times 5 \times 2 \times 5$$
$$1,000 = 10 \times 10 \times 10 = 2 \times 5 \times 2 \times 5 \times 2 \times 5$$

Ending zeros are created by 10's, each of which is the product of one 2 and one 5. So, to answer this question, determine how many pairs of 2's and 5's are in the expression:

$$125^{14}48^8 = (5^3)^{14} \times (2^4 \times 3)^8 = 5^{42} \times 2^{32} \times 3^8$$

Even though there are 42 powers of 5, there are only 32 powers of 2, so you can only form 32 pairs of one 5 and one 2.

# Chapter 15 *of*

5 lb. Book of GRE® Practice Problems

# Number Properties

## *In This Chapter...*

Number Properties

*Number Properties Answers*

# Number Properties

For questions in the Quantitative Comparison format ("Quantity A" and "Quantity B" given), the answer choices are always as follows:

(A)   Quantity A is greater.
(B)   Quantity B is greater.
(C)   The two quantities are equal.
(D)   The relationship cannot be determined from the information given.

For questions followed by a numeric entry box [     ], you are to enter your own answer in the box. For questions followed by a fraction-style numeric entry box $\dfrac{\boxed{\phantom{xx}}}{\boxed{\phantom{xx}}}$ , you are to enter your answer in the form of a fraction. You are not required to reduce fractions. For example, if the answer is $\dfrac{1}{4}$ , you may enter $\dfrac{25}{100}$ or any equivalent fraction.

All numbers used are real numbers. All figures are assumed to lie in a plane unless otherwise indicated. Geometric figures are not necessarily drawn to scale. You should assume, however, that lines that appear to be straight are actually straight, points on a line are in the order shown, and all geometric objects are in the relative positions shown. Coordinate systems, such as $xy$-planes and number lines, as well as graphical data presentations, such as bar charts, circle graphs, and line graphs, *are* drawn to scale. A symbol that appears more than once in a question has the same meaning throughout the question.

On a number line, the distance from $A$ to $B$ is 4 and the distance from $B$ to $C$ is 5.

| **Quantity A** | **Quantity B** |
|---|---|
| 1. The distance from $A$ to $C$ | 9 |

$a, b, c,$ and $d$ are consecutive integers such that $a < b < c < d$.

| **Quantity A** | **Quantity B** |
|---|---|
| 2. The average (arithmetic mean) of $a, b, c,$ and $d$ | The average (arithmetic mean) of $b$ and $c$ |

3. $w, x, y,$ and $z$ are consecutive odd integers such that $w < x < y < z$. Which of the following statements must be true?

Indicate all such statements.

☐   $wxyz$ is odd
☐   $w + x + y + z$ is odd
☐   $w + z = x + y$

| **Quantity A** | **Quantity B** |
|---|---|
| 4. The sum of all the odd integers from 1 to 100, inclusive | The sum of all the even integers from 1 to 100, inclusive |

$$x > 0 > y$$

| **Quantity A** | **Quantity B** |
|---|---|
| 5. $x - y$ | $(x + y)^2$ |

$$a < b < c < d < 0$$

| **Quantity A** | **Quantity B** |
|---|---|
| 6. $a - d$ | $bc$ |

7. If set $S$ consists of all positive integers that are multiples of both 2 and 7, how many numbers in set $S$ are between 140 and 240, inclusive?

$$ab > 0$$
$$bc < 0$$

| **Quantity A** | **Quantity B** |
|---|---|
| 8. $ac$ | $0$ |

$$abc < 0$$
$$b^2 c > 0$$

| **Quantity A** | **Quantity B** |
|---|---|
| 9. $ab$ | $0$ |

$a$, $b$, and $c$ are integers such that $a < b < c$.

| **Quantity A** | **Quantity B** |
|---|---|
| 10. $\dfrac{a + b + c}{3}$ | $b$ |

11. If $x^2 = y^2$, which of the following must be true?

- ☐ $x = y$
- ☐ $x^2 - y^2 = 0$
- ☐ $|x| - |y| = 0$

**MANHATTAN**
PREP

12. If $0 < a < \dfrac{1}{b} < 1$, then which of the following must be true?

    (A) $a^2 > a > b > b^2$

    (B) $b > a > a^2 > b^2$

    (C) $b^2 > a > a^2 > b$

    (D) $b^2 > a^2 > b > a$

    (E) $b^2 > b > a > a^2$

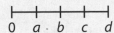

|  | **Quantity A** | **Quantity B** |
|---|---|---|
| 13. | $a \times c$ | $b \times d$ |

|  | **Quantity A** | **Quantity B** |
|---|---|---|
| 14. | The number of distinct factors of 32 | The number of distinct factors of 20 |

15. If $y^2 = 4$ and $x^2 y = 18$, which of the following values could equal $x + y$?

    Indicate **two** such values.

    ☐  −5

    ☐  −1

    ☐  1

    ☐  5

    ☐  6

|  | **Quantity A** | **Quantity B** |
|---|---|---|
| 16. | The remainder when $10^{11}$ is divided by 2 | The remainder when $3^{13}$ is divided by 3 |

$q$ is odd.

|  | **Quantity A** | **Quantity B** |
|---|---|---|
| 17. | $(-1)^q$ | $(-1)^{q+1}$ |

$n$ is a positive integer.

|  | **Quantity A** | **Quantity B** |
|---|---|---|
| 18. | $(-1)^{4n} \times (-1)^{202}$ | $(3)^3 \times (-5)^5$ |

19. If $x$ is a positive integer, which one of the following could be the remainder when $73^x$ is divided by 10?

    Indicate all such remainders.

    ☐ 0
    ☐ 1
    ☐ 2
    ☐ 3
    ☐ 4
    ☐ 5
    ☐ 6
    ☐ 7
    ☐ 8
    ☐ 9

20. If $x$, $y$, and $z$ are integers, $y + z = 13$, and $xz = 9$, which of the following must be true?

    (A) $x$ is even
    (B) $x = 3$
    (C) $y$ is odd
    (D) $y > 3$
    (E) $z < x$

|                        Quantity A                        |                     Quantity B                     |
| -------------------------------------------------------- | -------------------------------------------------- |
| 21. The least prime number greater<br>than 13            | The greatest prime number less<br>than 16          |

22. The average (arithmetic mean) of 11 integers is 35. What is the sum of all the integers?

    ┌─────────────┐
    │             │
    └─────────────┘

23. What is the sum of all the integers from 1 to 80, inclusive?

    (A) 3,200
    (B) 3,210
    (C) 3,230
    (D) 3,240
    (E) 3,450

**MANHATTAN**
PREP

24. If $p$ is the sum of all the integers from 1 to 150, inclusive, and $q$ is the sum of all the integers from 1 to 148, inclusive, what is the value of $p - q$?

25. If $m$ is the product of all the integers from 2 to 11, inclusive, and $n$ is the product of all the integers from 4 to 11, inclusive, what is the value of $\dfrac{n}{m}$?

    Give your answer as a fraction.

26. If $\sqrt{x}$ is an integer and $xy^2 = 36$, how many values are possible for the integer $y$?

    (A) Two
    (B) Three
    (C) Four
    (D) Six
    (E) Eight

    $a$, $b$, and $c$ are positive even integers such that $8 > a > b > c$.

    **Quantity A**              **Quantity B**
27.  The range of $a$, $b$, and $c$    The average (arithmetic mean)
                                        of $a$, $b$, and $c$

28. If $x$ is a non-zero integer and $0 < y < 1$, which of the following must be greater than 1?

    (A) $x$
    (B) $\dfrac{x}{y}$
    (C) $xy^2$
    (D) $x^2 y$
    (E) $\dfrac{x^2}{y}$

$a$, $b$, and $c$ are consecutive integers such that $a < b < c < 4$.

| | Quantity A | Quantity B |
|---|---|---|
| 29. | The range of $a$, $b$, and $c$ | The average of $a$, $b$, and $c$ |

$\sqrt{xy}$ is a prime number, $xy$ is even, and $x > 4y > 0$.

| | Quantity A | Quantity B |
|---|---|---|
| 30. | $y$ | 1 |

$x$ is even, $\sqrt{x}$ is a prime number, and $x + y = 11$.

| | Quantity A | Quantity B |
|---|---|---|
| 31. | $x$ | $y$ |

The product of positive integers $f$, $g$, and $h$ is even and the product of integers $f$ and $g$ is odd.

| | Quantity A | Quantity B |
|---|---|---|
| 32. | The remainder when $f$ is divided by 2 | The remainder when $h$ is divided by 2 |

33.  If $x$ is odd, all EXCEPT which one of the following must be odd?

(A)   $x^2 + 4x + 6$
(B)   $x^3 + 5x + 3$
(C)   $x^4 + 6x + 7$
(D)   $x^5 + 7x + 1$
(E)   $x^6 + 8x + 4$

$$x^2 > 25 \text{ and } x + y < 0$$

| | Quantity A | Quantity B |
|---|---|---|
| 34. | $x$ | $y$ |

The positive integer $a$ is divisible by 2 and $0 < ab < 1$.

| | Quantity A | Quantity B |
|---|---|---|
| 35. | $b$ | $\dfrac{1}{2}$ |

**MANHATTAN**
PREP

p and w are single-digit prime numbers such that $p + w < 6$.
$p^2$ is odd.

|  | **Quantity A** | **Quantity B** |
|---|---|---|
| 36. | w | 3 |

$$x^2 > y^2 \text{ and } x > -|y|$$

|  | **Quantity A** | **Quantity B** |
|---|---|---|
| 37. | x | y |

The sum of four consecutive integers is –2.

|  | **Quantity A** | **Quantity B** |
|---|---|---|
| 38. | The smallest of the four integers | –2 |

39. If $g$ is an integer and $x$ is a prime number, which of the following must be an integer?

Indicate all such expressions.

☐  $\dfrac{g^2 x + 5gx}{x}$

☐  $g^2 - x^2\left(\dfrac{1}{3}\right)$

☐  $6\left(\dfrac{g}{2}\right) - 100\left(\dfrac{g}{2}\right)^2$

# Number Properties Answers

1. **(D).** Whenever a question looks this straightforward ($4 + 5 = 9$, so the quantities initially appear equal), be suspicious. Draw the number line described. If the points $A$, $B$, and $C$ are in alphabetical order from left to right, then the distance from $A$ to $C$ will be 9. However, alphabetical order is not required. If the points are in the order $C$, $A$, and $B$ from left to right, then the distance from $A$ to $C$ is $5 - 4 = 1$. Therefore, the relationship cannot be determined.

2. **(C).** When integers are consecutive (or just evenly spaced), the average equals the median. Since the median of this list is the average of the two middle numbers, Quantity A and Quantity B both equal the average of $b$ and $c$. Alternatively, try this with real numbers. If the set is 2, 3, 4, 5, both quantities equal 3.5. No matter what consecutive integers are tested, the two quantities are equal.

3. ***wxyz* is odd and $w + z = x + y$ only.** This question tests the properties of odd numbers as well as of consecutives.

The first choice is TRUE, as multiplying only odd integers together (and no evens) always yields an odd answer.

However, when adding, the rule is "an odd number of odds makes an odd." Summing an even number of odds produces an even, so the second choice is FALSE.

The third choice is TRUE. Since $w$, $x$, $y$, and $z$ are consecutive odd integers, all can be defined in terms of $w$:

$$w = w$$
$$x = w + 2$$
$$y = w + 4$$
$$z = w + 6$$

Thus, $w + z = w + (w + 6) = 2w + 6$, and $x + y = (w + 2) + (w + 4) = 2w + 6$

Therefore, $w + z = x + y$. Alternatively, try real numbers, such as 1, 3, 5, and 7. It is true that $1 + 7 = 3 + 5$. This would hold true for any set of four consecutive, ordered odd numbers tested.

4. **(B).** No math is required to solve this problem. Note that the numbers from 1 to 100 include 50 even integers and 50 odd integers. The first few odds are 1, 3, 5, etc. The first few evens are 2, 4, 6, etc. Every even is 1 greater than its counterpart (2 is 1 greater than 1, 4 is 1 greater than 3, 6 is 1 greater than 5, etc.) Not only is Quantity B greater, it's greater by precisely 50.

5. **(D).** From the constraint, $x$ is positive and $y$ is negative. So Quantity A is definitely positive: $x - y = $ positive $-$ negative $=$ positive. Quantity B is the square of a number, which cannot be negative. Quantity B could be zero, if, for example, $x = 2$ and $y = -2$: $(x + y)^2 = (2 + -2)^2 = (0)^2$. In this case, Quantity A is greater. But if $x = 100$ and $y = -1$, Quantity A is $100 - (-1) = 101$ and Quantity B is $(100 + -1)^2 = 99^2$, which is much greater (close to 10,000). The relationship cannot be determined from the information given.

6. **(B).** This problem can be approached either conceptually or by picking values. For the former, anytime a greater number is subtracted from a smaller one, the result will be negative. Thus, $a - d < 0$. Conversely, since the product of two negatives is positive, $bc > 0$. Because any positive value is greater than all negative values, Quantity B must be greater. Alternatively, picking simple values for the variables would also lead to the same result.

7. **8.** A positive integer that is a multiple of both 2 and 7 is a multiple of 14. Since 140 is a multiple of 14, start listing there and count the terms in the range: 140, 154, 168, 182, 196, 210, 224, 238.

Alternatively, note that 140 is the 10th multiple of 14, and $240/14 \approx 17.143$ (use the calculator). Therefore, the 10th through the 17th multiples of 14, inclusive, are in this range. The number of terms is $17 - 10 + 1 = 8$ ("add one before you are done" for an inclusive list).

8. **(B).** If $ab > 0$, then $a$ and $b$ have the same sign. If $bc < 0$, then $b$ and $c$ have opposite signs. Therefore, $a$ and $c$ must have opposite signs. Therefore, $ac$ is negative, so Quantity B is greater.

If you find the logic difficult ($a$ and $b$ are same sign, $b$ and $c$ are opposite signs, therefore $a$ and $c$ are opposite signs), you could make a quick chart of the possibilities using plus and minus signs:

| $a$ | $b$ | $c$ | |
|---|---|---|---|
| + | + | − | ← First possibility, $a$ and $c$ have different signs. |
| − | − | + | ← Second possibility, $a$ and $c$ have different signs. |

9. **(B).** If $abc$ is negative, then either exactly 1 of or all 3 of the values $a$, $b$, and $c$ are negative:

| | | | |
|---|---|---|---|
| − | − | − | ← First possibility, all are negative. |
| − | + | + | ← Second possibility, 1 negative and 2 positives (order can vary). |

If $b^2c$ is positive, then $c$ must be positive, since $b^2$ cannot be negative. If $c$ is positive, eliminate the first possibility since all 3 variables cannot be negative. Thus, only one of $a$, $b$, and $c$ are negative, but the one negative cannot be $c$. Either $a$ or $b$ is negative, and the other is positive. It doesn't matter which one of $a$ or $b$ is negative—that's enough to know that $ab$ is negative and Quantity B is greater.

10. **(D).** Note that $\dfrac{a+b+c}{3}$ is just another way to express "the average of $a$, $b$, and $c$." The average of $a$, $b$, and $c$ would equal $b$ if the numbers were evenly spaced (such as 1, 2, 3 or 5, 7, 9), but that is not specified. For instance, the integers could be 1, 2, 57 and still satisfy the $a < b < c$ constraint. In that case, the average is 20, which is greater than $b = 2$. The relationship cannot be determined from the information given.

11. $x^2 - y^2 = 0$ **and** $|x| - |y| = 0$ **only.** When you take the square root of $x^2 = y^2$, the result is not $x = y$. Actually, it is $|x| = |y|$. After all, if $x^2 = y^2$, the variables could represent 2 and −2, 5 and 5, −1 and −1, etc. The information about the signs of $x$ and $y$ is lost when the numbers are squared; thus, taking the square root results in absolute values, which allow both sign possibilities for $x$ and $y$. Thus, the first choice is not necessarily true.

From $x^2 = y^2$, subtract $y^2$ from both sides to yield the second choice, providing algebraic proof that it must be true.

To prove the third choice, take the square root of both sides of $x^2 = y^2$ to get $|x| = |y|$, then subtract $|y|$ from both sides.

12. **(E).** The goal in this question is to order $a$, $a^2$, $b$, and $b^2$ by magnitude. Based on the original inequality $0 < a < \frac{1}{b}$ $< 1$, several things are true. First, $a$ and $\frac{1}{b}$ are positive, and thus $b$ itself is positive. If $\frac{1}{b} < 1$ and b is positive, multiply both sides of the inequality by $b$ to get $1 < b$, and then again to get $b < b^2$. (Multiplying by a positive value both times meant there was no need to flip the inequality sign.) Two of the expressions in the answer choices have been ordered: $b < b^2$. Eliminate choices that contradict this fact: choices (A) and (B) are wrong.

Second, note that $a < 1$ in the given inequality. Since $a$ is a positive number less than 1, $a^2 < a$. Show this either by multiplying both sides of $a < 1$ by $a$ (again, no need to flip the inequality sign when multiplying by a positive value) or by number properties (squaring positive fractions less than 1 always yields a smaller fraction). Eliminate choices that contradict the fact that $a^2 < a$: choices (A) and (D) are wrong.

Now, what is the relationship between the terms with a and the terms with $b$? From the first paragraph above, $1 < b$. From the second paragraph (and the given inequality), $a < 1$. Put these together: $a < 1 < b$, or just $a < b$. Eliminate the choices that contradict this fact: choices (A) and (C) are wrong.

At this point, choice (A) has been eliminated for three reasons, and (B), (C), and (D) for one reason each. The only choice remaining is (E), so it must be right by elimination.

(E) can be proven right by putting together the three separate inequalities $(b < b^2)$ and $(a^2 < a)$ and $(a < b)$ into a single inequality: $a^2 < a < b < b^2$. This is equivalent to choice (E): $b^2 > b > a > a^2$.

13. **(B).** The exact values of $a$, $b$, $c$, and $d$ are unknown, as is whether they are evenly spaced (do not assume that they are, just because the figure looks that way). However, it is known that all of the variables are positive such that $0 < a < b < c < d$.

Because $a < b$ and $c < d$ and all the variables are positive, $a \times c < b \times d$. In words, the product of the two smaller numbers is less than the product of the two greater numbers. Quantity B is greater.

You could also try this with real numbers. You could try $a = 1$, $b = 2$, $c = 3$, and $d = 4$, or you could mix up the spacing, as in $a = 0.5$, $b = 7$, $c = 11$, $d = 45$. For any scenario that matches the conditions of the problem, Quantity B is greater.

14. **(C).** This question asks for the greater number of distinct factors, not prime factors. The approach to determine the number of distinct factors is to create a chart that systematically lists all the combinations of two integers that equal the number in question. When you find the same pair in reverse order, the chart is done.

| **Quantity A (32)** | **Quantity B (20)** |
| --- | --- |
| $1 \times 32$ | $1 \times 20$ |
| $2 \times 16$ | $2 \times 10$ |
| $4 \times 8$ | $4 \times 5$ |

Each has 6 distinct factors and the two quantities are equal.

15. **– and 5 only.** From the first equation it seems that $y$ could equal either 2 or $-2$, but if $x^2y = 18$, then $y$ must equal only 2 (otherwise, $x^2y$ would be negative). Still, the squared $x$ indicates that $x$ can equal 3 or $-3$. So the possibilities for $x + y$ are:

$$3 + 2 = 5$$
$$(-3) + 2 = -1$$

16. **(C).** It is not necessary to calculate $10^{11}$ or $3^{13}$. Because 10 is an even number, so is $10^{11}$, and 0 is the remainder when any even is divided by 2. Similarly, $3^{13}$ is a multiple of 3 (it has 3 among its prime factors), and 0 is the remainder when any multiple of 3 is divided by 3. Therefore, the quantities are equal.

17. **(B).** The negative base $-1$ to any odd power is $-1$, and the negative base $-1$ to any even power is 1. Since $q$ is odd, Quantity A $= -1$ and Quantity B $= 1$.

18. **(A).** Before doing any calculations on a problem with negative bases raised to integer exponents, check to see whether one quantity is positive and one quantity is negative, in which case no further calculation is necessary. Note that a negative base to an even exponent is positive, while a negative base to an odd exponent is negative.

Since $n$ is an integer, $4n$ is even. Thus, in Quantity A, $(-1)^{4n}$ and $(-1)^{202}$ are both positive, so Quantity A is positive. In Quantity B, $(3)^3$ is positive but $(-5)^5$ is negative, and thus Quantity B is negative. Since a positive is by definition greater than a negative, Quantity A is greater.

19. **1, 3, 7, and 9 only.** As with multiplication, when an integer is raised to a power, the units digit is determined solely by the product of the units digits. Those products will form a repeating pattern. Here, $3^1 = \underline{3}$, $3^2 = \underline{9}$, $3^3 = 2\underline{7}$, $3^4 = 8\underline{1}$, and $3^5 = 24\underline{3}$. Here the pattern returns to its original value of 3 and any larger power of 3 will follow this same pattern: 3, 9, 7, and then 1. Thus, the units digit of $73^x$ must be 1, 3, 7, or 9. When dividing by 10, the remainder is the units digits, so those same values are the complete list of possible remainders.

20. **(D).** If $xz = 9$ and $x$ and $z$ must both be integers, then they are 1 and 9 (or $-1$ and $-9$) or 3 and 3 (or $-3$ and $-3$). Therefore, they are both odd. More generally, the product of two integers will only be odd if the component integers themselves are both odd. Because $z$ is odd, and $y + z$ equals 13 (an odd), $y$ must be even.

(A): $x$ is NOT even. Eliminate.
(B): $x$ could be 3 but doesn't have to be. Eliminate.
(C): $y$ is NOT odd. Eliminate.
(E): $z$ does not have to be less than $x$ (for instance, they could both be 3). Eliminate.

At this point, only (D) remains, so it must be the answer. To prove it, consider the constraint that limits the value of $y$: $y + z = 13$. Since $z$ could be $-1$, 1, $-3$, 3, $-9$, or 9, the maximum possible value for $z$ is 9, so $y$ must be at least 4. All values that are at least 4 are also greater than 3, so (D) must be true.

**MANHATTAN**
PREP

21. **(A).** This question draws upon knowledge of the smaller prime numbers. It might be helpful to list out the first few prime numbers on your paper: 2, 3, 5, 7, 11, 13, 17, 19…

The smallest prime number greater than 13 is 17, and the greatest prime number less than 16 is 13. Therefore, Quantity A is greater.

22. **385.** To find the sum of a set of numbers, given the average and number of terms, use the average formula.

$\text{Average} = \dfrac{\text{Sum}}{\text{Number of Terms}}$, so Sum = Average × Number of Terms = 35 × 11 = 385.

23. **(D).** To find the sum of a set of evenly spaced numbers, multiply the median (which is also the average) by the number of terms in the set. The median of the numbers from 1 to 80 inclusive is 40.5 (the first 40 numbers are 1 through 40, and the second 40 numbers are 41 through 80, so the middle is 40.5). You can also use the formula $\dfrac{\text{First} + \text{Last}}{2}$ to calculate the median of an evenly spaced set: $\dfrac{1+80}{2} = 40.5$. Multiply 40.5 times 80 to get the answer: 3,240.

24. **299.** $p$ is a large number, but it consists entirely of $q + 149 + 150$. Thus, $p - q$ is what's left of $p$ once the common terms are subtracted: $149 + 150 = 299$.

25. $\dfrac{1}{6}$. There is a trick to this problem—all of the integers in the product $n$ will be canceled out by the same integers appearing in the product $m$:

$$\frac{n}{m} = \frac{4 \times 5 \times 6 \times 7 \times 8 \times 9 \times 10 \times 11}{2 \times 3 \times 4 \times 5 \times 6 \times 7 \times 8 \times 9 \times 10 \times 11} = \frac{1}{2 \times 3} = \frac{1}{6}$$

26. **(E).** If $\sqrt{x}$ is an integer, then $x$ must be a perfect square. If $x$ is a perfect square and $xy^2 = 36$, then $x$ could actually equal *any* of the perfect square factors of 36, which are 1, 4, 9, or 36. (Only consider positive factors, because in order to have a valid square root, $x$ must be positive.) Thus, $y^2$ could equal 36, 9, 4, or 1, respectively.

If $y^2$ is positive, $y$ itself could be positive or negative. Thus, $y = \pm 6, \pm 3, \pm 2,$ or $\pm 1$, for a total of 8 possible values.

27. **(C).** Integers $a$, $b$, and $c$ must be 6, 4, and 2, respectively, as they are positive even integers less than 8 and ordered according to the given inequality. The range of $a$, $b$, and $c$ is $6 - 2 = 4$. The average of $a$, $b$, and $c$ is $\dfrac{6 + 4 + 2}{3} = \dfrac{12}{3} = 4$. The two quantities are equal.

28. **(E).** Find the choices that do not have to be greater than 1. It is possible that $x$ could be negative, which eliminates (A), (B), and (C). For choice (D), if $x^2 = 1$, that times the positive fraction $y$ would be less than 1. In choice (E), $x^2$ must be positive and at least 1, so dividing by the positive fraction $y$ increases the value.

29. **(D).** If the variables were also constrained to be positive, they would have to be 1, 2, and 3, making the quantities both equal to 2. However, the variables could be negative, for example, $a = -10$, $b = -9$, $c = -8$. The range of $a$, $b$, and $c$ will always be 2 because the integers are consecutive, but the average can vary depending on the specific values. There is not enough information to determine the relationship.

**MANHATTAN**
PREP

30. **(B).** If $\sqrt{xy}$ is a prime number, $\sqrt{xy}$ could be 2, 3, 5, 7, 11, 13, etc. Square these possibilities to get a list of possibilities for $xy$: 4, 9, 25, 49, 121, 169, etc. However, $xy$ is even, so $xy$ must equal 4.

Finally, $x > 4y > 0$, which implies that both $x$ and $y$ are positive. Solve $xy = 4$ for $x$, then substitute to eliminate the variable $x$ and solve for $y$:

If $xy = 4$, then $x = \dfrac{4}{y}$.

If $x > 4y$, then $\dfrac{4}{y} > 4y$.

Because $y$ is positive, you can multiply both sides of the inequality by $y$ and you don't have to flip the sign of the inequality: $4 > 4y^2$

Finally, divide both sides of the inequality by 4: $1 > y^2$

Thus, $y$ is a positive fraction less than 1 (it was already given that $y > 0$). Quantity B is greater.

31. **(B).** If $\sqrt{x}$ is a prime number, $x = \left(\sqrt{x}\right)\left(\sqrt{x}\right)$ is the square of a prime number. Squaring a number does not change whether it is odd or even (the square of an odd number is odd and the square of an even number is even). Since $x$ is even, it must be the square of the only even prime number. Thus, $\sqrt{x} = 2$ and $x = 4$. Since $x + y = 11$, $y = 7$ and Quantity B is greater.

32. **(A).** If $fg$ is odd and both $f$ and $g$ are positive integers, both $f$ and $g$ are odd. The remainder when odd $f$ is divided by 2 is 1. Since $fgh$ is even and $f$ and $g$ are odd, integer $h$ must be even. Thus, when $h$ is divided by 2, the remainder is 0. Quantity A is greater.

33. **(C).** For even and odd questions, you can either think it out logically or plug in a number. Since one choice requires raising the number to the 6th power, pick something small! Plug in $x = 1$:

(A) $x^2 + 4x + 6 = 1 + 4 + 6 = 11$
(B) $x^3 + 5x + 3 = 1 + 5 + 3 = 9$
(C) $x^4 + 6x + 7 = 1 + 6 + 7 = 14$
(D) $x^5 + 7x + 1 = 1 + 7 + 1 = 9$
(E) $x^6 + 8x + 4 = 1 + 8 + 4 = 13$

For the logic approach, remember that an odd number raised to an integer power is always odd, an odd number multiplied by an odd number is always odd, and an odd number multiplied by an even number is always even:

> (A) $x^2 + 4x + 6 = $ odd + even + even = odd
> (B) $x^3 + 5x + 3 = $ odd + odd + odd = odd
> (C) $x^4 + 6x + 7 = $ odd + even + odd = even
> (D) $x^5 + 7x + 1 = $ odd + odd + odd = odd
> (E) $x^6 + 8x + 4 = $ odd + even + even = odd

34. **(D).** If $x^2 > 25$, then $x > 5$ OR $x < -5$. For instance, $x$ could be 6 or −6.

If $x = 6$:

> $6 + y < 0$
> $y < -6$

$x$ is greater than $y$.

If $x = -6$:

> $-6 + y < 0$
> $y < 6$

$y$ could be less than $x$ (e.g., $y = -7$) or greater than $x$ (e.g., $y = 4$). Therefore, you do not have enough information.

35. **(B).** If the positive integer $a$ is divisible by 2, it is a positive even integer. Thus, the minimum value for $a$ is 2. Therefore, since $ab < 1$, $b$ must be less than $\frac{1}{2}$.

36. **(B).** If the sum of two primes is less than 6, either the numbers are 2 and 3 (the two smallest unique primes), or both numbers are 2 (just because the variables are different letters doesn't mean that $p$ cannot equal $w$). Both numbers cannot equal 3, though, or $p + w$ would be too great. If $p^2$ is odd, $p$ is odd, and therefore $p = 3$, so $w$ can only be 2.

37. **(A).** If $x^2 > y^2$, $x$ must have a greater absolute value than $y$. For instance:

|            | $x$ | $y$ |
|------------|-----|-----|
| Example 1  | 3   | 2   |
| Example 2  | −3  | 2   |
| Example 3  | 3   | −2  |
| Example 4  | −3  | −2  |

If $x > -|y|$ must also be true, which of the examples continue to be valid?

|  | $x$ | $y$ | $x > -|y|?$ |  |
|---|---|---|---|---|
| Example 1 | 3 | 2 | $3 > -|2|$ | TRUE |
| Example 2 | −3 | 2 | $-3 > -|2|$ | FALSE |
| Example 3 | 3 | −2 | $3 > -|-2|$ | TRUE |
| Example 4 | −3 | −2 | $-3 > -|-2|$ | FALSE |

Only Example 1 and Example 3 remain.

|  | $x$ | $y$ |
|---|---|---|
| Example 1 | 3 | 2 |
| Example 3 | 3 | −2 |

Thus, either $x$ and $y$ are both positive and $x$ has a greater absolute value (Quantity A is greater) or $x$ is positive and $y$ is negative (Quantity A is greater). In either case, Quantity A is greater.

38. **(C).** Write an equation: $x + (x + 1) + (x + 2) + (x + 3) = -2$. Now solve:

$$4x + 6 = -2$$
$$4x = -8$$
$$x = -2$$

Thus, the integers are −2, −1, 0, and 1. The smallest of the four integers equals −2, so the quantities are equal.

39. $\dfrac{g^2 x + 5gx}{x}$ and $6\left(\dfrac{g}{2}\right) - 100\left(\dfrac{g}{2}\right)^2$ **only.** In the first choice, $x$ can be factored out and canceled:

$$\frac{g^2 + 5gx}{x} = \frac{x(g^2 + 5g)}{x} = g^2 + 5g$$

Since $g$ is an integer, so too is $g^2 + 5g$.

In the second choice, $g^2$ is certainly an integer, but $x^2\left(\dfrac{1}{3}\right)$ is only an integer if $x = 3$ (since 3 is the only prime number divisible by 3), so the second choice is not necesarily an integer.

When the third choice is simplified, $6\left(\dfrac{g}{2}\right) - 100\left(\dfrac{g}{2}\right)^2 = 3g - \dfrac{100g^2}{4} = 3g - 25g^2$ results; since $g$ is an integer, $3g - 25g^2$ is also an integer.

# Chapter 16

## of

## 5 lb. Book of GRE® Practice Problems

# Word Problems

# In This Chapter...

Word Problems

Word Problems Answers

# Word Problems

For questions in the Quantitative Comparison format ("Quantity A" and "Quantity B" given), the answer choices are always as follows:

(A)   Quantity A is greater.
(B)   Quantity B is greater.
(C)   The two quantities are equal.
(D)   The relationship cannot be determined from the information given.

For questions followed by a numeric entry box [        ], you are to enter your own answer in the box. For questions followed

by a fraction-style numeric entry box $\frac{\boxed{\phantom{xx}}}{\boxed{\phantom{xx}}}$, you are to enter your answer in the form of a fraction. You are not required to

reduce fractions. For example, if the answer is $\frac{1}{4}$, you may enter $\frac{25}{100}$ or any equivalent fraction.

All numbers used are real numbers. All figures are assumed to lie in a plane unless otherwise indicated. Geometric figures are not necessarily drawn to scale. You should assume, however, that lines that appear to be straight are actually straight, points on a line are in the order shown, and all geometric objects are in the relative positions shown. Coordinate systems, such as $xy$-planes and number lines, as well as graphical data presentations, such as bar charts, circle graphs, and line graphs, *are* drawn to scale. A symbol that appears more than once in a question has the same meaning throughout the question.

1.   If a taxi charges $8.00 for the first mile, and $1.00 for each additional quarter mile, how much does the taxi charge for a 4.5 mile ride?

   (A)   $16.00
   (B)   $18.00
   (C)   $22.00
   (D)   $24.00
   (E)   $26.00

2.   If Nash had 12 grandchildren and three times as many granddaughters as grandsons, how many granddaughters did he have?

   (A)   3
   (B)   4
   (C)   6
   (D)   8
   (E)   9

3.   If Deepak pays 30% of his income in taxes and his take-home pay after taxes is $2,800 per month, how much does Deepak make per month, before taxes?

   $ [              ]

4.  A movie theater charges $6 per ticket, and pays $1,750 of expenses each time a movie is shown. How many tickets must be sold each time a movie is shown for the theater to make $1 of profit per ticket?

    (A)  300
    (B)  325
    (C)  350
    (D)  375
    (E)  400

5.  Arnaldo earns $11 for each ticket that he sells, and a bonus of $2 per ticket for each ticket he sells beyond the first 100 tickets. If Arnaldo was paid $2,400, how many tickets did he sell?

    (A)  120
    (B)  160
    (C)  180
    (D)  200
    (E)  250

6.  Attendees at a charity dinner each gave at least $85 to the charity. If $6,450 was collected, what is the maximum number of people who could have attended?

    (A)  73
    (B)  74
    (C)  75
    (D)  76
    (E)  77

7.  Eva meditates for 20 minutes at a time, with a 5-minute break in between sessions. If she begins meditating at 10:10, what time will it be when she completes her third 20-minute meditation session?

    (A)  11:20
    (B)  11:25
    (C)  11:50
    (D)  11:55
    (E)  12:25

8. A washing machine takes 35 minutes to wash one load of laundry, and in between washing different loads of laundry it takes Derek 2 minutes to unload and another 4 minutes to reload the machine. If the washing machine begins washing one load of laundry at 12:30pm, how many loads of laundry can Derek wash and unload before 6:35pm?

   (A) 8
   (B) 9
   (C) 10
   (D) 14
   (E) 15

Kendra is more than 5 years old.

| Quantity A | Quantity B |
|---|---|

9.   Five years less than twice        Twice what Kendra's age was
         Kendra's age                          five years ago

10. Each day that the drama club washes cars to raise money, the club's only expense is a fixed amount for supplies. If the club charged $12 for each car washed and earned a total profit of $190 in one day by washing 20 cars, how much did the club pay for supplies?

   $ [          ]

11. A store owner pays her assistant $22 per hour for every hour the store is open. If all other expenses for the store are $160 per day, and the store is open for 8 hours on Monday and sells $720 worth of merchandise on that day, what is the store's profit for the day?

   (A) $384
   (B) $396
   (C) $530
   (D) $538
   (E) $560

12. Regular gas costs $3.00 a gallon and is consumed at a rate of 25 miles per gallon. Premium costs $4.00 a gallon and is consumed at a rate of 30 miles per gallon. How much more will it cost to use premium rather than regular for a 300-mile trip?

   (A) $ 1
   (B) $ 4
   (C) $ 5
   (D) $36
   (E) $40

13. A retailer sold toys at a regular selling price of 25% greater than the retailer's cost to buy the toys. If the retailer reduces the regular selling price by 80%, what is then the loss on each toy sold as a percent of the retailer's cost?

    (A) 25%

    (B) 30%

    (C) 40%

    (D) 75%

    (E) 80%

14. Mr. Choudury's fourth-grade class consists of 20 students: 12 boys and 8 girls. If the boys weigh an average of 80 pounds each and the girls weigh an average of 70 pounds each, what is the average weight, in pounds, of all 20 students?

    (A) 71

    (B) 74

    (C) 75

    (D) 76

    (E) 79

15. It costs a certain bicycle factory a fixed amount of $11,000 to operate for one month, plus $300 for each bicycle produced during the month. Each of the bicycles sells for a retail price of $700. What is the minimum number of bicycles that the factory must sell in one month to make a profit?

    (A) 26

    (B) 27

    (C) 28

    (D) 29

    (E) 30

16. The yoga company Yoga for Life offers 45-minute classes at $12 per class. If the number of minutes Randolf spent doing yoga this month was 132 greater than the number of dollars he paid, how many classes did he attend?

    (A) 3

    (B) 4

    (C) 5

    (D) 6

    (E) 8

**MANHATTAN**
PREP

17. An online merchant sells wine for $20 for an individual bottle or $220 for a case of 12. Either way, the merchant's cost for the wine is $10 per bottle. Shipping costs the merchant $5 for a bottle and $40 for a case. If 12 cases and 60 individual bottles were sold, and there were no other revenue or expenses, the merchant's profit was equal to which of the following?

 (A) $  780
 (B) $1,020
 (C) $2,160
 (D) $2,640
 (E) $3,840

18. If every donor to a charity drive contributed at least $14 and $237 was collected, what is the maximum number of donors?

 (A) 13
 (B) 14
 (C) 15
 (D) 16
 (E) 17

In a certain barter system, 1 sack of rice can be traded for 2.5 pounds of beans or $\frac{1}{3}$ of a bushel of tomatoes.

| Quantity A | Quantity B |
|---|---|
| 19. The number of sacks of rice equivalent to 1 pound of beans | The number of sacks of rice equivalent to 1 bushel of tomatoes |

20. Francisco's MP3 player with a capacity of 64 gigabytes (GB) was three-quarters full. He then deleted 25% of the data saved on the device before saving another 20 GB of new data to the device. The resulting amount of data saved is what percent of the capacity of Francisco's MP3 player?

 (A) 62.5 %
 (B) 70 %
 (C) 75 %
 (D) 87.5 %
 (E) 95 %

21. Last year, a magazine charged a $50 subscription fee. This year, the price will be increased by $10. If the magazine could lose 4 subscribers this year and still collect the same revenue as it did last year, how many subscribers did the magazine have last year?

    (A) 20
    (B) 21
    (C) 22
    (D) 23
    (E) 24

22. A rectangular public park has an area of 3,600 square feet. It is surrounded on three sides by a chain link fence. If the entire length of the fence measures 180 feet, how many feet long could the unfenced side of the rectangular park be?

    Indicate all such lengths.

    ☐ 30
    ☐ 40
    ☐ 60
    ☐ 90
    ☐ 120

    The corner store sells yams and plantains by the pound. A pound of plantains cost $0.30 less than twice the cost of a pound of yams.

    |  | Quantity A | Quantity B |
    |---|---|---|
    | 23. | The cost of two pounds of yams and two pounds of plantains | The cost of three pounds of plantains |

24. The perimeter of a rectangular patio is 268 feet and its length is 168% of its width. What is the area of the patio, in square feet?

    (A) 4,000
    (B) 4,200
    (C) 4,320
    (D) 4,600
    (E) 4,760

**MANHATTAN**
PREP

25. Randall purchased a shirt for $19.44 using a $20 bill. If his correct change was returned in only dimes ($0.10) and pennies ($0.01), how many coins could Randall have received?

    (A)   9
    (B)   21
    (C)   29
    (D)   37
    (E)   44

26. In the modern era, the global population of humans has increased by 1 billion people approximately every 13 years. If that rate were to continue, approximately how many years would it take for the Earth's population to double from its current population of 7 billion people?

    (A)   26
    (B)   52
    (C)   91
    (D)   104
    (E)   169

Gerald bought a used motorcycle for $1,200 and spent $305 repairing it. He then sold the motorcycle for 20% more than the total amount he spent for purchase and repairs.

|  | **Quantity A** | **Quantity B** |
|---|---|---|
| 27. | The final selling price of the motorcycle | $1,800 |

A turbine salesman earns a commission of $x$% of the purchase price of every turbine he sells, where $x$ is a constant. His commission for a $300,000 turbine was $1500.

|  | **Quantity A** | **Quantity B** |
|---|---|---|
| 28. | The commission earned on a turbine that sold for $180,000. | $800 |

# Word Problems Answers

1. **(C).** Break the trip into two parts: the first mile and the final 3.5 miles. The first mile costs $8, and the final 3.5 miles cost $1 per $\frac{1}{4}$ mile, or $4 per mile. The total cost is $8 + 3.5(4) = 8 + 14 = \$22$.

2. **(E).** Rather than assigning separate variables to the granddaughters and grandsons, define them both in terms of the same unknown multiplier, based on the ratio given:

> Number of granddaughters = $3m$
> Number of grandsons = $m$

Note that you are solving for $3m$, not for $m$!

$$3m + m = 12$$
$$4m = 12$$
$$m = 3$$
$$3m = 9$$

Alternatively, suppose that Nash had exactly one grandson and three granddaughters. That would sum to four grandchildren altogether. Triple the number of grandsons and granddaughters to triple the number of grandchildren.

3. **$4,000.** If Deepak pays 30% in taxes, his take-home pay after taxes is 70%. Since this amount is equal to $2,800:

$$0.70x = 2,800$$
$$x = 4,000$$

4. **(C).** This problem requires the knowledge that profit equals revenue minus cost. Memorize the formula: Profit = Revenue − Cost (or Profit = Revenue − Expenses), but you could just think about it logically—a business has to pay its expenses out of the money it makes: the rest is profit.

The cost each time a movie is shown is $1,750. If the theater charges $6 per ticket and $t$ is the number of tickets, the revenue is $6t$. In order for the profit to be $1 per ticket, the profit must be $t$ dollars.

Plug these values into the equation Profit = Revenue − Cost:

$$t = 6t - 1,750$$
$$-5t = -1,750$$
$$t = 350$$

**MANHATTAN**
PREP

5. **(D).** Let $x$ = the total number of tickets sold. Therefore, $(x - 100)$ = the number of tickets Arnaldo sold beyond the first 100. Using the information given, set up an equation and solve:

$$11x + 2(x - 100) = 2,400$$
$$11x + 2x - 200 = 2,400$$
$$13x = 2,600$$
$$x = 200$$

6. **(C).** Divide \$6,450 by \$85 to get 75.88… But don't just round up! Each person gave at least \$85. If 76 people attended and each gave the minimum of \$85, then \$6,460 would have been collected. Since only \$6,450 was collected, that 76th person could not have attended. Instead, round down to 75. (This means at least one person gave more than the minimum.)

7. **(A).** List Eva's meditation sessions and breaks:

| | |
|---|---|
| 10:10–10:30 | session 1 |
| 10:30–10:35 | break |
| 10:35–10:55 | session 2 |
| 10:55–11:00 | break |
| 11:00–11:20 | session 3 |

Note that the question asks for the time when she will complete her third session, so do not add a third break!

A quicker way to do this problem would be to add 20(3) + 5(2) to get 70 minutes, and 70 minutes after 10:10 is 11:20.

8. **(B).** You *could* list Derek's activities:

| | |
|---|---|
| 12:30–1:05 | load 1 |
| 1:05–1:11 | unload/reload |
| 1:11–1:46 | load 2 |
| 1:46–1:52 | unload/reload |
| 1:52–2:27 | load 3 |
| Etc. | |

However, completing this rather tedious list all the way up to 6:35pm is not a good expenditure of time on the GRE. A better approach would be to determine how many minutes are available for Derek to do laundry. From 12:30 to 6:35 is 6 hours and 5 minutes, or 365 minutes.

It takes 41 minutes to do one load of laundry and then switch to the next one (34 + 4 + 2 minutes).

Divide 365 minutes by 41 to get 8.9… So, Derek can definitely do 8 total loads of laundry plus switching time.

What about that extra 0.9...? You need to figure out whether Derek can fit in one more laundry load. Importantly, for this last load he needs only 2 extra minutes to unload, since he will not be reloading the machine.

Multiply 8 (the total number of loads Derek can definitely do) by 41 minutes to get 328 minutes. Subtract 328 from the 365 available minutes to get 37 minutes. That is *exactly* how much time it takes Derek to do one load of laundry (35 minutes) and then unload it (2 minutes). So, Derek can wash and unload 9 total loads of laundry.

9. **(A).** This is an algebraic translation, meaning you need to translate the text into algebra. Use $k$ to represent Kendra's age, and the problem states that $k > 5$ (this is important only because Quantity B requires you to consider Kendra's age five years ago, and if she were younger than 5 years old, that would create an impossible negative age!).

> Quantity A $= 2k - 5$
> Quantity B $= 2(k - 5) = 2k - 10$

Since 2k is common to both quantities it can be subtracted from both without affecting their relative values.

> Quantity A $= -5$
> Quantity B $= -10$

Quantity A is less negative, so it is greater.

10. **$50.** Since Profit = Revenue − Expenses, and $12 for a car wash multiplied by 20 car washes = $240:

> $190 = 240 - E$
> $-50 = -E$
> $\$50 = E$

11. **(A).** Since Profit = Revenue − Expenses, and revenue = $720:

> $P = 720 - E$

Expenses are equal to $22 per hour times 8 hours, plus a fixed $160, or 22(8) + 160 = $336. Thus:

> $P = 720 - 336$
> $P = \$384$

12. **(B).** 12 gallons of regular gas are needed to go 300 miles (300 divided by 25 miles per gallon), costing $36 (12 gallons × $3 per gallon). 10 gallons of premium would be needed to go 300 miles (300 divided by 30 miles per gallon), costing $40 (10 gallons × $4 per gallon). The question asks for the difference, which is $40 − $36 = $4.

13. **(D).** For problems that ask for percents and use no real numbers, it is almost always possible to use 100 as a starting number. Suppose the retailer buys each toy for $100, and thus sells it for a regular price of $125. A reduction of this regular selling price by 80% drops the price to $25. The loss on each toy sold as a percent of the retailer's cost is:

$$\left(\frac{100 - 25}{100 \times 100}\right)\% = 75\%$$

14. **(D).** The most straightforward approach is to determine the total weight of all 20 students, and divide that total by 20:

> 12 boys × 80 pounds per boy = 960 pounds
> 8 girls × 70 pounds per girl = 560 pounds
> Total = 1,520 pounds
>
> $$\frac{1,520}{20} = 76$$

Alternatively, many or even most GRE multiple-choice weighted average problems have the same five answers:

> Much closer to the lesser value
> A little closer to the lesser value
> The unweighted average of the two values
> A little closer to the greater value
> Much closer to the greater value

Any of these five choices *could* be correct, but the correct answer is usually "a little closer to the lesser value" or "a little closer to the greater value." In this case, because there are a few more boys than girls, the average for the whole class will be a little closer to the boys' average weight than to the girls'.

15. **(C).** The question asks how many bicycles the factory must sell to make a profit. One way of phrasing that is to say the profit must be greater than 0. Since Profit = Revenue − Cost, you can rewrite the equation to say:

> Revenue − Cost > 0

Let $b$ equal the number of bicycles sold. Each bike sells for $700, so the total revenue is $700b$. The cost is equal to $11,000 plus $300 for every bicycle sold.

> $$(700b) - (11,000 + 300b) > 0$$

Isolate $b$ on one side of the inequality:

> $700b - 11,000 + 300b > 0$
> $400b - 11,000 > 0$
> $400b > 11,000$
> $b > 27.5$

If $b$ must be greater than 27.5, then the factory needs to sell at least 28 bicycles to make a profit.

16. **(B).** The typical way to do this problem would be to assign variables and set up equations, using $x$ to represent the number of classes Randolf took, $12x$ to represent the amount he paid, and $45x$ to represent the number of minutes he spent.

A quicker way might be to notice that with every class Randolf takes, the difference between the number of minutes he spends and the amount he pays increases by 33. If Randolf takes 1 class, then the number of minutes he spends is 33 greater than the number of dollars he pays. If he takes 2 classes, the number of minutes is 66 greater than the number of dollars, and so on. Since $132 = 4 \times 33$, Randolf must have taken 4 classes.

17. **(B).** Profit is equal to Revenue − Expenses. First, calculate revenue:

> 12 cases sold for \$220 each = \$2,640
> 60 bottles sold for \$20 each = \$1,200
> Total Revenue = \$3,840

Now, calculate expenses. How many total bottles of wine were sold? 12 cases × 12 bottles, plus 60 individual bottles = 204 bottles. Note that the bottles sold individually versus those sold in cases have the same purchase cost (\$10), but different shipping costs. Thus:

> 204 bottles at \$10 each = \$2,040
> Shipping on bottles = $60 \times \$5 = \$300$
> Shipping on cases = $12 \times \$40 = \$480$
> Total Expenses = \$2,820
>
> Profit = Revenue − Expenses
> Profit = \$3,840 − \$2,820
> Profit = \$1,020

18. **(D).** This is a maximization question. To solve maximization questions, you often have to minimize something else. In order to find the maximum number of donors, minimize the donation per person. In this case, everyone could pay exactly \$14:

$$\frac{237}{14} = 16.92$$

Rounding up to 17 is not right, because it is not possible that 17 people donated \$14 each (the total contributions would be \$238, which is greater than \$237). The answer is (D), or 16.

19. **(B).** If 1 sack of rice is worth $\frac{1}{3}$ of a bushel of tomatoes, buying the whole bushel would require 3 sacks of rice. Quantity B is equal to 3. The math is a bit tougher in Quantity A, but no calculation is really required—if a sack trades for 2.5 pounds of beans, a single pound of beans is worth less than a sack of rice. Quantity A is less than 1.

20. **(D).** If Francisco's MP3 player is three-quarters full, the current content equals $\frac{3}{4} \times 64$ GB = 48 GB. He then deleted 25%, or 12 GB, of that data, reducing the amount of data saved to 48 − 12 = 36 GB. After saving 20 GB of new data to the device, it holds 36 + 20 = 56 GB. This is $\left(\frac{56}{64} \times 100\right)\% = 87.5\%$ of the total capacity.

21. **(E).** Assign the variable $s$ for the number of subscribers last year:

> Last year:
> $50 per subscription
> $s$ subscribers

> This year:
> $60 per subscription
> $s - 4$ subscribers

The question states that the magazine "could" lose 4 subscribers and that the magazine would then collect the same revenue as last year—don't let the "could" throw you off. Calculate using this hypothetical situation:

$$50s = 60(s - 4)$$
$$50s = 60s - 240$$
$$-10s = -240$$
$$s = 24$$

22. **60 and 120 only.** The two values given are the area of the park and three out of the four sides of the perimeter of the park. If the side without fencing is a length, the equation for the overall length of the existing fence is $180 = 2W + L$, so $L = 180 - 2W$. The equation for the area of the park is $LW = 3,600$. With two variables and two equations, it is now possible to solve for the possible values of $L$:

$$L \times W = 3,600$$
$$L = 180 - 2W$$

$$(180 - 2W)W = 3,600$$
$$180W - 2W^2 = 3,600$$
$$90W - W^2 = 1,800$$
$$0 = W^2 - 90W + 1,800$$
$$0 = (W - 60)(W - 30)$$

So $W = 30$ or $60$. Plug each value back into either of the original two equations to solve for the corresponding length, which is 120 or 60, respectively.

23. **(A).** Represent the cost per pound of the vegetables by their first letters. The given information translates to $p = 2y - 0.30$ because "twice" means multiply by two and "less" indicates subtraction. Then, translate the quantities into algebraic expressions:

> Quantity A $= 2y + 2p$
> Quantity B $= 3p$

Since $2p$ is common to both quantities, it can be subtracted without changing their relative values:

> Quantity A $= 2y$
> Quantity B $= p$

Since $p = 2y - 0.30$, Quantity B is 0.30 less than Quantity A.

24. **(B)**. This rectangle problem requires applying the perimeter and area formulas. The area of a rectangle is equal to length times width ($A = LW$) and the perimeter is $2L + 2W = 268$. The question states that the length equals 168% of the width, $L = 1.68W$.

$$2L + 2W = 268$$
$$L + W = 134$$
$$1.68W + W = 134$$
$$2.68W = 134$$
$$W = 50$$

Solve for $L$ by plugging 50 in for $W$ in either equation:

$$L + 50 = 134$$
$$L = 84$$
$$A = 84(50) = 4,200$$

25. **(C)**. From the first sentence, calculate Randall's change ($20.00 - 19.44 = 0.56$). Then it's a matter of systematic tests to determine the various combinations of dimes and pennies that Randall could have received, stopping when one matches an answer choice listed:

| | |
|---|---|
| 5 dimes (0.50) + 6 pennies (0.06) = 11 coins | Not an option in the choices |
| 4 dimes (0.40) + 16 pennies (0.16) = 20 coins | Not an option in the choices |
| 3 dimes (0.30) + 26 pennies (0.26) = 29 coins | Correct answer |

26. **(C)**. To double from the current population of 7 billion people, the population would need to increase by 7 billion. If the population increases by 1 billion every 13 years, an increase of 7 billion would take $7 \times 13 = 91$ years.

27. **(A)**. Gerald spent $1,200 + $305 = $1,505 total on purchase and repairs. The selling price was 20% more, or 1.2 times this amount. Either plug $1.2 \times 1,505$ into the calculator to get $1,806, or recognize that 1.2 of $1,500 is exactly $1,800, so Quantity A is a little more than that.

28. **(A)**. There are a few options for solving the given problem. First, you could find out exactly what $x$ equals by setting up an equation: "1,500 is $x$ percent of 300,000" translates algebraically to $1,500 = \left(\dfrac{x}{100}\right)(300,000)$. Solving the equation will reveal that $x = 0.5$, so the commission is 0.5%. Taking 0.5% of $180,000 gives $900 for Quantity A, which is greater than Quantity B.

Alternatively, you could reason by proportion: $\dfrac{1500}{300,000} = \dfrac{c}{180,000}$. This works because the commission the salesman earns represents the same proportion of the total in all cases, so any changes to the total will be reflected in changes to the commission. This gives the same value for Quantity A, $900, and is still greater than Quantity B.

**MANHATTAN**
PREP

# Chapter *of* 17

5 lb. Book of GRE® Practice Problems

# Two-Variable Word Problems

# In This Chapter...

Two-Variable Word Problems

Two-Variable Word Problems Answers

# Two-Variable Word Problems

For questions in the Quantitative Comparison format ("Quantity A" and "Quantity B" given), the answer choices are always as follows:

(A)  Quantity A is greater.
(B)  Quantity B is greater.
(C)  The two quantities are equal.
(D)  The relationship cannot be determined from the information given.

For questions followed by a numeric entry box [        ], you are to enter your own answer in the box. For questions followed by a fraction-style numeric entry box [        ], you are to enter your answer in the form of a fraction. You are not required to reduce fractions. For example, if the answer is $\frac{1}{4}$, you may enter $\frac{25}{100}$ or any equivalent fraction.

All numbers used are real numbers. All figures are assumed to lie in a plane unless otherwise indicated. Geometric figures are not necessarily drawn to scale. You should assume, however, that lines that appear to be straight are actually straight, points on a line are in the order shown, and all geometric objects are in the relative positions shown. Coordinate systems, such as $xy$-planes and number lines, as well as graphical data presentations, such as bar charts, circle graphs, and line graphs, *are* drawn to scale. A symbol that appears more than once in a question has the same meaning throughout the question.

1.  Two parking lots can hold a total of 115 cars. The Green lot can hold 35 fewer cars than the Red lot. How many cars can the Red lot hold?

    (A)  35
    (B)  40
    (C)  70
    (D)  75
    (E)  80

2.  Three friends ate 14 slices of pizza. If two of the friends ate the same number of slices, and the third ate two more slices than each of the other two, how many slices were eaten by the third friend?

    (A)  3
    (B)  4
    (C)  5
    (D)  6
    (E)  7

    In 8 years, Polly's age, which is currently $p$, will be twice Quan's age, which is currently $q$.

    | **Quantity A** | **Quantity B** |
    |---|---|
    | $p - 8$ | $2q$ |

3.

4.  Pens cost 70 cents each and pencils cost 40 cents each. If Iris spent $5.20 on a total of 10 pens and pencils, how many pencils did she purchase? ($1 = 100 cents)

    (A)   4
    (B)   6
    (C)   8
    (D)  10
    (E)  13

5.  Jack downloaded 10 songs and 2 books for $48, Jill downloaded 15 songs and 1 book for $44. How much did Jack spend on books, if all songs are the same price and all books are the same price?

    (A)  $14
    (B)  $20
    (C)  $28
    (D)  $29
    (E)  $30

6.  Marisa has $40 more than Ben, and Ben has one-third as much money as Marisa. How many dollars does Ben have?

    $ [        ]

7.  Norman is 12 years older than Michael. In 6 years, he will be twice as old as Michael. How old is Michael now?

    (A)   3
    (B)   6
    (C)  12
    (D)  18
    (E)  24

8.  Krunchy Kustard sells only two kinds of doughnuts: glazed and cream-filled. A glazed doughnut has 200 calories, and a cream-filled doughnut has 360 calories. If Felipe ate 5 doughnuts totaling 1,640 calories, how many were glazed?

    (A)  1
    (B)  2
    (C)  3
    (D)  4
    (E)  5

9.  The "aspect ratio" of a computer monitor is the ratio of the monitor's width to its height. If a particular monitor has an aspect ratio of 16 : 9, and a perimeter of 100 inches, how many inches wide is the monitor?

    (A)  18
    (B)  25
    (C)  32
    (D)  36
    (E)  64

10. Cindy bought 48 containers of soda, all either 12-ounce cans or 20-ounce bottles. If the number of ounces she purchased in cans was equal to the number of ounces she purchased in bottles, how many bottles of soda did Cindy buy?

    (A)  18
    (B)  21
    (C)  24
    (D)  27
    (E)  30

11. Two runners' race times sum to 170 seconds and one of the race times is 10 seconds less than twice the other. What is the faster race time, in seconds?

    (A)  40
    (B)  50
    (C)  60
    (D)  70
    (E)  110

12. Beth is 12 years younger than Alan. In 20 years, Beth will be 80% of Alan's age. How old is Beth now?

    ┌──────────┐
    │          │ years old
    └──────────┘

13. Rey is 12 years younger than Sebastian. Five years ago, Rey was half Sebastian's age. How old will Sebastian be next year?

    (A)  15
    (B)  20
    (C)  25
    (D)  30
    (E)  35

14. During a sale, the local outlet of the Chasm sold three times as many jeans as chinos. If they made twice as much profit for a pair of chinos as for a pair of jeans, and sold no other items, what percent of their profits during the sale came from chinos?

    (A)  $16\frac{2}{3}\%$

    (B)    20%

    (C)    40%

    (D)    60%

    (E)  $83\frac{1}{3}\%$

15. Marisol is twice as old as Vikram. Eight years ago, Marisol was 6 years younger than three times Vikram's age at that time. How old will Marisol be in 5 years?

16. The length of a rectangle is two more than twice its width, and the area of the rectangle is 40. What is the rectangle's perimeter?

17. Marcy bought one pair of jeans at 70% off and one blouse at 40% off. If she paid $12 more for the blouse than for the jeans, and she spent a total of $84, what was the original price of the jeans?

    (A)   $76

    (B)   $96

    (C)  $100

    (D)  $120

    (E)  $124

18. Wall-to-wall carpeting is installed in a certain hallway. The carpeting costs $4.25 per square foot. If the perimeter of the hallway (in feet) is equal to 44% of the area of the hallway (in square feet) and the hallway is 50 feet long, how much did the carpeting cost?

    (A)  $182.50

    (B)  $212.50

    (C)  $505.25

    (D)  $1,062.50

    (E)  $1,100.00

**MANHATTAN**
PREP

19. Jamal got three monthly electric bills over the course of three months. If his average monthly bill over these three months was $44 more than the median bill, and the sum of the largest and the smallest bills was $412, what was the total amount of the three electric bills Jamal got over the course of the three months?

    (A) $456
    (B) $552
    (C) $600
    (D) $824
    (E) $1,000

20. A certain dog kennel houses only collies, labs, and golden retrievers. If the ratio of collies to labs is 5:9, there are 66 golden retrievers, and 12 more golden retrievers than labs in the kennel, what percent of the dogs in the kennel are collies?

    (A)   5%
    (B)   9%
    (C)  12%
    (D)  20%
    (E)  25%

21. If Mason is now twice as old as Gunther was 10 years ago, and $G$ is Gunther's current age in years, which of the following represents the sum of Mason and Gunther's ages 4 years from now?

    (A)  $\dfrac{3G}{2} + 3$
    (B)  $3G + 28$
    (C)  $3G - 12$
    (D)  $8 - G$
    (E)  $14 - \dfrac{3G}{2}$

22. A baker made a combination of chocolate chip cookies and peanut butter cookies for a school bake sale. His recipes only allow him to make chocolate chip cookies in batches of 7, and peanut butter cookies in batches of 6. If he made exactly 95 cookies for the bake sale, what is the minimum possible number of chocolate chip cookies that he made?

    (A)   7
    (B)  14
    (C)  21
    (D)  28
    (E)  35

23.  Anke has 5 fewer candies than Conrad. If Anke gives Conrad 5 candies, Conrad will then have 4 times as many candies as Anke. How many candies does Anke have?

    (A)   5

    (B)   10

    (C)   15

    (D)   20

    (E)   25

24.  Lou has three daughters: Wen, Mildred, and Tyla. Three years ago, when Lou was twice as old as Tyla, he was 30 years older than Mildred. Now, he is 47 years older than Wen. In 4 years, Wen will be half as old as Tyla. What is the sum of the current ages of Lou and his three daughters?

    (A)   138

    (B)   144

    (C)   154

    (D)   166

    (E)   181

25.  Dwayne planted 70 acres with two types of beans: navy and pinto. Each acre of navy beans yielded 27 bushels and each acre of pinto beans yielded 36 bushels. If Dwayne grew twice as many bushels of pinto beans as navy beans, how many acres of pinto beans did he plant?

    (A)   28

    (B)   30

    (C)   35

    (D)   40

    (E)   42

**MANHATTAN**
PREP

# Two-Variable Word Problems Answers

1. **(D).** Let $g$ = the number of cars that the Green lot can hold. Let $r$ = the number of cars that the Red lot can hold.

The first two sentences can be translated into two equations:

$$g + r = 115$$
$$g = r - 35$$

The question asks for $r$, so substitute $(r - 35)$ for $g$ in the first equation:

$$(r - 35) + r = 115$$
$$2r - 35 = 115$$
$$2r = 150$$
$$r = 75$$

2. **(D).** Let $P$ = the number of slices of pizza eaten by each of the two friends who eat the same amount. Let $T$ = the number of slices of pizza eaten by the third friend.

$$T = P + 2$$
$$P + P + T = 14$$

Substitute $(P + 2)$ for $T$ in the second equation:

$$P + P + (P + 2) = 14$$
$$3P + 2 = 14$$
$$3P = 12$$
$$P = 4$$

Solve for $T$:

$$T = P + 2 = 4 + 2 = 6$$

3. **(C).** This is an algebraic translation question, so start by translating the given information into equations. Remember to add 8 to both Polly and Quan's ages, because they will *both* be 8 years older in 8 years!

$$p + 8 = 2(q + 8)$$
$$p + 8 = 2q + 16$$
$$p = 2q + 8$$
$$p - 8 = 2q$$

The two quantities are equal.

4. **(B).** Assign one variable to the pencils and another variable to the pens:

> Number of pencils $= x$
> Number of pens $= y$
>
> $x + y = 10$
> $70y + 40x = 520$

The question asks for the number of pencils, $x$, so isolate $y$ in the first equation and substitute into the second:

> $y = 10 - x$
>
> $70(10 - x) + 40x = 520$
> $700 - 70x + 40x = 520$
> $700 - 30x = 520$
> $180 = 30x$
> $x = 6$

Alternatively, test the answer choices. Starting with the middle choice, if Iris bought 8 pencils and therefore 2 pens, she spent $(8 \times 40) + (2 \times 70) = 320 + 140 = 460$. That's 60 cents too little, so Iris must have bought fewer pencils and more pens. Try 6 pencils and 4 pens: $(6 \times 40) + (4 \times 70) = 240 + 280 = 520$. (You might also have noticed that every time Iris swaps a pencil for a pen, she spends an extra 30 cents.)

5. **(C).** The equations are $10s + 2b = 48$ and $15s + b = 44$. The easiest next move would be to solve the second equation for $b$:

> $b = 44 - 15s$

Substitute that into the first equation:

> $10s + 2(44 - 15s) = 48$
> $10s + 88 - 30s = 48$
> $-20s + 88 = 48$
> $-20s = -40$
> $s = 2$

Plug $s = 2$ back into either original equation to get that $b = 14$, and thus the two books that Jack bought cost $28.

6. **20.** Translate the given information. Let $M$ equal Marisa's money and $B$ equal Ben's:

> $M = B + 40$
> $B = \dfrac{1}{3}M$

The question asks for $B$, so solve the second equation for $M$ and substitute into the first equation:

**MANHATTAN**
PREP

$$3B = M$$

$$3B = B + 40$$
$$2B = 40$$
$$B = 20$$

Check the answer. If Ben has $20 and Marisa has $40 more than Ben, she has $60. It is true that Ben has one-third as much money as Marisa.

7. **(B).**   Let $N$ = Norman's age now; $(N + 6)$ = Norman's age in 6 years.
Let $M$ = Michael's age now; $(M + 6)$ = Michael's age in 6 years.

Translate the first two sentences into equations. Note that the second equation deals with Norman and Michael's ages in 6 years:

$$N = M + 12$$
$$(N + 6) = 2(M + 6)$$

The question asks for $M$, so substitute $(M + 12)$ for $N$ in the second equation:

$$(M + 12) + 6 = 2(M + 6)$$
$$M + 18 = 2M + 12$$
$$M + 6 = 2M$$
$$6 = M$$

8. **(A).** Assign variables to the two types of doughnuts, and write equations based on the given information:

Number of glazed = $G$
Number of cream-filled = $C$

$G + C = 5$            (the number of doughnuts)
$1{,}640 = 200G + 360C$   (the number of calories)

The question asks for $G$, so isolate $C$ in first equation and substitute into the second equation:

$$C = 5 - G$$

$$1{,}640 = 200G + 360(5 - G)$$
$$1{,}640 = 200G + 1{,}800 - 360G$$
$$1{,}640 = 1{,}800 - 160G$$
$$-160 = -160G$$
$$G = 1$$

Check the answer. If Felipe at 1 glazed doughnut, he ate 4 cream-filled doughnuts. He ate
$(1 \times 200) + (4 \times 360) = 200 + 1{,}440 = 1{,}640$ calories.

9. **(C).** Rather than assigning separate variables to the width and height, define them both in terms of the same unknown multiplier, based on the ratio given:

$$\text{Width} = 16m$$
$$\text{Height} = 9m$$

Remember that the question asks for the width, so answer for $16m$, not for $m$!

The perimeter of a rectangle is equal to 2(length + width), or in this case 2(width + height):

$$100 = 2 \times (16m + 9m)$$
$$100 = 50m$$
$$m = 2$$
$$16m = 32$$

An alternative method depends on the same underlying logic, but forgoes the algebra. Suppose the dimensions were 16 inches and 9 inches. This would yield a perimeter of 50 inches. Double the width and height to double the perimeter.

10. **(A).** Define variables and translate equations from the given information:

Number of bottles = $b$
Number of cans = $c$

$b + c = 48$ (Number of containers purchased)
$12c = 20b$ (Equal number of ounces in bottles purchased and cans purchased)

The question asks for $b$, so isolate $c$ in the first equation and substitute into the second equation:

$$c = 48 - b$$

$$12(48 - b) = 20b$$
$$576 - 12b = 20b$$
$$576 = 32b$$
$$b = 18$$

Check the answer. If Cindy bought 18 bottles, she bought 30 cans. The number of ounces in the bottles was $18 \times 20 = 360$. The number of ounces in the cans was $30 \times 12 = 360$.

11. **(C).** Call the race times $x$ and $y$. The question provides a sum: $x + y = 170$.

One of the race times is 10 seconds less than twice the other: $x = 2y - 10$.

Since the second equation is already solved for $x$, plug $(2y - 10)$ in for $x$ in the first equation:

**MANHATTAN**
PREP

$$2y - 10 + y = 170$$
$$3y - 10 = 170$$
$$3y = 180$$
$$y = 60$$

If $y = 60$ and the times sum to 170, then $x = 110$.

Note that the question asks for the *faster* race time—that means the smaller number! The answer is 60.

12. **28.** Since Beth is 12 years younger than Alan, you can write:

$$B = A - 12$$

To translate "in 20 years, Beth will be 80% of Alan's age," make sure that Beth becomes $B + 20$ and Alan becomes $A + 20$ (if you will be doing other operations to these values, put parentheses around them to make sure the rules of PEMDAS are not violated):

$$B + 20 = 0.8(A + 20)$$
$$B + 20 = 0.8A + 16$$
$$B + 4 = 0.8A$$

Since the first equation is already solved for $B$, plug $(A - 12)$ into the simplified version of the second equation in place of $B$:

$$B + 4 = 0.8A$$
$$(A - 12) + 4 = 0.8A$$
$$A - 8 = 0.8A$$
$$0.2A - 8 = 0$$
$$0.2A = 8$$
$$A = 40$$

Alan is 40. Since $B = A - 12$, Beth is 28.

Check the answer. In 20 years, Beth will be 48 and Alan will be 60, and it is true that 48 is 80% of 60.

13. **(D).** Assign variables and translate equations from the given information:

$r =$ Rey's age NOW
$s =$ Sebastian's age NOW

$$r = s - 12$$
$$(r - 5) = \frac{1}{2}(s - 5)$$

Multiply the second equation by 2 to eliminate the fraction and simplify:
$$2r - 10 = s - 5$$
$$2r = s + 5$$

Since the question asks for Sebastian's age next year and $r$ is already isolated in the first equation, substitute for $r$ in the adjusted second equation and solve:

$$2(s - 12) = s + 5$$
$$2s - 24 = s + 5$$
$$2s = s + 29$$
$$s = 29$$

If Sebastian is 29 now, he will be 30 next year.

Check the answer. If Sebastian is 29 now, Rey is 17 now. Five years ago, they were 24 and 12, respectively, and 12 is half of 24.

14. **(C).** If all the values given in a problem and its answers are *percents*, *ratios*, or *fractions of* some unknown, then the problem will probably be easiest to solve by stipulating values for the unknowns. In this problem, the two ratios given are 3 : 1 (jeans sold : chinos sold) and 2 : 1 (profits per pair of chinos : profits per pair of jeans). The easiest numbers to stipulate are:

    3 pairs of jeans sold
    1 pair of chinos sold
    $2 profit/pair of chinos
    $1 profit/pair of jeans

This yields $2 profit from the chinos out of a total $5 in profit: 2/5 = 40%.

15. **49.** Write each sentence as its own equation:

$$M = 2V$$
$$(M - 8) = 3(V - 8) - 6$$

Simplify the second equation before substituting for $M$ from the first equation into the second:

$$M - 8 = 3V - 24 - 6$$
$$M - 8 = 3V - 30$$
$$(2V) + 22 = 3V$$
$$22 = V$$

Thus, $M = 44$, and Marisol will be 49 years old in 5 years.

Check the answer. Eight years ago, Marisol was 36 and Vikram was 14. Three times Vikram's age at that time was 42, and Marisol was 6 years younger than that.

16. **28.** Convert this word problem into two equations with two variables. "The length is two more than twice the width" can be written as:

$$L = 2W + 2$$

Since the area is 40 and area is equal to length × width:

$$LW = 40$$

Since the first equation is already solved for $L$, plug $(2W + 2)$ in for $L$ into the second equation:

$$(2W + 2)W = 40$$
$$2W^2 + 2W = 40$$

Since this is now a quadratic (there are both a $W^2$ and a $W$ term), get all terms on one side to set the expression equal to zero:

$$2W^2 + 2W - 40 = 0$$

Simplify as much as possible—in this case, divide the entire equation by 2—before trying to factor:

$$W^2 + W - 20 = 0$$
$$(W - 4)(W + 5) = 0$$
$$W = 4 \text{ or } -5$$

Since a width cannot be negative, the width is equal to 4. Since $LW$ is equal to 40, the length must be 10. Now use the equation for perimeter to solve:

$$\text{Perimeter} = 2L + 2W$$
$$\text{Perimeter} = 2(10) + 2(4)$$
$$\text{Perimeter} = 28$$

Note that it might have been possible for you to puzzle out that the sides were 4 and 10 just by trying values. However, if you did this, you got lucky—no one said that the values even had to be integers! The ability to translate into equations and solve is very important for the GRE.

17. **(D).** To solve this problem, establish the following variables:

$J$ = original jean price
$B$ = original blouse price

Next, establish a system of equations, keeping in mind that "70% off" is the same as $100\% - 70\% = 30\%$, or 0.3, of the original price:

$$0.3J + 12 = 0.6B$$
$$0.3J + 0.6B = 84$$

Now use whatever strategy you're most comfortable with to solve a system of equations—for example, aligning the equations and then subtracting them:

$$0.3J + 12 = 0.6B$$
$$\underline{0.3J - 84 = -0.6B}$$
$$0 + 96 = 1.2B$$

$$B = \frac{96}{1.2}$$

$$B = 80$$

You can plug the price of the blouse back into the original equation to get the price of the jeans:

$$0.3J + 12 = 0.6B$$
$$0.3J + 12 = 48$$
$$0.3J = 36$$
$$J = 120$$

Alternatively, you could first figure out the price of the discounted jeans, $x$, with this equation:

$$x + (x + 12) = 84$$
$$2x + 12 = 84$$
$$2x = 72$$
$$x = 36$$

Then plug that discounted price into the equation *discounted price = original price × (100% − percent discount):*

$$36 = 0.3P$$
$$360 = 3P$$
$$120 = P$$

18. **(D).** The equation for the perimeter of a space is $2W + 2L = P$, where $W$ is width and $L$ is length.

The equation for the area is $A = W \times L$. Thus,

$$0.44(W \times L) = 2W + 2L$$
$$0.44(50W) = 2W + 2(50)$$
$$22W = 2W + 100$$
$$20W = 100$$
$$W = 5$$

If $W = 5$ and $L = 50$, then the area of the hallway is 250 sq. ft., and the total cost is: $4.25 × 250 = $1,062.50.

19. **(B).** Call the smallest bill $S$, the middle bill $M$, and the largest bill $L$.

$M$ is the same as the median, since there are only three values. The equation for average is:

**MANHATTAN**
PREP

$$\frac{\text{Sum of bills}}{\text{Number of bills}} = \text{Average}$$

Incorporate the equation for averages into the following equation:

$$\frac{S+M+L}{3} = M + 44$$
$$S + M + L = 3M + 132$$
$$S + L = 2M + 132$$

While the individual values of $S$ and $L$ are not given, their sum is:

$$412 = 2M + 132$$
$$280 = 2M$$
$$140 = M$$

Finally, add $M$ to the sum of $S$ and $L$:

$$140 + 412 = 552$$

20. **(D).** Start by assigning variables:

$C$ = Number of collies
$L$ = Number of labs
$G$ = Number of golden retrievers

According to the given information:

$$G = 66$$
$$L = 66 - 12$$
$$L = 54$$

Ratios work like fractions, and you can set them up accordingly:

$$\frac{5}{9} = \frac{C}{54}$$

Cross-multiplying and simplifying, you get:

$$C = 30$$

Now take the number of collies and express it as a percent of the total number of dogs:

Total # of Dogs = $30 + 54 + 66 = 150$

$$\left(\frac{30}{150} \times 100\right)\% = 20\%$$

21. **(C).** The sum of Mason and Gunther's ages 4 years from now requires adding 4 to both ages.

The question asks for the following, the sum of Mason and Gunther's ages 4 years from now:

$$(M + 4) + (G + 4) = ?$$
$$M + G + 8 = ?$$

Since Mason is twice as old as Gunther was 10 years ago, put $(G - 10)$ in parentheses and build the second equation from there (the parentheses are crucial):

$$M = 2(G - 10)$$
$$M = 2G - 20$$

Note that the answer choices ask for the sum of the ages 4 years from now, in terms of $G$, so substitute for $M$ (the variable you substitute for is the one that drops out).

Substituting from the second equation into the first:

$$(2G - 20) + G + 8 = ?$$
$$3G - 12 = ?$$

This matches choice (C).

Alternatively, you could write the second equation, $M = 2(G - 10)$, and then come up with two values that "work" in this equation for $M$ and $G$. The easiest way to do this is to make up $G$, which will then tell you $M$. For instance, set $G = 12$ (use any number you want, as long as it's over 10, since the problem strongly implies that Gunther has been alive for more than 10 years):

$$M = 2(12 - 10)$$
$$M = 4$$

If Gunther is 12, then Mason is 4. In four years, they will be 16 and 8, respectively. Add these together to get 24.

Now, plug $G = 12$ into each answer choice to see which yields the correct answer (for this example), 24. Only choice (C) works.

22. **(E).** The equation for the situation described is $7x + 6y = 95$, where $x$ stands for the number of batches of chocolate chip cookies and $y$ stands for the number of batches of peanut butter cookies.

It looks as though this equation is not solvable, because there are two variables and only one equation. However, since the baker can only make whole batches, $x$ and $y$ must be integers, which really limits the possibilities.

Furthermore, the question asks for the *minimum* number of chocolate chip cookies the baker could have made. So, try 1 for $x$ and see if you get an integer for $y$ (use your calculator when needed!):

**MANHATTAN**
PREP

$$7(1) + 6y = 95$$
$$6y = 88$$
$$y = 14.6...$$

Since this did not result in an integer number of batches of peanut butter cookies, this situation doesn't work. Try 2, 3, 4, etc. for $x$. (Don't try values out of order—remember, there might be more than one $x$ value that works, but you need to be sure that you have the smallest one!)

The smallest value that works for $x$ is 5:

$$7(5) + 6y = 95$$
$$6y = 60$$
$$y = 10$$

Remember that you need the minimum number of chocolate chip *cookies*, not *batches of cookies*. Since the minimum number of batches is 5 and there are 7 cookies per batch, the minimum number of chocolate chip cookies is 35.

23. **(B).** First, translate the problem into two equations, writing "Anke after she gave Conrad 5 candies" as $(A - 5)$ and "Conrad after receiving 5 more candies" as $(C + 5)$:

$$A = C - 5$$
$$4(A - 5) = C + 5$$

Since $A = C - 5$, plug $C - 5$ in for $A$ in the second equation:

$$4(C - 5 - 5) = C + 5$$
$$4(C - 10) = C + 5$$
$$4C - 40 = C + 5$$
$$4C = C + 45$$
$$3C = 45$$
$$C = 15$$

If $C = 15$, then, since Anke has 5 fewer candies, she has $A = 10$.

Check the answer. If Anke starts with 10 candies, after giving 5 to Conrad she has 5. If Conrad starts with 15 candies, he has 20 after receiving 5 from Anke. It is true that 20 is 4 times 5.

24. **(A).** The key to this tricky-sounding problem is setting up variables correctly and ensuring that you subtract or add appropriately for these variables when representing their ages at different points in time:

$L$ = Lou's age now
$W$ = Wen's age now
$M$ = Mildred's age now
$T$ = Tyla's age now

**MANHATTAN**
PREP

Two equations come from the second sentence of the problem:

> Equation 1: $(L - 3) = 2(T - 3)$
> Equation 2: $(L - 3) = (M - 3) + 30$

Another two equations come from the third sentence of the problem:

> Equation 3: $L = W + 47$
>
> Equation 4: $(W + 4) = \dfrac{(T + 4)}{2}$

In order to solve this problem effectively, look for ways to get two of the equations to have the same two variables in them. If you have two equations with only two variables, you can solve for both of those variables. Equation 4 has a $W$ and a $T$; the only other equation with a $T$ is Equation 1. If you substitute the $L$ in Equation 1 with the $W$ from Equation 3, you will have two equations with just $W$'s and $T$'s.

> Equation 1: $(L - 3) = 2(T - 3)$
>
> $(W + 47) - 3 = 2(T - 3)$
> $\qquad W + 44 = 2T - 6$
> $\qquad W + 50 = 2T$
>
> Equation 4: $(W + 4) = \dfrac{(T + 4)}{2}$
>
> $2W + 8 = T + 4$
> $2W + 4 = T$

Now combine the equations to solve for $W$.

> $W + 50 = 2(2W + 4)$
> $W + 50 = 4W + 8$
> $W + 42 = 4W$
> $\qquad 42 = 3W$
> $\qquad 14 = W$

Now that you know Wen's age, you can solve for the rest.

> Equation 3: $L = W + 47$
>
> $L = 14 + 47$
> $L = 61$
>
> Equation 1: $(L - 3) = 2(T - 3)$
>
> $(61 - 3) = 2(T - 3)$
> $\qquad 58 = 2T - 6$

**MANHATTAN**
PREP

$$64 = 2T$$
$$32 = T$$

Equation 2: $(L - 3) = (M - 3) + 30$

$$(61 - 3) = (M - 3) + 30$$
$$58 = M + 27$$
$$31 = M$$

Now that you know that $L = 61$, $W = 14$, $M = 31$, and $T = 32$, sum them to find the answer:

$$61 + 14 + 31 + 32 = 138$$

25. **(E).** This question is difficult to translate. Begin by finding two things that are equal, and build an equation around that equality. *Dwayne grew twice as many bushels of pinto beans as navy beans*:

2(bushels of navy beans) = (bushels of pinto beans)

Break that down further:

bushels of navy beans = acres of navy beans × bushels per acre of navy beans
bushels of pinto beans = acres of pinto beans × bushels per acre of pinto beans

So:

2(acres of navy beans × bushels per acre of navy beans) =
(acres of pinto beans × bushels per acre of pinto beans)

"Each acre of navy beans yielded 27 bushels and each acre of pinto beans yielded 36 bushels":

$2 \times 27 \times$ (acres of navy beans) $= 36 \times$ (acres of pinto beans)

Number of acres planted with pinto beans $= p$
Number of acres planted with navy beans $= 70 - p$

$$2 \times 27(70 - p) = 36p$$
$$54(70 - p) = 36p$$
$$3{,}780 - 54p = 36p$$
$$3{,}780 = 90p$$
$$p = 42$$

Check the answer. If Dwayne planted 42 acres of pinto beans, he planted 28 acres of navy beans. The yield of pinto beans was $42 \times 36 = 1{,}512$ bushels. The yield of navy beans was $28 \times 27 = 756$ bushels, which was half the yield of pinto beans.

# Chapter 18

## *of*

## 5 lb. Book of GRE® Practice Problems

# Rates and Work

# In This Chapter...

Rates and Work

Rates and Work Answers

# Rates and Work

For questions in the Quantitative Comparison format ("Quantity A" and "Quantity B" given), the answer choices are always as follows:

(A)  Quantity A is greater.
(B)  Quantity B is greater.
(C)  The two quantities are equal.
(D)  The relationship cannot be determined from the information given.

For questions followed by a numeric entry box [       ], you are to enter your own answer in the box. For questions followed

by a fraction-style numeric entry box ▭, you are to enter your answer in the form of a fraction. You are not required to

reduce fractions. For example, if the answer is $\frac{1}{4}$, you may enter $\frac{25}{100}$ or any equivalent fraction.

All numbers used are real numbers. All figures are assumed to lie in a plane unless otherwise indicated. Geometric figures are not necessarily drawn to scale. You should assume, however, that lines that appear to be straight are actually straight, points on a line are in the order shown, and all geometric objects are in the relative positions shown. Coordinate systems, such as $xy$-planes and number lines, as well as graphical data presentations, such as bar charts, circle graphs, and line graphs, *are* drawn to scale. A symbol that appears more than once in a question has the same meaning throughout the question.

1.  Running on a 10-mile loop in the same direction, Sue ran at a constant rate of 8 miles per hour and Rob ran at a constant rate of 6 miles per hour. If they began running at the same point on the loop, how many hours later did Sue complete exactly 1 more lap than Rob?

    (A)  3
    (B)  4
    (C)  5
    (D)  6
    (E)  7

2.  Svetlana ran the first 5 kilometers of a 10-kilometer race at a constant rate of 12 kilometers per hour. If she completed the entire 10-kilometer race in 55 minutes, at what constant rate did she run the last 5 kilometers of the race, in kilometers per hour?

    (A)  15
    (B)  12
    (C)  11
    (D)  10
    (E)  8

3.  A standard machine fills paint cans at a rate of 1 gallon every 4 minutes. A deluxe machine fills gallons of paint at twice the rate of a standard machine. How many hours will it take a standard machine and a deluxe machine, working together, to fill 135 gallons of paint?

    (A)  1
    (B)  1.5
    (C)  2
    (D)  2.5
    (E)  3

4.  Wendy can build a birdhouse in 15 hours and Miguel can build an identical birdhouse in 10 hours. How many hours will it take Wendy and Miguel, working together at their respective constant rates, to build a birdhouse? (Assume that they can work on the same birdhouse without changing each other's work rate.)

    (A)  5
    (B)  6
    (C)  7
    (D)  8
    (E)  9

5.  Machine A, which produces 15 golf clubs per hour, fills a production lot in 6 hours. Machine B fills the same production lot in 1.5 hours. How many golf clubs does machine B produce per hour?

    ☐ golf clubs per hour

    Davis drove from Amityville to Beteltown at 50 miles per hour, and returned by the same route at 60 miles per hour.

    | Quantity A | Quantity B |
    |---|---|
    6.  Davis's average speed for the round trip, in miles per hour | 55

7.  If a turtle traveled $\frac{1}{30}$ of a mile in 5 minutes, what was its speed in miles per hour?

    (A)  0.02
    (B)  0.1$\overline{6}$
    (C)  0.4
    (D)  0.6
    (E)  2.5

Akilah traveled at a rate of x miles per hour for 2x hours.

|  | **Quantity A** | **Quantity B** |
|---|---|---|
| 8. | The number of miles Akilah traveled | $3x$ |

9. Claudette traveled the first $\dfrac{2}{3}$ of a 60-mile trip at 20 miles per hour (mph) and the remainder of the trip at 30 mph. How many minutes later would she have arrived if she had completed the entire trip at 20 mph?

   [_____] minutes

10. Rajesh traveled from home to school at 30 miles per hour. Then he returned home at 40 miles per hour, and finally he went back to school at 60 miles per hour, all along the same route. What was his average speed for the entire trip, in miles per hour?

    (A) 32
    (B) 36
    (C) 40
    (D) 45
    (E) 47

11. Twelve workers pack boxes at a constant rate of 60 boxes in 9 minutes. How many minutes would it take 27 workers to pack 180 boxes, if all workers pack boxes at the same constant rate?

    (A) 12
    (B) 13
    (C) 14
    (D) 15
    (E) 16

12. To service a single device in 12 seconds, 700 nanorobots are required, with all nanorobots working at the same constant rate. How many hours would it take for a single nanorobot to service 12 devices?

    (A) $\dfrac{7}{3}$
    (B) 28
    (C) 108
    (D) 1,008
    (E) 1,680

13. If a baker made 60 pies in the first 5 hours of his workday, by how many pies per hour did he increase his rate in the last 3 hours of the workday in order to complete 150 pies in the entire 8-hour period?

    (A) 12
    (B) 14
    (C) 16
    (D) 18
    (E) 20

14. Nine identical machines, each working at the same constant rate, can stitch 27 jerseys in 4 minutes. How many minutes would it take 4 such machines to stitch 60 jerseys?

    (A) 8
    (B) 12
    (C) 16
    (D) 18
    (E) 20

15. Brenda walked a 12-mile scenic loop in 3 hours. If she then reduced her walking speed by half, how many hours would it take Brenda to walk the same scenic loop two more times?

    (A) 6
    (B) 8
    (C) 12
    (D) 18
    (E) 24

16. A gang of criminals hijacked a train heading due south. At exactly the same time, a police car located 50 miles north of the train started driving south toward the train on an adjacent roadway parallel to the train track. If the train traveled at a constant rate of 50 miles per hour, and the police car traveled at a constant rate of 80 miles per hour, how long after the hijacking did the police car catch up with the train?

    (A) 1 hour
    (B) 1 hour and 20 minutes
    (C) 1 hour and 40 minutes
    (D) 2 hours
    (E) 2 hours and 20 minutes

**MANHATTAN**
PREP

Each working at a constant rate, Rachel assembles a brochure every 10 minutes and Terry assembles a brochure every 8 minutes.

|     | **Quantity A** | **Quantity B** |
| --- | --- | --- |
| 17. | The number of minutes it will take Rachel and Terry, working together, to assemble 9 brochures | 40 |

18. With 4 identical servers working at a constant rate, a new Internet search provider processes 9,600 search requests per hour. If the search provider adds 2 more identical servers, and server work rate never varies, the search provider can process 216,000 search requests in how many hours?

   (A)  15
   (B)  16
   (C)  18
   (D)  20
   (E)  24

19. If Sabrina can assemble a tank in 8 hours, and Janis can assemble a tank in 13 hours, then Sabrina and Janis working together at their constant respective rates can assemble a tank in approximately how many hours?

   (A)  21
   (B)  18
   (C)  7
   (D)  5
   (E)  2

20. Phil collects virtual gold in an online computer game and then sells the virtual gold for real dollars. After playing 10 hours a day for 6 days, he collected 540,000 gold pieces. If he immediately sold this virtual gold at a rate of $1 per 1,000 gold pieces, what were his average earnings per hour, in real dollars?

   (A)  $5
   (B)  $6
   (C)  $7
   (D)  $8
   (E)  $9

21. After completing a speed training, Alyosha translates Russian literature into English at a rate of 10 more than twice as many words per hour as he was able to translate before the training. If he was previously able to translate 10 words per minute, how many words can he now translate in an hour?

   (A)  30
   (B)  70
   (C)  610
   (D)  1,210
   (E)  1,800

22. Jenny takes 3 hours to sand a picnic table; Laila can do the same job in $\frac{1}{2}$ hour. Working together at their respective constant rates, Jenny and Laila can sand a picnic table in how many hours?

   (A)  $\frac{1}{6}$

   (B)  $\frac{2}{9}$

   (C)  $\frac{1}{3}$

   (D)  $\frac{3}{7}$

   (E)  $\frac{5}{6}$

One worker strings 2 violins in 3 minutes. All workers string violins at the same constant rate.

|  | Quantity A | Quantity B |
|---|---|---|
| 23. | The number of minutes required for 12 workers to string 720 violins | The number of violins that 5 workers can string in 24 minutes |

24. Riders board the Jelly Coaster in groups of 4 every 15 seconds. If there are 200 people in front of Kurt in line, in approximately how many minutes will Kurt board the Jelly Coaster?

   (A)  5
   (B)  8
   (C)  10
   (D)  13
   (E)  20

A team of 8 chefs produce 3,200 tarts in 5 days. All chefs produce tarts at the same constant rate.

|  | **Quantity A** | **Quantity B** |
|---|---|---|
| 25. | The number of chefs needed to produce 3,600 tarts in 3 days | The number of days that 4 chefs need to produce 4,800 tarts |

26. Working together at their respective constant rates, robot A and robot B polish 88 pounds of gemstones in 6 minutes. If robot A's rate of polishing is $\frac{3}{5}$ that of robot B, how many minutes would it take robot A alone to polish 165 pounds of gemstones?

    (A) 15.75
    (B) 18
    (C) 18.75
    (D) 27.5
    (E) 30

27. Car A started driving north from point $X$ traveling at a constant rate of 40 miles per hour. One hour later, car B started driving north from point $X$ at a constant rate of 30 miles per hour. Neither car changed direction of travel. If each car started with 8 gallons of fuel, which is consumed at a rate of 30 miles per gallon, how many miles apart were the two cars when car A ran out of fuel?

    (A) 30
    (B) 60
    (C) 90
    (D) 120
    (E) 150

28. One robot, working independently at a constant rate, can assemble a doghouse in 12 minutes. What is the maximum number of <u>complete</u> doghouses that can be assembled by 10 such identical robots, each working on <u>separate</u> doghouses at the same rate for $2\frac{1}{2}$ hours?

    (A) 20
    (B) 25
    (C) 120
    (D) 125
    (E) 150

29. Working continuously 24 hours a day, a factory bottles Soda Q at a rate of 500 liters per second and Soda V at a rate of 300 liters per second. If twice as many bottles of Soda V as of Soda Q are filled at the factory each day, what is the ratio of the volume of a bottle of Soda Q to a bottle of Soda V?

(A) $\dfrac{3}{10}$

(B) $\dfrac{5}{6}$

(C) $\dfrac{6}{5}$

(D) $\dfrac{8}{3}$

(E) $\dfrac{10}{3}$

**MANHATTAN**
PREP

# Rates and Work Answers

1. **(C).** If Sue completed exactly one more lap than Rob, she ran 10 more miles than Rob. If Rob ran $d$ miles, then Sue ran $d + 10$ miles. Rob and Sue began running at the same time, so they ran for the same amount of time. Let $t$ represent the time they spent running. Fill out a chart for Rob and Sue, using the formula Distance = Rate × Time (D = RT):

|  | $D$ (miles) | = | $R$ (miles per hour) | × | $T$ (hours) |
|---|---|---|---|---|---|
| Rob | $d$ | = | 6 | × | $t$ |
| Sue | $d + 10$ | = | 8 | × | $t$ |

There are two equations:

$$d = 6t \qquad\qquad d + 10 = 8t$$

Substitute $6t$ for $d$ in the second equation and then solve for $t$:

$$6t + 10 = 8t$$
$$10 = 2t$$
$$5 = t$$

2. **(D).** To calculate Svetlana's speed during the second half of the race, first calculate how long it took her to run the first half of the race. Svetlana ran the first 5 kilometers at a constant rate of 12 kilometers per hour. These values can be used in the $D = RT$ formula:

| $D$ (km) | = | $R$ (km per hr) | × | $T$ (hr) |
|---|---|---|---|---|
| 5 | = | 12 | × | $t$ |

Svetlana's time for the first part of the race is $\dfrac{5}{12}$ hours, or 25 minutes.

She completed the entire 10-kilometer race in 55 minutes, so she ran the last 5 kilometers in $55 - 25 = 30$ minutes, or 0.5 hours. Now create another chart to find the rate at which she ran the last 5 kilometers:

| $D$ (km) | = | $R$ (km per hr) | × | $T$ (hr) |
|---|---|---|---|---|
| 5 | = | $r$ | × | 0.5 |

$$5 = 0.5r$$
$$10 = r$$

Svetlana ran the second half of the race at a speed of 10 kilometers per hour.

3. **(E).** The question asks for the amount of time in hours, convert the work rates from gallons per minute to gallons per hour. First, calculate the rate of the standard machine:

$$\frac{1\ \text{gallon}}{4\ \text{minutes}} \times \frac{60\ \text{minutes}}{1\ \text{hour}} = \frac{60\ \text{gallons}}{4\ \text{hours}} = 15\ \text{gallons per hour}$$

Since the deluxe machine's rate is twice the standard machine's rate, the deluxe machine can fill $15 \times 2 = 30$ gallons of paint per hour. Together, the machines can fill $15 + 30 = 45$ gallons of paint per hour. Now apply the formula for work, $W = RT$:

$$135 = 45 \times T$$
$$3 = T$$

4. **(B).** Use two separate lines in a $W = RT$ chart, one for Wendy and one for Miguel, to calculate their respective rates. Building 1 birdhouse equals doing 1 unit of work:

| | $W$ (birdhouses) | $=$ | $R$ (birdhouses per hour) | $\times$ | $T$ (hours) |
|---|---|---|---|---|---|
| Wendy | 1 | $=$ | $R_W$ | $\times$ | 15 |
| Miguel | 1 | $=$ | $R_M$ | $\times$ | 10 |

Thus, Wendy's rate is $\frac{1}{15}$ birdhouses per hour, and Miguel's rate is $\frac{1}{10}$ birdhouses per hour. Since Wendy and Miguel are working together, add their rates:

| | $W$ (birdhouses) | $=$ | $R$ (birdhouses per hour) | $\times$ | $T$ (hours) |
|---|---|---|---|---|---|
| Wendy + Miguel | 1 | $=$ | $\frac{1}{15} + \frac{1}{10}$ | $\times$ | $t$ |

Now solve for $t$ by first combining the fractions:

$$1 = \left(\frac{1}{15} + \frac{1}{10}\right)t$$
$$1 = \left(\frac{2}{30} + \frac{3}{30}\right)t$$
$$1 = \left(\frac{5}{30}\right)t$$
$$\frac{30}{5} = t$$
$$6 = t$$

**MANHATTAN**
PREP

5. **60 golf clubs per hour.** First, calculate the size of a production lot. Machine A works at a rate of 15 golf clubs per hour and completes a production lot in 6 hrs. Plug this information into the $W = RT$ formula:

| $W$ (clubs) | $=$ | $R$ (clubs per hour) | $\times$ | $T$ (hours) |
|---|---|---|---|---|
| $w$ | $=$ | 15 | $\times$ | 6 |

$w = 15$ clubs per hour $\times$ 6 hours $= 90$ clubs

Therefore, a production lot consists of 90 golf clubs. Since machine $B$ can complete the lot in 1.5 hours, use the $W = RT$ chart a second time to calculate the rate for machine B:

| $W$ (clubs) | $=$ | $R$ (clubs per hour) | $\times$ | $T$ (hours) |
|---|---|---|---|---|
| 90 | $=$ | $r$ | $\times$ | 1.5 |

Make the calculation easier by converting 1.5 hours to $\frac{3}{2}$ hours:

$$90 = \frac{3}{2}r$$
$$\frac{2}{3} \times 90 = r$$
$$2 \times 30 = r$$
$$60 = r$$

6. **(B).** Never take an average speed by just averaging the two speeds (50 mph and 60 mph). Instead, use the formula Average Speed = Total Distance ÷ Total Time. Fortunately, for Quantitative Comparisons, you can often sidestep actual calculations.

Davis's average speed can be thought of as an average of the speed he was traveling at every single moment during his journey—for instance, imagine that Davis wrote down the speed he was going during every second he was driving, then he averaged all the seconds. Since Davis spent more *time* going 50 mph than going 60 mph, the average speed will be closer to 50 than 60, and Quantity B is greater. If the distances are the same, average speed is always weighted towards the *slower* speed.

To actually do the math, pick a convenient number for the distance between Amityville and Beteltown—for instance, 300 miles (divisible by both 50 and 60). If the distance is 300 miles, it took Davis 6 hours to drive there at 50 mph, and 5 hours to drive back at 60 mph. Using Average Speed = Total Distance ÷ Total Time (and a total distance of 600 miles, for both parts of the journey), you get the following:

$$\text{Average Speed} = \frac{600 \text{ miles}}{11 \text{ hours}}$$

Average Speed = 54.54… (which is less than 55)

The result will be the same for any value chosen. Quantity B is greater.

7. **(C).** The turtle traveled $\frac{1}{30}$ of a mile in 5 minutes, which is $\frac{1}{12}$ of an hour. Using the $D = RT$ formula, solve for $r$:

| $D$ (mile) | $=$ | $R$ (miles per hour) | $\times$ | $T$ (hours) |
|:---:|:---:|:---:|:---:|:---:|
| $\frac{1}{30}$ | $=$ | $r$ | $\times$ | $\frac{1}{12}$ |

$$\frac{1}{30} = \frac{1}{12}r$$
$$\frac{12}{30} = r$$
$$0.4 = r$$

8. **(D).** Use $D = RT$:

Distance $= x(2x)$

Distance $= 2x^2$

Which is greater, $2x^2$ or $3x$? If $x = 1$, then $3x$ is greater. But if $x = 2$, then $2x^2$ is greater.

Without information about the value of $x$, the relationship cannot be determined.

9. **20 minutes.** First, figure out how long it took Claudette to travel 60 miles under the actual conditions. The first leg of the trip was $\frac{2}{3}$ of 60 miles, or 40 miles. To travel 40 miles at a rate of 20 miles per hour, Claudette spent $\frac{40}{20} = 2$ hours = 120 minutes. The second leg of the trip was the remaining $60 - 40 = 20$ miles. To travel that distance at a rate of 30 miles per hour, Claudette spent $\frac{20}{30} = \frac{2}{3}$ hour = 40 minutes. In total, Claudette traveled for $120 + 40 = 160$ minutes.

Now consider the hypothetical trip. If Claudette had traveled the whole distance of 60 miles at 20 miles per hour, the trip would have taken $\frac{60}{20} = 3$ hours = 180 minutes.

Finally, compare the two trips. The real trip took 160 minutes, so the hypothetical trip would have taken $180 - 160 = 20$ minutes longer.

10. **(C).** Do not just average the three speeds, as Rajesh spent more time at slower rates than at higher rates, weighting the average toward the slower rate(s). To compute the average speed for a trip, figure out the total distance and divide by the total time.

Pick a convenient distance from home to school, one that is divisible by 30, 40, and 60—say 120 miles (tough for Rajesh, but easier for you).

**MANHATTAN**
PREP

The first part of the journey (from home to school) took $\frac{120}{30} = 4$ hours. The second part of the journey took $\frac{120}{40} = 3$ hours. The third part of the journey took $\frac{120}{60} = 2$ hours.

The total distance Rajesh traveled is $120 + 120 + 120 = 360$ miles. The total time was $4 + 3 + 2 = 9$ hours. Finally, his average speed for the entire trip was $\frac{360}{9} = 40$ miles per hour.

11. **(A).** To solve a Rates & Work problem with multiple workers, modify the standard formula *Work = Rate × Time* to this:

$$Work = Individual\ Rate \times Number\ of\ Workers \times Time$$

Use the first sentence to solve for an individual worker's rate. Plug in the fact that 12 workers pack boxes at a constant rate of 60 boxes in 9 minutes:

$$Work = Individual\ Rate \times Number\ of\ Workers \times Time$$

$$60\ boxes = (R)(12)(9\ minutes)$$

$$R = \frac{5}{9}\ boxes\ per\ minute$$

In other words, each worker can pack $\frac{5}{9}$ of a box per minute. Plug that rate back into the formula, but use the details from the second sentence in the problem:

$$Work = Individual\ Rate \times Number\ of\ Workers \times Time$$

$$180 = \left(\frac{5}{9}\right)(27)(T)$$
$$180 = 15T$$
$$12 = T$$

12. **(B).** To solve a Rates & Work problem with multiple workers, modify the standard formula *Work = Rate × Time* to this:

$$Work = Individual\ Rate \times Number\ of\ Workers \times Time$$

Solve for an individual nanorobot's rate, using the fact that 700 nanorobots can service 1 device in 12 seconds. Notice that the "work" here is 1 device:

$$Work = Individual\ Rate \times Number\ of\ Workers \times Time$$

$$1\ device = (R)(700)(12\ seconds)$$
$$R = \frac{1}{8,400}\ devices\ per\ second$$

That is, each nanorobot can service $\dfrac{1}{8,400}$ of a device in 1 second. Plug that rate back into the formula, but using the details from the second sentence in the problem:

$$Work = Individual\ Rate \times Number\ of\ Workers \times Time$$

$$12\ devices = \left( \dfrac{1}{8,400}\ devices\ per\ second \right)(1)(T)$$

$$T = 100,800\ seconds$$

The answer is 100,800 seconds. Divide by 60 to convert this time to 1,680 minutes; divide by 60 again to get 28 hours.

13. **(D).** The question asks by how many pies per hour the baker's rate of pie-making increased, so determine his rate for the first 5 hours and his rate in the last 3 hours. The difference is the ultimate answer:

Rate for last 3 hours − Rate for first 5 hours = Increase

The rate for the first 5 hours was 60 pies ÷ 5 hours = 12 pies per hour.

In the last 3 hours, the baker made 150 − 60 = 90 pies. The rate in the last 3 hours of the workday was thus 90 pies ÷ 3 hours = 30 pies per hour.

Now find the difference between the two rates of work:

30 pies per hour − 12 pies per hour = 18 pies per hour

14. **(E).** To solve a Rates & Work problem with multiple workers, modify the standard formula *Work = Rate × Time* to this:

$$Work = Individual\ Rate \times Number\ of\ Workers \times Time$$

Solve for an individual machine's rate, using the fact that 9 machines can stitch 27 jerseys in 4 minutes:

$$Work = Individual\ Rate \times Number\ of\ Workers \times Time$$

$$27\ jerseys = (R)(9)(4\ minutes)$$
$$R = \dfrac{3}{4}\ jersey\ per\ minute$$

That is, each machine can stitch $\dfrac{3}{4}$ of a jersey in 1 minute. Plug that rate back into the formula, but using the details from the second sentence in the problem:

$$Work = Individual\ Rate \times Number\ of\ Workers \times Time$$

$$60 = \left( \dfrac{3}{4} \right)(4)(T)$$

$$T = 20$$

**MANHATTAN**
PREP

15. **(C).** This question compares an actual scenario with a hypothetical one. Start by figuring out the rate (speed) for Brenda's actual walk. Since she walked 12 miles in 3 hours, she walked at a rate of $12 \div 3 = 4$ miles per hour.

Now, in the hypothetical situation, she would walk the loop two more times, for a total additional distance of $12 \times 2 = 24$ miles. Her hypothetical speed would be half of 4 miles per hour, or 2 miles per hour.

Walking 24 miles at a rate of 2 miles per hour would take Brenda $24 \div 2 = 12$ hours.

Alternatively, note that both of the changes—doubling the distance and halving the rate—have the same effect: Each change makes the trip take twice as long as it would have before. So the time required for this hypothetical situation is multiplied by four: $3 \times 4 = 12$ hours.

16. **(C).** In this "chase" problem, the two vehicles are moving in the same direction, with one chasing the other. To determine how long it will take the rear vehicle to catch up, *subtract* the rates to find out how quickly the rear vehicle is gaining on the one in front.

The police car gains on the train at a rate of $80 - 50 = 30$ miles per hour. Since the police car needs to close a gap of 50 miles, plug into the $D = RT$ formula to find the time:

$$50 = 30t$$
$$\frac{5}{3} = t$$

The time it takes to catch up is $\frac{5}{3}$ hours, or 1 hour and 40 minutes.

17. **(C).** "Cheat" off the easier quantity. In 40 minutes (from Quantity B), Rachel would assemble $40 \div 10 = 4$ brochures and Terry would assemble $40 \div 8 = 5$ brochures, for a total of $4 + 5 = 9$ brochures. Thus, Quantity A is also 40, and the two quantities are equal.

18. **(A).** If the search provider adds 2 identical servers to the original 4, there are now 6 servers. Because $6 \div 4 = 1.5$, the rate at which all 6 servers work is 1.5 times the rate at which 4 servers work:

$$9{,}600 \text{ searches per hour} \times 1.5 = 14{,}400 \text{ searches per hour}$$

Now apply this rate to the given amount of work (216,000 searches), using the $W = RT$ formula:

$$216{,}000 = 14{,}400 \times T$$
$$216{,}000 \div 14{,}400 = 15 \text{ hours}$$

19. **(D).** Since Sabrina and Janis are working together, add their rates. Sabrina completes 1 tank in 8 hours, so she works at a rate of $\frac{1}{8}$ tank per hour. Likewise, Janis works at a rate of $\frac{1}{13}$ tank per hour. Now, add these fractions:

$$\frac{1}{8} + \frac{1}{13} = \frac{13}{104} + \frac{8}{104} = \frac{21}{104} \text{ tanks per hour, when working together.}$$

Next, plug this combined rate into the $W = RT$ formula to find the time. You might also notice that since the work is equal to 1, the time will just be the reciprocal of the rate:

|  | Work (tank) | = | Rate (tanks per hour) | × | Time (min) |
|---|---|---|---|---|---|
| Sabrina & Janis: | 1 | = | $\dfrac{21}{104}$ | × | $\dfrac{104}{21}$ |

At this point, you do not need to do long division or break out the calculator! Just approximate: $\dfrac{104}{21}$ is about $100 \div 20 = 5$.

Alternatively, use some intuition to work the answer choices and avoid setting up this problem at all! You can immediately eliminate (A) and (B), since these times exceed either worker's individual time. Also, since Sabrina is the faster worker, Janis's contribution will be less than Sabrina's. The two together won't work twice as fast as Sabrina, but they will work *more* than twice as fast as Janis. Therefore, the total time should be more than half of Sabrina's individual time, and less than half of Janis's individual time. $4 < t < 6.5$, which leaves (D) as the only possible answer.

20. **(E).** To solve for average earnings, fill in this formula:

Total earnings ÷ Total hours = Average earnings per hour

Since the gold-dollar exchange rate is $1 per 1,000 gold pieces, Phil's real dollar earnings for the 6 days were $540,000 \div 1,000 = \$540$. His total time worked was 10 hours per day × 6 days = 60 hours. Therefore, his average hourly earnings were $\$540 \div 60$ hours $= \$9$ per hour.

21. **(D).** To find the new rate in words per hour, start by setting up an equation to find this value:

New words per hour = 10 + 2(Old words per hour)

The old rate was given in words per minute, so convert to words per hour:

10 words per min × 60 min per hour = 600 words per hour

Now plug into the equation:

New words per hour = 10 + 2(600) = 1,210

Note that it would be dangerous to start by working with the rate per minute. If you did so, you might calculate 10 + 2(10) = 30 words per minute, then 30 × 60 = 1,800 words per hour. This rate is inflated because you added an additional 10 words per minute instead of per hour. Perform the conversions right away!

22. **(D).** Since the two women are working together, add their rates. To find their individual rates, divide work by time. Never divide time by work! (Also, be careful when dividing the work by $\dfrac{1}{2}$. The rate is the reciprocal of $\dfrac{1}{2}$, or 2 tables per hour.)

**MANHATTAN**
PREP

Find Jenny and Laila's combined rate, then divide the work required (1 table) by this rate: 1 table ÷ $\frac{7}{3}$ table per hour = $\frac{3}{7}$ hour.

|  | Work (tables) | = | Rate (table per hour) | × | Time (hours) |
|---|---|---|---|---|---|
| Jenny | 1 | = | $\frac{1}{3}$ | × | 3 |
| Laila | 1 | = | 2 | × | $\frac{1}{2}$ |
| Jenny & Laila | 1 | = | $\frac{1}{3} + 2 = \frac{7}{3}$ | × | $\frac{3}{7}$ |

23. **(A).** First, figure out the individual rate for 1 worker: 2 violins ÷ 3 minutes = $\frac{2}{3}$ violin per minute. (Always divide work by time to get a rate.) Now apply $W = RT$ separately to Quantity A and Quantity B.

Quantity A:

$R = 12 \times$ the individual rate $= 12 \times \frac{2}{3} = 8$ violins per minute

$W = 720$ violins

Solve for $T$ in $W = RT$:

$720 = 8T$

$90 = T$

Quantity B:

$R = 5 \times$ the individual rate $= 5 \times \frac{2}{3} = \frac{10}{3}$ violins per minute

$T = 24$ minutes

Solve for $W$ in $W = RT$:

$W = \left(\frac{10}{3}\right)(24)$

$W = 80$

Since 90 > 80, Quantity A is greater.

24. **(D).** To find Kurt's wait time, determine how long it will take for 200 people to board the Jelly Coaster. The problem states that 4 people board every 15 seconds. Since there are four 15-second periods in one minute, this rate converts to 16 people per minute. To find the time, divide the "work" (the people) by this rate:

200 people ÷ 16 people per minute = 200 ÷ 16 = 12.5 minutes.

The question asks for an approximation, and the closest answer is (D). In theory there may be an additional 15 seconds while Kurt's group is boarding (the problem doesn't really say), but Kurt's total wait time would still be approximately 13 minutes.

25. **(C).** To solve a Rates & Work problem with multiple workers, modify the standard formula *Work = Rate × Time* to this:

*Work = Individual Rate × Number of Workers × Time*

Solve for an individual chef's rate, using the fact that 8 chefs produce 3,200 tarts in 5 days:

*Work = Individual Rate × Number of Workers × Time*
3,200 tarts = (*R*)(8)(5 days)
*R* = 80 tarts per day

That is, each chef can produce 80 tarts per day. Plug that rate back into the formula for each of the quantities:

Quantity A
*Work = Individual Rate × Number of Workers × Time*
3,600 = (80)(*Number of Workers*)(3)
*Number of Workers* = 15

Quantity B
*Work = Individual Rate × Number of Workers × Time*
4,800 = (80)(4)(*Time*)
*Time* = 15 days

The number of chefs in Quantity A is equal to the number of days in Quantity B.

26. **(E).** When rate problems involve multiple situations, it can help to set up an initial "skeleton" *W = RT* chart for the solution. That way, you can determine what data is needed and fill in that data as you find it. Since the question asks how long robot A will take alone, the chart will look like this:

|  | Work (pounds) | = | Rate (pounds per min) | × | Time (min) |
|---|---|---|---|---|---|
| Robot A | 165 | = | *A*'s rate | × | *t* |

Work is known and the question asks for time, so robot *A*'s rate is needed. Call the rates *a* and *b*. Now set up another chart representing what you know about the two robots working together.

|  | Work (pounds) | = | Rate (pounds per min) | × | Time (min) |
|---|---|---|---|---|---|
| Robot A | 6*a* | = | *a* | × | 6 |
| Robot B | 6*b* | = | *b* | × | 6 |
| A & B together | 6(*a* + *b*) = 88 | = | *a* + *b* | × | 6 |

**MANHATTAN**
PREP

Now, $6(a + b) = 88$ and, from the question stem, robot A's rate is $\frac{3}{5}$ of B's rate. This can be written as $a = \frac{3}{5}b$. To solve for $a$, substitute for $b$:

$$a = \left(\frac{3}{5}\right)b$$

$$\left(\frac{5}{3}\right)a = b$$

$$6\left(a + \left(\frac{5}{3}\right)a\right) = 88$$

$$6\left(\frac{8}{3}\right)a = 88$$

$$\left(\frac{48}{3}\right)(a) = 88$$

$$a = 88\left(\frac{3}{48}\right)$$

$$a = 88\left(\frac{1}{16}\right) = \left(\frac{88}{16}\right) = \frac{11}{2}$$

So A's rate is $\frac{11}{2}$ pounds per minute. Now just plug into the original chart:

| | Work (pounds) | = | Rate (pounds per min) | × | Time (min) |
|---|---|---|---|---|---|
| Robot A | 165 | = | $\frac{11}{2}$ | × | 30 |

The time robot A takes to polish 165 pounds of gems is $165 / \frac{11}{2} = \frac{330}{165} = 30$ minutes.

27. **(C).** The question asks (indirectly) how far the two cars traveled, as those distances are necessary to find the distance between them. Since the cars go in the same direction, the skeleton equation is as follows:

Car A's distance − Car B's distance = Distance between cars
All distances refer to the time when car A ran out of fuel.

Since the limiting factor in this case is A's fuel supply, calculate how far the car is able to drive before running out of fuel. This in itself is a rate problem of sorts:

30 miles per gallon × 8 gallons = 240 miles

So car A will end up 240 miles north of its starting point, which happens $240 \div 40 = 6$ hours after it started. What about car B? It started an hour later and thus traveled (30 miles per hour)(6 hours − 1 hour) = 150 miles by that time.

Therefore, the two cars were $240 - 150 = 90$ miles apart when car A ran out of fuel.

**MANHATTAN PREP**

28. **(C).** Note that choice (D) is a trap. This issue is relatively rare, but it's worthwhile to be able to recognize it if you see it. In this case, each robot is *independently* assembling complete doghouses. Since the question asks for the number of *completed* doghouses after $2\frac{1}{2}$ hours, any *incomplete* doghouses must be removed from the calculations.

Since one robot completes a doghouse in 12 minutes, the individual hourly rate is $60 \div 12 = 5$ doghouses per hour. Therefore, each robot produces $5 \times 2.5 = 12.5$ doghouses in $2\frac{1}{2}$ hours. (Or just divide the 150 total minutes by 12 minutes per doghouse to get the same result.)

However, the questions asks about *completed* doghouses, and the robots are working independently, so drop the decimal. Each robot completes only 12 complete doghouses in the time period, for a total of $12 \times 10 = 120$ doghouses.

29. **(E).** If twice as many bottles of Soda V as of Soda Q are filled at the factory each day, then twice as many bottles of Soda V as of Soda Q are filled at the factory each second.

Use smart numbers for the number of bottles filled each second. Since twice as many bottles of Soda V are produced, the output in one second could be 100 bottles of Soda V and 50 bottles of Soda Q. Using these numbers, the volume of the Q bottles is 500 liters $\div$ 50 bottles = 10 liters per bottle and the volume of the V bottles is 300 liters $\div$ 100 bottles = 3 liters per bottle. The ratio of the volume of a bottle of Q to a bottle of V is 10 liters $\div$ 3 liters = $\frac{10}{3}$.

# Chapter 19

## of

## 5 lb. Book of GRE® Practice Problems

# Variables-in-the-Choices Problems

# In This Chapter...

# Variables-in-the-Choices Problems

For questions in the Quantitative Comparison format ("Quantity A" and "Quantity B" given), the answer choices are always as follows:

(A)   Quantity A is greater.
(B)   Quantity B is greater.
(C)   The two quantities are equal.
(D)   The relationship cannot be determined from the information given.

For questions followed by a numeric entry box [ ⬚ ], you are to enter your own answer in the box. For questions followed

by a fraction-style numeric entry box [ ⬚/⬚ ], you are to enter your answer in the form of a fraction. You are not required to

reduce fractions. For example, if the answer is $\frac{1}{4}$, you may enter $\frac{25}{100}$ or any equivalent fraction.

All numbers used are real numbers. All figures are assumed to lie in a plane unless otherwise indicated. Geometric figures are not necessarily drawn to scale. You should assume, however, that lines that appear to be straight are actually straight, points on a line are in the order shown, and all geometric objects are in the relative positions shown. Coordinate systems, such as $xy$-planes and number lines, as well as graphical data presentations, such as bar charts, circle graphs, and line graphs, *are* drawn to scale. A symbol that appears more than once in a question has the same meaning throughout the question.

1.   If Josephine reads $b$ books per week and each book has, on average, 100,000 words, which best approximates the number of words Josephine reads per day?

(A)   $100{,}000b$

(B)   $\dfrac{100{,}000b}{7}$

(C)   $\dfrac{700{,}000}{b}$

(D)   $\dfrac{7b}{100{,}000}$

(E)   $\dfrac{100{,}000b}{(7)(24)}$

2.   The width of a rectangle $w$ is twice the length of the rectangle. Which of the following equals the area of the rectangle in terms of $w$?

(A)   $w$

(B)   $2w^2$

(C)   $3w^2$

(D)   $\dfrac{w^2}{2}$

(E)   $\dfrac{w^2}{4}$

3. A clothing store bought 100 shirts for $x. If the store sold all of the shirts at the same price for a total of $50, what is the store's profit per shirt, in dollars, in terms of $x$?

(A) $50 - \dfrac{x}{100}$

(B) $50 - x$

(C) $5 - x$

(D) $0.5 - x$

(E) $0.5 - \dfrac{x}{100}$

4. Two trees have a combined height of 60 feet, and the taller tree is $x$ times the height of the shorter tree. How tall is the shorter tree, in terms of $x$?

(A) $\dfrac{60}{1+x}$

(B) $\dfrac{60}{x}$

(C) $\dfrac{30}{x}$

(D) $60 - 2x$

(E) $30 - 5x$

5. Louise is three times as old as Mary. Mary is twice as old as Natalie. If Louise is $L$ years old, what is the average (arithmetic mean) age of the three women, in terms of $L$?

(A) $\dfrac{L}{3}$

(B) $\dfrac{L}{2}$

(C) $\dfrac{2L}{3}$

(D) $\dfrac{L}{4}$

(E) $\dfrac{L}{6}$

6. Toshi is four times as old as Kosuke. In $x$ years Toshi will be three times as old as Kosuke. How old is Kosuke, in terms of $x$?

(A) $2x$

(B) $3x$

(C) $4x$

(D) $8x$

(E) $12x$

**MANHATTAN**
PREP

7.   A shirt that costs $k$ dollars is increased by 30%, then by an additional 50%. What is the new price of the shirt in dollars, in terms of $k$?

   (A)  $0.2k$
   (B)  $0.35k$
   (C)  $1.15k$
   (D)  $1.8k$
   (E)  $1.95k$

8.   Carlos runs a lap around the track in $x$ seconds. His second lap is five seconds slower than the first lap, but the third lap is two seconds faster than the first lap. What is Carlos's average (arithmetic mean) number of <u>minutes</u> per lap, in terms of $x$?

   (A)  $x - 1$
   (B)  $x + 1$
   (C)  $\dfrac{x - 1}{60}$
   (D)  $\dfrac{x + 1}{60}$
   (E)  $\dfrac{x + 3}{60}$

9.   Andrew sells vintage clothing at a flea market at which he pays $150 per day to rent a table plus $10 per hour to his assistant. He sells an average of $78 worth of clothes per hour. Assuming no other costs, which of the functions below best represents profit per day, $P$, in terms of hours, $h$, that the flea market table is open for business?

   (A)  $P(h) = 238 - 10h$
   (B)  $P(h) = 72 - 10h$
   (C)  $P(h) = 68h - 150$
   (D)  $P(h) = 78h - 160$
   (E)  $P(h) = -160h + 78$

10.  If $a$, $b$, $c$, and $d$ are consecutive integers and $a < b < c < d$, what is the average (arithmetic mean) of $a$, $b$, $c$, and $d$ in terms of $d$?

   (A)  $d - \dfrac{5}{2}$
   (B)  $d - 2$
   (C)  $d - \dfrac{3}{2}$
   (D)  $d + \dfrac{3}{2}$
   (E)  $\dfrac{4d - 6}{7}$

11. Cheese that costs $c$ cents per ounce costs how many dollars per pound? (16 ounces = 1 pound and 100 cents = 1 dollar)

    (A) $\dfrac{4c}{25}$

    (B) $\dfrac{25c}{4}$

    (C) $\dfrac{25}{4c}$

    (D) $\dfrac{c}{1,600}$

    (E) $1,600c$

12. A bag of snack mix contains 3 ounces of pretzels, 1 ounce of chocolate chips, 2 ounces of mixed nuts, and $x$ ounces of dried fruit by weight. What percent of the mix is dried fruit, by weight?

    (A) $\dfrac{x}{600}$

    (B) $\dfrac{100}{6x}$

    (C) $\dfrac{100x}{6}$

    (D) $\dfrac{100x}{6+x}$

    (E) $\dfrac{x}{100(6+x)}$

13. At her current job, Mary gets a 1.5% raise twice per year. Which of the following choices represents Mary's current income $y$ years after starting the job at a starting salary of $s$?

    (A) $s(1.5)^{2y}$

    (B) $s(0.015)^{2y}$

    (C) $s(1.015)^{2y}$

    (D) $s(1.5)^{\frac{y}{2}}$

    (E) $s(1.015)^{\frac{y}{2}}$

**MANHATTAN**
PREP

14. Phone plan A charges $1.25 for the first minute and $0.15 for every minute thereafter. Phone plan B charges a $0.90 connection fee and $0.20 per minute. Which of the following equations could be used to find the length, in minutes, of a phone call that costs the same under either plan?

    (A)  $1.25 + 0.15x = 0.90x + 0.20$

    (B)  $1.25 + 0.15x = 0.90 + 0.20x$

    (C)  $1.25 + 0.15(x - 1) = 0.90 + 0.20x$

    (D)  $1.25 + 0.15(x - 1) = 0.90 + 0.20(x - 1)$

    (E)  $1.25 + 0.15x + 0.90x + 0.20 = x$

15. If powdered drink mix costs $c$ cents per ounce and $p$ pounds of it are purchased by a supplier who intends to resell it, what will be the total revenue, in dollars, in terms of $c$ and $p$ if all of the drink mix is sold at a price per ounce equivalent to three times what the supplier paid? (16 ounces = 1 pound and 100 cents = 1 dollar)

    (A)  $48cp$

    (B)  $\dfrac{32cp}{100}$

    (C)  $\dfrac{100(32)}{cp}$

    (D)  $\dfrac{12cp}{25}$

    (E)  $\dfrac{25cp}{12}$

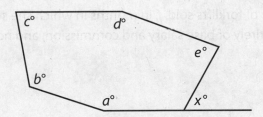

16. If $d = 2c$ and $e = \dfrac{1}{2}a$, what is $x$ in terms of $a$, $b$, and $c$?

    (A)  $\dfrac{3}{2}a + b + 3c - 540$

    (B)  $\dfrac{3}{2}a + b + 3c$

    (C)  $720 - \dfrac{3}{2}a - b - 3c$

    (D)  $720 - \dfrac{1}{2}a - b - 2c$

    (E)  $540 - \dfrac{1}{2}a - b - \dfrac{3}{2}c$

17. $a$, $b$, and $c$ are three consecutive odd integers such that $a < b < c$. If $a$ is halved to become $m$, $b$ is doubled to become $n$, $c$ is tripled to become $p$, and $k = mnp$, which of the following is equal to $k$ in terms of $a$?

    (A)  $3a^3 + 18a^2 + 24a$

    (B)  $3a^3 + 9a^2 + 6a$

    (C)  $\dfrac{11}{2}a + 16$

    (D)  $6a^2 + 36a + 24$

    (E)  $a^3 + 6a^2 + 4a$

18. If $m$ pencils cost the same as $n$ pens, and each pencil costs 20 cents, what is the cost, in dollars, of 10 pens, if each pen costs the same amount? (100 cents = 1 dollar)

    (A)  $\dfrac{200n}{m}$

    (B)  $\dfrac{2n}{100m}$

    (C)  $\dfrac{2m}{n}$

    (D)  $\dfrac{2n}{m}$

    (E)  $200mn$

19. Randi sells forklifts at a dealership where she makes a base salary of $2,000 per month, plus a commission equal to 5% of the selling price of the first 10 forklifts she sells that month, and 10% of the value of the selling price of any forklifts after that. If all forklifts have the same sale price, $s$, which of the choices below represents Randi's monthly pay, $P$, as a function of number of forklifts sold, $f$, in months in which she sells more than 10 forklifts? (Assume Randi's pay is made up entirely of base salary and commission, and no deductions are taken from this pay.)

    (A)  $P = 2,000 + 0.05sf + 0.10sf$

    (B)  $P = 2,000 + 0.05sf + 0.10s(f - 10)$

    (C)  $P = 2,000 + 0.05s + 0.10s(f - 10)$

    (D)  $P = 2,000 + 0.5s + 0.10sf - 10$

    (E)  $P = 2,000 + 0.5s + 0.10s(f - 10)$

**MANHATTAN**
PREP

20. If the width of a rectangle is $w$, the length is $l$, the perimeter is $p$, and $w = 2l$, what is the area in terms of $p$?

(A) $\dfrac{p^2}{18}$

(B) $\dfrac{p^2}{36}$

(C) $\dfrac{p}{9}$

(D) $\dfrac{p^2}{9}$

(E) $\dfrac{p}{6}$

# Variables-in-the-Choices Problems Answers

1. **(B).** Since Josephine reads $b$ books per week and each book has an average of 100,000 words, she reads $100,000b$ words per week. However, the question asks for words per *day*, so divide this quantity by 7.

Alternatively, you could try picking numbers. Notice that the question talks about weeks and days, so think about a number that is divisible by the 7 days in the week. If $b = 14$, for instance, then Josephine would read 14 books per week, or 2 books per day. This is equivalent to reading 200,000 words each day. Plug 14 in for $b$ in each answer choice, and only (B) results in 200,000.

2. **(D).** Since width is twice length, write $w = 2L$. However, the question requires an answer in terms of $w$, so solve for $L$:

$$L = \frac{w}{2}$$

Since area is $L \times W$ and $L = \frac{w}{2}$:

$$A = \frac{w}{2} \times W$$

Therefore, $A = \frac{w^2}{2}$, or choice (D).

Alternatively, pick values. If width were 4, length would be 2. The area would therefore be $4 \times 2 = 8$. Plug in 4 for $w$ to see which answer choice yields 8. Only (D) works.

3. **(E).** This problem requires the knowledge that profit equals revenue minus cost. You could memorize the formula Profit = Revenue − Cost (or Profit = Revenue − Expenses), or just think about it logically—a business has to pay its expenses out of the money it makes: the rest is profit.

The revenue for all 100 shirts was $50, and the cost to purchase all 100 shirts was $x$. Therefore:

Total profit = $50 - x$

The question does not ask for the total profit, but for the profit per shirt. The store sold 100 shirts, so divide the total profit by 100 to get the profit per shirt:

Profit per shirt $= \dfrac{50 - x}{100}$

None of the answer choices match this number, so you need to simplify the fraction. Split the numerator into two separate fractions:

$$\frac{50 - x}{100} = \frac{50}{100} - \frac{x}{100} = 0.5 - \frac{x}{100}$$

**MANHATTAN**
PREP

4. **(A).** First, define variables. Let $s$ = the height of the shorter tree. Let $t$ = the height of the taller tree.

If the combined height of the trees is 60 feet, then:

$$s + t = 60$$

The question also states that the height of the taller tree is $x$ times the height of the shorter tree:

$$t = xs$$

In order to solve for the height of the shorter tree, substitute ($xs$) for $t$ in the first equation:

$$s + (xs) = 60$$

Then isolate $s$ by factoring it out of the left side of the equation:

$$s(1 + x) = 60$$

$$s = \frac{60}{1 + x}$$

5. **(B).** First, express all three women's ages in terms of $L$. If Louise is three times as old as Mary, then Mary's age is $\frac{L}{3}$.

You also know that Mary is twice as old as Natalie. If Mary's age is $\frac{L}{3}$, then Natalie's age is $\frac{1}{2}$ of that, or $\frac{L}{6}$.

Now plug those values into the average formula. The average of the three ages is:

$$\text{Average} = \frac{L + \frac{L}{3} + \frac{L}{6}}{3}$$

To eliminate the fractions in the numerator, multiply the entire fraction by $\frac{6}{6}$ :

$$\frac{6}{6} \times \left( \frac{L + \frac{L}{3} + \frac{L}{6}}{3} \right) = \frac{6L + 2L + L}{18} = \frac{9L}{18} = \frac{L}{2}$$

6. **(A).** Let $T$ = Toshi's age; $(T + x)$ = Toshi's age in $x$ years
Let $K$ = Kosuke's age; $(K + x)$ = Kosuke's age in $x$ years

If Toshi is four times as old as Kosuke, then $T = 4K$.

To translate the second sentence correctly, remember to use $(T + x)$ and $(K + x)$ to represent their ages:

$$(T + x) = 3(K + x)$$

The question asks for Kosuke's age in terms of $x$, so replace $T$ with $(4K)$ in the second equation:

$$(4K) + x = 3K + 3x$$
$$K + x = 3x$$
$$K = 2x$$

7. **(E).** If the cost of the shirt is increased 30%, then the new price of the shirt is 130% of the original price. If the original price was $k$, then the new price is $1.3k$.

Remember that it is this new price that is increased by 50%. Multiply $1.3k$ by 1.5 (150%) to get the final price of the shirt:

$$1.3k \times 1.5 = 1.95k$$

8. **(D).** Carlos's lap times can be expressed as $x$, $x + 5$, and $x - 2$. (Remember, *slower* race times are *greater* numbers, so "five seconds slower" means *plus* 5, not *minus* 5!) Average the lap times:

$$\frac{x + (x + 5) + (x - 2)}{3} = \frac{3x + 3}{3} = x + 1$$

His average time is $x + 1$ *seconds*. But the question requires *minutes*. Since there are 60 seconds in a minute, divide by 60 to get $\frac{x + 1}{60}$, or choice (D).

Alternatively, pick values. If $x$ were 60 seconds, for example, Carlos's lap times would be 60, 65, and 58. His average time would be 61 seconds, or 1 minute and 1 second, or $1\frac{1}{60}$ minutes, or $\frac{61}{60}$ minutes. Plug in $x = 60$ to see which value yields $\frac{61}{60}$. Only (D) works.

9. **(C).** For every hour Andrew's business is open, he sells $78 worth of clothes but pays $10 to his assistant. Thus, he is making $68 an hour after paying the assistant. He also must pay $150 for the whole day.

Using Revenue − Expenses = Profit and $h$ for hours he is open, you get the following equation:

$$\text{Profit} = 68h - 150$$

Written as a function of profit in terms of hours, this is $P(h) = 68h - 150$, or choice (C).

Be careful that you are reading the answer choices as *functions*. $P$ is not a variable that is being multiplied by $h$! $P$ is the *name* of the function and $h$ is the variable on which the output of the function depends.

Note that (D) is a very good trap—this formula represents what the profit would be if Andrew only had to pay the assistant $10 *total*. However, he pays the assistant $10 *per hour*.

**MANHATTAN**
PREP

Alternatively, pick numbers. If Andrew were open for an 8-hour day (that is, test $h = 8$), he would make $68 an hour ($78 of sales minus $10 to the assistant), or $544 total. Subtract the $150 rental fee to get $394.

Then, plug 8 into the answer choices in place of $h$ to see which answer yields 394. Only (C) works.

10. **(C).** Since $a$, $b$, $c$, and $d$ are consecutive and $d$ is largest, you can express $c$ as $d - 1$, $b$ as $d - 2$, and $a$ as $d - 3$. Therefore, the average is:

$$\frac{(d-3)+(d-2)+(d-1)+d}{4} = \frac{4d-6}{4} = d - \frac{6}{4} \text{ or } d - \frac{3}{2}\text{ , which matches choice (C).}$$

Alternatively, plug in numbers. Say $a$, $b$, $c$, and $d$ are 1, 2, 3, and 4. (Generally, you want to avoid picking the numbers 0 and 1, lest *several* of the choices appear to be correct and you have to start over, but since only $d$ appears in the choices, it's no problem that $a$ is 1 in this example.)

Thus, the average would be 2.5. Plug in 4 for $d$ to see which choice yields an answer of 2.5. Only (C) works.

11. **(A).** If cheese costs $c$ cents per ounce, it costs $16c$ cents per pound. To convert from cents to dollars, divide by 100:

$$\frac{16c}{100} = \frac{4c}{25}\text{ , or choice (A).}$$

Alternatively, pick numbers. If $c = 50$, a cheese that costs 50 cents per ounce would cost 800 cents, or $8, per pound. Plug in $c = 50$ and select the answer that gives the answer 8. Only (A) works.

12. **(D).** To figure out what *fraction* of the mix is fruit, put the amount of fruit over the total amount of the mix: $\frac{x}{6+x}$. To convert a fraction to a percent, multiply by 100: $\frac{x}{6+x}(100) = \frac{100x}{6+x}$, or answer choice (D).

Alternatively, pick smart numbers. For instance, say $x = 4$. In that case, the total amount of mix would be 10 ounces, 4 of which would be dried fruit. Since $\frac{4}{10} = 40\%$, the answer to the question for your example would be 40%. Now, plug $x = 4$ into each answer choice to see which yields 40%. Only choice (D) works: $\frac{100(4)}{6+(4)} = \frac{400}{10} = 40$. This will work for any number you choose for $x$, provided that you correctly calculate what percent of the mix would be dried fruit in your particular example.

13. **(C).** To increase a number by 1.5%, first convert 1.5% to a decimal by dividing by 100 to get 0.015.

Do *not* multiply the original number by 0.015—this approach would be very inefficient, because multiplying by 0.015 would give you only the increase, not the new amount (you would then have to add the increase back to the original amount, a process so time-wasting and inefficient that it would not likely appear in a formula in the answer choices).

Instead, multiply by 1.015. Multiplying by 1 keeps the original number the same; multiplying by 1.015 gets you the original number plus 1.5% more.

**MANHATTAN**
PREP

Finally, if you want to multiply by 1.015 twice per year, you will need to do it $2y$ times. This $2y$ goes in the exponent spot to give you $s(1.015)^{2y}$, or choice (C).

**14. (C).** Write an equation to find the cost of a call under plan A, using $x$ as the number of minutes:

$$\text{Cost} = 1.25 + 0.15(x - 1)$$

Note that you need to use $x - 1$ because the caller does *not* pay $0.15 for every single minute—the first minute was already paid for by the $1.25 charge.

Now write an equation to find the cost of a call under plan $B$, using $x$ as the number of minutes:

$$\text{Cost} = 0.90 + 0.20x$$

Note that here you do *not* use $x - 1$ because the connection fee does not "buy" the first minute—the plan costs $0.20 for every minute.

To find the length of a call that would cost the same under either plan, set the two equations equal to one another:

$$1.25 + 0.15(x - 1) = 0.90 + 0.20x$$

This is choice (C). Note that you are not required to solve this equation, but you might be required to solve a similar equation in a different problem on this topic:

$$
\begin{aligned}
1.25 + 0.15x - 0.15 &= 0.90 + 0.20x \\
1.1 + 0.15x &= 0.90 + 0.20x \\
0.20 &= 0.05x \\
20 &= 5x \\
4 &= x
\end{aligned}
$$

A 4-minute call would cost the same under either plan. To test this, calculate the cost of a 4-minute call under both plans: it's $1.70 either way.

**15. (D).** The mix costs $c$ cents per ounce. Since you want the final answer in dollars, convert right now:

$$c \text{ cents per ounce} = \frac{c}{100} \text{ dollars per ounce}$$

The supplier then purchases $p$ pounds of mix. You cannot just multiply $p$ by $\frac{c}{100}$, because $p$ is in pounds and $\frac{c}{100}$ is in dollars per *ounce*. Since there are 16 ounces in a pound, it makes sense that a pound would cost 16 times more than an ounce:

$$\frac{c}{100} \text{ dollars per ounce} = \frac{16c}{100} \text{ dollars per pound}$$

Reduce to get $\frac{4c}{25}$ dollars per pound.

**MANHATTAN**
PREP

Multiply by $p$, the number of pounds, to get what the supplier paid: $\dfrac{4cp}{25}$ dollars.

Now, the supplier is going to sell the mix for three times what he or she paid. (Don't worry that the problem says three times the "price per ounce"—whether you measure in ounces or pounds, this stuff just got three times more expensive.)

Thus, $\dfrac{4cp}{25} \times 3 = \dfrac{12cp}{25}$, or answer choice (D).

Note: Make sure to calculate for revenue, not profit! The question did not require subtracting expenses (what the supplier paid) from the money he or she will be making from selling the mix.

Alternatively, plug in smart numbers. An easy number to pick when working with cents is 50 (or 25—whatever is easy to think about and convert to dollars). Write a value on your paper along with what the value means in words:

$c = 50$            mix costs 50¢ per ounce

Now, common sense (and the fact that 16 ounces = 1 pound) will allow you to convert:

50¢ per ounce = $8.00 per pound

The supplier bought $p$ pounds. Pick any number you want. For example:

$p = 2$            bought 2 pounds, so spent $16

Notice that no one asked for this $16 figure, but when calculating with smart numbers, it's best to write down next steps in the reasoning process.

Finally, the supplier is going to sell the mix for three times what he or she paid, so the supplier will sell it for $48.

Plug in $c = 50$ and $p = 2$ to see which answer choice generates 48. Only (D) works.

16. **(A).** Since the figure has six sides, use the formula $(n - 2)(180)$, where $n$ is the number of sides, to figure out that the sum of the angles inside the figure is equal to $(6 - 2)(180) = 720$.

The angle supplementary to $x$ can be labeled as $180 - x$ (since two angles that make up a straight line must sum to 180). Thus:

$$a + b + c + d + e + 180 - x = 720$$
$$a + b + c + d + e - x = 540$$

Solve for $x$. Since $x$ is being subtracted from the left side, it would be easiest to add $x$ to both sides, and get everything else on the opposite side.

$$a + b + c + d + e - x = 540$$
$$a + b + c + d + e = 540 + x$$
$$a + b + c + d + e - 540 = x$$

Since $d = 2c$ and $e = \frac{1}{2}a$ and the answers are in terms of $a$, $b$, and $c$, you need to make the $d$ and $e$ drop out of $a + b + c + d + e - 540 = x$.

Fortunately, $d = 2c$ and $e = \frac{1}{2}a$ are already solved for $d$ and $e$, the variables that need to drop out. Substitute:

$$a + b + c + 2c + \frac{1}{2}a - 540 = x$$

$$\frac{3}{2}a + b + 3c - 540 = x$$

This is a match with answer choice (A).

Alternatively, pick numbers. To do this, use the formula $(n - 2)(180)$, where $n$ is the number of sides, to figure out that the sum of the angles inside the figure: $(6 - 2)(180) = 720$. Then, pick values for $a$, $b$, $c$, $d$, and $e$, so that $d = 2c$ and $e = \frac{1}{2}a$:

$a = 100$
$b = 110$
$c = 120$
$d = 240$ (This is twice the value picked for $c$.)
$e = 50$ (This is $\frac{1}{2}$ the value picked for $a$.)

Subtract all of these values from 720 to get that the unlabeled angle, for this example, is equal to 100. This makes $x$ equal to $180 - 100 = 80$.

Now plug $a = 100$, $b = 110$, and $c = 120$ into the answers to see which formula yields a value of 80. (A) is the correct answer.

17. **(A).** One algebraic solution involves defining all three terms in terms of $a$. Since the terms are consecutive odd integers, they are 2 apart from each other, as such:

$a$
$b = a + 2$
$c = a + 4$

Then, $a$ is halved to become $m$, $b$ is doubled to become $n$, and $c$ is tripled to become $p$, so:

$$\frac{1}{2}a = m$$

**MANHATTAN**
PREP

$$2b = n$$
$$2(a + 2) = n$$
$$2a + 4 = n$$

$$3c = p$$
$$3(a + 4) = p$$
$$3a + 12 = p$$

Since $k = mnp$, multiply the values for $m$, $n$, and $p$:

$$k = \left(\frac{1}{2}a\right)(2a + 4)(3a + 12)$$

$$k = \left(\frac{1}{2}a\right)(6a^2 + 24a + 12a + 48)$$

$$k = \left(\frac{1}{2}a\right)(6a^2 + 36a + 48)$$

$$k = 3a^3 + 18a^2 + 24a$$

This is a match with answer choice (A).

A smart numbers solution would be to pick three consecutive odd integers for $a$, $b$, and $c$. When picking numbers for a Variables-in-the-Choices problem, avoid picking 0, 1, or any of the numbers in the problem (this can sometimes cause more than one answer to appear to be correct, thus necessitating starting over with another set of numbers). So:

$$a = 3$$
$$b = 5$$
$$c = 7$$

Then, $a$ is halved to become $m$, $b$ is doubled to become $n$, and $c$ is tripled to become $p$, so:

$$1.5 = m$$
$$10 = n$$
$$21 = p$$

Since $k = mnp$, multiply the values for $m$, $n$, and $p$:

$$k = (1.5)(10)(21)$$
$$k = 315$$

Now, plug $a = 3$ (the value originally selected) into the answer choices to see which choice equals 315. Only (A) works.

Because the correct answer is a mathematical way of writing the situation described in the problem, this will work for any value you pick for $a$, provided that $a$, $b$, and $c$ are consecutive odd integers and you calculate $k$ correctly.

18. **(C).** The phrase "*m* pencils cost the same as *n* pens" can be written as an equation, using *x* for the cost per pencil and *y* for the cost per pen:

$$mx = ny$$

Keep in mind here that *m* stands for the *number* of pencils and *n* for the *number* of pens (not the cost). Now, since pencils cost 20 cents, or $0.2 (the answer needs to be in dollars, so convert to dollars now), substitute in for *x*:

$$0.2m = ny$$

Solve for *y* to get the cost of 1 pen:

$$y = \frac{0.2m}{n}$$

Since *y* is the cost of 1 pen and $y = \frac{0.2m}{n}$, multiply by 10 to get the cost of 10 pens:

$$10y = 10\left(\frac{0.2m}{n}\right)$$
$$10y = \frac{2m}{n}$$

Thus, the answer is $\frac{2m}{n}$, or (C).

Alternatively, plug in smart numbers. Since pencils cost 20 cents, maybe pens cost 40 cents (you can arbitrarily pick this number). The question states that "*m* pencils cost the same as *n* pens"—pick a number for one of these variables, and then determine what the other variable would be for the example you've chosen. For instance, if *m* = 10, then 10 pencils would cost $2.00. Since 5 pens can be bought for $2.00, *n* would be 5. Now, answer the final question as a number: the cost of 10 pens in this example is $4.00, so the final answer is 4. Plug in *m* = 10 and *n* = 5 to all of the answer choices to see which yields an answer of 4. Only (C) works. For any working system you choose in which "*m* pencils cost the same as *n* pens," choice (C) will work.

19. **(E).** One way to do this problem is to construct a formula. Randi's pay is equal to $2,000 plus commission:

$$P = 2000 + \ldots$$

The question only asks about Randi's pay in months in which she sells more than 10 forklifts, so she will definitely be receiving 5% commission on 10 forklifts that each cost *s*. Since the revenue from the forklifts would then be 10*s*, Randi's commission would be 0.05(10*s*), or 0.5*s*:

$$P = 2,000 + 0.5s + \ldots$$

Now, add the commission for the forklifts she sells above the first 10. Since these first 10 forklifts are already accounted for, denote the forklifts at this commission level by writing *f* − 10. Since each forklift still costs *s*, the revenue from

**MANHATTAN**
PREP

these forklifts would be $s(f-10)$. Since Randi receives 10% of this as commission, the amount she receives would be $0.10s(f-10)$:

$$P = 2,000 + 0.5s + 0.10s(f-10)$$

It is possible to simplify further by distributing $0.10s(f-10)$, but before doing more work, check the answers—answer choice (E) is already an exact match.

Alternatively, plug in numbers. Say forklifts cost $100 (so, $s = 100$). Randi makes $5 each for the first 10 she sells, so $50 total. Then she makes $10 each for any additional forklifts. Pick a value for $f$ (make sure the value is more than 10, since the question asks for a formula for months in which Randi sells more than 10 forklifts). So, in a month in which she sells, for example, 13 forklifts (so, $f = 13$), she would make $2,000 + $50 + 3($10) = $2,080.

In this example:

$s = 100$
$f = 13$

Plug in these values for $s$ and $f$ to see which choice yields $2,080. Only choice (E) works:

$$P = 2,000 + 0.5(100) + 0.10(100)(13-10)$$
$$P = 2,000 + 50 + 10(3)$$
$$P = 2,080$$

20. **(A).** This question can be solved either with smart numbers or algebra. First, consider plugging in smart numbers.

Set $l = 2$, so $w = 4$. The perimeter will be $2l + 2w = 2(2) + 2(4) = 12$. The answer is the area, which is $wl = (2)(4) = 8$ based on these numbers. Now plug $p = 12$ into the choices to see which choice equals 8:

(A)  $\dfrac{144}{18} = 8$

(B)  $\dfrac{144}{36} = 4$

(C)  $\dfrac{12}{9} = \dfrac{4}{3}$

(D)  $\dfrac{144}{9} = 16$

(E)  $\dfrac{12}{6} = 2$

The correct answer is (A).

Though smart numbers are easier and faster here, an algebra solution is also possible. If $w = 2l$:

$$a = l \times w = l \times 2l = 2l^2$$
$$p = 2l + 2w = 2l + 4l = 6l$$

Solve the second equation for $l$:

$$l = \frac{p}{6}$$

And plug back into the first equation:

$$2\left(\frac{p}{6}\right)^2 = 2\left(\frac{p^2}{36}\right) = \frac{2p^2}{36} = \frac{p^2}{18}$$

# Chapter *of* 20

5 lb. Book of GRE® Practice Problems

# Ratios

# In This Chapter...

# Ratios

For questions in the Quantitative Comparison format ("Quantity A" and "Quantity B" given), the answer choices are always as follows:

(A)   Quantity A is greater.
(B)   Quantity B is greater.
(C)   The two quantities are equal.
(D)   The relationship cannot be determined from the information given.

For questions followed by a numeric entry box [＿＿＿], you are to enter your own answer in the box. For questions followed by a fraction-style numeric entry box $\frac{\boxed{\phantom{xx}}}{\boxed{\phantom{xx}}}$, you are to enter your answer in the form of a fraction. You are not required to reduce fractions. For example, if the answer is $\frac{1}{4}$, you may enter $\frac{25}{100}$ or any equivalent fraction.

All numbers used are real numbers. All figures are assumed to lie in a plane unless otherwise indicated. Geometric figures are not necessarily drawn to scale. You should assume, however, that lines that appear to be straight are actually straight, points on a line are in the order shown, and all geometric objects are in the relative positions shown. Coordinate systems, such as $xy$-planes and number lines, as well as graphical data presentations, such as bar charts, circle graphs, and line graphs, *are* drawn to scale. A symbol that appears more than once in a question has the same meaning throughout the question.

The ratio of men to women in a garden club is 5 to 4.

|      | **Quantity A** | **Quantity B** |
|------|----------------|----------------|
| 1.   | The smallest possible number of garden club members | 20 |

2.   A pantry holds $x$ cans of beans, twice as many cans of soup, and half as many cans of tomato paste as there are cans of beans. If there are no other cans in the pantry, which of the following could be the total number of cans in the pantry?

Indicate two such numbers.

☐   6
☐   7
☐   36
☐   45
☐   63

3.  If there are 20 birds and 6 dogs in a park, which of the following represents the ratio of dogs to birds in the park?

    (A)  3:13
    (B)  3:10
    (C)  10:3
    (D)  13:3
    (E)  1:26

4.  If there are 7 whole bananas, 14 whole strawberries, and no other fruit in a basket, what is the ratio of strawberries to the total pieces of fruit in the basket?

    Give your answer as a fraction.

    $$\frac{\boxed{\phantom{000}}}{\boxed{\phantom{000}}}$$

5.  The ratio of cheese to sauce for a single pizza is 1 cup to $\frac{1}{2}$ cup. If Bob used 15 cups of sauce to make a number of pizzas, how many cups of cheese did he use on those pizzas?

    $\boxed{\phantom{0000}}$ cups of cheese

6.  Laura established a new flower garden, planting 4 tulip plants for every 1 rose plant, and no other plants. If she planted a total of 50 plants in the garden, how many of those plants were tulips?

    $\boxed{\phantom{0000}}$ tulip plants

7.  A certain automotive dealer sells only cars and trucks, and the ratio of cars to trucks on the lot is 1 to 3. If there are currently 51 trucks for sale, how many cars does the dealer have for sale?

    (A)  17
    (B)  34
    (C)  68
    (D)  153
    (E)  204

8.  A steel manufacturer combines 98 ounces of iron with 2 ounces of carbon to make one sheet of steel. How many ounces of iron were used to manufacture $\frac{1}{2}$ of a sheet of steel?

    (A)  1
    (B)  49
    (C)  50
    (D)  198
    (E)  200

9.  Maria uses a recipe for 36 cupcakes that requires 8 cups of flour, 12 cups of milk, and 4 cups of sugar. How many cups of milk would Maria require for a batch of 9 cupcakes?

    (A)  2
    (B)  3
    (C)  4
    (D)  6
    (E)  8

10. In a certain orchestra, each musician plays only one instrument and the ratio of musicians who play either the violin or the viola to musicians who play neither instrument is 5 to 9. If 7 members of the orchestra play the viola and four times as many play the violin, how many play neither?

    (A)  14
    (B)  28
    (C)  35
    (D)  63
    (E)  72

11. The ratio of 0.4 to 5 equals which of the following ratios?

    (A)  4 to 55
    (B)  5 to 4
    (C)  2 to 25
    (D)  4 to 5
    (E)  4 to 45

12. On a wildlife preserve, the ratio of giraffes to zebras is 37 : 43. If there are 300 more zebras than giraffes, how many giraffes are on the wildlife preserve?

    (A) 1,550
    (B) 1,850
    (C) 2,150
    (D) 2,450
    (E) 2,750

13. At a certain company, the ratio of male to female employees is 3 to 4. If there are 5 more female employees than male employees, how many male employees does the company have?

    (A) 12
    (B) 15
    (C) 18
    (D) 21
    (E) 24

14. On Monday, a class has 8 girls and 20 boys. On Tuesday, a certain number of girls joined the class just as twice that number of boys left the class, changing the ratio of girls to boys to 7 to 4. How many boys left the class on Tuesday?

    (A) 5
    (B) 6
    (C) 11
    (D) 12
    (E) 18

15. If a dak is a unit of length and 14 daks = 1 jin, how many squares with a side length of 2 daks can fit in a square with a side length of 2 jins?

    (A) 14
    (B) 28
    (C) 49
    (D) 144
    (E) 196

In a group of adults, the ratio of women to men is 5 to 6, while the ratio of left-handed people to right-handed people is 7 to 9. Everyone is either left- or right-handed; no one is both.

| **Quantity A** | **Quantity B** |
|---|---|
| 16. The number of women in the group | The number of left-handed people in the group |

Party Cranberry is 3 parts cranberry juice and 1 part seltzer. Fancy Lemonade is 1 part lemon juice and 2 parts seltzer. An amount of Party Cranberry is mixed with an equal amount of Fancy Lemonade.

| **Quantity A** | **Quantity B** |
|---|---|
| 17. The fraction of the resulting mix that is cranberry juice | The fraction of the resulting mix that is seltzer |

The ratio of 16 to $g$ is equal to the ratio of $g$ to 49.

| **Quantity A** | **Quantity B** |
|---|---|
| 18. $g$ | 28 |

19. In a parking lot, $\frac{1}{3}$ of the vehicles are black and $\frac{1}{5}$ of the remainder are white. How many vehicles could be parked on the lot?

(A) 8

(B) 12

(C) 20

(D) 30

(E) 35

20.  Oil, vinegar, and water are mixed in a 3 to 2 to 1 ratio to make salad dressing. If Larry has 8 cups of oil, 7 cups of vinegar, and access to any amount of water, what is the maximum number of cups of salad dressing he can make with the ingredients he has available, if fractional cup measurements are possible?

    (A)  12
    (B)  13
    (C)  14
    (D)  15
    (E)  16

21.  With $y$ dollars, 5 oranges can be bought. If all oranges cost the same, how many dollars do 25 oranges cost, in terms of $y$?

    (A)  $\dfrac{y}{5}$
    (B)  $y$
    (C)  $y + 5$
    (D)  $5y$
    (E)  $25y$

22.  A woman spent $\dfrac{5}{8}$ of her weekly salary on rent and $\dfrac{1}{3}$ of the remainder on food, leaving $40 available for other expenses. What is the woman's weekly salary?

    (A)  $160
    (B)  $192
    (C)  $216
    (D)  $240
    (E)  $256

23.  In a certain rectangle, the ratio of length to width of a rectangle is 3:2 and the area is 150 square centimeters. What is the perimeter of the rectangle, in centimeters?

    (A)  10
    (B)  15
    (C)  25
    (D)  40
    (E)  50

At a certain college, the ratio of students to professors is 8:1 and the ratio of students to administrators is 5:2. No person is in more than one category (for instance, there are no administrators who are also students).

|  | **Quantity A** | **Quantity B** |
|---|---|---|
| 24. | The fractional ratio of professors to administrators | $\dfrac{5}{8}$ |

25.  In a certain country, 8 rubels are worth 1 schilling, and 5 schillings are worth 1 lemuw. In this country, 6 lemuws are equivalent in value to how many rubels?

(A)  $\dfrac{20}{3}$

(B)  30

(C)  40

(D)  48

(E)  240

26.  Team A and team B are raising money for a charity event. The ratio of money collected by team A to money collected by team B is 5:6. The ratio of the number of students on team A to the number of students on team B is 2:3. What is the ratio of money collected per student on team A to money collected per student on team B?

(A)  4:5

(B)  5:4

(C)  5:6

(D)  5:9

(E)  9:5

27.  Jarod uses $\dfrac{2}{3}$ of an ounce of vinegar in every 2 cups of sushi rice that he prepares. To prepare 7 cups of sushi rice in the same proportion, how many ounces of vinegar does Jarod need?

(A)  $\dfrac{3}{2}$

(B)  $\dfrac{4}{3}$

(C)  $\dfrac{7}{3}$

(D)  $\dfrac{7}{2}$

(E)  $\dfrac{14}{3}$

The total cost of 3 bananas, 2 apples, and 1 mango is $3.50. The total cost of 3 bananas, 2 apples, and 1 papaya is $4.20. The ratio of the cost of a mango to the cost of a papaya is $3:5$.

|  | **Quantity A** | **Quantity B** |
|---|---|---|
| 28. | The cost of a papaya | $2.00 |

29. In a certain town, $\frac{2}{5}$ of the total population is employed. Among the unemployed population, the ratio of males to females is $5:7$. If there are 40,000 employed people in the town, how many females are unemployed?

   (A)  16,000
   (B)  25,000
   (C)  35,000
   (D)  65,000
   (E)  75,000

30. On a certain map of the United States, $\frac{3}{5}$ of an inch represents a distance of 400 miles. If Oklahoma City and Detroit are separated on the map by approximately $\frac{3}{2}$ of an inch, what is the approximate distance between them in miles?

   (A)  240
   (B)  360
   (C)  600
   (D)  800
   (E)  1,000

31. A machine can manufacture 20 cans per hour, and exactly 10 such cans fit into every box. Maria packs cans in boxes at a constant rate of 3 boxes per hour. If the machine ran for 2 hours and was then turned off before Maria started packing the cans in boxes, how many minutes would it take Maria to pack all the cans that the machine had made?

   (A)  40
   (B)  45
   (C)  80
   (D)  160
   (E)  800

**MANHATTAN**
PREP

32. If Beth has $\frac{1}{4}$ more money than Ari, and each person has an integer number of dollars, which of the following could be the combined value of Beth and Ari's money?

    Indicate all such values.

    ☐   $12
    ☐   $54
    ☐   $72
    ☐   $200

33. If salesperson A sold 35% more motorcycles than salesperson B, which of the following could be the total number of motorcycles sold by both salespeople?

    Indicate all such total numbers of motorcycles.

    ☐   47
    ☐   70
    ☐   135
    ☐   235

34. A zoo has twice as many zebras as lions and four times as many monkeys as zebras. Which of the following could be the total number of zebras, lions, and monkeys at the zoo?

    Indicate all such totals.

    ☐   14
    ☐   22
    ☐   28
    ☐   55
    ☐   121

35. In nation Z, 10 terble coins equal 1 galok. In nation Y, 6 barbar coins equal 1 murb. If a galok is worth 40% more than a murb, what is the ratio of the value of 1 terble coin to the value of 1 barbar coin?

    (A)  $\frac{3}{5}$

    (B)  $\frac{11}{13}$

    (C)  $\frac{3}{7}$

    (D)  $\frac{21}{23}$

    (E)  $\frac{21}{25}$

36. Autolot has a 2 : 1 ratio of blue cars to red cars and a 6 : 1 ratio of red cars to orange cars on the lot. What could be the total number of blue, red, and orange cars on the lot?

    (A)　38
    (B)　39
    (C)　40
    (D)　41
    (E)　42

# Ratios Answers

1. **(B).** The ratio of men to women is 5 to 4. Since both 5 and 4 are whole numbers, they could actually *be* the number of men and women, respectively. These are also the *lowest* possible numbers of men and women, because reducing the ratio of 5 to 4 any further is impossible without making one part a non-integer (e.g., 2.5 to 2) or both parts negative, and the numbers of men and women must be positive integers.

Therefore, the smallest possible number of garden club members is 5 + 4 = 9. Quantity B is greater.

2. **7 and 63 only.** Write the number of each type of can:

$$\text{Cans of beans} = x \qquad \text{Cans of soup} = 2x \qquad \text{Cans of tomato paste} = 0.5x$$

Since each number of cans must be an integer, $x$ must be even or there would be partial cans of tomato paste. The total number of cans is $x + 2x + 0.5x = 3.5x$ and since $x$ must be even, the total number of cans could be 7, 14, 21, etc. Thus, the total number of cans must be a multiple of 7. Of the answer choices, only 7 and 63 are multiples of 7.

3. **(B).** If there are 6 dogs and 20 birds in the park, the ratio of dogs to birds is $6:20$, which reduces to $3:10$.

4. $\dfrac{2}{3}$ **or any equivalent fraction.** If there are 7 bananas and 14 strawberries, then there are 7 + 14 = 21 total pieces of fruit. The ratio of strawberries to the total is therefore $14:21$. Write this ratio as a fraction and cancel the common factor of 7 from top and bottom: $\dfrac{14}{21} = \dfrac{2 \times 7}{3 \times 7} = \dfrac{2}{3}$. The original ratio of $\dfrac{14}{21}$ would also be counted as correct if entered as is.

5. **30 cups of cheese.** Bob used cheese to sauce in a $1:1/2$ ratio, which could be multiplied by 2 to yield the equivalent cheese to sauce ratio of $2:1$. In words, there are twice as many cups of cheese as there are cups of sauce in the pizzas. Bob actually used 15 cups of sauce, so he used $2 \times 15 = 30$ cups of cheese.

6. **40 tulip plants.** To solve for the number of tulips, work with the Part:Part:Whole ratio. The ratio of tulips to roses is $4:1$, so the Tulip:Rose:Total relationship is $4:1:5$. This ratio can be written as $4x:1x:5x$, with $x$ as the unknown integer multiplier. There are 50 total plants in the garden, so set $5x$ equal to 50 and solve for $x$:

$$5x = 50$$
$$x = 10$$

Now plug this value into the expression for the actual number of tulips: $4x = 4(10) = 40$. Laura planted 40 tulip plants in the garden.

7. **(A).** Focus on the given Part : Part ratio. The ratio of cars to trucks is $1:3$, or $x:3x$ with $x$ as the unknown multiplier. Since there are 51 trucks for sale, set $3x$ equal to 51 and solve for $x$.

$$3x = 51$$
$$x = 17$$

Since $x$ also represents the number of cars, the dealer has 17 cars for sale.

8. **(B).** Iron and carbon combine to make steel in a specific given ratio. The ratio of iron (ounces) to carbon (ounces) to steel (sheets) is $98:2:1$. Because there are different units (ounces and sheets), the Part numbers do not sum to the Whole number as they typically do, but don't be concerned.

This ratio can be written as $98x:2x:x$, with $x$ as the unknown multiplier, which is also the number of sheets. To make 1/2 a sheet of steel, set $x$ equal to 1/2.

Now plug this value into the expression for the number of iron ounces: $98x = (98)(1/2) = 49$. To make 1/2 a sheet of steel, 49 ounces of iron are required.

9. **(B).** As a ratio, Flour : Milk : Sugar : Cupcakes is equal to $8:12:4:36$, where the first three numbers are in cups. Because there are different units (cups and cupcakes), the Part numbers do not sum to the Whole number, but don't be concerned.

This ratio can be written as $8x:12x:4x:36x$, with $x$ as the unknown multiplier. To make 9 cupcakes, set $36x$ equal to 9 and solve for $x$.

$$36x = 9$$
$$x = \frac{1}{4}$$

In words, for a batch of 9 cupcakes, Maria would make $\frac{1}{4}$ of the original recipe.

Now plug this value into the expression for cups of milk: $12x = (12)\left(\dfrac{1}{4}\right) = 3$. Maria would need 3 cups of milk.

10. **(D).** Since 7 members of the orchestra play the viola and four times as many play the violin, then $(7)(4) = 28$ people must play the violin. Altogether, $7 + 28 = 35$ musicians in the orchestra play either the viola or the violin.

The ratio of *either* to *neither* is $5:9$, or $5x:9x$ using the unknown multiplier. Since 35 people play either instrument, set $5x$ equal to 35 and solve for $x$.

$$5x = 35$$
$$x = 7$$

Now plug this value into the expression for *neither*: $9x = 9(7) = 63$. There are 63 people in the orchestra who play neither instrument.

11. **(C).** You can rewrite ratios as fractions and then multiply or divide top and bottom by the same number, keeping the ratio (or fraction) the same.

First, multiply top and bottom by 10, to remove the decimal: $\dfrac{0.4}{5} = \dfrac{0.4 \times 10}{5 \times 10} = \dfrac{4}{50}$

Next, cancel the common factor of 2: $\dfrac{4}{50} = \dfrac{2 \times 2}{25 \times 2} = \dfrac{2}{25}$

Finally, the fraction $\dfrac{2}{25}$ is the same as the ratio of 2 to 25, which is therefore equivalent to the original ratio of 0.4 to 5.

12. **(B).** The ratio of giraffes to zebras is $37:43$. Introduce the unknown multiplier $x$: the number of giraffes is $37x$, and the number of zebras is $43x$, where $x$ is a positive integer.

Now translate the second sentence of the problem into algebra. "There are 300 more zebras than giraffes" becomes Zebras − Giraffes = 300, or $43x - 37x = 300$. Solve for $x$:

$$43x - 37x = 300$$
$$6x = 300$$
$$x = 50$$

Finally, substitute into the expression for the number of giraffes: $37x = 37(50) = 1,850$. There are 1,850 giraffes.

Alternatively, the right answer must be a multiple of 37, because the giraffe number in the ratio is 37, and there must be a positive whole number of giraffes. Test the answer choices in the calculator to find that only 1,850 is divisible by 37. This shortcut doesn't always work this well, of course!

13. **(B).** The ratio of male to female employees is $3:4$. Introduce the unknown multiplier $x$, making the number of males $3x$ and the number of females $4x$, where $x$ is a positive integer.

Now translate the second sentence of the problem into algebra. "There are 5 more female employees than male employees" becomes Females − Males = 5, or $4x - 3x = 5$. Solve for $x$:

$$4x - 3x = 5$$
$$x = 5$$

Finally, substitute into the expression for the number of male employees: $3x = 3(5) = 15$. There are 15 male employees.

14. **(D).** Call the number of girls who joined the class $x$, so the new number of girls in the class is $8 + x$. Twice as many boys left the class, so the number of boys who left the class is $2x$, and the new number of boys in the class is $20 - 2x$.

The resulting ratio of boys to girls is 7 to 4. Since there is already a variable in the problem, don't use an unknown multiplier. Rather, set up a proportion and solve for $x$:

$$\frac{\text{Girls}}{\text{Boys}} = \frac{8+x}{20-2x} = \frac{7}{4}$$

$$4(8+x) = 7(20-2x)$$
$$32 + 4x = 140 - 14x$$
$$18x = 108$$
$$x = 6$$

Finally, the question asks for the number of boys who left the class. This is $2x = 2(6) = 12$ boys.

Check: There were 8 girls in the class, then 6 joined for a total of 14 girls. There were 20 boys in the class until 12 left the class, leaving 8 boys in the class. The resulting ratio of girls to boys is $\frac{14}{8} = \frac{7 \times 2}{4 \times 2} = \frac{7}{4}$, as given.

15. **(E).** Since 14 daks = 1 jin, a length measured in daks is 14 times the same length measured in jins. In other words, the ratio of the length in daks to the length in jins is 14 to 1.

Write this relationship as a fraction: $\frac{14 \text{ daks}}{1 \text{ jin}}$. You can also write $\frac{1 \text{ jin}}{14 \text{ daks}}$. You can convert a measurement from one unit to the other by multiplying by one of these unit conversion factors.

Side of big square: $(2 \text{ jins})\left(\frac{14 \text{ daks}}{1 \text{ jin}}\right) = 28$ daks. Since the small square has a side length of 2 daks, the number of small sides that will fit along a big side is $28 \div 2 = 14$.

However, 14 is not the right answer; 14 is the number of small squares that will fit along *one wall* of the big square, in one row. There will be 14 rows, so in all there will be $(14)(14) = 196$ small squares that fit inside the big square.

16. **(A).** Write two different Part : Part : Whole relationships. In each relationship, the two parts sum to the whole.

Women : Men : Total = 5 : 6 : 11, so Women : Total = 5 : 11.

Left-handed : Right-handed : Total = 7 : 9 : 16, so Left-handed : Total = 7 : 16.

In other words, women account for $\frac{5}{11} = 45.\overline{45}\%$ of the group, left-handed people for $\frac{7}{16} = 43.75\%$ of the group.

Since the total number of people is the same (it's the same group, whether divided by gender or handedness), the percents can be compared directly. There must be more women than left-handed people in the group. Quantity A is greater.

17. **(B).** Be careful—don't just add the "parts" from the different mixtures, because the parts will generally not be the same size! Start by writing Part : Part : Whole relationships for each glass. In each relationship, the whole is the sum of the parts:

For Party Cranberry, *Cranberry*: *Seltzer*: *Whole* = 3 : 1 : 4

For Fancy Lemonade, *Lemon*: *Seltzer*: *Whole* = 1 : 2 : 3

Since the two amounts that are mixed are the same size, choose a smart number to represent the total volume for both Party Cranberry and Fancy Lemonade. This number should be a multiple of both 4 and 3, according to the ratios above, so it is convenient to say that the amount of each is 12 ounces. Multiply the Party Cranberry ratio by 3 and the Fancy Lemonade ratio by 4, in both cases to get 12 total ounces:

For Party Cranberry, *Cranberry*: *Seltzer*: *Whole* = 9 : 3 : 12

For Fancy Lemonade, *Lemon*: *Seltzer*: *Whole* = 4 : 8 : 12

Finally, when the two glasses are mixed, the resulting total is 24 ounces, of which 9 ounces are cranberry juice but 3 + 8 = 11 ounces are seltzer. There is more seltzer in the resulting mix, so its fraction of the mix is greater than cranberry juice's fraction of the mix. Quantity B is greater.

18. **(D).** Write the ratios as fractions and set them equal to each other:

$$\frac{16}{g} = \frac{g}{49}$$

Cross-multiply to get $16 \times 49 = g^2$.

Remember that when "unsquaring" an equation with a squared variable, you must account for the negative possibility. The value of $g$ could be *either* $4 \times 7 = 28$ *or negative* 28. Nothing in the problem indicates that $g$ must be positive. Since Quantity A might equal Quantity B *or* be less than Quantity B, the relationship cannot be determined from the information given.

19. **(D).** Since vehicles must be counted with whole numbers and $\frac{1}{3}$ of the cars are black, the total number of cars must be divisible by 3. Otherwise, $\frac{1}{3}$ of the total would not be a whole number. The answer must be (B) or (D).

The remainder of the cars is $1 - \frac{1}{3} = \frac{2}{3}$ of the total. Of these, $\frac{1}{5}$ are white, so $\frac{1}{5}$ of $\frac{2}{3}$, or $\frac{2}{15}$ of the total number of vehicles are white. Again, because the white cars must be countable with whole numbers, $\frac{2}{15}$ of the total must be an integer. You can write the equation using fractions:

$$\left(\frac{2}{15}\right)(\text{Total}) = \text{Integer}$$

To get an integer outcome, the total must be divisible by 15. Of the answer choices, only (D) is divisible by 15.

20. **(E).** Since the ratio of ingredients is 3 : 2 : 1 in the recipe, imagine that Larry works in cups. Then a recipe makes 3 + 2 + 1 = 6 cups of dressing. To figure out the "limiting factor," take each available amount of ingredient and figure out how many times he could make the recipe, permitting fractions, if he had more than enough of the other ingredients.

Oil: 8 cups available ÷ 3 cups needed per recipe $= \frac{8}{3}$ recipes (in other words, $2\frac{2}{3}$ times the recipe). There is no need to round down, because fractional cups of ingredients are allowed.

Vinegar: 7 cups available ÷ 2 cups needed per recipe $= \frac{7}{2}$ recipes (in other words, $3\frac{1}{2}$ times through the recipe).

Water availability is not limited, so ignore it.

Oil is the limiting factor, because Larry can make the fewest recipes with it. Thus, he can only make $\frac{8}{3}$ recipes. To find the total cups of salad dressing, multiply this fraction by the total number of cups that a recipe makes:

$$\frac{8}{3} \text{ recipe} \times 6 \text{ cups per recipe} = 16 \text{ cups}$$

21. **(D).** Create a unit conversion factor using the given ratio of oranges to dollars. The conversion factor will look like either $\frac{5 \text{ oranges}}{y \text{ dollars}}$ or $\frac{y \text{ dollars}}{5 \text{ oranges}}$. Which one to use depends on how you want to convert the units.

The question asks how many dollars, in terms of $y$, 25 oranges cost. Since the given is oranges and the question asks for dollars, choose the conversion unit that cancels oranges and leaves dollars on top: $\frac{y \text{ dollars}}{5 \text{ oranges}}$. Then multiply:

$$(25 \text{ oranges})\left(\frac{y \text{ dollars}}{5 \text{ oranges}}\right) = \frac{25y}{5} \text{ dollars} = 5y \text{ dollars}$$

Intuitively, a total of 25 oranges is the same as 5 sets of 5 oranges each. Each set costs $y$ dollars. Therefore, the total cost for 5 sets of oranges is $5 \times y = 5y$.

22. **(A).** The total amount of money left over after paying rent and buying food is $40. From this number, you can find the woman's total weekly salary by determining what fraction this is of her total salary.

Since the woman spent $\frac{5}{8}$ of her salary on rent, she had $1 - \frac{5}{8} = \frac{3}{8}$ of her salary remaining. Of the remainder, she spent $\frac{1}{3}$ on food and had $\frac{2}{3}$ left over. So, $\frac{2}{3}$ of $\frac{3}{8}$ of her total weekly salary was left over for other expenses:

$$\left(\frac{2}{3}\right)\left(\frac{3}{8}\right) = \frac{2}{8} = \frac{1}{4}$$

One-quarter of her salary was the $40 left over. Now you can find $T$, her total weekly salary:

$$\left(\frac{1}{4}\right)T = \$40$$

$$T = \$160$$

**MANHATTAN**
PREP

23. **(E).** Rewrite the given ratio using the unknown multiplier $x$, so that the length of the rectangle is $3x$, while the width is $2x$. Now express the area of the rectangle in these terms, set it equal to 150 square centimeters, then solve for $x$:

$$\text{Area} = (\text{Length})(\text{Width})$$
$$150 = (3x)(2x)$$
$$150 = 6x^2$$
$$25 = x^2$$
$$5 \text{ cm} = x$$

In this case, you don't need to worry about the negative possibility for the square root, since lengths cannot be less than zero. The length is $3x = 15$ centimeters, while the width is $2x = 10$ centimeters.

Finally, the perimeter of a rectangle is twice the length, plus twice the width:

$$\text{Perimeter} = 2 \times \text{length} + 2 \times \text{width}$$
$$\text{Perimeter} = 2 \times 15 \text{ cm} + 2 \times 10 \text{ cm}$$
$$\text{Perimeter} = 30 \text{ cm} + 20 \text{ cm}$$
$$\text{Perimeter} = 50 \text{ cm}$$

24. **(B).** One way to approach this problem is to pick a smart number for the number of students, which shows up in both ratios. In the first ratio, students are represented by 8, so you want the smart number of students to be a multiple of 8. Likewise, in the second ratio, students are represented by 5, so you want the smart number of students to be a multiple of 5 as well. So pick 40 for the number of students.

From here, solve for the number of professors:

$$\frac{\text{Students}}{\text{Professors}} = \frac{40}{\text{Professors}} = \frac{8}{1}$$
$$40 = 8 \times \text{Professors}$$
$$5 = \text{Professors}$$

Likewise, solve for the number of administrators:

$$\frac{\text{Students}}{\text{Administrators}} = \frac{40}{\text{Administrators}} = \frac{5}{2}$$
$$40 \times 2 = 5 \times \text{Administrators}$$
$$16 = \text{Administrators}$$

Therefore, the ratio of professors to administrators is $5 : 16$. In fractional ratio form, this is $\dfrac{5}{16}$. Comparing the two quantities, both have the same numerator, but the denominator of Quantity A is greater, making it the smaller value. In fact, Quantity B is exactly twice as great as Quantity A.

25. **(E).** The question requires converting an amount of money in "lemuws" to "rubels." Conceptually, there are two steps: first convert lemuws to schillings, then convert schillings to rubels. The fast way to do this two-step conversion is to multiply the money by the right conversion factors, which express identities (such as 8 rubels = 1 schilling) in the form of ratios: $\dfrac{8 \text{ rubels}}{1 \text{ schilling}}$ or $\dfrac{1 \text{ schilling}}{8 \text{ rubels}}$. If you make sure that the units cancel correctly, then you can always be sure under pressure whether to multiply or divide by 8.

Here is the conversion, done all in one line:

$$\left(6 \text{ lemuws}\right)\left(\frac{5 \text{ schillings}}{1 \text{ lemuw}}\right)\left(\frac{8 \text{ rubels}}{1 \text{ schilling}}\right) = 240 \text{ rubels}$$

Both lemuws and schillings cancel on the left, leaving rubels. 6 lemuws are worth 240 rubels.

26. **(B).** To solve this ratios problem, choose smart numbers for the money collected for each team and the number of students on each team. Choose multiples of the ratios given, such as the following:

> Money collected by team A = $10
> Money collected by team B = $12
> Number of students in team A = 2
> Number of students in team B = 3

Then compute the money per student:

> Money per student in team A = $10 ÷ 2 = $5 per student
> Money per student in team B = $12 ÷ 3 = $4 per student

Thus, the ratio of money per student in team A to money per student in team B is 5 : 4.

27. **(C).** To find how much vinegar Jarod needs, think about how many multiples of his original recipe Jarod wants to make. The original recipe makes 2 cups of sushi rice, so 7 cups of rice is $\dfrac{7}{2}$ times his original recipe.

Since Jarod is scaling proportionally, to make $\dfrac{7}{2}$ times the usual amount of rice, he must also use $\dfrac{7}{2}$ times as much vinegar. Therefore, Jarod must use:

$$\left(\frac{7}{2}\right)\left(\frac{2}{3} \text{ ounces}\right) = \frac{7}{3} \text{ ounces of vinegar}$$

**MANHATTAN**
PREP

Alternatively, you can start with 7 cups of rice and multiply by the recipe's ratio of vinegar to rice, canceling cups of rice and producing ounces of vinegar:

$$\left(7 \text{ cups of rice}\right)\left(\frac{\frac{2}{3}\text{ ounces of vinegar}}{2\text{ cups of rice}}\right) = \frac{7}{3}\text{ ounces of vinegar}$$

28. **(B).** Solve for the cost of a papaya by translating the information given into mathematical statements. The first sentence states that 3 bananas, 2 apples, and 1 mango cost \$3.50. Letting $B$ represent the cost of a banana, $A$ the cost of an apple, and $M$ the cost of a mango, set up an equation:

$$3B + 2A + M = \$3.50$$

Similarly, for the second sentence, you get the following equation:

$$3B + 2A + P = \$4.20 \text{ (where } P \text{ is the cost of a papaya)}$$

The problem requires finding the cost of a papaya and provides the ratio of the costs of a mango and papaya. To use this information, remove bananas and apples from the list of unknowns. Here's how: try elimination. Specifically, subtract the first equation from the second:

$$
\begin{array}{r}
3B + 2A + P = \$4.20 \\
-\ (3B + 2A + M = \$3.50) \\
\hline
P - M = \$0.70
\end{array}
$$

Now, since the ratio of the cost of a mango to a papaya is $3 : 5$, write a proportion:

$\dfrac{M}{P} = \dfrac{3}{5}$, which becomes $M = \dfrac{3}{5}P$ if you isolate $M$. Now substitute back into the equation above, to eliminate $M$ and solve for $P$:

$$P - M = \$0.70$$

$$P - \frac{3}{5}P = \$0.70$$

$$\frac{5}{5}P - \frac{3}{5}P = \$0.70$$

$$\frac{2}{5}P = \$0.70$$

$$P = \frac{5}{2}(\$0.70) = \$1.75$$

Quantity B is greater.

29. **(C).** To solve for the number of unemployed females, first compute the total number of people who are unemployed. You need to represent the total number of people in the town. Call this number $x$. Since $\frac{2}{5}$ of the town is employed, a total of 40,000 people, write the ratio:

$$\frac{\text{Employed}}{\text{Total population}} = \frac{40,000}{x} = \frac{2}{5}$$

Cross-multiply and solve for $x$:

$$5(40,000) = 2x$$
$$200,000 = 2x$$
$$100,000 = x$$

If 40,000 people in the town are employed, then $100,000 - 40,000 = 60,000$ people are unemployed.

Finally, the ratio of unemployed males to females is $5:7$. In other words, out of every $5 + 7 = 12$ unemployed people, there are 7 unemployed females. Therefore, the fraction of unemployed females in the total unemployed population is 7 out of 12, or $\frac{7}{12}$. Set $y$ as the number of unemployed females:

$$\frac{\text{Unemployed females}}{\text{Total unemployed}} = \frac{y}{60,000} = \frac{7}{12}$$

To get the number of unemployed females, solve for $y$: $y = \frac{7 \times 60,000}{12} = 7 \times 5,000 = 35,000$

30. **(E).** According to the problem, $\frac{3}{5}$ of an inch on the map is equivalent to 400 miles of actual distance. So you can set up a ratio of these two measurements to use as a conversion factor: $\frac{\frac{3}{5}\ \text{inch}}{400\ \text{miles}}$ or $\frac{400\ \text{miles}}{\frac{3}{5}\ \text{inch}}$. Which one you use depends on which way you're converting: from miles to inches or vice versa.

The question states that Oklahoma City is separated from Detroit by approximately $\frac{3}{2}$ inches on the map, and asks how many real miles, approximately, lie between the two cities. To go from inches to miles, multiply the given measurement $\left(\frac{3}{2}\ \text{inches}\right)$ by the conversion factor that will cancel out inches and leave miles:

$$\left(\frac{3}{2}\ \text{inches}\right)\left(\frac{400\ \text{miles}}{\frac{3}{5}\ \text{inch}}\right) = \left(\frac{3}{2}\right)(400)\left(\frac{5}{3}\right)\ \text{miles} = 1,000\ \text{miles}$$

31. **(C).** First, figure out how many boxes worth of cans the machine produced in the 2 hours that it was on. The first step is to find the number of cans produced in 2 hours. Use the formula Work = Rate × Time. The question tells you 20 cans per hour is the rate and 2 hours is the time:

$$\text{Work} = (20\ \text{cans per hour}) \times (2\ \text{hours}) = 40\ \text{cans}$$

**MANHATTAN**
PREP

Now, since there are 10 cans per box, compute the number of boxes:

$$\text{Number of boxes} = 40 \text{ cans} \times \left( \frac{1 \text{ box}}{10 \text{ cans}} \right) = 4 \text{ boxes}$$

So Maria must pack 4 whole boxes to accommodate all the cans that the machine had made.

One more time, use the formula Work = Rate × Time. Maria's rate is 3 boxes per hour, while the total work as 4 boxes. Rearrange and plug in:

$$\text{Time} = \frac{\text{Work}}{\text{Rate}} = \frac{4 \text{ boxes}}{3 \text{ boxes per hour}} = \frac{4}{3} \text{ hours}$$

Finally, convert from hours to minutes as the question requires:

$$\text{Time} = \frac{4}{3} \text{ hours} \times \left( \frac{60 \text{ minutes}}{1 \text{ hour}} \right) = 80 \text{ minutes}$$

32. **$54 and $72 only.** If Beth has $\frac{1}{4}$ more money than Ari, their money is in a ratio of $5:4$ (because 5 is $\frac{1}{4}$ more than 4). Another way to see this result is with algebra:

$$B = A + \frac{1}{4}A = \frac{5}{4}A \text{, so } \frac{B}{A} = \frac{5}{4}.$$

As a result, for every $9 total, Beth has $5 and Ari has $4. To keep both Ari and Beth in integer dollar values, the answer needs to be a multiple of 9. Among the answer choices, only 54 and 72 are multiples of 9.

33. **47 and 235 only.** Since salesperson A sold 35% more motorcycles than salesperson B, their sales are in a ratio of $135:100$. You can reduce this ratio to $27:20$ by canceling a common factor of 5.

As a result, for every 47 motorcycles sold, salesperson A sold 27 and salesperson B sold 20. The number of motorcycles sold must be integer multiples of these numbers (because you can't sell partial motorcycles—not legally anyway), so the total needs to be a multiple of 47. Among the answer choices, only 47 and 235 are multiples of 47.

34. **22, 55, and 121 only.** First, figure out which animal there are fewest of. "Twice as many zebras as lions" means Zebras > Lions and "four times as many monkeys as zebras" means Monkeys > Zebras. So lions are found at the zoo in smallest numbers. To make the calculation straightforward, pick 1 lion as a smart number. Since there are twice as many zebras, there are 2 zebras. Finally, there are four times as many monkeys as zebras, so there are $4 \times 2 = 8$ monkeys. Putting all of that together:

Lions : Zebras : Monkeys = 1 : 2 : 8

So, for every 11 animals (1 + 2 + 8), there are 1 lion, 2 zebras, and 8 monkeys. To preserve integer numbers of lions, zebras, and monkeys, the total number of animals could only be a multiple of 11. Among the answer choices, only 22, 55, and 121 fit the bill.

35. **(E).** To tackle this question, rewrite all these ridiculously named currencies in terms of just one currency, ideally a real currency. Use whatever real currency you like, but here's an example with dollars.

Say that 1 murb is worth $1.

A galok is worth 40% more than a murb, or 40% more than $1. A galok is worth $1.40.

Since 10 terble coins equal 1 galok, then 10 terble coins are worth a total of $1.40. Each terble coin therefore, is worth $1.40 ÷ 10 = $0.14, or 14 cents.

Since 6 barbar coins equal 1 murb, then 6 barbar coins equal $1. Each barbar coin is worth $\$\frac{1}{6}$ or $\frac{100}{6}$ cents.

The ratio of the value of 1 terble coin to the value of 1 barbar coin:

$$\frac{1 \text{ terble}}{1 \text{ barbar}} = \frac{14 \text{ cents}}{100 \big/ 6 \text{ cents}} = 14 \times \frac{6}{100} = \frac{21}{25}$$

36. **(A).** Manipulate the given ratios to create one ratio that includes all three colors. You might use a table:

| R | B | O |
|---|---|---|
| 1 | 2 |   |
| 6 |   | 1 |

The problem here is the red car: that column contains both a 1 and a 6. In order to fix this issue, create a common term. Multiply the entire first ratio (the first row) by 6:

| R | B | O |
|---|----|---|
| 6 | 12 |   |
| 6 |    | 1 |

Now that the same number is in both rows of the red column, you can combine the two rows into a single ratio:

R : B : O = 6 : 12 : 1

For every 19 cars (6 + 12 + 1), there are 6 red cars, 12 blue cars, and 1 orange car. To maintain whole numbers of cars in each color, the correct answer has to be a multiple of 19. Only 38 is a multiple of 19.

# Chapter 21 *of*

## 5 lb. Book of GRE® Practice Problems

# Averages, Weighted Averages, Median, and Mode

# In This Chapter...

*Averages, Weighted Averages, Median, and Mode*

*Averages, Weighted Averages, Median, and Mode Answers*

# Averages, Weighted Averages, Median, and Mode

For questions in the Quantitative Comparison format ("Quantity A" and "Quantity B" given), the answer choices are always as follows:

(A)  Quantity A is greater.
(B)  Quantity B is greater.
(C)  The two quantities are equal.
(D)  The relationship cannot be determined from the information given.

For questions followed by a numeric entry box [    ], you are to enter your own answer in the box. For questions followed

by a fraction-style numeric entry box $\overline{\phantom{xxxx}}$, you are to enter your answer in the form of a fraction. You are not required to

reduce fractions. For example, if the answer is $\frac{1}{4}$, you may enter $\frac{25}{100}$ or any equivalent fraction.

All numbers used are real numbers. All figures are assumed to lie in a plane unless otherwise indicated. Geometric figures are not necessarily drawn to scale. You should assume, however, that lines that appear to be straight are actually straight, points on a line are in the order shown, and all geometric objects are in the relative positions shown. Coordinate systems, such as $xy$-planes and number lines, as well as graphical data presentations, such as bar charts, circle graphs, and line graphs, *are* drawn to scale. A symbol that appears more than once in a question has the same meaning throughout the question.

1.  Husain and Dino had an average (arithmetic mean) of $20 each. Dino then won a cash prize, which increased the average amount of money they had to $80. If no other changes occurred, how many dollars did Dino win?

$ [          ]

Janani is 6 centimeters taller than Preeti, who is 10 centimeters taller than Rey.

|  | **Quantity A** | **Quantity B** |
|---|---|---|
| 2. | The average (arithmetic mean) height of the three people | The median height of the three people |

The average (arithmetic mean) of $x$ and $y$ is 55.
The average of $y$ and $z$ is 75.

|  | **Quantity A** | **Quantity B** |
|---|---|---|
| 3. | $z - x$ | 40 |

4. What is the average (arithmetic mean) of $x$, $x - 6$, and $x + 12$?

    (A) $x$

    (B) $x + 2$

    (C) $x + 9$

    (D) $3x + 6$

    (E) It cannot be determined from the information given.

$$ab < 0$$

| Quantity A | Quantity B |
|:---:|:---:|
| $\dfrac{a+b}{2}$ | 0 |

5.

6. If $x$ is negative, what is the median of the list 20, $x$, 7, 11, 3?

    (A) 3

    (B) 7

    (C) 9

    (D) 11

    (E) 15.5

7. If the average (arithmetic mean) of $n$ and 11 is equal to $2n$, what is the average of $n$ and $\dfrac{13}{3}$?

    (A) 4

    (B) 8

    (C) 11

    (D) 14

    (E) 19

| Quantity A | Quantity B |
|:---:|:---:|
| The average (arithmetic mean) of $x - 3$, $x$, $x + 3$, $x + 4$, and $x + 11$ | The median of $x - 3$, $x$, $x + 3$, $x + 4$, and $x + 11$ |

8.

9. John bought 5 books with an average (arithmetic mean) price of $12. If John then buys another book with a price of $18, what is the average price of all 6 books?

    (A) $12.50

    (B) $13

    (C) $13.50

    (D) $14

    (E) $15

**MANHATTAN**
PREP

10. Every week, Renee is paid $40 per hour for the first 40 hours she works, and $80 per hour for each hour she works after the first 40 hours. How many hours would Renee have to work in one week to earn an average (arithmetic mean) of $60 per hour that week?

(A) 60
(B) 65
(C) 70
(D) 75
(E) 80

At a certain school, all 118 juniors have an average (arithmetic mean) final exam score of 88 and all 100 seniors have an average final exam score of 92.

| | **Quantity A** | **Quantity B** |
|---|---|---|
| 11. | The average (arithmetic mean) final exam score for all of the juniors and seniors combined | 90 |

| | **Quantity A** | **Quantity B** |
|---|---|---|
| 12. | The average (arithmetic mean) of $x$, $y$, and $z$ | The average (arithmetic mean) of $0.5x$, $0.5y$, and $0.5z$ |

13. Aaron's first three quiz scores were 75, 84, and 82. If his score on the fourth quiz reduced his average (arithmetic mean) quiz score to 74, what was his score on the fourth quiz?

[    ]

Four people have an average (arithmetic mean) age of 18, and none of the people are older than 30.

| | **Quantity A** | **Quantity B** |
|---|---|---|
| 14. | The range of the four people's ages | 25 |

Dataset A consists of 5 numbers, which have an average (arithmetic mean) value of 43. Dataset B consists of 5 numbers.

15.

| Quantity A | Quantity B |
|---|---|
| The value of $x$ if the average of $x$ and the 5 numbers in dataset A is 46. | The average of dataset B if the average of the 10 numbers in datasets A and B combined is 52. |

16. The average (arithmetic mean) of 7 numbers in a certain list is 12. The average of the 4 smallest numbers in this list is 8, while the average of the 4 greatest numbers in this list is 17. How much greater is the sum of the 3 greatest numbers in the list than the sum of the 3 smallest numbers in the list?

(A)  4

(B)  14

(C)  28

(D)  36

(E)  52

17. If the average (arithmetic mean) of $a$, $b$, $c$, 5, and 6 is 6, what is the average of $a$, $b$, $c$, and 13?

(A)  8

(B)  8.5

(C)  9

(D)  9.5

(E)  It cannot be determined from the information given.

18. A group consists of both men and women. The average (arithmetic mean) height of the women is 66 inches, and the average (arithmetic mean) height of the men is 72 inches. If the average (arithmetic mean) height of all the people in the group is 70 inches, what is the ratio of women to men in the group?

(A)  1:1

(B)  1:2

(C)  2:1

(D)  2:3

(E)  3:2

**MANHATTAN**
PREP

19. The average (arithmetic mean) of 13 numbers is 70. If the average of 10 of these numbers is 90, what is the average of the other 3 numbers?

    (A) −130
    (B) $\frac{10}{3}$
    (C) 30
    (D) 90
    (E) 290

20. Town A has 6,000 citizens and an average (arithmetic mean) of 2 radios per citizen. Town B has 10,000 citizens and an average of 4 radios per citizen. What is the average number of radios per citizen in both towns combined?

    Give your answer as a fraction.

The average (arithmetic mean) weight of 4 people is 85 kilograms.
Two of the people weigh 75 and 90 kilograms, respectively.

|  | **Quantity A** | **Quantity B** |
|---|---|---|
| 21. | The average (arithmetic mean) weight of the other two people, in kilograms | 85 kilograms |

22. Fiber X cereal is 55% fiber. Fiber Max cereal is 70% fiber. Sheldon combines an amount of the two cereals in a single bowl of mixed cereal that is 65% fiber. If the bowl contains a total of 12 ounces of cereal, how much of the cereal, in ounces, is Fiber X?

    (A) 3
    (B) 4
    (C) 6
    (D) 8
    (E) 9

23. The average (arithmetic mean) population in town X was recorded as 22,455 during the years 2000–2010, inclusive. However, an error was later uncovered: the figure for 2009 was erroneously recorded as 22,478, but should have been correctly recorded as 22,500. What was the average population in town X during the years 2000–2010, inclusive, once the error was corrected?

While driving from city A to city B, a car got 22 miles per gallon and while returning on the same road, the car got 30 miles per gallon.

|   | **Quantity A** | **Quantity B** |
|---|---|---|
| 24. | The car's average gas mileage for the entire trip, in miles per gallon | 26 |

$$S_n = 3n + 3$$
Sequence S is defined for each integer $n$ such that $0 < n < 10,000$.

|   | **Quantity A** | **Quantity B** |
|---|---|---|
| 25. | The median of sequence S | The mean of sequence S |

26. The bar graph below displays the number of temperature readings at each value from a sample, measured in degrees Fahrenheit. What was the average (arithmetic mean) temperature reading?

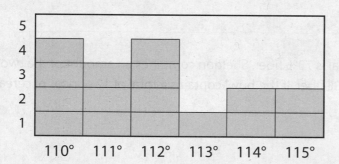

[____] degrees Fahrenheit

27. Score results on a college mathematics proficiency exam

| | Freshmen | Sophomores |
|---|---|---|
| Number of students taking the exam | 120 | 80 |
| Average (arithmetic mean) score on the exam | 78 points | 84 points |

What was the average (arithmetic mean) score for all the freshmen and sophomores taking the exam? Give your answer rounded to the <u>nearest 0.1 points</u>.

| | points

28. Set A:   1, 3, 5, 7, 9
    Set B:   6, 8, 10, 12, 14

For the sets of numbers above, which of the following statements are true?

Indicate <u>all</u> such statements.

☐   The mean of set B is greater than the mean of set A.
☐   The median of set B is greater than the median of set A.
☐   The standard deviation of set B is greater than the standard deviation of set A.
☐   The range of set B is greater than the range of set A.

29. Three people have $32, $72, and $98, respectively. If they pool their money then redistribute it among themselves, what is the maximum possible value for the median amount of money?

    (A)   $72
    (B)   $85
    (C)   $98
    (D)   $101
    (E)   $202

30.

**Weekly Revenue Per Product Category at Office Supply Store X**

| Product Category | Weekly Revenue |
|---|---|
| Pens | $164 |
| Pencils | $111 |
| Legal pads | $199 |
| Erasers | $38 |
| Average (arithmetic mean) of categories above | $128 |

According to the chart above, the average (arithmetic mean) revenue per week per product category is $128. However, there is an error in the chart; the revenue for Pens is actually $176, not $164. What is the new, correct average revenue per week per product category?

(A)  $130

(B)  $131

(C)  $132

(D)  $164

(E)  $176

Set *M* consists of 20 evenly spaced integers, 10 numbers of which are positive and 10 of which are negative.

|  | **Quantity A** | **Quantity B** |
|---|---|---|
| 31. | The average (arithmetic mean) of all the numbers in set *M* | 0 |

The average (arithmetic mean) of 3*x*, *x*, and *y* is equal to 2*x*.

|  | **Quantity A** | **Quantity B** |
|---|---|---|
| 32. | 2*x* | *y* |

**MANHATTAN**
PREP

33.  The average (arithmetic mean) age of the buildings on a certain city block is greater than 40 years old. If four of the buildings were built two years ago and none of the buildings are more than 80 years old, which of the following could be the number of buildings on the block?

Indicate all such numbers.

☐  4
☐  6
☐  8
☐  11
☐  40

34.  Four students contributed to a charity drive, and the average (arithmetic mean) amount contributed by each student was $20. If no student gave more than $25, what is the minimum amount that any student could have contributed?

$ [          ]

The average (arithmetic mean) of seven distinct integers is 12, and the least of these integers is −15.

|  | **Quantity A** | **Quantity B** |
|---|---|---|
| 35. | The maximum possible value of the greatest of these integers | 84 |

36.  The average (arithmetic mean) of fifteen consecutive integers is 88. What is the greatest of these integers?

[          ]

Three numbers have a range of 2 and a median of 4.4.

|  | **Quantity A** | **Quantity B** |
|---|---|---|
| 37. | The greatest of the numbers | 5.4 |

# Averages, Weighted Averages, Median, and Mode Answers

1. **$120.** If the two people had an average of $20 each, they held a sum of 2($20) = $40. After Dino won a cash prize, the new sum is $40 + p$ and the new average is 80. Plug into the average formula:

$$\text{Average} = \frac{\text{Sum}}{\text{Number of Terms}}$$

$$80 = \frac{40 + p}{2}$$

$$160 = 40 + p$$

$$120 = p$$

Dino won $120.

2. **(B).** Pick numbers that agree with the given height constraints. Rey is the shortest person, and if Rey is 100 cm tall, Preeti is 110 cm tall, and Janani is 116 cm tall. The average height is $\dfrac{100 + 110 + 116}{3} = 108.67$ cm (rounded to nearest 0.01 cm). The median height is the middle height, which is 110 cm. Quantity B is greater.

Alternatively, note that Preeti's height is the median. Preeti's height is closer to Janani's than to Rey's. Since the average of Janani and Rey's heights would be midway between those heights, and Preeti's height is greater than that middle, the median is greater than the average.

3. **(C).** Since the average of $x$ and $y$ is 55, $\dfrac{x + y}{2} = 55$, so $x + y = 110$.

Since the average of $y$ and $z$ is 75, $\dfrac{y + z}{2} = 75$, so $y + z = 150$.

Stack the two equations and subtract to cancel the $y$'s and get $z - x$ directly:

$$\begin{array}{r} z + y = 150 \\ -\,(x + y = 110) \\ \hline z - x = 40 \end{array}$$

The two quantities are equal.

4. **(B).** The average formula can be applied to algebraic expressions, just as to arithmetic ones:

$$\text{Average} = \frac{\text{Sum}}{\text{Number of Terms}}$$

$$\text{Average} = \frac{(x) + (x - 6) + (x + 12)}{3}$$

$$\text{Average} = \frac{3x + 6}{3} = x + 2$$

5. **(D).** The best way to solve Quantitative Comparisons problems with variables is to plug in multiple values for the variables, trying to prove (D).

If $ab < 0$, then one of the variables is positive and the other negative.

Try $a = 2$ and $b = -3$

$$\frac{2 + -3}{2} = -\frac{1}{2}$$ and Quantity B is greater. Therefore, the answer cannot be (A) or (C).

Try $a = 3$ and $b = -2$:

$$\frac{3 + -2}{2} = \frac{1}{2}$$ and now Quantity A is greater. Therefore, the answer cannot be (B) or (C). If you plug in two

different sets of numbers and get two different results for which quantity is greater, the answer must be (D).

6. **(B).** The easiest way to start thinking about a question like this is to plug in a value and see what happens. If $x = -1$, the list looks like this when ordered from least to greatest:

$$-1, 3, 7, 11, 20$$

The median is 7. Because any negative $x$ used will be the least term in the list, the order of the list won't change, so the median will always be 7.

7. **(A).** This question can be solved with the average formula:

$$\text{Average} = \frac{\text{Sum}}{\text{Number of terms}}$$

$$2n = \frac{n + 11}{2}$$

$$4n = n + 11$$

$$3n = 11$$

$$n = \frac{11}{3}$$

Since $n = \frac{11}{3}$, the average of $n$ and $\frac{13}{3}$ is:

$$\frac{\frac{11}{3} + \frac{13}{3}}{2} = \frac{\frac{24}{3}}{2} = \frac{8}{2} = 4$$

Alternatively, just notice that the midpoint between $\frac{11}{3}$ and $\frac{13}{3}$ is $\frac{12}{3}$, just as 12 is the midpoint between 11 and 13.

The average is $\frac{12}{3} = 4$.

8. **(C).** To find the median of the numbers, notice that they are already in order from least to greatest: $x - 3$, $x$, $x + 3$, $x + 4$, $x + 11$.

The median is the middle, or third, term: $x + 3$.

Now find the average of the numbers:

$$\frac{(x-3)+(x)+(x+3)+(x+4)+(x+11)}{5} = \frac{5x+15}{5} = x + 3$$

The median and the mean are both $(x + 3)$, therefore, the two quantities are equal.

9. **(B).** First, calculate the cost of the first 5 books.

Sum = (Average cost)(Number of books) = ($12)(5) = $60

Total cost of all 6 books = $60 + $18 = $78
Total number of books = 6

Average = $78/6 = $13 per book.

10. **(E).** Let $h$ = number of hours Renee would have to work. The average rate Renee gets paid is equal to the total wages earned divided by the total number of hours worked. Rene earns $40 per hour for the first 40 hours, so she makes $40 \times 40 = \$1,600$ in the first 40 hours. She also earns $80 for every hour after 40 hours, for additional pay of $80(h - 40)$. Therefore, her total pay can be calculated as:

$$\frac{1,600+80(h-40)}{h} = 60$$
$$1,600 + 80h - 3,200 = 60h$$

Now isolate $h$:

$$80h - 1,600 = 60h$$
$$-1,600 = -20h$$
$$80 = h$$

You could also notice that 60 is exactly halfway between 40 and 80. Therefore, Renee needs to work an equal number of hours at $40 per hour and $80 per hour. If she works 40 hours at $40 per hour, she also needs to work 40 hours at $80 per hour, yielding 80 hours of total work.

11. **(B).** This is a weighted average problem. Because the number of juniors is greater than the number of seniors, the overall average will be closer to the juniors' average than the seniors' average. Since 90 is halfway between 88 and 92, and the weighted average is closer to 88, Quantity B is greater.

It is not necessary to do the math because this is a Quantitative Comparison question with a very convenient number as Quantity B. However, you can actually calculate the overall average by summing up all 218 scores and dividing by the number of people: $\dfrac{118(88) + 100(92)}{118 + 100} = 89.83...$

12. **(D).** The average of $x$, $y$, and $z$ is $\dfrac{x+y+z}{3}$. Calculated similarly, the average of $0.5x$, $0.5y$, and $0.5z$ is exactly half that. If the sum of the variables is positive, Quantity A is greater. However, if the sum of the variables is negative, Quantity B is greater. If the sum of the variables is zero, the two quantities are equal.

13. **55.** To find Aaron's fourth quiz score, set up an equation:

$$\frac{75 + 84 + 82 + x}{4} = 74$$
$$241 + x = 296$$
$$x = 55$$

14. **(D).** If 4 people have an average age of 18, then the sum of their ages is $4 \times 18 = 72$. Since the question is about range, try to minimize and maximize the range. Minimizing the range is easy—if everyone were exactly 18, the average age would be 18 and the range would be 0. So clearly, the range can be smaller than 25.

To maximize the range, make the oldest person the maximum age of 30, and see whether the youngest person could be just 1 year old while still obeying the other rules of the problem: the sum of the ages is 72 and, of course, no one can be a negative age.

One such set: 1, 20, 21, 30

This is just one example that would work. In this case, the range is $30 - 1 = 29$, which is greater than 25.

15. **(C).** If the average of the 5 numbers in dataset A is 43, the sum of dataset A is $(5)(43) = 215$.

For Quantity A, use the average formula and sum all 6 numbers and divide by 6:

$$\frac{\text{Sum of the 5 numbers in dataset A} + x}{6} = 46$$
$$\frac{215 + x}{6} = 46$$
$$215 + x = 276$$
$$x = 61$$

For Quantity B, use the average formula again:

$$\frac{\text{Sum of dataset A} + \text{Sum of dataset B}}{10} = 52$$

$$215 + \text{Sum of dataset B} = 520$$

$$\text{Sum of dataset B} = 305$$

The average of the 5 numbers in dataset B is $\frac{305}{5} = 61$.

Alternatively, note that each dataset of 5 numbers has the same "weight" in the average of all 10 numbers. The average of dataset A is 43, which is $52 - 43 = 9$ below the average of all 10 numbers. The average of dataset B must be 9 above the average of all 10 numbers: $52 + 9 = 61$.

16. **(D).** Using the average formula, $\text{Average} = \dfrac{\text{Sum}}{\text{Number of terms}}$, build three separate equations:

All 7 numbers:

$$12 = \frac{\text{Sum of all 7 numbers}}{7}$$

$$\text{Sum of all 7 numbers} = 84$$

The 4 smallest numbers:

$$8 = \frac{\text{Sum of the 4 smallest numbers}}{4}$$

$$\text{Sum of the 4 smallest numbers} = 32$$

The 4 greatest numbers:

$$17 = \frac{\text{Sum of the 4 greatest numbers}}{4}$$

$$\text{Sum of the 4 greatest numbers} = 68$$

There are only 7 numbers, yet information is given about the 4 smallest and the 4 greatest, which is a total of 8 numbers! The middle number has been counted twice—it is included in both the 4 greatest and the 4 smallest.

The sum of all 7 numbers is 84, but the sum of the 4 greatest and 4 smallest is $68 + 32 = 100$. The difference can only be attributed to the double counting of the middle number in the set of 7: $100 - 84 = 16$.

The middle number is 16, so subtract it from the sum of the 4 smallest numbers to get the sum of the 3 smallest numbers: $32 - 16 = 16$.

Now subtract the middle number from the sum of the 4 greatest numbers to get the sum of the 3 greatest numbers: $68 - 16 = 52$.

The difference between the sum of the 3 greatest numbers and the sum of the 3 smallest numbers is $52 - 16 = 36$.

**MANHATTAN**
PREP

17. **(A).** Since Average $= \dfrac{\text{Sum}}{\text{Number of terms}}$ :

$$6 = \frac{a+b+c+5+6}{5}$$

$$30 = a+b+c+11$$

$$19 = a+b+c$$

It is not necessary, or possible, to determine the values of $a$, $b$, and $c$ individually. The second average includes all three variables, so the values will be summed again anyway.

$$\text{Average} = \frac{a+b+c+13}{4}$$

$$\text{Average} = \frac{19+13}{4}$$

$$\text{Average} = \frac{32}{4} = 8$$

18. **(B).** Use the weighted average formula:

$$\text{Average height of all} = \frac{(\text{Total height of all women})+(\text{Total height of all men})}{(\text{Number of women})+(\text{Number of men})}$$

From the average formula, Sum = Average × Number of terms. If $w$ is the number of women and $m$ is the number of men, the total heights of women and men respectively are:

Total height of all women = $66w$

Total height of all men = $72m$

Plug into the average formula, recalling that the average height for the entire group is 70 inches:

$$\text{Average height of all} = \frac{66w+72m}{w+m} = 70$$

Cross-multiply and simplify:

$$66w+72m = 70(w+m)$$

$$66w+72m = 70w+70m$$

$$72m = 4w+70m$$

$$2m = 4w$$

$$m = 2w$$

At this point, it might be tough to determine whether the answer is (B) or (C). This is an ideal time to plug in numbers. For instance, if $w = 3$, then $m = 6$. Now, the ratio of women to men is 3:6 or 1:2, answer choice (B).

Alternatively, continue with the algebra, solving for the $\dfrac{w}{m}$ ratio:

$$m = 2w$$

$$\frac{m}{2m} = \frac{2w}{2m}$$

$$\frac{1}{2} = \frac{w}{m}$$

19. **(B).** Remember the Average formula, Average $= \dfrac{\text{Sum}}{\text{Number of terms}}$ , can also be rewritten as: Sum $=$ Average $\times$ Number of Terms.

The average of 13 numbers is 70, so:

$$\text{Sum of all 13 terms} = 70 \times 13 = 910$$

The average of 10 of these numbers is 90, so:

$$\text{Sum of 10 of these numbers} = 90 \times 10 = 900$$

Subtract to find the sum of "the other 3 numbers": $910 - 900 = 10$.

$$\text{Average of the other 3 numbers} = \frac{\text{Sum}}{\text{Number of terms}} = \frac{10}{3}.$$

20. $\dfrac{13}{4}$ **(or any equivalent fraction).** To find this weighted average, first find the sum of all the radios in towns A and B, and then divide by the total number of people in both towns:

$$\text{Average} = \frac{6,000(2) + 10,000(4)}{16,000}$$

Cancel three zeros from each term:

$$\text{Average} = \frac{6(2) + 10(4)}{16}$$

$$\text{Average} = \frac{52}{16}$$

This reduces to $\dfrac{13}{4}$, though reduction is not required.

**MANHATTAN**
PREP

21. **(A).** The formula for averages is:  $\text{Average} = \dfrac{\text{Sum}}{\text{Number of terms}}$.

The sum of the weights of the people in this group is:

$$\text{Sum} = \text{Average} \times \text{Number of terms} = 85 \times 4 = 340$$

If two of the people weigh 75 and 90 kilograms, subtract them from the total to see what the other two people weigh, combined:

$$340 - 75 - 90 = 175 \text{ kg}$$

If the total weight of the other two people is 175, their average weight is:

$$\frac{175}{2} = 87.5 \text{ kg.}$$

Quantity A is greater.

22. **(B).** Use the weighted average formula to get the ratio of Fiber X to Fiber Max:

$$\frac{0.55x + 0.70m}{x + m} = 0.65, \text{ where } x \text{ is the amount of Fiber X and } m \text{ is the amount of Fiber Max.}$$

This is not that different from the regular average formula—on the top, there is the total amount of fiber (55% of Fiber X and 70% of Fiber Max), which is divided by the total amount of cereal $(x + m)$ to get the average. Simplify by multiplying both sides by $(x + m)$:

$$0.55x + 0.70m = 0.65(x + m)$$
$$0.55x + 0.70m = 0.65x + 0.65m$$

To simplify, multiply both sides of the equation by 100 to eliminate all the decimals:

$$55x + 70m = 65x + 65m$$
$$55x + 5m = 65x$$
$$5m = 10x$$

$$\frac{m}{x} = \frac{10}{5} \text{ or } \frac{2}{1}$$

Since $m$ and $x$ are in a 2 to 1 ratio, 2/3 of the total is $m$ and 1/3 of the total is $x$. Since the total is 12 ounces, Fiber X accounts for $\frac{1}{3}(12) = 4$ ounces of the mixed cereal.

One shortcut to this procedure is to note that the weighted average (65%) is 10% away from Fiber X's percent and 5% away from Fiber Max's percent. Since 10 is twice as much as 5, the ratio of the two cereals is 2 to 1. However, it is a 2 to 1 ratio of Fiber Max to Fiber X, not the reverse! Whichever number is closer to the weighted average (in this case, 70% is closer to 65%) gets the larger of the ratio parts. Since the ratio is 2 to 1 (Fiber Max to Fiber X), again, 1/3 of the cereal is Fiber X and $\frac{1}{3}(12) = 4$.

23. **22,457.** There is a simple shortcut for a change to an average. The figure for 2009 was recorded as 22,478, but actually should have been recorded as 22,500, meaning 22 people in that year were not counted. Thus, the sum should have been 22 higher when the average was originally calculated.

2000–2010, inclusive, is 11 years (subtract low from high and then add 1 to count an inclusive list of consecutive numbers). When taking an average, divide the sum by the number of things being averaged (in this case, 11). So the shortcut is to take the change to the sum and "spread it out" over all of the values being averaged by dividing the change by the number of things being averaged.

Divide 22 by 11 to get 2. The average should have been 2 greater. Thus, the correct average for the 11-year period is 22,457.

Alternatively, use the traditional method: 22,455 × 11 years = 247,005, the sum of all 11 years' recorded populations. Add the 22 uncounted people, making the corrected sum 247,027. Divide by 11 to get the corrected average: 22,457. (Note that while the traditional method is faster to explain, the shortcut is faster to actually execute!)

24. **(B).** One trap is to mistakenly pick (C), thinking that the car got a simple average of 22 and 30 miles per gallon. However, the trip from *A* to *B* required *more* gallons of gas, therefore, the average will be "weighted" more to the side of 22 (same number of miles, but *more* gallons), and wind up less than 26 mpg. Quantity (B) is therefore greater.

To show this explicitly, use a smart number of miles from city A to B, for example, a multiple of 22 and 30, such as 660 miles. Set up a chart using the formula

(Miles per gallon) × (Gallons) = (Miles)

|         | Miles per gallon | × | Gallons | = | Miles |
|---------|------------------|---|---------|---|-------|
| *A* to *B* | 22 | × | 30 | = | 660 |
| *B* to *A* | 30 | × | 22 | = | 660 |
| Total   | *x* | × | 52 | = | 1,320 |

The average miles per gallon for the whole trip is the total number of miles (1,320) divided by the total number of gallons (52):

$\frac{1,320}{52} = 25.38\ldots$ , which is less than 26.

Quantity B is greater.

**25. (C).** Sequence *S* is an evenly spaced set, which can be seen by plugging in a few *n* values:

$$S_1 = 3(1) + 3 = 6$$
$$S_2 = 3(2) + 3 = 9$$
$$S_3 = 3(3) + 3 = 12\ldots$$

Terms increase by 3 every time *n* increases by 1; this meets the definition of an evenly spaced set. For *any* evenly spaced set, the median equals the mean.

**26. 112.** This is a weighted average problem. *Do not* simply average 110, 111, 112, 113, 114, and 115. Instead, take into account how many times each number appears. The chart is really another way of writing:

110, 110, 110, 110
111, 111, 111
112, 112, 112, 112
113
114, 114
115, 115

In other words, the average temperature reading is really an average of 16 numbers. The easiest way to do this is:

$$\frac{4(110) + 3(111) + 4(112) + 1(113) + 2(114) + 2(115)}{16}$$

Use the calculator—the correct answer is 112.

**27. 80.4.** In order to determine the average score for *all* the freshman and sophomores combined, compute the total points for everyone, and divide by the total number of students.

Because $\text{Average} = \dfrac{\text{Sum}}{\text{Number of terms}}$ , it can also be written as the Sum = Average × Number of terms. Use the formula to compute the total number of points for all the freshmen and all the sophomores as individual groups:

Freshman total points = 78 points × 120 = 9,360
Sophomore total points = 84 points × 80 = 6,720

Combined, the freshmen and sophomores scored 9,360 + 6,720 = 16,080 points.

The total number of students is 120 + 80 = 200.

Now, apply the average formula, $\text{Average} = \dfrac{\text{Sum}}{\text{Number of terms}}$ , to the combined group:

$$\text{Average} = \frac{16,080}{200} = 80.4$$

**MANHATTAN**
PREP    669

**28. 1st and 2nd only.** In both sets, the numbers are evenly spaced. Moreover, both sets are evenly spaced by the same amount (adjacent terms increase by 2) and have the same number of terms (5 numbers in each set). The difference is that each term in set $B$ is 5 greater than the corresponding term in set $A$ (i.e., $6 - 1 = 5$, $8 - 3 = 5$, etc.).

In evenly spaced sets, the mean = median. Also, if an evenly spaced set has an odd number of numbers, the mean and median both equal the middle number. (When such a set has an even number of numbers, the mean and median both equal the average of the two middle numbers).

So, set $A$ has mean and median of 5 and set B has mean/median of 10. The first and second statements are true.

Since sets $A$ and $B$ are equally spaced and have the same number of elements, their standard deviations are equal (that is, set $A$ is exactly as spread out from its own mean as set $B$ is from its own mean), so the third statement is false.

Since $9 - 1 = 8$ and $14 - 6 = 8$, the ranges are equal and the fourth statement is false.

**29. (D).** The pool of money is $\$32 + \$72 + \$98 = \$202$. After the redistribution, each person will have an amount between $\$0$ and $\$202$, inclusive. Call the amounts $L$, $M$, and $H$ (low, median, high). To maximize $M$, minimize $L$ and $H$.

The minimum value for $H$ is $M$. The "highest" of the three values can be equal to the median (if $H$ were lower than $M$, the term order and therefore which number is the median would change, but if $H = M$, $M$ can still be the median). Draw it out

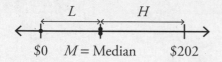

Minimum $L = \$0$
Minimum $H = M$

Maximum $M$ = Total pool of money − Minimum $L$ − Minimum $H$
$M = \$202 - \$0 - M$
$2M = \$202$
$M = \$101$

The correct answer is (D).

**30. (B).** The chart provides the average and the number of product categories. If the incorrectly calculated average was $\$128$ for the 4 categories, then the sum was $4 \times 128 = \$512$. Since the revenue for pens was actually $\$176$, not $\$164$, the sum should have been $\$12$ higher. Thus, the correct sum is $\$524$. Divide by 4 to get $\$131$, the answer.

Alternatively, notice that the $\$128$ average given in the question stem actually does a lot of work for you. If $\$164$ jumps up to $\$176$, that's an increase of $\$12$. Distributed over the four categories, it will bring the overall average up by $\$3$, from $\$128$ to $\$131$.

31. **(D).** "Evenly spaced" means ascending by some regular increment (each number greater than the next by some value). If 10 of the integers are positive and 10 are negative, then none of the numbers in the set are 0. Therefore, the 10th number must be less than 0 and the 11th greater than 0. To better understand this, try listing values for set $M$, starting in the middle. If the middle numbers are

   ... −1, +1 ...

then the spacing between the numbers is 2 and set M would look like:

   −19, −17, −15, −13, −11, −9, −7, −6, −5, −4, −3, −2, −1, 1, 3, 5, 7, 9, 11, 13, 15, 17, 19

The sum and the average of all the numbers in this set are both 0, so (A) and (B) cannot be the answer. However, is the average always 0? If the middle two numbers were offset a little:

   ... −1, 4 ...

then the spacing between the numbers is 5 and set M would look like:

   −46, −41, −36, −31, −26, −21, −16, −11, −6, −1, 4, 9, 14, 19, 24, 29, 34, 39, 44, 49

The first and the last terms sum to $-46 + 49 = 3$. The second term and penultimate term sum to $-41 + 44 = 3$, and so on. Each term can be paired with another for a sum of 3. There are 10 such pairs, so the total sum is $3 \times 10 = 30$ and the average is $30/20 = 1.5$.

The relationship cannot be determined from the information given.

32. **(C).** Write "the average of $3x$, $x$, and $y$ is equal to $2x$" as an equation and solve:

$$\frac{3x + x + y}{3} = 2x$$
$$4x + y = 6x$$
$$y = 2x$$

The two quantities are equal.

33. **8, 11, and 40 only.** Because Average $= \dfrac{\text{Sum}}{\text{Number of terms}}$, this question about averages depends both on $x$, the total number of buildings on the block, and on the sum of the building ages. The 4 buildings that are 2 years old have a total age of $4(2)$, and the $(x - 4)$ other buildings have a total age of $(x - 4)$(no more than 80). Set up an equation to find the average age:

$$\text{Average age} = \frac{4(2) + (x - 4)(\text{no more than } 80)}{x}$$

Having many 80-year-old buildings on the block would raise the average much closer to 80. (For instance, if there were a million 80-year-old buildings and four 2-year-old buildings, the average would be very close to 80 years old.) So, there is some minimum number of older buildings that could raise the average above 40.

Ignore the "greater than" 40 years old constraint on the average building age for a moment. What is the minimum $x$ needs to be to make the average age exactly 40 when the age of the other buildings is maximized at 80?

$$40x = 8 + (x - 4)(80)$$
$$40x = 8 + 80x - 320$$
$$-40x = -312$$
$$x = \frac{312}{40} = 7.8$$

Because there can't be a partial building, and the age of the buildings can't be greater than 80, $x$ must be at least 8 to bring the average age up over 40. (More buildings would be required to bring the average above 40 if those older buildings were only between 50 and 70 years old, for example.)

Alternatively, test the answer choices. Try the first choice, 4 buildings. Since 4 of the buildings on the block are only 2 years old, this choice can't work—the average age of the buildings would be 2.

Try the second choice. With 6 total buildings, there would be four 2-year-old buildings, plus two others. To maximize the average age, maximize the ages of the two other buildings by making them both 80 years old:

$$\frac{4(2) + 2(80)}{6} = 28$$

Since the average is less than 40 years old, this choice is not correct.

Try the third choice. With 8 total buildings, there would be the four 2-year-old buildings, plus four others. To maximize the average age, maximize the ages of the four other buildings by making them each 80 years old:

$$\frac{4(2) + 4(80)}{8} = 41$$

Since the average age is greater than 40 years old, this choice is correct. Since the other, greater choices allow the possibility of even more 80-year-old buildings, increasing the average age further, those choices are also correct.

34. **$5.** The average of four values is $20. Thus, the sum of the four values is $80. To determine the minimum contribution one student could have given, maximize the contributions of the other three students. If the three other students each gave the maximum of $25, the fourth student would only have to give $5 to make the sum equal to $80.

35. **(A).** If the average of 7 integers is 12, then their sum must be $7 \times 12 = 84$. To maximize the largest of the numbers, minimize the others.

The smallest number is −15. The integers are distinct (that is, different from each other), so the minimum values for the smallest 6 integers are −15, −14, −13, −12, −11, and −10. To find the maximum value for the 7th integer, sum −15, −14, −13, −12, −11, −10, and $x$, while setting that sum equal to 84:

**MANHATTAN**
PREP

$$-15 + (-14) + (-13) + (-12) + (-11) + (-10) + x = 84$$
$$-75 + x = 84$$
$$x = 159$$

Quantity A is greater.

36. **95.** In any evenly spaced set, the average equals the median. Thus, 88 is the middle number in the set. Since the set has 15 elements, the 8th element is the middle one:

| | | | | | | | |
|---|---|---|---|---|---|---|---|
| Lowest seven integers: | 81 | 82 | 83 | 84 | 85 | 86 | 87 |
| Middle integer: | 88 | | | | | | |
| Greatest seven integers: | 89 | 90 | 91 | 92 | 93 | 94 | 95 |

The largest integer in the list is 95. Confidence in this process allows you to skip the counting process. Instead reason that to go from 8th integer to the 15th integer, simply add 7: $88 + 7 = 95$.

37. **(D).** If the set has an odd number of terms, then the median is the middle number, so the middle number is 4.4. The set has a range of 2. The other two numbers could be 2 apart and also equally distributed around 4.4:

Example 1: 3.4, 4.4, 5.4

Here, the two quantities are equal.

Or, the two other numbers could be 2 apart but both a bit higher, or both a bit lower.

Example 2: 4.3, 4.4, 6.3
Example 3: 2.5, 4.4, 4.5

Thus, Quantity A could be equal to, less than, or greater than Quantity B. The relationship cannot be determined from the information given.

# Chapter 22
## *of*

5 lb. Book of GRE® Practice Problems

# Standard Deviation and Normal Distribution

# In This Chapter...

Standard Deviation and Normal Distribution

Standard Deviation and Normal Distribution Answers

# Standard Deviation and Normal Distribution

For questions in the Quantitative Comparison format ("Quantity A" and "Quantity B" given), the answer choices are always as follows:

(A)  Quantity A is greater.
(B)  Quantity B is greater.
(C)  The two quantities are equal.
(D)  The relationship cannot be determined from the information given.

For questions followed by a numeric entry box [        ], you are to enter your own answer in the box. For questions followed

by a fraction-style numeric entry box ⬚/⬚, you are to enter your answer in the form of a fraction. You are not required to

reduce fractions. For example, if the answer is $\frac{1}{4}$, you may enter $\frac{25}{100}$ or any equivalent fraction.

All numbers used are real numbers. All figures are assumed to lie in a plane unless otherwise indicated. Geometric figures are not necessarily drawn to scale. You should assume, however, that lines that appear to be straight are actually straight, points on a line are in the order shown, and all geometric objects are in the relative positions shown. Coordinate systems, such as *xy*-planes and number lines, as well as graphical data presentations, such as bar charts, circle graphs, and line graphs, *are* drawn to scale. A symbol that appears more than once in a question has the same meaning throughout the question.

1.  Set *S*: {5, 10, 15}

    If the number 15 were removed from set *S* and replaced with the number 1,000, which of the following values would change?

    Indicate all such values.

    ☐   The mean of the set
    ☐   The median of the set
    ☐   The standard deviation of the set

    Dataset *W*:   −9, −3, 3, 9
    Dataset *X*:   2, 4, 6, 8
    Dataset *Y*:   100, 101, 102, 103
    Dataset *Z*:   7, 7, 7, 7

2.  Which of the following choices lists the four datasets above in order from least standard deviation to greatest standard deviation?

    (A)  *W, X, Y, Z*
    (B)  *W, Y, X, Z*
    (C)  *W, X, Z, Y*
    (D)  *Z, Y, X, W*
    (E)  *Z, X, Y, W*

Set N is a set of $x$ distinct positive integers where $x > 2$.

|  | **Quantity A** | **Quantity B** |
|---|---|---|
| 3. | The standard deviation of set N | The standard deviation of set N if every number in the set were multiplied by −3 |

The 75th percentile on a test corresponded to a score of 700, while the 25th percentile corresponded to a score of 450.

|  | **Quantity A** | **Quantity B** |
|---|---|---|
| 4. | A 95th percentile score | 800 |

A species of insect has an average mass of 5.2 grams and a standard deviation of 0.6 grams. The mass of the insects follows a normal distribution.

|  | **Quantity A** | **Quantity B** |
|---|---|---|
| 5. | The percent of the insects that have a mass between 5.2 and 5.8 grams | The percent of the insects that have a mass between 4.9 and 5.5 grams |

The lengths of a certain population of earthworms are normally distributed with a mean length of 30 centimeters and a standard deviation of 3 centimeters. One of the worms is picked at random.

|  | **Quantity A** | **Quantity B** |
|---|---|---|
| 6. | The probability that the worm is between 24 and 30 centimeters, inclusive | The probability that the worm is between 27 and 33 centimeters, inclusive |

Home values among the 8,000 homeowners of Town X are normally distributed, with a standard deviation of $11,000 and a mean of $90,000.

|  | **Quantity A** | **Quantity B** |
|---|---|---|
| 7. | The number of homeowners in Town X whose home value is greater than $112,000 | 300 |

**MANHATTAN**
PREP

Exam grades among the students in Ms. Harshman's class are normally distributed, and the 50th percentile is equal to a score of 77.

| Quantity A | Quantity B |
|---|---|
| The number of students who scored less than 80 on the exam | The number of students who scored greater than 74 on the exam |

8.

9.  The length of bolts made in factory Z is normally distributed, with a mean length of 0.1630 meters and a standard deviation of 0.0084 meters. The probability that a randomly selected bolt is between 0.1546 meters and 0.1756 meters long is between

    (A)  54% and 61%.
    (B)  61% and 68%.
    (C)  68% and 75%.
    (D)  75% and 82%.
    (E)  82% and 89%.

10. Which of the following sets of data applies to this box-and-whisker plot?

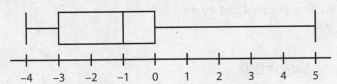

    (A)  −4, −4, −2, 0, 0, 5
    (B)  −4, 1, 1, 3, 4, 4
    (X)  −4, −4, −3, 1, 5
    (Δ)  −5, 3, 4, 5
    (E)  −4, −4, −2, −2, 0, 0, 0, 5

11. If a set of data consists of only the first ten positive multiples of 5, what is the interquartile range of the set?

    (A)  15
    (B)  25
    (C)  27.5
    (D)  40
    (E)  45

12. On a given math test with a maximum possible score of 100 points, the vast majority of the 149 students in a class scored either a perfect score or a zero, with only one student scoring within 5 points of the mean. Which of the following logically follows about dataset $T$, made up of the scores on the test?

Indicate all such statements.

☐ Dataset $T$ is not normally distributed.

☐ The range of dataset $T$ would be significantly smaller if the scores had been more evenly distributed.

☐ The mean of dataset $T$ is not equal to the median.

Jane scored in the 68th percentile on a test, and John scored in the 32nd percentile.

|  | Quantity A | Quantity B |
|---|---|---|
| 13. | The proportion of the class that received a score less than John's score | The proportion of the class that scored equal to or greater than Jane's score |

In a class with 20 students, a test was administered and was scored only in whole numbers from 0 to 10. At least one student got every possible score, and the average score was 7.

|  | Quantity A | Quantity B |
|---|---|---|
| 14. | The lowest score that could have been received by more than one student | 4 |

A test is scored out of 100 and the scores are divided into five quintile groups. Students are not told their scores, but only their quintile group.

|  | Quantity A | Quantity B |
|---|---|---|
| 15. | The scores of two students in the bottom quintile group, chosen at random and added together. | The score of a student in the top quintile group, chosen at random. |

16. In a set of 10 million numbers, one percentile would represent what <u>percent</u> of the total number of terms?

    (A) 1,000,000
    (B) 100,000
    (C) 10,000
    (D) 100
    (E) 1

17. What is the range of the dataset of numbers comprised entirely of $\{1, 6, x, 17, 20, y\}$ if all terms in the dataset are positive integers and $xy = 18$?

    (A) 16
    (B) 17
    (C) 18
    (D) 19
    (E) It cannot be determined from the information given.

18. On a particular test whose scores are distributed normally, the 2nd percentile is 1,720, while the 84th percentile is 1,990. What score, rounded to the nearest 10, most closely corresponds to the 16th percentile?

    (A) 1,750
    (B) 1,770
    (C) 1,790
    (D) 1,810
    (E) 1,830

A dataset contains at least two different integers.

| **Quantity A** | **Quantity B** |
| --- | --- |
| 19. The range of the dataset | The interquartile range of the dataset |

Some rock samples are weighed, and their weights are determined to be normally distributed. One standard deviation below the mean is 250 grams and one standard deviation above the mean is 420 grams.

| **Quantity A** | **Quantity B** |
| --- | --- |
| 20. The median weight, in grams | 335 grams |

In a normally distributed set of data, the mean is 12 and the standard deviation is less than 3.

|  | **Quantity A** | **Quantity B** |
|---|---|---|
| 21. | The number of data points in the set between 9 and 15 | 60% of the total number of data points |

|  | **Quantity A** | **Quantity B** |
|---|---|---|
| 22. | The standard deviation of the dataset 10, 20, 30 | The standard deviation of the dataset 10, 20, 20, 20, 20, 20, 30 |

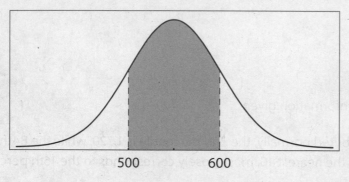

The graph represents the normally distributed scores on a test. The shaded area represents approximately 68% of the scores.

|  | **Quantity A** | **Quantity B** |
|---|---|---|
| 23. | The mean score on the test | 550 |

24.

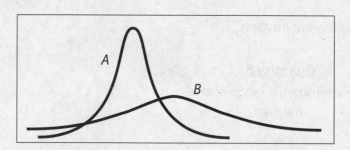

A and B are graphical representations of normally distributed random variables X and Y, respectively, with relative positions, shapes, and sizes as shown. Which of the following must be true?

Indicate <u>all</u> such statements.

☐  Y has a greater standard deviation than X.

☐  The probability that Y falls within 2 standard deviations of its mean is greater than the probability that X falls within 2 standard deviations of its mean.

☐  Y has a greater mean than X.

The outcome of a standardized test is an integer between 151 and 200, inclusive. The percentiles of 400 test scores are calculated, and the scores are divided into corresponding percentile groups.

|  | **Quantity A** | **Quantity B** |
|---|---|---|
| 25. | The minimum number of integers between 151 and 200, inclusive, that include more than one percentile group | The minimum number of percentile groups that correspond to a score of 200 |

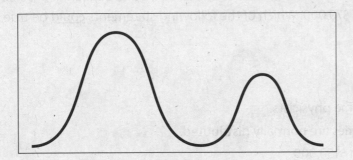

26.  Which of the following would the data pattern shown above best describe?

(A)  The number of grams of sugar in a selection of drinks is normally distributed.

(B)  A number of male high school principals and a larger number of female high school principals have normally distributed salaries, distributed around the same mean.

(C)  A number of students have normally distributed heights and a smaller number of taller, adult teachers also have normally distributed heights.

(D)  The salary distribution for biologists skews to the left of the median.

(E)  The maximum-weight bench presses for a number of male athletes are normally distributed and the maximum-weight bench presses for a smaller number of female athletes are also normally distributed, although around a smaller mean.

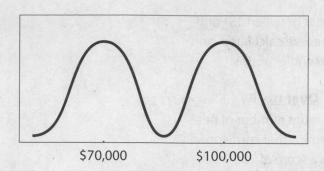

$70,000          $100,000

27.  A number of scientists' salaries were reported; physicists' salaries clustered around a mean of $100,000 and biologists' clustered around a mean of $70,000. Which of the following statements could be true, according to the graph above?

Indicate all such statements.

- ☐  Some biologists earn more than some physicists.
- ☐  Both biologists' and physicists' salaries are normally distributed.
- ☐  The range of salaries is greater than $150,000.

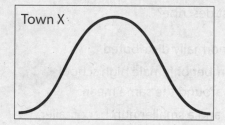  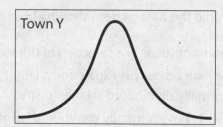

28.  The graph on the left above represents the number of family members per family in Town X, while the graph on the right above represents the number of family members per family in Town Y. The median family size for Town X is equal to the median family size for Town Y. The horizontal and vertical dimensions of the boxes above are identical and correspond to the same measurements. Which of the following statements must be true?

Indicate all such statements.

- ☐  The range of family sizes measured as the number of family members is larger in Town X than in Town Y.
- ☐  Families in Town Y are more likely to have sizes within 1 family member of the mean than are families in Town X.
- ☐  The data for Town X has a larger standard deviation than the data for Town Y.

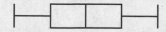

**MANHATTAN**
PREP

29. The box-and-whisker plot shown above could be a representation of which of the following sets?

    (A)  −2, 0, 2, 4
    (B)  3, 3, 3, 3, 3, 3
    (C)  1, 25, 100
    (D)  2, 4, 8, 16, 32
    (E)  1, 13, 14, 17

30. Which of the following statements <u>must</u> be true about the data described by the box-and-whisker plot above?

    Indicate <u>all</u> such statements.

    ☐  The median of the whole set is closer to the median of the lower half of the data than it is to the median of the upper half of the data.
    ☐  The data is normally distributed.
    ☐  The set has a standard deviation greater than zero.

31. The earthworms in sample A have an average length of 2.4 inches, and the earthworms in sample B have an average length of 3.8 inches. The average length of the earthworms in the combined samples is 3.0 inches. Which of the following must be true?

    Indicate <u>all</u> such statements.

    ☐  There are more earthworms in sample A than in sample B.
    ☐  The median length of the earthworms is 3.2 inches.
    ☐  The range of lengths of the earthworms is 1.4.

# Standard Deviation and Normal Distribution Answers

1. **"The mean of the set" and "The standard deviation of the set".** The word *mean* is a synonym for the average. Because an average is calculated by taking the sum of the terms in the set and dividing by the number of numbers in the set, changing *any* one number in a set (without adjusting the others) will change the sum and, therefore, the average. The median is the middle number in a set, so making the biggest number even bigger won't change that (the middle number is still 10). Standard deviation is a measure of how *spread out* the numbers in a set are—the more spread out the numbers, the larger the standard deviation—so making the biggest number *really far away* from the others would greatly increase the standard deviation.

2. **(D).** Standard deviation is a measure of how "spread out" the numbers in a set are—in other words, how far are the individual data points from the average of all of the data points? The GRE will not ask you to calculate standard deviation—in problems like this one, you will be able to eyeball which sets are more spread out and which are less spread out.

Since dataset $Z$'s members are identical, the standard deviation is zero. Zero is the smallest possible standard deviation for any set, so it must be the smallest here. You can eliminate answer choices (A), (B), and (C). Dataset $Y$'s members have a *spread* of 1 between each number, dataset $X$'s members are 2 away from each other, and dataset $W$'s members are 6 away from each other, so dataset $Y$ has the next-smallest standard deviation (note that this is enough to eliminate answer choice (E) and choose answer choice (D)). The correct answer is (D) $Z, Y, X, W$.

3. **(B).** "Set $N$ is a set of $x$ distinct positive integers where $x > 2$" just means that the members of the set are all positive integers different from each other, and that there are at least 3 of them. Nothing is given about the standard deviation of the set other than that it is not zero. (Because the numbers are different from each other, they are at least a little spread out, which means the standard deviation must be greater than zero. The only way to have a standard deviation of zero is to have a "set" of identical numbers, which would be referred to as a list or a dataset because all of the elements of a proper set (in math) must be different).

In Quantity B, multiplying each of the distinct integers by −3 would definitely spread out the numbers and thus increase the standard deviation. For instance, if the set had been 1, 2, 3, it would become −3, −6, −9. The negatives are irrelevant—multiplying any set of *different* integers by 3 will spread them out more.

Thus, whatever the standard deviation is for the set in Quantity A, Quantity B must represent a larger standard deviation because the numbers in that set are more spread out.

4. **(D).** Scoring scales on a test are not necessarily linear, so do not line up the difference in percentiles with the difference in score; it is not possible to make any predictions about *other* percentiles. For all you know, 750 could be the 95th percentile score—or 963 could be. All that is certain is that 25% of the scores are ≤ 450, while 50% of the scores are > 450 and ≤ 700, and 25% of the scores are > 700.

5. **(B).** Whenever the words "Normal distribution" appear on the GRE, draw a bell-curve diagram that approximates the one below. Memorize the numbers 34 : 14 : 2.

**MANHATTAN**
PREP

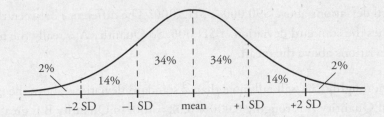

The middle of the bell curve is the average, or mean, so place 5.2 underneath the 0 in the center; 34%, 14%, and 2% represent the approximate percentages that fall between the standard deviation lines. For instance, 14% of the population falls between 1 and 2 standard deviations below the mean. Now, use the standard deviation of 0.6 grams to figure out the exact dividing lines between the marked regions of the normal curve. The mass of an insect that is exactly 1 standard deviation above the mean is 5.2 + 0.6 = 5.8, and the mass of one that is 1 standard deviation below the mean is 5.2 − 0.6 = 4.6. Similarly, the mass at exactly 2 standard deviations above the mean is 6.4 and at 2 below is 4.0.

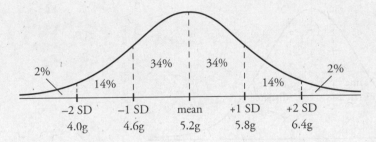

Quantity A, the percent between 5.2 and 5.8 grams, is 34%.

However, Quantity B will require some estimating. Note that 4.9 is halfway between 4.6 and 5.2, while 5.5 is halfway between 5.2 and 5.8. Therefore, the area between 4.9 and 5.5, while still a range of 0.6, is under the bigger part of the bell curve in the center. Since the area under the center is bigger than the area between 0 and 1 standard deviations, the percentage of the area under the center must also be greater. Therefore, Quantity B is greater.

6. **(B).** Normal distributions are always centered on and symmetrical around the mean, so the chance that the worm's length will be within a certain 6-centimeter range (or any specific range) is highest when that range is centered on the mean, which in this case is 30 centimeters.

More specifically, Quantity A equals the area between −2 standard deviations and the mean of the distribution. In a normal distribution, roughly 34 + 34 + 14 + 14 = 96% of the sample will fall within 2 standard deviations above or below the mean. Limit yourself only to the 2 standard deviations below the mean, then half of that, or 96%÷2 = 48%, falls in this range. In contrast, Quantity B equals the area between −1 standard deviation and +1 standard deviation. In a normal distribution, roughly 34 + 34 = 68% of the sample falls within 1 standard deviation above or below the mean. Since 68% is greater than 48%, Quantity B is greater.

Note that exact figures are not required to answer this question! Picture any bell curve—the area under the "hump" (that is, centered around the middle) is bigger! Thus, it has more members of the dataset (in this case, worms) in it.

7. **(B).** How many standard deviations above $90,000 is $112,000? The difference between the two numbers is $22,000, which is two times the standard deviation of $11,000. So Quantity A is really the number of home values greater than 2 standard deviations above the mean.

In any normal distribution, roughly 2% will fall more than 2 standard deviations above the mean (this is something to memorize). The value of Quantity A is roughly $8,000 \times 0.02 = 160$, so Quantity B is greater.

8. **(C).** The normal distribution is symmetrical around the mean. For any symmetrical distribution, the mean equals the median (also known as the 50th percentile). Thus, the number of students who scored *less* than 3 points *above* the mean ($77 + 3 = 80$) must be the same as the number of students who scored *greater* than 3 points *below* the mean ($77 - 3 = 74$). As long as the boundary scores (80 and 74) are placed symmetrically around the mean, the distribution will have equal proportions. Draw the normal distribution plot if it is at all confusing:

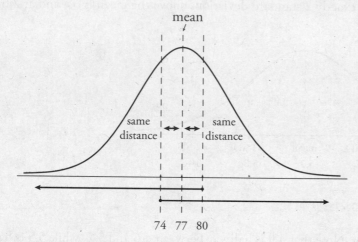

Notice that the two conditions overlap and are perfectly symmetrical. Each number consists of a short segment between it and the 50th percentile mark, as well as half of the students (either above or below the 50th percentile mark). That is, the "less than 80" category consists of the segment between 80 and 77, as well as all students below the 50th percentile mark (below 77). The "greater than 74" category consists of the segment between 74 and 77, as well as all students above the 50th percentile mark (above 77). Therefore, the quantities are equal.

9. **(D).** First, make the numbers easier to use. Either multiply every number by the same constant or move the decimal the same number of places for each number. In the case of moving the decimal four places, the mean becomes 1,630, the standard deviation becomes 84, and the two other numbers become 1,546 and 1,756.

Next, "normalize" the boundaries. That is, take 1,546 meters (the lower boundary) and 1,756 meters (the upper boundary) and convert each of them to a number of standard deviations away from the mean. To do so, subtract the mean. Then divide by the standard deviation.

Lower boundary: $1546 - 1630 = -84$

$$-84 \div 84 = -1$$

**MANHATTAN**
PREP

So the lower boundary is −1 standard deviation (that is, 1 standard deviation less than the mean).

Upper boundary: 1756 − 1630 = 126

$$126 \div 84 = 1.5$$

So the upper boundary is 1.5 standard deviations above the mean.

You need to find the probability that a random variable distributed according to the standard normal distribution falls between −1 and 1.5.

Use the approximate areas under the normal curve. Approximately 34% + 34% = 68% falls within one standard deviation above or below the mean, so 68% accounts for the −1 to 1 portion of the standard normal distribution. What about the portion from 1 to 1.5?

Approximately 14% of the bolts fall between 1 and 2 standard deviations above the mean. You are not expected to know the exact area between 1 and 1.5; however, since a normal distribution has its hump around 0, *more* than half of the area between 1 and 2 must fall closer to 0 (between 1 and 1.5). So the area under the normal curve between 1 and 1.5 must be greater than half of the area, or greater than 7%, but less than the full area, 14%.

Put it all together. The area under the normal curve between −1 and 1.5 is approximately 68% + (something between 7% and 14%). The lower estimate is 68% + 7% = 75% and the upper estimate is 68% + 14% = 82%.

10. **(E).** In a box-and-whisker plot, the middle line in the box represents the median, or middle, of the dataset. The outsides of the box are the medians of the data below and above the median, respectively, which mark the first and third quartile boundaries, or $Q_1$ and $Q_3$.

The median is −1; now check the medians of the answer choices. The median of (A) is the average of 0 and −2, which is −1; (A) could be the right answer. The median of (B) is 2, of (C) is −3, and of (D) is 3.5, so none of these are the correct answers. The median of (E) is between −2 and 0, which is −1; (E) could also be the right answer.

$Q_1$ is −3; check $Q_1$ for both (A) and (E). The median of the smaller three numbers (−4, −4, −2) for (A) is −4, which is wrong; you want $Q_1$ to be −3. Choice (E) is the only answer choice left; choose it without checking if you're confident in your previous work. Here's the actual proof: the median of the smaller four numbers (−4, −4, −2, −2) is −3.

11. **(B).** The interquartile range of a dataset is the distance between $Q_1$ (quartile marker 1, the median of the first half of the dataset) and $Q_3$ (quartile marker 3, the median of the second half of the dataset).

The first ten positive multiples of 5 are: 5, 10, 15, 20, 25, 30, 35, 40, 45, 50. $Q_1$ is the median of the first five terms, or 15. $Q_3$ is the median of the last five terms, or 40.

Take the difference between $Q_3$ and $Q_1$: 40 − 15 = 25.

12. **"Dataset *T* is not normally distributed" only.** The definition of "normally distributed" is that about two-thirds of the data falls within 1 standard deviation of the mean. If only one person scored close to the mean (and most people were at the top or bottom of the curve), that dataset is not normally distributed, so the first statement is true.

The second statement is false—the range of the data would not necessarily change if the dataset were more evenly distributed. For instance, as long as one person still had a zero and one person still had a score of 100, the other scores could fall anywhere without changing the range.

The third statement is also false. The mean of dataset $T$ might or might not be equal to the median. For instance, the one student within 5 points of the mean could have a score equal to the mean; of the remaining 148 students, half could have scores of 0 and half could have scores of 100. In this case, the mean would equal the median. However, the same scenario with *unequal* numbers of students scoring 0 and 100 would result in the mean *not* equaling the median.

13. **(C).** Percentiles define the proportion of a group that scores below a particular benchmark. Since John scored in the 32nd percentile, by definition, 32% of the class scored worse than John. Quantity A is equal to 32%.

Jane scored in the 68th percentile, so 68% of the class scored worse than she did. Since $100 - 68 = 32$, 32% of the class scored equal to or greater than Jane. Quantity B is also equal to 32%.

14. **(A).** Since the average is 7, use the average formula to find the sum of the scores in the class:

$$\text{Average} = \text{Sum} \div (\text{\# of terms})$$
$$7 = \text{Sum} \div 20$$
$$\text{Sum} = 140$$

At least one student got every possible score. There are eleven possible scores: $0 + 1 + 2 + 3 + 4 + 5 + 6 + 7 + 8 + 9 + 10$. This is an evenly spaced set, so calculate the sum by multiplying the average of the set by the number of terms in the set. The average is $(10 + 0)/2 = 5$ and the number of terms is 11, so the sum of the set is $5 \times 11 = 55$. Subtract this from the earlier sum; the remaining 9 students had to score $140 - 55 = 85$ points.

Quantity A is the lowest score that could have been received by more than one student. If 9 students scored a total of 85 points, and any one student could not score more than 10 points, then what is the lowest possible score that one of these 9 students could have received? In order to minimize that number, maximize the numbers for the other students. If 8 students scored 10 points each, for a total of 80 points, then the 9th student must have scored exactly 5. Quantity A must be greater than Quantity B. Notice that the average score of 7 forces a lot of the scores to be 10 in order to to balance out the very low scores of 0, 1, 2, etc., that are required in the class (at least one of each). The lowest score that could have been received by 2 students is 5, so Quantity A is 5.

15. **(D).** Quintiles ("fifths" of the data) define relative scores, not absolute scores. Imagine two possible score distributions:

Example 1: The class's scores are 1, 2, 3, 4, 5 (20% of the class scored each of these). In this case, adding up the two lowest quintile students would be $1 + 1 = 2$, which is less than 5, the score of a top quintile student.

Example 2: The class's scores are 10, 11, 12, 13, 14 (20% of the class scored each of these). In this case, adding up the two lowest quintile students would be $10 + 10 = 20$, which is greater than 14, the score of a top quintile student.

The relationship cannot be determined from the information given.

16. **(E).** A percentile *always* represents 1% of a set of data. If the question had asked how many *terms* one percentile represented, that would be a different question (with a different answer).

17. **(D).** The values of $x$ or $y$ are unknown, but since they are both positive integers, they can only be 1 and 18, 2 and 9, or 3 and 6 (because they have a product of 18). So the smallest number in the set is 1 and the greatest is 20. Since $20 - 1 = 19$, the range is 19.

18. **(D).** The diagram below shows the standard distribution curve for any normally distributed variable. The percent figures correspond roughly to the standard percentiles both 1 and 2 standard deviations (SD) away from the mean:

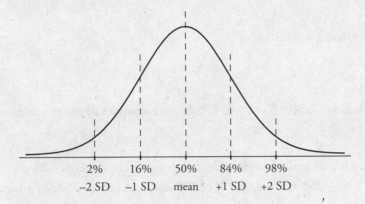

|  2%  |  16%  |  50%  |  84%  |  98%  |
| -2 SD | -1 SD | mean | +1 SD | +2 SD |

The 2nd percentile is 1,720, roughly corresponding to two standard deviations below the mean. Therefore, the mean −2 standard deviations = 1,720.

Likewise, the 84th percentile is 1,990: 84% of a normally distributed set of data falls below the mean + 1 standard deviation, so the mean + 1 standard deviation = 1,990.

Call the mean $M$ and the standard deviation $S$. Solve for these variables:

$$M - 2S = 1,720$$
$$M + S = 1,990$$

Subtract the first equation from the second equation:

$$3S = 270$$
$$S = 90$$

The question asks for the 16th percentile, which is the mean − 1 standard deviation or $M - S$. (It's a fact to memorize that approximately 2% of normally distributed data falls below $M - 2S$, and approximately 14% of normally distributed data falls between $M - 2S$ and $M - S$.)

Since $M - 2S = 1,720$, add another $S$ to get $M - S$:

$$(M - 2S) + S = 1,720 + 90 = 1,810$$

Notice that the percentiles are *not* linearly spaced. The normal distribution is hump-shaped, so percentiles are bunched up around the hump and spread out farther away.

19. **(D).** In most datasets, the range is larger than the interquartile range because the interquartile range ignores the smallest and largest data points. That's actually the purpose of interquartile range—to get a good picture of where *most* of the data is (think of the "big hump" on a bell curve). For instance:

Example set *A*:   1, 2, 3, 4, 5, 6, 7, 100

Here, the range is $100 - 1 = 99$.

The interquartile range is $Q_3 - Q_1$, or the median of the upper half of the data minus the median of the lower half of the data: $6.5 - 2.5 = 4$.

In this example, the range is much larger. However, consider this set:

Example set *B*:   4, 4, 4, 4, 5, 5, 5, 5

In this set, the range is $5 - 4 = 1$. The interquartile range is also $5 - 4 = 1$. While the interquartile range can never be *greater* than the range, they can certainly be equal.

20. **(C).** Since 1 standard deviation below the mean is 250 and 1 standard deviation above the mean is 420, the mean/median must be halfway in between. Since $420 - 250 = 170$ and half of 170 is 85, add 85 to 250 (or subtract it from 420) to get the mean/median of 335. (Note that in a normal distribution, the mean is equal to the median, so the two terms can be used interchangeably.)

21. **(A).** If the standard deviation is 3, then 1 standard deviation below the mean is 9 and 1 standard deviation above the mean is 15, so about 68% of the data is between 9 and 15 (in a normal distribution, it is always the case that about 68% of the data is within 1 standard deviation of the mean).

Since the *actual* standard deviation is *less than* 3, about 68% of the data is found within an *even smaller range* than 9 to 15. For instance, the standard deviation could be 1, and then about 68% of the data would be between 11 and 13. Or the standard deviation could be 2.5, and then about 68% of all the data would be found between 9.5 and 14.5.

Since 68% of the data is found within an *even smaller range* than 9 to 15, the range from 9 to 15 contains *more than* 68% of the data, so it definitely contains more than 60% of all the data points.

Don't be confused by the use of "number of data points." While the actual total number of data points is still unknown, it is definitely true that Quantity A is equal to a larger percent of that total than is Quantity B.

22. **(A).** Standard deviation is a measure of the data's spread from the mean. While the two sets have the same range $(30 - 10 = 20)$, they do *not* have the same spread. The four extra terms in Quantity B are identical to the mean, meaning that, on average, the data in Quantity B is closer to the mean than the data in Quantity A. Thus, Quantity A is more spread out, on average, and has the larger standard deviation. Do not compute the actual standard deviations to find the answer here.

23. **(D).** While the shaded area may appear to be evenly located on either side of the mean, it isn't necessarily. For example, the 68% could be more lopsided, like so:

**MANHATTAN**
PREP

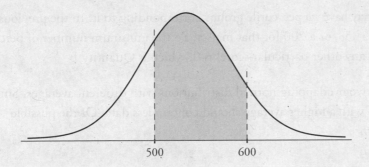

This area could still represent 68% of the scores, even if it's not 1 standard deviation to either side of the mean. In order to determine that the mean is 550, the problem would need to state explicitly that 500 and 600 each represent 1 standard deviation from the mean (or at least that 500 and 600 are equally far from the mean).

The fact that 68% of the data is located between 500 and 600 is a trick implying that 500 and 600 are −1 and +1 standard deviation from the mean, but this is not necessarily true. While it is always true that, in a normal distribution, about 68% (some people memorize the approximation as two-thirds) of the data is within 1 standard deviation of the mean, the reverse is not true: do not assume that any chunk of data that is about 68% of the whole is therefore within 1 standard deviation of the mean.

### 24. **1st and 3rd only.**

The first statement is true. Standard deviation describes how much a set of data diverges from the mean. Curve $B$ is more widely spread than curve $A$, and thus $Y$ has a greater standard deviation than $X$.

The second statement is not true. The probability that *any* normally distributed variable falls within 2 standard deviations of its mean is the same, approximately $0.14 + 0.34 + 0.34 + 0.14 = 0.96$, or 96%. Memorize this value for the GRE.

The third statement is true. The mean of a normal curve is the point along the horizontal axis below the "peak" of the curve. The highest point of curve $B$ is clearly to the right of the highest point of curve $A$, so the mean of $Y$ is larger than the mean of $X$. Notice that the mean has nothing to do with the *height* of the normal curve, which only corresponds to how tightly the variable is gathered around the mean (i.e., how small the standard deviation is).

### 25. **(A).** There are 400 test scores distributed among 50 possible outcomes (integers between 151 and 200, inclusive, which number $200 − 151 + 1 = 50$ integers). There is an average of $400 \div 50 = 8$ scores per integer outcome, and there are $400 \div 100 = 4$ scores in each percentile. So, if all the scores were completely evenly distributed with exactly 8 scores per integer, there would be two percentile groups per integer outcome (0th and 1st percentiles at 151, 2nd and 3rd percentiles at 152, etc.). In that case, all 50 integers from 151 to 200 would correspond to more than one percentile group.

Reduce the number of integers corresponding to more than one percentile group by bunching up the scores. Imagine that everyone gets a 157. Then that integer is the only one that corresponds to more than one percentile group (it corresponds to all 100 groups, in fact). However, don't reduce further this way. This gives exactly 1 integer, so the minimum number of integers corresponding to more than one percentile group is 1, which is Quantity A.

As for Quantity B, though, a particular integer may have *no* percentile groups corresponding to it. In the previous example, if everyone gets a 157, then no one gets a 158, or a 200 for that matter. So the minimum number of percentile groups corresponding to a score of 200 (or to any other particular score) is 0, which is Quantity B.

26. **(C).** A two-humped shape could come from two overlapping normal distributions with different averages. Since the hump on the right is smaller, the distribution with a higher average should contain less data. Of the possible answer choices, only (C) describes such a scenario.

27. **1st, 2nd, and 3rd.**

The first statement could be true. Although biologists' salaries cluster around a lower number than physicists' salaries do, do not assume that *every* biologist's salary is lower than *every* physicist's salary. Some biologists' salaries can be high, and some physicists' salaries can be low. The graph shows a small area of overlap between the two means.

The second statement could be true. Normal distributions are consistent with the hump shapes you see in the graph. While it's not possible to *prove* that they're normal, it's also not possible to prove that they're definitely not—they certainly *could* be normal.

The third statement could be true. From real-world normal distributions of an unknown amount of data, there's no way to tell the maximum or minimum values of the data. So the range certainly could be more than $150,000.

28. **2nd and 3rd only.**

The first statement is not necessarily true. Range is calculated this way: *Largest value – Smallest value*. From the graphs as shown (assuming that they do not continue "off screen" left and right), it is possible that the two distributions have the *same* range, because the distributions are above zero on both the far left and the far right. (In the real world, the graphs might even continue off screen, leading to even less confidence about the range of each distribution.)

The second statement is true. The graph on the right (Town Y) has a smaller standard deviation (it is less spread out around its mean). So families in Town Y are more likely to be within 1 family member of the mean than families in Town X are.

The third statement is true. The graph on the left is more spread out, so it has a larger standard deviation.

29. **(A).** The plot is symmetrical, so you can eliminate any non-symmetrical datasets (such as (C), (D), and (E)). In (B), all the data points are the same, so there would be no width to the box-and-whisker plot. Choice (A) is the only remaining possibility: the data is evenly spaced, leading to equal widths for each segment of the plot, as shown.

**MANHATTAN**
PREP

30. **3rd only.**

The first statement is not true. The median of the whole set is the line in the middle of the box. As shown, it is closer to the *right* side of the box (the median of the upper half of the data) than to the *left* side of the box (the median of the lower half of the data)—the opposite of what this statement claims.

The second statement is not true. This non-symmetrical plot could never represent a symmetrical distribution such as the normal distribution. In fact, a *true* normal distribution cannot be represented by a box-and-whisker plot at all, because such a distribution stretches infinitely to the right and to the left, in theory.

The third statement is true. Any set represented by a box-and-whisker plot has a standard deviation greater than zero, because the plot displays some spread in the data. The only set that has a zero standard deviation is a set containing identical data points with zero spread between them, such as {3, 3, 3, 3}.

31. **1st only.** Since the overall average length of all the earthworms is closer to the average length of earthworms in sample A than to the average for sample B, there are more earthworms in sample A.

However, without individual values, the mean and the range of the dataset are still unknown. For instance, the lengths of all the worms in sample *A* could be exactly 2.4, or they could be spread out quite a bit from 2.4. Similarly, the worms in sample B could measure exactly 3.0, or they could have a variety of different lengths that average to 3.0. Thus, the median and range could vary quite a bit.

# Chapter 23 *of*

5 lb. Book of GRE® Practice Problems

# Probability, Combinatorics, and Overlapping Sets

# In This Chapter...

Probability, Combinatorics, and Overlapping Sets

Probability, Combinatorics, and Overlapping Sets Answers

# Probability, Combinatorics, and Overlapping Sets

For questions in the Quantitative Comparison format ("Quantity A" and "Quantity B" given), the answer choices are always as follows:

(A)  Quantity A is greater.
(B)  Quantity B is greater.
(C)  The two quantities are equal.
(D)  The relationship cannot be determined from the information given.

For questions followed by a numeric entry box [＿＿＿＿], you are to enter your own answer in the box. For questions followed

by a fraction-style numeric entry box $\frac{\square}{\square}$, you are to enter your answer in the form of a fraction. You are not required to

reduce fractions. For example, if the answer is $\frac{1}{4}$, you may enter $\frac{25}{100}$ or any equivalent fraction.

All numbers used are real numbers. All figures are assumed to lie in a plane unless otherwise indicated. Geometric figures are not necessarily drawn to scale. You should assume, however, that lines that appear to be straight are actually straight, points on a line are in the order shown, and all geometric objects are in the relative positions shown. Coordinate systems, such as $xy$-planes and number lines, as well as graphical data presentations, such as bar charts, circle graphs, and line graphs, *are* drawn to scale. A symbol that appears more than once in a question has the same meaning throughout the question.

1.  A number is randomly chosen from a list of 10 consecutive positive integers. What is the probability that the number selected is greater than the average (arithmetic mean) of all 10 integers?

    (A)  $\frac{3}{10}$

    (B)  $\frac{2}{5}$

    (C)  $\frac{1}{2}$

    (D)  $\frac{7}{10}$

    (E)  $\frac{4}{5}$

2.  A number is randomly chosen from the first 100 positive integers. What is the probability that it is a multiple of 3?

    (A)  $\frac{32}{100}$

    (B)  $\frac{33}{100}$

    (C)  $\frac{1}{3}$

    (D)  $\frac{34}{100}$

    (E)  $\frac{2}{3}$

3. A restaurant menu has several options for tacos. There are 3 types of shells, 4 types of meat, 3 types of cheese, and 5 types of salsa. How many distinct tacos can be ordered assuming that any order contains exactly one of each of the above choices?

4. A history exam features five questions. Three of the questions are multiple-choice with four options each. The other two questions are true or false. If Caroline selects one answer for every question, how many different ways can she answer the exam?

5. The probability is $\frac{1}{2}$ that a certain coin will turn up heads on any given toss and the probability is $\frac{1}{6}$ that a number cube with faces numbered 1 to 6 will turn up any particular number. What is the probability of turning up a heads and a 6?

(A) $\frac{1}{36}$

(B) $\frac{1}{12}$

(C) $\frac{1}{6}$

(D) $\frac{1}{4}$

(E) $\frac{2}{3}$

6. An integer is randomly chosen from 2 to 20 inclusive. What is the probability that the number is prime?

Give your answer as a fraction.

7. An Italian restaurant boasts 320 distinct pasta dishes. Each dish contains exactly 1 pasta, 1 meat, and 1 sauce. If there are 8 pastas and 4 meats available, how many sauces are there to choose from?

**MANHATTAN**
PREP

8.  A 10-student class is to choose a president, vice president, and secretary from the group. If no person can occupy more than one post, in how many ways can this be accomplished?

    ☐

9.  BurgerTown offers many options for customizing a burger. There are 3 types of meats and 7 condiments: lettuce, tomatoes, pickles, onions, ketchup, mustard, and special sauce. A burger must include meat, but may include as many or as few condiments as the customer wants. How many different burgers are possible?

    (A) 8!
    (B) (3)(7!)
    (C) (3)(8!)
    (D) (8)($2^7$)
    (E) (3)($2^7$)

10. The probability of rain is $\frac{1}{6}$ for any given day next week. What is the probability that it will rain on both Monday and Tuesday?

    (A) $\frac{1}{36}$

    (B) $\frac{1}{12}$

    (C) $\frac{1}{6}$

    (D) $\frac{1}{3}$

    (E) $\frac{2}{3}$

11. How many five-digit numbers can be formed using the digits 5, 6, 7, 8, 9, 0 if no digits can be repeated?

    (A) 64
    (B) 120
    (C) 240
    (D) 600
    (E) 720

12. A bag contains 3 red, 2 blue, and 7 white marbles. If a marble is randomly chosen from the bag, what is the probability that it is <u>not</u> blue?

   Give your answer as a fraction.

   $$\boxed{\phantom{XXXX}} \over \boxed{\phantom{XXXX}}$$

13. A man has 3 different suits, 4 different shirts, 2 different pairs of socks, and 5 different pairs of shoes. If an outfit consists of exactly 1 suit, 1 shirt, 1 pair of socks, and 1 pair of shoes, how many different outfits can be made with the man's clothing?

   $$\boxed{\phantom{XXXX}}$$

   A state issues automobile license plates that begin with two letters selected from a 26-letter alphabet, followed by four numerals selected from the digits 0 through 9, inclusive. Repeats are permitted. For example, one possible license plate combination is GF3352.

|  **Quantity A**  |  **Quantity B**  |
| --- | --- |
| 14.   The number of possible unique license plate combinations | 6,000,000 |

15. A bag contains 6 black chips numbered 1–6 respectively and 6 white chips numbered 1–6 respectively. If Pavel reaches into the bag of 12 chips and removes 2 chips, one after the other, without replacing them, what is the probability that he will pick black chip #3 and then white chip #3?

   Give your answer as a fraction.

   $$\boxed{\phantom{XXXX}} \over \boxed{\phantom{XXXX}}$$

Tarik has a pile of 6 green chips numbered 1 through 6 respectively and another pile of 6 blue chips numbered 1 through 6 respectively. Tarik will randomly pick 1 chip from the green pile and 1 chip from the blue pile.

| **Quantity A** | **Quantity B** |
|---|---|
| 16. The probability that both chips selected by Tarik will display a number less than 4. | $\dfrac{1}{2}$ |

17. A bag contains 6 red chips numbered 1 through 6, respectively, and 6 blue chips numbered 1 through 6, respectively. If 2 chips are to be picked sequentially from the bag of 12 chips, without replacement, what is the probability of picking a red chip and then a blue chip with the same number?

Give your answer as a fraction.

In a school of 150 students, 75 study Latin, 110 study Spanish, and 11 study neither.

| **Quantity A** | **Quantity B** |
|---|---|
| 18. The number of students who study only Latin | 46 |

19. How many 10-digit numbers can be formed using only the digits 2 and 5?

(A)  $2^{10}$

(B)  $(22)(5!)$

(C)  $(5!)(5!)$

(D)  $\dfrac{10!}{2}$

(E)  $10!$

20. A 6-sided cube has faces numbered 1 through 6. If the cube is rolled twice, what is the probability that the sum of the two rolls is 8?

    (A) $\dfrac{1}{9}$

    (B) $\dfrac{1}{8}$

    (C) $\dfrac{5}{36}$

    (D) $\dfrac{1}{6}$

    (E) $\dfrac{7}{36}$

21. A certain coin with heads on one side and tails on the other has a $\dfrac{1}{2}$ probability of landing on heads. If the coin is flipped 5 times, how many distinct outcomes are possible if the last flip must be heads? Outcomes are distinct if they do not contain exactly the same results in exactly the same order.

    ┌─────────┐
    │         │
    └─────────┘

In a class of 25 students, each student studies either Spanish, Latin, or French, or two of the three, but no students study all three languages. 9 study Spanish, 7 study Latin, and 5 study exactly two languages.

|  | **Quantity A** | **Quantity B** |
|---|---|---|
| 22. | The number of students who study French | 14 |

23. Pedro has a number cube with 24 faces and an integer between 1 and 24 on each face. Every number is featured exactly once. When he rolls, what is the probability that the number showing is a factor of 24?

    Give your answer as a fraction.

**MANHATTAN**
PREP

24. A baby has *x* total toys. If 9 of the toys are stuffed animals, 7 of the toys were given to the baby by her grandmother, 5 of the toys are stuffed animals given to the baby by her grandmother, and 6 of the toys are neither stuffed animals nor given to the baby by her grandmother, what is the value of *x*?

25. How many integers between 2,000 and 3,999 have a ones digit that is a prime number?

26. A group of 12 people who have never met are in a classroom. How many handshakes are exchanged if each person shakes hands exactly once with each of the other people in the room?

    (A)  12

    (B)  22

    (C)  66

    (D)  132

    (E)  244

27. A class consists of 12 girls and 20 boys. One quarter of the girls in the class have blue eyes. If a child is selected at random from the class, what is the probability that the child is a girl who does not have blue eyes?

    (A)  $\dfrac{3}{32}$

    (B)  $\dfrac{9}{32}$

    (C)  $\dfrac{3}{8}$

    (D)  $\dfrac{23}{32}$

    (E)  $\dfrac{29}{32}$

28. A certain coin with heads on one side and tails on the other has a $\frac{1}{2}$ probability of landing on heads. If the coin is flipped three times, what is the probability of flipping 2 tails and 1 head, in any order?

    (A) $\frac{1}{8}$

    (B) $\frac{1}{3}$

    (C) $\frac{3}{8}$

    (D) $\frac{5}{8}$

    (E) $\frac{2}{3}$

29. A number cube has six faces numbered 1 through 6. If the cube is rolled twice, what is the probability that at least one of the rolls will result in a number greater than 4?

    (A) $\frac{2}{9}$

    (B) $\frac{1}{3}$

    (C) $\frac{4}{9}$

    (D) $\frac{5}{9}$

    (E) $\frac{2}{3}$

30. 100 tiles are labeled with the integers from 1 to 100 inclusive; no numbers are repeated. If Alma chooses one tile at random, replaces it in the group, and chooses another tile at random, what is the probability that the product of the two integer values on the tiles is odd?

    (A) $\frac{1}{8}$

    (B) $\frac{1}{4}$

    (C) $\frac{1}{3}$

    (D) $\frac{1}{2}$

    (E) $\frac{3}{4}$

31. If the word "WOW" can be rearranged in exactly 3 ways (WOW, OWW, WWO), how many different arrangements of the letters in "MISSISSIPPI" are possible?

> [                    ]

The probability of rain is $\frac{1}{2}$ on any given day next week.

|   | **Quantity A** | **Quantity B** |
|---|---|---|
| 32. | The probability that it rains on at least one of the 7 days next week | $\frac{127}{128}$ |

33. Two number cubes with six faces numbered with the integers from 1 through 6 are tossed. What is the probability that the sum of the exposed faces on the cubes is a prime number?

Give your answer as a fraction.

34. Jan and 5 other children are in a classroom. The principal of the school will choose two of the children at random. What is the probability that Jan will be chosen?

(A) $\frac{4}{5}$

(B) $\frac{1}{3}$

(C) $\frac{2}{5}$

(D) $\frac{7}{15}$

(E) $\frac{1}{2}$

The probability that Maria will eat breakfast on any given day is 0.5. The probability that Maria will wear a sweater on any given day is 0.3. The two probabilities are independent of each other.

|   | **Quantity A** | **Quantity B** |
|---|---|---|
| 35. | The probability that Maria eats breakfast or wears a sweater | 0.8 |

The probability of rain in Greg's town on Tuesday is 0.3. The probability that Greg's teacher will give him a pop quiz on Tuesday is 0.2. The events occur independently of each other.

|  | **Quantity A** | **Quantity B** |
|---|---|---|
| 36. | The probability that either or both events occur | The probability that neither event occurs |

37. A certain city has a $\frac{1}{3}$ chance of rain occurring on any given day. In any given 3-day period, what is the probability that the city experiences rain?

   (A) $\frac{1}{3}$

   (B) $\frac{8}{27}$

   (C) $\frac{2}{3}$

   (D) $\frac{19}{27}$

   (E) 1

38. Five students, Adnan, Beth, Chao, Dan, and Edmund are to be arranged in a line. How many such arrangements are possible if Beth is not allowed to stand next to Dan?

   (A) 24
   (B) 48
   (C) 72
   (D) 96
   (E) 120

39. A polygon has 12 edges. How many different diagonals does it have? (A diagonal is a line drawn from one vertex to any other vertex inside the given shape. This line cannot touch or cross any of the edges of the shape. For example, a triangle has zero diagonals and a rectangle has two.)

   (A) 54
   (B) 66
   (C) 108
   (D) 132
   (E) 144

**MANHATTAN**
PREP

| | **Quantity A** | **Quantity B** |
|---|---|---|
| 40. | The number of possible 4-person teams that can be selected from 6 people | The number of possible 2-person teams that can be selected from 6 people |

| | **Quantity A** | **Quantity B** |
|---|---|---|
| 41. | The number of ways 1st, 2nd, and 3rd place prizes could be awarded to 3 out of 6 contestants | The number of ways 1st, 2nd, 3rd, 4th, and 5th place prizes could be awarded to 5 contestants |

An inventory of coins contains 100 different coins.

| | **Quantity A** | **Quantity B** |
|---|---|---|
| 42. | The number of possible collections of 56 coins that can be selected (the order of the coins does not matter) | The number of possible collections of 44 coins that can be selected (the order of the coins does not matter) |

An office supply store carries an inventory of 1,345 different products, all of which it categorizes as "business use," "personal use," or both. There are 740 products categorized as "business use" only and 520 products categorized as both "business use" and "personal use."

| | **Quantity A** | **Quantity B** |
|---|---|---|
| 43. | The number of products characterized as "personal use" | 600 |

44. Eight women and two men are available to serve on a committee. If three people are picked, what is the probability that the committee includes at least one man?

   (A) $\dfrac{1}{32}$

   (B) $\dfrac{1}{4}$

   (C) $\dfrac{2}{5}$

   (D) $\dfrac{7}{15}$

   (E) $\dfrac{8}{15}$

45. At Lexington High School, each student studies at least one language — Spanish, French, or Latin — and no student studies all three languages. If 100 students study Spanish, 80 study French, 40 study Latin, and 22 study exactly two languages, how many students are there at Lexington High School?

   (A) 198
   (B) 220
   (C) 242
   (D) 264
   (E) 286

   Of 60 birds found in a certain location, 20 are songbirds and 23 are migratory. (It is possible for a songbird to be either migratory or not migratory.)

| **Quantity A** | **Quantity B** |
|---|---|
| 46. The number of the 60 birds that are neither migratory nor songbirds | 16 |

# Probability, Combinatorics, and Overlapping Sets Answers

1. **(C).** In a list of 10 consecutive integers, the mean is the average of the 5th and 6th numbers. Therefore, the 6th through 10th integers (five total integers) is greater than the mean. Since probability is determined by the number of desired items divided by the total number of choices, the probability that the number chosen is greater than the average of all 10 integers is $\dfrac{5}{10} = \dfrac{1}{2}$.

Another approach to this problem is to create a set of 10 consecutive integers; the easiest such list contains the numbers {1, 2, 3, 4, 5, 6, 7, 8, 9, 10}. The mean is one-half the sum of the first element plus the last element, or $\dfrac{1+10}{2} = 5.5$. Therefore, there are 5 numbers greater than the mean in the list: 6, 7, 8, 9 and 10. Again, the probability of choosing a number greater than the average of all 10 integers is $\dfrac{5}{10} = \dfrac{1}{2}$.

2. **(B).** The first 100 positive integers comprise the set of numbers containing the integers 1 to 100. Of these numbers, the only ones that are divisible by 3 are {3, 6, 9, ..., 96, 99}, which adds up to exactly 33 numbers. This can be determined in several ways. One option is to count the multiples of 3, but that's a bit slow. Alternatively, compute $\dfrac{99}{3} = 33$ and realize that there are 33 multiples of 3 up to and including 99. The number 100 is not divisible by 3, so the correct answer is $\dfrac{33}{100}$.

Alternatively, use the "add one before you're done" trick, subtracting the first multiple of 3 from the last multiple of 3, dividing by 3 and then adding 1: $\dfrac{(99-3)}{3} + 1 = 33$. Then, since probability is determined by the number of desired options divided by the total number of options, the probability that the number chosen is a multiple of 3 is $\dfrac{33}{100}$.

3. **180.** This problem tests the fundamental counting principle, which states that the total number of choices is equal to the product of the independent choices. Therefore, the total number of tacos is (3)(4)(3)(5) = 180 tacos.

4. **256.** This question tests the fundamental counting principle, which states that the total number of choices is equal to the product of the independent choices. The five separate test questions means there are five independent choices. For the three multiple-choice questions there are four options each, whereas for the two true/false questions there are two options each. Multiplying the independent choices yields (4)(4)(4)(2)(2) = 256 different ways to answer the exam.

5. **(B).** The probability of independent events A *and* B occurring is equal to the product of the probability of event A and the probability of event B. In this case, the probability of the coin turning up heads is $\dfrac{1}{2}$ and the probability of rolling a 6 is $\dfrac{1}{6}$. Therefore, the probability of heads *and* a 6 is equal to $\left(\dfrac{1}{2}\right)\left(\dfrac{1}{6}\right) = \dfrac{1}{12}$. Alternatively, list all the possible outcomes: H1, H2, H3, H4, H5, H6, T1, T2, T3, T4, T5, T6. There are 12 total outcomes and only 1 with heads and a 6. Therefore, the desired outcome divided by the total number of outcomes is equal to $\dfrac{1}{12}$.

6. $\frac{8}{19}$ **(or any equivalent fraction).** Among the integers 2 through 20, inclusive, there are 8 primes: 2, 3, 5, 7, 11, 13, 17, and 19. From 2 to 20, inclusive, there are exactly $20 - 2 + 1 = 19$ integers; remember to "add one before you're done" to include both endpoints. Alternatively, there are 20 integers from 1 to 20, inclusive, so there must be 19 integers from 2 to 20, inclusive. Since probability is defined as the number of desired items divided by the total number of choices, the probability that the number chosen is prime is $\frac{8}{19}$.

7. **10.** This problem tests the fundamental counting principle, which states that the total number of choices is equal to the product of the independent choices. Let the number of sauces be represented by the variable $S$. The total number of possible pasta dishes can be represented by each separate choice multiplied together: $(8)(4)(S)$, or $32S$. The problem also indicates that the total number of pasta dishes must be equal to 320. Therefore, $32S = 320$, so $S = 10$.

8. **720.** One possible approach is to ask, "How many choices do I have for each of the class positions?" Begin by considering the president of the class. Since no one has been chosen yet, there are 10 students from whom to choose. Then, for the vice president there are 9 options because now one student has already been chosen as president. Similarly, there are 8 choices for the secretary. Using the fundamental counting principle, the total number of possible selections is $(10)(9)(8) = 720$.

Alternatively, use factorials. In this case, order matters because people are selected for specific positions. This problem is synonymous to asking, "How many different ways can you line up 3 students as first, second, and third from a class of 10?" The number of ways to arrange the entire class in line is 10!. However, the problem is only concerned with the first 3 students in line, so exclude rearrangements of the last 7. The way in which these "non-chosen" 7 students can be ordered is 7!. Thus, the total number of arrangements for 3 students from a class of 10 is $\frac{10!}{7!} = (10)(9)(8) = 720$ choices.

9. **(E).** This problem tests the fundamental counting principle, which states that the total number of choices is equal to the product of the independent choices. The key to this problem is realizing how many choices there are for each option. For the meat, there are 3 choices. For each of the condiments there are exactly 2 choices: yes or no. The only real choice regarding each condiment is whether to include it at all. As there are 7 condiments, the total number of choices is $(3)(2)(2)(2)(2)(2)(2)(2) = (3)(2^7)$.

Note: the condiment options cannot be counted as 8! (0 through 7 = 8 options) because, in this case, the order in which the options are chosen does not matter; a burger with lettuce and pickles is the same as a burger with pickles and lettuce.

10. **(A).** For probability questions, always begin by separating out the probabilities of each individual event. Then, if all the events happen (an "*and* question"), multiply the probabilities together. If only one of the multiple events happens (an "*or* question"), add the probabilities together.

In this case, there are two events: rain on Monday and rain on Tuesday. The question asks for the probability that it will rain on Monday *and* on Tuesday, so multiply the individual probabilities together:

$$\frac{1}{6} \times \frac{1}{6} = \frac{1}{36}$$

**MANHATTAN**
PREP

11. **(D).** This problem relies on the fundamental counting principle, which says that the total number of ways for something to happen is the product of the number of options for each individual choice. The problem asks how many five-digit numbers can be created from the digits 5, 6, 7, 8, 9, and 0. For the first digit, there are only five options (5, 6, 7, 8, and 9) because a five-digit number must start with a non-zero integer. For the second digit, there are 5 choices again, because now zero can be used but one of the other numbers has already been used, and numbers cannot be repeated. For the third number, there are 4 choices, for the fourth number there are 3 choices, and for the fifth number there are 2 choices. Thus, the total number of choices is (5)(5)(4)(3)(2) = 600.

Alternatively, use the same logic and realize there are 5 choices for the first digit. (Separate out the first step because you have to remove the zero from consideration.) The remaining five digits all have an equal chance of being chosen, so choose four out of the remaining five digits to complete the number. The number of ways in which this second step can be accomplished is $\dfrac{(5!)}{(1!)} = (5)(4)(3)(2)$. Thus, the total number of choices is again equal to (5)(5)(4)(3)(2) = 600.

12. $\dfrac{5}{6}$ **(or any equivalent fraction).** In the bag of marbles, there are 3 red marbles and 7 white marbles, for a total of 10 marbles that are not blue. There are a total of 3 + 7 + 2 = 12 marbles in the bag. Since probability is defined as the number of desired items divided by the total number of choices, the probability that the marble chosen is *not* blue is $\dfrac{10}{12} = \dfrac{5}{6}$.

13. **120.** This problem utilizes the fundamental counting principle, which states that the total number of choices is equal to the product of the independent choices. Since the man must choose one suit, one shirt, one pair of socks, and one pair of shoes, the total number of outfits is the number of suits times the number of shirts times the number of socks times the number of shoes: (3)(4)(2)(5) = 120.

14. **(A).** This is a combinatorics problem. The license plates have 2 letters followed by 4 numbers, so make 6 "slots" and determine how many possibilities there are for each slot. There are 26 letters in the alphabet and 10 digits to pick from, so:

$$\underline{\phantom{x}26\phantom{x}} \quad \underline{\phantom{x}26\phantom{x}} \quad \underline{\phantom{x}10\phantom{x}} \quad \underline{\phantom{x}10\phantom{x}} \quad \underline{\phantom{x}10\phantom{x}} \quad \underline{\phantom{x}10\phantom{x}}$$

Multiply 26 × 26 on the calculator to get 676. Add four zeros for the four 10's to get 6,760,000. Quantity A is greater.

15. $\dfrac{1}{132}$ **(or any equivalent fraction).** The probability of picking black chip #3 is $\dfrac{1}{12}$. Once Pavel has removed the first chip, only 11 chips remain, so the probability of picking white chip #3 is $\dfrac{1}{11}$. Multiply $\dfrac{1}{12} \times \dfrac{1}{11} = \dfrac{1}{132}$.

16. **(B).** In this problem, Tarik is *not* picking 1 chip out of all 12. Rather, he is picking 1 chip out of 6 green ones, and then picking another chip out of 6 blue ones. There are 3 green chips with numbers less than 4, so Tarik has a $\dfrac{3}{6}$ chance of selecting a green chip showing a number less than 4. Likewise, Tarik has a $\dfrac{3}{6}$ chance of selecting a blue chip showing a number less than 4. Therefore, Quantity A is equal to $\dfrac{3}{6} \times \dfrac{3}{6} = \dfrac{1}{2} \times \dfrac{1}{2} = \dfrac{1}{4}$. Quantity B is greater.

17. $\frac{1}{22}$ **(or any equivalent fraction).** The trap answer in this problem is $\frac{1}{6} \times \frac{1}{6} = \frac{1}{36}$. This is *not* the answer to the question being asked—rather, this is the answer to the question, "What is the probability of picking a red chip and then a blue chip that both have #3?" (or any other specific number). This is a more specific question than the one actually asked. In the question, asked, there are six possible ways to fulfill the requirements of the problem, not one, because the problem does not specify whether the number should be 1, 2, 3, 4, 5, or 6.

Thus, *any* of the 6 red chips is acceptable for the first pick. However, on the second pick, only the blue chip with the same number as the red one that was just picked is acceptable (the chip must "match" the first one picked). Thus:

$$\frac{6}{12} \times \frac{1}{11} = \frac{1}{2} \times \frac{1}{11} = \frac{1}{22}$$

18. **(B).** Use the overlapping sets formula for two groups: Total = Group 1 + Group 2 − Both + Neither. (Adding the two groups—in this case Latin and Spanish—double-counts the students who study both languages, so the formula subtracts the "both" students.) Set up your equation:

$$150 = 75 + 110 - B + 11$$
$$150 = 196 - B$$
$$46 = B$$

Careful! This is not the value of Quantity A. Since 46 students study both Latin and Spanish, subtract 46 from the total who study Latin to find those who study only Latin:

$$75 - 46 = 29$$

Thus, Quantity A is 29. Therefore Quantity B is greater.

19. **(A).** This problem relies on the fundamental counting principle, which says that the total number of ways for something to happen is the product of the number of options for each individual choice. For any digit of the 10-digit number there are exactly two options, a 2 or a 5. Thus, since there are two choices for each digit and it is a 10-digit number, there are $(2)(2)(2)(2)(2)(2)(2)(2)(2)(2) = 2^{10}$ total choices.

20. **(C).** The probability of any event equals the number of ways to get the desired outcome divided by the total number of ways for the event to happen. Starting with the denominator, use the fundamental counting principle to compute the total number of ways to roll a cube twice. There are 6 possibilities (1, 2, 3, 4, 5, or 6) for the first roll and 6 for the second, giving a total of $(6)(6) = 36$ possibilities for the two rolls. For the numerator, determine the number of possible combinations that will sum to 8. For example, rolling a 2 the first time and a 6 the second time. The full set of options is (2, 6), (3, 5), (4, 4), (5, 3), and (6, 2). Thus, there are 5 possible combinations that sum to 8, yielding a probability of $\frac{5}{36}$.

21. **16.** This problem utilizes the fundamental counting principle, which states that the total number of choices is equal to the product of the independent choices. For the first flip, there are 2 options: heads or tails. Similarly, for the second flip, there 2 options; for the third, there are 2 options; for the fourth, there are 2 options; and for the fifth there is only one option because the problem restricts this final flip to heads. Therefore, the total number of outcomes

**MANHATTAN**
PREP

is $(2)(2)(2)(2)(1) = 16$. A good rephrasing of this question is, "How many different outcomes are there if the coin is flipped 4 times?" The fifth flip, having been restricted to heads, is irrelevant. Therefore, the total number of ways to flip the coin five times with heads for the fifth flip is equal to the total number of ways to flip the coin four times; either way, the answer is 16.

22. **(C).** The problem specifies that no one studies all three languages. In addition, a total of 5 people study two languages. Thus, 5 people have been double-counted. Since the total number of people who have been double-counted (5) and triple-counted (0) is known, use the standard overlapping sets formula:

Total = Spanish + French + Latin − (Two of the three) − 2(All three)

$25 = 9 + \text{French} + 7 - 5 - 2(0)$
$25 = 11 + \text{French}$
$14 = \text{French}$

The two quantities are equal.

23. $\dfrac{1}{3}$ **(or any equivalent fraction).** Probability equals the number of desired outcomes divided by the total number of possible outcomes. Among the integers 1 through 24, there are four factor pairs of 24: (1, 24), (2, 12), (3, 8), and (4, 6), for a total of 8 factors. The total number of possible outcomes when rolling the cube once is 24. The probability that the number chosen is a factor of 24 is $\dfrac{8}{24} = \dfrac{1}{3}$.

24. **17.** Use the overlapping sets formula for two groups: Total = Group 1 + Group 2 − Both + Neither. Here, the groups are "stuffed animal" and "given by the baby's grandmother." The problem indicates that the "both" category is equal to 5 and that the "neither" number is 6. The total is $x$.

Total = Group 1 + Group 2 − Both + Neither

$x = 9 + 7 - 5 + 6$
$x = 17$

25. **800.** This is a combinatorics problem. Make four "slots" (since the numbers are all four-digit numbers), and determine how many possibilities there are for each slot:

___  ___  ___  ___

Since the number must begin with 2 or 3, there are two possibilities for the first slot. Because the ones digit must be prime and there are only four prime one-digit numbers (2, 3, 5, and 7), there are four possibilities for the last slot:

_2_  ___  ___  _4_

The other slots have no restrictions, so put 10 in them, since there are ten digits from 0–9:

$$\underline{\phantom{2}2\phantom{2}} \quad \underline{\phantom{2}10\phantom{2}} \quad \underline{\phantom{2}10\phantom{2}} \quad \underline{\phantom{2}4\phantom{2}}$$

Multiply to get 800.

Alternatively, figure out the pattern and add up the number of qualifying four-digit integers. In the first ten numbers, 2000–2009, there are exactly four numbers that have a prime units digit: 2002, 2003, 2005, and 2007. The pattern then repeats in the next group of ten numbers, 2010–2020, and so on. In any group of ten numbers, then, four qualify. Between 2,000 and 3,999 there are $3,999 - 2,000 + 1 = 2,000$ numbers, or $\dfrac{2,000}{10} = 200$ groups of ten numbers, so there are a total of $400 \times 2 = 800$ numbers that have a prime units digit.

26. **(C).** Multiple approaches are possible here. One way is to imagine the scenario and count up the number of handshakes. How many hands does everyone need to shake? There are 11 other people in the room, so the first person needs to shake hands 11 times. Now, move to the second person: how many hands must he shake? He has already shaken one hand, leaving him 10 others with whom to shake hands. The third person will need to shake hands with 9 others, and so on. Therefore, there are a total of $11 + 10 + 9 + 8 + 7 + 6 + 5 + 4 + 3 + 2 + 1$ handshakes. The fastest way to find the sum of a group of consecutive numbers is to take the average of the first and last terms and multiply it by the number of terms. The average is $\dfrac{(11+1)}{2} = 6$ and there are $11 - 1 + 1 = 11$ terms (find the difference between the terms and "add one before you're done"). The sum is $6 \times 11 = 66$.

Alternatively, rephrase the question as "How many different ways can any 2 people be chosen from a group of 12?" (This works because the problem ultimately asks you to "choose" each distinct pair of 2 people one time.) The key here is to realize that handshakes are independent of order, that is, it doesn't matter if A shakes hands with B or if B shakes hands with A; it's the same outcome. Thus, it only matters how many pairs you can make. Any time a question presents a group of order-independent items selected from a larger set, apply the formula $\dfrac{\text{total!}}{\text{in!out!}}$ to arrive at the total number of combinations. Thus: $\dfrac{12!}{2!10!} = \dfrac{12 \times 11}{2} = 66$.

27. **(B).** The probability of any outcome is equal to the number of desired outcomes divided by the total number of outcomes. There are 12 girls and 20 boys in the classroom. If one-quarter of the girls have blue eyes, then there are $(12)\left(\dfrac{1}{4}\right) = 3$ girls with blue eyes. Therefore, there are $12 - 3 = 9$ girls who do *not* have blue eyes. The total number of ways in which a child could be chosen is the total number of children in the class, namely $12 + 20 = 32$. Therefore, the probability of choosing a girl who does not have blue eyes equals the number of girls without blue eyes divided by the total number of children, which is $\dfrac{9}{32}$.

28. **(C).** There are only 2 possible outcomes for each flip and only 3 flips total. The most straightforward approach is to list all of the possible outcomes: {HHH, HHT, HTH, HTT, TTT, TTH THH, THT}. Of these 8 possibilities, 3 of the outcomes have one head and two tails, so the probability of this event is $\dfrac{3}{8}$.

Alternatively, count the total number of ways of getting 1 head without listing all the possibilities. If the coin is flipped 3 times and you want only 1 head, then there are 3 possible positions for the single head: on the first flip

**MANHATTAN**
PREP

alone, on the second flip alone, or on the third flip alone. Since there are 2 possible outcomes for each flip, heads or tails, there are $(2)(2)(2) = 8$ total outcomes. Again, the probability is $\frac{3}{8}$.

Finally, another alternative is to compute the probability directly. The probability of flipping heads is $\frac{1}{2}$ and the probability of flipping tails is also $\frac{1}{2}$. The probability of getting heads in the first position alone, or HTT, is $\left(\frac{1}{2}\right)\left(\frac{1}{2}\right)\left(\frac{1}{2}\right) = \frac{1}{8}$, multiplied because the coin was flipped heads *and* tails *and* tails. This represents the probability of heads in position 1, but heads could also be in position 2 alone or in position 3 alone. Since there are 3 possible positions for the heads, multiply by 3 to get the total probability $(3)\left(\frac{1}{8}\right) = \frac{3}{8}$.

29. **(D).** Because this problem is asking for an "at least" solution, use the $1 - x$ shortcut. The probability that at least one roll results in a number greater than 4 is equal to 1 minus the probability that both of the rolls result in numbers 4 or lower. For one roll, there are 6 possible outcomes (1 through 6) and 4 ways in which the outcome can be 4 or lower, so the probability is $\frac{4}{6} = \frac{2}{3}$. Thus, the probability that both rolls result in numbers 4 or lower is $\left(\frac{2}{3}\right)\left(\frac{2}{3}\right) = \frac{4}{9}$. This is the result that you do *not* want; subtract this from 1 to get the probability that you do want. The probability that at least one of the rolls results in a number greater than 4 is $1 - \left(\frac{4}{9}\right) = \frac{5}{9}$.

Alternatively, write out the possibilities. The total number of possibilities for two rolls is $(6)(6) = 36$. Here are the ways in which at least one number greater than 4 can be rolled:

     51, 52, 53, 54, 55, 56
     61, 62, 63, 64, 65, 66
     15, 25, 35, 45 (note: 55 and 65 have already been counted above)
     16, 26, 36, 46 (note: 56 and 66 have already been counted above)

There are 20 elements (be careful not to double-count any options). The probability of at least one roll resulting in a number greater than 4 is $\frac{20}{36} = \frac{5}{9}$.

30. **(B).** Use both probability and number properties concepts in order to answer this question. First, in order for two integers to produce an odd integer, the two starting integers must be odd. An odd times an odd equals an odd. An even times an odd, by contrast, produces an even, as does an even times an even.

Within the set of tiles, there are 50 even numbers (2, 4, 6, …, 100) and 50 odd numbers (1, 3, 5, …, 99). One randomly-chosen tile will have a $\frac{50}{100} = \frac{1}{2}$ probability of being even, and a $\frac{1}{2}$ probability of being odd. The probability of choosing an odd tile first is $\left(\frac{1}{2}\right)$ and the probability of choosing an odd tile second is also $\left(\frac{1}{2}\right)$, so the probability of "first odd *and* second odd" is $\left(\frac{1}{2}\right)\left(\frac{1}{2}\right) = \frac{1}{4}$.

Alternatively, recognize that there are only four options for odd/even pairs if two tiles are chosen: OO, OE, EO, EE. The only one of these combinations that yields an odd product is OO. Since all of these combinations are equally likely, and since OO is exactly one out of the four possibilities, the probability of choosing OO is $\frac{1}{4}$.

31. **34,650.** This is a combinatorics problem, and the WOW example is intended to make it clear that any W is considered identical to any other W—switching one W with another would *not* result in a different combination, just as switching one S with another in MISSISSIPPI would not result in a different combination.

Therefore, solve this problem using the classic combinatorics formula for accounting for subgroups among which order does not matter:

$$\frac{\text{Total number of items!}}{\text{First group! Second group! Etc.}}$$

Because MISSISSIPPI has 11 letters, including 1 M, 4 S's, 4 I's, and 2 P's:

$$\frac{11!}{1!\,4!\,4!\,2!}$$

Now expand the factorials and cancel; use the calculator for the last step of the calculation:

$$\frac{11\times10\times9\times8\times7\times6\times5\times\cancel{4!}}{\cancel{1}\cancel{4!}(4\times3\times2\times1)(2\times1)} = \frac{11\times10\times9\times\cancel{8}\times7\times\cancel{6}\times5}{(\cancel{4}\times\cancel{3}\times\cancel{2}\times\cancel{1})(\cancel{2}\times\cancel{1})} = 11\times10\times9\times7\times5 = 34{,}650$$

32. **(C).** Since Quantity A is an "at least" problem, use the $1 - x$ shortcut. Rather than calculate the probability of rain on exactly 1 day next week, and then the probability of rain on exactly 2 days next week, and so on (after which you would still have to add all of the probabilities together!), instead calculate the probability of no rain at all on any day, and then subtract that number from 1. That will give the combined probabilities for any scenarios that include rain on at least 1 day.

Probability of NO rain for any of the 7 days $= \dfrac{1}{2}\times\dfrac{1}{2}\times\dfrac{1}{2}\times\dfrac{1}{2}\times\dfrac{1}{2}\times\dfrac{1}{2}\times\dfrac{1}{2}=\dfrac{1}{128}$

Subtract this probability from 1:

$$1-\frac{1}{128}=\frac{128}{128}-\frac{1}{128}=\frac{127}{128}$$

Quantities A and B are equal.

33. $\dfrac{5}{12}$. First think about the prime numbers less than 12, the maximum sum of the numbers on the cube. These primes are 2, 3, 5, 7, 11.

The probability of rolling 2, 3, 5, 7, or 11 is equal to the number of ways to roll any of these sums divided by the total number of possible rolls. The total number of possible cube rolls is $6\times6=36$. Make a list:

Sum of 2 can happen 1 way: $1+1$.
Sum of 3 can happen 2 ways: $1+2$ or $2+1$.
Sum of 5 can happen 4 ways: $1+4$, $2+3$, $3+2$, $4+1$.
Sum of 7 can happen 6 ways: $1+6$, $2+5$, $3+4$, $4+3$, $5+2$, $6+1$.

Sum of 11 can happen 2 ways: $5 + 6, 6 + 5$.

That's a total of $1 + 2 + 4 + 6 + 2 = 15$ ways to roll a prime sum.

Thus, the probability is $\frac{15}{36} = \frac{5}{12}$.

34. **(B).** The probability of any event equals the number of ways to get the desired outcome divided by the total number of outcomes.

Start with the denominator, which is the total number of ways that the principal can choose two children from the classroom. Use the fundamental counting principle. There are 6 possible options for the first choice and 5 for the second, giving $(6)(5) = 30$ possibilities. However, this double-counts some cases; for example, choosing Jan and then Robert is the same as choosing Robert and then Jan. Divide the total number of pairs by 2: $\frac{(6)(5)}{2} = 1$. Alternatively, use the formula for a set in which the order doesn't matter: $\frac{\text{total!}}{\text{in! out!}}$. In this case: $\frac{6!}{2!4!} = \frac{6 \times 5 \times 4!}{(2)(4!)} = \frac{6 \times 5}{2} = 15$.

Now compute the numerator, which is the number of pairs that include Jan. Since the pair only includes two children and one is already decided (Jan), there are exactly 5 options for the other child. Thus, there are 5 total pairs that include Jan: Jan with each of the other students.

The probability of choosing a pair with Jan is $\frac{5}{15} = \frac{1}{3}$.

Alternatively, you can calculate the probability of not choosing Jan and use the $1 - x$ shortcut. The probability of not choosing Jan as the first student is $\frac{5}{6}$, and the probability of choosing again and not choosing Jan is $\frac{4}{5}$ so

$$1 - \left(\frac{5}{6} \times \frac{4}{5}\right) = 1 - \frac{20}{30} = \frac{10}{30} = \frac{1}{3}.$$

As a final alternative, list all the pairs of students and count how many of them include Jan. Label the students in the class as J, 1, 2, 3, 4, and 5, where J is Jan. Then all the pairs can be listed as (J1), (J2), (J3), (J4), (J5), (12), (13), (14), (15), (23), (24), (25), (34), (35), and (45). (Be careful not to include repeats.) There are 15 total elements in this list and 5 that include Jan, yielding a probability of $\frac{5}{15} = \frac{1}{3}$.

35. **(B).** The problem indicates that the events occur independently of each other. Therefore, in calculating Quantity A, the first step is to calculate the "or" situation, but don't stop there. Adding $0.5 + 0.3 = 0.8$ double counts the occurrences when both events occur. To compensate, subtract out the probability of both events occurring in order to get rid of the "double counted" occurrences.

Notice that this is a Quantitative Comparison. Because the 0.8 figure includes at least one "both" occurrence, the real figure for Quantity A must be less than 0.8. Therefore, Quantity B must be greater.

To do the actual math, find the probability of both events occurring (breakfast *and* sweater): $(0.5)(0.3) = 0.15$. Subtract the "and" occurrences from the total "or" probability: $0.8 - 0.15 = 0.65$.

Thus, Quantity B is greater.

36. **(B).** The problem indicates that the events occur independently of each other. Therefore, in calculating Quantity A, do not just add both events, even though it is an "or" situation. Adding $0.3 + 0.2 = 0.5$ is incorrect because the probability that both events occur is counted twice. (Only add probabilities in an "or" situation when the probabilities are mutually exclusive.)

While Quantity A's value should include the probability that both events occur, make sure to count this probability only once, not twice. Since the probability that both events occur is $0.3(0.2) = 0.06$, subtract this value from the "or" probability.

Quantity A: Add the two probabilities (rain *or* pop quiz) and subtract *both* scenarios (rain *and* pop quiz):

$$0.3 + 0.2 - (0.3)(0.2) = 0.44$$

Quantity B: Multiply the probability that rain does *not* occur (0.7) and the probability that the pop quiz does *not* occur (0.8):

$$0.7(0.8) = 0.56$$

Alternatively, note that the two quantities, collectively, include every possibility and are mutually exclusive of one another (Quantity A includes "rain and no quiz," "quiz and no rain," and "both rain and quiz," and Quantity B includes "no rain and no quiz"). Therefore, the values of Quantities A and B must sum to 1. Calculating the value of either Quantity A or Quantity B would automatically indicate the value for the other quantity.

If you do this, calculate Quantity B first (because it's the easier of the two quantities to calculate) and then subtract Quantity B from 1 in order to get Quantity A's value. That is, $1 - 0.56 = 0.44$.

37. **(D).** In essence, the question is asking, "What is the probability that one or more days are rainy days?" since any single rainy day would mean the city experiences rain. In this case, employ the $1 - x$ shortcut, where the probability of rain on one or more days is equal to 1 minus the probability of no rain on any day. Since the probability of rain is $\frac{1}{3}$ on any given day, the probability of no rain on any given day is $1 - \frac{1}{3} = \frac{2}{3}$. Therefore, the probability of no rain on three consecutive days is $\left(\frac{2}{3}\right)\left(\frac{2}{3}\right)\left(\frac{2}{3}\right) = \frac{8}{27}$. Finally, subtract from 1 to find the probability that it rains on one or more days: P(1 or more days) $= 1 - $ P(no rain) $= 1 - \frac{8}{27} = \frac{19}{27}$.

38. **(C).** The number of ways in which the students can be arranged with Beth and Dan separated is equal to the total number of ways in which the students can be arranged minus the number of ways they can be arranged with Beth and Dan together. The total number of ways to arrange 5 students in a line is $5! = 120$. To compute the number of ways to arrange the 5 students such that Beth and Dan are together, group Beth and Dan as "one" person, since they must be lined up together. Then the problem becomes one of lining up 4 students, which gives $4!$ possibilities. However, remember that there are actually two options for the Beth and Dan arrangement: Beth first and then Dan or Dan first and then Beth. Therefore, there are $(4!)(2) = (4)(3)(2)(1)(2) = 48$ total ways in which the students can be lined up with Dan and Beth together. Finally, there are $120 - 48 = 72$ arrangements in which Beth is separated from Dan.

Alternatively, compute the number of ways to arrange the students directly by considering individual cases. In this case, investigate how many ways there are to arrange the students if Beth occupies each spot in line and sum them to find the total. If Beth is standing in the first spot in line, then there are 3 options for the second spot (since Dan cannot occupy this position), 3 options for the next spot, 2 options for the next spot, and finally 1 option for the last spot. This yields $(3)(3)(2)(1) = 18$ total possibilities if Beth is first. If Beth is second, then there are 3 options for the first person (Dan cannot be this person), 2 options for the third person (Dan cannot be this person either), 2 options for the fourth person, and 1 option for the fifth. This yields $(3)(2)(2)(1) = 12$ possibilities. In fact, if Beth is third or fourth in line, the situation is the same as when Beth is second. Thus, there are 12 possible arrangements whether Beth is 2nd, 3rd, or 4th in line, yielding 36 total arrangements for these 3 cases. Using similar logic, the situation in which Beth is last in line is exactly equal to the situation in which she is first in line. Thus, there are $(18)(2) = 36$ possibilities in which Beth is first or last. In total, this yields $36 + 36 = 72$ possible outcomes when considering all of the possible placements for Beth.

39. **(A).** A diagonal of a polygon is an internal line segment connecting any two unique vertices; this line segment does not lie along an edge of the given shape. Consider a polygon with 12 vertices. Construct a diagonal by choosing any two vertices and connecting them with a line. Remember that this is order independent; the line is the same regardless of which is the starting vertex. Therefore, this is analogous to choosing any 2 elements from a set of 12, and can be written as $\dfrac{12!}{10!2!} = \dfrac{12 \times 11 \times 10!}{10!(2)(1)} = \dfrac{12 \times 11}{2} = 6 \times 11 = 66$. However, this method includes the vertices connected to their adjacent vertices, which form edges instead of diagonals. In order to account for this, subtract the number of edges on the polygon from the above number: $66 - 12 = 54$.

Alternatively, choose a random vertex of the 12-sided shape. There are $12 - 1 = 11$ lines that can be drawn to other vertices since no line can be drawn from the vertex to itself. However, the lines from this vertex to the two adjacent vertices will lie along the edges of the polygon and therefore cannot be included as diagonals (see the figure of a pentagon below for an example):

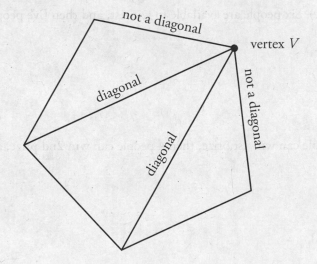

Thus, there are $12 - 1 - 2 = 9$ diagonals for any given vertex. Since there are 12 vertices, it is tempting to think that the total number of diagonals is equal to $(12)(9) = 108$. However, this scheme counts each diagonal twice, using each side of the diagonal once as the starting point. Therefore, there are half this many different diagonals: $\dfrac{108}{2} = 54$.

40. **(C).** This is a classic combinatorics problem in which *order doesn't matter*—that is, picking Javier and Sonya is the same as picking Sonya and Javier. A person is either on the team or not. Use the standard "order doesn't matter" formula:

$$\frac{total!}{in!\,out!}$$

For Quantity A:

$$\frac{6!}{2!\,4!} = \frac{6 \times 5 \times 4!}{(2)(1)4!} = \frac{6 \times 5}{2} = 15$$

For Quantity B:

$$\frac{6!}{4!\,2!} = \frac{6 \times 5 \times 4!}{4!(2)(1)} = \frac{6 \times 5}{2} = 15$$

The two quantities are equal. Note that it is not actually necessary to reduce each quantity. The factorials are the same in each, so the resulting quantities must be equal.

This will always work—when order doesn't matter, the number of ways to pick 4 and leave out 2 is the same as the number of ways to pick 2 and leave out 4. Either way, it's one group of 4 and one group of 2. What actually happens to those groups (getting picked, not getting picked, getting a prize, losing a contest, etc.) is irrelevant to the ultimate solution.

41. **(C).** In this problem, order matters; if Mari comes in 1st place and Rohit comes in 2nd, there is a different outcome than when Rohit places 1st and Mari places 2nd. Use the fundamental counting principle to solve. To determine Quantity A, make three slots (one for each prize). Six people are available to win 1st, and then five people could win 2nd, and four people could win 3rd:

$$\underline{\quad 6 \quad} \quad \underline{\quad 5 \quad} \quad \underline{\quad 4 \quad}$$

Multiply: (6)(5)(4) = 120.

For Quantity B, make 5 slots, one for each prize. Five people can win 1st prize, then 4 people can win 2nd prize, and so on:

$$\underline{\quad 5 \quad} \quad \underline{\quad 4 \quad} \quad \underline{\quad 3 \quad} \quad \underline{\quad 2 \quad} \quad \underline{\quad 1 \quad}$$

Multiply (5)(4)(3)(2)(1) = 120. The two quantities are equal.

42. **(C).** This is a classic combinatorics problem in which *order doesn't matter*—in fact, the problem states that explicitly. Use the standard "order doesn't matter" formula:

$$\frac{total!}{in!\,out!}$$

**MANHATTAN**
PREP

For Quantity A:

$$\frac{100!}{56!44!}$$

Because the numbers are so large, there must be a way to solve the problem without actually simplifying (even with a calculator, this is unreasonable under GRE time limits). Try Quantity B and compare:

$$\frac{100!}{44!56!}$$

The quantities are equal. Note that this will always work—when order doesn't matter, the number of ways to pick 56 and leave out 44 is the same as the number of ways to pick 44 and leave out 56. Either way, it's one group of 56 and one group of 44. What actually happens to those groups (being part of a collection, being left out of the collection, etc.) is irrelevant to the ultimate solution.

43. **(A).** Use the overlapping sets formula for two groups: Total = Group 1 + Group 2 − Both + Neither. But first, add 740 ("business use" *only*) + 520 ("business use" and "personal use") to get 1,260, the total number of products categorized as "business use."

Also note that the problem indicates that *all* of the products fall into one or both of the two categories, so "neither" in this formula is equal to zero:

Total = Business + Personal − Both + Neither
1,345 = 1,260 + $P$ − 520 + 0
1,345 = 740 + $P$
    605 = $P$

Quantity A is greater. Note that the question asked for the number of products characterized as "personal use" (which includes products in the "both" group). If the problem had asked for the number of products characterized as "personal use" *only*, you would have had to subtract the "both" group to get 605 − 520 = 85. In this problem, however, Quantity A equals 605.

44. **(E).** Because this is an "at least" question, use the $1 - x$ shortcut:

(The probability of picking at least one man) + (The probability of picking no men) = 1

The probability of picking no men is an *and* setup: woman *and* woman *and* woman.

For the first choice, there are 8 women out of 10 people: $\frac{8}{10} = \frac{4}{5}$.

For the second choice, there are $\frac{7}{9}$ (because one woman has already been chosen).

For the third choice, there are $\frac{6}{8} = \frac{3}{4}$.

Multiply the three probabilities together to find the probability that the committee will be comprised of woman *and* woman *and* woman:

$$\frac{4}{5} \times \frac{7}{9} \times \frac{3}{4} = \frac{1}{5} \times \frac{7}{3} \times \frac{1}{1} = \frac{7}{15}$$

To determine the probability of picking at least one man, subtract this result from 1:

$$1 - \frac{7}{15} = \frac{8}{15}$$

45. **(A).** This overlapping sets question can be solved with the following equation:

Total # of people = Group 1 + Group 2 + Group 3 − (# of people in two groups) − (2)(# of people in all three groups) + (# of people in no groups)

The problem indicates that everyone studies at least one language, so the number of people in no groups is zero. The problem also indicates that nobody studies all three languages, so that value is also zero:

Total # of students = 100 + 80 + 40 − 22 − (2)(0) + 0 = 198.

46. **(A).** It is not possible to solve for a single value for Quantity A, but it is possible to tell that Quantity A will always be greater than 16. Since 20 birds are songbirds and 23 are migratory, the total of these groups is 43, which is less than 60. It is possible for the overlap (the number of migratory songbirds) to be as little as 0, which would result in 20 songbirds, 23 non-songbird migratory birds, and 60 − 20 − 23 = 17 birds that are neither songbirds nor migratory.

It is also possible that there could be as many as 20 birds that overlap the two categories. (Find this figure by taking the number of birds in the smaller group; in this case, there are 20 songbirds). In the case that there are 20 migratory songbirds, there would also be 3 migratory birds that are not songbirds, in which case there would be 60 − 20 − 3 = 37 birds that are neither migratory nor songbirds.

Thus, the number of birds that are neither migratory nor songbirds is at least 17 and at most 37. No matter where in the range that number may be, it is greater than Quantity B, which is only 16.

# Chapter 24
## of
### 5 lb. Book of GRE® Practice Problems

# Data Interpretation

# In This Chapter...

# Data Interpretation

For questions in the Quantitative Comparison format ("Quantity A" and "Quantity B" given), the answer choices are always as follows:

(A) Quantity A is greater.
(B) Quantity B is greater.
(C) The two quantities are equal.
(D) The relationship cannot be determined from the information given.

For questions followed by a numeric entry box ⬚, you are to enter your own answer in the box. For questions followed by a fraction-style numeric entry box ⬚, you are to enter your answer in the form of a fraction. You are not required to reduce fractions. For example, if the answer is $\frac{1}{4}$, you may enter $\frac{25}{100}$ or any equivalent fraction.

All numbers used are real numbers. All figures are assumed to lie in a plane unless otherwise indicated. Geometric figures are not necessarily drawn to scale. You should assume, however, that lines that appear to be straight are actually straight, points on a line are in the order shown, and all geometric objects are in the relative positions shown. Coordinate systems, such as $xy$-planes and number lines, as well as graphical data presentations, such as bar charts, circle graphs, and line graphs, *are* drawn to scale. A symbol that appears more than once in a question has the same meaning throughout the question.

## Problem Set A

### 9th Grade Students at Millbrook High School

|                        | Boys | Girls |
|------------------------|------|-------|
| Enrolled in Spanish    | 12   | 13    |
| Not Enrolled in Spanish| 19   | 16    |

1.  Approximately what percent of the 9th grade girls at Millbrook High School are enrolled in Spanish?

    (A) 21%

    (B) 37%

    (C) 45%

    (D) 50%

    (E) 57%

2.   What fraction of the students in 9th grade at Millbrook High School are boys who are enrolled in Spanish?

    (A)  $\dfrac{1}{5}$

    (B)  $\dfrac{19}{60}$

    (C)  $\dfrac{5}{12}$

    (D)  $\dfrac{12}{31}$

    (E)  $\dfrac{12}{25}$

3.   What is the ratio of 9th grade girls not enrolled in Spanish to all 9th grade students at Millbrook Middle School?

    (A)  1:16
    (B)  13:60
    (C)  4:15
    (D)  19:60
    (E)  16:29

4.   If x percent more 9th grade students at Millbrook High School are not enrolled in Spanish than are enrolled in Spanish, what is the value of x?

    (A)  20
    (B)  25
    (C)  30
    (D)  40
    (E)  50

5.   If two of the 9th grade boys at Millbrook High school who are not enrolled in Spanish decided to enroll in Spanish, and then eight additional girls and seven additional boys attended the 9th grade at Millbrook Middle School and also enrolled in Spanish, what percent of 9th grade students at Millbrook would then be enrolled in Spanish?

    (A)  52%
    (B)  53%
    (C)  54%
    (D)  55%
    (E)  56%

**MANHATTAN**
PREP

## Problem Set B

**Number of Hours Worked per Week per Employee at Marshville Toy Company**

| # of Employees | Hours Worked Per Week |
|---|---|
| 4 | 15 |
| 9 | 25 |
| 15 | 35 |
| 27 | 40 |
| 5 | 50 |

6.  What is the median number of hours worked per week per employee at Marshville Toy Company?

    (A)  25
    (B)  30
    (C)  35
    (D)  37.5
    (E)  40

7.  What is the average (arithmetic mean) number of hours worked per week per employee at Marshville Toy Company?

    (A)  32
    (B)  33
    (C)  35
    (D)  $35\frac{2}{3}$
    (E)  $36\frac{1}{3}$

8.  What is the positive difference between the mode and the range of the number of hours worked per week per employee at Marshville Toy Company?

    (A)  0
    (B)  4
    (C)  5
    (D)  8
    (E)  26

## Problem Set C

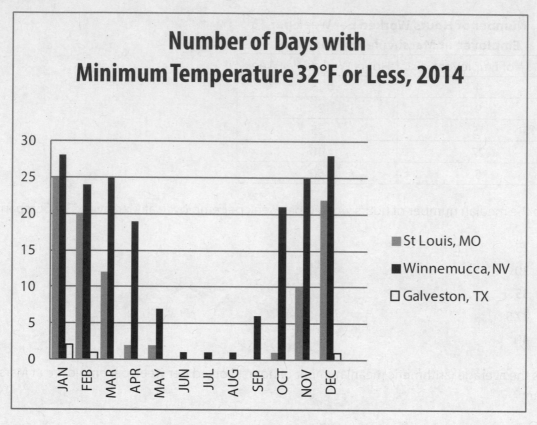

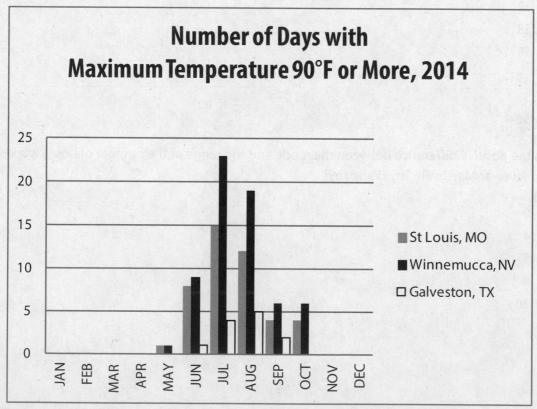

**MANHATTAN**
PREP

9.   In how many months of the year were there more than 20 days with temperatures 32°F or less in
     Winnemucca?

     (A)  2
     (B)  3
     (C)  4
     (D)  6
     (E)  7

10.  On how many days in the entire year did the temperature in Galveston rise to at least 90°F or fall at least
     as low as 32°F?

     (A)  11
     (B)  16
     (C)  28
     (D)  42
     (E)  59

11.  Approximately what percent of the days with maximum temperature of 90°F or more in St. Louis occurred
     in July?

     (A)  6%
     (B)  15%
     (C)  17%
     (D)  34%
     (E)  44%

12.  The number of freezing January days in Winnemucca was approximately what percent more than the
     number of freezing January days in St. Louis? (A "freezing" day is one in which the minimum temperature
     is 32°F or less.)

     (A)  3%
     (B)  6%
     (C)  12%
     (D)  24%
     (E)  28%

## Problem Set D

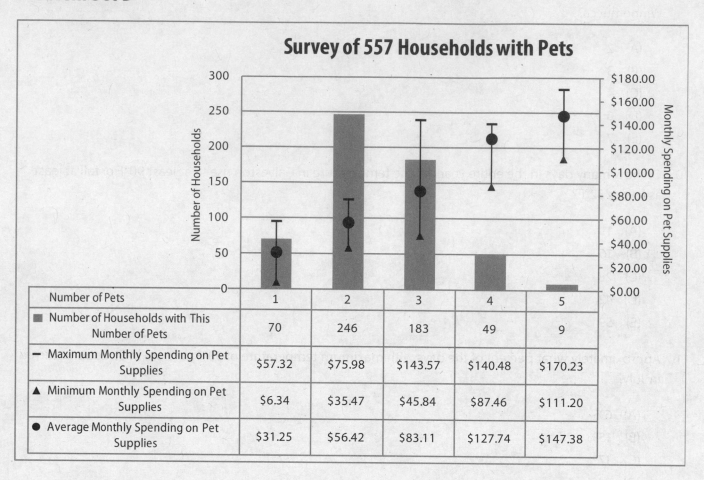

**Survey of 557 Households with Pets**

| Number of Pets | 1 | 2 | 3 | 4 | 5 |
|---|---|---|---|---|---|
| ■ Number of Households with This Number of Pets | 70 | 246 | 183 | 49 | 9 |
| — Maximum Monthly Spending on Pet Supplies | $57.32 | $75.98 | $143.57 | $140.48 | $170.23 |
| ▲ Minimum Monthly Spending on Pet Supplies | $6.34 | $35.47 | $45.84 | $87.46 | $111.20 |
| ● Average Monthly Spending on Pet Supplies | $31.25 | $56.42 | $83.11 | $127.74 | $147.38 |

13. Approximately what percent of the surveyed households have more than three pets?

    (A) 10%
    (B) 20%
    (C) 30%
    (D) 40%
    (E) 50%

14. Which of the following is the median number of pets owned by the households in the survey?

    (A) 1
    (B) 2
    (C) 3
    (D) 4
    (E) 5

**MANHATTAN**
PREP

15. What is the range of monthly spending on pet supplies for the household group with the largest such range?

    (A) $69.03

    (B) $97.73

    (C) $116.13

    (D) $138.98

    (E) $170.23

16. The household group with which number of pets had the greatest average (arithmetic mean) monthly spending per pet?

    (A) 1 pet

    (B) 2 pets

    (C) 3 pets

    (D) 4 pets

    (E) 5 pets

## Problem Set E

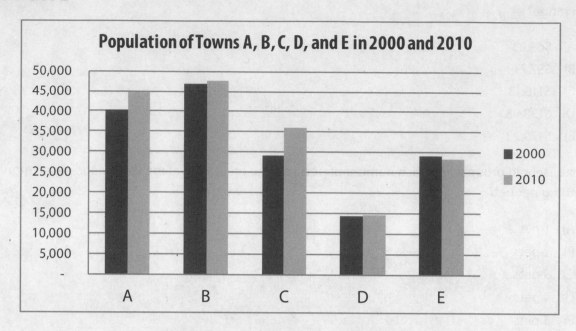

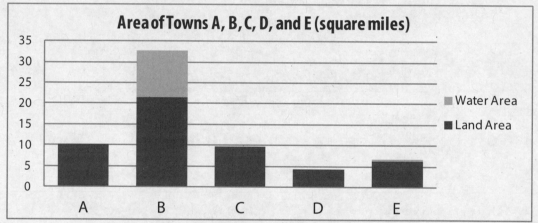

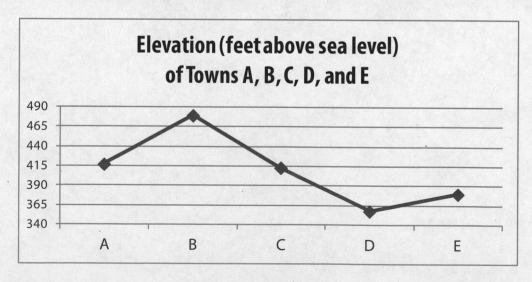

**MANHATTAN**
PREP

17. In what town did the population increase by the greatest percent between 2000 and 2010?

    (A) Town A
    (B) Town B
    (C) Town C
    (D) Town D
    (E) Town E

18. The water area of town B is most nearly equal the to the sum of the land areas of which two towns?

    Indicate <u>two</u> such towns.

    ☐ Town A
    ☐ Town B
    ☐ Town C
    ☐ Town D
    ☐ Town E

19. Which two towns have approximately the same elevation in feet above sea level?

    Indicate <u>two</u> such towns.

    ☐ Town A
    ☐ Town B
    ☐ Town C
    ☐ Town D
    ☐ Town E

## Problem Set F

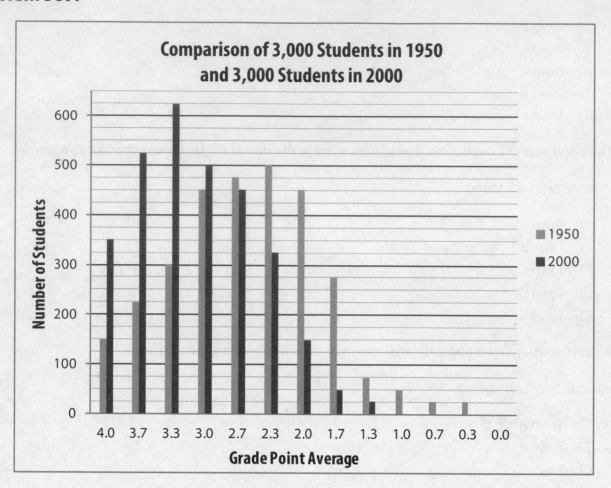

20. What was the mode for grade point average of the 3,000 students in 2000?

    (A)  3.7
    (B)  3.3
    (C)  3.0
    (D)  2.7
    (E)  2.3

21. What was the median grade point average of the 3,000 students in 1950?

    (A)  3.7
    (B)  3.3
    (C)  3.0
    (D)  2.7
    (E)  2.3

**MANHATTAN**
PREP

22. Approximately what percent of the students in 2000 earned at least a 3.0 grade point average?

    (A)  25%

    (B)  50%

    (C)  67%

    (D)  80%

    (E)  97.5%

23. Approximately what percent of the students in 1950 earned a grade point average less than 3.0?

    (A)  33%

    (B)  37.5%

    (C)  50%

    (D)  62.5%

    (E)  75%

## Problem Set G

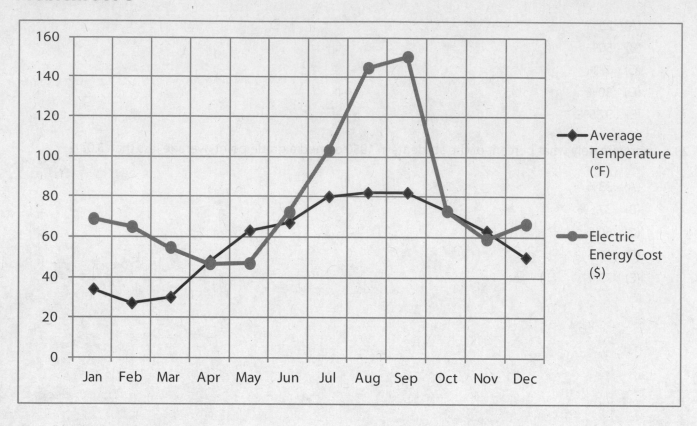

24. According to the chart, which two-month period had the greatest increase in electric energy cost?

    (A)  Between January and February
    (B)  Between May and June
    (C)  Between June and July
    (D)  Between July and August
    (E)  Between November and December

25. According to the chart, in which two-month period did electric energy cost increase the least?

    (A)  Between January and February
    (B)  Between April and May
    (C)  Between May and June
    (D)  Between June and July
    (E)  Between November and December

26. Approximately what was the average (arithmetic mean) electric energy cost per month for the first half of the year?

    (A)  $45
    (B)  $50
    (C)  $60
    (D)  $70
    (E)  $75

27. In which month was the electric energy cost per Fahrenheit degree (°F) of average temperature the least?

    (A)  April
    (B)  May
    (C)  October
    (D)  November
    (E)  December

# Problem Set H

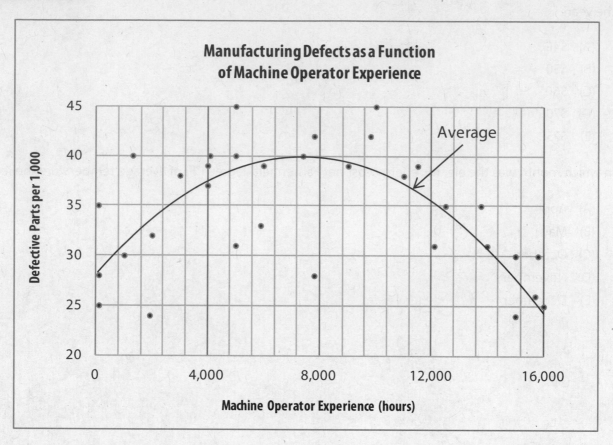

**Manufacturing Defects as a Function of Machine Operator Experience**

28. On average, the machine operators that produce the fewest defective parts per 1,000 have how many hours of experience?

    (A)  40
    (B)  4,000
    (C)  8,000
    (D)  12,000
    (E)  16,000

29. On average, the machine operators with approximately how many hours of experience have the same defective part rate as those with 12,000 hours of experience?

    (A)  2,000
    (B)  2,700
    (C)  4,400
    (D)  8,400
    (E)  12,800

**MANHATTAN**
PREP

30. On average, approximately how many hours of experience do machine operators who produce the most defective parts per 1,000 have?

    (A) 40
    (B) 4,000
    (C) 8,000
    (D) 12,000
    (E) 16,000

31. Of the individual machine operators who recorded a defective part rate of 4.2%, approximately how many hours of experience did the least experienced operator have?

    (A) 2,300
    (B) 5,000
    (C) 7,700
    (D) 9,800
    (E) 15,100

## Problem Set I

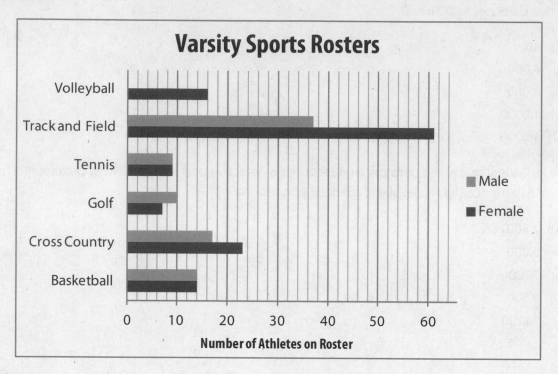

32. What is the ratio of male athletes to female athletes on the track and field roster?

    (A) $\dfrac{37}{61}$

    (B) $\dfrac{9}{14}$

    (C) $\dfrac{17}{23}$

    (D) $\dfrac{14}{9}$

    (E) $\dfrac{61}{37}$

33. All athletes are on only one varsity sports roster EXCEPT those who are on both the Track and Field team and the Cross Country team. If there are 76 male athletes in total on the varsity sports rosters, how many male athletes are on both the Track and Field team and the Cross Country team?

    (A) 11

    (B) 17

    (C) 37

    (D) 54

    (E) 76

**MANHATTAN**
PREP

34. On which varsity sports rosters do male athletes outnumber female athletes?

    Indicate <u>all</u> such rosters.

    ☐   Volleyball
    ☐   Track and Field
    ☐   Tennis
    ☐   Golf
    ☐   Cross Country
    ☐   Basketball

35. What is the ratio of female tennis players to male basketball players on the varsity sports rosters?

    (A)  $\dfrac{5}{12}$

    (B)  $\dfrac{9}{14}$

    (C)  $\dfrac{7}{8}$

    (D)  $\dfrac{14}{9}$

    (E)  $\dfrac{12}{5}$

## Problem Set J

| | Change in Total Revenue (2011–2012) | Percent Change in Number of Distinct Customers (2011–2012) | Percent Change in Total Costs (2011–2012) |
|---|---|---|---|
| **Store W** | −$400,000 | +2% | +15% |
| **Store X** | +$520,000 | +14% | +4% |
| **Store Y** | −$365,000 | +5% | +12% |
| **Store Z** | +$125,000 | −7% | −20% |

36. For which store was the revenue per distinct customer greatest in 2012?

    (A) Store W

    (B) Store X

    (C) Store Y

    (D) Store Z

    (E) It cannot be determined from the information given.

37. Between 2011 and 2012, total costs per distinct customer increased by the greatest percent at which store?

    (A) Store W

    (B) Store X

    (C) Store Y

    (D) Store Z

    (E) It cannot be determined from the information given.

38. At which of the following stores could the profit in 2012 have been less than that same store's profit in 2011?

Indicate <u>all</u> such stores.

    ☐ Store W

    ☐ Store X

    ☐ Store Y

    ☐ Store Z

    ☐ None of the above

**MANHATTAN**
PREP

39. Which of the following statements must be true?

    (A)  Of the four stores, store X had the greatest percent increase in revenue from 2011 to 2012.

    (B)  Per customer revenue increased at store Z from 2011 to 2012.

    (C)  Of the four stores, store W had the greatest increase in total costs from 2011 to 2012.

    (D)  Of the four stores, store Y had the highest percentage of repeat customers.

    (E)  In 2012, store W and store Z combined had fewer distinct customers than did store X.

## Problem Set K

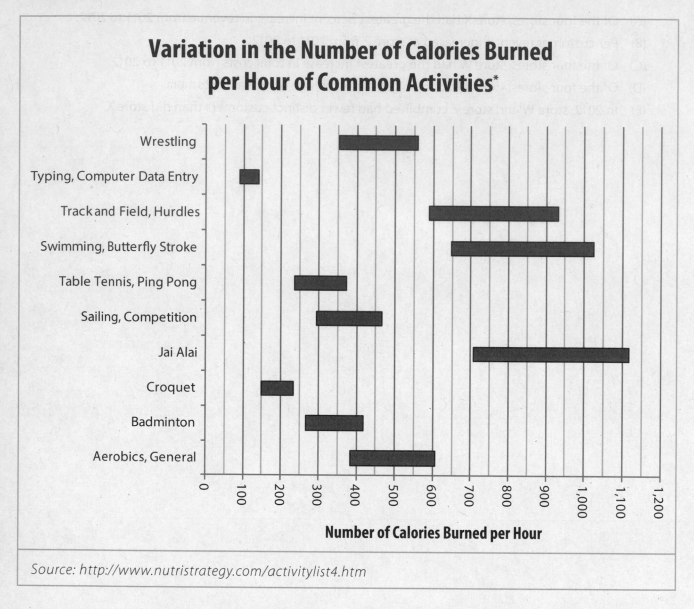

### Variation in the Number of Calories Burned per Hour of Common Activities*

Number of Calories Burned per Hour

Source: http://www.nutristrategy.com/activitylist4.htm

* Based on body weight of exercise subject. The lower limit represents the calories burned by a person weighing 130 pounds, while the upper limit represents the calories burned by a person weighing 205 pounds.

**MANHATTAN**
PREP

40. Which of the following statements could be true?

    Indicate all such statements.

    ☐ A person weighing between 130 and 205 pounds performs one of the above activities
      for 10 hours yet burns fewer calories than another person in the same weight range
      performing another activity for 1 hour.

    ☐ A 175-pound person playing jai alai for 1 hour burns fewer calories than a 180-pound
      person swimming the butterfly stroke for 1 hour.

    ☐ If all the people in question weigh between 130 and 205 pounds, the average calories
      burned by one person playing table tennis for 1 hour is more than the total calories
      burned by two people typing for 3 hours.

41. Which combination of activities burns the fewest calories total?

    (A) A 130-pound person playing badminton for 1 hour and a 205-pound person playing table
        tennis for 1 hour

    (B) A 130-pound person wrestling for 1 hour and a 205-pound person running track and field,
        hurdles for 1 hour

    (C) A 130-pound person typing for 1 hour and a 205-pound person swimming the butterfly
        stroke for 1 hour

    (D) A 130-pound person sailing in a competition for 1 hour and a 205-pound person doing
        aerobics for 1 hour

    (E) A 130-pound person typing for 1 hour and a 205-pound person playing croquet
        for 1 hour

# Problem Set L

| Population and GDP for 50 African Countries | | | | | | |
|---|---|---|---|---|---|---|
| | **Population** | | | | | |
| **Gross Domestic Product** | **More Than 50 Million** | **20–50 Million** | **10–20 Million** | **2–10 Million** | **Less Than 2 Million** | **Total** |
| **More Than $100 Billion** | 3 | 2 | 0 | 0 | 0 | 5 |
| **$20–100 Billion** | 1 | 7 | 1 | 1 | 0 | 10 |
| **$10–20 Billion** | 1 | 3 | 3 | 3 | 3 | 13 |
| **Less Than $10 Billion** | 0 | 0 | 7 | 8 | 7 | 22 |
| **Total** | 5 | 12 | 11 | 12 | 10 | 50 |

42. Among the 50 African countries represented in the chart above, how many countries have a population between 10 million and 50 million people and a GDP between $10 billion and $20 billion?

    (A)  6
    (B)  7
    (C)  13
    (D)  16
    (E)  23

43. Among the 50 African countries represented in the chart above, what percent of the countries have a population of less than 20 million people and a GDP of less than $20 billion?

    (A)  38%
    (B)  44%
    (C)  62%
    (D)  68%
    (E)  90%

**MANHATTAN**
PREP

44. Approximately what percent of the African countries in the chart above that have a GDP between $10 billion and $20 billion also have a population between 10 million and 20 million?

    (A)  6%
    (B)  23%
    (C)  26%
    (D)  30%
    (E)  51%

45. According to the chart above, which of the following is greatest?

    (A)  The number of countries with more than $10 billion of GDP and a population of less than 20 million
    (B)  The number of countries with less than $20 billion of GDP and a population of more than 10 million
    (C)  The number of countries with more than $20 billion of GDP
    (D)  The number of countries with less than $100 billion of GDP and a population of less than 10 million
    (E)  The number of countries with less than $100 billion of GDP and a population between 10 million and 50 million

## Problem Set M

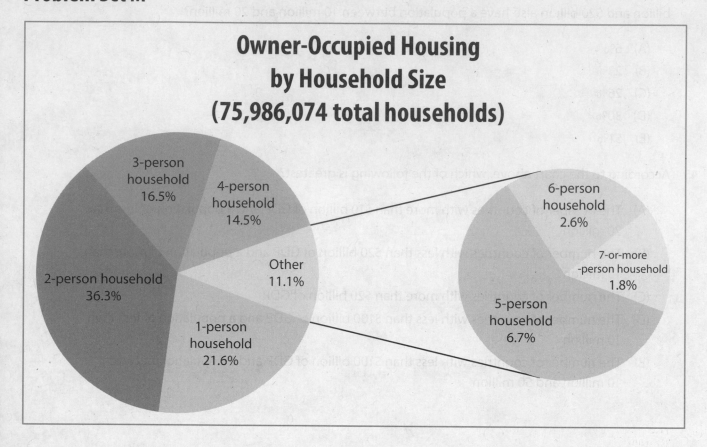

**Owner-Occupied Housing by Household Size (75,986,074 total households)**

46. What percent of owner-occupied housing units are households with fewer than four people?

    (A)  11.1%
    (B)  14.5%
    (C)  25.6%
    (D)  74.4%
    (E)  88.9%

47. Among the owner-occupied housing units represented in the chart above, approximately how many households are 5-person households?

    (A)  1 million
    (B)  2 million
    (C)  3 million
    (D)  4 million
    (E)  5 million

48. Based on the total number of people living in all such households, which of the following is a correct ordering, from least to greatest, of 1-person households, 3-person households, and 5-person households?

    (A)  1-person households, 3-person households, 5-person households
    (B)  1-person households, 5-person households, 3-person households
    (C)  3-person households, 1-person households, 5-person households
    (D)  3-person households, 5-person households, 1-person households
    (E)  5-person households, 3-person households, 1-person households

49. Which combination of household sizes accounts for more than 50% of all owner-occupied housing units?

    (A)  2- and 3-person
    (B)  3- and 4-person
    (C)  4- and 5-person
    (D)  5- and 6-person
    (E)  6- and 7-person

# Data Interpretation Answers

***Problem Set A:*** The title of the chart indicates that the total population is the total number of 9th graders at Mill-brook Middle School.

When given a chart that depends on addition (boys + girls = total students, and also those enrolled in Spanish + those not enrolled in Spanish = total students), it can be helpful to sketch a quick version of the chart and add a total column. For example:

|  | Boys | Girls | TOTAL |
|---|---|---|---|
| **Enrolled in Spanish** | 12 | 13 | |
| **Not Enrolled in Spanish** | 19 | 16 | |
| **TOTAL** | | | |

Now add down and across:

|  | Boys | Girls | TOTAL |
|---|---|---|---|
| **Enrolled in Spanish** | 12 | 13 | 25 |
| **Not Enrolled in Spanish** | 19 | 16 | 35 |
| **TOTAL** | 31 | 29 | 60 |

1. **(C).** There are 29 total girls and 13 are enrolled in Spanish. The fraction of girls enrolled in Spanish is $\frac{13}{29}$.

Convert to a percent: $\left(\frac{13}{29} \times 100\right)\% = 44.827...\%$, or about 45%.

2. **(A).** There are 60 total students and 12 boys enrolled in Spanish. The answer is $\frac{12}{60}$, which reduces to $\frac{1}{5}$. (Read carefully! "What fraction of the students … are boys who are enrolled in Spanish?" is *not* the same as "What fraction of the boys are enrolled in Spanish?")

3. **(C).** There are 16 girls not enrolled in Spanish and 60 total students. The ratio is $\frac{16}{60}$, which reduces to $\frac{4}{15}$ or 4 : 15.

4. **(D).** There are 35 students not enrolled in Spanish and 25 who are. The question can be rephrased as, "35 is what percent greater than 25?" Using the percent change formula:

$$\text{Percent Change} = \left(\frac{Difference}{Original} \times 100\right)\%$$

$$\text{Percent Change} = \left(\frac{10}{25} \times 100\right)\% = 40\%$$

Thus, *x* is 40.

**5. (E).** Sketch a new chart to reflect the changes. Switch 2 of the boys from "not enrolled" to "enrolled." Then, add 8 new girls and 7 new boys to the "enrolled" groups:

|  | Boys | Girls | TOTAL |
|---|---|---|---|
| **Enrolled in Spanish** | 12 + 2 + 7 = 21 | 13 + 8 = 21 | 42 |
| **Not Enrolled in Spanish** | 19 − 2 = 17 | 16 | 33 |
| **TOTAL** | 38 | 37 | 75 |

Update the Total rows and columns as well. Both "Boys" and "Girls," as well as "Enrolled in Spanish" and "Not Enrolled in Spanish," now sum to 75.

What percent of 9th grade students at Millbrook would then be taking Spanish? Since 42 out of 75 students would be enrolled in Spanish, calculate $\frac{42}{75}$ (with the calculator) and multiply by 100 to convert it to a percent. The answer is 56%.

***Problem Set B:*** This chart shows the frequency with which certain values—numbers of hours worked per week—appear. That is, the chart is a short way of showing a list of values that would begin: 15, 15, 15, 15, 25, 25, 25, 25, 25, 25, 25, 25, 25... (then the number 35 fifteen times, then the number 40 twenty-seven times, then the number 50 five times). Add the numbers in the left-hand column to determine that the total workforce is 60 people.

**6. (E).** The median of any list is the middle number, if there is an odd number of terms, or the average of the two middle numbers, if there is an even number of terms. However, here the median number of hours worked per week is not the middle number in the list 15, 25, 35, 40, 50 because this does not account for the frequency with which each of those numbers occurs. The actual list includes the value 15 four times (once for each of the 4 employees who works 15 hours per week), the value 25 nine times (once for each of the 9 employees who works 25 hours per week), and so on.

There are 60 employees. Thus, the middle of this list is the average of the 30th and 31st values. Since 4 + 9 + 15 = 28, the 30th and 31st values fall into the next highest group—the group of 27 people who work 40 hours per week. The median number of hours worked per week per employee is 40.

**7. (D).** The average number of hours worked per week is not the average of 15, 25, 35, 40, and 50. The calculation must account for how many people work each number of hours:

$$\frac{4(15)+9(25)+15(35)+27(40)+5(50)}{60} = 35.\overline{6} \text{ hours}$$

The answer is $35.\overline{6}$ or $35\frac{2}{3}$.

**8. (C).** The mode is the number that appears in the list with the greatest frequency. Since 27 people worked 40 hours a week and every other group has fewer than 27 people, the mode is 40. The range is the highest value in the list minus the lowest value in the list: 50 − 15 = 35. The positive difference between 40 and 35 is 40 − 35 = 5.

**Problem Set C:** The two charts show how often daily temperature extremes occurred in each month of the year for three cities. For the sake of simplicity, you can think of the top chart as "cold" and the bottom chart as "hot."

Note that there is no information about exactly how hot or how cold the days tallied are: a day with a minimum temperature of 27°F counts as a "cold" day, just as a day with minimum temperature of −10°F would. Therefore, it is likely that questions will just reference one or both of the two temperature categories broadly (≥ 90 and ≤ 32).

9. **(D).** From the "cold" chart, the black bar referring to Winnemucca rises above 20 in Jan, Feb, Mar, Oct, Nov, and Dec, for a total of 6 months.

10. **(B).** This question asks about number of days with both temperature extremes in Galveston. Galveston had 1 "hot" day in June, 4 in July, 5 in August, and 2 in September, for a total of 12. It had 2 "cold" days in January and 1 each in February and December, for a total of 4. The total number of days with either extreme temperature is 16 days.

11. **(D).** From the grey bars on the "hot" day chart, St. Louis had a total of $1 + 8 + 15 + 12 + 4 + 4 = 44$ days when the temperature reached at least 90°F, and 15 of those were in July. These July days account for $\left(\frac{15}{44} \times 100\right)\% \approx 34\%$ of all the hot days in St. Louis (approximately).

12. **(C).** In January, Winnemucca had 28 freezing days, while St. Louis had 25. So the question is asking, "28 is what percent more than 25?" Use the percent change formula: $\left(\frac{Difference}{Original} \times 100\right)\% = \left(\frac{3}{25} \times 100\right)\% = 12\%$.

**Problem Set D:** This table tallies the number of households, according to number of pets in the household, and each column captures information about these households. For example, the left most column with numbers indicates that there are 70 households that have one pet, and these households spend an average of $31.25 per month on pet supplies. In that group, the households that spent the least spent $6.34 on pet supplies, while the households that spent the most spent $57.32. Notice that the bars and the max/min/average range lines duplicate the information in the table. For exact calculations, rely on the chart numbers. For broader questions, such as "which is greater," the more visual representation of the data can often provide a quick answer.

13. **(A).** There are 557 households, of which 49 have four pets and 9 have five pets. Thus, a total of 58 households have more than three pets. To express this as a percent, divide this number by the total number of households:

$$\frac{58}{557} \approx 10\%$$

14. **(B).** Since there are 557 households, the median household would be midway between the 1st and 557th households on the list if the households are ranked by how many pets they own. The midpoint between the 1st and 557th households is the $\frac{(1+557)}{2} = 279$th household. Check: There are 278 households below this one, and 278 households above (because 279 + 278 = 557). Ranked by number of pets, households 1 through 70 (the first 70 households) have one pet, which means households 71 through 316 (in other words, the next 246 households) have two pets. Since the 279th household falls in this interval, the median household owns two pets.

15. **(B).** The group with the largest range of monthly spending is the group of households that own three pets. This can be seen by looking at the length of the vertical line between the maximum spending bar and the minimum spending triangle. Within this group, the maximum amount spent is $143.57 and the minimum is $45.84, so the range is $143.57 − $45.84 = $97.73.

16. **(D).** The group with one pet spent an average of $31.25 per pet, as indicated in the chart. The group with two pets spent an average of $56.42 on two pets, which is $28.21 per pet $\left(\dfrac{\$56.42}{2}\right)$. The 3rd group spent an average of $83.11 on three pets, or $\dfrac{\$83.11}{3}$ = $27.70 per pet (approximately). The 4th group spent an average of $127.74 on four pets, or $\dfrac{\$127.74}{4}$ = $31.94 per pet (approximately). The 5th group spent an average of $147.38 on five pets, or $\dfrac{\$147.38}{5}$ = $29.47 per pet (approximately). The highest average is among the group that has four pets.

**Problem Set E:** The three charts give information about the same five towns A, B, C, D, and E: population (2000 and 2010), area (water and land, given in square miles), and elevation (in feet above sea level).

17. **(C).** The difference in population between 2000 and 2010 is the difference in the heights of the dark- and light-gray bars in the population bar chart. Population decreased in town E, and barely changed in towns B and D. Thus towns *A* and *C* remain. The difference is about 5,000 for town A (45,000 − 40,000), but more than 5,000 for town C (more than 35,000—less than 30,000). The question asks for the town with greatest percent increase in population, so use the percent change formula: Percent Change = $\left(\dfrac{\text{Difference}}{\text{Original}} \times 100\right)\%$. Not only is the population increase greatest for town C, the population of town C is smaller than for town A. The percent increase in population for town A was $\left(\dfrac{5,000}{40,000} \times 100\right)\% = 12.5\%$, but the percent increase in population for town C was about $\left(\dfrac{7,000}{29,000} \times 100\right)\% \approx 24\%$.

18. **Town D and Town E only.** In the bar chart for area, dark gray represents the land area and light gray (stacked on top) represents the water area. Thus, to find water area, subtract the height of the dark-gray land area bar from the total height of the stacked bars.

Water area of town B is about 32− 21 = 11, although the vertical scale is admittedly not that precise. Water area for town B is a little more than 10, since the top of the dark-gray bar is slightly *closer* to the horizontal line for 20 than the top of the light-gray bar is to the horizontal line for 30. Similarly, water area for town B must be less than 12.5, as the top of the light-gray bar is halfway between 30 and 35, but the top of the dark-gray bar is clearly higher than 20.

Towns C, D, and E all have land area less than 10 square miles (i.e. all are below horizontal grid line for 10). Adding the land area of town C (a bit less than 10) to that of town D (about 4), the result is too high. The sum of land area in towns D and E is about 4 + about 6 (certainly less than 7.5), for a result closest to 11.

19. **Town A and Town C only.** In the elevation chart, the towns are on the *x*-axis and the elevation (in feet above sea level) is on the *y*-axis. Two towns have the same elevation if marked at the same *y* value, that is, if their data points are on the same horizontal line. Towns A and C are both close to the horizontal line for 415.

*Problem Set F:* The dark gray bars indicate the number of students with various grade point averages in 2000, and the light gray bars indicate number of students in the same categories in 1950. The title states that the surveys consist of 3,000 students.

Note the general contrast between students in the two years. Connecting the top of each light gray bar with a smooth line, the result would be a sort-of bell curve that peaks at grade point average of 2.3. Similarly, the dark gray bars form a similar bell curve, but its peak is at grade point average of 3.3, so the grades in general are clustered at the higher end of the scale in 2000.

20. **(B).** The mode of a list of numbers is the number that occurs most frequently in the list. In the bar graph for grade point average, dark gray bars represent the students in 2000, and the mode of that dataset is indicated by the tallest dark gray bar. This is at grade point average of 3.3. There were 625 students with a grade point average of 3.3 in the year 2000.

21. **(D).** The median is the middle value of an ordered list of numbers. For the 3,000 students in 1950, the median grade point average is the average of the 1,500th highest grade point average and the 1,501st highest grade point average. The students in 1950 are represented by the light gray bars. From the chart, you know the following:

> 150 students had a 4.0 grade point average.
> 225 students had a 3.7 grade point average. (Total with this GPA and higher = 150 + 225 = 375)
> 300 students had a 3.3 grade point average. (Total with this GPA and higher = 375 + 300 = 675)
> 450 students had a 3.0 grade point average. (Total with this GPA and higher = 675 + 450 = 1,125)
> 475 students had a 2.7 grade point average. (Total with this GPA and higher = 1,125 + 475 = 1,600)

The 1,500th and 1,501st students fall between the 1,125th and 1,600th students. Thus, the 1,500th and 1,501st highest grade point averages are both 2.7.

22. **(C).** The students in 2000 are represented by the dark gray bars:

> 350 students had a 4.0 grade point average.
> 525 students had a 3.7 grade point average.
> 625 students had a 3.3 grade point average.
> 500 students had a 3.0 grade point average.

There were 350 + 525 + 625 + 500 = 2,000 students who earned at least a 3.0 grade point average in the year 2000, out of a total of 3,000 students. This is $\frac{2}{3}$ of the students, or about 67% of the students.

23. **(D).** The students in 1950 are represented by the light gray bars:

> 150 students had a 4.0 grade point average.
> 225 students had a 3.7 grade point average.
> 300 students had a 3.3 grade point average.
> 450 students had a 3.0 grade point average.

**MANHATTAN**
PREP

In 1950, $150 + 225 + 300 + 450 = 1{,}125$ students had a grade point average of 3.0 or higher. Thus, $3{,}000 - 1{,}125 = 1{,}875$ students earned a grade point average *less than* 3.0. As a percent of the class, this is equal to $\left( \dfrac{1{,}875}{3{,}000} \times 100 \right) \% = 62.5\%$.

***Problem Set G:*** The vertical number scale on the left side of the graph applies to both datasets, but for Average Temperature the units are °F and for Electric Energy Cost the units are dollars (\$). For example, in January the average temperature was between 30°F and 40°F and the electric energy cost was about \$70. Be careful to read data from the correct set.

**24. (D).** Electric energy cost is represented by the light gray line and circular data points. A cost increase from one month to the next would mean a positive slope for the line segment between the two circular data points. The greater the slope of the light gray line segment, the greater the cost increase between those two months. There was an increase each month between May and September, and again between November and December. But the steepest positive slope is between July and August.

The cost increase from July to August was approximately $\$145 - \$103 = \$42$. For comparison, the cost increase from June to July was only about $\$103 - \$70 = \$33$. The correct answer is between July and August.

**25. (B).** Electric energy cost is represented by the light gray line and circular data points. A cost increase from one month to the next would mean a positive slope for the line segment between the two data points, and a cost decrease would mean a negative slope. The steeper the slope of the line segment, the greater the cost change between two consecutive months. A cost change of \$0 would mean the line segment has a slope of 0 (i.e., it is horizontal).

To find the two consecutive months with the smallest electric energy cost change, look for the light gray line segment that is most horizontal. The line segment between April and May is nearly horizontal. The correct answer is between April and May.

**26. (C).** There are two ways to approximate average electric energy cost per month in the first half of the year.

One way is to use the electric energy costs on the chart and compute the average for the first six months, using the light gray circular data points:

$$\text{Approximate average cost} = \frac{\$70 + \$65 + \$55 + \$47 + \$47 + \$70}{6} = \frac{\$354}{6} = \$59$$

Answer choice (C) \$60 is closest.

The other method is more visual. Consider choice (A), \$45, and imagine a horizontal line at \$45. All six cost data points for the first half of the year are above this horizontal line, so the average must be more than \$45. Similarly, imagine a horizontal line at \$75 for choice (E). All six cost data points for the first half of the year are below this horizontal line, so the average must be less than \$75. When a horizontal line at \$60 is considered, the six cost data points "balance": three are above the line and three are below, by approximately the same amount.

27. **(B).** To minimize $\dfrac{\text{Electric Energy Cost (\$)}}{\text{Average Temperature (°F)}}$, minimize cost (light gray circular data points) while maximizing average temperature (black diamond data points). Only in April, May, October, and November is the black data point equal to or greater than the gray data point (i.e., the $\dfrac{\text{Electric Energy Cost (\$)}}{\text{Average Temperature (°F)}}$ ratio is equal to or less than 1). In April, October, and November, this ratio is close to 1. In May, the difference between the cost and the average temperature is greatest, so the electric energy cost per °F of average temperature is least. The correct answer is May.

***Problem Set H:*** The chart shows defective parts per 1,000 as a function of machine operator experience. The dots indicate individual machine operators, and there is quite a bit of variance by individual. The line labeled "Average" shows the average performance of the group as a whole. A trend emerges: inexperienced machine operators and very experienced machine operators make fewer mistakes than those with medium level of experience. Also, certain individual machine operators produce defective parts at a lower rate than others with similar levels of experience.

28. **(E).** Because the question specifies "on average," refer to the curve marked "Average" rather than the individual data points. At the lowest point on this average curve, operators with 16,000 hours of experience produce slightly fewer than 25 defective parts per 1,000. Another low point is for operators with minimal experience, but even they produce between 25 and 30 defective parts per 1,000. In contrast, the defective part rate is maximized at the top of the curve: operators with 8,000 hours of experience produce about 40 defective parts per 1,000.

29. **(B).** Because the question specifies "on average," refer to the curve marked "Average" rather than the individual data points. Machine operators with 12,000 hours of experience produce an average of about 36 defective parts per 1,000.

The other group of machine operators that produces about 36 defective parts per 1,000 has a little less than 3,200 hours of experience. (Note that there are 5 grid lines for every 4,000 hours, so each vertical grid line is 800 hours apart. The grid mark to the left of the 4,000 mark represents $4,000 - 800 = 3,200$ hours.) Choice (B) is close to and less than 3,200.

Alternatively, check the average defective part rate for machine operators with the hours of experience listed in the choices:

    (A) 2,000 hours (around 33 or 34 defective parts per 1,000)
    (B) 2,700 hours (a bit over 35 defective parts per 1,000) CORRECT.
    (C) 4,400 hours (around 38 defective parts per 1,000)
    (D) 8,400 hours (a bit less than 40 defective parts per 1,000)
    (E) 12,800 (around 34 defective parts per 1,000)

30. **(C).** Because the question specifies "on average," refer to the curve marked "Average" rather than the individual data points. The defective part rate is maximized at the top of the curve: operators with 8,000 hours of experience produce about 40 defective parts per 1,000.

31. **(C).** Because the question refers to "individual machine operators," refer to the individual data points rather than the curve marked "Average."

A defective part rate of 4.2% equates to $\frac{4.2}{100} \times 1,000 = 42$ defective parts per 1,000. The chart has only two data points at approximately 42 defective parts per 1,000. The less experienced of these two machine operators had just under 8,000 hours of experience.

**Problem Set I:** Note that there are five vertical grid lines for every 10 athletes, so each vertical grid line accounts for 2 people.

32. **(A).** On the Track and Field roster, there are between 36 and 38 men (therefore 37) represented by the light gray bar. On the Track and Field roster, there are between 60 and 62 women (therefore 61) represented by the dark gray bar. In fraction form, the "ratio of men to women" is $\frac{\text{men}}{\text{women}}$. The correct answer is $\frac{37}{61}$.

33. **(A).** Male athletes are represented by the light gray bars for each sport. Sum the male athletes on each of the separate varsity sports rosters:

> Males on Volleyball roster: 0
> Males on Track and Field roster: between 36 and 38 (therefore 37)
> Males on Tennis roster: between 8 and 10 (therefore 9)
> Males on Golf roster: 10
> Males on Cross Country roster: between 16 and 18 (therefore 17)
> Males on Basketball roster: 14

There are $0 + 37 + 9 + 10 + 17 + 14 = 87$ male names on all of the rosters combined, but there are only 76 male athletes total. Since tennis, golf, and basketball players are all on only one roster, there must be $87 - 76 = 11$ male athletes who are counted twice, on both the Track and Field team and the Cross Country team. The correct answer is 11.

34. **Golf only.** Male athletes are represented by the light gray bars, female athletes by the dark gray bars. A sport in which male athletes outnumber female athletes will have a shorter dark gray bar than light gray bar.

This is only the case for Golf; there are 10 male athletes and 7 female athletes. Volleyball only has female athletes, so they outnumber the zero male athletes on the roster. In Tennis and Basketball, there are equal numbers of men and women. Female athletes outnumber male athletes on the Cross Country and Track and Field rosters.

35. **(B).** There are between 8 and 10 female tennis players (therefore 9) represented by the dark gray bar. There are 14 male basketball players represented by the light gray bar. In fraction form, the "ratio of female tennis players to male basketball players" is $\frac{\text{female tennis players}}{\text{male basketball players}}$. Thus, the answer is $\frac{9}{14}$.

**Problem Set J:** This chart compares four stores, providing information about change from 2011 to 2012 in three metrics: total revenue, number of distinct customers, and total costs. It is essential to note that change in total revenue is given in terms of dollars, whereas changes in number of distinct customers and in total costs are given only in percentages. In general, percents provide less information than absolute numbers, as the total (i.e., percent of what?) is needed for context.

36. **(E).** It may be tempting to select store Z, as revenue increased from 2011 to 2012 while the number of distinct customers decreased, but be careful when mixing absolute numbers and percents. Without knowing the revenue in 2012 (only the change from the previous year is known) or the number of customers (only the percent change from the previous year is known) for any of the stores, it cannot be determined from the information given.

37. **(A).** Because the question concerns costs per customer, given in percent change terms in the chart, and the question asks about percent change for this ratio, a comparison can be made among the stores.

The percent change formula in general is $\left( \dfrac{\text{Difference}}{\text{Original}} \times 100 \right)\%$. Thus, the percent change in total costs per distinct customer at a particular store is:

$$\left( \frac{\dfrac{\text{cost}_{2012}}{\text{customer}_{2012}} - \dfrac{\text{cost}_{2011}}{\text{customer}_{2011}}}{\dfrac{\text{cost}_{2011}}{\text{customer}_{2011}}} \times 100 \right)\%$$

This looks like a mess, but remember that both $\text{cost}_{2012}$ and $\text{customer}_{2012}$ can be written in terms of $\text{cost}_{2011}$ and $\text{customer}_{2011}$, respectively, based on the percent changes given in the table. Then $\text{cost}_{2011}$ and $\text{customer}_{2011}$ are in each term of the fraction and can be canceled. For example, for store W, the percent change in total costs per distinct customer is:

$$\left( \frac{\dfrac{1.15 \times \text{cost}_{2011}}{1.02 \times \text{customer}_{2011}} - \dfrac{\text{cost}_{2011}}{\text{customer}_{2011}}}{\dfrac{\text{cost}_{2011}}{\text{customer}_{2011}}} \times 100 \right)\% = \left( \frac{\dfrac{1.15}{1.02} - 1}{1} \times 100 \right)\% = \left( \left( \frac{1.15}{1.02} - 1 \right) \times 100 \right)\%$$

In other words, the magnitude of percent change in total costs per distinct customer depends only on the ratio of (1 + Percent change in total costs) to (1 + Percent change in number of distinct customers). Perform this comparison for all of the stores:

(A) Store W: $\dfrac{1.15}{1.02} = 1.12745$ *Greatest.*

(B) Store X: $\dfrac{1.04}{1.14} = 0.91228$

(C) Store Y: $\dfrac{1.12}{1.05} = 1.06667$

(D) Store Z: $\dfrac{0.80}{0.93} = 0.86022$

**MANHATTAN**
PREP

38. **Store W, Store X, and Store Y only.** Profit = Revenue − Cost.

Store W: Revenue decreased by $400,000, and costs increased by 15%. Both changes negatively affect profit. CORRECT.

Store X: Revenue increased by $520,000, but costs also increased by 4%. Profit in 2012 could be greater than, less than, or equal to profit in 2011, depending on the store's cost structure. Try sample numbers to show that profit could have decreased. If in 2011, revenue was $20,000,000 and costs were $15,000,000, the profit was $5,000,000. In 2012, revenue would be $20,520,000 and costs $15,600,000, making profit $4,920,000, less than in the previous year. CORRECT.

Store Y: Revenue decreased by $365,000, and costs increased by 12%. Both changes negatively affect profit. CORRECT.

Store Z: Revenue increased by $125,000 and costs decreased by 20%. Both changes positively affect profit.

39. **(B).** Consider each statement individually:

(A) While store X had the greatest increase in revenue, in dollars, it is impossible to calculate percent change in revenue $\left( \dfrac{\text{Difference}}{\text{Original}} \times 100 \right)$% for any of the stores without information about the actual dollar amount of their revenue in either year. Not necessarily true.

(B) Per customer revenue is $\dfrac{\text{Revenue}}{\text{Number of customers}}$. Store Z experienced an increase in revenue and a decrease in number of distinct customers, both of which increase per customer revenue. TRUE.

(C) While store W had the greatest percent increase in total costs, it is impossible to say whether this was the greatest increase in dollars without knowing the actual dollar amount of total costs for each of the stores that experienced a cost increase. Not necessarily true.

(D) The chart says nothing about repeat customers, only "distinct" customers. Not necessarily true.

(E) The chart says nothing about absolute numbers of distinct customers at any of the stores, only percent change from 2011 to 2012. Not necessarily true.

**Problem Set K:** Much of the detail in this chart is given in the title and other text. According to the title and the * note below, the chart shows the range of calories burned per hour by people in the 130- to 205-pound weight range in the course of performing various activities.

40. **First and second statements only.** Consider each statement individually.

The first statement could be true. A 130-pound person typing for 10 hours would burn less than 1,000 calories, which is less than the number of calories burned by a 205-pound person doing one of several activities on the chart for 1 hour (certainly jai alai and swimming the butterfly stroke burn more than 1,000 calories).

The second statement could be true. In general, the range of calories burned per hour is greater for jai alai than for swimming the butterfly stroke. The people in question are about the same weight, but it cannot be assumed that the number of calories burned is a function of weight in this range or that the relationship is linear. All that matters is that the calorie burning ranges for the two activities overlap, and both people fall in the weight range, so it could be true that a 175-pound person playing jai alai for 1 hour burns fewer calories than a 180-pound person swimming the butterfly stroke for 1 hour.

The third statement must be false. The average calories burned by one person playing table tennis for 1 hour is a maximum of about 375. Two people typing for 3 hours burn as many calories total as one person typing for $2 \times 3 = 6$ hours, which is a minimum of about 550. "At most 375" cannot be greater than "at least 550."

41. **(E).** For each combination of activities, look at the minimum value on the chart for the 130-pound person and the maximum value on the chart for the 205-pound person:

(A) Badminton (minimum) + Table tennis (maximum) = 275 + 375 = 650
(B) Wrestling (minimum) + Track and field, hurdles (maximum) = 350 + 925 = 1,275
(C) Typing (minimum) + Swimming, butterfly stroke (maximum) = under 100 + 1025 = under 1,125
(D) Sailing, competition (minimum) + Aerobics (maximum) = 300 + 600 = 900
(E) Typing (minimum) + Croquet (maximum) = under 100 + over 225 = about 325 CORRECT.

Alternatively, note that typing and croquet are the two activities that burn the fewest calories per hour overall. A 130 pound person and a 205-pound person each doing 1 hour of an activity shown on the chart would only burn fewer calories total if both people were typing.

**Problem Set L:** The table categorizes 50 African countries according to GDP (rows) and population (columns). Notice that each row sums to a subtotal number of countries in that GDP range, and each column sums to a subtotal number of countries in that population range. Both the subtotal row and subtotal column sum to 50, the grand total. Moreover, notice that both population and GDP are shown in descending order: high population/high GDP countries are in the upper left corner of the table, while low population/low GDP countries are in the lower right corner of the table.

42. **(A).** GDP between $10 billion and $20 billion is a single row in the table. Population between 10–50 million people includes two columns in the table. Look at the intersections between this row and two columns. There are three countries with populations of 10–20 million and GDPs of $10 billion to $20 billion. There are also three countries with populations of 20–50 million and GDPs of $10 billion to $20 billion GDP, for a total of six countries.

43. **(C).** Adding the entries that are in both the bottom two rows (less than $20 billion GDP) and the last three columns (population less than 20 million), the number of countries is $3 + 3 + 3 + 7 + 8 + 7 = 31$. Out of 50 countries, 31 fit this description, so the percent is $\left(\frac{31}{50} \times 100\right)\%$, or 62%.

44. **(B).** There are 13 countries with GDPs between $10–$20 billion, and of these, 3 have populations between 10–20 million. Thus, the percent is $\left(\frac{3}{13} \times 100\right)\%$, or approximately 23%.

45. **(D).** For each choice, carefully find the row(s)/column(s) that fit the description, and sum all table entries that apply.

(A) More than $10 billion GDP (the top three rows) and a population of less than 20 million (the three columns on right, before the subtotal column): $0 + 0 + 0 + 1 + 1 + 0 + 3 + 3 + 3 = 11$

(B) Less than $20 billion GDP (the bottom two rows above the subtotal row) and a population of more than 10 million (the three columns on left): $1 + 3 + 3 + 0 + 0 + 7 = 14$

(C) More than $20 billion GDP (the entire top two rows): $5 + 10 = 15$

(D) Less than $100 billion GDP (the bottom three rows above the subtotal row) and a population of less than 10 million (the two columns on the right before the subtotal column): $1 + 0 + 3 + 3 + 8 + 7 = 22$

(E) Less than $100 billion GDP (the bottom three rows above the subtotal row) and a population between 10–50 million (the second and third columns): $7 + 1 + 3 + 3 + 0 + 7 = 21$ *Greatest.*

Choice (D), 22, is the greatest.

***Problem Set M:*** This pie chart represents about 76 million owner-occupied housing units, categorized by household population. The smaller pie chart on the right further subdivides the households with at least 5 people. These categories could have been shown as small slivers in the pie chart on the left in the "Other" slice (notice that 6.7% + 2.6% + 1.8% = 11.1%).

46. **(D).** Sum the households with one, two, or three people (i.e., "fewer than four people"). Together these account for 21.6% + 36.3% + 16.5% = 74.4% of the total.

47. **(E).** According to the chart, 6.7% of the 75,986,074 households are 5-person households. Multiply 0.067 by 76 (keep "million" in mind). The result is about 5, so the answer is 5 million households.

48. **(B).** Approximate the total number of households as 76 million (close enough to 75,986,074).

One-person households are 21.6% of the total, or approximately 16.4 million. Since each such household has only one person, this represents about 16.4 million people.

Three-person households are 16.5% of the total, or approximately 12.5 million. Since each of these households has three people, that is about 37.5 million people.

Five-person households are 6.7% of the total, or approximately 5.1 million. Since each of these households has five people, that is about 25.5 million people.

Since 16.4 million < 25.5 million < 37.5 million, the correct ranking is 1-person households, 5-person households, 3-person households.

49. **(A).** The 2- and 3-person households account for 36.3% + 16.5% = 52.8% of all households, so this is the correct answer. Quickly rule out the other choices as a check:

(B) The 3- and 4-person households account for 16.5% + 14.5% = 31.0% of all households.

(C) The 4- and 5-person households account for 14.5% + 6.7% = 21.2% of all households.

(D) The 5- and 6-person households account for 6.7% + 2.6% = 9.3% of all households.

(E) The 6- and 7-person households account for at most 2.6% + 1.8% = at most 4.4% of all households (remember that some of the 1.8% could consist of households with more than 7 people).

All of the choices other than (A) are less than 50%.

# Chapter *of* 25

5 lb. Book of GRE® Practice Problems

# Polygons and Rectangular Solids

# In This Chapter...

Polygons and Rectangular Solids

Polygons and Rectangular Solids Answers

# Polygons and Rectangular Solids

For questions in the Quantitative Comparison format ("Quantity A" and "Quantity B" given), the answer choices are always as follows:

(A)   Quantity A is greater.
(B)   Quantity B is greater.
(C)   The two quantities are equal.
(D)   The relationship cannot be determined from the information given.

For questions followed by a numeric entry box [    ], you are to enter your own answer in the box. For questions followed

by a fraction-style numeric entry box $\frac{\quad}{\quad}$, you are to enter your answer in the form of a fraction. You are not required to

reduce fractions. For example, if the answer is $\frac{1}{4}$, you may enter $\frac{25}{100}$ or any equivalent fraction.

All numbers used are real numbers. All figures are assumed to lie in a plane unless otherwise indicated. Geometric figures are not necessarily drawn to scale. You should assume, however, that lines that appear to be straight are actually straight, points on a line are in the order shown, and all geometric objects are in the relative positions shown. Coordinate systems, such as *xy*-planes and number lines, as well as graphical data presentations, such as bar charts, circle graphs, and line graphs, *are* drawn to scale. A symbol that appears more than once in a question has the same meaning throughout the question.

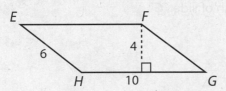

1.   What is the area of parallelogram *EFGH*?

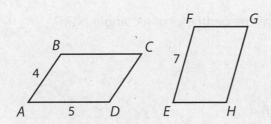

2.   The two parallelograms pictured above have the same perimeter. What is the length of side *EH*?

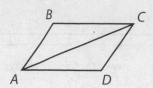

3.   In parallelogram *ABCD*, triangle *ABC* has an area of 12. What is the area of triangle *ACD*?

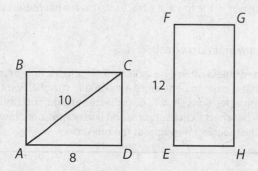

4.   Rectangles *ABCD* and *EFGH* have equal areas. What is the length of side *FG*?

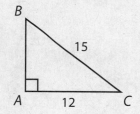

5.   Triangle *ABC* and rectangle *JKLM* have equal areas. What is the perimeter of rectangle *JKLM*?

<table>
<tr><td>**Quantity A**</td><td>**Quantity B**</td></tr>
</table>

6.   The area of a rectangle with          30
     perimeter 20

7.    What is the area of a square with a diagonal measuring $6\sqrt{2}$ ?

| |
|---|

|  | **Quantity A** | **Quantity B** |
|---|---|---|
| 8. | The area of a parallelogram with a base of length 4 and height of 3.5 | The area of a trapezoid with two parallel sides of lengths 5 and 9 and a height of 2 |

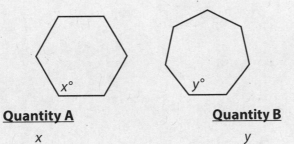

|  | **Quantity A** | **Quantity B** |
|---|---|---|
| 9. | $x$ | $y$ |

The perimeter of square $W$ is 50% of the perimeter of square $D$.

|  | **Quantity A** | **Quantity B** |
|---|---|---|
| 10. | The ratio of the area of square $W$ to the area of square $D$ | $\dfrac{1}{4}$ |

11.   A 10-inch by 15-inch rectangular picture is displayed in a 16-inch by 24-inch rectangular frame. What is the area, in inches, of the part of the frame not covered by the picture?

    (A)   150
    (B)   234
    (C)   244
    (D)   264
    (E)   384

A rectangular box has edges of length 2, 3, and 4.

|  | **Quantity A** | **Quantity B** |
|---|---|---|
| 12. | Twice the volume of the box | The surface area of the box |

13. What is the maximum number of 2-inch by 2-inch by 2-inch solid cubes that can be cut from six solid cubes that are 1 foot on each side? (12 inches = 1 foot)

(A)  8

(B)  64

(C)  216

(D)  1,296

(E)  1,728

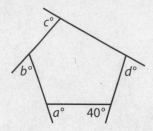

14. What is the value of $a + b + c + d$?

(A)  240

(B)  320

(C)  360

(D)  500

(E)  540

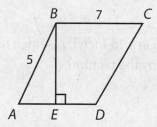

In the trapezoid above, $AE = ED = 3$ and $BC$ is parallel to $AD$.

|  Quantity A  |  Quantity B  |
| --- | --- |
| 15. The area of the trapezoid | 35 |

**MANHATTAN**
PREP

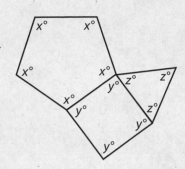

| **Quantity A** | **Quantity B** |
|:---:|:---:|
| 16. $\quad x + y + z$ | 270 |

17. A 2-meter by 2-meter sheet of paper is to be cut into 2-centimeter by 10-centimeter rectangles. What is the maximum number of such rectangles that can be cut from the sheet of paper? (1 meter = 100 centimeters)

A parallelogram has two sides with length 10 and two sides with length 5.

| **Quantity A** | **Quantity B** |
|:---:|:---:|
| 18. $\quad$ The area of the parallelogram | 30 |

19. What is the area of a regular hexagon of side length 4?

    (A)  $4\sqrt{3}$

    (B)  $6\sqrt{3}$

    (C)  $12\sqrt{3}$

    (D)  $24\sqrt{3}$

    (E)  $36\sqrt{3}$

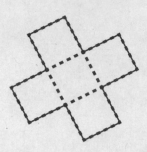

The figure above is composed of 5 squares of equal area, as indicated by the dotted lines. The total area of the figure is 45.

|     | Quantity A | Quantity B |
| --- | --- | --- |
| 20. | The perimeter of the figure | 48 |

21. A 2-foot by 2-foot by 2-foot solid cube is cut into 2-inch by 2-inch by 4-inch rectangular solids. What is the ratio of the total surface area of all the resulting smaller rectangular solids to the surface area of the original cube? (1 foot = 12 inches)

    (A)  2:1
    (B)  4:1
    (C)  5:1
    (D)  8:1
    (E)  10:1

22. If a cube has the same volume (in cubic units) as surface area (in square units), what is the length of one side?

    (A)  1
    (B)  3
    (C)  $\dfrac{5}{3}$
    (D)  6
    (E)  No such cube is possible.

# Polygons and Rectangular Solids Answers

1. **40.** The area of a parallelogram is base × height. In this parallelogram, the base is 10 and the height is 4 (remember, base and height need to be perpendicular). So the area is $10 \times 4 = 40$.

2. **2.** First find the perimeter of parallelogram *ABCD*. If two sides have a length of 4, and two sides have a length of 5, the perimeter is $2(4 + 5) = 8 + 10 = 18$. That means parallelogram *EFGH* also has a perimeter of 18. Because *EF* is labeled 7, *GH* also is 7. The lengths of the other two sides are unknown but equal to each other, so for now say the length of each side is *x*. The parallelogram now looks like this:

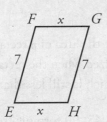

Therefore, the perimeter is:

$$2(7 + x) = 18$$
$$2x + 14 = 18$$
$$2x = 4$$
$$x = 2$$

The length of side *EH* is 2.

3. **12.** One property that is true of any parallelogram is that the diagonal will split the parallelogram into two equal triangles. If triangle *ABC* has an area of 12, then triangle *ACD* must also have an area of 12.

4. **4.** Triangle *ACD* is a right triangle and two of the side lengths are labeled, so the length of *CD* can be determined. Either use the Pythagorean theorem or recognize that this is one of the Pythagorean triplets: a 6–8–10 triangle. The length of side *CD* is 6. The area of rectangle *ABCD* is $8 \times 6 = 48$.

The area of rectangle *EFGH* is also 48, so $12 \times FG = 48$. The length of side *FG* is 4.

5. **30.** To find the area of right triangle *ABC*, use the Pythagorean theorem to first find the length of side *AB*:

$$12^2 + AB^2 = 15^2$$
$$144 + AB^2 = 225$$
$$AB^2 = 81$$
$$AB = 9$$

(A 9–12–15 triangle is a 3–4–5 triangle, with all the measurements tripled.)

The area of triangle $ABC$ is $\frac{1}{2}(12)(9) = \frac{108}{2} = 54$.

Rectangle $JKLM$ also has an area of 54. One side of the rectangle is labeled, so solve for the other: $6 \times JM = 54$. The length of side $JM$ is 9, so the perimeter of $JKLM$ is $2(6 + 9) = 12 + 18 = 30$.

6. **(B).** While a rectangle with perimeter 20 could have many different areas, all of these areas are less than 30:

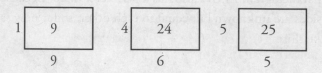

How can you be sure this will always be the case? It would be helpful to know the rule that the area of a rectangle with constant perimeter increases as length and width become more similar, and is maximized when the rectangle is a square. Thus, the 5-by-5 version of the rectangle represents the maximum possible area, which is still less than 30.

7. **36.** When a square is cut by a diagonal, two 45–45–90 triangles are created. Use the 45–45–90 formula (sides in the ratio $1 : 1 : \sqrt{2}$) to determine that the sides are equal to 6, and thus the area is $6 \times 6 = 36$. Alternatively, label each side of the square x (since they're the same) and use the Pythagorean theorem:

$$x^2 + x^2 = \left(6\sqrt{2}\right)^2$$
$$2x^2 = 72$$
$$x^2 = 36$$
$$x = 6$$

If each side of the square is 6, the area is $6 \times 6 = 36$.

8. **(C).** The formula for area of a parallelogram is *base* × *height*, so Quantity A is $4 \times 3.5 = 14$.

The formula for area of a trapezoid is $A = \frac{(b_1 + b_2)}{2} \times h$, where $b_1$ and $b_2$ are the lengths of the parallel sides, so Quantity B is $\frac{(5 + 9)}{2} \times 2 = 14$.

The two quantities are equal.

9. **(D).** Do not assume that any polygon is a regular figure unless the problem explicitly or implicitly says so. (For instance, if *every* angle in the hexagon were labeled with the same variable, you could be sure the hexagon was regular.)

Using the formula $(n - 2)(180°)$ where $n$ is the number of sides, calculate that the sum of the angles in the 6-sided figure is 720° and the sum of the angles in the 7-sided figure is 900°. However, those totals could be distributed any number of ways among the interior angles, so either $x$ or $y$ could be greater.

10. **(C).** If one square has twice the perimeter, it has twice the side length, so it will have four times the area. Why is this? Doubling only the length doubles the area. Then, doubling the width doubles the area *again*.

**MANHATTAN**
PREP

Alternatively, prove this with real numbers. Say square $W$ has perimeter 8 and square $D$ has perimeter 16. Thus, square $W$ has side 2 and square $D$ has side 4. The areas are 4 and 16, respectively. As a ratio, $\dfrac{4}{16}$ reduces to $\dfrac{1}{4}$. The two quantities are equal.

11. **(B).** The area of the picture is $10 \times 15 = 150$. The area of the frame is $16 \times 24 = 384$. Subtract to get the answer: $384 - 150 = 234$.

12. **(B).** The volume of a rectangular box is length × width × height. Therefore: $2 \times 3 \times 4 = 24$. Quantity A is double this volume, or 48.

The surface area of a rectangular box is 2(length × width) + 2(width × height) + 2(length × height). Therefore: $2(6) + 2(12) + 2(8) = 52$.

Quantity B is greater.

13. **(D).** Each large solid cube is 12 inches × 12 inches × 12 inches. Each dimension (length, width, and height) is to be cut identically at 2 inch increments, creating 6 smaller cubes in each dimension. Thus, $6 \times 6 \times 6$ small cubes can be cut from each large cube. There are 6 large cubes to be cut this way, though, so the total number of small cubes that can be cut is $6(6 \times 6 \times 6) = 6 \times 216 = 1{,}296$.

14. **(B).** The interior figure shown is a pentagon, although an irregular one. The sum of the interior angles of any polygon can be determined using the formula $(n - 2)(180°)$, where $n$ is the number of sides:

$$(5 - 2)(180°) = (3)(180°) = 540°$$

Using the rule that angles forming a straight line sum to 180°, the interior angles of the pentagon (starting at the top and going clockwise) are $180 - c$, $180 - d$, 140, $180 - a$, and $180 - b$. The sum of these angles can be set equal to 540:

$$540 = (180 - c) + (180 - d) + 140 + (180 - a) + (180 - b)$$
$$540 = 140 + 4(180) - a - b - c - d$$
$$540 - 140 - 720 = -(a + b + c + d)$$
$$-320 = -(a + b + c + d)$$

So, $a + b + c + d = 320$.

15. **(B).** While the figure may *look* like parallelogram, it is actually a trapezoid, as it has two parallel sides of unequal length ($AD = AE + ED = 6$ and $BC = 7$). The two parallel sides in a trapezoid are referred to as the bases. The formula for the area of a trapezoid is $A = \dfrac{(b_1 + b_2)}{2} \times h$, where $b_1$ and $b_2$ are the lengths of the parallel sides and $h$ is the height, which is the distance between the parallel sides ($BE$ in this figure).

Triangle $ABE$ is a 3–4–5 special right triangle, so $BE$ is 4. (Alternatively, use the Pythagorean theorem to determine this.)

Thus, the area is $\dfrac{(6 + 7)}{2} \times 4 = 26$. Quantity B is greater.

**MANHATTAN**
PREP          775

16. **(B).** Each angle in the pentagon is labeled with the same variable, so this is a regular pentagon. Using the formula $(n - 2)(180°)$, where n is the number of sides, the sum of all the interior angles of the pentagon is $(3)(180°) = 540°$. Divide by 5 to get $x = 108$.

Now, the quadrilateral. All four-sided figures have interior angles that sum to 360°. Alternatively, use the formula $(n - 2)(180°)$ to determine this. Divide 360 by 4 to get $y = 90$.

Now, the triangle. It is equilateral, so $z = 60$. (The sum of angle measures in a triangle is always 180°; if the angles are equal, they will each equal 60°.)

Thus, $x + y + z = 108 + 90 + 60 = 258$. Quantity B is greater.

17. **2,000.** Since the sheet of paper is measured in meters and the small rectangles in centimeters, first convert the measures of the sheet of paper to centimeters. The large sheet of paper measures 200 centimeters by 200 centimeters. The most efficient way to cut 2-centimeter by 10-centimeter rectangles is to cut vertically every 2 centimeter and horizontally every 10 centimeter (or vice versa; the idea is that all the small rectangles should be oriented the same direction on the larger sheet). Doing so creates a grid of $\dfrac{200}{2} \times \dfrac{200}{10} = 100 \times 20 = 2,000$ small rectangles.

18. **(D).** The formula for the area of a parallelogram is base × height, where height is the perpendicular distance between the parallel bases, not necessarily the other side of the parallelogram. However, if the parallelogram is actually a rectangle, the height *is* the other side of the parallelogram and is thereby maximized. So, if the parallelogram is actually a rectangle, the area would be equal to 50, but if the parallelogram has more extreme angle measures, the height could be very, very small, making the area much less than 30.

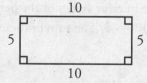 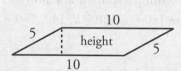

19. **(D).** Divide the hexagon with three diagonals (running through the center) to get six triangles. Since the sum of the angles in any polygon is $(n - 2)(180°)$, the sum for a hexagon is 720°. Divide by 6 to get that each angle in the original hexagon is 120°. When the hexagon is divided into triangles, each 120° angle is halved, creating two 60° angles for each triangle. Any triangle that has two angles of 60° must have a third angle of 60° as well, since triangles always sum to 180°. Thus, all six triangles are equilateral. Therefore, all three sides of each triangle are equal to 4.

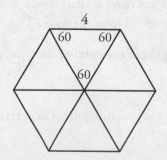

**MANHATTAN**
PREP

For any equilateral triangle, the height equals half the side times $\sqrt{3}$. Therefore, the height is $2\sqrt{3}$. Since $A = \frac{1}{2}bh$, the area of each equilateral triangle is $A = \frac{1}{2}(4)(2\sqrt{3}) = 4\sqrt{3}$. Since there are six such triangles, the answer is $24\sqrt{3}$.

20. **(B).** If a figure with area of 45 is composed of 5 equal squares, divide to get that the area of each square is 9 and thus the side of each square is 3.

Don't make the mistake of adding up *every* side of every square to get the perimeter—only count lengths that are actually part of the perimeter of the overall figure. (Note that the central square does not have any lengths that are part of the perimeter), as shown below:

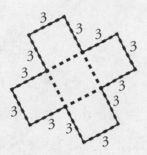

The perimeter is made of 12 segments, each with length 3. The perimeter is 36.

Incorrect choice (A) comes from reasoning that 5 squares have 20 total sides, each of length 3, and thus the combined length would be 60. Do not just subtract the four dotted line lengths, as each of these was actually counted twice, as part of the central square and one of the others. This mistake would incorrectly yield choice (C). The best approach here is to make a quick sketch of the figure, label the sketch with the given information, and count up the perimeter.

21. **(E).** To find the surface area of the original cube, first convert the side lengths to inches (it is NOT okay to find surface area or volume and then convert using 1 foot = 12 inches; this is only true for straight-line distances). The equation for surface area is $6s^2$, so, the surface area of the large original cube is $6(24 \text{ inches})^2 = 3{,}456$ square inches.

Each large solid cube is 24 inches × 24 inches × 24 inches. To cut the large cube into 2-inch by 2-inch by 4-inch rectangular solids, two dimensions (length and width, say) will be sliced every 2 inches, while one dimension (height, say) will be sliced every 4 inches. Thus, $\frac{24}{2} \times \frac{24}{2} \times \frac{24}{4} = 12 \times 12 \times 6 = 864$ small rectangular solids can be cut from the large cube.

The equation for the surface area of a rectangular solid is $2lw + 2wh + 2lh$. In this case, that is $2(2 \times 2) + 2(2 \times 4) + 2(2 \times 4) = 8 + 16 + 16 = 40$ square inches per small rectangular solid. There are 864 small rectangular solids, so the total surface area is $40 \times 864 = 34{,}560$ square inches.

Finally, the ratio of the total surface area of all the resulting smaller rectangular solids to the surface area of the original cube is the ratio of 34,560 to 3,456. This ratio reduces to 10 to 1.

22. **(D).** To solve this question, use the equations for the volume and the surface area of a cube:

Volume $= s^3$          Surface area $= 6s^2$

If a cube has the same volume as surface area, set these equal:

$s^3 = 6s^2$
$s = 6$

# Chapter 26
## *of*

5 lb. Book of GRE® Practice Problems

# Circles and Cylinders

# In This Chapter...

Circles and Cylinders

Circles and Cylinders Answers

# Circles and Cylinders

For questions in the Quantitative Comparison format ("Quantity A" and "Quantity B" given), the answer choices are always as follows:

(A)   Quantity A is greater.
(B)   Quantity B is greater.
(C)   The two quantities are equal.
(D)   The relationship cannot be determined from the information given.

For questions followed by a numeric entry box [    ], you are to enter your own answer in the box. For questions followed

by a fraction-style numeric entry box $\dfrac{\phantom{xxxx}}{\phantom{xxxx}}$, you are to enter your answer in the form of a fraction. You are not required to

reduce fractions. For example, if the answer is $\dfrac{1}{4}$, you may enter $\dfrac{25}{100}$ or any equivalent fraction.

All numbers used are real numbers. All figures are assumed to lie in a plane unless otherwise indicated. Geometric figures are not necessarily drawn to scale. You should assume, however, that lines that appear to be straight are actually straight, points on a line are in the order shown, and all geometric objects are in the relative positions shown. Coordinate systems, such as $xy$-planes and number lines, as well as graphical data presentations, such as bar charts, circle graphs, and line graphs, *are* drawn to scale. A symbol that appears more than once in a question has the same meaning throughout the question.

1.   A circle has an area of $16\pi$. What is its circumference?

   (A)   $4\pi$
   (B)   $8\pi$
   (C)   $16\pi$
   (D)   $32\pi$
   (E)   It cannot be determined from the information given.

2.   A circle has a circumference of 16. What is its area?

   (A)   $\dfrac{8}{\pi}$

   (B)   $\dfrac{8}{\pi^2}$

   (C)   $\dfrac{64}{\pi}$

   (D)   $\dfrac{64}{\pi^2}$

   (E)   $64\pi$

3.    A circle has a diameter of 5. What is its area?

  (A) $\dfrac{25\pi}{4}$

  (B) $\dfrac{25\pi}{2}$

  (C) $\dfrac{25\pi^2}{2}$

  (D) $10\pi$

  (E) $25\pi$

4.    A circle's area equals its circumference. What is its radius?

  (A)  1
  (B)  2
  (C)  4
  (D)  8
  (E)  16

Circle C has a radius r such that $1 < r < 5$.

|  | **Quantity A** | **Quantity B** |
|---|---|---|
| 5. | The area of circle C | The circumference of circle C |

6.    A circle has radius 3.5. What is its area?

  (A) $\dfrac{7}{2}\pi$

  (B) $9.5\pi$

  (C) $10.5\pi$

  (D) $\dfrac{49}{4}\pi$

  (E) $\dfrac{49}{2}\pi$

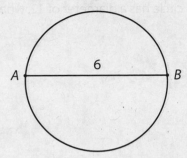

AB is <u>not</u> a diameter of the circle.

| **Quantity A** | **Quantity B** |
|---|---|
7. | The area of the circle | $9\pi$ |

8.   A circle has radius 0.001. What is its area?

   (A)  $\pi \times 10^{-2}$

   (B)  $\pi \times 10^{-3}$

   (C)  $\pi \times 10^{-4}$

   (D)  $\pi \times 10^{-6}$

   (E)  $\pi \times 10^{-9}$

9.   A circle has an area of $4\pi$. If the radius were doubled, the new area of the circle would be how many times the original area?

   (A)  2

   (B)  3

   (C)  4

   (D)  5

   (E)  It cannot be determined from the information given.

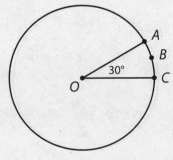

The radius of the circle with center O is 6.

| **Quantity A** | **Quantity B** |
|---|---|
10. | The length of arc ABC | 3 |

11. A sector of a circle has a central angle of 120°. If the circle has a diameter of 12, what is the area of the sector?

   (A) $4\pi$
   (B) $8\pi$
   (C) $12\pi$
   (D) $18\pi$
   (E) $36\pi$

Within a circle with radius 12, a sector has an area of $24\pi$.

|  **Quantity A** | **Quantity B** |
|---|---|
| 12. The measure of the central angle of the sector, in degrees | 90 |

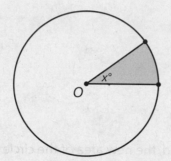

In the circle with center $O$, the area of the shaded sector is $\dfrac{1}{10}$ of the area of the full circle.

|  **Quantity A** | **Quantity B** |
|---|---|
| 13. $2x$ | 75 |

**MANHATTAN**
PREP

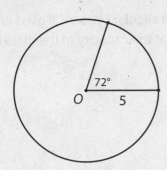

14. If $O$ is the center of the circle, what is the perimeter of the sector with central angle 72°?

    (A) $5 + 2\pi$

    (B) $10 + 2\pi$

    (C) $10 + 4\pi$

    (D) $10 + 5\pi$

    (E) $20 + 2\pi$

15. A sector of a circle has a radius of 10 and an area of $20\pi$. What is the arc length of the sector?

    (A) $\pi$

    (B) $2\pi$

    (C) $4\pi$

    (D) $5\pi$

    (E) $10\pi$

    Sector $A$ and sector $B$ are sectors of two different circles.
    Sector $A$ has a radius of 4 and a central angle of 90°.
    Sector $B$ has a radius of 6 and a central angle of 45°.

|  | **Quantity A** | **Quantity B** |
|---|---|---|
| 16. | The area of sector $A$ | The area of sector $B$ |

17. What is the height of a right circular cylinder with radius 2 and volume $32\pi$?

    A right circular cylinder has volume $24\pi$.

|  | **Quantity A** | **Quantity B** |
|---|---|---|
| 18. | The height of the cylinder | The radius of the cylinder |

19. If a half-full 4-inch by 2-inch by 8-inch box of soymilk is poured into a right circular cylindrical glass with radius 2 inches, how many inches high will the soymilk reach? (Assume that the capacity of the glass is greater than the volume of the soymilk.)

(A)  8

(B)  16

(C)  $\dfrac{4}{\pi}$

(D)  $\dfrac{8}{\pi}$

(E)  $\dfrac{16}{\pi}$

20. If a right circular cylinder's radius is halved and its height doubled, by what percent will the volume increase or decrease?

(A)  50% decrease

(B)  0%

(C)  25% increase

(D)  50% increase

(E)  100% increase

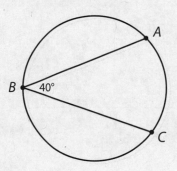

21. If the diameter of the circle is 36, what is the length of arc *ABC*?

(A)  8

(B)  $8\pi$

(C)  $28\pi$

(D)  $32\pi$

(E)  $56\pi$

**MANHATTAN**
PREP

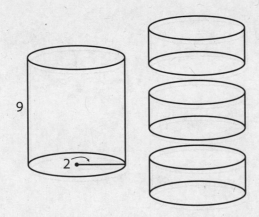

22. If a solid right circular cylinder with height 9 and radius 2 is cut as shown into three new cylinders, each of equal and uniform height, how much new surface area is created?

    (A)  $4\pi$

    (B)  $12\pi$

    (C)  $16\pi$

    (D)  $24\pi$

    (E)  $36\pi$

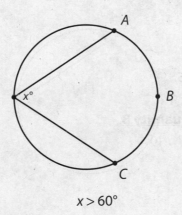

$x > 60°$

| **Quantity A** | **Quantity B** |
|---|---|
| 23.   The ratio of the length of arc *ABC* to the circumference of the circle | $\dfrac{1}{3}$ |

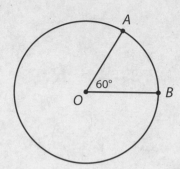

Point *O* is the center of the circle above.

| **Quantity A** | **Quantity B** |
| --- | --- |
| 24. The ratio of the length of minor arc *AB* to major arc *AB* | $\dfrac{1}{6}$ |

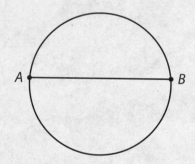

The circle above has area 25.

| **Quantity A** | **Quantity B** |
| --- | --- |
| 25. The length of chord *AB* | 10 |

# Circles and Cylinders Answers

1. **(B).** Since the area formula for a circle is $A = \pi r^2$:

$$16\pi = \pi r^2$$
$$16 = r^2$$
$$4 = r$$

Since the circumference formula is $C = 2\pi r$ and $r = 4$:

$$C = 2\pi(4)$$
$$C = 8\pi$$

2. **(C).** Since the circumference formula is $C = 2\pi r$:

$$16 = 2\pi r$$

Note that the circumference is just 16, not $16\pi$, so the radius is going to look a bit unusual. Divide both sides by $2\pi$ to solve for $r$:

$$\frac{16}{2\pi} = r$$
$$\frac{8}{\pi} = r$$

Now, plug the radius $\dfrac{8}{\pi}$ into the area formula for a circle:

$$A = \pi\left(\frac{8}{\pi}\right)^2$$
$$A = \pi \times \frac{64}{\pi^2}$$
$$A = \frac{64}{\pi}$$

3. **(A).** If a circle's diameter is 5, its radius is $\dfrac{5}{2}$. Plug this into the area formula:

$$A = \pi\left(\frac{5}{2}\right)^2$$
$$A = \pi \times \frac{25}{4}$$
$$A = \frac{25\pi}{4}$$

4. **(B).** To find the radius that would make the area and the circumference of a circle equal, set the area and circumference formulas equal to one another:

$$\pi r^2 = 2\pi r$$

Since both sides have both $r$ and $\pi$, divide both sides by $\pi r$:

$$r = 2$$

5. **(D).** Picking numbers is the easiest way to prove (D). If the radius is 3, the area is $9\pi$ and the circumference is $6\pi$, so Quantity A is greater. If the radius is 4, the area is $16\pi$ and the circumference is $8\pi$, so once again Quantity A is greater. But if the radius is 2, both the area and the circumference equal $4\pi$. Therefore, Quantity A is not always greater. Note also that $r$ is not required to be an integer. If you try a radius close to the minimum, such as 1.1, Quantity B would be greater.

6. **(D).** The area formula for a circle is $A = \pi r^2$, so plug the radius in. Since the decimal will be unwieldy, it is easier to plug the fractional version of 3.5 $\left(\text{i.e., } \dfrac{7}{2}\right)$ into the formula:

$$A = \pi \left(\frac{7}{2}\right)^2$$
$$A = \frac{49\pi}{4}$$

7. **(A).** Since a diameter is the longest straight line you can draw from one point on a circle to another (that is, a diameter is the longest chord in a circle), the actual diameter must be *greater* than 6.

If the diameter were exactly 6, the radius would be 3, and the area would be:

$$A = \pi(3)^2$$
$$A = 9\pi$$

However, since the diameter must actually be greater than 6, the area must be greater than $9\pi$. Do *not* make the mistake of picking (D) for Quantitative Comparison geometry questions in which you cannot "solve." There is often still a way to determine which quantity is greater.

8. **(D).** The formula for the area of a circle is $A = \pi r^2$, so plug radius 0.001 into the formula. However, since the answers are in exponential form, it would be easier to first convert 0.001 to $1 \times 10^{-3}$, or just $10^{-3}$, and use that in the formula:

$$A = \pi(10^{-3})^2$$
$$A = \pi(10^{-6})$$

9. **(C).** To begin, find the original radius of the circle: Area $= \pi r^2 = 4\pi$, so $r = 2$. Once doubled, the new radius is 4. A circle with a radius of 4 has an area of $16\pi$. The new area of $16\pi$ is 4 times the old area of $4\pi$.

**MANHATTAN**
PREP

10. **(A).** If the sector has a central angle of 30°, then it is $\frac{1}{12}$ of the circle, because $\frac{30}{360} = \frac{1}{12}$. To find the arc length of the sector, first find the circumference of the entire circle. The radius of the circle is 6, so the circumference is $2\pi(6) = 12\pi$. That means that the arc length of the sector is $\frac{1}{12}(12\pi) = \pi$. Since $\pi$ is about 3.14, Quantity A is greater.

11. **(C).** The sector is $\frac{1}{3}$ of the circle, because $\frac{120}{360} = \frac{1}{3}$. To find the area of the sector, first find the area of the whole circle. The diameter of the circle is 12, so the radius of the circle is 6, and the area is $\pi(6)^2 = 36\pi$. That means the area of the sector is $\frac{1}{3}(36\pi) = 12\pi$.

12. **(B).** First find the area of the whole circle. The radius is 12, which means the area is $\pi(12)^2 = 144\pi$. Since the sector has an area of $24\pi$ and $\frac{24\pi}{144\pi} = \frac{1}{6}$, the sector is $\frac{1}{6}$ of the entire circle. That means that the central angle is $\frac{1}{6}$ of 360, or 60°. Quantity B is greater.

13. **(B).** If the area of the sector is $\frac{1}{10}$ of the area of the full circle, then the central angle is $\frac{1}{10}$ of the degree measure of the full circle, or $\frac{1}{10}$ of 360° = 36° = $x$°. Thus, Quantity A = 2(36) = 72, so Quantity B is greater.

14. **(B).** To find the perimeter of a sector, first find the radius of the circle and the arc length of the sector. Begin by determining what fraction of the circle the sector is. The central angle of the sector is 72°, so the sector is $\frac{72}{360} = \frac{1}{5}$ of the circle. The radius is 5, so the circumference of the circle is $2\pi(5) = 10\pi$. The arc length of the sector is $\frac{1}{5}$ of the circumference: $\frac{1}{5}(10\pi) = 2\pi$. The perimeter of the sector is this $2\pi$ plus the two radii that make up the straight parts of the sector: $10 + 2\pi$.

15. **(C).** Compare the given area of the sector to the calculated area of the whole circle. The radius of the circle is 10, so the area of the whole circle is $\pi(10)^2 = 100\pi$. The area of the sector is $20\pi$, or $\frac{20\pi}{100\pi} = \frac{1}{5}$ of the circle. The radius is 10, so the circumference of the whole circle is $2\pi(10) = 20\pi$. Since the sector is $\frac{1}{5}$ of the circle, the arc length is $\left(\frac{1}{5}\right)(20\pi) = 4\pi$.

16. **(B).** Sector $A$ is $\frac{90}{360} = \frac{1}{4}$ of the circle with radius 4. The area of this circle is $\pi(4)^2 = 16\pi$, so the area of sector $A$ is $\frac{1}{4}$ of $16\pi$, or $4\pi$.

Sector $B$ is $\frac{45}{360} = \frac{1}{8}$ of the circle with radius 6. The area of this circle is $\pi(6)^2 = 36\pi$, so the area of sector $B$ is $\frac{1}{8}$ of $36\pi$, or $4.5\pi$.

Since $4.5\pi$ is greater than $4\pi$, Quantity B is greater.

17. **8.** Use the formula for the volume of a right circular cylinder, $V = \pi r^2 h$:

$$32\pi = \pi(2)^2 h$$
$$32 = 4h$$
$$8 = h$$

18. **(D).** Plugging into the formula for volume of a right circular cylinder, $V = 24\pi = \pi r^2 h$. However, there are many combinations of $r$ and $h$ that would make the volume $24\pi$. For instance, $r = 1$ and $h = 24$, or $r = 4$ and $h = 1.5$. Keep in mind that the radius and height don't even have to be integers, so there truly are an infinite number of possibilities, some for which $h$ is greater and some for which $r$ is greater.

19. **(D).** A box is a rectangular solid whose volume formula is $V =$ length $\times$ width $\times$ height. Thus, the volume of the box is 4 inches $\times$ 2 inches $\times$ 8 inches $= 64$ inches³. Since the box is half full, there are 32 inches³ of soymilk. This volume will not change when the soymilk is poured from the box into the cylinder. The formula for the volume of a cylinder is $V = \pi r^2 h$, so:

$$32 = \pi(2)^2 h, \text{ where } r \text{ and } h \text{ are in units of inches.}$$

$$\frac{32}{4\pi} = h$$
$$\frac{8}{\pi} = h$$

The height is $\dfrac{8}{\pi}$ inches. Note that the height is "weird" (divided by $\pi$) because the volume of the cylinder did *not* have a $\pi$.

20. **(A).** According to the formula for the volume of a right circular cylinder, the original volume is $V = \pi r^2 h$. To halve the radius, replace $r$ with $\dfrac{r}{2}$. To double the height, replace $h$ with $2h$. The only caveat: be sure to use parentheses!

$$V = \pi \left(\frac{r}{2}\right)^2 (2h) = \frac{2\pi r^2 h}{2^2} = \frac{\pi r^2 h}{2}$$

Thus, the volume, which was once $\pi r^2 h$, is now $\dfrac{\pi r^2 h}{2}$. In other words, it has been cut in half, or reduced by 50%.

Alternatively, plug in numbers. If the cylinder originally had radius 2 and height 1, the volume would be $V = \pi(2)^2(1) = 4\pi$. If the radius were halved to become 1 and the height were doubled to become 2, the volume would be $V = \pi(1)^2(2) = 2\pi$. Again, the volume is cut in half, or reduced by 50%.

21. **(C).** Note that a *minor* arc is the "short way around" the circle from one point to another, and a *major* arc is the "long way around." Arc $ABC$ is thus the same as major arc $AC$.

For a given arc, an inscribed angle is always half the central angle, which would be 80° in this case. The minor arc $AC$ is thus $\dfrac{80}{360} = \dfrac{2}{9}$ of the circle. Since the circumference is $36\pi$:

$$\text{minor arc } AC = \frac{2}{9}(36\pi) = 8\pi$$

**MANHATTAN**
PREP

Arc *ABC*, or major arc *AC*, is the entire circumference minus the minor arc:

$$36\pi - 8\pi = 28\pi$$

22. **(C).** One method is to find the surface area of the large cylinder, then the surface areas of the three new cylinders, then subtract the surface area of the large cylinder from the combined surface areas of the three new cylinders. However, there is a much faster way. When the large cylinder is cut into three smaller ones, only a few *new* surfaces are created—the bottom base of the top cylinder, the top and bottom bases of the middle cylinder, and the top surface of the bottom cylinder.

Thus, these four circular bases represent the new surface area created. Since the radius of each base is 2, use the area formula for a circle, $A = \pi r^2$:

$$A = \pi(2)^2$$
$$A = 4\pi$$

Since there are 4 such bases, multiply by 4 to get $16\pi$.

23. **(A).** If $x°$ were equal to 60°, arc *ABC* would have a central angle of 120°. (Inscribed angles, with the vertex at the far side of the circle, are always half the central angle.) A 120° arc is $\frac{120}{360} = \frac{1}{3}$ of the circumference of the circle.

Since $x$ is actually greater than 60°, the arc is actually greater than $\frac{1}{3}$ of the circumference. Thus, the ratio of the arc length to the circumference is greater than $\frac{1}{3}$.

24. **(A).** Since the angle that determines the arc is equal to 60 and $\frac{60}{360} = \frac{1}{6}$, minor arc *AB* is $\frac{1}{6}$ of the circumference of the circle. (There are always 360° in a circle. Minor arc *AB* is the "short way around" from *A* to *B*, while major arc *AB* is the "long way around.")

Since minor arc $AB$ is $\dfrac{1}{6}$ of the circumference, major arc $AB$ must be the other $\dfrac{5}{6}$. Therefore, the ratio of the minor

arc to the major arc is 1 to 5 (*not* 1 to 6). You could calculate this as $\dfrac{\frac{1}{6}}{\frac{5}{6}} = \dfrac{1}{6} \times \dfrac{6}{5} = \dfrac{1}{5}$, or you could just reason the

ratio of 1 of *anything* (such as sixths) to 5 of the same thing (again, sixths) is a 1 to 5 ratio.

The trap answer here is (C). This is a common mistake: $\dfrac{1}{6}$ of the total is not the same as a 1 to 6 ratio of two parts.

25. **(B).** The equation for the area of a circle is $A = \pi r^2$. Note that the given area is just 25, *not* $25\pi$! So:

$$\pi r^2 = 25$$
$$r^2 = \frac{25}{\pi} \approx 8$$
$$r = \text{a bit less than 3.}$$

So the diameter of the circle is a bit less than 6. The diameter is the chord with maximum length, so wherever $AB$ is on this circle, it's significantly shorter than 10.

**MANHATTAN**
PREP

# Chapter 27

## 5 lb. Book of GRE® Practice Problems

# Triangles

# In This Chapter...

# Triangles

For questions in the Quantitative Comparison format ("Quantity A" and "Quantity B" given), the answer choices are always as follows:

(A)  Quantity A is greater.
(B)  Quantity B is greater.
(C)  The two quantities are equal.
(D)  The relationship cannot be determined from the information given.

For questions followed by a numeric entry box [        ], you are to enter your own answer in the box. For questions followed

by a fraction-style numeric entry box $\frac{\phantom{xx}}{\phantom{xx}}$, you are to enter your answer in the form of a fraction. You are not required to

reduce fractions. For example, if the answer is $\frac{1}{4}$, you may enter $\frac{25}{100}$ or any equivalent fraction.

All numbers used are real numbers. All figures are assumed to lie in a plane unless otherwise indicated. Geometric figures are not necessarily drawn to scale. You should assume, however, that lines that appear to be straight are actually straight, points on a line are in the order shown, and all geometric objects are in the relative positions shown. Coordinate systems, such as $xy$-planes and number lines, as well as graphical data presentations, such as bar charts, circle graphs, and line graphs, *are* drawn to scale. A symbol that appears more than once in a question has the same meaning throughout the question.

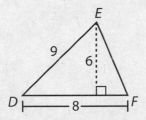

1.  What is the area of triangle *DEF*?

    (A)  23

    (B)  24

    (C)  48

    (D)  56

    (E)  81

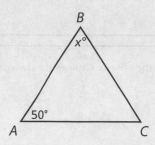

2.   If *AB* and *BC* have equal lengths, what is the value of *x*?

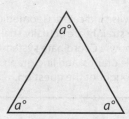   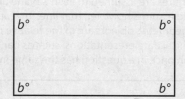

|   | **Quantity A** | **Quantity B** |
|---|---|---|
| 3. | $2a + b$ | $3a + \dfrac{b}{3}$ |

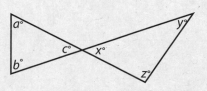

|   | **Quantity A** | **Quantity B** |
|---|---|---|
| 4. | $a + b + x$ | $c + y + z$ |

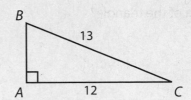

5.   What is the area of right triangle *ABC*?

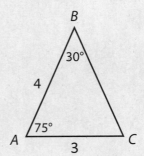

6.   What is the perimeter of triangle *ABC*?

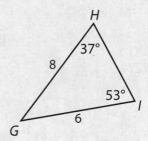

7.   What is the length of side *HI*?

8.    If the hypotenuse of an isosceles right triangle is $8\sqrt{2}$, what is the area of the triangle?

   (A)   18
   (B)   24
   (C)   32
   (D)   48
   (E)   64

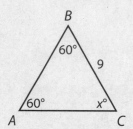

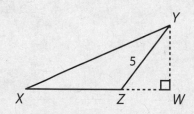

| **Quantity A** | **Quantity B** |
| --- | --- |
| Perimeter of triangle *ABC* | Perimeter of triangle *DEF* |

9.

10.   *ZW* has a length of 3 and *XZ* has a length of 6. What is the area of triangle *XYZ*?

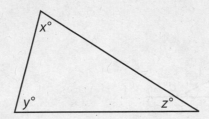

In the figure above, $x + z$ equals 110.

|  | **Quantity A** | **Quantity B** |
|---|---|---|
| 11. | $x$ | $y$ |

Two sides of an isosceles triangle are 8 and 5 in length, respectively.

|  | **Quantity A** | **Quantity B** |
|---|---|---|
| 12. | The length of the third side | 8 |

Two sides of an isosceles triangle are 2 and 11 in length, respectively.

|  | **Quantity A** | **Quantity B** |
|---|---|---|
| 13. | The length of the third side | 11 |

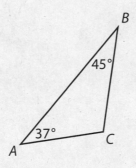

|  | **Quantity A** | **Quantity B** |
|---|---|---|
| 14. | $AC$ | $BC$ |

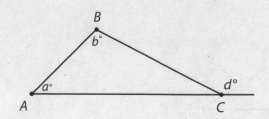

|              | **Quantity A** | **Quantity B** |
|--------------|----------------|----------------|
| 15.          | $a + b$        | $d$            |

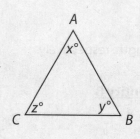

$$y < z$$
$$y > 60$$

|     | **Quantity A**          | **Quantity B**          |
|-----|-------------------------|-------------------------|
| 16. | The length of side $AC$ | The length of side $BC$ |

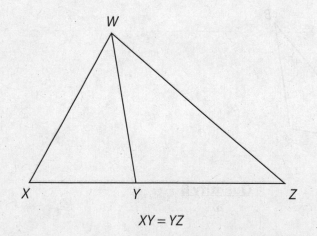

$$XY = YZ$$

|     | **Quantity A**       | **Quantity B**       |
|-----|----------------------|----------------------|
| 17. | The area of $XWY$    | The area of $YWZ$    |

**MANHATTAN**
PREP

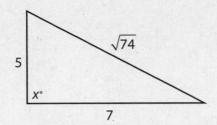

|  | **Quantity A** | **Quantity B** |
|---|---|---|
| 18. | $x$ | 90 |

19. If $p$ is the perimeter of a triangle with one side of 7 and another side of 9, what is the range of possible values for $p$?

   (A)  $2 < p < 16$
   (B)  $3 < p < 17$
   (C)  $18 < p < 32$
   (D)  $18 < p < 33$
   (E)  $17 < p < 63$

A right triangle has a hypotenuse of 12 and legs of 9 and $y$.

|  | **Quantity A** | **Quantity B** |
|---|---|---|
| 20. | $y$ | 15 |

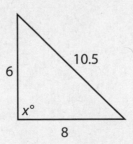

|  | **Quantity A** | **Quantity B** |
|---|---|---|
| 21. | $x$ | 90 |

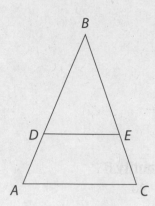

In the figure above, *DE* is parallel to *AC*.

$$BE = 2EC$$
$$DE = 12$$

|  Quantity A | Quantity B |
|---|---|
| 22. | | |

**Quantity A**: *AC*    **Quantity B**: 18

Two sides of a triangle are 8 and 9 long.

**Quantity A**     **Quantity B**

23.   The length of the third side of       $\sqrt{290}$
       the triangle

24. What is the area of an equilateral triangle with side length 6?

   (A)  $4\sqrt{3}$
   (B)  $6\sqrt{2}$
   (C)  $6\sqrt{3}$
   (D)  $9\sqrt{2}$
   (E)  $9\sqrt{3}$

**MANHATTAN**
PREP

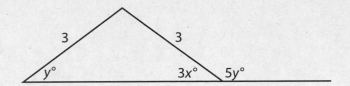

25.  What is the value of *x* in the figure above?

    (A)  5
    (B)  10
    (C)  18
    (D)  30
    (E)  54

26.  An isosceles right triangle has an area of 50. What is the length of the hypotenuse?

    (A)  5
    (B)  $5\sqrt{2}$
    (C)  $5\sqrt{3}$
    (D)  10
    (E)  $10\sqrt{2}$

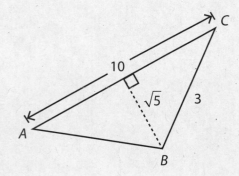

27.  In the figure above, what is the length of side *AB*?

    (A)  5
    (B)  $\sqrt{30}$
    (C)  $5\sqrt{2}$
    (D)  8
    (E)  $\sqrt{69}$

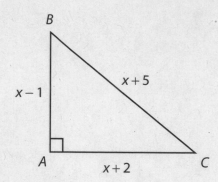

28. In the right triangle above, what is the length of *AC*?

   (A)  9

   (B)  10

   (C)  12

   (D)  13

   (E)  15

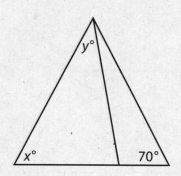

|  | **Quantity A** | **Quantity B** |
|---|---|---|
| 29. | $x + y$ | 110 |

**MANHATTAN**
PREP

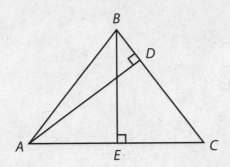

|  | **Quantity A** | **Quantity B** |
| --- | --- | --- |

30.   The product of *BE* and *AC*          The product of *BC* and *AD*

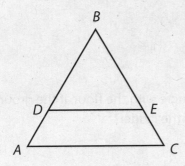

31.   In the figure above, *DE* and *AC* are parallel lines. If *AC* = 12, *DE* = 8, and *AD* = 2, what is the length of *AB*?

(A)  2
(B)  3
(C)  4
(D)  5
(E)  6

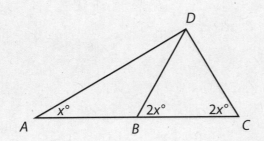

|  | **Quantity A** | **Quantity B** |
| --- | --- | --- |

32.              *DC*                          *AB*

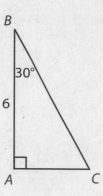

33. What is the perimeter of right triangle *ABC* above?

    (A)  $6 + 4\sqrt{3}$
    (B)  $6 + 6\sqrt{3}$
    (C)  $6 + 8\sqrt{3}$
    (D)  $9 + 6\sqrt{3}$
    (E)  $18 + 6\sqrt{3}$

34. A 10-foot ladder leans against a vertical wall and forms a 60-degree angle with the floor. If the ground below the ladder is horizontal, how far above the ground is the top of the ladder?

    (A)  5 feet
    (B)  $5\sqrt{3}$ feet
    (C)  7.5 feet
    (D)  10 feet
    (E)  $10\sqrt{3}$ feet

**MANHATTAN**
PREP

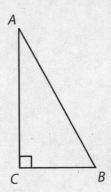

35.  Triangle *ABC* has an area of 9. If *AC* is three times as long as *CB*, what is the length of *AB*?

    (A)  6

    (B)  $3\sqrt{6}$

    (C)  $2\sqrt{15}$

    (D)  $4\sqrt{15}$

    (E)  15

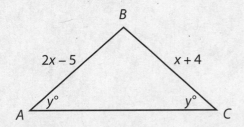

| **Quantity A** | **Quantity B** |
|---|---|
| 36.      *CB* | 7 |

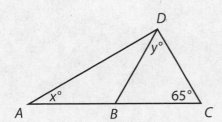

In the figure above, side lengths *AB*, *BD*, and *DC* are all equal.

| **Quantity A** | **Quantity B** |
|---|---|
| 37.      *x* | *y* |

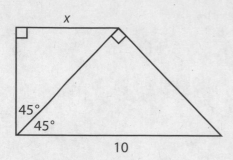

38. In the figure above, what is the value of x?

    (A)   2.5

    (B)   $\dfrac{5}{\sqrt{2}}$

    (C)   5

    (D)   $5\sqrt{2}$

    (E)   $\dfrac{10}{\sqrt{2}}$

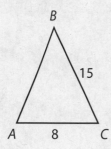

39. Which of the following statements, considered independently, provide sufficient information to calculate the area of triangle *ABC*?

    ☐   Angle *ACB* equals 90°

    ☐   *AB* = 17

    ☐   *ABC* is a right triangle

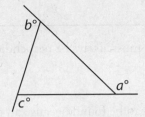

### Quantity A
### Quantity B

40.
$a + b + c$                                  180

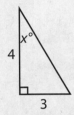
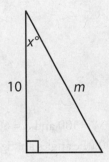

### Quantity A
### Quantity B

41.
$m$                                          15

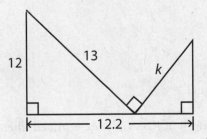

42. What is the length of hypotenuse $k$?

# Triangles Answers

1. **(B).** The area of a triangle is equal to $\dfrac{bh}{2}$. Base and height must always be perpendicular. Use 8 as the base and 6 as the height: $A = \dfrac{(8)(6)}{2} = 24$.

2. **80.** If two of the angles in a triangle are known, the third can be found because all three angles must sum to 180°. In triangle $ABC$, sides $AB$ and $BC$ are equal. That means their opposite angles are also equal, so angle $ACB$ is 50°.

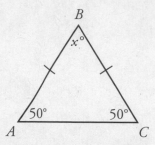

Because $50 + 50 + x = 180$, $x = 80$.

3. **(C).** The three angles in a triangle must sum to 180°, so $3a = 180$ and $a = 60$ (the triangle is equilateral). The four angles in a quadrilateral must sum to 360°, so $4b = 360$ and $b = 90$ (the angles are right angles, so the figure is a rectangle).

Substitute the values of $a$ and $b$ into Quantity A to get $2(60) + 90 = 120 + 90 = 210$. Likewise, substitute into Quantity B to get $3(60) + \dfrac{90}{3} = 180 + 30 = 210$. The two quantities are equal.

4. **(C).** Since $c$ and $x$ are vertical angles, they are equal. This means their positions in the quantities can be switched to put all the angles in the same triangle together:

**Quantity A**        **Quantity B**

$a + b + c$          $x + y + z$

The three angles inside a triangle sum to 180°, so the two quantities are equal.

5. **30.** To find the area of a triangle, a base and height are needed. If the length of $AB$ can be determined, then $AB$ can be the height and $AC$ can be the base, because the two sides are perpendicular to each other.

Use the Pythagorean theorem to find the length of side $AB$: $(a)^2 + (12)^2 = (13)^2$, so $a^2 + 144 = 169$, which means that $a^2 = 25$, and finally $a = 5$. Alternatively, recognize that the triangle is a Pythagorean triple 5–12–13.

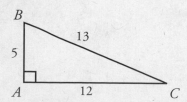

Base and height are known, so Area $= \dfrac{(12)(5)}{2} = 30$.

**MANHATTAN** PREP

6. **11.** To find the perimeter of triangle *ABC*, sum the lengths of all three sides. Side *BC* is not labeled, so inferences must be made from the given in the question.

Given the degree measures of two of the angles in triangle *ABC,* the degree measure of the third can be determined. If the third angle is *x*°, then $30 + 75 + x = 180$ and therefore $x = 75$.

Angle *BAC* and angle *BCA* are both 75°, which means triangle *ABC* is an isosceles triangle. If those two angles are equal, their opposite sides are also equal. Side *AB* has a length of 4, so *BC* also has a length of 4:

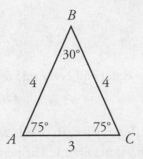

To find the perimeter, sum the lengths of the three sides: $4 + 4 + 3 = 11$.

7. **10.** Side *HI* is not labeled, so inferences will have to be drawn from other information provided in the figure. Two of the angles of triangle *GHI* are labeled, so if the third angle is *x*°, then $37 + 53 + x = 180$. That means $x = 90$, and the triangle really looks like this:

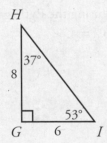

You should definitely redraw once you discover the triangle is a right triangle!

Now you can use the Pythagorean theorem to find the length of *HI*. *HI* is the hypotenuse, so $(6)^2 + (8)^2 = c^2$, which means $36 + 64 = 100 = c^2$, so $c = 10$. The length of *HI* is 10.

Alternatively, recognize the Pythagorean triple: triangle *GHI* is a 6–8–10 triangle.

8. **(C).** All isosceles right triangles (or 45–45–90 triangles) have sides in the ratio of $1 : 1 : \sqrt{2}$. Thus, an isosceles right triangle with hypotenuse $8\sqrt{2}$ has sides of 8, 8, and $8\sqrt{2}$. Use the two legs of 8 as base and height of the triangle in the formula for area:

$$A = \frac{bh}{2} = \frac{(8)(8)}{2} = 32$$

9. **(B).** To determine which triangle has the greater perimeter, find all three side lengths of both triangles. Begin with triangle $ABC$, in which two of the angles are labeled, so the third can be calculated. If the unknown angle is $x°$, then $60 + 60 + x = 180$ and, therefore, $x = 60$.

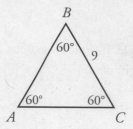

All three angles in triangle $ABC$ are 60°. If all three angles are equal, all three sides are equal and every side of triangle $ABC$ has a length of 9. The perimeter of $ABC$ is $9 + 9 + 9 = 27$.

Now look at triangle $DEF$, which is a right triangle. Use the Pythagorean theorem to find the length of side $EF$, which is the hypotenuse, so $(5)^2 + (12)^2 = c^2$, which means $25 + 144 = 169 = c^2$ and, therefore, $c = 13$. The perimeter of $DEF$ is $5 + 12 + 13 = 30$. Alternatively, 5–12–13 is a Pythagorean triple.

Because $30 > 27$, triangle $DEF$ has a greater perimeter than triangle $ABC$. Quantity B is greater.

10. **12.** Start by redrawing the figure, filling in all the information given in the text. To find the area of triangle $XYZ$, a base and a height are required. If side $XZ$ is a base, then $YW$ can act as a height, as these two are perpendicular.

Because triangle $ZYW$ is a right triangle with two known sides, the third can be determined using the Pythagorean theorem: $ZY$ is the hypotenuse, so $(a)^2 + (3)^2 = (5)^2$, meaning that $a^2 + 9 = 25$ and $a^2 = 16$, so $a = 4$.

Alternatively, recognize the Pythagorean triple: $ZYW$ is a 3–4–5 triangle:

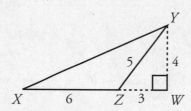

The area of triangle $XYZ$ is $\dfrac{bh}{2} = \dfrac{(6)(4)}{2} = 12$.

11. **(D).** The problem indicates that $x + z = 110$. Since the angles of a triangle must sum to 180°, $x + y + z = 180$. Substitute 110 for $x + z$ on the left side:

$y + 110 = 180$
$y = 70$

The problem compares $x$ and $y$. Although $y$ is known, the exact value of $x$ is not known, only that it must be greater than 0 and less than 110. The relationship cannot be determined from the information given.

12. **(D).** An isosceles triangle has two equal sides, so this triangle must have a third side of either 8 or 5. Use the Third Side Rule (any side of a triangle must be greater than the difference of the other two sides and less than their sum) to check whether both options are actually possible.

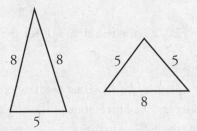

Since $8 - 5 = 3$ and $8 + 5 = 13$, the third side has to be greater than 3 and less than 13. Therefore, that side could indeed be either 5 or 8. The two quantities could be equal, or Quantity A could be less than Quantity B, so the relationship cannot be determined from the information given.

13. **(C).** An isosceles triangle has two equal sides, so this triangle must have a third side of either 2 or 11. Because one side is so long and the other so short, it is worth testing via the Third Side Rule (any side of a triangle must be greater than the difference of the other two sides and less than their sum) to see whether both possibilities are really possible.

From the Third Side Rule, a triangle with sides of 2 and 11 must have a third side greater than $11 - 2 = 9$ and less than $11 + 2 = 13$. Since 2 is not between 9 and 13, it is just not possible to have a triangle with sides of length 2, 2, and 11. However, a 2–11–11 triangle is possible. So the third side must be 11.

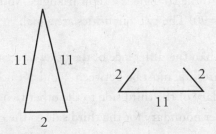

The two quantities are equal.

14. **(A).** Within any triangle, the following is true: the larger the angle, the longer the side opposite that angle.

The side opposite the 45° angle ($AC$) must be longer than the side opposite the 37° angle ($BC$): $AC > BC$. Quantity A is greater.

15. **(C).** By definition, the exterior angle $d$ is equal to the sum of the two opposite interior angles. Thus, $d = a + b$.

Alternatively, label the interior angle at vertex $C$ as $c°$. The sum of the angles in a triangle is 180°, so $a + b + c = 180$. The sum of angles that form a line is also 180, so $c + d = 180$, or $c = 180 - d$. Substitute into the first equation:

$$a + b + c = 180$$
$$a + b + (180 - d) = 180$$

$$a + b - d = 0$$
$$a + b = d$$

(This, incidentally, is the proof of the rule stated in the first line of this explanation.)

16. **(A).** Putting the constraints together, $60 < y < z$. That means that $y + z > 120$, leaving less than 60° for the remaining angle $x$. The angles can now be ordered by size: $x < y < z$.

The shortest side is across from the smallest angle, which is $x$, so the shortest side must be $BC$. The median length side is across from the median angle, which is $y$, so the median length side must be $AC$. Since none of the angles are equal, none of the sides are equal, and the length of $AC$ is greater than the length of $BC$. Quantity A is greater.

17. **(C).** The area of a triangle is equal to $\dfrac{bh}{2}$. The two triangles have equal bases, since $XY = YZ$. They also have the same height, since they both have the same height as the larger triangle $XWZ$. The two quantities are equal.

18. **(C).** Do not *assume* that $x = 90$. Instead, since all three side lengths are labeled, *test* whether the triangle is a right triangle by plugging into the Pythagorean theorem and seeing whether the result is a true statement:

$$5^2 + 7^2 = \left(\sqrt{74}\right)^2$$
$$25 + 49 = 74$$
$$74 = 74$$

Since 74 equals 74, the Pythagorean theorem does apply to this triangle. So the triangle is a right triangle. Notice also that the side across from $x$ was used as the hypotenuse. It must be that $x = 90$. The two quantities are equal.

19. **(C).** From the Third Side Rule, any side of a triangle must be greater than the difference of the other two sides and less than their sum. Since $9 - 7 = 2$ and $9 + 7 = 16$, the unknown third side must be between 2 and 16, not inclusive. To get the lower boundary for the perimeter, add the lower boundary of the third side to the other two sides: $2 + 7 + 9 = 18$. To get the upper boundary for the perimeter, add the upper boundary for the third side to the other two sides: $16 + 7 + 9 = 32$. Thus, $p$ must be between 18 and 32, not inclusive—in other words, $18 < p < 32$.

20. **(B).** You may have memorized the 3–4–5 Pythagorean triple, of which 9–12–15 is a multiple. This question is trying to exploit this—don't be tricked into thinking that $y = 15$. In a 9–12–15 triangle, 15 would have to be the hypotenuse. In any right triangle, the hypotenuse must be the longest side.

Since the given triangle has 12 as the hypotenuse, the leg of length $y$ must be less than 12, and thus less than 15. At this point, it is safe to choose (B). Although unnecessary, to get the actual value of $y$, apply the Pythagorean theorem:

$$9^2 + y^2 = 12^2$$
$$81 + y^2 = 144$$
$$y^2 = 63$$

So $y$ is a little less than 8, which is definitely less than 15. Quantity B is greater.

**MANHATTAN**
PREP

21. **(A).** One good approach here is to test the value in Quantity B. If angle $x$ equals 90°, then this is a right triangle. Use the legs of 6 and 8 to find the hypotenuse using the Pythagorean theorem: $6^2 + 8^2 = c^2$ will tell you that $c$ equals 10 in this case. (Or, memorize the 6–8–10 multiple of the 3–4–5 Pythagorean triple, since it appears often on the GRE.) Since the hypotenuse is slightly longer than 10, the angle across from the "hypotenuse" must actually be slightly larger than 90°. Therefore, $x$ is greater than 90.

22. **(C).** If $AC$ is parallel to $DE$, then triangles $DBE$ and $ABC$ are similar. If $BE = 2EC$ then if $EC$ is set to equal $x$, $BE$ would equal $2x$ and $BC$ would equal $x + 2x$, or $3x$. That means that the big triangle is in a 3 : 2 ratio with the small triangle (since $BC : BE = 3x : 2x$).

Set up the proportion for the bottom sides of these triangles, both of which are opposite the shared vertex at $B$:

$$\frac{2}{3} = \frac{DE}{AC}$$

$$\frac{2}{3} = \frac{12}{AC}$$

$$2(AC) = 36$$

$$AC = 18$$

The two quantities are equal.

23. **(B).** From the Third Side Rule, a triangle with sides of 8 and 9 must a have a third side greater than $9 - 8 = 1$ and less than $8 + 9 = 17$. Since $17^2$ is 289, which is less than 290, the measure of the third side is definitely less than $\sqrt{290}$. Quantity B is greater.

24. **(E).** An equilateral triangle with side length 6 can be drawn as:

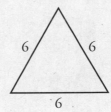

In order to find the area, recall that the area of a triangle is $A = \dfrac{bh}{2}$. The base of the triangle is already known to be 6, so find the height in order to solve for area. The height is the straight line from the highest point on the triangle dropped down perpendicular to the base:

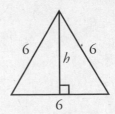

The angle opposite $h$ must be 60°, since it is one of the three angles of the original equilateral triangle. Thus, the triangle formed by $h$ is a 30–60–90 triangle as shown below.

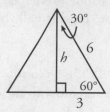

Using the properties of 30–60–90 triangles, $h$ is equal to the shortest side multiplied by $\sqrt{3}$. Thus $h = 3\sqrt{3}$ and the area is

$$A = \frac{bh}{2} = \frac{6 \times 3\sqrt{3}}{2} = 9\sqrt{3}$$

25. **(B).** Since there are two unknowns, look for two equations to solve. The first equation comes from the fact that $3x$ and $5y$ make a straight line, so they must sum to 180:

$$3x + 5y = 180$$

A triangle with at least two sides of equal length is called an isosceles triangle. In such a triangle, the angles opposite the two equal sides are themselves equal in measure. In this case, the two sides with length 3 are equal, so the angles opposite them ($y$ and $3x$) must also be equal:

$$y = 3x$$

Substitute for $y$ in the first equation:

$$3x + 5(3x) = 180$$
$$3x + 15x = 180$$
$$18x = 180$$
$$x = 10$$

26. **(E).** If the area of the triangle is 50, then $\dfrac{bh}{2} = 50$. In an isosceles right triangle, the base and height are the two perpendicular legs, which have equal length. Since base = height, substitute another $b$ in for $h$:

$$\frac{b^2}{2} = 50$$
$$b^2 = 100$$
$$b = 10$$

An isosceles right triangle follows the 45–45–90 triangle formula, so the hypotenuse is $10\sqrt{2}$.

**MANHATTAN**
PREP

Alternatively, use the Pythagorean theorem to find the hypotenuse:

$$10^2 + 10^2 = c^2$$
$$200 = c^2$$

Thus, $c = \sqrt{200} = \sqrt{100 \times 2} = 10\sqrt{2}$.

27. **(E).** For convenience, put the letter $D$ on the point at the right angle between $A$ and $C$, as shown:

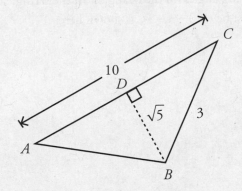

Solve this multi-step problem by working backwards from the goal. To find the length of $AB$, use the Pythagorean theorem on triangle $ADB$, since angle $ADB$ must be a right angle. In order to use the Pythagorean theorem, find the lengths of the two legs. $BD$ is known, so $AD$ needs to be determined. Since $AD$ and $DC$ sum to a line segment of length 10, $AD = 10 - DC$.

Finally, to find $DC$, apply the Pythagorean theorem to triangle $BDC$:

$$(\sqrt{5})^2 + (DC)^2 = 3^2$$
$$5 + (DC)^2 = 9$$
$$(DC)^2 = 4$$
$$DC = 2$$

Therefore, $AD = 10 - DC = 10 - 2 = 8$. Now apply the Pythagorean theorem to $ADB$:

$$(\sqrt{5})^2 + 8^2 = (AB)^2$$
$$5 + 64 = (AB)^2$$
$$69 = (AB)^2$$
$$AB = \sqrt{69}$$

28. **(C).** Because this is a right triangle, the Pythagorean theorem applies to the lengths of the sides. The Pythagorean theorem states that $a^2 + b^2 = c^2$, where $c$ is the hypotenuse and $a$ and $b$ are the legs of a right triangle. Plug the expressions into the theorem and simplify:

$$(x - 1)^2 + (x + 2)^2 = (x + 5)^2$$
$$(x^2 - 2x + 1) + (x^2 + 4x + 4) = x^2 + 10x + 25$$
$$2x^2 + 2x + 5 = x^2 + 10x + 25$$
$$x^2 - 8x - 20 = 0$$

$$(x - 10)(x + 2) = 0$$
$$x = 10 \text{ or } x = -2$$

However, $x = -2$ is not an option; side lengths can't be negative. So $x$ must equal 10. This is *not* the final answer, however. The question asks for side length $AC$:

$$AC = x + 2 = 10 + 2 = 12$$

29. **(B).** The question compares $x + y$ with 110. To do so, fill in the missing angles on the triangles. In the triangle on the left, all three angles must sum to 180°. Therefore, the missing angle must be $(180 - x - y)$, as shown here:

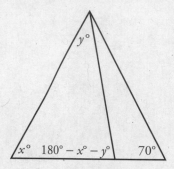

Now consider the angle next to the one you just solved for. These two angles sum to 180°, forming a straight line. So the adjacent angle must be $x + y$:

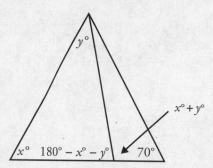

Alternatively, notice also that $x + y$ is the exterior angle to the triangle on the left, so it must be the sum of the two opposite interior angles (namely, $x$ and $y$).

Now, the three angles of a triangle must sum to 180°, and no angle can equal 0. So any *two* angles in a triangle must sum to *less* than 180°. Consider the triangle on the right side, which contains angles of $x + y$ and 70°. Their sum is less than 180°:

$$(x + y) + 70 < 180$$

Subtract 70 from both sides:

$$x + y < 110$$

Quantity B is greater.

**MANHATTAN**
PREP

30. **(C).** First determine how the quantities relate to the triangle. For instance, examine Quantity A, the product of *BE* and *AC*. Notice that *BE* is the height of the largest triangle *ABC*, while *AC* is the base. This product should remind you of the formula for area: $A = \dfrac{bh}{2}$.

Plug in $b = AC$ and $h = BE$, then move the 2:

$$2 \times \text{Area} = (AC)(BE)$$

What about Quantity B, the product of *BC* and *AD*? If you consider *BC* the base, then *AD* is the height to that base. So you can put $b = BC$ and $h = AD$ into the area formula, as before:

$$2 \times \text{Area} = (BC)(AD)$$

Both Quantity A and Quantity B are twice the area of the big triangle *ABC*. The two quantities are equal.

31. **(E).** If *DE* and *AC* are parallel lines, triangles *ABC* and *DBE* are similar. That means that there is a fixed ratio between corresponding sides of the two triangles. Since $AC = 12$ and $DE = 8$, that ratio is 12 : 8 or 3 : 2. This means that each side of triangle *ABC* (the larger triangle) is 1.5 times the corresponding side of triangle *DBE* (the smaller triangle), as shown below:

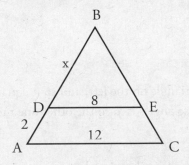

Assign a value of *x* to line *DB*, in order to set up the following proportion:

$$\frac{AB}{DB} = \frac{3}{2} = \frac{2+x}{x}$$

$$3x = 2(2 + x)$$
$$3x = 4 + 2x$$
$$x = 4$$

Since the question is asking for the value of *AB*, the answer is $2 + 4 = 6$.

32. **(C).** To compare *DC* and *AB*, first solve for the unlabeled angles in the diagram. The two angles at point *B* make a straight line, so they sum to 180°, and the unlabeled angle is $180 - 2x$, as shown:

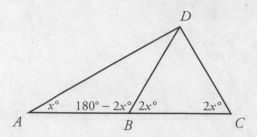

Now ensure that the angles of triangle *ADB* on the left sum to 180°. The top vertex of triangle *ADB* must measure $180 - x - (180 - 2x) = 180 - x - 180 + 2x = x$.

Therefore, the figure becomes:

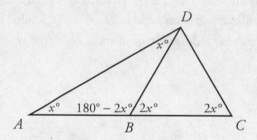

Alternatively, notice that angle *DBC* (equal to $2x$) is the exterior angle to the triangle on the left, and so it equals the sum of the two opposite interior angles in that triangle on the left. One of those angles is *x*, so the other one must be *x* as well.

Now apply the properties of isosceles triangles. The two angles labeled *x* are equal, so the triangle that contains them (triangle *ADB*) is isosceles, and the sides opposite those equal angles are also equal. Put a slash through those sides (*AB* and *BD*) to mark them as the same length.

Likewise, the two angles labeled $2x$ are equal, so the triangle that contains them (triangle *BDC*) is isosceles, and the sides opposite those angles (*BD* and *DC*) are equal. Add one more slash through *DC* in the figure:

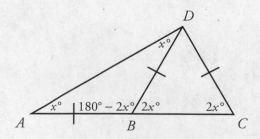

Thus, sides *AB* and *DC* have the same length. The two quantities are equal.

**MANHATTAN**
PREP

**33. (B).** To compute the perimeter of this triangle, sum the lengths of all three sides. Because one angle is labeled as a right angle and another as 30°, right triangle $ABC$ is a 30–60–90 triangle. For any 30–60–90 triangle, the sides are in these proportions:

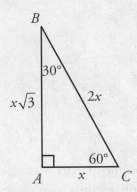

Match up this universal 30–60–90 triangle to the given triangle, in order to find $x$ in this particular case. The only labeled side in the given triangle (6) matches the $x\sqrt{3}$ side in the universal triangle (they're both opposite the 60° angle), so set them equal to each other:

$$6 = x\sqrt{3}$$

$$x = \frac{6}{\sqrt{3}}$$

Rationalize the denominator by multiplying by $\frac{\sqrt{3}}{\sqrt{3}}$ (which does not change the value of $x$, as $\frac{\sqrt{3}}{\sqrt{3}}$ is just a form of 1):

$$x = \frac{6}{\sqrt{3}}\left(\frac{\sqrt{3}}{\sqrt{3}}\right)$$

$$x = \frac{6\sqrt{3}}{3}$$

$$x = 2\sqrt{3}$$

Now figure out all the sides in the given triangle. The length of side $AC$ is $x = 2\sqrt{3}$, the length of side $AB$ is given as 6, and the length of side $BC$ is $2x = 2(2\sqrt{3}) = 4\sqrt{3}$.

Finally, sum all the sides to get the perimeter:

$$\text{Perimeter} = 6 + 2\sqrt{3} + 4\sqrt{3}$$
$$\text{Perimeter} = 6 + 6\sqrt{3}$$

34. **(B).** First, draw a diagram and label all the givens:

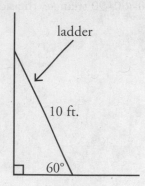

Since the wall is vertical and the floor is horizontal, the angle where they meet is 90°. So the triangle is 30–60–90. The question asks for the vertical distance from the top of the ladder to the floor, so represent this length as $x$:

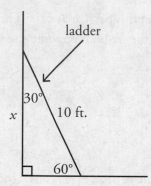

In any 30–60–90 triangle, the short leg (opposite the 30° angle) is the hypotenuse divided by 2, making the floor side equal to $10 \div 2 = 5$ feet. The longer leg (opposite the 60° angle) is $\sqrt{3}$ times the short leg. So $x = 5\sqrt{3}$ feet.

35. **(C).** Draw a diagram and label the sides of the triangle with the information given. Since $AC$ is three times as long as $CB$, label $CB$ as $x$ and $AC$ as $3x$, as shown:

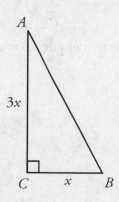

Use the area of the triangle, which is given as 9, to find the base $x$ and the height $3x$. The formula for area is $A = \dfrac{bh}{2}$. Plug in and solve for $x$:

$$9 = \frac{x(3x)}{2} = \frac{3x^2}{2}$$

**MANHATTAN**
PREP

$$18 = 3x^2$$
$$6 = x^2$$
$$\sqrt{6} = x$$

So $CB = \sqrt{6}$ and $AC = 3\sqrt{6}$. Use the Pythagorean theorem to find $AB$:

$$(AB)^2 = (\sqrt{6})^2 + (3\sqrt{6})^2$$
$$(AB)^2 = 6 + 54 = 60$$
$$AB = \sqrt{60} = 2\sqrt{15}$$

36. **(A).** Since the bottom left and bottom right angles are both equal to $y°$, the triangle is isosceles, and the sides opposite those angles ($AB$ and $BC$) must also be equal:

$$2x - 5 = x + 4$$
$$x - 5 = 4$$
$$x = 9$$

$BC$ is therefore equal to $9 + 4 = 13$. Quantity A is greater.

37. **(B).** Redraw the figure and label the equal sides:

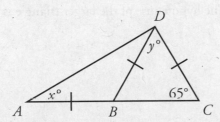

The small triangle on the left ($ADB$) is isosceles as it has two sides of equal length. Likewise for the small triangle on the right ($BDC$) within it. In an isosceles triangle, the angles opposite the two equal sides are themselves equal in measure. Accordingly, label more angles on the figure:

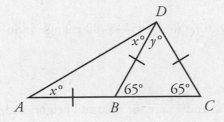

The three angles in the triangle on the right must sum to 180°:

$$65 + 65 + y = 180$$
$$130 + y = 180$$
$$y = 50$$

The two angles at point $B$ make a straight line, so they sum to 180°. So the unlabeled angle must be $180 - 65 = 115°$.

Finally, the three angles in the triangle on the left must sum to 180°:

$$x + x + 115 = 180$$
$$2x = 65$$
$$x = 32.5$$

So $y$ is greater than $x$. Quantity B is greater.

38. **(C).** Redraw the figure and label all angles, applying the rule that the angles in a triangle sum to 180°:

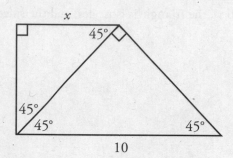

These are two separate 45–45–90 triangles. In a 45–45–90 triangle, the sides are in a $1 : 1 : \sqrt{2}$ ratio. Thus, the length of each leg equals the length of the hypotenuse divided by $\sqrt{2}$. The hypotenuse of the larger triangle is 10, so each leg of that triangle is $\dfrac{10}{\sqrt{2}}$.

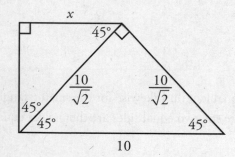

The hypotenuse of the smaller triangle is $\dfrac{10}{\sqrt{2}}$. Divide by $\sqrt{2}$ again according to the 45–45–90 triangle ratio $(1 : 1 : \sqrt{2})$ to see that $x = \dfrac{10}{\sqrt{2}\sqrt{2}} = \dfrac{10}{2} = 5$.

39. **Angle $ACB$ equals 90° and $AB = 17$ only.** If angle $ACB = 90°$, then 8 and 15 are the base and height, and you can calculate the area. The first statement is sufficient.

If $AB = 17$, you can plug 8, 15, and 17 into the Pythagorean theorem to see whether you get a true statement. Use 17 as the hypotenuse in the Pythagorean theorem because 17 is the longest side:

$$8^2 + 15^2 = 17^2$$
$$64 + 225 = 289$$
$$289 = 289$$

Since this is true, the triangle is a right triangle with the right angle at $C$. If angle $ACB = 90°$, then 8 and 15 are the base and height, and you can calculate the area. (Since 8–15–17 is a Pythagorean triple, if you had that fact memorized, you could skip the step above.) The second statement is sufficient.

Knowing that $ABC$ is a right triangle (the third statement) is *not* sufficient to calculate the area because it's not specified which angle is the right angle. A triangle with sides of 8 and 15 could have hypotenuse 17, but another scenario is possible: perhaps 15 is the hypotenuse. In this case, the third side is shorter than 15, and the area is smaller than in the 8–15–17 scenario.

40. **(A).** The three interior angles of the triangle sum to 180°. Try an example: say each interior angle is 60°. In that case, $a$, $b$, and $c$ would each equal 120° (since two angles that make up a straight line sum 180), and Quantity A would equal 360°.

It is possible to prove this result in general by expressing each interior angle in terms of $a$, $b$, and $c$, and then setting their sum equal to 180°:

$$(180 - a) + (180 - b) + (180 - c) = 180$$
$$540 - a - b - c = 180$$
$$360 = a + b + c$$

Quantity A is greater.

41. **(B).** Since both triangles have a 90° angle and an angle $x°$, the third angle of each is the same as well (because the three angles in each triangle sum to 180°). All the corresponding angles are equal, so the triangles are similar, and the ratio of corresponding sides is constant.

The smaller triangle is a 3–4–5 Pythagorean triple (the missing hypotenuse is 5). Set up a proportion that includes two pairs of corresponding sides. The words "4 is to 10 as 5 is to $m$" become this equation:

$$\frac{4}{10} = \frac{5}{m}$$
$$4m = 50$$
$$m = 12.5$$

Quantity B is greater.

42. **7.8.** Begin by noting that the triangle on the left is a 5–12–13 Pythagorean triple, so the bottom side is 5. Subtract $12.2 - 5 = 7.2$ to get the bottom side of the triangle on the right.

Next, the two unmarked angles that "touch" at the middle must sum to 90°, because they form a straight line together with the right angle of 90° between them, and all three angles must sum to 180°. Mark the angle on the left $x$. The angle on the right must then be $90 - x$.

Now the other angles that are still unmarked can be labeled in terms of $x$. Using the rule that the angles in a triangle sum to 180°, the angle between 12 and 13 must be $90 - x$, while the last angle on the right must be $x$, as shown:

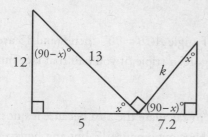

Since each triangle has angles of 90, $x$, and $90 - x$, the triangles are similar. This observation is the key to the problem. Now you can make a proportion, carefully tracking which side corresponds to which. The 7.2 corresponds to 12, since each side is across from angle $x$. Likewise, $k$ corresponds to 13, since each side is the hypotenuse. Write the equation and solve for $k$:

$$\frac{7.2}{12} = \frac{k}{13}$$

$$\frac{(13)7.2}{12} = k$$

$$7.8 = k$$

**MANHATTAN**
PREP

# Chapter 28

## of

5 lb. Book of GRE® Practice Problems

# Coordinate Geometry

# In This Chapter...

Coordinate Geometry

Coordinate Geometry Answers

# Coordinate Geometry

For questions in the Quantitative Comparison format ("Quantity A" and "Quantity B" given), the answer choices are always as follows:

(A)   Quantity A is greater.
(B)   Quantity B is greater.
(C)   The two quantities are equal.
(D)   The relationship cannot be determined from the information given.

For questions followed by a numeric entry box [      ], you are to enter your own answer in the box. For questions followed

by a fraction-style numeric entry box $\frac{\phantom{xx}}{\phantom{xx}}$, you are to enter your answer in the form of a fraction. You are not required to

reduce fractions. For example, if the answer is $\frac{1}{4}$, you may enter $\frac{25}{100}$ or any equivalent fraction.

All numbers used are real numbers. All figures are assumed to lie in a plane unless otherwise indicated. Geometric figures are not necessarily drawn to scale. You should assume, however, that lines that appear to be straight are actually straight, points on a line are in the order shown, and all geometric objects are in the relative positions shown. Coordinate systems, such as $xy$-planes and number lines, as well as graphical data presentations, such as bar charts, circle graphs, and line graphs, *are* drawn to scale. A symbol that appears more than once in a question has the same meaning throughout the question.

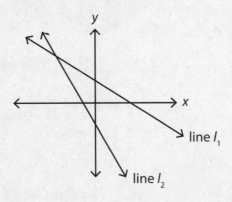

|   | **Quantity A** | **Quantity B** |
|---|---|---|
| 1. | The slope of line $l_1$ | The slope of line $l_2$ |

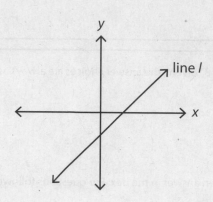

2.   If the figure above is drawn to scale, which of the following could be the equation of line *l*?

(A)  $y = 4x + 4$

(B)  $y = 4x - 4$

(C)  $y = x - 6$

(D)  $y = x + \dfrac{1}{2}$

(E)  $y = -x - 3$

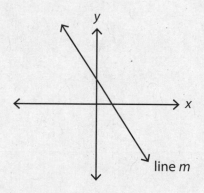

3.   If the figure above is drawn to scale, which of the following could be the equation of line *m*?

(A)  $6y + 6x = 7$

(B)  $3y = -4x - 3$

(C)  $5y + 10 = -4x$

(D)  $y = 2$

(E)  $x = -2$

**MANHATTAN**
PREP

4.  What is the slope of a line that passes through the points (−4, 5) and (1, 2)?

    (A)  $-\dfrac{3}{5}$

    (B)  −1

    (C)  $-\dfrac{5}{3}$

    (D)  $-\dfrac{7}{3}$

    (E)  −3

5.  Which of the following could be the slope of a line that passes through the point (−2, −3) and crosses the y-axis above the origin?

    Indicate <u>all</u> such slopes.

    ☐  $-\dfrac{2}{3}$

    ☐  $\dfrac{3}{7}$

    ☐  $\dfrac{3}{2}$

    ☐  $\dfrac{5}{3}$

    ☐  $\dfrac{9}{4}$

    ☐  4

6.  If a line has a slope of −2 and passes through the points (4, 9) and (6, y), what is the value of y?

    ┌─────────────┐
    │             │
    └─────────────┘

7.  What is the distance between the points (−2, −2) and (4, 6)?

    (A)  6

    (B)  7

    (C)  8

    (D)  10

    (E)  $8\sqrt{2}$

8. Which of the following points in the coordinate plane lies on the line $y = 2x - 8$?

   Indicate all such points.

   ☐   $(3, -2)$

   ☐   $(-8, 0)$

   ☐   $\left(\dfrac{1}{2}, -7\right)$

9. Which of the following points in the coordinate plane does not lie on the curve $y = x^2 - 3$?

   (A)   $(3, 6)$

   (B)   $(-3, 6)$

   (C)   $(0, -3)$

   (D)   $(-3, 0)$

   (E)   $(0.5, -2.75)$

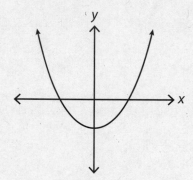

10. Which of the following could be the equation of the figure above?

    (A)   $y = x - 3$

    (B)   $y = 2x^2 - x$

    (C)   $y = x^2 - 3$

    (D)   $y = x^2 + 3$

    (E)   $y = x^3 - 3$

**MANHATTAN**
PREP

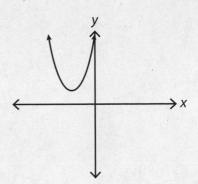

11.  Which of the following could be the equation of the parabola in the coordinate plane above?

   (A)  $y = x^2 + 3$
   (B)  $y = (x - 3)^2 + 3$
   (C)  $y = (x + 3)^2 - 3$
   (D)  $y = (x - 3)^2 - 3$
   (E)  $y = (x + 3)^2 + 3$

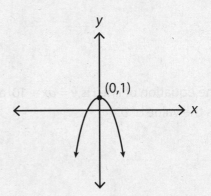

12.  Which of the following could be the equation of the parabola in the coordinate plane above?

   (A)  $y = -x - 1$
   (B)  $y = x^2 + 1$
   (C)  $y = -x^2 - 1$
   (D)  $y = -x^2 + 1$
   (E)  $y = -(x - 1)^2$

**MANHATTAN**
PREP          835

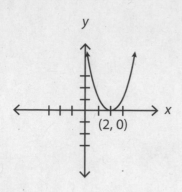

13. If the equation of the parabola in the coordinate plane above is $y = (x - h)^2 + k$ and $(-3, n)$ is a point on the parabola, what is the value of $n$?

In the coordinate plane, the equation of line $p$ is $3y - 9x = 9$.

| **Quantity A** | **Quantity B** |
|---|---|
| The slope of line $p$ | The $x$-intercept of line $p$ |

14.

15. In the $xy$-coordinate plane, lines $j$ and $k$ intersect at point $(1, 3)$. If the equation of line $j$ is $y = ax + 10$, and the equation of $k$ is $y = bx + a$, where $a$ and $b$ are constants, what is the value of $b$?

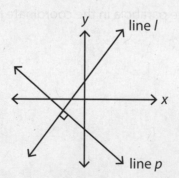

The slope of line $l$ is greater than 1.

| **Quantity A** | **Quantity B** |
|---|---|
| The slope of line $p$ | $-1$ |

16.

**MANHATTAN**
PREP

Lines $l_1$ and $l_2$ are parallel, and their respective slopes sum to less than 1.

| **Quantity A** | **Quantity B** |
|---|---|
| 17. The slope of a line perpendicular to lines $l_1$ and $l_2$ | $-\dfrac{1}{2}$ |

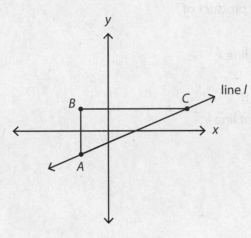

18. In the coordinate system above, the slope of line $l$ is $\dfrac{1}{3}$ and the length of line segment $BC$ is 4, how long is line segment $AB$?

(A) $\dfrac{3}{4}$

(B) $\dfrac{4}{3}$

(C) 3

(D) 4

(E) 12

19. What is the area of a triangle with vertices $(-2, 4)$, $(2, 4)$ and $(-6, 6)$ in the coordinate plane?

Lines $m$ and $n$ are perpendicular, neither line is vertical, and line $m$ passes through the origin.

| **Quantity A** | **Quantity B** |
|---|---|
| 20. The product of the slopes of lines $m$ and $n$ | The product of the $x$-intercepts of lines $m$ and $n$ |

In the coordinate plane, points $(a, b)$ and $(c, d)$ are equidistant from the origin.

$$|a| > |c|$$

| **Quantity A** | **Quantity B** |
|---|---|
| $|b|$ | $|d|$ |

21.

In the coordinate plane, lines $j$ and $k$ are parallel and the product of their slopes is positive.

The $x$-intercept of line $j$ is greater than the $x$-intercept of line $k$.

| **Quantity A** | **Quantity B** |
|---|---|
| The $y$-intercept of line $j$ | The $y$-intercept of line $k$ |

22.

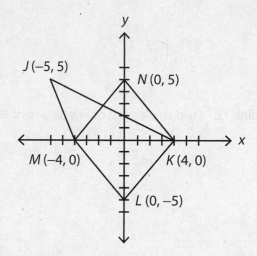

| **Quantity A** | **Quantity B** |
|---|---|
| The area of parallelogram $KLMN$ | The area of quadrilateral $JKLM$ |

23.

24. Which of the following could be the equation of a line parallel to the line $3x + 2y = 8$?

(A) $y = \dfrac{2}{3}x + 7$

(B) $y = -\dfrac{2}{3}x + 7$

(C) $y = \dfrac{3}{2}x + 7$

(D) $y = -\dfrac{3}{2}x + 7$

(E) $y = \dfrac{3}{2}x - 7$

**MANHATTAN**
PREP

# Coordinate Geometry Answers

1. **(A).** Both slopes are negative (pointing down when reading from left to right), and line $l_2$ is steeper than line $l_1$. Thus, the slope of $l_2$ has a greater *absolute value*. But since the values are both negative, the slope of $l_1$ is a greater number. For instance, the slope of $l_1$ could be $-1$ and the slope of $l_2$ could be $-2$. Whatever the actual numbers are, the slope of $l_1$ is closer to 0 and therefore greater.

2. **(C).** Since there are no numbers on the graph, the exact equation of the line cannot be determined, but the line has a positive slope (it points upward when reading from left to right) and a negative $y$-intercept (it crosses the $y$-axis below the origin). All of the answers are already in slope-intercept form ($y = mx + b$, where $m$ = slope and $b$ = $y$-intercept). Choices (A), (B), (C), and (D) have positive slope. Of those, only choices (B) and (C) have a negative $y$-intercept.

Now, is the slope closer to positive 4 or positive 1? A slope of 1 makes 45° angles when it cuts through the $x$ and $y$ axes, and this figure looks very much like it represents a slope of 1. A slope of 4 would look much steeper than this picture. Note that $xy$-planes are drawn to scale on the GRE, and units on the $x$-axis and on the $y$-axis are the same, unless otherwise noted.

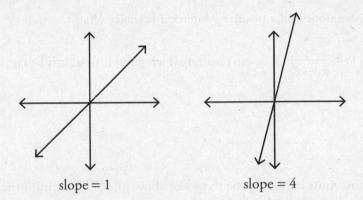

slope = 1                    slope = 4

The correct answer is (C). Note that the GRE would only give questions in which the answers are far enough apart that you can determine the intended answer.

3. **(A).** Since there are no numbers on the graph, the exact equation of the line cannot be determined, but the line has a negative slope (it points down when reading from left to right) and a positive $y$-intercept (it crosses the $y$-axis above the origin).

Change the answers to slope-intercept form ($y = mx + b$, where $m$ = slope and $b$ = $y$-intercept). First note that (D) and (E) cannot be the answers—choice (D) represents a horizontal line crossing through (0, 2), and choice (E) represents a vertical line passing through (−2, 0).

Choice (A):

$$6y + 6x = 7$$
$$6y = -6x + 7$$
$$y = -x + \frac{7}{6}$$

This line, choice (A), has a slope of $-1$ and $y$-intercept of $\frac{7}{6}$.

Choice (B):

$$3y = -4x - 3$$
$$y = -\frac{4}{3}x - 1$$

This line, choice (B), has a slope of $-\frac{4}{3}$ and $y$-intercept of $-1$.

Choice (C):

$$5y + 10 = -4x$$
$$5y = -4x - 10$$
$$y = -\left(\frac{4}{5}\right)x - 2$$

This line, choice (C), has a slope of $-\frac{4}{5}$ and $y$-intercept of $-2$.

The only choice with a negative slope and a positive $y$-intercept is choice (A).

4. **(A).** The slope formula is $m = \frac{y_2 - y_1}{x_2 - x_1}$. It doesn't matter which point is first; just be consistent. Using $(-4, 5)$ as $x_1$ and $y_1$ and $(1, 2)$ as $x_2$ and $y_2$:

$$m = \frac{2 - 5}{1 - (-4)} = -\frac{3}{5}$$

5. $\frac{5}{3}$, $\frac{9}{4}$, **and 4 only.** The line must hit a point on the $y$-axis above $(0, 0)$. That means the line could include $(0, 0.1)$, $(0, 25)$, or even $(0, 0.00000001)$. Since the $y$-intercept could get very, very close to $(0, 0)$, use the point $(0, 0)$ to calculate the slope—and then reason that since the line can't *actually* go through $(0, 0)$, the slope will actually have to be steeper than that.

The slope formula is $m = \frac{y_2 - y_1}{x_2 - x_1}$. Using $(0, 0)$ as $x_1$ and $y_1$ and $(-2, -3)$ as $x_2$ and $y_2$ (you can make either pair of points $x_1$ and $y_1$, so make whatever choice is most convenient):

$$m = \frac{-3 - 0}{-2 - 0} = \frac{-3}{-2} = \frac{3}{2}$$

**MANHATTAN**
PREP

Since the slope is positive and the line referenced in the problem needs to hit the $x$-axis above $(0, 0)$, the slope of that line will have to be greater than $\frac{3}{2}$, as in the gray lines below:

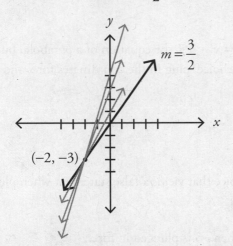

Select all answers with a slope greater than $\frac{3}{2}$. Thus, only $\frac{5}{3}$, $\frac{9}{4}$, and 4 are correct.

6. **5.** The slope formula is $m = \frac{y_2 - y_1}{x_2 - x_1}$. Using $(4, 9)$ as $x_1$ and $y_1$ and $(6, y)$ as $x_2$ and $y_2$, and plugging in $-2$ for the slope:

$$-2 = \frac{y - 9}{6 - 4}$$
$$-2 = \frac{y - 9}{2}$$
$$-4 = y - 9$$
$$5 = y$$

7. **(D).** Use the distance formula, $d = \sqrt{(x_2 - x_1)^2 + (y_2 - y_1)^2}$:

$$d = \sqrt{(4 - (-2))^2 + (6 - (-2))^2}$$
$$d = \sqrt{(6)^2 + (8)^2}$$
$$d = \sqrt{36 + 64}$$
$$d = \sqrt{100}$$
$$d = 10$$

Alternatively, recognize the Pythagorean triple 6–8–10.

8. **(3, –2) and $\left(\frac{1}{2}, -7\right)$ only.** For the point $(3, -2)$ to lie on the line $y = 2x - 8$, $y$ needs to equal $-2$ when 3 is plugged in for $x$:

$$y = 2(3) - 8$$
$$y = 6 - 8 = -2$$

**MANHATTAN**
PREP                                                                      841

Since $y$ does equal $-2$ when $x$ equals 3, the point $(3, -2)$ does lie on the line. However, when $-8$ is plugged in for $x$, $y$ does not equal 0, so $(-8, 0)$ is not a point on the line. When $\frac{1}{2}$ is plugged in for $x$, $y$ equals $-7$, so point $\left(\frac{1}{2}, -7\right)$ lies on the line.

9. **(D).** The problem asks for the point that does <u>not</u> lie on the curve. $y = x^2 - 3$ is the equation of a parabola, but you don't need to know that fact in order to answer this question. For each choice, plug in the coordinates for $x$ and $y$. For instance, try choice (A):

$$6 = (3)^2 - 3$$
$$6 = 6$$

Since this is a true statement, choice (A) lies on the curve. The only choice that yields a false statement when plugged in is choice (D), the correct answer.

For the point $(-3, 0)$ to lie on the curve $y = x^2 - 3$, $y$ needs to equal 0 when $-3$ is plugged in for $x$:

$$y = (-3)^2 - 3$$
$$y = 9 - 3 = 6$$

$y$ does not equal 0 when $x$ equals $-3$, so the point does not lie on the curve.

10. **(C).** The graph is of a parabola, so its equation must be in the general form of $y = ax^2 + bx + c$. That eliminates choices (A) and (E). Of the remaining answer choices, only answer choice (C) gives a negative $y$ value when $x = 0$ is plugged in. Also, it should be noted that when a parabola lacks a $bx$ term, that is $b = 0$, it will be centered around the $y$-axis, just as this graph is.

11. **(E).** The standard equation of a parabola in vertex form is $y = a(x - h)^2 + k$, where the vertex is $(h, k)$. Here is the vertex of the parabola described by each answer choice:

|     |          |                   |
|-----|----------|-------------------|
| (A) | (0, 3)   | On the axis       |
| (B) | (3, 3)   | Incorrect quadrant |
| (C) | (−3, −3) | Incorrect quadrant |
| (D) | (3, −3)  | Incorrect quadrant |
| (E) | (−3, 3)  | Correct           |

Only choice (E) places the vertex in the correct quadrant.

12. **(D).** The standard equation of a parabola in vertex form is $y = a(x - h)^2 + k$, where the vertex is $(h, k)$. Eliminate choice (A), as it is not the equation of a parabola. Here is the vertex of the parabola described by each remaining answer choice:

|     |          |           |
|-----|----------|-----------|
| (B) | (0, 1)   | Correct   |
| (C) | (0, −1)  | Incorrect |
| (D) | (0, 1)   | Correct   |
| (E) | (1, 0)   | Incorrect |

**MANHATTAN**
PREP

Both (B) and (D) have the correct vertex. However, choice (B) describes a parabola pointing upward from that vertex, because the $x^2$ term is positive. The negative in front of choice (D) indicates a parabola pointing downward from that vertex.

13. **25.** The equation of the given parabola is $y = (x - h)^2 + k$. The standard equation of a parabola in vertex form is $y = a(x - h)^2 + k$, where the vertex is $(h, k)$. (Since the equation of this particular parabola does not have constant $a$, $a$ must be equal to 1.)

Using $y = (x - h)^2 + k$ and the vertex $(2, 0)$ shown in the graph:

$$y = (x - 2)^2 + 0$$
$$y = (x - 2)^2$$

Since $(-3, n)$ is a point on the parabola, plug in $-3$ and $n$ for $x$ and $y$, respectively:

$$n = (-3 - 2)^2$$
$$n = (-5)^2$$
$$n = 25$$

14. **(A).** In slope intercept form ($y = mx + b$, where $m$ is the slope and $b$ is the $y$-intercept):

$$3y - 9x = 9$$
$$3y = 9x + 9$$
$$y = 3x + 3$$

The slope is 3. The $y$-intercept is also 3, but the problem asks for the $x$-intercept. To get an $x$-intercept, substitute 0 for $y$:

$$0 = 3x + 3$$
$$-3 = 3x$$
$$-1 = x$$

Thus, the slope is 3 and the $x$-intercept is $-1$. Quantity A is greater.

15. **10.** If lines $k$ and $m$ intersect at the point $(1, 3)$, then 1 can be plugged in for $x$ and 4 plugged in for $y$ in either line equation.

For line $j$:

$$y = ax + 10$$
$$3 = a(1) + 10$$
$$-7 = a$$

For line $k$, plug in not only $x = 1$ and $y = 3$, but also the fact that $a = -7$:

$$y = bx + a$$
$$3 = (b)(1) + (-7)$$
$$10 = b$$

16. **(A).** If the slope of line $l$ is greater than 1 and line $p$ is perpendicular (because of the right angle symbol on the figure), then line $p$ has a negative slope between $-1$ and 0, because perpendicular lines have negative reciprocal slopes—that is, the product of the two slopes is $-1$.

Try a few examples to better illustrate this: line $l$ could have a slope of 2, in which case line $p$ would have a slope of $-\dfrac{1}{2}$. Line $l$ could have a slope of $\dfrac{3}{2}$, in which case line $p$ would have a slope of $-\dfrac{2}{3}$. Or line $l$ could have a slope of 100, in which case line $p$ would have a slope of $-\dfrac{1}{100}$.

All of these values $(-\dfrac{1}{2}, -\dfrac{2}{3},$ and $-\dfrac{1}{100})$ are greater than $-1$. This will work with any example you try. Since line $l$ has a slope greater than 1, line $p$ has a slope with an absolute value less than 1. Because that value will also be negative, it will always be the case that $-1 <$ the slope of line $p < 0$.

17. **(D).** Since lines $l_1$ and $l_2$ are parallel, they have the same slope. Call that slope $m$. Since the slopes sum to less than 1:

$$m + m < 1$$
$$2m < 1$$
$$m < \dfrac{1}{2}$$

Thus, lines $l_1$ and $l_2$ each have the same slope that is less than $\dfrac{1}{2}$. A line perpendicular to those lines would have a negative reciprocal slope. However, there isn't much more you can do here. Lines $l_1$ and $l_2$ could have slopes of $\dfrac{1}{4}$ (in which case a perpendicular line would have slope $= -4$) or slopes of $-100$ (in which case a perpendicular line would have slope $= \dfrac{1}{100}$). Thus, the slope of the perpendicular line could be less than or greater than $-\dfrac{1}{2}$.

18. **(B).** The slope of line $l$ is $\dfrac{1}{3}$. Since slope $= \dfrac{\text{rise}}{\text{run}}$ (or "change in $y$" divided by "change in $x$"), for every 1 unit the line moves up, it will move 3 units to the right.

Since the *actual* move to the right is equal to 4, create a proportion:

$$\dfrac{1}{3} = \dfrac{AB}{4}$$

Cross-multiply to get $3AB = 4$ or $AB = \dfrac{4}{3}$.

**MANHATTAN**
PREP

19. **4.** Make a quick sketch of the three points, joining them to make a triangle. Since (–2, 4) and (2, 4) make a horizontal line, use this line as the base. Since these two points share a *y*-coordinate, the distance between them is the distance between their *x*-coordinates: 2 – (–2) = 4, as shown below:

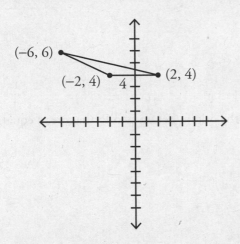

The height of a triangle is always perpendicular to the base. Drop a height vertically from (–6, 6). Subtract the *y*-coordinates to get the distance: 6 – 4 = 2.

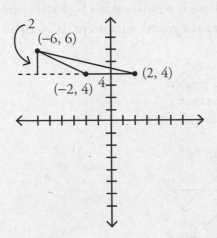

The formula for area of a triangle is $\frac{bh}{2}$. Thus, the area is $\frac{(4)(2)}{2}$, or 4.

20. **(B).** The slopes of perpendicular lines are the negative inverse of each other, so their product is –1. For example, perpendicular lines could have slopes of 2 and $-\frac{1}{2}$, or $-\frac{5}{7}$ and $\frac{7}{5}$. In all of these cases, Quantity A is –1. (The only exception is when one of the lines has an undefined slope because it's vertical, but that case has been specifically excluded.) If line *m* passes through the origin, its *x*-intercept is 0, so regardless of the *x*-intercept of line *n*, Quantity B is 0. Quantity B is greater.

21. **(B).** A point's distance from the origin can be calculated by constructing a right triangle in which the legs are the vertical and horizontal distances. Sketch a diagram in which you place (*a*, *b*) and (*c*, *d*) anywhere in the coordinate plane that you wish; then construct two right triangles using (0, 0) as a vertex.

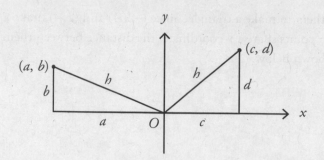

Both hypotenuses are labeled $h$, since the points are equidistant from the origin. Set up two Pythagorean equations:

$$a^2 + b^2 = h^2$$
$$c^2 + d^2 = h^2$$

So $a^2 + b^2 = c^2 + d^2$.

Since $|a| > |c|$, it is true that $a^2 > c^2$. (Try it with test numbers.) To make the equation $a^2 + b^2 = c^2 + d^2$ true, you must have $b^2 < d^2$. This means that $|b| < |d|$, and Quantity B is greater.

22. **(D).** Parallel lines have the same slope. Since the product of the two slopes is positive, either both slopes are positive or both slopes are negative. Here are two examples in which line $j$ has a greater $x$-intercept, as specified by the problem:

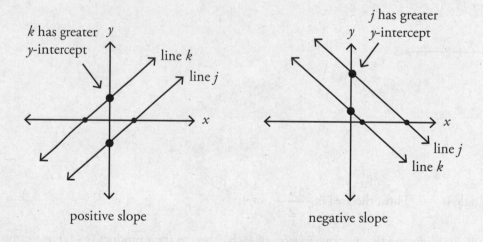

If the slopes are positive, $k$ will have the greater $y$-intercept, but if the slopes are negative, $j$ will have the greater $y$-intercept. The relationship cannot be determined from the information given.

23. **(C).** Both figures share triangle $MLK$, so there is no need to calculate anything for this part of the figure. Parallelogram $KLMN$ and quadrilateral $JKLM$ each have a "top" (the part above the $x$-axis) that is a triangle with base $MK$ ($= 8$) and height 5. If two triangles have the same base and equal heights, their areas are equal. No calculation is needed to pick (C).

**MANHATTAN**
PREP

24. **(D).** Rearrange the equation to get it into $y = mx + b$ format, where $m$ is the slope:

$$3x + 2y = 8$$
$$2y = -3x + 8$$
$$y = -\frac{3}{2}x + 4$$

The slope is $-\frac{3}{2}$. Parallel lines have the same slope, so only choice (D) is parallel.

# Chapter 29
## *of*
### 5 lb. Book of GRE® Practice Problems

# Mixed Geometry

# In This Chapter. . .

Mixed Geometry

Mixed Geometry Answers

# Mixed Geometry

For questions in the Quantitative Comparison format ("Quantity A" and "Quantity B" given), the answer choices are always as follows:

(A)   Quantity A is greater.
(B)   Quantity B is greater.
(C)   The two quantities are equal.
(D)   The relationship cannot be determined from the information given.

For questions followed by a numeric entry box [        ], you are to enter your own answer in the box. For questions followed

by a fraction-style numeric entry box $\frac{\quad}{\quad}$, you are to enter your answer in the form of a fraction. You are not required to

reduce fractions. For example, if the answer is $\frac{1}{4}$, you may enter $\frac{25}{100}$ or any equivalent fraction.

All numbers used are real numbers. All figures are assumed to lie in a plane unless otherwise indicated. Geometric figures are not necessarily drawn to scale. You should assume, however, that lines that appear to be straight are actually straight, points on a line are in the order shown, and all geometric objects are in the relative positions shown. Coordinate systems, such as *xy*-planes and number lines, as well as graphical data presentations, such as bar charts, circle graphs, and line graphs, *are* drawn to scale. A symbol that appears more than once in a question has the same meaning throughout the question.

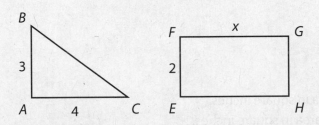

1.   Right triangle *ABC* and rectangle *EFGH* have the same perimeter. What is the value of *x*?

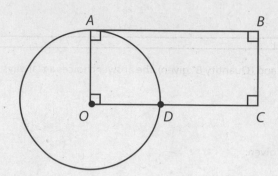

Point $O$ is the center of the circle.

2. If the area of the circle is $36\pi$ and the area of the rectangle is 72, what is the length of $DC$?

3. The center of a circle is $(10, -3)$. The point $(10, 9)$ is outside the circle, and the point $(6, -3)$ is inside the circle; neither point is on the circle. If the radius, $r$, is an integer, how many possible values are there for $r$?

    (A) Seven
    (B) Eight
    (C) Nine
    (D) Ten
    (E) Eleven

    A square's perimeter in inches is equal to its area in square inches.
    A circle's circumference in inches is equal to its area in square inches.

|      | __Quantity A__ | __Quantity B__ |
|------|----------------|----------------|
| 4.   | The side length of the square | The diameter of the circle |

**MANHATTAN**
PREP

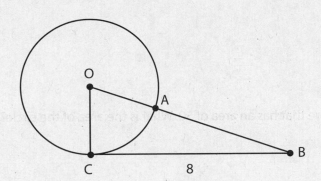

5.   In the figure above, point *O* is the center of the circle, points *A* and *C* are located on the circle, and line segment *BC* is tangent to the circle. If the area of triangle *OBC* is 24, what is the length of *AB*?

     (A)   2
     (B)   4
     (C)   6
     (D)   8
     (E)   10

In the figure above, the circle is inscribed in the square.
The area of the circle is $9\pi$.

| **Quantity A** | **Quantity B** |
|---|---|
| The area of the square | 30 |

6.

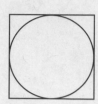

7.   In the figure above, the circle is inscribed in a square that has an area of 50. What is the area of the circle?

   (A)  $\dfrac{25\pi}{4}$

   (B)  $\dfrac{25\pi}{2}$

   (C)  $25\pi$

   (D)  $50\pi$

   (E)  $\dfrac{625\pi}{16}$

8.   What is the area of the square in the figure above?

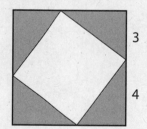

9.   In the 7-inch square above, another square is inscribed. What fraction of the larger square is shaded?

   (A)  $\dfrac{3}{12}$

   (B)  $\dfrac{24}{49}$

   (C)  $\dfrac{1}{2}$

   (D)  $\dfrac{25}{49}$

   (E)  $\dfrac{7}{12}$

**MANHATTAN**
PREP

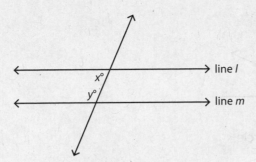

Lines *l* and *m* are parallel.

|   | **Quantity A** | **Quantity B** |
|---|---|---|
| 10. | $x + 2y$ | 180 |

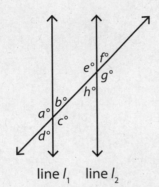

line $l_1$     line $l_2$

Lines $l_1$ and $l_2$ are parallel.

$a > 90$

|   | **Quantity A** | **Quantity B** |
|---|---|---|
| 11. | $a + f + g$ | $b + e + h$ |

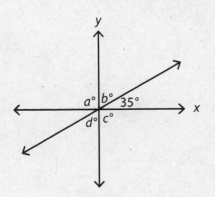

12. What is the value of $a + b + c + d$?

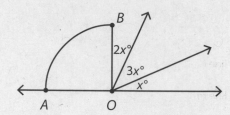

Sector *OAB* is a quarter-circle.

|  **Quantity A**  |  **Quantity B**  |
| :---: | :---: |
| 13. | *x* | 15 |

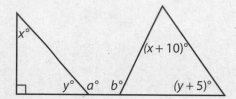

14.   What is *a* in terms of *b* and *y*?

    (A)  $b + y + 65$

    (B)  $b - y + 65$

    (C)  $b + y + 75$

    (D)  $b - 2y + 45$

    (E)  $b - y + 75$

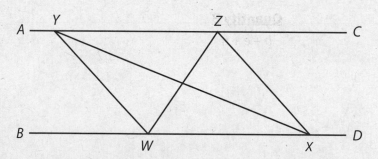

In the figure above, line segments *AC* and *BD* are parallel.

|  **Quantity A**  |  **Quantity B**  |
| :---: | :---: |
| 15. | The area of triangle *WYX* | The area of triangle *WZX* |

**MANHATTAN**
PREP

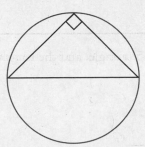

In the figure above, a right triangle is inscribed in a circle with an area of $16\pi$ cm$^2$.

| **Quantity A** | **Quantity B** |
|---|---|
| 16.    The hypotenuse of the triangle, in centimeters | 8 |

17. A rectangular box has a length of 6 centimeters, a width of 8 centimeters, and a height of 10 centimeters. What is the length of the diagonal of the box, in centimeters?

    (A)  10
    (B)  12
    (C)  $10\sqrt{2}$
    (D)  $10\sqrt{3}$
    (E)  24

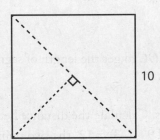

18. Julian takes a 10-inch by 10-inch square piece of paper and cuts it in half along the diagonal. He then takes one of the halves and cuts it in half again from the corner to the midpoint of the opposite side. All cuts are represented in the figure with dotted lines. What is the perimeter of one of the smallest triangles, in inches?

    (A)  10
    (B)  $10\sqrt{2}$
    (C)  20
    (D)  $10 + 10\sqrt{2}$
    (E)  $10 + 20\sqrt{2}$

# Mixed Geometry Answers

**1. 4.** Triangle *ABC* is a right triangle, so this must be a 3–4–5 triangle, and the length of side *BC* is 5. That means the perimeter of triangle *ABC* is $3 + 4 + 5 = 12$.

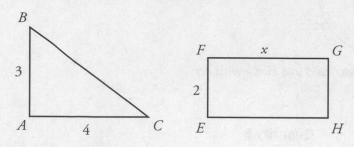

Thus, the perimeter of rectangle *EFGH* is also 12. Using that information, find *x*:

$$2 \times (2 + x) = 12.$$
$$4 + 2x = 12$$
$$2x = 8$$
$$x = 4.$$

**2. 6.** The area of this circle is $36\pi$ and the area of any circle is $\pi r^2$, so the radius of this circle is 6. Label both radii (*OA* and *OD*) as 6. Because *ABCO* is a rectangle, its area is equal to base times height, where radius *OA* is the height.

$$\text{Area of a rectangle} = bh$$
$$72 = b(6)$$
$$12 = b$$

Since *OC* is a base of the rectangle, it is equal to 12. Subtract radius *OD* from base *OC* to get the length of segment *DC*: $12 - 6 = 6$.

**3. (A).** This problem does not actually require any special formulas regarding circles. Calculate the distance between the center point $(10, -3)$ and point $(10, 9)$. Since the *x*-coordinates are the same and $9 - (-3) = 12$, the two points are 12 apart. Because $(10, 9)$ is outside of the circle, the radius must be less than 12. Similarly, calculate the distance between the center point $(10, -3)$ and point $(6, -3)$. Since the *y*-coordinates are the same, the distance is $10 - 6 = 4$. Because $(6, -3)$ is inside the circle, the radius must be more than 4. The radius must be an integer that is greater than 4 and less than 12, so it can only be 5, 6, 7, 8, 9, 10, or 11. Thus, there are seven possible values for *r*.

**4. (C).** The perimeter of a square is $4s$ and the area of a square is $s^2$ (where *s* is a side length). If the square's perimeter equals its area, set the two expressions equal to each other and solve:

$$4s = s^2$$
$$0 = s^2 - 4s$$
$$0 = s(s - 4)$$
$$4 \text{ or } 0 = s$$

**MANHATTAN**
PREP

Only $s = 4$ would result in an actual square, so $s = 0$ is not a valid solution.

The circumference of a circle is $2\pi r$ and the area of a circle is $\pi r^2$ (where $r$ is the radius). If the circle's circumference equals its area, set the two expressions equal to each other and solve:

$$2\pi r = \pi r^2$$
$$2r = r^2$$
$$0 = r^2 - 2r$$
$$0 = r(r - 2)$$
$$2 \text{ or } 0 = r$$

Only $r = 2$ would result in an actual circle, so $r = 0$ is not a valid solution.

If the radius of the circle is 2, then the diameter is 4. Thus, the two quantities are equal.

5. **(B).** Because $BC$ is tangent to the circle, angle $OCB$ is a right angle. Thus, radius $OC$ is the height of the triangle. If the area of the triangle is 24, use the area formula for a triangle (and 8 as the base, from the figure) to determine the height:

$$A = \frac{bh}{2}$$
$$24 = \frac{8 \times OC}{2}$$
$$48 = 8 \times OC$$
$$6 = OC$$

Thus, the radius of the circle is 6 (note that there are two radii on the diagram, $OC$ and $OA$). Since two sides of the right triangle are known, use the Pythagorean theorem to find the third:

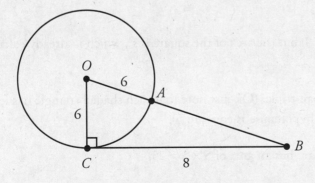

$$6^2 + 8^2 = (OB)^2$$
$$36 + 64 = (OB)^2$$
$$100 = (OB)^2$$
$$10 = OB$$

(The 6–8–10 triangle is one of the special right triangles you should memorize for the GRE!)

Since the hypotenuse $OB$ is equal to 10 and the radius $OA$ is equal to 6, subtract to get the length of $AB$. The answer is $10 - 6 = 4$.

6. **(A).** If the area of the circle is $9\pi = \pi r^2$, the radius must be 3. The radius represents half the side of the square, so the square is 6 on each side. The area of the square is thus $A = s^2 = 36$, which is greater than 30. Quantity A is greater.

7. **(B).** If the area of the square is 50, the sides of the square are $\sqrt{50} = \sqrt{25}\sqrt{2} = 5\sqrt{2}$.

If the square is $5\sqrt{2}$ "tall," so is the circle. That is, the side of the square is equal to the diameter of the circle. Since the diameter of the circle is $5\sqrt{2}$, the radius is $\dfrac{5\sqrt{2}}{2}$. Using the formula for the area of a circle, $A = \pi r^2$:

$$A = \pi \left( \frac{5\sqrt{2}}{2} \right)^2$$

$$A = \pi \left( \frac{25 \times 2}{4} \right)$$

$$A = \frac{25\pi}{2}$$

Note that even if you got a bit lost in the math, you could estimate quite reliably! The square is a bit larger than the circle, so the circle area should be a bit less than 50. Put all the answers in the calculator, using 3.14 as an approximate value for $\pi$, and you will quickly see that choice (A) is equal to 19.625, which is too small, and choice (B) is equal to 39.25, while the other three choices are much too large (larger than the square).

8. **50.** One way to solve this problem is by using the Pythagorean theorem. All sides of a square are equal to $s$, so:

$$s^2 + s^2 = 10^2$$
$$2s^2 = 100$$
$$s^2 = 50$$

Note that you *could* solve for $s$ ($s = \sqrt{50} = \sqrt{25 \times 2} = 5\sqrt{2}$), but the area of the square is $s^2$, which is already calculated above. The area of the square is 50.

9. **(B).** Each of the shaded triangles is a 3–4–5 Pythagorean triple. (Or, just note that each shaded triangle has legs of 3 and 4; the Pythagorean theorem will tell you that each hypotenuse is equal to 5).

Since each hypotenuse is also a side of the square, the square has an area of $5 \times 5 = 25$.

The larger square (the overall figure) has an area of $7 \times 7 = 49$.

Subtract to find the area of the shaded region: $49 - 25 = 24$.

The fraction of the larger square that is shaded is therefore $\dfrac{24}{49}$.

**MANHATTAN**
PREP

10. **(A).** When two parallel lines are cut by a transversal, same-side interior angles are supplementary. Thus, $x + y = 180$. Since $y$ is not 0 (the transversal and line $m$ do not "overlap"), $x + 2y$ is greater than $x + y$, which also means that $x + 2y$ is greater than 180.

11. **(A).** While the exact measures of any of the angles are not given, when parallel lines are cut by a transversal, only two angle measures are created: all the "big" angles are the same and all the "small" angles are the same. Further, the sum of a "small" and a "big" angle is 180°. (These angles are said to "form a line.") Use this fact to simplify both quantities.

Quantity A: $a + f + g = a + (f + g) = a + (180)$
Quantity B: $b + e + h = b + (e + h) = b + (180)$

Subtract 180 from each quantity, and the question is really asking for the comparison of $a$ and $b$. Since $a > 90$ and $a + b = 180$, $b = 180 - a = 180 - $ (greater than 90) = less than 90. If $a$ is greater than 90 and $b$ is less than 90, Quantity A is greater.

12. **290.** Angles that "go around in a circle" sum to 360°. It may be tempting to just subtract 35 from 360 and answer 325, but don't overlook the unlabeled angle, which is opposite and therefore equal to 35°. Therefore, subtract $35 + 35 = 70$ from 360 to get the answer, 290.

13. **(C).** If sector $OAB$ is a quarter-circle, then the angle inside the quarter-circle at $O$ measures 90°. Since angles that make up a straight line must sum to 180, $2x + 3x + x$ must sum to 90:

$2x + 3x + x = 90$
$6x = 90$
$x = 15$

The two quantities are equal.

14. **(E).** An exterior angle of a triangle is equal to the sum of the two opposite interior angles. From the left triangle, $a = x + 90$. From the right triangle, $b = (x + 10) + (y + 5) = x + y + 15$.

Alternatively, you could use the facts that the interior angles of a triangle sum to 180, as do angles that form a straight line. From the left triangle, $x + y + 90$ and $y + a$ both equal 180, so $x + y + 90 = y + a$, or $x + 90 = a$. From the right triangle, $180 = (x + 10) + (y + 5) + (180 - b)$, or $b = x + y + 15$.

The question asks for $a$ in terms of $b$ and $y$, so $x$ is the variable that needs to be eliminated. Eliminate the variable by solving one equation for $x$, and substituting this expression for $x$ in the other equation. From the right triangle:

$b = x + y + 15$
$x = b - y - 15$

From the left triangle:

$a = x + 90$
$a = (b - y - 15) + 90$
$a = b - y + 75$

15. **(C).** Both triangles, *WYX* and *WZX*, share a common base of segment *WX*. Consider the formula for the area of a triangle:

$$\text{Area} = \left(\frac{1}{2}\right)(\text{base})(\text{height})$$

If two triangles have equal bases, the triangle with the greater area is the one with the greater height. The height is a perpendicular line drawn from the highest point on the triangle to the base. In this case, the heights would be the gray lines below:

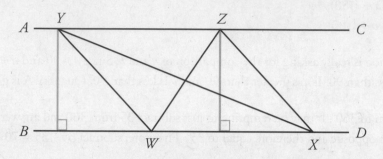

By the definition of parallel lines, *AC* and *BD* are uniform distance apart. Therefore, the heights shown are the same. Because these triangles have equal bases and heights, they must have equal areas.

16. **(C).** To solve this problem, recall that a triangle inscribed in a semicircle will be a right triangle *if and only if* one side of the triangle is the diameter (i.e., the center of the circle must lie on one side of the triangle). Because this is a right triangle, the hypotenuse must be the diameter of the circle.

To find the diameter of the circle, recall the formula for area, Area = $\pi r^2$, and set up an equation:

$$16\pi \text{ cm}^2 = \pi r^2$$
$$16 \text{ cm}^2 = r^2$$
$$r = 4 \text{ cm}$$

Given that diameter is twice the radius, the diameter (i.e., the hypotenuse of the triangle) is 8 cm. Quantity A is 8, so the two quantities are equal.

17. **(C).** A fast approach to solving this problem is to use the "Super Pythagorean theorem," which states that the diagonal of any rectangular box is *d* in the following formula:

$$d^2 = l^2 + w^2 + h^2$$

where *l*, *w*, and *h* are the length, width, and height of the box, respectively. Plugging in the given information yields:

$$d^2 = 6^2 + 8^2 + 10^2$$
$$d^2 = 36 + 64 + 100$$
$$d^2 = 200$$
$$d = 10\sqrt{2}$$

**MANHATTAN**
PREP

Alternatively, if you don't remember the Super Pythagorean, apply the normal Pythagorean theorem twice. To find the diagonal of the box, first find the diagonal of one of the sides. Use the bottom side of the figure below as the base:

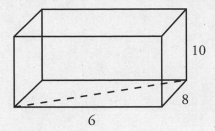

where the dashed line represents the diagonal of the base. Applying the Pythagorean theorem:

$$c^2 = a^2 + b^2$$
$$c^2 = 6^2 + 8^2$$
$$c^2 = 36 + 64$$
$$c^2 = 100$$
$$c = 10$$

From here, draw the diagonal of the box and apply the Pythagorean theorem again to the vertically oriented triangle with legs 10 and 10 again as shown:

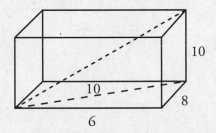

$$d^2 = 10^2 + 10^2$$
$$d^2 = 100 + 100$$
$$d^2 = 200$$
$$d = 10\sqrt{2}$$

18. **(D).** In order to compute the perimeter of one of the smaller triangles, first compute the length of the diagonal. For a square with side length 10 inches, the length of the diagonal can be computed by the Pythagorean theorem, (diagonal)$^2$ = (side)$^2$ + (side)$^2$:

$$d^2 = 10^2 + 10^2$$
$$d^2 = 200$$
$$d = 10\sqrt{2}$$

Alternatively, recognize that the diagonal of a square is always $\sqrt{2}$ times the side length.

The second cut goes from the corner to the midpoint of the diagonal, so that slice is half as long as the diagonal of the square: $\frac{10\sqrt{2}}{2} = 5\sqrt{2}$. This can be seen as

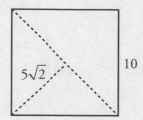

Similarly, because the remaining line in each of the smaller triangles is half of a diagonal, each is of length $5\sqrt{2}$ inches:

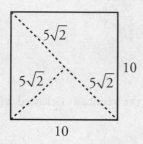

Summing the lengths of the sides, the perimeter of the smallest triangle is:

$$\text{Perimeter} = 10 + 5\sqrt{2} + 5\sqrt{2}$$
$$\text{Perimeter} = 10 + 10\sqrt{2}$$

**MANHATTAN**
PREP

# Chapter 30 *of* 30

5 lb. Book of GRE® Practice Problems

# Advanced Quant

# In This Chapter...

Advanced Quant

Advanced Quant Answers

# Advanced Quant

The following questions are *extremely* advanced for the GRE. We have included them by popular demand—students who are aiming for perfect math GRE scores often wish to practice on problems that may be even harder than any seen on the real GRE. We estimate that a GRE test-taker who does well on the first math section and therefore is given a difficult second section might see one or two problems, at most, of this level of difficulty.

**If you are *not* aiming for a perfect math score, we absolutely recommend that you skip these problems!**

If you are taking the GRE for business school or another quantitative program, you may wish to attempt some of these problems. For instance, you might do one or two of these problems—think of them as "brain teasers"—to cap off a study session from elsewhere in the book. (For reference, getting 50% of these problems correct would be a pretty incredible performance!)

Even if you *are* aiming for a perfect math score, though, please make sure you are *flawless* at the types of math problems in the *rest* of this book before you work on these. You will gain far more points by reducing minor mistakes (through practice, steady pacing, and good organization) on easy and medium questions than you would by focusing on ultra-hard questions.

For more such problems, visit the Manhattan Prep GRE blog for our monthly Challenge Problem. (Access to the archive of over fifteen dozen Challenge Problems is available to our course and Guided Self-Study students for free and to anyone else for a small fee.)

That said, attempt these Advanced Quant problems—if you dare!

1.  21 people per minute enter a previously empty train station beginning at 7:00:00 pm (7 o'clock and zero seconds). Every 9 minutes beginning at 7:04:00 pm, a train departs and everyone who has entered the station in the last 9 minutes gets on the departing train. If the last train departs at 8:25:00 pm, what is the average number of people who get on each of the trains leaving from 7:00:00 pm to 8:25:00 pm, inclusive?

    (A)  84

    (B)  136.5

    (C)  178.5

    (D)  189

    (E)  198.5

2.  The random variable $x$ has the following continuous probability distribution in the range $0 \le x \le \sqrt{2}$, as shown in the coordinate plane with $x$ on the horizontal axis:

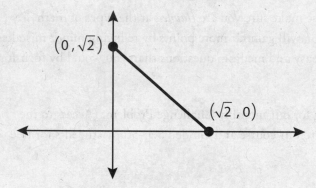

    The probability that $x < 0$ = the probability that $x > \sqrt{2} = 0$.

    What is the median of $x$?

    (A)  $\dfrac{\sqrt{2}-1}{2}$

    (B)  $\dfrac{\sqrt{2}}{4}$

    (C)  $\sqrt{2}-1$

    (D)  $\dfrac{\sqrt{2}+1}{4}$

    (E)  $\dfrac{\sqrt{2}}{2}$

$$x < 0$$

|  | **Quantity A** | **Quantity B** |
|---|---|---|
| 3. | $x^2 - 5x + 6$ | $x^2 - 9x + 20$ |

**MANHATTAN**
PREP

4.  If $x$ is a positive integer, what is the units digit of $(24)^{5+2x}(36)^6(17)^3$?

    (A)  2
    (B)  3
    (C)  4
    (D)  6
    (E)  8

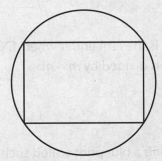

5.  In the figure above, the circumference of the circle is $20\pi$. Which of the following is the maximum possible area of the rectangle?

    (A)  80
    (B)  200
    (C)  300
    (D)  $100\sqrt{2}$
    (E)  $200\sqrt{2}$

6.  The length of each edge of a cube equals 6. What is the distance between the center of the cube to one of its vertices?

    (A)  $3\sqrt{2}$
    (B)  $6\sqrt{2}$
    (C)  $3\sqrt{3}$
    (D)  $4\sqrt{3}$
    (E)  $6\sqrt{3}$

7.  If $c$ is randomly chosen from the integers 20 to 99, inclusive, what is the probability that $c^3 - c$ is divisible by 12?

    Give your answer as a fraction.

    ```
    ┌─────────────┐
    │             │
    └─────────────┘
    ─────────────────
    ┌─────────────┐
    │             │
    └─────────────┘
    ```

8.  The remainder when 120 is divided by single-digit integer $m$ is positive, as is the remainder when 120 is divided by single-digit integer $n$. If $m > n$, what is the remainder when 120 is divided by $m - n$?

    ```
    ┌─────────────┐
    │             │
    └─────────────┘
    ```

9.  A circular microchip with a radius of 2 centimeters is manufactured following a blueprint scaled such that a measurement of 1 centimeter on the blueprint corresponds to a measurement of 0.8 millimeters on the microchip. What is the diameter of the blueprint representation of the microchip, in centimeters? (1 centimeter = 10 millimeters)

    ```
    ┌─────────────┐
    │             │ centimeters
    └─────────────┘
    ```

    For a certain quantity of a gas, pressure $P$, volume $V$, and temperature $T$ are related according to the formula $PV = kT$, where $k$ is a constant.

|  | **Quantity A** | **Quantity B** |
|---|---|---|
| 10. | The value of $P$ if $V = 20$ and $T = 32$ | The value of $T$ if $V = 10$ and $P = 78$ |

**MANHATTAN**
PREP

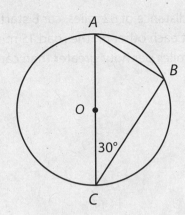

11.  The circle with center $O$ has a circumference of $12\pi\sqrt{3}$. If $AC$ is a diameter of the circle, what is the length of line segment $AB$?

    (A)  $3\sqrt{2}$
    (B)  6
    (C)  $6\sqrt{3}$
    (D)  18
    (E)  $18\sqrt{3}$

12.  A batch of widgets costs $p + 15$ dollars for a company to produce and each batch sells for $p(9 - p)$ dollars. For which of the following values of $p$ does the company make a profit?

    (A)  3
    (B)  4
    (C)  5
    (D)  6
    (E)  7

13.  If $k$ is the sum of the reciprocals of the consecutive integers from 41 to 60 inclusive, which of the following are less than $k$?

Indicate <u>all</u> such statements.

    ☐  $\dfrac{1}{4}$

    ☐  $\dfrac{1}{3}$

    ☐  $\dfrac{1}{2}$

14. Half an hour after car A started traveling from Newtown to Oldtown, a distance of 62 miles, car B started traveling along the same road from Oldtown to Newtown. The cars met each other on the road 15 minutes after car B started its trip. If car A traveled at a constant rate that was 8 miles per hour greater than car B's constant rate, how many miles had car B driven when they met?

    (A)  14

    (B)  12

    (C)  10

    (D)  9

    (E)  8

15.

$x$ and $y$ are positive integers such that $x^2 5^y = 10{,}125$

| Quantity A | Quantity B |
|:---:|:---:|
| $x^2$ | $5^y$ |

16. Which of the following is equal to $\dfrac{-2}{\sqrt{n-1}-\sqrt{n+1}}$ for all values of $n > 1$?

    (A)  $-1$

    (B)  $1$

    (C)  $2\left(\sqrt{n-1}+\sqrt{n+1}\right)$

    (D)  $\sqrt{n-1}+\sqrt{n+1}$

    (E)  $\dfrac{\sqrt{n-1}}{\sqrt{n+1}}$

17. Bank account A contains exactly $x$ dollars, an amount that will decrease by 10% each month for the next two months. Bank account B contains exactly $y$ dollars, an amount that will increase by 20% each month for the next two months. If A and B contain the same amount at the end of two months, what is the ratio of $\sqrt{x}$ to $\sqrt{y}$?

    (A)  $4:3$

    (B)  $3:2$

    (C)  $16:9$

    (D)  $2:1$

    (E)  $9:4$

**MANHATTAN**
PREP

Body Mass Index (BMI) is calculated by the formula $\dfrac{703w}{h^2}$, where $w$ is weight in pounds and $h$ is height in inches.

| Quantity A | Quantity B |
|---|---|
| 18. The number of pounds gained by a 74-inch-tall person whose BMI increased by 1.0. | The number of pounds lost by a 65-inch-tall person whose BMI decreased by 1.2. |

19. How many times does the digit grouping "57" (in that order) appear in all of the five-digit positive integers? For instance, "57" appears once in 12,357, twice in 57,057, and does not appear in 24,675.

    (A)  279

    (B)  3,091

    (C)  3,519

    (D)  3,671

    (E)  4,077

| Quantity A | Quantity B |
|---|---|
| 20. The average of all the multiples of 5 between 199 and 706 | The average of all the multiples of 10 between 199 and 706 |

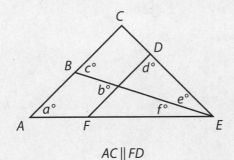

$AC \parallel FD$

| Quantity A | Quantity B |
|---|---|
| 21. $a + d - c - 90$ | $90 - e - b - f$ |

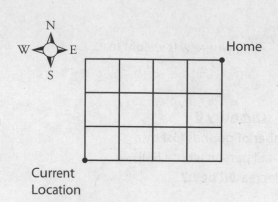

Current
Location

22. A man travels to his home from his current location on the rectangular grid shown above. If he may choose to travel north or east at any corner, but may never travel south or west, how many different paths can the man take to get home?

(A) 12
(B) 24
(C) 32
(D) 35
(E) 64

23. A bag contains 3 white, 4 black, and 2 red marbles. Two marbles are drawn from the bag. If replacement is <u>not</u> allowed, what is the probability that the second marble drawn will be red?

(A) $\dfrac{1}{36}$

(B) $\dfrac{1}{12}$

(C) $\dfrac{7}{36}$

(D) $\dfrac{2}{9}$

(E) $\dfrac{7}{9}$

$$x < 0$$

| **Quantity A** | **Quantity B** |
|---|---|
| 24. $\left(\left(25^{x}\right)^{-2}\right)^{3}$ | $\left(\left(5^{-3}\right)^{2}\right)^{-x}$ |

| **Quantity A** | **Quantity B** |
|---|---|
| 25. The sum of all the multiples of 6 between −126 and 342, inclusive | 8,502 |

**MANHATTAN**
PREP

$x$ is an integer.

|  | **Quantity A** | **Quantity B** |
|---|---|---|
| 26. | $(-1)^{x^2}+(-1)^{x^3}+(-1)^{x^4}$ | $(-1)^{x}+(-1)^{2x}+(-1)^{3x}+(-1)^{4x}$ |

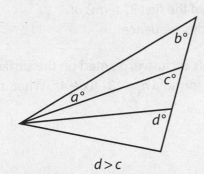

$d > c$

|  | **Quantity A** | **Quantity B** |
|---|---|---|
| 27. | $a$ | $d - b$ |

The circumference of a circle is $\dfrac{7}{8}$ the perimeter of a square.

|  | **Quantity A** | **Quantity B** |
|---|---|---|
| 28. | The area of the square | The area of the circle |

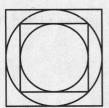

|  | **Quantity A** | **Quantity B** |
|---|---|---|
| 29. | The ratio of the area of the larger square to the area of the smaller square | Twice the ratio of the area of the smaller circle to the area of the larger circle |

$$m = 2^{16}3^{17}4^{18}5^{19}$$
$$n = 2^{19}3^{18}4^{17}5^{16}$$

|  | **Quantity A** | **Quantity B** |
|---|---|---|
| 30. | The number of zeros at the end of $m$ when written in integer form | The number of zeros at the end of $n$ when written in integer form |

The sequence of numbers $a_1, a_2, a_3, \ldots, a_n, \ldots$ is defined by

$a_n = 2^n - \dfrac{1}{2^{n-33}}$ for each integer $n \geq 1$.

| **Quantity A** | **Quantity B** |
|---|---|
| 31. The sum of the first 32 terms of this sequence | The sum of the first 31 terms of this sequence |

32. Each of 100 balls has an integer value from 1 to 8, inclusive, painted on the surface. The number $n_x$ of balls representing integer $x$ is defined by the formula $n_x = 18 - (x - 4)^2$. What is the interquartile range of the 100 integers?

 (A)  1.5
 (B)  2.0
 (C)  2.5
 (D)  3.0
 (E)  3.5

The operator ! is defined such that $a!b = a^b \times b^{-a}$.

| **Quantity A** | **Quantity B** |
|---|---|
| 33. $\dfrac{(x!4)}{(4!x)}$ | $\dfrac{x^8}{16^x}$ |

34. What is the ratio of the sum of the odd positive integers between 1 and 100, inclusive, and the sum of the even positive integers between 100 and 150, inclusive?

 (A)  2 to 3
 (B)  5 to 7
 (C)  10 to 13
 (D)  53 to 60
 (E)  202 to 251

**MANHATTAN**
PREP

35. For integer $n \geq 3$, a sequence is defined as $a_n = (a_{n-1})^2 - (a_{n-2})^2$ and $a_n > 0$ for all positive integers $n$. The first term $a_1$ is 2, and the fourth term is equal to the first term multiplied by the sum of the second and third terms. What is the third term, $a_3$?

   (A)   0
   (B)   3
   (C)   5
   (D)   10
   (E)   16

36. In a certain sequence, each term beyond the second term is equal to the average of the previous two terms. If $a_1$ and $a_3$ are positive integers, which of the following is <u>not</u> a possible value of $a_5$?

   (A)   $-\dfrac{9}{4}$

   (B)   0

   (C)   $\dfrac{9}{4}$

   (D)   $\dfrac{75}{8}$

   (E)   $\dfrac{41}{2}$

37. The operator @ is defined by the following expression: $a@b = \left|\dfrac{a+1}{a}\right| - \dfrac{b+1}{b}$ where $ab \neq 0$. What is the sum

   of the solutions to the equation $x@2 = \dfrac{x@(-1)}{2}$?

   (A)   −1
   (B)   −0.75
   (X)   −0.25
   (D)   0.25
   (E)   0.75

   $x$ is a non-negative number and the square root of $(10 - 3x)$ is greater than $x$.

   |  | **Quantity A** | **Quantity B** |
   |---|---|---|
   | 38. | $|x|$ | 2 |

The area of an equilateral triangle is greater than $25\sqrt{3}$ but less than $36\sqrt{3}$.

|  | Quantity A | Quantity B |
|---|---|---|
| 39. | The length of one of the sides of the triangle | 9 |

40. The inequality $|8 - 2x| < 3y - 9$ is equivalent to which of the following?

   (A)  $2x < \dfrac{(17 - 3y)}{2}$

   (B)  $3y + 2x > 1$

   (C)  $6y - 2 < 2x$

   (D)  $1 - y < 2x < 17 + y$

   (E)  $3y - 1 > 2x > 17 - 3y$

In the sport of mixed martial arts, more than 30% of all fighters are skilled in both the Muy Thai and Brazilian Jiu Jitsu styles of fighting. 20% of the fighters who are not skilled in Brazilian Jiu Jitsu are skilled in Muy Thai. 60% of all fighters are skilled in Brazilian Jiu Jitsu.

|  | Quantity A | Quantity B |
|---|---|---|
| 41. | The percent of fighters who are skilled in Muy Thai | 37% |

The rate of data transfer, $r$, over a particular network is directly proportional to the bandwidth, $b$, and inversely proportional to the square of the number of networked computers, $n$.

|  | Quantity A | Quantity B |
|---|---|---|
| 42. | The resulting rate of data transfer if the bandwidth is quadrupled and the number of networked computers is more than tripled | $\dfrac{4}{9}r$ |

**MANHATTAN**
PREP

# Advanced Quant Answers

1. **(C).** From 7 pm to 7:04, 84 people enter the station (21 per minute). These 84 people will get on the 7:04 train.

After that, for each 9-minute period, 9(21) = 189 people will enter the station and then get on a train. These trains will leave at 7:13, 7:22, 7:31, 7:40, 7:49, 7:58, 8:07, 8:16, and 8:25.

Since 9 trains each have 189 people and the first train has 84 people, the average is:

$$\frac{9(189) + 1(84)}{10} = 178.5$$

Note that the strange time format (minutes and seconds) doesn't make the problem any harder—the problem is actually clearer because the train comes at 7:04 and 0 seconds, rather than 7:04 and 30 seconds, at which point more people would have entered the station.

2. **(C).** A continuous probability distribution has a total area of 100%, or 1, underneath the entire curve. The median of such a distribution splits the area into two equal halves, with 50% of the area to the left of the median and the other 50% to the right of the median:

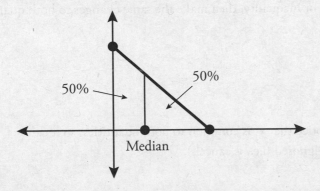

In simpler terms, the random variable $x$ has a 50% chance of being above the median and a 50% chance of being below the median. You can ignore the regions to the right or the left of this triangle, since the probability that $x$ could fall in either of those regions is zero. So the question becomes this: what point on the $x$-axis will divide the large right triangle into two equal areas?

One shortcut is to note that the area of the large isosceles right triangle must be 1, which equals the total area under any probability distribution curve. Confirm by means of the area formula for this right triangle:

$$\frac{1}{2}bh = \frac{1}{2}\left(\sqrt{2}\right)\left(\sqrt{2}\right) = \frac{2}{2} = 1.$$

The quickest way to find the median is to consider the *small* isosceles right triangle, *ABC*, as shown:

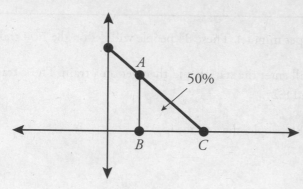

Triangle *ABC* must have an area of $\frac{1}{2}$. So what must be the length of each of its legs, *AB* and *BC*? From the formula $\frac{1}{2}bh = \frac{1}{2}$, and noting that the base *BC* equals the height *AB*, the base *BC* must be 1 (the same as the height). Since the coordinates of point *C* are ($\sqrt{2}$, 0), the coordinates of point *B* must be ($\sqrt{2} - 1$, 0). That is, the median is $\sqrt{2} - 1$.

3. **(B).** One way to solve is to set up an implied equation or inequality, then make the same changes to both quantities, and finally compare after simplifying:

| Quantity A | | Quantity B |
|:---:|:---:|:---:|
| $x^2 - 5x + 6$ | ? | $x^2 - 9x + 20$ |
| $-(x^2 - 5x + 6)$ | | $-(x^2 - 5x + 6)$ |
| 0 | ? | $-9x - (-5x) + 20 - 6$ |
| 0 | ? | $-9x + 5x + 14$ |
| 0 | < | $-4x + 14$ |

Notice that $x^2$ is common to both quantities, so it can be ignored (i.e., it cancels).

Because *x* is negative, $-4x + 14 = -4(neg) + 14 = pos + 14$, which is greater than 0.

Another way to solve is to factor and then compare based on number properties. Quantity A factors to $(x - 2)(x - 3)$. Quantity B factors to $(x - 4)(x - 5)$. Because *x* is negative, "*x* minus a positive number" is also negative. Each quantity is the product of two negative numbers, which is positive:

> Quantity A: $(x - 2)(x - 3) = (neg)(neg) = pos$
> Quantity B: $(x - 4)(x - 5) = (more\ neg)(more\ neg) = more\ pos$

Quantity B is greater.

4. **(A).** 24 to any power ends in the same units digit as 4 to the same power (if considering only the last digit of the product, consider only the last digits of the numbers being multiplied).

**MANHATTAN**
PREP

4 to any power ends in either 4 or 6 ($4^1 = 4$, $4^2 = 16$, $4^3 = 64$, etc.). If the power is odd, the answer ends in 4; if the power is even, the answer ends in 6. Since the exponent $5 + 2x$ is odd for any integer $x$, $24^{5+2x}$ ends in 4.

36 to any power ends in the same units digit as 6 to the same power. Powers of 6 always end in 6, so $36^6$ ends in 6.

17 to any power ends in the same units digit as 7 to the same power. While the units digits of the powers of 7 do indeed create a pattern, $7^3$ is just 343, which ends in 3. Thus:

$24^{5+2x}$ ends in 4
$36^6$ ends in 6
$7^3$ ends in 3

Multiplying three numbers that end in 4, 6, and 3 yields answer that ends in 2, because $(4)(6)(3) = 72$, which ends in 2.

**5. (B).** What are the possibilities for the inscribed rectangle?

The inscribed rectangle can be stretched and pulled to extremes: extremely long and thin, extremely tall and narrow, and somewhere in between:

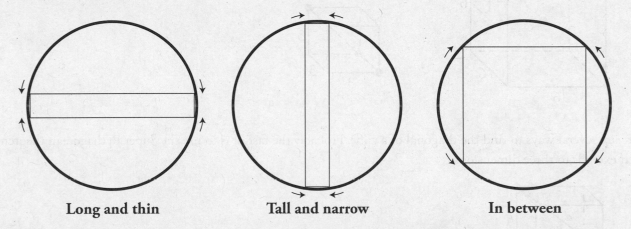

**Long and thin**         **Tall and narrow**         **In between**

The "long and thin" and "tall and narrow" rectangles have a very small area, and the "in between" rectangle has the largest possible area. In fact, the largest possible rectangle inscribed inside a circle is a square:

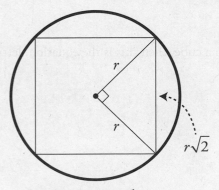

**Square: maximal area**

In this problem, the circumference is equal to $20\pi = 2\pi r$. Thus $r = 10$. The square then has a side length of $10\sqrt{2}$ and an area of $\left(10\sqrt{2}\right)^2 = 200$.

6. **(C).**

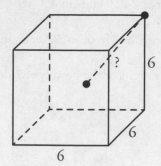

The length of any side of the cube is 6, and the question asks for the distance between the center of the cube and any of its vertices (corners). Chopping up the cube into 8 smaller cubes, the distance from the center of the $6 \times 6 \times 6$ cube to any corner is the diagonal of a $3 \times 3 \times 3$ cube.

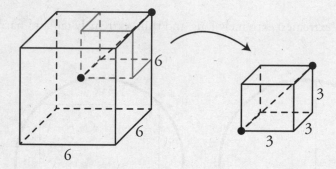

There are several ways to find the diagonal of a cube. Probably the fastest is to use the Super Pythagorean theorem, which extends to three dimensions:

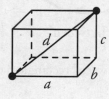

$$a^2 + b^2 + c^2 = d^2$$

In the special case when the three sides of the box are equal, as they are in a cube, then this is the equation, letting $s$ represent any side of the cube:

$$s^2 + s^2 + s^2 = d^2$$
$$3s^2 = d^2$$
$$s\sqrt{3} = d$$

Since $s = 3$, $d = 3\sqrt{3}$.

**MANHATTAN**
PREP

7. $\frac{3}{4}$ **(or any equivalent fraction).** Probability is $\frac{\left(\text{favorable outcomes}\right)}{\left(\text{total \# of possibilities}\right)}$. There are $99 - 20 + 1 = 80$ possible values for $c$, so the unknown is how many of these $c$ values yield a $c^3 - c$ that is divisible by 12.

The prime factorization of 12 is $2 \times 2 \times 3$. There are several ways of thinking about this: numbers are divisible by 12 if they are divisible by 3 and by 2 twice, or if they are multiples of both 4 and 3, or if half of the number is an even multiple of 3, etc.

The expression involving $c$ can be factored:

$$c^3 - c = c(c^2 - 1) = c(c - 1)(c + 1)$$

These are consecutive integers. It may help to put them in increasing order: $(c - 1)c(c + 1)$. Thus, this question has a lot to do with *consecutive integers*, and not only because the integers 20 to 99 themselves are consecutive.

In any set of three consecutive integers, a multiple of 3 will be included. Thus, $(c - 1)c(c + 1)$ is always divisible by 3 for any integer $c$. This takes care of part of the 12. So the question becomes "How many of the possible $(c - 1)c(c + 1)$ values are divisible by 4?" Since the prime factors of 4 are 2's, it makes sense to think in terms of odds and evens.

$(c - 1)c(c + 1)$ could be (E)(O)(E), which is definitely divisible by 4, because the two evens would each provide at least one separate factor of 2. Thus, $c^3 - c$ is divisible by 12 whenever $c$ is odd, which are the cases $c = 21, 23, 25, \ldots, 95, 97,$ 99. That's $\left(\frac{(99 - 21)}{2}\right) + 1 = \left(\frac{78}{2}\right) + 1 = 40$ possibilities.

Alternatively, $(c - 1)c(c + 1)$ could be (O)(E)(O), which will only be divisible by 4 when the even term itself is a multiple of 4. Thus, $c^3 - c$ is also divisible by 12 whenever $c$ is a multiple of 4, which are the cases $c = 20, 24, 28, \ldots,$ 92, 96. That's $\left(\frac{(96 - 20)}{4}\right) + 1 = \left(\frac{76}{4}\right) + 1 = 20$ possibilities.

The probability is thus $\frac{(40 + 20)}{80} = \frac{60}{80} = \frac{3}{4}$.

8. **0.** Since the remainder is defined as what is left over after one number is divided by another, it makes sense that the leftover amount would be positive. So why is this information provided, if the remainder is "automatically" positive? Because there is a third possibility: that the remainder is 0. If the remainder when 120 is divided by $m$ is positive, the salient point is that $\frac{120}{m}$ does not have a remainder of 0. In other words, 120 is not divisible by $m$, or $m$ is not a factor of 120. Similarly, $n$ is not a factor of 120.

Another constraint on both $m$ and $n$ is that they are single-digit positive integers. So $m$ and $n$ are integers between 1 and 9, inclusive, that are not factors of 120. Only two such possibilities exist: 7 and 9.

Since $m > n$, $m = 9$ and $n = 7$. Thus, $m - n = 2$, and the remainder when 120 is divided by 2 is 0.

9. **50 centimeters.** Microchip radius = (2 cm) $\left(10\dfrac{mm}{cm}\right)$ = 20 mm. Microchip diameter = 40 mm.

Blueprint diameter = 1 cm on blueprint per every 0.8 mm on the microchip:

$$= \left(\frac{1 \text{ cm on blueprint}}{0.8 \text{ mm on microchip}}\right)\left(40 \text{ mm diameter on microchip}\right)$$

$$= \left(1 \text{ cm on blueprint}\right)\left(\frac{40}{0.8}\right)$$

$$= \left(1 \text{ cm on blueprint}\right)\left(\frac{400}{8}\right)$$

$$= 50 \text{ cm on blueprint}$$

10. **(D).** If $PV = kT$, then $P = \dfrac{kT}{V}$. Quantity A is $P = \dfrac{k(32)}{(20)} = \dfrac{8}{5}k$.

If $PV = kT$, then $T = \dfrac{PV}{k}$. Quantity B is $T = \dfrac{(78)(10)}{k} = \dfrac{780}{k}$.

Don't rush to judgment, thinking that $780 > \dfrac{8}{5}$ means that Quantity B is greater. Notice that the $k$ term is in the numerator of one quantity (so Quantity A increases with $k$) and the denominator of the other (so the larger $k$ is, the smaller Quantity B is).

If $k = 1$, then Quantity B is greater $\left(780 > \dfrac{8}{5}\right)$. But if $k = 100$, Quantity A is greater ($160 > 7.8$). The relationship cannot be determined from the information given.

11. **(C).** Since $AC$ is a diameter of the circle, triangle $ABC$ is a right triangle and angle $ABC$ is a right angle. This means that angle $CAB$ is 60°, and the ratios of a 30–60–90 triangle can be used to solve the problem.

The circumference of the circle, $\pi d = 12\pi\sqrt{3}$, so the diameter, which is also $AC$, is $12\sqrt{3}$.

Now use ratios (specifically via the unknown multiplier $x$ to find $AB$):

|  | **AB** | **BC** | **AC** |
|---|---|---|---|
| Basic Ratio | $1x$ | $x\sqrt{3}$ | $2x$ |
| Known Side |  |  | $12\sqrt{3}$ |
| Unknown Multiplier |  |  | $x = \dfrac{12\sqrt{3}}{2} = 6\sqrt{3}$ |
| Compute Sides | $6\sqrt{3}$ | $\left(6\sqrt{3}\right)\left(\sqrt{3}\right) = 18$ | $12\sqrt{3}$ |

Line segment $AB$ has a length of $6\sqrt{3}$.

**MANHATTAN**
PREP

Alternatively, you could use estimation here if you forgot the ratios for 30–60–90 triangles. Since the longest side is always opposite the largest angle (and the shortest opposite the smallest), the sequence of sides must be $AC > BC > AB$. The diameter $AC = 12\sqrt{3} \approx 12(1.7) \approx 20.4$. From the looks of it, $AB$ is about $\frac{1}{2}$ of $AC$'s length (definitely not close to the length of $AC$), so answer choices (D) and (E) seem too long. Choices (A) and (B) are each less than $\frac{1}{3}$ of $AC$, which doesn't seem long enough.

12. **(B).** Profit equals revenue minus cost. The company's profit is:

$$
\begin{aligned}
p(9 - p) - (p + 15) &= 9p - p^2 - p - 15 \\
&= -p^2 + 8p - 15 \\
&= -(p^2 - 8p + 15) \\
&= -(p - 5)(p - 3)
\end{aligned}
$$

Profit will be zero if $p = 5$ or $p = 3$, which eliminates answers (A) and (C). For $p > 5$, both $(p - 5)$ and $(p - 3)$ are positive. In that case, the profit is negative (i.e., the company loses money). The profit is only positive if $(p - 5)$ and $(p - 3)$ have opposite signs, which occurs when $3 < p < 5$.

Alternatively, plug in the answer choices to see which value corresponds to a revenue that is higher than cost.

(A)  Cost = 18, Revenue = 18, Profit = 0   Incorrect
(B)  Cost = 19, Revenue = 20, Profit = 1   Correct
(C)  Cost = 20, Revenue = 20, Profit = 0   Incorrect
(D)  Cost = 21, Revenue = 18, Profit < 0   Incorrect
(E)  Cost = 22, Revenue = 14, Profit < 0   Incorrect

13. $\frac{1}{4}$ and $\frac{1}{3}$ only. The sum $\left( \frac{1}{41} + \frac{1}{42} + \frac{1}{43} + \frac{1}{44} + \cdots + \frac{1}{57} + \frac{1}{58} + \frac{1}{59} + \frac{1}{60} \right)$ has 20 fractional terms. It would be nearly impossible to compute if you had to find a common denominator and solve without a calculator and a lot of time. Instead, look at the maximum and minimum possible values for the sum.

Maximum: The largest fraction in the sum is $\frac{1}{41}$; $k$ is definitely smaller than $20 \times \frac{1}{41}$, which is itself smaller than $20 \times \frac{1}{40} = \frac{1}{2}$.

Minimum: The smallest fraction in the sum is $\frac{1}{60}$; $k$ is definitely larger than $20 \times \frac{1}{60} = \frac{1}{3}$.

Therefore, $\frac{1}{3} < k < \frac{1}{2}$ .

I.   $\frac{1}{4} < \frac{1}{3} < k$   YES

II.  $\frac{1}{3} < k$       YES

III. $\frac{1}{2} > k$       NO

14. **(A).** Draw a diagram to illustrate the moment at which car A and car B pass each other moving in opposite directions:

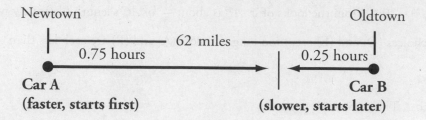

You could test the answer choices:

| | B's distance (miles) | B's rate (mph) $=\dfrac{D}{T}=\dfrac{D}{0.25}$ | A's rate (mph) = B's Rate + 8 | A's distance (miles) $= R \times T$ $= R \times 0.75$ | Total distance |
|---|---|---|---|---|---|
| **(A)** | **14** | **56** | **64** | **48** | **62** |
| (B) | 12 | 48 | 56 | 42 | 54 |
| (C) | 10 | 40 | 48 | 36 | 46 |
| (D) | 9 | 36 | 44 | 33 | 42 |
| (E) | 8 | 32 | 40 | 30 | 38 |

Or solve algebraically, using an *RTD* chart. Convert 15 minutes to $\dfrac{1}{4}$ (or 0.25) hours:

| | Rate | Time | Distance |
|---|---|---|---|
| Car A | $(r + 8)$ mph | 0.75 hours | $(0.75)(r + 8)$ miles |
| Car B | $r$ mph | 0.25 hours | $0.25r$ miles |
| Total | | | 62 miles |

Set up and solve an equation for the total distance:

$$(0.75)(r + 8) + (0.25r) = 62$$
$$0.75r + 6 + 0.25r = 62$$
$$r = 56$$

Therefore, car B traveled a distance of $0.25r = (0.25)(56) = 14$ miles.

15. **(D).** Factor 10,125 to its prime factors: $10{,}125 = 3^4 5^3$.

So, $x^2 5^y = 3^4 5^3$.

In order to have $5^3$ on the right side, there have to be three factors of 5 on the left side. All three could be in the $5^y$ term (i.e., $y$ could equal 3). Or, one of the 5's could be in the $5^y$ term, and two of the 5's in the $x^2$ term (i.e., $y$ could equal 1 and $x$ could have a single factor of 5).

In order to have $3^4$ on the right side, $x^2$ must have $3^4 = \left(3^2\right)^2$ as a factor. In other words, $x$ must have $3^2$ as a factor, because $3^2$ is certainly not a factor of 5. Thus, $x$ is a multiple of 9.

The possibilities:

| Quantity A: $x^2$ | | Quantity B: $5^y$ | Check: The product must be 10,125 | Check: Quantity A must be a perfect square | Check: Quantity B must be a power of 5 |
|---|---|---|---|---|---|
| $x^2 = 9^2 = 81$ | < | $5^y = 5^3 = 125$ | $(81)(125) = 10{,}125$ | Yes | Yes |
| $x^2 = (9 \times 5)^2 = 2{,}025$ | > | $5^y = 5^1 = 5$ | $(2{,}025)(5) = 10{,}125$ | Yes | Yes |

In one case, Quantity A is greater. In the other, Quantity B is greater. The relationship cannot be determined from the information given.

16. **(D).** Since there are variables in the answer choices, pick a number and test the choices. If $n = 2$, then

$$\frac{-2}{\sqrt{n-1}-\sqrt{n+1}} = \frac{-2}{\sqrt{2-1}-\sqrt{2+1}} = \frac{-2}{1-\sqrt{3}} \approx \frac{-2}{1-1.7} \approx \frac{-2}{-0.7}$$, which is greater than 2 (around 2.86). Now test the

answer choices to see which one matches the target:

(A) $-1$                                                Too low

(B) $1$                                                 Too low

(C) $2\left(\sqrt{n-1}+\sqrt{n+1}\right) = 2\left(\sqrt{2-1}+\sqrt{2+1}\right) \approx 2(1+1.7)$      Too high

(D) $\sqrt{n-1}+\sqrt{n+1} = \sqrt{2-1}+\sqrt{2+1} \approx 1+1.7 \approx 2.7$      Correct

(E) $\dfrac{\sqrt{n-1}}{\sqrt{n+1}} = \dfrac{\sqrt{2-1}}{\sqrt{2+1}} \approx \dfrac{1}{1.7}$      Too low

Alternatively, solve this problem algebraically. The expression is in the form of $\dfrac{-2}{a-b}$, where $a = \sqrt{n-1}$ and $b = \sqrt{n+1}$.

Either simplify or cancel the denominator, as none of the answer choices have the same denominator as the original, and most of the choices have no denominator at all. To be able to manipulate a denominator with radical signs, first try to eliminate the radical signs entirely, leaving only $a^2$ and $b^2$ in the denominator. To do so, multiply by a fraction that is a convenient form of 1:

$$\frac{-2}{a-b} = \frac{-2}{a-b} \times \frac{(a+b)}{(a+b)} = \frac{-2(a+b)}{a^2-b^2}$$

Notice the "difference of two squares" special product created in the denominator with the choice of $(a + b)$.

Substitute for $a$ and $b$:

$$\frac{-2}{\sqrt{n-1}-\sqrt{n+1}} \times \frac{\sqrt{n-1}+\sqrt{n+1}}{\sqrt{n-1}+\sqrt{n+1}} = \frac{-2\left(\sqrt{n-1}+\sqrt{n+1}\right)}{(n-1)-(n+1)} = \frac{-2\left(\sqrt{n-1}+\sqrt{n+1}\right)}{-2} = \sqrt{n-1}+\sqrt{n+1}$$

The correct answer is (D).

17. **(A).** First, note the answer pairs (A) and (C), and (B) and (E), in which one ratio is the square of the other. This represents a likely trap in a problem that asks for the ratio of $\sqrt{x}$ to $\sqrt{y}$ rather than the more typical ratio of $x$ to $y$. It is fairly safe to eliminate (D) as it is not paired with a trap answer and therefore probably not the correct answer. You should also suspect that the correct answer is (A) or (B), the "square root" answer choice in their respective pairs.

For problems involving successive changes in amounts—such as population growth problems, or compound interest problems—it is helpful to make a table:

|               | **Account A** | **Account B** |
|---------------|---------------|---------------|
| Now           | $x$           | $y$           |
| After 1 month | $\left(\dfrac{9}{10}\right)x$ | $\left(\dfrac{12}{10}\right)y$ |
| After 2 months | $\left(\dfrac{9}{10}\right)\left(\dfrac{9}{10}\right)x = \left(\dfrac{81}{100}\right)x$ | $\left(\dfrac{12}{10}\right)\left(\dfrac{12}{10}\right)y = \left(\dfrac{144}{100}\right)y$ |

If the accounts have the same amount of money after two months, then:

$$\left(\frac{81}{100}\right)x = \left(\frac{144}{100}\right)y$$

$$81x = 144y$$

This can be solved for $\dfrac{\sqrt{x}}{\sqrt{y}}$:

$$\frac{x}{y} = \frac{144}{81}$$

$$\frac{\sqrt{x}}{\sqrt{y}} = \frac{\sqrt{144}}{\sqrt{81}} = \frac{12}{9} = \frac{4}{3}$$

18. **(A).** First, note that the height of each person in question is fixed (no one grew taller or shorter); only weights changed. Second, note that BMI is always positive and is proportional to $w$; as weight increases, BMI increases, and vice versa. So the language of the quantities—"pounds gained … BMI increased" and "pounds lost … BMI decreased"—is aligned with this proportionality. Both quantities are a positive number of pounds.

Since $\text{BMI} = \dfrac{703w}{h^2}$, change in $\text{BMI} = \dfrac{703w_{before}}{h^2} - \dfrac{703w_{after}}{h^2} = \dfrac{703}{h^2}\left(w_{before} - w_{after}\right)$.

To simplify things, you can write this in terms of $\Delta BMI$ and $\Delta w$, the positive change in BMI and weight, respectively:

$$\Delta BMI = \frac{703}{h^2}\Delta w$$

**MANHATTAN**
PREP

(The triangle symbol indicating positive change in a quantity does not appear on the GRE—it is used here for convenience in notating an explanation.)

Since the quantities both refer to $\Delta w$, rewrite the relationship as $\Delta w = \dfrac{h^2}{703}\Delta BMI$. Both $\Delta BMI$ and $h$ are given in each quantity, so $\Delta w$ can be calculated and the relationship between the two quantities determined. (The answer is definitely not (D).)

| **Quantity A** | **Quantity B** |
|---|---|
| $\Delta w = \dfrac{h^2}{703}\Delta BMI = \dfrac{74^2}{703}(1.0) = \dfrac{74^2}{703}$ | $\Delta w = \dfrac{h^2}{703}\Delta BMI = \dfrac{65^2}{703}(1.2)$ |

Since the 703 in the denominator is common to both quantities, the comparison is really between $74^2 = 5{,}476$ and $65^2(1.2) = 4{,}225(1.2) = 5{,}070$. Quantity A is greater.

19. **(D).** There are four different cases that you must count: 5 7 _ _ _ ; _ 5 7 _ _ ; _ _ 5 7 _ ; and _ _ _ 5 7. In the case of 5 7 _ _ _, all three of the empty spaces can have any digit from 0–9, which is 10 possibilities, for a total of $10 \times 10 \times 10 = 1{,}000$ possible numbers. In the case of _ 5 7 _ _, there are only 9 choices for the first digit since you cannot put a zero there if it is to be a five-digit positive integer. For the last two digits any number from 0–9 is still allowed, for a total of $9 \times 10 \times 10 = 900$ possible numbers for the second case. The third and fourth cases are similar to the second; both include 900 possible numbers. Summing up the four cases, there are $1{,}000 + 900(3) = 3{,}700$ such integers. This result double-counts, however, the cases with two 57's in them: 5757X, 57X57, and X5757. The first two cases yield 10 numbers each, while the last case yields only 9 (because 05757 doesn't count as a 5-digit number, by convention). Subtracting these 29 numbers, you get 3,671.

20. **(A).** To find the average of any evenly spaced set, take the average of the first and last values. For the case of Quantity A, the first multiple of 5 is 200 and the last multiple of 5 is 705. The average then is $\dfrac{200 + 705}{2} = 452.5$.

For Quantity B, the first multiple of 10 is also 200, however, the last multiple is 700, thus the average is $\dfrac{200 + 700}{2} = 450$. Quantity A is greater.

21. **(C).** Set up an implied inequality and perform identical operations on each quantity, grouping variables:

| **Quantity A** | | **Quantity B** |
|---|---|---|
| $a + d - c - 90$ | ? | $90 - e - b - f$ |
| $a + d - c$ | ? | $180 - e - b - f$ |
| $a + d - c + e + b + f$ | ? | $180$ |
| $(a + d + e + f) + (b - c)$ | ? | $180$ |

In the last step above, only the order of the variables was changed and parentheses added to group certain terms. Notice that the angle at point $C$ and point $D$ is the same, as $AC$ and $FD$ are parallel lines intersected by the transversal $CE$. So, the first set of parentheses holds the sum of the interior angles of the biggest triangle $ACE$, which is 180. Also because $AC$ and $FD$ are parallel lines intersected by transversal $BE$, $b = c$, so $b - c = 0$ in the second set of parentheses.

| **Quantity A** | | **Quantity B** |
|---|---|---|
| $(a + d + e + f) + (b - c)$ | ? | 180 |
| $(180) + (0)$ | = | 180 |

The two quantities are equal.

22. **(D).** Given that the man can only move north and east, he must advance exactly 7 blocks from his current location to get home regardless of which path he takes. Of these 7 blocks, 4 must be moving east and 3 must be moving north. An example path is shown below:

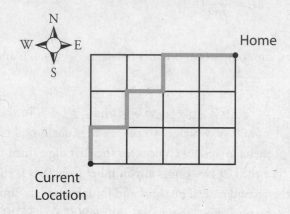

Current
Location

The problem can then be rephrased as follows: "Of the 7 steps, when does the man choose to go east and when does he choose to go north?" Labeling each step as N for north and E for east, you can see the problem as the number of unique rearrangements of NNNEEEE (e.g., this arrangement corresponds to going north 3 times and then east 4 times straight to home). This is determined by $\dfrac{total!}{repeats!} = \dfrac{7!}{3!\,4!} = 35$.

23. **(D).** There are 2 red marbles and 7 not-red marbles. (It is irrelevant whether white or black is drawn; the question is about red or not.) There are two ways in which the second marble drawn is red: either not-red first, then red second OR red first, and then red again. Using $P(R)$ to indicate the probability of drawing red and $P(\text{not } R)$ to indicate the probability of drawing not-red, we have:

$$P\left(\text{not } R\right) \times P(R) = \left(\frac{7}{9}\right)\left(\frac{2}{8}\right) = \frac{14}{72}$$

$$P(R) \times P(R) = \left(\frac{2}{9}\right)\left(\frac{1}{8}\right) = \frac{2}{72}$$

Since a red on the second draw could happen one way or the other, sum these probabilities:

$\dfrac{14}{72} + \dfrac{2}{72} = \dfrac{16}{72} = \dfrac{2}{9}$ .

**MANHATTAN**
PREP

24. **(A).** Simplify both quantities, remembering that a power to a power means multiply the exponents. Also, 25 is 5 squared, so you can substitute, putting both quantities in terms of a base of 5:

$$\text{Quantity A: } \left(\left(25^x\right)^{-2}\right)^3 = 25^{-6x} = \left(5^2\right)^{-6x} = 5^{-12x}$$

$$\text{Quantity B: } \left(\left(5^{-3}\right)^2\right)^{-x} = 5^{6x}$$

Typically, when comparing exponents with the same base, the one with the larger exponent is greater. It might be tempting to conclude that $6x > -12x$, but be careful with negative variables.

If $x = -1$, Quantity A $= 5^{12}$ and Quantity B $= 5^{-6}$, or $\dfrac{1}{5^6}$. In this case, Quantity A is much greater.

If $x = -\dfrac{1}{2}$, Quantity A $= 5^6$ and Quantity B $= 5^{-3}$, or $\dfrac{1}{5^3} = \dfrac{1}{125}$. Again, Quantity A is much greater.

If $x = -10$, Quantity A $= 5^{120}$ and Quantity B $= 5^{-60}$. The more negative $x$ gets, the greater the difference between Quantity A and Quantity B becomes. Quantity A is always greater.

Another way to look at it:

$$\text{Quantity A: } 5^{-12x} = 5^{-12 \times negative} = 5^{positive}$$
$$\text{Quantity B: } 5^{6x} = 5^{6 \times negative} = 5^{negative}$$

Even if $|x|$ is a tiny fraction, that is, the expression is some high order root of 5 such as $\sqrt[8]{5}$ or $\sqrt[100]{5}$, these quantities would approach 1 such that Quantity A is $5^{positive} > 1$ and Quantity B is $5^{negative} < 1$.

Since Quantity A is greater than 1 and Quantity B is less than 1, Quantity A is greater.

25. **(A).** First, note that some of the positive multiples of 6 in Quantity A are canceled out by the negative multiples of 6 in Quantity A (e.g., $-126 + 126 = 0$, $-120 + 120 = 0$, etc.).

To find the sum of the remaining multiples of 6 (i.e., 132 through 342, inclusive), find both the number of terms and the average of those terms: sum = (average) × (number of terms).

To find the number of terms, take the last multiple of 6 minus the first multiple of 6, divide by 6 and then add 1:

$$\text{Number of terms (multiples of } n) = \frac{last\ mult\ of\ n - first\ mult\ of\ n}{n} + 1$$

$$= \frac{342 - (132)}{6} + 1 = \frac{210}{6} + 1 = 35 + 1 = 36$$

To find the average of any evenly spaced set, take the average of the first and last values:

$$\text{Average} = \frac{First + Last}{2} = \frac{132 + 342}{2} = 237$$

Therefore, the sum is equal to (Average) × (Number of terms) = (237)(36) = 8,532. Quantity A is greater.

**26. (B).** When a negative base is raised to an integer power, the question is about positives and negatives and odds and evens: $(-1)^{odd} = -1$ and $(-1)^{even} = +1$.

If $x$ is even, all of the exponents in this question are even:

Quantity A: $(-1)^{even^2} + (-1)^{even^3} + (-1)^{even^4} = (-1)^{even} + (-1)^{even} + (-1)^{even} = 1 + 1 + 1 = 3$

Quantity B: $(-1)^{even} + (-1)^{2 \times even} + (-1)^{3 \times even} + (-1)^{4 \times even} = 1 + 1 + 1 + 1 = 4$

If $x$ is odd, *some* of the exponents in this question are odd:

Quantity A: $(-1)^{odd^2} + (-1)^{odd^3} + (-1)^{odd^4} = (-1)^{odd} + (-1)^{odd} + (-1)^{odd} = (-1) + (-1) + (-1) = -3$

Quantity B: $(-1)^{odd} + (-1)^{2 \times odd} + (-1)^{3 \times odd} + (-1)^{4 \times odd} = (-1)^{odd} + (-1)^{even} + (-1)^{odd} + (-1)^{even}$

$$= (-1) + 1 + (-1) + 1$$
$$= 0$$

In both cases, Quantity B is greater than Quantity A.

**27. (B).** Because an exterior angle of a triangle is equal to the sum of the two opposite interior angles of the triangle (in this case, the top small triangle), $c = a + b$.

Therefore, $d > c$ and $a + b = c$ taken together imply that $d > a + b$.

Subtract $b$ from both sides: $d - b > a$.

Quantity B is greater.

**28. (A).** This problem introduces a square and a circle, and states that the circumference of the circle is $\dfrac{7}{8}$ the perimeter of the square.

This is license to plug in. Both a square and a circle are regular figures—that is, all squares are in the same proportion as all other squares and all circles are in the same proportion as all other circles—plugging in only *one* set of values yields the same result as would plugging in *any* set of values. Because the figures are regular and related in a known way (circumference is equal to $\dfrac{7}{8} \times$ square perimeter), there is no need to repeatedly try different values as is often necessary on Quantitative Comparisons.

Because the circumference of a circle depends on $\pi$ ($C = \pi d$), it is best to pick values for the square. If the side of the square is 2, the perimeter is $4(2) = 8$ and the area is $(2)(2) = 4$. Then, circumference of the circle is $\left(\dfrac{7}{8}\right)(8) = 7$. Since circumference is $2\pi r = 7$, the radius of the circle is $r = \dfrac{7}{2\pi}$.

Using these numbers:

Quantity A: The area of the square = 4.

Quantity B: The area of the circle = $\pi r^2 = \pi \left(\dfrac{7}{2\pi}\right)^2 = \pi \left(\dfrac{49}{4\pi^2}\right) = \dfrac{49}{4\pi} \approx 3.9$.

(Use the calculator and the approximation 3.14 for $\pi$ to determine that Quantity A is greater.)

**MANHATTAN**
PREP

**29. (A).** One good way to work through this problem is to pick a number, ideally starting with the innermost shape, the small circle. Say this circle has radius 1 and diameter 2, which would also make the side of the smaller square equal to 2.

If the small square has side 2, its diagonal would be $2\sqrt{2}$ (based on the 45–45–90 triangle ratios, or you could do the Pythagorean theorem using the legs of 2 and 2). If the diagonal is $2\sqrt{2}$, then the diameter of the larger circle is also $2\sqrt{2}$ (and the radius of the larger circle is one-half of that, or $\sqrt{2}$), making the side of the larger square also equal to $2\sqrt{2}$. Therefore:

> Small circle: radius = 1, area = $\pi$
> Large circle: radius = $\sqrt{2}$, area = $2\pi$
>
> Small square: side = 2, area = 4
> Large square: side = $2\sqrt{2}$, area = 8

Thus, the large circle has twice the area of the small circle, and the large square has twice the area of the small square. This will work for any numbers you choose. In fact, you may wish to memorize this as a shortcut: if a circle is inscribed in a square that is inscribed in a circle, the large circle has twice the area of the small circle; similarly, if a square is inscribed in a circle that is inscribed in a square, the large square has twice the area of the small square.

In Quantity A, the ratio of the area of the larger square to the smaller square is $\dfrac{2}{1} = 2$.

In Quantity B, twice the ratio of the area of the smaller circle to the area of the larger circle is equal to $2\left(\dfrac{1}{2}\right) = 1$.

**30. (A).** This problem is not as bad as it looks! Of course, the integers are much too large to fit in your calculator. However, all you need to know is that a pair consisting of one 2 and one 5 has a product of 10 and therefore adds a zero to the end of a number. For instance, a number with two 2's and two 5's in its prime factors ends with two zeros, because the number is a multiple of 100.

Quantity A has nineteen 5's and many more 2's (since $2^{16}$ and $4^{18}$ together is more than nineteen 2's — if you really want to know, it's $2^{16}$ and $(2^2)^{18}$, or $2^{16}$ and $2^{36}$, or $2^{52}$, or fifty-two 2's). Considering *pairs* made up of one 2 and one 5, exactly nineteen pairs can be made (the leftover 2's don't matter), and the number ends in 19 zeros.

Quantity B has sixteen 5's and many more 2's (specifically, there are fifty-three 2's, but there's no need to calculate this). Considering *pairs* made up of one 2 and one 5, exactly sixteen pairs can be made (the leftover 2's don't matter), and the number ends in 16 zeros. Thus, Quantity A is greater.

31. **(A).** Calculate several terms of the sequence defined by $a_n = 2^n - \dfrac{1}{2^{n-33}}$ and look for a pattern:

$$a_1 = 2^1 - \frac{1}{2^{-32}} = 2^1 - 2^{32}$$

$$a_2 = 2^2 - \frac{1}{2^{-31}} = 2^2 - 2^{31}$$

...

$$a_{16} = 2^{16} - \frac{1}{2^{-17}} = 2^{16} - 2^{17}$$

$$a_{17} = 2^{17} - \frac{1}{2^{-16}} = 2^{17} - 2^{16}$$

...

$$a_{31} = 2^{31} - \frac{1}{2^{-2}} = 2^{31} - 2^2$$

$$a_{32} = 2^{32} - \frac{1}{2^{-1}} = 2^{32} - 2^1$$

Notice that the 16th and 17th terms (the two middle terms in a set of 32 terms) are arithmetic inverses, that is, their sum is zero. Likewise, the 1st and 32nd terms sum to zero, as do the 2nd and 31st terms. In the first 32 terms of the sequence, there are 16 pairs that each sum to zero. Thus, Quantity A is zero.

For the sum of the first 31 terms, you could either:

1.  Subtract $a_{32}$ from the sum of the first 32 terms: $0 - (2^{32} - 2^1) = 2^1 - 2^{32} = 2 -$ (a very large number) = negative, or
2.  realize that in the first 31 terms, all terms except $a_1$ can be paired such that the pair sums to zero, so the sum of the first 31 terms $= a_1 = 2^1 - 2^{32} = 2 -$ (a very large number) = negative.

Thus, Quantity B is negative, which is less than zero. Quantity A is greater.

32. **(C).** The "interquartile range" of a group of 100 integers is found by splitting the 100 integers into two groups, a lower 50 and an upper 50. Then find the median of each of those groups. The median of the lower group is the first quartile ($Q_1$), while the median of the upper group is the third quartile ($Q_3$). Finally, $Q_3 - Q_1$ is the interquartile range.

The median of a group of 50 integers is the average (arithmetic mean) of the 25th and the 26th integers when ordered from smallest to largest. Order the list of 100 integers from smallest to largest, then, find #25 and #26 and average them to get the first quartile. Likewise, find #75 and #76 and average them to get the third quartile. Then perform the subtraction.

**MANHATTAN**
PREP

| $x$ = the integer label on the ball | $n_x = 18-(x-4)^2$ = the number of balls with this label | Cumulative number of balls |
|---|---|---|
| 1 | $18-(1-4)^2 = 18-(-3)^2 = 18-9=9$ | 9 |
| 2 | $18-(2-4)^2 = 18-(-2)^2 = 18-4=14$ | $9+14=23$ |
| 3 | $18-(3-4)^2 = 18-(-1)^2 = 18-1=17$ | $23+17=40$ |
| 4 | $18-(4-4)^2 = 18-(0)^2 = 18$ | $40+18=58$ |
| 5 | $18-(5-4)^2 = 18-(1)^2 = 18-1=17$ | $58+17=75$ |

Stop here. Ball #75 has a 5 on it (in fact, the last 5), while ball #76 must have a 6 on it (since 6 is the next integer in the list). Thus, the third quartile $Q_3$ is the average of 5 and 6, or 5.5. Count carefully—if you are off by even just one either way, you'll get a different number for the third quartile. Balls #25 and #26 both have a 3 on them. So the first quartile $Q_1$ is the average of 3 and 3, namely 3.

Finally, $Q_3 - Q_1 = 5.5 - 3 = 2.5$.

33. **(C).** Compute the expressions for each of the terms:

$$x!4 = x^4 \times 4^{-x} \quad \text{and} \quad 4!x = 4^x \times x^{-4}$$

Dividing the first by the second yields:

$$\frac{x^4 4^{-x}}{4^x x^{-4}} = \frac{x^4}{x^{-4}} \times \frac{4^{-x}}{4^x} = x^8 4^{-2x}$$

There are a number of ways to write $x^8 4^{-2x}$:

$$x^8 4^{-2x} = \frac{x^8}{4^{2x}} = \frac{x^8}{16^x}$$

The two quantities are equal.

34. **(C).** First find each of the sums. To find a sum of an evenly spaced set, use the formula:

$$\text{sum} = (\text{average}) \times (\text{number of terms})$$

For the odd positive integers between 1 and 100, inclusive (use "2" as the multiple; while odds are not multiples of two per se, they are evenly spaced every two numbers):

$$\text{Number of terms (odds)} = \frac{\textit{last mult of n} - \textit{first mult of n}}{n} + 1$$

$$= \frac{99 - 1}{2} + 1$$

$$= 50$$

To find the average of any evenly spaced set, take the average of the first and last values:

$$\text{Average (odds)} = \frac{\textit{First} + \textit{Last}}{2} = \frac{1 + 99}{2} = 50$$

Sum of the odd integers between 1 and 100, inclusive is equal to (average) × (number of terms) = 50 × 50 = 2,500.

For the even positive integers between 100 and 150, inclusive:

$$\text{Number of terms (evens)} = \frac{\textit{last mult of n} - \textit{first mult of n}}{n} + 1$$

$$= \frac{150 - 100}{2} + 1$$

$$= 26$$

$$\text{Average (evens)} = \frac{\textit{First} + \textit{Last}}{2} = \frac{100 + 150}{2} = 125$$

Therefore, the sum of the even integers between 100 and 150, inclusive is equal to (average) × (number of terms) = 125 × 26 = 3,250.

The ratio of the sum of the odd positive integers between 1 and 100, inclusive, to the sum of the even positive integers between 100 and 150, inclusive is equal to $\frac{2,500}{3,250} = \frac{250}{325} = \frac{(25)(10)}{(25)(13)} = \frac{10}{13}$, or 10 to 13.

35. **(C).** The problem gives two ways to calculate the fourth term: (1) the definition of the sequence tells you that $a_4 = a_3{}^2 - a_2{}^2$ and (2) the words indicate that $a_4 = a_1(a_2 + a_3) = 2(a_2 + a_3)$. Setting these two equal gives $a_3{}^2 - a_2{}^2 = 2(a_2 + a_3)$. Factor the left side: $(a_3 + a_2)(a_3 - a_2) = 2(a_2 + a_3)$. Since $a_n > 0$ for all possible $n$'s, $(a_3 + a_2)$ does not equal 0 and you can divide both sides by it: $a_3 - a_2 = 2$ and $a_3 = a_2 + 2$. Using the definition of $a_3$, you know $a_3 = a_2{}^2 - a_1{}^2 = a_2{}^2 - 4$. Substituting for $a_3$ yields: $a_2 + 2 = a_2{}^2 - 4$ and $a_2{}^2 - a_2 - 6 = 0$. Factor and solve: $(a_2 - 3)(a_2 + 2) = 0$; $a_2 = 3$ or $-2$. $a_n$ must be positive, so $a_2 = 3$ and $a_3 = a_2 + 2 = 3 + 2 = 5$.

36. **(D).** Since $a_1$ and $a_3$ are integers, $a_2$ must also be an integer: $a_3 = \frac{(a_1 + a_2)}{2}$ or INT $= \frac{(\text{INT} + a_2)}{2}$ so 2(INT) = INT $+ a_2$ and $a_2 = 2(\text{INT}) - \text{INT}$, which is itself an integer. $a_4$ is thus the average of two integers. If $a_2 + a_3$ is even, $a_4$ will be an integer. If $a_2 + a_3$ is odd, $a_4$ will be a decimal ending in 0.5. If $a_4$ is an integer, $a_5$ can be an integer or can be a decimal ending in 0.5. If $a_4$ is a decimal ending in 0.5, $a_5$ must be a decimal ending in 0.25 or 0.75. $a_5$ cannot be a decimal ending in 0.375 such as $\frac{75}{8} = 9.375$. Note that $a_5$ can be negative: even if $a_1$ and $a_3$ are positive, that does not rule out the possibility that $a_2$ (and subsequent terms) could be negative.

**MANHATTAN**
PREP

37. **(D).** Use the definition of @ to rewrite the equation: $\left|\dfrac{x+1}{x}\right| - \dfrac{2+1}{2} = \dfrac{1}{2}\left(\left|\dfrac{x+1}{x}\right| - \dfrac{-1+1}{-1}\right)$. Simplifying yields:

$\left|\dfrac{x+1}{x}\right| - \dfrac{3}{2} = \dfrac{1}{2}\left|\dfrac{x+1}{x}\right|$. Let $z = \left|\dfrac{x+1}{x}\right|$. Substitute $z$ into the equation: $z - \dfrac{3}{2} = \left(\dfrac{1}{2}\right)z$ or $z = 3$. To solve $\left|\dfrac{x+1}{x}\right| = 3$, take two cases:

1. $\dfrac{x+1}{x} > 0$, so $\dfrac{x+1}{x} = 3$ or $x = 0.5$.

2. $\dfrac{x+1}{x} < 0$, so $\dfrac{x+1}{x} = -3$ or $x = -0.25$.

The sum of the solutions is $0.5 + (-0.25) = 0.25$.

38. **(B).** Expressed algebraically, $\sqrt{10 - 3x} > x$. Because both sides of this inequality are non-negative, you can square both sides to result in the following:

$$10 - 3x > x^2$$
$$0 > x^2 + 3x - 10$$
$$0 > (x + 5)(x - 2)$$

Now, because the product of $(x + 5)$ and $(x - 2)$ is negative, you can deduce that the larger of the two expressions, $(x + 5)$, must be positive, and the smaller expression, $(x - 2)$, must be negative. Therefore, $x > -5$ and $x < 2$. Combining these yields $-5 < x < 2$.

However, because the question indicates that $x$ is non-negative, $x$ must be 0 or greater. Therefore, $0 \leq x < 2$. The absolute value sign in Quantity A doesn't change anything—$x$ is still greater than or equal to zero and less than 2, and Quantity B is larger.

Alternatively, plug the value from Quantity B into $\sqrt{10 - 3x} > x$:

$$\sqrt{10 - 3(2)} > 2$$
$$\sqrt{4} > 2$$
$$2 > 2$$

This is FALSE, so $x$ cannot be 2.

Now, plug in a smaller or larger value to determine whether $x$ needs to be greater than or less than 2. If $x = 1$:

$$\sqrt{10 - 3(1)} > 1$$
$$\sqrt{7} > 1$$

$\sqrt{7}$ is between 2 and 3, so this is true.

Trying values will show that only values greater than or equal to zero and less than 2 make the statement true, so Quantity A must be less than 2.

**MANHATTAN**
PREP

**39. (A).** The area of an equilateral triangle is $\dfrac{b^2\sqrt{3}}{4}$ where $b$ is the length of one side. Since this area is between 25 $\sqrt{3}$ and $36\sqrt{3}$, substitute to get $25\sqrt{3} < \dfrac{b^2\sqrt{3}}{4} < 36\sqrt{3}$. Dividing all sides by $\sqrt{3}$ yields $25 < \dfrac{b^2}{4} < 36$. Multiplying all sides by 4 yields $100 < b^2 < 144$, and taking the square root of all sides yields $10 < b < 12$. Since every possibility for $b$ is greater than 9, Quantity A is greater.

**40. (E).** When dealing with absolute values, consider two outcomes. First determine the outcome if the expression within the absolute value sign is positive. So, if $8 - 2x > 0$, then $|8 - 2x| = 8 - 2x$, and therefore $8 - 2x < 3y - 9$ or $2x > 17 - 3y$.

You also must determine the outcome if the expression within the absolute value sign is negative. So if $8 - 2x < 0$, then $|8 - 2x| = 2x - 8$, and therefore $2x - 8 < 3y - 9$ or $2x < 3y - 1$. Combining these two inequalities yields $3y - 1 > 2x > 17 - 3y$.

Now a quick sanity check to make sure the inequality makes sense: $3y - 9$ must be greater than 0 or the absolute value could not be less than $3y - 9$. So $y > 3$. This means $17 - 3y < 8$, and $3y - 1 > 8$, so there is definitely room for $2x$ to fit between those values. If the potential values of $17 - 3y$ and $3y - 1$ had overlapped, this would be an indication either that a mistake had been made or that the problem required further investigation to refine the result.

**41. (A).** This is an overlapping set problem. Matrix 1 shows an initial setup for a double-set matrix. The columns are headed "Skilled in BJJ" and "Not Skilled in BJJ." The rows are headed "Skilled in Muy Thai" and "Not Skilled in Muy Thai." There is also a total row and a total column.

When dealing with overlapping sets, consider whether the question is giving information regarding the population as a whole or regarding a subset of the population. While the first statement ("30% of all fighters") refers to the whole population, the second statement ("20% of the fighters who are not skilled in Brazilian Jiu Jitsu") refers to a subset of the population, in this case the 40% who are not skilled in Brazilian Jiu Jitsu. Thus, 8% are skilled in Muy Thai but not in Brazilian Jiu Jitsu, as seen in Matrix 1:

| Matrix 1 | | Skilled in BJJ | Not Skilled in BJJ | Total |
| --- | --- | --- | --- | --- |
| | Skilled in Muy Thai | > 30 | 8 | |
| | Not Skilled in Muy Thai | | | |
| | Total | 60 | 40 | 100 |

Matrix 2 shows how to fill out additional cells. Notably, there are some ranges of values that are possible for the cells in the first column. These ranges are limited by 0 on the low end and 60 on the high end:

| Matrix 2 | | Skilled in BJJ | Not Skilled in BJJ | Total |
|---|---|---|---|---|
| | **Skilled in Muy Thai** | > 30 but ≤ 60 | 8 | |
| | **Not Skilled in Muy Thai** | ≤ 0 but < 30 | 32 | |
| | **Total** | 60 | 40 | 100 |

Matrix 3 sums across the rows to get subtotals. Particularly, the percent of fighters who are skilled in Muy Thai is greater than 38 but less than or equal to 68. Thus, Quantity A is greater:

| Matrix 3 | | Skilled in BJJ | Not Skilled in BJJ | Total |
|---|---|---|---|---|
| | **Skilled in Muy Thai** | > 30 but ≤ 60 | 8 | > 38 but ≤ 68 |
| | **Not Skilled in Muy Thai** | ≤ 0 but < 30 | 32 | ≤ 32 but < 62 |
| | **Total** | 60 | 40 | 100 |

42. **(B).** Express this situation with the equation $r = \dfrac{kb}{n^2}$, where $k$ is a constant. Quadrupling $b$ and more than tripling $n$ yields the following equation: $r_1 = \dfrac{k \times 4b}{(\text{"greater than } 3n\text{"})^2}$, where $r_1$ represents the new rate of data transfer.

Squaring a value that is greater than 3 produces a value that is greater than 9, allowing the equation to be rewritten as $r_1 = \dfrac{k \times 4b}{\text{"greater than } 9n^2\text{"}}$. Rearranging this equation yields $r_1 = \dfrac{4}{\text{"greater than 9"}} \times \dfrac{k \times b}{n^2} = \text{less than } \dfrac{4}{9} r$. Thus, Quantity B is greater.

# Chapter 31

## of

### 5 lb. Book of GRE® Practice Problems

# Essays

# In This Chapter...

How to Study for the AWA Using This Book

Issue Essay Topics

Argument Essay Topics

Issue Essay Guidelines and Sample Responses

Argument Essay Guidelines and Sample Responses

# How to Study for the AWA Using This Book

Included in the AWA (Analytical Writing Assessment) section of the GRE are two essays—an Issue Essay and an Argument Essay—with a time limit of 30 minutes each.

If you feel extremely confident about your writing and just want to get a feel for GRE-specific essay writing, feel free to simply read over the topics and some of the sample essays and comments that appear in the *sample responses*.

However, if you need to seriously improve your AWA performance, do NOT read all of the essay topics at once.

Instead, set yourself up with a word processing program on a computer (any text program is fine—the simpler the program, the more the experience will be like the GRE) and a timer. Turn off any spellchecking or grammar-checking feature in your word processing program.

Bookmark the pages in this book that contain the Issue and Argument Essay topics. Set the timer for 30 minutes. When the clock begins, read Issue Topic #1 and plan and write an essay on this topic. STOP when the 30 minutes are up.

Then, without pausing or taking a break, turn to the Argument Essay topics, reset the timer for 30 minutes, read Argument Topic #1 and plan and write an essay on that topic. STOP when the 30 minutes are up.

To review your work, read the commentary and sample essays on these essay topics (found in *Issue Essay Guidelines and Sample Responses* and *Argument Essay Guidelines and Sample Responses*). Compare your essays to the samples. While obviously there are many positions you can take on a particular topic, ask whether your own essays are as well-structured, persuasive, and on-topic as the examples. (We find that Issue Essays on the same topic tend to differ quite a bit from each other, but good Argument Essays on the same topic are often quite similar—each Argument topic has several flaws planted by the writers of the test for test-takers to analyze.)

Practice with the other topics in the same way. You may decide after a few rounds of practice that you only want to practice Issue topics or only want to practice Argument topics. This is fine. But please do observe good practice habits—always time yourself, and keep in mind that reading and thinking about the topic is included in the 30 minutes. Ideally, you should spend about 2–5 minutes reading and thinking about the topic, which will give you 25–28 minutes to write and revise.

Finally, should you exhaust the resources in this book, you may wish to know that ETS, the organization that makes the GRE, has actually released all of its actual Issue and Essay topics! You can read and practice with hundreds of such topics at ETS.org.

# Issue Essay Topics

The GRE's AWA (Analytical Writing Assessment) includes two essays—an Issue Essay and an Argument Essay—to be written in 30 minutes each. There is no break in between the essays or after the AWA.

On the computer-based GRE, the Issue Essay prompt will appear on the screen above a text box in which you may write as much as you wish, or as much as you are able, in the 30-minute time limit. Most top-scoring essays tend to be 4–6 full paragraphs long (although this is not a requirement). You should write an introductory paragraph, 2 or more body paragraphs with one main point per paragraph, and a concluding paragraph.

You will have scratch paper on which to plan your essay (or you may make notes in the text box and then delete them). The system does not have any type of spell check, but it does allow you to cut and paste.

According to ETS: Trained GRE readers will evaluate your response for its overall quality based on how well you:

- respond to the specific task instructions
- consider the complexities of the issue
- organize, develop, and express your ideas
- support your ideas with relevant reasons and/or examples
- control the elements of standard written English

Here are the official instructions from the test screen:

> You have 30 minutes to plan and compose a response to the issue below. A response to any other issue will receive a score of zero. Make sure that you respond according to the specific instructions and support your position on the issue with reasons and examples drawn from such areas as your reading, experience, observations, and/or academic studies.

To practice your essay writing, we suggest typing your work into any word processing program on your computer. Start a timer for 30 minutes BEFORE READING THE TOPIC. The time you spend reading the topic and planning your work is part of the 30 minutes. Before you take the real GRE, you need to be able to read a GRE essay topic and plan your work in less than 5 minutes, so you have enough time to actually write the essay.

Discussions of the topics and sample essays are located in the sample responses for this section of the book.

**MANHATTAN**
PREP

### Issue Topic #1

Claim: In order to help small businesses thrive, government should play a minimal role in private business matters.

Write a response in which you discuss the extent to which you agree or disagree with the claim. In developing and supporting your position, be sure to address the most compelling reasons and/or examples that could be used to challenge your position.

### Issue Topic #2

Schools should do more to prepare students for the non-academic aspects of adulthood.

Write a response in which you discuss the extent to which you agree or disagree with the recommendation and explain your reasoning for the position you take. In developing and supporting your position, be sure to address the most compelling reasons and/or examples that could be used to challenge your position.

### Issue Topic #3

People should question the rules of authority as opposed to accepting them passively.

Write a response in which you discuss the extent to which you agree or disagree with the statement and explain your reasoning for the position you take. In developing and supporting your position, you should consider the reasons for which the statement may or may not be true and explain how these considerations shape your position.

### Issue Topic #4

If two applicants for a job are otherwise equally qualified, the job should go to the applicant with more experience.

Write a response in which you discuss the extent to which you agree or disagree with the statement and explain your reasoning for the position you take. In developing and supporting your position, you should consider the specific circumstances in which adopting the position would or would not be advantageous and explain how these examples shape your position.

### Issue Topic #5

Schools should cut funding for extracurricular activities such as sports and the arts when school buildings are in need of repair.

Write a response in which you discuss the extent to which you agree or disagree with this recommendation and explain your reasoning for the position you take. In developing and supporting your position, describe specific circumstances in which adopting the recommendation would or would not be advantageous and explain how these examples shape your position.

## Issue Topic #6

Creativity should be used as the only true measure of intelligence.

Write a response in which you discuss the extent to which you agree or disagree with the claim. In developing and supporting your position, be sure to address the most compelling reasons and/or examples that could be used to challenge your position.

## Issue Topic #7

Government funding for purely scientific endeavors, such as space exploration, should be reduced in order to direct more funding toward humanitarian science projects.

Write a response in which you discuss the extent to which you agree or disagree with the claim. In developing and supporting your position, be sure to consider specific instances for which this statement may or may not be true.

## Issue Topic #8

The fact that technology is outpacing the needs of those in cultures that can afford the technology creates cultures of excess consumerism.

Write a response in which you discuss the extent to which you agree or disagree with the claim. In developing and supporting your position, be sure to address the most compelling reasons and/or examples that could be used to challenge your position.

## Issue Topic #9

Luck plays more of a role in determining success than work ethic does.

Write a response in which you discuss the extent to which you agree or disagree with the claim. In developing and supporting your position, be sure to address the most compelling reasons and/or examples that could be used to both support and challenge your position.

## Issue Topic #10

Some people believe that competition drives young athletes to perform at their best, while others believe that competition discourages those who are not athletically talented from participating in organized sports.

Write a response in which you discuss which view more closely aligns with your own and explain your reasoning for your position. In developing and supporting your position, be sure to address both views presented.

**MANHATTAN**
PREP

# Argument Essay Topics

The GRE's AWA (Analytical Writing Assessment) includes two essays—an Issue Essay and an Argument Essay—to be written in 30 minutes each. There is no break in between the essays or after the AWA.

On the computer-based GRE, the Argument Essay prompt will appear on the screen above a text box in which you may write as much as you wish, or as much as you are able, in the 30-minute time limit. Most top-scoring essays tend to be 4–6 full paragraphs long (although this is not a requirement). You should write an introductory paragraph, 2 or more body paragraphs with one main point per paragraph, and a concluding paragraph.

You will have scratch paper on which to plan your essay (or you may make notes in the text box and then delete them). The system does not have any type of spell check, but does allow you to cut and paste.

According to ETS:

> Trained GRE readers will evaluate your response for its overall quality based on how well you:

- respond to the specific task instructions
- consider the complexities of the issue
- organize, develop, and express your ideas
- support your ideas with relevant reasons and/or examples
- control the elements of standard written English

Here are the official instructions from the test screen:

> You have 30 minutes to plan and compose a response to the issue below. A response to any other issue will receive a score of zero. Make sure that you respond according to the specific instructions and support your position on the issue with reasons and examples drawn from such areas as your reading, experience, observations, and/or academic studies.

To practice your essay writing, we suggest typing your work into any word processing program on your computer. Start a timer for 30 minutes BEFORE READING THE TOPIC. The time you spend reading the topic and planning your work is part of the 30 minutes. Before you take the real GRE, you need to be able to read a GRE essay topic and plan your work in less than 5 minutes, so you have enough time to actually write the essay.

Discussions of the topics, as well as sample essays, are in the sample responses for this section of the book.

## Argument Topic #1

A recent study by the Centers for Disease Control and Prevention found that employees with paid sick leave are 28% less likely to be involved in a work-related accident than employees who do not receive payment for sick leave. Researchers hypothesize that employees with unpaid sick leave feel pressured to work during time of illness for fear of lack of pay. On-the-job accidents are then spurred by impaired judgment or motor skills due to illness or illness-related medications. The highest-risk occupations, such as construction, showed the highest discrepancy in incidents based upon paid and unpaid leave.

Write a response in which you discuss what questions would need to be answered in order to determine whether the researchers' hypothesis is reasonable. Be sure to explain what effects the answers to these questions would have on the validity of the hypothesis.

## Argument Topic #2

The city council of Town X has proposed reducing the city's electric expenses by switching all the lights in public buildings from incandescent bulbs to light-emitting diodes (LEDs). The switch would be made gradually as the old incandescent bulbs burn out, and the city council reasons that since LED lights burn brighter and cost no more to purchase, the switch would help Town X save money on electrical costs in the future.

Write a response in which you discuss what questions would need to be answered to help evaluate the efficacy of the city council's proposal to save money on electrical costs. Be sure to explain how the answers to these questions would help to evaluate the council's prediction.

## Argument Topic #3

Company X has just switched to a 4-day workweek, mandating that employees work 10 hours per day from Monday to Thursday instead of 8 hours per day from Monday to Friday. Although the policy is new, Company X claims that the policy will help to increase profits by shutting down offices on Fridays and to boost employee morale by reducing commuting time to and from work each week.

Write a response in which you examine the stated and/or unstated assumptions of the argument. Be sure to explain how the argument depends on these assumptions and what the implications are for the argument if the assumptions prove unwarranted.

**MANHATTAN**
PREP

## Argument Topic #4

Five years ago, the local university built two new dormitories through different contractors: Aleph Construction and Gimmel Builders. The buildings were nearly identical, though it cost Gimmel Builders approximately 20% more to construct its dormitory. Aleph's dormitory, however, has required approximately 10% more in maintenance costs per year over the past five years. Therefore, to construct another new dormitory with the lowest overall cost, the local university should hire Aleph Construction.

Write a response in which you examine the stated and/or unstated assumptions in the expert's claim. Be sure to explain how the argument depends on these assumptions and what the implications are for the argument if the assumptions prove unwarranted.

## Argument Topic #5

Airline industry representatives have recently argued that flying is safer than driving, citing two separate studies. First, U.S. statistics show that each year there are approximately 40,000 deaths in automobile accidents versus only approximately 200 in flight accidents. Second, studies indicate that pilots are four times less likely than average to have accidents on the road.

Write a response in which you discuss what questions would need to be answered in order to determine whether the argument is reasonable. Be sure to explain what effects the answers to these questions would have on the validity of the argument.

## Argument Topic #6

In a laboratory study of two different industrial cleansers, CleanAll was found to remove 40% more dirt and kill 30% more bacteria than the next best cleanser. Furthermore, a study showed that employees working at buildings cleaned with CleanAll used far fewer sick days than employees working in buildings cleaned with other cleansers. Therefore, to prevent employee illness, all companies should use CleanAll as their industrial cleanser.

Write a response in which you examine the stated and/or unstated assumptions of the argument. Be sure to explain how the argument depends on these assumptions and what the implications are for the argument if the assumptions prove unwarranted.

## Argument Topic #7

Downtown Zurzi is becoming increasingly congested with traffic, increasing commuting time for those who work downtown or near downtown. The nearby city of Loft was faced with the same problem several years ago and implemented a small weekly tax for driving one's car downtown. Downtown traffic almost immediately subsided in Loft and the local government also raised much-needed money for fixing roads elsewhere. Obviously, this plan should be implemented in Zurzi in order to solve the brewing traffic congestion problem.

Write a response in which you discuss what specific evidence is needed to evaluate the argument and explain how the evidence would weaken or strengthen the argument.

## Argument Topic #8

In last year's mayoral election in Town T, candidate Miller led candidate Keating by a substantial margin in the polls leading up to the election. At the last minute, Keating launched a widely viewed series of television advertisements that focused on preserving the natural environment of Town T, a topic neglected by Miller. Subsequently, Keating won the election by a narrow margin. This year, if candidate Miller hopes to win the upcoming mayoral election, he must increase his coverage of the topic of preserving the natural environment of Town T.

Write a response in which you examine the stated and/or unstated assumptions of the argument. Be sure to explain how the argument depends on these assumptions and what the implications are for the argument if the assumptions prove unwarranted.

## Argument Topic #9

Last year, PrepUp had record enrollment in its test prep courses, but yearly profits fell by nearly 30%. In contrast, TopPreparation had comparable enrollment to the year before, with profits rising by approximately 20%. This discrepancy most likely results from the fact that PrepUp teaches only live, in-person classes, which require expensive rental spaces and teaching equipment. Although TopPreparation's total enrollment remained unchanged, its online enrollment increased by 50%, and online classes have much lower overhead costs. In order to address these issues of profitability in the coming year, PrepUp will begin offering online test prep courses.

Write a response in which you discuss what questions would need to be answered in order to decide whether PrepUp's plan for the coming year and the argument on which it is based are reasonable. Be sure to explain how the answers to these questions would help to evaluate the plan.

## Argument Topic #10

Cot-Ten, a cotton production company, has recently faced profitability issues based on the use of Chemical X in its manufacturing process. The main by-product produced when using Chemical X is covered under stringent environmental regulations, making it very difficult and expensive to dispose of. A similar processing product, Chemical Y, has recently been discovered, and can be used by Cot-Ten at a minimal cost of switching. The CEO of Cot-Ten has declared that the company will increase profits by switching to Chemical Y by the end of the month.

Write a response in which you discuss what specific evidence is needed to evaluate the argument and explain how the evidence would weaken or strengthen the argument.

**MANHATTAN**
PREP

# Issue Essay Guidelines and Sample Responses

## Issue Topic #1

Claim: In order to help small businesses thrive, government should play a minimal role in private business matters.

Write a response in which you discuss the extent to which you agree or disagree with the claim. In developing and supporting your position, be sure to address the most compelling reasons and/or examples that could be used to challenge your position.

**Here's a take on this topic—followed by an actual essay—from Manhattan Prep instructor Jennifer Dziura:**

Unlike some Issue Essay topics, this one isn't too extreme. If a topic says "never" or "always," you almost have to disagree with it. But this topic says "a minimal role," so you really could agree or disagree without taking too extreme a position. Since you are being asked for your opinion—inasmuch as you can back it up with reasons and examples!—there's no reason you *can't* take an extreme position, but extreme positions are simply much harder to defend with solid reasons and examples. There are usually exceptions to any extreme position, and nuanced positions both look a little more sophisticated and are easier to defend.

I can see that government meddling too much in the affairs of small businesses could make it really hard to start a small business (big businesses have people whose entire job it is to do paperwork, but smaller operations can be seriously burdened by complicated systems of permits and permissions). But obviously (to me, anyway!) the government needs to keep businesses from discriminating against employees, polluting the environment, and selling dangerous products (for companies that sell food, vitamins, beauty products, baby products, cars, etc.).

But wait! Before I write about how it's important for government to regulate product safety, pollution, etc.—*actually, I don't think that's on-topic!* I was asked to write about how the government should act "in order to help small business thrive" not "in order to make the world a better place." (I guess I care more about the second part!)

Okay, in order to make sure I stay on-topic, I'm going to argue that the government should regulate small businesses *so the public will trust small businesses, which will help small businesses thrive.*

It's important to make sure that every reason or example you use ADDRESSES THE TOPIC, and that all of your argumentation is unified under a coherent and on-topic main point.

Note: I also had some other ideas about how maybe the government should protect small business from big business. I was thinking about Wal-Mart putting local shops out of business or Chick-fil-A (a U.S. fast food joint that uses the slogan "Eat More Chicken") suing a man in Vermont who makes t-shirts that say "Eat More Kale." I think this could also make a good point for this essay topic (or a good focus for a whole essay on this topic!), but it doesn't really fit into my other idea (that the government should leave small businesses alone except to protect the public), so I'm not going to use this.

Finally, the topic says "be sure to address the most compelling reasons and/or examples that could be used to challenge your position," so I'll make that my third body paragraph. What would my opponents say? I'm thinking here about people who argue that corporations have the legal status of people, and that people have the right to voluntarily transact as they wish. Honestly, I was just arguing about this on Facebook ("We'd be paying private companies for the privilege of driving over bridges that don't have to meet any government safety standards! There'd be mice in our sausages! Children working 12-hour days in factories! Lunch counters in the South could still be segregated!"), so I feel very prepared. (As well as extremely opinionated!)

Okay, I'm ready to start writing. Here are the notes I'd type into the text box (and then delete as I was writing the real essay):

> thesis: gov should stay out of small business affairs but should protect human rights and safety
> I.   staying out: too many regulations can hamper entrepreneurship
> II.  protecting the public is important so public trusts small business
> III. challenges to my position: if people want to freely trade money for services, no one should get in their way (my response: governments always provide services that are impractical for people to provide for themselves, like safety testing)

Note: One good essay time-saver is to copy and paste your introduction into the conclusion spot, and then re-word it as your conclusion. It's easier than writing from scratch!

## Essay:

Small businesses need many conditions in place in order to thrive: startup capital, a suitable location and physical infrastructure, shrewd founders who can adapt to changing circumstances—and also, of course, customers. While, in general, a government's hands-off policy towards small business can help small businesses by freeing owners from time-consuming and cumbersome regulations, it is also the case that some government regulations are needed to protect the public from unscrupulous business owners. This type of regulation not only helps the public, but helps small businesses thrive by increasing consumer confidence in small businesses, as well as protecting ethical small businesses from unfair competition from businesses that break the rules.

The United States has one of the highest rates of entrepreneurship in the developed world—much higher than the rates in Western Europe. Why? In the U.S., virtually anyone can start a business. For about $35, you can obtain a business license, and then you're officially in business. Hiring the first employee or two is also relatively simple, and some workers can be paid as contractors, which eliminates the need to administer payroll taxes. In contrast, in Western European nations where you need employment papers (and sometimes references) to even open a simple checking account, naturally, the regulations and paperwork needed to start an enterprise can be daunting. Furthermore, laws intended to protect workers mean that it is virtually impossible to fire anyone, which can be a real burden for a small business that simply cannot survive with employees who are not up to the task. The lack of regulation in the U.S. is a strong contributor to the burgeoning of small business in that country.

On the other hand, a pure laissez-faire policy would be disastrous for small business, as well as for society. Should we allow small businesses to sell "health cures" that actually make people sick, or car seats for babies that haven't been through safety testing? Of course not—even if requiring safety testing puts a burden on small business. The safety of the public is important, to be sure, but public confidence is also important if small businesses are to have any customers. Furthermore, some small business owners (just

**MANHATTAN**
PREP

like large business owners) practice racial discrimination, sexual harassment, and other abuses of workers, such as paying undocumented workers less than minimum wage. It is important for human rights to curtail these abuses; it also helps small businesses for the government to put a check on such practices, because then legitimate, ethically run businesses can compete on a fair playing field.

While this essay propounds a system of minimal to moderate regulation of small businesses, some might argue that government has no right to intrude on the private dealings of businesses and their customers. According to this view, if someone wants to offer unlicensed cosmetic injections, and budget-minded consumers are willing to have their wrinkles filled with who-knows-what, then it is the right of both parties to transact as they wish. However, in developed nations, governments take on, at very least, the provision of services that individuals cannot provide for themselves—military defense, the creation of highways and other infrastructure, and the testing of food and medicine on a wide scale, among others. Individuals do not have the ability to test every can of baby food for botulism or to evaluate the credentials of a "doctor." Thus, in industries in which human health and safety are at issue, some regulation is justified.

How should governments best help small businesses thrive? In some sense, the answer is that governments should back off and let people do as they will. In a free market, many small businesses will be launched, many will fail, and the best will survive. However, some government intervention is required to protect the public from dangerous products and harmful business practices. These regulations ultimately help small business as a whole by encouraging consumer confidence in these businesses.

**Here is a second opinion from Manhattan Prep instructor Emily Sledge:**

Concerning government involvement in private business matters, we might imagine a scale from "total" on the left to "none" on the right. Jen has successfully argued for slightly right of center on this scale, making her position clear and taking a more easily defensible position than either extreme would be. Notice some of her techniques: the second paragraph explains her most "extreme" position, giving the United States as an example of how thriving small businesses are correlated with less regulation. So if less regulation is good, wouldn't no regulation be even better? Not so fast! The remaining body paragraphs swing the essay back toward the center, offering examples of why various and diverse stakeholders (the public, small business owners, employees) benefit from some regulation, and why certain situations require some government involvement. The reiteration of her thesis at the beginning of the fourth paragraph is a nice touch; Jen gives many detailed examples in the third and fourth paragraphs, so it is wise to remind the reader of the big picture periodically.

## Issue Topic #2

Schools should do more to prepare students for the non-academic aspects of adulthood.

Write a response in which you discuss the extent to which you agree or disagree with the recommendation and explain your reasoning for the position you take. In developing and supporting your position, be sure to address the most compelling reasons and/or examples that could be used to challenge your position

**Here's a take on this topic—followed by an actual essay—from Manhattan Prep instructor Tommy Wallach:**

This is a pretty juicy prompt, as they go, because it's about education. Prompts about business experience or scientific endeavors require a lot more hypothesizing on my part, as I've never been in business or conducted scientific research. But for this prompt, I can draw on personal experience. Everyone's been to school!

While you can rest an entire essay on your own experience, I like to mix it in with at least one fact/hypothetical example, so it doesn't feel like I'm writing some kind of personal essay. However, don't be afraid to use the first person in your essays; it will not cause you to lose points. I would certainly draw on my own opinion of how my academic and non-academic education served me in order to write this essay.

Maybe because I'm the artsy type, I'm going to choose to agree with the prompt, though this one is definitely open enough that you could go either way. My thesis will be that most of post-scholastic life is non-academic, so actually the non-academic should be the *focus* of school. This is slightly more extreme than necessary, but I feel confident that I can support it.

Finally, the topic says "be sure to address the most compelling reasons and/or examples that could be used to challenge your position," so I'll make that my third body paragraph. Providing a straw man argument (defined as a sham argument you set up just to knock it down) is never a bad idea in the Issue Essay, but it is of course required with a prompt like this.

Alright. Next, I'd type up a brief outline to make sure I had enough meat for a good essay. Don't forget to delete it from the box before you submit the essay. It probably wouldn't kill you either way, but why confuse your reader?

Thesis: life after school is non-academic, so non-academic > academic

P1: Economic crisis because of financial illiteracy

P2: My experience: private school with math/science focus

P3: Challenges to my position: specialized tech jobs require serious academics: response = Microsoft hiring riddle

**Essay:**

Education is certainly the hot-button issue of the moment, with national policies like Race to the Top and No Child Left Behind changing the way we teach, measure academic success, and even learn. At the heart of the debate over the future of education is the question broached in this prompt: are academic subjects, such as mathematics and history, more worthy of students' time than life skills, such as critical thinking, ethics, and self-expression? Many refuse to let go of the system of rote memorization and strict quantitative evaluation that has long characterized education in America, yet in a fast-paced world characterized by huge systemic problems and constant seismic shifts in science, business, and technology, this system is no longer functional. Adulthood is primarily non-academic, and school is meant to prepare students for adulthood. Thus, schools should indeed do more to prepare students for the non-academic aspects of life.

At the heart of the recent financial crisis was the proliferation of sub-prime mortgages, in which people without any capital were able to procure a mortgage the payments of which they would never be able to afford. How were so many people hoodwinked by predatory loans? It is because their education, in spite of all of its math classes, did not prepare them in any way for the mathematics of the real world. What use is calculus, which only a tiny subset of students will ever use in their lives or jobs, in comparison to lessons in reading contracts or investing intelligently, something that every person will need to do at one point or another? It is not too extreme to suggest that if our schools spent more of their time focused on finance as it actually affects people's lives, the crisis could have been avoided, or at least significantly mitigated.

And non-academic skills are as important on the micro level as they are on the macro level. I attended a private school in Seattle, Washington with a firm focus on mathematics and science; we were required to take both a math and a science class every year, and most of us were encouraged to take AP and honors classes in these subjects. While there is something to be said for working outside of your comfort zone, the intense attention paid to academics came at the expense of those subjects that most interested me. During high school, I competed as a concert pianist and performed in professional theater productions in Seattle. Like me, the vast majority of my classmates did not go into fields involving either math or science, and those years we spent studying academic subjects to advanced levels caused us to lose out on time we could have spent developing passions from which we might have derived joy for the rest of our lives. Studies show that playing an instrument provides numerous benefits relevant to the non-academic aspects of adulthood, such as managing stress, persevering in the face of failure, and maintaining focus.

Of course, many educational theorists argue that the workforce is increasingly being channeled into either the service economy, comprised primarily of jobs requiring no education at all, or those jobs that require a high level of technical proficiency and thus a specialized academic education. These theorists believe that our only hope of remaining competitive in the world economy is to ensure that our schools focus on academics such as math and science, so that America's children will be prepared to step into those highly specialized jobs. However, it turns out that even the most advanced tech companies in the world claim that mental flexibility is far more important to their hiring decisions than pure knowledge (much of which they would rather pass on through training on-site, in order to promote their own methodologies). At interviews for Microsoft, potential candidates are said to have been asked the following riddle: "Why is a sewer grate round, rather than square?" The answer is that a round grate can never fall down the hole (a square can if you tilt it up and rotate it into the diagonal). Surely no amount of purely academic education would prepare one to answer a question such as this; only an educational regimen that propounded critical and flexible thinking about real world problems would be of any use.

   An academic education is inarguably important. No student should be allowed to leave school without a solid understanding of basic mathematics and the ability to read critically and write coherently. But these skills are merely one part of what makes a well-rounded individual. For too long, American schools have been overly focused on quantifiable metrics of achievement; if we are to compete in the global economy, as well as fix some of the terrible problems afflicting our world, it will be necessary to design a new education premised on preparing students for the lives they are most likely to lead, rather than some idealistic concept.

**Here is a second opinion from Manhattan Prep instructor Emily Sledge:**

I thought this essay was strongest when Tommy used even-handed language, as he did in his summation, writing that an academic education is "inarguably important," and that certain basic skills are a minimum educational requirement, but that "these skills are *merely one part* of what makes a well-rounded individual." That's much tougher to dispute than the more extreme language Tommy used in the preceding paragraph: "Surely *no* amount of purely academic education would prepare one to answer a ques tion such as this; *only* an educational regimen that propounded … *thinking about real world problems* would be of *any* use." Fortunately, Tommy's thesis—agreeing with the prompt—is fairly moderate, arguing that we should "do more" to prepare students for the non-academic aspects of life.

While Tommy did an admirable job in a 30-minute essay, an ideal essay might have countered certain objections. Tommy asks, "What use is calculus … in comparison to lessons in reading contracts or investing intelligently?" But aren't academic topics such as reading comprehension, grammar, vocabulary, and algebra fundamental to these real life skills? One could make the case that calculus requires and teaches the very "critical and flexible thinking" skills Tommy later cites as important. The sewer grate question is a good one—intriguing if you've never given it any thought. Yet he cites geometry concepts in the answer to the puzzle, suggesting that academic topics are at the core of this "mental flexibility" exercise.

In summary, I liked the mix of personal, business, and education examples, and thought they were well-suited to an argument that academic and non-academic skills are both important to learn.

In general, I would recommend toning down strong assertions (such as those about the relative value of academic and non-academic study) to make your GRE essays more credible and more difficult to dispute.

**MANHATTAN**
PREP

## Issue Topic #3

People should question the rules of authority as opposed to accepting them passively.

Write a response in which you discuss the extent to which you agree or disagree with the statement and explain your reasoning for the position you take. In developing and supporting your position, you should consider the reasons for which the statement may or may not be true and explain how these considerations shape your position.

**Here's a take on this topic—followed by an actual essay—from Manhattan Prep instructor Stephanie Moyerman:**

First, I must establish my "take" on the statement. Paying careful attention to the exact wording, I notice that the statement suggests that people should only *question* the rules of authority, but does not imply or suggest any necessary actions. As I can see no harm in merely questioning the rules of authority, I initially decide that I agree with the prompt. After all, great milestones in modern history, such as the Enlightenment and the American Revolution, have resulted from the questioning of authority.

I must remember, however, that I am not to explain whether I agree or disagree with the prompt, but the *extent* to which I agree or disagree. Any essay in which I express 100% agreement with the statement will be very difficult to defend. Therefore, I decide that my position will be to mainly agree with the statement, but to consider at least one situation in which the statement may not be true. I decide that in the case of elected officials and a government with a system of checks and balances, such as the United States, it would become very difficult to pass any law if all constituents questioned each and every rule. Further, the idea of elected leaders is that they best represent their constituents as a whole. Countries with a varied body of constituents that follow this statement could experience people questioning the laws that obviously benefit the society as a whole. This could lead to disorder, a more segregated society, or, in the very least, the hindrance of governmental progress.

With these points in mind, I type the following notes into the text box:

> Main Idea: In most instances, people should question the rules of authority as opposed to accepting them passively. However, there are specific cases in which adhering strictly to this statement could have negative effects.

> I.   Questioning the rules of authority, in and of itself, does not suggest necessary actions, just thought.
> II.  The French and American Revolutions both resulted from questioning the rules of authority.
> III. Questioning the rules of authority can lead to disorder, segregation, and/or hindrance of progress in a varied nation with elected officials.

**Essay:**

Glancing back through modern history, one will undoubtedly notice that many remarkable changes have been sparked by people questioning the rules of authority. One might argue that the outcomes of these changes have weighed on both the good and bad side of human history and that questioning authority can be wrong or dangerous. But it is not the questioning of authority that caused these end results; it is the action of the people involved. Questioning the rules of authority only reveals the necessity for change within an established institution. Thus, I strongly agree with the statement that people should question the rules of authority as opposed to accepting them passively. The questioning of authority incites necessary social and political change without implying any necessary action.

Take, for example, the formation of the United States of America. For years under British rule citizens in the colonies were unfairly taxed and treated in accordance with British law. Not until some very powerful men questioned British rule and stood up to defend their beliefs did the colonies come to think of themselves as an independent entity. Years later, when released from British rule, their original questioning of the rules of authority led the leaders of the United States to take a different authoritative stance than the British. The United States became a democracy ruled by the people. The questioning of authority not only brought about social change, but also had a strong influence on the shaping of future events. In fact, one of our famous forefathers, Benjamin Franklin, famously quoted that, "It is the first responsibility of every citizen to question authority."

Similarly, but more extreme, the citizens of France in the 18th century lived under the delusion that their monarchy was ordained by God for many years. These years were filled with hardship, starvation, and greed, where the monarchy and those around them lived untainted palatial lives while their citizens lay hungry in the streets. It was not until the masses came to question the monarchy's rules that social change was brought about and the government was overthrown. In this instance, however, many radical groups came to power after the monarchy collapsed, each reacting to the harsh rules of the previous authority. Eventually, by continuing to question these rules, the French were able to remove their tyrannical rulers and form a republic.

Some might claim that questioning the rules of authority necessarily implies violent action in the case of civil change: that one cannot exist without the other. This is certainly not the case. Take, for example, Mahatma Gandhi and his fight for India's independence. His questioning of authority not only inspired others to do so, but also inspired them to affect social change via non-violent protest. The questioning of authority, coupled with moral actions, led to the end of much tyranny and injustice throughout the world all through non-violent means.

This is not to say that I think that this statement is the best course of action in every situation and for every person. There are certain situations in which questioning authority could lead to consequences such as segregation, disorder, and/or a hindrance of progress. Take, for instance, the government of the United States, one with elected officials and a system of established checks and balances. When citizens independently elect their leaders, one must bear in mind that these officials are elected to service the needs of the constituents as a whole. In a system where every person questions each new rule, as the statement implies, political leaders must cater to many different viewpoints, hindering progress. Further, natural divisions arise from people with differing views on the laws, such as Democrats and Republicans. These divisions segregate populations and hinder progress as well.

**MANHATTAN**
PREP

In essence, I agree with this statement as long as it is not taken to the extreme. One cannot achieve social or political change without questioning the authority, and certainly changes have been necessary in our history and will be necessary in our future. However, certain situations do exist where an entire population adhering strictly to this statement could find itself hindering progress and drawing somewhat arbitrary lines among people.

**Here is a second opinion from Manhattan Prep instructor Jennifer Dziura:**

What an interesting take on this topic! As an American, my first thought when I read this topic was, "Of *course* people should question the rules of authority!" After all, questioning the rules doesn't mean you have to break them— sometimes questioning the rules leads a person to start a political movement or write an article or just sign a petition, and sometimes it causes a person to grow up, major in political science, and then run for office. Questioning the rules is the basis of critical thinking and citizenship!

So, I was pretty surprised to see Stephanie argue that too much questioning of the rules could lead to disorder. While Stephanie made the decision to write a more nuanced essay by taking a middle-ground point of view, I would have written a more hard-hitting essay in favor of questioning the rules all the time. I might have used examples of the civil rights movement in the United States (in which Martin Luther King, Jr. and many others went to jail for breaking the rules in a fight for justice) versus countries in which no dissent is tolerated (such as North Korea). I also tend to use John Stuart Mill's concept of the marketplace of ideas in many essays, and that would have fit very nicely here.

Overall, though, Stephanie has written a well-structured and well-developed essay. Bonus points for the Ben Franklin quote!

## Issue Topic #4

> If two applicants for a job are otherwise equally qualified, the job should go to the applicant with more experience.
>
> Write a response in which you discuss the extent to which you agree or disagree with the statement and explain your reasoning for the position you take. In developing and supporting your position, you should consider the specific circumstances in which adopting the position would or would not be advantageous and explain how these examples shape your position.

**Here's a take on this topic—followed by an actual essay—from Manhattan Prep instructor Stephanie Moyerman:**

As a relatively young person in America's workforce, I read this statement and my gut disagrees. However, I must be careful not to write a personal reaction essay, but instead to qualify the reasons for my disagreement and use them to shape my writing. In addition, the prompt states that I should consider the specific circumstances in which adopting the position would or would not be advantageous and discuss how these shaped my position.

To brainstorm my essay, I first try to pinpoint exactly why being young gives me such a strong personal reaction to this statement. Adhering to this prompt would certainly put younger applicants at a disadvantage, as they, by virtue of their fewer years on the planet, tend to have less work experience. In fact, if this were taken to the extreme and every company adhered strictly to this statement, it would become difficult for any young person to be hired into any competitive job due to the sheer number of applicants in today's job market. This would lead to a self-perpetuating cycle: young people lack experience, they miss job opportunities based on their lack of experience, and then are dismissed from future job opportunities because they cannot gain valuable job experience. I am not, however, advocating that jobs should be given to younger applicants, simply stating that judging by experience alone presents a bias against a certain group.

To claim that two people are "otherwise equally qualified" is also extremely vague. In every situation, a less arbitrary test could be constructed. Surely, if experience is that important, it should play a role in the test that decides the outcome. For instance, a coding challenge for otherwise equally qualified candidates for a computer programming job should favor the candidate with more experience, as their experience should equate to being better at such a task. However, if it does not, they should not be chosen for the job simply because their experience is greater.

After careful consideration, I realize that I strongly disagree with the statement. The job should not be given to the candidate with more experience, but should be decided on a case-by-case basis. Perhaps in the extreme case of budget or time constraints a concrete test such as experience would be helpful. Here are the notes I would write:

> Thesis: The job should not go to the applicant with more experience, but should be evaluated on a case-by-case basis.
>
> (A)  "Otherwise equally qualified" is a vague term. Can a distinction still be made? Situation dependent—the job itself, colleagues, overall goals, etc., play a rather large role.
>
> (B)  The number of applicants for competitive jobs would limit a young person's ability to achieve said job, creating a perpetual cycle.
>
> (C)  Extreme cases to favor the other side.

## Essay:

In 2006, more than 1,200 applicants applied for a single professorship opening at Harvey Mudd College, a small, liberal arts college in Southern California. The sheer number of applicants, all with PhDs in physics, made the application process extremely competitive. Judging only by resumes, transcripts, statements of intent, and recommendations, the teaching staff of the college narrowed the pool down to three finalists. With so many applicants for such a competitive position, it became all but impossible to distinguish between those that were most highly rated. In essence, these people were all equally qualified for the job. However, marked distinctions among the finalists remained. They were comprised of a late-twenties recent PhD graduate from CalTech, a late-thirties professor from the University of North Carolina, and an early-thirties post-doctoral fellow from Stanford. The school did not defer to their differences in age or experience to decide. Instead, each candidate was flown to the college and presented a prepared lecture to the freshman class of approximately 200 students. The students evaluated each candidate in categories such as clarity and likability. One might imagine that lecturing experience might favor the professor, but in the end, the recent CalTech graduate achieved the highest ratings and was hired by the college. All three finalists had a fair and equal chance at the job upon final decision, though experience was not disregarded by the test. Had the college deferred to experience alone, our CalTech graduate would have been eliminated.

Harvey Mudd College is not unique in its hiring process. Almost all schools defer to another means of judgment for incoming candidates. The sheer number of applicants meeting the benchmark

**MANHATTAN**
PREP

requirements for every open professorship guarantees two or more equally qualified applicants at the top. And, if every professorship nationwide were decided from this point based on experience, it would be all but impossible for young people to break into college and university teaching positions. Allowing experience to be the deciding factor would create a perpetual cycle—young applicants would be turned down due to their lack of experience, limiting their ability to gain experience and denying them access to future jobs if decided in the same fashion. There is, of course, nothing special about a university teaching position. Many lusted-after job openings experience a similar number of applicants. Judging identically equal applicants by experience appears to be an unnecessary bias against the young, especially when impartial tests remain that could aid in the decision making process.

There are circumstances, however, in which it would be advantageous to simply choose the job applicant with more experience. For instance, had the hiring budget for Harvey Mudd College been much lower, it would have been impossible to fly the candidates out and give them the impartial test that was mentioned. Or, if an applicant had to be chosen on a very short, strict time schedule, such tests of merit would not be feasible. In said cases, it seems acceptable to use experience as the deciding criteria between otherwise identically equal candidates.

Ultimately, unbiased hiring tests appear to be the best option for deciding between otherwise identically equal candidates. Experience factors into candidate performance, but does not become the only deciding factor. However, extreme circumstances, such as short time-scales and limited financial resources, may limit the ability to perform unbiased hiring tests. In these cases, hiring based on experience alone does appear to have its merits.

**Here is a second opinion from Manhattan Prep instructor Jennifer Dziura:**

I love the unusual introduction of this essay! While many Issue Essays tend to begin with a restatement of the topic, a developing sentence or two, and then a thesis, this essay begins with a story and actually builds a bit of suspense! Who will get the job? As it turns out, not the most experienced candidate. A fantastic and appropriate story.

While Stephanie disagrees with the prompt, she offers a bit (just a bit!) of ground to the other side—she acknowledges that experience should be the determining factor *if* there are budgetary or time limitations. This is ceding very little ground indeed! She's basically saying, "I guess you could do it *your* way—if you don't have time to do it the *right* way."

I love that the essay doesn't just go against the prompt—it also offers a suitable alternative ("unbiased hiring tests"). As such, this essay was very persuasive.

## Issue Topic #5

Schools should cut funding for extracurricular activities such as sports and the arts when school buildings are in need of repair.

Write a response in which you discuss the extent to which you agree or disagree with this recommendation and explain your reasoning for the position you take. In developing and supporting your position, describe specific circumstances in which adopting the recommendation would or would not be advantageous and explain how these examples shape your position.

**Here's a take on this topic—followed by an actual essay—from Manhattan Prep instructor Stacey Koprince:**

This is a tricky little topic because we can interpret the circumstances in so many different ways. If we take the phrase "in need of repair" literally, then we might think, "Well, if you *need* to repair it, you have to! What else can we do?"

Real life is never quite this black and white, though. "In need of repair" can mean anything from the imminent collapse of the walls to, hey, there's a dent in this wall over here.

As I thought this through, I realized that, first, I needed to articulate when you would actually need to make a certain type of repair and when you would have more leeway to let something go. In this case, I came up with the idea that a school, first and foremost, delivers academic services. So, if neglecting to make a certain repair would prevent a school from delivering those academic services (or otherwise significantly impair the school's ability to do so), then that repair probably does need to be made. On the other, hand, something of a more aesthetic nature that would not interfere with academics, such as that dent in the wall, may or may not be more important than funding the tennis team.

Ultimately, then, a blanket policy is too heavy-handed. There needs to be a more nuanced ability to decide on a case-by-case basis. At this point, I'd typed up some notes for paragraphs 1 through 3, and I thought, "Hmm. What am I going to do for paragraph 4?" I realized that there was something else bothering me about the statement: why is it a choice between repairs and extracurriculars? Are there no other possible sources of funding? Maybe not, but let's actually establish that before we cut off Friday night football and Monday afternoon debate club.

And voila! I had my paragraph 4 and was able to start writing. Here are my notes:

P1: Disagree that this should be a blanket policy. Depends on other considerations… General principle: academics come first

P2: Do repairs and cut extracurric's: if interferes with academic (heat doesn't work; roof is caving in)

P3: Don't repair if doesn't interfere (paint is fading but not in any way problematic; cosmetic)

P4: Is it really either/or? Alternative sources of funding? Special bonds when major repairs/renovations are needed?

P5: Conclusion

**MANHATTAN**
PREP

**Essay:**

The author claims that, when school buildings are in need of repair, the schools should do two things: prioritize these repairs over extracurricular activities and use the funds from those extracurricular activities to pay for the repairs. It is entirely possible that school districts will have to make a difficult choice such as this one, but it would be hasty to put into place a blanket policy without first examining the goals and priorities of the schools. Do schools serve solely to deliver academic services? I would argue no—athletics and art programs are very important as well, though academics are clearly the first priority. A school faced with such a choice might instead base such a decision upon whether the needed repair is one that would interfere with academics if it were not made.

For example, if a school's heating system breaks down in the winter or the roof weakens and is in danger of caving in, then clearly the school will need to make the necessary repairs immediately. If the necessary funding can be obtained only from curtailing extracurricular activities, then those activities must go by the wayside. If the school cannot deliver on its fundamentals (academics), then it cannot (or should not!) offer additional programs that are designed to enrich the core offering but are not a part of the core offering themselves. Note that there are two levels of decision to be made here: whether the problem, if not repaired, will interfere with academics, and whether the funds must come specifically from the after-school activities budget.

Alternatively, suppose that the school could use re-painting but there is nothing dangerous or otherwise problematic about the current paint job; the issue is, in other words, aesthetic. Suppose, again, that the funds for re-painting would have to come from the extracurricular activities fund. Is it more important for the school to be aesthetically pleasing or to offer after-school programs? Reasonable people may disagree as to the answer, and this is the whole point: all repairs are not equal, and it is not necessarily the case that any repair trumps all extracurricular activities.

The examination of these two hypotheticals allows us to uncover a problematic assumption with the original assertion. Is it the case that the school must make an either/or choice: either school repair or extracurricular funding? If significant, necessary repairs are needed, there are perhaps other avenues for funding: government grants, bonds voted for by the local community, even a fundraising drive. At the same time, for ongoing maintenance issues of a more aesthetic nature, schools might reasonably decide to make some minor compromises—re-paint every 6 years instead of every 4, say—in order to stretch their money to cover extracurricular programs. After all, everyone has to stick to a budget, and we all make trade-offs every day in deciding how to spread our limited funds.

In conclusion, the author's assertion is too narrowly drawn. It is entirely possible that a school may have to cut funding to some extra programs when it finds itself faced with a costly maintenance problem that would interfere with academics if not addressed. After all, the school must first deliver on its mission to educate its students. There are many shades of grey, however, in distinguishing between necessary and "nice to have" maintenance, and it is by no means a foregone conclusion that any kind of maintenance trumps any kind of after-school program. In fact, there are many circumstances in which a school might reasonably defer or minimize long-term maintenance in order to maintain adequate funding for additional activities that can immeasurably enrich a student's life and learning.

**Here is a second opinion from Manhattan Prep instructor Jennifer Dziura:**

I think that this essay would score a 6 because it questions the definition of terms within the argument ("in need of repair") and then *actually addresses the entire topic*—both the idea about repairs and the idea about extracurriculars. I've read enough mediocre essays to tell you what most test-takers would do with this topic—they would write a whole essay about how sports and the arts are really important. That type of essay is unsophisticated, not entirely on-topic, and quite frankly, childish. Adult life is full of hard decisions: sure, extracurriculars are important, but so are functional school buildings. So, now what? How do we decide between two important things? That's where a good essay should start.

By the way, Stacey writes "grey" in the final paragraph. This is a Canadian/UK spelling (in the United States, "gray" is more commonly used). I mention that because the official graders for the GRE see essays from students around the globe—they see American English, British English, Indian English, and other varieties, and they're used to seeing things phrased or spelled in slightly different ways. These varieties are perfectly acceptable.

## Issue Topic #6

> Creativity should be used as the only true measure of intelligence.
>
> Write a response in which you discuss the extent to which you agree or disagree with the claim. In developing and supporting your position, be sure to address the most compelling reasons and/or examples that could be used to challenge your position.

**Here's a take on this topic—followed by an actual essay—from Manhattan Prep instructor Stacey Koprince:**

I really struggled to think of examples for this topic. I knew immediately that the position was too extreme and I couldn't possibly agree with it—but specific arguments or examples to support my position? Ugh. So I did something extremely unusual (for me) here. I wrote notes for my first paragraph but, after banging my head against the wall for a minute or so, I then wrote my entire first paragraph without any notes written down for the other paragraphs, hoping that the act of writing would help the brainstorming side of my brain to kick into gear.

And it worked! I was able to keep writing. About halfway through the third paragraph, I went back to my notes to type up a very brief outline of what I was in the midst of doing, just to make sure that it made sense and that I wouldn't forget what I wanted to do in paragraph four when I got there.

You'll also see that I have three capitalized words in my notes for paragraph one. I wrote this in response to the second sentence of the instructions: we have to address the ways in which others could "challenge [our] position." I always make it a point to acknowledge the other main point of view in my Issue Essays, but because they specifically requested it, I'm going to spend more time on this than usual—likely a paragraph rather than just a sentence or two.

> P1: Examples. ACKNOWLEDGE OTHER SIDE!!! "Only" is extreme—one measure, not "only."
> P2: ?
> P3: ?
> P4: protest by author: this is just creativity in disguise
> P5: concl

**Essay:**

Intelligence can be measured in many forms—so many, in fact, that while the concept of intelligence has been around for millennia, we're still debating how to define, let alone measure, such a nebulous concept. Is it a measure of how much someone learns in school? How well someone performs on standardized tests, such as the SAT, or IQ tests, such as the Stanford-Binet? Surely the author of the essay prompt would protest that these are not valid measures of intelligence because an artistic genius—Picasso or Mozart—might not perform very well on such "standard" measures of intelligence. And I agree with the author to this extent: a standardized test should not be the measure by which we seek to quantify or classify intelligence in general—not the only measure, that is. To the extent that we do need to quantify intelligence, we must first answer the question: what particular type of intelligence are we trying to measure?

A standardized test designed for admission to a certain educational program can be a valid measure for someone seeking to quantify how well someone has learned the material tested on that exam, as well as how flexibly someone can apply that knowledge to the particular types of questions seen on the exam. Such an exam, if well-constructed, could help the makers to ascertain how well the person is able to reason through various ideas or solution paths for a narrowly-defined set of material, and we might call that a form of intelligence. But is this the only measure of intelligence? Certainly not, as this is not the only type of intelligence.

Let's examine another concept entirely: the EQ, or emotional quotient. In recent decades, researchers have developed this concept to describe how well an individual assesses, expresses, and manages her own emotions as well as those of others. We've all known or heard of at least one "genius" who has an off-the-charts IQ but cannot interact productively with others. We've also likely all known someone who is extremely good with people, though he or she may not have graduated near the top of the class. Which is more intelligent? We haven't even begun to address other types of genius—the comedic genius of Lucille Ball, the gymnastic perfection of Nadia Comaneci, the marketing acumen of Steve Jobs, the "street smarts" of someone with little formal education and none of the "typical" signs of success who has nevertheless developed a strong, stable, and satisfying life despite hardship.

The author of the prompt might argue that all of these examples are ultimately a manifestation of creativity—that creative thinking allows someone to perform well on a standardized test, or to "read" the emotions or expressions of others and react accordingly, or to dream up the perfect marketing campaign that goes viral in a matter of minutes. If we define creativity that broadly, then I will agree with the author that creativity should always be considered when assessing intelligence. But I maintain that it is only one factor among many, including knowledge, expertise, flexibility, and observation.

If I had to propose one concept to cover all, I would propose that what we're really measuring is the ability to solve problems (within the context and parameters of whatever the particular "problem" is)—how to capture those water lilies on canvas to best effect, how to time a certain joke to draw the biggest laughs, how to recognize and best respond to an expression of dismay, or disgust, or grief on another's face. I would prefer, however, not to limit the discussion at all. I am content to let intelligence rest as a complicated, difficult to define, and nearly impossible to measure concept that nonetheless exists in everyone to some degree or another.

**Here is a second opinion from Manhattan Prep instructor Jennifer Dziura:**

My first thought when I read this topic was, "Wow, a lot of people might be tempted to write a whole essay about how the GRE is dumb and they should be able to submit an art portfolio or something instead." (I can't cite any official rule against it, but you probably shouldn't submit a GRE essay about how you don't like the GRE.)

In any case, I like several things about Stacey's essay—she takes a very fair and balanced position (Lucille Ball, Nadia Comaneci, Steve Jobs), but also follows a rather unique essay structure, leading us through several types of intelligence before synthesizing her ideas in the final paragraph, where she concludes that the best definition of intelligence is the ability to solve problems. I think all of my own GRE essays have given a clear thesis in the first paragraph; this essay flips that structure very effectively, making the conclusion an actual *conclusion*, rather than just a summarization of what came before.

I also liked that Stacey shared her reasoning process with us—who among us doesn't know the feeling of *freaking out* because you can't think of what to write? Sometimes you just have to start writing and work it out as you go.

## Issue Topic #7

> Government funding for purely scientific endeavors, such as space exploration, should be reduced in order to direct more funding toward humanitarian science projects.
>
> Write a response in which you discuss the extent to which you agree or disagree with the claim. In developing and supporting your position, be sure to consider specific instances for which this statement may or may not be true.

**Here's a take on this topic—followed by an actual essay—from Manhattan Prep instructor Stacey Koprince:**

I found it easy to come up with my "take" on this one but difficult to come up with specific examples. I knew in general that technologies originally developed for space exploration are now being used in a whole host of things here on Earth, but I wasn't 100% sure about the details. In particular, as I wrote my essay, I realized that healthcare examples would relate best to my other examples, but I was also the most shaky on the healthcare details. So, honestly, I sort of guessed—I wrote in some details as though I were confident, but I could be wrong. (And, no, I did not go back and correct them before publishing this! I want you to see what I really did.)

We're actually allowed to do this; the essays are not fact-checked. I'm not going to say that man first landed on the moon in 1842, because I know that's completely not true, but if I do have some details that aren't quite right, I'm not going to be penalized for that. If you think about it, it makes perfect sense: the essay graders can't possibly take the time to fact check every last thing, and so they check nothing.

I want to point out one more thing: my final essay is a bit shorter than usual (although still longer than many high-scoring Issue Essays), and that reflects that fact that it took me longer than usual to work out what I wanted to write. At some point, though, I had to cut off my planning and start writing or I wouldn't have had enough time to finish—and that's when I realized that I needed to "fudge" on my details a little.

Here are my original notes. After I wrote my opening paragraph, I realized that I should switch paragraphs 2 and 3 in order to provide a better transition into paragraph 4:

P1: Specific examples. Prioritize humanitarian science over pure science. Why? Benefits? Goals?

P2: Techs developed via space expl. projects are used extensively on earth (communications: cell phone; healthcare: robotic components that help in surgery; energy: solar cell panels)

P3: "humanitarian" = broad, but let's say health and education projects? Sometimes we do want to prioritize these

P4: But find a balance between the two, b/c "pure science" can result in "humanitarian" help

P5: conclusion

## Essay:

The author claims that humanitarian science projects should be prioritized over pure science projects, to the point of redirecting funding from pure science to humanitarian science. There are perhaps some instances in which this would be judicious, but in the absence of any discussion of the goals for such funding and the possible benefits to be obtained, such a black-and-white policy is likely too simplistic. Further, the author appears to assume that this is a zero-sum game: that such funding must go to one or the other and that the same amount of funding will be "worth more" by some (unspecified) measure if spent on humanitarian projects.

It would be helpful to examine specific cases in order to make this abstract argument a bit more concrete. "Humanitarian" is a broad term, but let's assume that the author is referring to projects that will provide healthcare or education to communities currently lacking such services in some significant way. (The term humanitarian could, of course, refer to many other types of research, community outreach programs, and so on—but we're trying to discuss one tangible example.) Vaccinating children against smallpox and measles is an obviously high-priority task: the technology exists, it is not prohibitively expensive, and it will both save lives and improve quality of life immeasurably. In any prioritization of funds, this particular usage must be near the top.

It is also the case, though, that many technologies originally developed during space exploration projects are now used in mission-critical "humanitarian" arenas. For instance, remote monitoring of vital statistics (such as heart rate and blood pressure) via miniature devices that can be affixed to or implanted in the body—or even swallowed!—allows us to monitor someone's health when that person is not physically in a healthcare setting. Other miniature remote-controlled devices (robots, if you will) are used in surgical settings to minimize the invasiveness of the procedure, or even to perform a maneuver that is impossible with traditional surgery. Satellite networks allow us to monitor weather patterns and broadcast information about the approaching hurricane immediately, potentially saving tens of thousands of lives.

Further, it isn't necessarily sufficient to look at the goals and expected benefits in the short-term. When NASA scientists were developing ways to monitor the health and manage the treatment of astronauts from afar, they likely weren't anticipating the myriad ways in which the technology would ultimately be used "on Earth." Early photovoltaic technology was developed almost exclusively in space because access to the sun's rays was free and easy. Decades later, solar cells are a leading source of terrestrial "clean" energy and one of the leading candidates to replace fossil fuel energy should we one day find ourselves in the position of running out of Earth-based energy sources.

Any approach, then, that paints all "humanitarian" projects with one broad stroke ("worthwhile") and "pure science" projects with another ("less important") is too crude an approach to make such very nuanced decisions. Given limited funds, of course priorities will have to be determined and a tough balance struck. History demonstrates convincingly, however, that what begins as a "pure science" project might one day prove to be a "humanitarian" effort that can affect the lives of every person on the planet.

**Here is a second opinion from Manhattan Prep instructor Tommy Wallach:**

In spite of Stacey's claim that she struggled to come up with ideas for the prompt, you certainly wouldn't know it from reading this essay! In truth, you should never look like you're at a loss for facts, because any details you're unsure about can be fictionalized, as long as you'd be willing to bet good money that your *overall concept* is correct. In other words, you may not know exactly why sugar is bad for the body, but you can feel free to say, "Sugar is bad for the body because the calories are burned quickly—causing the notorious sugar rush—leaving the body starved for nutrients in the long term." Are you sure that's exactly how it goes down? Nope. But it's more than good enough for your purposes. That being said, if you *can* write an essay entirely with stuff you know is true, you're likely to be more confident, and thus sound more confident.

If you wanted to take the other side of this essay, you could start by discussing the enormous amount of federal money that goes to weapons development, and argue that this investment has paid very little dividends in terms of raising our standard of living. In the next paragraph, you could discuss a small investment that has paid huge dividends in this regard, such as vaccination research in the 19th century, research into antibiotics, or agricultural improvements that have allowed for the production of greater and greater amounts of food to be grown on the same amount of land. Finally, because the prompt asks you to consider the other side, you could use Stacey's example, discussing how research conducted by NASA often results in practical products and techniques used in a more humanitarian way down the line. You could then argue that this is all well and good, but surely it would be more efficient to simply invest that money in those humanitarian projects in the first place.

## Issue Topic #8

The fact that technology is outpacing the needs of those in cultures that can afford the technology creates cultures of excess consumerism.

Write a response in which you discuss the extent to which you agree or disagree with the claim. In developing and supporting your position, be sure to address the most compelling reasons and/or examples that could be used to challenge your position.

**Here's a take on this topic—followed by an actual essay—from Manhattan Prep instructor Roman Altshuler:**

This is a pretty broad statement. Supposedly, it applies to *all* cultures that are affluent enough to afford technology. The claim looks really obvious, so my first thought is this: GRE essays are supposed to show complexity. If you agree with a prompt that says something obvious, it's going to be pretty difficult to say anything complex about it. On the other hand, if you disagree with a prompt that says something that seems obvious, you have an easy way to make your essay complex: you just explain that what the prompt claims is *too* obvious. It's based on a superficial understanding of the facts.

Notice, also, that the prompt asks you to "address the most compelling reasons and/or examples that could be used to challenge your position." The strategy of explaining why the claim is too obvious does that automatically: I just describe why the appearances are misleading, and by describing them I am already listing reasons that could be used to challenge my position.

So now I am thinking about content. What am I going to write about? I don't want to write about technology in general, because it seems like that will be too broad. So instead I am going to pick a particular instance of technology that I'll focus on for most of the essay as an especially salient example (and I'll call it an "especially salient example" in the essay, because that sounds fancy and uses a GRE word). How about cell phones? I just got a new one, so I have a bunch of thoughts about cell phones that I can draw on. The example seems a little too banal, but that's okay, as long as I can say things about it that aren't.

So now what about my argument? I think about whether people would buy crap they don't need if it didn't exist. Well, obviously not. But all that crap wouldn't exist if people didn't want to buy stuff. So maybe the prompt gets things backwards: it's not that the existence of lots of unnecessary technology makes people buy it. It's that people in a consumer culture want to have more stuff to buy, and that's why there is so much unnecessary stuff.

The prompt's mention of "cultures that can afford the technology" makes me think of affluent cultures and the poor societies their consumerism exploits. Maybe I can say something about that. I put that thought on the back burner; I'll try to get something out of it if I need an extra paragraph.

The prompt also mentions that the problem is with technology that is "outpacing the needs" of people in certain consumer cultures. How do we know when technology "outpaces needs"? I see a few problems right off the bat. First of all, needs change. It's easy to say that something is unnecessary or frivolous when looking from the outside, but from the inside the growth of technology creates its own needs. For example: I *need* a tablet, because I read a lot and want to carry large amounts of reading material with me everywhere. Also, we don't always know that a culture "needs": technology often *seems* unnecessary, but turns out to satisfy needs in hindsight. I remember how cell phones, with their access to social networks, were crucial in mobilizing protesters in the revolution in Egypt. I'll use that as an example.

And anyway, is it really clear that there *is* lots of technology that outpaces needs driving consumer culture? Some people will buy anything that's new, but maybe most people don't buy stuff that they really don't need. I could be wrong about that, but it's worth making an argument for it.

Now I clearly have enough to write about, so I won't need to talk about affluent vs. disadvantaged cultures after all. Instead, I'll focus on the idea that technology outpaces needs. By questioning the premise of the prompt, I can give a nuanced, somewhat unusual take on the issue. And then I'll wrap up that approach by insisting that *even if the premise is right*—that there is lots of technology on the market that nobody needs—it's *still* not true that this causes people to buy stuff they don't need.

I've been jotting notes as I go, so at this point I have the following written:

> Intro: cell phones. Thesis: it looks like tech nobody needs drives consumerism, but this gets things backwards and mistakenly assumes that people are buying stuff they don't need
> 1.   people don't buy things that nobody needs
> 2.   needs change. sometimes tech satisfies needs nobody knows about yet. Arab Spring example.
> 3.   consumer culture leads to new technology, not the reverse

As I get to each point, I delete it. And it's important to always keep the broader picture in mind, so when I develop the points, I have to explain what they have to do with the overall theme.

### Essay:

    As a result of constant competition and innovation, technology evolves at a staggering rate. Fifteen years ago mobile phones were a novelty for the privileged few; now they are the possession of roughly 70 percent of the world's population. And, of course, it is not enough simply to release a new kind of product and sell it: the product must be constantly updated, developed, and marketed in a new form. Better battery life and reception, global positioning, access to the internet, the ability to download music from the "cloud," or to take photographs and immediately share them across one's social network; all these are developments that have sprung sequentially from manufacturers in relatively short order, each one used to market a new generation of phone to eager consumers. And, of course, cell phones are only one example among many, though an especially salient one. The constant release of updated forms of the same technology, combined with the existence of a ready market to adopt these upgrades, conveys the appearance that the updates drive purchasing for the sake of purchasing; that if not for the oncoming tides of new products, the waves of spending would abate. But the appearance gets the relation backwards, and it relies on too simplistic a view of what the relation between technology and the needs of a culture might be.

    First of all, it is far from obvious that technology that genuinely outpaces the needs of its consumers retains a consumer base. Items that fail to find a public often vanish without a trace. Consider the push on the part of a number of computer manufacturers at the dawning of the last decade to market expensive tablet computers. The attempt went nowhere, and tablets vanished from the market to return only ten years later when a need for them appeared. The history of technology is replete with such market failures which, precisely because they were failures, rarely make it into public memory. This tendency to forget where the market has failed is perhaps the best explanation for the tendency to believe that unnecessary technological advances drive consumers' tendency to purchase every new bit of technology, no matter how little needed. But in fact, it seems, technology that outpaces the needs of a culture simply vanishes from that culture without taking hold. Of course every affluent culture has a wave of so-called "early adopters," who will buy the newest gadget, no matter how useless. But segments of the population who will spend on items they cannot even fathom needing are, unsurprisingly, small.

    Granting that technology that outpaces the needs of its market base sometimes fails, it may still seem as if this is often not the case; that, in fact, frequently technological advances are purchased and adapted on a wide scale by a culture, even when ostensibly no need for such a technology is present. The judgment that occurrences of this sort are common, however, faces serious objections. What, first of all, can we mean by the idea of technology "outpacing the needs" of its users? If we think of needs in the most basic terms, as universally shared by all human beings, then the list of genuine needs will be quite small:

**MANHATTAN**
PREP

food, shelter, clothing, and companionship. But even this small list of basics requires supplementation. Medicine, for example, seems like a basic need; but the need for medical technology is in principle limitless as long as human beings remain mortal. It is not so clear, then, that—at least in some areas—technology really can outpace need. It is also worth considering that technological advances in some seemingly frivolous fields may transfer to advancements of vital necessity. Finally, just as basic needs appear in some respects infinite, so the advancement of technology can create new needs, perhaps ones unforeseen prior to its development. A technologically advanced culture, for example, may well have needs far beyond those of its less affluent analogues; such needs may well appear trivial to outsiders. And, of course, the fact that some bit of technology does not satisfy a clear need at present does not show that it satisfies no need of the culture: one need only consider the role played by mobile technology—which may have appeared excessive when it first appeared—in the recent events of the Arab Spring.

Just as we find it difficult to definitely declare that any particular technological upgrade has outpaced the needs of its culture, so we should be suspicious that such outpacing, where it occurs, genuinely drives the consumerism. Affluent cultures constantly demand new outlets for their affluence; technology is merely one of the many industries that responds to that demand. It is not hard to imagine that those with money to spend will want to spend it. Thus, it seems reasonable to assume that excess consumerism drives the demand for new products, not the reverse. Moreover, the consumerism is fanned by any number of marketing techniques, themselves produced by companies eager to increase their profit margin. Often, new developments in technology, as in other industries, come about in response to the need to market new products. But again, it is the marketing and the cultural response to it that drives innovation here. The innovation exists for the sake of the marketing and consumerism, not the other way around. That new, seemingly frivolous technology is constantly produced, marketed, and purchased may give the appearance that it is new technology that causes the consumerism, but the reverse may well be the case.

We should be skeptical, then, of the view that unnecessary technology creates cultures of excess consumerism. While often this is how things may look on the surface, in reality the complex relations between technological innovation, need, and consumerism are far more complex. New technology creates new needs, and the consumers' demand for new products creates those products. To blame technology, especially technology that seems to have no necessary application, for the increase in consumerism is to misdiagnose the situation; it is to mistake the symptom for the underlying cause.

**Here is a second opinion from Manhattan Prep instructor Jennifer Dziura:**

When I read this essay, I almost laughed—"This incredibly lengthy, well-reasoned, well-argued essay is going to intimidate the heck out of our students!" It's worth mentioning that the friendly GRE instructor we know as Roman is known in some circles as "Dr. Altshuler, philosophy professor." So, consider this essay an ideal—not a standard most test-takers would be able to meet in a mere 30 minutes!

One thing that's especially excellent about this essay is the complex argumentative structure. Roman didn't just argue yes or no. Rather, he broke the topic into two claims: "technology is outpacing needs" and "this creates cultures of excess consumerism." He then questions the definition of "needs," argues against the first claim, and then argues that *even if the first claim is right*, the second claim still doesn't work.

This is a thorough way to attack an argument! (You say A will lead to B? A isn't true, but EVEN IF IT WERE, it wouldn't lead to B.) It's like you're winning the argument *twice*.

I also really enjoyed the example about the Arab Spring. This is a perfect example of a seeming "luxury" serving a noble and important purpose. (If I were writing this example, though, I'd include at least a sentence explaining what the Arab Spring is, just in case the grader hasn't heard of this historical event.) This is also a good reason to keep up with current events—students who complain they have "nothing to write about" would generally benefit from a daily dose of news coverage.

Finally, keep in mind that there's no requirement that you take such an argumentative approach—this is the Issue Essay, not the Argument Essay. So, you could certainly choose instead to agree with the prompt and give examples of technology leading to excess consumerism.

## Issue Topic #9

> Luck plays more of a role in determining success than work ethic does.

> Write a response in which you discuss the extent to which you agree or disagree with the claim. In developing and supporting your position, be sure to address the most compelling reasons and/or examples that could be used to both support and challenge your position.

**Here's a take on this topic—followed by an actual essay—from Manhattan Prep instructor Chris Berman:**

The stimulus asks that the response address the evidence for both positions—this must be accomplished while establishing a clear and defensible position. To receive a top score, the essay must consider defining the terms ("success") used in such broad statements. Precisely understanding the statement presented is also very important; this one revolves around luck playing *more* of a role, and an essay that argued that success was due entirely to one or the other would not be completely responsive.

Finally, note any assumptions underlying either position that could be utilized. For instance, if I were to argue in favor of the preeminence of work ethic, I could discuss the assumption that luck does or doesn't even out in the long run. However, when all is said and done, I have to argue the position for which points and examples leap to mind. I will posit the greater importance of luck, as my notes show:

> Main point—the importance of luck is supported by the vast majority of the historical evidence, and the opposing position rests on questionable assumptions and less compelling evidence.
> 1.   Examples that support this point.
> 2.   Opposing points and their flaws
> 3.   Opposing assumptions and their flaws
> 4.   Brief summation

**MANHATTAN**
PREP

**Essay:**

While no one should deny the utility of a strong work ethic in pursuit of material success and professional recognition, luck has a greater power and can deliver or destroy the dreams of both the earnest and the slothful. The truth of this perhaps ironic or even tragic aspect of life is borne out by the historical record. Military history is rife with examples of how fortune changes "the affairs of men." One such example would be Frederick the Great, the 18th century Prussian king. Famous both for his personal work ethic and for his imposition of the same on his soldiers, he is virtually universally acknowledged as the foremost military leader of his time. Yet, he was only saved from utter defeat by the unexpected death of the Empress of Russia. Sports history is also rife with examples of luck trumping effort. "Hollywood" also provides a plethora of examples of how good or bad luck determines the fate of hard working actors—Lana Turner, a star of the 1940's, was "discovered" at Schwab's drugstore. More quotidian lives follow the same pattern—inventors who lose the fruits of their labors through chance, and countless industrious people whose lives were undone by chance accidents or disease.

This aspect of life is also frequently mirrored in literature, plays, and songs. The deus ex machina of Greek tragedy is the beginning of a long lineage of art describing the superiority of fate to human will. Some would counter by arguing that fiction embraces the triumph of hard work and point to the Horatio Alger stories and similar works. However, not only are such examples smaller in number, but many of them were crafted expressly to tout that virtue in the service of building a society rather than to accurately depict the realities of life. Furthermore, it could also be argued that those who strived and succeeded against obstacles merely had enough good luck to dodge a fatal blow in one form or another. While Puritan and Lutheran philosophies laud the worth of work ethic, these essays were based on theological rather than pragmatic grounds. In fact, many were expressly composed to explain and counter the reality of the preeminence of random fortune.

Additionally, dubious assumptions underlie some of the main arguments in favor of the primacy of work ethic. Implicitly, the opposing view equates work ethic with the quality of the work. While there is certainly a correlation, there is no causation between effort and excellence. No matter how hard I were to work, I will never be a professional athlete of any sort. Also, the counterargument assumes that there is sufficient demand for the supposed excellence derived from effort. To return to the "Hollywood" example, there it is glaringly obvious that there is an oversupply of capable and objectively similarly skilled actors; thus, logically enough, random factors and good fortune become the primary determinants. I have personally seen actors cast because they remind the directors of their brothers. I have also seen actors not cast for exactly the same reason. Such oversupply is a characteristic of many, albeit not all, fields. Finally, the assumption that an individual's luck will return to the mean, as it were, is dubious. Again, history, the arts, and most people's anecdotal evidence point to the conclusion that some are luckier than others, even if no one lives an absolutely charmed life. Perhaps one lifetime is too small a sample size.

To reiterate, while a strong work ethic is sometimes necessary for and usually contributes to success, luck is the more powerful factor. The record of human activity leads to no other conclusion. To that point, there is an old saying that remains only too relevant: "If you want to make God laugh, tell him your plans."

**Here is a second opinion from Manhattan Prep instructor Jennifer Dziura:**

Great essay! Chris writes in a literary and somewhat formal style, which I think makes a powerful first impression ("luck … can deliver or destroy the dreams of both the earnest and the slothful"). Because of the writing style, I can say I wasn't surprised at all to see the essay introduce examples about literature, from Greek tragedy to Horatio Alger.

I also very much enjoyed the essay's critical takedown of Alger as an example of work ethic being more important than luck and of Protestant denominations' propounding of work ethic (which some people still call "Protestant work ethic"). In both cases, Chris argues that these do *not* make good examples of the primacy of work ethic over luck, because the sources had ulterior motives. The argument about an oversupply of talent was also persuasive (if there are more hard workers than there are jobs for those hard workers, luck will end up being the deciding factor).

If I had been writing an essay on this topic, I would have also argued in favor of luck, although I'm sure it would have been a very different essay. I probably would've written a lot about how what country you're born in has a lot more to do with your success than the efforts you put in. In a developed nation, you benefit from health care, roads, infrastructure, public education, and some kind of safety net for hard times, whereas none of these are reliably available in many of the nations of the world. Some people are born in war zones or refugee camps; some people think they're signing up for a job opportunity and end up becoming victims of human trafficking. Hard work is irrelevant in these cases.

If you wanted to go the other way on this topic and argue that work ethic is more important than luck, you can't *just* write about the importance of hard work. You also need to address the obvious objections—what about all the people who obviously got lucky (or unlucky)? I think that would be a hard essay to write. However, you could pursue some kind of middle ground approach, perhaps something like, "Good luck is an essential ingredient of success, but most strokes of luck are useless without the work ethic to pursue those opportunities."

## Issue Topic #10

> Some people believe that competition drives young athletes to perform at their best, while others believe that competition discourages those who are not athletically talented from participating in organized sports.
>
> Write a response in which you discuss which view more closely aligns with your own and explain your reasoning for your position. In developing and supporting your position, be sure to address both views presented.

**Here's a take on this topic—followed by an actual essay—from Manhattan Prep instructor Jesse Cotari:**

When I look at this prompt, my first thought is: *How do I take a side when both sides are pretty accurately describing facts, rather than offering opinions?* But instead of dwelling on that issue, I kick the question to my subconscious and get to work thinking about each side of the issue. I do some brainstorming, write the first sentence of the introduction, and then start in on the first two paragraphs. My goal at this point is to establish both sides' validity with examples of how they could both be correct, which will set up for whatever twist is coming that will drive my later paragraphs.

(I'm a big believer in giving my unconscious mind something to work on while I'm focusing attention forward. Typing takes mostly time and attention, whereas figuring out a creative "take" on an idea sometimes just takes right-brained inspiration. Instead of sitting around waiting for inspiration to strike, I get working on less creative processes like typing out an already-outlined paragraph.)

By the time I finish the first body paragraph, I have a pretty good idea of where the rest of the essay is going, so I take a moment to do a little more outlining, focusing on the deeper implications of either viewpoint.

If it were necessary to take an unqualified view in support of one side, I would have had a hard time. However, the possibility of including nuance makes this much easier. First, I decide to define the "unspoken assumption" behind each argument. Why would someone say one or the other of those statements? Probably to push a particular type of sports program. Okay, so let's talk about that.

At this point, despite the fact that I see the validity of both sides, I take a qualified side with "everybody wins!" This means positing that collaboration is more important than perseverance. Do I believe that that's 100% true all of the time? No, but I can make a case for other sources of perseverance in addition to sports, so I'll go with it. I finish up the introductory paragraph, write the second body paragraph, and then, the conclusion.

OF NOTE: I know that my process in this case is risky. Since I'm writing the essay in a non-linear way, I leave a little time to go back and be sure that everything flows.

## Essay:

The statement above presents two conflicting presentations of the same true facts: It is unquestionable that athletic competition both drives and discourages young athletes. However, unspoken assumptions as to the purpose of organized sports underlie significant differences in the implications of either statement. By understanding these underlying assumptions, it is possible to decide which aspect of organized sports is most beneficial to potential young athletes. While being driven to one's best through competition certainly has its benefits, the values of teamwork and collaboration that can be derived from any athletic participation are more important to success in the rest of life.

The first view, that competition drives young athletes to perform at their best, can be clearly examined through the lens of track and field. The immediate feedback received from watching a competitor pull ahead makes a direct psychological impact on any runner. In head-to-head competition, the direct ability to compare one's performance with that of one's rivals can be intensely motivational. Even after the race, the knowledge that with a little more practice victory could have been achieved can impel a young competitor to run those extra miles in preparation. This direct comparison with the abilities of others is one factor that can drive young athletes to be their best, but also makes the opposing viewpoint valid as well. Those who are not "athletically talented" make the comparison and instead of seeing reasons to put in more hours of practice, see reasons not to bother. Constantly failing to win can indeed be highly discouraging. Thus it is unquestionably true that both discouragement and personal drive are potential side effects of organized sports.

At a more fundamental level, however, it is not the viewpoints themselves, but the unspoken assumptions as to the purpose of organized sports that are incompatible and make siding against competition possible. The first view, that competition drives athletes to be their best, is a valid aim if being good at sports is a useful end goal. Does being able to run 400 meters faster than anyone else in the country serve any practical purpose? In a world generally free from the necessity to escape large predators, probably not. Nonetheless, it is true that the perseverance and dedication necessary to achieve that goal are worthy skills. The ends of development of dedication should, however, be compared with the opposing assumption: that playing a team sport is valuable, regardless of the level of success. Through participating in a team sport, young athletes can develop the ability to work with others to a common purpose. In the modern work-place—focused on teams, interactivity and collaboration—this life skill offers a clear advantage. While perseverance can be developed in other areas (particularly academic ones, where the benefits are more tangible), few pursuits offer the ability to develop the skills required to participate in a team. Deemphasiz-ing the competitive aspect of team sports (or at least providing the option to play team sports in a less competitive environment) allows the development of collaboration to reach a wider youth population and spreads the benefits of organized sports to more young athletes.

In the end, the statements present two true facts that have different implications. Both perseverance and teamwork are vital to the success of any adult, and are worthy goals of an athletic program. However, by reducing the emphasis on competition, the benefits of working with a team can accrue to a larger cohort of young athletes.

**Here is a second opinion from Manhattan Prep instructor Jennifer Dziura:**

Essays on very specific topics are challenging! Personally, I would be very annoyed to get this topic—as a reasonably educated person, I feel like I have a lot of fields to draw on for relevant and persuasive examples, but here I cannot use any of my knowledge because I am pretty much forced to write about children's sports.

Jesse does a great job with this topic, correctly identifying that both statements about youth sports have some truth to them, and so we must decide what we most value if we are to decide which truth is most important.

I was also *fascinated* by Jesse's writing process, in which he uses his subconscious mind to do some processing while he does the more tedious work of typing. If you wonder how some people think through an essay topic and write such long and well-developed essays all in 30 minutes, well…this is one way to do it!

Personally, I find that I'm able to think of and write so much in half an hour because I have a lot of practice. But maybe more importantly, I have a structure in mind before I begin writing (intro, 3 body paragraphs, conclusion), so I feel almost like I'm just dropping some details into a form or something. Finally, successful essay writers are often people who read a *lot,* on a variety of topics—and people who look things up when they don't know something! It can be frustrating when you want to write about the electric car because it perfectly fits the topic, but you realize you don't actually know anything about electric cars. Prepared test-takers are people who do a lot of reading (world news, science news, business news, the *New York Times Review of Books,* etc.), and whose natural curiosity leads them to Google or Wikipedia to fill in the gaps in their knowledge.

Of course, when you get a topic about children's sports, it's hard to make a lot of that knowledge base fit, but it can be done—off the top of my head, Rousseau's *Emile* and the theories of Piaget on child development could be used in an essay on this topic, even though they have nothing specifically to do with sports. Similarly, an example about the history of the Olympics could apply—as long as you explain how an example about adults applies to children. Also keep in mind that there isn't actually a requirement to bring in outside examples or information, as long as you can find enough to write about just making general/hypothetical arguments about the prompt itself. Jesse's essay is an excellent example of this approach.

**MANHATTAN**
PREP

# Argument Essay Guidelines and Sample Responses

## Argument Topic #1

A recent study by the Centers for Disease Control and Prevention found that employees with paid sick leave are 28% less likely to be involved in a work-related accident than employees who do not receive payment for sick leave. Researchers hypothesize that employees with unpaid sick leave feel pressured to work during time of illness for fear of lack of pay. On-the-job accidents are then spurred by impaired judgment or motor skills due to illness or illness-related medications. The highest-risk occupations, such as construction, showed the highest discrepancy in incidents based upon paid and unpaid leave.

Write a response in which you discuss what questions would need to be answered in order to determine whether the researchers' hypothesis is reasonable. Be sure to explain what effects the answers to these questions would have on the validity of the hypothesis.

**Here's a take on this topic—followed by an actual essay—from Manhattan Prep instructor Stacey Koprince:**

I read the instructions first, then the argument. The instructions focus on the "questions" needed to evaluate the argument; because I knew this when I started making notes, I was able to put as many as possible into question form. Later, when I began to write, I already had many questions that I could fold right into the argument.

The argument has two significant flaws. First, the study results (in sentences 1 and 4) do not address any part of the hypothesis (that is, whether people are working while ill and whether that then causes accidents). Second, the argument fails to address (and dismiss) any alternative explanations for the data.

My raw notes are fairly long, but notice how I've got them organized paragraph by paragraph. When I start writing, I actually type right underneath the notes for each paragraph, so that I can reuse exactly what I've already typed and then simply delete any extraneous words. This is similar to writing a detailed outline first and then fleshing out the first draft. The only thing I don't brainstorm is the conclusion—my conclusion will just be a restatement of everything I've already said. Here are my notes:

P1: Hypothesis = pressured to work. But evidence doesn't show WHY there are more accidents. Conjecture.

P2: Can the existing data be made to show actual causation? Study could poll people as to why they had the accident. Did they actually come to work sick?

P3: Other possible explanations? Differences based upon job title or level? Desk-job workers probably less likely to have accidents; are they also more likely to have paid sick leave? Blue-collar jobs more likely to cause accidents and also less likely to offer paid sick leave? Salary vs. hourly wage work?

P4: Other reasons why people feel pressured to work? Perhaps unpaid sick leave correlates with certain kinds of jobs where it's more problematic for a team if someone doesn't show up for work that day. *[Note: as I wrote the essay, I realized that this was already too much like paragraph 3—luckily, by then, I'd thought of something else to say in paragraph 4.]*

P5: conclusion

The instructions specifically ask me to "explain what effects the answers" would have on the argument. It's not enough to ask the questions—I also have to state how various responses might help or hurt the argument. Note that I did not necessarily say, "If the answer is yes, then this will happen; if the answer is no, then that will happen." It's enough to say something like "if X happens, this would support the hypothesis." I did, though, make sure that some questions were presented in a way that allowed me to say, "If so, this strengthens the hypothesis," and others were presented in a way that allowed me to say, "If so, this weakens the hypothesis."

### Essay:

The author provides two pieces of evidence in support of the researchers' contention that workers without paid sick leave are more likely to work when ill, and that such workers are more likely to experience a job-related accident as a result. The results of the study cannot be disputed—we must accept as true, for example, that those with paid sick leave are significantly less likely to have work-related accidents than those without paid sick leave. We might, however, question whether the study was large enough, or representative enough, to draw broad conclusions. Further, the study does not demonstrate causation: it does not tie the incidence of work-related accidents to illness. While the researchers' hypothesis is certainly one possibility, more research is needed to eliminate other possibilities and to bolster the strength of this argument.

The largest leap in the argument is the assumption that those without paid sick leave feel pressured to work when ill. No evidence is presented to establish this supposition. In order to strengthen this part of the argument, the researchers might ask study participants whether they have actually come to work ill during the same time frame covered by the original study and, if so, why they chose to come to work when ill. If the study participants who did experience a work-related accident were also more likely to come to work ill for fear of lack of pay, then the hypothesis would be much more strongly supported, particularly if this occurred with a correspondingly large proportion of workers (to match the 28% greater incidence of accidents in the original study).

The researchers would also strengthen their case by addressing alternative explanations for the data in the original study. For instance, are there differences between the two groups based upon industry or job performed that might explain the data? For example, are hourly workers more likely to lack paid sick leave, while salaried workers are more likely to receive it? Are hourly workers more likely to work in blue-collar or more manual occupations, where on-the-job accidents are more frequent? If so, then we would expect a correlation between unpaid sick leave and a higher incidence of workplace accidents because the work itself is inherently more dangerous, not because people are choosing to work when ill. Further, if it is the case that higher-risk occupations in general are more likely to lack paid leave, then the second piece of evidence also loses its significance. In such a case, the researchers' hypothesis would be significantly weakened.

The data presented also lacks a depth of detail that would help us to evaluate the significance of the study results. How many people were surveyed? What is the margin of error and how was the study conducted? Is the 28% figure statistically significant? If the study represented a large enough survey group to extrapolate to the general population, across regions, industries, and job responsibilities, then the study results may be conveying something significant. If, alternatively, few people were surveyed or the incidence of job-related accidents were very low, then perhaps the 28% difference represented a small number of people, well within the statistical variance expected.

**MANHATTAN**
PREP

While the argument presents an interesting hypothesis, the data presented is not strong enough to establish the validity of the conclusion to even a small degree. First, at a basic level, we need to know whether the existing data is statistically significant and sufficiently representative. There are also several gaps in the logic chain, assertions made without supporting evidence. Finally, the researchers could strengthen their case by examining, and dismissing, alternative explanations for the data presented thus far. These steps might not be enough to establish the validity of the hypothesis beyond a doubt, but they would allow the researchers to determine whether the pursuit of the hypothesis is a good use of time, funds, and attention.

**Here is a second opinion from Manhattan Prep instructor Tommy Wallach:**

Phew! Stacey has done a phenomenal job with this brutal Argument Essay. What makes it so hard? Well, the argument itself doesn't actually make a huge number of outright logical errors (e.g., "This burrito has guacamole, therefore it is the best burrito in Los Angeles!"). Instead, the majority of errors here are errors of *omission*. Stacey needs to use all the rules she knows about making a good argument in order to describe everything the author left out.

Generally, an Argument Essay presents you with a terrible argument, and it's up to you to explain why it's terrible. But in this case, the argument just isn't that bad as written. Thankfully, the prompt gives some hint of this. By asking what questions would need to be answered to justify the conclusion, it's more or less telling you that you'll need to consider things the prompt ignored. Make sure you take note of the special instructions on every essay, because they often provide helpful hints such as this one.

Honestly, I can't think of much I would do differently in this essay, though I do think Stacey missed one juicy low-hanging point. The Centers for Disease Control and Prevention is likely to have as its prime focus the desire to stop the spread of disease (it's not particularly interested in making sure random construction workers get good benefits). The best way to stop the spread of disease is to make sure sick people stay home, and the best way to get sick people to stay home is to ensure that they all get paid sick leave. Since the CDC's conclusion happens to coincide with that ulterior motive (getting sick people to stay home), we might have reason to doubt the CDC's conclusion.

## Argument Topic #2

> The city council of Town X has proposed reducing the city's electric expenses by switching all the lights in public buildings from incandescent bulbs to light-emitting diodes (LEDs). The switch would be made gradually as the old incandescent bulbs burn out, and the city council reasons that since LED lights burn brighter and cost no more to purchase, the switch would help Town X save money on electrical costs in the future.
>
> Write a response in which you discuss what questions would need to be answered to help evaluate the efficacy of the city council's proposal to save money on electrical costs. Be sure to explain how the answers to these questions would help to evaluate the council's prediction.

**Here's a take on this topic—followed by an actual essay—from Manhattan Prep instructor Stacey Koprince:**

As always, I read the prompt first, not the argument, so that I know what angles I need to take right from the start. This one's asking me to suggest "questions to help evaluate" the plan presented in the argument. I need to explain how the answers would help to evaluate the plan, not simply present the questions.

Great! My angle is "attack"—that is, I'm going to pick apart the plan, asking "Are you sure? Have you thought about XYZ? What about ABC? Is it really going to work that way?"

I also note that the prompt tells me what the goal is: "to save money on electrical costs." Okay, now I dive into the argument. The first paragraph of my essay is going to summarize the argument, so my argument notes will go there (I type these notes in as I'm reading; they'll become my outline). Then I start attacking, labeling all my questions P2, P3, or P4:

P1: Goal: reduce electric cost. Plan: gradual switch from IB to LED. LED brighter, cost same to purchase.

P2: Do they cost the same to use? Brighter, maybe use more energy? Do they last as long?

P3: Can they just be switched out directly? Will the new bulbs fit the existing fixtures? Etc.

P4: Other drawbacks? Unintended consequences?

P5: Conclusion

My P5 note is standard—I always write "Conclusion" (actually, "concl.", but I spelled out my notes above for you more than I would for myself) and worry about it later.

In this case, I notice that the argument offers no real "supporting" reasons to switch—but, hey, the new bulbs cost the same as the old ones. That doesn't help me *save* money. Plus, the initial cost to purchase is only part of the total cost—what about the electricity bill? And then I'm off and running.

Notice that I did actually think to myself: okay, what's the conclusion, and what evidence is the author trying to present in support of that conclusion? I can then ask myself, "Does each premise really support the conclusion?" and "Is the plan really going to work in the way that the author thinks?" In both cases, the answer is going to be no—I just have to figure out how each piece of the argument falls short.

Finally, I reminded myself that I need to have a neutral tone throughout. That is, I'm not trying to argue that the town council is wrong or its plan will not work; I'm simply pointing out flaws and indicating that the council has some more research to do in order to demonstrate that its plan is sound. I had to remind myself of that on this one because I think the town council's plan actually does sound pretty bad!

## Essay:

The council proposes reducing electric expenses by changing from one type of light bulb to another over time. While the council provides two reasons why this could help to save money, only one is a poten-tial support (the fact that the new bulbs burn more brightly). The other reason, that the LED bulbs cost no more to purchase, does not help to save money; rather, it only shows that the town will not spend more money to purchase the bulbs. Further, the one supporting fact may or may not result in a cost savings—we don't have enough information to tell for sure.

The initial cost to purchase the new bulbs is the same, but this is only one of the costs associated with lighting. The bulk of the cost is incurred over time, as the bulbs are used. Do the new bulbs use the same amount of electricity to run? The argument mentions that they're brighter; perhaps they use more energy? If so, then the electrical costs could actually increase over time, not decrease—the opposite of what the council expects. Further, do the new bulbs last as long as the old ones? If they last longer, then costs might decrease; if they burn out more quickly, however, then costs could increase.

The council's plan is to replace the incandescent bulbs with the new LEDs over time, as the old ones burn out. Is it possible to make a direct replacement without incurring any extra costs? Will the new bulbs fit into the old fixtures, and do they use the same type of electrical connection? If not, there could be a significant cost associated with retrofitting the fixtures in order to accommodate the new type of bulb—and that would be made more complicated by the plan to replace the bulbs gradually as they burn out. If one fixture has three incandescent bulbs, and one burns out, and if that fixture would need to be retrofitted in order to be able to take an LED, can you retrofit only one portion of the fixture? Likely not, so now, in addition to the cost of retrofitting, we will also be tossing out two perfectly good incandescent bulbs in order to switch to LEDs.

Finally, are there any other drawbacks associated with switching from the old bulbs to the new that might add to the costs or reduce the efficacy of the new bulbs? For instance, perhaps the new lights, which burn more brightly, also emit a larger amount of heat, which might cause the building to have to increase the usage of air conditioning, thereby increasing electricity costs (albeit from a different source). Possible unintended consequences need to be addressed before implementing such a plan, or the council might find itself with a surprise on its next electric bill.

The plan presented by the council includes just one piece of evidence intended to support the idea that electric costs will decrease, and even that piece of evidence is suspect (as we saw, the fact that the LEDs burn more brightly might mean that they actually use more energy!). While it may ultimately be the case that the plan is sound and will save Town X money, we cannot conclude this from the argument as it stands now. There are simply too many unexplored variables, including total cost, not just replacement cost, and possible drawbacks, including retrofitting or other unexpected consequences, that could actually result in increased costs.

**Here is a second opinion from Manhattan Prep instructor Jennifer Dziura:**

This is definitely NOT the only argument prompt I've read that says "B is better than A, so let's switch!" In fact, Topic #10 in this book also matches this format. With any topic of this type, switching time and cost are issues, which Stacey hit on in great detail in paragraph 3.

There is also always a danger in switching from a known thing to an unknown thing, which Stacey addresses in paragraph 4.

If I had gotten this topic, I would have written a pretty similar essay—the topic writers build a small set of flaws into each argument for you to find, so good essays on the same Argument topic tend to be pretty similar. I don't think I would have thought of the thing about fixtures having multiple bulbs, though!

It does occur to me that certain types of lighting can trigger migraines in some people, so that makes me think that there might be more health consequences related to a new type of lighting. If sitting under sun lamps is a treatment for depression, maybe really unnatural types of light could have the opposite effect? I'm not saying that that's true— just that more study is needed.

## Argument Topic #3

Company X has just switched to a 4-day workweek, mandating that employees work 10 hours per day from Monday to Thursday instead of 8 hours per day from Monday to Friday. Although the policy is new, Company X claims that the policy will help to increase profits by shutting down offices on Fridays and to boost employee morale by reducing commuting time to and from work each week.

Write a response in which you examine the stated and/or unstated assumptions of the argument. Be sure to explain how the argument depends on these assumptions and what the implications are for the argument if the assumptions prove unwarranted.

**Here's a take on this topic—followed by an actual essay—from Manhattan Prep instructor Stacey Koprince:**

The instructions specifically ask me to address assumptions made in the argument, so I first typed "P1: assumptions" and I also made a mental note to concentrate on that while I read the argument. Once I found the conclusion ("Company X claims that…"), I put it in my Paragraph 1 notes, and then I started brainstorming what assumptions would lead to that conclusion.

The best way to brainstorm assumptions is to figure out what premise leads to a particular claim. In this case, the argument says that "shutting down offices" will lead to an "increase [in] profits." Hmm, well, I know that profits are calculated by subtracting costs from revenues. This premise says the costs are going to go down, so the author must be assuming that revenues are going to stay the same. Now, I just need to brainstorm a couple of possibilities for why revenues might not stay the same if the company is closed down every Friday.

Next, the argument says that "reducing commuting time" will "boost employee morale." Here, I immediately thought, "What if someone's commute time is 10 minutes? He or she really isn't going to care much about commute time." That led me to the basic assumption here: that commute time is a significant source of concern for the vast majority of employees—and that told me what to think about next! It's possible that working an 8-hour day is just fine but 10 hours crosses a line in some way. If someone needs to pick a child up from daycare, or get a child onto the school bus in the morning, that person is not going to be thrilled with extended work hours. I have a Tae Kwon Do class after work one night a week; they're not going to change the time or day of the class just to accommodate my new work schedule!

See what I did at the end there? I put myself into the argument. What if my company were proposing this? Because the instructions specifically ask us to talk about what would happen "if the assumptions prove unwarranted," I put my critical thinking cap on. Why would this be annoying or problematic for me? (If you think it'd be great for you, then imagine a friend who would have legitimate problems with the proposal.)

**MANHATTAN**
PREP

Here are my notes for the argument (note: I type my notes in and then I write paragraph by paragraph, erasing each line of notes as I go):

> p1 Assumptions. Claim: increase profits, boost morale.
>
> p2 Assumes commute time = major pain point. Maybe 10h per day = bad for morale (kids, after-work activities?)
>
> p3 Assumes can make same revenues in 4 days as 5.
>
> p4 Assumes they can just shut down on Fri. Customers? Deliveries? Etc.
>
> p5 Conclusion

## Essay:

Company X claims that switching to a 4-day workweek will help the company to increase both profits and employee morale. While it is possible that the plan will work as stated, the company's argument depends upon several assumptions that may or may not be valid. It is possible that a 4-day workweek will have no effect on profits; however, under certain circumstances, a 4-day workweek could actually decrease profits. Further, while some employees will no doubt be thrilled to have a 3-day weekend every week, others may not appreciate a 10-hour work day.

The company assumes that commute time is a significant "point of pain" for most of its employees, and that those employees would be happy to work 10 hours rather than 8 in order to avoid one day of commute time. The company fails to address, however, how a 10-hour workday might alter the schedules and lives of the employees outside of work. Let's assume that employees work a standard 8am to 5pm schedule. Now, employees will have to start earlier or work later (or both). Those with partners and/or children may find that this new schedule disrupts the family dinner or the before-school morning routine. Those who participate in regularly scheduled activities—an exercise routine, a sports match, a book club—may find their personal and social activities curtailed. If so, the new plan is not likely to improve employee morale.

The company believes that profits will increase because the company will reduce expenses associated with keeping the office open on Fridays. The company assumes, then, that it will make the same amount of revenue in 4 days that it typically makes in 5. Perhaps the nature of the company's business allows this but it would be wise to validate this assumption before proceeding. For instance, the business model might require salespeople to call on customers. What hours do those customers work? If it is very difficult to call on customers before 8am or after 5pm, then extending the hours for salespeople while cutting off one workday a week could actually result in decreased revenues. Alternatively, employees may be more mentally fatigued by the end of a 10-hour day and lose productivity; it's entirely possible that four 10-hour days will produce less work than five 8-hour days, though both add up to 40 hours.

This brings us to our final assumption: the company appears to believe that there are no negative consequences relative to shutting down completely on Fridays. Does the company ever field customer inquiries or have to provide support for its products and services? If so, customers will be unhappy if they cannot reach the company on Fridays. Does the company receive deliveries of any kind or have to interact with vendors or suppliers in any way? In such a case, Friday closures could impact the company's efficiency, which could in turn impact revenues, expenses, or morale.

Company X has developed an interesting idea that may be worth further exploration, but committing to such a plan immediately would be rash. There are a number of variables that need to be examined before concluding that the plan is likely to achieve the stated goals without resulting in (possibly quite negative) unintended consequences. It would be prudent for the company to determine, via direct dialogue with workers, what measures in general are likely to improve employee morale. Further, the company must carefully examine the possible financial consequences associated with spreading 40 hours of work over 4 days rather than 5 and with closing its offices entirely on a day when businesses are typically expected to be open.

**Here is a second opinion from Manhattan Prep instructor Tommy Wallach:**

Great essay from Stacey here. You can see from her explanation of how she went about writing it that Stacey cares a lot about organization. The three major assumptions are listed in the introduction, and then you hit them one at a time in three nice long paragraphs. This is *always* the goal, as long as you can come up with enough material while you're outlining.

Notice how Stacey uses the real world without resorting to specific examples; this is a hallmark of a good Argument Essay. In the second paragraph, she brings up "an exercise routine, a sports match, a book club." These are simple, solid, real-world examples. There's no need to talk about specific companies, and you should try to avoid it, or you risk writing more about the issue than the argument itself. You should be able to hypothesize plenty of realistic situations ("employees may be more mentally fatigued by the end of a 10-hour day," "the business model might require salespeople to call on customers," etc.) without resorting to *actual* situations from history/current events. (Specific examples are great in the Issue Essay, but not so much in the Argument Essay.)

Stacey hits a million great points here, but you'd be surprised how much stuff is hidden inside each prompt. For example, Stacey did not mention the possibility that Friday is the most lucrative day of the week, and so losing it would be worse than losing another day. She also never discusses the fact that when people are forced onto a different schedule than most of their friends and family, that free time might not be worth as much. These aren't mistakes, by the way, as Stacey found *plenty* of great stuff to talk about here. It's just a reminder that essay prompts always provide more than enough material for you to write a solid three-paragraph essay.

## Argument Topic #4

> Five years ago, the local university built two new dormitories through different contractors: Aleph Construction and Gimmel Builders. The buildings were nearly identical, though it cost Gimmel Builders approximately 20% more to construct its dormitory. Aleph's dormitory, however, has required approximately 10% more in maintenance costs per year over the past five years. Therefore, to construct another new dormitory with the lowest overall cost, the local university should hire Aleph Construction.
>
> Write a response in which you examine the stated and/or unstated assumptions in the expert's claim. Be sure to explain how the argument depends on these assumptions and what the implications are for the argument if the assumptions prove unwarranted.

**Here's a take on this topic—followed by an actual essay—from Manhattan Prep instructor Chris Berman:**

No matter how the stimulus is phrased, a successful essay must correctly identify the conclusion and evidence topics. Usually, I note any central assumptions. Here, the stimulus expressly asks that I do so. Also, the specific question asks that the response discuss the implications if the assumptions are flawed—so, I must essentially note how to weaken the argument. The structure here is classic of the GRE. The premises involve percentages. Almost always with such a structure, there are flawed assumptions concerning the relationship between the percentages and actual numbers. This argument contains some other assumptions to question—for example, the supposed lifespan of the structures and the meaning of "nearly identical," to name two. Here are the notes for my response:

1. Identify the structural features of the argument.
2. Identify the questionable assumptions
3. Note how those assumptions, if unwarranted, would weaken the conclusion

## Essay:

The argument concludes that Aleph is the more cost efficient contractor because its building cost was a substantial percent less than the competition's, even though its maintenance costs were higher than Gimmel's, albeit by a smaller percentage. Besides the assumption that the facts are accurate, this argument hinges on several other assumptions of dubious currency. Most strikingly, the argument assumes that a lower percentage automatically indicates a lower numerical cost. This is mathematically untenable. The author merely assumes that the maintenance base price is low enough that a smaller percentage indicates a smaller cost. If this is incorrect, the conclusion becomes erroneous. Furthermore, the argument apparently assumes that the lifespan of these buildings is not long enough for the additional maintenance costs to outweigh the construction savings. A miscalculation here would also completely undermine the conclusion.

While the aforementioned assumptions are certainly enough to question the validity of the conclusion, this argument contains several other quite possibly unwarranted assumptions. First, the author assumes that the contractors' prices have not changed in the interim. Additionally, the argument states that the buildings are "nearly identical," but the author only assumes that those implied small differences do not account for the difference in price. Furthermore, the argument takes for granted that the costs of all other features of the buildings—the land, zoning costs, transportation, etc.—were identical. Another unsupported assumption is that the maintenance costs will not change. Similarly, the author blithely relates the higher maintenance costs to the contractor without providing evidence that the costs do not result from unrelated factors. Finally, the argument supposes that there is no other contractor that would prove the least costly of all.

This litany of unsupported assumptions seriously jeopardizes the certainty of the conclusion. If any one of the suppositions contained in the argument proved false, the conclusion would be factually wrong, as Aleph would then not be the most cost efficient option.

**Here is a second opinion from Manhattan Prep instructor Jennifer Dziura:**

I like that we've included in this book a shorter essay that still covers all the bases! Our instructors can tend to be a bit long-winded.

While my own Argument Essays tend to follow a set structure (short intro, three body paragraphs, short conclusion), and I tend to shoehorn whatever I have to say into that structure (if I have eight problems with the argument, I will logically group them into about three body paragraphs), Chris here sticks *exactly* to the instructions, which ask about assumptions. So he gives us a "litany" of them, and ends with a strong conclusion: "If any one of the suppositions contained in the argument proved false, the conclusion would be factually wrong."

I think that the structure Chris used here, in which he introduces many of his arguments in the introduction, might be a bit risky. In less adept hands, this could look unplanned or disorganized, although Chris makes it work nicely.

When in doubt in your own writing, I'd stick to "one main point per paragraph."

## Argument Topic #5

Airline industry representatives have recently argued that flying is safer than driving, citing two separate studies. First, U.S. statistics show that each year there are approximately 40,000 deaths in automobile accidents versus only approximately 200 in flight accidents. Second, studies indicate that pilots are four times less likely than average to have accidents on the road.

Write a response in which you discuss what questions would need to be answered in order to determine whether the argument is reasonable. Be sure to explain what effects the answers to these questions would have on the validity of the argument.

**Here's a take on this topic—followed by an actual essay—from Manhattan Prep instructor Daniel Yudkin:**

Crucial to writing a strong Argument essay is to refer consistently to the key words mentioned in the given prompt. The prompt in this case asks me to discuss which "questions would need to be answered" to make the argument more "reasonable," and what effect their answers would have on the argument's "validity." Keeping these key points in mind, I can turn to specifics.

What is wrong with this argument? At first blush, it may seem convincing to learn that so few people die in flight compared to in automobile accidents. This is indeed a strong start to an argument, but it is missing a key ingredient, a "question" that needs to be "answered" in order for this statistic to make any sense. I need to know more than objective quantities; I need to know *proportions*. To know that only 200 people die in planes isn't enough—I need to know what *fraction* this is of the entire amount. Suppose only 200 people took planes every year, and every single one of them died. Flying doesn't sound quite as safe anymore, does it? Therefore, an important question to be answered involves the total number of people who drive and fly every year.

Turning to the second supporting sentence, I learn that pilots are safer-than-average drivers. Of course, what this doesn't tell me is anything about how safe they are in the air. Therefore, in order for this sentence to add to the argument's validity, I would need to know the extent to which being a safe driver makes you a safe flier. Now, even with

this information, I still wouldn't know what impact this would have for the average airplane passenger—but at least it would be a start. My essay itself will explore this topic further.

One final question that may not be worth mentioning in the essay but is important to keep in mind is where the statistics came from—in other words, were the studies cited from reliable, reputable sources? Or were they conducted by organizations that had a vested interest in proving a particular point? When all else fails—when the argument seems sound and you're having trouble pinpointing its flaws—this is always a good idea to fall back on.

I can construct my essay now using my first two issues as the skeleton, expanding and using examples to illustrate these points, and taking care to refer repeatedly to the specific issues raised in the prompt. These are the questions from my notes:

> **Questions:**
> What is the relative proportion of deaths per year between driving and flying?
> To what extent does being a good driver make a good pilot?

## Essay:

The purpose of the airline industry's argument, elucidated in the passage above, is to convince the reader that flying is safer than driving. The industry representatives cite two pieces of evidence to support their conclusion—first, that fewer people die per year in flight; second, that airline pilots get into fewer driving accidents. To show that these arguments are reasonable, several questions need to be answered. The first question has to do with the proportion of deaths represented by the figures of annual deaths; the second has to do with the degree to which being a safe driver translates into being a safe pilot.

Suppose the CEO of a car company tried to convince shareholders that the company was succeeding in a marketing campaign to sell a certain kind of car by saying that over 10,000 cars had sold since the campaign began. The obvious question on the shareholders' minds should be the fraction of the total number of cars sold that this figure represents. If 10,000 cars represents less than 1% of the entire market on cars for this period, presumably they would not be very pleased with the campaign. Similarly, knowing that only 200 people, versus 40,000 people, died in flight versus on the road is not informative until we know the proportion of the total number of fliers and drivers that these numbers represent. If far fewer people fly than drive, 200 could represent a large fraction of all fliers. And if the proportion of flight-deaths is higher than the proportion of car-deaths, then regardless of the total number, it would be fair to say that flying is not safer than driving. The question that needs to be answered, in other words, is how many people fly and drive each year. This would then allow us to calculate the portion of the total that these figures represent.

Turning to the second piece of evidence used to support the argument that flying is safer than driving, we learn that airline pilots are safer-than-average drivers, having four times fewer accidents than the norm. In order for this fact to be convincing, several questions would need to be answered. First of all, we would need to know whether being a safe driver translates into being a safe pilot. But more than this, we would need to know what being a safe pilot *means*. Keep in mind that we are solely evaluating the argument that flying is safe *relative to driving*. So knowing that pilots are "safe fliers" is nonsensical unless we can evaluate that claim in the context of driving. Therefore, a question that needs to be answered to make this argument valid is what having a "safe pilot" means for airline passengers. An example of an answer to this question that would make the argument more valid would be that for any given hour of flight, pilots are vastly less likely to crash than for a given hour of driving. This is quite clearly a long distance away from the statement as initially phrased—evidence that the argument as-is is in need of serious revision.

In sum, we see in this passage the beginnings of a coherent argument, but more information is needed in order to fully evaluate the strength of the claims. Namely, we would need to know what fractions 200 and 40,000 represent of the entire population of fliers and drivers, respectively, and also what implications being a safe driver has for being a safe airline pilot.

**Here is a second opinion from Manhattan Prep instructor Jennifer Dziura:**

Some Argument prompts present you with frankly *ridiculous* arguments. Flying is safer because pilots are safer *drivers*? On what planet does that make any sense?! Don't toss aside your initial feeling of "What the heck?!" A ridiculous premise is like a gift from the GRE—you can easily write a whole paragraph (as Daniel did) about how pilots being safe drivers is not the same as flying being safer. Daniel adeptly points out that *even if* being a safe driver were highly correlated with being a safe pilot, it's not clear that having a safe pilot makes air travel all that safe (what if there's a tropical storm, or the plane's wings fall off?).

Note also that Daniel adopts a very natural structure here—the prompt gave two reasons why flying is supposedly safer. Daniel wrote an intro, a large body paragraph about each of those two reasons, and a short conclusion.

Finally, always check the instructions that come with your topic. The instructions here ask you to "discuss what questions would need to be answered in order to determine whether the argument is reasonable." Accordingly, Daniel's tone is more like "Here is exactly what information we would need," rather than "This argument is stupid." The graders like you to sound balanced, thoughtful, and reasonable.

## Argument Topic #6

> In a laboratory study of two different industrial cleansers, CleanAll was found to remove 40% more dirt and kill 30% more bacteria than the next best cleanser. Furthermore, a study showed that employees working at buildings cleaned with CleanAll used far fewer sick days than employees working in buildings cleaned with other cleansers. Therefore, to prevent employee illness, all companies should use CleanAll as their industrial cleanser.
>
> Write a response in which you examine the stated and/or unstated assumptions of the argument. Be sure to explain how the argument depends on these assumptions and what the implications are for the argument if the assumptions prove unwarranted.

**Here's a take on this topic—followed by an actual essay—from Manhattan Prep instructor Daniel Yudkin:**

Typically, when you are asked to examine the assumptions that drive an argument, you are presented with certain pieces of evidence that do not totally add up to the final conclusion. The job, then, is to point out which pieces of evidence are missing that would be necessary to generate the conclusion. This argument, states that all companies should adopt CleanAll. The reasons for this are that it's more effective than the "next best cleanser" and that when it's adopted employees seem to take fewer sick days.

The phrase "next best cleanser" should be a dead giveaway of a great discussion target. Since no objective standards are cited, I don't know if this cleanser is the second worst, or what. Next, the fact that employees take fewer "sick days" is insufficient evidence of the efficacy of the cleanser; there could be a variety of other causes for this. Finally, there may be other considerations that companies have in which cleanser they use, so even if the above two assumptions were satisfied, it wouldn't necessarily warrant the conclusion.

Here is my outline:

**Assumptions**
- "Next best cleanser" is something important.
- "Sick days" are a significant indicator of cleanliness.
- Effectiveness warrants adoption.

I will systematically describe these assumptions in my essay, taking care to indicate, as the prompt requests, the implications for the argument if the assumptions prove unwarranted.

## Essay:

In this argument, the author suggests that all companies should adopt CleanAll as their industrial cleanser. This is based on several facts that the author cites. The argument depends, however, on certain additional assumptions which are not explicitly stated and which, should they prove unfounded, may critically weaken the final conclusion.

For example, the author references the fact that CleanAll performed better than the next best cleanser in a laboratory study of two industrial cleansers. Before this piece of evidence can be used to support the argument that CleanAll should be adopted by all companies, several things need to be established. First of all, it is important to know the origin of this study. Is the organization that performed this study reliable? The argument assumes that it is, but if it is not this would greatly weaken its thrust. Additionally, and importantly, we are never told what this "next best cleanser" is. Suppose that CleanAll was the second-worst industrial cleanser. If it were compared with the worst cleanser, it may very well boast the same facts that it removes more dirt and bacteria. In order for this claim to have weight, then, it is crucial to know the scope of the comparison. As is, the assumption that this comparison cleanser is high-quality is unsupported.

Another assumption on which the argument depends is the notion that sick days are a valid measure of the effectiveness of an industrial cleaner. The study demonstrates that the employees of companies using CleanAll take far fewer sick days. But we must not jump immediately to the conclusion that this differences was *caused* by the effectiveness of CleanAll. Were the two companies randomly selected? Were other possible variables controlled for? And finally, does fewer sick days mean a better cleaner? As is, the argument assumes that each of these is the case—for if any of these *weren't* the case, it would be unwarranted to jump to the final conclusion that *all* companies should adopt the cleaner.

The final assumption the argument makes is that a sweeping claim can be made from limited evidence. Suppose that all the assumptions stated above were indeed correct—that CleanAll performed better than leading cleansers, not just low-quality ones, and that its use in a company does indeed cause employees to take fewer sick days. Even if these were all the case, it wouldn't necessarily indicate that all companies should adopt the product. Perhaps there are other considerations that influence companies' choices. Price is one example. Perhaps CleanAll is much more expensive than competitors. Even such seemingly inane factors as scent could influence companies' choice as to whether they should use CleanAll. In short, the argument assumes that sick days and dirt removal account for the entirety of the factors influencing companies' decision in which cleanser to adopt; if these assumptions prove unwarranted the argument will have far fewer grounds to stand on in its conclusions.

In sum, while the evidence cited in this argument does provide initial reasons to believe that CleanAll is a superior cleanser, the argument's conclusion rests on other assumptions—namely, that the cleaning studies it cites are valid and reliable, that the use of "sick days" is an appropriate measure of cleanser effectiveness, and that companies care about only these two things. Without concrete evidence that these assumptions can be satisfied, we must remain skeptical.

**Here is a second opinion from Manhattan Prep instructor Jennifer Dziura:**

This well-written, well-argued, and well-organized essay really hits all the marks!

Personally, it kind of occurred to me that killing *all* the bacteria isn't necessarily a plus for a cleaning product. Apparently (according to what I read in the news, anyway) excessive use of antibacterial products is causing resistant superbugs to evolve! These bugs could kill us all! And couldn't harsh cleaning products also aggravate people's allergies, chemical sensitivities, etc.? (Some offices actually ban perfume for this reason.)

Anyway, that's just my personal brainstorming—Daniel's essay certainly has more than enough to go on. I loved the point that performing better than the "next best" cleanser could just mean your product is second-worst. Daniel also astutely points out that cleaning power isn't the only determinant of which product is best for a particular buyer. After all, it's an office building, not an operating room.

## Argument Topic #7

Downtown Zurzi is becoming increasingly congested with traffic, increasing commuting time for those who work downtown or near downtown. The nearby city of Loft was faced with the same problem several years ago and implemented a small weekly tax for driving one's car downtown. Downtown traffic almost immediately subsided in Loft and the local government also raised much-needed money for fixing roads elsewhere. Obviously, this plan should be implemented in Zurzi in order to solve the brewing traffic congestion problem.

Write a response in which you discuss what specific evidence is needed to evaluate the argument and explain how the evidence would weaken or strengthen the argument.

**Here's a take on this topic—followed by an actual essay—from Manhattan Prep instructor Daniel Yudkin:**

When I read an Argument topic that makes a comparison, the first thing I think about is the degree to which that comparison is warranted. Sure enough, with this argument topic, I will be spending much of my time discussing the ways in which Zurzi and Loft may differ in their respective traffic situations. Because many assumptions are built into the notion that what works well for Loft will work well for Zurzi, this is a rich issue for discussion.

A second common assumption made in Argument topics is that something is a *good thing*. In this case, the argument assumes that it is a good thing that "traffic almost immediately subsided in Loft" and the town "raised much-needed money for fixing roads elsewhere." Of course, there may be downsides to these incidents, which I'll have to address in the essay.

The prompt asks me to discuss the "specific evidence" needed to decide whether the argument is good or bad, and how that evidence might strengthen or weaken the argument. With the above two thoughts in mind, I can now make a clear sketch of which issues my essay is going to address:

### Comparison (Loft & Zurzi)
- Is the driving population the same?
- Is the downtown traffic situation the same?

### Good Thing?
- Did the lack of traffic deprive local business owners of customers?
- Could those who paid the tax afford to pay it?
- Did the traffic simply move elsewhere, congesting other areas?

I now have five decent nuggets from which to craft an Argument Essay. I can start with a general introduction and then move on to discuss the specific examples in the subsequent paragraphs, making sure to point out how each example is directly relevant to the prompt. Then I will round it off with a conclusion that summarizes the points.

## Essay:

We learn in the above argument that a town, Zurzi, is confronted with a traffic problem, and we learn how another town, Loft, dealt with this problem. We are asked to subscribe to the notion that since Loft's efforts to curtail traffic were effective, Zurzi should enact similar measures. In order to better evaluate this argument, additional evidence is needed, falling generally into the categories of whether Loft's efforts were indeed effective, and, even if this is the case, whether there is reason to believe that Zurzi will enjoy similar success were it to follow suit.

Were Loft's efforts effective? To answer this question we would need to know more about the side effects of its actions. There are several possible negative side effects that could have occurred as a result of Loft's implementing a tax on cars that enter the downtown area. For example, if traffic is suddenly avoiding that area because of the tax, where is it going? Are people simply driving less, or have they merely moved to another part of town? Evidence showing that traffic is simply bypassing that area and congesting another part of town would weaken the argument. Additionally, we may want to know *who* this tax is most affecting. In many cities, people who live on the outskirts of town are less able to afford the more expensive real estate in the city center. They then drive to work downtown. If this is the case in Loft, then the tax may be putting financial strain on those who cannot afford it, but have no other choice. If we were to find evidence that this was the case, this would weaken the argument that Zurzi should enact a similar plan. Finally, another important side effect of the tax may be the impact on local business owners. If suddenly traffic downtown is drastically curtailed, local business owners may find themselves with a precipitous decline in business. Evidence to this effect would serve to undermine the original statement.

We turn next to the second big assumption of the prompt, which is that Zurzi should do as Loft does. Suppose we find evidence that Loft's measures were indeed successful—that traffic patterns aren't harmfully disrupted, that the tax isn't too great a financial burden, and that business owners are enjoying, say, an increasing influx of pedestrian clientele. Does this imply that Zurzi should necessarily do in kind? Not until we have evidence that Zurzi's situation is comparable to Loft's. For example, we would need to know whether Zurzi's driving population is the same, both geographically and financially, as Loft's. Just because Loft's drivers can afford to pay that tax doesn't mean that Zurzi's can—we need more information to confirm that this the case. Additionally, as with Loft, we would need evidence indicating that businesses are subject to similar conditions. Evidence to this effect—namely, evidence indicating that Zurzi faces conditions similar to Loft—would strengthen, and indeed are necessary to the logical thrust of, the argument.

In summary, we see two main pillars of evidence that would need to be established in order to better evaluate the argument. First, we'd need evidence that Loft's efforts were successful. Second, we'd need evidence that Zurzi is like Loft. With such confirming evidence, the argument begins to cohere. Without it, the argument is bereft of critical foundations.

**Here is a second opinion from Manhattan Prep instructor Jennifer Dziura:**

Great essay, Daniel! Any time you get a GRE essay topic that makes an analogy, you can pretty much write a whole essay (if you have to) about what a bad analogy it is. For Argument Essay purposes, all analogies are terrible analogies!

Daniel's third paragraph covers in detail all the things we'd need to know about Loft and Zurzi to make sure that what worked in Loft would be likely to work in Zurzi. Daniel's substantial second paragraph about the possible side effects of the plan makes for a very thorough essay. I especially liked the closing about the argument's being "bereft of critical foundations."

## Argument Topic #8

In last year's mayoral election in Town T, candidate Miller led candidate Keating by a substantial margin in the polls leading up to the election. At the last minute, Keating launched a widely viewed series of television advertisements that focused on preserving the natural environment of Town T, a topic neglected by Miller. Subsequently, Keating won the election by a narrow margin. This year, if candidate Miller hopes to win the upcoming mayoral election, he must increase his coverage of the topic of preserving the natural environment of Town T.

Write a response in which you examine the stated and/or unstated assumptions of the argument. Be sure to explain how the argument depends on these assumptions and what the implications are for the argument if the assumptions prove unwarranted.

**Here's a take on this topic—followed by an actual essay—from Manhattan Prep instructor Tommy Wallach:**

This is a nice, long argument topic. I generally find that the more words there are in the prompt, the more problems there are in the argument, which is good news if you want to pull together three solid body paragraphs. Remember that your thesis on any Argument Essay is more or less the same: "While the author comes to a plausible conclusion, the argument made to reach that conclusion is flawed."

My goal is to find three problems with this argument. Remember that they have been purposely placed in the prompt, so all I have to do is locate them. The first one I can see is that an error with time is being made here. Just because an issue is problematic one year doesn't mean it will be problematic another year. The natural environment issue may already have been resolved.

The next problem has to do with the comparison between the two elections. In the previous election, Miller went up against Keating and lost. But the prompt doesn't say that Miller is going up against Keating again. Miller's new opponent may have no plans to focus on that issue, or his opponent may have already staked out that territory early in the campaign.

The final problem I see is that a causal relationship has been implied between the TV ads and Miller's loss, yet this could just be a correlation. Miller could have lost for some other reason. I don't love this particular flaw, so I'm going to leave it for last. You should always do your best to find three flaws, but if one of them feels weak, leave it for last. Your reader will often begin to skim at the end if they think you're going strong.

Here's my outline:

> Thesis: Author comes to decent conclusion, argument no good.
> I. Issues are not the same every election.
> II. Candidates are not the same/polling situation not the same.
> III. No definitive evidence given that TV ads were deciding factor.

**Essay:**

The prompt above describes a mayoral election between Miller and Keating that Miller lost soon after a particular TV ad was run. From this, the author derives a conclusion about what Miller should do to win the election this year. In coming to this conclusion, the author makes a number of unfounded assumptions that undermine the validity of the argument. These assumptions are based on faulty comparisons—between candidates, topical issues, and other contextual elements—and a mistaking of correlation for causation. If the author wants to support his conclusion, he would need to provide evidence proving that these two elections are comparable, and that Miller's loss can factually be attributed to its implied cause.

The first error made by the author is in implying that just because an issue was topically relevant during one election, it will necessarily be relevant during the next election. For all we know, the natural environment could have been a major issue in the previous election because of some climatic issue, such as saving a particular waterway or passing a specific law to protect local wetlands, that has since been resolved (during Keating's mayoralty, for example, which would make logical sense given that she ran on a preserva-tionist platform). If the author wants to make this connection, he would need to provide evidence that the natural environment remains a hot-button issue that could decide the election one way or another.

The next faulty assumption in the argument also involves a comparison, namely between Miller and whoever his opponent is. The prompt seems to imply that Miller will be going up against Keating again, but there's no evidence to support this. This matters, because if Miller is running against a different candidate, then there's no reason to believe a strategy that would have served him well against Keating would still be useful. For example, he could be running against a park ranger, who will always be able to beat him on issues relevant to the natural environment, in which case increasing his coverage of those issues would be a waste of time. To fix this assumption, the author would need to tell us definitively that Miller is running against Keating again (or a very similar candidate).

Another major assumption the argument makes is in deciding that the television ads Keating ran were the sole or even primary reason that Miller lost the first election. This is a causation/correlation error, in that we have no reason to believe the two things didn't simply happen separately, rather than one causing the other. It's just as likely that Miller committed some terrible faux pas near the end of the election, and that turned out to be more of a deciding factor than the television ads. The author needs to provide evidence that the primary impetus behind so many people changing their vote between the time of the polling showing Miller in the lead and Keating's win was the television ads.

It's certainly plausible that Miller might fare better in the next election if he pays attention to a subject he is said to have neglected. However, we cannot know that for certain unless the author provides definitive evidence that the issue of environmental preservation is still in the forefront of constituents' minds, that Miller and Keating are the two candidates in the next election, and that the television ads and the issue they underscored were the primary reason Miller lost his lead in the previous election. With this information in place, the author's conclusion becomes not just plausible, but convincing.

**Here is a second opinion from Manhattan Prep instructor Jennifer Dziura:**

I was especially interested in Tommy's comment that his thesis is always pretty much, "While the author comes to a plausible conclusion, the argument made to reach that conclusion is flawed." Mine is always something like, "This argument has numerous logical flaws, rests on many unwarranted assumptions, and would be improved with the addition of more information." In other words, Tommy's approach is more middle-ground, and mine is more, "This argument is awful."

Tommy's approach works very well in this essay. We're certainly not called on to argue that Miller should *not* campaign on environmental issues—just that there are gaps in the particular reasoning presented in the argument for this conclusion.

## Argument Topic #9

> Last year PrepUp had record enrollment in its test prep courses, but yearly profits fell by nearly 30%. In contrast, TopPreparation had comparable enrollment to the year before, with profits rising by approximately 20%. This discrepancy most likely results from the fact that PrepUp teaches only live, in-person classes, which require expensive rental spaces and teaching equipment. Although TopPreparation's total enrollment remained unchanged, its online enrollment increased by 50%, and online classes have much lower overhead costs. In order to address these issues of profitability in the coming year, PrepUp will begin offering online test prep courses.
>
> Write a response in which you discuss what questions would need to be answered in order to decide whether PrepUp's plan for the coming year and the argument on which it is based are reasonable. Be sure to explain how the answers to these questions would help to evaluate the plan.

**Here's a take on this topic—followed by an actual essay—from Manhattan Prep instructor Jesse Cotari:**

The topic of this Argument Essay provides both advantages and risks for me. On the upside, I've recently been doing loads of business case studies that focus on profits, revenues, and competitive advantage. This means that I have a lot of familiarity with the types of analytical frameworks that go into tackling this type of situation, and hence loads of ideas! But this presents a number of risks. A bevy of ideas can be a burden when writing a timed essay, so it's going to be essential to brainstorm quickly, group common ideas together, prioritize the best, and discard the second-tier ideas. Furthermore, I felt the distinct draw to attack this problem as a business case, and not as an AWA essay. However, doing this the AWA way means identifying and focusing on the logical flaws in the argument, not just examining the issues involved in making a proper business decision. The last risk was jargon. Dropping a term like "allocated fixed cost" into the argument without definition is going to irritate a grader (with good reason). On the other hand, defining terms can eat up vital time and make an essay's logic drag. To attack this essay effectively therefore means keeping the *ideas* behind the jargon in mind while staying clear of any particularly economic or financial terms.

My first bit of processing is to outline the argument, to get a sense for the flow and identify common logical errors:

PrepUp had "record enrollment" whereas TopPrep had unchanged numbers.

PU:
High enrollment, dropping profits
Live in-person classes
Expensive rental spaces
expensive teaching equipment

TP:
same enrollment → 20% rise in profits
50% rise in online classes

The key flaws I see here are a lack of quantification (we're given percents, not numbers), vague terms ("record enrollment"?), "correlation isn't causation," and issues of "skill and will." I also have an idea that relates the sizes of the companies, the initial investment required for an online teaching system, and the comparative per-student cost of that initial investment. However, despite the fact that it's probably a solid idea, I dump it because I realize that the verbiage and chains of logic necessary to make the point would slow me down and potentially reduce the overall flow of the essay. I decide to lump lack of quantification and vague terms into one issue, and come up with the following outline:

Intro
Lack of numbers (% vs $)
Correlation is not causation: Profitability and in-person classes
Even if: Skill and will: Investment, training, → profit
Wrap up.

(I always like having an "even if" in the chain of my argument. It's usually my third body paragraph. At that point in my essay, I've pointed out a number of flaws in the logic. Then I say, *even if you fixed all of these problems, you **still** wouldn't be able to make your argument work*.)

Outline in hand (actually, typed on the screen, to be deleted at the end), the last thing I do is always to reread the prompt. Noting that it says "questions…to be answered," I make a mental note to phrase the essay in those terms, and begin writing.

With two minutes left, I go back and make a few last checks. In my fervor of ripping up the argument, I notice that I neglected to phrase "logical omissions" as "questions to be answered," so I fix that. I make my intro a little more pointed. The last thing I do is be sure to copy–paste to fix the places where I abbreviated TopPreparation as "TP."

## Essay:

At first glance, the recommendation appears obvious: If TopPreparation's business model is yielding large increases in profit, PrepUp should emulate this business model to improve profitability. However, the logic of the argument as it stands is utterly incomplete, and there are major questions that need to be answered before deciding whether undertaking a plan of offering online courses makes sense for PrepUp.

The first area of deficit in the argument lies in the numbers, or rather, in their absence. All of the profits are stated in percent increases or decreases, with no initial values to start from. If PrepUp had been insanely profitable in previous years, whereas TopPreparation barely made ends meet, emulating Top-Preparation's business model would be unwise. It would be essential to determine the starting profitability of both businesses to make any comparison.

A second major question stems from the assumed connection between increased enrollment and decreased profits at PrepUp. To make this connection, we would need to answer the question of whether per-student costs have actually increased. Without knowing the underlying causes, increased enrollment could positively or negatively affect profits, or could have absolutely no relationship to their present decline. If new classes have been held in new, more expensive classrooms, increasing enrollment could have indeed led to increased costs and the decline of profits. On the other hand, if increased enrollment has led to increases in average class sizes, the per-student cost would have actually gone down, while per-student income would have remained the same, leading to an increase in per-student profitability. It is equally possible that profits have declined because costs unrelated to instruction have increased. Perhaps the CEO decided to increase her pay by a large percentage. Perhaps PrepUp invested in new IT infrastructure. Without knowing the breakdown of the current income and expenses, it is impossible to impute the profitability decline solely to the expense of in-person teaching.

Even if PrepUp and TopPreparation were initially producing comparable profits, and increasing enrollment in classes has pushed up per-student costs, there is still a major question to be answered: How much is the new system going to cost compared to how much it will save? Development, implementation and personnel training are required for the roll-out of any new system, and these things are not free; there will likely be a large initial investment required to implement such a system. While "much lower overhead" sounds like an attractive goal, a savings of $10,000 per year for a system that costs $100,000 to implement would imply a minimum 10-year timeline for recovery of the initial investment. Without knowing the initial investment required to implement a new online system, it is impossible to assess the overall contribution to cost savings.

All told, while the online teaching system does appear attractive, exact quantitative data is lacking in the argument. Without a basis to compare the two companies, and without understanding the current drivers of profitability and the costs of the new system, it is impossible to properly evaluate the argument in favor of online classes.

**Here is a second opinion from Manhattan Prep instructor Jennifer Dziura:**

I enjoyed Jesse's strategy of always having an "even if" in the chain of the argument—in Jesse's case, in the third body paragraph.

A sophisticated Argument Essay doesn't just say, "Everything in the prompt is wrong." Rather, it addresses *relationships* among the components of the argument. Jesse writes two full paragraphs about problems in comparing Top-Preparation and PrepUp, and then says that *even if* the comparisons are valid and the assumptions true, the cost of switching might *still* eliminate any advantage to the plan to switch.

Note that Jesse doesn't come out against PrepUp's plan—he concludes that "the online teaching system does appear attractive," but that much more quantitative data is needed. Because Jesse has gone into great detail about *exactly* what data we would need, this conclusion is persuasive.

## Argument Topic #10

Cot-Ten, a cotton production company, has recently faced profitability issues based on the use of Chemical X in its manufacturing process. The main by-product produced when using Chemical X is covered under stringent environmental regulations, making it very difficult and expensive to dispose of. A similar processing product, Chemical Y, has recently been discovered, and can be used by Cot-Ten at a minimal cost of switching. The CEO of Cot-Ten has declared that the company will increase profits by switching to Chemical Y by the end of the month.

Write a response in which you discuss what specific evidence is needed to evaluate the argument and explain how the evidence would weaken or strengthen the argument.

**Here's a take on this topic—followed by an actual essay—from Manhattan Prep instructor Jennifer Dziura:**

Let's run through this argument: Disposing of Chemical X (well, the by-product of Chemical X) is expensive and is hurting profits.

But Chemical Y has just been discovered! Cot-Ten can use Chemical Y instead. (Hmmn, sketchy. Brand-new chemicals kind of freak me out. Maybe our clothes will start giving us cancer!)

We are then told that the cost of switching will be minimal. Um, okay, but that's hardly the point! Tell me something—anything!—about this mysterious Chemical Y!

OMG, so many unanswered questions! Such as:

- Are there also "stringent environmental regulations" about Chemical Y? (Or is it likely that there *will* be, since Chemical Y is new?) Or regulations on its by-products?
- Does Chemical Y *have* by-products? If so, are there *more* by-products? For instance, maybe it costs less per pound to dispose of Chemical Y's byproducts, but maybe Chemical Y makes *way more overall by-products,* so that the overall cost is higher.
- Does it cost more to *buy* Chemical Y in the first place???

- Is the cotton made with Chemical Y just as good? Might REVENUES go down even as expenses are slashed? THERE ARE TWO SIDES TO PROFIT: revenue and expenses, and revenue is kind of the more important one!
- Are there other reasons profits might not increase? Are consumers opposed to this relatively unknown new chemical? (I am! And this isn't even real!)

Okay, this is plenty for me to get started writing, especially since the instructions ask me to talk about "what specific evidence is needed." Easy! I know I need to shoehorn these points into three body paragraphs, but since my bullet points above have a lot of overlap…I'm just going to start writing and see how it goes. After I write the body paragraphs, I'll go back and revise my introduction to make sure my thesis reflects what I actually talked about.

Also—very important—I want to make sure that I stay ON-TOPIC. Keep in mind that writing a paragraph about how Chemical Y might destroy the environment and kill all the wildlife and give everyone diseases would NOT help me score well on this essay. In fact, this point would be IRRELEVANT, because the argument's conclusion is that Cot-Ten will be able to *increase its profits* (not just "do good stuff") by switching. So, if I wanted to argue that the new chemical might have all kinds of bad effects, I need to tie those bad effects back into "profitability," such as by pointing out that poisoning people is bad for the bottom line.

## Essay:

In response to its profitability problems, cotton production company Cot-Ten intends to switch from Chemical X, which requires expensive disposal of its by-products, to Chemical Y. However, Chemical Y is a truly unknown actor in this drama. To evaluate the argument at hand, we need far more information about Chemical Y, its by-products and disposal processes, its cost, and its efficacy in producing saleable cotton. Otherwise, Cot-Ten will be moving from a profitability deficit to a total unknown that could very well prove worse.

The reason provided for Cot-Ten's switch from Chemical X is that the by-product of that chemical falls under strict environmental regulations, and is thus expensive to dispose, thus impacting Cot-Ten's profitability. Then we are told that the newly discovered Chemical Y is "similar." Similar in what ways? Presumably, the chemical serves the same function in the manufacturing process, but the argument has done nothing to assure us that Chemical Y is not, in fact, similar in terms of environmental regulations and disposal costs. What if Chemical Y is actually more expensive to dispose of? To properly evaluate Cot-Ten's plans, we need to know how much by-product, if any, Chemical Y produces, and the cost and difficulty of that by-product's disposal. In order to know that, it would be helpful to know whether Chemical Y falls under any environmental regulations or whether—since Chemical Y is new—such environmental regulations are likely to be passed in the near future. In order to calculate any cost savings, we would also need to know whether the manufacturing process would use the same amount of Chemical Y as it did of Chemical X (even if Chemical Y's by-products are cheaper to dispose of, pound-for-pound, if much more Chemical Y is needed or if Chemical Y yields far more by-product, this cost savings could be easily canceled out).

Keep in mind, however, that the argument's conclusion relates not just to cutting expenses, but to profitability overall. What if the switch to Chemical Y causes revenue to fall? We are told that Chemical Y is a "similar processing product," but will the cotton produced with this chemical be identical (or better)? Even if the product produced is technically the same, will consumers be aware of the switch? If so, would

**MANHATTAN**
PREP

they have any reason to doubt the new product's quality or otherwise be opposed to the switch? The same factors that might cause environmental regulations to be levied against Chemical Y, as they were against Chemical X, could also cause environmentally-conscious consumers to oppose the new product, thus lowering revenues.

If it turned out that Chemical Y were truly an innocuous alternative to Chemical X, that it cost less to dispose of Chemical Y's by-products, and that consumers would purchase the new product for at least the same price and frequency as the old product, then the argument would be immeasurably strengthened. However, if Chemical Y were to have the same problems—high disposal costs due to environmental regulations—or introduce other costs, or if it were to reduce revenues, then the argument's conclusion would be unjustified. While Cot-Ten executives may have scored a coup by locating a cost-saving alternative, much research must be done before these executives can be congratulated. Whether Cot-Ten's profitability will rise, and whether switching from Chemical X to Chemical Y is a wise move, remains to be seen.

**Here is a second opinion from Manhattan Prep instructor Tommy Wallach:**

This is a really great essay from GRE superstar Jen Dziura. Notice how her introduction manages to be playful and professional at once ("Chemical Y is a truly unknown actor in this drama."). Don't be afraid to make your essays entertaining; those poor readers have to score dozens and dozens of these things every day, and they'll be grateful for a little bit of fun.

Jen focuses her big second paragraph on the primary assumption made in the passage, that Chemical Y is going to improve the whole by-product disposal issue. If I were writing this essay, I might break this paragraph into two smaller ones, just to give the reader a bit of a break. I might have the first paragraph focus on the issue of Chemical Y's own by-products and disposal costs, and the second paragraph on the issue of whether manufacturing/purchasing Chemical Y might cost more. Jen hits both of these points already, so the change would merely be an organizational one. (My OCD brain always strives for exactly five paragraphs, even though there's no rule about it!)

Notice also how many ideas Jen had before she started writing. There were so many, some of them had to get left by the wayside! If you know you have plenty of good ideas, don't hurt yourself trying to stretch the essay to fit them all in. Organization is key, so keeping your paragraphs focused is better, even if you leave out an idea or two (I might have grabbed on to the "minimal cost of switching" myself, but there's so much here, there's really no need). In this essay, it's easy to see that paragraph two is about the profit side of things, where paragraph three is about the revenue side of things. Jen knows that essay readers need to be able to see exactly what each paragraph is about, preferably within the first couple sentences of that paragraph.

# Chapter 32
## of
## 5 lb. Book of GRE® Practice Problems

# Verbal Practice Sections

# In This Chapter...

# Verbal Practice Section 1: Easy Difficulty

**20 Questions**
**Time: 30 Minutes**

> For questions 1–6, select one entry for each blank from the corresponding column of
> choices. Fill in the blank in the way that best completes the text.

1. A dry-farmed tomato raised in low-nitrogen soil will often have the nutrient value of a much larger
   conventionally grown tomato, and its flavor may be similarly _____.

   | |
   |---|
   | delicious |
   | healthful |
   | scanty |
   | concentrated |
   | shrunken |

2. Most viewers of today's reality television underestimate the degree of _____ with which the
   seemingly artless narrative of each episode is assembled: oftentimes, actors interviewed on camera are
   asked to repeat their story half a dozen times before producers are satisfied.

   | |
   |---|
   | dramaturgy |
   | opportunism |
   | fallacy |
   | contrivance |
   | histrionics |

3. Many (i) _____ have commentated that football reflects an industrial perspective because the game
   time is inflexibly determined by the clock, whereas baseball stems from an agrarian one, in which, the
   passage of time is more (ii) _____ and determined by events.

   | Blank (i) | Blank (ii) |
   |---|---|
   | pundits | amorphous |
   | amateurs | pacific |
   | dilettantes | asymmetrical |

4.  Ernest Hemingway, the novelist and proponent of traditional masculine virtues that were already considered (i) _____ by his more progressive peers, eventually lost currency with the general public; although his earlier literary works remained popular, his continuing adherence to that code drove him to disdain society, which, in turn, (ii) _____ him.

| Blank (i) | Blank (ii) |
| --- | --- |
| effeminate | shunned |
| anachronistic | eulogized |
| sardonic | murdered |

5.  While a (i) _____ , the smallest amount that can exist independently, of water could be said to be a single molecule, a (ii) _____ of dust could be made up of pollen, hair, human skin cells, minerals from soil, or even burnt meteor particles. Thus, one definition of dust is "solid particles with a diameter of less than 500 micrometers"—a (iii) _____ definition that is based only on size and state of matter rather than on structure.

| Blank (i) | Blank (ii) | Blank (iii) |
| --- | --- | --- |
| plethora | trove | precise |
| parameter | covey | loose |
| quantum | mote | deleterious |

6.  From the battle's opening (i) _____ to its (ii) _____ conclusion, the forces of destruction razed a path through the city, ultimately leaving behind a (iii) _____ stillness where there once had been streets and squares bustling with life.

| Blank (i) | Blank (ii) | Blank (iii) |
| --- | --- | --- |
| finale | sanguinary | blissful |
| salvo | celebrated | routine |
| error | blithe | disquieting |

**MANHATTAN**
PREP

For each of questions 7–10, select one answer choice unless otherwise instructed.

It is no revelation that people prefer immediate rewards. What is less well known is that people are willing to renounce a significant portion of a given reward in order to expedite delivery. This phenomenon is known as "discounting," because the value of a delayed reward is discounted, or reduced, in the mind of the receiver. Discounting helps explain the

5  straightforward "time value of money" (a dollar now is worth more than a dollar later), but its manifestations can be far more dramatic.

Behavioral economists have identified extreme discounting in experiments in which subjects were offered either a dollar immediately or three dollars the next day. Individuals who consistently choose significantly smaller rewards for their immediacy are described as

10  "present-biased." Present-bias may seem innocuous, but it has serious ramifications. In another experiment, young children were given a marshmallow, then told that if they could wait a few minutes to eat it, they would receive a second one. Those unable to endure the delay suffered from more behavioral problems in adolescence and scored markedly lower on standardized tests than the children who were able to wait and thereby earn another treat. Traits such

15  as indolence and apathy may indeed be manifestations of present-bias; material success is predicated on one's ability to recognize hedonistic impulses, understand their consequences, and delay or suppress gratification.

What was once known as "exponential discounting" (because the length of the delay before a reward was given seemed to correlate directly with the size of the perceived discount)

20  has been renamed "hyperbolic discounting," because the effects of time delay do not seem strictly linear. A study showed that people offered $50 now or $100 in a year were likely to choose the former. But when people were offered either $50 in 5 years or $100 in 6 years (the same choice 5 years in the future), the vast majority chose the latter. This experiment reveals the difficulty of making effective financial decisions about one's future priorities, just as the

25  choice to procrastinate requires the unlikely supposition that one's future self will have a greater set of resources to accomplish the postponed task than one's present self.

7.  The function of the second paragraph within the passage may be most appropriately characterized as

(A)  analyzing the psychological sources of the phenomenon introduced in the first paragraph

(B)  elaborating upon and qualifying the main proposition put forth in the first paragraph

(C)  providing an alternative point of view on the positions already established by the author

(D)  illustrating one aspect of the phenomenon named in the first paragraph and offering possible social implications

(E)  drawing general conclusions about specific examples presented earlier

8.  The passage suggests which of the following about the traits of indolence and apathy?

    (A)  They are predicated on one's material success.

    (B)  They may be regarded as the effects of a tendency toward extreme discounting.

    (C)  They may be manifested in present-bias.

    (D)  They may seem innocuous, but they have serious ramifications.

    (E)  They are the cause of one's ability to identify and suppress hedonistic impulses.

9.  It can be inferred that the word *hyperbolic* in the phrase "hyperbolic discounting" signifies, in this context,

    (A)  the nonlinearity of decision making based on various delays

    (B)  the exaggeration of the effects of time delay

    (C)  the direct correlation between a delay's duration and a perceived discount's magnitude

    (D)  the exponential growth of the size of the discounting

    (E)  the lack of certainty in one's perception of longer and shorter delays

10.  According to the passage, which of the following is true of the children described in the passage who were able to wait to eat their first marshmallow?

    (A)  They scored lower on standardized tests than children unable to wait.

    (B)  They suffered more frequently from behavior problems as adolescents.

    (C)  They each received a second marshmallow as part of the experiment.

    (D)  They could be characterized as indolent or apathetic.

    (E)  They can accurately be described as present-biased.

---

**Question 11 is based on the following reading passage.**

---

The female arkbird will lay eggs only when a suitable quantity of nesting material is available, and the climate is suitably moderate. This winter is the coldest on record, but somewhat counterintuitively, the temperature change has actually increased the amount of nesting material as trees and plants die, shedding twigs and leaves. However, although nesting material is abundant, _____ .

11.  Which of the following options for the blank above is best supported by the passage?

    (A)  the female arkbird will likely migrate to avoid the cold

    (B)  arkbird mortality rates increase as the weather becomes less moderate

    (C)  female arkbirds prefer the type of nesting material produced in warmer weather

    (D)  an abundance of nesting material provides increased protection for arkbird eggs

    (E)  the female arkbird will not lay eggs this winter

For questions 12–15, select the two answer choices that, when used to complete the
sentence, fit the meaning of the sentence as a whole and produce completed sentences
that are alike in meaning.

12.  Floodwaters had already breached the library's walls, but hopeful volunteers in hip boots worked tirelessly
to _____ the damage.

☐  exacerbate
☐  ameliorate
☐  recant
☐  forfeit
☐  recount
☐  mitigate

13.  Eleanor of Aquitaine, who married Henry II of England, was dead and forgotten for hundreds of years, until
Katherine Hepburn _____ her in "The Lion in Winter," injecting her own vitality into the depiction of
that queen.

☐  mummified
☐  mocked
☐  resurrected
☐  glamorized
☐  immortalized
☐  parodied

14.  However beneficent the intentions, if the civilian death toll continues to climb, ongoing contact with the
local populace may well prove _____ to the aim of normalizing relations.

☐  honorable
☐  bedazzling
☐  unpropitious
☐  inimical
☐  captivating
☐  incongruous

15. Despite numerous attacks on the witness's character, his testimony is supported by evidence and appears to be _____ .

☐ vociferous

☐ fallacious

☐ credible

☐ antagonistic

☐ assiduous

☐ sound

---

**Question 16 is based on the following reading passage.**

---

The chemicals division at Company M spent 4% of its 2008 budget on marketing. The consumer products division spent 35% of its 2008 budget on marketing, while the machinery division spent only 2% of its 2008 budget on marketing.

16. Which of the following conclusions is best justified by the data above?

(A) The consumer products division spent more on marketing in 2008 than the chemicals and machinery divisions combined.

(B) Consumers are more swayed by marketing than are the mostly corporate buyers of chemicals and machinery.

(C) On average, all three divisions combined spent less than 35% of their 2008 budgets on marketing.

(D) The company's overall spending on marketing is between 4% and 35%.

(E) The chemicals division spent 100% more on marketing in 2008 than did the machinery division.

**MANHATTAN**
PREP

**Questions 17–19 are based on the following reading passage.**

Maps are essential décor for any social studies class, and though they are helpful tools in beginning to understand geography, maps are merely 2-D representations of a 3-D world and will always carry certain inherent inaccuracies. Because of their flatness and size restrictions, maps require manipulation, rendering them incapable of showing the actual shape of the
5   Earth and the continents, nations, and other features upon it. Though these might seem like necessary concessions, the implications of such manipulations move beyond the blackboard and can have damaging effects; forcing students to see the world in 2-D each day has the attendant effect of teaching them to understand the world in two-dimensional terms.

Furthermore, maps present borders as fixed, unchanging entities, which is a misleading
10   implication to present in a history course. Borders have been changing throughout the history of civilization, and the United States is a perfect example of a country with borders that have blurred and bled into one another for decades as states continued to form and join as recently as the 20th century.

17. The author's main idea is that

   (A)   maps are a necessary evil
   (B)   maps present borders as static
   (C)   3-D representation of the world is impossible
   (D)   outdated information makes education less effective
   (E)   graphic representation can encourage cognitive misconceptions

18. Which of the following, if true, would most undermine part of the author's evidence?

   (A)   Some students exposed to maps grasp 3-D and dynamic concepts about the world.
   (B)   Most teachers rely very little on the maps displayed in their classrooms.
   (C)   Computer-generated map displays increasingly in use in classrooms show changes in boundaries almost instantaneously.
   (D)   Maps from hundreds of years ago contain errors.
   (E)   2-D maps do not indicate topographical features effectively.

19. The author does which of the following in the passage?

   (A)   Employs circular logic.
   (B)   Cites a historical case.
   (C)   Uses physical description to support an accusation.
   (D)   Discusses a hierarchy of problems with maps.
   (E)   Rebuts a commonly held view.

---

**Question 20 is based on the following reading passage.**

---

In 1928, Sir Alexander Fleming, working at St. Mary's Hospital in London, observed that a bluish-green mold had contaminated a culture of Staphylococcus, and that the areas of the Staphylococcus bacteria nearest to the mold were being destroyed. Upon testing a pure culture of this mold, Fleming discovered that the mold killed many types of bacteria. He named the substance *penicillin* and published his results in 1929.

It was not, however, until over a decade later that a team of researchers from Oxford, aided by an American laboratory, were able to increase the growth rate of penicillin—by then recognized to be the strongest antibacterial agent known at that time—such that enough of it could be produced to treat Allied soldiers wounded on D-Day, in 1944.

---

Consider each of the answer choices separately and indicate all that apply.

---

20. Which of the following can be inferred from the passage?

☐   Fleming did not fully appreciate the therapeutic value of penicillin.

☐   At some point prior to 1944, penicillin could not be grown fast enough.

☐   Since ancient times, antibacterial agents have been used to treat wounded soldiers.

# Answers to Verbal Practice Section 1

1. **Concentrated.** "Similarly" indicates that the relatively small "dry-farmed tomato" has all the flavor of a "conventionally grown" large tomato, just as it has all the nutrients. The blank requires a word that means something like condensed. Only "concentrated" works. "Shrunken" and even "scanty" might be attractive, but neither captures the idea that the tomato has a great deal packed into a small package. And while a dry-farmed tomato might be both "delicious" and "healthful," again, neither of these create a sentence that fits with the clue offered in the first part of the sentence.

2. **Contrivance.** This blank takes its clue from the phrase "seemingly artless." As is often the case in GRE questions, the word "seemingly" should set you up to be thinking of an opposite to "artless," which means genuine, not artificial. In this case, then, you want a word that denotes something deliberately constructed or fabricated: something "contrived." The other options denote opinions that might be assigned to reality television, but "dramaturgy" (the practice of dramatic composition), "opportunism" (exploitation), "fallacy" (misconception), and "histrionics" (theatrics) are not antonyms of artless and are therefore incorrect.

3. **Pundits, amorphous.** The clue for the first blank is "commentated." Neither "amateurs" nor "dilettantes" (a synonym of amateurs) are likely to make this kind of knowledgeable comment. The correct choice for the first blank is "pundits," or experts in a particular field. The pivot word *whereas* means that the second blank opposes "inflexibly determined." "Amorphous" fits this meaning. Nothing in the sentence suggests that the passage of time is "pacific" (peaceful) or "asymmetrical."

4. **Anachronistic, shunned.** The first blank must reflect the opinion of "progressive peers" regarding that which is "traditional" ("progressive" indicates wanting to move forward—away from traditions). The correct answer, "anachronistic," refers to something that is in the wrong period or era and often connotes something old-fashioned or behind the times. The incorrect answers, "effeminate" (feminine) and "sardonic" (mocking), do not contrast with "progressive." The second blank must match "disdain" because of the expression "in turn"; "shunned" is a good match. "Murdered" is too strong for the second blank while adhering to a behavior would not "eulogize" someone.

5. **Quantum, mote, loose.** A "quantum" is "the smallest amount that can exist independently" and is a perfect fit for blank (i). "Plethora" means a large amount of something, which is the opposite of what the clue suggests, and "parameter" is a boundary. For blank (ii), a "mote" is a speck or small amount; the word is specifically associated with dust. "Trove" means a collection of valuable things and "covey" means a small group of things. In blank (iii), since the definition is "based only on size and state of matter rather than on structure," it is "loose," rather than strict or "precise." Nowhere in the sentence is it suggested that this definition is "deleterious," meaning causing harm.

6. **Salvo, sanguinary, disquieting.** A "salvo" is a simultaneous release of bombs and is often used metaphorically to mean the start of some kind of fight; this is a better fit to describe the opening battle than either "finale" or "blissful." Every clue in the sentence is negative, so you want to describe the battle's conclusion in a negative way—only "sanguinary" (involving much bloodshed) matches. The other options, "celebrated" and "blithe" (untroubled happiness), are the opposite direction. Finally, a "stillness where there once had been streets and squares bustling with life" is neither "blissful" nor "routine," but very much disturbing, or "disquieting."

7. **(D).** The first paragraph introduces the phenomenon of "discounting": the reduction in the perceived value of a delayed reward. Discounting can account for "straightforward" effects such as the time value of money, but "more dramatic" manifestations are also hinted at. Some of these dramatic manifestations of "extreme discounting" are described in the second paragraph. That paragraph introduces "present-bias" by describing two experiments (one in which $1 now is preferred to $3 tomorrow, and another in which children struggle to resist marshmallows). The consequences of the marshmallow experiment are stated and ruminated upon in a larger social context (how present-bias may prevent material success). Thus, the second paragraph elaborates upon a particular, extreme version of the phenomenon introduced in the first paragraph and draws out a few larger implications.

Regarding choice (A), the second paragraph does not explain where discounting comes from psychologically. Regarding choice (B), the first paragraph does not really introduce a "proposition" per se, which would be a claim of some sort. Rather, the first paragraph simply defines a phenomenon. Additionally, the second paragraph does not "qualify" (limit) the first paragraph in any way. As for choice (C), the author has staked out no position in the first paragraph; he or she has only described a phenomenon. The second paragraph does not take an alternative point of view, either. As for choice (E), there are no true "specific examples" introduced in the first paragraph for the second paragraph to draw conclusions from.

8. **(B).** According to the passage, "traits such as indolence and apathy may indeed be manifestations of present-bias," so the correct answer choice will say more or less the same thing. Choice (A) mixes up words from the text ("predicated," "material success"), but does not match the meaning of the passage. The passage says that material success is predicated on the "ability to recognize hedonistic impulses," not that indolence and apathy are predicated on material success. Choice (B) is correct but is in disguise. The passage describes "manifestations of present-bias," but this answer choice talks about "the effects of a tendency toward extreme discounting." However, the beginning of the second paragraph defines "present-bias" in terms of "extreme discounting." That is, present-bias is really nothing more than a tendency toward extreme discounting. This disguise makes choice (B) tricky. Regarding choice (C), be careful with language! Saying that these traits "are manifested *in* present-bias" means exactly the reverse of "are manifestations *of* present-bias." In the former, the traits are somehow hidden, but they show up *in* or *through* something on the surface called present-bias. The passage, on the other hand, describes present-bias as the trait hidden inside of indolence and apathy. Choice (D), like choice (A), mixes up words from the text. Present-bias—not indolence and apathy—is what "may seem innocuous," but has "serious ramifications." Choice (E) also grabs language from the text but uses it in a mixed-up way. The language "traits such as indolence and apathy" shows up in the same sentence as the "ability to recognize hedonistic impulses…and delay or suppress gratification," but those two phrases are not connected in an "X causes Y" way.

9. **(A).** This Inference question asks what can be deduced about a particular word, "hyperbolic," as used in the phrase "hyperbolic discounting." Do not try to figure out the word's meaning in your head; wrong answer choices have been devised to play off of your possible knowledge of the word "hyperbolic." Rather, go to the text. The author says that "'exponential discounting'…has been renamed 'hyperbolic discounting,' because the effects of time delay do not seem strictly linear." The meaning of "hyperbolic" must have to do with this idea, that "the effects of time delay do not seem strictly linear." Only choice (A) works. Be careful of choice (B)—the use of the word *hyperbole* in everyday speech to mean exaggeration makes this a trap answer.

**MANHATTAN**
PREP

10. **(C).** Specific detail questions ask for something absolutely true according to the passage. This question asks specifically about the children who were able to wait. Choice (C) is correct; the second paragraph states that "if [the children] could wait a few minutes to eat [the first marshmallow], they would receive a second one." Incorrect choices (A), (B), (D), and (E) describe the children who *didn't* wait.

11. **(E).** When the question stem asks for the option "best supported by the passage," it is asking for a conclusion that is the logical synthesis of the premises in the argument. The argument gives two requirements for egg laying: there must be nesting material and the climate must be moderate. While "moderate" hasn't been specifically defined, it's safe to say that "the coldest winter on record" is the opposite of "moderate." Therefore, the bird will not lay eggs. The fact that the nesting material requirement has been filled—even above and beyond what is required—doesn't fix the problem. Choices (A), (B), (C), and (D) offer statements for which the passage does not offer enough information to evaluate.

12. **Ameliorate, mitigate.** Floodwaters had already entered the library, but the "hopeful" volunteers are working anyway—they hope to limit the damage. "Ameliorate" and "mitigate" both have the sense of making something better without completely solving it. Note that "exacerbate" means the opposite (to make worse), and "recant" and "forfeit" are negative words that don't fit the sentence (you could "recant" your former statements and "forfeit" an athletic competition, for instance). Finally, "recount" means to narrate and nothing in the sentence suggests that the volunteers were discussing the damage to the library.

13. **Resurrected, immortalized.** The answers must oppose "dead and forgotten." Both "resurrected" and "immortalized" fit. While "glamorized" might be tempting, it does not fit the clues from the sentence ("vitality" is not the same as "glamorous"). "Mocked" and "parodied" form an incorrect pair—the sentence gives no indication that Eleanor is being made fun of. Finally, "mummified" is another trap based on the theme that Eleanor of Aquitaine had been dead for years, but this word does not have a pair nor does it fit the clues given in the sentence. Note that "resurrected" and "immortalized" are not synonyms, but both certainly oppose the clue "dead and forgotten."

14. **Unpropitious, inimical.** Though there are good ("beneficent") motives, lots of people are dying. If this continues, then this "ongong contact" may end up harming the stated goal of "normalizing relations." "Unpropitious" and "inimical" both mean adverse or harmful. "Incongruous" means not incompatible or inconsistent. While this could be a match for the blank, meaning-wise—since contact with the locals may be incompatible with the aim of normalizing relations—it lacks a match among the answer choices. "Honorable" doesn't fit the desired meaning. And while "bedazzling" and "captivating" do form a pair, they provide a meaning that is not in line with what the sentence suggests.

15. **Credible, sound.** The testimony "is supported by evidence," so it must be believable. The correct answers are "credible" and "sound," which both mean believable. "Vociferous" (vehement and insistent) and "antagonistic" (feeling hostile towards) are a pair but do not mean believable. "Fallacious" means false, the opposite of what the blank requires. "Assiduous" describes something that is marked by careful attention or consistently applied effort and does not fit this sentence.

16. **(C).** Regarding choice (A), the consumer products division spent a higher "percentage" on marketing, but that doesn't mean it spent more actual dollars (maybe the consumer products division is much smaller than chemicals and machinery). Choice (B) should trip a red alert! The passage offers absolutely no information about consumer behavior. Choice (C) is correct—on average, all three divisions spent less than 35% of their budgets on marketing. 35% of any number, averaged in with less than 35% of some other numbers, will certainly generate an average under 35%. Note that on Logic Reading Comprehension questions, correct conclusions are often fairly obvious or are near paraphrases of information you've already read in the passage. Regarding choice (D), the passage does not indicate whether the company has other divisions besides chemicals, machinery, and consumer products, so this conclusion cannot be drawn. Choice (E) is wrong because while the chemicals division may have spent a higher percentage, this reveals nothing about the actual number of dollars spent or the relative sizes of the two departments' marketing budgets.

17. **(E).** The author's thrust is that 2-D representation warps students' perception; it pushes them to think of the world as flat and static rather than as 3-D and dynamic. The author does not say maps are necessary or evil, so choice (A) is too extreme. Choice (B) is a true detail from the passage but is more narrow than the author's overall point. Choice (C) might be implied but the purpose of the passage is to discuss the effect of such tools. Similarly, choice (D) might be inferred from the second paragraph but ignores the main issue of the essay.

18. **(C).** The second paragraph critiques the static quality of maps. Choice (C) eliminates that problem. As for choice (A), "some" means at least one, not a majority—the example of what may just be a few exceptional students does not do much damage to the evidence or the point that, in general, maps cause students to think about the world in 2-D. The author's evidence involves the presence of maps in the classroom, so the amount of use is irrelevant; eliminate choice (B). Choice (D) is also irrelevant, as the passage premises involve modern maps. Choice (E) is backwards; it strengthens the evidence that maps impede 3-D comprehension.

19. **(B).** In the second paragraph, the author uses the example of the 20th-century United States to buttress his or her argument. Choices (A) and (E) are incorrect; the passage contains neither circular logic nor a rebuttal. As for choice (C), the author does use physical description but not in support of an "accusation." Choice (D) is incorrect because the author listed problems but did not create a hierarchy.

20. **2nd only.** The passage states that Fleming discovered penicillin and that others developed it. His feelings or predictions about his discovery cannot be inferred. The passage does, however, say that "it was not until a decade later that a team of researchers from Oxford, with the help of an American laboratory, were able to increase the growth rate of penicillin...such that it could be produced in sufficient quantity to treat Allied soldiers wounded on D-Day, in 1944." Thus, at some point prior to 1944, penicillin was being grown too slowly. Finally, while penicillin was used to treat Allied soldiers in 1944, that does not mean antibacterial agents were used "since ancient times."

**MANHATTAN**
PREP

# Verbal Practice Section 2: Medium Difficulty

**20 Questions**
**Time: 30 Minutes**

> For questions 1–6, select one entry for each blank from the corresponding column of choices. Fill in the blank in the way that best completes the text.

1. Cormac McCarthy writes in an idiom both spare and flowery, with paragraphs of short, declarative sentences interspersed with long, _____ passages of description and philosophizing.

   | |
   |---|
   | boring |
   | floral |
   | baroque |
   | classical |
   | fictional |

2. Simony is one of the three primary (i) _____ in Joyce's *Dubliners*, recurring in almost every story in the collection. In some stories, the simony is more or less literal, with characters attempting to purchase salvation with money. In other stories, it arrives in a more (ii) _____ form.

   | Blank (i) | Blank (ii) |
   |---|---|
   | theses | spiritual |
   | leitmotifs | pecuniary |
   | characters | figurative |

3. Mixed-media artist Mae Chevrette begins each painting by affixing to canvas a photo from her travels, then embedding _____ such as used ticket stubs and concert posters before applying paint. The final works, emblazoned with quotes as well as evidence of Chevrette's extensive and wide-ranging travels, convey a sense of joyful _____.

   | Blank (i) | Blank (ii) |
   |---|---|
   | devices | philosophy |
   | apocrypha | wanderlust |
   | ephemera | anomie |

4. Taxation of legal substances known to be of a (i) _____ nature necessarily threads a thin line; it threatens to (ii) _____ government support for consumption of a product the use of which the government is rightly interested in curtailing.

| Blank (i) | Blank (ii) |
|-----------|------------|
| noxious | legitimize |
| salubrious | incentivize |
| solicitous | signify |

5. The newspaper's essay contest soliciting defenses of anti-vegetarianism yielded only a handful of entries that did not allow authors' (i) _____ to dictate their arguments: focusing on the seemingly universal human (ii) _____ for consuming animal products, these authors successfully navigated the gray area between simple self-justification and genuine apologia. The successful submissions argued not so much that desire or tradition could justify the current palate, but that the eradication of factory farming, the (iii) _____ , and the return to natural feed can blunt the evils caused by its excesses.

| Blank (i) | Blank (ii) | Blank (iii) |
|-----------|------------|-------------|
| erudition | penchant | effacement of resources |
| proclivities | salutation | imputation of ecology |
| tenacity | earmark | mitigation of suffering |

6. The long-term Senator began his career as an unrepentant (i) _____ for his party's excesses, defending policies that posterity has since judged to be reactionary, even (ii) _____ ; more recently he has taken (iii) _____ line, denying that those very policies ever reflected the party's values.

| Blank (i) | Blank (ii) | Blank (iii) |
|-----------|------------|-------------|
| critic | surreptitious | a restorative |
| apologist | illegal | an unconscionable |
| gadfly | retrograde | a revisionist |

**MANHATTAN**
PREP

> **Questions 7–9 are based on the following reading passage.**

The increasing number of published scientific studies ultimately shown to have been based on erroneous data threatens not only reputations of individual scholars but also perceptions of the field as a whole. Since the general public often interprets such debunkings as evidence of malicious or conspiratorial intentions on the part of researchers, these incidents

5  risk being construed as evidence that fraudulent practices pervade the discipline. Such conclusions are rendered all the more potent by the rousing prospect of exposing hypocrisy in a field that prides itself on its rigor. It would therefore behoove interested parties to go to lengths to demonstrate that such episodes, while incidentally regrettable, are not necessarily signs of malfeasance, and are in fact fully consistent with a healthy science. Indeed, the very

10  practices of hypothesis testing and scientific replication are in place precisely to redress such concerns. Spurious results may linger briefly in the communal ethos, but the more attention they garner for their ingenuity and impact, the more likely they are to be subjected to the crucible of attempted replication. Just as in a thriving garden, small weeds may crop up from time to time only to get pulled out at signs of trouble, so too in science do specious findings

15  occasionally attempt to infiltrate the canon only to get uprooted and tossed aside in the end by the inexorable process of scientific natural selection.

7.    In the context of the passage, the word *rousing* (line 6) is used to indicate that

      (A)  scientists often take deep satisfaction in adhering to their own rules

      (B)  people may find the chance to catch others in their own web to be galvanizing

      (C)  scientific non-experts are unaware that their criticisms of more specialized areas of study could be construed as exposing hypocrisy

      (D)  uncertainty itself can be something that the general public finds exciting

      (E)  scientific revolutions often happen when most experienced academics least expect them

> Consider each of the answer choices separately and indicate all that apply.

8.    The author of the passage would most likely defend which of the following scenarios as instances of "healthy science"?

      ☐  A young researcher discovers an important error in an established text and makes careful note of it in her personal logbook.

      ☐  A highly influential scholar publishes a controversial finding in a well-regarded journal only to be shown by follow-up studies to have inadvertently relied on an invalid statistical method.

      ☐  Unbeknownst to his collaborators, a scientist tweaks his data to be more consistent with a theory that has already won much empirical support.

9.  Which of the following best describes the overall purpose of the passage?

    (A)  To develop a scientific hypothesis and then describe evidence refuting it

    (B)  To argue that a problem that many people believe to be endemic to a specific domain is in fact much more widespread

    (C)  To encourage more robust dialogue between scientific experts and laypeople

    (D)  To highlight a possible interpretation of a phenomenon and then point out how that interpretation is mistaken

    (E)  To build support for a position and then contend that that position is fundamentally flawed

---

**Question 10 is based on the following reading passage.**

---

Mayor of Middletown: Two years ago, in order to improve the safety of our town's youth, I led the charge for a law requiring all bicycle riders to wear helmets when riding within city limits. My opponents claim the law is a failure because, last year, we had a higher incidence of bicycle accident victims with severe head injuries than in the previous year. The more important statistic, however, is the bicycle accident fatality rate, which has dropped nearly 30% since the law passed. Clearly, the helmet law has been a success.

10. Which of the following, if true, would best support the mayor's claim that the helmet law has been a success?

    (A)  If accident victims do not die as a result of a head injury, they often suffer from permanent brain damage.

    (B)  While only 15% of all bicycle accidents resulting in injury occur as a result of a collision with a motor vehicle, those accidents represent 90% of fatal accidents.

    (C)  In bicycle accidents, injuries to hands, knees, and elbows are far more common than head injuries.

    (D)  Typically, fatality rates for bicycle accident victims who sustain serious head injuries are twice as high when the victims are not wearing helmets as when they are.

    (E)  The effect of the helmet law in Middletown is typical; other towns also experienced a higher incidence of head injuries but a lower fatality rate.

---

**Questions 11–12 are based on the following reading passage.**

---

Ultraviolet radiation (with a wavelength in the range of 290–400 nanometers), visible light (400–760 nm), and infrared radiation (760–3,000 nm) are the three forms of energy that the Earth receives from the sun. Within the ultraviolet spectrum, the three sub-categories are UVC (200–290 nm), UVB (290–320 nm), and UVA (320–400 nm). Most UVC rays do not reach the Earth

5  because ozone and other gases in the upper atmosphere absorb them, but exposure to this type of radiation from germicidal lamps and mercury lamps may still be hazardous. Excessive exposure to visible light is also thought to be harmful, but it is not of extreme importance with respect to prevention of skin damage. Most skin damage is caused by UVA and UVB radiation. Ten times more UVA than UVB reaches the Earth, but the amount of UVA needed to

10  produce sunburn in human skin is 800–1,000 times higher than the amount of UVB needed. Nevertheless, UVA intensifies the sunburn effects of UVB through delayed erythema and aids in cancer formation. Thus, effective sunscreens and sun blocks must protect throughout both the UVB and UVA ranges.

---

Consider each of the answer choices separately and indicate <u>all</u> that apply.

---

11.  Which of the following can be inferred from the passage?

☐  A form of energy with a wavelength in the range of 2,000–2,500 nanometers would not be categorized as ultraviolet radiation.

☐  UVB rays cannot cause cancer formation without the intensifying effects of UVA.

☐  Ultraviolet radiation is not a form of infrared radiation.

---

Consider each of the answer choices separately and indicate <u>all</u> that apply.

---

12.  The sentence "Nevertheless, UVA intensifies ... cancer formation" (lines 12–13) serves which of the following roles?

☐  It provides a factual basis for creating sunscreens and sun blocks with certain properties.

☐  It undermines an argument presented earlier in the passage.

☐  It suggests that, within the wavelength range of ultraviolet radiation, radiation with wavelength lower than 320 nm can exacerbate the carcinogenic properties of radiation with a wavelength higher than 320 nm.

**MANHATTAN**
PREP                                                                        979

> **For questions 13–16, select the two answer choices that, when used to complete the sentence, fit the meaning of the sentence as a whole and produce completed sentences that are alike in meaning.**

13. Even the most accomplished performers at times have difficulty with some of Rachmaninoff's more perilous passages—the composer seems often to have written his music with the deliberate intent to _____.

    □ confound
    □ unnerve
    □ transmute
    □ transmogrify
    □ distribute
    □ malign

14. Americans can scarcely suppose that all 100,000,000 speakers of Indian English are united in error; it is past time that we recognized that distinctively Indian constructions are not _____.

    □ fads
    □ solecisms
    □ idioms
    □ dialects
    □ pidgins
    □ lapses

15. The _____ adventurer James Brawnson spends the majority of his autobiography trying to make his life sound like something out of an Indiana Jones movie, but in the end, according to some reviewers, it all comes off rather forced and unconvincing.

    □ hapless
    □ bold
    □ self-styled
    □ unlucky
    □ so-called
    □ intrepid

**MANHATTAN**
PREP

16. One of the more bizarre powers of the U.S. presidency is the more or less _____ authority to grant pardons, negating months or even years of criminal litigation in an instant.

   ☐ impartial
   ☐ unqualified
   ☐ unbiased
   ☐ executive
   ☐ sweeping
   ☐ tyrannical

Questions 17–20 are based on the following reading passage.

Long regarded as a necessary evil, the royal mistress is a classic staple of the French court. It was hardly a new trick for a monarch to use mistresses and political advisors as scapegoats, but the Bourbons did it with their own particular flare and brand of ceremony. Much of life in the French court was dictated by tradition, ritual, and custom, and the role of the mistress was

5    no exception to this. Mistresses were there to please the king and be the target for unwanted criticism, but they were also expected to stay out of political affairs.

This, of course, was hardly ever the case. The mistresses of Louis XIV, however, were rather well behaved in comparison to those of the future kings. Louis XIV fathered 13 illegitimate children with his mistresses over the course of his life. Thus, his many mistresses were often

10   more concerned with securing rights for their illegitimate offspring than with meddling in affairs of the state. This lack of political meddling made them somewhat less prone to the tremendously harsh scrutiny faced later by those of Louis XV. Additionally, Louis XIV's absolutist rule certainly had much to do with his mistresses remaining in their "proper places." Furthermore, Louis's strict control of the presses kept much of the harshest criticism at bay.

15   Nevertheless, there was still a steady stream of underground literature and cartoons that demonstrated abhorrence for many of Louis's paramours. What was important about the criticism that did proliferate against his mistresses, however, was that it was used to great advantage by Louis XIV. Indeed, he used it to deflect criticism from himself. By having an easily disposable female to shoulder the blame for various monarchical mishaps, Louis was able to

20   retain his appearance of absolute control and otherworldly perfection.

There would, however, be consequences for such skillful puppet-mastery in the coming century. Louis XIV was the singular architect of a vast veil of fictive space inlaid between him and his people, creating a dangerous precedent of masterful manipulation that could not be maintained to the same degree by later monarchs. It was clear that Louis XIV crafted this fictive

25   space cleverly and with great skill, peppering it with self-promoting propaganda to control his image in the collective imagination of his people. His progeny, however, were simply not as adept at doing so. Even more problematic, although future monarchs were not able to dexterously manipulate this fictive space themselves, it did not go away. Instead, it was the satirists, pamphleteers, and playwrights who took over its construction in the years leading up

30   to the Revolution. In short, though it was Louis XIV who wrote his own mythology, Louis XVI would have his written for him.

17.  The primary purpose of the passage is to

    (A)  critique the morals of the court of Louis XIV

    (B)  discuss the popular opinion of French royal mistresses

    (C)  contrast the mistresses of Louis XIV and Louis XV

    (D)  suggest the main cause of the French Revolution

    (E)  describe the utility and flaws of a political tradition

18.  According to the passage, all of the following were reasons that the mistresses of Louis XIV were less problematic than those of Louis XV EXCEPT:

    (A)  They were more concerned with securing the futures of their offspring.

    (B)  There was little freedom for the press under Louis XIV.

    (C)  They produced more offspring than did those of Louis XV.

    (D)  Louis XIV was a skillful politician.

    (E)  They were relatively uninterested in affairs of state.

> Consider each of the answer choices separately and indicate <u>all</u> that apply.

19.  The passage suggests which of the following?

    ☐  Necessary evils are part of monarchies.

    ☐  Writing one's own mythology can be good statesmanship.

    ☐  Louis XIV viewed Louis XV as an unsatisfactory heir.

20.  The passage implies that

    (A)  Louis XIV made mistakes that led to the Revolution

    (B)  Louis XIV was a member of the Bourbon family

    (C)  Louis XV wrote his own mythology

    (D)  the most troublesome mistresses were those of Louis XVI

    (E)  Louis XIV had more mistresses than Louis XVI

# Answers to Verbal Practice Section 2

**1. Baroque.** Because the description of "short, declarative sentences" matches up with the word *spare* in the first part of the sentence, you need something in the blank that matches up with "flowery," meaning full of elaborate literary words or phrases. "Boring" is judgmental, and "floral" just means "of flowers." Both "classical" and "fictional" might work, but the sentence does not provide clues to suggest the meaning of either. "Baroque," meaning highly ornate and extravagant in style, fits the sentence.

**2. Leitmotifs, figurative.** A theme that reappears throughout a work of art is called a "leitmotif" (simony—"attempting to purchase salvation with money"—is not a "thesis" in *Dubliners*, nor is it a "character"). You are told "Simony is more or less literal" in some stories, but "in other stories," it must be the opposite, or "figurative." The other options, "spiritual" and "pecuniary" (related to money) do not contrast with literal.

**3. Ephemera, wanderlust.** "Used ticket stubs and concert posters" are not "devices," nor are they "apocrypha" (fake). Rather, they are "ephemera," printed matter not intended to be saved. In the second blank, "wanderlust" describes a love of travel, matching much better with the rest of the sentence than either "philosophy" or "anomie" (lack of ethical standards).

**4. Noxious, incentivize.** If "the government is rightly interested in curtailing" the use of a product, this suggests that the product is somehow harmful, or of a "noxious" nature, so that's the first blank. Both "salubrious" (healthful) and "solicitous" (expressing concern) are positive words. By taxing such products, the government gains a profit from their consumption. That the government is "threading a thin line" suggests that there is a conflict: on the one hand, the government has an interest in increasing profits, and on the other hand, it has an interest in curtailing the use of the taxed substance. So the problem is that the taxation provides a reason to encourage, or "incentivize," use of the product. This taxation would neither "legitimize" nor "signify" government support for this product consumption.

**5. Proclivities, penchant, mitigation of suffering.** The clue for the first two blanks is given in the claim that "authors successfully navigated the gray area between simple self-justification and genuine apologia." "Apologia" means defense, so the authors were defending eating meat. But they did not allow their desire to eat meat to derail their arguments. The first two blanks require something like desires or tendency, and both "proclivity" and "penchant" mean that. "Erudition" (knowledge) is tempting, but it doesn't fit because saying that someone did not allow his knowledge to drive his arguments is a way of saying that the arguments were bad, and that would not describe the "successful" arguments that won the contest. "Tenacity" (persistence) is also a trap because it looks like tendency. "Salutation" (greeting) and earmark (identifying feature or characteristic) are good GRE vocabulary words but have the wrong meaning. The third blank requires something that can blunt the evils of eating meat, and that goes along with "the eradication of factory farming" and "the return to natural feed," so you are looking for something that contributes to the well-being of or detracts from the harms done to animals raised for food. "Mitigation of suffering" (easing of suffering) fits this bill. "Effacement of resources" (wiping out of resources) and "imputation of ecology" (blaming of ecology) would both increase harm done to animals and so cannot be correct.

**6. Apologist, retrograde, revisionist.** For the first blank, you want a word that means to defend. Surprisingly, that's precisely what "apologist" means (the word apology once meant a speech offered to defend or justify). "Critic" and "gadfly" (a particularly annoying critic) are both opposite to the desired meaning. For the second blank, something similar to "reactionary," but even stronger and more negative, is needed. Since "reactionary" means opposed to change, you want a word that means very opposed to change. "Retrograde" will do, since it suggests a retreat to some earlier state. "Surreptitious" (secretive) has the wrong meaning and "illegal" goes too far. The third blank describes an approach that recasts history or challenges a conventional history. That sort of recasting is called "revisionist." "Restorative" can't be correct because the denial isn't restoring anything. "Unconscionable" (unreasonable or immoral) goes too far; denying that policies reflected the party's values could just indicate wishful thinking or a lack of perceptiveness.

7. **(B).** As the passage states, some mistakes in scientific results "risk being construed as evidence that fraudulent practices" are going on. Non-science people are "rous[ed]" by the "prospect of exposing hypocrisy in a field that prides itself on its rigor." The author, then, believes that there is no fraud, but that laypeople may mistakenly believe such fraud exists and be excited by the prospect of calling out, or exposing the hypocrisy of, these scientists who claim to be so rigorous and objective. Answer (B) best matches this idea. Choices (A), (D), and (E) could be true in the real world but are not mentioned in the passage. Choice (C) contains many words from the right area of the passage, but the passage does not suggest that laypeople are unaware; if anything, the passage suggests that they are likely aware.

8. **2nd only.** The author of the passage argues that erroneous findings will be eventually corrected via the process of "scientific natural selection," or being subjected to scrutiny. "The very practices of hypothesis testing and scientific replication are in place precisely to redress such concerns," the author writes. The first statement is incorrect, since there is no such scrutiny—no one else will read the researcher's logbook. The third statement is incorrect because the scientist tweaks his data deliberately—this is more like the "fraudulent practices" described earlier in the passage than the "healthy science" described later—and because no scrutiny takes place.

9. **(D).** The passage points out that the discovery of erroneous findings *could* be seen as malfeasance by researchers, then goes on to show how these same findings are actually a healthy and natural part of the scientific process. Choice (A) isn't correct because the author does not develop a scientific hypothesis. Choice (B) is incorrect because the author shows that the purported problem isn't actually a problem at all. Choice (C) is tempting but the author is not actually trying to promote dialogue. The author does build a certain position but never tries to tear that position down, as choice (E) states.

10. **(D).** The mayor claims the law is a success because the accident fatality rate has dropped nearly 30% since the law passed. Opponents claim the law is a failure because more people have suffered from severe head injuries since the law passed. The answer choice that supports the mayor's claim will rebut the opponents' claim or somehow weaken its effect. While choice (A) may be true, it does not address the mayor's claim that the helmet law in particular has been successful in its goal to protect bicycle riders. Choice (B) is tempting because it offers a compelling reason why the town might want to enact a helmet law in the first place. However, reasons to enact the law are out of the argument's scope, which concerns the success of the already enacted law. This choice does not provide any information allowing you to assess the success (or failure) of the helmet law. Furthermore, choice (B) introduces "motor vehicles," which are also out of scope. Choice (C) may be tempting because the goal of the law is to protect the town's youth, and, presumably, it is desirable to limit all kinds of injuries. However, the focus of the argument is on a helmet law.

Choice (D) is correct—when bicyclists suffer serious head injuries, the chances of dying are twice as high for those not wearing helmets. The converse is that people with head injuries are less likely to die from those injuries if they were wearing a helmet. In other words, some of the injured would have been on the fatality list instead had they not been wearing helmets. This supports the mayor's case by showing that the premise used by the mayor's opponents does not actually indicate a failure in the law. Regarding choice (E), the fact that the results are similar in other towns means merely that the outcome is predictable in some way; it does not necessarily indicate success.

11. **1st and 3rd only.** The passage states that ultraviolet radiation is in the range of 290–400 nm, so energy with a wavelength of 2,000–2,500 nm would not fall in that range (in fact, it would fall into the range of infrared radiation). The passage additionally states that UVA rays intensify UVB damage and can aid in cancer formation, but it cannot be inferred that UVA rays are *necessary* for cancer to form. Finally, since ultraviolet radiation has a wavelength in the range of 290–400 nanometers and infrared radiation is in the range of 760–3,000 nm, ultraviolet radiation is not a form of infrared radiation.

12. **1st only.** That UVA rays can intensify sunburn and aid in cancer formation "provides a factual basis" for the recommendation in the next sentence that sunscreens block both UVB and UVA rays. The highlighted sentence does not "undermine an argument"—in fact, no "argument" exists in the passage, which is informative and factual. Finally, the third statement is the opposite of what is given: UVA (above 320 nm) "exacerbates the carcinogenic properties" of UVB (below 320 nm), not the other way around.

13. **Confound, unnerve.** Very experienced performers have so much difficulty with some of Rachmaninoff's "more perilous [difficult] passages" that it sometimes seems as though the music was intentionally designed to [blank]. The blank must mean something like confuse or cause people to struggle. "Confound" means confuse and so is a good match. "Unnerve," which means to cause someone to lose confidence, also works. "Transmute" and "transmogrify" both mean to transform, which doesn't mean difficult. Neither "distribute" nor "malign" (say bad things about or slander) has a match and so cannot be correct.

14. **Solecisms, lapses.** That which "Americans *can scarcely suppose*" is false, so "distinctively Indian constructions" are not errors. The blank should mean something like errors. "Lapses" are errors and "solecisms" are grammatical errors. "Dialects" and "pidgins" (simplified versions of a language) have close to the same meaning, but that meaning is the wrong one; Indian English is indeed a dialect of English. "Idioms" are also related to language, but you could describe some "distinctly Indian constructions" as idioms, so it is not correct. "Fads" doesn't have a match and so also cannot be correct.

15. **Self-styled, so-called.** The most important words here are "forced" and "unconvincing," used to describe Brawnson's account of his adventures. That means that Brawnson is decidedly not Indiana Jones, so the blank must in some way negate "adventurer." "Self-styled" and "so-called" both imply that Brawnson may call himself an adventurer, but other people might not, which is exactly what the blank needs. "Hapless" and "unlucky" form a pair, but this answer isn't correct because adventurers can certainly be unlucky and the story of an unlucky adventurer would not necessarily be "forced and unconvincing." "Bold" and "intrepid" also form a pair, but they would enhance Brawnson's reputation as an "adventurer."

16. **Unqualified, sweeping.** The key here is that the power to grant pardons can negate "months or years of criminal litigation in an instant." That implies the power is quick and absolute. "Sweeping" correctly captures the absolute nature of this power. Although "unqualified" can mean without qualifications, it is also used to mean without limits. Using the less common second meaning of an everyday word like "unqualified" is a typical GRE test writer trick. "Unbiased" and "impartial" form another pair, but the meaning is not correct because although a person or a selection process could be described as "unbiased," the authority to do something cannot be. "Tyrannical" is going too

far—nothing in the sentence suggests that the president is an oppressive dictator—and "executive" doesn't mean much of anything in this context because all presidential powers are, technically, "executive."

17. **(E).** In the first paragraph, the author outlines the political role of royal mistresses in France and goes on to discuss the virtues and pitfalls of this system. Choice (A) is out of scope, as the author avoids moral judgments. Choice (B) is too narrow; popular opinion is a detail, one of the pitfalls. Choice (C) is wrong because the passage does not contrast the mistresses—about whom there is very little information—but rather their effect on French politics. Choice (D) is incorrect (and too extreme) because the author does not say it was the *main* cause.

18. **(C).** This issue is largely discussed in the second paragraph, which provides support for the four incorrect choices. Choice (C) is correct because, though the author does mention the number of Louis XIV's illegitimate children, the passage does not mention the number for Louis XV or compare those numbers.

19. **2nd only.** In the last paragraph, the passage describes the success Louis XIV had in writing "his own mythology" and compares that to the less satisfactory attempts by his successors. The first statement is out of scope as the author only states that it was a staple of the French court, not all courts. Similarly, no indication is given of Louis's opinion of his successor.

20. **(B).** In the first paragraph, the author states that the Bourbons brought a unique "flare" to the French custom of royal mistresses. Regarding answer (A), the passage discusses the success and skill of Louis XIV; mistakes are only attributed to his successors. Choice (C) is unsupported—the passage notes that Louis XVI did not write his own mythology but Louis XV is not mentioned. Answers (D) and (E) are wrong for similar reasons—the passage compares the volume of and problems caused by the mistresses of Louis XIV and Louis XV. But nothing is mentioned in that regard for Louis XVI.

# Verbal Practice Section 3: Hard Difficulty

**20 Questions**
**Time: 30 Minutes**

> For questions 1–6, select one entry for each blank from the corresponding column of choices. Fill in the blank in the way that best completes the text.

1.  While it is tempting to think that artists like Picasso literally see the world in a markedly different way, examination of the artist's creative process reveals _____ movement from roughly realist sketches toward his famous Cubist style through a series of ever more abstract steps.

    | |
    |---|
    | an obsessive |
    | an iterative |
    | a random |
    | a historical |
    | a dicey |

2.  Researchers from the University of Southampton concluded that ethnic differences are likely not the cause of mutual mistrust, citing government surveys that show that cooperation and trust are no higher in racially _____ neighborhoods than in mixed communities.

    | |
    |---|
    | militant |
    | parochial |
    | provincial |
    | homogeneous |
    | sectarian |

3.  Though in her home country of Denmark the singer always enjoyed an outpouring of support verging on the (i) _____ , she continues overseas to confront certain impediments to success—evidence, perhaps, that not all art is (ii) _____ .

    | Blank (i) | Blank (ii) |
    |---|---|
    | evanescent | fully decipherable |
    | adulatory | universally translatable |
    | totalitarian | entirely tractable |

**MANHATTAN**
PREP

4. That (i) _____ rhetoric is so easily (ii) _____ the language of patriotism is perhaps one of the greatest dangers of relying too heavily on the latter to bolster public morale.

| Blank (i) | Blank (ii) |
| --- | --- |
| pacifist | phased in |
| obsequious | couched in |
| bellicose | implied by |

5. The very title of Evelyn Waugh's Sword of Honour trilogy suggests a robust and (i) _____ tale, and the bare outline seems to fit, as the protagonist Guy Crouchback serves as a commando, trains as a paratrooper, and is dispatched to Yugoslavia to aid the partisans. In fact, however, Crouchback is an extraordinarily (ii) _____ man, ill-at-ease with his younger and more (iii) _____ fellow officers, and almost never motivated by appetite or impulse.

| Blank (i) | Blank (ii) | Blank (iii) |
| --- | --- | --- |
| pell-mell | effete | vigorous |
| red-blooded | venerable | puerile |
| avant-garde | literary | timorous |

6. In the contemporary climate of academic specialization, the typical university lecturer of only two centuries ago, who was expected to (i) _____ views on subjects as diverse as geography, physics, and the fine arts, seems a veritable (ii) _____, and we forget at our peril that it was precisely such breadth of learning that led to some of the great discoveries and even (iii) _____ shifts in the sciences, as when Darwin drew upon his knowledge of philosophy and economics to articulate his famous theory of evolution.

| Blank (i) | Blank (ii) | Blank (iii) |
| --- | --- | --- |
| propound | astrophysicist | hegemonic |
| gainsay | polymath | paradigmatic |
| demarcate | autodidact | minuscule |

---

**Questions 7–10 are based on the following reading passage.**

---

Without a doubt, one of the pinnacle achievements of modern physics is the development of Maxwell's equations. Their beauty lies in their elegant simplicity, while the breadth and depth of Maxwell's equations speak for themselves. These four simple equations, coupled with the Lorenz Force Equation, form a full basis for modeling the behavior of an
5    entire branch of physics: classical electrodynamics and optics. Further, despite their deceptive simplicity, Maxwell's equations have withstood the test of time. While equations modeling most other fields of physics have been modified to accommodate new experimental results and theories, Maxwell's equations have not been altered since their original conception in 1861. Take, for instance, Einstein's theory of general relativity, first published in 1916. Although the
10   equation governing general relativity was also elegant and powerful, and laid the framework for most modern astrophysics, Einstein himself did not realize and correct an error within his equation until nearly fifteen years later. Newtonian mechanics has given way to more powerful theoretical frameworks and analytical mechanics has bent under the weight of quantum theory, but Maxwell's equations stand as originally written, tried and true.
15       Maxwell's four equations, the majority of which are less than twenty characters, are the mathematical formulation of four very simple ideas. First, any free electric charge will result in an electric field. Second, magnets do not have free charges, but are always paired together with a positive and negative end, yielding a magnetic field that has a looped structure. Third, a magnetic field that changes in time will result in an electric field and, fourth, an electric current
20   or changing electric field will produce a magnetic field. It is truly amazing that these four simple rules, unmodified, have been used to model all electric, magnetic, and optics studies for more than 150 years.

7.    Which of the following best expresses the author's intent in writing the passage?

   (A)  To argue that Maxwell's equations are the most important equations in all of physics
   (B)  To explain the significance and meaning of Maxwell's equations
   (C)  To argue that Maxwell is a more important name in physics than Einstein
   (D)  To describe the implications of each of Maxwell's four equations
   (E)  To advocate further studies in the field of electromagnetism and optics

8.  The author references Einstein's theory of general relativity for which of the following reasons?

    (A)  To argue that the equations of electricity and magnetism are more important than the equations of relativity

    (B)  To provide an example of an equation that has been unwavering in time

    (C)  To advocate that Maxwell was a more important historical figure than Einstein

    (D)  To show that the implications of Maxwell's equations are far more powerful than general relativity

    (E)  To provide an example of an important equation that has been modified over time

9.  Which of the following is <u>not</u> mentioned as a rule in any of Maxwell's four equations?

    (A)  The looped structure of a magnetic field results from coupled charges.

    (B)  A magnetic field that changes in time results in an electric field.

    (C)  Any free electric charge results in an electric field.

    (D)  Magnetic fields are generated by unpaired magnetic charges.

    (E)  An electric current will produce a magnetic field.

Consider each of the answer choices separately and indicate <u>all</u> that apply.

10. Which of the following can be correctly inferred from the passage?

    ☐  Maxwell's four equations form a full basis for modeling the behavior of classical electrodynamics and optics.

    ☐  Einstein's equations of general relativity were incorrect as originally written in 1916.

    ☐  Newtonian mechanics has been modified by quantum theory.

---

**Question 11 is based on the following reading passage.**

When people are told that some behavior is common, they are more likely to indulge in that behavior even when society disapproves of it. For example, if many people are shown littering in an anti-litter advertisement, observers may subconsciously feel that littering is a normal, accepted activity. Thus, in order to influence behavior effectively, it is critical not to show or discuss anyone engaging in an activity that the advertisement seeks to discourage.

11.  Which of the following, if true, most undermines the argument's conclusion?

   (A)  In a study, the most effective anti-smoking advertisement featured a person smoking amidst a disapproving crowd.

   (B)  The most effective way to influence behavior is for parents to teach their children not to litter.

   (C)  People who watch public service advertisements are typically aware that actors are merely pretending to engage in the disapproved behavior.

   (D)  Teenagers are more likely to litter than the general population and less likely to be influenced by anti-litter advertisements.

   (E)  In a study, the most effective anti-littering advertisement featured a pristine public park with children playing in the background.

---

**For questions 12–15, select the two answer choices that, when used to complete the sentence, fit the meaning of the sentence as a whole and produce completed sentences that are alike in meaning.**

---

12.  Although bonobos are a good deal more gregarious than chimpanzees, they do not hesitate to _____ those whose continued presence would otherwise undermine the safety or even equanimity of the group.

   ☐  patronize
   ☐  imperil
   ☐  oust
   ☐  jeopardize
   ☐  safeguard
   ☐  ostracize

13. Perhaps because his military training discouraged indirection, the National Incident Commander sought a _____ and open conversation with the Governor.

☐ plain

☐ profane

☐ frank

☐ brusque

☐ pert

☐ boisterous

14. Though croquet is proverbially a genteel game, it is not enough to play your own ball well—you must _____ your opponent's play as well, even when impeding his or her progress costs you strokes.

☐ scotch

☐ anticipate

☐ obviate

☐ underscore

☐ eliminate

☐ stymie

15. A report in General Hospital Psychiatry finds that panic attacks _____ the effects of diabetes, probably by interfering with patients' self-care, leading to a 75% increase in the frequency of symptoms.

☐ exacerbate

☐ hinder

☐ impede

☐ aggravate

☐ indemnify

☐ degrade

---

**Question 16 is based on the following reading passage.**

---

A certain medication used to treat migraine headaches acts by blocking pain receptors in the brain. When a person takes the medication within one hour after ingesting grapefruit or grapefruit juice, however, the effectiveness of the medication is significantly diminished. Researchers have determined that the grapefruit contains a compound that alters the shape of the pain receptors, with the result that the medication can no longer bind with them completely.

16. Which of the following conclusions could be most properly drawn from the information given above?

    (A)  If one takes the medication more than an hour after ingesting grapefruit, its effectiveness is not diminished.

    (B)  Ingesting grapefruit after taking the medication does not diminish the effectiveness of the medication.

    (C)  There is only one type of pain receptor in the brain.

    (D)  The medication is fully effective only when it properly binds with its target pain receptors.

    (E)  It is not possible to design a medication for migraine headaches that can bond with the altered receptors.

**MANHATTAN**
PREP

> **Questions 17–19 are based on the following reading passage.**

Jeffrey C. Goldfarb suggests public-spirited dialogue need not happen after a traditional theater show, as it is most successful when it happens during a show. He believes that the live component of the theater distinguishes it from other media objects, and allows meaning to arise from the interaction between performers and audience as the performance is happening.

5 Whereas television or film, for instance, has no room for active dialogue, theater does because the performers and audience are present in the space together. The theatrical text becomes the medium, and the performers speak through the way in which they perform the text, while the audience does so through a number of culturally sanctioned actions: applause, laughter (both laughing with and laughing at), sighing, gasping, cheering, and booing. Goldfarb

10 recounts a particular occurrence surrounding a production of *Dziady* (Forefather's Eve) in Poland in 1968. The show had been ordered to close and, on its last night, the theater was overcrowded with supporters. They were an enthusiastic, vocal audience who entered into "dialogue" with the actors and read into the play's anti-czarist language a critique of Soviet government. When the performance ended, the crowd went into the streets to protest. The

15 play's content became political through dialogue and, in a way, the theater building held a public sphere where an anti-Soviet audience gathered to affirm their political sentiment before taking it to the street in open, public protest.

What Goldfarb does not write about is how uncommon such an event is, especially for today's American theatergoers. Augusto Boal was probably closer to the reality of current

20 Western theater when he complained about how still everyone is expected to keep during any performance, constantly policed by other audience members. The high prices on professional theater tickets and an elitist value on cultural tradition (versus popular, technology-based mass media) combine to produce an aristocratic culture surrounding theater. In this manner, a "high class" code of etiquette is imposed upon the performance space, dictating that

25 audience members are to remain quiet: the actors speak, the audience listens. As Boal criticizes in *Legislative Theatre*, traditional form sets up a relationship where "everything travels from stage to auditorium, everything is transported, transferred in that direction—emotions, ideas, morality!—and nothing goes the other way." He argues that this relationship encourages passivity and thus cancels theater's political potential.

17.  The primary purpose of the passage is to

    (A)  Lay out a viewpoint and present a perceived omission

    (B)  Articulate an original thesis

    (C)  Deride an established tradition

    (D)  Contrast two opposing ideas

    (E)  Reconcile two opposing ideas

Consider each of the answer choices separately and indicate <u>all</u> that apply.

18. The author implies which of the following about American theater?

☐ In some social settings, passivity is considered a virtue.

☐ Augusto Boal would approve of the events of the closing performance of *Dziady*.

☐ Physical presence has a bearing on the creation of active dialogue.

Consider each of the answer choices separately and indicate <u>all</u> that apply.

19. Which of the following must be true according to the passage?

☐ By contemporary American social mores, the Polish audience described would be exhibiting other than "high class" behavior.

☐ *Dziady* criticized the Soviet regime.

☐ Theater is more educational than film.

---

**Question 20 is based on the following reading passage.**

---

In the 1930's, Pablum, the first pre-cooked, dried baby food, was sold in America. Pablum took its name from the Latin word *pabulum*, which meant "foodstuff," and was also used in medicine to refer to a passively absorbed source of nutrition. While Pablum contained vitamin D and thus helped to prevent rickets in an era in which child malnutrition was still widespread, ironically, the word *pablum*—undoubtedly influenced by the negative connotation of the word *pabulum* as well as the physical reality of a mushy, bland, rehydrated cereal—today means "trite, naïve, or simplistic ideas or writings; intellectual pap."

20. Which of the following best describes the irony of the shifting meanings of the word *pablum*?

(A) A word for a passively absorbed source of nutrition is used for a substance actively fed to babies.

(B) Many babies would have died of malnutrition without Pablum.

(C) A word derived from Latin is still in use in modern English, although the meaning has changed somewhat.

(D) A cereal designed to be nourishing now lends its name to a word for something lacking in substance.

(E) Just as babies are fed bland food, *pablum* today means "bland writing or ideas."

# Answers to Verbal Practice Section 3

1. **An iterative.** Although one might think that Picasso "[saw] the world" in an unusual way, his artistic process actually progressed from style to another "through a series of ever more abstract steps." The correct answer, "iterative" means involving repetition or reiteration. None of the other choices fits the idea of a movement that both takes place in steps and has a definite direction—it cannot be "random" or "dicey," since it has a clear aim and structure, and neither "obsessive" nor "historical" reflects the required meaning.

2. **Homogeneous.** According to the sentence, "ethnic differences" are not the root cause of "mutual mistrust" because surveys show that trust is no higher in [blank] neighborhoods than in racially mixed neighborhoods. The blank must describe areas without many differences. If you borrow those very words, you might anticipate something like unmixed, the same throughout. "Homogeneous" has just this meaning. "Militant" and "sectarian" (partisan) are a pair, but it would be expected that trust would be lower in racially partisan or combative neighborhoods, so these answers are traps for anyone who misses the contrast that the sentence sets up with "mixed communities." Similarly, "parochial" and "provincial," which both mean unsophisticated or narrow-minded, are also traps.

3. **Adulatory, universally translatable.** If the singer enjoys an "outpouring of support," you'd expect it to "verge" on extremely positive support—in this case, "adulation," which means extreme adoration. "Evanescent" (fleeting) and "totalitarian" (dictatorial) don't fit the desired meaning. The fact that her art is not as well received in other places means that it might not carry over, or "translate," to those places. The two wrong answers for the second blank, which contain two words related to being understandable or usable, "decipherable" and "tractable," are close, but do not capture the sense of artistic adaptation implied in the second clause.

4. **Bellicose, couched in.** Since the "rhetoric" (persuasive language) presents a danger, you are looking for something dangerous: "bellicose," meaning aggressive or warlike, is a perfect fit. "Obsequious" means servile and "pacifist" means favoring or supporting peace, so neither of those seems particularly dangerous. The bellicose rhetoric is expressed in, phrased in, or laid out in the language of patriotism; "couched in" means the same thing as laid out in. This is a better fit than "implied by," since to say that patriotism implies bellicose rhetoric is to make the assumption that patriotism is aggressive in itself, rather than simply yielding easily to aggression. It doesn't make logical sense to say "phased in the language of patriotism," so this choice looks like a trap for someone reading quickly who might misread it as "phrased in."

5. **Red-blooded, effete, vigorous.** The first word should echo "robust" and fit the military derring-do described in the "bare outline." "Red-blooded" suggests virility and heartiness. "Pell-mell" (jumbled or disorderly) and "avant-garde" (innovative) are great GRE words, but don't echo "robust." "In fact, however" suggests that Crouchback is not actually robust, and he is further described as "ill-at-ease," and "never motivated by appetite or impulse." These suggest something like feeble or impotent. "Effete" is even better, as it describes someone lacking vigor and energy. "Venerable" (deserving of reverence) cannot be correct because it is strongly positive, which doesn't fit with the sentence's description of Crouchback. "Literary" is a theme trap. Although the sentences are describing a book, the second blank is specifically describing a character in the book, and the character is not a person concerned with literature. For the third blank, the phrasing "and more" suggests a contrast with Crouchback; you're not looking, then, for something that is a pure synonym for "younger" but for something that goes against the description of Crouchback as "effete." The best answer is "vigorous." "Puerile" (immature) is a trap—it seems to echo "younger," but the sentence

does not suggest that these younger officers are immature. "Timorous" (timid) is a reversal trap. It is a match for the description of Crouchback, not the desired contrast, and so cannot be correct.

6. **Propound, polymath, paradigmatic.** The "university lecturer of two centuries ago" was expected to have, or to set out, views on diverse subjects. To "propound" a view is to set it forward or lay it out. "Demarcate" (mark the boundaries of) is not a good fit; "gainsay" means to contradict, and while the lecturer may have the ability to contradict views on diverse subjects, this doesn't make as much sense as laying them out. A person with a wide, practically encyclopedic breadth of knowledge is a "polymath." "Astrophysicist" doesn't fit, since it is only the name of one specialized branch of study; an "autodidact" is someone who is self-taught. In the final blank, you are looking for something stronger than "great discoveries": something like a change (or shift) in the way science is done, or the way scientific theories are understood—the theory of evolution is an example of such a change. A paradigm is a model or template for doing something, so "paradigmatic" is an excellent match for this blank. "Hegemonic" (describing a dominant or ruling power) is too strong. "Minuscule" (tiny) is a trap for anyone who didn't notice the "and even," which indicates that the blank has to be filled by a word that goes further than "great discoveries."

7. **(B).** The author uses the first paragraph of the passage to explain why Maxwell's equations are so significant. The second paragraph discusses the meaning of each of Maxwell's equations. Answer choice (B) presents both of these ideas. Further, choice (A) incorrectly states that this passage argues that Maxwell's equations are the most important in physics. Choice (C) incorrectly compares Maxwell to Einstein. Choice (D) is too narrow; it fails to address the author's intent in writing the first paragraph. Finally, the author does not advocate for further studies as described in answer choice (E).

8. **(E).** Before introducing Einstein's theory of general relativity, the author states that Maxwell's equations have "withstood the test of time." The author goes on to say that, in contrast, although Einstein's equations are "elegant and powerful," they had to be modified not long after their postulation. Therefore, the author uses Einstein's theory of general relativity to provide an example of an important equation that has been modified over time, as answer choice (E) describes. Answer (A) is incorrect as the author does not directly compare the fields of electricity and magnetism and relativity. Answer (B) is incorrect as it states the opposite of what is mentioned in the paragraph. Choice (C) incorrectly compares Maxwell to Einstein as opposed to their equations. Finally, choice (D) is incorrect because the implications of Maxwell's equations are never compared to those of Einstein's general relativity.

9. **(D).** The passage states that magnets do not have free charges but are always paired together with a positive and negative end. Therefore, answer choice (D) is not mentioned, as it claims that magnetic fields are generated by unpaired magnetic charges. Answer choice (A) is presented in Maxwell's second equation: paired, or coupled, charges yield a looped magnetic field. Answer (B) is presented in Maxwell's third equation, choice (C) is presented in Maxwell's first equation, and choice (E) is presented in Maxwell's fourth equation.

10. **2nd only.** The passage states that Einstein did not realize and correct an error in his theory of general relativity until 15 years after the theory was postulated in 1916. Therefore, Einstein's original equations of general relativity must have been incorrect as written in 1916. The first statement cannot be inferred as the passage says that Maxwell's equations, coupled with the Lorenz Force Equation, form the full basis for electrodynamics and optics. The third statement incorrectly infers that Newtonian mechanics has been modified by quantum theory, whereas the last sentence in the first paragraph states that it is analytical mechanics, and not Newtonian mechanics, that has been modified by quantum theory.

11. **(A).** According to the argument, if "many" people are shown littering in an anti-litter ad, then those watching the ad "may" feel that littering is normal or accepted. The author concludes from this that the "bad" behavior should not be shown or discussed at all in an ad that seeks to discourage this "bad" behavior. The question asks for a piece of information that weakens the author's conclusion. Choice (A) illustrates that the author's assumption is not valid: a very effective anti-smoking ad featured one person smoking. That is, an effective ad did feature someone engaging in the negative behavior. While answer (B) may be true, the conclusion is not concerned with the most effective way to influence a particular type of behavior. Regarding choice (C), the conclusion focuses on what not to do (show or discuss the discouraged behavior) in order to influence behavior in an effective manner. That observers are aware that the ads may feature actors does not influence that particular conclusion. Regarding choice (D), the conclusion is not concerned with whether advertisements are more or less effective than other means for influencing teenagers. Finally, answer choice (E) strengthens the author's position: the best advertisement does not show the behavior that the ad seeks to discourage, however, the question asks for a weakener, not a strengthener.

12. **Oust, ostracize.** "Although" implies an action that you wouldn't ordinarily expect from "gregarious," or friendly, animals; they would be unfriendly. The "otherwise" in "continued presence would otherwise undermine" implies that bonobos sometimes do something to exclude others. "Oust" (expel) and "ostracize" (exclude from a group) have slightly different meanings but work because they give the sentence the same overall meaning. "Imperil" and "jeopardize" both mean something like "endanger," but this pair does not oppose "continued presence" as directly as do "oust" and "ostracize." Neither "patronize" nor "safeguard" means anything similar to exclude, so they are not correct either.

13. **Plain, frank.** Since his training "discouraged indirection," you can expect a word like direct. The word "open" suggests that the Commander wanted to be candid. "Plain" and "frank" both suggest unornamented but not necessarily unfriendly speech. "Brusque," on the other hand, suggests a discourteous bluntness. "Profane" (irreverent or disrespectful), "pert" (attractive in a neat and stylish way), and "boisterous" (rowdy or rambunctious) do not fit with the desired meaning.

14. **Scotch, stymie.** "Though" suggests that the word is opposed to gentility, and so you might expect something like behave coarsely toward. The word "impeding" provides a more precise idea: the blank requires something like aggressively block. "Scotch," which means abruptly end, and "stymie," which means thwart, are both good. "Obviate" (prevent or preclude), and "eliminate" are tempting, but don't quite have the right meaning because they imply preventing the other player from playing, rather than impeding his or her progress." The word "anticipate" is also tempting, because it is often helpful to be able to anticipate an opponent's play in a game, but this word has no match and so cannot be correct. "Underscore" (emphasize) doesn't have a match either but also doesn't fit meaning-wise.

15. **Exacerbate, aggravate.** Since panic attacks eventually lead to "a 75% increase in the frequency of symptoms," they make the effects of diabetes much worse. "Exacerbate" and "aggravate" have precisely this meaning. In some contexts, "hinder" and "impede," which mean to block something, would mean to make worse, but blocking the symptoms of a disease would actually help. "Degrade" is a negative word, meaning demote, debase, or impair, but none of its meanings work here. "Indemnify," which means to secure against hurt or loss, doesn't fit either.

16. **(D).** The passage says that the medication has been shown to be less effective when taken after grapefruit consumption because grapefruit consumption has been shown to affect the binding of the medication to pain receptors. It can be concluded that effective binding is needed to enable the full effectiveness of the medication, as answer choice (D) states. Regarding choice (A), the passage says that grapefruit or grapefruit juice ingested within an hour will "significantly" diminish the effectiveness of the medication. This does not mean that grapefruit or grapefruit juice ingested more than an hour before the medication is ingested will have no effect on the medication; it may have a mild effect. Regarding choice (B), the passage speaks only of taking the medication after ingesting grapefruit; it says nothing about what might happen when eating grapefruit after taking the medication. As for choice (C), while the passage discusses one kind of pain receptor, this does not mean that these are the only pain receptors in the brain. Answer (E) is out of scope. The passage offers no information about possible research or design of new migraine medications.

17. **(A).** The author presents Goldfarb's view in the first paragraph and then highlights an omission in Goldfarb's thesis in the second paragraph. Answer choice (B) is incorrect because "original" contradicts the text—the author recounts the opinions of Goldfarb and Boal. Choice (C) is wrong, as the author does not "deride" anything, and the word "established" is not supported by the text. Answer (D) is eliminated because there is no contrast nor opposing ideas—Goldfarb neglected to mention that something he discussed was quite uncommon, but Goldfarb's ideas do not oppose Boal's. Similarly, regarding choice (E), no reconciliation is attempted and there are still no opposing ideas.

18. **1st, 2nd, and 3rd.** The first statement must be true, as the second paragraph indicates that some American audiences consider passive behavior polite. The second statement must be true since, according to the last sentence of the second paragraph, Boal criticized passivity because it "cancels theater's political potential." The third statement is a good match for this sentence from the first paragraph: "Whereas television or film, for instance, has no room for active dialogue, theater does because the performers and audience are present in the space together."

19. **1st only.** In the first paragraph, the passage describes the interaction between the Polish audience and the cast; in the second paragraph, the author states that American "high class" behavior involves remaining quiet in the theater. Together, these two pieces of information support the first statement. The second statement is incorrect—the passage states that the audience "read into," or interpreted, the anti-czarist language as a critique of the Soviet regime; while the play may very well have been intended that way, this cannot be inferred from the given information. The comparison concerning education in the third statement is unjustified because the passage only states that the live element is unique to theater.

20. **(D).** The word "irony" is an outcome of events contrary to what was, or might have been, expected. Choice (A) is not ironic—the medical term *pablum* means a passively absorbed nutrition, and babies receive the baby food Pablum in a passive way. Choices (B), (C), and (E) may be true, but also do not fit the definition of ironic. Answer (D) is indeed ironic—the word now means nearly the opposite of what was originally intended. Only answer choice (D) presents this kind of ironic twist.

# Chapter 33 *of*

## 5 lb. Book of GRE® Practice Problems

# Math Practice Sections

# In This Chapter. . .

# Math Practice Section 1: Easy Difficulty

**Math Practice Section: Easy**

**20 Questions**

**35 Minutes**

For questions in the Quantitative Comparison format ("Quantity A" and "Quantity B" given), the answer choices are always as follows:

(A)    Quantity A is greater.
(B)    Quantity B is greater.
(C)    The two quantities are equal.
(D)    The relationship cannot be determined from the information given.

For questions followed by a numeric entry box [    ], you are to enter your own answer in the box. For questions followed by a fraction-style numeric entry box ▭, you are to enter your answer in the form of a fraction. You are not required to reduce fractions. For example, if the answer is $\frac{1}{4}$, you may enter $\frac{25}{100}$ or any equivalent fraction.

All numbers used are real numbers. All figures are assumed to lie in a plane unless otherwise indicated. Geometric figures are not necessarily drawn to scale. You should assume, however, that lines that appear to be straight are actually straight, points on a line are in the order shown, and all geometric objects are in the relative positions shown. Coordinate systems, such as $xy$-planes and number lines, as well as graphical data presentations such as bar charts, circle graphs, and line graphs, *are* drawn to scale. A symbol that appears more than once in a question has the same meaning throughout the question.

$x$, $y$, and $z$ are consecutive integers such that $x < y < z$.

|  | **Quantity A** | **Quantity B** |
|---|---|---|
| 1. | $y$ | $\dfrac{x+z}{2}$ |

|  | **Quantity A** | **Quantity B** |
|---|---|---|
| 2. | $(-3)^4$ | $(-3)^{-3}$ |

|  | **Quantity A** | **Quantity B** |
|---|---|---|
| 3. | $x$ | $5$ |

|  | **Quantity A** | **Quantity B** |
|---|---|---|
| 4. | $y^7 \times y^8 \times y^{-6}$ | $3y^9$ |

$xy > 0$ and $yz < 0$

|        | **Quantity A** | **Quantity B** |
|--------|----------------|----------------|
| 5.     | $xz$           | 0              |

In 2011, it cost Tammy $1.30 to manufacture each copy of her magazine, which she sold for $2.30. In 2012, it cost Tammy $1.50 to manufacture each copy of the same magazine, which she sold for $3.00.

|        | **Quantity A** | **Quantity B** |
|--------|----------------|----------------|
| 6.     | The percent by which Tammy's profit per copy of the magazine changed from 2011 to 2012. | $33\frac{1}{3}\%$ |

List X consists of the numbers 4, 7, 9, 11, 24, 32.

List Y (not shown) consists of six unique numbers, each computed from the corresponding term in list X by dividing the number in list X by 2, then adding 5 to the result.

|        | **Quantity A** | **Quantity B** |
|--------|----------------|----------------|
| 7.     | The range of list Y | 6 less than the greatest number in list Y |

8.  Which of the following represents the length of the diagonal $d$ of a square with area $a$?

   (A)  $d = a^2$
   (B)  $d = \sqrt{2a}$
   (C)  $d = 2\sqrt{a}$
   (D)  $d = a\sqrt{2}$
   (E)  $d = a\sqrt{3}$

9.  In an apartment complex, 60% of the apartments contain at least one television, and 20% of these apartments are equipped with cable. If every apartment that is equipped with cable contains at least one television, what percent of the apartments in the complex are not equipped with cable?

   (A)  8%
   (B)  12%
   (C)  16%
   (D)  88%
   (E)  92%

**MANHATTAN**
PREP

> **Questions 10–12 are based on the following chart.**

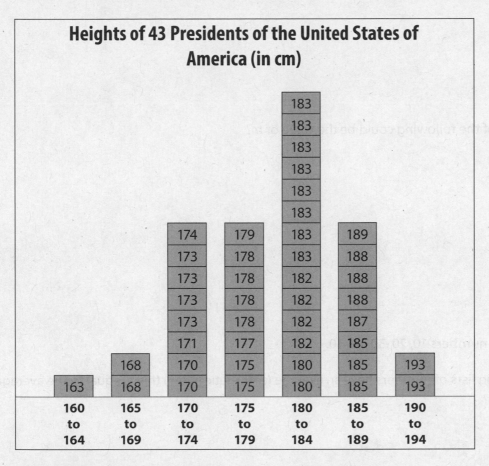

### Heights of 43 Presidents of the United States of America (in cm)

| | | 174 | 179 | 183 | 189 | |
| 160 to 164 | 165 to 169 | 170 to 174 | 175 to 179 | 180 to 184 | 185 to 189 | 190 to 194 |

10. What is the range of heights of the 43 U.S. presidents in the chart?

    (A) 30 cm
    (B) 34 cm
    (C) 35 cm
    (D) 163 cm
    (E) 178 cm

11. What is the median height of the 43 U.S. presidents in the chart, in centimeters?

    (A) 175
    (B) 177
    (C) 178
    (D) 180
    (E) 182

12. Approximately what percent of U.S. presidents are 185 centimeters or taller?

    (A)  10%
    (B)  23%
    (C)  29%
    (D)  43%
    (E)  50%

13. If $m + 5 < \dfrac{3}{2}$, which of the following could be the value of $m$?

    (A)  $-\dfrac{15}{4}$
    (B)  $-\dfrac{7}{2}$
    (C)  $-2$
    (D)  $\dfrac{7}{2}$
    (E)  $2$

14. List M consists of the numbers 10, 20, 30, 40, 50.

    Which of the following lists of numbers have an average (arithmetic mean) that is equal to the average of the numbers in list M?

    Indicate all such lists.

    ☐   0, 30, 60
    ☐   10, 20, 30, 35, 50
    ☐   10, 22, 30, 38, 50
    ☐   0, 0, 0, 0, 150

**MANHATTAN**
PREP

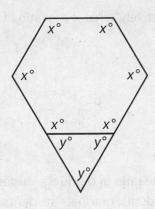

15. What is the value of *xy*?

**Buying Habits of Customers Buying Toothpaste X at Chan's Grocery Store**

| Discount Type | Manufacturers' Coupon | Store Coupon | No Coupon |
|---|---|---|---|
| Percent of Customers | 54% | 43% | x% |

16. The table above summarizes all possible discount types for customers buying toothpaste X at a certain grocery store. No one used both types of coupon. If a person is selected randomly from among the customers buying toothpaste X at Chan's Grocery Store, what is the probability that this customer did not use a coupon?

   (A)  0.003
   (B)  0.03
   (C)  0.3
   (D)  0.33
   (E)  3.3

17. Company A can pave 500 feet of sidewalk in 6 hours, and company B can pave 1,000 feet of sidewalk in 8 hours. At these rates, how many more <u>yards</u> of sidewalk can company B pave in 9 hours than company A can pave in 9 hours? (3 feet = 1 yard)

   (A)  125
   (B)  166
   (C)  333
   (D)  375
   (E)  500

18.  If the three sides of an equilateral triangle are equal to 4x, 6y, and 24, respectively, what is the ratio of x to y?

Give your answer as a fraction.

19.  If the ratio of undergraduate students to graduate students is 7 to 4 and the ratio of graduate students to professors is 2 to 1, which could be the total number of undergraduate students, graduate students, and professors?

Indicate all such numbers.

☐   520

☐   640

☐   2,600

☐   10,000

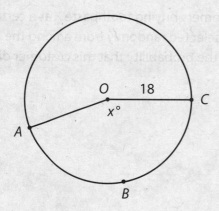

20.  If O is the center of the circle and x = 160, what is the perimeter of sector ABCO?

(A)  $18 + 8\pi$

(B)  $18 + 16\pi$

(C)  $36 + 8\pi$

(D)  $36 + 16\pi$

(E)  $36 + 24\pi$

# Answers to Math Practice Section 1

**1. (C).** The average of three consecutive integers is always equal to the middle value and is always equal to the average of the smallest and largest terms. Since Quantity B represents the average of the smallest and largest terms, it is equal to the middle term $y$.

Alternatively, pick numbers. If $x$, $y$, and $z$ are 1, 2, and 3, then Quantity A = 2 and Quantity B = $\dfrac{1+3}{2} = 2$. The two quantities are equal. Any other example of three consecutive numbers will also yield equal quantities.

**2. (A).** In Quantity A, $(-3)^4 = (-3)(-3)(-3)(-3) = 81$. In Quantity B, $(-3)^{-3} = \dfrac{1}{(-3)^3} = \dfrac{1}{-27}$. Quantity A is greater.

Note that you can stop calculating as soon as you realize that one quantity is positive and one is negative. The negative base in both quantities suggests that you should check whether the exponents are odd or even. Even exponents "hide the sign" of the base, so a negative base to a even exponent is positive. On the other hand, a negative base to an odd exponent remains negative (even if the exponent is a *negative* odd).

**3. (D).** If this were a right triangle, the Pythagorean theorem would indicate the following:

$$3^2 + 4^2 = x^2$$
$$9 + 16 = x^2$$
$$25 = x^2$$
$$5 = x$$

However, the triangle is not known to be right (the Pythagorean theorem only applies to right triangles) as none of the angles are labeled. The Third Side Rule, which applies to all triangles regardless of angle measures, states that the third side of any triangle must be greater than the difference between the other two sides and less than the sum of the other two sides. So $x$ must be greater than $4 - 3 = 1$ and less than $4 + 3 = 7$. Since $x$ could be less than, greater than, or equal to 5, it cannot be determined which quantity is greater.

**4. (D).** Since the terms in Quantity A have the same base and are multiplied together, simplify by adding the exponents:

$$y^7 \times y^8 \times y^{-6} = y^9$$

While $y^9$ may *seem* smaller than $3y^9$, this is only true if $y$ is positive. If $y = 0$, the two quantities are equal. If $y$ is negative, so is $y^9$, and $3y^9$ is more negative than $y^9$. Therefore, the relationship cannot be determined from the information given.

**5. (B).** Since $xy > 0$, $x$ and $y$ have the same sign. Since $yz < 0$, $y$ and $z$ have opposite signs. Therefore, $x$ and $z$ have opposite signs. If $x$ and $z$ have opposite signs, their product is negative, which is less than 0. Quantity B is greater.

**6. (A).** In order to calculate the percent change in profit from 2011 to 2012, first calculate the profits in each year based on the formula: Profit = Revenues − Costs.

Therefore,

> Profit per each copy of the magazine in 2011 = $2.30 − $1.30 = $1.00
> Profit per each copy of the magazine in 2012 = $3.00 − $1.50 = $1.50

To find the percent increase, use the percent change formula:

$$\text{Percent Change} = \left( \frac{Difference}{Original} \times 100 \right)\%$$

$$\text{Percent Change} = \left( \frac{0.50}{1.00} \times 100 \right)\% = 50\%$$

Be careful not to put the 2012 profit in the denominator. Mistakenly doing so would lead you to pick (C) erroneously. The "Original" profit is that for 2011.

Quantity A is greater.

7. **(B).** Since the terms in list Y are "each computed from the corresponding term in list X by dividing the number in list X by 2, then adding 5 to the result," list Y consists of 7, 8.5, 9.5, 10.5, 17, 21. Therefore, you can solve:

> Quantity A: The range is 21 − 7 = 14.
> Quantity B: 6 less than the greatest number in list Y = 21 − 6 = 15.

Quantity B is greater.

8. **(B).** A square with area $a$ has sides of $\sqrt{a}$. Use the Pythagorean theorem with $\sqrt{a}$ for each leg and $d$ for the hypotenuse:

$$\left(\sqrt{a}\right)^2 + \left(\sqrt{a}\right)^2 = d^2$$
$$a + a = d^2$$
$$2a = d^2$$
$$\sqrt{2a} = d$$

This is a match with choice (B). Alternatively, plug in numbers. If a square has side length 4, the area equals 16 and the diagonal would be:

$$4^2 + 4^2 = d^2$$
$$32 = d^2$$
$$\sqrt{32} = d$$

Plug $a = 16$ into each choice to see which yields $d = \sqrt{32}$. Only choice (B) works.

**MANHATTAN**
PREP

9. **(D).** The easiest way to solve this problem is to choose a smart number for the total number of apartments in the apartment complex. As this is a percents problem, choose a total of 100 apartments. Since 60% of these apartments have at least one television, 60 apartments contain a television (or more than one television—it doesn't matter how many—only television at all vs. no television matters) and 40 apartments do not contain a television.

Since 20% of the apartments that contain a television are equipped with cable, 20% of 60 = 0.2 × 60 = 12 apartments have both television and cable.

"Every apartment that is equipped with cable contains at least one television" means that none of the 40 apartments without a television are equipped with cable. Thus, only 12 apartments are equipped with cable, meaning 100 − 12 = 88 are not. Alternatively, 48 + 40 = 88 apartments are not equipped with cable.

Since 88 out of 100 apartments are not equipped with cable, the answer is 88%.

Alternatively, you can assign the variable $x$ to the total number of apartments in the apartment complex. Following the steps from above, $0.6x$ apartments contain a television and $(0.2)(0.6x) = 0.12x$ apartments are equipped with cable. From here, $x − 0.12x = 0.88x$ apartments, or 88% of the apartments in the complex, do not have cable.

10. **(A).** The shortest U.S. president is 163 centimeters tall and the tallest is 193 centimeters tall. The range is the difference between the highest and lowest values, so 193 cm − 163 cm = 30 cm.

11. **(E).** The median is the middle value if all the data points are arranged from least to greatest. With 43 data points, the median is the 22nd data point, because there are 21 data points that are less than or equal to that point, and 21 that are greater than or equal to that point. Counting up from the least value (or down from the greatest value), the 22nd data point is 182 cm.

12. **(B).** From the chart, 10 U.S. presidents are 185 cm or taller, out of a total of 43. As a percent, this is $\left( \frac{10}{43} \times 100 \right)$%, or approximately 23%.

13. **(A).** Solve the inequality:

$$m + 5 < \frac{3}{2}$$

$$m < \frac{3}{2} - 5$$

$$m < \frac{3}{2} - \frac{10}{2}$$

$$m < -\frac{7}{2}$$

Answer choice (A) is the only one that is less than $-\frac{7}{2}$. If needed, plug each answer choice into the calculator and compare decimal values to −3.5.

14. **{0, 30, 60} and {10, 22, 30, 38, 50} and {0, 0, 0, 0, 150} only.** Certainly, you could average the list 10, 20, 30, 40, 50 (the average is 30) and then average the lists in all the answer choices to see which also averages to 30. However, you cannot afford to waste any time on the GRE.

Instead, note that the average of an evenly spaced set is equal to the median. Thus, the average of 10, 20, 30, 40, 50 is the median, or middle term, 30. In the first choice, the list 0, 30, 60 is also evenly spaced, so the average is 30.

In the second choice, the list 10, 20, 30, 35, 50 is the same as the original list (10, 20, 30, 40, 50) except for one number—the 40 has been changed to 35. Thus, the averages cannot be the same.

In the third choice, the list 10, 22, 30, 38, 50 is the same as the original list (10, 20, 30, 40, 50), but with 2 taken away from the fourth number and added to the second number. Since the sum didn't change, the average didn't either.

In the fourth choice, the average is the sum divided by the number of items, or $\frac{150}{5} = 30$.

15. **7,200.** Since every angle in the hexagon is labeled $x°$, the hexagon is equiangular. To find the sum of the degree measures in a polygon, use the formula $(n - 2)(180)$, where $n$ is the number of sides. Since $n = 6$, then $(6 - 2)(180) = 720$, so the sum of the degrees in the hexagon is 720. Thus, $6x = 720$ and $x = 120$.

Since the triangle is equiangular, $3y = 180$ and $y = 60$.

Thus, the value of $xy = 120 \times 60 = 7,200$.

16. **(B).** Add 54% + 43% = 97% to get the percent of customers who used a coupon. Only 100% − 97% = 3% of customers did not use a coupon. Thus, for a person selected randomly from among the customers buying toothpaste X at Chan's Grocery Store, there is a 3%, or 0.03, probability that he or she did not use a coupon.

17. **(A).** Company A can pave 500 feet of sidewalk in 6 hours, and thus $\frac{500}{6}$ feet per hour. In 9 hours, company A can pave $\frac{500}{6} \times 9 = 750$ feet of sidewalk.

Company B can pave 1,000 feet of sidewalk in 8 hours, and thus $\frac{1000}{8} = 125$ feet per hour. In 9 hours, company B can pave $125 \times 9 = 1,125$ feet of sidewalk.

Thus, in 9 hours, company B can pave 1,125 − 750 = 375 feet of sidewalk more than company A. Since 3 feet = 1 yard, divide by 3 to get the answer in the correct units: 375 feet ÷ 3 feet per yard = 125 yards.

18. $\frac{3}{2}$ **(or any equivalent fraction).** Since the sides of an equilateral triangle are all equal, $4x = 6y = 24$. With a three part equation, you can equate any two parts you wish.

For instance:

$$4x = 24$$
$$x = 6$$
$$6y = 24$$
$$y = 4$$

Thus, the ratio of $x$ to $y$ is 6 to 4, which reduces to 3 to 2. On the GRE, you do not need to reduce the answers to fraction numeric entry questions.

19. **520 and 2,600 only.** If the ratio of undergraduate students to graduate students is 7 to 4 and the ratio of graduate students to professors is 2 to 1:

| Undergraduate | Graduate | Professors |
|---------------|----------|------------|
| 7 | 4 | |
| | 2 | 1 |

Equate the ratios by making the two numbers under "Graduate" equal. To do this, double the second ratio. (If you change one number in the ratio 2 : 1, you must perform the same operation to the other number in that ratio.)

| Undergraduate | Graduate | Professors |
|---------------|----------|------------|
| 7 | 4 | |
| | 4 | 2 |

Now, collapse the ratios onto one line:

| Undergraduate | Graduate | Professors |
|---------------|----------|------------|
| 7 | 4 | 2 |

The ratio is 7 to 4 to 2. Since $7 + 4 + 2 = 13$ and numbers of people must be integers, the total number of people must be a multiple of 13. Only 520 and 2,600 qualify.

20. **(D).** If $x = 160$, then the sector is $\dfrac{160}{360} = \dfrac{4}{9}$ of the circle. Thus, arc $ABC$ is $\dfrac{4}{9}$ of the circumference. Since the circumference is equal to $2\pi r = 2\pi(18) = 36\pi$, take $\dfrac{4}{9}(36\pi)$ to yield $16\pi$.

Thus, the perimeter of the sector is equal to two radii plus $16\pi$, or $36 + 16\pi$.

# Math Practice Section 2: Medium Difficulty

Math Practice Section: Medium
20 Questions
35 Minutes

For questions in the Quantitative Comparison format ("Quantity A" and "Quantity B" given), the answer choices are always as follows:

(A)    Quantity A is greater.
(B)    Quantity B is greater.
(C)    The two quantities are equal.
(D)    The relationship cannot be determined from the information given.

For questions followed by a numeric entry box [        ], you are to enter your own answer in the box. For questions followed

by a fraction-style numeric entry box $\frac{\boxed{\phantom{xx}}}{\boxed{\phantom{xx}}}$, you are to enter your answer in the form of a fraction. You are not required to

reduce fractions. For example, if the answer is $\frac{1}{4}$, you may enter $\frac{25}{100}$ or any equivalent fraction.

All numbers used are real numbers. All figures are assumed to lie in a plane unless otherwise indicated. Geometric figures are not necessarily drawn to scale. You should assume, however, that lines that appear to be straight are actually straight, points on a line are in the order shown, and all geometric objects are in the relative positions shown. Coordinate systems, such as xy-planes and number lines, as well as graphical data presentations such as bar charts, circle graphs, and line graphs, are drawn to scale. A symbol that appears more than once in a question has the same meaning throughout the question.

Set M consists of all the integers between −2 and 12, inclusive.
Set N consists of all the integers between 9 and 15, inclusive.

|  | **Quantity A** | **Quantity B** |
|---|---|---|
| 1. | The smallest integer in set M that is also in set N | 9 |

17% of $p$ is equal to 18% of $q$, where $p$ and $q$ are positive.

|  | **Quantity A** | **Quantity B** |
|---|---|---|
| 2. | $p$ | $q$ |

Circle A has area $a$. Semicircle B has area $\frac{a}{2}$.

|  | **Quantity A** | **Quantity B** |
|---|---|---|
| 3. | The circumference of circle A | Twice the perimeter of semicircle B |

**MANHATTAN**
PREP

|                          | **Quantity A**                              | **Quantity B**                              |
|--------------------------|---------------------------------------------|---------------------------------------------|

4. 

| **Quantity A** | **Quantity B** |
|----------------|----------------|
| The standard deviation of the set 1, 5, 7, 19 | The standard deviation of the set 0, 5, 7, 20 |

An isosceles triangle has a perimeter of 28. The shortest side has length 8.

| **Quantity A** | **Quantity B** |
|----------------|----------------|
| 5. The length of the longest side of the triangle | 12 |

$$(3 - z)(z + 4) = 0$$

| **Quantity A** | **Quantity B** |
|----------------|----------------|
| 6. $z$ | 5 |

$$a > b > c > d$$
$$ab > 0$$
$$ad < 0$$

| **Quantity A** | **Quantity B** |
|----------------|----------------|
| 7. $ac$ | $cd$ |

8. If $12b = 2g$ and $4g - 3b = 63$, what is the value of $\dfrac{g}{b}$ ?

Give your answer as a fraction.

9. $81^3 + 27^4$ is equivalent to which of the following expressions?

Indicate __all__ such expressions.

- ☐ $3^7(2)$
- ☐ $3^{12}(2)$
- ☐ $9^6(2)$
- ☐ $9^{12}$
- ☐ $3^{24}$

Questions 10–12 are based on the following chart.

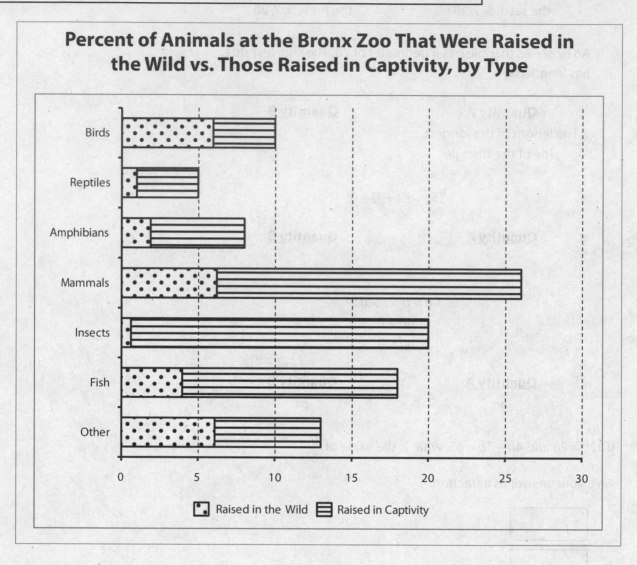

### Percent of Animals at the Bronx Zoo That Were Raised in the Wild vs. Those Raised in Captivity, by Type

Raised in the Wild    Raised in Captivity

10. Approximately what percent of all the zoo's animals are either mammals that were raised in the wild or amphibians raised in captivity?

   (A)  8
   (B)  12
   (C)  18
   (D)  34
   (E)  100

**MANHATTAN**
PREP

11. If the Bronx Zoo donated all of its insects and fish to other zoos, approximately what percent of the animals in the zoo would be birds raised in the wild?

   (A) 5
   (B) 9
   (C) 24
   (D) 32
   (E) 60

12. If the zoo currently has 80 total birds, what is the smallest number of birds that could be added such that at least 20% of the animals at the zoo would be birds?

   (A) 10
   (B) 80
   (C) 100
   (D) 125
   (E) 200

13. Trail mix is made by combining 3 pounds of nuts that cost $x$ dollars per pound with 1 pound of chocolate that costs $y$ dollars per pound and 2 pounds of dried fruit that costs $z$ dollars per pound. What is the cost in dollars per pound for the trail mix?

   (A) $\dfrac{3x+y+2z}{xyz}$

   (B) $3x+y+2z$

   (C) $\dfrac{3x+y+2z}{6}$

   (D) $6(3x+y+2z)$

   (E) $\dfrac{x}{3}+y+\dfrac{2}{z}$

14. If $z = 3^4$, then $\left(3^z\right)^z =$

   (A) $3^{16}$
   (B) $3^{81}$
   (C) $3^{324}$
   (D) $3^{405}$
   (E) $3^{6,561}$

15. Maurice entered a number into his calculator and erroneously divided the number by 0.03 instead of 0.0003, resulting in an incorrect result. Which of the following is a single operation that Maurice could perform on his calculator to correct the error?

    Indicate <u>all</u> such operations.

    ☐ Multiply the incorrect product by 100
    ☐ Divide the incorrect product by 100
    ☐ Multiply the incorrect product by 0.01
    ☐ Divide the incorrect product by 0.01

16. A company's annual expenses are composed entirely of a fixed amount in costs, plus a variable amount that is directly proportional to the number of clients served. In 2009, the company served 450 clients and its total expense was $830,000. In 2010, the company served 510 clients and its total expense was $896,000. What is the company's fixed annual expense, in dollars?

    (A) 1,757
    (B) 1,844
    (C) 335,000
    (D) 485,000
    (E) 830,000

17. Which of the following lines is perpendicular to $4x + 5y = 9$ on the $xy$-plane?

    (A) $y = \dfrac{5}{4}x + 2$

    (B) $y = -\dfrac{5}{4}x + 9$

    (C) $y = -4x + \dfrac{9}{5}$

    (D) $y = \dfrac{4}{5}x - \dfrac{4}{5}$

    (E) $y = -\dfrac{4}{5}x$

18. The tens digit is missing from the three-digit number 8 __ 9. If the tens digit is to be randomly selected from the ten different digits from 0 to 9, what is the probability that the resulting three-digit number will be a multiple of 9?

    (A) 0.1
    (B) 0.2
    (C) 0.4
    (D) 0.9
    (E) 1

**MANHATTAN**
PREP

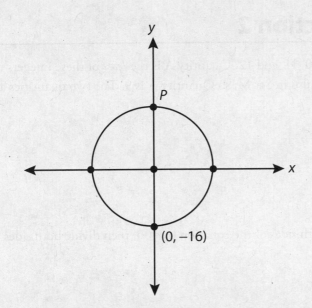

19. In the figure above, the circle is centered at (0, 0). What is the distance between point $P$ and the point (−10, −8) (not shown on the graph)?

    (A)  18

    (B)  20

    (C)  22

    (D)  24

    (E)  26

20. If $f(-0.5) = 0$, which of the following could be $f(x)$?

    (A)  $2x + 2$

    (B)  $4x - 2$

    (C)  $4x^2 - 1$

    (D)  $x^2 - 1$

    (E)  $(-x)^2 - 2.5$

# Answers to Math Practice Section 2

**1. (C).** Set M consists of −2, −1, 0, 1, 2, 3, 4, 5, 6, 7, 8, 9, 10, 11, and 12. Quantity A is the *least* of these integers that is also in set N. The smallest integer in set N is 9, which is also in Set M, so Quantity A is 9. The two quantities are equal.

**2. (A).** Written out as algebra, "17% of $p$ is equal to 18% of $q$" is:

$$\frac{17}{100}p = \frac{18}{100}q$$

Solve for $p$. The easiest way to do this is to first multiply both sides of the equation by 100, then divide both sides by 17:

$$p = \frac{18}{17}q$$

Since $\frac{18}{17}$ is greater than 1 and both variables are positive, $p$ is greater than $q$.

(Note that it was necessary to know that both variables were positive! If they were negative, $p = \frac{18}{17}q$ would imply that $p$ is more negative than $q$, so $q$ would have been greater than $p$. Without information about sign, the answer would have been (D).)

**3. (B).** If the given semicircle has half the area of the circle, then the semicircle $B$ is just one of the pieces you get after cutting circle $A$ exactly in half through its center. However, that does *not* mean that the semicircle has half the perimeter. Observe:

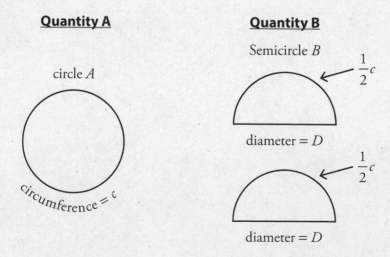

**Quantity A**

circle $A$

circumference $= c$

**Quantity B**

Semicircle $B$

$\frac{1}{2}c$

diameter $= D$

$\frac{1}{2}c$

diameter $= D$

The semicircle is drawn twice, as Quantity B refers to "twice the perimeter of semicircle $B$." Note that Quantity A is equal to the circumference $c$, while Quantity B is equal to this same circumference, plus twice the length of the diameter. Quantity B is greater.

**MANHATTAN**
PREP

**4. (B).** Standard deviation measures the variance from the mean; the more spread out a set is, the higher the deviation. The set in Quantity B is the same as the one in Quantity A, but with the smallest number *even smaller* and the largest number *even larger*, so the set in Quantity B is more spread out and thus has a greater standard deviation.

**5. (D).** An isosceles triangle has two sides that are equal and a third side that is a different length. The isosceles triangle in this question has a perimeter of 28 and shortest side of length 8. Now, suppose that the shortest side is the one that is repeated, such that the triangle has two sides of length 8 and one other side of length $x$. This would mean:

$$8 + 8 + x = \text{Perimeter}$$
$$16 + x = 28$$
$$x = 12$$

This triangle would have lengths 8, 8, and 12 as the three legs. Test this triangle via the Third Side Rule: the length of any side of a triangle must be greater than the difference between the other two sides and less than the sum of the other two sides. The third side ($x$) must be greater than $8 - 8 = 0$ and less than $8 + 8 = 16$. Since 12 is between 0 and 16, this is a legal triangle.

On the other hand, consider the possibility that the other side, $x$, is repeated and the length 8 is used only once. In this case:

$$x + x + 8 = 28$$
$$2x = 20$$
$$x = 10$$

The sides of this triangle are 10, 10, and 8. Test this triangle via the Third Side Rule: the third side (8) must be greater than $10 - 10 = 0$ and less than $10 + 10 = 20$. Since 8 is between 0 and 20, this is a legal triangle.

For one triangle, the quantities in Quantity A and Quantity B would be equal, but for the other, Quantity B would be greater than Quantity A. Therefore, the relationship cannot be determined from the information given.

**6. (B).** $(3 - z)(z + 4) = 0$, so either $(3 - z)$ or $(z + 4)$ must equal 0:

$$3 - z = 0$$
$$z = 3$$

OR

$$z + 4 = 0$$
$$z = -4$$

Thus, $z$ is either 3 or $-4$. Either way, Quantity B is greater.

**7. (D).** If $ad < 0$, $a$ and $d$ have opposite signs. Because $a > d$, $a$ must be positive and $d$ must be negative. Similarly, if $ab > 0$, $a$ and $b$ have the same sign, so $a$ and $b$ are both positive. The remaining variable $c$ can be positive, 0, or negative and still fall between $b$ and $d$. If $c$ is 0, the two quantities are equal. If $c$ is positive, Quantity A is positive and

Quantity B is negative. If $c$ is negative, Quantity B is positive and Quantity A is negative. The relationship cannot be determined from the information given.

Alternatively, pick numbers. If $a = 4$, $b = 3$, $c = 2$, and $d = -1$, then all the criteria of the problem are fulfilled and Quantity A is greater. But if $a = 4$, $b = 3$, $c = -5$, and $d = -10$, then all the criteria of the problem are still fulfilled, but Quantity B is greater.

8. $\dfrac{6}{1}$ **(or any equivalent fraction).** Solve one equation for a single variable, and substitute into the other equation:

| Eq. (1): $12b = 2g$ | Eq. (2): $4g - 3b = 63$ |
|---|---|
| $6b = g$ | Isolate $g$ in Eq. (1). Divide by 2. |
| $4(6b) - 3b = 63$ | Substitute $(6b)$ for $g$ in Eq. (2). |
| $24b - 3b = 63$ | Solve for $b$. Simplify. |
| $21b = 63$ | Combine like terms. |
| $b = 3$ | Divide by 21. |
| $12(3) = 2g$ | Substitute (3) for $b$ in Eq. (1). Solve for $g$. |
| $36 = 2g$ | Simplify. |
| $g = 18$ | Divide by 2. |

Since $b = 3$ and $g = 18$, $\dfrac{g}{b} = \dfrac{6}{1}$.

9. $3^{12}(2)$ **and** $9^6(2)$ **only.** To simplify $81^3 + 27^4$, note that both bases are powers of 3. Rewrite the bases and combine:

$$81^3 + 27^4 =$$
$$(3^4)^3 + (3^3)^4 =$$
$$3^{12} + 3^{12} =$$
$$3^{12}(1 + 1) =$$
$$3^{12}(2)$$

Since $3^{12}(2)$ appears in the choices, this is one answer. However, this is an "indicate <u>all</u>" question, so you should check whether any other choices are equivalent. One other choice, $9^6(2)$, also qualifies, since $9^6(2) = (3^2)^6(2) = 3^{12}(2)$.

10. **(B).** Of the animals, 26% are mammals and about a quarter *of those* were raised in the wild: $\dfrac{1}{4}$ of 26% = about 6.5%.

Of the animals, 8% are amphibians and about three quarters *of those* were raised in captivity: $\dfrac{3}{4}$ of 8% = about 6 %.

In total, these two categories account for about 12% of all the zoo's animals.

11. **(B).** To solve this question, imagine that there were originally 100 animals in the zoo. If the zoo gives away all the insects and fish, then there are 38 fewer animals (20 + 18) in the zoo, or 62. But there are still 10 birds, which now make up about 16% of the zoo's animals (use your calculator to find this if you don't feel comfortable estimating). Of those, a little more than half were raised in the wild. Among the choices, only 9% is a little more than half of 16%.

**MANHATTAN**
PREP

12. **(C).** If the zoo has 80 birds, which make up 10% of the total number of animals at the zoo, then there are 800 animals total. To correctly calculate how many birds must be added, realize that any birds added increases not only the subtotal of 80 birds but also the total of 800 animals. If adding new animals (rather than trading reptiles for birds, for example), you cannot just double the number of birds to double the percent of the animals that are birds!

Thus, use the following inequality:

$$\frac{80+x}{800+x} \geq \frac{20}{100}$$

$$100(80+x) \geq 20(800+x)$$

$$8{,}000+100x \geq 16{,}000+20x$$

$$80x \geq 8{,}000$$

$$x \geq 100$$

At least 100 birds must be added such that at least 20% of the animals at the zoo would be birds (check: there would be 180 birds among 900 animals, or 20% of the total).

13. **(C).** This question is a tricky one, because even though it never uses the word *average* or the word *ratio*, it's more or less a combined ratio and averages question. The trail mix is nuts, chocolate, and dried fruit in a ratio of 3 : 1 : 2. For every 6 pounds of trail mix, there are 3 pounds of nuts, 1 pound of chocolate, and 2 pounds of dried fruit.

The cost of 6 pounds of trail mix is $3x + y + 2z$. However, to solve for the cost of one pound, divide by 6. You could also think of this as a kind of average:

$$\text{Average} = \frac{(\text{Sum})}{(\#\text{ of terms})} = \frac{(3x+y+2z)}{6}, \text{ where each "term" is a pound.}$$

This is choice (C). Alternatively, pick numbers. For example:

$$x = 6$$
$$y = 5$$
$$z = 2$$

In this example, 3 pounds of nuts that cost $x = 6$ dollars per pound plus 1 pound of chocolate that costs $y = 5$ dollars per pound plus 2 pounds of dried fruit that costs $z = 2$ dollars per pound would cost:

$$3(6) + 1(5) + 2(2) = 27$$

Thus, 6 pounds of trail mix (3 lbs. nuts + 1 lb. chocolate + 2 lbs. dried fruit) would cost $27. So, 1 pound would cost one-sixth of that: $\frac{27}{6}$ or $\frac{9}{2}$ dollars, which is $4.50.

Now, plug $x = 6$, $y = 5$, and $z = 2$ into the choices to see which answer yields $4.50. Only (C) works.

14. **(E).** Since $3^4 = 81$, $z = 81$. So, $\left(3^z\right)^z$ is equal to $\left(3^{81}\right)^{81} = 3^{81 \times 81} = 3^{6{,}561}$.

15. **"Multiply the incorrect product by 100" and "Divide the incorrect product by 0.01" only.** Since 0.03 is 100 times greater than 0.0003, when Maurice accidentally divided by 0.03 instead of 0.0003, he divided by a number 100 times too big. Thus, multiplying by 100 will correct the error. Thus, the first choice is correct.

However, dividing by any quantity is the same as multiplying by its reciprocal. So, multiplying by 100 is the same as dividing by 0.01. Thus, the fourth choice is also correct.

Alternatively, pick a number. Divide by both 0.03 and 0.0003, and then check each answer to see which correct the error. Choose 12 as the original number.

|  |  |
|---|---|
| 12 divided by 0.03 = 400 | INCORRECT RESULT |
| 12 divided by 0.0003 = 40,000 | CORRECT RESULT |

Now, perform the operation in each answer choice on the incorrect product, 400, to see which operations turn that product into 40,000. The first and the fourth operations listed as choices both work.

16. **(C).** Begin by constructing a function describing the situation in the problem. Using $E$ for expenses, $x$ for the number of clients, $c$ for the expense per client, and $f$ for fixed costs:

$$E(x) = xc + f$$

In words, expense as a function of the number of clients equals the number of clients multiplied by the variable cost per client, plus the fixed cost.

In 2009, the company served 450 clients and its total expense was \$830,000. Thus:

$$830,000 = 450c + f$$

In 2010, the company served 510 clients and its total expense was \$896,000. Thus:

$$896,000 = 510c + f$$

Since it is easier to isolate $f$ than $c$ in each equation, get $f$ by itself for each equation and then set the opposite sides equal:

$$830,000 = 450c + f$$
$$f = 830,000 - 450c$$

$$896,000 = 510c + f$$
$$f = 896,000 - 510c$$

$$830,000 - 450c = 896,000 - 510c$$
$$830,000 + 60c = 896,000$$
$$60c = 66,000$$
$$c = 1,100$$

**MANHATTAN**
PREP

Plug $c = 1,100$ into either equation to find $f$:

$$f = 830,000 - 450(1,100)$$
$$f = 335,000$$

Alternatively, subtract \$896,000 − \$830,000 to get \$66,000, which must be the cost difference between serving 450 clients and serving 510 clients (a difference of 60 clients). Divide \$66,000 by 60 clients to get \$1,100, the variable cost per client. Then, multiply \$1,100 × 450 = \$495,000 to get the variable cost of serving 450 clients, not counting the fixed cost. Finally, subtract this figure from the total cost of serving 450 clients to get the fixed cost: \$830,000 − \$495,000 = \$335,000. The numbers should look familiar; the point is that you can "reason through it" without strictly setting up equations.

17. **(A).** First, algebraically manipulate $4x + 5y = 9$ into $y = mx + b$ format, where $m$ is the slope and $b$ is the $y$-intercept:

$$4x + 5y = 9$$
$$5y = -4x + 9$$
$$y = -\frac{4}{5}x + \frac{9}{5}$$

Since $m = -\frac{4}{5}$, the slope is $-\frac{4}{5}$. Perpendicular lines have negative reciprocal slopes. Thus, the correct answer has a slope of $\frac{5}{4}$. Only choice (A) qualifies.

18. **(A).** If the tens digit is to be randomly selected from the digits 0 to 9, there are ten possibilities for the completed number. Using your calculator, divide each by 9 to see which ones are multiples of 9:

| | | |
|---|---|---|
| 809 | ← | not a multiple of 9 |
| 819 | ← | MULTIPLE OF 9 |
| 829 | ← | not a multiple of 9 |
| 839 | ← | not a multiple of 9 |
| 849 | ← | not a multiple of 9 |
| 859 | ← | not a multiple of 9 |
| 869 | ← | not a multiple of 9 |
| 879 | ← | not a multiple of 9 |
| 889 | ← | not a multiple of 9 |
| 899 | ← | not a multiple of 9 |

The answer is $\frac{1}{10}$, or 0.1.

Alternatively, a number is divisible by 9 if the sum of its digits is a multiple of 9. The existing digits sum to $8 + 9 = 17$, so the addition of 0 through 9 means that the sum of all three digits could be 17 through 26, inclusive. Only one multiple of 9 (i.e., 18) is found in this range.

19. **(E).** Because the circle is centered at (0, 0) and passes through (0, −16), the radius of the circle is 16. Point *P* lies on the circle and the *y*-axis, so it lies exactly one radius above the origin. Point *P*'s coordinates are therefore (0, 16). To find the distance between (0, 16) and (−10, −8), either use the distance formula, or draw a graph and make a right triangle on which you can use the Pythagorean theorem.

From the distance formula, $d = \sqrt{(x_2 - x_1)^2 + (y_2 - y_1)^2}$ :

$$d = \sqrt{(-10 - 0)^2 + (-8 - 16)^2}$$
$$d = \sqrt{(-10)^2 + (-24)^2}$$
$$d = \sqrt{676}$$
$$d = 26$$

To use the triangle method, plot (0, 16) and (−10, −8), then drop a line down from (0, 16) to make a right triangle. To do so, you will need to add the third point (0, −8):

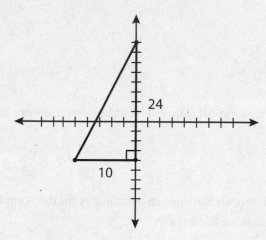

Use the coordinates to determine the lengths of the legs, then use the Pythagorean theorem (the hypotenuse is *d*):

$$24^2 + 10^2 = d^2$$
$$576 + 100 = d^2$$
$$676 = d^2$$
$$d = 26$$

20. **(C).** If $f(-0.5) = 0$, then the answer is 0 when $x = -0.5$. For each choice, plug in −0.5 for *x*. Only if the result is 0 could the choice be $f(x)$:

(A) $2x + 2 = 2(-0.5) + 2 = -1 + 2 = 1$
(B) $4x - 2 = 4(-0.5) - 2 = -2 - 2 = -4$
(C) $4x^2 - 1 = 4(-0.5)^2 - 1 = 4(0.25) - 1 = 1 - 1 = 0$          CORRECT
(D) $x^2 - 1 = (-0.5)^2 - 1 = 0.25 - 1 = -0.75$
(E) $(-x)^2 - 2.5 = (-(-0.5))^2 - 2.5 = (0.5)^2 - 2.5 = 0.25 - 2.5 = -2.25$

**MANHATTAN**
PREP

# Math Practice Section 3: Hard Difficulty

**Math Practice Section: Hard**
**20 Questions**
**35 Minutes**

For questions in the Quantitative Comparison format ("Quantity A" and "Quantity B" given), the answer choices are always as follows:

(A)    Quantity A is greater.
(B)    Quantity B is greater.
(C)    The two quantities are equal.
(D)    The relationship cannot be determined from the information given.

For questions followed by a numeric entry box [          ], you are to enter your own answer in the box. For questions followed

by a fraction-style numeric entry box $\frac{\quad}{\quad}$, you are to enter your answer in the form of a fraction. You are not required to

reduce fractions. For example, if the answer is $\frac{1}{4}$, you may enter $\frac{25}{100}$ or any equivalent fraction.

All numbers used are real numbers. All figures are assumed to lie in a plane unless otherwise indicated. Geometric figures are not necessarily drawn to scale. You should assume, however, that lines that appear to be straight are actually straight, points on a line are in the order shown, and all geometric objects are in the relative positions shown. Coordinate systems, such as *xy*-planes and number lines, as well as graphical data presentations such as bar charts, circle graphs, and line graphs, *are* drawn to scale. A symbol that appears more than once in a question has the same meaning throughout the question.

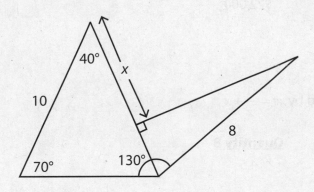

|   | **Quantity A** | **Quantity B** |
|---|---|---|
| 1. | $x$ | 6 |

|   | **Quantity A** | **Quantity B** |
|---|---|---|
| 2. | $(z^6)^x \times z^{3x}$ | $z^{9x}$ |

For a group of test-takers, the scores on an aptitude test were normally distributed, had a mean of 154, and a standard deviation of 3.

| | **Quantity A** | **Quantity B** |
|---|---|---|
| 3. | The fraction of test-takers in the group who scored greater than 158 | $\dfrac{1}{3}$ |

$$3x + 5y + 2z = 20$$
$$6x + 4z = 10$$

| | **Quantity A** | **Quantity B** |
|---|---|---|
| 4. | $y$ by itself | 2 |

Romero Automobiles sells cars only from manufacturer X and manufacturer Y. The range of the list prices of the cars from manufacturer X is $22,000. The range of the list prices of the cars from manufacturer Y is $15,000.

| | **Quantity A** | **Quantity B** |
|---|---|---|
| 5. | The range of the list prices of all automobiles sold by Romero Automobiles | $22,000 |

The operation # is defined by $x\# = \dfrac{1}{x} + x$.

| | **Quantity A** | **Quantity B** |
|---|---|---|
| 6. | (4#)# | 4.5 |

**MANHATTAN**
PREP

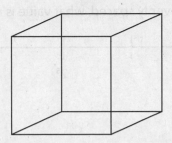

The cube above has side length of 4.

|   | **Quantity A** | **Quantity B** |
|---|---|---|
| 7. | After selecting one vertex of the cube, the number of straight line segments longer than 4 that can be drawn from that vertex of the cube to another vertex of the cube. | When the cube is placed on a flat surface, the maximum number of edges of the cube that can be touching the flat surface at once. |

8.  If $160^2 = 16x$, then $x$ is equivalent to which of the following?

    (A)  10
    (B)  $2^3 5$
    (C)  $2^2 5^2$
    (D)  $2^6 5^2$
    (E)  $2^6 5^3$

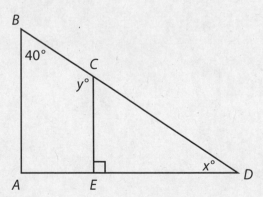

9.  In the triangle shown above, *BA* is parallel to *CE*. What is the value of $x + y$?

| |
|---|
|   |

10. If the tick marks on the number line below are evenly spaced, what value is represented by $x$?

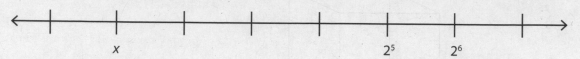

    (A)  $2^0$

    (B)  2

    (C)  $(-2)2^5$

    (D)  $(-3)2^5$

    (E)  $(-4)2^5$

11. If the volume of a cube is $v$, what is the surface area of the cube in terms of $v$?

    (A)  $6\sqrt{v}$

    (B)  $\left(\sqrt[2]{v}\right)^3$

    (C)  $6\left(\sqrt[2]{v}\right)^3$

    (D)  $\left(\sqrt[3]{v}\right)^2$

    (E)  $6\left(\sqrt[3]{v}\right)^2$

12. What is the area of an equilateral triangle with vertices at $(-1, -3)$, $(9, -3)$, and $(m, n)$ where $m$ and $n$ are both positive numbers?

    (A)  $25\sqrt{2}$

    (B)  $50\sqrt{2}$

    (C)  $10\sqrt{3}$

    (D)  $25\sqrt{3}$

    (E)  $50\sqrt{3}$

**MANHATTAN**
PREP

Questions 13–15 are based on the following charts.

## Marital Status of Military Personnel by Gender and Branch

| Marital Status | | Army | Navy | Air Force | Marines |
|---|---|---|---|---|---|
| Single, no children less than 18 years old | Men | 164,513 | 107,349 | 94,800 | 90,949 |
| | Women | 27,492 | 24,757 | 25,247 | 6,338 |
| Single, with children less than 18 years old | Men | 26,571 | 10,506 | 9,544 | 4,807 |
| | Women | 11,037 | 5,859 | 6,313 | 1,263 |
| Married, spouse is also military personnel or retired military | Men | 15,058 | 8,638 | 20,760 | 4,719 |
| | Women | 14,633 | 8,832 | 18,574 | 3,676 |
| Married, spouse is a civilian | Men | 275,953 | 147,255 | 142,573 | 88,233 |
| | Women | 21,687 | 11,175 | 13,982 | 1,858 |

## Number of Military Personnel by Gender and Branch

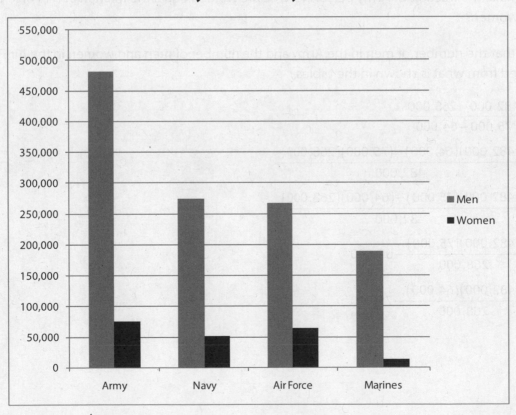

13. Women who are single with children less than 18 years old are the greatest percent of all women within which military branch?

    (A)  Army
    (B)  Navy
    (C)  Air Force
    (D)  Marines
    (E)  It cannot be determined from the information given.

14. If a man whose spouse is also military personnel or retired military were to be selected at random, what would the probability be that he was <u>not</u> in the Air Force?

    (A)  72%
    (B)  58%
    (C)  42%
    (D)  24%
    (E)  13%

15. Which of the following expressions approximates the number of women who would have to enlist in the Army to make the fraction of Army personnel who are women equal the fraction of Air Force personnel who are women?

    (Assume that the number of men in the Army and the number of men and women in the Air Force remain unchanged from what is shown in the tables.)

    (A)  $\dfrac{482,000 - 268,000}{75,000 - 64,000}$

    (B)  $\dfrac{(482,000)(64,000) - (75,000)(268,000)}{482,000}$

    (C)  $\dfrac{(482,000)(75,000) - (64,000)(268,000)}{482,000}$

    (D)  $\dfrac{(482,000)(75,000)}{268,000} - 64,000$

    (E)  $\dfrac{(482,000)(64,000)}{268,000} - 75,000$

16. A cable car travels from Seabreeze to Resortville, making two stops in between. Between Seabreeze and the first stop, the cable car travels $\frac{1}{3}$ of the total distance between Seabreeze and Resortville. Between the first stop and the second stop, the cable car travels $\frac{3}{5}$ of the remaining distance between the first stop and Resortville. What fraction of the entire distance from Seabreeze to Resortville remains between the second stop and Resortville?

    (A)  $1 - \frac{1}{3} - \frac{3}{5}$

    (B)  $1 - \frac{1}{3} - \frac{3}{5}\left(\frac{1}{3}\right)$

    (C)  $1 - \frac{1}{3} - \frac{3}{5}\left(1 - \frac{1}{3}\right)$

    (D)  $1 - \frac{1}{3} - \frac{1}{3}\left(1 - \frac{3}{5}\right)$

    (E)  $1 - \frac{1}{3} - \frac{1}{5}\left(1 - \frac{1}{3} - \frac{1}{5}\right)$

17. If $p$ and $q$ are integers and $20p + 3q$ is odd, which of the following must be odd?

    (A)  $p - q$
    (B)  $p + 2q$
    (C)  $3p + q$
    (D)  $2p + q^2$
    (E)  $3p + 3q$

18. In a study, 4,400 participants were surveyed regarding side effects of a new medication, and $x$ percent reported experiencing drowsiness. If $x$ is rounded to the nearest integer, the result is 8. Which of the following could be the number of survey participants who reported experiencing drowsiness?

Indicate <u>all</u> such values.

    ☐   325
    ☐   330
    ☐   352
    ☐   375

19. $\dfrac{5^3(4^{45}-4^{43})27}{225^2}$ is equivalent to which of the following?

    (A)  $4^{43}$

    (B)  $4^{45}$

    (C)  $4^{90}5^3$

    (D)  $4^{86}5^3 3^3$

    (E)  $4^{90}5^3\,3^3$

20. The following table shows the price of a plane ticket for an April 1st flight, based on the date of purchase.

| Price | When Purchased On |
| --- | --- |
| $210 | March 16 |
| $168 | March 2 |
| $140 | March 1 |

Harpreet purchased a ticket on March 1st. If he had purchased the ticket on March 2nd, he would have paid x percent more. If he had purchased the ticket on March 16th, he would have paid y percent more than he would have paid on March 2nd. What is the positive difference between x and y?

    (A)  5

    (B)  14

    (C)  20

    (D)  25

    (E)  28

# Answers to Math Practice Section 3

1. **(C).** The leftmost triangle has two angles labeled 40° and 70°. Subtract these from 180° (the sum of the angles in any triangle) to determine that the third angle is 70°. Subtract $130 - 70 = 60°$ to get the measure of the adjoining angle in the rightmost triangle.

Since the leftmost triangle is isosceles, the two long sides are each equal to 10.

Since the rightmost triangle is a 30–60–90 triangle, the sides are in the proportion $x : \sqrt{3}\,x : 2x$. Because the hypotenuse is 8 and also the $2x$ in the ratio, the shortest leg of this triangle is $x = 4$.

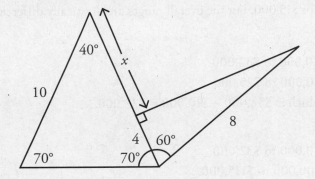

To calculate $x$, subtract: $10 - 4 = 6$. The two quantities are equal.

2. **(C).** The terms in Quantity A have the same base, so add the exponents: $(z^6)^x \times z^{3x} = z^{6x} \times z^{3x} = z^{9x}$. The two quantities are equal. Note that $(z^6)^x$ is interchangeable with $(z^x)^6$ and $z^{6x}$.

3. **(B).** For a normal distribution, approximately two-thirds of the values are within one standard deviation of the mean. Thus, roughly $\frac{1}{6}$ of the population is more than a deviation above the mean, and $\frac{1}{6}$ is more than a deviation below. Thus, about $\frac{1}{6}$ of the test-takers would score greater than 157 ($154 + 3 = 157$, one standard deviation above the mean), so an even smaller fraction of the test-takers would score greater than 158.

4. **(A).** In order to isolate $y$, eliminate both $x$ and $z$. Because there are only two equations, both $x$ and $z$ must be eliminated at the same time if the value of $y$ is to be determined.

Notice that the coefficients for $x$ and $z$ in the second equation (6 and 4, respectively) are exactly double their coefficients in the first equation (3 and 2, respectively). Divide the second equation by 2, making the coefficients the same.

$$3x + 5y + 2z = 20 \qquad \longrightarrow \qquad 3x + 5y + 2z = 20$$
$$6x + 4z = 10 \qquad \longrightarrow \qquad 3x + 2z = 5$$

Now subtract the second equation from the first:

$$3x + 5y + 2z = 20$$
$$\underline{-(3x + 2z = 5)}$$
$$5y = 15$$
$$y = 3$$

Quantity A is greater.

5. **(D).** The range of list prices of automobiles is found by subtracting the price of the least expensive automobile from the price of the most expensive automobile. Given just the range, there is not enough information to determine the maximum and minimum list price vehicles from either manufacturer. Before selecting (D), though, you should try to prove (D). Construct two examples in which the list prices of the cars from manufacturer X have a range of $22,000 and the list prices of the cars from manufacturer Y have a range of $15,000, but the overall ranges are drastically different:

EXAMPLE 1:
List prices of manufacturer X's cars range from $10,000 to $32,000.
List prices of manufacturer Y's cars range from $10,000 to $25,000.
Here, the overall range is the same as X's range, which is $32,000 − $10,000 = $22,000.

EXAMPLE 2:
List prices of manufacturer X's cars range from $10,000 to $32,000.
List prices of manufacturer Y's cars range from $100,000 to $115,000.
Here, the overall range is $115,000 − $10,000 = $105,000.

In Example 1, the range = $22,000 and the quantities are equal. In Example 2, Quantity A is much greater than Quantity B. It is not possible to make the range any smaller than $22,000 (the minimum range of all the prices cannot be *smaller* than the larger of the two ranges of each manufacturer's prices), but it can get much, much larger.

Note that the testing done above was very important! If Quantity B had read "$21,999," the answer would be (A) rather than (D).

6. **(B).** Start inside the parentheses (according to PEMDAS, always deal with parentheses first).

$$4\# = \frac{1}{4} + 4, \text{ or } \frac{17}{4}.$$

Since $4\# = \frac{17}{4}$, plug $\frac{17}{4}$ in for $x$ to get $(4\#)\#$.

Thus, $(4\#)\# = \dfrac{1}{\frac{17}{4}} + \dfrac{17}{4} = \dfrac{4}{17} + \dfrac{17}{4}.$

While you could find a common denominator, it is more efficient to ballpark the value or use the calculator. Ballparking, $\frac{4}{17}$ is less than 0.25 and $\frac{17}{4}$ is exactly 4.25, so the sum is less than 4.5. Using the calculator, $\frac{4}{17} + \frac{17}{4}$ is about 4.485. Quantity B is greater.

7. **(C).** If a cube has side length of 4, all of the "straight line segments" connecting vertices of the cube *along an edge of the cube* will have length of 4. The only straight line segments between vertices that are longer than 4 are those that go diagonally through the cube or diagonally across a face. From a selected vertex of the cube, there are 3 diagonals across the adjacent faces of the cube, and 1 diagonal through the cube to the opposite vertex:

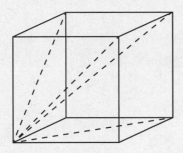

Thus, Quantity A is 4.

If a cube is placed on a flat surface, the maximum contact occurs when one cube face abuts the surface—and thus 4 cube edges touch the surface. There is no way to make more than 4 cube edges touch the flat surface at once. The two quantities are equal.

8. **(D).** The easiest first step is to divide both sides by 16. To do that, make sure you separate out $160^2$ first. Notice that $160^2 = 160 \times 160 = 16 \times 10 \times 160$:

$$16 \times 10 \times 160 = 16x$$
$$10 \times 160 = x$$
$$1{,}600 = x$$

None of the answer choices match this, so break 1,600 down into its primes ($1{,}600 = 100 \times 16 = 25 \times 4 \times 16 = 5^2 \times 2^2 \times 2^4 = 5^2 \times 2^6$) and see which choice is equivalent. Alternatively, multiply out the answer choices to see which equals 1,600. The correct choice is (D).

9. **190.** Redraw the figure, labeling all information given:

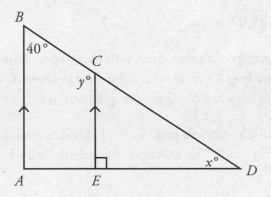

Since *BA* and *CE* are parallel, angle *B* and minor angle *C* are equivalent, as shown:

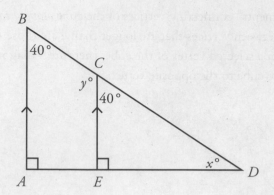

The two angles that meet at *C* make up a straight line, so they sum to 180°:

$$180 = y + 40$$
$$y = 140$$

The three angles of triangle *CDE* must sum to 180°, so:

$$180 = 40 + 90 + x$$
$$180 = 130 + x$$
$$x = 50$$

Therefore, $x + y = 140 + 50 = 190$.

10. **(D).** At first glance, you might be tempted to think that each tick mark on this number line corresponds to a power of 2, but remember that powers grow exponentially (i.e., the distance between $2^5$ and $2^6$ is not the same as the distance between $2^1$ and $2^2$), whereas the tick marks in the diagram are evenly spaced. So, start by finding the distance between $2^5$ and $2^6$.

Since $2^5 = 32$ and $2^6 = 64$, the difference between them is 32. That means the distance between each tick mark on the number line is 32. So to get from $2^5$ to *x*, "walk back," or subtract, four intervals of 32: $32 - 4(32) = -96$.

Multiply out the answers to see which one equals −96. Only choice (D) works.

11. **(E).** There are two ways to solve this question, with smart numbers or algebra. Start with plugging-in. First, set a value for the volume. In this case, pick a perfect cube, so the side length and all other values will be integers. The smallest perfect cube (other than 1, which you should try never to use when doing plug-in questions) is 8.

A cube with a volume of 8 has a side length of 2, meaning each side has an area of 4. A cube has 6 faces, making the total surface area 24. (The equation for surface area is Surface Area = $6s^2$). The answer to this question is 24, based on these numbers.

Immediately eliminate any answer choices that have the square root of 8, as the result will not be an integer. The answer must be either (D) or (E). The cube root of 8 is 2. Answer choice (D) only squares it, yielding 4. In answer choice (E), that result is multiplied by 6, producing 24, which is the required answer. Thus, the answer is (E).

If you wanted to solve with algebra, you'd need to start by solving for a side of a cube with volume $v$:

$$v = s^3 \qquad \text{so} \qquad s = \left(\sqrt[3]{v}\right)$$

The equation for the surface area of a cube is $6s^2$. In this case, substitution for $s$ results in exactly the expression written in answer choice (E).

12. **(D).** To find the area of an equilateral triangle with vertices at $(-1, -3)$, $(9, -3)$, and $(m, n)$, you do not need to find the values of $m$ and $n$. To find the area of an equilateral triangle, you only need one side. First, find the distance between $(-1, -3)$ and $(9, -3)$.

Since these two points are on a horizontal line together (they share a $y$-coordinate), the distance is just the difference between their $x$-coordinates: $9 - (-1) = 10$.

An equilateral triangle with side 10 will have the same area regardless of where it is placed on an $xy$-coordinate plane, so the location of $m$ and $n$ is irrelevant. Instead, draw an equilateral triangle with sides equal 10. Drop a height down the middle:

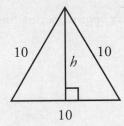

Dividing a 60–60–60 triangle in this way creates two 30–60–90 triangles. The bottom side of the triangle is bisected by the height:

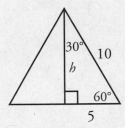

Using the properties of 30–60–90 triangles, $h$ is equal to the shortest side multiplied by the square root of 3. Thus, $h = 5\sqrt{3}$. (You may also wish to memorize that the height of an equilateral triangle is *always* equal to half the side multiplied by $\sqrt{3}$.)

Find the area of the triangle, using 10 as the base:

$$A = \frac{bh}{2} = \frac{10(5\sqrt{3})}{2} = 25\sqrt{3}$$

13. **(A).** Women who are single with children less than 18 years old as a fraction of all women is:

$$\frac{\text{\# single women with children}}{\text{\# women}}$$

Find the number of single mothers in each of the four services by looking at the first table, ***Martial Status of Military Personnel by Gender and Branch.*** The number of women who are single with children is given as:

| | |
|---|---|
| Army | 11,037 |
| Navy | 5,859 |
| Air Force | 6,313 |
| Marines | 1,263 |

There are two ways to find the total number of women in each service, though. Either sum the exact number of women in each branch of the service across each of the marital statuses given in the first chart, or read an approximate number of women from the second bar chart, ***Number of Military Personnel by Gender and Branch***, then only bother to sum from the detailed chart if the two answers are very close to each other.

Since using the chart will be faster and GRE problems are designed to be solved quickly, try approximating from the bar chart first. The total number of women in each of the four services is approximately

| | |
|---|---|
| Army | 75,000 |
| Navy | 50,000 |
| Air Force | 60,000 |
| Marines | 10,000 |

Now calculate the approximate percent of women who are single mothers in each branch of the service:

| | |
|---|---|
| Army | $\frac{11,000}{75,000} \approx 14.7\%$ |
| Navy | $\frac{5,900}{50,000} \approx 11.8\%$ |
| Air Force | $\frac{6,300}{60,000} \approx 10.5\%$ |
| Marines | $\frac{1,300}{10,000} \approx 13\%$ |

The percent looks highest in the Army. At least, reason that the number of single mothers in the Army is about double the number of single women in either the Navy or Air Force, yet the total number of women in the Army is definitely less than double the total number of women in either the Navy or Air Force, making their percentage of women greater in the Army.

Just quickly check the actual totals for the Army and the Marines:

**MANHATTAN**
PREP

Army: single mothers = 11,037 and total women = 74,849. The percent is 14.7%.

Marines: single mothers = 1,263 and total women = 13,135. The percent is 9.6%.

Thus, the Army has the greatest percentage of women who are single and have dependents under the age of 18.

14. **(B).** The probability that a man whose spouse is also military personnel or retired military is NOT in the Air Force is given by the formula:

$$\frac{\text{\# of men in the "married, military spouse" category who are NOT in the Air Force}}{\text{total \# men in the "married, military spouse" category}}$$

All of the information needed to calculate both of these numbers is in the first table, ***Martial Status of Military Personnel by Gender and Branch.***

The total number of men married to a military spouse or retired military in each of the four services:

$$15,058 + 8,638 + 20,760 + 4,719 = 49,175$$

Then just subtract the number of Air Force men in this category to get the number of men in such marriages who are not in the Air Force:

$$49,175 - 20,760 = 28,415$$

And finally:

$$\frac{28,415}{49,175} = 0.5778 \approx 58\%$$

15. **(E).** In order to solve this problem, make the two ratios equal. The ratio in question is $\frac{\text{Women}}{\text{Total}}$, but $\frac{\text{Women}}{\text{Men}}$ is simpler and works also because Total depends only on Women and Men):

$$\frac{\text{resulting \# of women in Army}}{\text{\# of men in Army}} = \frac{\text{\# of women in Air Force}}{\text{\# of men in Air Force}}$$

There are two ways to find the number of women and men in the Army and Air Force. Either sum the exact number of women and men in each marital status for each branch of the service in question, or read an approximate number from the second bar chart, ***Number of Military Personnel by Gender and Branch.***

Since the problem says to approximate and gives numbers in the answer choices that can serve as guidelines, approximation from the bar chart will be good enough.

The important thing is to focus on the *structure* of the math. Since adding women to the Army will change the number of women in the Army, use a variable to represent the additional women. Let *x* represent the number of women who would have to enlist in the Army in order to make the ratios equal.

$$\frac{\text{current \# of women in Army} + x}{\text{\# of men in Army}} = \frac{\text{\# of women in Air Force}}{\text{\# of men in Air Force}}$$

From the bar chart, look up the approximate numbers:

|             | Army    | AF      |
|-------------|---------|---------|
| # of women  | 75,000  | 60,000  |
| # of men    | 475,000 | 270,000 |

The next step is to plug these approximate numbers into the equation and solve for $x$:

$$\frac{75{,}000 + x}{475{,}000} = \frac{60{,}000}{270{,}000}$$

$$\rightarrow 75{,}000 + x = 475{,}000 \times \frac{60{,}000}{270{,}000}$$

$$\rightarrow x = 475{,}000 \times \frac{60{,}000}{270{,}000} - 75{,}000$$

Looking at the answer choices, structurally, the answer must be (D) or (E), and the numbers in (E) are a better fit to the numbers approximated from the chart.

16. **(C).** Since the question concerns the "fraction of the entire distance from Seabreeze to Resortville," think of the entire distance as equal to 1. Between Seabreeze and the first stop, the cable car travels $\frac{1}{3}$, leaving $\frac{2}{3}$ left to travel.

Between the first stop and the second stop, the cable car travels $\frac{3}{5}$ of the remaining $\frac{2}{3}$, or $\frac{3}{5} \times \frac{2}{3} = \frac{2}{5}$.

So far, the cable car has gone $\frac{1}{3} + \frac{2}{5} = \frac{11}{15}$. Thus, the remaining distance is $1 - \frac{11}{15} = \frac{4}{15}$. Only choice (C) is equal to $\frac{4}{15}$, although this takes some manipulation of the choices to check.

Alternatively, construct a formula. The first leg of the journey leaves $1 - \frac{1}{3}$ left to travel. The second leg of the journey subtracts another $\frac{3}{5}$ of the remaining $1 - \frac{1}{3}$, or $\frac{3}{5}\left(1 - \frac{1}{3}\right)$. Thus, the correct expression is $1 - \frac{1}{3} - \frac{3}{5}\left(1 - \frac{1}{3}\right)$.

17. **(D).** If $p$ and $q$ are integers, then $20p$ is even regardless of whether $p$ is even or odd. Since $20p + 3q$ is odd, $3q$ must be odd. If $3q$ is odd, then $q$ is odd. Thus, $q$ is odd, but $p$ could be odd or even. The correct answer must be odd regardless of whether $p$ is odd or even.

If $p$ is odd, (A) is even, (B) is odd, (C) is even, (D) is odd, and (E) is even. Since the correct answer choice is the one that *must* be odd, only (B) and (D) are possibilities.

**MANHATTAN**
PREP

If $p$ is even, (B) is even and (D) is odd. Thus, choice (D) is definitely odd and is the correct answer.

18. **330 and 352 only.** Using your calculator, convert each choice to a percent, and determine whether that percent would round up or down to 8%:

$$\frac{325}{4,400} \times 100 = 7.386...\%$$ This number would round down to 7%, not up to 8%.

$$\frac{330}{4,400} \times 100 = 7.5\%.$$ This number rounds up to 8%, and thus this choice is correct.

$$\frac{352}{4,400} \times 100 = 8\%$$ exactly, and thus this choice is correct.

$$\frac{375}{4,400} \times 100 = 8.522...\%$$ This number would round up to 9%, not down to 8%.

19. **(A).** When dealing with exponents, try to get (almost) everything in terms of common prime bases. Since all the answer choices have a base 4, leave those terms alone for now:

$5^3$ (already simplified)

$27 = 3^3$

$225^2 = 25^2 \times 9^2 = (5^2)^2 \times (3^2)^2 = 5^4 \times 3^4$

Replacing all of these in the equation yields: $\dfrac{5^3(4^{45} - 4^{43})3^3}{5^4 3^4}$.

Cancel 5's and 3's in the top and bottom: $\dfrac{(4^{45} - 4^{43})}{5 \times 3} = \dfrac{(4^{45} - 4^{43})}{15}$.

Factor $4^{43}$ out of both terms in the numerator and simplify: $\dfrac{4^{43}(4^2 - 4^0)}{15} = \dfrac{4^{43}(16 - 1)}{15} = \dfrac{4^{43}(15)}{15} = 4^{43}$.

20. **(A).** On March 1st, the ticket cost $140. If he had purchased it on March 2nd, Harpreet would have paid $168, which is $28 more. To find $x$, use the percent change formula:

$$\text{Percent Change} = \left(\frac{Difference}{Original} \times 100\right)\% = \left(\frac{28}{140} \times 100\right)\% = 20\%$$

Thus, $x = 20$. If he had purchased the ticket on March 16th, he would have paid $210, which is $42 more than the $168 he would have paid on March 2nd. Again, use the Percent Change formula:

$$\left(\frac{42}{168} \times 100\right)\% = 25\%$$

Thus, $y = 25$ and the positive difference between $x$ and $y$ is 5. ("Positive difference" just means to subtract the smaller number from the bigger one, or to subtract either number from the other and then take the absolute value.)

# Appendix A

### of

## 5 lb. Book of GRE® Practice Problems

# Vocabulary List

# In This Chapter...

Vocabulary List

# Vocabulary List

The following is a list of all the vocabulary words—as well as some expressions—used in this book.

A few words are marked (n.) for noun, (adj.) for adjective, or (v.) for verb. We have done this in cases where a word has a common meaning (*pan*, noun—a metal container for cooking food in) as well as a less common one (*pan*, verb—to criticize harshly), and we want you to learn the less common one.

While you can look up words on online dictionary sites such as dictionary.com, m-w.com, and thefreedictionary.com, we also like learnersdictionary.com, which offers simple definitions intended for English Language Learners, as well as wordnik.com, which offers sample sentences and in-context usage for each word.

If you need to look up a phrase, try idioms.thefreedictionary.com, or simply Google the phrase in quotation marks, followed by the word "idiom." For instance:

Note for English Language Learners: In selecting which words to include, we've assumed you already know words like *merge, simultaneous, considerate, dampen, saturate, mandatory, innovation, delusion, juvenile, dictate, catastrophe, hysteria, enduring, generalize, superstitious, penalize, suitable, controversial, contemporary, dismiss, insightful, mystified, peculiar, detest, wit, literally.* If not, please visit www.manhattanprep.com/gre, create a free membership, and download our Basic Vocab List.

| | | | |
|---|---|---|---|
| abasement | amicable | arcades | baneful |
| abated | amicably | arcadian | baroque |
| aberrant | amity | archaically | base |
| abhor | amorality | arduous | baseless |
| abhorrent | amorphous | arid | bask |
| abjured | amortized | aristocratic | bedazzling |
| abolition | anachronistic | arresting | bedlam |
| abreast of | anarchist | artful | beguiled |
| abridge | anathema | artfully | belie |
| abstruse | anecdotal | articulate | belletristic |
| accolades | anecdote | artifacts | bellicose |
| accrue | anemic | artifices | beneficent |
| acculturation | annotated | artisans | benign |
| acerbic | anomalies | artless | beseeched |
| acrimony | anomalous | ascension | besmirch |
| actuarial | anomaly | ascent | besotted |
| acumen | anomie | ascertain | bifurcated |
| adherants | antagonism | ascetic | bipartisan |
| adherence | antagonistic | asceticism | blandishments |
| adroit | antedated | askance to | blatant |
| adulatory | antediluvian | asperity | blissful |
| aesthetic (adj.) | anticipate | assent | blithe |
| aesthetics (n.) | antipathy | asserts | bloodthirsty |
| affability | antiquated | assiduous | blunt (v.) |
| affectless | antithetical to | assimilation | bodes |
| affinity | apathetic | assuage | bogged down |
| affirm | apathy | asylum | bogus |
| affluent | ape (v.) | asymmetrical | boisterous |
| agglomerated | apex | attest to | bolster |
| aggrieve | aphorism | audit | bombastic |
| aghast | apocalyptic | aurora | bon-mots |
| agrarian | apocrypha | austerity | bonobos |
| akimbo | apocryphal | autodidact | boondoggle |
| albatross | apologia | auxiliary | boorish |
| alienation | apologist | avant garde | boosterish |
| allegorical | appease | avaricious | botched |
| alluring | appellations | aver | brandishes |
| amalgamate | apportioned | averse | breach |
| amateurs | approbation | aversion | bridge |
| ameliorate | appropriate (v.) | balkanized | brook |
| amenable | appropriation | banal | brusque |
| amended | aptitudes | banality | brutality |
| amiable | aquiline | bane | bucolic |

**MANHATTAN**
PREP

| | | | |
|---|---|---|---|
| buoyancy | commando | cornerstone | deft |
| burgeoning | commentated | corroborate | deftly |
| bustling | commune | corroborating | deftness |
| buttress | communism | cosmopolitan | degrade |
| buttressed | compatriots | couched in | deification |
| byzantine | compel | counterfactual | deified |
| cabal | complaints | counterpoint | deify |
| cajole | complement | coup | deleterious |
| callous | complementary | covey | deliberate |
| calumnies | complicit | crane | delimit |
| candor | comprehension | credence | delineate |
| canny | conceded | credible | delinquent |
| canonization | conceit | credulous | delves |
| capricious | concessionary | croquet | demagogic |
| castigate | concomitant | crouchback | demarcate |
| catalyst | concrete | cubist | demeaning |
| catharsis | condoned | culminate | dementia |
| caustic | confers | culmination | demonized |
| cauterizes | confound | culpable | denial |
| cavalier | congeal | cultivate | denigrate |
| celebrated | congenial | cultivation | depicted |
| cerebral | conglomerates | cumbersome | deplorable |
| chaff | congress | cunning | deposed |
| chagrin | congruent | curbed | deprecating |
| charade | conjectural | curt | depreciated |
| charismatic | consanguineous | curtailing | deprivation |
| chary | consecration | dame | derivative |
| chide | constitution | daunting | desiccated |
| chided | contemptible | dauntless | designation |
| chronicling | contention | dearth | despots |
| chronology | contest | debacle | desultory |
| circumscribing | contraband | debased | detest |
| cite | contrary | debauchery | detriment |
| citing | contravening | decamped | deviation |
| clairvoyant | contribute | decipherable | devoid |
| clamor | contrite | declarative | dialectical |
| clandestine | contrivance | deem | diameter |
| coalesced | contrived | defame | diatribes |
| coda | conundrums | defeasible | dicey |
| cogent | conversance | defer | didactic |
| collusive | convivial | deficient | diffident |
| coltish | convoluted | defile | dilettante |
| comestible | copious | definitive | diligence |

| | | | |
|---|---|---|---|
| dire | dwindled | epoch | explicit |
| disaffection | dystopian | equable | explicitly |
| disclaim | earmark | equanimity | exploits |
| disconcertingly | earthy | equilibrium | extemporaneous |
| discounted (v.) | ebullient | equitable | extirpated |
| discourse | eclectic | equivocal | extrapolate |
| discreet | ecologies | equivocate | exuded |
| discrepancy | ecology | equivocations | fabricate |
| discretionary | effacement | eradication | facetious |
| disinclination | effect (v.) | ergonomic | facile |
| disingenuous | effeminate | ernest | factions |
| disinterested | effete | erode | falacious |
| disparage | efficacious | ersatz | fallacy |
| dispatch | effusive | erstwhile | fanciful |
| dispensations | egoist | erudite | fantastical |
| dispersal | egregious | erudition | farce |
| disquieting | eliminate | eschew | farcical |
| dissemble | elite | esteemed | fascism |
| disseminate | elitist | estrangement | fascist |
| dissent | eloquence | etymologies | fastidious |
| dissipation | eloquent | eulogized | fatuous |
| dissolute | elude | euphemistically | fealty |
| dissolution | emblazoned | euphony | feckless |
| dissonance | emblematic | evanescent | fecund |
| dissuaded | eminence | evasions | fervent |
| distension | empirical | evasive | fester |
| distinction | emulate | evinced | fetid |
| distort | enamored | evoked | fettered |
| divergent | encumbrances | evoking | fickle |
| divisive | enervate | exacerbate | fidelity |
| doggedly | enigmatic | exacting | fiduciary |
| dogmatic | enraged | excise | figurative |
| doyenne | enraptured | excoriation | finale |
| draconian | enshrine | excruciating | flabbergast |
| drafted | enshrinement | exculpate | flag (v.) |
| dramaturgy | ensues | exegetic | flagrancy |
| dry | entail | exemplars | flamboyant |
| dulcet | entreaty | exemplary | fledgling |
| dull | eons | exhaustive | flouted |
| duplicitous | ephemera | exorbitant | flummox |
| duplicitously | ephemeral | expatiation | foibles |
| duplicity | epicurean | expatriate | forfeit |
| dust | epitomized | explicate | formalism |

**MANHATTAN**
PREP

| | | | |
|---|---|---|---|
| forté | hedonism | immaterial | indisputably |
| fortuitous | heeding | immoderate | indolence |
| foster | hegemonic | immolate | ineffectual |
| frank | hegemony | immortalized | ineptness |
| fruition | helmsmanship | immutable | inevitably |
| fulmination | hemorrhaging | impact | inexorably |
| futile | heralded | impartial | infinitesimal |
| gadfly | hermeneutic | impartiality | infirmity |
| gaffe | hermetic | impasse | infuses |
| gainsay | heterodox | impeccable | ingenious |
| galleys | heterogeneous | impecunious | ingenuity |
| galvanize | heuristic | impede | ingenuous |
| gambits | hierarchical | impediments | inherently |
| gamut | hierarchy | impenetrable | inimical |
| garrulous | hindered | imperil | injecting |
| gauche | hindrance | imperious | inkling |
| gauntlet | hinging | impervious | innocuous |
| genial | hinterland | impious | innovative |
| genteel | hirsute | implacability | innuendos |
| germane | histrionic | implicit | innumerable |
| gilt | hobble | important | inquisitions |
| gist | hodgepodge | importunate | inscribing |
| grandiloquent | homogeneous | impotent | insensibly |
| gregarious | honed | impressed | insidious |
| grizzled | honeycombed | improvident | insightful |
| grotesque | honorific | impudent | insights |
| guileless | horrific | imputation | insinuated |
| guise | house | incendiary | insipid |
| gunning | humanize | incensed | insolent |
| guru | husband (v.) | incentivize | insolvent |
| habituated | hyperboles | inchoate | insouciance |
| hackneyed | hysteria | incipient | instigating |
| hadron | iconoclasm | incite | instigation |
| hale | iconoclastic | incongruous | insurmountable |
| hallmark | idealogues | inconsequential | intentions |
| hamlet | ideological | incorrigible | inter |
| hamstring | idioms | incumbent | interlocutors |
| hapless | idiosyncratic | indecipherable | interlude |
| happenstance | idle | indemnify | interpolate |
| harbingers | ignominious | indeterminable | interspersed |
| hardy | illiberal | indeterminate | intransigence |
| heads (v.) | illicit | indifference | intrepid |
| hector | imbues | indignant | inundates |

inured to
inveigle
investiture
iota
irascible
irate
ironically
irony
irredeemable
irrefutable
iteration
iterative
jaundiced
jeopardize
jibes
jingoistic
joviality
jurisprudent
keen
kinetic
kudos
labile
labyrinthine
lackey
lackluster
laconic
language
languid
lapses
lard
lascivious
lassitude
laud
laudable
laudatory
laurels
lavishness
lax
laxity
leery
legume
leitmotifs
licentious

limelight
lionize
lissome
listlessly
literary
literati
lithe
litigation
loath (v.)
loathsome
lofty
logistical
longtime
lubricious
lucid
luminary
macabre
magnanimity
magnitude
maladies
maladjusted
maladroitness
malicious
malign
malleable
manacled
manifest
manumit
marginalize
martial
maudlin
maxim
mead
meddlesome
medley
melancholy
mélange
mellifluous
menacing
mendacious
mercantilist
mercenary
mercurial

messianic
metastasize
meticulous
meticulousness
militant
millennia
mimetic
mindfulness
minuscule
minutiae
mirthful
mishmash
misnomers
mitigate
mitigation
moderate (v.)
modicum
modishness
mollifies
momentum
mongers
monolithic
monological
moot
moralizing
morbidities
mordant
mores
moribund
morose
mote
motivation
motley
mummified
mundane
munificent
munitions
musings
mutiny
myopic
myriad
mystics
nadir

naïve
narcissists
nascent
national
nave
neanderthals
nebulous
negating
nemesis
nettled
nonchalance
nonplussed
normalizing
nose
notorious
novel
novice
noxious
nugatory
obliterated
obloquies
obscure
obsequious
obtuse
obviate
ode
officious
ominously
omissions
omnipotent
onerous
opportunism
opprobrium
opulent
orthodox
orthodoxy
ostensibly
ostentatious
ostracize
oust
outright
override
overseer

**MANHATTAN**
PREP

| | | | |
|---|---|---|---|
| overt | pedagogy | politic | propriety |
| pacific | pedantic | politicized | proscribe |
| pacifist | pedantry | polymath | prose |
| paean | peddle | ponderous | protagonist |
| painstaking | pedestrian | populace | protean |
| palatable | peer | populist | proverbially |
| pale | peers | posit | providential |
| palettes | penchant | posited | provincial |
| palliate | perennially | posterity | prudent |
| pallid | peril | postmodern | prudish |
| panacea | perilous | posture | prurient |
| pander | pernicious | poultices | psyche |
| panned (v.) | perpetuate | pragmatic | puckish |
| pantheon | perpetuity | pragmatists | puerile |
| parables | personable | precocious | pulchritude |
| paradigmatic | perspicacious | predilection | punctilious |
| paradigms | pert | preordained | pundits |
| paradox | pertinent | preposterous | puritanical |
| paragon | perturbing | presage | purported |
| parameter | pervades | prescient | putative |
| parcel | phased in | presentation | pynchon |
| parlay | philandering | presumptuous | quaint |
| parlous | phlegmatic | preternatural | qualified |
| parochial | piddling | priggish | quanta |
| parodied | pidgins | primacy | quantum |
| parsimoniousness | piecemeal | primal | quarks |
| parsimony | piety | probity | quips |
| partiality | pillory | proclivity | quixotic |
| partisan | piques | procure | quotidian |
| partisanship | pitch (v.) | prodigal | radiative |
| partition | pith | prodigies | railed |
| passable | pithy | profane | rancorous |
| patent | placid | profligate | rapier |
| paternal | plastic | profound | rash |
| pathologize | plaudits | profundity | raucous |
| patriarch | plethora | progeny | razed |
| patrician | pliant | prolific | reactionary |
| patronize | plodding | prolix | realist |
| patrons | plunder | prologue | recanted |
| paucity | poignant | promulgates | recapitulated |
| peasant | polarized | prophetic | reciprocal |
| peccadilloes | polemic | proponent | recoiling |
| peculiarly | polemical | propound | redacted |

redoubtable
redresses
redundant
referents
regressive
rejoinder
relished
reminiscences
render
rendered
reneged
renowned
repentant
repertory
repulsed
requisite
requite
resilience
restitution
restorative
resurrected
retching
retort
retrograde
retrospective
reverent
revisionist
revivification
rhetoric
riddled
rife with
risqué
robust
rout
rue
saccharine
sagacious
sages (n.)
salubrious
salutation
salvo
sanctioned
sangfroid

sanguinary
sanguine
sardonic
sartorial
satiric
satisfies
savvy
scandal
scanty
scarcity
scintillating
scotch (v.)
scrutinized
seasoned
sectarian
seditious
sedulous
seemingly
seething
selfless
semblance
semiotic
sensibilities
sentiments
sentries
serendipitous
serendipity
seriously
shaman
shunned
shuttered (v.)
signify
similes
simony
simpatico
simulacrum
sinecure
singular
skittish
skulk
slanderous
slipstream
sloth

smitten
sobriquets
socialist
solace
sole
solecisms
solemnity
soliciting
solicitous
solicitousness
solipsistic
solvent
somber
sophistry
sophomoric
sound (adj.)
spartan
specious
specter
spectroscopy
spontaneous
spooked
spurious
squalid
stagnant
stanchion
statute
staunch
stem (v.)
stems
steward
stipulate
stoic
stolid
stouter
strapping
stratagem
stridency
strife
strive
stymie
subterfuge
subversion

subverted
suffrage
superficial
superfluous
supersede
supplants
supplement
supplicated
surreptitious
sussing
sweeping
sycophant
syncopated
synergetic
synoptic
tacit
taciturn
taciturnity
tangential
tangible
tantamount to
tarry
tat
taut
taxonomy
teeming (adj.)
temper (v.)
temperate
tenaciously
tenacity
tendentious
tenets
tepid
terseness
tethered
theology
theses
timorous
tirade
titillation
toil
tonality
tony

torpid
torpor
tortuous
torturous
totalitarian
touchstone
tout
touted
tractable
transgressor
transient
transmogrify
transmute
tremulous
trenchant
trepidation
triage
tribute
trilobites
truculent
truisms
turbines
turpitude
tyrannical
ubiquitous
unabashed
unbridled
unconscionable
uncouth
undermined
underscore
unflappable
unilateral
unkempt
unnerve
unpropitious
unqualified
unscrupulous
unseemly
unwavering
unwieldy
upend
urbane

urbanity
utilitarian
utopia
vacillating
vacuity
vainglorious
vapid
variegated
venal
venerability
venerable
venerate
veracity
verdant
verged
verges
verging
veritable
vestigial
vexing
viable
vicissitude
vigorous
vindicated
vindictiveness
virulence
vitality
vitreous
vituperations
vivacious
vociferous
volatile
voluble
vulgar
wag
waning
ward off
wax (v.)
whet
whimsical
whitewash
winsome
witticisms

wracked
wry
xenophobia
zeal
zealots

# STUDY ANYWHERE!

## WITH MANHATTAN PREP'S GRE FLASH CARDS

**coterie**
(noun)
COH-ter-ee

587

**Definition:** Close or exclusive group, clique

**Usage:** The pop star never traveled anywhere without a **coterie** of assistants and managers.

**Related Words:** *Cabal* (conspiracy, group of people who plot), *Entourage* (group of attendants)

**More Info:** In French, a *coterie* was a group of tenant farmers.

*These cards go above and beyond providing abstract, out-of-context definitions—the backs of all cards contain a word "network" designed to help the student develop a lasting understanding of the word in a GRE-relevant context.*

*We offer both a 500 Essential Words and a 500 Advanced Words deck, each complete with definitions, example sentences, pronunciations, and related words. The 2-volume set comprises the most comprehensive vocabulary study tool on the market.*

2nd Edition

For the Revised GRE

MANHATTAN PREP
GRE® FLASH CARDS

### 500 Essential Words

✓ Designed specifically for the vocabulary question types found on the Revised GRE
✓ Cards include definitions, example sentences, pronunciations, and related words
✓ Want more? Check out our second flash card set: *500 Advanced Words*

**Written by Jennifer Dziura**

*GRE is a registered trademark of the Educational Testing Service (ETS), which neither sponsors nor endorses this test product.*

2nd Edition

For the Revised GRE

MANHATTAN PREP
GRE® FLASH CARDS

### 500 Advanced Words

✓ Designed specifically for the vocabulary question types found on the Revised GRE
✓ Cards include definitions, example sentences, pronunciations, and related words
✓ Want more? Check out our first flash card set: *500 Essential Words*

**Written by Jennifer Dziura**

*GRE is a registered trademark of the Educational Testing Service (ETS), which neither sponsors nor endorses this test product.*

## CHECK OUT THESE CARDS AND MORE AT

MANHATTANPREP.COM/GRE